Twentieth-Century Literary Criticism

Topics Volume

Guide to Gale Literary Criticism Series

For criticism on	Consult these Gale series
Authors now living or who died after December 31, 1959	*CONTEMPORARY LITERARY CRITICISM (CLC)*
Authors who died between 1900 and 1959	*TWENTIETH-CENTURY LITERARY CRITICISM (TCLC)*
Authors who died between 1800 and 1899	*NINETEENTH-CENTURY LITERATURE CRITICISM (NCLC)*
Authors who died between 1400 and 1799	*LITERATURE CRITICISM FROM 1400 TO 1800 (LC)* *SHAKESPEAREAN CRITICISM (SC)*
Authors who died before 1400	*CLASSICAL AND MEDIEVAL LITERATURE CRITICISM (CMLC)*
Authors of books for children and young adults	*CHILDREN'S LITERATURE REVIEW (CLR)*
Dramatists	*DRAMA CRITICISM (DC)*
Poets	*POETRY CRITICISM (PC)*
Short story writers	*SHORT STORY CRITICISM (SSC)*
Black writers of the past two hundred years	*BLACK LITERATURE CRITICISM (BLC)*
Hispanic writers of the late nineteenth and twentieth centuries	*HISPANIC LITERATURE CRITICISM (HLC)*
Native North American writers and orators of the eighteenth, nineteenth, and twentieth centuries	*NATIVE NORTH AMERICAN LITERATURE (NNAL)*
Major authors from the Renaissance to the present	*WORLD LITERATURE CRITICISM, 1500 TO THE PRESENT (WLC)*

ISSN 0276-8178

Volume 90

Twentieth-Century Literary Criticism

Topics Volume

**Excerpts from Criticism of Various Topics
in Twentieth-Century Literature, including Literary
and Critical Movements, Prominent Themes and
Genres, Anniversary Celebrations, and Surveys
of National Literatures**

Jennifer Baise
Editor

Thomas Ligotti
Associate Editor

GALE GROUP

Detroit
New York
San Francisco
London
Boston
Woodbridge, CT

STAFF

Jennifer Baise, *Editor*

Thomas Ligotti, *Associate Editor*

Maria Franklin, *Permissions Manager*
Kimberly F. Smilay, *Permissions Specialist*
Kelly A. Quin, *Permissions Associates*
Sandy Gore, *Permissions Assistant*

Victoria B. Cariappa, *Research Manager*
Andrew Guy Malonis, Barbara McNeil, Gary J. Oudersluys, Maureen Richards, Cheryl L. Warnock, *Research Specialists*
Patricia T. Ballard, Tamara C. Nott, Tracie A. Richardson, *Research Associates*
Phyllis Blackman, Corrine Stocker, *Research Assistant*

Mary Beth Trimper, *Production Director*
Stacy L. Melson, *Buyer*

Gary Leach, *Graphic Artist*
Randy Bassett, *Image Database Supervisor*
Robert Duncan, Michael Logusz, *Imaging Specialists*
Pamela Reed, *Imaging Coordinator*

Library of Congress Catalog Card Number 76-46132
ISBN 0-7876-2748-8
ISSN 0276-8178

Printed in the United States of America
10 9 8 7 6 5 4 3 2 1

Contents

Preface vii

Acknowledgments xi

Preface

Since its inception more than fifteen years ago, *Twentieth-Century Literary Criticism* has been purchased and used by nearly 10,000 school, public, and college or university libraries. *TCLC* has covered more than 500 authors, representing 58 nationalities, and over 25,000 titles. No other reference source has surveyed the critical response to twentieth-century authors and literature as thoroughly as *TCLC*. In the words of one reviewer, "there is nothing comparable available." *TCLC* "is a gold mine of information—dates, pseudonyms, biographical information, and criticism from books and periodicals—which many libraries would have difficulty assembling on their own."

Scope of the Series

TCLC is designed to serve as an introduction to authors who died between 1900 and 1960 and to the most significant interpretations of these author's works. The great poets, novelists, short story writers, playwrights, and philosophers of this period are frequently studied in high school and college literature courses. In organizing and reprinting the vast amount of critical material written on these authors, *TCLC* helps students develop valuable insight into literary history, promotes a better understanding of the texts, and sparks ideas for papers and assignments. Each entry in *TCLC* presents a comprehensive survey of an author's career or an individual work of literature and provides the user with a multiplicity of interpretations and assessments. Such variety allows students to pursue their own interests; furthermore, it fosters an awareness that literature is dynamic and responsive to many different opinions.

Every fourth volume of *TCLC* is devoted to literary topics. These topic entries widen the focus of the series from individual authors to such broader subjects as literary movements, prominent themes in twentieth-century literature, literary reaction to political and historical events, significant eras in literary history, prominent literary anniversaries, and the literatures of cultures that are often overlooked by English-speaking readers.

TCLC is designed as a companion series to Gale's *Contemporary Literary Criticism,* which reprints commentary on authors now living or who have died since 1960. Because of the different periods under consideration, there is no duplication of material between *CLC* and *TCLC*. For additional information about *CLC* and Gale's other criticism titles, users should consult the Guide to Gale Literary Criticism Series preceding the title page in this volume.

Coverage

Each volume of *TCLC* is carefully compiled to present:

- criticism of authors, or literary topics, representing a variety of genres and nationalities

- both major and lesser-known writers and literary works of the period

- 6-12 authors or 3-6 topics per volume

- individual entries that survey critical response to each author's work or each topic in literary history, including early criticism to reflect initial reactions; later criticism to represent any rise or decline in reputation; and current retrospective analyses.

Organization of This Book

An author entry consists of the following elements: author heading, biographical and critical introduction, list of principal works, reprints of criticism (each preceded by an annotation and a bibliographic citation), and a bibliography of further reading.

- The **Author Heading** consists of the name under which the author most commonly wrote, followed by birth and death dates. If an author wrote consistently under a pseudonym, the pseudonym will be listed in the author heading and the real name given in parentheses on the first line of the biographical and critical introduction. Also located at the beginning of the introduction to the author entry are any name variations under which an author wrote, including transliterated forms for authors whose languages use nonroman alphabets.

- The **Biographical and Critical Introduction** outlines the author's life and career, as well as the critical issues surrounding his or her work. References to past volumes of *TCLC* are provided at the beginning of the introduction. Additional sources of information in other biographical and critical reference series published by Gale, including *Short Story Criticism, Children's Literature Review, Contemporary Authors, Dictionary of Literary Biography,* and *Something about the Author,* are listed in a box at the end of the entry.

- Some *TCLC* entries include **Portraits** of the author. Entries also may contain reproductions of materials pertinent to an author's career, including manuscript pages, title pages, dust jackets, letters, and drawings, as well as photographs of important people, places, and events in an author's life.

- The **List of Principal Works** is chronological by date of first book publication and identifies the genre of each work. In the case of foreign authors with both foreign-language publications and English translations, the title and date of the first English-language edition are given in brackets. Unless otherwise indicated, dramas are dated by first performance, not first publication.

- Critical essays are prefaced by **Annotations** providing the reader with information about both the critic and the criticism that follows. Included are the critic's reputation, individual approach to literary criticism, and particular expertise in an author's works. Also noted are the relative importance of a work of criticism, the scope of the essay, and the growth of critical controversy or changes in critical trends regarding an author. In some cases, these annotations cross-reference essays by critics who discuss each other's commentary.

- A complete **Bibliographic Citation** designed to facilitate location of the original essay or book precedes each piece of criticism.

- Criticism is arranged chronologically in each author entry to provide a perspective on changes in critical evaluation over the years. All titles of works by the author featured in the entry are printed in boldface type to enable the user to easily locate discussion of particular works. Also for purposes of easier identification, the critic's name and the publication date of the essay are given at the beginning of each piece of criticism. Unsigned criticism is preceded by the title of the journal in which it appeared. Some of the essays in *TCLC* also contain translated material. Unless otherwise noted, translations in brackets are by the editors; translations in parentheses or continuous with the text are by the critic. Publication information (such as footnotes or page and line references to specific editions of works) have been deleted at the editor's discretion to provide smoother reading of the text.

- An annotated list of **Further Reading** appearing at the end of each author entry suggests secondary sources on the author. In some cases it includes essays for which the editors could not obtain reprint rights.

Cumulative Indexes

- Each volume of *TCLC* contains a cumulative **Author Index** listing all authors who have appeared in Gale's Literary Criticism Series, along with cross references to such biographical series as *Contemporary Authors* and *Dictionary of Literary Biography*. For readers' convenience, a complete list of Gale titles included appears on the first page of the author index. Useful for locating authors within the various series, this index is particularly valuable for those authors who are identified by a certain period but who, because of their death dates, are placed in another, or for those authors whose careers span two periods. For example, F. Scott Fitzgerald is found in *TCLC*, yet a writer often associated with him, Ernest Hemingway, is found in *CLC*.

- Each *TCLC* volume includes a cumulative **Nationality Index** which lists all authors who have appeared in *TCLC* volumes, arranged alphabetically under their respective nationalities, as well as Topics volume entries devoted to particular national literatures.

- Each new volume in Gale's Literary Criticism Series includes a cumulative **Topic Index,** which lists all literary topics treated in *NCLC, TCLC, LC 1400-1800,* and the *CLC* yearbook.

- Each new volume of *TCLC,* with the exception of the Topics volumes, includes a **Title Index** listing the titles of all literary works discussed in the volume. In response to numerous suggestions from librarians, Gale has also produced a **Special Paperbound Edition** of the *TCLC* title index. This annual cumulation lists all titles discussed in the series since its inception and is issued with the first volume of *TCLC* published each year. Additional copies of the index are available on request. Librarians and patrons will welcome this separate index; it saves shelf space, is easy to use, and is recyclable upon receipt of the following year's cumulation. Titles discussed in the Topics volume entries are not included *TCLC* cumulative index.

Citing Twentieth-Century Literary Criticism

When writing papers, students who quote directly from any volume in Gale's literary Criticism Series may use the following general forms to footnote reprinted criticism. The first example pertains to materials drawn from periodicals, the second to material reprinted from books.

> [1]William H. Slavick, "Going to School to DuBose Heyward," *The Harlem Renaissance Reexamined,* (AMS Press, 1987); reprinted in *Twentieth-Century Literary Criticism,* Vol. 59, ed. Jennifer Gariepy (Detroit: Gale Research, 1995), pp. 94-105.

> [2]George Orwell, "Reflections on Gandhi," *Partisan Review,* 6 (Winter 1949), pp. 85-92; reprinted in *Twentieth-Century Literary Criticism,* Vol. 59, ed. Jennifer Gariepy (Detroit: Gale Research, 1995), pp. 40-3.

Suggestions Are Welcome

In response to suggestions, several features have been added to *TCLC* since the series began, including annotations to critical essays, a cumulative index to authors in all Gale literary criticism series, entries devoted to criticism on a single work by a major author, more extensive illustrations, and a title index listing all literary works discussed in the series since its inception.

Readers who wish to suggest authors or topics to appear in future volumes, or who have other suggestions, are cordially invited to write the editors.

Acknowledgments

The editors wish to thank the copyright holders of the criticism included in this volume and the permissions managers of many book and magazine publishing companies for assisting us in securing reproduction rights. We are also grateful to the staffs of the Detroit Public Library, the Library of Congress, the University of Detroit Mercy Library, Wayne State University Purdy/Kresge Library Complex, and the University of Michigan Libraries for making their resources available to us. Following is a list of the copyright holders who have granted us permission to reproduce material in this volume of *TCLC*. Every effort has been made to trace copyright, but if omissions have been made, please let us know.

COPYRIGHTED ESSAYS IN *TCLC*, VOLUME 90, WERE REPRODUCED FROM THE FOLLOWING PERIODICALS:

American Literature, v. XXVII, November, 1955. Copyright © 1955 Duke University Press, Durham, NC. Reproduced by permission.—*American Quarterly*, v. IX, Fall, 1957. Copyright 1957, renewed 1985, American Studies Association. Reproduced by permission of The Johns Hopkins University Press./ v. XXV, December, 1973. Copyright 1973, American Studies Association. Reproduced by permission of The Johns Hopkins University Press.—*boundary 2*, v. V, 1977. Copyright © *boundary 2*, 1977. Reproduced by permission.—*The Centennial Review*, v. XVI, Summer, 1972 for "Sin and the City: The Uses of Disorder in the Urban Novel" by Alan Henry Rose. © 1972 by *The Centennial Review*. Reproduced by permission of the publisher and the author.—*Chicago Review*, v. 27, Summer, 1975. Copyright © 1975 by *Chicago Review*. Reproduced by permission.—*CLIO*, v. 16, Winter, 1987 for "Postmodern Theory/ Postmodern Fiction" by John Johnston. © 1987 by Robert H. Canary and Henry Kozicki. Reproduced by permission of the author.—*Contemporary Literature*, v. 11, Summer, 1970; v. 32, Spring, 1991. © 1970, 1991 by the Board of Regents of the University of Wisconsin. Reproduced by permission of The University of Wisconsin Press.—*Critical Inquiry*, v. 13, 1986 for "Pluralism in Postmodern Perspective" by Ihab Hassan; v. 22, Summer, 1996 for "What Is Living and What Is Dead in American Postmodernism: Establishing the Contemporaneity of Some American Poetry" by Charles Altieri. Copyright © 1986 by The University of Chicago. Both reproduced by permission of the publisher and the respective authors.—*Critical Quarterly*, v. 32, Spring, 1990. © Manchester University Press 1990. Reproduced by permission.—*Critique: Studies in Modern Fiction*, v. 15, 1974; v. XXXIV, Fall, 1992. Copyright © 1974, 1992 Helen Dwight Reid Educational Foundation. Both reproduced with permission of the Helen Dwight Reid Educational Foundation, published by Heldref Publications, 119 18th Street, N. W., Washington, DC 20036-1802.—*The Hudson Review*, v. VII, Autumn, 1954. Copyright 1954, renewed 1982 by The Hudson Review, Inc. Reproduced by permission.—*Journal of Popular Culture*, v. IX, Winter, 1975; v. XI, Summer, 1997. Copyright © 1975, 1997 by Ray B. Browne. Both reproduced by permission.—*Kentucky Foreign Language Quarterly*, v. XIII, Second Quarter, 1966. Reproduced by permission.—*Meanjin Quarterly*, v. 30, December, 1971 for "Violence in the Eternal City: 'Catch-22' as a Critique of American Culture" by Lucy Frost. Reproduced by permission of the author.—*The Midwest Quarterly*, v. XXXV, Winter, 1994. Copyright © 1994 by *The Midwest Quarterly*, Pittsburgh State University. Reproduced by permission.—*MLN*, v. 97, January, 1982. © copyright 1982 by The Johns Hopkins University Press. All rights reserved. Reproduced by permission.—*Modern Fiction Studies*, v. 32, Spring, 1986; v. 36, Summer, 1990. Copyright © 1986, 1990 by Purdue Research Foundation, West Lafayette, IN 47907. All rights reserved. Both reproduced by permission of The Johns Hopkins University.—*The New England Quarterly*, v. XLVI, December, 1973 for "Classical Vision and the American City: Henry James's 'The Bostonians'" by R. A. Morris. Copyright 1973 by *The New England Quarterly*. Reproduced by permission of the publisher and the author.—*New England Review and Bread Loaf Quarterly*, v. XII, Summer, 1990 for "The Poetry Lab: Science in Contemporary American Poetry" by Maura High. Copyright © 1990 by Middlebury College. Reproduced by permission of the author.—*New Literary History*, v. 20, 1988 for "The Problem of the Postmodern" by C. Barry Chabot. Copyright © 1988 by New Literary History. Reproduced by permission of The Johns Hopkins University Press./ v. 20, Winter, 1989. Copyright © 1989 by New Literary History. Reproduced by permission of The Johns Hopkins University Press.—*Nineteenth-Century Fiction*, v. 4, December, 1949 for "The Wheel and the Beast: The Influence of London and Thomas Hardy" by George Witter Sherman. Copyright 1949, renewed 1977 by The Regents of the University of California. Reproduced by permission of the Regents.—*Novel: A Forum on Fiction*, v. 21, Winter-Spring, 1988. Copyright NOVEL Corp. © 1988. Reproduced with permission.—*Partisan Review*, v. LX, No. 3, 1973 for "Surfiction: A Postmodern Position" by Raymond Federman. Copyright © 1973 by *Partisan Review*. Reproduced by permission of the publisher and the author.—*Phylon: The Atlanta University Review of Race and Culture*, v. XXXII, No. 1, Winter, 1971. Copyright, 1971, by Atlanta University. Reproduced by permission of PHYLON.—*The Phylon Quarterly*, v. XX. No. 1, Winter, 1959. Copyright by Atlanta University. Reproduced by permission of *PHYLON*.—*Poetics Today*, v. 3, Summer, 1982. © *Poetics Today*. Reproduced by permission.—*The Sewanee Review*, v. LXXXVI, Spring, 1978 for "The Dilemma of Literature in an Age of Science" by David J. Gordon; v. XCIX, Winter, 1991 for "Postmodernism and American Literary History" by David H. Hirsch. Copyright © 1978, 1991 by the respective authors. Both reproduced with permission of the editor.—*The South Atlantic Quarterly*, v. 89, Spring, 1990. Copyright © 1990 by Duke University Press, Durham, NC. Reproduced by permission.—*Studies in Short*

Fiction, v. 15, Spring, 1978; v. 32, Spring, 1995. Copyright 1978, 1995 by Newberry College. Both reproduced by permission.—*Sub-stance,* 27, 1980. Reproduced by permission.—*Theatre Journal,* v. 45, May, 1993. © 1993, University and College Theatre Association of the American Theatre Association. Reproduced by permission of The Johns Hopkins University Press.—*Theatre Research International,* v. 18, Autumn, 1993. Reproduced by permission of Oxford University Press.—*TriQuarterly,* v. 33, Spring, 1975 for "The Self-Conscious Moment: Reflections on the Aftermath of Modernism" by Robert Alter. © 1975 by *TriQuarterly,* Northwestern University. Reproduced by permission of the author.—*Virginia Quarterly Review,* v. 65, Summer, 1989. Copyright, 1989, by *The Virginia Quarterly Review,* The University of Virginia. Reproduced by permission of the publisher.—*The Yale Review,* v. LXIV, October, 1974. Copyright 1974, by Yale University. Reproduced by permission of the editors and Blackwell Publishers.

COPYRIGHTED ESSAYS IN *TCLC,* VOLUME 90, WERE REPRODUCED FROM THE FOLLOWING BOOKS:

Barth, John. From *Further Fridays: Essays, Lectures, and Other Nonfiction: 1984-94.* Little, Brown and Company, 1995. Copyright © 1995 by John Barth. All rights reserved. Reproduced by permission.—Fischer-Lichte, Erika. From "Postmodernism: Extension or End of Modernism? Theater Between Cultural Crisis and Cultural Change" in *Zeitgeist in Babel: The Postmodernist Controversy.* Edited by Ingeborg Hoesterey. Indiana University Press, 1991. © 1991 by Indiana University Press. All rights reserved. Reproduced by permission.—Gelfant, Blanche Housman. From *The American City Novel.* University of Oklahoma Press, 1954. Copyright 1954 by the University of Oklahoma Press. Renewed 1982 by Blanche Housman Gelfant. Reproduced by permission.—Goist, Park Dixon. From *From Main Street to State Street: Town, City, and Community in America.* Kennikat Press, 1977. Copyright © 1977 by Kennikat Press Corp. All rights reserved. Reproduced by permission of the author.—Graff, Gerald. From "The Myth of the Postmodern Breakthrough" in *Literature Against Itself: Literary Ideas in Modern Society.* Ivan R. Dee, Inc. 1995. © 1979 by The University of Chicago. All rights reserved. Reproduced by permission of the author.—Hakutani, Yoshinobu. From "The City and Richard Wright's Quest for Freedom" in *The City in African-American Literature.* Edited by Yoshinobu Hakutani. Fairleigh Dickinson University Press, 1995. © 1995 by Associated University Presses, Inc. All rights reserved. Reproduced by permission.—Hassan, Ihab. From "Cities of Mind, Urban Words" in *Literature and The Urban Experience.* Rutgers University Press, 1981. All rights reserved. Reproduced by permission of the author.—Kurz, Paul Konrad. From *On Modern German Literature,* Vol. I. Translated by Sister Mary Frances McCarthy. The University of Alabama Press, 1967. Copyright © 1967 by Paul Konrad Kurz. English translation copyright © 1970 by The University of Alabama Press. Reproduced by permission of the author.—Levin, Harry. From "Science and Fiction" in *Bridges to Science Fiction.* George E. Slusser, George R. Guffey, Mark Rose, eds. Southern Illinois University Press, 1980. Copyright © 1980 by Southern Illinois University Press. All rights reserved. Reproduced by permission.—McLaren, Peter L. and Colin Lankshear. From "Critical Literacy and the Postmodern Turn" and "Postscript to 'Critical Literacy and the Postmodern Turn'" in *Critical Literacy: Politics, Praxis, and the Postmodern.* Edited by Colin Lankshear and Peter L. McLaren. State University of New York Press, 1993. © 1993 State University of New York. All rights reserved. Reproduced by permission.—Parker, Mark. From "'The Name of the Rose' as a Postmodern Novel" in *Naming the Rose: Essays on Eco's 'The Name of Rose.'* Edited by M. Thomas Inge. University Press of Mississippi, 1988. Copyright © 1988 by the University Press of Mississippi. All rights reserved.—Strehle, Susan. From *Fiction in the Quantum Universe.* The University of North Carolina Press, 1992. Copyright © 1992 by The University of North Carolina Press. All rights reserved. Used by permission of the publisher.

The City and Literature

INTRODUCTION

Literary depictions of urban areas range from the painstakingly detailed descriptions of Dublin in James Joyce's *Ulysses* to the bleak cityscapes of the post-apocalyptic futurist scenarios of H. G. Wells, Philip K. Dick, and Samuel Delany. As humanity increasingly became more urbanized, the image writers portrayed of its cities became more diverse. A contemporary of King Henry VIII, Sir Thomas More created *Utopia*, an idealized, fictional island country that is centered around the capital of Amaurote, with fifty-four cities of equal size each containing approximately six thousand homes. Samuel Pepys's diary details London during the plague years and the Great Fire of 1666. The English Romantic movement began a literary tradition of disparaging the city. Such poets as William Blake wrote that the increased industrialization of the cities served to degrade its inhabitants. The Industrial Revolution in England, France, and the United States spurred writers to write of the inhumane living conditions in the countries' capitals. In *Walden* American Transcendentalist writer Henry David Thoreau wrote of how the effects of urban living crush the spirit. During the late nineteenth and early twentieth centuries, such writers as Theodore Dreiser and Stephen Crane wrote about the city as a malevolent force toward their protagonists. Modernist, existentialist, and postmodernist writers of the twentieth century continued to depict the city as an usurper of the human spirit that inherently destroys humanity's essence.

REPRESENTATIVE WORKS*

S. Y. Agnon
  Sippur Pashut 1935
Horatio Alger
  Helen Ford 1866
  Ragged Dick; or, Street Life in New York with the Bootblacks 1868
Nelson Algren
  The Neon Wilderness (short stories) 1947
  The Man with the Golden Arm 1950
Sherwood Anderson
  Dark Laughter 1925
Sholem Asch
  East River 1946
Paul Auster
  City of Glass 1985
  Ghosts 1986
  The Locked Room 1986

Donald Barthelme
  City Life (short stories) 1970
Saul Bellow
  The Victim 1947
  The Adventures of Augie March 1953
Leonard Bishop
  Down All Your Streets 1952
  Days of My Love 1953
Thomas Boyd
  In Time of Peace 1935
Charles Brockden Brown
  Arthur Mervyn 1800
Claude Brown
  Manchild in the Promised Land 1965
Eugene Brown
  Trespass 1952
William Burroughs
  Naked Lunch 1959
Abraham Cahan
  Yekl: A Tale of the New York Ghetto 1896
Italo Calvino
  Invisible Cities 1972
Albert Camus
  The Plague 1947
Winston Churchill
  The Dwelling-Place of Light 1917
Stephen Crane
  Maggie: A Girl of the Streets 1896
Edward Dahlberg
  Bottom Dogs 1930
Marcia Davenport
  East Side, West Side 1947
Samuel Delany
  The Towers of Toron 1964
  City of a Thousand Suns 1965
Floyd Dell
  The Briary Bush 1921
Henry Denker
  My Son, the Lawyer 1950
Thomas Disch
  334 1976
John Dos Passos
  One Man's Initiation—1917 1920
  Three Soldiers 1921
  Streets of Night 1923
  Manhattan Transfer 1925
  The 42nd Parallel 1930
  1919 1932
  The Big Money 1936
  Adventures of a Young Man 1939
Theodore Dreiser
  Sister Carrie 1900
  The Financier 1912
  An American Tragedy 1925

Ralph Ellison
  The Invisible Man 1952
James T. Farrell
  Studs Lonigan 1935
  No Star Is Lost 1938
Edna Ferber
  Nobody's in Town 1939
Nat Ferber
  New York: A Novel 1929
Rudolf Fisher
  The Walls of Jericho 1928
F. Scott Fitzgerald
  This Side of Paradise 1920
  The Beautiful and Damned 1922
  The Great Gatsby 1925
Waldo Frank
  City Block 1922
Henry B. Fuller
  The Cliff Dwellers 1893
Albert Halper
  Union Square 1943
Thomas Hardy
  Desperate Remedies 1871
  A Pair of Blue Eyes 1873
  Jude the Obscure 1896
Joseph Heller
  Catch 22 1961
Robert Herrick
  A Life for a Life 1910
William Dean Howells
  A Hazard of New Fortunes 1889
Evan Hunter
  Blackboard Jungle 1954
Fanny Hurst
  Mannequin 1926
Henry James
  The Bostonians 1886
  The American Scene 1907
James Joyce
  Dubliners (short stories) 1914
  Ulysses 1922
MacKinlay Kantor
  Diversity 1928
Day Kellogg Lee
  The Master Builder 1852
Meyer Levin
  The Old Bunch 1937
Sinclair Lewis
  Main Street 1920
  Babbitt 1922
Andre Malraux
  The Human Condition 1933
Thomas Mann
  Death in Venice 1912
Claude McKay
  Home to Harlem 1928
  A Long Way from Home 1937
Henry Miller
  Tropic of Cancer 1934
  Black Spring 1936
  Tropic of Capricorn 1939
Frederic Morton
  Asphalt and Desire 1952

Willard Motley
  Knock on Any Door 1947
Frank Norris
  McTeague 1899
John O'Hara
  Butterfield 8 1935
Marge Piercy
  Woman on the Edge of Time 1976
Ann Petry
  The Street 1946
Ernest Poole
  The Voice of the Street 1906
Thomas Pynchon
  The Crying of Lot 49 1966
Elmer Rice
  Imperial City 1937
Dorothy Richardson
  *The Long Day: The Story of a New York Working Girl
    as Told by Herself* 1905
Rainer Maria Rilke
  Malte Laurids Brigge 1924
Ethel Rosenberg
  Go Fight City Hall 1946
J. D. Salinger
  The Catcher in the Rye 1951
Irving Schulman
  The Amboy Dukes 1947
Upton Sinclair
  The Jungle 1906
  The Metropolis 1908
Tess Slesinger
  The Unpossessed 1934
Betty Smith
  A Tree Grows in Brooklyn 1943
Bayard Taylor
  John Godfrey's Fortunes 1864
Wallace Thurman
  The Blacker the Berry 1929
Carl Van Vechten
  Nigger Heaven 1926
Edith Wharton
  The House of Mirth 1905
  The Age of Innocence 1920
Thomas Wolfe
  You Can't Go Home Again 1940
Herman Wouk
  City Boy 1952
Richard Wright
  Native Son 1940
  The Outsider 1953
  Lawd Today 1963

*All works are novels unless otherwise noted.

OVERVIEWS

Ihab Hassan

SOURCE: "Cities of Mind, Urban Words," in *Rumors of Change: Essays of Five Decades,* University of Alabama Press, 1995, pp. 68-84.

[In the following excerpt, originally written in 1981, Hassan discusses depictions of urban life from Plato to Samuel Delany.]

> *The city is a fact in nature, like a cave, a run of mackerel or an ant-heap. But it is also a conscious work of art, and it holds within its communal framework many simpler and more personal forms of art. Mind takes form in the city; and in turn, urban forms condition mind. . . . With language itself, [the city] remains man's greatest work of art.*

—*Lewis Mumford*

> *With cities, it is as with dreams: everything imaginable can be dreamed, but even the most unexpected dream is a rebus that conceals a desire or, its reverse, a fear. Cities, like dreams, are made of desire and fears, even if the thread of their discourse is secret, their rules are absurd, their perspectives deceitful, and everything conceals something else.*

—*Italo Calvino*

> *Our language can be seen as an ancient city: a maze of little streets and squares, of old and new houses, and of houses with additions from various periods; and this surrounded by a multitude of new boroughs with straight regular streets and uniform houses.*

—*Ludwig Wittgenstein*

I

The city: grime, glamour, geometries of glass, steel, and concrete. Intractable, it rises from nature, like proud Babel, only to lie athwart our will, astride our being, or so it often seems. Yet immanent in that gritty structure is another: invisible, imaginary, made of dream and desire, agent of all our transformations. I want here to invoke that other city, less city perhaps than inscape of mind, rendered in that supreme fiction we call language. Immaterial, that city in-formed history from the start, molding human space and time ever since time and space molded themselves to the wagging tongue.

And so to commence, I shall tersely review the founding of that ideal city, which even the naturalist tradition in American fiction—from Frank Norris, Upton Sinclair, Theodore Dreiser, through James Farrell, Henry Roth, Nelson Algren, to Willard Motley, Hubert Selby, and John Rechy—failed to make into mortar and stone. I shall regard it as concept, project, field, a magic lantern through which the human condition may be viewed. Next, I shall consider some examples of fiction, largely postwar, uniquely American, omitting, alas, both international trends and historical antecedents. Last, from this special perspective, I shall assay some in-conclusion, which my brief scope must make even briefer.

II

In its earliest representations, the city—Ur, Nineveh, Thebes, or that heaven-defying heap turned into verbal rubble that we call Babel—symbolized the place where divine powers entered human space. The sky gods came, and where they touched the earth, kings and heroes rose to overwhelm old village superstitions and build a city. As Lewis Mumford says: "All eyes now turned skywards. . . . Those who made the most of the city were not chagrined by the animal limitations of human existence: they sought deliberately, by a concentrated act of will, to transcend them." And so they did, with language, "with glyphs, ideograms, and script, with the first abstractions of number and verbal signs." All cities, it seems, are sacred, symbolic, heavenly at their origin, made of unconscious promptings as they grow into mind, made of mind that grows into purer mind through the power of language.

Thus the dematerializing metropolis coincides with the first temple or palace stone and dimly evokes, farther back, the burial mound, around which village life fearfully gathered. The "twin cities," biopolis and necropolis, stand for the visible and invisible demesnes that all human endeavor, however profane, assumes. Arnold Toynbee, we recall, thought that cities helped to "etherialize" history. But etherialization, as Mumford knows, carries also its counterpoint—"The rhythm of life in cities seems to be an alternation between materialization and etherialization: the concrete structure, detaching itself through a human response, takes on a symbolic meaning, uniting the knower and the known; while subjective images, ideals, intuitions . . . likewise take on material attributes. . . . City design is thus the culminating point of a socially adequate process of materialization."

Yet as the universe became conscious of itself in Homo sapiens, so do we now reflect upon the city through abstractions the city itself generates. To see a city whole is also to apprehend its theoretical nature, its hidden functions and ideal forms. For the city acts as mediator between the human and natural orders, as a changing network of social relations, as a flux of production and consumption, as a labyrinth of solitudes, as a system of covert controls, semiotic exchanges, perpetual barter, and, withal, as an incipient force of planetization. In short, at once fluid and formal, the city apprehends us in its vital grid.

Modern theoreticians of the city variously recognize this aspect of its character. Max Weber, for instance, conceives the city not as a large aggregate of dwellings but as a complex "autocephalic" system of self-maintaining forces, while Robert E. Park, founder of urban "ecological" sociology in America, describes it as "a state of mind, a body of customs and traditions, and of organized attitudes and sentiments." Practical and streetwise, Jane Jacobs still insists that the "ubiquitous principle" of cities is their need "for a most intricate and close-grained diversity of uses that give each other a constant mutual support," a need that dishonest city planning invariably conceals. Raymond Williams, though historically alert to the forces of production and consumption in the city, also perceives it as a "form of shared consciousness rather than merely a set of techniques," about which everything "from the magnificent to the apocalyptic—can be believed at once."

As for Marshall McLuhan, we know his theme: the old metropolitan space must eventually dissolve into electric information, a "total field of inclusive awareness." Similarly, Charles Jencks considers the urban environment as a communicating system, a cybernetic or semiotic mesh; hence the efforts of such architects as Nicholas Negroponte to use computers (URBAN 5) in designing cities. Finally, stretching the cybernetic metaphor to its limit, Paolo Soleri speculates that in "the urban organism, the mind remains in independent but correlated parcels divided spatially and coincidental with the parceled brains, the whole forming the mental or thinking skin of the city." His "arcology" presages no less than the passage from matter to spirit.

Such visions may seem intolerably angelic to citizens inured to the diabolic occulsions and exigencies of the modern metropolis. Yet the city remains an alembic of human time, perhaps of human nature—an alembic, to be sure, employed less often by master alchemists than by sorcerer's apprentices. Still, as a frame of choices and possibilities, the city enacts our sense of the future; not merely abstract, not mutable only, it fulfills time in utopic or dystopic images. This expectation strikes some thinkers as peculiarly American. Nearly half a century ago, Jean-Paul Sartre remarked, "For [Europeans], a city is, above all, a past; for [Americans], it is mainly a future; what they like in the city is everything it has not yet become and everything it can be." But Sartre was never the most reliable observer of America, and what he perceives as an American impatience merely avows the city's own high-handedness with history.

Utopia, dystopia, futuropolis: these cities of mind have occupied a space in the Western imagination since Plato's republic. In Christian times, the city of God, the heavenly city, even the medieval church triumphant, became structures of a pervasive spiritual energy whose absence in nether regions suffered the infernal city to rise. (Pieter Brueghel's paintings of Babel attest to this doubleness in their equivocation between heaven and hell.) But the great architects of the Italian Renaissance (Filippo Brunelleschi, Rafael Alberti, Bramante, and Leonardo da Vinci), its painters (notably Ambrogio Lorenzetti, Piero della Francesca, and Francesco di Giorgio), and its authors (especially Tommaso Campanella in *City of the Sun*) turned to the dream of reason; circular or square, radial or polygonal, their urban visions revealed logic, will, clarity, purest tyranny of the eye.

English utopian writers, like Sir Thomas More and Francis Bacon, also implicated their utopic concepts into urban space. So did, later, the pictorial architects of the eighteenth century, Etienne-Louis Boullée and Claude Nicholas Ledoux, the nineteenth-century planners of Garden City, inspired by Ebenezer Howard, and those eccentric designers of the early twentieth century, Tony Garnier and Antonio Sant' Elia, who ushered in the austere shapes of futurism and constructivism, of the Bauhaus and Le Corbusier. Closer to our time still, "plug-in cities" of Archigram illustrate the immanent structuralist principle; Buckminster Fuller's geodesic forms enclose us all in nearly invisible technology; and Constantinos Doxiadis's "entopias" offer blueprints of "the city of dreams that can come true." Abstract urbs all, bright geometries of desire, they share with Disneyland and Disney World—indubitably our two most solvent cities—a commitment to effective fantasy.

Yet as Jane Jacobs warns: "Designing a dream city is easy; rebuilding a living one takes imagination." Since our cities seem still to beggar the imagination of planners, our urban afflictions persistently defy our sense of a feasible future. Thus, dystopia becomes a synonym of megalopolis. Disneyland will not rescind Harlem, and against the visions of Soleri, Doxiadis, or Fuller, those of Fritz Lang in *Metropolis* or of Jean-Luc Godard in *Alphaville* may yet prevail. Writers and illustrators of speculative fiction certainly continue to envisage island cities in space—mobile, radiant, noetic, all Ariel and no Caliban, communicating with each other and the universe by means of unique mental powers. Yet these mind-cities yield, in darker speculations, to vast conurbations of discorporate brains, floating in innumerable cubicles, ruled all by a sublime computer or despot brain. Here time and space, transcended by mind, betray the ultimate terror of dematerialization—complete control.

III

I have not strayed altogether from my subject, the city in fiction; I have tried rather to perceive it from a certain angle that reveals the city as a fiction composing many fictions. Baudelaire, perhaps first among moderns, knew this well enough, though some might claim for Restif de la Bretonne or Eugène Sue earlier knowledge of nocturnal streets. Baudelaire, at any rate, allegorized Paris in various poems; one in particular, "Les Sept Vieillards," found an echo in T. S. Eliot's poem about another "unreal city":

> Fourmillante cité, cité pleine de rêves,
> Où le spectre en plein jour raccroche le passant!
> Les mystères partout coulent comme des sèves.

This spectral note pervades, in diverse timbres, all modern as well as postmodern literature—fiction, poetry, or drama, naturalist, symbolist, or absurd. Certainly, the city as a formal dream or internal shape of consciousness emerges in fiction before the postwar period. Marcel Proust's Paris, James Joyce's Dublin, Alfred Döblin's Berlin, Robert Musil's Vienna, the London of Virginia Woolf, the Manhattan of John Dos Passos, Henry Miller's Brooklyn, and Nathanael West's Los Angeles attest to a longer historical view. Perhaps I can make the point by adverting to the last two.

In *Black Spring* (1963), Miller declares himself a patriot of the fourteenth ward, where he was raised, to which he continually returns "as a paranoiac returns to his obsessions":

> We live in the mind, in ideas, in fragments. We no longer drink in the wild outer music of the streets— we remember only. . . . Here there is buried legend after legend of youth and melancholy, of savage nights and mysterious bosoms dancing on the wet mirror of the pavement, of women chuckling softly as they scratch themselves, of wild sailors' shouts, of long queues standing in the lobby, of boats brushing each other in the fog and tugs snorting furiously against the rush of tide. . . .

> The plasm of the dream is the pain of separation. The dream lives on after the body is buried.

After the city vanishes too, one might add. For Miller really dissolves the city into his emotions, into remembrances more vivid than the city ever was, splashing his words on the page as Jackson Pollock threw colors on a canvas, exorcising his death in images drenched in nostalgia. Sensations, perceptions, observances of the city thus obey, in the fourteenth ward, the imperative of his soft need.

The absorption or ingestion of the object—a whole borough here—typifies the romantic sensibility. But Miller could suddenly exchange the romantic egoist for the selfless cosmologist, perhaps no less romantic. Thus, in the surrealist section of *Black Spring* entitled "Megalopolitan Maniac," he collapses the city not into the self but into the universe: "The city is loveliest when the sweet death racket begins. Her own life lived in defiance of nature, her electricity, her frigidaires, her soundproof walls. Box within box she rears her dry walls, the glint of lacquered nails, the plumes that wave across the corrugated sky. Here in the coffin depths grow the everlasting flowers sent by telegraph. . . . This is the city, and this the music. Out of the little black boxes an unending river of romance in which the crocodiles weep. All walking toward the mountain top. All in step. From the power house above God floods the street with music. It is God who turns the music on every evening just as we quit work."

The city as self, the city as cosmos: thus Miller draws the far limits of urban conceptualization. Nathanael West, however, conceptualizes the city with cooler art: in *The Day of the Locusts* (1939), Los Angeles finds its consummation in a painting that Tod Hackett wants to create. West—employing throughout various devices of style and impersonal narration to distance himself from the lunatic scene—ends his novel with a vision of chaos within another vision of chaos, rendered in the very act of experiencing that chaos amid the crowds assaulting Kahn's Persian Palace Theatre. Here is the passage depicting Andrews's apocalypse within apocalypse:

> Despite the agony in his leg, he was able to think clearly about his picture, "The Burning of Los Angeles." After his quarrel with Faye, he had worked on it continually to escape tormenting himself, and the way to it in his mind had become almost automatic.

> As he stood on his good leg, clinging desperately to the iron rail, he could see all the rough charcoal strokes with which he had blocked it out on the big canvas.

A description of the fiery and phantasmic picture ensues, as Andrews imagines himself at work on his painting. Thus, West gives us in his novel the work of art that Andrews fails to complete. Can this mean that Hollywood, city of dreams, lends itself to our apprehension only as another kind of dream (the painting) within still another form of art or dream (West's fiction)? The question offends our sense of the real. Yet how different, finally, does Hollywood seem from all those modern cities that drive us to fictions of survival amidst their desperate confusions?

IV

The modern city compels certain idealizations of its orders or disorders. Moreover, all art selects, abstracts, and so must further conceptualize its objects, dense or ethereal. The great naturalists, I suspect, knew this subliminally, as did symbolists and modernists to a fuller degree. In the postwar period, however, fabulism, irrealism, absurdism abet the conceptual tendency further. I have no leisure here to survey the entire fictional landscape; nor should I endeavor to do so, since the urban element in many novels seems sometimes extraneous. In certain works, though, urban setting and fictive form are inseverable. I cite—all too cursorily, I fear—two early examples: Ralph Ellison's *Invisible Man* (1952) and Saul Bellow's *The Adventures of Augie March* (1953).

Ellison's novel transmutes Harlem into a dance of characters, a music of ideas and illusions; realism and surrealism here are seamless. Thus, the protagonist always moves between an act and its shadow: "I leaped aside, into the street, and there was a sudden and brilliant suspension of time, like the last ax stroke and the felling of a tall tree." All New York becomes the image, the sound, the very texture of a dramatic theme, and the coal cellar, in which Invisible Man at last confronts his invisibility, burns with an ironic intelligence more luminous than the 1369 light bulbs improbably affixed to its ceiling. Similarly, Bellow's Chicago shapes Augie's high call to freedom, his quest for the fabled "axial lines." Deadly, fluent like money, omnific like love, the city becomes the very form of American experience in midcentury. And when Augie wonders in a dejected moment if cities, once cradles of civilization, can ever become wholly barren of it, he thus refutes himself: "An inhuman thing, if possible, to have so many people together who beget nothing on one another. No, but it is not possible, and the dreary begets its own fire, and so this never happens."

To the classic fictions of Ellison and Bellow one may add others that variously render or vivify the American city.

But I should turn now to another kind of novel, more shadowy in its urban inscapes, more cunning. I allude to William Burroughs's *Naked Lunch* (1959), Thomas Pynchon's *The Crying of Lot 49* (1966), and Donald Barthelme's *City Life* (1970).

In Burroughs's entropic world, whether earthly or galactic, the city becomes a machine for dying. Fueled on sex, junk, and money, this infernal machine invariably regulates, violates, exterminates; in short, it both controls and negates, relying on the calculus of absolute human need. The need, beyond eroticism, is for forgetfulness, a final lubricity. This lubricity, in the metabolism of the addict, aspires to "Absolute ZERO." But if Burroughs's spectral city finds its center in the human body, locus of desire and decay, it meets its circumference in language. Death enters the erotic body and spreads through the body politic carried by the virus Word. Hence the cure: Rub Out the Word! Or if it proves impractical, then let the word, testifying against the world, testify also against itself. Cut up, desiccated, phantasmagoric, Burroughs's language reaches heights of savage poetry, grisly humor, metaphysical outrage, grotesque conceit, yet must finally expend itself, as the city must, in prophetic waste. Thus *Naked Lunch* attempts to become itself the feculent city, an expanse of shameful words, deeds, deaths, dreams. The shame of cities? It is of existence itself.

Pynchon, another wizard of words and waste, offers, in *The Crying of Lot 49,* a city ruled by the expectation of WASTE (We Await Silent Tristero's Empire) and DEATH ("Don't Ever Antagonize The Horn"). His Los Angeles, indeed the whole of urban California if not of the United States, seems a lunatic semiotic system, both immanent and indeterminate, the breath of some universal paranoia. The mystery that Oedipa Maas pursues through the labyrinths of signs remains a mystery; for self and society in America have dissolved into these same esoteric signs— hieroglyphs of concealed meaning or meaninglessness (we never know which).

Still, though entropy affects the physical, the social, the linguistic universes—pace Maxwell's demon—the mind insists on weaving and unweaving patterns, creating and decreating fictions, including Pynchon's own. Consider these communicative devices the author devises to guide or misguide his heroine through the book: a cryptic will, stamp collections, the mails, telephone, television, radio, graffiti and drawings, plays, movies, lapel buttons, wrecked cars, hallucinogens, maps, transistor circuits, motel signs, rock music, inaudible voice frequencies, striptease shows, impressions on a dirty mattress, footnotes, forged editions, doodles, puns, typographic errors, sign languages, children's games, tapes, armbands, bullet shots, epileptic fits, sex, silence, and so forth. Semiosis unending: can we wonder that the city, that all existence, turns for Oedipa into a cryptogram? Here she muses the nature of language: "Behind the initials was a metaphor, a delirium tremens, a trembling unfurrowing of the mind's plowshare. The saint whose water can light lamps, the clairvoyant whose lapse in recall is the breath of God, the

true paranoid for whom all is organized in spheres joyful or threatening about the central pulse of himself, the dreamer whose puns probe ancient fetid shafts and tunnels of truth all act in the same special relevance to the word, or whatever it is the word is there, buffering, to protect us from. The act of metaphor then was a thrust at truth and a lie, depending where you were: inside, safe, or outside, lost. Oedipa did not know where she was."

The world, the city, the book: all promise some hierophany, always deferred. But is a malignant Logos or the encapsulated human self here at fault? Locked in an imaginary tower, Oedipa once dreams of letting her hair down to serve as ladder for another, only to discover that her hair is a wig. Narcissism, then, defines our city's limit, as in San Narciso. And the opposite of narcissism, which we call love, breaks through these limits and in so doing releases "the unnamable act, the recognition, the Word." In short, Pynchon's city of treacherous signs may stand in the void or hold some occult meaning that only love can yield. Or perhaps only the "unimaginable Pacific," the "hole left by the moon's tearing-free and monument to her exile," can redeem it. But which?

Burroughs's and Pynchon's are cities of entropy and mystery; Barthelme's, no less entropic or mysterious, is one of parody. *City Life,* of course, tells us nothing overtly about New York City. A collage of stories, a catena of fragments, it provides rather an experience of urban being, under the aspects of parody, pastiche, parataxis, under the aspect of the most delicate irony. The experience resists interpretation, battens on absurdity and irrelevance; and so we fasten on such words as *dreck, detritus, trash, waste,* and *sludge,* which Barthelme slyly supplies. "It's that we want to be on the leading edge of this trash phenomenon," he writes, "the everted sphere of the future, and that's why we pay particular attention, too, to those aspects of language that may be seen as a model of the trash phenomenon." And again: "We like books that have a lot of *dreck* in them, matter which presents itself as not wholly relevant (or indeed, at all relevant) but which, carefully attended to, can supply a kind of 'sense' of what is going on. This 'sense' is not be to obtained by reading between the lines (for there is nothing there, in those white spaces) but by reading the lines themselves." The dreck, sludge, or trash, may strike us as the unassimilable detritus of an urban mass civilization; yet they become available to us as epistemic units of city life, parodies of parodies—and parodies of parodies of parodies—that finally inhabit the mind as a unique mode of urban consciousness.

The transformation of dreck into mind is style in action. Barthelme's consummately ironic style employs catalogues, drawings, photographs, puns, vignettes, aphorisms, clichés, neologisms, jokes, innuendos, stutters, fragments, metafictions, non sequiturs, recondite allusions, odd juxtapositions, asides, absurd humor, and typographic horseplay, not only to defamiliarize his art but also to dematerialize his city. (Defamiliarization and dematerialization have been for nearly a century concomitants in various arts—cubist, surrealist, and abstract.) Above all, Barthelme's rhetoric of irony deconstructs, displaces, defers urban reality—to use three voguish terms—precisely because it declines to make it whole. The city, radically discontinuous, becomes a mental construct, reconstructed from verbal shards, sad, zany, or wise. As Barthelme remarked in an interview: "New York City is or can be regarded as a collage, as opposed to, say, a tribal village in which all the huts (or yurts, or whatever) are the same hut, duplicated. The point of collage is that unlike things are stuck together to make, in the best case, a new reality." This is more urbane than Ramona's urban statement near the end of *City Life*: "Ramona thought about the city.—I have to admit we are locked in the most exquisite mysterious muck. This muck heaves and palpitates. It is multidirectional and has a mayor. To describe it takes many hundreds of thousands of words. Our muck is only a part of a much greater muck—the nation-state—which is itself the creation of that muck of mucks, human consciousness. Of course all these things also have a touch of sublimity." And so the city, "dreck," "collage," or "palpitating muck," leads directly to the problem of the nation-state in the twentieth century and to "that muck of mucks, human consciousness"—touched with sublimity, of course.

v

The city conceived as a machine for dying (Burroughs), as a paranoiac semiotic system (Pynchon), and as mental dreck or palpitating muck (Barthelme), presumes on the novelist's freedom from verisimilitude. Such freedom becomes constitutive in a number of works that we may unabashedly call fantasy or science fiction.

Marge Piercy's *Woman on the Edge of Time* (1976) stands at the edge of this genre. Poised between three worlds—the desolate present, a utopic future, a dystopic alternative—the book refracts reality in the lens of several mental institutions; the madhouse becomes both metaphor and microcosm of the modern city, which ruthlessly exploits the poor, the powerless, and the deviant. At its core, Piercy's book seethes with poetic outrage, in the honored naturalist mode, threatening to explode its fantastic frame. Yet the frame holds because the present does contain all versions of its future; the modern city does enact the convulsions of its fate. Thus, the incarceration of Connie Ramos in Rockover Mental Hospital not only betrays the violence of our civilization; it further tests its potential for survival.

Connie communes mentally with two futures. One seems ideal, arcadian, impeccable in its advanced views of sex, race, ecology, technology, education, political life, yet earthy withal. The other looms like an urban nightmare of windowless skyscrapers, gray suns, fetid air, cyborg police, and unspeakable vulgarity. But the crucial insight of the novel identifies the war between these two possible futures with the actual war between Connie and her captors—that is, the struggle between two cities, one of human fulfillment, the other of inhuman deprivation. Here

is Connie's cry of pain: "Whoever owned this place, these cities, whoever owned those glittering glass office buildings in midtown filled with the purr of money turning over, those refineries over the river in Jersey with their flames licking the air, they gave nothing back. They took and took and left their garbage choking the air, the river, the sea itself. Choking her. A life of garbage. Human garbage."

Garbage (or dreck) this city really is not, but rather something more sinister: electroencephalic control through brain implants. Thus, the good doctor explains: "You see, we can electrically trigger almost every mood and emotion—the fight-or-flight reaction, euphoria, calm, pleasure, pain, terror! We can monitor and induce reactions through the microminiaturized radio under the skull."

The novel, as I have said, tells a tale of two cities. To their struggle—a struggle also between unborn futures, virtual worlds clashing in a crux of time—the novel can offer no denouement except the rage of Connie, her poisoned will to survive. Relentlessly ideological in parts—all the men, for instance, seem nasty or brutish—*Woman on the Edge of Time* still projects a powerful image of human courage and city madness. Barely removed from the present, it reveals us to ourselves all the more savagely in the urban mirror of our distortions.

Set only half a century hence, once more in New York, Thomas Disch's *334* (1976) also stands at the threshold of fantasy, revealing us to ourselves implacably. Again, life there seems so close to our own that we scarcely recognize it as alien. Yet violence and hebetude, garishness and despair, mingle easily in this crammed city of the imminent future; everything there seems a grotesque parody of our best hopes. Still, many characters—whether engaged in the cryonics black market or the no less deadening market of sex—strike us as vibrantly human, and their will to endure miraculously endures. As Lottie in Bellevue Hospital broods: "And anyhow the world doesn't end. Even though it may try to, even though you wish to hell it would—it can't. There's always some poorjerk who thinks he needs something he hasn't got, and there goes five years, ten years getting it." The same Lottie, however, in the same year, 2026, says: "The end of the world. Let me tell you about the end of the world. It happened fifty years ago. Maybe a hundred. And since then it's been lovely."

Indeed, the dominant structures and metaphors of the work suggest both perplexity and decadence. Composed of interrelated fragments, vignettes, tableaus, the book is a labyrinth of miseries—smog, lupus, television, eugenics, overcrowding, sadomasochism, artificial foods—each preternaturally vivid, all absurd. Centered on a dismal building at 344 East Eleventh Street, the various families accept historical decline within their spatial frame. Thus the titular number 334 evokes an address as well as the imaginary "birthdate" of Alexa, a character in the section called "Everyday Life in the Later Roman Empire"; her imaginary "death" in 410, the year Alaric sacked Rome, terminates her "alternate historical existence" under the influence of a drug, Morbihanine. And so Alexa dreams of bloody ritual sacrifices at the Metropolitan Museum and wakes to wonder, in Spenglerian gloom, if civilization still warrants the human effort. Clearly, the city of Disch, Pynchonesque, emanates a subtle insanity: ourselves.

This theme is brilliantly prefigured in Samuel Delany's trilogy, *The Fall of the Towers* (1977), which includes *Captives of the Flame* (1963), *The Towers of Toron* (1964), and *City of a Thousand Suns* (1965). The city here, at last, realizes its fabulous potential; it emerges as a cosmic frame of mind, an extension of intelligences both terrestrial and extraterrestrial. In fact, the trilogy contains not one but many cities. There is, first, silent Telphar, deserted, with spires and high looping roadways, ruled by a "psychotic" computer, symbolizing mind turned against itself, symbolizing death. There is, next, the island capital, Toron, like "a black gloved hand, ringed with myriad diamonds, amethysts by the score, turquoises, rubies," rising with its towers "above the midnight horizon, each jewel with its internal flame," yet all too human, with kings, ministers, tycoons, circuses, rabble, a city conspiring against itself in a wholly imaginary war that projects its own civic corruptions until all its towers come tumbling down.

There is also that rough, utopic City of a Thousand Suns, salvaged by malcontents from death and rubble, rooted in earth, reaching beyond its forest clearing for the stars. Then, halfway across the universe, there is a nameless city, provisional home of the Triple Being, built twelve million years ago by a vanished civilization yet so made as to continue recreating itself into time. As the Triple Being, supernal spirit, explains: *"The city responds to the psychic pressures of those near, building itself according to the plans, methods, and techniques of whatever minds press it into activity."*

In that city, beneath a double sun immeasurably distant from our own, a conference of sentient beings convenes. Delany depicts the scene marvelously. He begins, "What is a city?" and the conferees begin thus to answer, each according to its nature: "To one group at the meeting, immense thirty-foot worms, the city seemed a web of muddy tunnels and the words came as vibrations through their hides. . . . A metallic cyst received the words telepathically; for him the city was an airless, pitted siding of rock. . . . To the fifty-foot eyestalks of one listener the atmosphere of the city was tinged methane green. . . . To one living crystal in the city the words of the Triple Being came as a significant progression of musical chords. . . . A sentient cactus shifted its tentacles and beheld the city almost as it was in reality, a stretch of pastel sand; but, then, who can say what was the reality of the city." And so it continues, while the Triple Being unfolds the cosmic conflict centered now on cities of the Earth, a conflict of men engaged in phantasmic wars against themselves, which hence attract the Lord of the Flames: a roaming, curious, amoral force in the universe, negative by human reckoning, strange by the reckoning of all.

But I risk to make trite the exuberant inventions of Delany's work, which raises the question of the city radically—that is, at an imaginative limit. What is upolis? The good city eschews inversions of the (human) will and turns randomness not into uniformity but choice. "It is a place where the time passes as something other than time"; and the one and the many attain to a harmony that only time can yield. More empathic than telepathic—for Delany's characters know that communicating minds can jar and clash and still remain isolated—the good city grants its citizens time to touch, "experience and perception weighed against experience and perception, the music their minds made free in the double sound of their names." No wonder then that even the Lord of the Flames finds something to learn on bungling Earth. Though collective in his consciousness, dispersive in his influence, reversed in his polarities of love and death, matter and antimatter, this everted intergalactic creature realizes at last his kinship with creation.

Again, what is Delany's upolis? Both arcadian and utopian, in time and also out of it, at once cosmic, social, and personal, material as well as immaterial, founded on work and boundless in mind, concrete no less than universal, this city, unfinished, absorbs cosmic randomness into the ever-widening circles of its awareness, which may also be called—however shyly—love.

VI

Given the human propensity for endings, what may we conclude about the city, fiction, or the city in fiction? Nothing conclusive, I fear.

Fiction and the city have been complicit, if not from the rise of Babel, then since Picaresque and bildungsroman. In these early genres, the novel often portrayed the innocent young man from the country come to experience urban sins and pleasures. In so doing, the novel recovered an ancient debate between nature and civilization, arcadia and polis, earth and fire, two mythic modes of human being in the world that still strain the sensibilities of our ironic age. It is as if the original sin of race were not only disobedient knowledge (Adam and Eve in the garden) but also disobedient artifice (Prometheus and his fire, Daedalus and his maze, the babbling builders of Babel).

I insist on this old complicity of language, knowledge, and artifice because I believe that it constitutes the central archetype of the city, its ambiguous gnosis. For the city has always been a crime against nature, against the pleromatic condition of some fabled disalienation, and it remains the crime that consciousness itself perpetrates, perpetuates, against creation. Mythically, then, and prophetically too, the city is less city than a moment in that human project realized by mind, a mind, as Friedrich Nietzsche knew, that can think only in fictions, a mind, as so many modern gnostics think, seeking ever-wider—and more problematic—expression of itself in the universe. Hence, the dematerialization of metropolis, often associated with the emergence of extraordinary human powers, finally depends on psychic even more than technic resources.

Such dematerialization, though, can prove horrendous, as the examples of Rotterdam, Coventry, Dresden, Hiroshima—of Auschwitz and Gulag and all those other cities of night in our land, including Watts—have shown. Can we wonder that the city has become another name for bedlam, slum, prison camp, asphalt jungle, every kind of dystopia we know? Certainly, the contemporary novel provides no reassurance on this score; with rare exceptions, the city in fiction embodies an imagination of disaster, which, as Susan Sontag remarked of science fiction films, responds to "seemingly opposed destinies: unremitting banality and inconceivable terror." Far richer in response to these threats than celluloid, the novel still admits no bright and exacting vision, no luminous trope.

Perhaps our dreams themselves have lost the edge of hope. For the city is itself desire, as I have persistently argued, as well as trope. But perhaps, also, history has begun to veer from the city, swerve. Oswald Spengler, we recall, thought that although world history was the history of cities, a time came at the end of a civilization when, "empty receptacles of an extinguished soul," these doomed world-cities would move on "to final self-destruction." Yet our destiny need not hinge on such dubious exercises in cyclicism and gloom. The city may simply cede the initiative to another organization of human energies, another definition or disposition of what we have hitherto called civilization, and so open new vistas for our earth. Here is Kenneth Boulding's roseate vision: "We may very well ask ourselves, therefore, whether we visualize a period in the not very distant future when in postcivilized societies, the city will really have disappeared altogether as an entity. We can even visualize a society in which the population is spread very evenly over the world in almost self-sufficient households . . . each basking in the security of an invisible and cybernetic world state in which each man shall live under his vine and his own fig tree and none shall make him afraid."

Yet the time is neither dusk nor dawn in the West but the present. We stand as ever between history and hope. And standing there I perceive the postmodern city as a place of ecumenism, open to the universe. Nervous, mindful, turbulent, it intensifies alienation as well as planetization. The process derives from no mystic doctrine or Teilhardian intuition but rather from human interactions that Ralph Waldo Emerson presaged more than a century ago: "Our civilization and these ideas," he observed, "are reducing the earth to a brain. See how by telegraph and steam the earth is anthropolized." Such reductions of the earth seem, at times, to threaten us with homogeneity if not baleful constraints. But the city is variousness itself inscribed in steel and stone. Terrorism and totalitarianism in it are but extreme revisions of the one and the many, neither of which we can ignore. Thus, we distrust utopic uniformity precisely because each of

us needs to quicken the city with some image of his or her dream. Happy Babel: immaterial in its languages, diverse in its desires, projected to some end still obscure to us that yet menaces the gods.

THE CITY IN AMERICAN LITERATURE

Blanche Housman Gelfant

SOURCE: "The City Novel as Literary Genre," in *The American City Novel,* University of Oklahoma Press, 1954, pp. 3-24.

[*In the following essay, Gelfant traces the development of the modern American urban novel as a distinct literary form.*]

INTENTION

In Ben Hecht's *A Thousand and One Afternoons in Chicago,* a newspaperman dreams of writing a great novel about the American city. He wants to discover the inmost and essential meaning of city life so that his novel can say definitively: "The city is so and so. Everyone feels this and this. No matter who they are or where they live, or what their jobs are they can't escape the mark of the city that is on them."[1] While the newspaperman is a thin, sentimentalized character, the literary impulse he is expressing is a real and urgent one: for out of the desire to define the city and reveal its essential "mark" upon its people the twentieth-century American novel has developed as a generic literary form. Behind the rise of the modern city novel has been the awareness—always growing stronger and more clearly articulated—that city life is distinctive and that it offers the writer peculiarly modern material and demands of him literary expression in a modern idiom. As a shaping influence upon the modern American literary mind, the city has made its impression not only as a physical place but more important as a characteristic and unique way of life. In order to give literary expression to this way of life—to re-create its tensions and tempos, its institutional patterns, its economic structure, its system of tenuous and yet complex social relationships, its manners and moral temper, its breathless, sometimes stultifying, atmosphere, its immediate daily routines and mechanized monotony, and its total impact upon the mind, imagination, and spirit—the American novelist has drawn upon the methods of European and English writers. But his social vision and emotional complex, which are the intrinsic material of his art, derive from an experience of American life. This experience has developed an awareness of the distinctive qualities of the American city as a modern creation of industrialism, a melting pot, still inchoate and lacking in the rich historical and emotional associations that the centuries have built up about a London or Paris. Central to the city writer's interest in the distinctiveness, the American-ness, and urgent modernity of a Chicago or New York is his concern over the personal impact of urban life. His fundamental intention, phrased by Hecht's character, is to show what the American city is by revealing how it creates and definitively marks the people living in it.

This intention is realized within the novel as the city becomes a key actor in a human drama. It participates in the action as a *physical place,* which makes a distinctive impression upon the mind and senses; as an *atmosphere,* which affects the emotions; and as a total *way of life*— a set of values and manners and a frame of mind—which molds character and destiny. In Robert Herrick's *A Life for a Life,* there is an explicit, if rather dramatic, statement of the shaping influence of the city: "The City was man! And already it was sowing its seed in the heart of the youth, this night. It was moulding him as it moulds the millions, after its fashion, warming his blood with desire,—the vast, resounding, gleaming City. . . . "[2]

Usually the city plays the role of antagonist. It exists as the obstacle to the fulfillment of the hero's desires, while, ironically, it may promote and encourage them. Sometimes it may itself be protagonist, emerging in such novels as John Dos Passos' *Manhattan Transfer* and Elmer Rice's *Imperial City* as a vital personality with an identity and life of its own, distinct from that of its people.

This active participation of the city in shaping character and plot distinguishes the city novel from what might be called urban local color fiction. In a local color city novel, the characters act against a static urban setting that is not the vital and necessary condition for their acts. The substitution of another backdrop might alter details within the novel but not the essential patterns of plot, characterization, theme, and language. An O. Henry short story, "The Defeat of the City," amusingly dramatizes the difference between the intrinsic and the spurious urban product.[3] (O. Henry, incidentally, for all the unwarranted praise that the social historian Henry Steele Commager[4] has given him as the authentic American city writer, is an excellent example of the writer exploiting urban material primarily for local color.) The hero of this story has come to New York from an upstate farm and has been transformed by the city: New York has "remodelled, cut, trimmed and stamped him to the pattern it approves."[5] When he visits the farm, however, he is overcome by a "rural atavism": he tears off his stylish clothes, wrestles buffoonishly, strums an old banjo, dances the buck-and-wing, and becomes so completely the "yokel" that no trace is left of "the immaculate Robert Walmsley, courted clubman and ornament of select circles." He stands unmasked as a "peasant gambolling indecorously in the valley"—this is his real self. Now, just as Walmsley seemed to be a real urbanite because he displayed the clothes and manners of the city man, so local color city fiction seems to be authentic urban literature because it uses urban settings and dialects; but this urban paraphernalia does not create city fiction, just as Walmsley's clothes did not create a New Yorker. The ruling theme of O. Henry's work, for example, is the

irony of coincidences, which do not depend for their occurrence upon a particular locale; in *The Four Million* and *The Voice of the City,* the coincidences only happen to occur in New York.

Unlike a local color writer, the city novelist sees urban life as an organic whole, and he expresses a coherent, organized, and total vision of the city. As he is not concerned simply with details of local color, he is also not concerned only with the anecdotal value of city incidents (as O. Henry is in his stories). In creating a unified impression, he uses particularized incidents as a means of arriving at underlying truths about city life. He offers an interpretation and a judgment of the city—a way of seeing and evaluating it as an ordered pattern of experiences consistent with the inner principles of its being. While the interpretation inheres in the total formal structure of the novel, the experiences that develop and comment upon the meaning of city life are contained in the episode.

The death of little Arty in Farrell's *No Star is Lost* is a case in point. When little Arty becomes ill, the O'Neills call Dr. Geraghty, but even though the doctor realizes that the child has diphtheria, he refuses to care for him. Arty dies; but the children at the O'Flahertys', given careful medical attention, quickly recover. The episodes dealing with Arty's illness and death have suspense and human interest. But while each episode is a link in the narrative structure, it serves also as an instrument of social commentary. Because of the circumstances surrounding this death, one begins to understand the structure and meaning of a social system. As Jim O'Neill realizes, his son is victimized by poverty. Dr. Geraghty will not come to a poor man's home,[6] but he arrives quickly enough at the O'Flahertys', not because Al O'Flaherty is his special friend, but because he knows he will collect his fee. Money is the arbiter of life and death in the South Side—this is what the unnecessary waste of Arty's life clearly reveals.

Almost invariably the city novel contains social implications. Yet its intention is not exhortatory. As a form of creative expression rather than propaganda, it is distinguishable from what may be called city *problem* fiction, fiction which presents a particular *social evil* in order to show the need for immediate reform. The purpose of a problem novel is rhetorical; its end is a call for social action. The standard for judging the problem novel is its exactness in *reproducing* the social facts and its influence upon public opinion. It is a good problem novel if, like good journalism, it presents facts clearly and correctly and if it leads to social reform. Perhaps the best example of problem literature is Upton Sinclair's *The Jungle.* It presents an accurate, if heightened, picture of social conditions that demand to be reformed. The exposé of the scandalously unsanitary conditions in the Chicago stockyards led to a government investigation and a federal pure foods act. The novel proposes a specific remedy for social evils, that is, a socialistic system. The affinity between problem literature and journalism is strong: in spirit, purpose, and material, *The Jungle* is a fictional counterpart of the muckraking journalism of Ida Tarbell, Ray Stannard Baker, and Lincoln Steffens.

Sometimes a fictional account of actual situations has been so close to journalism that it has almost defied classification. For example, *The Long Day* by Dorothy Richardson, a social worker, is a fictional statement of the author's experiences as a working-girl in New York.[7] As its conclusion it summarizes the young girl's problems and temptations in the city and outlines a program of social reforms. The difference between such problem fiction (and journalism) and the city novel can be seen by a comparison between *The Long Day* and Dreiser's *Sister Carrie.* Both depict the working-girl's struggles to find work, to maintain economic independence, and to protect herself against temptation. But *Sister Carrie* does not present a solution to the isolated problems of the young girl in the city because the novel is not limited to these specific problems. Rather it is concerned with a total way of life. It explores the values and manners of the modern city and reveals its total impact upon human character and destiny. It has also an intrinsic interest in the city as a unique place and atmosphere. In other words, the intention of the novel is to explore the city, to show what it is, what values it lives by, and what effect it has upon the individual's character and destiny. Consequently, it is broader in scope than the problem novel; it interprets city life as a social structure, while the problem novel records, in a more photographic manner, only the symptoms of a particular urban disorder.

City novelists have themselves pointed out that their intention is to give a personal impression of the city and not a solution to its problems. Dreiser, for example, recalls how his brother Paul had once shown him about New York and suggested that he write a novel to expose corruption and inequality in the city.[8] Because he was then "youthful, inexperienced, unlettered," Dreiser had thought that he could "show up some of these things" and perhaps help to prevent them; but his mature reflection was that "picturing or indicating life" was no guarantee of changing it. He understood the purpose of the novel to be the *expression* of a personal vision of life, and not *exhortation.* In a preface to a bibliography of his work, Dreiser pointed out that his purpose was that of the creative artist—to re-create his "vision of life": "This is what living in my time has seemed like. . . . You may not like my vision . . . but it is the only one I have seen and felt . . . therefore it is the only one I can give."[9]

Later writers have become more aware of a complexity of motives behind the city novelist's act of creation. Farrell, for example, believed like Dreiser that the writer's purpose is to communicate a personal discovery about his world and that the primary function of the novel, as "a branch of the fine arts," is to provide "aesthetic pleasure."[10] Although the city novel deals with social disorder and personal failure, it produces aesthetic pleasure by virtue of the form it imposes upon the disorganized experiences of life. But Farrell also pointed out that as the writer reveals the confusions and disorder of modern life, his art

becomes "an instrument of social influence."[11] The subject matter of the novel makes its claim upon the social conscience of the reader; he may be aroused to action as he is troubled by the vision of life contained within the novel. If the city novel exerts social influence, then, it is because of its social implications rather than because of a direct attack upon an urban problem.

A study of the literary methods of city novelists brings into sharp focus the integral relationship between their social vision and aesthetic technique. In the past some critics (Granville Hicks, for example)[12] have taken the novelists' social ideas out of their novelistic context and judged them as social philosophy, while others (Mark Schorer in his comments on Farrell)[13] have taken a single formal element out of context and judged it as technique. But the city novel is an organic whole in which material and form have become one aesthetic integer. The material is the writers' particular social vision of city life; their techniques are the instruments through which they have crystallized and expressed this vision. The formal elements in their work—style, plot, tone, theme, and structure—give literary expression to their specific attitudes towards the city as a place, an atmosphere, and a way of life. To judge Dreiser's structure, for example, without relating it to his view of the city's economic structure, or Dos Passos' complex aesthetic design without relating that to his comprehensive view of a complex urban society, or Farrell's style without evaluating it as an instrument that reveals his characters' sensibility is to ignore the fundamental unity of the city novel as a work of art. It is only as we examine the relationship between material and form, between the vision of city life and technique, that we can evaluate city fiction as literary art; and then we also can see that its artistic achievement has been a considerable one. For not only has the city novel shown a keen insight into the social meaning of the city's complex and turbulent life: it has also developed a form for recreating that life in imaginative terms that reveal its essential meanings.

FORM, SETTING, AND LANGUAGE

Through literary practice, if not through theory, three forms of the city novel have emerged: the "portrait" study, which reveals the city through a single character, usually a country youth first discovering the city as a place and manner of life; the "synoptic" study, a novel without a hero, which reveals the total city immediately as a personality in itself; and the "ecological" study, which focuses upon one small spatial unit such as a neighborhood or city block and explores in detail the manner of life identified with this place.

The portrait novel belongs in the literary tradition of the novel of initiation—that is, a novel tracing a young hero's discovery of life and growth to maturity. In the portrait novel, the hero is typically a naïve and sensitive newcomer to the city, usually a country youth, as in the fiction of Dreiser, Herrick, and Wolfe, although in Howell's *A Hazard of New Fortunes,* he is an older man.

Structurally, the novel is built upon a series of educating incidents in which the city impresses upon the hero its meanings, values, and manners. As the hero responds to the insistent pressures of city life, his character undergoes a change: he learns what the city is, and this is his achievement of sophistication and maturity. He may adjust himself to an urban way of life and conform to its standards and seek its goals, or once he becomes aware of its social implications, he may repudiate it. The change in character, as a younger person either suffers inner defeat, achieves material success, or arrives at social wisdom, reflects the personal impact of urbanism. Dreiser's protagonists submit to the city: they learn to want that which it obviously values—money, fashion, and ease. The heroes of portrait novels of the thirties and forties usually repudiate city life for its injustices and materialism and dedicate themselves to the cause of social change.

Since the portrait study traces a process of social conditioning—the hero is gradually illuminated and conditioned to the city's way of life—the narrative pace may be slow and the effect documentary. Whatever the form and results of the conditioning, the forces acting upon the hero must be commensurate with the changes in his character. In Dreiser's novels, the city impresses itself upon the hero's mind and sensibility in a few climactic experiences, which are moments of recognition when the protagonist realizes what the city has to offer. But the preparation for these moments has been carefully laid, for example, in the studied account of Carrie's job-hunting or in the descriptions of Clyde's home environment. The potential weakness of the portrait novel is that the portrayal of environmental forces may be made at the expense of the interior drama, so that the hero seems an automaton, too much acted upon and not enough an actor. But at its best, the form allows for a revelation of a way of life in its greatest personal significance, that is, in its effect upon human character and destiny. It permits the reader to see and feel the environmental pressures that help mold, if they do not entirely determine, the moral identity of modern city man.

The ecological novel differs from the portrait study by having as its protagonist not a single person but a spatial unit—a city neighborhood, block, or even an apartment house. Interest thus focuses upon the social relationships and manners within a close group, although one figure may come to prominence, as Danny O'Neill does in Farrell's novels of the South Side. The title of the ecological novel often specifies the spatial unit: for example, there is Waldo Frank's *City Block,* Albert Halper's *Union Square,* Ann Petry's *The Street,* Sholem Asch's *East River,* and John Kafka's *Sicilian Street.* Sometimes the locale is implied in the title; Willard Motley's *Knock on Any Door* refers (as the epigraph states) to any door in the city's back alley and slum; and Nelson Algren's *The Neon Wilderness* (a collection of stories) refers to Chicago's Skid Row. Sometimes the title designates the social group, as in Meyer Levin's *The Old Bunch.*

While the ecological form limits the range of the novel, it permits an intensive study of urban manners and of idiosyncratic urban types. The breakdown of the city into small, self-contained, and distinctive social worlds gives a sociological justification to the ecological approach. The fact that most recent writers have been born into a particular neighborhood and know its way of life intimately explains the increasing popularity of the form. This inmost kind of knowledge of a society within the city is the writer's equipment: it can make him, as it has made Farrell, a city novelist of manners. The ecological novel can reveal city life as it exists for the native city-dweller—perhaps devoid of its surface glamour, perhaps merely monotonous as in Farrell's South Side Chicago, or bitter and cruel as in the slums of Michael Gold's, Joseph Gollomb's and Isidor Schneider's East Side New York, or superficial and conventionalized as in Edith Wharton's "fashionable New York." Perhaps no city fiction gives the reader so immediate a sense of the familiar world of everyday experiences as the novels of Farrell. His ecological approach permits a detailed exploration of the manners and morals of a cohesive group of city people. Time moves slowly in his works—four novels are required to show Danny O'Neill's emergence from childhood and adolescence—and this slowing down of time in combination with the strict circumscription of space allows for a minute and comprehensive portrayal of how urban people think, act, and feel. The reader comes to understand the inner life of a community in terms of the perceptions of its people. In Farrell's works the reader can see the forces of environment slowly and inexorably shaping the youth, giving them the content of their experiences and determining their attitudes, actions, and destinies.

The synoptic novel makes the city itself protagonist. It is an inclusive form that presents the complex pattern of city life—its contrasting and contiguous social worlds (the ironic union of gold coast and slum, of gangland and bohemia, of Harlem and Chinatown), its multifarious scenes, its rapid tempos and changing seasons, its tenuous system of social relationships, meetings, and separations, and its total impact as a place and atmosphere upon the modern sensibility. Because it intends to be all-inclusive, the synoptic novel requires special techniques of condensation, integration, and characterization. The massive material of city life must be ordered and condensed to fit within a formal framework. Urban symbolism, used so prominently in *Manhattan Transfer,* is one method of condensing statement, atmosphere, and judgment. The awkwardness of Elmer Rice's *Imperial City* can be explained in part by his failure to develop successful methods of condensation. Unless the separate scenes and incidents of the synoptic novel are also integrated within a clearly defined formal frame, the novel will collapse into a loose series of incidents. Mood unifies *Manhattan Transfer,* but more important, an underlying interpretation of modern city life relates the varied incidents and characters to a unifying theme. Since the protagonist in the synoptic novel is the city itself, the technique of individual characterization raises a crucial artistic problem, for if the people do not emerge with sufficient importance and vitality, the novel loses the appeal of human drama. In *Imperial City,* Elmer Rice inserts biographical sketches within the narrative structure when the focus is upon the action of a particular character. But this is a crude device that results in awkward pauses within the novel and an undramatic exposition of character. *Manhattan Transfer* also does not successfully solve the problem of characterization, although it is the outstanding example of the synoptic city novel and of experimental technique. In its elaborate symbolism, its dissociated urban images, its dramatization of color in the cityscape, its experimentation with syncopated rhythms, and its impressionistic method, it reveals an artist's conscious effort to re-create the modern city through innovations in language and form.

The form of the city novel has important implications for the language as well as the setting. Since the ecological form limits the setting to a circumscribed and usually peculiar area, it may use this area's characteristic speech as a means of creating character and scene. The synoptic form, on the other hand, may rely heavily upon metaphor and symbol as a language that condenses description and social judgment. If in the portrait novel the hero makes a sweeping exploration of the city, a panoramic approach to setting may lead to symbolism as a technique of implicit social commentary and to the use of vulgar speech patterns as a technique for realizing atmosphere and character.

The urban setting may be created through three distinguishable elements: the physical facts of the scene (actual streets, structures, topography), the aesthetic impression that the scene makes upon a sensitive mind, and the urban atmosphere. Early writers felt called upon to give a detailed account of the physical facts—partly because they could not assume the reader's familiarity with them, partly because they themselves had only recently discovered these facts and found them exciting, partly because they felt that a literary theory of realism demanded close description, and partly because they believed it important to preserve the facts as a matter of historical record. Their difficulty layin incorporating information about the setting into the narrative structure. Usually, they relied upon exposition, which was awkwardly set apart from the narrative. Dreiser, for example, sometimes halts his story and addresses the reader directly in order to inform him about the facts of the scene. But while this intrusion of exposition is awkward, the facts are significant, for the physical scene affects the characters and produces in them attitudes and emotions that help explain their actions. Later writers have been able to incorporate facts into the structure more successfully not only because they have felt themselves less under the necessity of describing physical details but also because innovations in novelistic technique make it possible for them to project external facts through the minds of the character.

The facts themselves have changed with the historical development of the city. And the writer's response to them has also changed as he sees them from the perspective of his own time and his own personal relationship to them. The physical city of Dreiser's novels, described in

expository passages, is a growing and vigorous world in which is heard constantly the noise of construction. There are grand mansions that thrill the newly arrived country youth, streaming crowds of well-dressed people who arouse their admiration and envy, tall and impressive office buildings that inspire wonder and awe. And in its very immensity the city also brings youth to a recognition of their smallness and essential helplessness in the modern world. In the beginning of *Manhattan Transfer,* New York is like Dreiser's Chicago a young and vigorous city with promises of a great destiny, but at the end of the novel its promise is left unfulfilled. The vision of the architects in the novel of a magnificent city of steel, concrete, and glass, beautiful in a modern way, never comes to life. New York has become a place of incessant movement, clamorous noise, stench, oppressive heat or biting wind, of dirt and garbage and grit. The physical city of Farrell's novels is a narrow and confining neighborhood far different from Dreiser's immense city of glittering contrasts. The boys play in small alleys or narrow streets, and the women live out their days in cluttered apartments. The only spot of beauty in this dismal world is a small artificial park.

When the objective scene is presented as subjective experience, it usually becomes not a statement of fact but an aesthetic impression. The setting is no longer described: it is dramatized as an inner experience. The emphasis is therefore not upon the facts of perception: it is upon the fact *of* perception—upon the way one sees the scene, the way it seems to be. The aesthetic impression reflects the quality of mind of the observer, whether it be the novelist or one of his characters. Because it gives a personal reaction, in which the selective element is significant, it also contains an implicit judgment. Whether one finds the city a place of beauty or ugliness, of harmony or discord, may be expressed through the selective process that determines the details of the aesthetic impression.

Like the aesthetic impression, the atmosphere realizes the setting as a physical place and comments on it. The difference in atmosphere between an early and later city novel is partly a historical one; but also it reflects a change in attitude towards the city and a change in the writer's knowledge. Dreiser saw the city as it was going through an exhilarating period of growth, and he saw it as a newcomer. In his novels the atmosphere plays an important part in a pattern of defeat: it arouses in youth hopes that are to be unrealized. His characters move in an atmosphere of vigor, strength, and excitement, and only gradually are they made aware of undercurrents of struggle and tensions in the atmosphere. When they begin to appreciate these currents, their hopes have already been doomed to defeat. Dos Passos' characters also move in an atmosphere of excitement and tension, but it is one that has lost its power to inspire dreams. The contrast between the atmosphere of Dreiser's city and that of Farrell's is a sharp and significant one. Farrell's young men do not step out into a city whose vigorous mood stimulates and excites them; they live in an atmosphere of stagnation in which are hidden currents of brutality. The city that inspired in characters like Carrie, Eugene Witla, or Cowperwood enthusiasm and a vast eagerness to live has now become a place that makes the young people weary with the emptiness of time.

In giving expression to the city as a place and a way of life, city novelists have been concerned with the development of an idiom appropriate to their material. Because the world they deal with is a mechanized world of man-made structures, a language that draws heavily upon metaphors and symbols taken from nature seems incongruous and outmoded. Rather, the city itself has provided a vocabulary for the urban novel. While early novels like _Sister Carrie, A Life for a Life,_ and _The Voice of the Street_ employed urban symbols, the need for an appropriate idiom was not explicitly discussed. But a more recent novelist like Farrell, who has become fully aware of his role as city novelist, has pointed out in critical writings the need for a metaphorical and symbolic language derived from the facts of modern urban life. In a review of Edward Dahlberg's novel _Those Who Perish,_ he wrote:

> . . . an author does not pick his images out of a grab bag, but rather they grow out of his own background and changing experiences. . . . it is apparent that romantic literary conventions have already passed their efflorescence and that they reflect an ideology of dualism completely dead and antiquated for many of us.
>
> Contemporary American writers, in many cases, I believe, have . . . perceived this fact about the use of romantic symbolisms. Many of them are the products of urban life. In their immediate sensory experiences they have been most affected by the sights, sounds, odors, and objects of an industrial city. In their first stages of reading particularly, they have absorbed much of the romantic poets, and in their early writing there has been some imitation of the romantics. Generally speaking, the charms and attractions of nature have been peripheral if not non-existent in their lives. Hence they often have sensed a dichotomy between the objects and sensations they have sought to describe and the language and symbolism they have inherited.[14]

Perhaps one of the most conscious experimenters with urban imagery is Dos Passos in _Manhattan Transfer._ His use of the dissociated or fragmentalized image is particularly effective in creating the sense of rapid movement within the city, while it suggests also a peculiarly modern kind of perception. In very recent fiction, the most evocative and stirring use of urban imagery has been made by Nelson Algren.

Urban symbolism equates physical elements in the setting with social or psychological characteristics of city life. The symbol not only suggests an interpretation of urban society but it usually contains an implicit moral judgment. Thus, symbolism is one of the city novelist's means of introducing his evaluation of modern life without, however, intruding himself as direct commentator. Early novels which use urban characters as symbols are

H. B. Fuller's _The Cliff-Dwellers_ and Ernest Poole's _The Voice of the Street._ In the former, the elusive figure of a beautiful pampered wife of a Chicago titan symbolizes the materialistic impulse within competitive Chicago, as well as the injustices and social inanities that result from this materialism. In _The Voice of the Street,_ the hero, who might be taken for a kind of urban "Everyman," vacillates between two characters, who together personify the dual forces of good and evil in the city. Herrick's _A Life for a Life_ makes a simple linear equation between a huge glittering sign that says "Success" and the materialistic and competitive drives within urban society. Beneath the sign there takes place an accident which indicates the high human cost of success. As in _Manhattan Transfer,_ fire is symbolic of the destructive element in modern life. Dreiser made most effective symbolic use of fashion: in a society where people were anonymities, the outward signs of dress became a kind of symbolic language that communicated one's social and economic position. Perhaps no writer translated the facts of city life into symbolic gestures as much as Thomas Wolfe, although his symbolism was not always conscious and controlled; and perhaps no writer has so consciously controlled his urban symbols as John Dos Passos in _Manhattan Transfer._ In Meyer Levin's _The Old Bunch,_ the Chicago World's Fair becomes an interesting symbolic counterpart to the city itself: its flimsy façades and glittering spectacles are destroyed in a final collapse, just as, Levin implies, the false values and deceptive foundations of urban society are also doomed to destruction. These are only a few examples of how the city novelist has assimilated the physical facts of the urban setting into his language.

Another development has been the use of vulgar city speech as a medium for creating character and scene. This development can be explained in part as the result of a shift in narrative point of view. When the early novelist like Dreiser or Herrick put himself in the position of omniscient author, he spoke in his own language. Dreiser characteristically shifted from a most extravagant romantic idiom to journalese and to scientific jargon. This was his own vocabulary. But once the writer projected the scene from within the consciousness of his characters, he began to employ their speech patterns, intonations, and rhythms. Particularly in the ecological novel, an idiosyncratic language—whether that of the Chicago Irish or the New York East Side Jews—has been an aesthetic medium. The effectiveness of this language depends upon the novelist's ability to make it a revelation of a state of mind and a way of life; and contrary to common critical opinion, this is the achievement of Farrell's language—it creates and comments upon the South Side and its people.

THEMES

Twentieth-century life has thrust upon the modern artist certain obsessive concerns—to name some, a concern over man's aloneness and alienation, over the collapse of his community and the breakdown of tradition, the ineffectuality of love and religion, the impact of mechanization, the materialism of modern life, and the conflict between artist and society. These are the themes of modern art; they are also the themes of city fiction. Because the modern American city abstracts and concentrates the social forces that have given the artist his themes, the city novel can develop and project these themes against the background that most clearly illuminates their social origins and implications. The modern experience of alienation and aloneness is thus related to a breakdown of tradition and community nowhere so striking and definitive as in the city. The materialistic temper of the age, as well as the mechanistic basis of our modern way of life, is also most intensely expressed in the city. And the tempo and tensions of the twentieth-century world of speed and hectic amusement are revealed in the rhythms and pace of big city life. In the same way that the city epitomizes the twentieth century, city fiction focalizes the main themes of twentieth-century literature.

The comprehensive theme of city fiction is personal dissociation: the prototype for the hero is the self-divided man. Dissociation is a pathological symptom which results from, and reflects, a larger social disorder. The dissociated person has not found a way to integrate motive and act and so to organize his life's activities towards a continuous and progressive fulfillment of his desires. In contrast to inhibition, which implies coercive pressures from an organized society, dissociation arises mainly because of a lack of social unanimity: the community has failed to provide a cohesive tradition that can guide the individual in his choice of goals and moral alternatives. Dissociation is also distinguishable from frustration. One experiences frustration when he is prevented from attaining his goal; but one is dissociated when he cannot even clearly define what his goal is.

In *Manhattan Transfer,* Jimmy Herf articulates most clearly the confused and indecisive feelings of personal dissociation. He is discussing his failure to achieve fulfillment with his friend Stan Emery (who expresses his own inner dissociation by seeking escape from reality in alcohol):

> "The trouble with me [Jimmy says] is I cant decide what I want most, so my motion is circular, helpless and confoundedly discouraging."

> "Oh but God decided that for you. You know all the time but you wont admit it to yourself."

> "I imagine what I want most is to get out of this town [New York] preferably first setting off a bomb under the Times Building."

> "Well why don't you do it? It's just one foot after another."

> *"But you have to know which direction to step."*[15]

In Dreiser's characters, desire is urgent and intense, but dissociation manifests itself because the character does not really understand the nature of his desire—and consequently, he seldom makes the right decision for his own

happiness. With Carrie, for example, desire and action remain essentially unintegrated: while she really wants beauty, she acts to attain only its false appearances in fashion and fame. And her dream of personal happiness and fulfillment remains as elusive at the end of the novel as it was at the beginning.

The irony, pathos, and tragedy of city fiction lie in the fact of dissociation. Ironically, the city novel shows that the chaotic conditions of urban society create man's intense need for conscious self-integration while they also constitute the obstacles to personal fulfillment. Thus, from *Sister Carrie,* the first city novel of the century, to such recent works as Nelson Algren's *The Man with the Golden Arm,* city fiction has portrayed man searching for a complete self in an urban world where personal integration or completeness seems to have become impossible. The pathos and tragedy of urban fiction lie in the inner defeat that man suffers as he becomes self-divided and perhaps even self-destructive. The "stranger motif" is another expression of the pathetic and tragic implications of dissociation. The characters in urban fiction typically feel that they are strangers moving in an alien world. Their subjective experience is one of loss and confusion: they feel as though they have lost hold of their identity, that they have failed to define and objectify themselves, and that any course of action may involve them in serious self-contradictions, if not indeed in self-destruction. The failure of personal love is both cause and consequence of an inner dissociation. As Sherwood Anderson tried to show, an incomplete man cannot love; and a man who cannot objectify himself through relationships of love cannot be sure of the reality of his identity. If the failure to conciliate motive, perceptions, and acts is final, defeat is inevitable. But if a character recognizes the cause of his floundering, he may decide upon some course of action. Like Jimmy Herf in *Manhattan Transfer,* he may leave the city for an unknown destination, or, like Farrell's Danny O'Neill, he may dedicate himself to the task of changing society.

In Tess Slesinger's *The Unpossessed,* another aspect of dissociation is very specifically revealed, and that is its relationship to a new kind of personal freedom, the freedom that results from the collapse of binding social conventions. It is partly because the individual is free—free, it seems, from coercive moral restraints, from clearly defined social responsibilities, from the forces of convention and the ties to family and community—that he suffers inner confusions and feels himself somehow lost in a social void. The heroine of *The Unpossessed,* the modern liberated woman, articulates her feelings of isolation, impotence, and sterility in an interior monologue, and significantly, she ties these together with her sense of personal freedom. She recalls that when she separated from her lover, "We wept because we could not weep, we wept because we could not love, we wept because . . . we care about nothing, believe in nothing, live for nothing, because we are free, free, free, like empty sailboats lost at sea."[16]

Although dissociation takes form as a personal failure, it has been related in both literary and sociological pictures of the city to the social context of urbanism as a way of life. This relationship between personal and social systems of disorder is expressed in the formal terms of the novel as an interaction between character and setting or milieu. It is expressed in other terms in a sociological theory of urbanism that defines the collective characteristics of the city as a way of life and describes their personal consequences for the individual. While the sociology of city life cannot validate the art of the city novel, it can illuminate the social backgrounds with which the novel is concerned and out of which it has emerged. Because the actualities of city life have shaped the city novelist's vision of life and given him the material, themes, symbols, setting, and language of his art, an understanding of the modern city's essential characteristics can further our understanding of the city novel. The following chapter gives a selective summary of these characteristics as they have been formulated and systematized in the sociological theory of urbanism.

NOTES

[1] Ben Hecht, *A Thousand and One Afternoons in Chicago* (New York, Covici-Friede, 1922), 286.

[2] Robert Herrick, *A Life for a Life* (New York, The Macmillan Company, 1910), 44.

[3] O. Henry, "The Defeat of the City," *The Voice of the City* (Garden City, New York, Doubleday, Page and Company, 1919), 85-94.

[4] Henry Steele Commager, *The American Mind: An Interpretation of American Thought and Character Since the 1880's* (New Haven, Yale University Press, 1950), 62.

[5] O. Henry, "The Defeat of the City," *The Voice of the City,* 85.

[6] James T. Farrell, *No Star Is Lost* (Cleveland, World Publishing Company, 1947 reprint), 602, 627.

[7] Dorothy Richardson, *The Long Day: The Story of a New York Working Girl as Told By Herself* (New York, The Century Company, 1905).

[8] Theodore Dreiser, *A Book About Myself* (New York, Boni and Liveright, 1922), 449.

[9] Theodore Dreiser, Preface to Edward McDonald, *A Bibliography of the Writings of Theodore Dreiser* (Philadelphia, Centaur Book Shop, 1928), 12.

[10] James T. Farrell, *A Note on Literary Criticism* (New York, Vanguard Press, 1936), 11.

[11] *Ibid.,* 177.

[12] See Granville Hicks, *The Great Tradition* (New York, The Macmillan Company, 1935).

[13] See Mark Schorer, "Technique as Discovery," *Forms of Modern Fiction* (ed. by William Van O'Connor, Minneapolis, University of Minnesota Press, 1948), 283-300.

[14] James T. Farrell, "In Search of an Image," *The League of Frightened Philistines* (New York, Vanguard Press, 1945), 156f.

[15] John Dos Passos, *Manhattan Transfer* (New York and London, Harper and Brothers, 1925), 176. Italics mine.

[16] Tess Slesinger, *The Unpossessed* (New York, Simon and Schuster, 1934), 136.

Alan Henry Rose

SOURCE: "Sin and the City: The Uses of Disorder in the Urban Novel," in the *Centennial Review*, Vol. XVI, No. 3, Summer, 1972, pp. 203-20.

[*In the following excerpt, Rose examines the use of urban settings in novels from various periods of American literature, beginning with Charles Brockden Brown's novel* Arthur Mervyn, *and ending with J. D. Salinger's* Catcher in the Rye.]

I

Since the beginning of the American novel its young hero has been drawn inexorably to the city. Financial success is rarely his goal, and amidst the continuous charges of evil and corruption one is hard pressed to find other motivation commensurate with the lure of the place. Yet the urban obsession dominates novels taken from widely different periods of our culture; in Charles Brockden Brown's *Arthur Mervyn* (1800), Bayard Taylor's *John Godfrey's Fortunes* (1864), Theodore Dreiser's *Sister Carrie* (1900), F. Scott Fitzgerald's *The Great Gatsby* (1925), and J. D. Salinger's *The Catcher in the Rye* (1951), the protagonist repeats the same journey toward crime and degradation. If we shift our traditional rurally oriented point of view, if we approach the common denominator of the urban experience, the city's devious complexity, its amorality, positively, as an essential if unspoken component of the young hero's development, we can account for the city's recurrent role in the American novel. For in a culture committed to rural innocence, dominated by a variant of the initiation pattern defined by the first and finalized letter of our earliest primer, "In Adam's Fall, We sinned all," the young hero has no alternative but the city in which to find the raw experience, the complexity and disorder which traditionally in the ancient metaphor of initiation, the Fortunate Fall, comprise the crucial step to maturity.

The deviations in the American version of the Fall extend further than its unusually intimate association with sin and crime. In the general pattern, as R. W. B. Lewis suggests, "the human personality fulfilled itself only through a classic drama of a fall and a regeneration . . . [yet Puritan] orthodoxy insisted [so] heavily on the Fall that it held the creature wholly passive in the process of redemption. Redemption, for the orthodox, was effected by a single shattering blast from heaven."[1] The Fortunate Fall in American fiction involves this unique paradox: to become reborn "as a social being," in Henry James, Sr.'s words, to mature, the protagonist has not merely to have "an encounter with 'Evil,'" he must share it, become criminal, usually commit a crime. But once he has himself experienced corruption within our pattern he is powerless to save himself; he must await an inexplicable act of external intervention. If, as Lewis and Herbert Weisinger maintain, we are dealing with a "metaphor in the area of human psychology [with] immense potential,"[2] an unconscious pattern of action whose power is defined by its component of irrationality, this is indeed a central archetype of our culture. For the city novel through its first century can be recognized, astonishingly, by its mystical overtones, its hidden areas of fantasy and abandon, and the unique failure of reason in its plot action. While remaining, as Leslie Fiedler puts it, "unexamined," the archetype assuming the different forms of a changing culture retains its efficacy; it continues to offer the possibility of regeneration. But as the novel becomes "psychological," as it turns to subjective analysis, the Fall as a source of resolution weakens, and fragments.[3] In the twentieth century American novel the city is a place offering not fruitful maturity but confusion, frustration, and barrenness.

II

The Philadelphia of *Arthur Mervyn* is an emerging city; accordingly its role in the novel, its influence upon the young protagonist is sketchy and blurred. Mervyn journeys toward it with doubts; he wonders, for example, "whether the city would afford me employment."[4] He is the first of our heroes to feel the lure of its power; still outside its limits, *before* sensing the painful trials it is to impose upon him, Mervyn prematurely sets up the equation of mature resolution with success which we shall see will only become a reality later, *after* the experience of urban disorder: "Now, said I, I am mounted into man. I must build a name and a fortune for myself." (22) As Mervyn nears the city, however, the corruption which characterizes it in the archetype begins to influence his behavior and expression. The city symbolizes sin in the Fall; it is surrounded in secular terms by crime. At the moment he enters the city, Mervyn's naiivité fades; he cheats the toll collector at the Schuylkill River Bridge, and rationalizes his crime: "All that honor enjoins," he concludes, "is to pay when I am able." (25)

Once in Philadelphia the full effects of its complexity begin to be felt. In the eastern city trade with Europe and the Far East was increasing, and the waves of European immigration were beginning. The city already seemed exotic. Its foreignness, reflecting the source of much of the wealth and culture, gave form to the complexity, and to the corruption, which the city offered. Immediately upon entering Philadelphia, Mervyn is made "the victim of malicious artifice" (33); forced to witness a convoluted, morally ambiguous scene which poses a distinctly foreign quality for him. If he were to "tell the tale [he would be ranked] with the story tellers of Shirauz and Bagdad." (32) Before his first full day in the city is over, Mervyn's descent into urban degradation has begun. He has met with Welbeck, a morally corrupt foreigner, and been made to shed his simple country garments and clothe himself in French livery. Losing his early, hollow maturity, Mervyn begins his experience of the city an apprentice, subjected to the lessons of a complex, urbane, and criminal master.

The general abandon of the city tends to focus in a disordered center. As the city crystallized, its nucleus took the form of an established area of intense social depravity. In the less defined terms of *Arthur Mervyn,* the city is momentarily overcome by its moral and social malaise during the yellow fever epidemic of 1793. At the center of the plague lies the Hospital, normally ordered, but now a place of "mortal stenches . . . debauchery and riot . . . malignancy and drunkenness" (165), in which subterranean corruption dominates, and the dissipated attendants enact their criminal debauchery below the prostrate bodies of the helpless patients. In this inverted milieu Mervyn, stripped of conventional social attitudes, experiences as evil the coalescent disorder offered by the city: "Now the calamity had entered my own doors, imaginary evils were supplanted by real, and my heart was the seat of commiseration and horror." (127)

The importance of this experience can be gauged by Mervyn's compulsion to be in Philadelphia during the plague, and his inexorable movement toward the Hospital: "I harboured not a momentary doubt that the course which I had taken [into the plague] was prescribed by duty." (132) But once sharing the corruption Mervyn, tellingly, is powerless to save himself: "I closed my eyes, and dismissed all fear, and all fore-sight of futurity . . . and should probably have expired on this spot." (206) But he is saved by the chance appearance of one Dr. Stevens who, reflecting the irrational nature of the pattern, is unaccountably drawn to Mervyn: "I scarcely ever beheld an object which laid so powerful and sudden a claim to my affection and succour." (5) It is this same Stevens who, besides performing the providential act of external intervention which saves Mervyn, also provides the reward which follows the protagonist's immersion in disorder and defines his success. He introduces Mervyn to Achsa Fielding, who is not only rich and socially prominent, she is mature, a widow, and foreign, a Jew. In her, resolution and maturity are translated into economic and social rewards. Because of the relative tentativeness of this early expression, Mervyn's success, and the efficacy of our archetype, can best be measured not by the linguistic and imagistic development which will come to characterize the initiation process, but by the distance the protagonist has come from his status at the beginning of the novel. There, at his arrival in the city, Mervyn is apprenticed to the foreign and experienced Welbeck. After his journey through urban disorder, at the end of the cycle, he is about to become husband and master of this foreign, experienced, and mature woman.

III

Between the formative years sketched in *Arthur Mervyn*, and the mid-nineteenth century of *John Godfrey's Fortunes*, the American city had crystallized. It sees the culmination of the division of labor, a place where "man responds to the industrial process with only part of his personality: segmentalization . . . characterizes his work;"[5] where the old myth that industriousness leads to personal fulfillment and economic advancement is exploded. In fact, "in the novels one can hardly find a single instance where industriousness, frugality and piety are the operative factors in the hero's rise in society."[6] But if the emergent city gives the lie to an old, hollow myth of success, it provides an abundance of materials to support a psychologically far more valid one. For it is when the protagonist is *not* working that he is free to share the complexity that the new city, the focal point for "all the new economic forces . . . the generating center for social and intellectual progress,"[7] has to offer. And the nucleus of its complexity, tentatively disordered in *Arthur Mervyn,* is now emphatically defined by foreignness; for example "four out of every five residents of Greater New York were foreigners or of foreign parentage,"[8] and by the squalor of the new slums which by 1888 comprised "over thirty-two thousand tenements with a population exceeding a million."[9] By the mid-nineteenth century the city offers a place where in reality "community organization breaks down and there is an especially good opportunity for personal disorganization to occur, [where] vagrant and normally inhibited impulses are permitted free reign."[10] No wonder for authors like William Dean Howells it seems based on a savage and primal disorder: "Ravening beasts and poisonous reptiles lurk in those abodes of riches and poverty . . . [among] sewers that rolled their loathsome tides under the streets, amidst a tangle of gas pipes, steam pipes, . . . all without a plan."[11] All without a plan—the American city has indeed emerged as a metaphor for chaos, a place where the dangerous but potentially life-giving descent into the irrational underworld can occur.

So when the hero of *John Godfrey's Fortunes* comes to the city in 1864 to find fame and success, the New York in which he arrives impresses him with a complexity which he sees in terms of foreignness: "I knew not which was most remarkable—the never-ending crowd that filled the chief thoroughfare, the irregular splendor of the shops, or the filthiness of the pavement. . . . I could with difficulty comprehend that I had not passed into some foreign country."[12] The city's role in the novel, offering an opening into an initiatory descent into disorder for the inexperienced, is now clearly defined by the ominous contrasts within Godfrey's first residential neighborhood: "The rooming house was two or three blocks removed from the noise of the bowery, and its neighborhood wore

an aspect both of quiet and decay. . . . Not far off, on the opposite side of the street, there was a blind alley, leading to some hidden cluster of tenements, whence issued swarms of dirty, ragged, and savage children." (195)

Although Godfrey comes to the city to seek success, it is the psychological nature of his poverty which counts: "I had never experienced any marked unkindness or injustice . . . and I did not imagine the human race to be otherwise than honest, virtuous, and reciprocally helpful." (8) As long as he remains in the city and works industriously, without gaining experience from it, success remains elusive. He has a menial job on the *Daily Wonder* which ironically prevents him from experiencing the wonders which daily occur around him: "For months I strictly performed my appointed duties . . . acquiring no experience which seems worthy of being recorded." (221) Without moving toward the initiatory center of the city Godfrey's early immature equation of maturity with wealth, his goal of "Love, Manhood, and Money" (225), tellingly similar to Mervyn's, remains unchanged and ineffectual. Although he has met a rich heiress, Isabel Haworth, she continues inaccessible.

Godfrey's descent into degradation begins when he moves from Mrs. Very's plain American boarding house to Mrs. De Peyster's foreign one. The back room of the nearby bar "Ichneumon" acts as a symbol of the foreign, complex, disordered center of the city. It is run by a foreigner, its den is smoky, like the "salon des nuages," it is called "the Cave." To enter this potentially regenerative place Godfrey's "initiation fee is beer through the evening." (326) In fact his initiation begins when "a Delphic voice exclaimed, 'The offering is accepted . . . welcome and acceptance from the mystic brotherhood.'" Godfrey soon begins to share "the lawless recklessness of the utterance to which it was dedicated." (331)

The language which the Cave offers, its "utterance," embraces the primacy of raw experience. Significantly, its terminology is not abstract and theoretical as are the later attempts to analyze the pattern, but consists of a powerful imagistic language of regeneration which reflects the unconscious vitality contained in the archetype. As Godfrey is immersed deeper into the lawlessness of the Cave he comes to reject the apparent relationship of work with reward, his immature equation of money and manhood: "economy . . . practical talent . . . industry . . . work, and the worry that comes with it are . . . relics." (329) As Godfrey draws near to the underlying center of the archetype, toward experiential abandon, the meaning attached to cash, one of the society's most cherished beliefs, begins to shift. Money becomes significant only as a means of realizing psychological fulfillment: "Money is an empty form—a means of transfer, being nothing in itself—like the red flame, which is no substance, only representing the change of one substance into another. . . . They only who turn it to the enrichment of their lives— who use it as a gardener does manure, for the sake of flowers—have the abstract right to possess it." (328) Money to manure. There is a ring of Freud for us that lends a special impact to the protagonist's epiphany, deep within the city's disorder, that success is based upon an organic process of psychological development.

Godfrey does come to share an abandoned thirst for experience: "My life naturally took on, more and more, a reckless, vagabondizing character. . . . My stomach, like my brain, craved variety, piquancy, excitement." (418) His crucial experience of disorder occurs while drunk in the Cave. He "had never [before] lost the control of brain or body." After one and a half bottles of Sauterne "a partial paralysis crept over my body. . . . My mental vision turned inwards and was fixed upon myself with wonderful sharpness and power. . . . I was in a condition resembling catalepsy rather than intoxication . . . in a luminous revelation of my own nature that I was forced to read." (434) In the midst of disorder, this is Godfrey's moment of self-insight. It carries the seeds of resolution; normally it would bring about a rebirth. Yet the shadow of Puritan predestination in the Fall in America precludes an effective individual act of will. In spite of his descent into regenerating experience Godfrey, like Mervyn, is incapable of emerging mature from his moment of insight without an external intervention: "I struggled to find the trace of some path which might lead me out of the evil labyrinth,—but I could not think or reason: it was blind, agonizing groping in the dark." (437)

The irrationality basic to the archetype is reflected in the absence of a reasonable account for the external intervention which does save Godfrey and brings about his resolution. Deep in his stupor, Godfrey mystically hears a footstep, which is outside of the bar and must be close to a mile away. Somehow it seems that "its cessation were the beginning of deeper disgrace, and its approach that of a regenerated life!" (437) He staggers out of the bar and finds that he had been hearing "Bob Simmons! Dear old [boyhood] friend, God has sent you to save me!" (439) Simmons seems to symbolize the regenerative qualities of the city. He has come from the country to settle there, as has Godfrey, and he is a bricklayer, apparently enjoying his creative role in adding to the physical complexity of the place.

Godfrey's progress seems measured by his ability to see his rebirth clearly, as a psychological experience. At first he interprets Simmons' appearance religiously: "In the Providence which led him to me at that hour and in that crisis of my fortunes, my fears of a blind chance or a baleful pursuing Fate were struck down forever." (433) But soon the idea grows that his regeneration was part of a more secular, psychological pattern. He makes a rather casual attempt to reject the heresy: "I *prefer not* to think that my restoration to health was already assured by the previous struggle through which my mind had passed, that from the clearer comprehension of myself, I should have worked up again by some other path. [Rather,] it is *pleasant* to remember that the hand of a brother-man lent its strength to mine, and to believe that it was the chosen instrument of my redemption from evil ways." (439, italics mine) Finally, he discards the religious interpretation and

views his descent and regeneration entirely in terms of secular experience: "Those months of vagabondage seemed like a dark uneasy dream, in the steady light of resolution which now filled my life; it was as if a sultry haze in which the forms of Good and Evil were blended, and the paths of order and of license become an inextricable labyrinth, had been blown away, leaving the landscape clearer than ever before." (465)

The "struggle through which [his] mind had passed," and the consequent "steady light of resolution which now filled [his] life," suggest that Godfrey has attained the insight which marks maturity. He can now see through appearances: "I was able to recognize them under whatever mask they approach." (465) When he finally win his heiress, Isabel Haworth and her $80,000, she is seen as something more than just a cash reward: "Thank God! I whispered to myself, money is her slave, not her deity." (371) Godfrey ends by living the lesson learned in the Cave: his urban experience has taught him to interpret the abstract economic language of his era's success myth in a manner which allows him to realize its underlying psychological content.

IV

John Godfrey's Fortunes is a unique example of the "success novel"; it begins to explore the meanings of success in the city while retaining the simple form and the irrational content of the dozens of less sensitive works from its genre. Its rudimentary probings make it an unusually rich subject, yet they also carry the seeds of dissolution. A half-century later, at the time *Sister Carrie* was written, the impulse toward fictional analysis of cultural forces had strengthened. Dreiser's book is an exercise in myth-breaking; it separates out the major components of the success myth, the Fall and resolution, balances Hurstwood's decline against Carrie's rise, and subjects them each to theoretical discussion. In the process the unconscious integrity of the myth is undercut; it is deprived of the irrational components responsible for its regenerative qualities, and the pattern begins to produce only destruction and sterility. Hurstwood's story, expressing only the fragment of the fall, demonstrates the disaster which results when the protagonist is denied the irrational luck, the external act of intervention which traditionally occurred to save the hero from disintegration. His lack of resolution to raise himself from the descent into the hideous poverty of the Bowery reflects the individual's inability to effect his own salvation by an act of will within the context of the archetype. Hurstwood's decline into poverty, his loss of mental control, and his final suicide reveal the destruction which accompanies the violation of the traditional pattern.

It is, however, Carrie's book; her role in the city myth comes under closest scrutiny, and consequently moves toward the most telling incompleteness. Carrie begins as the previous protagonists had; she comes from the country to the city and "submits to a solemn round of industry and [is told to] see the need of hard work without longing for play."[13] Carrie soon rejects the Hansons' hard working home, her $4.50 per week job, and this joyless theory. But a hint to the meaning of the novel lies in the fact that it *is* a theory. The "industry" that Carrie turns from is for the first time extensively analyzed, and while it is unlikely that she "would get in one of the great shops and do well enough until—well, until something happened . . . and Carrie would be rewarded for coming and toiling in the city" (16), the new awareness that "something" must precede the reward undermines the unconscious resolving force of the act of luck, the irrational intervention when it does occur.

Enacting a fragmentalized pattern, Carrie is denied its central component, the experience of evil and corruption. While the New York Carrie and Hurstwood journey to, the city which Dreiser considered the center of experience in America, is again entered after a crime, it is Hurstwood who steals the $10,000. And, as has been discussed, it is around Hurstwood that accrues all the crime, degradation, and corruption that the myth had required the quester to experience. Carrie is untouched by degradation; consequently she does not learn the psychological lesson of the Cave that John Godfrey comes to understand: "only the long strain of starvation would have taught her that in some cases [money] could have no value." (57) It is not so much that Carrie is not capable of learning the nature of experience, but that the lesson is unavailable to her. Carrie's view of experience is as immature at the end of *Sister Carrie,* when she has wealth, as it was at the beginning: "And now Carrie had attained that which in the beginning seemed life's object . . . yet she was lonely. In her rocking-chair she sat . . . singing and dreaming. . . . She was still waiting for that halcyon day when she should be led forth among dreams become real." (418) Inviolate in spite of her liaisons, still inexperienced, her name in fire-letters hovering above the city but never part of it, Carrie may as well sit in a convent as in her tower over New York. Missing her fall she indeed remains a secular American nun, a Sister Carrie.

v

The structure of *The Great Gatsby,* our document of illusions shattered, of myths seen with ruthless clarity, is even more emphatically fragmented; Gatsby's fall is balanced against Nick Carraway's development. The sense of loss, the longing which reflects weakness in our pattern in *Sister Carrie* is intensified in the later book. Gatsby does not sit "singing and dreaming." He stands, in a posture of exquisitely frustrated yearning: "He stretched out his arms toward the dark water in a curious way . . . I could have sworn he was trembling."[14] The dimensions of the myth's components in *The Great Gatsby* are "colossal," appropriately enough on the eve of the American success myth's explosion. Gatsby is not merely apprenticed to a Welbeck on his arrival in the city, he is formed by the titanic criminality of Meyer Wolfsheim: "'He's the man who fixed the World's Series back in 1919'. . . . [He] play[ed] with the faith of fifty million people—with the single-mindedness of a burglar

blowing a safe." (74) In the absence of the archetype's saving stroke of luck, Gatsby's experience of degradation grows uncontrollably: even his guests could not have "guessed at [the extent] of his corruption." (154) His "drug-store business was just small change . . . [compared to] something on now." (135) Without the old irrational intervention Gatsby's world can only go downhill, decay, "turn septic on the air now." (107) After rejecting his immature work "SCHEDULE," his development is irreversibly "down a desolate path of fruit rinds and discarded favors and crushed flowers" (111), where rebirth has been conclusively thwarted.

The gauge of Gatsby's failure, in terms of experience, is of course the inaccessibility of Daisy Fay. Earlier, in *John Godfrey's Fortunes,* salvation had been accompanied by a rich heiress, and she had been valuable because she translated money into experience. Daisy too offers such an equation: her voice, which is "a promise that she had done gay, exciting things . . . and that there were gay, exciting things hovering" (9-10), is also "'full of money.'" (120) Daisy is not the goal of Gatsby's quest; like Miss Haworth she would mark its success: "Daisy tumbled short of his dreams—not through her own fault, but because of the colossal vitality of his illusion. It had gone beyond her, beyond everything." (97) But Daisy, after a false hope, drifts further from Gatsby and the resolution that she symbolizes remains unrealized, a "hope, a romantic readiness . . . some heightened sensitivity to the promises of life." (2)

Nick Carraway comes closer to enacting the traditional pattern of initiation in the city, and by his failure reveals more clearly its dissolution. Nick has not come to New York for economic success, the "dozen volumes on banking . . . [remained] on my shelf." (4) Rather, Nick is "restless" for the experience that the eastern city offers. His journey is toward its vital complexity: "I began to like New York, the racy, adventurous feel of it at night, and the satisfaction that the constant flicker of men and women and machines gives to the restless eye." (57) The "satisfaction" that the city offers for Nick is based upon its intense experiential quality: its "wild promise of all the mystery and the beauty in the world." (69)

Accordingly, it is into this clearly-defined experiential city that Nick must descend if he is to share its initiatory center of degradation. Only one of Nick's commutations to New York is described with specific detail: his ride in with Gatsby to meet Meyer Wolfsheim. Again the entrance to the city is prefaced by a crime, the encounter with a "frantic policeman" (68) for speeding. At the bridge into Manhattan the foreignness and racial complexity of New York become apparent in "the tragic eyes and short upper lips of southeastern Europe," and the "haughty rivalry . . . [of] three modish negroes." (69) This journey to New York is pregnant with meaning: "Anything can happen now . . . anything at all." (69)

What does happen is Nick's meeting with Meyer Wolfsheim, who symbolizes the corruption which underlies the urban experience. Wolfsheim is found under the center of the city, in a "Forty-second Street cellar" (69), in "half-darkness." (70) The dark cave-like environment beneath the city is apparently Wolfsheim's milieu; accordingly his visual apparatus has shrunken: "After a moment [Nick] discovered his tiny eyes." (70) Wolfsheim is the priest of this subterranean world; "'a denizen of Broadway'" (74), he makes over it "a sort of benediction." (73) It is in his power to offer the momentary contact with corruption central to the protagonist's initiation: "I understand you're looking for a business gonnegtion." (71) But the offer is "startling" to Nick. He draws back, Gatsby confirms the reluctance, and when the crucial moment passes "Mr. Wolfsheim seemed disappointed." (71) In fact he and the resolving if painful experience he makes possible have been rejected; he cannot "impose" himself upon Nick, and he leaves. As he goes he seems a grotesque parody of evil, "his tragic nose . . . trembling" (73). But the tenacity of his hold, once established, and the strength remaining in our archetype are apparent in the most dramatic of his images, the "human molars" he wears on his sleeves.

The result of the encounter with the archetype, without the possibilities for regeneration offered by the intact pattern have already been suggested in the case of Gatsby. Without a saving intervention Gatsby's "gonnegtion" with corruption is not momentary; rather it is broken only with his death: "'Mr. Gatsby's dead.' There was a long silence on the other end of the wire, followed by an exclamation [from one of Gatsby's criminal contacts] . . . then a quick squawk as the connection was broken." (167) Without the contact Nick's search for maturity and fulfillment remains ambiguous. He is thirty when he leaves New York, past the age of initiation. As he leaves, Jordan Baker concludes he is a "bad driver." Significantly Nick's urban encounter has changed her opinion of him for the worst. Originally, she "'thought [him] rather an honest, straightforward person.'" (179) While Nick casts some doubt over Jordan's reliability, it must be remembered that her first word, and apparently her dominant characteristic as the only observer in the novel, is "'Absolutely!'" (11) Although his experience in New York appears to age Nick, meeting Tom Buchanan he "felt suddenly as though I were talking to a child" (181), it is not a fruitful maturity. Nick's withdrawal from "the abortive sorrows and short-winded elations of men" (2) is quite unlike the psychological resolution that the intact myth offered the protagonist. Nick's barrenness upon leaving the city reflects the collapse of the archetypal pattern of the Fall into urban experience as an effective initiation myth in America.

VI

The objectification and dissolution of the archetype appears conclusive by the early fifties, in novels such as J. D. Salinger's *Catcher in the Rye.* Salinger's book goes beyond the pessimistic sense of loss with which *The Great Gatsby* ends. In the fruitless search for the resolution that an aged myth can no longer offer, Holden

Caulfield is himself an image of enervation. Nick Carraway ends concerned with his own aging: a major characteristic of Holden Caulfield is his abundance of "gray hair."[15] Furthermore, the form of success the protagonist travels to the city to find, in flux in *Sister Carrie,* experiential in *The Great Gatsby,* has itself dissolved, become hopelessly inaccessible. Holden's question, suggesting the lost soul of the city, the missing ducks in Central Park, results not in fulfillment and resolution, but in frustration. The Jew he asks it of, "Old Horwitz," in contrast to Meyer Wolfsheim, is already remote and hostile, empty of any resolving knowledge. When he drives off "like a bat out of hell" (83), Holden is in effect abandoned in the city, already symbolically deprived of the knowledge that could make resolution possible. At that point, rather than beginning the regenerative period in the city that would result in his going home "all rested and feeling swell" (51), he embarks upon his fated quest leading only toward physical and mental collapse.

The hopelessness of making the necessary encounter in the city becomes apparent upon Holden's arrival in New York. Like previous protagonists, he has journeyed from the country, Agerstown, Pennsylvania, and has prefaced his entrance to the city with a moral offense, in this case the compulsive lie to Mrs. Morrow. But in New York his first impulse implies the thwarted nature of his relation with the city. In language even more explicit than that in *The Great Gatsby,* Holden immediately tries to establish a "connection" with the city: "The first thing I did when I got off at Penn Station, I went into this phone booth. I felt like giving somebody a buzz." (59) But the collapse of the myth, the emptiness of the city's role in it, renders the essential impulse futile: "But as soon as I was inside, I couldn't think of anybody to call up. . . . So I ended up not calling anybody. I came out of the booth, after twenty minutes or so." (59)

As has been suggested, the archetype comes under increasingly explicit analysis in its decline. The first person narrative technique of *Catcher in the Rye* precludes the sort of analytic discussion found in Dreiser's novel. Similarly, Holden's youth makes highly articulate insight such as Nick Carraway offers difficult. However, an image occurs in *Catcher in the Rye* which, in its explicit analytic intent and totally objective language, appears to encapsulate the subjectively shrunken state of the urban archetype. Near the end of Holden's unproductive journey through the city waits a figure unusually equipped to analyze the archetype of the city in literature, Mr. Antolini, a member of the English Department at an urban university. Antolini offers Holden an objective vision of his pattern of action: "I have a feeling that you're riding for some kind of a terrible, terrible fall." (186) Significantly, his fall is irreversible because the culture no longer offers the integral contact with disorder and the consequent irrational act of salvation: "This fall I think you're riding for—it's a special kind of fall, a horrible kind. The man falling isn't permitted to feel or hear himself hit bottom. He just keeps falling and falling. The whole arrangement's designed for men who, at some time or other in their lives, were looking for something their own environment couldn't supply them with." (187) Antolini's analytic expression is true; its accuracy acts as a gauge of the degree to which the myth has weakened. The archetypal pattern, previously so powerful as to be "unspeakable," is easily expressed here in its totality. Offered in explicit form to Holden as a substitute for the intimate psychological experience, its efficacy is suggested by Holden's reaction: "All of a sudden, I yawned. What a *rude bastard*, but I couldn't help it!" (190)

The results of Holden's quest, more than Nick Carraway's aging and withdrawal, reveal the enervated state of the archetype. Holden, too, finally comes face to face with a subterranean image of the city. Meyer Wolfsheim, below the center of New York, still offered some possibility of a contact with living corruption. The vision Holden encounters, and the prelude to his final collapse, is characterized by a totally unproductive abstraction and atrophication. Holden descends not into a hot, teeming restaurant, but into the Egyptian tombs, where the mummies are displayed, in the Metropolitan Museum of Art. And there, in the totally static environment, surrounded by figures of immeasurable agedness, Holden confronts the abstraction which symbolizes the decadence of a once fruitful pattern of initiation, an obscene distortion of the act of sexual maturity. In response the protagonist experiences not a sense of salvation and rebirth, but a vision of his own death, conclusively buried under a tombstone which associates his name with the obscenity symbolizing the failure of the initiation myth. It is this long delayed moment which finally realizes the full implications of the agedness which surrounds Holden. It is the death knell of a century and a half old, uniquely American, urban archetype.

NOTES

[1] *The American Adam* (Chicago, 1955), p. 58.

[2] Pp. 59-60. See also Weisinger, *Tragedy and the Paradox of the Fortunate Fall* (East Lansing, 1953).

[3] Fiedler's discussion of the archetype is found in "Come Back to the Raft Ag'n, Huck Honey!" from *An End to Innocence* (Boston, 1955).

[4] Charles Brockden Brown, *Arthur Mervyn* (New York, 1962), p. 20. Subsequent references from this, and the other easily available paperback editions used are included in the text.

[5] Blanche H. Gelfant, *The American City Novel* (Norman, Oklahoma, 1954), p. 32.

[6] John C. Cawelti, *The Apostles of the Self-Made Man* (Chicago, 1965), p. 62.

[7] Arthur M. Schlesinger, *The Rise of the City* (New York, 1938), p. 79.

[8] P. 72.

[9] P. 110.

[10] Gelfant, p. 40.

[11] The passage from *A Traveler from Altruria* is quoted in George Dunlap, *The City in the American Novel 1789-1900* (Philadelphia, 1934), p. 112.

[12] Bayard Taylor, *John Godfrey's Fortunes* (New York, 1889), p. 179.

[13] Theodore Dreiser, *Sister Carrie* (Boston, 1959), p. 31.

[14] F. Scott Fitzgerald, *The Great Gatsby* (New York, 1953), p. 21.

[15] J. D. Salinger, *The Catcher in the Rye* (New York, 1969), p. 57.

Adrienne Siegel

SOURCE: "When Cities Were Fun: The Image of the American City in Popular Books, 1840-1870," in *Journal of Popular Culture,* Vol. IX, No. 3, Winter, 1975, pp. 573-82.

[*In the following essay, Siegel focuses on depictions of urban life in popular novels of the mid-1800s.*]

From the Gothic horrors of Charles Brockden Brown's Philadelphia to the cinematic celebration of Frederico Fellini's *Roma,* the city has loomed in the popular imagination as a locale larger than life, a place of mystery and romance. The sociologist Robert Park early realized that what people thought of their cities existed as much as a social reality as what they did in them.

> The city . . . is something more than congeries of individual men and of social convenience . . . something more, also, than a mere constellation of institutions and administrative devices. . . . The city is, rather, a state of mind, a body of customs and traditions, and of the organized attitudes and sentiments that inhere . . . in this tradition.[1]

Yet only a handful of scholars have studied the ideological dimension of urban history.[2] None has investigated in more than shadowy sketches the images of urban life provided in media directed at a mass audience.

One of the most important examinations of the image of the American city is the pioneering book written by Morton and Lucia White, *The Intellectual versus the City.* In their opinion, America's literary heritage has consisted of a melange of fear and revulsion toward metropolitan life. Whether writers were romantics who rhapsodized the beauties of a natural landscape or urbane men who embraced the values of civilized society, the American city was a failure. It was either a depraved artifact that violated a benign nature or a stunted child of civilization that lacked the cosmopolitan charm of European urban centers. It would seem from the evidence they have assembled that any prospective migrant to the American city, after reading the books of the nation's literary giants, would have felt dread at the thought of leaving a benighted arcadia for "commerce, crime, crowds, and conventionalism" in the nightmarish metropolis.[3]

Yet the census returns would seem to belie such conclusions. One asks how succeeding generations could have kept coming to the city if there were no cultural forces at work to ease the pain of adjusting to a new home. One questions whether the attitudes of an alienated intellectual elite really reflected the opinions of society at large. Already historians are beginning to recognize the need to examine not only the works of recognized literary luminaries but also the writings of popular leaders of culture.[4] Frank Freidel has suggested that if the historian were to dig into a lower tier of intellectual activity, he would find an enthusiastic response to the city.[5] Charles N. Glaab has argued that in spite of the shibboleth that America has been saddled with an anti-urban tradition, examination of ordinary reading fare reveals an exuberant celebration of the American city as a symbol of progress and growth.[6] Blaine A. Brownell has gone so far as to contend that popular thought throughout American history, until most recently, has viewed the city as the best of all possible worlds.[7]

What is particularly revealing to the student of urban America is the iconography of American cities created by hack writers during the period 1840-1870. For it was during these crucial decades that people poured into cities in unprecedented proportions. At no other time in the history of the United States has such a large percentage of Americans voted with their feet for urban life. In 1840 the census registered a 63.7 percentage of increase in the number of urban dwellers as compared to 1830; in 1850, a startling 92.1 per cent; and in 1860, an increase of 75.4 per cent.[8] Thus it was not the fratricidal War between the States that marked the great watershed in American demography but rather the pre-industrial decades of economic take-off that brought the most dramatic shift in population from the farm to the city.

In what kind of psychological frame of mind did so many people uproot themselves from traditional moorings to face life in a startling new environment? In what way did they become acculturated to the traumatic displacement from a known universe to one unknown? To what extent did the media respond to the restless migration of the population to the urban frontier?

In a day that was without movies, television, radio, and comic strips, books provided the most common form of mass leisure entertainment. Already at mid-century *Harper's Magazine,* in a congratulatory mood, proclaimed, "Literature has gone in pursuit of the million, penetrated highways and hedges, pressed its way into cottages, factories, omnibuses, and railroad cars, and become the most cosmopolitan thing of the century."[9]

Reading was becoming a national habit. While population and national income nearly doubled during the decades of the forties and fifties, the value of books more than trebled.[10]

It was during these decades that a revamped publishing industry, alert to the needs of supplying a mass market with cheap books, churned out an extraordinary number of novels that presented a hungry readership with information about the burgeoning urban centers of America. In fact, while in the entire span from 1774-1839 only 46 urban novels were published, in the single decade of the 1840's writers flooded the market with 173 works of city fiction; in the 1850's, with yet another deluge of 167 books; and in the 1860's with still another 97 novels.[11] It would seem that these works, disseminated to a mass audience, exerted a more powerful influence on fashioning the popular conception of the American city than the remote philosophical and literary disquisitions of intellectual men of letters. In all probability they served as a significant psychological force that pulled people to the city.

Indeed, in contrast to the sombre images of urban life projected by writers of *belles lettres,* the pop-book of the mid-19th century quite frequently pictured the city as an enticing haven, a refuge from the drudgery and monotony of an isolated rural existence. Sin City was also Fun City, offering the spirited a chance for gay amusement, interesting associations, and material splendor. The metropolis might contain all sorts of physical hazards and moral blemishes, but it nevertheless was a place of intense emotions, feverish animation, unrivaled vitality. Pulp literature describing the city depicted it as a locale of unbelievable contrasts, its human complexity representing all classes, all interests, all nationalities. "Saints and sinners, mendicants and millionaires, priests and poets, courtesans and chiffoniers, burglars and bootblacks, move side by side in the multiform throng."[12] Always varying, always new, every day and every hour, the city seemed to enlarge the mind, sharpen the faculties, and quicken the wit. "Everybody likes to be in a crowd; perceives [its] electric influence, . . . thinks better and brighter and faster, talks quicker and shrewder, feels more acutely, enjoys more keenly."[13] In fact, for an age of romanticism, the city, as well as nature, could provide a sense of vitality and feelings of wild excitement.

Epitomizing the youth, vigor, and opportunity of the nation, the American metropolis was the dream machine of an acquisitive society, promising prosperity to stifled country youth. It could demand what was difficult, extraordinary, fabulous, impossible.[14] A place where millions were to be commanded, with no limits, no bounds upon action, it provided the natural arena for those with ambition and daring to test their strength. Unlike the drowsy atmosphere of the country, the mighty current of urban life animated men to speedy accomplishment of some grand design.[15]

Even a critic of urban society like the prolific popular writer of city exposés, George G. Foster, was forced to admit

A great city is the highest result of human civilization. Here the Soul . . . has put forth its most wonderful energies—energies developed to their utmost power, and excited to their highest state of activity by constant contact with other souls, each emulating, impelling, stimulating, rivaling, outdoing the others. . . . It is only in a large city, where some hundreds of thousands combine their various powers, that the human mind can effectively stamp itself on every thing by which it is surrounded.[16]

No matter how one might detest the clamorous city, there was no denying that the American metropolis vibrated with a piquancy that could serve as a magnet to restless souls from the countryside. For those outside the enchanted circle of urban life, the city was a place of processions, gay shops, blazing lights, glare and glitter, fun and noise. To an excited youth about to enter what, to him, was a land of magic, the metropolis exuded a mysterious hum that "fell like music on his ears, and in the thought that he should soon be there, all his sadness vanished, and when the bell rang out warning to be off . . . he could scarcely refrain from shouting out his joy and delight."[17]

According to literary salesmen, the urbanite could enjoy a freedom from meddlers that would be the envy of overly scrutinized village folk. "The right to do 'as you d—n please' . . . is nowhere so universally recognized, or less curbed by authority" as in the great metropolitan centers of the nation.[18] The city resident could dwell in a mansion or in a garret, dine elegantly or not at all, get up early or late, live in the latest mode or scorn the fashions of the day, with no small-town busybodies to gossip or interfere.[19] Yet the city offered not only independence but also companionship. In its surging tide of citizens, literary supporters boasted, it allowed people to feel a fellowship unknown to isolated individuals in some rural retreat.[20]

As the nation became absorbed with relentless expansion, the city conjured up a cherished image of growth. If hardy pioneers, rolling on an irresistible tide of manifest destiny, were pushing forward the frontiers of the Republic, enterprising urbanites were energetically crowding the wharves with giant ships and tirelessly choking city space with the engines of commerce. In fact, to contemporary witnesses, the bursting sense of life which characterized the American nation of the mid-19th century found its sharpest focus in the tumultuous, expanding cities of the Union.[21]

With its fond descriptions of palaces of pleasure and its thrilling narrations of danger and rescue, the urban pop-novel at mid-century can be considered America's tales of the Arabian Nights. Offering the writer the possibility of presenting a perpetual panorama of glittering splendor and exquisite wonder, it is not surprising that many chose to spin "one thousand and one" stories out of this intriguing new material. The amusements of urban life, especially, seemed to cast a spell over the reading public. Beautiful people, living in a make-believe world of

voluptuous magnificence, became familiar figures to an audience who sought stimulation for their fancy in leisure hours.[22] Those readers weighed down by the deadening routine of store and office and farm could find in fictional scenes of cosmopolitan entertainment a passport into a glamorous and exciting world. They could delight in scenes of "starlight and flowers," of balls where wealth, art, taste, and luxury stirred the senses and intoxicated the imagination.[23] They could be transported through the printed page into parties where enchanting rooms garlanded with flowers and wafted with heady perfumes, echoed with the laughter of a carefree throng.[24]

Not only could the metropolis boast of its bedazzling balls but also of its beautiful women. Nowhere else, it would seem, could such dresses and bonnets, shawls and jewelry be seen. No other place gave fair creatures such free rein to promenade and be admired.[25] It exhibited "gay girls" dressed in glorious silks and laces who fetchingly strolled along the avenues.[26] Compared to the predictable, calico-frocked country lass, the sight of a city belle filled the eye and brain with a sense of intoxication. Woman-watching was, in the estimation of many popular experts, one of the titillating attractions of metropolitan life.[27]

The urban novel also portrayed scenes of sumptuous feasts available in city restaurants that must have made a rural readership pine for a trip to the metropolis. Glimpses into rooms where tables were resplendent with fragrant tropical flowers, cut glass, and silver service perhaps made the "meat and potato" crowd long to enter the sophisticated world of urban gourmandise.[28] How their imagination must have boggled at descriptions of dinners at Delmonico's where food became a masterpiece of culinary art! How their appetite must have been whetted by visions of the city's stylish set stimulating their palates on oysters and Chablis, turtle soup and iced punch, fish and sherry and glasses of Cliquot, Lafitte, and Rüdesheimer. What cultivation they must have attributed to urbane gourmets who knew that a single clove of garlic had to be laid on a plate with *cotelettes en papillotes* for exactly five minutes and that the *riz de veau* had to be accompanied with a particular kind of pea which only grew in the neighborhood of Arras, or that a "'34" Lafitte had to be procured from the lower part of the hill![29] And how ecstatic it must have been for those who dined more simply to take an excursion by book to an ice-cream palace like Taylor's sumptuous establishment, adorned on all sides with gleaming mirrors, where they could indulge their taste for delicate desserts or luxurious liqueurs.[30] Over and over, the reader was apprised that no one could enjoy the basic human requirement of food like the city dweller. Farmers, unable to afford the products of their own gardens, stripped the countryside of its harvests to provision the people of the metropolis who liberally paid for the gratification of their gustatory senses.[31]

Not only did the city offer a "grand bouffe" of culinary indulgence, it also afforded the opportunity for elegant dress. Nowhere else, it would seem from pulp urban literature of this period, was such an abundance of goods available. Stores cascaded with fabrics, covering every available foot of space with textiles of every color, cost, and texture.[32] In marbled palaces of trade, customers were regaled with a medley of merchandise that could satisfy the most demanding taste and the most commanding purse.[33] Shops like Stewart's, Lord and Taylor's, and Arnold Constable became story book names to ladies limited in their luxuries to poorly stocked local general stores.[34]

Nor was it to be imagined that the brick and mortar of the metropolis shut out the urbanite from the pleasures of the green grass, tall tree, and singing birds. He could have his cake and eat it, too. All the joys of the man-made world were at his command as well as the beauties of nature. In popular books the urban resident was shown attending the theater at night and refreshing himself in the pastoral scenery provided by a public park during the day.[35] If the man with a hoe could feast his eyes on some rushing stream, the New Yorker could gratify his senses with wild and romantic views of a magnificent bay and the dancing waters of the Croton Reservoir.[36] If the tiller of the soil could thrill to the bleating of his sheep and the song of the birds, the city dweller could be captivated with the exotic mélange of animal life presented for his pleasure at zoological parks.[37] Country folk who congratulated themselves on the incomparable glories of their clear air and sparkling waters could soon learn from pulp urban books that the denizens of the metropolis could find in the magnificent pleasure grounds of Central Park pure air and beautiful lakes.[38]

The festivity of the metropolis made it, as portrayed in popular prose, a magnet for those seeking merriment. At holiday times, its joyous exuberance linked its inhabitants in warm ties of good fellowship, reminiscent of any country hamlet. On New Year's Day in New York City people visited friends and neighbors, and could even enter the homes of strangers if they simply accompanied the corner grocer or local merchant. No sea of floating anonymity or alienation, the urban population wished each other well, and those who were financially comfortable opened their homes, offering a surging tide of guests a magnificent tablé of delicacies and wines.[39] Elegant ladies in gorgeous clothes welcomed all visitors and pressed the free flowing bottles upon their guests.[40] Mrs. Lydia Maria Child, cookbook author and editor of the *National Anti-Slavery Standard,* commented in her highly popular book, *Letters from New York* (1843), on the practices of New Year's Day in Gotham:

> No lady, that *is* a lady, will be out in the streets on the first of January. Every woman, that *is* "anybody," stays at home, dressed in her best, and by her side is a table covered with cakes, preserves, wines, oysters, hot coffee, etc.; and as every gentleman is honour bound to call on every lady, whose acquaintance he does not intend to cut, the amount of eating and drinking done by some fashionable beaux must of course be very considerable. The number of calls is a matter of

pride and boasting among ladies, and there is, of course, considerable rivalry in the magnificence and variety of the eating tables.[41]

Not only did the city provide conviviality, it also created a man-made world of taste and refinement. After all, only in the metropolis could one gratify the needs of the higher faculties. Only an urban community offered the aesthetic delights of professional music, art, and theater. Popular prose celebrated the numerous facilities for artistic satisfactions. The Empire City, especially, was viewed as the cultural capital of the nation. No other place could support the sheer quantity and variety of its houses of entertainment. In New York one could attend the Academy of Music and Pike's Opera for music, Booth's Theatre and Wallach's for legitimate drama, Brougham's for comedy and still Niblo's, the Olympic, the Broadway, the Old Bowery, the Stadt, and Wood's theaters for exciting spectacles. For those not yet satisfied, there were minstrel halls, concert rooms, and dance houses. There was even the ethnic stage presenting specialized fare for Irish and German immigrants.[42] And for budding talents, the "at-home" offered a theater in-the-round for amateur musical and literary performances.[43] But this was not all. For those less high-minded, the appeal of the urban stage was spiced by references to comedies that indulged in suggestions of seduction and adultery. The urban dweller must have appeared privileged, indeed, in his easy access to piquant theatrical performances enlivened with a liberal allowance of *double entendres* and spiced with a carefree disregard of Victorian propriety![44]

Nor did popular writing at mid-century leave the impression that the fascinating amusements of the metropolis were confined to the privileged few. The expansive city held out the possibility of rousing fun for one and all. For the sturdy street urchin there was oyster stew mixed with raucous music at Tony Pastor's, festive exhibitions of freaks and animals at Barnum's, and theatrical "happenings" at the Bowery Theatre.[45] Here, in an atmosphere heavy with the fumes of gin and tobacco, he could hiss at villains, shout at the approach of danger, and stir the hero to victory by a riotous chorus of applause.[46] For the "Plug Uglies" there was the Pit Theatre where for the price of 15 cents they could forget their troubles in thrilling blood-and-thunder scenes of stabbing, throat-cutting, and tomahawking;[47] and for the salacious, there were the *"tableaux vivants,"* performed by unclad *"model artistes."*[48]

In the inexhaustible storehouse of city wonders, celebrated by a host of mid-19th century cheap books, there seemed to be no end of occasions to stimulate interest and excitement. If high society found pleasure in art galleries and boxes at the opera, the city's low life was portrayed indulging its fancies in underground pits where it could savor a gory cockfight or relish a bloody rat combat. At Kit Burns a savage audience could thrill at the sight of rats, picked up from the New York harbor, being devoured by dogs. The object of the sport was to wager which canine could kill the most rodents in a given number of minutes. The rousing performance was, of course, habitually punctuated with oaths, shouts, and demonstrations of delight. When the human beasts tired of that spectacle, they could always work up a new frenzy over a blood-curdling combat between two huge bull dogs.[49]

The city, a place of never-ending pageantry, sparkled with a gaiety that could never be found in a quiet country nook.[50] With its gaudy concert-saloons, bowling alleys, billiard parlors, ornate "temples of Bacchus," gambling dens, and tawdry houses of prostitution, the metropolis offered possibilities for all kinds of enjoyment. Along its streets sauntered fashionable exquisites and fluttering belles.[51] Wherever one looked, there were sights to delight the eye and quicken the pulse.[52] A stroll along Broadway, suggested popular authors, could provide a pleasure unknown to country villagers confined to a much too familiar Main Street. For Broadway pulsated, throbbed with a feverish intensity.[53] "A walk through [it was] like a voyage round the Globe."[54] A promenade on the Bowery provided another kind of fascination. The "birds" of the Bowery, in all their extravagant plumage, plump and noisy, brought a gaiety on Saturday night that could not belong to those isolated in a quiet country retreat. For though the farmer might have tranquility, how could that compare to Christy's garden, the bursting shops, the "crack" ice-cream saloons, and theater with a 15 cent price of admission?[55] The Bowery with its swaggering "b'hoys" and gaudy "g'hals," its noise and tumult, vibrated with an excitement, a variety of life that made it as much as any freeholder's farm the home of a great social democracy.[56]

So replete were many popular novels with a sense of the wonder of urban pageantry that they might well have served as "hard-sell" commercials for city life. A man who has lived all his life in a small town expresses his delight with the metropolis in Day Kellogg Lee's novel, *The Master-Builder* (1852).

> I shall never get used to the roar of these streets, nor see an end of all the city wonders. But do not imagine from this, that I am home-sick. Far from it. . . . I like the excitement of all this roar, and all this sight-seeing, and hope I may not get so used to it as ever to meet it with indifference.[57]

As readers perused the popular pulp of the mid-19th century, the lure of the city must have become more and more enticing. For those fed up with the humdrum existence of farm and village, fiction of this sort might well have provided a tantalizing inducement to migrate to the metropolis. For those bewildered by the psychological trauma of having already shifted their habitation from a rural to an urban setting, the cheap book of this period perhaps helped to ease the pain of acculturation by persuading readers to see the commotion of the city as a healthy stimulus to creative energy. By cataloguing the charms of the metropolis, popular authors built up a case for an alternative life-style of fun and freedom. A move to an urban center would mean living in a society of abundance. It would provide a longed-for passport to pleasure. Perhaps the satirist Allen Gazlay in his book, *The Races of Mankind* (1856), best summarized for contemporaries compelling motives for urban migration:

> greater facilities in the pursuit of wealth; a more intimate enjoyment of social intercourse; intelligence, amusements, the arts, commerce, among which, fashions, taste, and the pomp and vanity of display, are not the least exciting.[58]

NOTES

[1] Robert Park, *The City* (Chicago: Univ. of Chicago Press, 1925), p. 1.

[2] A treatment from the point of view of literary analysis can be found in George Arthur Dunlap, *The City in the American Novel, 1789-1900: A Study of American Novels Portraying Contemporary Conditions in New York, Philadelphia, and Boston* (New York: Russell and Russell Inc., 1965), and for the 20th century in Blanche Housman Gelfant, *The American City Novel* (Norman: Univ. of Oklahoma Press, 1954). A broad sociological analysis that employs a variety of sources can be found in Anselm L. Strauss, *Images of the American Cities* (New York: The Free Press of Glencoe, 1961). For an analysis of attitudes of leading American writers of belles lettres see Morton and Lucia White, *The Intellectual versus the City: From Thomas Jefferson to Frank Lloyd Wright* (New York: The New American Library, 1964), and for an investigation of the response of bards to the American city consult Robert H. Walker, "The Poet and the Rise of the City," *Mississippi Valley Historical Review* (June 1962), pp. 85-99.

[3] White, p. 62.

[4] Dwight H. Hoover, "The Diverging Paths of American Urban History," *American Quarterly,* XX (No. 2, Summer Supplement, 1968), p. 20.

[5] Frank Freidel, "Boosters, Intellectuals and the American City," in Oscar Handlin and John Burchard (eds.), *The Historian and the American City* (Cambridge, Mass.: The M.I.T. Press, 1966), pp. 115-120.

[6] Charles N. Glaab, "The Historian and the American Urban Tradition," *Wisconsin Magazine of History,* LVII (Autumn, 1963), p. 15.

[7] Blaine A. Brownell, "The Agrarian and Urban Ideals," *Journal of Popular Culture* (Winter, 1971), p. 579.

[8] George Rogers Taylor, "The Beginnings of Mass Transportation in Urban America," *The Smithsonian Journal of History,* I (Summer and Autumn, 1966), pp. 31-52.

[9] Quoted in James D. Hart, *The Popular Book: A History of America's Literary Taste* (New York: Oxford University Press, 1950), p. 86.

[10] Carl Bode, *The Anatomy of American Popular Culture, 1840-1861* (Berkeley and Los Angeles: Univ. of California Press, 1959), pp. 109-10; E. Douglas Branch, *The Sentimental Years, 1836-60* (New York: D. Appleton-Century Co., 1934), p. 119.

[11] Lyle Wright, *American Fiction 1774-1850: A Contribution toward a Bibliography* (San Marino, Calif.: The Huntington Library, 1969), *passim;* Lyle Wright, *American Fiction 1851-1875: A Contribution toward a Bibliography* (San Marino: The Huntington Library, 1965), *passim.* What seems particularly suggestive is the fact that in the heyday of the Western frontier, the "urban frontier" attracted so much more literary interest. In the 1840's only 54 novels were published on the West; in the 1850's, a meagre 61; and in the 1860's, a paltry 25.

[12] Junius Henri Browne, *The Great Metropolis; A Mirror of New York, A Complete History of Metropolitan Life and Society, with Sketches of Prominent Places, Persons and Things in the City, As They Actually Exist* (Hartford: American Publishing Co., 1869), p. 339.

[13] Adam Badeau, *The Vagabond* (New York: Rudd and Carleton, 1859), pp. 31-32.

[14] Richard Burleigh Kimball, *Was He Successful? A Novel* (New York: Carleton, 1863), pp. 164-65.

[15] Aziel S. Roe, *Looking Around. A Novel* (New York: Carleton, 1865), pp. 9-10.

[16] George G. Foster, *New York in Slices: By an Experienced Carver* (New York: W. F. Burgess, 1849), p. 3.

[17] Charles Gayler, *Out of the Streets, A Story of New York Life* (New York: Robert M. De Witt, 1869), p. 112.

[18] Thomas Butler Gunn, *The Physiology of New York Boarding-Houses* (New York: Mason Brothers, 1857), p. 12.

[19] Matthew Hale Smith, *Sunshine and Shadow in New York* (Hartford: J. B. Burr and Co., 1868), p. 27.

[20] Richard Burleigh Kimball, *To-Day: A Romance* (New York: Carleton, 1869), p. 114; Robert S. Clar, *The Metropolites; or, Know Thy Neighbor. A Novel* (New York: American News Co., 1864), pp. 16-17.

[21] Browne, p. 28.

[22] Mary Noel, *Villains Galore, The Heyday of the Popular Story Weekly* (New York: The Macmillan Co., 1954), p. 307.

[23] Sara Coolidge, *Ambition* (Boston: James French and Co., 1856), pp. 58-59.

[24] Augustus Franklin, *Anne Melbourne: or The Return to Virtue. A Tale of Boston* (Boston: H. L. Williams, 1846), p. 7; Mrs. Nancy Polk Lasselle, *Annie Grayson; or Life in Washington* (New York: Bunce and Brother, 1853), p. 127; Kimball, *To-Day,* p. 283.

[25] Browne, p. 24; M. Smith, p. 28.

[26] George Thompson, *The Gay Girls of New-York: or, Life on Broadway; Being the Mirror of the Fashions, Follies and Crimes of a Great City* (New York: George W. Hill, 1854), pp. 10-11.

[27] George G. Foster, *Celio: or New York Above-Ground and Under-Ground* (New York: Robert M. De Witt, 1850), pp. 80-81.

[28] Justin Jones, *The Belle of Boston: or, The Rival Students of Cambridge* (Boston: F. Gleason, 1844), p. 38.

[29] Bayard Taylor, *John Godfrey's Fortunes* (New York: G. P. Putnam; Hurd and Houghton, 1864), pp. 310-311.

[30] George G. Foster, *Fifteen Minutes around New York* (New York: De Witt and Davenport, 1854), p. 21.

[31] Browne, p. 391.

[32] Henry Morford, *The Days of Shoddy, A Novel of the Great Rebellion in 1861* (Philadelphia: T. B. Peterson and Brothers, 1863), p. 35.

[33] John Neal, *True Womanhood; A Tale* (Boston: Ticknor and Fields, 1859), p. 18; Henry Llewellyn Williams, *Gay Life in New York; or Fast Men and Grass Widows By an Old Traveler* (New York: Robert M. De Witt, 1866), p. 26.

[34] James Dabney McCabe, *The Secrets of the Great City; A Work Descriptive of the Virtues and Vices, the Mysteries, Miseries, and Crimes of New York City* (Philadelphia: National Publishing Co., 1868), pp. 168-71.

[35] Horatio Alger, *Ragged Dick* (New York: Collier Books, 1967), p. 73.

[36] Browne, p. 59; Lydia Maria Child, *Letters from New York* (New York: C. S. Francis and Co., 1845), p. 212.

[37] M. Smith, p. 361.

[38] McCabe, pp. 232-40. Yet praise of public parks was not confined to New York City. A recreational ground like Fresh Pond Park of Boston which allowed the city's residents to enjoy the great outdoors also won its share of literary accolades. See William B. English, *Gertrude Howard, The Maid of Humble Life: or, Temptations Resisted* (Boston: Redding Co., 1843), p. 4.

[39] St. Clar, p. 451.

[40] J. B. Bouton, *Round the Block. An American Novel* (New York: D. Appleton and Co., 1864), pp. 19-20; Osgood Bradbury, *Female Depravity; or, The House of Death* (New York: Robert M. De Witt, 1857), p. 23.

[41] Child, p. 87.

[42] McCabe, pp. 441-43.

[43] Timothy Shay Arthur, *Out in the World. A Novel* (New York: Carleton, 1864), p. 28; Badeau, p. 277; St. Clar, p. 77.

[44] George Foster, *New York in Slices*, p. 101; *Mary Beach: or, The Fulton Street Cap Maker* (New York: W. F. Burgess, 1849), pp. 42-43.

[45] Alger, *Ragged Dick,* pp. 43, 49, 54.

[46] George G. Foster, *New York Naked* (New York: Dewitt and Davenport, 1850), p. 143; Edward Zane Carroll, *Three Years After; A Sequel to the Mysteries and Miseries of New York* (New York: Dick and Fitzgerald, 1850), p. 43; Mrs. Elizabeth Oakes Smith, *The Newsboy* (New York: J. C. Derby, 1854), pp. 25-26.

[47] Horatio Alger, *Ben, The Luggage Boy; or Among the Wharves* (Philadelphia: Porter and Coates, 1870), pp. 12, 165; Wirt Sikes, *One Poor Girl: The Story of Thousands* (Philadelphia: J. B. Lippincott and Co., 1869), pp. 208-13.

[48] These "naked Olympians" performed to an enthusiastic crowd, who, when not crackling peanut shells, cheered on the performers with yells, whistles, and the stamping of feet. See John D. Vose, *Seven Nights in Gotham* (New York: Bunnell and Price, 1852), p. 48.

[49] McCabe, pp. 388-92.

[50] A typical Alger hero is appalled at the thought of foresaking a hobo existence on the city's streets for a comfortable home on a Western farm. He fears that he would be lonesome and miss the varied scenes and daily excitement of urban thorough fares. See Alger, *Ben,* pp. 161-62.

[51] Augustine Joseph Hickey Duganne, *The Daguerrotype Miniature; or Life in the Empire City* (Philadelphia: G. B. Zieber and Co., 1846), p. 5.

[52] John Donaldson, *Jack Datchett, The Clerk: An Old Man's Tale* (Baltimore: H. Colburn, 1846), p. 5.

[53] Thomas Low Nichols, *Ellen Ramsey; or the Adventures of a Greenhorn, in Town and Country* (New York: For Sale by Booksellers and Periodical Agents Generally, 1843), p. 22.

[54] Browne, p. 339.

[55] Alger, *Ben,* p. 165.

[56] George G. Foster, *New York by Gas-Light; with Here and There a Streak of Sunshine* (New York: Dewitt and Davenport, 1850), p. 123.

[57] D. K. Lee, *The Master-Builder; or, Life at a Trade* (Redfield: Clinton Hall, 1852), p. 311.

[58] A. W. Gazlay, *Races of Mankind; with Travels in Grubland* (Cincinnati: Longley, Brothers, 1856), p. 214.

Marcus Klein

SOURCE: "San Francisco and Her Hateful Ambrose Bierce," in the *Hudson Review,* Vol. VII, No. 3, Autumn, 1954, pp. 392-407.

[*In the following essay, Klein explores Ambrose Bierce's relationship to the city of San Francisco.*]

In December of 1913 Ambrose Bierce, seventy-one years old and a self-designated battle correspondent, just disappeared into a war in Mexico. He was even then obscure, having grossly outlived his career and hence his publicity, but his suicide, presuming it was a suicide, aroused a certain kind of interest. He died very well, in terms of the magazine thriller. Indeed, the real mystery of Ambrose Bierce is that he managed his death so much more gracefully and so much more logically than he ever did his life. His death rightly compelled attention, a thing he had for many years missed. But it was at the same time an attention unliterary, rather ghoulish, and at best trivial. The public felt no loss, and despite a multiplicity of biographies and literally scores of inflamed appreciations, justice has not subsequently been done.

Bierce had never been famous, but he was more than curious, and he had had in his day a peculiar, often cultist, always local, but nonetheless gaudy notoriety. He had been "Bitter Bierce" and "The Wickedest Man in San Francisco". He had been celebrated, even adored, with the ready and effervescent civic spirit of the San Franciscans, as their very own. Delightful in sarcasm, splendid in heresy, he was in fact the court jester, to whom impudence was allowed. He had created merriment by shooting dogs. He would but for an ordinance have shot all dog-lovers, and he was loved because he roared with mirth at the mention of a minister. He told off-color stories about the dead and, as a matter of journalistic integrity, advocated violence towards well-enough-meaning anti-evolutionists, feminists, Socialists, regionalists, sports fans, fat babies, and democracy. He had argued long and wittily in favor of suicide (an interesting number of literary San Franciscans seem to have been convinced) and warmly, on high eugenic principles, for the castration of all criminals. As a journalist, daily columnist (the first in America), and as a professional gossip, hatchet-man and literary critic, he had lived for some thirty years a scandal, which was hotly admired but not precisely a success, of exceptionally constant abuse and ridicule. He had been impertinent for a population anxious for thrills.

"And at the end of it," Bierce wrote in one of his many quasi suicide notes, "all we see is that nothing matters." He was referring in the particular instance to his literary career, in which he was disappointed, but he had said the same thing often before and in various circumstances, and in two words it completely, as he wrote to George

Sterling, expressed his philosophy. It was no philosophic contribution. Bierce had not thought things out, but he was neither being facile nor striking a cheaply amazing pose. That nothing mattered was for him revealed and conspicuous truth, the consequences of which he quite accepted, and what passed for his impertinence derived from it. But true or not, and neurotic, as has to monotony been suggested, or not, that fearfully codified hostility described an attitude in America and in his time exceptional to the point of blunt unsociability. What was and is undiscovered is that Bierce was almost alone in his ability to say, as epitaph and as dogma—almost, at the end, casually—that really nothing mattered, and what is unnoted is that this attitude, a premature rebellion combining energy and disenchantment, was, in that twilight time of American letters, a premonition of a new freedom.

The period after the Civil War (Bierce, with De Forest, is one of the two writers of even moderate consequence who were in the War) gave that attitude some legitimacy. But it was not voiced, by at least implied assent, until it became actually, after the turn of the century and especially after the First World War, even respected. There was suddenly a new tone in American letters, generated of no school and in its instances specifically so dissimilar as Jack London, Theodore Dreiser, *Three Soldiers,* and the metaphysical revival. But the instances shared an identity. There flowered a new attention to facts, stubborn and inelegant, and at the same time a reaction, often lost in the bloom of its own fury, against decades of progressively less meaningful idealism. Writers of the new generation celebrated, beyond narrow inspirations like naturalism and the seventeenth-century conceit, the will to think toughly, lucidly, and, if need be, disagreeably. Truth became a problem, and was found not necessarily to exist in what had conventionally been named beauty. There was a new attitude, issuing from many circumstances, but in great part from the revolt against the Romantic Movement, its prison, its decay, its conspicuous inadequacy and the oppression of its legacy to late-nineteenth-century America. The new attitude, calling for compact realities, was characterized abroad by T. E. Hulme, who suddenly saw the "World as finite, and so there was no longer any refuge in infinites of grandeur", and who with the clarity and authority of the man who finally buries the corpse, described the necessity for it:

> Each field of artistic activity is exhausted by the first great artist who gathers a full harvest from it. This period of exhaustion seems to me to have been reached in romanticism. We shall not get any new efflorescence of verse until we get a new technique, a new convention, to turn ourselves loose in.

The new convention actually, by the time Hulme called for it, was in advanced development, but the formulation, given a few years, was exact. Hulme could observe conservatively, ironically, with studied superfluity, "I think that there is an increasing proportion of people who simply can't stand Swinburne." It was a truism, and a sentiment that twenty-five years earlier no writer in America

who valued his popularity would have dared affect. (And indeed even Bierce, who was vain in other ways and who logically should have objected, thought *Atalanta in Calydon* "one of the noblest poems in our language.") Bierce was actively sarcastic through the last three decades of the century, which may well enough be defined as that period of exhaustion. It was not a period merely of questionable taste, but of bad taste unyielding, of a popular appetite enforced—if not by Swinburne, by Tennyson and then by Kipling and Robert Louis Stevenson. The commercially successful poet of Bierce's generation was supremely James Whitcomb Riley; the most respected was the sedate and powerful editor of the *Atlantic Monthly,* Thomas Bailey Aldrich.

Bierce practised journalism—never quite literature—in San Francisco, which was not like the rest of the country but which shared with it, discounting perhaps significant but minor eruptions, its adoration of unreasoning optimism (large enough, in the nineties, to include Omar Khayyam's hedonism), benevolence, beauty, sadness, and tremulous sentiment. One has only, to discover what the country thought good, thought poetry, to turn the pages of Edmund Clarence Steadman's *An American Anthology,* published at the turn of the century. By far the most popular poet in the West was Joaquin Miller; his closest rival was Edwin Markham, who had given socialism to Tennyson and who had in "The Man with the Hoe" made beautiful the peasants' revolt in a way that somehow had nothing to do with incipient and bloody unionism, the thievery of the railroads, the problem of Chinese immigration, the fantastic civic corruption, and the abominations of the waterfront. The period was delivered to goodness beyond need of light and beyond the possibility of vitality. In such a republic, the rejection Bierce dared, if itself romantically inflated beyond belief, was phenomenal. It was to Americans and much more to San Franciscans, though discounted by their disbelief, frightening.

The time had, of course, its other critics, both literary and social. If it was the age of gilt, the time of Morgan and Mark Hanna and of the great fortunes, it was the time also of difficult industrial transition, of economic crisis, and of the Populist revolt. The old order lingered on, Emerson and Melville and Whitman, and at the same time there were Howells and Mark Twain. Edward Eggleston had broken ground for realism with *The Hoosier Schoolmaster* in 1871 and in 1880 Henry Adams had published anonymously his unromantic *Democracy,* and there had been Ed Howe and Henry Fuller and Joseph Kirkland and then Harold Frederic, but they constituted only the opposition. One cannot say they were not read, but Eggleston was proud of his book's having sold in twenty years as many copies as a contemporary success had sold in one season, and if he gave comfort to a few who found unbearable the manic phase of the nation's literature, he was largely overlooked. Those who *were* regarded were Mrs. E. D. E. N. Southworth, whose *Ishmael* and *Self-Raised,* though written more than thirty years before, were through the eighties and nineties to sell over two million copies each; Mrs. Burnett, who was guilty of *Little Lord Fauntleroy;* Ouida, Blackmore, and the Reverend Mr. E. P. Roe; and finally Henri DuMaurier, whose *Trilby* appeared in *Harper's* for January, 1893, and became promptly a pestilence, inspiring even Dreiser to remember moodily that "it had a strange psychologic effect on me at the time". The spokesmen for the era were rather the early Howells who, despite honesty and splendid intentions, had given the novel over to the American girl, and then Aldrich who declined to "vivisect the nightingale". And if Howells' resignation in 1881 from the editorship of the *Atlantic Monthly* was a symbolic episode in the struggle for realism on native grounds, the succession to that pontificate of American letters by Aldrich is also not without significance. It was Aldrich who was the "Enamored architect of airy rhyme", and who pitied

> A twilight poet, groping quite alone,
> Belated, in a sphere where every nest
> Is emptied of its music and its wings

and to whom realism was almost as offensive as foreigners. It was he who united a decaying Brahminism to an anachronistic romanticism, and it was he, despite self-pity, and not the later Howells, who was heard.

The attitude in letters he exploited he also compelled, and it was against that, from which so few escaped, that Bierce so ferociously rebelled. It was a pose of gentility sustained and somehow coupled with ecstasy; the poet was rare and delicate and aesthetic; he did not think and he above all did not hurt. It was a distinguished generation if there is included in it Emily Dickinson who, knowing the unacceptability of her work, did not choose to be of it, and Walt Whitman, who had written of it as early as 1871 in unequivocal terms of anger and despair, and Henry James, who abandoned the disorder and took lessons in reality from Balzac. But the poets accepted by the commoners were Riley and Eugene Field and, for a slightly more cloistered audience, the established poets were of the kind of John Bannister Tabb and the lost Madison Julius Cawein of Kentucky, he who discovered that "There is no rhyme that is half so sweet / As the song of the wind in the rippling wheat." ("Smoothness", Hulme was to declare to the next generation. "Hate it. This is the obsession that starts all my theories.") The attitude of the poet who was both serious and acceptable was expressed at the end of the era by William Winter: "The deadliest foe of the creative impulse is criticism. Genius is something that comes without effort and impels its possessor to heroic labor." Genius had the character of a hot spring and it was not to be disciplined. And as it was only artistic discipline that could be criticized, the response of the generation was uncritical and amounted when it was positive, as it often was, to generalized but nonetheless febrile adulation.

Or so it was in the great world, of Boston and New York—but the little world of San Francisco, cunningly made of gold and railroads and Mumm's Champagne, differed only in quantity. It restricted Bierce, who after all wrote for the newspapers, but its attitudes were by Bierce's time less unusual than San Franciscans liked to think.

When Bierce, on September 21, 1867, made his first poetic contribution to San Francisco culture, a series of twenty-two grisly stanzas in terza rima suffused with imagery of " . . . bloody death of stricken day / And ocean's leprous agony", the city was but eighteen years of age and no longer chaste. The great day was gone, and the world of Bret Harte, the Indians, the banditry, the bad men, the Vigilantes, the "heathen Chinee", the Donner Pass, the Gentleman from Pike. The Native Sons of the Golden West had already organized and when, in 1869, the transcontinental railroad was completed, there came the day of the railroad kings and an era of gaudy civic corruption, fantastic speculation, rococo "Society", Nob Hill, race wars, unionism (the leaders of which soon became rich and docile), and unlikely devotion to culture. The memory of its classical period was jostled by devoted imitation and institutionalized celebration (as the melancholy founding of the Bohemian Club in 1872), but the vigor and the masculinity were gone. What was left was incredible wealth—there was the gold and then the silver and the Big Bonanza, and then the railroads and the ranches and the port—a city with a greater proportion of college graduates than any other in the country, and the "tradition", which was great sport and which sustained a civic Bohemianism. The result was an ardor for luxury unparalleled in the country, and poetry and the arts were, like the terrapin, considered local delicacies, conspicuously consumed and conspicuously produced.

What San Francisco saw and heard and read was, inevitably, what was coming to the attention of everyone else in America, but San Francisco seems to have given this culture of the seventies ("It was in the seventies," Parrington commented, "that good taste reached its lowest ebb"), and of the next two decades, a special tribute. Bierce was heroic in his attitude towards an enthusiasm which made discrimination superfluous, but the city remained ineluctably blithe. The period, which was to be drenched in joy, was baptized perhaps by the Great Musical Festival of February 22-26, 1870, a tribute to genius which combined the talents of fifty soloists lent free by Sacramento, the Marysville Philharmonic and Liederkrantz Societies, fifteen hundred adult and three thousand children's voices, three hundred instrumentalists, thirty guardsmen from Company A, First California Guard, with six ten-pound fieldpieces, and one hundred firemen to strike upon fifty anvils with sledge-hammers. And it was only the beginning. Sarah Bernhardt came and was accorded frank and magnificent love, though at least half her audience did not understand French, as was Lillie Langtry, who had already had an affair with New Jersey, Modjeska, Lotta Crabtree, who was overwhelmed and gave San Francisco a fountain, Adelina Patti, and multitudes of lesser singers, dancers, musicians, actors, readers, and poets.

Wilde came in the eighties and inspired the Decorative Arts Club, which flourished with tropical rankness. When

Patti came in March of 1884 there were street battles, the glass doors of the theater were broken, and the box office was demolished. "She has become a spectacle," declared the *Argonaut,* "like Jumbo or any other freak." Lillie Langtry later the same year was a similar wonder. And Emma Nevada, a local girl who had done well, was greeted in *La Sonnambula* by "a steady rain of lilies, roses, marguerites and marigolds pour (ing) through the air and pelt(ing) the singer." Audiences paid their fifty or seventy cents and yelled themselves hoarse when Tetrazzini came to the Tivoli in *Lucia* and yelled themselves hoarse again when Laura E. Dainty, in a white nun's-veiling gown puffed at the back, recited "Little Jim" at Moody and Sankey congregations. Grand Opera, sung in English, had arrived as early as 1868 (Mrs. Amelia Neville, an older citizen, thought that "This was an interesting novelty. Italian opera had always before been sung in Italian.") and made a fortune, and a song called "One Fish-Ball" ("We give no bread with o-ne fish-ball") became at the same moment a social sentiment; and in the nineties San Franciscans packed a score of theaters, whether for Coquelin in *Tartuffe,* Ibsen's Nora, or Captain Francis Levison, the villain of Mrs. Wood's *East Lynne.*

San Franciscans also wrote poetry. It was not Bierce, as has been said, who was the poet-missionary or the gauleiter of the local creative impulse. He was responsible for neither the spiritedness of San Francisco's poets nor for their numbers. As early, according to Franklin Walker, as that fateful April morning in 1847 when Mr. Edward C. Kemble's poem, "Blowing up the Winds", appeared in the *California Star,* the poet's corner was sanctified on the front page of all news-sheets, and in the following decades it was continued, in the metropolitan dailies, with respect close to zest. In 1893 Ella Sterling Cummins discovered for purposes of immortality in *The Story of the Files: A Review of California Writers and Literature,* two hundred and forty-one famous men, or not quite five for every year of San Francisco's proper existence.

The literary spirit partook of the general craze for Art and was exuberant. But in attitude and form it was seldom, as Bierce saw, distinctively "Western", and it did not have the excuse of freshness. Its gusto was inescapably conditioned by Riley in Indiana and predirected by Aldrich in Boston and by Tennyson almost—after 1892 literally—from the other side of the grave. Literature had prestige among the citizens and poets were respected, a civic condition that cannot be held to imply dishonor except insofar as it corrupted the poets themselves. But poetry became a matter of social competition, and it was the *Poet,* that restless, hollow-cheeked wanderer in another ether, who was recognized too often as alone legitimate. Thus accumulated that monstrous quantity of dull, derivative, and awkward when not simply absurd poetic exercise which constitutes the burden of the Files. The San Franciscans were not more stupid—quite the contrary—but they were more energetic than other Americans and so they intensified the sin, and the intolerable result was sublimity over-nourished.

The national propaganda for goodness and light was enormous and stifling. What was required was a concerted action toward a new and a more expensive faith, and as its agent a literature willing to flaunt before the wide public the contrary facts of existence, willing to be tough, ugly, antagonistic, shocking. So Hulme declared for a new genre and so Ezra Pound, heroically, in 1913 was praying: "If America should bring forth a real pessimist—not a literary pessimist—I should almost believe."

Bierce, by coincidence, in that very year withdrew his efforts. But Bierce had thirty years before—and, what is more, in San Francisco—found strength to stir under the similar but more unrelieved burden and to be, pugnaciously, a pessimist. Just how much of the burden he dislocated it is impossible to say. He made a hostile gesture, when others dared not, and so struck a blow for the sanity of men, and it is in terms of that service that Bierce is important and astonishing.

He was not, after all, Pound or Hulme. Those thirty years worked a difference in the possibility of sophistication, and certain allowances must be made. He had not a sufficient sense of literary history. There is no evidence that he understood in very wide context what he was doing. His objection was intuited, and it existed in individual instances, and it was not subtle. The agent provocateur in the midst of the convention, if he was to be felt at all, could not afford subtlety; and so Bierce, as has often been said, expended unnecessary effort, shot at the mice with a Winchester and put butterflies on the rack. He perceived in practice, with rare accuracy, the weaknesses of a vitiated convention; he was extraordinarily clever; and he was bold. But he was the author of no movement, and he was not the one to stimulate a theory.

He was moreover embarrassingly uneducated—at twenty-five a kind friend introduced him to Shakespeare—and he too apparently lacked the profit of academic training. He never put in order what he knew, and what happens often to self-instructed men happened to him: he dared to rebel against the authorities of the moment, but, despite fury, he could not escape from them. His education acted, for the entire period of his professional life, against his intelligence, and so the standards he spoke from and the visions of truth he saw were often confused and often conspicuously illogical, as inconsistent, no matter how wholesome in attitude, as the persons and prejudices they were to expose. He could on one occasion, submitting to socially authorized Toryism, convict the American socialist of "congenital insurgency" and of rebelling "against pretty nearly everything that takes his attention and enlists his thought, though not many things do," and on another denounce, and with equal dedication, those who ridiculed socialism for its charitable aims and beshrewed it as a threat to the stability of government—and remain all the while equally unaware of the generality of his own rage. He could denounce alike the "enormous majority" of American newspapers, "conducted by rogues and dunces for dunces and rogues," for their opposition to every attempt at political and social reform and, tranquil to dilemma, the reformers themselves for an absurd belief in reform and the possibility of progress. He could observe, with an aloofness fairly outrageous, that "the man in jail for publication of immoralities is always a socialist" and that socialist newspapers—he usually disliked socialists—had always "a profitable 'line' of indecent advertisements," stand muscularly for the good against all literary obscenity, and finally devastate the prissiness of a women's literature, "the cartilaginous virgins of Miss Mary Wilkins, and the inspired he-prudes of Miss Mary William Dean Howells". He was not one of Emerson's men. He wrote in a tone neither ecstatic nor transcendental and he made some show of logical strenuousness; and so inconsistency in him was a grave fault.

It was a fault which also infected his principles, so far as he had any, of literary production and criticism. His contemporaries existed for him in irritating detail and with remarkable precision he exposed their excesses, but he succumbed in his moments of general aesthetics, and without knowing it, to the very taste he was most engaged in detesting. He fired his comment at those who continued to disseminate an emotional set which, for the purposes of poetry, had been too long codified and which had lost all vitality, but he recanted always before authority, and by applying his insult, which was his method, to the critics of Tennyson and to the contemners of Swinburne, he sought grace. The defect was the more regrettable in that he had many readers—he was the most popular journalist in the West—and because he offered himself and was too often received as infallible in matters of literary judgement. "Pupils," as he delighted to call them, submitted manuscripts by the hundreds and swarmed to him, to give him adulation and to receive his pronouncements—and they heard him proscribe all poetry but that which rhymed exactly, had meter, and dealt with the past, and all novels because the novel was dead. There wasn't a line of poetry in *Leaves of Grass,* he told Bailey Millard, and "Out of the Cradle, Endlessly Rocking" was "sentimental twaddle of the worst order".

So he compromised his force. Had he had the proper historical equipment he might have been a very great critic indeed, the herald of a new order, the effective conscience to his generation. As he was, he abused individuals. He dusted the jackets, by his own words, not of folly and vice but of the fools and the vicious, which meant inevitably that his satire was to exist in instances and not in general, and also, incidentally, that its time of direct relevance was to be extremely brief. The fools passed quickly, in the natural way, to utterest oblivion, and while his writings retain verbal pungency, Bierce's volumes seem at the end like nothing so much as monuments in marble to the pigmies. Bierce, moreover, wrote for immediate publication almost every day of his adult life, and therefore much of the work was dull and a considerable part was unfortunately pompous.

But taking it all in one piece, the abuse, though sometimes gross, was frank, fresh, and zestful, and in the tone it took and the insult it dared, it was undeniably bracing.

And, in spite of what it must seem today, it was not trivial. The fools, their facades and their fads, cluttered a possible landscape, and so there was reason to oppose the New Woman, the Poet of the Day, bicycling, balls, bloomers, the Bloomer Girl, and William Jennings Bryan—who "a week before the convention of 1896 . . . had never heard of himself":

> . . . upon his natural obscurity was superposed the opacity of a Congressional service that effaced him from the memory of even his faithful dog, and made him immune to dunning. . . . To the dizzy elevation of his candidacy he was hoisted out of the shadow by his own tongue, the longest and liveliest in Christendom. Had he held it—which he could not have done with both hands—there had been no Bryan. His creation was the unstudied act of his own larynx; it said, "Let there be Bryan," and there was Bryan.

And, because they contributed to the same condition, there was cause to afflict the Fourth of July orators, the people who christened ships, the persons who introduced a Congressional bill to make the pansy the national flower—why not a national soup? Bierce proposed—those who glibly idealized death, talked of heroism and such things as fields of honor. The fools existed, in multitudes, and by aiding history in the good work of disposing of them, Bierce set himself in opposition to the great sins become principle, of softness and insincerity and sentimental absurdity.

The literary fools Bierce persecuted were peace-loving and gentle, most often local offenders like persons named Madge Morris and William Greer Harrison and David Lesser Lezinsky, lost quickly and forever, and others, of wider reputation, were in themselves not more than innocuous. They might well have been permitted to exist. The evil, however, lay in the fact that they were popular, that they were, in a literary setting which demanded adherence, compelled to exist. When one attacked them, one attacked the judgment of society, and so one was justified. "In the world of letters, at least," Bierce offered, "nothing is more intolerable than tolerance." When out of good nature or any other reprehensible motive one commended them or their work or whatever else in letters was false and popular, one "had a hand in the dirty work of debasing the intellectual coin of his country. . . . " It was an illiberal creed to which Bierce gave consistent loyalty, if not consistent insight, but illiberalism had the justification of any purgative.

And Bierce gave good doses. So one morning he confronted a Mr. H. L. who had sent Bierce a manuscript:

> You were not born to write stories. Stories are not true and you are too conscientious to make them seem true, and so mislead your fellow creatures. Try writing sermons, which are all true.

And John Lambie, a poet, he advised with hearty brevity to "try oleating in prose". Madge Morris, who drew tribute from Joaquin Miller and who "harp in hand . . . smote the rebel wire, and lifting up her noise addressed that prodigious dryness," the Colorado Desert, had years of Bierce, and Miller himself, of the hairy-chested prosody and the tom-tom rhythms, alone on his mountain suffered "The Mormon Question", by J-qu-n M-ll-r:

> I said I will shake myself out of my clothes,
> I will roll up my sleeves, I will spit on my hands
> (The hands that I kissed to the sun in the lands
> To the north, to the east, to the south, and the
>   west
> Of every sea that is under the sun,)
>
>   . . . . .
>
> And I rose in the strongest strength of my strength
> With my breast of brass and my hair's full length,
> And I shook myself out of my clothes in the land
> Of the Mormons, and stood there and kissed my
>   hand.

And Bierce, democratic in intolerance, slashed class lines and found equally unbearable the queasy tenderness of David Starr Jordan, president of Stanford University, who confessed:

> Beyond the sea, I know not where,
> There is a town called Viverols;
> I know not if 'tis near or far,
> I know not what its features are,
> I only know 'tis Viverols . . .

and the melancholy of a self-styled radical who had seen:

> Oh, Oh, Oh! Beautiful Emma taking a stroll with
>   her beau
> Out on the meadow in the moonlight yonder,
>   proving herself untrue,

which for Bierce was an interesting illustration of an anarchist in love, "a spectacle hardly inferior to that of a soaring squid." And then, for a moment, at the end of his career, he noted the national literary situation, "the infantese of the late Eugene Field, the coagulated vulgarity of Mr. James Whitcomb Riley, the impossible nigger lore of Mr. Joel Chandler Harris, the proprietary syntax of Mr. Stephen Crane, the phonetic mephiticisms of Mrs. Amelie Rives Chandler," and "the hill tribe detestables of Miss Mary Murfree. . . . "

These critical explorations were too often merely sarcasm, but in this age of enchantment disrespect was good, and in this context sarcasm implied realities.

So Bierce spelled his uncertain glory, to be able to imply realities, as it was his fate only by occasional accident to achieve them. He had no "ideas". His insights, literary, social, political, moral, were too often and too apparently, as we see it now, stunted in conception by what seem foolish antagonisms. His engagements lacked wisdom and his arguments quite simply lacked intellect. But they masqueraded. They somehow made up for intellect. With an energy unaccounted for by mere perversity, by simple

petulance, Bierce *delivered* his antagonisms, delivered them with the shock of belligerent, intruding, undeniable truth. It was no small artistic achievement. He brought to the low uses of sarcasm an amazing, even, considering its uses, a too-perfect technique. He sometimes overshot, but when he didn't he brought his sentences to the rare thing, precision. They were dearly wrought and finely balanced and arranged, and they were impenetrable. Any unit larger than the sentence would have exposed him, and he consequently worked too exclusively at it, but with an imagination adapted to chiseling. He mastered it. He reduced it to a tense, subtle finality, and *it* imposed the authority he in himself lacked.

Bierce had learned his style where and as he could, in the boisterous but narrow school of Western journalism, in a short intermediate career in Fleet Street, in unmethodical reading and home-improvement; and he had little idea what he had learned. In fact Bierce brought to his journalism a literary—and by implication a social—ideal greater than ever he knew. He might hold Swinburne up to the admiration of his "pupils" and he might hasten, crushed by the mob, to the throne of Tennyson, but he was all the while, in spite of himself and much more to the necessary point, reading to the same mob the lesson of the Augustans—a lesson to the effect that gardens were to be trimmed, that wings were to be clipped, that poesy had a function more divine than flight, that reality was not a spree. Bierce contradicted the lesson of his own stylistic achievement, but the achievement remained. It interrupted the revels, it suggested truth to the point of brutality, and it confused the enemy.

Bierce paid the price for his inability finally to detect the real truth; he paid to some extent in his critical encounters, where he too frequently just missed or even missed entirely the real general point, never more copiously than in his short stories. Those sixty-five stories, less occasional than his arguments, naturally constitute his memorial—and indeed it is by one or two of them, ubiquitously anthologized, that he is regularly remembered. Their failure, in the Jamesian vocabulary, is that they do not represent; they fail to create and to fulfill the actuality that, paradoxically, they suggest. Ingeniously plotted, they are constrictingly schematic, they are paralyzed by ingenuity. They are compact. They are clever—genuinely clever. They are efficient little machines. But they are lifeless, two-dimensional, oppressed with a dialogue all syntax and, in their eternal game of grisly irony, finally monotonous. They make the single claim to art that they reveal a working craft: they have concision and they are well-arranged.

Craft, on the other hand, in a time when it was facility that tended to be honored, had its value—and the stories, for the same reason and despite what they lack, are still admirable. But to Bierce's audience there was something greater: they were, in fact, appalling. They irresistibly asserted themselves because, more than craft, they had boldness, they had the courage even to be offensive. What must seem to us today an obstinate, not to say a deranged concern with war, madness, the menace of the supernatural, literally assaulted the public imagination. To a public for whom beauty was joy and tragedy wistful, the story, "Chickamauga," of a child, a deaf mute, romping among dying soldiers and screaming at the sight of its murdered parents, had the impact of a blow. The story of the instant of desperate fantasy of an already hanging man, "An Occurrence at Owl Creek Bridge," had the force almost of truth! The story, "A Son of the Gods," of the gallant young officer whose very courage, excessive and magnetic, provokes a mass slaughter, undermined a public morality. Courage is foolhardy; the hanging man, despite your sentiment and in the nature of things, hangs. These are bearable themes, but they were unexpected. What Bierce precociously revealed was the reader, a reader who hadn't realized the imprisonment of his own romantic inclination; and therein was concealed the shock. It was not realism he committed, but outrage, immediate engagement with a literature and an audience. So he adapts the cheap nostalgia made popular by Riley and Eugene Field to a lyrical tale of parricide; the narrator of "An Imperfect Conflagration" soliloquizes: "Early one June morning in 1872 I murdered my father—an act which made a deep impression on me at the time. This was before my marriage, while I was living with my parents in Wisconsin." So, in the terrible "Oil of Dog," he perverts the worn and oppressive charm of "Little Orphant Annie" to a story of abortion: "My name is Boffer Bings. I was born of honest parents in one of the humbler walks of life, my father being a manufacturer of dog-oil and my mother having a small studio in the shadow of the village church, where she disposed of unwelcome babes." And so in "The Famous Gilson Bequest"—a story which with curious exactness anticipates "The Man That Corrupted Hadleyburg"—the horse-thief Gilson, while exposing the profounder degeneracy of his townsmen, in and out of life remains unrepentingly a thief. With wit real if sometimes mannered, with the good callousness of his intelligence, with skill, Bierce corrupted his contemporaries: death was possible and unlovely when it came; courage is ridiculous; murder and thievery and other activities of the human spirit are evil only according to a hypocritical ethic. The stories were often gratuitously revolting, but, unlike the satin horrors of Poe, they did a job. They drew an indictment. They served; they broke barriers to show possibilities beyond sentimentality.

Finally the superannuated dogma was broken, and Bierce might have had his day. But if by the time Bierce went into Mexico there was some sign of a change in the American temper, it was not because of him and he didn't recognize it. He had had his self-confessed disciples, most notably George Sterling, but none followed in the attitude that made him important, and there is no matter of his influence. He had been given, in his best days, the tribute of much enthusiasm, but as his audience was flushed with nothing so much as its own enthusiasms, the tribute was not a great one. Had the tendency of his objection been recognized he would have had neither popularity nor the cultural authority which he was granted, and in fact his career on any but a superficial level was one of profound alienation, a fact he came more and more to realize. He was at the end certainly disappointed; he was the better man and he must have known that the day had gone to the James Whitcomb Rileys and the Thomas Bailey Aldriches, and that he was not to be mourned. And yet—and it is the finest thing to be said of him—he did not submit; he did not bow to easy sentiment or, allowing charity for intellectual contradictions, assume values not his own. He went to unreasonable extremes in vilifying that sentiment and those values and often to an attitude so inflexibly negative that it approached the unreason against which it was conceived. "So," he wrote to Sterling, "—you have my entire philosophy in two words: 'Nothing matters.'" It was not, as Bierce said it, a wise thing to say. But in a culture where so much that was so worthless seemed to matter a great deal, it took courage and a ruthless, acidulous honesty to say it. It was a sentiment shocking to the sentimental mind.

Sam S. Baskett

SOURCE: "Jack London on the Oakland Waterfront," in *American Literature,* Vol. XXVII, No. 3, November, 1955, pp. 361-71.

[*In the following excerpt, Baskett focuses on Jack London's treatment of Oakland, California, and life on its docks in his work* John Barleycorn.]

In ten chapters of *John Barleycorn,* almost a third of the book, Jack London gives a convincing, colorful description of his experiences on the Oakland waterfront during the early 1890's, stealing oysters, drinking grandly and, later, enforcing the fish laws. London's principal biographers (his wife, Charmian; his daughter, Joan; and Irving Stone) have all incorporated into their works a number of the experiences described in *John Barleycorn,* frequently even to the extent of echoing the phrasing of that book. Moreover, perhaps because of this apparent verification of so much of London's self-portrait, almost all summaries of his life and commentaries on his work draw on *John Barleycorn* as a satisfactorily accurate record of London's life.[1]

To be sure, many have commented that *John Barleycorn* must be used with caution. The exaggeration and bombast which characterize the book have been recognized, of course; and the accuracy of some of the specific incidents related in the book has been challenged, including London's version of the cramming-school incident, the loan from the bartender, and the heroic drinking. Despite the obvious minor discrepancies and distortions in *John Barleycorn,* however, London's essential description of himself as "Prince of the Oyster Pirates," peer of the waterfront drunkards and Deputy Fish Patrolman, scourge of his erstwhile comrades, has been generally accepted. The uncritical acceptance of this description specifically and *John Barleycorn* generally has resulted in a somewhat inaccurate picture of London: for the validity of young London's claim to the title of

"Prince" of a thriving group of oyster pirates is rather doubtful; his account of the drunken brawl of the Hancock Fire Brigade, the one drinking incident I have been able to check with other reports, is almost certainly exaggerated beyond recognition; and very probably he had no official or recognized connection with the Fish Patrol.

London asserted in *John Barleycorn* that he began his career as an oyster pirate when he was fifteen. In 1899, however, London had written to Cloudesley Johns that "When I was just sixteen [January 12, 1892] I broke loose and went off on my own hook. Took unto myself a mistress of the same age, lived a year of wildest risk in which I made more money in one week than I do in a year now . . . ," and presumably this earlier statement is more accurate.[2] If so, this period in London's life began during January, 1892. The culminating episode of this year, as described in *John Barleycorn,* was the election-parade drinking spree. The author and "Young Scratch" Nelson assembled with the Hancock Fire Brigade and, upon obtaining firemen's helmets, red shirts and torches, boarded the train for Haywards. Having paraded, the marchers received their pay—free liquor. According to London, the drinkers completely took over the saloons, every man helped himself to several bottles and went outside where "we knocked the necks of the bottles off against the concrete curbs, and drank." London went to other saloons, drank perhaps "two quarts or five," and finally was hustled "in the very last rank of a disorderly parade" to the Oakland train. Once aboard the train, London, crazed and suffocating from the raw whiskey he had consumed, seized a torch and broke a window, setting off a frenzied drunken brawl, "and they say there were few unbroken windows in the wreckage of the car that followed as the free-for-all fight had its course."

This Haywards election parade was reported in both Oakland papers on October 24, 1892, as occurring on Saturday, October 22. The *Times* gave the fullest and most sympathetic account.

> The Democrats of Haywards held a ratification meeting in one of the largest halls in the town and the uniformed clubs of this city sent down and took part in the torch light parade that preceded the meeting. . . . The Hancock Fire Brigade . . . turned out about 200 members, and, composed as they are, of a fine body of men, received much applause as they marched along.

The *Tribune,* supporting the Republicans, omitted the commendation, but did print a story about the affair. Neither paper, however, made any reference to the wrecking of the train car on the return trip; there is no suggestion of any actions of an unusually rowdy or destructive nature. This negative evidence is not complete proof, of course, but it seems safe to assume that if a fracas of the heroic proportions described by London had taken place, some evidence of it would at least have reached the newspaper of the rival political party.[3]

The Haywards election party establishes a terminal date for London's "year of wildest risk." Following this escapade, London wrote, "I lived more circumspectly, drank less deeply and went home more frequently." And he described no more incidents between this date, October 22, and his shipping out on a sealing schooner the following January. Thus, in the nine months between January and October, 1892, occurred all the events on which London's fame as "Prince of the Oyster Pirates" and Deputy Fish Patrolman must rest. According to London's statement in *John Barleycorn,* his fame as a pirate was considerable:

> My reputation grew. When the story went around the water-front of how French Frank had tried to run me down with his schooner, and of how I had stood on the deck of the *Razzle Dazzle,* a cocked double-barreled shotgun in my hands, steering with my feet and holding her to her course, and compelled him to put up his wheel and keep away, the water-front decided that there was something to me despite my youth. And I continued to show what was in me. There were the times I brought the *Razzle Dazzle* in with a bigger load of oysters than any other two-man craft; there was the time when we raided far down in Lower Bay and mine was the only craft back at daylight to the anchorage off Asparagus Island; there was the Thursday night we raced for market and I brought the *Razzle Dazzle* in without a rudder, first of the fleet, and skimmed the cream of the Friday morning trade; and there was the time I brought her in from Upper Bay under a jib, when Scotty burned my mainsail.

While possibly and even probably London did engage in a number of wild and illegal adventures, there are several reasons for doubting the accuracy of his description of himself as the dominating figure of the Oakland waterfront.

(1) London made clear a number of times that he felt no compunction about giving as his experiences what he thought would be believable and marketable, rather than what had actually happened. Writing in the *Cosmopolitan Magazine* of his life as a tramp, London said,

> I have often thought that to this training of my tramp days is due much of my success as a story-writer. In order to get the food whereby I lived, I was compelled to tell tales that rang true. At the back door, out of inexorable necessity, is developed the convincingness and sincerity laid down by all authorities on the art of the short story. . . . Realism constitutes the only goods one can exchange at the kitchen door for grub.[4]

And later in the same series he told of fabricating experiences that gained him back-door meals from maiden ladies, although "if those maiden ladies had been less trustful and guileless they could have tangled me up beautifully in my chronology."

(2) London's report of his adventures seems less authentic when we follow his warning and check the chronology

of *John Barleycorn.* London described the purchase of the *Razzle Dazzle,* which, according to the Johns letter, probably could not have occurred earlier than January, 1892, and then related several experiences of the period he was on this boat. Soon, however, he joined Nelson aboard the latter's *Reindeer*[5] and spent "months of mad deviltry" with him. After this, he had "longer spells ashore," and an undesignated amount of time "fooling with salmon fishing and making raids up and down bay and rivers as a deputy fish patrolman," including one "three solid weeks" when he never "drew a sober breath." Somewhat shaken by a reconsidered attempt to drown himself when he fell off a dock in a drunken stupor, he left the bay area, made his way to Sacramento and fell in with some "road kids." Joan London states that he was with this gang "several weeks," going to Nevada and back with them. Returning to Oakland, he loafed around the waterfront for some time, "only occasionally going for cruises of several days on the bay to help out on short-handed scow-schooners"—all before October 22. In these nine months there is too little time for London to have participated successfully, and to the extent he claims, in all the adventures mentioned in *John Barleycorn.* It is not easy to "untangle" London's chronology, for he, perhaps intentionally, included no specific dates in his narration; but unless he has exaggerated his participation in all of these undertakings, by checking backward from the date of the election parade, we can ascertain that he could have spent only a very few months—possibly not more than two—aboard the *Razzle Dazzle.*

(3) London's statements about his career as an oyster pirate are inconsistent. In the *Cosmopolitan Magazine* for November, 1907, he commented that the road kids with their tales of riding the rods "made my oyster piracy look like thirty cents." On the following page he claimed "as an oyster pirate I had already earned conviction at the hands of justice which, if I had to serve them, would have required a thousand years in state's prison." Recognizing that London may have wished to change the emphasis for the purpose of making different points, one still finds some difficulty in believing that these two statements indicate London has firmly in mind an irreducible body of events that actually occurred.

This same troubling facility in adjusting his focus is exhibited by London in references to his title. In *John Barleycorn* he says, "What completed everything and won for me the title of 'Prince of the Oyster Beds,' was that I was a good fellow ashore with my money, buying drinks like a man." And yet he told Charmian London in the same year he wrote *John Barleycorn* that he had been called "Prince" because he sailed the *Razzle Dazzle* with a woman aboard, who as the mistress of French Frank had been known as "Queen of the Oyster Pirates."

(4) London's attitude toward money and toward his family, and the attitude of his family toward him and toward law-breaking all tend to conflict with the assertion that he obtained huge sums through the sale of stolen oysters, sums which were irresponsibly squandered in riotous

carousing. At fifteen, London stated in *John Barleycorn,* he was working in a cannery ten hours a day, ten cents an hour, and giving a substantial portion of his wages to his mother. At sixteen, he was making hundreds of dollars per week and admitting little or no responsibility to his family. It is not surprising, of course, that London would break away from the heavy obligations apparently imposed upon him by his mother. It is surprising, however, that during the few months he could have been an oyster pirate there is no record that his family protested about either his life of reckless danger (his stepfather, John London, had served for several years up to about this time as a deputy constable, special officer, and watchman) or his failure to turn over some of his gains from the oyster raids. At seventeen, when London returned from the sealing voyage he turned over most of his accumulated wages. Shortly afterwards he obtained a job in a jute mill, ten hours a day, ten cents an hour. "Then, too, my mother said I had sown my wild oats and it was time I settled down to a regular job. Also the family needed the money." London apparently was considerably tamer at seventeen than he had been at sixteen. One can reconcile the two pictures only if he assumes that the "wild oats" sown were those of a lusty young waterfront bum, drifting around trying to get his bearings, rather than those of the pre-eminently successful oyster thief of the bay area.

(5) London did not write fully about his experiences as an oyster pirate until twenty years after those experiences had occurred. Throughout his writing career London was particularly successful in working up all phases of his life into publishable form. For example, the essays collected in *The Road* (1907) dealt fully and seriously with his life as a tramp in 1892 and 1893-1894; and London thoroughly exploited in print every aspect of his Klondike venture. Yet his writings prior to *John Barleycorn* do not document the claim made in the *Cosmopolitan Magazine* for November, 1907, that at sixteen "I had attained a dizzying reputation in my chosen circle of adventurers by whom I was known as the 'Prince of the Oyster Pirates.'" The one extensive description of oyster piracy occurs in *The Cruise of the "Dazzler"* (1902), like *Tales of the Fish Patrol* an adventure book for adolescents, but this fiction is so obviously fashioned for juvenile readers that any autobiographical identification seems unwise.[6] If London's adventures as an oyster pirate were as successful and extensive as he has claimed, if they were the dominating experiences of his seventeenth year, why did he not write up these experiences on an adult level, perhaps in the form of easily marketable autobiographical-sociological essays, as he did almost every other phase of his early life? Actually, London never did publish these experiences in detail—for the references to oyster piracy in *John Barleycorn* are vague and general, as well as incidental to the central concern with alcohol.

(6) London's picture of a "fleet" manned by perhaps dozens of swashbuckling, heavy-drinking, hardfisted oyster pirates is not fully verified by contemporary accounts.[7] *The Biennial Report of the State Board of Fish Commissioners of the State of California* for the relevant

years, while discussing law enforcement problems in some detail, does not single out oyster pirates for specific emphasis. Nor do the Oakland papers substantiate London's representation of continual violence and theft along the oyster beds. It may be, of course, that the editors preferred to look the other way. One reference made to the oyster industry is rather different from London's description, however, the Oakland *Tribune* for January 21, 1891, reporting:

> The abandoned oyster beds of the Morgan Oyster Company on Bay Farm Island present a very busy scene, hundreds of persons going there in search of oysters, and last night there was oyster hunting by moonlight. It is estimated that during the past week more than $5000 worth of oysters have been carried away. . . . They are fast disappearing, however, and it will not be many days until the beds are exhausted. All that a person needs to go hunting for them is a pair of rubber boots, as there is much mud in the beds. They can be reached by land, but more directly by a boat from the county bridge.

The abandonment of these and other oyster beds was an indication that the transplanting of oysters in the bay area had not been successful. Perhaps the fifteen-year-old London shared in the plunder to be obtained from these beds. This is not to imply, certainly, that no oyster piracy took place in Oakland in the 1890's. However, in at least this one instance, free oysters were legitimately available to the man who knew how to handle a small boat.

There are several reasons, then, for viewing with some skepticism the accepted picture of young London as a most dashingly successful oyster thief whose exploits shocked and intrigued the entire community. His own references to those exploits, in *John Barleycorn* and elsewhere, while convincing at first seem much less compellingly authentic when examined closely. The "Prince of the Oyster Pirates" tends to be reduced in size to sixteen-year-old Jack, a boy on his own for the first time, at loose ends, learning how to be a sailor, how to drink, how to exchange credible tales with the waterfront riffraff, and how to steal.

Concerning London's role as a Deputy Fish Patrolman, even more skepticism is justifiable. In *John Barleycorn* London only mentions in passing that he had made "raids up and down bay and rivers as a deputy fish patrolman," but this reference has undoubtedly served to give greater autobiographical weight to the adventure book for adolescents, *Tales of the Fish Patrol*. London wrote in a copy of this work, "Find here, sometimes hinted, sometimes told, and sometimes made different, the days of my boyhood when, I, too, was on the Fish Patrol."[8] His biographers, with the exception of Joan London, have largely ignored this warning, considering the *Tales* as a factual record. They have even noted that he supported himself at this time from the fines collected. On the contrary, the evidence is rather conclusive that London had no official connection with the Fish Patrol and received

no money as a patrolman. In the *Biennial Report of the State Board of Fish Commissioners* for 1891-1892, there is a directory of deputy patrolmen who served without pay and there is also a list of payments to the deputies, payment by payment. London is not included in either list. This and the subsequent biennial report both contain excerpts from the daily reports of deputies and there is no mention of London. Apparently so far as the official records of the California Fish Patrol are concerned, Jack London did not exist.[9]

Thus it is difficult to verify at least three of the incidents described by London in *John Barleycorn;* in fact, the evidence I have been able to uncover rather sharply contradicts London's version of his early adventures. Just how much London exaggerated, or fabricated, it is hard to say, for, as T. K. Whipple wrote in 1938, "to disentangle the facts from his [London's] phantasy of himself would be almost impossible."[10] This much can be said, however. We are much more likely to learn what London was actually like—as opposed to what London thought he was like or wished his reader to think—if we begin with the recognition that *John Barleycorn* cannot be trusted as autobiography.

NOTES

[1] For example, Edward Wagenknecht in *Cavalcade of the American Novel* (New York, 1952), p. 224 n., says that *John Barleycorn*, "though often spoken of as a novel, is a factual record, with some manipulation for literary effectiveness, of London's experiences with alcohol. . . . " Maxwell Geismar in *Rebels and Ancestors* (Boston, 1953), in the first two pages of a short biographical sketch of London uses material from *John Barleycorn* eight times, actually quoting from it five times.

[2] Charmian London, *The Book of Jack London* (New York, 1921), I, 86. Mrs. London, reporting a conversation with London "twenty years thereafter" concerning his relations with the "Queen of the Oyster Pirates," quotes him as saying "I was a husky man at sixteen" (*ibid.*, I, 84).

[3] In 1916 Oliver Madox Hueffer wrote that "Among the apocryphal legends attached to his [London's] name and founded very possibly on his own statements was that of his almost superhuman drunkenness" ("Jack London, A Personal Sketch," *New Statesman*, VIII, 206, 1916). There are numerous examples in *John Barleycorn* of London's obvious exaggeration of his drinking feats. Surely no boy of sixteen could drink "two or five" quarts of whiskey in a short time and then walk to a train, as London claimed to have done after the Haywards parade. London said, on another occasion, that he spent "all of one hundred and eighty dollars for drinks" in twelve hours. At the going price of ten cents for whiskey and five cents for beer, thus he claimed to have bought 1800 whiskeys or 3600 beers for his friends in one night of carousing.

[4] "A Reminiscence and a Confession," *Cosmopolitan Magazine*, XLIII, 19 (May, 1907).

[5] It seems rather strange that the young superman who has become the terror and wonder of the Oakland waterfront, who has been making hundreds of dollars a week, would let a burned mainsail of the *Razzle Dazzle* cause him to abandon that craft and sink to partnership with another oyster pirate.

[6] Actually, *The Cruise of the "Dazzler"* tends to refute London's later claims. "'Frisco Kid" (the nickname used by London) and "French Pete" (London in *John Barleycorn* buys the *Razzle Dazzle* from "French Frank") are oyster pirates, but we have the following description of their activities from the point of view of a young boy: French Pete is captain and "lord and master" of 'Frisco Kid; they work the abandoned oyster beds, the procedure being described in some detail; they do not steal any oysters from private beds, although they talk about a raid and do steal, or attempt to steal other items; the sailing exploits of the pirates receive the principal stress in the book.

[7] If the oyster pirates went almost as they pleased about the Oakland waterfront in 1892 as London's account in *John Barleycorn* seems to suggest, by London's own statement their day was soon to be abruptly terminated. When London returned in July, 1893, from his voyage to the North Pacific he "took a look at the death road." The pirates were all gone—in prison, in hiding or dead.

[8] Joan London, *Jack London and His Times* (New York, 1939), p. 44.

[9] In *Tales of the Fish Patrol,* London stated that when he was sixteen the Fish Commission had chartered his sloop, the *Reindeer* (in *John Barleycorn* the *Reindeer* is Nelson's boat), "and I became for the time being a deputy patrolman." Again, the reports do not confirm London's statement. The report for 1891-1892 mentions a launch, the "Rustler"; and the following report adds that the patrol have found it to their advantage to make use of the launch "Hustler," and "her Captain, Henry Rowson, and thus have been able to cover the ground in a much more expeditious manner than would have been possible under any other circumstances."

[10] "Jack London—Wonder Boy," *Saturday Review of Literature,* VIII, 3 (Sept. 24, 1938).

Peter Buitenhuis

SOURCE: "Aesthetics of the Skyscraper: The Views of Sullivan, James and Wright," in *American Quarterly,* Vol. IX, No. 3, Fall, 1957, pp. 316-24.

[*In the following essay, Buitenhuis discusses the twentieth-century urban skyscraper in an examination of Frank Lloyd Wright, Louis Sullivan, and the fiction of Henry James.*]

When a new form is invented, whether it be in art, literature or architecture, a new aesthetic has to be created so that the form, in its various manifestations, can be evaluated and criticized. Some of the worst and most misguided criticism is always written during the infancy of a new form, but also some of the most original and incisive. The views of Louis Sullivan, Henry James and Frank Lloyd Wright on the typically American innovation of the skyscraper are not only constructive but also show how far men of different generations, backgrounds and temperaments can agree on aesthetic judgments.

Before the evolution of the steel skeleton frame, the weight and relatively low tensile strength of masonry limited the height of the office building to about twelve floors. The demand for taller buildings became stronger and stronger, however, as American cities rapidly grew in the closing years of the nineteenth century and commercial land values soared. The steel frame was a direct response to this demand. The first office building to utilize the technique was constructed in 1885. It soon became obvious that a steel-framed building could rise at least four times as high as a masonry building. In little over ten years the technique had revolutionized tall office-building design.

The center of development of this new architectural form was Chicago. It was a place peculiarly well-suited to the idea of the skyscraper. The bustling, booming city, with a tremendous sense of its destiny as the future metropolis of the Midwest, was the city in America most individualistic in its enterprise. In the tall building the American tycoon found a fitting symbol for his restless drive and buoyant hopes. In the 1880's and 1890's large numbers of skyscrapers were built in Chicago. The impetus rapidly spread to other cities, especially New York. Many of the architects called upon to design skyscrapers worked within established forms, merely elongating these forms to fit the needs of the tall building. The wealth of their clients stimulated them also to decorate their designs with lavish copies of classical and Gothic models. Some Chicago architects were, however, dissatisfied with this approach to a new form. One of the most visionary of these was Louis Sullivan.

Frank Lloyd Wright, who worked in Sullivan's office between 1887 and 1894, recounts how one day Sullivan entered his cubicle, placed a piece of manila paper on Wright's desk, and left without a word. On the paper was an elevation of the Wainwright Building, "the very first human expression," Wright called it, "of a tall steel office-building as Architecture."[1] Wright pointed out that Sullivan had hit upon the fundamental principle of skyscraper design in his replacement of the broken, opaque walls of previous tall buildings with sheer, transparent screens. The only part of the building that Wright disliked was the elaborate cornice. In such designs as that for the Reliance Building (1895), Sullivan corrected this tendency toward ornamentation and produced soaring, well-proportioned, curtain-walled skyscrapers.[2]

Sullivan himself first raised the aesthetic problem of the skyscraper in an article that appeared in March, 1896, called "The Tall Office Building Artistically Considered."

How shall we impart to this sterile pile, this crude, harsh, brutal agglomeration, this stark, staring exclamation of eternal strife, the graciousness of those higher forms of sensibility and culture that rest on the lower and fiercer passions? How shall we proclaim from the dizzy heights of this strange, weird, modern housetop the peaceful evangel of sentiment, of beauty, the cult of a higher life?[3]

The answer to this question lay in his own famous apothegm: "form follows function."

The function of the office-building, as Sullivan saw it, was to supply a large number of identical, well-lit offices. He therefore proposed a modular unit on which the design of the skyscraper should be based.

> The practical horizontal and vertical division or office unit is naturally based on a room of comfortable area and height, and the size of this standard office room as naturally predetermines the standard structural unit, and, approximately, the size of window openings. In turn, these purely arbitrary units of structure form in an equally natural way the true basis of the artistic development of the exterior.[4]

The building was to be, simply, a tier of identical floors, except for a main entrance floor and an attic for tanks, pipes and machinery. Sullivan denied the need for cornice or frieze or any other embellishment of the building. He pointed out that although nine out of ten skyscrapers then being built were used as a display for "architectural knowledge in the encyclopaedic sense," it was obvious that such decoration was mere folly. The architect was in this way only speaking "a foreign language with a noticeable American accent," instead of expressing with "native instinct and sensibility" that which was in him to say in "the simplest, most modest, most natural way. . . . "[5]

In a style that savors of Walt Whitman, Sullivan justified the form of the skyscraper.

> What is the chief characteristic of the tall office building? And at once we answer, it is lofty. This loftiness is to the artist nature its thrilling aspect. It is the very organ-tone in its appeal.It must be in turn the dominant chord in his expression of it, the true excitant of his imagination. It must be tall, every inch of it tall. The force and power of altitude must be in it, the glory and pride of exaltation must be in it. It must be every inch a proud and soaring thing, rising in sheer exultation that from bottom to top it is a unit without a single dissenting line—that it is the new, the unexpected, the eloquent peroration of most bald, most sinister, most forbidding conditions.[6]

From the start, Sullivan was well aware of these "forbidding conditions" in which skyscrapers were built. He saw that they were a response to a selfish commercial need, and a direct result of the rapidly rising value of city lots in good business locations. In his skyscrapers he sought to transmute these drives into a soaring form which signified

the endeavor but made no concessions to the "lower passions" which provided the original impetus for the form. The steel frame was boldly outlined on the exterior of the building. It provided both the frame for the huge windows and the unit of construction. In the Carson Pirie Scott Department Store (1899) and the McClurg Building (1900), the form is seen at its best. The soaring vertical piers of steel are regularly and cleanly intersected by the horizontal girders which mark the level of floors and ceilings.[7]

While the Chicago skyline soon revealed the results of the work of Sullivan and like-minded architects, that of New York showed no such change. Although New York architects lost no time in adopting the steel frame principle, they retained the thick masonry construction of the old tall buildings on the exterior, to give the illusion that the stone was securely bearing the weight. There was no grace in the heavy vertical stone pillars nor in the horizontal bands of masonry and cast iron of these new skyscrapers. They struggled up into the sky encumbered by layers of brick, stone, iron and marble. For them, "rising in sheer exultation" was out of the question.

These were the skyscrapers that Henry James saw when he sailed into the harbor in 1904, after an absence of more than twenty years, and looked across at what he called in *The American Scene* the "serried, bristling city" of New York. Nearly thirty years earlier, in 1878, James had written a story, *An International Episode,* in which an English nobleman, visiting New York, is to his surprise shot up in an elevator to the seventh floor of a "fresh, light, ornamental structure, ten stories high." He looks out of the window of the office in which he finds himself to see the weather vane of a church steeple on a line with his eyes.[8] It is probable that this is a fictional account of a visit that James himself paid to an office on Wall Street. The weather vane surely belonged to the spire of Trinity Church. He returned to the scene on his visit of 1904-5 and gazed in astonishment at "the special sky-scraper that overhangs poor old Trinity to the north—a south face as high and wide as the mountainwall that drops the alpine avalanche, from time to time, upon the village, and the village spire, at its foot. . . . "[9] The difference between the "ornamental structure, ten stories high" and this "mountain-wall" must have been a measure to James of the difference made by the intervening years to his "old" New York.

James found many reasons to dislike these new skyscrapers. To him the "flash of innumerable windows and flicker of subordinate gilt attributions" seemed like "the flare, up and down their long, narrow faces, of the lamps of some general permanent 'celebration.'"[10] The windows of most New York skyscrapers at this time were set deeply into the thick masonry, as if the buildings had been thought of as substantial houses extended almost indefinitely upwards. As a result, the skyline was dense with the flashing, broken facades that James found so distasteful.

It was natural that he should seek to compare the skyscraper with some analogous structure in European architecture, deeply versed as he was in this aspect of the older civilization. He found his analogy in the Renaissance bell-towers of Italy. Yet how different they were from these "towers of glass"! "Such a structure," he wrote, "as the comparatively windowless bell-tower of Giotto, in Florence, looks supremely serene in its beauty. You don't feel it to have risen by the breath of an interested [money] passion that, restless beyond all passions, is for ever seeking more pliable forms." In the Giotto tower James found a successful solution to the eternal quest for form. "Beauty," he continued, "has been the object of its creator's idea, and, having found beauty, it has found the form in which it splendidly rests."[11] We have seen that Sullivan started his quest from another quarter—a quarter typically American in its pragmatism. Function had been his first objective; form was to follow it, and beauty was to be the result. Paradoxically, Sullivan's finest curtain-walled skyscrapers have in them much of the sheer elegance of the Italian windowless towers.

Implicit in Sullivan's justification for the form of the skyscraper is the premise that the building should stand in isolation. A lofty building has little "force and power of altitude" if it is crowded by other tall buildings. The New York skyscrapers seemed to James to be "extravagant pins in a cushion already overplanted, and stuck in as in the dark, anywhere and anyhow . . ."[12] Land values had soared so rapidly in Manhattan at the end of the nineteenth century that landowners had competed among themselves to put up tall buildings. Already, in 1904, they huddled together and hemmed in the streets. "Quiet interspaces." James wrote, "always half the architectural battle, exist no more in such a structural scheme."[13] However, on a few occasions, Henry James saw skyscrapers as Louis Sullivan intended them to be seen, when tricks of light softened their broken outlines. In the later afternoons of some summer and winter days, a "refinement of modelling," James observed, "descends from the skies and lends the white towers, all new and crude and commercial and over-windowed as they are, a fleeting distinction."[14] Even when, one foggy morning, he had been gazing up at the skyscraper that had "extinguished" Trinity, he had been aware that "the vast money-making structure quite horribly, quite romantically justified itself, looming through the weather with an insolent cliff-like sublimity."[15]

James's most radical criticism of the New York skyscrapers was that the commercial motive which had caused them to be built, the motive which Sullivan had successfully sublimated, dominated the form. *"They,"* James ironically and balefully observed, "ranged in this terrible recent erection, were going to bring in money—and was not money the only thing a self-respecting structure could be thought of as bringing in?"[16] Convinced as he was that the mercenary spirit was, of all, the most restless, he saw little chance that the form should remain as it was.

> Crowned not only with no history, but with no credible possibility of time for history, and consecrated by no uses save the commercial at any

cost, they are simply the most piercing notes in that concert of the most expensively provisional into which your supreme sense of New York resolves itself. They never begin to speak to you, in the manner of the builded majesties of the world as we have heretofore known such—towers or temples or fortresses or palaces—with the authority of things of permanence or even of things of long duration. One story is good only till another is told, and sky-scrapers are the last word of economic ingenuity only till another word be written. This shall be possibly a word of still uglier meaning, but the vocabulary of thrift at any price shows boundless resources, and the consciousness of that truth, the consciousness of the finite, the menaced, the essentially *invented* state, twinkles ever, to my perception, in the thousand glassy eyes of these giants of the mere market.[17]

Even the windows themselves seemed to James to have a sinister purpose. "Doesn't it," he asked, "take in fact acres of window-glass to help even an expert New Yorker to get the better of another expert one, or to see that the other expert one doesn't get the better of *him?*" The answer was apparently self-evident. "It is easy to conceive," he went on, "that, after all, with this origin and nature stamped upon their foreheads, the last word of the mercenary monsters should not be their address to our sense of formal beauty."[18]

Frank Lloyd Wright's observations on the New York skyscrapers, written twenty-five years later, are remarkably similar in ideas, if not in language, to those of Henry James. As a basis for his criticism, however, were the principles of skyscraper construction that he had learned from Sullivan. Looking back in 1930 to those visionary designs by his old master, he could see how little they had affected the designs of the contemporary skyscrapers. In his lecture "The Tyranny of the Skyscraper," given at Princeton, he said: "The light that shone in the Wainwright Building as a promise, flickered feebly and is fading away."[19]

By this time, skyscrapers had clustered so thickly that the city had been forced to pass some "set-back" laws, so that some light should filter down into the street canyons and into the lower offices. Set-back skyscrapers lose of course that single soaring line that Sullivan postulated as the basis for design. Wright pointed out:

> The Skyscraper of today is only the prostitute semblance of the architecture it professes to be. The heavy brick and stone that falsely represents walls is, by the very set-back laws, unnaturally forced onto the interior steel stilts to be carried down by them through twenty, fifty or more stories to the ground. The picture is improved, but the picturesque element in it all is false work built over a hollow box. These new tops are shams, too—box-balloons.[20]

James had used the same image as Wright, characteristically muted, to call all the gilding on the skyscrapers the efforts of a "compromised charmer" to cover up the temporary nature and insincerity of the building.[21] Also in the same vein as James, Wright observed: "The skyscraper envelope is not ethical, beautiful or permanent. It is a commercial exploit or a mere expedient. It has no higher ideal of unity than commercial success." Wright also recognized that the congestion of the skyscrapers had robbed them of what distinction they might have gained from their height. "Utterly barbaric," he wrote, "they rise regardless of special consideration for environment or for each other, except to win the race or get the tenant. Space as a becoming psychic element of the American city is gone."[22] As Sullivan had before him, Wright scorned those native architects who had tried to bring Beaux-Arts ideas to bear on the design of the skyscraper and to see it as a column, with base, shaft and capital. He derided those architects who saw it as "Gothic—commercial competitor to the Cathedral."[23] He demanded integrity and sanity in the design and erection of skyscrapers in American cities.

Sullivan had treated the skyscraper as a form without taking into consideration the rest of the city scene. Both Wright and James, however, realized that it was impossible to deal with the skyscraper apart from the aesthetic and utilitarian aspects of the whole city. Both saw in what James called "the original sin of longitudinal avenues perpetually, yet meanly intersected" and Wright "the original village grid-iron" the root of New York's trouble. James wrote darkly:

> There is violence outside, mitigating sadly the frontal majesty of the monument, leaving it exposed to the vulgar assault of the street by the operation of those dire facts of absence of margin, of meagreness of site, of the brevity, of the block, of the inveteracy of the near thoroughfare, which leave 'style,' in construction, at the mercy of the impertinent cross-streets, make a detachment and independence, save in the rarest cases, an insoluble problem, preclude without pity any element of court or garden, and open to the builder in quest of distinction the one alternative, and the great adventure, of seeking his reward in the sky.[24]

Wright observed:

> Barely tolerable for a village, the grid becomes a dangerous criss-cross check to all forward movements even in a large town where horses are motive power. But with the automobile and skyscraper that opposes and kills the automobile's contribution to the city, stop-and-go attempts to get across to somewhere or to anywhere, for that matter, in the great Metropolis, are inevitable waste— dangerous and maddening to a degree where sacrificial loss, in every sense but one, is for everyone.
>
> Erstwhile village streets become grinding pits of metropolitan misery. Frustration of all life, in the village-that-became-a-city, is imminent in this, the great unforeseen Metropolis. . . . "[25]

Unlike James, however, Frank Lloyd Wright believed that the skyscraper as form had great possibilities. He was

strongly of the opinion that the commercial motive behind the building of skyscrapers was a force for good. "Business ethics," he wrote, "make a good platform for true Aesthetics in this Machine Age or in any other." In Wright's eyes, the trouble was that the dominating force in the construction of the New York skyscrapers was not business ethics alone but "a conscious yearn, a generosity, a prodigality in the name of taste and refinement" that led only to pretension and artificiality. Were this mummery only dropped, Wright believed (as had Sullivan) that "space-manufacturing-for-rent," as he called it, "might become genuine architecture and be beautiful as standardization in steel, metals and glass."[26] Perhaps to prove this point, Wright built his superb skyscraper for the Johnson Wax Company at Racine, Wisconsin. The building is suspended from a central core of steel and concrete, and the sheer glass walls, accented with vertical metal strips, are banded by the parapets of the alternate floors which are cantilevered out from the core. The intermediate floors, which are circular, do not reach the exterior walls, so that the horizontal planes are not over-emphasized. Equally important, this skyscraper stands apart from other tall buildings, so that its "force and power of altitude" can be seen and appreciated.[27]

To bring order out of the chaos of New York, Wright recommended that immediate action be taken to control the erection of further skyscrapers. He also urged the broadening of roadbeds and the removal of pedestrians to a higher level. James made no such specific recommendation. He only reflected wryly on the endless abuse of natural beauty and constant scorn of opportunity in New York. As he looked at the tall buildings that marched relentlessly northwards up Manhattan and along the Hudson, he came to what was for him, a life-long conservative and individualist, a remarkable conclusion.

> The whole thing is the vividest of lectures on the subject of individualism, and on the strange truth, no doubt, that this principle may in the field of art—at least if the art be architecture—often conjure away just that mystery of distinction which it sometimes so markedly promotes in the field of life. . . . And yet why *should* the charm ever fall out of the 'personal,' which is so often the very condition of the exquisite? Why should conformity and subordination, that acceptance of control and assent to collectivism in the name of which our age has seen such dreary things done, become on a given occasion the one *not* vulgar way of meeting a problem?[28]

Henry James expressed in this question the whole dilemma of the city-planner. The irony of the situation is that the skyscraper, symbol of American individual enterprise, should be that form of construction most necessary to control in order to bring back not only some measure of convenience to the American city, but also to restore to it the aesthetic appeal of its own loftiness.

In the views of Sullivan, James and Wright, we can see then a spectrum of architectural criticism. Firstly, there is the definition and the justification of the form, secondly the criticism of the misuses of the form, and lastly an attempt to relate the special problems that the skyscraper raises to the planning of the city. Although James was, basically, opposed to the idea of the skyscraper, he yet gave it the benefit of the consideration due any significant new form, as few had done before him. In criticizing the form, however, he sought always to find in it the expression of the "money-passion" which he came to believe was corrupting so much of twentieth-century American life. Sullivan and Wright were both aware of this commercial motive in the form, but they turned their critical and creative talents to separating what they considered to be the gold of American enterprise and endeavor from the dross of prodigality, ostentation and historicism. All three recognized in the skyscraper a peculiarly American form and strove to evaluate it in terms of their vision of American life.

NOTES

[1] Frank Lloyd Wright, "The Tyranny of the Skyscraper," *Modern Architecture* (Princeton: Princeton University Press, 1931), p. 85.

[2] William Alex, "The Skyscraper: USA," *Perspectives 8,* Summer 1954, Plate 10.

[3] Louis Sullivan, "The Tall Office Building Artistically Considered," *Kindergarten Chats* (rev. ed.), ed., Isabella Athey (New York: Wittenborn, Schultz, 1947), p. 202.

[4] Sullivan, *Kindergarten Chats,* p. 203.

[5] *Ibid.,* pp. 208, 213.

[6] *Ibid.,* p. 206.

[7] Alex, "The Skyscraper: USA," plates 12 & 13.

[8] Henry James, "An International Episode," *The Great Short Novels of Henry James,* ed. Philip Rahv (New York: Dial Press, 1944), p. 157.

[9] Henry James, *The American Scene* (London: Chapman & Hall, 1907), p. 83.

[10] *Ibid.,* p. 76.

[11] James, *The American Scene,* pp. 77-78.

[12] *Ibid.,* p. 76.

[13] *Ibid.,* p. 95.

[14] *Ibid.,* p. 81.

[15] *Ibid.,* p. 83.

[16] James, *The American Scene,* p. 94.

[17] *Ibid.,* p. 77.

[18] *Ibid.,* p. 96.

[19] Wright, *Modern Architecture,* p. 98.

[20] Wright, *Modern Architecture,* pp. 94-95.

[21] James, *The American Scene,* pp. 110-11.

[22] Wright, *Modern Architecture,* p. 98.

[23] *Ibid.,* p. 94.

[24] James, *The American Scene,* p. 100.

[25] Wright, *Modern Architecture,* pp. 90-91.

[26] *Ibid.,* p. 96.

[27] Alex, "The Skyscraper: USA," plates 31-33.

[28] James, *The American Scene,* pp. 141-42.

R. A. Morris

SOURCE: "Classical Vision and the American City: Henry James's *The Bostonians,*" in the *New England Quarterly,* Vol. XLVI, No. 4, December, 1973, pp. 543-57.

[*In the following excerpt, Morris explores urban settings in Henry James's* The Bostonians.]

A number of recent studies have stressed the great problems which the modern city has posed to the sensibilities of imaginative writers during the nineteenth and twentieth centuries—writers such as Dickens, Dostoevski and Baudelaire, Dreiser and Crane, Kafka, Fitzgerald, Celine, Orwell, and even that apologist for the technological era, H. G. Wells.[1] This essay will consider a late nineteenth-century American view of the city, by Henry James, and his efforts to invest the American urban scene with an aesthetic significance which, in James's opinion, it sorely needed.

One view holds that James was principally a "realist" who sought, in his fiction, to give a faithful transcription of contemporary life. The difficulties in this view are worth considering briefly. It is this sense of James as a realist which informs a study by Daniel Lerner and Oscar Cargill.[2] In writing of the development, in *The Bostonians,* of an extended classical comparison drawn from the *Antigone* of Sophocles, the authors conclude that James recognized his novel to be a failure because he had violated the criteria of realism to which he normally subscribed; and they remark that elsewhere James "deliberately suppressed classical allusion in the bulk of his fiction, feeling perhaps that it was inappropriate to the contemporary tone he wished to give his writing" (317). If it is indeed the mark of a realist to suppress extensive historical or literary analogies, then James cannot be termed a strict realist. But Cargill and Lerner's belief that the "realistic" James tended to suppress classical allusion in the bulk of his fiction is itself very much open to question. Classical themes such as the one mentioned in *The Bostonians* figure in a number of his stories and novels. In a chapter on *The Europeans,* Peter Buitenhuis observes that James's imagery "draws heavily from the pastoral tradition."[3] J. A. Ward has noted a somewhat similar pattern in *The Princess Casamassima,* where London momentarily takes on the appearance of a pastoral landscape, provoking the hero, Hyacinth Robinson, to dreams of release from his "anonymity" and of escape from the "urban murkiness and congestion" prevailing in that novel.[4] It also seems a question whether James really believed that classical allusion would be inappropriate to the contemporary tone of his writing. Ward's view of *The Princess Casamassima* might suggest that the novelist consciously employed classical comparisons to underscore the blight of industrial London. Moreover, as this discussion will show, James appears to have used classical allusions in a surprisingly sustained fashion in his descriptions of contemporary American life. It would seem, in fact, that James was as much an allusive or an aesthetic novelist as a writer of realistic fiction. It is the aesthetic dimension of James's art— specifically, the accretions of figurative detail on his pictures of contemporary life—which will bear most heavily on the subject treated here.

As late as 1904, when James returned to America after nearly two decades spent in Europe, he was tantalized by the resemblance of the American landscape to an idealized pastoral world. In the opening chapter of *The American Scene,* the idea which informs his vision of New England is that of a classical pastoral, "exquisitely and ideally Sicilian, Theocritan, poetic"; and he is led to ask: "Why was the whole connotation so delicately *Arcadian,* like that of the Arcadia of an old tapestry, an old legend, an old love-story in fifteen volumes. . . . "[5] If this classicized vision of New England fails as a controlling idea in *The American Scene,* it is because James recognizes that the real actors on the American scene are not the bucolic remains of old New England, but "the monstrous form of Democracy" and the looming shapes of a new and unsettling urban technology. Glimpsed by the returning traveler from across New York Harbor, the city appeared as a "monstrous organism . . . some colossal set of clockworks, some steel-souled machine-room of brandished arms and hammering fists and opening and closing jaws. The immeasurable bridges are but as the horizontal sheaths of pistons working at high pressure, day and night, and subject, one apprehends with perhaps inconsistent gloom, to certain, to fantastic, to merciless multiplication" (75). Apparently conceived as an imaginative alternative to this enormous urban geography in *The American Scene,* the pastoral ideal still could offer no real defense against the new urban technology. James frankly admits that failure. And yet it is significant that, not so very long before, he had sought to infuse his description of the American city itself with

a classical sense. In focusing upon *The Bostonians* (1886), this essay will show how James was driven by a need to impose order upon the chaos which he believed to exist in American urban life. This discussion will reveal several lines of classical pastoral imagery and landscape imagery, which are not always directly related, but which bear upon James's attempt to set the American city in a harmonious aesthetic context.

Criticism does not seem very precisely to have located the center of James's interests in *The Bostonians.* Recent interpretations have tended to regard the ideological struggle between Basil Ransom and Olive Chancellor as the subject of the novel. Maxwell Geismar, for example, is sure that Ransom is "close to being the Jamesian spokesman" and equates Ransom ("a Post-Civil War Southern Conservative, a traditionalist who is almost a royalist") with the arch-"Royalist," James himself, whose position in this "satire" on New England intellectual life was "conservative, traditional or reactionary."[6] Irving Howe, on the other hand, has denied that Ransom is James's spokesman and sees him figuring in a "harsh comedy in which both sides . . . are scored off by James."[7] Criticism appears to have fastened rather fruitlessly upon the question of competing ideologies. Perhaps what interested James more is the odd similarity of Olive's and Ransom's positions rather than their opposed philosophies of life. Both are represented as *déracinés,* Olive because of her "nervous" and "morbid" modernity (she is a women's-rights zealot), and Ransom because he is an up-rooted Southerner. Both suffer recognizably from anomie, engendered by their experience in a society which often seems mechanical and cruel. James appears to take considerable trouble in order to suggest the similitude of their experience. Olive, suffering agonies in a crowd, sees "a barrier of broad male backs," dumbly registers laughter "that verged upon coarseness," and feels insanely oppressed by the "glancing smiles" directed at her across the room, "which seemed rather to disconnect her with what was going forward on that side than to invite her to take part in it."[8] Ransom similarly is frequently described at moments of extreme discomfort, as at the Burrages' crowded evening party, where he feels caught up in a tide of people, who "edged about, advanced and retreated," whose faces seem animated "with sudden nods and grimaces," and whose effect upon him is strangely Kafkaesque. Even the room itself is made to accentuate Ransom's intense awareness of the crowd: "The walls of the room were covered with pictures—the very ceiling was painted and framed. The people pushed each other a little . . ." (254). Given this context, we should perhaps see *The Bostonians* as grounded in a painful sense of the pressures and the spiritual emptiness of contemporary urban life.

But if the ideological contest between the characters is less crucial than it has been made out to be, what was James seeking to accomplish in writing the novel? The clue to his purpose seems to lie in the imagery, especially its extensive use of classical imagery, and its often stylized contrasts of urban and rural landscape scenes. Earlier it was indicated that James used classical allusion in his fiction in a complicated way, mixing together a classical and a contemporary sense of life. In effect, it seems that James was seeking to enrich the contemporary world, in an attempt not wholly unlike what James Joyce later sought to accomplish through his use of *The Odyssey* in *Ulysses*. Or to put it somewhat differently, James was groping towards the creation of an urban mythology, a means of imaginatively interpreting his increasingly technological era. If James failed, and he did fail, he nevertheless provides an interesting early illustration of the problem which Hart Crane defined, in the 1920's, as central to his own time: " . . . unless poetry can absorb the machine, i.e., *acclimatize* it as naturally and casually as trees, cattle, galleons, castles . . . [it] has failed of its full contemporary function."[9] Put most simply, James's purpose in *The Bostonians* was to "acclimatize" the American city, a task, however, which was not to be easily accomplished.

James's impressions of urban life are described repeatedly through the imagery of extreme sensory exacerbation—" . . . the relaxed and disjoined roadway, enlivened at the curb-stone with an occasional ash barrel or with gas-lamps drooping from the perpendicular, and westward, at the end of the truncated vista, of the fantastic skeleton of the Elevated Railway, over-hanging the transverse longitudinal street . . ." (191). The countryside, which in antithetical fashion he idealizes, becomes powerfully suggestive of his feeling that modern American life required some kind of readjustment. Before showing the use James was to make of a classical vision in describing that readjustment, it may be helpful to demonstrate his use in the novel of a strain of landscape imagery embodying distinct ideas about the superiority of the country to the city.

At the opening of the third section of *The Bostonians*, James has Ransom meditate on vacations during a train ride down Cape Cod in pursuit of Verena Tarrant, whom he wants to marry. Ransom's contrast of the city and the countryside is extreme in a comic way: "it had been described to him as the drowsy Cape, the languid Cape, the Cape not of storms, but of eternal peace. He knew that the Bostonians had been drawn thither, for the hot weeks, by its sedative influence, by the conviction that its toneless air would minister to perfect rest. In a career in which there was so much nervous excitement as in theirs they had no wish to be wound up when they went out of town . . ." (356). But the contrast is grim by implication, because the "refreshment" Ransom finds in tasting "the breath of nature" at seaside Marmion allows him to measure all the painfulness in "his long grind in New York, without a vacation, with the repetition of the daily movement up and down the long, straight, maddening city, like a bucket in a well or a shuttle in a loom" (357). James clearly has so much to say about the countryside in the novel that one supposes he was exploring it as a symbol of man's relief from the nervous tensions generated by urban life. But he also appears to have had a more ambitious use for the countryside than as the single vital contrast to an essentially negative vision of

the city. At points in the narration, James can be seen trying to incorporate the city itself within this rural vision. It is this motive which seems to explain the presence of an aestheticized "landscape sense" in some parts of the description of the cities of Boston and New York.

The function of James's landscape imagery appears to have been rendering the city aesthetically harmonious. Yet there is a sense, running through much of the narrative, of the city's resistance to such an attempt. James's first efforts to harmonize the city are strangely qualified, indeed, partially vitiated by a satiric impulse. Frequently his characters engage in urban "view hunting," which, initially at any rate, James ridicules. Early in the novel, in the first of several scenes where characters are made to look from Olive Chancellor's drawing room window upon the Charles River basin, Ransom considers "a brackish expanse of an anomalous character" and finds the view rather "picturesque" (15). In a later instance, the Charles River and the industrial wasteland visible from Olive's windows are seen as " . . . desolate suburban horizons, peeled and made bald by the rigor of the season . . . straight sordid tubes of factories and engine-shops. . . . There was something inexorable in the poverty of the scene, shameful in the meanness of its details, which gave a collective impression of boards and tin and frozen earth . . ." (178). These items are presented in their oppressive detail to form a basis for James's parody of the excessively aesthetic interest taken in this scene at twilight by Olive and Verena: "There were pink flushes on snow, 'tender' reflections in patches of stiffened marsh, sounds of car-bells, no longer vulgar, but almost silvery. . . . They admired the sunsets, they rejoiced in the ruddy spots projected upon the parlor wall . . ." (178-179). These were "agreeable effects," James observes, and then allows the ladies to return to "the glittering tea tray and more and more talk about the long martyrdom of women . . ." (179). From such instances, it appears that James had strong doubts whether the city legitimately could be viewed in an aesthetic context. Nevertheless, the frequency with which landscape imagery is applied to urban scenes in the novel suggests that James was determined to impose some degree of aesthetic form upon the chaotic ugliness of the city.

However, the results of James's attempt at using landscape imagery in his descriptions of the city often are unfortunate. Here is a view of Basil Ransom's neighborhood in New York: " . . . an immense penthouse shed, which projected over a greasy pavement. Beneath it, on the dislocated flags, barrels and baskets were freely and picturesquely grouped . . . and a smart, bright wagon, with the horse detached from the shafts, drawn up on the edge of the abominable road (it contained holes and ruts a foot deep, and immemorial accumulations of stagnant mud), imparted an idle, rural, pastoral air to a scene otherwise perhaps expressive of a rank civilization" (189-190). The "picturesque," the "idle," the "rural," and the "pastoral" are, rather weakly, made to combat the oppressiveness of "rank civilization." The laboriousness, and the uncertainty, of this attempt to give the urban scene a rural and picturesque tone are apparent, but it should be recognized that what James was attempting was the idealization and enrichment of the urban environment.

James is far more successful when he can regard the city directly in terms of an actual landscape. When Ransom eventually goes to Central Park with Verena, James's description shifts with relief into a celebration of nature. The park "bristled with the raw delicacy of April, and, in spite of its rockwork grottos and tunnels, its pavilions and statues, its too numerous paths and pavements, lakes too big for the landscape and bridges too big for the lakes, expressed all the fragrance and freshness of the most charming moment of the year" (333). The scene is rendered both comic and beautiful, for the city no longer makes itself felt in a threatening way. Although the architecture in Central Park certainly is ungainly ("lakes too big for the landscape and bridges too big for the lake"), the disproportion is merely amusing and does not interfere with the "freshness and fragrance" which James's lovers encounter.

As James proceeds to develop the scene in Central Park, a number of motifs and thematic concerns—originally introduced at earlier points in the narrative—begin to coalesce imaginatively for the first time. The city blends harmoniously with nature: "The bowers and boskages stretched behind them, the artificial lakes and cockneyfied landscapes, making all the region bright with the sense of air and space, and raw natural vegetation too diminutive to overshadow" (348). Even the houses bounding the park are described as "chocolate-colored" and contrast, appetitively, with the sad, metallic appearance of the "red, rusty face" of Ransom's house earlier in the narrative (189). The whole urban landscape now appears balanced and harmonious, and it is even made to divide smoothly into painterly "grounds": " . . . streetcars rattled in the foreground, changing horses while the horses steamed . . . and the beer-saloons, with exposed shoulders and sides, which in New York do a great deal toward representing the picturesque, the 'bit' appreciated by painters . . . and on the other side the commercial vistas of Sixth Avenue stretched away with a remarkable absence of aerial perspective" (348-349). Here, even the hectic business of the city presents itself softly to the eye, with "a remarkable absence of aerial perspective." The swing away from ugliness in James's description makes us recall, earlier in the novel, the contrasting "truncated vista" created by the Elevated Railway, which "darkened and smothered" the city streets and made a "queer barrier" to vision itself (191, 302). James observes that even Verena Tarrant's dogmatically held opinions concerning democracy and women's rights begin to melt as she listens to Ransom in this setting, while the two characters themselves suggestively merge with the landscape and take on the first vague outlines of pastoral figures in an idealized landscape: "Strange I call the nature of [Verena's] reflections, for they softly battled with each other as she listened, in the warm, still air, touched with the faraway hum of the immense city, to his deep, distinct voice, expressing monstrous opinions with exotic

cadences and mild familiar laughs, which, as he leaned toward her, almost tickled her cheek and ear" (336-337). Elsewhere, Ransom and Verena are depicted explicitly as pastoral figures. Somewhat later, at Cape Cod, James again focuses elaborately upon the landscape: " . . . here all the spirit of a ripe summer afternoon seemed to hang in the air. There were wood-walks too; they sometimes followed bosky uplands, where accident had grouped the trees with odd effects of 'style,' and where in grassy intervals and fragrant nooks of rest they came upon sudden patches of Arcady" (395). The place itself is termed Arcadian. At other points in the narrative, James will view his characters themselves as classical Arcadians.

The difference between these two lush scenes and the earlier one where James had tried to find an aesthetic interest in Ransom's squalid neighborhood is, of course, great. But it should be remembered that James's methods of description are essentially similar in these contrasting instances. The city street scene, the scenery of Central Park, and the county landscape all are described with a significant degree of super-added aesthetic detail. The three scenes are depicted lavishly in "painterly" or "picturesque," as well as pastoral terms. It is in this context that James's intimately connected landscape and pastoral imagery may be seen deriving from the novelist's craving for an aesthetically satisfying vision of the largely urban world in which he lived.

The readjustment of modern urban life which James sought in *The Bostonians* was not merely a substitution of rural beauty for the exacerbation, blight, and "modern fatigue" (26) produced by urban life. What it involved was a simplification, and an imaginative enrichment of contemporary life. And yet it is clear from the novel that James found himself unable finally to arrive at such an imaginative vision. This failure is suggested by the continual tendency of his aesthetic and classical schemata to break down in the face of the intractable realities of urban life. Still, despite a tendency to collapse, the classical pastoral imagery of *The Bostonians* can be seen as an especially daring element in James's attempt at enriching modern life, daring because the novelist tries to use it to idealize both his characters and the natural and urban environment. This attempt at combining the classical and the modern proved as difficult for James as for any modern writer. It is clear from the novel that James's aesthetic needs often jarred with his artistic discretion and with his awareness of the inevitable falseness in any attempt to interpret the modern age through a historically remote classical ideal. The initial, satirical use of pastoral imagery reflects that strain markedly: "[Verena] has appeared to [Ransom] before as a creature of brightness, but now . . . she made everything that surrounded her of no consequence; dropping upon the shabby sofa with an effect as charming as if she had been a nymph sinking on a leopard-skin . . ." (228-229). The narrative eye here is Basil Ransom's, and the "nymph" and the "shabby sofa" transformed into a "leopard-skin" would seem to indicate that Ransom is indulging in a romantic fantasy. The balance between

Ransom's imagery and the shabbiness of the scene merely serves to define Ransom's sentimentality. His "pastoral" idea of Verena appears rather different from (and less truthful than) his initial impression of her at Miss Birdseye's, when she had an air "of belonging to a troupe, of living in the gaslight": "If she had produced a pair of castanets or a tambourine, he felt that such accessories would have been quite in keeping" (59). It seems likely, from this instance, that James did not find it all that easy to idealize his characters so that they might fit a classical mold. And yet the novelist's subsequent use of pastoral motifs suggests that he had a less satirical purpose in mind than commenting upon Ransom's sentimentality. Later it is James himself who places Ransom and Verena in a much more idealized pastoral setting and combines the pastoral motif with a general interest in the aesthetic possibilities afforded by the New England landscape: " . . . accident had grouped the trees with odd effects of 'style'" (395). But as we noticed in his treatment of landscape imagery and of the "picturesque," James appears to have experienced great difficulty in working-up his motifs to a formal beauty. To speak more generally, James evidently was torn between a desire to find a harmonious order in modern life and a contrary, skeptical awareness of the flatness and ugliness of his characters' lives and of their world.

Throughout the novel, James's handling of pastoral metaphors appears to reflect a fundamental ambivalence. Towards the end of *The Bostonians,* he depicts an angry crowd at the Boston Music Hall in order to suggest a parallel to a Virgilian thunderstorm: "The storm was now raging in the hall" (461). At one point in the prolonged uproar, caused by Verena's mysterious non-appearance on stage, the Burrages are depicted simultaneously (and ludicrously) as pastoral figures and ruffled sophisticates: " . . . the arrival of the Burrages who had quitted the stage and who swept into the room in the manner of people seeking shelter from a thunderstorm. The mother's face expressed the well-bred surprise of a person who should have been asked out to dinner and seen the cloth pulled off the table . . ." (463). Here, where the pastoral and the modern seem not quite to jibe, it is as though James is mocking his own comparisons and calling attention, comically, to the impossibility of redeeming the modern world merely by evoking a classical past. Apparently reflecting that ironic awareness, a number of other classical allusions in the novel are made to focus on the absurd aspects (103), or on the sordidness of James's characters. Selah Tarrant, for instance, is regarded ironically as a modern postulant; the newspapers are his "temple," and he hopes to penetrate to the "inmost shrine" (L. *penetralia*): "The *penetralia* of the daily press were, however, still more fascinating, and the fact that they were less accessible, that here he found barriers in his path, only added to the zest of forcing an entrance" (106). Similarly, in the episode which closes the novel, Ransom's image for the Boston Music Hall is the Roman Colosseum: "The place struck him with a kind of Roman vastness; the doors which opened out of the upper balconies, high aloft, and which were constantly swinging to and fro with the passage of the spectators and the ushers, reminded him of the *vomitoria* that he had read about in descriptions of the Colosseum" (442). It is a metaphor appropriate to a troubled mind, such as Ransom's own, for it recalls not the classical world so much as the anomie, the hostile impersonality which rests with an iron weight upon the whole body of James's novel of modern city life. Some of his pastoral and classical comparisons are unattractive indeed, because they seem unable to help enliven modern life. We can more precisely examine the relation between the difficulties James faced in *The Bostonians* and his employment of a classical theme if we turn to the treatment of Ransom and Verena, who, like the whole urban environment, are often described in terms which prove resistant to a classical vision.

James has Ransom fall in love with Verena Tarrant in a way which seems designed to typify the randomness of encounters in urban life. Verena first appears, then disappears for a year, and then reappears with the same abruptness. Only then does Ransom fall in love with her. The moment occurs, in fact, even before he has seen her again, during a conversation between Ransom and Mrs. Luna in New York. James establishes the scene in a context of money worries and anxiety, and with the added complication for Ransom of having to ward-off Mrs. Luna's amorous "exhuberant provocation." Ransom, barely managing to escape from Mrs. Luna, "exhaled a soft vague sigh . . . such as a man might utter who had seen himself on the point of being run over and yet felt that he was whole" (213). What is most significant is that James makes a point of showing us this deracinated man in love as a figure which becomes almost eccentrically "strong." Verena, for instance, speaks repeatedly, and rather morbidly, about Ransom's formidable "will" (340, 346). But Ransom's description of being in love is especially interesting, because curiously unromantic. What it actually defines is less being-in-love than Ransom's struggle to keep his "balance" in a world which he finds disconcertingly complicated: " . . . he had a purpose which swallowed up . . . inanities and he was so full of it that it kept him firm, balanced him, gave him assurance . . ." (376). It is being in love that gives Ransom his forcefulness, and it is interesting to notice, later in the novel, what radical effects a loss of love has upon this character when James shows him trying, almost hopelessly, to track-down Verena in the labyrinths of Boston and New York: "He had been roaming in very much the same desperate fashion, at once eager and purposeless, for many days before he left New York, and he knew that his agitation and suspense must wear themselves out. At present they pressed him more than ever; they had become tremendously acute" (440). Thus, Ransom is depicted as a man on a pendulum. His strength has its roots in fearful anxieties, and his love in an exaggerated need for security. James describes him literally as a "modern" man, for Ransom is made to reveal the very same "modern" and "morbid" traits which he believed he detected in Olive Chancellor. The point is driven home for the reader when James pauses ironically over that "Boetian" thought of Ransom's, as he sat in Olive's Cambridge drawing room, to observe wryly that "morbidness" was somehow "typical" of the whole age (11). And so it was, in an age almost unrelievedly urban and mechanical.

To return to James's classical theme. Ransom's sentimentality in thinking Verena a pastoral "nymph" is understandable, because it is a product of the character's need to escape from an intolerable environment. Ransom needs the "simplicity" and freedom from neurosis which he imagines he sees in Verena. James indicates that this need was at the back of the character's mind throughout the first long conversation between Ransom and Verena at Cambridge: "Verena struck Ransom as constantly simple, but there were moments when her candor seemed to him preternatural" (251). Ransom's figure of the "nymph" is the result of that feeling. A disoriented urban man, Ransom sees Verena as the embodiment of a pastoral simplicity, the anti-type in short, of his own uncomfortable life. During the first moment of that scene at Cambridge, Ransom is shown feeling an intense discomfort, which he cannot quite fathom. He is surprised to discover how naturally Verena behaves, while he feels, in contrast, clumsily "ceremonious" and unable to explain what he wants from her (229). This discomfort can be interpreted as an instance of the anomie, the rootlessness which we noticed earlier. Ransom then becomes increasingly aware of Verena's "affable" smile in the face of his discomfort, and this results in a second, more extended pastoral figure: " . . . the listening smile, innocent as it was in the Arcadian manner of Mockery, seemed to accuse him of not having the courage of his inclinations" (229). Although not precisely aware of the fact, Ransom thus defines himself as an inhibited modern man wishing that his behavior were less subject to complication and inhibitions. In his fantasy, Verena (an "Arcadian") mocks him for that awkwardness. Several moments later James makes it clear that Verena has utterly "startled and confounded her visitor" with her naturalness (230). A third pastoral suggestion then occurs to Ransom, who receives a nostalgic echo of the "golden age" from Verena's conversation: "She added in her gay, friendly trustful tone—the tone of facile intercourse, the tone in which happy, flower-crowned maidens may have talked to sunburnt young men in the golden age" (230). Although James employs an extended pastoral metaphor in this scene to reveal his character's feelings of anomie, Ransom's fantasy on the golden age becomes oddly compelling. Ransom can be seen straining towards a more imaginative vision of life than what his own world offered. And so, in spite of his reservations, can James.

James does not greatly extend that vision of a pastoral time when "flower-crowned maidens . . . talked to sunburnt young men in the golden age." As the ambiguous tone suggests with reference to Ransom's pastoral fantasy, the vision is "facile" because modern conditions of life no longer jibe with it. Ransom is not permitted to speculate further on the golden age, although the novelist does. At the end of the novel, Ransom's hasty flight

with Verena during a pseudo-Virgilian storm scene at the Music Hall, where even the guard at the dressing room door appears exaggerated, like some pastoral "butting animal" (448), merely indicates James's melancholy sense of the disruption of modern life. Ransom and Verena pass through the confused streams of people in the "outer labyrinth" of the Music Hall (463)—and in that image we recall their earlier passage through the slums of Cambridge, "a sightless, soundless, interspersed, embryonic region" (240)—to step out onto the street, bound nowhere very definite. The classical vision which we have been tracing through *The Bostonians* does not lead, finally, to a new urban mythology, but it does show that one of James's major concerns was the effort to come to grips imaginatively with the difficult, anomic facts of contemporary American urban life.

NOTES

[1] See the following: Walter Benjamin, "On Some Motifs in Baudelaire," in *Illuminations,* Hannah Arendt, editor, trans. Harry Zohn (New York, 1968), 157-202; Donald Fanger, *Dostoevsky and Romantic Realism: A Study of Dostoevsky in Relation to Balzac, Dickens, and Gogol* (Cambridge, Mass., 1965); John Fraser, "Photography and the City," *Yale Review,* LIX, 228-241; Leo Marx, *The Machine in the Garden* (New York, 1964); David R. Weimer, *The City as Metaphor* (New York, 1966).

[2] Daniel Lerner and Oscar Cargill, "Henry James at the Grecian Urn," *PMLA,* LXVI, 316-331.

[3] Peter Buitenhuis, *The Grasping Imagination* (Toronto, 1970), 89-102.

[4] J. A. Ward, *The Search for Form: Studies in the Structure of James's Fiction* (Chapel Hill, N.C., 1967), 138-140.

[5] Henry James, *The American Scene,* Leon Edel, editor (Bloomington, 1968), 14.

[6] Maxwell Geismar, *Henry James and the Jacobites* (Boston, 1963), 61-63.

[7] Irving Howe, editor, *The Bostonians* (New York, 1956), xxvi.

[8] Henry James, *The Bostonians,* Irving Howe, editor (New York, 1956), 130. Later quotations will refer to this edition.

[9] Quoted in Marx, *The Machine in the Garden,* 240.

Glen A. Love

SOURCE: "New Pioneering on the Prairies: Nature, Progress, and the Individual in the Novels of Sinclair Lewis," in *American Quarterly,* Vol. XXV, No. 5, December, 1973, pp. 558-77.

[*In the following essay, Love discusses social criticism in the urban novels of Sinclair Lewis .*]

"It's just that I have some kind of an unformulated idea that I want to be identified with Grand Republic—help in setting up a few stones in what may be a new Athens. It's this northern country— you know, stark and clean—and the brilliant lakes and the tremendous prairies to the westward—it may be a new kind of land for a new kind of people, and it's scarcely even started yet."

Cass Timberlane

Perhaps no American writer of modern times has so insistently presented an ambivalent and divided artistic self to his readers and critics as has Sinclair Lewis. Participant and enthusiast as well as observer and critic, the scourge of American villages, doctors, preachers, businessmen, as well as—so Lewis later assured us—their heartiest well-wisher, he remains a compelling figure for the student of our culture. T. K. Whipple, in his well-known essay in *Spokesmen* over forty years ago, concluded that "Lewis is the most successful critic of American society because he is the best proof that his charges are just."[1] And more recently, Mark Schorer, Sheldon Grebstein and D. J. Dooley, in their books on Lewis, all demonstrate convincingly that he was a writer possessed of eternally warring qualities, that on almost any level of personal or artistic performance he reflected a persistent split in sensibility: lonely introvert versus mad exhibitionist, coy romancer versus satiric realist, defender versus derider of intellect and art, alternately ridden by, and rejecting, material success.[2] From this welter of contrarieties hopelessly yoked emerges what Schorer calls "the real enigma of his novels, a persistent conflict of values that clashed no less within him" (p. 4).

In this opposition of values, it is Lewis the nay-sayer, the tormentor of middle America, who has received the most attention. "The fact is," one typical judgment runs, "that Lewis is dull when being positive but delightful when being negative."[3] Yet in attempting to understand more clearly the paradox which Schorer describes we are driven back to a fuller consideration of the other Lewis, the Lewis who would seem to claim a place in the main current of American idealism, who with Emerson and Whitman would project upon a native landscape the values of democratic individualism and a sublime conception of the future, and who would present in his fiction idealized alternatives to the society whose chronicler he was. This is the Lewis who scored the "contradiction between pioneering myth and actual slackness" in America, and who wrote of himself that he "mocked the cruder manifestations of Yankee Imperialism because he was, at heart, a fanatic American."[4] While these counterforces of affirmation in Lewis' work have received scholarly attention, their function as a compelling, and at best controlling, set of ideas in the body of his novels is, I believe, open to further examination.[5] Such examination may not only clarify our understanding of the main strands of Lewis' idealism and their interrelationships, but may also reveal how these patterns of affirmation pervade Lewis' fiction, emerging in his early novels,

shaping his major books of the 1920s and finally dissolving into incoherence and frustration in his later works.

Cass Timberlane's speech, above, serves as illustration and starting point.[6] It presents the reader with a unique cluster of images and ideas which may be seen to function prominently in Lewis' novels: an exalted Midwestern natural landscape, against which is set forth a visionary future (objectified as a modern creation, often a city), and a figure indigenous to this landscape—appropriate here even to his name—who stands as a harbinger or creator of this future. Characteristically, however, he is a potential rather than an actual creator of this new age. Associated with this grouping—idealized natural setting, city of the future and creative individual—are revealing aspects of style. Most notable is the metaphorical cast of the speaker's utterance, "setting up a few stones in what may be a new Athens." Even the actual name, "Grand Republic," calls up the utopian rhetoric of earlier Cass Timberlanes. And although Lewis may mock such Founding Father manifest-destinyism elsewhere in this novel (as well as in setting *Kingsblood Royal* in a racist Grand Republic and *Babbitt* in "Zenith") he is clearly sympathetic here to his speaker's conception. Related to this metaphorical distancing of subject is the tentativeness of the entire statement: "Some kind of an unformulated idea . . . what may be . . . you know . . . it may be. . . . " From what we come to know of the speaker, his lack of specificity suggests not a casual disregard for what he is saying, but rather the opposite. As with a Hemingway hero, the speaker's avoidance of a more precise articulation of his ideas is a measure of their potency to him, an appeal to the listener for a psychic response, an assumption of agreement below the word-surface. Even the use of dashes rather than conventional punctuation or transitions which would clarify the logical progression may be seen as a stylistic device to emphasize both the interrelatedness of these notions within the speaker's mind and the urgency behind them. Setting aside for the moment considerations of *Cass Timberlane* as novel, what Lewis provides in this passage is a prototype whose development and significance may be profitably examined.

This characteristic pattern of images and ideas emerges falteringly in the five early Lewis novels which antedate the publication of *Main Street* in 1920. Lewis' treatment of nature and landscape in these works, to begin with, seems to offer little opportunity for development. Despite his claim that *Walden* was the chief influence upon his formative years, and his high praise of Thoreau, Lewis' early version of pastoral is often, unlike Thoreau's, merely the sentimental countryside rapture which has always flourished in our popular literature, to which category the early works may, on the face of it, be consigned.[7] Nature in these novels is commonly simply an escape, albeit a beneficial and restorative one, and the urbanite ennobled and revivified by an Arcadian interlude is to become a stock figure for Lewis. The milquetoast, citified hero of his first novel, *Our Mr. Wrenn* (1914), is, for example, propelled into self-reliance partly as a result of his walking trip through the

English countryside. Similarly in *The Innocents* (1917) an elderly New York couple set out upon a walking trip across the country, and en route are rather incredibly transformed from shy nonentities into aggressive and successful go-getters.[8] City girls like Ruth Winslow of *The Trail of the Hawk* (1915) and Claire Boltwood of *Free Air* (1919) change, through contact with nature, from Eastern, or "indoor," to Western, or "outdoor," women, thus completing a required rite of passage for Lewis heroines. As Lewis' sympathetic treatment of them prepares us for his later favorable view of "outdoor" women like Carol Kennicott in *Main Street,* Edith Cortright in *Dodsworth,* and Ann Vickers, so his dismissal of the "indoor" Gertie Cowles of *The Trail of the Hawk* presages his later unsympathetic treatment of "indoor" women like Joyce Lanyon of *Arrowsmith,* Fran Dodsworth and Jinny Timberlane, Cass' young wife, whose moral lapse accompanies her transition from "outdoor" to "indoor" woman.

Alert to the worst excesses of sentimental pastoral in these early works, Lewis tempers his treatment of nature by the inclusion of realistic or even satiric detail. For example, a country-engendered euphoria mistakenly causes Una Golden of *The Job* (1917) to succumb to "the thwarted boyish soul that persisted in Mr. Schwirtz's barbered, unexercised, coffee-soaked, tobacco-filled, whiskey-rotted, fattily-degenerated city body."[9] In *The Trail of the Hawk* Lewis at one point spoofs the clichés of popular wilderness fiction at the same time that he repeats its basic values:

> "If this were a story," said Carl, knocking the crusted snow from dead branches and dragging them toward the center of a small clearing, "the young hero from Joralemon would now remind the city gal that 'tis only among God's free hills that you can get an appetite, and then the author would say, 'Nothing had ever tasted so good as those trout, yanked from the brook and cooked to a turn on the sizzling coals.'" She looked at the stalwart young man, so skilfully frying the flapjacks, and contrasted him with the effeminate fops she had met on Fifth Avenue.[10]

This alternate milking and mocking of the conventions of the wilderness novel is a practice which Lewis carries on throughout *Free Air* as well as in the later *Mantrap* (1926). In *Free Air* Lewis includes realistic treatments of the primitive roads, temperamental automobiles, the occasional filthy hotel and backroad degenerate, the debunking of Milt Daggett's pulp-fiction stereotype of aggressive lumberjacks wooing and winning reticent maidens. Nevertheless, the larger conception of nature and the West which emerges from the novel is not Claire Boltwood's early impression of "rocks and stumps and socks on the line," but rather is that familiar mythic territory for which Milt serves as emblem.[11]

Indeed, Lewis has a firmer grasp on these early characters whose linkage with nature is the result not of escape but of birthright. Carl Ericson of *The Trail of the Hawk* and Milt Daggett of *Free Air* are presented as authentic native heroes, clear-eyed rural Midwesterners who have absorbed the sources of strength and vitality in the land itself. Such origins will be the means of legitimizing the aims and ennobling the character of later Lewis figures like Martin Arrowsmith, Sam Dodsworth, Cass Timberlane and Neil Kingsblood, as well as such minor but significant characters as Bone Stillman of *The Trail of the Hawk* and Miles Bjornstam of *Main Street,* both of whose association with wilderness—rather than simply rural—images is an index to their more radical individualism.[12] Still it is not merely in their origins but in their futures that Carl Ericson and Milt Daggett emerge as the most prophetic of Lewis' early heroes. Ericson, in particular, typifies Lewis' new American:

> Carl was second-generation Norwegian; American-born, American in speech, American in appearance save for his flaxen hair and china-blue eyes. . . . When he was born the "typical Americans" of earlier stocks had moved to city palaces or were marooned on run-down farms. It was Carl Ericson, not a Trowbridge or a Stuyvesant or a Lee or a Grant, who was the "typical American" of his period. It was for him to carry on the American destiny of extending the western horizon; his to restore the wintry Pilgrim virtues and the exuberant, October, partridge-drumming days of Daniel Boone; then to add, in his own or another generation, new American aspirations for beauty. (p. 6)

Once again the problem with Lewis' characterization of this first of his visionary Westerners is that his validity as an archetypal figure is weakened by an occasionally effusive romantic overlay. To the young Carl Ericson, we are told, for example,

> it was sheer romance to parade through town with a tin haversack of carbons for the arc-lights, familiarly lowering the high-hung mysterious lamps, while his plodding acquaintances "clerked" in stores on Saturdays or tended furnaces. Sometimes he donned the virile—and noisy—uniform of an electrician: army gauntlets, a coil of wire, pole-climbers strapped to his legs. Crunching his steel spurs into the crisp pine wood of the lighting-poles, he carelessly ascended to the place of humming wires and red crossbars and green-glass insulators, while crowds of two and three small boys stared in awe from below. (p. 26)

Still, despite his tendency to veer off into cuteness, Lewis has discovered a figure of potentiality for him in a young Westerner who reads *Scientific American,* finds inspiration in his high school laboratory, and lusts after an automobile. Both in *The Trail of the Hawk* and in *Free Air* Lewis begins to turn his treatment of nature and the West—virtual synonyms for Lewis, as for Thoreau—away from a simplistic celebration of its potentialities for escape and toward an alliance with scientific progress. Carl Ericson and Milt Daggett are more than just two more in a procession of nature's noblemen; in addition to their irreproachable natural credentials they are both creative technologists, "new" men. Milt not only wins Claire

Boltwood out west but prepares himself there for accession into the technological age, as represented by his study of engineering at the University of Washington. Beyond that lies what he envisions as a challenging career as a builder in Alaska. Carl becomes not only a famous pioneer aviator but also the inventor of a camping automobile called the Touricar, and an early version of the more substantial later designer and industrialist, Sam Dodsworth. Both young men, then, emerge as seminal heroes for Lewis, figures whose alliances both to the land and the technological future might qualify them as new American pioneers. Like Mark Twain's Connecticut Yankee, these Lewis heroes cross the threshold from an agrarian past into an industrial future and their ability to mechanize successfully serves to demonstrate their claim to an appropriate role in the new age. Nature by itself was irrelevant, and the Westerner bound to the soil an anachronism. If "the American destiny of extending the western horizon" was to be advanced, as Lewis believed, it would be by the native Westerner who had grasped the new tools of science. Thus the old stalemate between machine and garden might be transformed into a progressive synthesis.[13] In this important sense, Lewis is not merely lavishing exquisite praise upon nature, as T. K. Whipple accused him of doing (p. 227). Rather, Lewis reaches toward the awareness of his culture-hero Thoreau that nature exists most meaningfully in relationship to the civilization of its time rather than apart from it.

As novels, however, neither *The Trail of the Hawk* nor *Free Air* can be taken as seriously as their controlling theme would seem to require. Both are mired in the excesses of popular romance, and while *Free Air* ends before Milt Daggett's new pioneering actually begins, *The Trail of the Hawk*, instead of engaging seriously Carl Ericson's proposed archetypal role, diffuses it into a series of "adventures." It remained for *Main Street*, published in 1920, the year following *Free Air*, to manifest these early ideas in an imaginative work of primary importance, and to open a decade in which Lewis' new pioneers would occupy the center of most of his major works.

Although *Main Street* represented a critical and popular advance over the earlier novels, it bears important similarities to them in the figure of Carol Milford Kennicott. Like Milt Daggett she sees great work to be done in the future and eagerly anticipates her own part in it. Like Carl Ericson she is depicted as a representative new American: "The days of pioneering, of lassies in sunbonnets, and bears killed with axes in piney clearings, are deader now than Camelot; and a rebellious girl is the spirit of that bewildered empire called the American Middlewest."[14] And once again the heritage of the young seeker is an America still in the process of becoming, "bewildered" by the speed of its cultural change. The hill upon which Carol stands in the novel's opening sentences, "where Chippewas camped two generations ago," now looks out upon flour mills and the skyscrapers of Minneapolis and St. Paul. It is a land, she realizes later, whose work has scarcely begun, "the newest empire of the world. . . . They are pioneers, these sweaty wayfarers . . . and for all

its fat richness, theirs is a pioneer land. What is its future? she wondered. . . . What future and what hope?" (pp. 28-29).

Like both Carl and Milt, Carol is a Midwesterner who is closely identified with the natural world. In the opening she stands beside the Mississippi, "in relief against the cornflower blue of Northern sky," and although Lewis playfully diminishes her pose by listing the random contents of her mind, he consistently identifies her eagerness of spirit with the potentiality for hope and beauty in the wide Midwestern landscape. Even when Gopher Prairie's ugliness and pettiness threaten to overwhelm her she can find in the land itself, as she does after a day spent hunting and walking with her husband, Will, "the dignity and greatness which had failed her in Main Street" (p. 61). She is first attracted to Will by those qualities of his personality closest to her own: his fondness for tramping and the outdoors, his sense of the heroic Midwestern past, his occasional awareness of its possibilities for the future. His proposal of marriage is presented in the only the terms which Carol would have accepted: "'It's a good country, and I'm proud of it. Let's make it all that those old boys dreamed about'" (p. 22), and it is his failure to recognize the seriousness of this vow for Carol that lies at the base of their later misunderstandings. Failing to take Carol seriously, as Daniel Aaron has pointed out, is also a mistake for those, like H. L. Mencken, who see Carol only as a featherbrained romantic.[15] It is, of course, just the visionary propensity which made her ridiculous to Mencken and others which defines her an an appropriate Lewis heroine.

What had begun for Carol during college as a reading assignment in a sociology class—a text on town-improvement—and a resolution to "'get my hands on one of these prairie towns and make it beautiful'" (p. 11), seems to offer itself as actual opportunity through Will's proposal.[16] But she soon finds that what Will and the townspeople have in mind by town-improvement is cosmetic rather than surgical. Her plans for social amelioration extend beyond that of rebuilding prairie towns (Will complains that she is "always spieling about how scientists ought to rule the world" [p. 381], and she espouses typical progressivist ideas) but it is primarily as a thwarted builder and planner that she is presented to the reader. In the famous passage in which she walks down Main Street for the first time, only The Farmer's National Bank ("An Ionic temple of marble. Pure, exquisite, solitary" [p. 40]) escapes her catalogue of the town's ugliness, "planlessness" and "temporariness," where "each man had built with the most valiant disregard of all the others" (p. 41).[17] Later when she analyzes more carefully the town's appearance it is with the eye of the builder and planner:

> She asserted that it is a matter of universal
> similarity; of flimsiness of construction, so that
> the towns resemble frontier camps; of neglect of
> natural advantages, so that the hills are covered
> with brush, the lakes shut off by railroads, and the

creeks lined with dumping grounds; of depressing sobriety of color; rectangularity of buildings; and excessive breadth and straightness of the gashed streets, so that there is no escape from gales and from sight of the grim sweep of land, nor any windings to coax the loiterer along, while the breadth which would be majestic in an avenue of palaces makes the low shabby shops creeping down the typical Main Street the more mean by comparison. (p. 260)

Another credulous Western innovator like Carl Ericson and Milt Daggett, Carol is a more compelling figure than either of her predecessors because of the extraordinary tension between the eager expectancy of her hopes and the forces of dullness and smugness which oppose her. Shut off from any meaningful work by her position as woman and wife, by her shallow education, by her own sentimentalism and flightiness, and by her sense of inadequacy to her task, she is finally resigned to her defeat at the close of the novel:

> "She looked across the silent fields to the west. She was conscious of an unbroken sweep of land to the Rockies, to Alaska; a dominion which will rise to unexampled greatness when other empires have grown senile. Before that time, she knew, a hundred generations of Carols will aspire and go down in tragedy devoid of palls and solemn chanting, the humdrum inevitable tragedy of struggle against inertia." (p. 431)

At the end, no longer even the potential creator, she remains a frustrated figure living under a self-imposed truce in a community which she might have transformed into something distinctive and beautiful, had she possessed the technical skill and the nerve to match her idealism.[18] Technical skill and nerve are, of course, the attributes of her doctor-husband, Will, but without vision he remains merely the severed half of her incomplete self. What is called for in the wider design of *Main Street* is a sublime architect, a figure whose pragmatic technological mastery and courage to innovate are equal to the force of his, or her, dream.[19]

If *Main Street* shows us the incipient builder deprived of the realization of her goal—a new town on the prairie—*Babbitt* (1922) reverses the presentation to reveal the shining Midwestern city achieved, but without an appropriate creator to shape or interpret its destiny. Both novels are concerned with defining humane life for the citizens of a community; both ask at what point in the process of development this humane life can best be realized. Zenith has clearly gone beyond that point, as Gopher Prairie has failed to reach it. Instead of *Main Street*'s heroic natural landscape blighted by human incompetence and pettiness, *Babbitt* presents a man-created world of immense technological dazzle, but finally devoid of meaningful relationships, not only among its inhabitants, but between man and landscape and between man and the products of his technology. It is a kind of upside-down *Walden,* where the buildings, houses, porcelain and tile bathrooms, and electric cigar-lighters overwhelm the

human figures and reduce their actions to insignificance. As he did in *Main Street,* Lewis was dramatizing, in *Babbitt,* Lewis Mumford's contemporary observation that "architecture and civilization develop hand in hand: the characteristic buildings of each period are the memorials to their dearest institutions."[20] Lewis establishes the pattern at once as the novel opens: "The towers of Zenith aspired above the morning mist; austere towers of steel and cement and limestone sturdy as cliffs and delicate as silver rods. They were neither citadels nor churches, but frankly and beautifully office-buildings."[21]

From this panoramic view of a city "built—it seemed—for giants" (p. 6), the camera eye moves down, in a characteristically ironic Lewis juxtaposition, to focus upon the helpless figure of George F. Babbitt, asleep in his Dutch Colonial house in Floral Heights, and from there down to the alarm clock, the bathroom gadgets "so glittering and so ingenious that they resembled an electrical instrument-board" (p. 8), the eyeglasses, the suit, the contents of Babbitt's pockets—all of the wares by which the new city asserts its mastery over its inhabitants. As the opening chapter ends, Lewis turns his reader's attention back to the encompassing city as Babbitt stands looking out his window over the city, where his attention is drawn to the Second National Bank Tower:

> Its shining walls rose against April sky to a simple cornice like a streak of white fire. Integrity was in the tower, and decision. It bore its strength lightly as a tall soldier. As Babbitt stared, the nervousness was soothed from his face, his slack chin lifted in reverence. All he articulated was "That's one lovely sight!" but he was inspired by the rhythm of the city; his love of it renewed. He beheld the tower as a temple spire of the religion of business, a faith passionate, exalted, surpassing common men; and as he clumped down to breakfast he whistled the ballad "Oh, by gee, by gosh, by jingo" as though it were a hymn melancholy and noble. (pp. 14-15)

Lewis is of course satirizing that form of technological progress which is born of inadequate goals, which masks the emptiness and confusion of its inhabitants with a façade of gleaming limestone. Integrity, decision, strength—the proper qualities of the shapers of this new city—are possessed only by its commercial buildings. Whereas in *Main Street* we are shown the dream of a new civilization without the reality, in *Babbitt* we have the reality without the dream, a humming dynamo of a modern city whose external intimations of heroic accomplishment mock the meager-hearted underachievers who inhabit it. Babbitt, its representative man, can only barter its structures; he cannot create them.

Lewis clearly expects something more from his main figure. For George F. Babbitt is more than just the typical American businessman. He is also a Westerner, and the distinction, as the earlier works have demonstrated, is an important one for Lewis. As he explained it elsewhere, the Westerners may look like Easterners, "both groups are chiefly reverent toward banking, sound Republicanism, the playing of golf and bridge, and the possession of large motors. But whereas the Easterner is content with these symbols and smugly desires nothing else, the Westerner, however golfocentric he may be, is not altogether satisfied. . . . secretly, wistfully he desires a beauty that he does not understand."[22] Hence Babbitt's vague but insistent yearnings, perhaps the most important of which lead him away from the city and toward nature. Even his romantic fantasies with the "faery child" of his dreams occur in a series of natural settings—groves, gardens, moors, the sea. But more striking are those occasions when, seeking the balms of nature and male camaraderie, Babbitt heads off to the Maine woods to repeat the familiar American gesture of nonurban renewal. Even in Maine, of course, he cannot shake off the city which claims him. His dress and behavior in the woods are absurdly out of place: "[Babbitt] came out . . . in khaki shirt and vast and flapping khaki trousers. It was excessively new khaki; his rimless spectacles belonged to a city office; and his face was not tanned but a city pink. He made a discordant noise in the place. But with infinite satisfaction he slapped his legs and crowed, "Say, this is getting back home, eh?" (p. 124).

His conception of his Maine guide, Joe Paradise, as an incorruptible Leatherstocking and an appropriate model for his own revivification is destroyed when Joe reveals himself as a backwoods Babbitt, one who will walk or canoe in to the best fishing places if the sports insist, but who prefers a flat-bottom boat with an Evinrude, and who looks forward to the day when he can open a shoe store in town. Thus Babbitt—too addled by his Zenith existence to absorb the regenerative silence of the woods, bereft by the loss of his friend Paul Riesling, and deprived, by Joe Paradise's abdication, of an appropriate model of conduct toward nature—finds himself drawn back to his city as one who "could never run away from Zenith and family and office, because in his own brain he bore the office and the family and every street and disquiet and illusion of Zenith" (p. 242). Babbitt's retreat into nature fails as do his escapes into bohemianism and liberalism because Zenith has drained him of the values of hope and freedom which are his Western birthright, and he is thus incapable of grasping the terms of his dilemma. The call of the wild is indubitably real to Babbitt, as it has perhaps always been to Americans, but his fragmentary and childish conception of it ("moccasins—six-gun—frontier town—gamblers—sleep under the stars—be a regular man, with he-men like Joe Paradise—gosh!" [p. 238]) renders him vulnerable to confusion and failure. The novel ends, as did Main Street, with a chastened rebel, but Babbitt remains at last a more pathetic figure than Carol Kennicott, for unlike her he is never able to formulate coherently the dream which he is finally forced to deny. Only Babbitt's son Ted, the rebellious would-be inventor and mechanic, emerges at the end as an emblem of the hopeful future, a potential new technocrat who may rise out of Babbitt's ashes.

In *Arrowsmith* (1925) Lewis for the first time in a major novel presents a main character whose consequence as an agent of cultural progress matches his technical mastery and his dedication to his goal. Martin Arrowsmith, the doctor turned researcher, is an amalgam of the earlier Doc Kennicott and the visionary Carol. "I desired," Lewis recalled later, "to portray a more significant medico than Kennicott—one who could get beneath routine practice into the scientific foundation of medicine; one who should immensely affect all life."[23] Along with his scientific credentials, Arrowsmith possesses in his Midwestern roots the requisite benisons of nature. The book opens with the scene of a wagon carrying his pioneer forebears through the Ohio wilderness, and with his great-great-grandmother-to-be saying portentously, "'Nobody ain't going to take us in. . . . We're going on jus' long as we can. Going West! They's a whole lot of new things I aim to be seeing!'"[24] Heavy-handed as it sometimes is, the novel's frequently noted pioneering theme is appropriate to Arrowsmith in the realistic as well as mythic sense: that is, as a heroic explorer of unknown frontiers, he is not quite the perfect social being. In this sense, nature has a double function in the novel, not only to ennoble the hero but to humanize him, as is seen in the description of his early summer spent stringing telephone lines in Montana: "The wire-gang were as healthy and as simple as the west wind; they had no pretentiousness; though they handled electrical equipment they did not, like medics, learn a confusion of scientific terms and pretend to the farmers that they were scientists. They laughed easily and were content to be themselves, and with them Martin was content to forget how noble he was" (p. 33). From the linemen, admirable rustic technologists, Martin's cold idealism receives a lesson in humanity.

In the book's ending, Lewis provides the highest moral vindication of Martin's rejection of society by presenting it as a Thoreauvian retreat to the Vermont woods, complete with rough shack, pond, woodland neighbors, even a latter-day Thoreau himself in the abrasively individualistic Terry Wickett. Improbable as this conclusion may seem after the careful realism of the earlier sections, Martin Arrowsmith's cabin-laboratory is an unmistakable projection of Lewis' linked themes of scientific progress, creative individualism and nature.[25]

It should be added, however, that in its apparent denial of the possibilities for reconciliation between the questing individual and society, the ending of *Arrowsmith* is uncharacteristic of Lewis. With this exception, it is not the wilds but the middle landscape between raw nature and the city which comprises the appropriate terrain for the Lewis hero.[26] And that hero will not again be a scientist, that is, an essentially abstract creator whose purpose and function is to add to, rather than to apply, new knowledge. Rather, Lewis will return to the pragmatic designer, builder and architect as his representative hero. Even Arrowsmith, of course, resists classification as a "pure" scientist in the category of a Max Gottlieb or Terry Wickett. Arrowsmith's humane impulses prevail over his scientific duties in the plague episode, and the experiment is a failure. Nevertheless, Arrowsmith remains as Lewis' only new pioneer who may justifiably be termed radical.

If *Arrowsmith* is the high point of Lewis' radical individu-alism, *Dodsworth* (1929) presents the fullest treatment of the more characteristic figure toward whom the earlier novels have been pointing.[27] In the opportunities for self-examination afforded by a trip to Europe with his wife, Fran, Sam Dodsworth, 50-year-old industrialist, decides that he wants to return to America and do something more with the rest of his life than build automobiles. Fran, conversely, selfishly worries over the loss of her youth and is increasingly attracted to aimless travel and super-ficial Europeans. After their separation, Sam meets Edith Cortright, a sympathetic widow whom, after various re-bounds to Fran, he is finally to marry. During the course of the novel he has become interested in the garden suburb movement, as typified historically by Forest Hills on Long Island and its more flamboyant imitations, as represented by Zenith's "Sans Souci Gardens":

> To the north of Zenith, among wooded hills above the Chaloosa River, there was being laid out one of the astonishing suburbs which have appeared in America since 1910. So far as possible, the builders kept the beauties of forest and hills and river; the roads were not to be broad straight gashes butting their way through hills, but winding byways. . . .
>
> It came to him that now there was but little pioneering in manufacturing motors; that he hadn't much desire to fling out more cars on the packed highways. To create houses, . . . noble houses that would last three hundred years, and not be scrapped in a year, as cars were—
>
> "That'd be interesting," said Sam Dodsworth, the builder.[28]

In pursuing this venture, Dodsworth prepares to become Lewis' most significant and characteristic new pioneer: a Western idealist who has mastered the technology nec-essary to achieve his goal, a goal which is sanctioned by its associations both with cultural progress and with nature. Dodsworth the automobile manufacturer is, in an age of automobiles, merely serving the social order with-out guiding or ameliorating its destiny. He cannot "im-mensely affect all life." The anticipated shift of his role to that of designer and builder of wooded suburbs promises to elevate him from mechanic to creator. A materialist who can yield to the dream that is his Western inheritance but who nevertheless retains his mastery of the industrial technology, a searcher who has weighed his native val-ues against the soft sophistication of Europe, Dodsworth, more than any other of Lewis' heroes, seems both prop-erly qualified and properly motivated to move society along the path toward its appropriate future.

It should be emphasized at this point that if Arrowsmith is Lewis' Thoreauvian hero, Dodsworth is his Emersonian hero, and the latter figure, despite Lewis' stated praise of Thoreau and disparagement of Emerson, is the more typi-cal of Lewis' work.[29] In his commitment to technological progress here and elsewhere Lewis comes into sharp conflict with Thoreau, who stood grimly on the side of nature in what he often depicted as a virtual state of warfare between country and city. Lewis, on the other hand, can hardly restrain his enthusiasm in the presence of advancing civilization:

> My delight in watching the small Middle Western cities grow, sometimes beautifully and sometimes hideously, and usually both together, from sod shanties to log huts to embarrassed-looking skinny white frame buildings to sixteen-story hotels and the thirty-story bank buildings, may be commented on casually. There is a miracle in the story of how all this has happened in two or three generations. Yet, after this period, which is scarcely a second in historic time, we have a settled civilization with traditions and virtues and foolishness as fixed as those of the oldest tribe of Europe. I merely submit that such a theme is a challenge to all the resources a novelist can summon.[30]

It is not Thoreau but Emerson who was Lewis' predeces-sor and who might have provided Lewis with a shock of recognition had he read Emerson more carefully. Lewis precisely echoes Emerson's belief that a civilization is to be judged by the extent to which it draws the most benefit from its cities. Like Emerson, Lewis sees nature and the city as ultimately reconciled through the city's being related more closely to its natural environment. Like Emerson, he envisions this reconciliation as the role of a heroic man of action who will fulfill his own destiny and that of the nation in carrying out this synthesis. Like Emerson, Lewis conceived of this figure as a Western "cosmopolitan," one who would combine within himself natural and urban attributes. Finally, like Emerson, Lewis' emblem for the American future is what Michael Cowan, in his study of Emerson, calls a "City of the West," a combining and reconciling of industrial and Arcadian values.[31]

Although *Dodsworth* is the culmination of Lewis' efforts to bring forth a visionary Western technologist, the work reveals a troublesome lessening of intensity toward the implications and consequences of his theme, an inability or unwillingness to follow it through to its novelistic conclusions. *Dodsworth* closes with the promise of a new life for Sam, but he has now bounced from wooded es-tates to travel trailers, which he has imagined as carrying urbanites in comfort into the forest. ("'Kind of a shame to have 'em ruin any more wilderness. Oh, that's just sentimentality,' he assured himself" [p. 27]). And houses or trailers, we are never witness to their creation, nor do they quite qualify for their role, however much they might widen the vistas of nature-hungry Americans. The earlier dream of a Carol Kennicott, hazy as it was, embraced the entire community in a gesture of democratic inclusive-ness, rather than just that comfortably well-off portion of it to which Sam Dodsworth has limited himself.

In such curiously diminished forms, Western builders will continue to appear in Lewis' later novels. Myron Weagle of *Work of Art* (1934), for example, actually achieves his version of a city in the West, but the reader has difficulty in taking it seriously. A New England hotelkeeper whose career is devoted to the creation of "the Perfect Hotel Inn," Weagle moves through a frustrating career, heads west, buys a small hotel in a Kansas town, and turns it into a "work of art," as opposed to the cheap and meretricious books turned out by his writer-brother. But after the larger design of Lewis' earlier works, an innkeeper, however proficient, scarcely qualifies as a pioneer of progress, nor does his Western inn begin to fill the expansive canvas which Lewis has prepared.

The same sorts of truncated dreamers and deflated visions are found in Lewis' four final novels. *Cass Timberlane* (1945) first establishes a panoramic West and a properly idealistic, if middle-aged, Westerner and then reverts almost entirely to domestic affairs. For Neil Kingsblood (*Kingsblood Royal,* 1947), the hopeful Western horizon has shrunk to his suburban home in Sylvan Park, a disquieting version of Sam Dodsworth's earlier dream suburb. Here, according to the brochure of Mr. William Stopple, realtor, "gracious living, artistic landscaping, the American Way of Life, and up-to-the-minute conveniences are exemplified in 'Dream o' Mine Come True' . . . ," while at the same time Mr. Stopple privately advises that Sylvan Park "is just as free of Jews, Italians, Negroes, and the exasperatingly poor as it is of noise, mosquitoes, and rectangularity of streets."[32] While Neil Kingsblood and his wife jeer at the rhetoric of the Stopple brochure, they nevertheless unabashedly regard Sylvan Park as "a paradise and a highly sensible paradise" (p. 10); and while they come to reject the racist values of suburbia, they finally take up guns to preserve their place within it. In *The God-Seeker* (1949), Lewis exchanges new pioneering for old, but the pattern of reduction remains. Aaron Gadd abandons the larger dream which has sent him west to the Minnesota frontier and returns to his trade of carpentry: "'There are many things I don't ever expect to know, and I'm not going to devote myself to preaching about them but to building woodsheds so true and tight that they don't need ivory and fine gold—straight white pine, cedar shingles, a door that won't bind—glorious!'"[33]

Finally, in Lewis' last novel, *World So Wide* (1951), the hopeful Western horizon has simply turned into blank wall. Once again, Lewis posits his familiar builder-hero, but here his dream does not survive even the opening chapter. Hayden Chart, an architect of the Western city of "Newlife," Colorado ("that big, huge place where you look up to the horizon") decides on page nine that, after his wife's accidental death, he must turn from the task which was to have been his life's work: "now he would never build that prairie village which was to have been housed in one skyscraper: the first solution in history of rural isolation and loneliness."[34] As Chart's prairie skyscraper-village diffuses into a world so wide, his life peters out into aimless travel, a pathetic following after Meaningful Experiences. As a final stroke, Lewis revives the figures of Sam and Edith Dodsworth, who befriend Chart in Europe. The Dodsworths, we learn, have left America after returning there for only a short time, having found, as Sam confides, that Europe has "spoiled" them

for life in America (p. 46). Even offstage Lewis' American dream cannot sustain itself.

These reformed visionaries of his later works demonstrate Lewis' difficulty in engaging fully the concept of new pioneering which engrossed him throughout his career as novelist. In one respect, these Wester pilgrims, forever diverting themselves from the shining city on a prairie which is their professed destination, may dramatize their creator's misjudgment of his own abilities: although Lewis' impulses were often romantic and idealistic, his talents did not extend beyond the rendering of the actual. He may thus be seen as the victim of an idea which compelled him even as its formulation resisted his efforts to bring it to fictional life. In another respect, the half-hearted builders may suggest a failure of will on Lewis' part, another manifestation of a familiar American failure, as Frederick I. Carpenter describes it: "The idealist, recognizing that his vision of perfection is impossible, renounces his vision and 'returns to reality.'"[35] Yet it is not Lewis' renunciation of his vision that is most striking, but rather that he clings to it long after it has ceased to be a working force in his fiction, that he finally *cannot* renounce the vision. While the dream goes slack or is vulgarized in the later works, we are nevertheless left with an assertion of, or preoccupation with, a basic belief which remains consistent throughout Lewis' novels and which seems to transcend the divided self which Schorer and others have portrayed. Whether Lewis defines the good life explicitly in the idealistic hopes of his characters, or implicitly in the objects he selects for attack, the satirist and idealist in him merge in the moral basis from which both modes proceed.

From what we know of the man it is difficult not to speculate that Lewis, who could write of himself that "there never was in private life a less attractive or admirable fellow," and who, in reality, never revealed a deep appreciation of nature, sought in the visionary plans and pastoral associations of his main characters the means of legitimizing himself as an artist and a man.[36] His tendency to identify himself publicly with his fictional creations (e.g., Carl Ericson, Carol Kennicott, Martin Arrowsmith) suggests strongly that we may find in the novels fictional surrogates for this restless and unattractive loner.[37] Ridden all of his life by a deep sense of inferiority to the doctors in his family, his father and his brother Claude, Lewis, through his Western builders, may have sought the means to vindicate himself as a creator, to authenticate his own personal worth and dignity, something which he felt his family never accorded him in his career as a writer.[38] If the speculation is valid, it cannot have escaped Lewis that in his Arrowsmiths and Dodsworths he possessed a potent challenge to the superiority of the Lewis family doctors, who, unlike the creators, had not the power to "immensely affect all life." Nor was it likely that he could overlook, in the impotence and failure of his later fictional heroes, the evidence of his own inability, at last, to validate his vision as a creator. Seen thus, the Lewis canon offers itself as an ironic affirmation of Leon Edel's claim, in writing of Willa Cather, that an artist's works constitute a kind of supreme biography of their creator.

Nevertheless, preoccupation with the long downward slope of Lewis' career in the years from the publication of *Dodsworth* to his death in 1951 should not, as Sheldon Grebstein reminds us, divert attention from his lasting achievements of the 1920s. In *Main Street, Arrowsmith* and *Dodsworth,* and in the brilliant inversions of *Babbitt,* Lewis demonstrated his rightful claim to a place among those writers who have examined the sources of validity in American idealism, and who have created in their works new emblems of possibility to be measured against the failures of the present. While it may be objected that we search almost without success for those changes actually wrought by Lewis' Western creators, the same criticism might be applied to nearly any of the visionary designs in our literature. Fragmentary and resistant to close scrutiny they may still propose fresh possibilities to the imagination while they miscarry in actuality. A more formidable objection is that Lewis' new pioneering fails not because it emphasizes the disparity between the real and the ideal but because it insists upon the possibilities for their reconciliation. To a generation of critics and readers securely beyond innocence and accustomed to the assumption that the frontier is closed and that the presence of the machine in the garden must cause the serious artist to turn inevitably in the direction of tragedy, Lewis' idealistic technologists must seem to have either naïvely misjudged the realities or sold out to them. In Lewis' defense it must be questioned whether such judgments are not too narrowly conceived if they rule out a figure of his literary significance. Somewhere, Lewis believed, between the sod shanty and the asphalt parking lot we had missed civilization, but perhaps it was still not too late. Like the older progressives of the turn of the century, he saw the historical process as a means of transcending the old paradox of industrial civilization destroying the American garden. Through his novels he continually asserts the prodigious speed with which the country was growing and changing, and his belief that the culture which emerged from this ferment of growth and change could be shaped and heightened by such fictional heroes and heroines as he created, and by such a writer as he himself wished to be. Thus we have his revealing assertion to Perry Miller that, "'I love America . . . I love it, but I don't like it'," and his repeated claim that he wanted to raise the cultural maturity of America by mocking its "cruder manifestations."[39] When he complained of and satirized the pioneer myth, he did so only when it became an empty memorializing of the past and an apology for present mediocrity, rather than an impetus toward advancing our cultural possibilities. To participate in the formulation and direction of this emerging culture was Lewis' aim as a writer. Hence his characteristic version of American pastoral calls for the cultivation rather than the rejection of progressive human aspirations, and in his new pioneers he found a unique means to combine the diverse aims of personal freedom and social obligation. The fundamental Lewis hero hopes thus, through the product of his creative endeavors— invention, building, town, city, medical discovery—to assert not only his own individuality but also his participation in the social order and his commitment to the shaping of the emerging new society.

If his best works embody this conception of the appropriate role for new leaders of America, the total body of his novels has an even wider significance for the student of our culture, for there he preserves an important record of the impact of modern technology upon the tenaciously held Arcadian myths of middle America. Indeed, his shortcomings as an artist may be a function of his appropriateness as a cultural representative. As an artist, he shared with many of his fictional characters an impatience with long-range goals, a propensity for being too easily diverted, a tendency, like the historical pioneer, to move on, leaving disordered and unfinished landscapes behind him, without pondering the consequences. In this sense do Lewis' artistic inadequacies constitute a kind of sardonic tribute to his superb gifts of mimicry and photographic realism, an ultimate stamp of corroboration upon his own, self-proclaimed "fanatic" Americanness.

NOTES

[1] *Spokesmen: Modern Writers and American Life* (New York: Appleton, 1928), p. 228. After the original note to a work, and in cases where its title is indicated in the text, page citations will be included in the text.

[2] Mark Schorer, *Sinclair Lewis: An American Life* (New York: McGraw-Hill, 1961); Sheldon Grebstein, *Sinclair Lewis* (New York: Twayne, 1962); D. J. Dooley, *The Art of Sinclair Lewis* (Lincoln: Univ. of Nebraska Press, 1967).

[3] Maurice Kramer, "Sinclair Lewis and the Hollow Center," *The Twenties: Poetry and Prose,* eds. Richard E. Langford and William E. Taylor (Deland, Fla.: Everett Edwards, 1966), p. 69.

[4] The "contradiction . . ." statement is from Lewis' unpublished "Introduction to *Babbitt,*" in *The Man from Main Street: Selected Essays and Other Writings: 1904-1950,* eds. Harry E. Maule and Melville H. Cane (New York: Pocket Books, 1963), p. 26. Hereafter cited as *MMS.* Lewis' self-description is from "The Death of Arrowsmith," *MMS,* p. 105.

[5] Two important earlier studies which treat aspects of Lewis' idealism are Frederick I. Carpenter's "Sinclair Lewis and the Fortress of Reality," in his *American Literature and the Dream* (New York: Philosophical Library, 1955), pp. 116-25, and Maxwell Geismar's "Sinclair Lewis: The Comic Bourjoyce," in his *The Last of the Provincials* (Boston: Houghton Mifflin, 1949), pp. 69-150. I have also found stimulating the final chapter of D. J. Dooley's work (note 2), as well as passing references in Grebstein and Schorer, especially pp. 810-11 in the latter's monumental critical biography.

[6] *Cass Timberlane* (New York: Random House, 1945), p. 28.

[7] For Lewis' praise of Thoreau and *Walden* see "Introduction to *Four Days on the Webutuck River*," *MMS*, pp. 169-70, and "One-Man Revolution," *MMS*, pp. 242-44.

[8] The wilderness rehabilitation at its most strained is found in Lewis' later work, *The Prodigal Parents* (1938), where Fred Cornplow rescues his dull-witted son from sloth and dissipation by forcing him into a canoe trip through the Canadian wilderness. With greater restraint, however, Lewis (himself an inveterate walker) will portray, in *Main Street* and *Dodsworth*, the hike through the countryside as a convincing effort by his characters to break away from destructive and inhibiting social pressures.

[9] *The Job* (New York: Harcourt, Brace, 1917), p. 203.

[10] *The Trail of the Hawk* (New York: Harcourt, Brace, 1915), pp. 316-17.

[11] *Free Air* (New York: Grosset & Dunlap, 1919), p. 190.

[12] In *Kingsblood Royal* (1947), Neil Kingsblood's discovery of his black ancestor, Xavier Pic, is cushioned for the hero (and, one suspects, for Lewis and his audience) by Pic's having been an intrepid *voyageur* and explorer of the Northern wilds.

[13] For a discussion of 19th century versions of the alliance of nature and technology, see Leo Marx's section on "the rhetoric of the technological sublime," in his *The Machine in the Garden* (New York: Oxford Univ. Press, 1964), pp. 195-207. I have assumed here and at the conclusion of my essay that the title and thesis of Marx's book are well enough known not to require documentation.

[14] *Main Street* (New York: New American Library, 1961), pp. 7-8.

[15] Daniel Aaron, "Main Street," in *The American Novel*, ed. Wallace Stegner (New York: Basic Books, 1965), p. 171.

[16] In attempting to find whether Lewis had an actual book in mind as the source for Carol's textbook, one is drawn back to Ebeneezer Howard's influential *Garden Cities of Tomorrow* (1902), first published in 1898 as *Tomorrow: A Peaceful Path to Real Reform*, and to the many books and periodicals which it spawned. Prof. Walter Creese, Dept. of Architecture, Univ. of Illinois, Urbana, a student of this and related town-planning movements, has suggested, in answer to my inquiry to him, that Carol's text is probably a blend of these. Carol's college years (approximately 1904-7, according to Schorer's chronology) were the period in which the Garden City movement was flourishing. Lewis' frequent references to town-planning and beautification in *Main Street* (see, e.g., pp. 129-30) and to garden suburbs and their historical development in *Dodsworth* demonstrate his familiarity with these movements.

[17] In excepting the classical bank from Carol's catalogue of Main Street's unrelieved ugliness, Lewis again reveals his architectural awareness. Every town was likely to have such a bank at the time, a tribute to ascendant capitalism; but, further, innovative architects like Louis Sullivan were building in bold, new designs, many small-town banks across the Middle West. Perhaps the most noteworthy of these, judging by the prominence it is given in architectural histories, is the National Farmer's Bank (the name a reversal of Gopher Prairie's bank) in Owatonna, in Lewis' home state, constructed in 1907-8, on Sullivan's design. See, e.g., Vincent Scully, *American Architecture and Urbanism* (New York: Praeger, 1969), pp. 126-29, and Christopher Tunnard and Henry Hope Reed, *American Skyline* (Boston: Houghton Mifflin, 1955), pp. 210, 222-23.

[18] Vida Sherwin's judgment against Carol that she is "an impossibilist. And you give up too easily" (p. 263), seems to have been shared by Lewis to some extent, if we consider external evidence in the form of a "sequel" to the novel, a visit by the author, after a lapse of four years, to his imaginary town, which Lewis published in *The Nation* in 1924 (*MMS*, pp. 312-30). In Gopher Prairie, a new school building "with its clear windows, perfect ventilation, and warm hued tapestry brick," stands as testimony to Vida's effective gradualist tactics. The Carol of the sequel, dumpy and defeated, has no such memorial to mark her fitful efforts at town improvement.

[19] Although the Lewis biographies (and a letter from Mark Schorer in response to my inquiry) indicate no direct evidence of Lewis' knowing Frank Lloyd Wright or his work, it is difficult to believe that Lewis, in whose works architecture is so often emphasized, would not be aware of Wright, or of the fact that Wright meets Lewis' requirements so admirably here, not only in Wright's radical innovativeness and technical skill, but in the extent to which, as the originator of "Prairie Architecture" at the turn of the century he gave architectural expression to the Middle Western landscape. See his *Writings and Buildings* (New York: Horizon, 1960), pp. 37 ff. See also the Wisconsin-born Wright's self-description as "grown up in the midst of a sentimental family planted on free soil by a grandly sentimental grandfather . . . the Welsh pioneer," and his claim that "the real American spirit, capable of judging an issue for its merits, lies in the West and Middle West, where breadth of view, independent thought and a tendency to take common sense into the realm of art, as in life, are characteristic. It is alone in an atmosphere of this nature that the Gothic spirit of building can be revived." (Quoted in Wayne Andrews, *Architecture, Ambition and Americans* [New York: Harper's, 1955]), p. 230.

[20] *Sticks and Stones*, 2d rev. ed. (New York: Dover, 1955), p. 193.

[21] *Babbitt* (New York: New American Library, 1962), p. 5.

[22] "Minnesota, the Norse State," *MMS*, p. 283.

[23] Quoted in Schorer's "Afterword," *Arrowsmith* (New York: New American Library, 1961), p. 432.

[24] *Arrowsmith*, p. 5.

[25] Arrowsmith's cabin-laboratory recalls the earlier shack of Miles Bjornstam in *Main Street,* where potbellied stove and bare pine floor share the scene with a workbench and assorted volumes, including a manual on gasoline engines and one by Thorstein Veblen (p. 117).

[26] It is worth noting that Lewis, in a 1941 mock obituary about himself entitled "The Death of Arrowsmith," suggests a softening of Martin's denial of society (*MMS,* pp. 104-8). After the title, Lewis uses his own name in the mock obituary but refers to himself in terms synonymous with Arrowsmith. We are told that for the last ten or fifteen years of his life, Lewis-Arrowsmith has lived in a modest country estate in northwestern Connecticut, with his cats, his garden and his work. Thus we are left with a pastoral rather than a primitive landscape and with, in this bit of external evidence, the suggestion of synthesis rather than alienation.

[27] Mention should be made at this point of Lewis' intervening "big" book, *Elmer Gantry* (1927). It stands as a kind of negative pole for all of Lewis' motivations toward social progress and heroic individualism. Without even the vague yearnings and abortive attempts of a Babbitt to invest his life with meaning, Gantry is the ultimate parasite, and Lewis' satire is correspondingly relentless. The book's only true Christian antithesis to Gantry is a backwoods cleric who finds his God—predictably—in nature. But the Rev. Pengilly is a minor character whose forest mysticism remains etherialized and private, useless in any combat of ideas. Even a more vital and significant foil for Gantry like Frank Shallard offers Lewis no model for a hero. An honest doubter like Shallard is to be preferred to a thorough hypocrite like Gantry, to be sure, but the genus is not promising for Lewis. The preachers, like the practicing physicians and the businessmen, are Lewis' second-class citizens, functionaries and servants of the social order rather than its designers and creators.

[28] *Dodsworth* (New York: New American Library, 1967), p. 182.

[29] See note 7. For Lewis' disparagement of Emerson, see *MMS,* pp. 15, 243.

[30] "A Note about *Kingsblood Royal,*" *MMS,* p. 37. Compare this, for example, with Emerson: "The history of any settlement is an illustration of the whole—first the emigrant's camp, then the group of log cabins, then the cluster of white wooden towns. . . . and almost as soon followed by the brick and granite cities, which in another country would stand for centuries, but which here must soon give way to enduring marble" (*Uncollected Lectures*), quoted in Michael Cowan, *City of the West: Emerson, America, and the Urban Metaphor* (New Haven: Yale Univ. Press, 1967), p. 26.

[31] I am indebted to Cowan's *City of the West* for my understanding of Emerson in this context.

[32] *Kingsblood Royal* (New York: Random House, 1947), p. 10.

[33] *The God-Seeker* (New York: Popular Library, 1949), p. 307.

[34] *World So Wide* (New York: Random House, 1951), p. 9.

[35] Carpenter, p. 124.

[36] The quotation is from "Self-Portrait (Berlin, Aug. 1927)," *MMS,* p. 47. For the account of a calamitous actual encounter between Lewis and nature, see Claude Lewis' description of a trip with his brother into the Canadian wilds: *Treaty Trip,* Donald Green and George Knox, eds. (Minneapolis: Univ. of Minnesota Press, 1959).

[37] For Lewis' identification of himself with Ericson and other of his characters, see "Self-Portrait," *MMS,* p. 46. For Lewis' admission that he was Carol, see Schorer, p. 286, and Grebstein, pp. 71, 171. His identification with Arrowsmith is the basis for his mock obituary, "The Death of Arrowsmith," *MMS,* pp. 104-8.

[38] Perry Miller, in his account of his friendship with Lewis at the end of the author's life, tells of Lewis' blowup when he, Miller, facetiously suggested in the presence of Lewis and his brother, Dr. Claude Lewis, that Claude would doubtless prefer visiting medical facilities in Leiden the following morning to hearing Lewis' lecture. Later, Miller says, Lewis apologized, saying, "'It's been that way from the beginning. . . . I wanted to write, and I've worked like hell at it, and the whole of Sauk Center and my family and America have never understood that it is work, that I haven't just been playing around, that this is every bit as important as Claude's hospital. When you said that Claude did not want to hear my lecture, . . . you set up all the resentments I have had ever since I can remember.'" Miller, "The Incorruptible Sinclair Lewis," *Atlantic,* 187 (Apr. 1951), 34.

[39] Miller, p. 34. For Lewis' conception of his role as an agent of cultural progress, see note 4, and also Alexander Manson, "The Last Days of Sinclair Lewis" (as told to Helen Camp), *Saturday Evening Post,* 223 (Mar. 31, 1951), 110. See also Lewis' disparaging of the false myth of pioneering quoted in Schorer, p. 300.

Eugen Arden

SOURCE: "The Early Harlem Novel," in the *Phylon Quarterly,* Vol. XX, No. 1, pp. 25-31.

[*In the following excerpt, Arden examines the first published fiction set in and inspired by Harlem, focusing on works by Paul Lawrence Dunbar, Claude McKay, Wallace Thurman, Rudolf Fisher, and Countee Cullen.*]

Three fine novels published within the past few years give eloquent testimony to the continued vigor of "the Harlem novel," as compared, for example, to the disappearing "immigrant novel." The variety alone impresses us: Eugene Brown's *Trespass*[1] delicately probes the implications of a Negro-white love affair; William Krasner's *North of Welfare* surveys the violence of the "dark ghetto's" slums and gangs; and Evan Hunter's *Blackboard Jungle* brings to dramatic focus all the vague stories we hear about teachers' problems in a "bad" neighborhood.

The Harlem novel has, in short, come of age. The setting now lends itself to good and bad fiction, to delicate psychological exploration or to social propaganda, and addresses itself both to special readership and to the general public.

I propose to look back, however, and describe something of the beginning of Harlem fiction, and to remind the reader of a nearly-forgotten but nearly-great novel which was the forerunner of the whole school. The novel I speak of is Paul Lawrence Dunbar's *The Sport of the Gods* (1902), the first novel to treat Negro life in New York seriously and at length.

A naturalistic novel, *The Sport of the Gods* embodies something of the "plantation-school concept,"[2] which implies that the Negro becomes homesick and demoralized in the urban North. The inexperienced youths in this novel, Joe and Kitty Hamilton, migrate from the South to a treacherous New York environment which deterministically produces their degeneration and disaster. When Joe Hamilton finally strangles his mistress after many sordid scenes, a character in the novel exclaims:

> Here is another example of the pernicious influences of the city on untrained negroes. Oh, is there no way to keep these people from rushing away from the small villages and country districts of the South up to cities, where they cannot battle with the terrible force of a strange and unusual environment?

The answer is that

> the stream of young negro life would continue to flow up from the South, dashing itself against the hard necessities of the city and breaking like waves against the rock,—that until the gods grew tired of their cruel sport.[3]

The attitude of the Hamiltons toward New York and their experiences in the city follow a familiar pattern, reminiscent of all "evil city" folklore. In *The Sport of the Gods,* New York at first represents a promised land of freedom, where the protagonists expect to shed their troubles and start a fresh happy life.

> They had heard of New York as a place vague and far away, a city that, like Heaven, to them had existed by faith alone. All the days of their lives they had heard about it, and it seemed to them like the centre of all the glory, all the wealth, and all the freedom in the world. New York. It had an alluring sound.[4]

But fate in this naturalistic novel is inexorable, and the forces of the city, so alluring and yet so disastrous to the inexperienced, quickly demoralize Joe and then his sister Kitty. A visit to the Banner Club—"a social cesspool"—starts Joe's decline, and a place in the chorus starts Kitty on a life which includes "experiences" obviously leading to no good end for her.

At the time Dunbar wrote this novel, there was not yet a Harlem as we know it today. Just after the turn of the century, most of New York's Negroes lived in cramped quarters near the Pennsylvania Railroad Station (the region to which the Hamilton family went on arrival), or else wedged in amongst the Irish on San Juan Hill. Another colony existed on West 53rd Street, but the Negroes there were mainly stage folk, musicians, and journalists—and even there the over-crowding was notorious.

By the turn of the century, more room somewhere on the island of Manhattan had to be made for the Negro. The needed space was found in Harlem, a district which had been by-passed by many of the white people expanding north into new sections. In 1905 an apartment in one nearly empty building on 134th Street near Fifth Avenue was rented to a Negro family, and soon the rest of the building was filled up by Negroes who followed. Other apartment buildings were then opened to Negro tenancy, the area spreading westward to Seventh Avenue by 1910. In the two decades that followed, the Negro population in New York grew from less than sixty thousand to more than two hundred thousand, most of the arrivals settling in Harlem. The greatest increase took place during the First World War, when many Southern Negroes flocked to Northern industrial centers and swelled the established Negro communities.

For a time, the white residents did everything possible to stem the tide. They attempted to buy up houses occupied by colored tenants and have them vacated; they strove to prevent white realtors from selling or renting to Negroes.[5] But it was all to no avail. One great factor, that of money, worked in the Negroes' favor. Needing the apartments so desperately, they paid two or three times as much rental as the whites. Downtown they were badly cramped for space, and repeated incidents of interracial strife were breaking out in Hell's Kitchen, the Tenderloin, and San Juan Hill. The Negroes arriving from the South served further to increase the pressure to expand the Harlem beachhead. By the end of the first Great War, the battle for Harlem was settled decisively in the Negroes' favor.

Their victory, however, was to prove a bitter one. Forced to pay exorbitant rents, families had to double up in apartments to meet the rentals, and even then extra boarders had to be taken in. Every space was utilized— sometimes even bathrooms were improvised to serve as extra bedrooms.[6] Thus did Harlem become the most densely settled Negro community in the world, extending from 125th Street to 147th Street between Fifth and Eighth Avenues, and soon to press downtown to meet the Puerto Ricans surging up from 110th Street.

In the 1920's Harlem and its celebrities began to attract wide attention, white folk swarming into the "back ghetto" in the search of "exuberant escape in the so-called exotic primitivism of Negro cabaret life."[7] In fiction, Carl Van Vechten was the first to capitalize successfully on the new, swarming Harlem, though he and his imitators were really following the lead of Dunbar in treating the comparatively unworked scenes of Harlem low-life. Indeed, Van Vechten expressed the indebtedness of his *Nigger Heaven* (1926) to Dunbar's *The Sport of the Gods* by writing that Dunbar

> described the plight of a young outsider who comes to the larger New York Negro world to make his fortune, but who falls a victim to the sordid snares of that world, a theme I elaborated in 1926 to fit a newer and much more intricate social system.[8]

That "intricate social system," however, gets lost in the sensationalism of *Nigger Heaven,* which paints Harlem with too obvious a gusto. Van Vechten must have been fascinated by the barbaric rhythms of Negro jazz, the intoxicating dances, and the wild abandon of cabaret life after midnight; or at any rate, he must have known that his readers would be. His book enjoyed immediate popularity and became, according to Hugh M. Gloster, "a sort of guide book for visitors who went uptown seeking a re-creation of the primitive African jungle in the heart of New York City." The songs and snatches of the "blues" by Langston Hughes incorporated into the text of *Nigger Heaven* also helped to enhance the reputation of the book. Roi Ottley, in another study of Harlem, joined in crediting the Van Vechten novel with doing much to establish Harlem as a great vogue; Ottley also points out, however, that the loose money and the jazziness of the 'Twenties were basically responsible for Harlem's short happy career as the Mecca of the thrill-seeker.[9]

But the sensational qualities of *Nigger Heaven* do not obscure the fact that Van Vechten had much of serious interest to say about the urban Negro. The major problem he discusses is the rejection of the Negro by a predominantly white society. There are no sermons pleading "tolerance," but the injustice of segregation is expressed by one character who bitterly remarks, "A white prostitute can go places where a coloured preacher would be refused admission."[10]

Much more subtle, however, is the whole conflict between the growing race consciousness of the Negro and the opposite pressure of the white society, a conflict which turned Negro against Negro. Reflecting the "Africa for Africans" movement led by Marcus Aurelius Garvey in the years just following the First World War, the Negro intelligentsia demonstrated a rousing enthusiasm for primitive African art pieces and Negro folk spirituals, matters which figure predominantly in the characterization of Mary Love in this novel. But in spite of all the outward signs of chauvinism, the Negro world of Harlem made frantic attempts to emulate white cultural values. Mary speaks heatedly, for example, of advertising statistics which showed that "her race spent more money on hair-straighteners and skin-lightening preparations than they did on food and clothing."[11] The

way to success for a Negro, to put it as plainly as possible, was to be as much a white as possible, to be something, in short, which he was not.

This pressure to conform and imitate was bound to produce all sorts of disruptive tensions, both personal and communal. The Negroes' problem, like the immigrants' problem, was that of the outsider. The "ghetto," both for immigrants and Negroes, was not only geographical but cultural. To leave one's own "kind" in favor of the great, white, "American" world was possible only after an intense conflict of loyalties. Van Vechten cleverly organized these tensions around one central and provocative consideration: that the Negroes have succumbed to white values to such a degree that amongst the Negroes themselves there is a pervasive system of color prejudice. The very dark, kinky-haired, negroid-featured of them were at the bottom of the social ladder, which was a situation not peculiar to New York alone or to the Jazz Age. Charles W. Chesnutt had earlier described a Cleveland "Blue Vein Club" among Negroes in *The Wife of His Youth and Other Stories of the Color Line* (1899). The protagonist of the title story in this collection must choose between the faithful black wife of his youth and a refined "light" woman of his own caste. The problem in each case is rooted in a compulsive urge to imitate white values and the attacks of conscience which inevitably follow.

At the top of the ladder were those Negroes for whom it was possible to pass as white, a decision often made on the basis of disillusionment. Dick Sill, a cynic who "passes," hotly defends his position to Byron, the young hero of Van Vechten's novel, who has just returned to Harlem from the University of Pennsylvania. Dick is a lawyer, but, he says, "the race doesn't want colored lawyers. If they're in trouble they go to white lawyers, and they go to white banks and white insurance companies. . . . Most of 'em . . . pray to a white God. You won't get much help from the race."[12]

Byron, living amongst such tensions, is himself a sorry figure of confusion. Outwardly, he is a model hero of fiction: he is handsome, well-educated, comes to Harlem with letters of introduction to influential leaders, and is loved by women both good and bad. Actually, his way of living becomes more and more dissolute, and he spends much time whining that the whole world is against him. He wants to be a writer and he is living in a Negro metropolis which is practically unknown in any real sense to the outside world; but he insists upon writing wild melodramatic tales of miscegenation completely outside the realm of his experience. We are not surprised that his stay in Harlem ends abruptly with an act of sordid, pointless violence.

Claude McKay's *Home to Harlem* (1928) bears many similarities to *Nigger Heaven,* though McKay has insisted that he is in no way indebted to Van Vechten. The germ of *Home to Harlem* was supposed to be a 1925 short story of McKay's which had been entered without success in a contest conducted by *Opportunity* magazine.

Although *Nigger Heaven* was published in 1926, McKay explains that he did not read it until 1927, by which time he had almost completed the expansion of his two-year-old short story into a novel.[13] To the reader in 1928, however, McKay's novel must have seemed very much a part of the Van Vechten vogue, in its descriptive tours through Harlem's cabarets, pool rooms, gambling dives, dance halls, and houses of prostitution.

As in *Nigger Heaven,* the more sensational elements of the novel are balanced by the treatment of serious racial questions. The two main characters are Jake, who deserts the United States Army in Brest because he is put to work in a labor battalion rather than allowed to fight, and his friend Ray, a sensitive, well-educated Negro who has an aversion for Harlem low-life. Confused by a social order under white domination, Ray can see no meaning to his existence, and can find none in his wide reading. Dimly he begins to feel that his education has shackled rather than freed him and that his greatest contentment would be to lose himself "in some savage culture in the jungles of Africa."[14]

Another novel of the Van Vechten type is Wallace Thurman's *The Blacker the Berry* (1929) about Emma Lou Morgan, whose black skin alienates her from a light-skinned family in Idaho, from her classmates at the University of Southern California, and finally from her Harlem lover, a mulatto-Filipino. There is the familiar exploitation of Harlem local color in scenes of midnight vaudeville shows, ballroom dances, and frenzied drinking in speakeasies. The very material, in other words, which had once been regarded as destructive in the "evil city" novel, was now manipulated to suggest a romantic view of the big city. Gaiety in New York came to mean living in a state just this side of hysteria; and the Harlem tour began to loom as large as the Rockies in the imagination of the tourists.

It is clear that by the end of the 1920's a stereotyped Negro of Harlem had been created, acknowledged, and assumed; his existence seemed confined to drink, sex, gambling, and brooding about racial matters, with an edge of violence always in view. In attempting to distinguish the new Negro from what had been the "typical Negro" in earlier fiction—"no minstrel coon off the stage, no Thomas Nelson Page's nigger, no Octavus Roy Cohen's porter, no lineal descendent of Uncle Tom"[15]—the Van Vechten–McKay–Thurman school created another type as damaging and unrepresentative as that which was replaced. Amongst the Harlem writers themselves, a counter-movement of realism in Negro fiction grew and was given impetus by Rudolf Fisher and the influential Countee Cullen. Less interested in the exotic and animalistic aspects of Negro life, Fisher and Cullen attempted to provide a more representative picture which would show that in Harlem, too, there was some regard for quiet living, hard work, serious thinking, and mature standards of morality.

The Walls of Jericho (1928) by Fisher realistically describes the general social life of Harlem, including glimpses of church life, the Sunday promenade on Seventh Avenue, and the annual costume ball of the General Improvement Association (an organization probably suggested by the National Association for the Advancement of Colored People) The Harlem scene is treated with considerable detachment, and Fisher masters the Harlem slang so skillfully that he has been called the peer of Ring Lardner in idiomatic writing.[16]

Countee Cullen's personal background fitted him admirably to write *One Way to Heaven* (1932), a novel which deals intimately with the place of church and religion in the lives of Negroes in Harlem. The son of Reverend Frederick A. Cullen, founder of the Salem Methodist Episcopal Church, Countee Cullen is able to include descriptions of watch-night meetings, conversions of sinners, and other services of the African Methodist Episcopal Church, all of which bear the mark of authenticity. The job of the Negro writer, Cullen once said, is to "create types that are truly representative of us as a people,"[17] thus explaining both the strength and the weakness of his novel. *One Way to Heaven* offers a sane, realistic picture of typical Negro urban life; but it also suffers by the creation of types rather than individuals, and by a looseness of construction which strings the events together in such a way as to make their sequence seem almost accidental. Cullen, for all his good intentions, thus emerges as a less compelling novelist than Van Vechten or even Claude McKay, though when taken together, the exotics and the realists were already suggesting that Harlem offered the materials for extraordinary fiction.

Perhaps the most important thing to say about the Harlem novel is the most obvious: a new character in American fiction was created. Just as the plantation Negro was typical of Nineteenth Century fiction, so in our own day the prototype was the Negro in an urban, industrial environment. There he was confronted with new pressures evolving from a new *mise en scène* and a set of social imperatives different from those which had once dominated his tradition. The process of choice sometimes proved ennobling and sometimes corrosive. The novels which sought to represent him found a need for newer and larger dimensions, for this urban Negro was more pliable, less likely to fit into stock categories than any of the earlier Negro characters. The Harlem novel, in short, has made possible the development of such variety in characterization that a third dimension has at last been added to the Negro in fiction.

NOTES

[1] Published in hard covers in 1952, but better known in the paperback of 1954.

[2] Hugh M. Gloster, *Negro Voices in American Fiction* (Chapel Hill, 1948), p. 46.

[3] Paul Lawrence Dunbar, *The Sport of the Gods* (New York, 1902), pp. 212, 213-14.

[4] *Ibid.,* pp. 77-78.

[5] Claude McKay, *Harlem: Negro Metropolis* (New York, 1940), pp. 16-20.

[6] *Ibid.*

[7] Gloster, *op. cit.,* p. 113.

[8] Carl Van Vechten, "Introduction," p. vii, in James W. Johnson, *Autobiography of an Ex-Coloured Man* (New York, 1928).

[9] Gloster, *op. cit.,* p. 158; and Roi Ottley, *New World A-Coming* (Boston, 1943), p. 66.

[10] Carl Van Vechten, *Nigger Heaven* (New York, 1926), p. 46.

[11] *Ibid.,* p. 11.

[12] *Ibid.,* p. 119.

[13] Claude McKay, *A Long Way from Home* (New York, 1937), pp. 282-83.

[14] Claude McKay, *Home to Harlem* (New York, 1928), p. 274.

[15] *Ibid.,* pp. 63-64.

[16] Gloster, *op. cit.,* p. 177.

[17] "The Negro in Art," *The Crisis,* XXXII (August, 1926), 193.

[*] Dissertations were not published then. The Alain Locke Memorial Committee plans a publication of Locke's thesis.

Lucy Frost

SOURCE: "Violence in the Eternal City: *Catch-22* as a Critique of American Culture," in *Meanjin Quarterly,* Vol. 30, December, 1971, pp. 447-53.

[*In the following excerpt, Frost examines Joseph Heller's depiction of urban violence in* Catch-22 *and discusses cultural criticism in the novel.*]

Catch-22 is and yet is not a war novel. Published in 1961, it bears the distinctive imprint of civilian America during the 'fifties, an America smugly uncritical and much better prepared for entertainment than for any disturbing illumination. Assessing the literary publications of 1961, Alfred Kazin placed Joseph Heller's work in 'the new category of studiously funny war books . . . the book is an entertainment, not a novel.'[1] As now seems transparently obvious, *Catch-22* entertains only so long as the sources of entertainment remain harmless. When they cease to be harmless, the reversals of expectation which had elicited laughter become more disturbing than amusing. Because the expectations reversed involve attitudes, values, and goals central to American culture,[2] *Catch-22* is a serious critique of the total culture, not just of war.

At the fulcrum of the critique, violence operates as a touchstone for cultural crisis. In American history, according to the nation's public rhetoric, violence that is extended, deliberate, and legally sanctioned has been occasioned by wars, and it is with such violence that the novel at first seems primarily concerned. Soon it becomes apparent, however, that this is a new kind of war novel. The foreign enemy has disappeared from the scene and is present only in the inanimate forms of machines, flak or lines on maps. The enemy exists within the Army itself. For a brief moment even the normally obtuse Clevinger recognizes his real enemies as he looks into the faces of the superior officers hearing his case before the Action Board: 'These three men who hated him spoke his language and wore his uniform, but he saw their loveless faces set immutably into cramped, mean lines of hostility and understood instantly that nowhere in the world, not in all the fascist tanks or planes or submarines, not in the bunkers behind the machine guns or mortars or behind the blowing flame throwers, not even among all the expert gunners of the crack Hermann Goering Anti-aircraft Division . . . were there men who hated him more.'[3] By dispensing with the foreign enemy, Heller opens up new metaphoric possibilities for the war novel. During the first half of the book the reader is rarely reminded of violence at all. The free enterprise system within a wartime setting seems to have become the non-violent equivalent of war. This in itself is a startling criticism of American culture, for Americans usually expect the activities of military and civilian life to be separate. In *Catch-22* the activities interpenetrate, with varying consequences.

Early in the novel the Army turns commercial under the direction of Milo Minderbinder and the M & M—Milo and Minderbinder—syndicate in which everyone has a share. The problems monopolizing attention in Army units stationed on Pianosa are largely problems of civilian life. In the face of Colonel Cathcart's personal ambitions, for example, military objectives recede from sight. The men fly more and more bombing missions not because enemy pressure is increasing, but because the colonel wants to be a general and so keeps boosting his unit's flight record as a means of boosting his own opportunities for promotion. Colonel Cathcart might easily be a Ford dealer urging his salesmen to fill higher and higher sales quotas so that he can get a desk in the district office. The Colonel seems to feel no more anxiety when involving his men in danger, violence, and perhaps death, than he would if he were demanding that they sell more cars. Clearly Heller is deriving from Army life a metaphor for society. With civilian impulses motivating the officers, the novel is comic until violence breaks through to stifle the laughter. One initial consequence of grafting civilian business values onto a military establishment is a gourmet mess hall; a later consequence is Milo's contract to bomb his own camp. When such violence surfaces, the novel's tone alters. There comes the reminder that because the cultural rhetoric of peace-loving America makes war, however justified, an aberration, it should be *impossible* for a novelist to use the Army as a metaphor for the United States, especially when the country is not even at war—as was true in 1961. The metaphor is possible, however, because of the changes in traditional conceptions of both the Army and the society, and it is through the depiction of these changes that Heller develops his critique.

In the past it has been widely believed that the military performed functions dictated by the society it served. In *Catch-22* the Army's goals are no longer shaped by a governing civilian society; they are predominantly internal and autonomous. The Army has become an independent society with its own goals and its own enemies. Civilian life—in the form of the M & M syndicate—is subordinated within the governing military structure. Civilian life without even the cohesion of the military structure is depicted briefly but vividly in a single chapter of concentrated nightmare during which Yossarian searches Rome for a young girl he wants to save. Within civilian society, law supposedly contains violence. In Rome, the operation of justice through laws has been replaced by the authority of physical power. This is the authority signified by the phrase, 'Catch-22'. It is the authority to determine right according to force, not cultural values: 'Catch-22 says they have a right to do anything we can't stop them from doing.' Any rhetoric of human rights is a sham. Yossarian recognizes with a shock that there is nothing to appeal to beyond the force itself. People who use 'Catch-22' as authority for their actions refer to no orders, no justifying documents, no law: 'Catch-22 did not exist, he was positive of that, but it made no difference. What did matter was that everyone thought it existed, and that was much worse, for there was no object or text to ridicule or refute, to accuse, criticize, attack, amend, hate, revile, spit at, rip to shreds, trample upon or burn up.'

This recognition marks a significant departure from earlier explanations of destructive force in society. Late in the nineteenth century Joseph Conrad grappled with a similar question about the origins of a society's violence when he wrote *Heart of Darkness*. In that novel Kurtz, alone at a remote African trading station, becomes a source of power similar to the source represented by 'Catch-22'. What Conrad seems to mean when he describes Kurtz as 'hollow' is close to what Heller suggests by saying that 'Catch-22' does not exist. Both Kurtz and 'Catch-22' are beyond those socially determined patterns establishing order by means of law. Kurtz cuts himself off from other men, becomes hollow, 'his unlawful soul' beguiled 'beyond the bounds of permitted aspirations.' In the end he could no longer be appealed to in any human terms, 'in the name of anything high or low.' And yet there is an important difference between being hollow and not existing. Marlow can argue with Kurtz, while Yossarian cannot argue with the 'Catch'. Because Kurtz has the physical shape of a man, Marlow's struggle with the intangible thing that is Kurtz's soul is not a struggle with the amorphous power of 'Catch-22'. And that makes all the difference. Marlow can struggle and win, however qualified may be his victory. Since Yossarian is struggling against an enemy he cannot even locate, much less confront, winning is impossible, indeed, an irrelevant concept. Yossarian can only escape, for the power of darkness now emanates from an entire culture. It is no longer localized within a man, and culture lacks the power to restrain it.

Walking through Rome, Yossarian witnesses the embodiment of 'Catch-22' in the life of a city. Physical force is the mode of human contact: people chase one another, attack, reduce humanity to its physical components. Such reduction banishes everything associated in Western culture with what traditionally has been called man's higher nature. The reader is kept aware of loss because he is responding to the brutal city through the humanitarian values inherent in Yossarian's perspective. He sees, for example, as Yossarian does, that with justice gone, Rome's law enforcement officers are in a position similar to that of the Army officers. Like their military counterparts they use force ungoverned by its original social function. This Yossarian learns after he comes upon 'a single civilian Italian with books and a slew of civilian policemen with armlocks and clubs. The screaming, struggling civilian was a dark man with a face white as flour from fear . . ."Help!" he shrieked shrilly in a voice strangling on its own emotion, as the policemen carried him to the open doors in the rear of the ambulance and threw him inside. "Police! Help! Police!" ' The scene becomes a Joycean epiphany for Yossarian. First he 'smiled wryly at the futile and ridiculous cry for aid, then saw with a start that the words were ambiguous, realized with alarm that they were not, perhaps, intended as a call for police but as a heroic warning from the grave by a doomed friend to everyone who was *not* a policeman with a club and a gun and a mob of other policemen with clubs and guns to back him up. "Help! Police!" the man had cried, and he could have been shouting of danger.' This epiphany gives to Yossarian the awareness that society is not organized according to humanitarian values, that its protective institutions such as laws and law-enforcement agencies are no longer subordinate to these values, and that in their place are the brute connections made by the power of physical force. Violence is the new connective bond between people.

In place of social conduct modelled on rational and humanitarian principles, Yossarian views a scene of grotesque images reminiscent of paintings by Bruegel. The source for the grotesque is suggested by the chapter's title, 'The Eternal City'. Rome has been called the 'Eternal City' since its proud days of cultural achievement when it seemed that man had built a city which would endure forever. Even after its fall from the glorious days of the Empire, Rome has remained the very symbol of Western civilization. Joseph Heller, juxtaposing that symbol against Yossarian's vision of Rome, suggests that man is cut off from the *secular* source of his spiritual life because the inherited culture with its humanistic ideals is no longer operative in the life of the city. The techniques of the grotesque upon which Heller relies to portray this severance are in the tradition of a painter like Bosch, whose altarpieces portray an earlier severance—that of man cut off from the *religious* source of his spiritual life. In such grotesque worlds, whatever the source of the grotesque, man is shown adrift without meaning in a sea of absurdity. The absence of meaning is a source of the enduring terror produced by a true grotesque. Those violent aspects of life which are ignored, assimilated, or purged in the everyday world familiar to us, catch our attention immediately in the grotesque world where attempts to contain violence—often successful in the familiar world—inevitably fail. When this happens, as it does in Heller's vision of 'The Eternal City', violence becomes the basic ingredient in life, both individual and social. The violence is terrifying not so much because the individual actions are of great magnitude as because there is no reason for the violence of the actions. There is no reason for anything in the 'abidingly strange'[4] world of the grotesque.

Yossarian's journey through Rome's underworld of the doomed is to him a nightmarish revelation of a truth previously there but hidden from his sight because he had been so absorbed in himself. For the first time Yossarian has gone to Rome looking not for exploitable sex, but for a young girl he hopes to save from exploitation. Consequently, he is for the first time a spectator rather than a participant, and he sees what was there all along. He discovers that his cultural assumptions do not fit reality. This discovery creates a crisis of belief in culture, a crisis experienced by many Americans today. The magnitude of the crisis is probably accentuated by the importance attached to the belief. During the nineteenth century, as J. Hillis Miller has said,[5] many Victorian intellectuals became convinced that God had disappeared from their world, and they tried desperately to replace their loss of His presence with aspects of their secular life. Their answer to the intellectual crisis which accompanied God's withdrawal was to substitute culture for religion. Precisely because that substitute has moulded Yossarian's assumptions about life, he is ill-fitted for existence in the world of *Catch-22*. Yossarian's stance as misfit is funny until the final chapters of the novel when his world is judged.

The effect of this judgment is to transform his rôle of misfit into that of victim. Heller portrays Yossarian as a man whose innate goodness withstands the pressures of exposure to a corrupting environment. Yossarian's final response is to resist by turning his back on his society. In all this, of course, he follows the old American pattern of which Huck Finn is the classic prototype. Still, Yossarian is different from his nineteenth century counterpart. Because their societies differ, the concluding attitudes to American culture differ. Huck travels through a sparsely populated, agrarian world, unsophisticated and uncomplicated by our present standards. As he floats down the river with Jim, the very sparsity of population makes it possible to identify victims and assailants. Behind the acts of violence and the threats of

violence lies a bevy of deadly sins, all readily recognizable. Even in the feud between the Grangerfords and the Shepherdsons, which might seem to prefigure Heller's preoccupation with 'senseless' violence, the violence is fitted to a pattern and follows the predictable steps of a family feud. Twain attacks the foibles of men, the driving passions that make them weak creatures, and certainly his vision would make one doubt the possibility that culture could ever perform the functions once performed by religion, simply because one cannot depend on humanity where lofty tasks are concerned. Yet Twain does not give up hope entirely. With the territory ahead goes the hope that Huck might find some life better than society along the river. And that life would be on the American continent.

Yossarian, on the other hand, lives in a society which seems to concentrate its energies on making life an ever more impersonal experience. Victims and assailants rarely face each other. Bureaucratic organizations separate commands from the men commanded. Purveyors of abstraction manipulate language in order to manipulate reality. Language used in this fashion lacks moral aspect in any humanistic terms. It is directed not to individual men but to groups, and, more often, merely to the group's social function. Colonel Cathcart uses language in this way when he issues commands that change the number of missions to be flown. His concern in designating the number is with other numbers—those set by his rival officers at other bases—and not with the men who fly the missions, with Orr, Dunbar, Yossarian, and the rest. And as Cathcart is separated from the men he sometimes sends to their deaths, so also are the men separated from the victims on the ground who receive their bombs. Cathcart is separated from his victims by the abstract, non-human language of official notices; the men are separated from their victims by the literal distance between their aircraft and the ground. Both separations are clearly those of distance between men who are joined together as assailant and victim. In these, as well as the many other similar instances in the novel, the distance between assailant and victim makes violence decidedly easier. As distance increases, any emotional and psychological—to say nothing of moral—reaction on the part of the assailant decreases. Under such conditions, a man's responsibility to and for other men rarely influences behavior. The distance between men is convenient for violence, but not for humane life, especially in a highly organized, densely populated environment which in itself encourages impersonality.

Even when he lights out for the territory ahead of the rest, Yossarian's situation is different from Huck's on the frontier, although the impulses behind the flights have much in common. By offering Sweden as an alternative for Yossarian, Heller suggests that there is a way to escape the dehumanizing forces at work in Yossarian's own culture. By avoiding any suggestion of how life in Sweden, another urbanized Western nation, will be fundamentally different, Heller does not make the alternative convincing. Only the desire for the alternative rings true. Heller, like so many of his contemporaries, arrives at a cultural impasse. After damning the present he clings precariously to the values espoused by nineteenth century humanism. The way out of violence and out of the 'Catch' is to be humane. In a society governed by force, where authorities are ready to use violence with little, sometimes no, provocation, to be humane is to be a victim of that impersonal force. Yossarian seems to opt for the alternative provided, ironically, by the threats of Nately's whore. This is the alternative of personal, passionate violence by a woman who blames Yossarian for her lover's death because Yossarian brought her the news. Nately's whore is not deterred by the impersonality of the actual assailant; she embodies the abstract assailant in a man with whom she can contend. By making Yossarian responsible for Nately's death, she finds her own way for humanizing impersonal violence. Her way, we know, is to create an illusion, and we are left wondering whether Yossarian, too, has solved his problems by creating an illusion.

These are scarcely optimum conditions for realizing nineteenth century hopes for culture. Indeed, these are conditions running counter to humanitarian ideals. In the world of *Catch-22* these conditions destroy culture. They do so because while culture may be propelled by humane impulses, War and the Army are not. The destruction is not immediately apparent within the Army, where a rigid hierarchical system of rank with power staves off chaos. In civilian society no such hierarchy exists. The cultural cornerstones removed, the fragile edifice topples. When Yossarian wanders the streets of Rome looking for a particular girl, he finds instead a barrage of people without names or faces. These people have only the impersonality of violent physical actions, actions which have no explanations, no motives, not even the greed of Huck's notorious companions, the King and the Duke. Yossarian sees a city where culture has disappeared as the binding force by which an impersonal environment is humanized. The effect of this disappearance becomes clear to Yossarian in the stark and unequivocal terms of Snowden's secret: 'Man was matter, that was Snowden's secret. Drop him out the window and he'll fall. Set fire to him and he'll burn. Bury him and he'll rot like other kinds of garbage. The spirit gone, man is garbage.'

Heller's use of the war novel as a genre appropriate for a serious critique of American culture is not original. Earlier novelists including Stephen Crane, e. e. cummings, John Dos Passos and Ernest Hemingway used the genre to expose their culture's failure to provide ideals appropriate to the actual experience of war. After World War II several novelists, for whom the war years constituted an initiation into adult life, took this accusation much further. For them the War was—and continues to be— the event that destroyed their belief in America as a society with a culture shaped by humanistic traditions. The first war novel to express this disillusionment was Norman Mailer's *The Naked and the Dead* (1948). Both *The Naked and the Dead* and *Catch-22* use World War II for their settings, and yet the central conflict in each

involves not the armies that the War made enemies, but men made enemies within the American Army and, more broadly, within American culture. The vision of the United States created by these two novels is that of a country with conflicting sets of cultural norms. One set has as its aims the acquisition of inanimate objects, and of the power to treat other men as if they were the abstract progeny of a computer. The other is dedicated above all else to humanizing life. If the rhetoric of the nation supports the second, the actions of its leaders together with its institutions—political, economic, and social—are directed toward the first. And thus exposure to the phenomenon of war does not seem to have been in itself as important to novelists in World War II as to their counterparts in World War I, but exposure to life in a highly organized society, in a military establishment which clearly has a goal of destruction and openly values force, was more important. Experiencing the shock of army life during war, the novelists learned that in the opinion of the men whom their culture's values designated heroes, 'life is not the remarkable, the precious, or necessary thing we think it is,' as a character says in John Hawkes's superb war novel, *The Cannibal* (1949).

Behind the literary treatments of the War, then, lies the assumption not that World War II altered the nature of Western civilization, but that, to those who would look closely, it revealed what was already there. In the extreme situation of war, things concealed in humanistic rhetoric during peacetime existed without the rhetoric because the period of war, ironically, permitted honesty about the culture's aims. The War justified the use of force in any form to achieve goals, whatever the price paid by individuals. It worked according to the principle of 'Catch-22', and almost everyone accepted the 'Catch' without doubting its validity, much less its existence. The novel's most terrifying implication is that the 'Catch' still operates in 'peacetime' America today.

NOTES

[1] Alfred Kazin, 'Literature,' in 'The Year's Developments in the Arts and Sciences,' *The Great Ideas Today: 1962* (Chicago: Encyclopaedia Britannica, Inc., 1962), p. 148.

[2] 'Culture' is being used throughout this article in its sociological, rather than strictly artistic, meaning.

[3] Joseph Heller, *Catch-22* (N.Y.: Simon and Schuster, Inc., 1961).

[4] Wolfgang Kayser, *The Grotesque in Art and Literature* (Bloomington, Indiana University Press, 1963), p. 183. In his history of the development of the grotesque Kayser isolates distinguishing characteristics, and it is upon his discussion that my remarks about the function of the grotesque in *Catch-22* are based.

[5] See especially his introduction to *The Disappearance of God* (N.Y.: Schocken Books, 1965).

Park Dixon Goist

SOURCE: "The City as Noncommunity," in *From Main Street to State Street: Town, City, and Community in America,* Kennikat Press, 1977, pp. 68-79.

[*In the following essay from her book-length study of urban settings in American literature, Goist discusses the works of Theodore Dreiser and Henry Blake Fuller.*]

Though he lived in cities and even wrote one "urban novel," Hamlin Garland remained essentially a writer of the frontier or middle border. But the locale of his one effort at city fiction has been the focal point of a good deal of novelistic effort. At the turn of the nineteenth century two of the outstanding novelists of Chicago were Theodore Dreiser (1871-1945) and Henry Blake Fuller (1857-1929). Their backgrounds were quite different, as were both their literary and life styles. Dreiser came from the hinterlands and spent a good portion of his career attempting to come to terms with America's largest cities, Chicago and New York. Fuller was born and lived all his life in Chicago, and after an initial effort to deal with his native city he turned largely to other kinds of work. Given these and other differences to be discussed in this chapter, it is interesting to note that both Dreiser and Fuller share a structure of feeling with Garland in regard to individualism and community in the city.

In her study *The American Urban Novel* (1954), Blanche Gelfant maintains that "with the publication of *Sister Carrie,* the twentieth-century American city novel came into being" (p. 63). It is significant to note that Theodore Dreiser, the author of this important urban novel, like his contemporaries Booth Tarkington, Zona Gale, Sherwood Anderson, and Sinclair Lewis, grew up in small town America. Like Tarkington he was from Indiana, and like Anderson he knew small town poverty at first hand. But unlike these members of his generation Dreiser became a novelist of the city, and in his books he attempted to define the meaning of large cities for American life.

Forty years after Dreiser's *Sister Carrie* appeared in 1900, the Chicago sociologist Louis Wirth wrote a now classic essay entitled "Urbanism as a Way of Life," in which he argued that the uniqueness of a big city lifestyle results from the interaction of the large size, diversity, and heterogeneity of its population. Theodore Dreiser was not a sociologist consciously measuring the relative weight of certain given variables, but he was a participant observer who, like Wirth, sought in his aesthetic rendering of the metropolis to explain what urbanism meant as a way of life.[1]

Before writing *Sister Carrie* Dreiser was a successful newspaper and free-lance magazine writer. Only reluctantly, at the urging of a close friend, did he take a hand at writing a novel. But once he set to work, he was able to complete the book in seven months (probably only four of which were actually spent on *Sister Carrie*). In that relatively short period he produced an American literary classic. Dreiser was able to achieve this feat in part because he had spent the preceding seven years writing prodigiously for newspapers and magazines, thus learning his craft. Also, when he turned to fiction he drew on his own personal encounters with the city. As the experiences of George Willard and Felix Fay in the towns of Ohio, Iowa, and Illinois encouraged them to look to Chicago as the next step in their ventures, so Dreiser and his fictional characters were drawn to that metropolis of the Midwest to find the meaning of life. The adventures of Carrie take up where the stories of George and Felix leave off: in her the meaning and impact of the city upon the half-formed small town youngster is traced. Dreiser's volume is an urban novel precisely because it reveals how the city environment shaped the lives of its individual characters.[2]

The book's plot revolves around the fortunes of three people and covers the period from August, 1889, to January, 1897. Caroline Meeber comes to Chicago from Columbia City, Wisconsin, and gets a physically exhausting, low-paying job in a cheap shoe factory. She lives with her sister and brother-in-law, whose pinched existence is determined largely by his menial job cleaning refrigerator cars at the city's stockyards. Following a short illness, Carrie loses her job and, without an income from which to pay the rent or buy clothes for the winter, accidentally runs into Charles Drouet, a flashy traveling salesman she had met on the train to Chicago. Disheartened by the restrictive life at her sister's flat, unable to secure a job, convinced of Drouet's concern for her, and desirous of the lifestyle he can provide, she accepts his offer and the two begin living together.

Soon thereafter Drouet introduces his "wife" to George Hurstwood, the suave manager of Fitzgerald and Moy's, a fashionable downtown bar. Hurstwood has a comfortable life, a substantial home, and a respectable wife who has conventional social ambitions for her two children. But he falls in love with Carrie, who does not yet know he is married, wins her away from Drouet, who, when he finds out what has been going on, tells her about Hurstwood's marital status. As his own marriage collapses, Hurstwood, in a moment of wine-confused panic, takes almost $11,000 from his employer's safe, and by a ruse tricks Carrie into going to Montreal with him. He is forced to return most of the money; then he and Carrie, who has reconciled herself to the situation (she does not know about the theft of the money), change their name, get married, and go to New York. There Hurstwood experiences a decline of fortunes that eventually leads him to the Bowery where he resorts to panhandling. In contrast, his wife (now Carrie Medenda) launches a stage career which brings her wealth and prominence, abandoning Hurstwood in the process. At the end of the novel Hurstwood, now a completely defeated individual, crawls away into a flophouse, turns on the gas, and ends his life. Carrie, unfulfilled by her success, sits alone in her rocking-chair, amidst luxurious surroundings, unhappy, yearning for something she is unable to attain.[3]

The plot and characters in the novel were drawn largely from Dreiser's own family experiences. In 1885 his sister Emma began an affair with a man some fifteen years her senior who was a cashier at a swank Chicago bar. She soon learned that he was married and had three children. Nonetheless, she joined him and they went to Montreal; on the way he revealed that while drunk he had stolen money from his employers. He returned most of the $3,500, the employers did not prosecute, and he and Emma settled in New York as managers of a rather shady rooming house. In the novel Dreiser's sister becomes Sister Carrie and the Chicago cashier is Hurstwood. The figure of Drouet was based on a clever, popular, and well-dressed student Dreiser had envied at the University of Indiana, which he attended in 1889-90. More important than these close parallels between fiction and fact is the way the events and characters are recreated to reflect Dreiser's understanding of the meaning of city life.

The first thing one notices about Carrie is how little influence a small town background contributes in her adjustments to the metropolis. A reader learns almost nothing about her parents (except that her father works in a flour mill) and nothing at all about her eighteen years in Columbia City. When she leaves, "the threads which bound her so lightly to girlhood were irretrievably broken" (p. 1), and only rarely does she have "a far-off thought of Columbia City" (p. 58). When she does have a fleeting memory of her home town, it is because she is disturbed or confused over some moral and/or economic issue: as she begins living with Drouet (p. 86), as she contrasts North Shore Drive elegance with Drouet's Ogden Place rooms (p. 128), or just after she has left Drouet and learned that Hurstwood is married (p. 271). But even when she has lost her job in the shoe factory and her sister suggests that she return home, although Carrie agrees, this is never a real alternative. "Columbia City, what was there for her? She knew its dull, little round by heart." Like Rose Dutcher she has seen Chicago, and here she wants to stay and experience life. "Here was the great, mysterious city which was still a magnet for her. What she had seen only suggested its possibilities. Now to turn her back on it and live the little old life out there . . ." seemed impossible (pp. 73-74). In the next scene Carrie allows Drouet to buy her clothes and set her up in an apartment. The glittering possibilities of the city have overcome whatever moral hesitation still lingers "lightly" from her Columbia City girlhood.

As Carrie enters the city, although she is eighteen, her character is essentially unformed. Self-interest is her guiding characteristic; enjoying "the keener pleasures of life," she is "ambitious to gain in material things." She is "a fair example of the middle American class—two generations removed from the emigrant" (p. 2). What impact does the city have on this young, half-formed middle American? It impresses itself on Carrie, as it had on Dreiser himself, as a place of sharp contrasts between drudgery, poverty, and anonymity on the one hand, ease, wealth, and prominence on the other. Carrie quickly responds to the latter. The joyless, relentless, laboring, and

humdrum existence of her sister and brother-in-law represent one urban reality. In contrast to this narrowness is the more luxurious life of Drouet, Hurstwood, and her female acquaintances Mrs. Hale and Mrs. Vance. That life revolves around fine clothes and jewelry, the fashion promenades in Chicago (and later in New York), social contacts, good restaurants, and the excitement of the theater—all made possible by money. "Money: something everybody else has and I must get . . ." (p. 70). If the city measures one's worth by what one has, then she intends to get. Carrie's capacity to understand what society values and her spirit in pursuing those goals are her inherited characteristics; the specific values she accepts are acquired from the city environment. Urbanism as a way of life for Carrie means attempting to achieve a lifestyle marked by prominence and wealth.

The irony is that Carrie does achieve success, as a noted actress, and yet she is unfulfilled. She seems as little responsible for her rise to stardom as Hurstwood is for his plunge from an upper class position ("the first grade below the luxuriously rich") to being a street beggar. At the end of the novel, as Hurstwood ends his life by his own hand, finally defeated by circumstances over which he has no control, Carrie sits idly rocking in her chair, successful according to the terms she has accepted but in her way also trapped, dreaming vaguely of something beyond her elegant surroundings. Carrie has recently been stirred by the urgings of Robert Ames of Indianapolis that she give up comedy and turn to serious drama. Ames argues that her face reflects a longing which many people feel and are struggling to express, and that she should (indeed, has an obligation to) use this genius on the stage so that people can express themselves through her. Carrie does not understand the import of what Ames is urging, and as the world represented by Drouet and Hurstwood loses its allure she is left confused and uncertain about life.

Dreiser's point here is important in understanding his interpretation of the city. When Carrie comes to Chicago, she has the imagination and capacity to respond to beauty, but her vague aesthetic yearnings have as yet no guiding principle or definite focal point for realization. The urban ideal of beauty held up so alluringly before her is one of glitter and show, and being an imaginative and impressionable person she responds accordingly and makes the city's goals her own. Dreiser is not criticizing Carrie for her choice, for it was a choice he had himself made when first encountering the city. But when she achieves the earthly success represented by Hurstwood and offered by the city, she senses that it somehow does not bring happiness. She is, Dreiser tells us, "an illustration of the devious ways by which one who feels, rather than reasons, may be led in the pursuit of beauty" (p. 557). The realization of the material success valued in Chicago and New York does not bring emotional and human fulfillment, but on the contrary leaves one emotionally drained and spiritually confused.

In his use of symbols and imagery, as in his manipulation of plot and characters, Dreiser's conception of the city is discerned. Carrie is seen as "a waif amid forces," "half-equipped little knight," "a soldier of fortune," "a pilgrim," "a wisp in the wind," and "a harp in the wind"—in other words, a wanderer at the mercy of arbitrary gods. As she is bounced hither and yon, her shifting identity is reflected in various names: Caroline Meeber becomes in the course of her wanderings "Sister Carrie, "Cad," "Mrs. Drouet," "Mrs. G. W. Murdock," "Mrs. Wheeler," and finally "Carrie Medenda." Her real entry into the cherished "walled city" (the world of wealth and luxury) is attained by her discovery of "the gate to the world," the theater. The stage, as so often in novels of this period, represents not only the show and glamour of city life, but is also pictured as providing a means for actors and audiences alike to play a role in life. It is a way, so Dreiser and other authors imply, for the many estranged urbanites to gain the illusion that they are a part of things, for a moment at least. For Carrie, then, her way of entering into the swirl of life around her means having a role to play. "Oh if she could only have such a part, how broad would be her life! She too could act appealing" (p. 345). In this "elfland" world of Aladdin her success is, arbitrarily, assured. A final recurring symbol, that of the rocking chair, captures this note of the ceaseless yet meaningless urban movement, a to-and-fro motion with no apparent direction: the rise and fall of individual lives has as much reason as the back-and-forth rocking of Carrie's chair.

If community involves, as recent sociologists argue, the meaningful interaction of people who share certain socially sanctioned norms and behavior, then there is no community in the city world of *Sister Carrie*. People in the novel live and die alone. Personal relationships are of only the most tenuous nature. Hurstwood leaves his family with startling ease, with no twinge of conscience. His wife's main concern over her husband's departure is of a strictly monetary nature. Hurstwood's "friends" at the bar are merely casual acquaintances, whose "hail fellow well met" élan is but a facade. Drouet is a man with no permanent home and no lasting relationships, a traveling salesman who flits easily from place to place, woman to woman. Carrie finds it only slightly more difficult to break family ties and intimate relationships with Drouet and Hurstwood.

Dreiser's city is a world where even the closest and most intimate relationships are easily abandoned. Here there is no hope of developing and maintaining the bonds which traditionally have held community together. The city of Theodore Dreiser is the epitome of noncommunity.

In 1928 Theodore Dreiser wrote of a little-known author, Henry B. Fuller, that he was "the man who led the van of realism in America." Dreiser praised Fuller's novel *With the Procession* (1895), calling it "as sound and agreeable a piece of American realism as that decade, or any since, produced."[4] Not widely known even in his own lifetime, though highly respected by a few style-conscious writers and critics, Fuller has recently been the focus of renewed interest, evidenced most clearly by the publication of a combined biography and critical study in 1974. Bernard

Bowron, Jr.'s, *Henry B. Fuller of Chicago* carried the appropriate subtitle "The Ordeal of a Genteel Realist in Ungenteel America." Appropriate because Fuller, though a native Chicagoan whose grandfather had come to the city in 1849 and made a sizable fortune, was a recluse who did not share the booster attitude and aggressive business values which dominated his city. Yet Fuller did not flee America to become a literary expatriate, but sought in some of his early work to deal with the "formulation of American society" as exemplified in Chicago.[5]

With the Procession is the story of one of Chicago's Old Settler families, the Marshalls, whose commitment to the standards of a bygone day has left them "out of things," the social parade having passed them by. The novel involves the efforts of a younger generation of Marshalls to lift the family into "the procession."[6]

David Marshall, the father, has built up a successful grocery business through thirty-five years of steady work and conservative economic practices. He performs his role in life with "an air of patient, self-approving resignation" (p. 17). He works on from year to year at his business, with no particular goal in mind, because this is what he knows and what he does best. He has lost interest in "society," and he understands his obligation to be to his family and to his employees and their families, but not to the public at large. In his life and outlook David Marshall exemplifies an individualism and privatism which Fuller implies was more appropriate to an earlier day. A good part of the efforts on the part of other characters in the novel is aimed at persuading David Marshall of his duty to the broader society of Chicago.

The elder Marshall resists these overtures largely because the Chicago "public" he is becoming aware of is not at all the same "society" that his daughters wish to join. In the first place, it is eventually revealed that Marshall's business practices have not always been as decorous as he might have wished them to be. His partner Gilbert Belden follows the more aggressive, extralegal practices of the day. How did such a man become an associate of the more staid and cautious Marshall? Belden was taken into the firm during the financial panic of 1873, just two years after the great Chicago fire, when Marshall & Co. was on the brink of ruin. Marshall is forced to resort to tactics "quite outside the lines of mercantile morality, and barely inside the lines of legality itself," and Belden is hired away from a rival firm to accomplish the maneuver (p. 100). Once established, he pushes ahead to become a full partner, eventually attempts to wrest control from Marshall and transform the business into a stock company. But Fuller is not simply attributing all good to the Old Settlers and all bad to the newcomers: there is obviously a closer relationship between the sharp practices of the new businessmen and the "conservatism" of the Old Settlers than David Marshall might at times like to admit to himself.

Near the end of the novel, with David on his deathbed, Marshall & Belden is in receivership. But the family fortune (some $3,000,000) is not lost. David's oldest son Roger has successfully invested his father's money in speculative real estate ventures, which represents another break with the professed practices of the past. Roger Marshall is a lawyer, also involved with the seamier aspects of the family business. In the process of these dealings he becomes familiar with the rapidly changing social character of the city.

Roger participates in one set of events, the details of which take place "offstage" and are revealed only piecemeal in snatches of conversation. They reflect the inescapable entanglement of the Marshalls with a newer Chicago. An immigrant woman, Mrs. Van Horn, has purchased goods from David and is reselling them from her residence, which is only two blocks from the Marshall home. A writ is issued to halt the practice, but the woman is alerted by a relative connected with the police court, and when the search takes place no goods are found. Her son is an alderman, her nephew a bailiff, and when the matter gets to court it is continued (delayed) three times. When Roger presses the issue in the lower court, two of the woman's nephews break into the Marshall stable and beat the coachman. When these ruffians go before the court, the alderman's son writes out a fictitious bail bond, then the two muggers jump bail and the bond is forfeited.

Roger's function in all this, and other such matters, is to act as an intermediary, a sort of buffer, between the Marshalls and the changing world of Chicago which is engulfing them. At the unsatisfactory conclusion of the Van Horn affair, Roger tells his father, who is gradually becoming aware of the implications of such incidents:

> You have lifted off the cover and looked in. Do you want to go deeper? You'll find a hell-broth—thieves, gamblers, prostitutes, pawnbrokers, saloon-keepers, aldermen, heelers, justices, bailiffs, policemen—all concocted for us within a short quarter of a century. . . . I never felt so cheap and filthy in my life. (p. 145)

David wonders if he himself isn't to blame as he sees his son coarsening under the impact of such activities. Again, the "new" Chicago is impinging forcefully upon David Marshall and his family. The survival of the family is due in no small part to its ability, in the person of Roger, to understand change and adapt to new conditions.

Eliza Marshall, David's wife, is initially even more immune to the changing world in which she lives than her husband. She is, the narrator tells us, "a kind of antiquated villager—a geological survival from an earlier age" (p. 7). Her Chicago is still the town of 1860 (a "town," incidentally, with a population of 190,000 in that year), "an Arcadia which, in some dim and inexplicable way, had remained for her an Arcadia still—bigger, noisier, richer, yet different only in degree, and not essentially in kind" (p. 10). The Marshall home had been built in 1860 in a sedate residential area on Michigan Avenue, but thirty years later the neighborhood has changed drastically. By 1893 the local church has moved and old neighbors gone to more fashionable areas. Hotels, business offices, boarding houses, even a cheap music hall, have replaced the former homes. A suburban railway which runs close by spews its smoke and cinders over the yard into the house. Finally the family experiences urban violence when the Van Horn ruffians break into the Marshall stable.

Eliza clings tenaciously to her aging possessions and old ways amidst all this hectic change. This trait is effectively symbolized in her annual jelly making, which takes place every July, despite the fact that the "smoke and cinders of metropolitan life" have killed all her currant bushes. She now cans store-bought currants. The urban smoke has also killed Eliza's cherry tree and the rest of the garden as well. Successful efforts to effect a move from this "dear old place" to a new, more fashionable house are one of the key indications that the Marshalls have indeed begun once again to march "with the procession."

Jane Marshall is the daughter responsible for bringing about the family's entrance into the mainstream of Chicago's upper class social procession. She is also the family member most marked by the Old Settler spirit. Jane, thirty-three and single, launches her younger sister Rosy into the social limelight, and even succeeds in pushing her reluctant father into the role of an after-dinner speaker. Once in society, Rosy becomes insufferable, marries a somewhat nebulous Englishman because his father has a title, and cuts her mother's old friends from the wedding list, making sure her new "society" acquaintances are invited. Jane is also successful in convincing the elder Marshall that a move "further out" is called for, and the new house is nearing completion as the novel ends (the old home to be knocked down and replaced by a warehouse). Jane has twinges of remorse: "If it hadn't been for me we should never have left our old home and given up our old life" . . . (p. 261). But she is consoled by a proposal of marriage from Theodore Brower, a progressive, reform-minded insurance man.

Jane is forcefully assisted in her successful social maneuvers on behalf of the Marshall family by the wealthy and socially prominent Mrs. Granger Bates. The daughter of a "boss-carpenter," she and her husband have struggled up to a position of financial, cultural, and philanthropic leadership in Chicago. She is proud of this achievement and her position. "We have fought the fight—a fair field and no favor—and we have come out ahead. And we shall stay there too; keep up with the procession is my motto, and head it if you can. I *do* head it, and I feel that I'm where I belong" (p. 58). Years before, David Marshall was one of her favorite suitors, and though they have not seen one another in years she is now eager to help Jane with her plans.

Mrs. Bates has a strong streak of nostalgia for the earlier times and simpler ways of her childhood, but, as Bowron points out, she is not a sentimentalist (p. 156). She has a good sense of just how much of the procession is mere show and how much is of cultural value. If the dominant values of "privatism," of laissez-faire business enterprise, can give rise to socially valuable and culturally worthwhile creations, Fuller suggests that it will be due to people of the kind represented by Mrs. Granger Bates and Jane Marshall. They do not want to see the Old Settler spirit give way before the onslaught of the Beldens and other newcomers. Thus, Mrs. Bates is willing to help Jane, in whom she finds "one of *us*."

In contrast to the artistic and social hopes for a business culture which Mrs. Bates represents, is the almost complete disdain for Chicago expressed by Truesdale, Jane's younger brother. Truesdale leaves Yale to study art and music in Europe, or more correctly, "on the Continent." He returns to Chicago, where he observes there is "so little taste . . . so little training, so little education, so total an absence of any collective sense of the fit and proper" (p. 73). In Chicago Truesdale deplores the lack of promenades, cafes, journals, and the absence of an atmosphere of leisure he believes conducive to art and culture. American cities are too big, too noisy, too dirty, and too confusing and disordered to serve as an environment in which a true culture could flourish. Truesdale's pretentious ridicule of Chicago is based on his self-consciously acquired appreciation of the picturesque Gothic in France and Italy. At the end of the novel Truesdale is on his way to Japan, after it has been discovered that while in Europe he had an affair with an Alsatian girl whose father is now working for Marshall & Belden. The resolution of this sordid matter by Roger (which includes buying off the girl's family by providing a willing husband for her) is just one more element driving David Marshall to his deathbed.

In sharp contrast to Truesdale stands the engineer-architect Tom Bingham, president of Bingham Construction Company. Bingham (who may have been based on Fuller's friend Daniel Burnham, a famous Chicago architect and city planner) thoroughly accepts Chicago values and gives them form in the ornate residences and steel-frame business towers which he builds. He is the architect and builder of the Marshalls' new home. Also in contrast to Truesdale, but from a different angle, is Theodore Brower, the man Jane chooses over Bingham as a husband. Brower's role in the novel is somewhat ambiguous. His is the one voice of near-dissent in the book, but his interesting reform suggestion of a legal-aid justice center for the poor is dropped. Instead it is decided to have a college building serve as a monument to David Marshall. In leading up to his original suggestion, Brower observes:

> This town of ours labors under one peculiar disadvantage: it is the only great city in the world to which all its citizens have come for one common, avowed object of making money. . . . In this Garden City of ours every man cultivates his own little bed and his neighbor his, but who looks after the paths between? . . . The thing to teach the public is this: the general good is a different thing from the sum of the individual goods. Over in the settlements we are trying to make these newcomers realize that they are a part of the body politic; perhaps we need another settlement to remind some of the original charter-members of the same fact. (pp. 203-4)

What Brower is talking about is community and, as Larzer Ziff points out, Fuller seems to put more stock in this approach to Chicago's future than in the hopes many people placed in the transforming power of the example of planned orderliness represented by the buildings of the famous "White City" built for the Chicago World's Fair in 1893. This seems to be confirmed in Jane Marshall's choice of Brower as a husband rather than Bingham, an architect whose hopes for the future are akin to those of the City Beautiful advocate who designed the buildings and grounds for that famous fair.[7]

As far as Fuller would go with the reform theme was to suggest that in some vague way the Old Settler spirit of Mrs. Granger Bates would be melded with the liberal concerns of Brower. This was, at least, a step beyond the limitations of David Marshall's individualism, Eliza's nostalgic blindness, Truesdale's superciliousness, and Bingham's entrepreneurism. But Fuller, with one exception, dropped Chicago from his future literary subject matter, abandoning the difficult task of giving creative shape to a society he was so ambiguous toward. And yet, as Bowron has pointed out, "his inability to escape Chicago, both as fact and symbol, is, ironically, the essence of his art" (p. xxvii). What Fuller attempted and could not do was to cope with the contradictions, caused by rapid growth and change, which were so characteristic of Chicago in the 1890s and after.

Guy Szuberla, in his study of Fuller's vision of Chicago as a "cityscape," has indicated one important aspect of *With the Procession* as an urban novel. Szuberla argues that Fuller is probably the first American novelist to discard the agrarian myth as an adequate mode of perception for dealing with the modern machine-made city environment. In this interpretation Fuller's work "reflects a new idea of urban space" akin to Hart Crane's later directive that literature "absorb the machine" and "surrender . . . temporarily, to the sensations of urban life" (pp. 83-84).[8] What this means in *With the Procession* is that both the Arcadian perception of Mrs. Marshall and the pseudosophisticated view of the picturesque and pastoral held by her son Truesdale are rejected as ways of seeing the city. The lesson is clear: "The pastoral myth, which has served to define the America of the past, has lost its relevance in the modern city" (p. 90).

Szuberla's point is convincing, but in the context of the present discussion it needs to be supplemented by a further observation. Though the pastoral myth *had* been abandoned by Fuller as a way of seeing the city, he was unable to come to terms with the growing social contradictions of Chicago. He could not resolve the dilemma between his respect for the individualistic Old Settler spirit and the vague community consciousness of Brower. For an instant Brower becomes a spokesman for the immigrants and poor of the city. Fuller's awareness of the impact of social change is shown in the Van Horn affair and in Brower's response to it. But the author's inability to cope with the meaning of these events is reflected in the fact that the action of the Van

Horn affair takes place offstage and is revealed to the reader only indirectly. Instead, Fuller emphasizes the more traditional literary motif of tension between an older established class, the Marshalls, and social parvenus like the Beldens. Thus, one of the final scenes is the putdown of Mrs. Belden by Eliza Marshall (who conveys the false impression that daughter Rosy has been "presented at court"). Fuller was, at the same time, aware of the much more important conflict between the immigrant poor and the Old Settlers. But by inclination and social position (he was manager of his family's business affairs after his father's death in 1885) he ultimately shied away from the issue. Clearly, however, for all the ambiguities he felt, his final vote was cast for the individualism of the Old Settlers.

The city of Theodore Dreiser lacks community in the sense that the word is being used in the present study. People in Dreiser's Chicago and New York lack the basic social interaction and sharing which are now so frequently understood to be primary characteristics of community. *Sister Carrie* suggests that such traits have always been lacking in the city. In Henry Blake Fuller's Chicago, on the other hand, an older "style" of upper class community is being challenged by significant social changes resulting from industrialization and immigration. This older way of living is also being shattered by a growing materialistically oriented effort to keep up with the procession, and by those new to the game who don't always follow the established rules. It is not suggested by Fuller that all was peace and harmony in the past, but among a certain stratum of society there was a distinct "us" feeling, a sense of belonging based on social and economic position. An exclusive community, the Old Settlers' Chicago involved social interaction and shared experiences among a class operating in a given geographic locale. But the locale was rapidly changing after 1860, in physical dimension, population size, and social composition. The older sense of community and the lifestyle it represented were being undermined both by the "immigrant hordes" and by aggressive middle class social climbers. If for Dreiser the city was just naturally always anticommunity, from Fuller's perspective it had become so by the 1890s.

NOTES

[1] Louis Wirth, "Urbanism as a Way of Life," *American Journal of Sociology* 44 (July 1938): 1-24; Blanche Housman Gelfant, *The American City Novel,* pp. 42-94.

[2] Biographical material on Dreiser in this chapter is based on Robert H. Elias, *Theodore Dreiser;* W. A. Swanberg, *Dreiser;* Theodore Dreiser, *A Book about Myself,* and *Dawn.*

[3] Theodore Dreiser, *Sister Carrie.*

[4] Theodore Dreiser, introduction, Frank Norris, *McTeague* (New York, 1928), p. vii-xi; "The Great American Novel," *American Spectator* 1 (December 1932): 1.

[5] Biographical material on Fuller in this chapter is based on Bernard R. Bowron, Jr., *Henry Blake Fuller of Chicago,* and John Pilkington, *Henry Blake Fuller.*

[6] Henry Blake Fuller, *With the Procession.*

[7] Larzer Ziff, *The American 1890s,* pp. 112-13. See also Thomas Hines, *Burnham of Chicago.*

[8] Guy Szuberla, "Making the Sublime Mechanical." I would like to thank Professor Szuberla for his helpful suggestions in regard to this chapter.

Eric Monkkonen

SOURCE: "Socializing the New Urbanites: Horatio Alger Jr.'s Guidebooks," in *Journal of Popular Culture,* Vol. XI, No. 1, Summer, 1997, pp. 77-87.

[*In the following excerpt, Monkkonen pursues the urban themes of the Horatio Alger novels.*]

The rapid urbanization of the United States during the last half of the nineteenth century is a phenomenon which demands our continued scrutiny if we are to understand its social meaning. It would be unfortunate if we continued only examining urban problems and the negative social effects of burgeoning cities without asking what the beneficial aspects were. Hopefully, the sad and defensive families described so well in Richard Sennett's work on Chicago were not the models for everyone's reaction to the changing city.[1] What about the new urban migrants? And more specifically, what about the native born, white, rural migrants to the city? If the urban migrants in Theodore Dreiser's urban novels provide accurate models, the urban prospects were indeed grim, but perhaps we should look elsewhere for literary advice because rural folk continued to migrate to the city.

Too often these native born migrants to the city have been overlooked; and we forget that while the cities had many immigrants in them, they also had many born in the United States who faced an urban world as alien to them as that with which the most recent immigrants dealt. The table below gives minimum estimates of native born migrants to the fifty largest U.S. cities, and it reveals a surprising trend. Native born migrants were increasing their proportion of the city's population, whether compared to all of the native born in cities or to the total city populations. Thus, although we may never know their absolute size, we must conclude that these folk represented a sizable and growing group in the urban landscape.

How did these people learn to cope with cities made up largely of other migrants? How did they respond to the city's psychological and economic incentives, both positive and negative? In some ways, the native born white migrants to the city faced their new environment with more social pressures and less community support than did their European or Black counterparts. The rural middle class whites, especially, faced a world in which they were expected to achieve success, a world where men could be "self-made."[2] Unlike any other group, the mantle of the American ethic of upward mobility fell upon them. The attempts of the white middle class to conform to this ethical prescription can be studied in many ways, but one place to start is by looking at their guidebooks, their how-to-do-it manuals. Here, I use the novels of Horatio Alger, Jr., as an example of the kind of guidebook available to the urban migrant, a guidebook which provided both exhortative advice—struggle and succeed—and practical advice—how to get around the city, especially New York City, without being swindled.

NATIVE BORN MIGRANTS TO THE 50 LARGEST CITIES*

	NUMBER	% OF ALL CITY INHABITANTS	% OF ALL NATIVE BORN INHABITANTS
1870	749,398	13.0%	19.7%
1880	1,076,920	13.9%	29.6%
1890	1,753,186	15.6%	24.2%

Source: Calculated from the *Compendium of the Ninth Census* (1870), Table XIX, *Compendium of the Tenth Census* (1880), Table XXII, and from the *Eleventh Census* (1890), V. 1,Table 29.

* These estimates are designed to describe a lower limit and serve for the purposes of an index. They were calculated by subtracting the population born in the United States, but outside the state in which the city they inhabited was located, from the total native born population for each city. Thus the estimate totally neglects those rural persons who migrated to a city within their home state—probably a large number—while it assumes that persons from other states were born in rural places. Hopefully, the estimate makes up in consistency what it loses in accuracy. Washington, D.C., provides an interesting example where we can estimate accurately the number of native born newcomes to a city, although, again, we have no hint as to their urban or rural origins. For Washington, 48% of all inhabitants were born outside of the city but within the United States in 1870, 46% in 1880, and 47% in 1890. These figures contradict the trend of the largest fifty cities, and are most important for showing the size of the non-locally born population.

Usually the name of Horatio Alger, Jr. is considered only in connection with the ethic of upward mobility; doing so misses the real value and function of his children's novels. For though titles like *Bound to Rise* or *Up the Ladder* may proclaim that the subject is occupational mobility, the form and content shows another subject—how to manipulate the environment and avoid being victimized by it. Rather than looking at Alger's explicit advice, we need to attend to the implicit advice; rather than listening to his exhortations to climb the ladder of success, we must examine his much more extensive advice on how to survive and master the urban world.

Alger's family background and upbringing remind one of people like Theodore Parker or William Ellery Channing and provide surprising contrast with his later career as a hack writer in New York City. The son of a Harvard Divinity School graduate and Unitarian minister, a Harvard and Harvard Divinity School graduate himself, he left his pastorate in the tiny town of Brewster, Massachusetts in 1866 and headed for New York City.[3] Early in 1850 Alger had written in his diary: "Am reading *Moby Dick* and find it exciting. What a thrilling life the literary must be! Imagination and observation—these I take to be the important requisites. Would it be desirable for me to take up writing as a life work?"[4] One might have expected Alger to develop into a great name in American intellectual history, instead of a writer of formula stories for boys. But his move from Brewster, a town with a population of 1300 to New York City and its million people, his change from religious preaching to secular preaching, both symbolize the new role Alger was to assume as a guide to the city and to the social world of the urban middle class.

In this paper I discuss chiefly *Ragged Dick; or, Street Life in New York with the Bootblacks* (1868), Alger's eighth novel, his only best-seller, a novel that established the Alger formula and his reputation as a writer.[5] This novel is probably most representative of Alger and is better written than his subsequent novels. Publishers, after *Ragged Dick,* wanted only more of the same from Alger, and although he protested, it was profitable and easy for him to keep writing the same novel. This explains the comparative lack of vitality and freshness of his later work and allows us to use *Ragged Dick* as a model.

As a child, Horatio Alger, Jr.'s constant, compulsive pastime was to build towers with his building blocks. He would quietly place blocks one on top of the other until they tumbled and then he would start again.[6] At the age of fifty he was still trapped in repetitive patterns. As he was unable to escape the patterns of building block towers he was unable to write anything beyond his formula. He had a genuine desire to write an adult novel, he talked of his plans constantly, but he could not think of an idea and his plans never got beyond a title, *Tomorrow.* When he left New York to die at his sister's South Natick home he had his novels removed from his room: "if he could, he said, he intended to forget them."[7]

It was apparently little compensation for Alger to know that he was not alone in his fixation, that an estimated 200,000,000 of his books were sold. He probably would not be impressed by the fact that almost three-fourths of a century after his death, the discovery of one of his novels which had not been published would make the *New York Times.* Usually, the enormous popularity of Alger's work is attributed to "the deep and abiding homage they paid to success."[8] More perceptive critics point out that the novels are not about the fruits of success, but concern themselves with the struggle to attain success. John Tebbel argues that Alger's readers "could no more comprehend the world of success than

Alger himself, who had not the slightest understanding of the rich and successful."[9] But to argue, as Tebbel does, that the disappearance of Ragged Dick from the *Ragged Dick* series is because Alger's limited imagination would take him no farther into the meaning of occupational mobility is to miss the point. For Alger was a New Yorker first, and for him the main component of success lay simply in the mastery of the urban environment—survival, not an economic goal was his subject.

Alger's love of New York City and his fascination with its street life cannot easily be disentangled from his concern with the achievement of success. *Helen Ford* (1866) was Alger's first book written after he had left his country minister's position and come to the city. In the novel he dismisses the country as a good retreat for old folk who like monotony; he has obviously been caught up by New York City and excited by the possibilities of life in the city.[10] Early in the novel he juxtaposes Broadway's "shifting scenes" of life with pedantic declamations on the rough jostling of the world and exhortations on the world's possibilities for success. Alger writes: "Often they [Helen and her father] would walk up Broadway, and Helen, at least, found amusement in watching the shifting scenes which presented themselves to the beholder in that crowded thoroughfare. Life in all its varieties, from pampered wealth to squalid poverty, too often the fruit of a mis-spent life, jostled each other upon the sidewalk, or in the street. The splendid equipage dashes past the humble handcart: the dashing buggy jostles against the loaded dray."[11] For Alger, streets and street life are the symbolic of the essence of the city; not only do swindlers prowl the streets, but benevolent businessmen as well; it is up to the individual to differentiate between the two. And the constant visual images of the streets emphasize his view of urban life as process or movement.

As a child, his compulsive piling of building blocks until they tumbled was a manifestation of the same pattern seen in his continual thematic emphasis of the upward struggle. But it would not do for his heroes to fall as did his towers: it was therefore necessary for his plots to ultimately rely on luck. At various times he rationalizes this by claiming "what we call good luck, generally comes from greater industry, good judgement, and, above all, the prompt use of opportunities."[12] Luck saves all his heroes: Dick gets a job by saving the drowning daughter of a kindly businessman, Helen Ford suddenly receives an inheritance, Jed the Poorhouse Boy is a missing heir, etc. But in typical Algeresque didacticism the need for luck is not mentioned:

> For in the street-life of the metropolis a boy needs to be on the alert, and have all his wits about him, or he will find himself wholly distanced by his more enterprising competitors for popular favor. To succeed in his profession, humble as it is, a boot-black must depend on the same qualities which gain success in higher walks of life.[13]

The use of luck is the flaw in his model; it rescues his tower.

John M. Roberts, in his study on game involvement, points out that "a game of chance is a response to the passivity of the players' normal life role. . . . Benevolent fate, if not fantasy, may lift the routine worker out of his or her present life tasks with magical efficacy."[14] Alger's emphasis on struggle with his reliance on luck may be a subconscious admission of the futility of the struggle for most lower class Americans. His awareness that pluck alone will not prevail can be seen in his portrayal of Martha Gray in *Helen Ford*. Martha, in order to support her marginal existence, sews fifteen hours a day. When wages drop she is forced to work sixteen hours and eat less. Alger makes it clear she is slowly sinking under the strain and refers the reader to an article in the *Atlantic Monthly* to verify the bleak pictures he has painted. Martha is saved, of course, by luck, by her friend Helen's inheritance, but one wonders if Martha of New York City had time to bother with Alger's novels.

However, Alger did have more than wish-fulfillment to offer some of his readers. For the Martha Grays there was only wishing, but for middle class rural boys like Frank Whitney in *Ragged Dick* Alger provided a guide to survival and success in the city. Kenneth Burke, in discussing "Literature as Equipment for Living," says that, "proverbs [and by extension, all of literature] are strategies for dealing with *situations*."[15] Joseph Campbell finds a similar purpose in myth: "it is the business of mythology proper, and of the fairy tale, to reveal the specific dangers and techniques of the dark interior way from tragedy to comedy."[16] And although *Ragged Dick* has been criticized for being "little more than a guided tour of the city" and Alger called by a contemporary a "one-man Society for the Prevention of Getting Lost," one of the major functions of Alger was precisely that which his critics find a deficiency. The market for *Ragged Dick* was 300,000 twelve to sixteen year old boys, many like Theodore Drieser, who set out for the city at the age of sixteen "like a boy hero out of a Horatio Alger, Jr., novel."[17] These boys, motivated by visions of material success, brought to the city expectations and assumptions given them by Alger. Thus, one can look at *Ragged Dick* as a guidebook providing "strategies for dealing with situations," a guidebook which tells what the city is all about and how to handle it.

Ragged Dick has two parts, the first containing Dick's adventures with Frank during one day, and the second Dick's progress upward over the period of one year. These two sequences serve as two different kinds of guide books: the first a social and physical guide to New York City, the second a guide to success. This works well because in the first sequence Dick and presumably, the reader are motivated to succeed, while in the second Dick and the reader learn specifically how to succeed. Equally important, in the first sequence, Frank and the reader are initiated into the ways of the city, allowing the reader to participate symbolically with Dick in the second sequence in the use of the city. Thus the earlier part of the novel emphasizes the city, the later, success. Before Dick can succeed, he has learned to live in the city; before the reader can symbolically attain success with Dick, he must learn, with Frank, to master the city's threatening environment.

In the first part of the novel there are, within fifty pages, ten urban threat situations, taking the form of swindlers, mean people and dangerous traffic. Only once is Dick caught off guard and "startled," but even then he masters the situation; in every other situation he is "indignant" or, when he and Frank come across a swindled country bumpkin, "contemptuous." Frank, on the other hand, is "amazed" or "dismayed" or "astonished" and readily sympathizes with the countryman of whom Dick is so contemptuous. But Frank has, by this time, learned not to be taken aback by the countryman's experience; he is beginning to respond to city threats in a way that indicates he feels some understanding and control in the urban situation. Hopefully, by this point in the novel, the reader too has learned something about city threats and the techniques of handling them.

Of the ten challenges to Dick and Frank in the first part of the novel, seven involve money, establishing the relationship between mastery of the urban environment and financial success. Georg Simmel's classic analysis of "The Metropolis and Mental Life" emphasizes the importance of money in the psychic meaning of urban life, "How much?" becoming the basic interpersonal urban question.[18] Alger's model for responding to the psychosocial environment of the city recognizes the centrality of money and its importance as a vehicle for the interaction with much of the city's life. Thus the city in the first sequence threatens to take the individual's money; the individual must guard his purse with both head and hand or lose it. The city does not return money to those who have lost it; like Dick, it is contemptuous of the bumpkin who is so easily swindled. He does not deserve to keep his money. The city and money are good only for those who deserve them, those who can manipulate them.

In the second part of the novel, Alger emphasizes the details and techniques of getting ahead; however, one attempt at swindling reminds the reader of ever present dangers. The city, first seen as economically and physically threatening to the initiate, has become a controllable tool useful both for economic independence and the means to an exciting urban life. Alger gives the itemized details of Dick's life and rise, giving the novel verisimilitude through concrete detail. The figures convincingly demonstrate to both Alger and his readers that it can be done. When Dick earns sixty cents before breakfast, Alger shows what a nourishing breakfast should be:

Coffee	5 cents
Beefsteak	15 cents
A couple of rolls	5 cents
	25 cents[19]

There is an alternate breakfast for the days when Dick's business is not so good: two apples or cakes for five cents. At the end of thirty-nine weeks Dick has saved, by dint of hard work and "care for the future," one hundred and seventeen dollars.

Assessing the utility of *Ragged Dick* as a guide book proves difficult; the novel's popularity does not necessarily show its effects, but Theodore Dreiser's case may give some clues:

> Dreiser left home and went . . . 'to Chicago to seek his fortune.' The city seemed to him 'a land of promise, a fabled realm of milk and honey. . . . Here, as nowhere else, youth might make its way.' The luxury of the magnificent city seemed almost to speak to him: 'All that life or hope is or can be or do, this I am, and it is here before you! Take of it! Live, live, satisfy your heart!' . . . After four years in Chicago, Dreiser was still 'without trade or profession, or sort of nondescript dreamer without the power to earn a decent living. . . .'[20]

Dreiser's luck finally changed and he got into the newspaper business, but for the youth without his genius things might not have gone so well. Clearly, as far as financial success was concerned, Alger's advice proved to be of little value: without luck or genius poor Martha Grays would remain poor Martha Grays.[21]

But Alger's popularity did not rest upon utility in the late nineteenth century struggle for occupational mobility. Instead, Alger assured the middle class that the lower classes could rise if they wanted, thus assuaging uneasy consciences and allaying anxieties about increasing urbanization. And more important, he served as a guide for middle class boys to the city. Perhaps he inspired hopes within lower classes, portraying city life—like California gold fields—as filled with riches for those who were willing to work. His novels were deemed safe by Sunday School teachers who were a little suspicious of the more exotic adventure stories of W. T. Adams and E. Stratemeyer. Alger's boys had adventures because of their virtue, not in spite of it.

The post–Civil War United States was a nation facing its future in the city; yet a long tradition gave it a mythical future only in the country. As has been amply demonstrated, American popular culture was anti-urban, and the only back drop for epic American heroes was in the West. Going against the grain of popular culture, Alger tied his heroes' fortunes to the city; almost as though financial success was his token nod to popular demands and expectations, he really wrote stories of mythic juvenile heroes who realized their identities and found their roles in the city, not country. This can be best demonstrated with *Ragged Dick*.

The first fifty pages of *Ragged Dick* form what Campbell calls "the nuclear unit of the monomyth," where "the standard path of the mythological adventure of the hero is a magnification of the formula represented in the rites of passage: *separation—initiation—return*."[22] The reader is introduced to the hero, Dick, on the morning of the day that will change Dick's life. Dick is portrayed in his everyday life: he sleeps in a packing create; he spends his money on the theatre, cigars, liquor and gambling; he is dressed in rags and has no parents. Yet, he is a witty and cheery boy who "would not steal, or cheat, or impose upon younger boys, but was frank and straight-forward, manly and self reliant."[23] It is impossible to dislike Dick and difficult not to identify with this independent raga-muffin who is unafraid to look anyone in the eye. Dick is every boy's wish fulfillment.

Dick shines enough shoes to pay for breakfast and in-vites another lazy (and therefore poor) boot-black to eat with him. As they eat, Johnny tells Dick of his short and unsatisfactory attempt to live on a farm. Secure, with a real bed, good food and a generally easy time, Johnny found the rural life wanting; he says, "I felt lonely."[24] So he ran away and returned to the city. Thus early in the book both Dick and reader learn there is no reason to leave the city for the country. Alger makes sure the reader does not miss the point of Johnny's succinct statement by pointing out that the street vagabond "gets so at-tached to his precarious but independent mode of life, that he feels discontented in any other . . . and in the quiet scenes of the country misses the excitement in the midst of which he has always dwelt."[25] The city is the only place for our hero to live.

After his breakfast with Johnny, a counterfeiter tries to swindle Dick, but he is far too wise in city ways to be taken in—he is, the reader sees, a fit guide to initiate someone else into city ways. As Dick considers whether or not he should go to Barnum's to "see the bearded lady, the eight foot giant, the two foot dwarf, and other curiosities, too numerous to mention," he is suddenly given the job of showing fourteen year old Frank Whitney, a middle class country boy, the sights of New York City. This constitutes the point of separation the the old ways of life, both for our hero and his new compan-ion, Frank. Separation is characterized by Campbell as "exercises of severance, whereby the mind is radically cut away from the attitudes, attachments, and life patterns of the stage left behind."[26] the separation is frightening for both of the boys, for while Frank is separated from his middle class rural world of adult protection, Dick is sepa-rated from his lower class world of the streets.

Dick's separation from his old world is symbolized by the new suit of clothes Frank's uncle, Mr. Whitney, gives him. The new clothes create a new person, in a death and rebirth sequence, and also serve as an amulet with magic, protective powers. The epic journey of the hero begins when Mr. Whitney takes the boys to his room in the Astor House to give Dick his new clothes. Alger de-scribes this crucially important episode on the threshold of adventure thus:

'Follow me, my lad,' he [Whitney] said.

Dick in some surprise obeyed orders, following Mr. Whitney and Frank into the hotel, past the office, to the foot of the staircase. Here a servant

of the hotel stopped Dick, but Mr. Whitney explained that he had something for him to do, and he was allowed to proceed.

They entered a long entry, and finally paused before a door. This being opened a pleasant chamber was disclosed.

'Come in, my lad,' said Mr. Whitney.

Dick and Frank entered.[27]

This parallels the elements of the mythic hero's entrance to adventure delineated by Campbell:

The mythological hero, setting forth from his commonday hut or castle, is lured, carried away, or else voluntarily proceeds, to the threshold of adventure. There he encounters a shadow presence that guards the passage. The hero may defect or conciliate this power and go alive into the kingdom of the dark.[28]

Whitney's supernatural device—clothes—are put on by Dick, and he and Frank set out on their adventures, Dick's in a new white collar world, Frank's in the urban environment.

Their first challenge is encountered immediately. It is the "servant of the hotel" who had stopped Dick before. But the clothes amulet works, he does not even recognize Dick and lets him pass. On the street Dick accosts his boot-black friend Johnny who replies with a confused, "Who be you?" Dick, in appearance at least, is already a new person. Frank's first challenge is in crossing busy Broadway with its terrifying traffic, a feat which is no challenge to his urban guide Dick. And thus it goes, Dick's world challenging Frank and Frank's challenging Dick. Summarizing the challenges: a man attempts to swindle Dick but Dick bests him; Frank tells Dick there is still hope for a new life-style; another attempt to swindle Dick, again Dick wins and Frank watches; now, in Frank's first human encounter, he is accused of stealing a purse but with Dick's help is saved; Dick admits to Frank that he is not always happy with his life style of the street, that he has the "blues" sometimes; the boys come across a swindled countryman, and for the first time Frank com-prehends the situation and participates in the challenge; the final episode takes place on the Brooklyn–Wall Street ferry where the boys together recover the countryman's money. Alger's Bloomsday or Dicksday draws to an end; the boys return to the hotel and promise to write one another, Mr. Whitney encouraging Dick to strive upward, magically endowing him by "laying his hand persua-sively" on Dick's shoulder and Dick leaves the hotel.

"The return and reintegration with society," says Campbell, "the hero himself may find the most difficult requirement of all."[29] Dick, after leaving Frank, decides to "turn over a new leaf" and rents a room. He cannot sleep in the street anymore nor does he feel inclined to go back to wearing rags. He is no longer Ragged Dick and from this point forward the story is of Dick's upward struggle for success and respectability and entrance to the middle class. Time passes quickly in the second part of the novel and the new phase of Dick's life. He takes in a lodger, a middle class guide and companion for Dick, a younger boy who tutors him at night in exchange for rent, protection and Dick's guidance to the city. This new character is named Fosdick. Even though Dick still blacks boots he has not returned to his old way of living for he is now clean, dresses well, saves his money and studies with Fosdick. Of course other boot-blacks notice and resent the change but Dick defends himself and his new way of life, sometimes with his fists. Dick, with the guidance of Fosdick, is "struggling upward"; by the novel's end he has been lucky enough to get a clerking job. Both he and Fosdick are talking of starting night school. He now signs his name Richard Hunter, Esq., indicating that he has completed his rebirth and epic adventure.

Alger's father's hope that Horatio Jr. would continue the family name in religion was not in vain. His thorough religious training (his childhood nickname was "Holy Horatio") had instilled in him a religious cast of mind he could not leave behind in Brewster. But he could substitute new values or methods for those of Unitarianism and, in the process, articulate a new religious tradition for the growing urban groups dedicated to making money. He justified what the critics of Unitarianism had been claiming, that it was a religion for merchants, and signaled the final urban secularization of religion. It was no longer, "Get rich to glorify God," it was just, "Get rich." The sin of missing God-given opportunity to profit became the sin of missing opportunity.

Mircea Eliade says "the majority of men 'without religion' still hold to pseudo religions and degenerated mythologies."[30] Of course Alger would claim to be properly pious, but his novels, except for token gestures, are devoid of institutionalized religion. The substitute religion is urban success. Even the aspect of religious reverence has changed, for Alger's new religion declares that every man can become, if not a diety, at least an angel. The Astor House, used by Alger to symbolize the epitome of Mr. Whitney's success, is a new kind of cathedral that requires confidence, wit and boldness to enter. Alger's gods, lodging in a large urban hotel, the Astor House, are as far from nature as they are from humility; these new gods are in the last place Emerson would have looked.

For Alger's characters, nature no longer elicits the traditional sentiments. Of the mountains and countryside of California, a character says: "Now this is a new country—beautiful I grant, but without a history. Look around you, and you will see nothing to remind you of man. It is nature on a grand scale, I admit, but the soul is wanting."[31] Tom, the young miner digging for gold, is anxious to get money and go to where people are. He wants money, but "only for what it will bring" in the context of the city.

The struggles for Alger's heroes, expressed in mythic forms, have the effect Campbell says is the purpose of

rites of passage: "to conduct people across those difficult thresholds of transformation that demand a change in the patterns not only of conscious but also of unconscious life."[32] Alger, with all his faults, served as a guide to a growing urban environment, taking youth from the farm to the city, extolling values and virtues that hopefully assisted a rural society become urban.

NOTES

[1] Richard Sennett, *Families Against the City* (Cambridge, Mass., 1970).

[2] Much has been written of the nineteenth century ethic of the "self-made man." See, for instance, John Carvelti, *Apostles of the Self-Made Man* (Chicago, 1965); Irvin Wyllie, *Self-Made Man in America: The Myth of Rags to Riches* (New Brunswick, N.J., 1954).

[3] Brewster was clearly a declining village; its population fell from 1477 in 1860 to 1259 in 1870. Thus Alger's departure was part of a general trend.

[4] Quoted in John Tebbel, *From Rags to Riches* (New York, 1963), 40.

[5] *Ibid.,* 11

[6] *Ibid.,* 24

[7] *Ibid.,* 133.

[8] Horatio Alger, Jr., *Struggling Upward,* intro. by Russel Crouse, (New York, 1945), x.

[9] Tebbel, 13.

[10] Horatio Alger, Jr., *Helen Ford* (Boston, 1866), 205.

[11] *Ibid.,* 19.

[12] Horatio Alger, Jr., *The Young Miner* (Phila., 1879), 40.

[13] *Ragged Dick,* reprinted in Crouse, p. 273.

[14] John M. Roberts and Brian Sutton-Smith, "Child Training and Game Involvement," *Ethnology,* I (1962), 179. See also Michael Zuckerman's excellent article, "The Nursery Tales of Horatio Alger," *American Quarterly,* 24 (1972), 209, for another interpretation of Alger's reliance on chance.

[15] Kenneth Burke, *The Philosophy of Literary Form* (New York, 1957), 256.

[16] Joseph Campbell, *The Hero With a Thousand Faces* (New York, 1965), 29.

[17] Kenneth S. Lynn, *The Dream of Success* (Boston, 1955), 18.

[18] Kurt H. Wolff, *The Sociology of Georg Simmel* (London, 1950), 41.

[19] *Ragged Dick* in *Struggling Upward,* 211.

[20] Lynn, 18-19.

[21] See Zuckerman's comments on Alger's "steady undertone of desperation" (203).

[22] Campbell, 30.

[23] *Ragged Dick,* 155.

[24] *Ibid.,* 158.

[25] *Ibid.,* 158.

[26] Campbell, 10.

[27] *Ragged Dick,* 164.

[28] Campbell, 245.

[29] *Ibid.,* 36.

[30] Mircea Eliade, *The Sacred and the Profane* (New York, 1961), 209.

[31] Alger, *The Young Miner,* 132.

[32] Campbell, 10.

Houston A. Baker, Jr.

SOURCE: "The Environment as Enemy in a Black Autobiography: *Manchild in the Promised Land,*" in *Phylon: The Atlanta University Review of Race and Culture,* Vol. XXXII, No.1, Spring, 1971, pp. 53-9.

[*In the following essay, Baker focuses on environment in Claude Brown's* Manchild in the Promised Land.]

The concept of the environment as enemy is far from new; Zola and the naturalistic school of the nineteenth century took the concept as a starting point. Moreover, the concept is not new to black literature, for the Chicago of Bigger Thomas and the New York of the "invisible man" bring about the fall of the protagonists in *Native Son* and the *Invisible Man* just as surely as the mines in *Germinal* and the gin shops in *L'Assomoir* bring about the fall of the protagonists in those works. Like Zola and other naturalistic writers, Wright and Ellison have portrayed the vast web of forces surrounding man as inexorable; the environment ultimately brings either death or degradation to their respective protagonists. To deal with the environment as an injurious or hostile force in Claude Brown's *Manchild in the Promised Land,* therefore, is not to enter a world of strange literary conventions. However, the conventions here are somewhat modified.

In *Manchild in the Promised Land,* there is no ineluctable march of naturalistic events; there are no long and bitter tirades against a hostile universe, and no scenes where the protagonist is portrayed as the mangled and pitiable victim of negative forces. Brown's work, therefore, can neither be rigidly classified as "naturalistic" nor as an "angry" autobiography in the manner of the narrative of William Wells Brown. Brown has not only portrayed the negative aspects of the environment, but also the positive aspects: not only the defeats brought about by the antagonistic environment, but also the victories won and the beneficial changes that resulted from the battle.

Manchild in the Promised Land presents the struggle of one black male child to escape from the throes of a colonial system; Harlem, or the initial environment, is the colony whose codes and inimical effects the protagonist has to escape. The protagonist's struggle is defined in terms of various shifts in environment, and the reader emerges with a balanced view of his struggle due to the combination of romantic nostalgia and clinical realism in the narrator's technique of description. This *philos-a-philos* relationship between the narrator and the environment gives Brown's work a critical objectivity that makes the book useful for socio-historical purposes; moreover, the changes in environment that define the protagonist's struggle reflect a historical process with a degree of accuracy that also makes the work valuable as social history. An examination of the struggle presented in the work, therefore, will reveal not only how Brown's use of the environment as enemy constitutes a modification of a literary convention, but also will show what the work tells about the struggle of blacks in a recent epoch.

The picture of the environment as a hostile force begins to emerge in the first lines of *Manchild in the Promised Land;* the protagonist at the age of thirteen is fleeing an unknown assailant, and lodged in his stomach is a bullet, "trying to take my life, all thirteen years of it."[1] And the narrator's earliest memory is of the Harlem riot in 1943 when the population rebelled against the inimical environment surrounding it. The dark picture continues to unfold when the narrator reveals that his father has killed a man, and the landlord of the building in which he lives has clubbed a man to death for urinating in the hall. Both his father and the landlord represent the "old order" to the narrator, and the legacy of the old order consists of "liquor, religion, sex, and violence" (p. 291). In fact, the narrator says that "the Harlem tradition [of violence] had come from the backwoods" (p. 289), and he continues with the following reflection on the members of the old order: "They didn't seem to be ready for urban life" (p. 289).

The environment then is one conditioned by a violent past and overseen by men—both black and white (pp. 298-99)—who do not understand the generation to which the narrator belongs. This lack of understanding made life at home unbearable, and as a result, the protagonist took to the streets. He defines his early habitat in the following passage:

I always ran away [from youth shelters] to get back to the streets. I always thought of Harlem as home, but I never thought of Harlem as being in the house. To me home was the streets. I suppose there were many people who felt that. If home was so miserable, the street was the place to be. (p. 428)

The life of the streets consisted of fighting, stealing, smoking marijuana, and learning the "code" of the gang (p. 270). The narrator says: "Throughout my childhood in Harlem, nothing was more strongly impressed on me than the fact that you had to fight and that you should fight." (p. 263) The things he and his contemporaries fought for were "manhood, women, and money"; the code was simple, with its emphasis on violence drawn from the quality of life:

> By the time I was nine years old, I had been hit by a bus, thrown into the Harlem River (intentionally), hit by a car, severely beaten with a chain. And I had set the house afire. (p. 21)

It is the meaning of this violence, however, that is of significance in any consideration of the environment as enemy, and that meaning is given in the words of the narrator. When he is urged to join the Black Muslim movement in order to rebel against white society, the narrator says:

> The revolution that you're talking about, Alley, I've had it. I've had that revolution since I was six years old. And I fought it every day—in the streets of Harlem, in the streets of Brooklyn, in the streets of the Bronx and Lower Manhattan, all over—when I was there stealing, raising hell out there, playing hookey. I rebelled against school because the teachers were white. And I went downtown and robbed the stores because the store owners were white. I ran through the subways because the cats in the change booths were white. (p. 340)

The street life, therefore, is revealed as a form of rebellion against the environment, an environment which, in effect, constitutes a colony held in check by white society "downtown." The accuracy of the narrator's estimation is reinforced by a statement from John Henrick Clarke's *Harlem, A Community in Transition.* Clarke says:

> Harlem is not a self-contained community. It is owned and controlled by outsiders. It is a black community with a white economic heartbeat. Of the major retail outlets, national chains and local merchants, only a handful are Negro-owned. In the raging battle for integration and equal job opportunities for Negroes, little is heard about the Negroes' long fight to gain control of their community. A system of pure economic colonialism extends into politics, religion and every money-making endeavor that touches the life of a Harlem resident.[2]

Through violence, stealing, indeed all aspects of the street life, the protagonist pits his skill against the pressures of the environment, but so conceived, the rebellion is destined to failure: "It was doomed to fail, right from the word go." (p. 340)

Indeed the inevitable failure of rebellion against the antagonistic environment can easily be seen; it takes the form of a deterministic pattern through three changes of environment that occur in the early part of *Manchild in the Promised Land.* The first change occurs when the narrator is sent to the South for a year because he has refused to attend school; the second change occurs when he is sent to Wiltwyck, a correctional institution for boys; and the third when he is sent to Warwick, another correctional institution. By the time he was fifteen, the narrator had suffered "exile" or incarceration three times for his rebellious activities against the initial environment. If the battle was indeed between the narrator and his environment, clearly, the environment was the early victor.

And yet the paradox of the penal system does not fail to operate in *Manchild in the Promised Land,* for in all three of the "secondary" environments the protagonist became more skilled in the techniques of waging a battle against the initial environment. In the South, he learned to lie with proficiency; in Wiltwyck, he met companions who engaged in criminal activities with him on home visits; and in Warwick, he learned something new about crime from everyone he met. The irony of the penal system is captured by the narrator's statement that "We all came out of Warwick better criminals." (p. 146) The initial environment was thus a fiendishly insidious antagonist, for not only did it punish the rebel, but it also embodied the punishment in a form that made further sins unavoidable. The first three secondary environments, therefore, are little more than adjuncts—additional arms, if you will—of the enemy, and this can be seen in the code that characterized Wiltwyck and Warwick: it was the code of the streets from which the protagonist was sent. And the adverse effects of these secondary environments can be seen in the romantic nostalgia of the narrator.

The secondary environments bring about a mode of perception that proceeds out of the imaginative rather than the rational faculty, and this mode of perception conditions the nostalgia of the protagonist. For example, on returning home from the South, he says:

> When I came out of the subway at 145th Street and St. Nicholas Avenue, I thought there had never been a luckier person in the world than me. . . . I was so happy to see them, to see it, to see it all, to see Harlem again. (pp. 52-3)

There is a certain pathos in these lines when one reflects on what the environment actually means—what the "blood and vomit" that the narrator sees on his arrival at home actually mean; and the pathos of the romantic vision is seen again when the narrator speaks of Harlem on his return from Wiltwyck. He says: "Oh, Lord, Harlem, let me git to you! It was an exciting feeling—going home." (p. 107) Finally, the same romantic nostalgia is seen just before the narrator's return from Warwick:

> All I wanted to do was get back to Harlem. I wanted to get back to Jackie and pot and the

streets and stealing. This was my way of life. I couldn't take it for too long when I was there, but this was all I knew. (p. 156)

The already low aspirational level is further lowered by the secondary environments, and these environments simply increase the protagonist's desire to continue his futile rebellion. On leaving Wiltwyck, his only desire is to get high on heroin, and on leaving Warwick, his only desire is to get back to stealing and smoking marijuana. When the end result of the return to the place so nostalgically yearned for is considered, only the narrator's desire to return can be seen as romantic. Yet this romanticism helps to preserve a balanced point of view, for it keeps the book from falling to the level of a puerile denunciation of the environment. The romanticism, in other words, acts as the *philos* that removes *Manchild in the Promised Land* from the category of the "angry" autobiography. Moreover, this romanticism functioned as one motivation for the actions of the narrator's youth, and as such it has a place in his story and quite possibly in the stories of others of his generation. The world of the Harlem streets was glorious because it stood in contrast to the miserable homes and the correctional institutions, which seemed to be the only alternatives.

Nonetheless, the ultimate effect of romantic nostalgia was adverse, for it led the narrator to give up the idea of school altogether, to move out of his parents' home, and to adopt the code of the Hamilton Terrace environment at the age of sixteen. At the age of sixteen, therefore, he was dangerously close to being destroyed by the environment. He was living in the area where the worst criminals in Harlem lived, and he was selling drugs. He says, "I was going the crime way. That's all there was to it." (p. 173) The next stops that life held out to him at the time were Coxsackie, Woodburn, and then Sing Sing. Clearly the environment was the victor at this point, and it had taken its toll in human lives and suffering. As the narrator says, "Most of the cats I came up with were in jail or dead or strung out on drugs." (p. 179)

But it is at this point of ultimate despair, at this point of the "everlasting nay," that the advantage in the battle begins to shift to the protagonist, and it is this shift that removes *Manchild in the Promised Land* most decisively from the naturalistic category. Heretofore, there has been no linear development, only the inexorable pendulum of the narrator's moves from an antagonistic initial environment to equally antagonistic secondary environments and back again; the expansion has been simply vertical as the protagonist has become more deeply involved in the life of crime. Now, at the age of seventeen, the first horizontal expansion of the book occurs as the narrator moves to Greenwich Village. In effect, the movement is equal to a movement from the colony to the mainland; the narrator starts on the road to development outside the ghetto. The horizontal expansion is not only defined in terms of the physical move, but also in terms of the narrator's point of view toward life. In commenting on the change, he says:

I was free. For the first time in my life I didn't have the feeling that I had to go to Coxsackie, to Woodburn, and then to Sing Sing. I had the feeling now that anything could happen, anything that I decided to do. It seemed a little bit crazy, but I even had the feeling that if I wanted to become a doctor or something like that, I could go on and do it. (p. 185)

For the first time the narrator has a feeling of freedom and a higher aspirational level. Moreover, he is now able to reflect objectively on the enemy. There is no romantic nostalgia in his clinically realistic descriptions of the drug "plague" that swept through the community in the fifties, and he is far from romantic as he describes the lesbians, the homosexuals, the poor police protection, and the poor politicians who went to make up the colony.

In chapter eight he sees that the type of hero the community set up was a criminal such as Jim Goldie, and in chapter nine the narrator makes his first analysis of the "black reflection" that began in the early fifties.[3] In chapters ten, eleven, and twelve, the narrator reflects on the old order of the Southern black man, on the effects of drugs on the community, and on his own future as well as the future of his younger brother, who started taking drugs at an early age. All of these chapters reach a new high in objectivity; all of the inimical aspects of the Harlem environment are seen critically as the narrator adjusts his perspectives and grows to maturity. In chapter thirteen, there is a marvelous description of what Saturday night means to blacks, and in chapter fourteen, the narrator's view of the early era of "black reflection" continues as he describes the rise of the Muslim movement in Harlem. He concludes the chapter by saying: "If they [the Muslims] don't do any more than let the nation know that there are black men in this country who are dangerously angry, then they've already served a purpose." (p. 349)

Finally, in chapter fifteen, the point of farthest horizontal expansion occurs. The narrator's move to Greenwich Village has allowed him to withdraw from the hostile environment for a time, and he has been relatively successful in the white world. But when he pursues his retreat to its limits and attempts to have an affair with a Jewish girl, he is defeated by the white world. This defeat provokes a retreat to the initial environment, but that initial environment can no longer be as injurious as previously, since the narrator has adjusted his perspectives and matured. He says, "It was as though I had found my place and Harlem had found its place. We were suited for each other now." (p. 372) The narrator is surely the victor at this point; in chapters seventeen and eighteen, his victory is confirmed by his discovery of the beneficial forces in the initial environment. He meets Reverend James, and through the funds of a church council, he gets away from the environment altogether. The last chapter deals with the changing nature of the community, the new luxury apartment buildings, and the new brand of policeman who is interested in protecting the community. By the end of the last chapter, it not only seems as though the protagonist has escaped a hostile environment, but also that the environment itself is a tame and beneficent place. One is almost tempted to ask if the environment had ever been hostile, or if the environment was indeed the enemy. And it is precisely at this point that one can see just how superb a work the author has managed to produce for the social historian, for he has presented an unimpassioned, objective, and factual account of an epoch. By maintaining a balance between romantic nostalgia and clinical realism, by keeping the *philos-a-philos* relationship in balance, the author has been able to present a work that neither succumbs to the ideological rigidities of naturalistic conventions nor the subjective distortions of angry autobiography.

That the environment is the enemy, however, can clearly be seen by a statement made near the end of the book: "It seemed as though most of the cats that we'd come up with just hadn't made it. Almost everybody was dead or in jail." (p. 419) By the end of the work Alleybush, Kid, and K. B., all childhood friends of the narrator, are in jail; Jackie, Debbie, and Trixie, three of the main women in his life, are prostitutes, while a fourth, Sugar, is a drug addict. Butch and Tony, two of his best friends in youth, have died as a result of drug addiction; and Pimp, the narrator's younger brother, is in jail on an armed robbery charge. The price exacted by the environment is thus a monumental one, and if any message emerges clearly, it is that only the exceptional, only the few made it—many met death at an early age. Danny, one of those who made it out of the environment, was a man capable of miracles, for he was "strung-out" on drugs, accomplished his cure, and came back to the same environment where he had met his downfall.[4] Turk, the fighter who is the number two contender for the heavyweight crown at the end of the book, is also an exceptional figure, a person capable of the philosophical reflections seen throughout the last of the book.[5] But the most exceptional figure of all is, of course, the narrator himself. The fact that he was able by an act of will to turn around and follow the straight road after ten or eleven years of crime is truly remarkable. And even if allowance is made for a certain amount of egocentricity and exaggeration, yet clearly the narrator was ahead of a great number of his companions. In innumerable instances throughout the work, his leadership potential and above-average abilities are revealed.[6] Danny, Turk, and Sonny (the narrator)— these are the only ones left when *Manchild in the Promised Land* closes on a note of nostalgia with the narrator at five years of age describing the sights of the streets to his unbelieving father.

And one can sympathize with the father because it is hard to believe that in the ultra-civilized, twentieth century city such an environment could exist; yet it does exist, and one can only marvel at the restrained manner in which the author has presented his story. Though the environment described by the work is clearly the enemy, its landscapes are not totally bleak, and the possibility of victory exists. The tactics of Brown's victory should be of ultimate concern not only to the social historian, but to mankind in general.

NOTES

[1] Claude Brown, *Manchild in the Promised Land* (New York: Signet Books, 1965), p. 1. All citations from *Manchild in the Promised Land* in the text are from this edition. Hereafter referred to in the notes as *Manchild*.

[2] John Henrik Clarke, *Harlem, A Community in Transition* (New York, 1964), p. 8.

[3] *Manchild*, p. 172. The narrator says: "In the fifties, when 'baby' came around, it seemed to be the prelude to a whole new era in Harlem. It was the introduction to the era of black reflection. A fever started spreading. Perhaps the strong rising of the Muslim movement is something that helped to sustain or even usher in this era."

[4] *Manchild*, pp. 255-62. In response to Danny's plan to stay in Harlem after being cured, the narrator says that it would be a "miracle" if it could be done (p. 257).

[5] *Manchild*, pp. 368-72. The dialogue between the narrator and Turk at this point is particularly apt as an illustration of Turk's character.

[6] *Manchild*, pp. 82, 104, 141, and 155. On page 155, not only does the wife of the director of Warwick encourage the narrator to finish high school because he has a good head on his shoulders, but also the narrator says, "I just ran the place, and I kept it quiet." If he came even close to "running" an institution with 500 criminally inclined young men in it, he was clearly exceptional.

Yoshinobu Hakutani

SOURCE: "The City and Richard Wright's Quest for Freedom," in *The City in African-American Literature*, edited by Yoshinobu Hakutani, Fairleigh Dickinson University Press, 1995, pp. 50-63.

[*In the following essay, Hakutani explores the urban settings of Richard Wright's fiction.*]

One of the central themes in nineteenth-century American fiction was for a white man to leave his community in quest of pastoral peace of mind. Not only was he able to live in harmony with nature, but he would find a bosom friend in the stranger, a dark-skinned man from whom he learned the values of life he had never known. Natty Bumppo in James Fenimore Cooper's Leather-Stocking novels makes such friendship with Chingachgook and Hard-Heart, noble savages of the American wilderness. Ishmael in *Moby-Dick* is ritualistically wedded to Queequeg, a pagan from the South Seas. Huck Finn discovers a father figure in Jim, a runaway slave. In modern African-American fiction, on the contrary, a black man is deeply suspicious of the pastoral scene. He finds the rural South a living hell and dreams of the northern city as deliverance from racial prejudice and exclusion. Richard Wright, while being careful not to romanticize American urban life, shows that a black man who finds the city a better place to live in than the rural community which has defined his past can succeed in creating the self in the city.

Wright's desire to create the self in his own life is well documented in his autobiography *Black Boy*. His success in fictionalizing such an impulse is also evident in his other work, particularly *Native Son* and *The Outsider*. "Reduced to its simplest and most general terms," he asserts in "Blueprint for Negro Writing," "themes for Negro writers will rise from understanding the meaning of their being transplanted from a 'savage' to a 'civilized' culture in all of its social, political, economic, and emotional implications."[1] By what Wright calls the savage culture, he means the origin of black people in Africa as well as the history of slavery in the South. By the civilized culture, he implies the promised land of the American city in the North after the slaves' emancipation.

Although the motive for a white man's quest for the pastoral idylls has little to do with race, his urgent need, nonetheless, is to escape from some sort of social and emotional tension he suffers in living with other individuals. In *Moby-Dick* Ishmael confesses his motive for becoming a whale hunter: "especially whenever my hypos get such an upper hand of me, that it requires a strong moral principle to prevent me from deliberately stepping into the street, and methodically knocking people's hats off—then, I account it high time to get to sea as soon as I can."[2] The root of Ishmael's anxiety is the crush of individuals that occurs in a crowded community; Ishmael's action betrays the basic elements of national character—individualism and freedom.

If a white man wanted to exercise the rights of liberty and individuality, it would be nothing unusual in modern America that a black man also would desire to acquire such privileges. One of the causes for black men in Wright's work to move from a rural to an urban environment is precisely the absence of individuality and independence within the black community in the South. More than any other book, *Black Boy* is a criticism of the black community, where people are united by race and religion but they are not encouraged to generate the spirit of individualism. Clearly the young Wright rebelled against such tradition. For those who did not seek independence and freedom, such a community would be a haven. Ralph Ellison has observed:

> In some communities every one is "related" regardless of blood-ties. The regard shown by the group for its members, its general communal character and its cohesion are often mentioned. For by comparison with the cold impersonal relationships of the urban industrial community, its relationships are personal and warm.[3]

To Wright, however, such an environment in the South does not produce meaningful relationships among people and it is even detrimental to the creation of manhood.

The lack of individuality among black people in the South has taken a heavy toll on black character. The oppressive system, Wright observes in *12 Million Black Voices*, "created new types of behavior and new patterns of psychological reaction, welding us together into a separate unity with common characteristics of our own."[4] He provides an illustration of this behavior so familiar to plantation owners:

> If a white man stopped a black on a southern road and asked: "Say, there, boy! It's one o'clock, isn't it?" the black man would answer: "Yessuh."
>
> If the white man asked: "Say, it's not one o'clock, is it, boy?" the black man would answer: "Nawsuh."
>
> And if the white man asked: "It's ten miles to Memphis, isn't it, boy?" the black man would answer: "Yessuh."
>
> And if the white man asked: "It isn't ten miles to Memphis, is it, boy?" the black man would answer: "Nawsuh."
>
> Always we said what we thought the whites wanted us to say. (*Black Voices* 41)

What Wright calls "the steady impact of the plantation system" also was on the education of black children. In many southern states the white authorities edited the textbooks which black children were allowed to use. These textbooks automatically deleted any references to government, constitution, voting, citizenship, and civil rights. The school authorities uniformly stated that such foreign languages as French, Spanish, and Latin were not suitable for black children to learn. This provincial policy is reminiscent of the famous scene in *Adventures of Huckleberry Finn* in which Jim cannot understand why a Frenchman cannot speak English.[5] Failing to convince Jim that there are languages other than English and cultures other than English and American, Huck utters in frustration with a sense of irony: "I see it warn't no use wasting words—you can't learn a nigger to argue" (79). In *12 Million Black Voices*, Wright reports that white men "become angry when they think that we desire to learn more than they want us to" (64).

To Wright, the effect of white subjugation in the South was most visible in the black communities of the Mississippi delta. By the time he became fourteen he was able to read and write well enough to obtain a job, in which he assisted an illiterate black insurance salesman. On his daily rounds to the shacks and plantations in the area, he was appalled by the pervasiveness of segregated life: "I saw a bare, bleak pool of black life and I hated it; the people were alike, their homes were alike, and their farms were alike."[6] Such observations later infuriated not only white segregationists, but many black citizens who wrote letters to the FBI and denounced *Black Boy*. Some letters called him "a black Nazi" and "one of the biggest spreaders of race hatred." Another black protester complained: "I am an American Negro and proud of it because we colored people in America have come a long way in the last seventy years. . . . We colored people don[']t mind the truth but we do hate lies or anything that disturb[s] our peace of mind."[7]

This absence of individuality and self-awareness among black people in the South often leads to the compromise of their character. Individually, Fishbelly and his father in *The Long Dream* are powerless in asserting themselves. Although they are not forced to cooperate with the white police, greed often sacrifices their moral integrity. They are fully aware that their illicit political connections will make them as wealthy as the whites. What is worse, not only politics but sex is dealt with in its sordid context: the hero's ritual of initiation into manhood is performed in a house of prostitution.[8]

Even though some black men are able to escape the southern environment and move to the industrial city in the North, they find it difficult to rid themselves of the corrupting system they have learned in the South. Jake Jackson of *Lawd Today,* one of the most despicable black characters Wright ever created, is tempted to do anything if he can make money. Although he is not capable of reasoning or independent observation, he is capable of deceiving others. He approves of graft as a way of life in the city for anyone to get ahead; he admires people who can profit by accepting bribes. He even envies gangsters who can wield their power to intimidate the strong and the weak alike. "I always said," Jake boasts, "that we colored folks ought to stick with the rich white folks."[9] What unites people like Fishbelly Tucker and Jake Jackson is the fact that though they can escape and, like the protagonist of *Black Boy* and Big Boy in "Big Boy Leaves Home," can become considerably free from the racial strictures in their lives, they ultimately fail to find themselves. Even though they are physically free of the subjugating system, mentally they have failed to become individuals with autonomy and integrity.

Wright told Irving Howe that "only through struggle could men with black skins, and for that matter, all the oppressed of the world, achieve their humanity."[10] To Wright, freedom for black people can become a reality only when all black people acquire independent visions as outsiders. No matter how courageous Silas, a black farmer in "Long Black Song," may appear, his fight against the oppressors makes little impact on the black liberation as a whole because his rebellion is motivated by a private matter.[11] The black emancipation from the rural South, Wright warns, must be accompanied by the vision of the outsider. Ely Houston, New York district attorney, in *The Outsider* speaks as Wright's mouthpiece:

> Negroes, as they enter our culture, are going to inherit the problems we have, but with a difference. They are outsiders, and they are going to *know* that they have these problems. They are going to be self-conscious; they are going to be gifted with a double vision, for, being Negroes, they are going to be both *inside* and *outside* of our culture at the same time.[12]

Houston's admonition can be easily heeded by a black intellectual like Cross Damon, but to most of Wright's uneducated black men the fear of persecution is what threatens their freedom and existence. In *Black Boy* Wright is continually at pains to show that white people had a preconceived notion of a black man's place in the South: the black man serves white people, he is likely to steal, and he cannot read or write. A black man was not likely to be executed for petty theft; there were relatively few restrictions on the subjects he was allowed to discuss with white men. Even sex and religion were the most accepted subjects of conversation, for they were the topics that did not require positive knowledge or self-assertion on the part of the black man. Interracial sex, however, was taboo, and black men risked their lives if they were caught in the act. "So volatile and tense," Wright says in "How 'Bigger' Was Born," "are these relations that if a Negro rebels against rule and taboo, he is lynched and the reason for the lynching is usually called 'rape,' that catchword which has garnered such vile connotations that it can raise a mob anywhere in the South pretty quickly, even today."[13]

This fear of persecution is most poignantly expressed in *Lawd Today:* a group of southern-born black men gaze lasciviously at the carelessly exposed thighs of a white woman sitting obliquely across the aisle on a train. The taboo of interracial sex is defined in a quatrain improvised alternately by Jake and his three companions:

> Finally, Jake rolled his eyes heavenward and sang in an undertone: *"Oh, Lawd, can I ever, can I ever? . . ."*
>
> Bob screwed up his eyes, shook his head, and answered ruefully: *"Naw, nigger, you can never, you can never. . . . "*
>
> Slim sat bolt upright, smiled, and countered hopefully: *"But wherever there's life there's hope. . . . "*
>
> Al dropped his head, frowned, and finished mournfully: *"And wherever there's trees there's rope."* (96-97)

Although this scene is portrayed with humor, it represents the deepest fear any black man can have.[14]

It is well documented that the principal motive behind black people's exodus from the rural South to the industrial North is their quest for freedom and equality. Wright himself, a victim of racial prejudice and hatred in the South, fled to Chicago in search of the kind of freedom he had never experienced in the feudal South. "For the first time in our lives," he writes in *12 Million Black Voices,* "we feel human bodies, strangers whose lives and thoughts are unknown to us, pressing always close about us" (100). In stark contrast to the situation in the South where black people were not allowed to communicate freely with white citizens, the crowded and noisy apartments in the northern cities have become hubs of interracial mingling and communication, the place where the migrant black people come in close contact with "the brisk, clipped men of the North, the Bosses of Buildings." Unlike the southern landlords, the city businessmen, Wright discovered, are not "at all *indifferent*. They are deeply concerned about us, but in a new way" (100).

In the industrial city a black man functions as part of a "machine." Unlike his life in the rural South, which depends upon "the soil, the sun, the rain, or the wind," his life is controlled by what Wright calls "the grace of jobs and the brutal logic of jobs" (*Black Voices* 100). By living and working ever so closely with the white bourgeoisie, the minority workers in the city strive to learn the techniques of the bourgeoisie. Consequently, Wright notes, black workers "display a greater freedom and initiative in pushing their claims upon civilization than even do the petty bourgeoisie" ("Blueprint" 54). The harsh conditions under which black workers must produce and compete with white workers became an incentive to achieve a higher social and economic status. In short, the black man of the industrial North is given a chance to shape his own life. Economically man is a machine and his production is measured not by his race, but by his merit.

Clearly, the businessmen of the city are not concerned about the welfare of the black workers recently fled from the rural South. Like the self-proclaimed philanthropist Dalton in *Native Son,* they take an interest in the black people because their business would prosper if the black men's economic status improves. Focusing on such economic facts in the city. Wright carefully creates a character like Dalton, a symbol for the ambivalent and contradictory ways of the city. Mr. Dalton thus has given millions for social welfare, especially for the NAACP, and ostensibly donated money to buy ping-pong tables for black children. Bigger Thomas does not know this, nor is he aware that Mr. Dalton's contribution comes from the exorbitant rents charged to the black tenants living in his overcrowded and rat-infested apartments. However ironic this may be, the fact remains that Bigger feels grateful for getting a job and that, for him at least, his employer does not appear a racist. Despite the severe living conditions in which black people are placed, the fierce competitions they face,[15] and the traumas they suffer, the city nevertheless provides them with possibilities of freedom and equality.

What impressed Wright when he arrived in Chicago from the deep South was the relative absence of discrimination. "It was strange," he writes in *American Hunger,* "to pause before a crowded newsstand and buy a newspaper without having to wait until a white man was served."[16] Although he was allowed to sit beside white men and women on a streetcar as are Jake Jackson and his black companions in *Lawd Today,* he began to feel "a different sort of tension than I had known before. I knew that this machine-city was governed by strange laws" (2). *American Hunger* also intimates an episode which suggests that some white citizens were not as much obsessed with

the problems of race as southerners, and that a black man is often treated by the white citizens as an equal.[17] One time, Wright obtained employment as a porter in a Jewish delicatessen and felt he had to lie about his absence from that job to take his civil service examination for a better paying job in the post office. But it turned out that his employer would have gladly consented for him to take the examination and that he would not have had to lie about something so important and beneficial to the employee. In *The Outsider* the realistic details woven in the life of a postal worker, Cross Damon, are those of the problems caused by living in the city. Cross is not in any way handicapped in his life or work because he is a black man. He is physically and mentally a tired man; he is bored with routine work just as are his fellow workers, black or white. Because of an early and unfortunate marriage, he has to support a wife he does not love, and their children; he also has a pregnant mistress who is trying to force him to marry her. To forget his miseries he takes to drinking. But such problems have little to do with Cross's being a black man.

Earning a livelihood in industrialized society as does Cross Damon, however, takes a heavy toll of his life. Like Sartre's Mathieu, Cross finds himself in a state of incomprehensible disorder and meaninglessness. To black men such as Cross Damon and Fred Daniels of "The Man Who Lived Underground," the city takes the appearance of a labyrinthine metropolis, where the pervading mood is aimlessness, loneliness, and lack of communication. If man is treated as a machine, he is not expected to communicate or intermingle with his fellow human beings. The controlling image of Wright's city is that of a crowded place inhabited by the people, black and white, who are alienated by displacement and industrialization.

The dehumanizing influences of urban life upon nonintellectuals like Bigger Thomas make their personality warp and harden. In the heart of Chicago, Wright witnessed numerous examples of the Bigger Thomas type—nervous, fearful, frustrated. "The urban environment of Chicago," Wright recalls, "affording a more stimulating life, made the Negro Bigger Thomases react more violently than even in the South. More than ever I began to see and understand the environmental factors which made for this extreme conduct" ("How 'Bigger' Was Born" xv). These black youths, moreover, are alienated not only from the white civilization, but from their own race. Based on this reality, Bigger is depicted as "resentful toward whites, sullen, angry, ignorant, emotionally unstable, depressed and unaccountably elated at times, and unable even, because of his own lack of inner organization which American oppression has fostered in him, to unite with the members of his own race" ("How 'Bigger' Was Born" xxi).

While Bigger Thomas of *Native Son,* buttressed by Wright's own experience in Chicago, is depicted as a hero able to transcend these obstacles of city life and gain self-confidence, another black man, Jake Jackson of *Lawd Today,* is presented as a degenerate character largely unaware that industrialization and capitalism have hope-lessly corrupted his soul. Wright makes it clear that while Jake is not legally a criminal as is Bigger, Jake is a latter-day slave. If Jake is a victim of the economic system, he is also a worshiper of the shoddy values of the system that exploits him. Jake and Bigger are both the products of the same civilization, but Jake, unlike Bigger, is incapable of transcending the dreadful effects of the environment.[18]

Even though the dominant influences of the urban environment on the black men lead to dehumanization and isolation, the same environment can provide them with avenues for transcendence. In fact, Chicago, New York, and later Paris, unlike the southern cities, offered Wright education, free access to libraries, political affiliation, and introduction to realist writers such as Theodore Dreiser, Sinclair Lewis, and John Dos Passos, and French existentialist novelists such as Sartre and Camus. It is a well-known fact that Wright learned how to write fiction by associating with the John Reed Club of Chicago, a leftist writers' organization. Not only did he find intellectual stimulation in Communist philosophy, but also, as Blyden Jackson points out, he found among the members of the Communist party the warm and sustained relationships, the lack of which was the cause of his loneliness in the South.[19]

On the one hand, Wright's ideological fascination with communism is overtly expressed in such early short stories as "Fire and Cloud" and "Bright and Morning Star," which take place in the southern environment. The chief reason Wright joined the Communist party was not his belief in the economics of communism, nor his attraction to trade unionism, nor his curiosity about its underground politics. His vision was the possibility of uniting the isolated and oppressed people allover the world. His own experience in the cities had convinced him that industrialization and commercialization lead people to isolation and loneliness. On the other hand, his personal attraction to communism is alluded to in *The Outsider*. After accidentally gaining a new identity, Cross Damon leaves Chicago for New York, a cosmopolitan city, where he befriends a Communist couple, the Blounts, not because of sympathy for their ideology, but simply because he finds in them urbanity, liberalism, and lack of racial bigotry, the qualities he had not earlier found in white people. To a total stranger in a huge metropolis, the sudden appearance of the Blounts, who offer him food, shelter, and companionship, is indeed an oasis.

As an artist, however, Wright in his own life became disillusioned with the Communist party. To his dismay he learned that the Party insisted on discipline over truth, and that factionalism within the Party pre-empted dialogue and criticism. The Party was primarily interested in a fledgling writer as long as his imaginative ability would result in the writing of pamphlets acceptable to the Party principles. "It was inconceivable to me," he wrote, "though bred in the lap of southern hate, that a man could not have his say. I had spent a third of my life

travelling from the place of my birth to the North just to talk freely, to escape the pressure of fear" (*American Hunger* 92). Not only did he find the Party practice repressive, but he realized that blind adherence to Communist ideology would leave the artist little room for concentration and reflection. "The conditions under which I had to work," Wright felt, "were what baffled them. Writing had to be done in loneliness and Communism had declared war upon human loneliness" (123).

In *The Outsider* Cross Damon murders not only the Fascist landlord, but also the Communist associate, a symbolic act of terror in asserting himself. If his New York landlord is a painful reminder of the Ku Klux Klansmen of the South, his Communist companion equally stands in the way on the road to his freedom and independence. Now with Eva, the wife of the murdered Communist, in his arms, Cross reflects on this climactic action:

> They'll think I did it because of Eva! No; Communists were not unintelligent; they could not seriously think that. There was one thing of which he was certain: they would never credit him with as much freedom to act as they had. A certain psychological blindness seemed to be the hallmark of all men who had to own worlds. . . . All other men were mere material for them; they could admit no rivals, no equals, other men were either above them or below them. (369)

Unlike Clyde Griffiths in Dreiser's *An American Tragedy,* a victim of the materialistic civilization, Cross Damon has learned through his murders how to exercise his will. And before death he is finally able to declare his independence.

Similarly, the last word in *Native Son* is not expressed by the white authorities who hold Bigger in jail, nor the white liberals who are sympathetic to black people. The final statement is given not by the Communist lawyer Max, but by Bigger, a black man who has at last achieved his goal in life:

> "What I killed for must've been good!" Bigger's voice was full of frenzied anguish. "It must have been good! When a man kills, it's for something. . . . I didn't know I was really alive in this world until I felt things hard enough to kill for 'em. . . . It's the truth, Mr. Max. I can say it now, 'cause I'm going to die." (392)

Bigger's dismissal of the Reverend Hammond's attempt to console the accused before the trial is also a symbolic act, which suggests the black man's rejection of religion. In the same way, Cross rejects his mother, the product of southern Negro piety.[20] Cross, like Bigger, rejects the traditional Christianity in the South, for it taught black children subservient ethics. It is only natural that Cross should rebel against such a mother, who moans, "To think I named you Cross after the Cross of Jesus" (*Outsider* 23). Both men reject religion because in a complex modern society it functions only as a ritual; it offers only irrational escape, blind flight from reality. Both men, having conquered the forces of the urban environment, have now severed themselves from the last remnants of the religious and political influences upon them as well. They both have become rugged individualists, the willed creators of their past, present, and future in a chaotic and hostile world.[21]

But Cross's search for meaning in his life is a departure from Bigger's achievement of manhood. In Chicago, the problem of race, the avowed conflict between black and white people, becomes the catalyst for Bigger's manhood. In New York, the issue which torments Cross is not the conflict of race; the larger issue he faces is man's existence or annihilation. In creating Cross, Wright departed from the social issues confronting a black man and asked the universal question of what man is. In terms of plot, the accidental killing of a white woman in *Native Son* whets Bigger's creative impulses. To Cross, on the other hand, Eva, only incidentally a white woman, becomes an essence he tries to find in the meaningless existence. Cross has fallen in love with Eva because they both suffer from the same wound; she was forced to marry a man she did not love just as Cross was once married to a woman he did not love. For Cross the consummation of his love for Eva means the ultimate purpose of his new life. It is understandable that when that goal appears within reach and yet is taken away from him, he finds only "the horror" that he had dreaded all his life (*Outsider* 440).

Although both men seek freedom and independence in their lives, what they find at the end of their lives, the visions which they gain before death, are poles apart. Bigger's last words, "I didn't know I was really alive in this world until I felt things hard enough to kill for 'em" (*Native Son* 392), signal the affirmation of life. Cross, tasting his agonizing defeat and dying, utters:

> "I wish I had some way to give the meaning of my life to others. . . . To make a bridge from man to man . . . Starting from scratch every time is . . . is no good. Tell them not to come down this road. . . . Men hate themselves and it makes them hate others. . . . We must find some way of being good to ourselves. . . . Man is all we've got. . . . But certainly different . . . We're strangers to ourselves." (*Outsider* 439)

Whereas Bigger's vision is full of joy and hope, Cross's is tinged with sadness and estrangement.

In general, critics have regarded Wright's philosophy in *The Outsider* as existential. Noting Cross's action to kill without passion and his indifference to the emotions of others, they have called the philosophy of this metaphysical rebel most consistently nihilistic.[22] To some readers, moreover, Cross represents "the moral and emotional failure of the age."[23] The reason for calling Cross nihilistic lies in his uncharacteristic remark in the novel: "Maybe man is nothing in particular" (*Outsider* 135). Cross's statement, however, seems to be based upon Wright's world view, the philosophy of the absurd, which was in vogue after World War II. Existentialists, and nihilists in particular, are convinced of the essential

absurdity of human existence, but Cross is not. If one judges life as inherently meaningful as Cross does, then it follows that his action to seek love, friendship, and freedom on earth also is meaningful. Cross is passionately in search of order, eternity, and meaning. In the light of his actions in the novel, not in view of Wright's occasional philosophy, Cross ends his life as a failed humanist rather than a nihilist.

As Wright endowed Bigger Thomas with the capacity to assert his freedom and independence, Wright also endowed Cross Damon with the power to create an essence. On the one hand, Bigger, despite his lack of education, has challenged and transcended the unjust forces of the urban environment. On the other, placed under the cosmopolitan climate where he is able to shed the last vestiges of the obsolete Christian ethics as well as the stifling Marxist ideology, Cross stumbles onto the philosophy of existentialism. Rejecting such a philosophy, however, he has instead defined his own way of life. His revolt is not so much against the nothingness and meaninglessness of existence as it is against the inability of man's attempt to make illogical phenomena logical. Despite his own failure, the revelation he gains at the end of his life suggests the possibilities of harmony and love among all men. Bigger and Cross have walked different avenues in the city, but in the end they have both been able to "uphold the concept of what it means to be human" in America.[24]

NOTES

[1] Richard Wright, "Blueprint for Negro Writing," *New Challenge* 2 (Fall 1937): 62-63.

[2] Herman Melville, *Moby-Dick,* ed. Charles Fiedelson, Jr. (Indianapolis: Bobbs-Merrill, 1964), 23.

[3] Ralph Ellison, "Richard Wright's Blues," *Antioch Review* 5 (June 1945): 208.

[4] Richard Wright, *12 Million Black Voices* (New York: Viking, 1941), 41. Subsequent references to this book are given in parentheses.

[5] In an attempt to teach Jim that English is not the only language spoken on earth, Huck says:

> "S'pose a man was to come to you and say Polly-voo-franzy—what would you think?"
>
> "I wouldn't think nuffin' I'd take en bust him over de head—dat is, if he warn't white. I wouldn't 'low no nigger to call me dat."
>
> "Shucks, it ain't calling you anything. It's only saying, do you know how to talk French?"
>
> "Well, den, why couldn't he say it?"
>
> "Why, he is a-saying it. That's a Frenchman's *way* of saying it."

See *Adventures of Huckleberry Finn* (Boston: Houghton Mifflin, 1962), 79.

[6] Richard Wright, *Black Boy* (New York: Harper & Row, 1945), 151. Subsequent references to this book are given in parentheses.

[7] Addison Gayle, *Richard Wright: Ordeal of a Native Son* (Garden City, N.Y.: Anchor Press/Doubleday, 1980), 173-74. According to Gayle, Senator Bilbo of Mississippi condemned *Black Boy* on the floor of the U.S. Senate on 7 June 1954: it is "the dirtiest, filthiest, lousiest, most obscene piece of writing that I have ever seen in print . . . it is so filthy and dirty . . . it comes from a Negro, and you cannot expect any better from a person of his type" (173).

[8] "Fire and Cloud," Wright's earlier short story, also deals with the corruption of the black leadership in southern cities.

[9] Richard Wright, *Lawd Today* (New York: Walker, 1963), 160. Later references to this novel are given in parentheses.

[10] Irving Howe, "Black Boys and Native Sons," *A World More Attractive* (New York: Horizon, 1963), 109.

[11] I agree with Edward Margolies, who says: "Yet Silas's redemption is at best a private affair—and the Negro's plight is no better as a result of his own determination to fight his oppressors with their own weapons. He is hopelessly outnumbered." See Edward Margolies, *The Art of Richard Wright* (Carbondale: Southern Illinois University Press, 1969), 67.

[12] Richard Wright, *The Outsider* (New York: Harper & Row, 1953), 129. Subsequent references to this novel are given in parentheses.

[13] Richard Wright, "How 'Bigger' Was Born," in *Native Son* (New York: Harper & Row, 1940), xii.

[14] Horace Cayton, a sociologist and Wright's close friend and associate, observes that for a black man "punishment in the actual environment is ever present; violent, psychological and physical, leaps out at him from every side." See Horace Cayton, "Discrimination—America: Frightened Children of Frightened Parents," *Twice-a-Year* 12-13 (Spring/Summer/Fall/Winter 1945): 264.

[15] The competition the black man faces in the city creates a tension quite different in nature from the tension in the segregated South. One of Jake's friends in *Lawd Today* says: "The only difference between the North and the South is, them guys down there'll kill you, and those up here'll let you starve to death" (156).

[16] Richard Wright, *American Hunger* (New York: Harper & Row, 1977), 1-2. Subsequent references to this book are given in parentheses.

[17] Besides liberals such as the Hoffmans, the Jewish delicatessen owner, undergound gangsters also treated black people with equality and compassion, as Wright notes in *12 Million Black Voices:* "through the years our loyalty to these gangster-politicians remains staunch because they are almost the only ones who hold out their hand to help us, whatever their motives. . . . The most paradoxical gift ever tendered to us black folk in the city is aid from the underworld, from the gangster, from the political thief' (121-22).

[18] Jake Jackson among Wright's characters is often the object of disparaging remarks by critics, but there are some notable exceptions. Granville Hicks affectionately defended *Lawd Today,* calling it less powerful than *Native Son* and *Black Boy,* but uniquely interesting. What interested Hicks is that although Wright was an avowed Communist at the time he wrote the novel, he did not make a Communist out of Jake Jackson, Jake even despised communism, Hicks points out, and refused to become a victim of the capitalist system, either. Jake was delineated as uneducated, frustrated, and "erring but alive" (37-38). Lewis Leary, regarding Jake as a caricature of the white world, calls him "incongruously, enduringly alive." See Lewis Leary, "*Lawd Today:* Notes on Richard Wright's First/Last Novel," *CLA Journal* 15 (June 1972): 420.

[19] Blyden Jackson, "Richard Wright: Black Boy from America's Black Belt and Urban Ghettos," *CLA Journal* 12 (June 1969): 301.

[20] While Wright dismisses Christianity as useless for black people's freedom and independence, he values the black church in the city because it enhances their community life. In *12 Million Black Voices,* he observes: "Despite our new worldliness, despite our rhythms, our colorful speech, and our songs, we keep our churches alive. . . . Our churches are centers of social and community life, for we have virtually no other mode of communion and we are usually forbidden to worship God in the temples of the Bosses of the Buildings. The church is the door through which we first walked into Western civilization" (130-31).

[21] Margaret Walker, a fellow black novelist who knew Wright well, writes: "Wright's philosophy was that fundamentally all men are potentially evil. . . . Human nature and human society are determinants and, being what he is, man is merely a pawn caught between the worlds of necessity and freedom. . . . All that he has to use in his defense and direction of his existence are (1) his reason and (2) his will." See Margaret Walker, "Richard Wright," *New Letters* 38 (Winter 1971): 198-99.

[22] Charles I. Glicksberg, in "Existentialism in *The Outsider,*" *Four Quarters* 7 (January 1958): 17-26, and in "The God of Fiction," *Colorado Quarterly* 7 (Autumn 1956): 207-20, saw parallels between Wright and Camus in the treatment of their existential heroes. Michel Fabre, Wright's biographer, specifically indicates that Wright's

composition of *The Outsider* "was influenced in subtle ways by his reading of *The Stranger* in August 1947. He read the book in the American edition at a very slow pace, 'Weighing each sentence,' admiring 'its damn good narrative prose,' and remarked:

> It is a neat job but devoid of passion. He makes his point with dispatch and his prose is solid and good. In America a book like this would not attract much attention for it would be said that he lacks feeling. He does however draw his character very well. What is of course really interesting in this book is the use of fiction to express a philosophical point of view. That he does with ease. I now want to read his other stuff."

See Michel Fabre, "Richard Wright, French Existentialism, and *The Outsider*," in *Critical Essays on Richard Wright*, ed. Yoshinobu Hakutani (Boston: G. K. Hall, 1982), 191.

[23] Edward Margolies in his comparison of Damon and Meursault, the hero of *The Stranger*, points out the similarities between the two characters. See Edward Margolies, *The Art of Richard Wright*, 135.

[24] Quoted from Wright's unpublished journal, 7 September 1947, in which he wrote: "Sartre is quite of my opinion regarding the possibility of human action today, that it is up to the individual to do what he can to uphold the concept of what it means to be human" (Fabre 186).

THE CITY IN EUROPEAN LITERATURE

Peter Brooks

SOURCE: "Romantic Antipastoral and Urban Allegories," in the *Yale Review*, Vol. LXIV, No. 1, October, 1974, pp. 11-26.

[*In the following excerpt, Brooks compares and contrasts urban and rural settings as they are used by Baudelaire, Rousseau, and Balzac.*]

The artist of the modern, wrote Charles Baudelaire in 1859, is "tyrannized by the circumstance." In his article on Constantin Guys, the "painter of modern life," Baudelaire tries to define the distinguishing traits of modernity in art: "Modernity is the transitory, the fugitive, the contingent, one half of art, whose other half is the eternal and immutable." That is, the artist intent to represent the modern must attend not only to the immutable forms of the beautiful, but as well to the contingent modes of the fashionable, the particular styles and gestures which constitute the esthetically characteristic at any given moment of history. He is concerned with the artificial, the man-made, the particular happening and thing.

Baudelaire discovers here—as in other essays—the modern importance of the "accessory," which manufacture, advertising, and fashion propose to man as the necessary supplement to his nudity, as definition of role, status, image. The accessory is possessible: it is the objective world made available through acquisition. A significantly modern version of the relationship between man and things is in fact *acquisition*, the definition of self through the purchase of things. As Baudelaire suggests, this is particularly characteristic of life and art in the context of urbanization and industrial manufacture, where life has come in some measure—Baudelaire says "half"—to be determined by the life of commodities, of the made things which man surrounds himself with. The modern urban landscape is a clutter of things, made objects and costumes which the modern artist must render because they have become both expressive and determinative of man's behavior and character, which no longer can be described exclusively in a vocabulary of moral and psychological abstractions, as in the literary portraiture of the seventeenth and eighteenth centuries. Baudelaire's "artist of the modern" is also the artist of the urban, and Baudelaire states most explicitly what is apparent to the other great urban writers in the Romantic tradition—Balzac, Dickens, Gogol, Flaubert, Dostoevsky—that the artificial and the manufactured, man's made things, have become a new and total context for life, a factitious nature, complete with its iron and concrete flora, which supports and defines man's "nature."

If the portraiture of an earlier literature had no need for accessories and could talk in psychological essences, the literature of the city before the nineteenth century generally felt no need to paint the urban landscape. For the writers of the Enlightenment, from Montesquieu through Voltaire to Diderot, the city is in fact not a landscape but a social ethic. They conceive the city as a kind of cosmopolitan center of civilization, a space liberated from the narrow-mindedness of provincial life, a place of free commercial and social interchange where people come together in a spirit of enlightened self-interest and profit from mutual intercourse. The ideal center of the ideal city is the London Stock Exchange as described by Voltaire in his *Lettres philosophiques*: the place where men of different nationalities, religious beliefs, and languages come together from a motive of utility and bargain together to the profit of all. The Exchange is for Voltaire a kind of secular temple to the idea of utility and mutually beneficial commerce, in both the economic and human senses. For the *philosophes* and the Encyclopedists, for all those concerned with the spread of liberal ideas and social progress, the city was the progressive force and context because it most called upon men to be citizens, to partake in a life of social and intellectual interchange. The apology for luxury undertaken by Voltaire in his poem "Le Mondain" is a defense of more than material wealth: it is also an apology for the life of refined sociability made possible by the urban context alone. Outside the city is provincialism, prejudice, the dead weight of tradition. Jean-Jacques Rousseau's withdrawal from metropolitan life with his retreat to the Ermitage in 1756 was so vehemently attacked by Voltaire, Diderot, and the others because it symbolized desertion of the whole cause of progress and liberalism, renunciation of the sole context in which "enlightening" was possible, the choice of a benighted world severed from civilization. Diderot saw a contradiction in the fact that Rousseau, who liked to think of himself as the "citizen" (he signed his books "Citoyen de Genève") had deserted the city. In a letter that Rousseau never forgave, near the point of crisis in their quarrel, Diderot wrote: "Farewell citizen. Yet what a curious citizen is the hermit!" Hermitism is irresponsible: in an odd detail, Diderot asks what will happen to those Parisian beggars who have become accustomed to Rousseau's daily contribution now that he has left Paris. Rousseau is guilty of violating the community of man, of failing to play his part in the great human interrelationship that is the city.

Since the metropolis of the *philosophes* is a social ideal and ethic, the necessary context of a form of thought and a way of life, it is not a landscape: there are few instances, even in the novels of Parisian life, of an effort to see the city and describe it. If there are some examples of tableaux of Paris, impressions of its streets, buildings, passers-by—such as with the arrival in Paris of Marivaux's heroine in *La Vie de Marianne*—these are glimpses only, and the narrative quickly moves indoors, into the drawing room, because the city is essentially conceived as a social concentration, a world of salons and cafés where people meet and interact. There is no cityscape, no urban phenomenology, because no one steps back to view the city as an environmental phenomenon. Novelists write from within the context of the social ethic which corresponds to, supports, and is supported by, urban existence, and there is no need to problematize either the ethic or its physical framework. The norms of both are assumptions shared by writers and readers alike. For the city to be discovered literarily, an effect of alienation will have to take place. The social ethic will have to be opposed by another ideal, another vision of life, which will, by reflection, give a problematic status to the social and metropolitan ethic.

It is the passage from the city of the *philosophes* to the city of the "painter of modern life" that interests me here. What is involved is a discovery through which the whole way of *seeing,* and indeed of *reading,* the city changes radically. One must of course note that this transformation belongs in part to the city itself, in its evolution under the impact of industrialization and increased urban immigration. What is most notable about Paris in the first half of the nineteenth century is the greatly increased density of inhabitation, especially in the working-class districts: a large increase in population is not compensated by a comparable increase in construction, either of buildings or of such public services as sewers and water mains. So that if physically Paris (except in its suburban outskirts) does not undergo striking changes—as it will in the 1850's and 1860's, when Baron Haussmann sets to work under the orders of Napoleon III—it does deteriorate as an urban environment, feels more claustrophobic and forces on the attention of its middle classes the presence of crime, prostitution, and misery. Still, to

explain the difference in the way Paris is perceived purely in terms of its own changes seems to me the wrong approach: not only is the Parisian landscape not transformed, transformations in perception depend equally on the eye of the perceiver, its training, on literary conventions and traditions, on esthetics and ideology. What concerns me here is the birth of a new perceptual and literary convention for viewing the city.

I think that the mediation between the two images of the city comes, curiously, from the man who fled the city, from Rousseau. He sets in motion the process of passage from one image to the other, and the results have interesting implications. A first stage in understanding Rousseau's role in this process is indicated by Erich Auerbach in a suggestive passage of *Mimesis,* where he argues that Rousseau's "politicizing of the idyllic concept of Nature" created a wish-image of great persuasiveness, and one that rapidly laid bare its radical opposition to social reality. This opposition directed attention in a new way to the given, historical, social reality, with the result of problematizing what had hitherto been unproblematical. Auerbach writes: "The Rousseauist movement and the great disillusionment it underwent was a prerequisite for the rise of the modern conception of reality. Rousseau, by passionately contrasting the natural condition of man with the existing reality of life determined by history, made the latter a practical problem; now for the first time the eighteenth-century style of historically unproblematic and unmoved presentation of life became valueless." That is, Rousseau's "politicized pastoral"—his use of pastoral as a polemical ethico-political stance—marks the beginning of an end to innocence about the socio-ethical stance within the metropolis, politicizes *that* stance, and makes it subject to critical attention. If pastoral was always a convention used to contrast the merits of the civilized and the simple lives, the debate was carried on within a framework itself highly urbane. Rousseau literalizes and hence radicalizes the pastoral position, turns it from a convention into a political and moral demand.

But to say more precisely how Rousseauian pastoral leads to the particularized urban landscape of Baudelaire and Balzac, we have to go beyond Auerbach's argument, and beyond the political implications of Rousseau's pastoral to its primary imperatives. We should consider first of all Rousseau's relation to things, his feeling for the concrete world of objects which stands in such marked contrast to other writers of his time. Commenting on the *Confessions,* Sainte-Beuve once remarked with distaste that Rousseau had the sensibility of a peasant, and never omitted to tell us what he had to eat and drink. It is true that, in the *Confessions* and *La Nouvelle Héloïse,* the commonplace world, its events and its things, are represented with a sensuous detail and a feel for their place in man's life that simply cannot be found in contemporaneous French novels. Rousseau is fully aware of his difference in this, as in all things. In the Preface in dialogue form which he wrote for *La Nouvelle Héloïse,* his imaginary critic complains, "Is it worth the trouble of keeping a register of what anyone can see every day in his own home or that of his neighbor?"—which gives Rousseau an opportunity to defend his attention to the quotidian and ordinary, his attempt to render a sense of a place and its things as they impinge upon human existence. In a remarkable passage of the *Confessions,* Rousseau describes how, after creating the two imaginary and idealized protagonists of his novel and having begun to write the impassioned correspondence between them, he felt the necessity of establishing them and their tale in a real setting, one that he knew. It had to include a lake, he says, and he thought first of the Borromean Islands, in Lago Maggiore, but found them too far-off and "touristic" for his purpose. He returned, finally, to "the lake around which my heart has never ceased to wander," the Lake of Geneva, and this opened the way to the fictional realization of Vevai and Clarens. One has here the impression of a landscape, and the necessity *of* landscape, discovered emotionally: a certain real landscape needed to "hang on to," to anchor his imaginative conceptions. And although the pastoral landscapes of *La Nouvelle Héloïse* may to a degree be idealized, there is a strong sense of their presence and solidity, the necessity of their being there and being described in detail.

This sense of the emotional necessity of landscape is strong throughout Rousseau's writings. He needs its presence and solidity to save him from excessive idealism and the life of fantasy, to materialize and realize his reveries. The one moment of perfect happiness in his life, the idyll of Les Charmettes, has reality and continuity partly because it is anchored in a place, fused to a landscape which he has appropriated perfectly to his emotional needs. His love of botanizing must spring from the same need to anchor consciousness and meditation in the things of the natural world. He mentions in the *Rêveries* a German who was supposed to have written a whole book on a lemon peel. "I could have done a book," says Rousseau, "on each gramen of the fields, on each moss of the woods, on each lichen that carpets the rocks." Botany becomes a way of understanding and grasping the world through its detailed materiality, through what Balzac will call, in a passage inspired by Rousseau, a "rêverie matérielle"—a revery over matter, starting from and returning to the presence of the landscape, pressuring external reality so that it yields the meaning of its relationship to man. Mind "identifies" itself with natural objects and "appropriates" them to itself.

Rousseau's need for this new pastoral of the solid, palpable object is a direct result of his rejection of the social ethic of his time, and the expressive code associated with it. The dominant literary mode of the eighteenth century, I suggested, was sociable and worldly: a literature of man-in-society, concerned with normative standards of social comportment and psychology, situated in a metropolis conceived as a place of human "being together." With his rejection of this ethic and literary stance, Rousseau was left, existentially, morally, even rhetorically in a void, with the necessity to rediscover a reality, a moral frame of existence, and a medium of communication. All of these

would be based on the landscape rediscovered. Rousseau is in the position of having to start anew, *ex nihilo,* from radical nakedness, and to reconstruct an entire world of significance from pure, unmediated commerce with the world, from the bare confrontation of consciousness and things. With the loss of traditional expressive conventions, he is constantly fighting against something close to aphasia, a threat of inexpressivity. He writes in the *Confessions:* "My ideas arrange themselves with the most incredible difficulty. They circulate dumbly in my head; . . . until they move me, heat me, give me palpitations, and in the midst of all this emotion I see nothing clearly; I cannot write a word, I must wait. Insensibly this great movement quiets, this chaos clears; each thing comes to put itself in its place, but slowly and after a long and confused agitation." Creation, writing, the making of meaning is torture for Rousseau because everything must come out of this primitive chaos, must be derived *ex nihilo* rather than from the conventions of rhetoric.

The world, both in its physical presence and its ethical substance, must be recreated from mind's processing of the elemental building blocks of reality. This means that for Rousseau—as for Wordsworth and for other Romantic poets—landscape must be possessible by mind, and, even more, must be morally legible. Consciousness insists that it can find in landscape the concrete figurations of a natural ethics which will serve, in Wordsworth's terms, as "The guide, the guardian of my heart and soul / Of all my moral being." Indeed, in the absence of any other system of spiritual reference—traditional religion, social convention—it is the landscape itself, subjected to the interrogations of ethical consciousness, that becomes the frame and support of man's moral being. If traditional pastoral (as elaborated in the Renaissance) used a well-established set of metaphors which implied traditional Christian valuations of its properties and settings, this new Romantic pastoral is based on new, personal metaphors through which the visionary eye creates a vast network of analogies between the order of mind and the order of things.

We can begin to grasp how Rousseau's rejection of a social ethic and a literary convention based on the sociability of the metropolis stands as the paradoxical precondition of a new attention to the reality of the city, a discovery of its meaning as landscape. As Auerbach argues, this new attention derives in part from a deflection of the attention directed to Rousseau's politicized pastoral, the anti-image which, in its very deceptions, leads to an acute awareness of the lived reality of the nonpastoral. Beyond this construction of the anti-image, there is at work the process of Rousseau's new pastoral itself, which furnishes the terms of the new awareness of the urban landscape. Rousseau's insistent need to rediscover reality and the ethical substance of life in a personal confrontation of the landscape will be determinative for later writers, for whom the eighteenth-century social convention and ethic have been rendered historically problematic by Rousseau's example, by social upheaval, and finally by revolution. The writers of the succeeding

Romantic generations would also have to rediscover reality for themselves, in a direct confrontation with things that could no longer be mediated by the assumptions and conventions of the eighteenth-century social stance. Those who had best learned the lessons of Rousseau, who had attended both to his politicized pastoral and to his rediscovery of the physical landscape and its ethical import, would have to face the implications of man within the urban landscape. While there are some early prototypes of this confrontation at the end of the eighteenth century—in the works of Restif de la Bretonne and Sébastien Mercier, for instance—it would not be elaborated until considerably later, with the rise of the first true generations of Romantic writers that come of age in the 1820's and 1830's.

A primary demand upon art in the context of nineteenth-century urbanism, then, is that it perform an urban phenomenology, that it discover the reality of its context, not in any social or psychological abstractions, but in the particularity, the hardness and "thereness" of the world, which must be looked at and touched. The artist of the modern city must, like Rousseau on the Ile de Saint-Pierre, undertake the *flora peninsularis:* he must, as a kind of urban botanist, inventory the buildings, streets, lamp posts, carriages that make up the cityscape. Rousseau's state of nakedness in the Ile de Saint-Pierre is repeated with the arrival in Paris of each Balzacian hero: consciousness must begin again from point zero in the effort to register, to describe, to come to terms with the irreducible presence, the thereness and hardness of the landscape which this time is not natural but fabricated, a "valley of plaster" as Balzac calls it on page one of *Père Goriot.* To the protagonist placed within this landscape, the way of gaining leverage on it is through possession—the effort to appropriate to the self those pieces of the milieu defined as "accessories," offering themselves to acquisition. This scenario is played out over and over again in Balzac. Among many examples, one could choose the provincial Lucien de Rubempré's first promenade in the Tuileries Garden, in *Illusions perdues,* where he contrasts his own frowzy plainness to the elegant accessories sported by the young dandies. One of them dandles an ivory cane, another a riding crop, one pulls out a fine gold watch, another plays with his gold cuff-links—and Lucien, both alienated and fascinated, discovers, in the words of the narrator, the "world of necessary superfluities," acquisition of which must be his first step toward the conquest of Paris. But this kind of possession is insufficient, both for the most significant Balzacian protagonists and, especially, for the novelist himself. He can be content with nothing less than the visionary possession of the landscape in its totality.

This is to suggest that an urban phenomenology, if primary and necessary, is never sufficient. As the process of coming to the urban landscape by way of Rousseauian pastoral should in itself indicate, the observer of the modern city cannot remain at the level of "registering" surfaces and appearances. Rather—and it is here that we most feel the continuing force of the ethical motives

behind Rousseau's pastoral—the very premise of a Balzacian or a Baudelairian cityscape is the effort to move through and beyond phenomenology to total moral significance, to a vision of the landscape as an ethical framework and context for human life. The urban landscape undergoes a process of allegorization which allows it to assume the burden of the lost and destroyed conventions: it becomes a significant intellectual and moral framework in terms of which there can be dramatization and evaluation of the important issues in man's salvation and damnation. The landscape of the city becomes a *paysage moralisé,* an anti-pastoral or urban counter-pastoral in that its elements, moralized and made significant in human terms, constitute an embracing convention like that of an earlier pastoral. The terms of reference of traditional pastoral—shepherds, flocks, flowers, mowers, gardens—constituted a complete convention which allowed a sophisticated debate on man's choices of life and moral nature. By a long detour, through the social convention of the eighteenth century, through the personal pastoral of Rousseau, we have reached something that will constitute a similarly ambitious convention. The elements of reference of the cityscape, allegorized by the play of ethical mind on the landscape, will permit the same kind of debate.

The first of Balzac's "Scènes de la Vie Parisienne," *Ferragus,* shows this process at work in its opening pages. "There are in Paris," the narrator begins, "certain streets as dishonored as a man accused of infamy; then there are noble streets, then simply honest streets, then young streets on whose morality the public hasn't yet formed an opinion; then homicidal streets, streets older than old dowagers are old, estimable streets, streets which are always clean, streets which are always dirty, working, laboring, mercantile streets. Finally, the streets of Paris have human qualities, and by their physiognomy impress on us certain ideas in spite of ourselves." From this simple, primary assignment of moral qualifications, the narrator goes on to call Paris "the most delicious of monsters," which starts a new level of allegorization. The monster is anatomized vertically and horizontally: the garrets of Paris constitute a head, for they are full of thinkers; the second storeys are happy stomachs; the ground floor shops are active feet. Its activity is incessant: scarcely have the last carriages returned from the ball in the center of Paris than arms and legs start moving on the outskirts, as the workers begin their day: the city slowly shakes itself into life, moving like the articulations of a great lobster. Each man and each house, says the narrator, is a "lobe of cellular tissue" in this creature. It is notable that this tale ends in Père Lachaise cemetery which, with its streets and different economic sectors, its varied and pretentious funerary architecture, its preserved vanities, is like a Paris seen through the wrong end of a telescope: Paris on the scale of worms, the ultimate outcome of the monster's seductions.

Balzac's descriptions of the city rehearse over and over again the processing of the urban landscape, the effort of optical vision to become moral vision, so that the cityscape may serve as the stage for moral figurations, and the melodramatic struggle of vice and virtue. As the narrator sets the stage of *Père Goriot,* he calls the degraded sector of Paris he will evoke a "frame of bronze," and compares entry into the landscape of his story to a descent into the Parisian catacombs, "as, with each step, light diminishes and the song of the guide goes hollow." In the visionary sociology which introduces *La Fille aux yeux d'or,* the Parisian landscape is more explicitly Dantesque, with its three circles of increasing misery and feverish heat, its furnaces spewing forth distorted forms of the universal desideratum, "gold and pleasure." The escutcheon of the City of Paris (in the center of which is a ship on the Seine) becomes a representation of the Ship of Fools, plunging on the seas in exorbitant movement. I won't go on citing cases; they are omnipresent, and in each of them one can see the Balzacian narrator pressuring the details of reality, the elements of the urban landscape, to make them yield their symbolic content as counters in the human melodrama. All the things of urban existence—the things that Baudelaire cites as the object of attention for the painter of modern life—are made fully significant in human terms. The effort to find something hard and solid to define man's existence by is always doubled by the effort to give the elements discovered in the phenomenology the same significant, stated meaning as the elements of a stage set in popular melodrama. The narrator goes behind visible surfaces to open up moral depths, a space where the moral imagination can find its home.

Balzac's most successful and exemplary protagonists follow an itinerary which leads them—from alienation through possession of accessory objects—to total visionary possession of the landscape in its human significance. One of the best-known instances of landscape in Balzac records the end of that itinerary, and shows the transformation of landscape into allegorical stage-setting: with the completion of his "education" in the Parisian inferno, Eugène de Rastignac stands on the heights of Père Lachaise cemetery and—after burying in the earth his "last tear" of youth—looks out from his commanding position over the panorama of the "beaux quartiers" of Paris lying sinuously along the serpentine Seine. His glance, possessing the landscape, seems to "suck the honey from this murmuring hive." The city, so hypostasized, so seized as moral antagonist, becomes the object of the famous challenge, "A nous deux maintenant!" From his initial situation of deprivation and limited vision within the walls of the "valley of plaster," Rastignac rises to this commanding height on the mountain of the dead. Hence he can see the monster, see the landscape as endowed with a moral nature, and furbish his arms.

Rastignac's personal vision of Paris here, and the operation it allows him to perform on the urban landscape, is analogous to the narrator's effort throughout the "Scènes de la Vie Parisienne." He must make his *viewing* of the landscape into *vision.* Consciousness does not rest on the surfaces of objects and constructions; it claims to penetrate to their occult moral meanings. It subjects them to a processing, which establishes their metaphoric links

to consciousness, which invests the world with the ethical significances that man needs in order to feel that his environment is neither alien nor absurd, but intimately involved in the concerns of his moral life. The Balzacian description of Paris in fact always includes two movements, which may be simultaneous: a phenomenology of the world, a registering of its elements, and a pressuring of these elements to make them yield their moralized and allegorized meanings, an interrogation of things which are seen to be both irreducible in their physical presence and the vehicle of a grandiose metaphor pointing to the human drama. The passage from phenomenology to allegory is accomplished through visionary possession of the landscape: a visual putting into perspective which allows mind to locate and articulate the meanings of landscape.

This dual movement reveals Balzac at work creating, substantially, the Romantic anti-pastoral or counter-pastoral convention which will become an accepted framework in much nineteenth-century urban fiction. The same movement is found in its most accomplished form in Baudelaire. Indeed, the process I have been attempting to describe seems the very direction and intent of Baudelaire's poetry of the city. In one of the richest poems in the group called "Tableaux Parisiens," "Le Cygne," he describes how the heavy, irreducible elements of the urban landscape—"palais neufs, échafaudages, blocs, / Vieux faubourgs"—all become what he calls "allegory." The contemplating mind accommodates the city to its interior images, makes the cityscape figure a drama of loss and exile. It is this "figuration" that Baudelaire calls "allegory": phenomena are not merely themselves, but speak of man's condition, so that the poem can end with evocation of the numberless people of "captives and the vanquished." And since with Baudelaire we have moved into the Paris of Baron Haussmann's urban renewal, there is now a subtle play between the solidity and evanescence of urban phenomena, the way in which solid material blocks can suddenly be wiped out to give way to others, with new angles and façades. The very presence of the city comes to figure absence, the destruction of what it replaces, the loss of home that it has masked with its constructions.

Baudelaire is of course recognized as the most conscious and accomplished poet of the urban. He has accepted the city as the totality of "nature," a complete fauna and flora. Because of this acceptance, and his exploitation of the city as total context of life, he has come to be regarded as having first generated the image of the city as—to use the terms of Carl Schorske—an entity "beyond Good and Evil": a multifarious environment to be savored in all its aspects, infamous as well as sublime. This is true to the extent that for Baudelaire there is no world outside the city, which contains, in intensified form, all of experience. But to call Baudelaire's Paris a space beyond good and evil seems to me somewhat to miss the point. When, in the poem that stands as epilogue to *Le Spleen de Paris,* the Baudelairian narrator describes himself as "an old débauché" seeking his old mistress, Paris, and says: "I want to inebriate myself with the old whore whose infernal charm always rejuvenates me," he isn't situating the city beyond good and evil, but rather within the field of play of hyperbolical ethical forces. He loves and desires Paris, but precisely for the corruption of its civilization, the pleasures it offers, which are not understood by the "profane and common." Like Rastiganc, this narrator has climbed to a height above Paris (on Montmartre) and put the cityscape into perspective in order to seize its ethical import. He wants the reader's ethical reaction—not, of course, a naively moralistic reaction, but one that recognizes both the presence of evil and the beauty of evil, and sees that the city, in its very configuration, determines man's moral landscape. Baudelaire is a source of the petrified artificial landscapes of the *fin de siècle* Decadents(as of the stylized urban nature of Modern Style) but he does not stand with their somewhat facile amoralism. He is rather fully within the Romantic tradition in that the city is seen—must be seen—as the place of a moral drama.

Baudelaire may, however, mark an end-term in the Romantic reaction to the city. After him, in the poetry of Symbolists and Decadents, in the novels of Zola and the Naturalists, if the city may still be symbolic, even mythic, one senses less of a need to work out the relationship of consciousness to the urban landscape, and less of an effort to make it an allegorical setting for the human drama. We do not feel there is the same need to rediscover in the city an entire convention like that of pastoral. The city becomes more purely surface and plane; there is loss of the effort to go behind and beyond surface, to excavate an ethical living space. Perhaps there is a growing resignation to a perception that the urban landscape cannot be accommodated and assimilated to consciousness. This perception is given a striking contemporary enactment in Jean-Luc Godard's film, *Two or Three Things That I Know about Her.* (The "her" is both the heroine and Paris.) At the end of the film, Marina Vlady repeats a statement she had made at the outset: "Un paysage est un visage"—"A landscape is a face." Then the camera rotates slowly through 360 degrees, recording the anonymous, alien façades of the new apartment blocks where she lives. The sequence underlines what the whole film has tended to demonstrate: the difficulty of making the modern urban landscape into a "face": the difficulty of establishing any viable relationship between consciousness and the environment it has created for itself. *paysage* refuses the status of *visage* in much of the contemporary fiction that seems to us closest to our lived experience. To claim that *paysage is visage* may be to fall into a myth of interiority, the myth of what Alain Robbe-Grillet, citing Roland Barthes, calls "the Romantic Heart of Things." Robbe-Grillet's own fictions are of course the best example of a refusal to consider *paysage* as *visage,* the insistence that the landscape is neither meaningful nor absurd, but simply "there," and must be the object of a pure phenomenology, refusing any allegorization, any metaphorical links to the human domain.

It is the premise of all Romantic literature that the world cannot be nonsignificant, that there is a heart of things,

which may be a source of happiness or unhappiness, but can never simply be disregarded. If we have become suspicious of the postulate of a Romantic Heart, we should not lose sight of the importance of the effort and the claim that underlie it. The Romantic reaction to the city implicitly claims that man cannot live without the support of the landscape within which he lives, a support which comes from making the landscape morally legible, assimilable to the drama of human ethical consciousness. That the Romantic urban writers feel the need for an urban allegory as well as a phenomenology testifies to an unwillingness to abandon the moral decipherment of the world despite the destruction of traditional humanist assumptions and conventions.

The complexity of the Romantic reaction, I have tried to suggest, may derive from the passage through Rousseau: both his politicized pastoral ideal, and his rediscovery of the presence of landscape through an essentially ethical choice. Romantic anti-pastoral or counter-pastoral—that is, Romantic urbanism—strives toward making the unnatural world as significant, for good or ill, to man's moral being as the "presences" of nature are to Rousseau or Wordsworth. The Romantic reaction to the urban always includes at least subliminal awareness of the process of Rousseauian pastoral. It is no accident that Balzac's urban criminal mastermind, Vautrin—the man who has conquered the city from its underside up, who knows all its alleyways and boulevards, all its garrets and mansions—declares himself, at the moment of his arrest by the police in *Père Goriot,* a "disciple of Rousseau" who protests against "the deceptions of the social contract." He in fact carries in his heart a pastoral wish-image: the desire to flee Paris and establish himself as a planter in Virginia, in a patriarchal rural society. It is a measure of the inescapability of the urban context that he will never be allowed to realize this dream, and will instead become, eventually, chief of the Parisian secret police. There are no more worlds elsewhere. One must hence work within the urban landscape, on it, to make it yield the terms and relations needed by the ethical sensibility. This, of course, is not Vautrin's task, but that of Balzac and the other Romantic writers of the urban.

George Witter Sherman

SOURCE: "The Wheel and the Beast: The Influence of London on Thomas Hardy," in *Nineteenth-Century Fiction,* Vol. 4, No. 3, December, 1949, pp. 209-19.

[*In the following essay, Sherman explores the impact of Thomas Hardy's experiences in London on his later fiction.*]

To Thomas Hardy the city of London was a Wheel and a Beast. "This hum of the Wheel—the roar of London!" he comments on the spectacle from the Marble Arch. Despite its deafening noise, he knew what it was composed of: "Hurry, speech, laughters, moans, cries of little children. . . . All are caged birds; the only difference lies in the size of the cage. This too is part of the tragedy." The Wheel by day became a Beast at night, "a monster whose body had four million heads and eight million eyes," which produced insomnia in him from the eerie feeling of lying down in the presence of the Four Million, whom he had once also called "four million forlorn hopes."

One does not have to unearth Hardy's reading in the classics or philosophy to discover the origin of these images. They do not come from books, but from life itself, from the ever-increasing concentration of people in cities as the result of our industrial age. Neither do they belong exclusively to Hardy nor apply to London alone. Our own Sandburg has described Chicago, "Fierce as a dog with tongue lapping for action, cruel as a savage pitted against the wilderness." Lafcadio Hearn, reporter in Cincinnati and later in New Orleans during the 'eighties, noted, " . . . even before you see the smoky coronet that surrounds the modern city, you can hear a wild growl like that of some enraged beast." Thousands of city dwellers and workers have reacted in the same way to our industrialized and urbanized society; and probably no images portray more clearly or powerfully its brutalizing and destructive force than a Wheel and a Beast.

London was the commercial capital of the world. When Hardy, a youth commencing his twenties, went up to the city in 1862, the year of the Great Exhibition, he found the London of Dickens and Thackeray undergoing tremendous expansion and transformation. Hungerford Market stood where Charing Cross station now stands. "The Tube," or Subway, was still in its infancy. There was no Thames Embankment and no bridge across Ludgate Hill, and the huge block of buildings known as the Law Courts had not yet been erected. During his next five years in London Hardy came to have a knowledge of the metropolis, Mrs. Hardy says, like a born Londoner and as only a young man can get it.

Picture the youthful Hardy boarding the omnibus at Kilburn Gate, near Westbourne Park Villas, where he lived, with the cries of the conductors, "Any more passengers for London!" ringing in his ears. Imagine him in A. W. Blomfield's architectural offices at 8 Adelphi Terrace, drawing at the easternmost window on the second floor, or idling, when work was slack, on the balcony to watch the construction of the Thames Embankment and Charing Cross Bridge. Accompany him to the illuminated parade on the eve of the Prince of Wales's approaching marriage in the spring of 1863, when six people were killed in the Mansion Crush and he narrowly escaped with his life. Witness with him in the fall and winter of 1865-66, in a Poesque atmosphere behind high hoardings and by the flare of lamps, the removal of bodies in the Old St. Pancras Churchyard to permit the extension of the Midland Railway, and one of the coffins falling apart and revealing a skeleton and two skulls. Follow him to the Willis Rooms, where he was alternately attracted to and repulsed by the aristocratic Bayswater girls, with whom he danced, because of feelings of social and economic

inferiority; and, perhaps to compensate for them, imagined the presence of "powdered Dears from Georgian Years," who had danced quadrilles and polkas there in Johnson's and Addison's time. It was a fashionable and exclusive resort, little changed, since those days when it was known as Almack's, and later as Brooks's Club, where, according to Gibbon the historian, the Goddess of Terpsichore was second only in popularity to the Goddess of Chance. Stand with Hardy on a day in 1865 in Covent Garden when he listened to John Stuart Mill speak in behalf of his candidature for Westminster, and remember that he knew Mill's essay *On Liberty* almost by heart.

These are some of the main events in Hardy's life in London between 1862 and 1867. On the whole, they were busy and prosperous years for all classes. The building trades had won a victory in 1862 after three years' agitation for the nine-hour day. The same year the Lancashire cotton mills were idle on account of the Northern blockade of the South's cotton ports, and large-scale relief had to be organized for these unemployed workers. Liberals and Radicals were active in spreading pro-Northern and antislavery sentiments to prevent England from aiding the South. In 1864 the Italian liberator Garibaldi was accorded a tremendous working-class reception. In 1865 General William Booth was taking religion into the slums of London, and in spite of the general prosperity hundreds of people were without a place to eat and sleep. There was agitation for the extension of suffrage and all kinds of reform. Karl Marx was busy in London organizing international working-men's associations. The Reform League, a militant political organization, with a membership of some 20,000, largely recruited from the trade unions throughout England, was working for amelioration.[1] The Reform League was important in Hardy's life because it was on the ground floor below Blomfield's offices, and the members of the League were well known to Blomfield's pupils, who, "as became Tory and Churchy young men, indulged in satire at the League's expense," Mrs. Hardy says, and once indeed had to apologize to its bricklayer secretary, George Howell, for their conduct. Hardy, one may be sure, did not participate in this horseplay. His sympathies were on the other side, with the working class. We have evidence of that in Andrew Macmillan's letter returning the manuscript of Hardy's legendary novel *The Poor Man and the Lady,* "by The Poor Man," which was never published and was later lost or destroyed. Macmillan wrote: "The utter heartlessness of *all* the conversation you give in drawing-rooms and ballrooms about the working-classes has some ground of truth, I fear, and might justly be scourged as you aim at doing; but your chastisement would fall harmless from its very excess." One is somewhat skeptical of Macmillan's judgment when he remembers that Lowes in the House of Commons described the working class as "impulsive, unreflecting, violent people," guilty of "venality, ignorance, drunkenness, and intimidation." Macmillan praised the scene in Rotten Row and called "Will's speech to the workingmen" in Trafalgar Square "full of wisdom." Trafalgar Square was a popular place for speeches and demonstrations, and Hardy must have listened to a few of them himself. The Reform League staged a huge meeting in the square on June 29, 1867, and afterward paraded through Pall Mall to show their hostility to the new Tory ministry. Hardy left London in July of that year, and if he did not attend the meeting he certainly would have known about it. But neither the publishers nor the Victorian reading public were ready for a "socialistic, not to say revolutionary" novel such as Hardy's was reputed to have been. George Meredith, of Chapman and Hall, to whom Hardy next submitted the manuscript, advised him, Mrs. Hardy says, "'not to nail his colours to the mast' so definitely in a first book, if he wished to do anything practical in literature." Such criticism as this made Hardy apprehensive about his future. His fear of insecurity persisted long after there was any justification for it. In his diary, November 28, 1878, he wrote: "Woke before it was light. Felt that I had not enough staying power to hold my own in the world." Hardy did not have the crusading energy to fight the Wheel and the Beast. He instinctively recoiled against the inhuman materialism and ignoble rewards of his age as he observed it in London. "If I have seen one thing," he wrote in "A Young Man's Exhortation" (1867), "it is the passing preciousness of dreams." In his decision to leave London in the summer of 1867 and return to a simpler pattern of life in Wessex, there is a strain of ivory towerism. Since corruptibility had never been compulsory, he would retreat to his native heath and let the city lie at the monster's feet.

From the title alone of *The Poor Man and the Lady,* "by The Poor Man," Arthur Quiller-Couch says we may deduce something of Hardy's indignation at the remediable ills of society. "Thin-skinned" and uncertain of the future, he put away his sword of ink and wrote, as he afterward admitted, "to keep base life afoot." Henceforth, London was not material for a novel to him, but only for novel-padding. At music halls, police courts, horse races, slums, and other places, which he visited for this express purpose, he saw plenty of evidence of the Wheel and the Beast. There are passages in his novels and in his journal which disclose his sensitivity to poverty and misery in London. "Poverty in the country is a sadness," he comments in *The Hand of Ethelberta* (1876), "but poverty in town is a horror." Again, in his journal: "Rural life may reveal coarseness of considerable leaven, but that libidinousness which makes the scum of cities so noxious is not usually present." In *Desperate Remedies* (1871), his first published novel, he describes a rickety-furnished tenement apartment with its diaper-strung kitchen, and comments on the lives of the occupants: "Only for one short hour in the whole twenty-four did husband and wife taste genuine happiness. It was in the evening after the sale of some necessary article of furniture, they were under the influence of a quartern of gin." He records in his journal the remark of a man on the street corner to him: "When one is drunk, London seems a wonderfully enjoyable place, with its lamps and cabs, moving like fire-flies." In Piccadilly at night he observes: "A man on a stretcher, with bloody bandage round his head, was wheeled past by two policemen, stragglers following." At one of the music halls, he comments on "the round-hatted young men gaping at the stage with receding chins and rudimentary mouths"; and at Bizet's opera of *Carmen* he is struck by "the possessed, maudlin, distraught manner" of the players on the stage, "as if they lived on a planet whose atmosphere was intoxicating." The animalism and brutality of Manston in *Desperate Remedies,* and the couple in *Jude,* at the office of marriage licenses—the soldier, sullen, and his bride, sad over her black eye and her pregnancy,—are products of the city jungle and contain glimmers of Dreiser's later sociological studies. There is an impressionistic description in *A Pair of Blue Eyes* (1873) of a surging, bustling crowd, mostly of women, with the glaring gas lamps from butchers' stalls discoloring their lumps of flesh. Hardy is reminded of "the wild colouring in Turner's later pictures," which alone satisfied his awareness of the tragical mysteries of life. "The purl and babble of tongues of every pitch and mood," he writes, "was to the human wildwood what the ripple of a brook is to the natural forest." It is an urban voice, "Heart-halt and spirit lame," that seeks refuge from the city's oppression in the little poem "In a Wood," only to find in the forest the same combat as among men. It is interesting that Hardy, who was one of the first acclaimers of Darwin's *Origin of Species* (1859) should see the struggle for existence in uncultivated nature in terms of the competitive struggle in the city. In *The Hand of Ethelberta* and *Jude the Obscure,* however, he comments with ironic humor on the subdivision of labor in the city; and in *A Pair of Blue Eyes* he attributes the difference between the rural mechanic and the typical workingman to "that beach pebble attrition . . . which metamorphoses the unit Self into a fraction of the Unit Class." Not knowing Marx, Hardy was led by his observations of the distressing phenomena in London, as probably any young man would have been who had been kept regularly at church till he knew the morning and evening service by heart, into philosophical reflections about God and man. When Hardy saw "patient hundreds labouring on," a drunken or disorderly person with a bandaged head, men and women jammed into omnibuses, or charcoal trees in the square, he was moved to reflect: "Yes, man has done more with his materials than God has done with his." He began to wonder whether "the human race is too extremely developed for its corporeal conditions," and whether "Nature . . . so far back as when she crossed the line from invertebrates to vertebrates did not exceed her mission." Unable to get over the hurdle between reality and illusion, he tried to solve the contradiction in the existence of good and evil by stretching Darwin's hypothesis over the gigantic force which was slower to develop consciousness and morality than man.

Some of these philosophical reflections from London life, Hardy used in *Jude the Obscure* (1896) in the "vague and quaint imaginings" of Sue, "that at the framing of terrestrial conditions there seemed never to have been contemplated such a development of emotional perceptiveness among the creatures subject to those conditions as that reached by thinking and educated humanity," for instance, and "that the First Cause worked automatically like a somnambulist and not reflectively like a sage." Before Hardy wrote *Jude,* he was beginning to regard people in drawing rooms, art salons, on street corners, wherever he observed them in London, as automatons and somnambulists. When viewing the pictures at the Academy in May, 1890, he recollected the time "when there was a rail round Frith's pictures, and of the curious effect upon an observer of the fashionable crowd seeming like people moving about under enchantment, or as somnambulists." In the Grand Gallery of the Louvre, in Part II of *The Dynasts,* the Spirit of the Years comments to the Spirit of the Pities on Marie Louise's marriage to Napoleon: "Yet see it pass, as by a conjuror's wand." One never encounters in Hardy's writings comparisons of Wessex people to automatons or somnambulists.

The somnambulistic behavior of urban people was even more apparent to Hardy in the London of the Boer War. In the poem "Embarcation" depicting a scene on the Southampton docks in October, 1899, he writes: "Wives, sisters, parents, wave white hands and smile, / As if they knew not that they weep the while." The companion poem "Departure" contains two lines which read like a summary of *The Dynasts* in one sentence: "Must your wroth reasonings trade on lives like these, / That are as puppets in a playing hand?—" Some old notes written before he began working on *The Dynasts* indicate the military trend of his imagination: "Army as somnambulists.—not knowing what it is for." "London appears not to *see itself,*" he writes in his journal, March 28, 1888. "Each individual is conscious of *himself,* but nobody conscious of themselves collectively, except perhaps some poor gaper who stares round with half-idiotic aspect. There is no consciousness here," he adds, "of where anything comes from or goes to,—only that it is present." Hardy borrowed the term "Immanent Will" from Schopenhauer, it is true, but these traits which he ascribes to it, he observed on the stream of humanity in London long before he was acquainted with German philosophy. His description of the crowd in the Strand on the periphery of Manston's vision in *Desperate Remedies* (1871) precludes the influence of either Schopenhauer or von Hartmann, for *The World as Will and Idea* was not translated into English until 1883, and *The Philosophy of the Unconscious* not until 1884. Hardy sees

> . . . tall men looking insignificant; little men looking great and profound; lost women of miserable repute looking as happy as the days are long; wives happy by assumption looking careworn and miserable. Each and all were alike in this one respect, that they followed a solitary trail like the inwoven threads which form a banner, and all were equally unconscious of the significant whole they collectively showed forth.

Furthermore, the distinguishing trait of the Will, "groping tentativeness," seems to have risen out of the general experience of living and more particularly out of the discovery that the world is different from what he thought it was or wished it to be. At the age of forty-one: "Since I discovered several years ago, that I was living in a world where nothing bears out in practice what it promises incipiently, I have troubled myself very little about theories . . . where development according to perfect reason is limited to the narrow field of pure mathematics, I am content with *tentativeness* from day to day." Was he thinking possibly of his disappointments and frustration as a youth in London?

These urban human traits, his brooding imagination magnified to the dimension of the "unconscious, unweeting mind" of *The Dynasts,* just as he extended the wheel-like pattern of Piccadilly to cosmic proportions as the abode of "Man's counterfeit / That turns in some far sphere unlit / The Wheel which drives the Infinite."

Hardy employs the Beast image in *The Dynasts,* as well as the Wheel. The Beast seems to have become more graphic to him in the fall of 1879, when he and his wife viewed the Lord Mayor's show from the upstairs office of *Good Words,* a periodical published in Ludgate Hill. To Mrs. Hardy, who had never seen the spectacle before, the surface of the crowd seemed like "a boiling cauldron of porridge," but to Hardy it was the Beast which caused his insomnia:

> As the crowd grows denser it loses its character of an aggregate of countless units, and becomes an organic whole, a molluscous black creature having nothing in common with humanity, that takes the shape of the streets along which it has lain itself, and throws out horrid excrescences and limbs into neighbouring alleys; a creature whose voice exudes from its scaly coat, and who has an eye in every pore of its body. The balconies, stands, and railway bridge are occupied by smaller detached shapes of the same tissue, but of gentler motion, as if they were the spawn of the monster in their midst.

"The very turmoil of the streets has something repulsive," wrote Frederick Engels in *The Condition of the Working Class in England in 1844,* "something against which human nature rebels." Hardy's aerial view of the movements of London traffic bears a resemblance to the description of the Russian army whose "undulating columns twinkle as if they were scaly serpents" invading France; and also to the Allied armies, which "glide on as if by gravitation, in fluid figures, dictated by the conformation of the country, like water from a burst reservoir; mostly snake-shaped, but occasionally with batrachian and saurian outlines." One can see how much the view of the Lord Mayor's show from Ludgate Hill in 1879 contributed to the perspective and the images by which Hardy depicts military movements in Part III of *The Dynasts* in 1908. The monster glimpsed by the Spirit of the Pities following the battle of Ligny is recognizable by the Spirit of the Years as Devastation:

> . . . loosely jointed,
> With an Apocalyptic Being's shape,
> And limbs and eyes a hundred thousand strong,
> And fifty-thousand heads; which coils itself
> About the buildings there.

Hardy's harrowing experience in the Mansion Crush in 1863 may partly account for the origin of the Beast metaphor. It should not be forgotten that Hardy was a sensitive and immature youth who had scarcely been away from home before, and furthermore that he had been made apprehensive about the city and his chances of securing employment on his arrival there. If Wordsworth could write about feeling "in heart and soul the shock of the huge town's first presence," as he "paced her streets, a transient visitant," how much more powerful an impression must have been produced on Hardy by an experience as terrifying as his. It is very possible that the shock from it remained deep in Hardy's subconscious and increased his feeling of sensitivity to one of hypersensitivity. If one accepts this experience as the source of the Beast image, the less terrifying aspect of the monster Devastation in *The Dynasts* is readily explained by the interval of time in which the effect of the shock was diminished. Wordsworth's definition of poetry as "emotion recollected in tranquillity" has a peculiar application in Hardy's case. We know something of the working of Hardy's mind from his account of the poem "In Time of the Breaking of Nations." This poem, he tells us, was engendered by an emotion felt while he was observing an agricultural scene in Cornwall at the time of the Franco-Prussian War, but it was not written till 1915. Hardy says of himself, "I believe it would be said by people who knew me well that I have a faculty (possibly not uncommon) for burying an emotion in my heart or brain for forty years, and exhuming it at the end of that time as fresh as when interred." One would not wish either to exaggerate or to minimize the influence of the Mansion Crush on Hardy. Possibly he was not entirely aware of its influence himself, but his suffering from insomnia in the city lends some support to the theory.

In one respect these images of London as a Wheel and a Beast never seem to have emerged wholly from Hardy's subconscious. Consider the explicit significance that such a writer as George Gissing has given *The Whirlpool* or as Frank Norris *The Octopus*. Hardy might have realized his images of the Wheel and the Beast if he had not consented to the abortion of *The Poor Man and the Lady* "by The Poor Man"; but after he came to regard London life as a source for novel-padding instead of a thesis, there was little hope for his emancipation. If he had lived in the "Great Wen" of Cobbett's time and thrown his energies into working for the Reform Bill, or even if he had remained in the London of his own time and fought against some of the remediable ills at which he felt indignant instead of retreating to Wessex, his Wheel and Beast images might have become potent symbols of reality instead of philosophical masks for his reluctant atheism.

NOTES

[1] There is a reference to the Reform League in Marx's letter (January 15, 1866) to Dr. Kugelmann, when during the middle 'sixties political activities of the working classes took on for a while an international aspect. Marx writes: "We have succeeded in drawing into the movement the one really big workers' organization, the English Trades Unions, which formerly concerned themselves *exclusively* with wage questions. With their help the English Society (The Reform League) which we founded for achieving universal suffrage (half of its central committee consists of members—workers—of our Central Committee) held a monster meeting a few weeks ago, at which only workers spoke. You can judge of the effect by the fact that the *Times* dealt with the meeting in leading articles in two consecutive issues."—*Letters to Dr. Kugelmann* (New York: International Publishers, 1934), p. 33.

Constance Urdang

SOURCE: "Faust in Venice: The Artist and the Legend in *Death in Venice*," in *Accent: A Quarterly of New Literature*, Vol. XVIII, No. 4, Autumn, 1958, pp. 253-67.

[*In the following excerpt, Urdang discusses setting in Thomas Mann's* Death in Venice.]

> Every piece of work is in fact a realization—piecemeal if you like, but each complete in itself—of our own nature; they are stones on that harsh road which we must walk to learn of ourselves.
>
> —Mann

> . . . who would taste
> The medicine of immortality,
> And who would "be as God"?
> And in what way?
>
> —Shapiro

In his introduction to the American edition of the *Stories of Three Decades*, Thomas Mann says, about a group of early stories, that they "wear the impress of much melancholy and ironic reflection on the subject of art and the artist: his isolation and equivocal position in the world of reality, considered socially and metaphysically and as the result of his double bond with nature and spirit." The youthful melancholy may have lessened with the years, but the theme of the place of the artist in the world continued to occupy Mann's attention. All the artist-figures in his works share certain characteristics not shared by the non-artists—although they too, by reason of their very humanity, have the "double bond with nature and spirit."

Perhaps the most important characteristic of Mann's artist is his isolation, whether subjective (as in the case of Tonio Kröger) or objective (like Leverkühn's, expressed in the social isolation that results from his contraction of syphilis, the physical isolation of the house in the country to which he retires, the psychological isolation of his madness). Mann would certainly have agreed that isolation is not the peculiar prerogative of the artist—that it is one of the inescapable concomitants of the human condition. Nevertheless, essentially the artist remains for him the exile, the outsider, the stranger to normal, conventional human activity. The artist can observe life and the world of reality, can interpret it, can even understand it; but he cannot participate in it. If he does, disaster follows (Cipolla is shot for having thus misused his art, von Aschenbach dies of cholera because he has permitted himself to get involved in life, Leverkühn's attempts at human relationships are aborted by the deaths of those he loves).

These artists are all, in this sense, "marked men," whether or not the sign or stigma of their differentness is generally visible (interestingly, it is the artist manqué, the dilettante who shares some—but not all—of the characteristics of the truly creative artist-figure, who is most often physically marked; Herr Friedemann is a hunchback, Klaus Heinrich has a club foot).

Some further characteristics of Mann's artists, as at least one critic has pointed out, are their unusual sensitivity (producing that heightened perception necessary for the production of a work of art), their lack of adaptability (another aspect of the inability to conform to external values), and their general uselessness and incompetence in dealing with practical life (an ineffectuality sometimes even carried over into the sphere of their art: Spinell, in *Tristan,* is ineffectual in his role as artist as well as in his role as man).

Mann always sees the artist in his relation to the bourgeois. Sometimes, as in *Dr. Faustus,* the two are represented by separate characters (Leverkühn, artist; Zeitblom, bourgeois); more often, both aspects are contained within a single character. Tonio Kröger is the son of a respectable German consul father and a fiery, musical Italian mother; even Hans Castorp, in whom the bourgeois element is by far the stronger, had painted some pictures that were not without artistic merit; and von Aschenbach's ancestors "had all been officers, judges, departmental functionaries"—and northerners—except for his maternal grandfather, "a Bohemian musical conductor," and a southerner, for Mann frequently identifies the north with the bourgeois and the south with the artist (Kröger's father, too, was northern, his "artistic" mother southern). It is an awareness of the conflict that results from the presence of these two opposing forces (the one representing the bond with the world of reality, with nature; the other representing the bond with the spirit) within himself that tortures the artist and that has produced him. He both wants and does not want to share in the life that he recognizes as "the world of reality"; he both wants and does not want to rid himself of the sign or stigma of his isolation; but he can no more avoid his destiny than a giraffe can decide to become a horse and proceed to do so.

There is one quality above all that isolates Mann's artists from their fellow-men. It is a truism to apply to the artist the phrase "divine discontent," but perhaps it is as good a phrase as any to describe the impulse that urges him to persist—and the better because it can be used to

characterize as well the legendary Faust. For Mann's artist, like the Faust-figure, is driven—by something in himself that he does not understand—to seek knowledge beyond the humanly knowable. More than that; since in his relation to his work the artist is omnipotent, in his role as creator he becomes a true usurper of superhuman powers. For the sixteenth and seventeenth centuries that force which drove the symbolic Faust to estrange himself from both man and God would be explained only in terms of a literal pact with the devil. For later writers the devil had become a metaphor, the inferno raged within the mind; but the evil was no less real, and the imagery persisted. Particularly writers of the Romantic school recognized the existence of evil and made it concrete; the forces of darkness are never far from their dark landscapes, filled with gloomy castles, deserted roads, sinister forests, threatening storms, vampires, werewolves, satanic heroes and helpless heroines. Here nighttime, illness and sin form an unholy alliance. The discovery and exploitation of the Unconscious confirmed what these writers already knew. The old metaphors had not been wrong. The devil was real, and was still at work, although the language used to describe him had shifted from that of theology to that of psychiatry.

Several critics have pointed out Mann's indebtedness to the ideas of German Romanticism. They find evidence of this debt in his conception of genius as disease; in one of his persistent prejudices, that illness is more interesting and deeper than health; in his fascination with decadence and death; in his notion of the close relationship between pleasure and pain, between beauty and death; in his emphasis on the connection between the unnatural, unclean, sick, death-bound, sinful and diabolical, and the artist. His use of these ideas, Romantic as it was in essence, was not naive. His purpose, more than anything else, was to show that particularly for the artist it is necessary not only to recognize the existence of evil, but to seek it out and embrace it. To understand this process as one of "succumbing" to the fascination of death and disease (or, if you like, sin), is to misunderstand it; for there is nothing passive about it. The artist-heroes, like Baudelaire and the Decadents, must actively pursue evil. Like Faust, they must invite the devil.

Unlike more mystical writers, Mann does not claim either sainthood or salvation for these sinners. Their reward, if it is one, is the creation of works of art—and that very creation is at the same time the deepest manifestation of their sin, for the power to create is a prerogative of the divine, and not the human, and they have usurped that power. It is for this reason that, like Faust, Mann's creative artists must be punished. Tonio Kröger must watch life dancing past from behind the glass door; Cipolla must be shot; Aschenbach must die of cholera; Leverkühn must go mad, because each of them has signed his pact with the devil.

While it was not until *Dr. Faustus* (1947) that the devil appeared in his own person in Mann's books, we are told that he planned a Faust book as early as 1901, and hints of the Faustian story may be found again and again in earlier works. *The Magic Mountain,* with its many discussions of evil, its equating of sin with sickness and death, its frequent use of the trappings of mediaeval magic, its Walpurgisnacht—and its eventual ironic salvation of the hero (who, after all, was not an artist), which makes this work a comedy, rather than a tragedy[1]—is one of these. And *The Magic Mountain* was originally conceived as a "comic counterpart" to *Death in Venice.*

At first glance, the two works are entirely dissimilar. One is a novel in many "books"; the other is most often considered a "long short story." The hero of one is a young bourgeois; that of the other, an aging artist. The action of one covers many years; that of the other, a few weeks. One appears to be a novel of ideas, in which the youthful protagonist passes, picaresque-fashion, through a series of intellectual or ideological adventures; the other seems like a study of the disintegration of a man. And yet Mann must have felt that, seminally at least, some underlying theme or idea linked the two works. It may be that the overtones of the Faust legend which appear in *The Magic Mountain* can provide a thread leading to the untangling of that theme.

Since his earliest appearance in the sixteenth century the figure of Faust, representing the darkly questioning mind, the eternally unsatisfied spirit, the incurable thirst for knowledge which drives its victims to transgress human limitations, has engaged the thoughts and the imaginations of men. Based on the far older and virtually universal tradition of the magus, the god-priest-king of myth and the ancient world, with the coming of Christianity the central figure of the legend had become a sorcerer whose superhuman aspirations were implemented by the use of magic, the black art, and who, for his forbidden tampering with the forces of darkness, was condemned by orthodoxy to eternal damnation. Magus or magician, he owed his perennial existence to the fact that the problems and dilemmas made concrete in his story are those fundamental moral and philosophical questions which have been presented and represented throughout history: the relationship between man and the powers of good and evil; man's revolt against human limitations; the desire for knowledge beyond mere information; and the disparity between the sublimity and misery of human life.

The Faust-figure has stood for different things to different periods of history. To the viewers of the first Faust dramas and puppet-plays, derived from traditional retellings of the legend, his punishment was a warning against inordinate ambition, speculation about the unknowable, and any kind of league with evil spirits. In Marlowe's tragedy he had become the protagonist of an action which concentrated, intensified, and symbolized the doom brooding over the entire Christian world—for his sin, committed in time, was punished in eternity. For Goethe he became a symbol of the absolute incorruptibility of man, who can spend a lifetime sinning but will not finally be false to the divinity within himself. Essentially, however, Faust, whose sin consists in his

"divine discontent"—in wanting knowledge that transcends what can be humanly known—that is, in wanting for himself those qualities and powers reserved for the deity—is a special kind of sinner. He is one who has deliberately chosen evil, fully aware of the price he will have to pay. It was this sinner who caught the imagination and interest of the writers of *Sturm und Drang* and, later, the Romantics. Like Milton's Lucifer, the "sublime criminal" of Schiller's *Räuber,* the satanic heroes of the Gothic romances, and the "fatal men" of Byron, Faust, by reason of his "tragic stain," has taken the desperate, irremediable, fatal false step, and has chosen sin and darkness.

At first glance, Gustave von Aschenbach, the protagonist of *Death in Venice,* would seem to be the antithesis of the Faust-figure and of the artist as Mann usually sees him. He is a successful, middle-aged man, wealthy enough to own a house in the mountains as well as a town house in Munich, and to travel as he pleases; although his wife is dead, his marriage had been happy, and his married daughter is not a source of anxiety to him; fame had come to him early, and he was admired by both the general public and the connoisseur; although his best work is behind him, he is still "busy with the tasks imposed upon him by his own ego and the European soul," and he wants to live to a good old age. He is consciously a Classicist, an anti-Romantic. His achievement is the product of the "union of dry, conscientious officialdom and ardent, obscure impulse" personified in his parents; his favorite motto is *"Durchhalten!"*; the classic austerity of his style has disciplined every aspect of his life, and he is linked with a series of ascetics: Frederick the Great, Savonarola, St. Sebastian. And that is not all. His rejection of Romanticism, of "bohemianism and all its works," is entirely conscious. As a youth "he had done homage to intellect . . . had turned his back on the 'mysteries' . . ."; as a mature man, he "turned his back on the realm of knowledge." Further, we are told that "The Abject," his most famous story, "rejects the rejected, casts out the outcast. . . . Explicitly he renounces sympathy with the abyss, explicitly he refutes the flabby humanitarianism of the phrase, *'Tout comprendre c'est tout pardonner.'"* This series of rejections from which Aschenbach's life and art have sprung would seem to represent the opposite of that acceptance which is generally characteristic of Mann's artists. It is as if we are being presented with an artist who is truly superhuman—who by virtue of discipline and "austerity" and the Classic ideal has succeeded in evading the curse of his destiny, in avoiding the abyss, and in escaping the eternal damnation which is Faust's. But the story is not yet finished.

The first section concerns Aschenbach's walk in Munich, a walk which starts out prosaically enough but finishes with undertones of the dreamlike, the mysterious, the fantastic, even the sinister. He first observes the stonemason's yard, which forms a "supernumerary and untenanted graveyard opposite the real one," and then his attention is drawn to the figure of a man with a "pilgrim air" who stands on the portico of the mortuary chapel.

Thus the stranger's connection with death is obvious from the beginning. He is described in negative terms, as "not Bavarian" (as the painted old man on the steamship is "no youth at all," as the gondolier is of "non-Italian stock," as the street-musician is "scarcely a Venetian type"); he has that reddish hair associated in the German tradition with sinister figures (the hair of the painted old man is dyed brown, so we do not know its original color; the gondolier has a blond moustache; the street musician has "a great mop of red hair"); he has "long, white, glistening teeth laid bare to the gums" (the gondolier's efforts "bared his white teeth to the gums," the street-musician is described as "showing his strong white teeth in a servile smile"). Aschenbach does not know whether seeing the stranger produces in him the unrest which he immediately feels, but a longing to travel suddenly comes on him like "a seizure, almost a hallucination," and he has a vision of the jungle:

> a landscape, a tropical marshland, beneath a reeking sky, steaming, monstrous, rank—a kind of primeval wilderness-world of islands, morasses, and alluvial channels. Hairy palm-trunks rose near and far out of lush brakes of fern, out of bottoms of crass vegetation, fat, swollen, thick with incredible bloom. There were trees, mis-shapen as a dream, that dropped their naked roots straight through the air into the ground or into water that was stagnant and shadowy and glassy-green, where mammoth milk-white blossoms floated, and strange high-shouldered birds with curious bills stood gazing sidewise without sound or stir. Among the knotted joints of a bamboo thicket the eyes of a crouching tiger gleamed . . .

For an unaccountable reason, this vision inspires in him "a longing inexplicable," and while he is not so irrational as to contemplate a journey to the tigers, he decides almost at once to give up his quiet summer in the mountains and to travel to the south (invariably, for Mann, the source of art). When, safe in the tram, he thinks again of the man on the portico, the stranger has disappeared; "his whereabouts remained a mystery."

This early episode, then, foreshadows much of what is to come. Vernon Venable has interpreted the story as one in which,

> the treble is the simple narrative sequence of Aschenbach's voyage, his life on the Lido, his love for the boy Tadzio, and his death. The ground bass is the "life and death" theme, repeated as a sort of undertone to the story by those characters who seem to have no very obvious connection with the narrative content.[2]

He quite rightly points out that a clue to Mann's technique lies in the dualism or polarity which always characterizes his subject-matter; that the themes of his novels are generally constituted by such large antitheses as life-death, fertility-decay, flesh-spirit; that he "never prefers one term of his antithesis to the other, for his interest is not in arguing theses but in developing themes"; finally, that his irony is so deep-seated that even individual

symbols are ambiguous, and the jungle, for example, which represents life at its most lush, is seen also as the breeding-place of the plague. These general statements cannot be denied, but it would seem that in *Death in Venice* the life-death antithesis, which does pervade the story, is used not primarily for its own sake, but as a metaphor in the presentation of the true theme, that of the impossibility, for the artist, of avoiding his destiny, as Faust could not avoid his. The mysterious stranger, then, signifies life (as opposed to the cemetery, the crosses and monuments in the stone-mason's yard, and the mortuary); the vision of the jungle, seen by Aschenbach now as lush, rank fertility, is here opposed to his musings on the mystical meanings of the scriptural texts; Aschenbach's fear and his desire are opposed—three oppositions which do fall roughly into the three realms of physical things, of ideas, and of emotions, as Venable suggests; but there is more to it than that. The stranger, who reappears in various guises throughout the story, is not simply a symbolic human figure who happens to be there and unwittingly acts as a catalyst for Aschenbach's decisions (although, if we choose to take the entire story in its psychological interpretation only, we could say that none of the characters outside of Aschenbach himself has any "real" existence, beyond that which he gives them in his mind—just as we cannot know whether the devil did actually appear to Leverkühn or whether that scene was the product of a mind already diseased). He is the figure of the tempter who can assume any shape he pleases, and if we do not recognize him yet, we need only wait until he appears as the gondolier, an "obstinate, uncanny man," who says, "The signore will pay," and then vanishes before he has received any money; or as the street-musician, that suspicious figure that "seemed to carry with it its own suspicious odor" (carbolic, in terms of the naturalistic detail). The jungle, too, may be seen as standing for more than simply "life" or "death"; although Aschenbach is first drawn toward it as the one and is eventually destroyed by it as the other, at bottom it represents the "mysteries," the forces of darkness, the Romantic abyss which Aschenbach has successfully avoided throughout his life.

The second section of the story concerns Aschenbach's past life and discusses his works; it does not advance the narrative in any way. Here too, however, are disquieting hints of the inevitable ending. The classic austerity, the moral fibre of the man and the artist, which is the surviving principle around which he has built his life and his art after rejecting both knowledge and the "mysteries," is itself called into question:

> And yet: this moral fibre, surviving the hampering and disintegrating effect of knowledge, does it not result in its turn in a dangerous simplification, in a tendency to equate the world and the human soul, and thus to strengthen the hold of the evil, the forbidden, and the ethically impossible? Is it not moral and immoral at once . . . ?

In this section we learn that we know more about Aschenbach than he himself does. As he sees himself, by denying the existence of evil, renouncing sympathy with the abyss, he has escaped the destiny of the artist. But what he has attempted to deny, in refusing to acknowledge his guilt and attempting to escape the punishment of Faust, is his own humanity. "Development is destiny," Mann tells us, and there is no escaping it.

In the third section we travel with Aschenbach to Venice. He is going to meet his fate, but he does not go directly. First he tries an island in the Adriatic: "A blunder." Even after he has arrived on the Lido reality becomes dreamlike and distorted: "this right-about of his luggage sends him back, as if accidentally. But as soon as he sets foot on the steamer that is to take him to Venice, "reality" begins to fade—as it did when he first saw the mysterious stranger. The sailor who escorts him belowdecks is hunchbacked; the ticket-seller has "a beard like a goat's," he gives Aschenbach an "odd impression," he looks like a circus-director, is glib like a croupier, his bow is melodramatic. On the deck Aschenbach encounters the old fop from Pola, a caricature of what he himself is to become.

> He felt . . . as though the world were suffering a dreamlike distortion of perspective. . . . Strange figures passed and repassed—the elderly coxcomb, the goat-bearded man . . . there came over him a dazed sense, as though things about him were just slightly losing their ordinary perspective, beginning to show a distortion that might merge into the grotesque.

The sight of Venice at first dispels his morbid feelings, but it is followed immediately by the episode with the gondolier, a figure Aschenbach recognizes as somehow uncanny and threatening. "The signore will pay," says this sinister figure, and in his own mind Aschenbach identifies him with Charon, after a passage in which the Venetian gondola is compared to the black coffin and the bier.

The next significant episode is his first sight of the boy Tadzio, here already seen in terms of Greek sculpture, of Phaeax and Eros, accompanied by his sisters with their vacant, nunlike expressions and dresses of cloisterlike plainness. Aschenbach is at once conscious of his own grey hair, and makes the Romantic connection between beauty and death (which has already been foreshadowed by the description of Venice, followed by the gondola incident):

> "He is delicate, he is sickly," Aschenbach thought. "He will most likely not live to grow old." He did not try to account for the pleasure the idea gave him.

The final episode in this section is Aschenbach's abortive departure from a Venice which has somehow become a challenge to him.

> The hardest part . . . was the thought that he should never more see Venice again . . . he must henceforth regard it as a forbidden spot, to be forever shunned; senseless to try it again, after he had proved himself unfit.

The city has become a forbidden spot, not, he recognizes, because of anything intrinsic to itself, but because of some failure on his own part. But of course he does not leave. Again on his return to the Lido reality becomes dreamlike and distorted: "this right-about-face of destiny—incredible, humiliating, whimsical as any dream!" By the end of the episode he has come to a partial realization of his true motives in returning:

> he . . . sat hiding the panic and thrills of a truant schoolboy beneath a mask of forced resignation. . . . He felt rejoiced to be back, yet displeased with his vacillating moods, his ignorance of his real desires.

When he sees Tadzio again, "the casual greeting died away before it reached his lips, slain by the truth in his heart," and he makes a "gesture of welcome, a calm and deliberate acceptance of what might come."

In the fourth section, as in the second, little "happens" in a narrative, or dramatic, sense. Aschenbach sees Tadzio daily. Athens, Socrates, Phaedrus are key names. All the imagery is expressed in terms of Classic myth; but the cold clarity of the disciplined, austerely Classical—which Aschenbach has always opposed to the mysteries of the Romantic abyss—has become distorted. The clean, sharp outlines are blurred by a sensual, even a specifically sexual, grossness, and it is this very distortion which now draws Aschenbach. The sun is a naked god with cheeks aflame. There are references to Elysium; Oceanus; Achelous and the nymphs; Semele and Zeus; Eros; the Trojan shepherd borne aloft by an eagle; Eos; "the goddess, ravisher of youth, who stole away Cleitos and Cephalos and, defying all the envious Olympians, tasted beautiful Orion's love"; Poseidon's horses; Hyacinthus, doomed to die because two gods were rivals for his love; Zephyr; Narcissus—in the grip of his hopeless passion Aschenbach sees "a world possessed, peopled by Pan." It is a world soon to be possessed by panic.

The fifth, and longest, and last section deals with the coming of the plague to Venice, and with Aschenbach's final recognition of the relation between the cholera—with the vice and lawlessness that accompany it—and his own illicit passion; with his further recognition of the relation between beauty and death, here virtually identified; and with his perception of the connection between art and the abyss—with his final understanding of the nature of his guilt—of the Faustian role of the artist—and of his own destiny. It embodies a rejection, on Mann's part, of the Classic view of the artist, and an acceptance of the Romantic view.

The section opens with Aschenbach's earliest intimation of something gone wrong in the life of the Lido. The hotel barber is the first to mention "the sickness" to him and that afternoon, on his trip into Venice (now become an infernal region), he notices the "sweetish, medicinal smell, associated with wounds and disease," and makes the further connection between disease and the sinful, or diabolical:

> Passion is like crime . . . it welcomes every blow
> dealt the bourgeois structure, every weakening of
> the social fabric. . . . These things that were going
> on in the unclean alleys of Venice. . . gave Aschenbach
> a dark satisfaction. The city's evil secret mingled
> with the one in the depths of his heart . . .

Next come the street-musicians, among whom reappears
the sinister stranger, not a Venetian, with his mop of red
hair, his suspicious odor, his mocking laugh. But
Aschenbach, drinking pomegranate juice (another reminder of the dreamlike, the unreal, the subterranean) on
the hotel terrace, cannot elicit a direct statement from the
man on the subject that is troubling him. It is not until the
next day that the British travel agent enlightens him,
describing the source of the cholera in virtually the same
words that were used to describe Aschenbach's vision of
the jungle, showing that he had travelled farther than he
had intended in response to the "pilgrim air" of the now
nearly-forgotten stranger in Munich:

> Its source was the hot, moist swamps of the delta
> of the Ganges, where it bred in the mephitic air of
> that primeval island-jungle, among whose bamboo
> thickets the tiger crouches, where life of every sort
> flourishes in rankest abundance . . .

Aschenbach knows that he should leave, but he is kept
in Venice by the deeper knowledge that the guilty secret
of the city is less frightful than his own.

> His art, his moral sense, what were they in the
> balance beside the boons that chaos might confer?

That night he has a real Walpurgisnacht of a dream. "The
beginning was fear; fear and desire, with a shuddering
curiosity . . ." at the end, "in his very soul he tasted the
bestial degradation of his fall." When he awakes, panic is
in the air. But in the city of death and fear Tadzio, the
beautiful beloved, remains, and Aschenbach

> would follow him through the city's narrow streets
> where horrid death stalked too, and at such times
> it seemed to him as though the moral law were
> fallen in ruins and only the most monstrous and
> perverse held out a hope . . .

. . . strange thoughts for a man thought of by his contemporaries as the conqueror of decadence; but by this
time he has become its victim.

There is not much more he must do to demonstrate his
complete surrender to the forces of darkness that now
surround him, made visible in the ravages of the cholera, in the increase on the streets of Venice of intem-
perance, indecency, and crime. His disgust at the contrast between his own aging body and grey hair, and
the ideal youthful beauty he sees in the boy Tadzio
blinds him to the perversity of the impulse that leads
him to dye his hair and paint his face in hideous emula-
tion of the young-old man he had encountered on the
steamer. He gets lost in the maze of streets, and sinks
down, already stricken, although he does not realize it,

with the preliminary symptoms of the cholera, on the
steps of a well:

> There he sat, the master . . . who had . . . in a style
> of classic purity renounced bohemianism and all
> its works, all sympathy with the abyss and the
> troubled depths of the outcast human soul . . .

The irony is obvious. But it is an irony deeper than at
first appears, for this is not merely a depiction of the
personal degradation and downfall of an individual artist.
It is the picture of Faust on the midnight of his last day,
with nothing to do but wait until the devil comes to claim
him for eternal damnation; it is the picture of the artist-
figure who recurs again and again in Mann's work, here
seen at the point at which he must pay his debt to the
dark forces through which his art came into being. Now
that the end is in sight, Aschenbach realizes what Mann
has known all along:

> What good can the artist be as a teacher, when
> from his birth up he is headed direct for the pit?
> For knowledge . . . is all-knowing, understanding,
> forgiving; it takes up no position, sets no store
> by form. It has compassion with the abyss—it *is*
> the abyss . . .

He realizes that he has not escaped, that he cannot escape the artist's destiny—which is that of the damned
Faust. Beauty, simplicity, detachment, form—all the virtues of art—lead to the bottomless pit:

> Yes, they lead us thither, I say, us who are poets—
> who by our nature are prone not to excellence but
> to excess.

The final paragraph of the story is devoted to his death,
and here the final Romantic equation is made, for death
itself appears to him as the "pale and lovely summoner,"
in the image of his beautiful beloved.

What is Mann "saying," then, in *Death in Venice*?
What is it all "about"? More than anything else, it is
about the nature and destiny of the artist. As Henry
Hatfield has noted,

> The novella is . . . an expression of a gnawing
> anxiety about the cost in human terms, of playing
> the role of the "hero of creative work."[3]

Told in Romantic terms, in terms of the life-death antithesis and the Romantic beauty-death synthesis, it is a
demonstration of the thesis that

> true art can come only from a perception of all sides
> of life, and that the sick, the unclean, the unnatural,
> death itself, must be studied and understood.

More than that, it shows that, for the artist, cursed as
Faust was cursed, by his artist-nature, it is necessary
actively to seek out and embrace evil; and that there is
no escape from the inevitable punishment which must
follow on his guilt. That guilt consists, essentially, not in

committing any particular sin, but in being an artist, a creator, in reaching out beyond the humanly knowable and taking on himself the burden of superhuman power. This is the Romantic view of the artist as creator, rather than imitator. It is Faust's guilt. Throughout his long and successful life Aschenbach thought he had avoided that destiny, only to find at the end that it cannot be avoided. He renounced knowledge, bohemianism, "the abyss," in favor of discipline, classicism, and austerity—only to find that these are nothing more than the other side of the same coin. By choosing to be an artist he had sealed his pact with the devil, and now at the end of his life, after a period of more than twenty-four years' creativeness, the devil has collected his price.

The story is far from a literal transposition—a parody, in Mann's sense—of the Faust legend, as *Dr. Faustus* frankly is. In terms of time, it deals only with the culminating moment of the Faust legend. Aside from the dream Walpurgisnacht there is no overt reference to the legend's narrative; it is all implied. But many other less overt references to the Faust story remain: the mysterious stranger, always "uncanny," "suspicious," described in such a way as to relate him to the sinister supernatural figures of German tradition; the excursion through the streets of Venice (or the kingdom of Hell), when it seemed "the moral law were fallen in ruins and only the most monstrous and perverse held out a hope"—as would be true of Hell; even the details of Aschenbach's early career create some kind of parallel to Faust's researches into all branches of knowledge. Aschenbach's opportunities to get away from Venice—the first when he actually decides to leave, and is brought back by the "accidental" misdirection of his luggage, the second when the British travel agent urges him to leave and he consciously decides to remain—echo the damned Faust's belief in his inevitable damnation and his refusal to listen to the voices that speak to him of grace.

In view of the fact that Mann had planned a Faust book as early as 1901; that *Death in Venice* (1911) was followed by *The Magic Mountain,* with its Faustian echoes, originally conceived as a "comic counterpart" to it; that he did, so many years later, write *Dr. Faustus;* and that he tended to return again and again to ideas that appealed to him, it does not seem far-fetched to see in *Death in Venice* an initial statement of the Faust theme, particularly since every artist who appears in Mann's works seems to be related in some way to the Faust-figure. Without implying that this was always a conscious relation on Mann's part of the artist to an historical literary legend, one could say that for him the Faust stories held meanings valid generally for our time, and specifically for Mann himself, and that throughout his career as a writer he continued to feel out these meanings. As Mann himself said,

> Every piece of work is in fact a realization—piecemeal if you like, but each complete in itself—of our own nature; they are stones on that harsh road which we must walk to learn of ourselves.

NOTES

[1] Relevant here is Mann's idea of the "Parody," a term he uses to mean the re-telling of a myth or legend from a modern, self-conscious point of view; *Tristan,* a story written in 1902, is the first clear example of this, as the novel *Dr. Faustus* is the last. In this usage, a parody is neither burlesque nor allegory; it is a reworking of the substrata of meaning in the myth in terms of a contemporary story with naturalistic details.

[2] Vernon Venable, "Poetic Reason in Thomas Mann," *The Virginia Quarterly Review,* XIV (Winter 1938), 65.

[3] Henry Hatfield, *Thomas Mann,* p. 61.

Roy Jay Nelson

SOURCE: "Malraux and Camus: The Myth of the Beleaguered City," in *Kentucky Foreign Language Quarterly,* Vol. XIII, No. II, Second Quarter, 1966, pp. 86-94.

[*In the following excerpt, Nelson compares Albert Camus's depiction of Oran in* The Plague *with Andre Malraux's representation of Shanghai in* The Human Condition.]

"The philosopher must decide between alternatives," writes Austin Warren, "or reduce his thesis and antithesis to some underlying or overlying synthesis. But the novelist of a speculative turn need not push his position to a stand. He can divide his conflicting insights between his characters. . . . "[1] Here is indeed a precious liberty for the modern author who finds himself in a world devoid of absolutes, where truth is temporal. But the novel of multiple truths, none of which may, on moral grounds, dominate the others, raises severe structural problems for the author who still cares about coherence and unity in his art. The presentation of multiplicity within unity, the adaptation of the traditional novel to an absurd world, is a task which Malraux and Camus attacked and accomplished in a remarkably similar way— the former in *La Condition humaine* (1933),[2] and the latter in *La Peste* (1947).[3]

Critics have shown interest in the impression of unity which each of these novels produces despite a superficially episodic structure,[4] but they have usually been satisfied with demonstrating the existence of this unity and describing its nature. A deeper relationship of subject matter to form in these works remains relatively unexplored.

The two novels share a general subject: the confrontation of man's desire for absolute and eternal truth and the opposing multiplicity and contingency of the real world. This dichotomy is exemplified in numerous facets of man's existence. We find ourselves separate from others because we possess totally individual natures and because we must strive to make our uniqueness known to others through the use of a conventional language. We desire immortality for ourselves or for the causes we support, yet we know that we shall die, and so eventually will the values we uphold. We want reality to conform to a predictable pattern, and yet our hopes are constantly dashed by the surprise of the chance occurrence. These are all examples of a single central problem—the desire for parmenidean unity *versus* real multiplicity: the absurd. The man who accepts this world view will necessarily confront all phases of that fundamental conflict. But the struggle is vast, complex overpowering. To reduce it to human terms, we need to attack the absurd, element by element, in its own multiplicity. Might not a novelist be led in this way to create a whole city of differing characters, each seeking his peculiar solution to a single aspect of the great problem?

In this sense, the fictional Shanghai would be Malraux himself; and plague-stricken Oran, Camus. The various characters would be seen not as complete individuals but as fragments of the authors' mentalities, each one representing a part of the general struggle, a tentative solution to an element of a single central problem. To establish this notion, let us look first at the structural elements which tend to make these novels episodic, elements representative of the multiplicity of the chaotic world. Later we shall consider the forces of order, suggestive of the human aspiration for unity.

First, neither novel has a protagonist in the traditional sense. In *La Condition humaine,* Kyo is the leader of the communists, yet about half of the novel is taken up with matters not directly related to him. He is a man of action, strangely incomplete without his contemplative father. Although he is allowed to die for his cause in the end, it is Katow who appears, at least to Western eyes, more heroic in death, for he will sacrifice his cyanide to his young Chinese comrades and allow himself to be burned alive, while Kyo uses his cyanide tablets and dies quickly. Throughout the novel, our interest and our viewpoint are determined now by this character, now by that one: Clappique at the gaming tables, Tchen trying to assassinate Chiang Kai-shek, Ferral making love or experiencing the dissolution of the Consortium well after Kyo's demise.

La Peste, as well, is devoid of a true protagonist. Rieux is the narrator, of course, but Camus conceals this fact from us until the end, perhaps out of a desire not to make of him, by the use of first person narration, a conventional hero. Here again our interest flits from character to character: we follow the efforts of Rambert to flee the stricken city and the progress of Joseph Grand's literary sentence; we go to the opera with Cottard and Tarrou, and we witness the agony and death of Judge Othon's little boy. Rieux's story, like his life, is anecdotal: a succession of daily rounds, a series of relatively unrelated conversations, reports of general statistics and reactions to the disease. If indeed, then, we are to speak of unified plot structure in either novel, it must be in terms of a totality larger than any single character. What happens—that which has the traditional beginning, middle, and end—happens to the City.

A second major element of disorder is the absence of any stated scale of values. The warring characters dwell in relative peace with the author, their creator. Both authors strictly avoid commentary and explicit moral judgment. König, for example, Chiang Kai-shek's chief of police in *La Condition humaine,* sends the communists to their death in a locomotive's fire box. While giving this brutal deed a chance to speak for itself, Malraux is careful to give its perpetrator the opportunity to present his explanation (M, pp. 317-318), the mental and physical torture the communists once inflicted upon him by driving nails into his shoulders. Having wept before his torturers, he felt himself to have lost all human dignity, and now, "Ma dignité, à moi," he adds, "c'est de les tuer." Thus his cruelty stems from a desire for personal dignity, a source akin to that of the selfless struggle of Kyoshi Gisors, whom he will condemn to death. Furthermore, it is to Kyo's father, the opium addict seeking first of all his own inner peace, that Malraux attributes the most lucid wisdom. Clappique's inner struggle, as he negligently allows the communists to be arrested and slaughtered, is portrayed by Malraux with sympathetic interest.

A similar impartiality is evident in *La Peste.*[5] Rieux, as a doctor, early seeks the imposition of the severest quarantine and prophylactic measures to halt the advance of the epidemic. Yet he remains on friendly terms with those who combat the restrictions. While he will not sign a health certificate to help Rambert leave Oran, he will in no way seek to impede the reporter's efforts to flee illegally; indeed, it is at Rieux's apartment that Rambert encounters Cottard, whose underworld connections can arrange the escape (C, pp. 156-157). Rieux has harsh words for no one, throughout the book, except for Father Paneloux, and then only at a time of severe emotional strain and fatigue, and he hastens to apologize (C, p. 237). Since the narrator withholds judgment, characters remain unjudged. Rieux does not judge himself; we believe him to be good, since he heals the sick and fights the plague at personal risk, yet he is not presented as perfect: his marriage has been less than ideal, for he admits having neglected his wife (C, p. 21); sometimes, too, he seems indifferent to individual suffering, preferring to think in abstract, statistical terms (C, pp. 105-106). Here, as in *La Condition humaine,* the author eschews absolute, didactic judgment, each reaction being, for the author, at least a valid possibility.

Given a common danger and numerous reactions, all of them admissible, a series of episodes related to a general struggle becomes, then, the most likely sort of presentation. Furthermore, both authors have tended to fragment the general peril, to confront different characters with specific aspects of the City's problem. In this way, certain characters become, as it were, generals assigned to specific fronts in the universal combat. In *La Condition humaine,* for example, the problem of human isolation is recognized by Gisors, when Kyo speaks to him of the coded language records. It is Katow, however, who has a measure of success in dealing with this human limitation as his gift of the cyanide tablets produces a poignant instant of communion, of supra-linguistic understanding between himself and his young companions.

In *La Peste,* Joseph Grand fights the battle with language, as he struggles to make every element of his sentence perfect. It is significant that, thinking himself about to die of the plague, he scrawls across the bottom of his manuscript, "Ma bien chère Jeanne, c'est aujourd'hui Noël" (C, p. 284). The personal symbolism of Christmas, the moment when he and Jeanne had realized the existence of their love, touches the reader, and Rieux as well, before the pages are consumed by the flames. Thus Grand through the use of symbolism conquers for a moment his own isolation. But in a larger sense, if Oran is Camus himself, then the quarantine wall is the limit of his self, his skin, as it were, the point of contact and of separation in relation to the outside world. When letters can no longer be sent out of Oran because they are possible germ bearers, and when telephones are reserved for emergencies, the citizens are obliged to communicate with their loved ones outside in the conventional phrases of telegrams: "Vais bien. Pense à toi. Tendresse" (C, p. 83). Everyday language is hardly more adequate in conveying our own intimate feelings. Characters do pass through the wall once, on the occasion of the fraternal swim (C, pp. 277-278) when Tarrou and Rieux know a moment of physical, unspoken kinship reminiscent of Katow's brief victory.

Other characters wage war on other fronts. When Kyo decides that the Shanghai Communists should keep their arms and fight for their lives against Chiang, he is opposing death, struggling against all that is anti-eternal, as surely as is Rieux in combating the plague. Ferral, in Malraux's novel, is striving to be God, to be capable of restoring order to a chaotic situation. Similarly, Judge Othon in *La Peste* is striving for order through law in Oran, and for self-discipline in his own life. Some characters seek to escape their human condition simply by denying it. Rambert, in *La Peste,* keeps claiming, "Je ne suis pas d'ici" (C, pp. 101, 121). But one can never really escape, and Rambert's efforts are so often frustrated that he decides to end them. Malraux seems to admit escape through imagination and dreams, and indeed Gisors succeeds in fleeing by means of opium. However, his escape is only partial: his attachment to his son ties him to reality, and he must suffer at Kyo's death. Clappique escapes through imaginative role-playing. He claims he does not exist, which is indeed true; he has many different existences, none of which is real. He flees Shanghai in still another disguise, but it is Clappique the deckhand who escapes; the Clappique who was a Shanghai art dealer has ceased to be.

If the lack of a conventional protagonist, the absence of an explicit scale of values and the fragmentation of the struggle among vastly different characters tend to make these novels episodic, there are nonetheless forces for order. The individual dangers which threaten Tchen, Kyo, and Clappique have a common name: Chiang Kai-shek. In Camus' work, the plague is the destiny of Catholic and atheist, criminal, judge, and idealist. Though the danger

is fragmented in presentation, we are constantly aware of its common origin. Camus reinforces this notion particularly by the use of statistics and generalities about *"nos concitoyens"* in virtually every other chapter. It is the existence of this shared peril which unites the diversified characters in a single beleaguered City, and which makes of the City a true protagonist. If the danger is, in reality the simple fact of man's condition, as Malraux's title implies and as Camus' allegory suggests,[6] then the applicability of Austin Warren's notion to these novels is clear. The "conflicting insights" are, in this sense, possible reactions to the human condition, reactions which coexist in the mind of each author at the time of writing, and each of which takes the form of a character.

Another unifying technique is that of distanciation. Part III of *La Condition humaine* takes place outside Shanghai. Kyo goes to Hankow in search of an absolute—the Communist party line. Dissatisfied with the orders, he has a chance to reflect on motivations, to consider the human condition, as it were, from outside. Seen from a distance, Shanghai and its problems seem like a single entity to the reader. Distanciating sentences, like this one from Part II, also add to the effect of unity: "Coeur vivant de la Chine, Shanghai palpitait du passage de tout ce qui la faisait vivre; jusque du fond des campagnes, . . . les vaisseaux sanguins confluaient comme les canaux vers la ville capitale où se jouait le destin chinois" (M, p. 136). A similar unifying view from outside exists in *La Peste,* when Rieux and Tarrou go swimming. Perhaps even more important in this regard are the conversations between these two characters, which achieve a degree of aesthetic distance and generality of view. They take place on the terrace of the asthmatic old Father Time, who counts his endless chick-peas, high above the city.

Furthermore, there are implied universal values based on the relative success of the characters in coping with particular segments of the battle. Those who live on, somehow, are at least temporary conquerors. It is as if the authors were themselves trying out various solutions to the problems posed by the absurd in order to see which are most satisfactory. Malraux's life, when he wrote *La Condition humaine,* held indeed the possibility of many futures. Would he continue in revolutionary actions, perhaps dying a martyr's death like Kyo, to live on in the memory of man? Would he seek peace in opium and philosophical meditation like Gisors? Would he find the meaning of life in art like Kama? Would he turn to a search for order like Ferral and like him submit his own fate to the will of politicians?

Camus' novel is less speculative. He knows he wants to place himself on the side of the victims in the universal disaster. He knows, too, that he is a writer, and though he modestly makes Joseph Grand into something of a simpleton, he takes to heart the spirit of Grand's final advice:[7] to eliminate all the adjectives, those interpretive, subjective words which cannot be understood beyond the barrier of self. Indeed, instead of speculating about the future, Camus seems to look backward here, upon what he has been, and the life of Oran throughout the plague might be seen as a view of the history of one man's life. No somber skies, no dull rains presage the onset of the plague; it begins in the spring, reaches its hideous peak during the ardent summer, starts to diminish with the fall rains, and disappears in January. The traditional symbolism of the seasons here becomes a unifying device and might well suggest that the plague is one man's life, from birth to death.

It is perhaps this sensation of multiple insights arising from a single mind that produces the particular emotional effect which, to a degree, both novels share. While much can be said about the structure of classic tragedy as the informing principle[8] in these works, the central emotion in neither novel is tragic. While it is quite plausible to speak of cathartic release through heroic death in Malraux's novel, such emotion is present only, strictly speaking, in the death of Kyo. He lives on, in the minds of others, as a martyr at the end, but this represents only his particular victory. Tragedy is one way to organize one element of the absurd world. Malraux carefully attenuates the tragic effect of Kyo's decease by inserting, in Part VII, the long recital of Ferral's economic difficulties between the suicide and the final cathartic realization that Kyo lives on in memory. Camus, of course, consistently belittles heroic sacrifice: we all die, and the method seems, in comparison to that fact, unimportant. The old asthmatic expresses it best:

> —Dites, docteur, c'est vrai qu'ils vont construire un monument aux morts de la peste?
>
> —Le journal le dit. Une stèle ou une plaque.
>
> —J'en étais sûr. Et il y aura des discours. Le vieux riait d'un rire étranglé.
>
> —Je les entends d'ici. "Nos morts . . .", et ils iront casser la croûte (C, p. 330).

Indeed, the most persistent emotion in both works is that of poignant frustration arising from unresolved conflicts. Both Chiang Kai-shek and the plague bacillus remain alive at the end, as do the diversified populations of the cities. The world is not cleaner for having been swept by the breath of tragedy. Tension, a relatively modern emotion, is the basic aesthetic effect achieved through the device of the beleaguered City. There is tension between reality and symbolic meaning or abstraction, between the individual and the universal, between the citizen and the City, and between the City and the enemy. The author gives his characters the divergent tendencies of his own insights, but binds them together in the City with a compelling force like that which orders the atom.

If we have dwelt upon the similarities of these novels, it is not to suggest that Camus has imitated or attempted to improve upon his predecessor whom he admired so much.[9] The differences between the novels are manifest. But if we can note here a basic structural resemblance, if we can see that similar—not identical—preoccupations tend to suggest similar forms, then we can posit that we are, perhaps, in the presence of a modern myth, of a sort of archetypal structure for the novel of the absurd: a City-protagonist which is truly one unified entity, and numerous highly individualized characters representing the temptations or potentialities of that collectivity.[10]

Malraux's novel seems less purely allegorical, truer to the historical reality on which it rests, while *La Peste,* though containing allusions to Camus' wartime experience, retains a more rigid, one-for-one relationship between symbol and signification. This greater degree of stylization may indicate a minor advantage awarded to the forces for unity over the tendency toward fragmentation, but both works depend, for their effect, upon the maintenance of a delicate equilibrium upon similar tightropes.

NOTES

[1] Austin Warren, *Rage for Order* (Chicago: University of Chicago Press, 1948), p. 89.

[2] André Malraux, *La Condition humaine* (Paris: Gallimard, 1933). Page references in the text which are preceded by an "M" refer to this edition.

[3] Albert Camus, *La Peste* (Paris: Gallimard, 1947). Page references in the text which are preceded by a "C" refer to this edition.

[4] Bert M.-P. Leefmans, "Malraux and Tragedy: The Structure of *La Condition humaine,*" *The Romanic Review,* XLIV, 3 (Oct. 1953), 208-214; Jean R. Carduner; *La Création romanesque chez Malraux,* University of Minnesota dissertation (Ann Arbor: University Microfilms, 1959), pp. 35-36, 66-87; John Cruikshank, "The Art of Allegory in *La Peste,*" *Symposium* XI, 1 (Spring, 1957), 61-74; Alfred Noyer-Weidner; "Das Formproblem der *Pest* von Albert Camus," *Germanisch-Romanische Monatschrift,* VIII, 3 (Juli 1958), 260-285.

[5] Cruikshank notes, p. 67, the absence of obvious didacticism in *La Peste.*

[6] For interpretations of Camus' allegory, see especially Roger Quilliot: *La Mer et les prisons* (Paris: Gallimard, 1956), pp. 161-188, and Philip Thody: *Albert Camus* (London: Hamish Hamilton, 1957) pp. 29-46. On the allegorical implications of *La Condition humaine,* see W. M. Frohock: *André Malraux and the Tragic Imagination* (Stanford: Stanford University Press, 1952), pp. 58-89.

[7] See Camus: *Carnets, mai 1935-février 1942* (Paris: Gallimard, 1962), p. 127: "La véritable oeuvre d'art est celle qui dit moins . . ."

[8] On Malraux, see Leefmans, *op. cit.,* and Frohock, *loc. cit.;* the five parts of *La Peste* might be likened to the acts of a tragedy.

[9] Malraux did, however, seem to see the plague as symbolic of the human condition (M, pp. 79, 186).

[10] *Les Dieux ont soif* by Anatole France might also be shown to fit the same structural mold.

Frederick Garber

SOURCE: "Time and the City in Rilke's *Malte Laurids Brigge,*" in *Contemporary Literature,* Vol. 11, No. 3, Summer, 1970, pp. 324-39.

[*In the following essay, Garber employs Rilke's letters and personal history to illuminate the urban settings in his fiction.*]

In a letter of 1924 to Nora Purtscher-Wydenbruck, Rilke shapes out the contours of a *Bewusstseinspyramide,* a pyramid of consciousness which images for him the extent and dimensions of what we can know. At the point of the pyramid, he says, stands ordinary existence, but the base spreads deep within us until we move around in an area independent of time and space, an area where

> uns das einfache Sein könnte zum Ereignis werden, jenes unverbrüchliche Vorhanden-Sein und Zugleich-Sein alles dessen, was an der oberen "normalen" Spitze des Selbstbewusstseins nur als "Ablauf" zu erleben verstattet ist.[1]

Rilke comments further that at the time of writing *Malte* he had been searching for a form "die Vergangenes und noch nicht Entstandenes einfach als Gegenwärtigkeit letzten Grades aufzufassen fähig wäre."[2] Obviously one has to be cautious about depending on the accuracy of *post facto* remarks of this sort, especially remarks made at so great a distance from the labor on *Malte.* But with these retrospective assertions Rilke moved closer to defining the order and import of the world of Malte Laurids Brigge than he did in other comments, some in passing and some more extended, on the notebook form or on the difficult problem of Malte's success in pulling himself back into coherence. A strange realism prompted Rilke to speak of the *Aufzeichnungen* as artistically, perhaps, a poor unity but humanly a possible one.[3] Yet this view cannot account for the impressive symmetry of the novel or its overriding sense of direction, however much the presence or even the existence of a terminus may be brought into question. More useful and ultimately more successful is Rilke's own image of the pyramid pointed with the ordinary world.

As the letter of 1924 makes clear, *Die Aufzeichnungen des Malte Laurids Brigge* takes at least part of its origin from Rilke's search for a form that could organize temporal dimensions into a seamless order, an order which, because all points in time are present in it at once, liberates the observer from the prison-house of an exclusively immediate time. Were this order to be achieved within any work, that work would have to show, formally, the simultaneous presence of all areas in time and, further, would probably make that search for order into a central theme in its own dramatic movement. There seems no question that Rilke attempted, in the *Aufzeichnungen,* to unify theme and form in this way. If there is a sense in which the book is autobiography (and I do not mean the relatively insignificant fact that certain of Malte's experiences happened to Rilke), that sense emerges in the recognition that both writer and hero were attempting the same thing, the unification of the varieties of temporal strata into an order which could clarify and give some meaning to the painful disparities in human experience. Rilke must have been aware of this similarity. He must also have seen the paradox that in the very process of telling Malte's story, he was trying to bring about a more successful version of the ordering his hero had failed to accomplish.

Despite what Rilke implies about the random nature of the notebook entries, the book sets immediately into focus not only the search for order but the mode in which the search is to be accomplished and, gradually and increasingly, the material which has to be ordered. The *Aufzeichnungen,* as we know, have roots in Baudelaire, Dostoevsky, Jacobsen, and some aspects of the decadent nineties. The first entry locates Malte squarely in the center of a squalid city, the image which Baudelaire created once and for all for modern literature. This is part of what Malte must order. Two entries follow, the first an elaborate description of night sounds, to all of which Malte responds with frantic intensity, the next an awesome picture of a silence in which a sense of impending doom is figured through a wall about to crash down. With this background Rilke arranges a corner of Malte's untidy life, placing him here and now, in this city at this time in his own and the world's history. The first three entries, fervent in their involvement with sight, sound, and silence, show Malte's senses frenziedly at play, working to organize the materials of a world the very principles of which are alien to him but in which he must learn, somehow, to live. The mode of organization is vision: "Habe ich es schon gesagt? Ich lerne sehen. Ja, ich fange an. Es geht noch schlecht. Aber ich will meine Zeit ausnutzen."[4] Here, then, are the beginnings of a content and the establishment of a mode, crude matter which has to be shaped and the definition of the process of shaping. Malte's work is the work of an artist, the seer as maker trying to form coherence out of the chaos of impressions around him. But ironically and ominously, this artist has to learn his craft while he organizes material whose meaning to him he cannot yet understand. He will understand only after he has ordered it, that is, when he has mastered the mode and become the full visionary who can see where things belong and how they got there. Malte is, therefore, no passive hero: the activity of seeing absorbs and drives him from the immediate scene into a variety of difficult dimensions. (What he actually does comes somewhere between the compulsive passivity of Dostoevsky's Underground Man and the confused assertiveness of Raskolnikov.) The actions in the book are actions observed with all the intensity of one to whom the unknown order he is trying to make means coherence and life. From early to late, Malte is teaching himself to see; surely one of the more painful ironies of the novel is its quality as a *Selbstbildungsroman*.

The mode of seeing takes the form of a search for points of sight, images on which he can fasten and, once they are understood, from which he can move to others that have not yet been drawn into the order of his being. The pervasive concreteness of the *Aufzeichnungen* grows out of Malte's obsessive concern with things and actions, the facts of all the worlds he touches. He studies every object and event that comes into the periphery of his consciousness in order to find out what sort of ideas and patterns cluster around them, what they mean to themselves, to others, and, most important, to himself. Each image earns its full right to existence in his notes because it reveals something to him about what and where he is and has been. No fact is neutral for Malte, who has an eye for the minutiae of every kind of reality; each fact has a quality, a tone and color, and might have some relation to the order he is trying to shape. If the objects come at him too quickly when he looks at Paris or St. Petersburg, the images do drop eventually into place (probably without his full awareness but certainly with the reader's), and the city emerges as one great hospital. Paris is a place of sickness and corruption, a city only too real (cf. Eliot's "unreal city") where women come to be delivered only to have their infants grow fat and greenish with sores on their foreheads. Malte, like Hamlet, finds that imagery of decay and pollution defines most accurately the current stench of things, though with Malte the odor is not moral but psychological and metaphysical. Here is the modern landscape seen through the eyes of a figure out of another world. The city images the condition of the modern urbanized soul, a world not of the dead (that at least would be finished and bearable, perhaps even as beautiful as the mask of the drowned girl, *la noyée*), but of the nearly dead, those approaching extinction through some grotesque sickness which takes no account of their perishing individuality. The act of dying seems to frighten Malte more than the fact of death itself, partly because the change he is going through seems to him as radical in its shift of being as the act of dying, partly also because his fear of the loss of self sees that loss accomplished irrevocably as dying goes on. His *tableaux parisiens* grow gradually, thus, into a painfully coherent picture which echoes Baudelaire and prefigures T. S. Eliot. And, as with these poets, certain details of the city stand out from the others as seeing-points, images which, as he is learning to see, offer a special fascination because they embody the essential qualities of the city surrounding him: the woman with her face in her hands, the man with St. Vitus's dance, the flowers that stood up and said "red" in a frightened voice, the green covering of the armchair with the hollow in which innumerable heads had rested.

Rilke's skill in organizing the apparent disparateness of the notebook entries appears also with certain images which focus tentatively, with a strange combination of curiosity and dread, on some point of relationship with a fact out of Malte's past. Most obvious, of course, are the contrasted modes of dying to which Malte explicitly refers. But his instinct for survival sends him everywhere in search of contrasting images, some of which grow into and give substance to a variety of themes in the book. Indeed, contrasts, properly interpreted, shape a pattern and therefore an order, a kind of wholeness that can stabilize, if not entirely explain, how Malte gets to where he is. The hunt for images draws his apprehensive but meticulous eye into the most minute observations on Parisian street life and, perhaps many pages later, into finding a contrast and echo at another place, perhaps in another time when he and the world were newer and healthier.

Clothing, houses, illnesses—these especially cluster into patterns built on echoes ringing in time as well as space, echoes which cohere into the first notes of a harmony which Malte could never finish. The streets of Paris led him to a house or, more properly, to the wall of a house which was no longer there. Clinging to the wall were the obscenely frank remnants of the inside of the building, its intimate life whose objects draw him toward the edge of nausea: the water-closet pipe that wriggles like a stubbornly independent digestive tract, the spots on the wall which had kept their paint fresher because pictures or wardrobes had once covered them. The reek of the air surrounding the former tenants still lay on the wall, but most of all the life had never left:

> Das zähe Leben dieser Zimmer hatte sich nicht zertreten lassen. Es war noch da, es hielt sich an den Nägeln, die geblieben waren, es stand auf dem handbreiten Rest der Fussböden, es war unter den Ansätzen der Ecken, wo es noch ein klein wenig Innenraum gab, zusammengekrochen.[5]

"Die Hauptsache," he had said in the first entry, "war, dass man lebte. Das war die Hauptsache."[6] This wall which faces Malte has its exact, grotesque parallel in a sight he could not tolerate earlier, the woman at whom he could not stare because her face was in her hands and he could not bear to see the "blossen wunden Kopf ohne Gesicht."[7] Now, here, with this wall that confronts him, he has to stare at the flayed inside of a house, forced against all his resistance into a repulsive intimacy with its parts and with the smell of its air. Paris catches up with Malte and compels him to stare at the secret writhings of its life.

But in the *Aufzeichnungen* there is still another house that isn't there, a house which offers another kind of parallel opening up further dimensions of Malte's life and defining the mode of organization he needs to work the multiple segments of his reality into a stable coherence. The burned-out house of the Schulins, which Malte had visited before and after the fire, retained its presence for those who knew it, and it came back suddenly and briefly into the lives of its former inhabitants and their visitors. It rises invisibly within them, absorbed into the depths of their consciousness. The life of this house, though, is the life of the Schulins, whose style of existence reveals a different kind of anxiety from the desperate clamminess exuded by the inhabitants of the house in Paris. The Schulins' nervousness comes from their presence at a moment of change in a life style, the destruction of the old order symbolized by the gutting of their ancestral home. Malte, like Yeats, finds a fascination in ancestral houses and sees them as dramatic symbols of the passing—the destruction by burning—of the old order and its way of life. All through Malte's notes there runs the theme of change, dramatized in this contrast of the houses and frequently elsewhere: as, for example, in the knitting of the end of Book I, the lady in the tapestries, with the beginning of Book II, the young girls who come to museums to sketch, having left their families and houses to live the life of the city. The elements of these contrasts, the houses and the women, are points of sight, images Malte lights upon during the education of his vision. To see these points as not disparate but related, and to be able to draw a line from one seeing-point to another, means that Malte has begun to make the rudiments of order in his world. With luck and struggle he can sometimes come to see that between two points a continuum stretches, a movement in time and space which embodies the change he senses everywhere. Malte has, himself, been part of such a movement; but to be within it is not necessarily to understand it—indeed, perhaps quite the opposite might result. Only the activity of seeing can show that there is, in fact, a continuum and not merely a bewildering leap.

The problems of change, then, come down not so much to acceptance (that would occur long after all the other elements in the process are accomplished) as the need to recognize and define continuity. In order to do this, Malte has to sort out and learn to live with a variety of contradictory impulses and phenomena that press in on him simultaneously, particularly the revelation of contemporary fact, the maturing and adjusting process of his own selfhood, and a dazed, rarely coherent or objectified sense of loss. He is certain only that there has been a point where something stopped, what for him is the end of a line: "Aber nun war der Jägermeister tot, und nicht er allein. Nun war das Herz durchbohrt, unser Herz, das Herz unseres Geschlechts. Nun war es vorbei. Das war also das Helmzerbrechen: 'Heute Brigge und nimmermehr', sagte etwas in mir."[8] If Ulsgaard was an end, Paris is the new beginning. In fact, the hunting master had died in a strange city in unfamiliar surroundings, with Ulsgaard already gone. With an ironic overlap, the death had taken place in the new life. But Malte's own heart had already begun to do the shaping of continuity demanded by the new facts: "Es war ein einzelnes Herz. Es war schon dabei, von Anfang anzufangen."[9]

Out of this new beginning, impelled by it and in turn enriching it, comes Malte's complex sense of time and its manifold dimensions. What happened to Malte and the aristocratic culture he represents happened in time and (some would say) because of it. Thus, his impulse to turn to temporal questions is grounded in an accurate, instinctive grasp of the outline of his problems. He knows, for

example, that any moment he can observe is both self-contained, with its own difficult order, and also part of a process, the linear movement of time from one point to another, a process whose order is not at all apparent and which he must therefore learn to see. Each moment is a child of history and Malte becomes a genealogist, searching its lineal descent. Clearly involved with this problem, though—and Malte has some awareness of the involvement—is his current condition and its oppressive lack of order. His life seems fragmented and his self is apparently discontinuous. If he were to make sense out of the movement of his life from Ulsgaard to Paris, he would then be able to perceive it in sequential time, the measured movement from one temporal location to another. This, in turn, would make it possible for the movement to be comprehended in narrative form, the imaginative embodiment of the sense of time as an unfolding, coherent, and linear sequence, with no irrational leaps, no unexplained hiatuses. This is not to say that Malte wanted to write a novel about his life but that, as a writer, he was drawn initially toward the idea of time as linear sequence because of the relation of that aspect of time to narrative form. The impulse to draw lines between such seeing-points as the Schulin house and the house in Paris was an effort to overcome discontinuity in the manner most meaningful to him. Both Rilke and his hero sensed the relation of the order of the world and the order of art. But where Malte shores up fragments against his ruins, the fragments are disconnected for him and not for Rilke, who can see the movement and the order of the whole. As we shall see subsequently, though, another mode of understanding the shape of time, a mode opposed to the linear because it sought for simultaneity, was implicit in Malte's efforts. In his inability to reconcile the modes, indeed in his failure to accomplish them both, lay much of Malte's tragedy.

Drawn as always into the lives of others, Malte senses that even if he is not yet ready to write, and therefore to embody sequential time in narrative form, he can turn to another field of exploration, history, to which a similar approach would be possible. History, he knows, is another and potentially less subjective version of the experience and objectification of time as linear movement. His explorations, then, offer at least the possibility that he might be able to work around in the past in order to discover what it knew, to see its shape, that is, and to learn what he can from that. Further, in Malte's concern with history lies one of the central ordering patterns within the fragments: here, as elsewhere, theme and form reflect each other in the *Aufzeichnungen*. What Rilke has done is, first, to establish Malte's search for his role in contemporary urban phenomena and then send him back into history in order to find out what might help to clarify the meaning of things right now. Much of Part One and several entries in Part Two deal specifically with Malte's turn to the history closest to him, his own life in Ulsgaard and that of others allied to him in time and place. With varying degrees of success he attempts to look upon himself and those who were around him as he would look at historical figures. This is what he means by beginning at the beginning. The first attempts to move even further back in time occur with figures close to the history of his own family, such as his mother's sister Ingeborg, his grandmother Margaret Brigge, who had been betrothed to Felix Lichnowski, and, of course, the ghost who appears where she has every right to be, Christine Brahe. Some of these figures, such as Saint-Germain and Christine, serve as images of transition, connected both to Malte's private history (in the form of the history of his family) and also to the larger history of their times. The figures focus that overall movement in the *Aufzeichnungen* which goes from the personal to the public, from Malte's life to the life of his ancestors and then to that of Europe in general. Malte believes that only in these terms and with this kind of expanding development can he understand the full meaning of the decline of aristocracy—not that he comes to any other conclusion than that astonishing figures appeared now and then in his family and all through Europe.

Time, thus, becomes a mode of seeing for Malte, and in so doing it establishes one of the more curious paradoxes in this book of multiple truths. For, aware as he is that time is a process whose major result is the flux which has brought him to this pass, Malte still manages, with some success, to use time as an instrument with which he can probe his own concerns. Of the first element in the paradox, time as incessant and irrevocable movement, Malte is so aware that he can indulge in a rare, brilliantly grotesque self-parody in the story of the obsessions of Nikolaj Kusmitsch. Obviously influenced by Dostoevsky's *Double,* this episode mocks the idea of time as money—Kusmitsch, we remember, looked in the directory for a Time Bank— but it also shows Kusmitsch so horrified at his growing sense of time as hurried flux that he can feel the earth turning under him and the seconds passing like wind blowing on his face. With a piercingly accurate irony Malte tells of Nikolaj going to bed and reciting a poem with emphatically regular rhythmical stresses so that the order of art can conquer the flux of time:

> Und dann hatte er sich das ausgedacht mit den Gedichten. Man sollte nicht glauben, wie das half. Wenn man so ein Gedicht langsam hersagte, mit gleichmässiger Betonung der Endreime, dann war gewissermassen etwas Stabiles da, worauf man sehen konnte, innerlich versteht sich.[10]

Malte knows that Nikolaj's madness can be his own and that Nikolaj's fate is a bizarre but precise dramatization of his own obsessions:

> Ich erinnere mich dieser Geschichte so genau, weil sie mich ungemein beruhigte. Ich kann wohl sagen, ich habe nie wieder einen so angenehmen Nachbar gehabt, wie diesen Nikolaj Kusmitsch, der sicher auch mich bewundert hätte.[11]

But if time and its anxieties force the figure of Nikolaj Kusmitsch into a bitter role in Malte's self-exploration, the other element in this paradox—time as a tool of awareness—brings other characters more positively within the periphery of his concerns. Rilke's extraordinarily

sensitive understanding of other times and places affords him the opportunity of sending Malte back into history to look for other means by which he can organize his immediate difficulties. Rilke's compassion and insight combine with his deft craftsmanship to bring other periods and their people into vivid, present life, drawing into an elaborately depicted historical present some striking personage out of the past, setting that character in motion again on his own stage, and all this always with some comparison with Malte implicit in the meaning of his actions. Malte's move from personal to European history makes it possible for Rilke to bring the past into immediate being and at the same time to set up foils and doubles for his agonized hero.

For example, a figure like Grischa Otrepjow, the False Czar, fascinates Malte for a number of reasons. Grischa is an impostor who builds a mask in which he himself almost believes. Glorying in all the possibilities of self open for his experimentation, Grischa lives out a role which explores the manifold shapes a mask can take, and in this he is encouraged by the people: "Das Volk, das sich ihn erwünschte, ohne sich einen vorzustellen, machte ihn nur noch freier und unbegrenzter in seinen Möglichkeiten."[12] The relation to Malte's concerns with the establishment of a coherent self are obvious, as is Grischa's version of the idea of the mask, which always fascinated Malte even as it terrified him with the possibility of the loss of all identity. He admires in Grischa the courage which can take on voluntarily the dangerous task of building another self. (Duse had impressed him for much the same reason.) But Grischa means even more than this to Malte; other themes in the *Aufzeichnungen* weave in and out of the episode on the False Czar: Malte's speculations about Grischa's motivation prefigure the story of the Prodigal Son while simultaneously echoing the earlier passage on the girls in the museum:

> Ich bin nicht abgeneigt zu glauben, die Kraft seiner Verwandlung hätte darin beruht, niemandes Sohn mehr zu sein. (Das ist schliesslich die Kraft aller jungen Leute, die fortgegangen sind.)[13]

Malte stares into history and finds even in the person of the mad Charles the Sixth of France some aspect of himself, for the king "begriff, dass die wahre Konsolation erst begann, wenn das Glück vergangen genug und für immer vorüber war."[14] In history as well as in Paris, Malte studies ugliness, death, and love, all these themes and more, in terms of the fate of individual lives. When Paris repels it is because of the people there, what they are and go through. History fascinates because of the people he sees in it, the extraordinary personalities to which he, as old Count Brahe, was especially susceptible. When Brahe said of Saint-Germain that "Ich konnte damals natürlich nicht beurteilen, ob er geistreich war und das und dies, worauf Wert gelegt wird—: aber er *war,*"[15] he shows that same awed sense of a grand presence of self that Malte experienced in the evocation of these historical personalities. The historical scenes in the *Aufzeichnungen* are triumphs of Rilke's ability to imagine himself into the center of another's being, to explore and objectify with absolute convincingness what it must have felt like to be what that being was. His profound empathy with these figures out of the past prefigures the mode of the *Neue Gedichte* which were to follow.

For Malte, though, the excursions into history ultimately convince him that even for these figures time seemed to be inexorably linear and therefore deadly. Linear time is death time, and an awesome personality serves, finally, to ensure a spectacular demise or an impressive corpse like that of Charles the Bold, Duke of Burgundy, whose cleft skull still commanded an imposingly dressed cadaver, but a cadaver nevertheless. The difficulty was not so much in overcoming the inevitability of flux, since Malte saw no way out of that, as in finding a means of coming to terms with it that would make sequence more tolerable if no less fatal.

In a way, Malte's turn back into his own and Europe's history had been part of an effort to make peace with linear time. For Western man generally, time has usually been linear, whether in the progression from an old to a new Eden charted in the Judaeo-Christian Bible, or in an epic like the *Odyssey,* which ends at an old home but with a hero much older than when he had left it. Malte is no Odysseus but neither is he an orthodox Christian with his eyes fixed ecstatically on the New Jerusalem to which time is implacably driving him. What Malte can draw on, though, that neither Biblical nor Hellenic man had available, was a sense of the unconscious as the lair of memory, and therefore a conception of the past as always present and potentially immediate under circumstances which could bring it out. Malte, as modern man, is unceasingly aware of the realities, ugly perhaps but present nevertheless, which lie within him gathering strength until some accident drives them up to the surface and out into the light again:

> Mit einer somnambulen Sicherheit holt sie [diese Krankheit] aus einem jeden seine tiefste Gefahr heraus, die vergangen schien, und stellt sie weider vor ihn hin, ganz nah, in die nächste Stunde. . . . Und mit dem, was kommt, hebt sich ein ganzes Gewirr irrer Erinnerungen, das daranhängt wie nasser Tang an einer versunkenen Sache.[16]

If the past still lives in the unconscious and is available, however fragmented, to memory, it can be understood as contemporaneous with the present and not, therefore, lost and in back of him. Malte senses that, potentially at least, the divisions and boundaries of time might not be so absolute or inevitable that no recourse to their rigidity is possible.

With his first step into history, Malte drew on the past that lay within him in the form of his personal memory and began to bring it again into immediacy. As I indicated earlier, Malte as artist was attracted originally to the idea of time as linear sequence because of the relation of that kind of time to narrative form. He discovers, of course, that sequential time can be experienced only at the most

frightful cost. But implicit in the recovery of the past in present time is the possibility of a new mode of experiencing based on a sense that all time is simultaneous, a mode that asserts a unity transcending (because it ignores) all boundaries. Part of the shape of the *Aufzeichnungen* is based on this attempt and on the premises implied within it. If this attempt to establish simultaneity (*Zugleich-Sein*) fails—and it is not clear whether Malte saw all the contours of possibility—it does so for several reasons. First, in order to shape or to show a unity, Malte had eventually to make sense out of his childhood or, as he says, to finish it. That would mean finally to understand his childhood in relation to his present self; to create, in other words, the full narrative sequence between Ulsgaard and Paris. He could not get even that far: "Ich habe um meine Kindheit gebeten, und sie ist wiedergekommen, und ich fühle, dass sie immer noch so schwer ist wie damals und dass es nichts genützt hat, älter zu werden."[17] Clearly, Malte is unable to cohere his present experience of time into linear form, the form he concluded was death time. It would follow, then, that the more difficult mode of simultaneity was surely impossible for him, no matter to what degree he might have sensed what it could do. But even beyond this, given Malte's limitations, the simultaneity he saw as a possibility, both with his own memory and that of Europe's history, was fatally limited because it had no sense of the future but only of the present as the place where the past ends. To make radiant and harmonic wholeness out of a full sense of all dimensions in time was beyond what Malte could do: he could not bring into his potential unity what would have to come from the breaking of that ultimate boundary which is in no sense ordinarily available, the division between present and future. Ironically, Malte had known even as a child that the boundaries of any moment in time and space were not inviolable and that they could be shattered, sporadically for most people but regularly for some. Old Count Brahe would not permit chronological sequence, the distinctions between past, present, and future, to have any meaning for him: "Personen, die er einmal in seine Erinnerung aufgenommen hatte, existierten, und daran konnte ihr Absterben nicht das geringste ändern."[18] He had even been known to speak to a frightened girl, just pregnant for the first time, of the travels of one of her sons. For him, obviously, the pyramid of consciousness was an immediate and present fact in which he permanently lived. Indeed, the boundaries of reality had broken for Malte himself at several points, e.g., when a hand breached the wall under the table and reached out of another world groping to clasp his own hand. Shattered boundaries are everywhere in the *Aufzeichnungen*: ghosts walk out of the past into a dining room, houses that are no longer there rise suddenly, restlessly, into present consciousness and fade slowly again. Malte's attraction to the mode of simultaneous time arose naturally out of what he had been and where he had come from. The problems, the impossibilities, come from what and where he is now.

Yet at the end a solution seems to offer itself; not, it should be added, that Malte necessarily made use of the solution he had come to see. Individual seeing-points in his own and Europe's history—the girl at the party in Venice, Gaspara Stampa, the Portuguese nun—all cluster eventually into a pattern which unfolds at the end into the story of the Prodigal Son, "die Legende dessen . . .der nicht geliebt werden wollte."[19] With the idea of intransitive love Malte comes to see what for others had been a mode of organizing self which transcends all pain and loss; which, in fact, needs loss in order to accomplish itself fully. Intransitive love begins, as consolation began for the old mad king Charles, when all happiness is long and forever past. If such love shuns, even fears, reciprocity, that comes only because the receiving of love from any other lover than the Highest would negate the whole point of intransitive love, the meaning of its movement, which is the most complete fulfillment of self in the most exacting kind of loving. Any being other than the Ultimate Being would be lesser, and the love would therefore not be all that it could have been. From the human point of view, that is, from the lover's, God is so far away that the process of loving *towards* him becomes itself the center of contemplation:

> Manchmal früher fragte ich mich, warum Abelone die Kalorien ihres grossartigen Gefühls nicht an Gott wandte. Ich weiss, sie sehnte sich, ihrer Liebe alles Transitive zu nehmen, aber konnte ihr wahrhaftiges Herz sich darüber täuschen, dass Gott nur eine Richtung der Liebe ist, kein Liebesgegenstand? Wusste sie nicht, dass keine Gegenliebe von ihm zu fürchten war?[20]

Such love, then, can be accomplished only by an incessant drive forward, all passion channeled into this one obsessive loving which carries the whole being on with it toward a goal so distant that it can be understood only as a process, not as an ending. To stop is to perish: "Geliebtwerden ist vergehen, Lieben ist dauern."[21]

With this sense that God "nur eine Richtung der Liebe ist, kein Liebesgegenstand," there rises to the surface perhaps the most profound aspect of the idea of intransitive love. For that love is linear, inexorably and necessarily so. It is, in fact, so engrossed with implacable forward movement in time that it feels itself cheated when Christ comes to meet it, for the lovers had expected only the endless road, and they are somehow wronged. Their love, in other words, can be accomplished only in linear time, and they need all the linear time they can possibly get in order to fulfill what for them becomes the encompassing task of their being. Malte came to realize that for these women lovers (the Prodigal Son shows that men can be involved when the lover is God) the experience of intransitive love could be seen as their way of coming to terms with the problems of sequential time. If sequential temporal movement can be neither negated nor ignored, it can become the necessary framework within which a special kind of love unfolds and develops as it works its way toward God. Linear time might be death time, but for these lovers it is the most fruitful temporal mode, the only one which can give their love the shape it needs.

If Malte, here and now in the great hospital that is Paris, saw all this and saw it clearly, then he would have found what could have been a way out for himself. Whether he took that way seems doubtful indeed, for to see is not to do, and learning to see was all that Malte's strength would allow him. The book ends, though, with the fulfillment of the activity with which it began. If Malte never achieved the fullness of vision which brings life and death into a comprehensible harmony, he at least learned to see how the move toward death could also involve the fulfilling of love. The *Aufzeichnungen* end with everything yet to be done but with a way of doing now, at last, in sight.

NOTES

[1] From the letter of 11 August 1924 in Rainer Maria Rilke, *Gesammelte Briefe in Sechs Bänden,* ed. Ruth Sieber-Rilke and Carl Sieber (Leipzig, 1939-41), v, 292. The edition is hereafter cited as *Briefe*. The passage translates as follows: simple Being can become an event for us, that inviolable immediacy and simultaneity of everything which, at the upper "normal" point of self-consciousness, we are allowed to experience only as "termination."

[2] *Ibid.;* "which would be capable of comprehending the past and the not-yet-occurred simply as presence to the ultimate degree."

[3] From the letter of 11 April 1910 to Manon zu Salms-Laubach in *Briefe*, III, 99. This letter might well be the cause of the comparative scarcity of literary studies of the *Aufzeichnungen,* most commentaries confining themselves primarily, to a study of the book as a stage in Rilke's spiritual development. There are useful comments on the form of the *Aufzeichnungen* in Armand Nivelle, "Sens et structure des *Cahiers de Malte Laurids Brigge,*" *Revue d'esthétique,* XII (1959), iii-iv, 5-32, and in Ulrich Fülleborn, "Form und Sinn der 'Aufzeichnungen des *Malte Laurids Brigge'*. Rilkes Prosabuch und der moderne Roman," *Unterscheidung und Bewahrung. Festschrift für Hermann Kunisch,* ed. Klaus Lazarowicz and Wolfgang Kron (Berlin, 1961), pp. 147-169. There are suggestive remarks on the *aufzeichnungen* scattered throughout Maurice Betz, *Rilke in Paris* (Zürich, 1948), some of the remarks being retrospective comments by Rilke. See also *Rainer Maria Rilke. Inge Junghanns. Briefwechsel,* ed. Wolfgang Herwig (Leipzig, 1959), pp. 41-70, and Ernst Hoffmann, "Zum dichterischen Verfahren in Rilkes *Aufzeichnungen des Malte Laurids Brigge,*" in *Deutsche Vierteljahrsschrift für Literaturwissenschaft und Geistesgeschichte,* XLII (1967), 202-230.

[4] All quotations from the novel follow the text in the Insel-Verlag edition of the *Sämtliche Werke* (Leipzig, 1955-66), VI (1966). This quotation is from p. 711. Translation: Have I already said it? I am learning to see. Yes, I am beginning. But I intend to make good use of my time.

[5] P. 750; "The stubborn life of these rooms had not allowed itself to be trampled out. It was still there. It held

onto the nails which had been left, it stood on the remaining handsbreath of flooring, it huddled under the places where the corners began, where there was still a little bit of space within."

[6] P. 709; "The main thing was, being alive. That was the main thing."

[7] P. 712; "naked wounded head without a face."

[8] P. 855; "But now the master of the hunt was dead, and not he alone. Now the heart had been pierced through, our heart, the heart of our race. Now it was finished. This was, then, the breaking of the helmet: 'Today Brigge and nevermore,' something said within me."

[9] *Ibid.;* "It was an individual heart. It was already at the point of beginning from the beginning."

[10] P. 870; "And then he had devised that business with the poems. One would scarcely have believed how that helped. When one recited a poem thus, slowly and with even accentuation of the end-rhymes, then to a certain extent something stable was there on which one could gaze, inwardly of course."

[11] *Ibid.;* "I remember this story so accurately because it reassured me greatly. I may well say that I have never had so agreeable a neighbor as this Nikolaj Kusmitsch, who certainly would also have admired me."

[12] Pp. 882-883; "The people, who wanted him, without having anyone special in mind, made him only freer and more unbounded in his possibilities."

[13] P. 882; "I am not disinclined to believe that the strength of his transformation lay in his no longer being anyone's son. (That is finally the strength of all young people who have gone away.)"

[14] P. 910; "understood that true consolation began only when happiness was far enough gone and forever past."

[15] P. 850; "At that time, of course, I could not tell whether he was brilliant, or this and that to which people attach value—: but he *was*."

[16] P. 766; "With a somnambulistic certainty [this illness] hauls out of each person his deepest danger, which seemed passed, and places it again before him, quite near and imminent. . . . And with that which comes there arises a whole confusion of mad memories which hang on it like wet seaweed on some sunken thing."

[17] P. 767; "I have prayed for my childhood and it has come back, and I feel that it is still as difficult as it was then and that getting older has been no help."

[18] P. 735; "People whom he had once taken into his memory continued to exist, and their death could not change that in the slightest."

[19] P. 938; "the story of him . . . who did not want to be loved."

[20] P. 937; "I had sometimes wondered earlier why Abelone did not turn the calories of her magnificent feeling toward God. I know that she longed to remove everything transitive from her love, but could her truthful heart be deceived about God's being only a direction of love, not an object of love? Did she not know that she need fear no return of love from Him?"

[21] *Ibid.;* "To be loved is to pass away, to love is to endure."

William Cutter

SOURCE: "Setting as a Feature of Ambiguity in S. Y. Agnon's *Sippur Pashut*," in *Critique: Studies in Modern Fiction*, Vol. 15, No. 3, 1974, pp. 66-79.

[*In the following essay, Cutter discusses the town of Shibbush as it is depicted in S. Y. Agnon's novel Sippur Pashut.*]

Sippur Pashut (A Simple Story) is one of the five major novels of Nobel Laureate S. Y. Agnon. Written in 1935, it is set in Galicia in the declining world of Eastern European Jewish life some twenty-five years earlier.

The broad outlines of the story are indeed quite simple, although the novel is far more complex in its symbolic structure, character development, and potential "levels of meaning." A seventeen-year-old boy, Hirshel Horowitz, is trapped between the values of his bourgeois parents, Baruch Meir and Tsirel Klinger Horowitz, and his own spiritual needs in the changing world. The novel treats the conflicts and resolutions which grow out of his situation. Galician society of 1910 decreed that Hirshel would marry the respectable Minah Tsiemlich (meaning "so so") instead of the night blooming Blumah Nacht, whom he truly loves and who represents eros and freedom as well as personal fulfillment. The forced marriage and its implications for Hirshel's freedom contribute to what really amounts to a nervous breakdown which Agnon perceives in metaphysical terms. Hirshel's cure is coupled with his return to society, acceptance of his "so so" wife, and the regeneration of a new family. Hirshel strives throughout the novel to "correct his attributes" by breaking away from his family and establishing an independent ground of operation, and thus the conclusion of the novel is a surprise and, indeed, a disappointment. He rejects his idealistic gropings and settles down into the family business, inheriting his grandfather's store in the same way that he inherited a family curse, another cause of his mental disturbance.

For Agnon, no less than for Shakespeare, human events have metaphysical implications, and an incorrect marriage reflects a state of the universe, just as fixing what is wrong in the world has possible messianic implications. The time is definitely "out of joint" in Shibbush, Hirshel's town; something is rotten there, though the narrator hides the rottenness under layers of irony. The name "Shibbush" in Hebrew means something like "malfunction" and seems to be a distortion of the name of Agnon's own hometown, Bucacz.

A debate has been conducted around this novel with regard to the narrator's feelings about Hirshel's resolution. Scholars have suggested the levels of irony within the story; on the one hand, Hirshel's capitulation to bourgeois norms is disgusting, but on the other, it seems to be the only resolution. Is Hirshel to be scorned for having given up his ideals? Or is the world unfixable, in which case his capitulation is not only tolerable but appropriate? A line which appears throughout the novel is the narrator's assurance that "the bourgeoisie are the essence of the world"; and while the line strikes a biting tone each time it is said, one cannot help but feel that Agnon meant it in the most literal sense.

Although part of a larger argument that the entire novel resides in ambiguity, the discussion here is limited to a consideration of the ways in which setting is used to heighten that ambiguity. Setting enriches the problems of *Sippur Pashut* by adding layer upon layer of paradox to an already paradoxical and ambiguous world. Agnon is always implying that things are not what they seem. He means this, also, quite literally.

The psychiatrist Langsam and the narrator of *Sippur Pashut* comment on the treatment of Hirshel Horowitz's psychiatric condition:

> The most important thing is not to close the patient up in an insane asylum, nor to return him home immediately, for even a healthy person can become insane from an insane asylum, and in the city, the children will throw rocks at him and call him crazy.[1]

Langsam's description of two ways in which environments affect people parallels two of the ways in which setting influences Hirshel. He is, variously, attacked by his environment, or he takes on aspects of it, as the statement suggests; in most instances he is measured by how close he is to its standards. Problems relating to setting have been dealt with in Agnon criticism but not exclusively in terms of the total impact of setting on *Sippur Pashut* and its protagonist.

Sippur Pashut is in part a novel of manners and morals, as defined by Lionel Trilling,[2] and Hirshel's emotional disorder and subsequent "adjustment" is directly related to his ability or inability to "belong" to that setting in which those manners and morals find expression. The settings are rarely metaphoric in nature, rather they operate as extensions of the protagonist. The social environment yields synecdochic details which contribute to the recurring motifs that take the story beyond its social levels.[3] As a novel in which social environment plays such a great part, *Sippur Pashut* is replete with rich descriptions of setting. The specific settings may be viewed in terms of the larger backdrop of Shibbush and the ancillary locales, such as Lemberg and Malikrovik. The specific focus in many scenes constitutes a microcosm of that larger setting, and the details of these more intimate settings become synecdochic elements which contribute to characterization. Indeed, each of the locations in which action takes place builds "characterization" in the same measure that Tsirel believes that they build or destroy "character": the home of the Horowitzes, their store, the Zionist club, the home of Gildenhorn, the Tsiemlich farm, the apartment of Hirshel and Minah, Hirshel's synagogue, the streets of Shibbush, and Langsam's clinic in Lemberg. A consideration of varying aspects of setting will demonstrate that setting is used not to clarify the status of the protagonist, but to complicate it.

The city into which Hirshel is born is the city in which he is to finish out his life. It is a place in social transition, a major center of business and social affairs. It is large enough to have aspirations of being an important city but small enough to limit the choices which a young man has:

> In those days the glory of the Torah had departed, and Jewish young men left their books for business. The *bright* ones went to study that which yielded profit, and the average ones occupied themselves in commerce. There was yet another category not involved in Torah and not involved in business and who were supported by their parents while they occupied themselves with matters that were not of the community, either Zionism or Socialism. (65)

Shibbush is further characterized as a community whose people "know what the body needs, but do not know what the soul needs" (180), and in general the texture of the story suggests that an air of boredom pervades the town.[4] The question of people's bodily needs is presented with a measure of ambiguity in the narrator's discussion of Shibbush citizens who have gone to America. On the one hand, Shibbush does not meet all the physical needs of its people, for they are eager for the better material life in America. On the other: "To tell the truth, the air in America is not as nice as this here" (119).

The sequence in which the narrator treats the general atmosphere of Shibbush and Hirshel's place within it is telling. The apparent digression regarding the emigrants with the narrator's ironic pose regarding the preference of Shibbush by the native who has returned is followed by a brief paragraph which concludes Chapter 11:

> If the air of Shibbush which has no solidity is able to keep the natives of Shibbush in Shibbush, how much the *more so* can pillows and blankets do it. Hirshel intended to flee from Shibbush, but when he put his head on the pillow and covered himself with his blanket, he knew immediately that he would not leave Shibbush. (119)

In this instance, sequence helps us see how much a child of Shibbush Hirshel is. In a later instance, sequence teaches us the opposite. We learn (134) that Hirshel is settling into the business of the store, but then we learn

(135) that he and Shibbush really are not in accord on what makes a store successful. He is a son of Shibbush, only in part.

The society of Shibbush is not totally static, and yet the narrator does not see the changes as dramatically affecting anyone's life. The static mood prevails, even when he is telling us of dramatic changes:

> The times were changing, and opinions were being altered. Singers who at one time were treated with contempt had suddenly come to be treated with respect. Students went around with them and openly called them artists. . . . It is impossible to say that the singers had changed, and it is impossible to say that they hadn't changed. Hirshel certainly hadn't changed. The stamp of the *ba' 'al bayit* isn't erased easily. (78)

The two poles which are dealt with throughout the novel are thus reflected in this passage. The norms of the older generation are described ironically, while the norms of the new generation are not praised. And if "the stamp of the *ba' 'al bayit* isn't erased easily," then one can be certain that more young people than Hirshel are retaining bourgeois attitudes.

The store of the Horowitz family is, of course, the nucleus around which life revolves, and it helps the reader measure Hirshel. The store supports the family economically as well as architecturally, in that their living quarters are on the second floor. Through the store Baruch Meir met and married Tsirel and rejected Mirel, and by its standards Tsirel is able to evaluate her son:

> Hirshel returned to the store and behaved like a true shopkeeper. . . . Tsirel saw and her heart was happy. From the time that Hirshel entered the store he was never as occupied with business as he was in those days. Tsirel, who had forced him into the store, never hoped that he would fully commit himself to business. It was enough for Tsirel that Hirshel work in the store and not pursue things of no consequence, and now she saw that he acted like a real merchant. (79)

The store is very much like Shibbush, its city: aware of the physical needs of men but not their spiritual needs. The store is described in some detail, commensurate perhaps with its centrality to the levels of meaning within the novel:

> If there are three or four people inside, it seems as if the store is full of customers. But there is never a time in which there aren't more than five or six. The tables are laden with scales full of goods. Tsirel is seated at the door. She herself does not deal in sales but is speaking with customers. (133)

Hirshel variously fits into the mood of the store (or rather "seems" to fit) or is unable to adjust. The vacillation is spread throughout the novel; only after his return from Lemberg does he "seem" to fit in once and for all. The store as a barometer is not really consistent, and Hirshel's

various closeness or alienation from it obviously confuses and pleases Tsirel alternately. One image remains, however, which may complicate how the narrator feels about Hirshel's ultimate adjustment. Early in the novel:

> It never occurred to Hirshel that he would not leave there quickly, but the odor of the ginger, and the cinnamon, the raisins, and the wine and cognac and all the other smells of the store were sweeter to him than the smell of the Gemara. Similarly, the customers appealed to him more than the people of the *bet midrash*. (67)

Here, the smells are synecdochic details which suggest that life in the store is indeed sweeter. The narrator uses objective facts as part of his setting here, and no matter how much we would like the narrator to reject Hirshel's final decision, the fact is that the store smells sweet to the protagonist, the narrator, and the reader.

The home of Tsirel and Baruch Meir is not the major focus of their lives. We are introduced to the home quite early in the novel and familiarized with its norms almost immediately, though a lengthy description of the setting is missing. The narrator's periodic digression into domestic details (120, for example) does lend some concreteness to the home, but the lack of concern with the home is precisely the sense the narrator seems to want to convey. While specific images and synecdochic features of the store are distributed throughout the novel (smells, scales, customers, piles of money), the Horowitz home is to be pictured in a more generalized way. In a sense we know more about the home from what we know about the people in it, and then we view the characters in the light of what we can assume about the home. It is a good bourgeois home, accustomed to comfort and always served by a maid of some kind. It is a model of small town urban elegance, on the level of the Tsiemlich farm in Malikrovik which is described in greater detail. Agnon's greater emphasis on the Tsiemlich home as setting is consistent with the fact that, for the Tsiemlichs, home as well as farm is essential to their lives. The Horowitzes do not fully belong in their home, suggested by the fact that they are locked out by their cantankerous maid, who pretends she does not know who they are (114). On the next occasion of their departure, Tsirel has to make certain that she is not locked out again. (Note that "al Kapot ha' man'ul"—on the threshold—is the title of the collection in which *Sippur Pashut* is found.)

The Tsiemlich home is the scene of the Jewish country gentry, where food is the center of life. On a winter evening after the engagement, we experience a rather ironic entry into bucolic settings which are to play such a crucial role in the novel. The peacefulness of the scene is contrasted with its strangeness in a way which anticipates most of the other pastoral scenes in the novel (121). The dinner scene in Chapters 12 and 13 is truly impressive and begins with a description of how the table is laid: "The table was set with breads and three kinds of liqueurs, one simple, one seasoned with cumin, and one with a fruit base for women. Also on the table were marinated mushrooms" (125). The dinner scene describes the reactions of Baruch Meir and Tsirel to the Olympian feast. In many ways the Tsiemlich's meal belongs to Tsirel, as she dominates conversations, and because she is really characterized by food throughout the novel.[5] While she may not be able to take charge of her own house, she can take charge of almost any other situation. Here the narrator focuses on her concern that her son is not eating, and her voice is heard above all. We are reminded that the opening scene in the Horowitz house revolves around the cakes which Blumah has baked (60), so that in one sense Tsirel and Hirshel are connected by this concern. On the other hand, the banalities of conversation regarding the food place Hirshel farther and farther on the margin. Both food and talk repel him. The food as a synecdochic feature of this setting ties Tsirel to Bertha and thus alienates Hirshel from them both.

The appearance of a gravy boat in the grotesque shape of a goose (126) adds to the absurdity of the scene; and the goose is to return just as absurdly near the end of the novel (269). For Hirshel this society is bizarre, in which Jews behave grandly, goose-shaped ceramics crown the table, and a marriage broker has been invited to dinner even though the *shidduch* has been completed. Hirshel ruminates on the social patterns of his family: "Now there was time to think. It seemed strange to him that men leave their homes in order to eat in someone else's home" (126). His fasting and rejection of the food, especially on this occasion, annoy his mother. Food seems to represent the physicality from which Hirshel is trying to liberate himself.[6] Thus his eating only a few moments later (129) is a kind of capitulation which adds distance between Hirshel and the narrator. We must never forget that Hirshel is reported to be especially in need of the pillows and blankets of Shibbush.

The setting in Malikrovik is at one and the same time totally strange and yet familiar to Hirshel. It is familiar and yet strange to his parents, who are overwhelmed by the novelty of mushrooms in the winter. Hirshel is overwhelmed by a social custom which is really commonplace for him. Other settings, simultaneously natural and foreign to Hirshel, are partly responsible for crucial events within the novel. On the final night of Hanukkah, the entire Horowitz family is invited to the Gildenhorn home. The narrator uses a card game to describe the social surroundings and Hirshel's feeling of "not belonging" to them. The relationship of the people at the party to Hirshel is summed up briefly:

> and other guests whom Hirshel knew and didn't know. After returning his greeting they returned to their cards and paid no attention to him. Hirshel was left to himself and sat where he sat . . . Hirshel was dressed well, but as a man who was not accustomed to come into society; he fidgeted with his clothes lest his tie wasn't straight or his socks were falling. He was as one into whose clothes a moth had entered, and he was distracted. (104)

His feeling of not belonging is enhanced by the condescending way in which Balaban tosses him a cigarette (106). The party scene creates a sense of chaos, heightening the confusion which Hirshel brought with him to the party. The smoke confuses him, the card playing strikes him as foolish, and the people even look like cards. But his alienation here must be viewed in the light of the fact that he might indeed belong, for no detail in this setting is really foreign to him. He himself smokes, as we see on a number of occasions, and the "good life" suggested by the party is quite in consonance with his own life. In the confusion created by the setting, Hirshel clutches at Minah and has, really, one of his few satisfying conversations with her. The marginal feeling which both of them have at the party seems to draw them toward each other and more or less to seal their fate.

By the time of his wedding, Hirshel has related ambivalently to the family store, the Malikrovik setting, and the Gildenhorn home. Each of these settings is comprised of elements with which he is totally familiar, and yet each of them plays a part in creating his mood of estrangement and ultimate breakdown. "Ambivalent" is appropriate, for Hirshel accepts and rejects the values inherent in each of these settings. The same ambivalence is reflected in his relationship to Minah; through elements of the setting this ambivalence is sharpened, yet one must keep in mind Hirshel's positive feelings for Minah.

Hirshel explicitly wants to reject Minah almost immediately after their marriage, but the implicit difficulty in accomplishing that rejection is conveyed with the help of setting. They do share certain values,[7] and they are brought together in two of the specific settings which confound Hirshel. Principal among these shared norms is their mutual desire to live in an apartment separate from the Horowitz family. Prompted by Minah's desire not to live with Tsirel and Baruch Meir, Sofiah Gildenhorn impresses upon Tsirel the need for the young people to live alone (Chapters 16 and 17). The apartment, potentially a symbol of independence, becomes a symbol of the dependence which Minah and Hirshel retain: "It was good that Sofiah had said that Minah needed an apartment to herself, otherwise there would have been no room for her father's gifts" (164). This ambivalence is noted in the furnishings of the apartment itself. In one of their functions, they reflect a young well-to-do couple: their "home was in good order and had fine furnishings" (164). The description of the specific items within this well-furnished house supports one's expectations that the young couple are observing the social norms very nicely: "White curtains with a red sash in the middle hung over the windows" (164). But that Agnon chose this one detail of the window for the paragraph suggests that he is using synecdoche to reflect more on the totality of his characters' personality than on any part of it: "The world appears to them from the windows like a triangle. But Minah does not stand at the window. He whose house is pleasant from within, why should he look outside?" (164).

We move from the house as a symbol of independence to the house as a symbol of dependence and acceptance of norms. Ultimately, the details of the setting reflect a modified difference between the norms of the generations after all: "It is possible that the chairs of plush in the home of Baruch Meir were more comfortable for sitting than the bamboo chairs although one could move them to wherever one wishes to sit" (164). One can sense the uncomfortable parent squirming in the newly styled furniture of his children and being reminded of how much more comfortable the old style furniture is. In some way, however, even the assessment of the new style furniture is carried on in terms of bourgeois, practical standards. At least the bamboo chairs can be moved around.

Agnon rarely describes specific physical details without the addition of some commentary. In the section under scrutiny above, the narrator takes us through an entire life by way of the physical setting: we move from the information that the house is in good order, to a detail regarding the house's furnishings (the curtains), to a statement about windows on the world which are not used, to a return to a comment about how social norms affect one's attitudes regarding the world, and finally to a specific comment on the happiness of Hirshel and Minah. "It is impossible to say that Hirshel and Minah were happy, and it is impossible to say that they weren't happy; but their house was in good order, and they didn't lack anything" (164). The passage thus makes its point and helps create the novel's atmosphere through the combination of concrete objects and evaluative comments. The narrator's ironic attitude about the scene places the relationship of Minah and Hirshel in a rather gloomy context. It also creates a sense of confusion as to the authenticity of Hirshel's resistance to the values of his family and reinforces another ambiguity in Hirshel's resistance to the relationship with Minah. He is repelled by her but drawn to her family setting. Hirshel's nuptial home is another index of his increasing mental disturbance: "Why did Hirshel enjoy guests at first, because he saw himself through them as a *ba' 'al bayit;* when his house became sour to him, guests became sour to him" (174).

We must turn now to a type of setting which is unrelated to rooms, homes, furniture, food, and customers: the outside world where manners and morals are liberated, and where material values are not important. The various bucolic settings of the novel play a crucial part in the changes which take place within Hirshel. The walks which Hirshel is counselled to take for his health become a part of a ritual of lurking surreptitiously around Blumah's street (again he is "on the threshold"). At first Hirshel has difficulty in making this exercise a routine (182), but once the routine has some purpose (the visiting of Blumah's street), other pleasures and other experiences present themselves:

> It is pleasant to walk alone on summer nights in quiet streets. The store is behind you, and the boxes and cases don't poke out your eyes and the customers aren't obsequious to you and the odor

of their mouths doesn't come to your mouth and Tsirel your mother doesn't sit in front of you and jabber what she has to jabber and you don't have to run home to sit with Minah. (186)

Once again Agnon employs an accumulation of details to capture the sense of the store: once we saw cinnamon, ginger, raisins, and cognac; now we have the odor of mouths, boxes, cases, and jabbering. Thoughts about being free of the store clearly reflect the idea of breaking out of the parents' urban world and relate specifically to generational tension.[8] But the bucolic settings seem to have value as ends in themselves:

> It was Hirshel's preference to walk simply alone, where the streets were peacefully quiet, with houses set amidst the trees with the stars hanging on them above, with a light breeze brushing his face, the waters flowing gently and the forest giving off its smell. (186)

Bucolic settings enable Hirshel to escape from his environment, but perhaps most significantly, such settings seem to lead him into his "insanity" and out of it. After all, Hirshel's "fit" takes place in the woods, and yet his cure is effected in the peaceful countrified settings of the Langsam clinic. Not surprisingly, the forest in which Hirshel walks is hostile and friendly to him at the same time. When he begins his therapeutic walks in the woods, the dogs of the forest bark at him, but eventually they become accustomed to his presence (184). The link between his comfort in this setting and the woods as the locus of his insane behavior is clear, but it is a link of polarities and relates to similar polarities within the novel. The woods are friendly but are the scene of his insanity. The store is hostile, but its smells beckon, and it is the scene of sanity. Bourgeois homes are where Hirshel belongs, but they disgust him.

The streets where Hirshel walks serve to strengthen his ties to the history of the community, and his interest in its history is one of the things which alienates him from Minah. Akaviah Mazal is one of the town historians, and he lives in that part of town. Since his marriage to Tirzah in "biDmi Yamehah" Mazal has made peace with this provincial town, not so much in its present state but in its historically ideal form. The quarter is now occupied by no Jews except for Mazal, and yet it evokes more specifically Jewish memories than any other location. Mazal seems to have become a part of the town by being cut off from it. "Hirshel walked quietly in the street. What did Hirshel think about during all of his walks? Many things happened to our forefathers on that street, and there are many things there about which man from Israel might think" (184). The location, then, represents a part of the past which is irretrievable except by memory. Hirshel has very little narrated personal past, but Blumah, from his past, is here. History, pastoral moods, and eros thus join through the setting with which Hirshel tries to make contact. He never succeeds, however, and remains ultimately an urban man, leaving his first son to a more or less permanent life in the country with his in-laws.

In order to reach the resolution which brings him to a cure, Hirshel must move to another pastoral setting and there experience the unique cure of Dr. Langsam. The clinic at Lemberg is indeed peaceful and slow, a setting which is congenial to Langsam's laborious discussion of his childhood and to the sweet songs which he sings to Hershel. Langsam's clinic is contrasted so sharply with the Horowitz store that Hirshel's need of this bucolic mood in preparing himself to work in the family's business is indeed strange.

One of the important settings, once Hirshel has returned to his family, is the town synagogue, which plays an important social role in the novel and has all of the bourgeois associations of a contemporary synagogue in small town diaspora. Money is donated to it in due time, and lip service is paid. But for Hirshel it takes on special qualities. Like the street he frequents, the synagogue represents a place away from Minah and, like that street, is a place of history. Furthermore, it is linked to Hirshel's peculiar ruminations:

> And they still pray there as in earlier days and no one engages in idle speech, and they are careful to pray at the proper times and they do not change the accustomed reading of their forefathers, nor any prayer, nor melody, they neither add to them nor subtract from them. Mazal wrote a special chapter on the synagogue in his book. . . . It is good to Hirshel to be alone with his thoughts. . . . Hirshel had a thousand thoughts. God in heaven knows what those thoughts were. (177)

Indeed, a part of Hirshel's two stage emotional breakdown takes place in the synagogue (Chapter 26). It is interesting to compare the description of the synagogue with the narrator's comments about the changing social norms in Shibbush. If the synagogue does not change, but Hirshel does, can we say that now that he is married and settled with his wife, Hirshel will begin coming to the synagogue on special holidays and donating gifts for its support? The synagogue is a place which preserves norms, but those people who preserve norms support it only superficially. Shimon Hirsh Klinger understood, however, that the difference between the store and the synagogue lay in the idle talk which filled the latter.

Agnon uses his setting to maximum advantage, without forcing the reader to be aware of the importance of the role of setting within the novel. He creates metaphor, metonymic settings, and synecdochic details; often the detail becomes symbolic of Hirshel's changing personality at a given time. Setting in the novel is central to the descriptions of Hirshel's efforts to draw near to and away from his social surrounding; at the same time, it has the many elements of romance which Shaked discusses. The vacillating hostility and friendliness of a variety of settings suggests that Hirshel really belongs nowhere. His residence in Shibbush may be uncertain in the same ambiguous and paradoxical way in which setting (and indeed the entire universe) is treated throughout the novel. No evidence proves that any setting is really totally hostile or friendly to him, and we must examine Hirshel's apparently close relationship to the store as

only tentative once again. Is his return inevitable and thus for him the only solution? Does anything indicate that Hirshel really belongs in any setting? Is any setting used consistently enough to determine a fixed relationship between character and setting?

The characters' relationship to setting is one of the dynamic poles of *Sippur Pashut*. Atmospheres are as fixed as the family curse (66), but Hirshel's changing relationship to them promises no consistency. No setting represents him. At the beginning of the novel, in another context, we are told that "the man from the market place is not the same as the Tannaitic scholar who sat and studied Torah" (78). If we have learned anything from the setting in *Sippur Pashut,* we know that the man who might study Torah is not so different from the man who sits in the market place or store.

NOTES

[1] S. Y. Agnon, *Sippur Pashut* (Tel Aviv: Schocken, 1961), p. 222. Subsequent references are to this edition, Volume III of the Collected Works, eighth edition; the translation is my own.

[2] Lionel Trilling, *The Liberal Imagination* (New York, 1953), p. 200ff.

[3] Gershon Shaked, "Bat hamelekh use' 'udat ha'em" (The King's Daughter and the Feast of her Mother), *Gazit,* 24 (1966-7), 135-47. Shaked demonstrates the relationship between the "social" and "romance" elements within the novel.

[4] Arnold Band, *Nostalgia and Nightmare* (Los Angeles, 1969), p. 246. Note the many dialogues, the narrator's suggestions that people have little to do, and in general what people seem to do.

[5] Cf. Shaked.

[6] Cf. Shaked.

[7] On Hirshel's essential bourgeois nature, cf. Josef Ewen, "He' 'arot ahadot le Sippur Pashut le S. Y. Agnon" (Some Comments on Agnon's *Sippur Pashut*), *Moznayim,* 29 (1970), 400-14.

[8] Baruch Kurzweil, "Ba' 'ayat hadorot besippure Agnon" (The Problem of Generations in Agnon's Stories), in *Masot 'al Sippure S. Y. Agnon* (Essays on the Stories of S. Y. Agnon) (Jerusalem, 1970).

Carol P. James

SOURCE: "Seriality and Narrativity in Calvino's *Le Città invisibili,*" in *MLN,* Vol. 97, No. 1, January, 1982, pp. 144-61.

[*In the following excerpt, James discusses Italo Calvino's* The Invisible City.]

Forse del mondo è rimasto un terreno vago ricoperto da immondezzai, e il giardino pensile della reggia del Gran Kan. Sono le nostre palpebre che li separno, ma non si sa quale è dentro e quale è fuori.[1]

Keeping in mind that examples are always chosen for their pertinence and not at random, we can let Italo Calvino's novel *Le città invisibili* stand as an example of a work where postmodernism is both obvious and questionable. As if hesitating on some sort of threshold between the modern and the postmodern, the novel presents a double structure of narrativity and seriality: a story about Kublai Khan and Marco Polo surrounds eleven sets of five cities, grouped in arithmetically arranged series. The seriality of the cities defines the trait we shall treat as postmodern, while the framing device, the narrative of those cities which would put them into a certain perspective, relates to a modern, or in any case pre-postmodern, esthetic of a mise-en-abyme or "narrative context." Whether or not the frame actually recuperates the cities-series into the narrative will determine the final labeling of the novel as modern or postmodern. Our reading will attempt to clarify the necessity of this confrontation and its implications for reading in general.

Each of the nine sections of the book begins and ends in italics with a page or two of conversations between Polo and the Khan. These pre- and postfaces do not constitute a continuous narrative. The fifty-five cities, from a half page to three pages long, are divided among the nine sections, the first and last containing ten cities and the rest five each. There are eleven sets of five cities called, in order of their appearance, "Le città e la memoria," "Le città e il desiderio," "Le città e i segni," "Le città sottili," "Le città e gli scambi," "Le città e gli occhi," "Le città e il nome," "Le città e i morti," "Le città e il cielo," "Le città continue," and "Le città nascoste." In so far as possible each city is followed by one from the next set so that the sequencing forms a pattern of simultaneous forward and reverse movement. Sections 2 through 8 begin with the fifth and last city of a set and end with the first city of a new set. The movement works as follows in the fourth section: from the first to the fifth city, 1-2-3-4-5, the titles read, "Le città e i segni 5," "Le città sottili 4," "Le città e gli scambi 3," "Le città e gli occhi 2," "Le città e il nome l." Sections 1 and 9 are arranged 1, 2-1, 3-2-1, 4-3-2-1, and 5-4-3-2, 5-4-3, 5-4, 5, respectively, to accommodate the introduction and wrapping up of the series. While each city is doubly named by its position in its set and by its own proper name, the italicized passages are nameless, indicated only by ellipsis dots in the table of contents.

The cities, deployed geometrically as they are among shapeless narrative fragments, can be compared to a sculpture, perhaps one of Don Judd's series of cubes set up at precise distances one from another in a gallery where people may circulate freely around them. A comparison of the cities to postmodern works of art is apt. Functioning according to set theory in mathematics, seriality is a way of making art without concentrating on a object. The art

lies in relationships, not in material entities. Where formalist, modernist art seeks meaning in the deterministic relations among a composition's visible elements, the components of a series derive their value by creating their own ever-changing context.[2] The elements of a series are arranged numerically and no one part leads or takes precedence over any other(s). A systems esthetic functions on *différance*. Seriality is without paradigm, the "model" itself becoming part of the set.[3] Not only has seriality become a mark of the times, but, borrowing from Kuhn's concept of paradigms (not so far from Bachelard's *epistémè*), Jack Burnham writes that art now is between paradigms (*Great Western Salt Works,* p. 15). Serial arrangements generated from rules or chance procedures are based on logical operations rather than on the sort of privately invented signs or shapes we have attributed to inspiration or genius. Seriality is numerical; bypassing the ego, it embodies no values of beauty or taste. As used by the arts it is post-humanist. Having abandoned his or her work to the contextualizing of the consumer, the postmodern artist destabilizes the writer-reader roles, redefining the artistic experience as a shared one. As we shall see, the roles of listener and teller in *Le città invisibili* are exchangeable and the problem of narrator and narrated irresolvable. The notion of active reading, the leveling of the roles of creator and critic, necessarily follows in the wake of this change in mental processes. This revolution was necessitated by the end of teleology, that end which was worked out in modernist art with its concern with deaths—the death of God, of literature, of art—and with renewal—the avant-garde and the Poundian imperative "Make it New. If postmodernist thinking takes for granted the equality of artist and receiver and the ambivalence between creator and creation (see body art, for example), it is only because it has gone through the modernist backing away from representation or reflection of a world engaged in an end-seeking process, away from illusionism and mimesis, into and through the solipsism of self-generation, radical irony and their corollaries of emphasis on form and medium. The formalist aspect of modernism reposes on its urge to find meaning other than in content because the significance of content always stems from its referential function, and reference, always dependent on the metaphorical leap between sign and referent, poses a theology, a faith, necessarily grounded in an ultimate end or purpose.

Postmodernism has abandoned problem solving as a model (if not all models), has ceased the search for unity and/or stability, and has accepted the paradoxical picture physics provides of the universe: a universe whose laws are not laws but projections of relativity not really provable, a universe whose infinity is not eternity. The use of chance and indeterminacy as operators in art reflects these newer axioms of science. The anonymity of systems art and the devaluation of the "look" of things (the art object as fetish) follow from the physicists' disregard for any surface/depth distinction in favor of a knowledge of structure based on the incalculable movements of invisible subatomic particles. The topology of the postmodern rests on the slippery post-moebian surface, twisted in shape, undifferentiated from any depth or well-spring, without beginning or end. The arrangement of Calvino's cities is not one that builds up a story or anything at all except its own system. After Gödel's theorem we know numbers can only work if we accept certain unprovable axioms.[4] But nevertheless they work and seriality has become a concept useful in esthetic contexts where no proof is called for.

The reading of *Le città invisibili* is complicated by a double seriality, a double undecidability. First of all, the numbers set up a hierarchy of first to last which bears no relation whatsoever to the "story." The arithmetic arrangement misplaces the thematics of the groups—death, continuity, signs, desire, and so forth—by juxtaposing cities of different sets. Number, while belonging to the basics of logic and order, is also on the side of nonsense: numbers do not represent or relate the way that the names of things have meaning. Thus numbers, especially when associated with proper names which are also perceived as having no intrinsic meaning, make us uneasy when they are removed from their strictly arithmetic, symbolic terrain and used as ordering devices in a (fictional) context where the meanings of words and actions are overdetermined. Meeting up with a meaningless set of numbers in a novel is an experience of the uncanny which considerably upsets our novel-reading habits. Not accustomed to narrative in serial arrangement, the reader seeks transitions from one city to the next and resemblances among cities of the same rubric. The numerical arrangement of the cities which produces the palindromic aspects mentioned above (the 5-4-3-2-1, the 1-2-3-4-5, the 11 sets of 5 = 55) is symmetrical and unexpandable. The totalizing synthesis of the number system can also turn into a platonic metaphor, a *mathesis universalis,* which threatens to swallow the "realist" part of the narrative, the part whose rules of reading set up the book as a novel and not theology. In addition to these two types of naming (the thematic names of sets and the numbers which specify or "name" the linear order), each of the cities has its own name, a feminine-sounding name, which belongs to no set or order at all. The normal narrative-reading habit of searching for a mimetically motivated order in an arbitrary system (numbers) sets up a numerology, an intertextuality of finding meaning in numbers and their arrangements. The usual narrative-reading procedure of paronomasia, of reading proper names as common, signifying, nouns, is frustrated by the diversity of names (who can keep the cities straight?) within the named sets. The multiple-dimension grid readings (across the sets, across like numbers, in numerical order) which the seriality of *Le città invisibili* invites are frustrated by the disparateness, by the lack of connections—the silence—between the cities as well as by the wealth of symbols and emblems each city offers up to interpretation. The hermeneutic enterprise seems to rest in fitting the cities into the surrounding narrative where they are interspliced, that is, interjected artificially by a connection which remains essentially a break.

The seriality of the cities forms an aporia with respect to the narrative. The strict (reversible but not expandable) arrangement flouts the convention that narrative is going somewhere, is approaching an end or resolution. The cities are also holes in any presumed totality of narration. This aporetic position of the cities—at once blockage and lack—results from their seriality and engages postmodern questions about the nature of narrative and representation. If we consider the arbitrariness and perfection of numerical arrangements to be unnatural signs, then the signs used in narration are natural (or at least pseudo-natural) and they ought to recuperate or naturalize the arbitrary signs if the book is to be a novel. There is a tendency simply to disregard the numbers and sets or see them as the author's whim or mimic of a mapping procedure. If, however, we understand seriality to be different and irrecuperable, we acknowledge the aporia, the irreducible gap. By introducing into a novelistic context the use of an element foreign to language, Calvino sets *Le città invisibili* on the cusp between the modern and the postmodern.

Within the strict grammar of number, the thematic categories of the cities are not static; the individual cities are not examples or cases but nodes in a circulation of the themes throughout the sets. The naming of themes (the repetition of the set titles) retains the role of title and remains apart from the telling of the individual stories. For the reader, the mixture of the phenomenological (eyes, trade, sky), the metaphysical (death and desire), and the ambiguous ("sottili"—thin *and* subtle), complicates the texture of circulation. The cities refuse to give themselves over to a thematic pattern that would support, replicate, or mirror the numerical pattern. Seen from this perspective, the cities fragment themselves thematically because of the impossibility of reading any coherence into the various sets ("Le città e la memoria" have as much to do with desire as do "Le città e il desiderio"). The cities remain, or better put, are remainders or fragments at odds with their arrangement.

The novel and the city seem to have been born and bred together as products of mercantilism and capitalism. Ihab Hassan notes the postmodernist splintering of the modernist rubric of urbanism according to the multifarious manifestations of the City in the literary and political fictions of today: Global Village, minority movements, urban crime, Hiroshima.[5] Calvino's cities involve these disparate characteristics; they are deliberate impossibilities, exotic in the sense of never homey, always *unheimlich*, enticing but foreign. Individual cities mix the beautiful and the ugly, the fanciful and the lugubrious, life and death. Armilla consists only of a set of plumbing and bathroom fixtures (pp. 55-56); Ottavia is a spider-web city (p. 81); Bauci stands on stilts (p. 83); the people of Eusapia have so invested themselves in their fantasies that they have taken to imitating the scenes they have set up in their necropolis (pp. 115-116); in Fillide empty space is the site of imaginary points connected by invisible roads (p. 97); Argia is buried, with earth replacing its air (p. 133). The people of the cities are not characters; they seem more like decorations in a silent tapestry or figures in a myth; in other words, emblems or allegories of those cities they inhabit.

The cities do not combine to form a universe or nation or empire (the importance of these politics and their relation to the narrative will be examined subsequently) and even within themselves they are not one. The reading of each city shows it to contain its other. The doubling within the cities takes many forms: Laudomia, (pp. 147-149), is populated by its dead and its yet to be born as well as its living. Andria (pp. 156-157) duplicates the form of the constellations in its sky. Sofronia consists of two half-cities, a carnival and a brick and marble city, the latter dismantled and shipped away in off-season (p. 69). In Isaura "un passaggio invisibile condiziona quello visibile" (p. 28). The double images are often on the rhetorical plane: "Della città di Dorotea si può parlare in due maniere" (p. 17); in Tamara "la città . . . ti fa ripetere il suo discorso, e mentre credi di visitare Tamara non fai che registrare i nomi con cui essa definisce se stessa e tutte le sue parti" (p. 22). If at bottom the cities seem all alike, it is not because they add up to one city but because each must create itself as the paradigm of itself. Seriality permits only succession; there are no causal effects. The cities neither interact nor refer to one another. The doubling within each city denies it a single origin or essence. "A Eudossia . . . si conserva un tappeto in cui puoi contemplare la vera forma della città. . . . Ma allo stesso modo tu puoi trarne la conclusione opposta: che la vera mappa dell'universo sia la città d'Eudossia così com'è, una macchia che dilaga senza forma . . ." (pp. 103-104). Memory and origin are finally confused: Zirma is "ridondante: si ripete perché qualcosa arrivi a fissarsi nella mente. . . . La memoria è ridondante: ripete i segni perché la città cominci a esistere" (p. 27). All these chiastic movements in the reading of the cities replace the linear movements which motivate traditional narrative. The serial arrangement displaces thematics for a rhetorical pattern of non-origin and non-causality. The cities remain incomplete, forever moving from one state to another. "La città ti appare come un tutto in cui nessun desiderio va perduto e di cui tu fai parte," but you are submitting to the power of desire; "la tua fatica che dà forma al desiderio prende dal desiderio la sua forma, e tu credi di godere per tutta Anastasia mentre non nesei che lo schiavo" (p. 20). Such are the consequences of the lure of wholeness.

It is tempting to relegate the cities to the realm of dream. Their discontinuity and disembodiment, the strong currents of desire and fear, and their position apart from the diurnal conversations of Polo and the Khan set them up as experiences from the Other. Dreams, or the desire for dreams, are escapes; the Khan wants to hear of wondrous places of beauty: "E' tempo che il mio impero, già troppo cresciuto verso il fuori, . . . cominci a crescere al di dentro', e sognava boschi di melegranate . . ." (p. 79). But Polo reminds him that "< l >e città come i sogni sono costruite di desideri e di paure, anche se il filo del loro discorso è segreto, le loro regole assurde, le prospettive ingannevoli, e ogni cosa ne nasconde un'altra" (p. 50). The reader is led to consider that all the cities are Kublai Khan's dreams, like Lalage: "Ti racconterò cosa ho sognato stanotte, . . . vedevo di lontano elevarsi le guglie

d'una città dai pinnacoli sottili." And Polo replied, "La città che hai sognato è Lalage" (p. 80). Or that perhaps Polo has dreamed the cities. The cities might also be considered dream auguries of the fate of civilization. The overprocreation of Procopia (pp. 152-153), the ecological disaster brought about by a futile frenzy to extinguish pests in Teodora (pp. 164-165), the endless suburban blight of Trude (p. 134), and the throw-away culture of Leonia (pp. 119-121) stretch the Khan's empire into the twentieth century. But *Le città invisibili* seems hardly to be a cautionary tale built on a well-worn time shift topos. The topology working here is more truly like dream than like fantasy or day dream. The cities are places of desire and interdiction and their only real location is that in their set and in the series of sets. Seriality bears close relation to dream where, as Freud noted, sequence replaces cause and effect as a "logical relation" in the mechanism of dream formation.[6] Sequence and similarity—rhetorically we could speak of metonymy—define the grammar of dreams. The hesitancy between dream and wakefulness presents a further complication about the consciousness of the participants and the real place of the cities in their story. The possibility of dreams throws the reader off any straight course and forces the reinsertion of all the cities into another realm of mental process. Dream also provides a psychological accounting for a state of aporia and the rhetoric a novel can engage in to represent a simultaneous presence and absence or contradiction in modes of existence.

If the disconcerting numerical arrangement and the possibility that the cities are someone's dreams confuse the way toward interpretation, we must admit that this route has always already been broken up by the multiple deviations of the narrative. Who, we ask at the outset, is telling this story? The several types of narration frustrate the issue. The passages in italics are narrated in the third person, with the dialogue of Marco Polo and Kublai Khan in quotes except in the seventh section where the dialogue is presented dramatically, naming the character at each change of speaker. There is no self-named narrator here, but might we construe Italo's italics as a tease? The telling of the cities is even more complex. Already questioned in the suggestions that the cities are dreams or fictions Polo invents or has heard elsewhere, our certainty that Polo is recounting cities he has seen dissolves when we examine the use of the first person singular. Occurring first in the fourth city, the *I* debuts with the standard self-effacement of the storyteller: "Inutilmente, magnanimo Kublai, tenterò di descriverti la città di Zaira dagli alti bastioni" (p. 18). Other instances, such as that of Eutropia ("Vi dirò come," p. 70) and that of Ottavia ("Ora dirò come è Ottavia, città-ragnatela," p. 81) are also ancient devices, performative utterances which both announce their intention and initiate the storytelling. This directness, associated with the topos of sincerity, is undone by a caveat preceding the recounting of Olivia: "Nessuno sa meglio di te, saggio Kublai, che non si deve mai confonderela città col discorso che la descrive" (p. 67). Ipazia, the city which has more first person references than any other, is impossible to read: "Di tutti i cambiamenti di lingua che deve affrontare il viaggiatore in terre lontane, nessuno uguaglia quello che lo attende nella città di Ipazia, perché non riguarda le parole ma le cose" (p. 53). The voyager-storyteller finds that his only sure referent, his self-referent, is thrown into doubt and concludes, "Non c'è linguaggio senza inganno" (p. 54). These aphorisms then recall the novel's incipit, "Non è detto che Kublai Kan creda a tutto quel che dice Marco Polo quando gli descrive le città visitate nelle sue ambascerie" (p. 13), which sets up the cities as lies or metafictions but does not, at the outset, destroy storytelling as a conscious process. The text of the last of the cities and names, Irene, which begins with the name itself whose first letter is *I* also ends with a repetition of the name and an *I* telling of further narrative tricks: "Forse di Irene ho già parlato sotto altri nomi forse non ho parlato che di Irene" (p. 132). This *I* could never be that of Polo because a third-person narrator has already been inserted into the previous paragraph: "A questo punto Kublai Kan s'aspetta che Marco parli d'Irene com'è vista da dentro. E Marco non può farlo: . . . Irene è un nome di città da lontano, e se ci si avvicina cambia" (pp. 131-132). Where does this *I* who has seen the inside, who has a special knowledge, come from? The confusion about narrators, coupled with the suggestion that a city has multiple names, questions the numerical arrangement as well as the situating role of the italicized passages. It seems that perhaps, after all, the teller of the cities is not Polo but an anonymous "invisible" voice from nowhere.

The question of a narrator becomes crucial where the structure implies two narrators, an outer and an inner, but in the narration itself the unfolding of the cities denies the possibility of containment which a story-in-a-story, a narrative embedding, would provide. What Blanchot has called the narratorial voice ("voix narratrice")[7] becomes an impossibility in *Le città invisibili*. The narratorial voice is the voice of a subject that recounts something, knowing who and where it is: a conscious subject who keeps the story under control. Polo might be assumed to be the narratorial voice of the cities if we had not already seen that this cannot be. To this narratorial voice that poetics, in particular narratology, strives to systematize, Blanchot opposes the narrative voice ("voix narrative"), a neutral voice that, paradoxically, speaks from a place where the work is silent. The narrative voice has no place in the work, but neither does it look down upon it—it has no place, simply (*Entretien,* p. 565). The narrative voice places the fiction it narrates in a non-place, not in the idealistic sense of u-topia, but in the sense of residing in a fictional place, the *Unheimlich*. This no-place is always outside and missing, and as it cannot be part of the work but is nevertheless there, supplementarily: " . . . the 'it' . . . designates 'its' place both as that where it will always be missing and which therefore would remain empty, but also as a surplus of place, a place always in excess: *hypertopie*" (*Entretien,* pp. 563-564). The voicelessness (*aphonie*) and placelessness of the narrative voice render it mad, radical, unpoliceable: "it is

radically exterior, it comes from exteriority itself" (*Entretien*, p. 565); it is "the most critical which can, unheard, give over something to be heard" (*Entretien,* p. 567). The breakdown of the first person in the narration of the cities, as well as the serial arrangement—an arrangement which inhibits cogent narration and is not possibly the product of a narratorial voice—hints at the narrative voice which indeed comes from the radical elsewhere. The narrative voice exceeds the stories of the cities, invading the neuter of the surrounding italicized passages. We can no longer consider the Polo-Khan dialogues as a frame *surrounding* the cities. The possibilities of narrative deception—that the cities told might have no relation to Polo's voyages, for example—escape narratorial control and enrich reading in a sly way that complements the kind of mathematical probability and relativity set up by the serialization of the cities. The no-place of the narrative voice is concomitant with (does not symbolize or allegorize) the instability of substance and the irresolvable problem of telling (who is speaking, listening, inventing?) in a story about a vast empire that is fragmented and doomed to decline.

Polo's assertion at the beginning of the last section, "Chi comanda al racconto non è la voce: è l'orecchio" (p. 143), recognizes the narrative voice's importance in the economy of narration: the emperor Kublai Khan's enterprise is to get Polo to tell and tell and tell because by being the listener he thinks to direct the narration. The Khan means to establish his authority by bringing about (giving *place* to < *donner lieu à* >) a narrative that would be identifiable, wherein he could collect the cities of his empire into a connected whole; he tries to force the narrative voice to turn into a narratorial voice. The Khan has to have this sort of narrative because it is the narration which constitutes his empire and power: "Solo nei resoconti di Marco Polo, Kublai Kan riusciva a discernere, attraverso le muraglie e le torri destinate a crollare, la filigrana d'un disegno così sottile da sfuggire al morso delle termiti" (pp. 13-14). The Khan has power over his empire only if he turns it into fiction, even if he does not realize fiction's treacheries.

The telling of the stories, that is the cities, indeed results from Khan's desire to know his empire, when "to know" means "to possess." In the first quote in the italicized narrative he asks: "Il giorno in cui conoscerò tutti gli emblemi, . . . riuscirò a possedere il mio impero, finalmente?" (p. 30). Narrative is the demand for narrative[8] and it creates the economy, the power structure, of the work. The gap between the narrative and cities—they are not "interwoven" into the narration but exist in their serial elsewhere—is glimpsed by the Khan who at first has to interpret Polo's pantomimes or "logogriphs": "Il Gran Kan decifrava i segni, però il nesso tra questi e i luoghi visitati rimaneva incerto. . . . Nella mente del Kan l'impero si rifletteva in un deserto di dati labili e intercambiabili come grani di sabbia da cui emergevano per ogni città e provincia le figure evocate dai logogrifi del veneziano" (p. 30). The serial arrangement of the cities we read is not at all the description Polo gives Kublai piece by piece, each new piece of information turning the first piece of information about a place into an emblem. Polo's role as storyteller is further ironized within the dialogues: "Il veneziano sapeva che . . . le sue risposte e obiezioni trovavano il loro posto in un discorso che già si svolgeva per conto suo, nella testa del Gran Kan" (p. 33), as the Khan desires to take over the role he has assigned to another. The narrative escapes the totality of a closed form because it keeps on going as long as the Khan wants it to. The phatic motivation of the narrative undercuts the devices of verisimilitude which let the reader trust the representational value of the narration. The empire's winding down turns out to be its excuse for coming into fictional being. Polo invents cities only to satisfy the Khan's need to have evidence of what will inevitably slip away.

At a crucial point, at the beginning of the eighth (and final "regularly" numbered) section, just preceding the city Irene, the Khan comes upon a formula for stabilizing and dominating his empire: "Pensò: 'Se ogni città è come una partita a scacchi, il giorno in cui arriverò a conoscerne le regole possiederò finalmente il mio impero, anche se mai riuscirò a conoscere tutte le città che contiene'" (p. 127). This enunciates the rule of series, a mathematical projection of all possible moves and orders. Here, then, is a logic within the narrative that may justify the serial, number-rule bound arrangement of the cities. But the Khan forgets that chess is played with two kind of rules, the constitutive rules of the game and the unpredictable performative rules of strategy. Likewise, the natural laws of cities render their origins and being chaotic and, because these rules are not numerical or logical, the cities are always out of sight and hand both literally and figuratively.

> Al contemplarne questi paesaggi essenziali, Kublai rifletteva sull'ordine invisibile che regge le città, sulle regole cui risponde il loro sorgere e prender forma e prosperare e adattarsi alle stagioni e intristire e cadere in rovina. Alle volte gli sembrava d'essere sul punto di scoprire un sistema coerente e armonioso che sottostava alle infinite difformità e disarmonie, ma nessun modello reggeva il confronto con quello del gioco degli scacchi.

> (p. 128)

The serial arrangement is as impossible politically (imperialism is not like chess) as it is poetically (numbers break the rules of novelistic order). The arrangement is perfect, too symmetrical to be human.

The empire fails because it cannot enclose its cities, cannot define or find its property, proper-ness, own-ness, or character. The topology is never geographic, only mathematical becoming rhetorical by virtue of its role as an attempt at empire, at persuasion. The book does not form a narrative whole but exists on two rhetorical levels which constantly slip by each other. These two levels correspond to the modern and the postmodern:

the narrative which puts itself into question while seeking to recuperate its fragments into a whole—a dialectized economy of exchange and representation—as opposed to the numerically generated set of separates which do not add up but exist as being relative to one another. To return to the art analogy, we see that these two modes parallel Cubist art and multiple-modular systems: the one fragments a (still recognizable) representation of a whole while the other represents nothing and exists only as a kind of propositional thinking. The narrative of *Le città invisibili* does not put together a story but interrupts another discourse. Narrative as call for narrative is renewed and cut off at every moment.

To reiterate the essential difference of the two modes of narrative in *Le città invisibili* and the impossibility of closure or unity is not to deny an interplay which constitutes the force of the novel's significance. The cities' seriality, when related to the philosophical implications of the (lack of) paradigm, loses its numerical sterility and assumes its importance in the movement constituting meaning. Unlike the Khan's atlases which define and predict the emplacement of cities, the narrative voice does not map out the place of the cities; their location as parts of a series is set by the titles of the various sub-divided sets and, like any title or frame, the set names link the work to its outside. The outside here hesitates between the italicized passages which literally surround the cities and the outside of the work, the usual "world," "reality," or field of intertextuality. That which exists between the inside and the outside, the *parergonal* (as Derrida refers to it, taking up a term used to designate something accessory or subordinated to the main subject in painting and expanding it to "make the economy of the abyme"[9]) serves as a reminder of the hesitancy of the place of the text and its outside. *Le città invisibili* engages a multiple parergonality because the cities are surrounded by their numbers, their place in sets, by the italicized parts, and by the outside symbolized by the covers of the book. Parergonality does not imply sets of multiple parentheses but indeed abolishes context as a means of recuperation or stability and insists on the mobility and unhome-ness of the in-between.

The parergonality of the series—the series' place inside the narration and its external origin—derives from and sets up a problematic of origins. A traditionally thematic reading of *Le città invisibili* would unhesitatingly point to an origin of the cities in the humanistic themes which seem to motivate the Polo-Khan dialogue: death and desire sublimated as voyage, alienation, the clash of east and west, apocalypse—all emblematized as cities (human constructs) in varying stages of physical, moral, and rhetorical decay. Up-to-date strains of environmental doomsday and 1984 can be heard as poignant leit-motifs of the book, perhaps suggesting that only some new economic order can rescue narrative from the decaying empire of exchangeable signs that modernism spent out.

The way the cities and the narration work as a constant exchange of frames or outsides constitutes a bending in and out such as Derrida calls "invagination": "the inward refolding of *la gaine,* the inverted reapplication of the outer edge to the inside of a form where the outside then opens a pocket" ("Living on," 97). This operation is not one that begins or has a place of origin but is "possible from the first trace on." Invagination is related to seriality because the model or referent is missing. If the cities are understood as being motivated by an ultimate model or paradigm put forth in the conversations, the novel can be called modern. On the other hand, if the cities invaginate each other, *Le città invisibili* is postmodern.

An abundance of possible models can direct our reading of *Le città invisibili.* From the City of God to *Metropolis,* cities have been used as models and metaphors for man and his constructs. One city, Venice, the place Polo left behind, dominates the Khan's attempt at model building. Polo's repressed, invisible city of origin surely manifests its return in the multiplicity of the cities but also and more significantly in his desire to keep it out of the Khan's empire.

> "Ti è mai accaduto di vedere una città che assomigli a questa?" chiedeva Kublai a Marco Polo sporgendo la mano inanellata fuori dal baldacchino di seta del bucintoro imperiale, a indicare i ponti che s'incurvano sui canali, i palazzi principeschi le cui soglie di marmo s'immergono nell'acqua . . .
>
> "No, sire," rispose Marco, "mai avrei immaginato che potesse esistere una città simile a questa."
>
> L'imperatore cercò di scrutarlo negli occhi. Lo straniero abbassò lo sguardo.
>
> (p. 93)

Polo's lie is the basis of an anti-paradigm which directs his telling of the cities: "Per distinguere le qualità delle altre, devo partire da una prima città che resta implicita. Per me è Venezia" (p. 94). The Khan knows that a paradigm does not suffice: "Ma le città visitate da Marco Polo erano sempre diverse da quelle pensate dall'imperatore. 'Eppure io ho costruito nella mia mente un modello di città da cui dedurre tutte le città possibili,' disse Kublai" (p. 75). He needs Polo whose method is *other:*

> "Anch'io ho pensato un modello di città da cui deduco tutte le altre," rispose Marco. "È una città fatta solo d'eccezioni, preclusioni, contraddizioni, incongruenze, controsensi. Se una città cosîè quanto c'è di piú improbabile, diminuendo il numero degli elementi abnormi si accrescono le probabilità che la città ci sia veramente."
>
> (p. 75)

Polo disregards the Khan's empirical discourse for the realm of fiction in order to satisfy the need for narration. The emperor may "determine that each of these fantastic places is really the same place"[10] and thus

identify with the traditional paradigm-seeking reader, but it remains to Polo's unmodeled imagination to give substance to the work. It is the fictional process, the *écriture,* which keeps the cities from merging into one: "E Polo: 'Viaggiando ci s'accorge che le differenze si perdono: ogni città va somigliando a tutte le città, i luoghi si scambiano forma ordine distanze, un pulviscolo informe invade i continenti. Il tuo atlante custodisce intatte le differenze: quell'assortimento di qualità che sono come le lettere del nome'" (p. 145). The serial numbering and naming give the cities their individual being and what truth they have: "La menzogna non è nel discorso, è nelle cose" (p. 68).

At the very end of the book, Polo affirms, "la città cui tende il mio viaggio è discontinua nello spazio e nel tempo, ora piú rada ora piú densa" (p. 169). The last cities mentioned, "Enoch, Babilonia, Yahoo, Butua, Brave New World" (p. 169), are literary cities Kublai finds ready-made in his atlas, cities whose paradigm is an archetype we all know, "'la città infernale, ed è là in fondo che, in una spirale sempre piú stretta, ci risucchia la corrente'" (p. 170). So between the "real" Venice and Dante's fiction of hell lie all invisible cities, those unseen, unknown, and those that emerge from the dreamworld and its seriality. The book, fable and allegory that it is, ends with Polo's moral about escaping the inferno while living it: "cercare e saper riconoscere chi e cosa, in mezzo all'inferno, non è inferno, e farlo durare, e dargli spazio" (p. 170). The giving of space refuses closure and lets the search continue; the cities invaginate Polo and Khan and the narrative they are enmeshed in. The "città che minacciano negli incubi e nelle maledizioni" (p. 169), that is, all the cities, constitute "l'inferno che abitiamo tutti i giorni" (p. 170). The splitting of the paradigm between Venice and the Inferno and their clash within fifty-five cities reaffirm this reinsertion of hell into everywhere and the disappearance of heaven-purgatory-hell and all other hierarchies.

The cities and their telling represent "an apocalyptic superimprinting of texts: there is no paradigmatic text" (Derrida, "Living on," pp. 137-138). A serial text is always going to contain the apocalypse at every moment; rooted in the world of numbers, seriality lies beyond the human. If it seems that the humanist tenor of the last chapter serves to deny the post-humanism of the serial structure, we have only to glance back at the eighth chapter where Kublai Khan seeks unity in the chess metaphor. But he learns that, rather than the paradigmatic inferno, the motivator of the cities' structuring is a Nietzschean conception of "place" or "stance" based on rhetorical awareness. The last paragraph of the opening italicized part of this section is repeated as the opening of the closing part, and in it we see that the chess game, like all the Khan's other strategies of entrapment, escapes his intentions. "Il Gran Kan cercava d'immedesimarsi nel gioco: ma adesso era il perché del gioco a sfuggirgli. Il fine d'ogni partita à una vincita o una perdita: ma di cosa? Qual'era la vera posta?" (p. 139). His desire to seize his empire by reducing it to its structural components only deployed the deconstructive process of rhetoric: "A forza di scorporate le sue conquiste per ridurle all'essenza, Kublai era arrivato all'operazione estrema: la conquista definitiva, di cui i multiformi tesoridell'impero non erano che involucri illusori, si riduceva a un tassello di legno piallato" (pp. 129, 139; page 129 adds in conclusion, "il nulla . . ."—Calvino's ellipsis). Lest the Khan's desperation at the empty end be turned into the platonic satisfaction of having found an essence, he is further surprised to see that Polo is able to go on reading: the planed wood tells of "boschi d'ebano, delle zattere di tronchi che discendono i fiumi, degli approdi, delle donne alle finestre" (p. 140). The Khan's metaphor gives way to Polo's metonymy: "La quantità di cose che si potevano leggere in un pezzetto di legno liscio e vuoto sommergeva Kublai" (p. 140).

On the one hand, then, we find reductionism, the demand for a here and now, for the essential, for possession, and on the other the perpetual delay of understanding, inflation of the stakes, re-reading and re-understanding. The nothingness resulting at the end of the chess game unveils the absence of the paradigm, but the interpretive process can continue examining not the game or its rules but the parergons or supplements without which it could not exist. The invisible cities, like the squares on the chess board, are limited in number but permit, like the plain wood, continuous readings of the perpetual apocalypse that seriality writes within itself.

Seriality, whose order is mathematical, not geographic or human, is a sort of a-economy and as such aids the narrative voice in preventing a closed narrative economy—one regulating the author-reader exchanges—from taking (a) place. The privilege of generation is taken from the paradigm, from the paragon, and transferred to the parergon, the supplement or by-work. The radical exteriority of the narrative voice always destructures what paradigms attempt to enclose. Seriality and narrative voice work together in a logic of the cartouche. A cartouche is a drawn frame on an engraving or a tablet drawn in the form of a sheet of paper (this usually indicated by rolled or curled edges) such as those enclosing titles or legends on maps. The cartouches on Kublai's maps separate the words and the images but turn those words into images. As Derrida reminds us, "The logic of the cartouche is disconcerting, like that of a narration whose site would remain improbable" (*La verité,* p. 252). This logic tells us that origin is repetition; the paradigm is not the originator, neither producing nor generating because it itself has to be reproduced. The paradigm might as well be a copy or reproduction of one of its own descendents. The series proves this logic: "serial practice trades in the execution of paradigm or the decline of the model" (*La verité,* p. 235). The seriality of the cities ruins any claim Venice or the Inferno have to being models for any or all the cities. They too become part of the series; there are no paradigms but "paradigm effects" which circulate the parergonal effects continually reinserted into the series.

As soon as the cartouche is no longer in force it cannot claim to *tell < réciter >* the truth except by giving way *< donnant lieu >* to the conditions of doubt, it enters into the series as one simulacrum among others. Part of the series without paradigm, without a father. . . . It transforms the paradigm into a *paradigm effect* (without eliminating it, for there is always some left). (*La vérité,* p. 255)

In attempting to explain the invisibility of the cities—why they cannot be assigned a place—we have considered two types of discourse which operate by undercutting each other. The cities are arranged in series, a numerical arrangement which stands outside narrative structure, structure which orders fictional events in a more or less realist, *human,* way. In conclusion we will recall briefly how the two modes tend to recuperate each other and how they fail to do so—to the profit of postmodern fiction. Both novelistic narrative and number are systems which tend toward linearity. In *Le città invisibili* the series are set up in a closed form. The perfection of numbers represents a threat to always hesitant, always slippery language. The numbers, along with the proper names of the cities, set up a nominalistic system of empty signifiers whose only exchange value or meaning is their place in their own system. Unlike mathematics, where numbers and symbols have to be supported by metalanguage, the number and order of series are self-contained. The conversations of Marco Polo and Kublai Khan somehow contain the series of cities, but they neither contextualize nor economically dominate the cities: no narratorial voice can assign places to the invisible cities within Kublai's empire. The dialogues, while implying that the cities are only examples of those in the vast unknowable empire, constantly question the location and very existence of the cities and the empire. The dialogues, even if they never contain the cities in their narrative structure, use their seriality to put into motion the paradigm effects which are constantly in movement to tell the story. While the novel's putting itself into question can be called a trait of modernism and the serial-modular deconstruction of paradigm postmodern, *Le città invisibili* rejects categorization. This flight from containment and refusal to follow a pattern tend to tip the literary-historical scale toward the postmodern where definitions and categories will always elude us. Calvin Tompkins recently remarked that "Postmodernism, the term being advanced these days, is no more than a stop-gap, a reminder of the problem."[11] If we misread "reminder" as "remainder," I think we come closer to understanding the shift from modernist thinking. The "remainder" keeps in circulation the paradigm effects of modernism that continue to inform our reading of narrative strategies.

NOTES

[1] Italo Calvino, *Le città invisibili* (Torino: Giulio Einaudi, 1972), p. 110. Subsequent page references will be in the text.

² See Jack Burnham, *Great Western Salt Works* (N.Y.: Braziller, 1974), pp. 21-22.

³ See Jacques Derrida's study of Titus-Carmel's *The Pocket Size Tlingit Coffin* where he works out this paradox of the model in the series. "Cartouches," in *La vérité en peinture* (Paris: Flammarion, 1978), pp. 213-284. Quotations from this work are my translations.

⁴ Kurt Gödel's theorem or "proof," published in 1931, established the undecidability of certain laws and statements. For an exploration of its implications, see Douglas R. Hofstadter, *Gödel, Escher, Bach* (N.Y.: Basic Books, 1979), especially pp. 17-19. Hofstadter succinctly restates the theorem as, "All consistent axiomatic formulations of number theory include undecidable propositions" (p. 17).

⁵ Ihab Hassan, *Paracriticisms* (Urbana: Univ. of Ill. Press, 1975), p. 54. It is significant that he proposes modernist "rubrics" (types, categories, unities) and postmodernist "notes" (fragments, incomplete thoughts).

⁶ S. Freud, *On Dreams* (N.Y.: Norton, 1952), p. 64.

⁷ Maurice Blanchot, "La voix narrative (le 'il', le neutre)," in *L'entretien infini* (Paris: Gallimard, 1969), pp. 556-567. My translation. See also Derrida, "Living On: Border Lines," trans. J. Hulbert, in H. Bloom et al., *Deconstruction and Criticism* (N.Y.: Seabury Press, 1979), pp. 104-107.

⁸ Derrida, "Living On," p. 87 and passim.

⁹ See Derrida, "Parergon," in *La vérité en peinture* pp. 19-168, here p. 44.

¹⁰ Gore Vidal, *New York Review of Books* and jacket copy for *Invisible Cities,* trans. Wm. Weaver (N.Y.: Harcourt Brace Jovanovich, 1974).

¹¹ C. Tompkins, "Matisse's Armchair," *New Yorker,* Feb. 25, 1980, p. 108.

FURTHER READING

Secondary Sources

Harmon, Maurice, ed. *The Irish Writer and the City*. Gerrards Cross, Buckshire, England: Colin Smyth, 1984, 203 p.
    Collection of essays on the depiction of Irish cities by such authors as Flann O'Brien, Brian Friel, Thomas Kilroy, and James Stephens.

Herron, Ima Honaker. *The Small Town in American Literature*. Durham, N.C.: Duke University Press, 1939, 477 p.
    Traces the literary treatment of American urban life from the colonial period to Sinclair Lewis.

Hutchins, Patricia. *James Joyce's Dublin*. London: Grey Walls Press, 1950, 101 p.
    An illustrated guide to Dublin as described by Joyce in *Portrait of the Artist as a Young Man* and *Ulysses*.

Sizemore, Christine Wick. *A Female Vision of the City: London in the Novels of Five British Women*. Knoxville: University of Tennessee Press, 1989, 307 p.
    Examines the works of Doris Lessing, Margaret Drabble, Iris Murdoch, P. D. James, and Maureen Duffy, comparing and contrasting the novelists' urban depictions.

Squier, Susan Merrill, ed. *Women Writers and the City: Essays in Feminist Literary Criticism*. Knoxville: University of Tennessee Press, 1984, 306 p.
    Discusses the works of Flora Tristan, Marguerite Duras, George Eliot, Virginia Woolf, Rebecca West, Margaret Atwood, Doris Lessing, Willa Cather, Adrienne Rich, and others.

Timms, Edward, and Kelley, David, eds. *Unreal City: Urban Experience in Modern European Literature and Art*. New York: St. Martin's Press, 1985, 268 p.
    Examines urban themes and depictions in the works of such twentieth-century authors as T. S. Eliot, Ezra Pound, Guilliame Appollinaire, Bertolt Brecht, Andre Breton, and Franz Kafka.

Postmodernism

INTRODUCTION

The term postmodernism has been defined in many different ways, and many critics and authors disagree on even its most basic precepts. However, many agree that, in literature, postmodernism represents the rejection of the modernist tenets of rational, historical, and scientific thought in favor of self-conscious, ironic, and experimental works. In many of these works, the authors abandon the concept of an ordered universe, linear narratives, and traditional forms to suggest the malleability of truth and question the nature of reality itself, dispensing with the idea of a universal ordering scheme in favor of artifice, temporality and a reliance on irony. Many postmodern writers believe that language is inherently unable to convey any semblance of the external world, and that verbal communication is more an act of conflict than an expression of rational meaning. Therefore, much work classified as postmodern displays little attention to realism, characterization, or plot. Time is often conveyed as random and disjointed; commonplace situations are depicted alongside surreal and fantastic plot developments, and the act of writing itself becomes a major focus of the subject matter. Many works feature multiple beginnings and endings. Much postmodern fiction relies on bricolage, which is the liberal use of fragments of preexisting literary material to create a work that places a higher value on newness than on originality. Postmodernism is generally considered to emanate from the social and political ferment of the 1960s. The Prague Spring of 1968 in Czechoslovakia, the Algerian War of Independence, and student protests in France and the United States are believed by critics to indicate a profound distrust in historical and cultural traditions, as well as modernist notions of progress, objectivity, and reason. French philosopher Jacques Derrida is credited as the foremost proponent of postmodern thought, particularly for his concept of deconstructionism. Any work that relies on words to convey meaning, according to Derrida, can be interpreted in many, often contradictory, ways. A thorough textual analysis of such a work reveals that the original author's perception, what he or she declares, is inherently different from what the author describes. Because the term is open to many different interpretations, many diverse works are classified as postmodern. While many works labeled postmodern do not strictly adhere to any formal tenets, a great number of them borrow postmodern techniques and devices, including discontinuous time, recurring characters, irony, and authorial intrusions. Postmodern works also evidence the belief that there is no distinction between reality and fiction, much like there is no inherent relationship between words and the objects they are meant to signify.

REPRESENTATIVE WORKS

John Ashbery
Self-Portrait in a Convex Mirror (poetry) 1975
Houseboat Days (poetry) 1977
John Barth
The Sot-Weed Factor (novel) 1960; revised 1967
Giles Goat-Boy; Or, The Revised Syllabus (novel) 1966
Donald Barthelme
The Teachings of Don B.: Satires, Parodies, Fables, Illustrated Stories, and Plays of Donald Barthelme (short stories and plays) 1998
Roland Barthes
Writing Degree Zero (criticism) 1967
Critical Essays (criticism) 1972
Mythologies (criticism) 1973
The Pleasure of the Text (criticism) 1975
Jean Baudrillard
The Mirror of Production (criticism) 1975
In the Shadow of the Silent Majorities; Or, The End of the Social, and Other Essays (essays) 1983
Simulations (criticism) 1983
Walter Benjamin
Illuminations (criticism) 1968
Thomas Berger
Little Big Man (novel) 1964
Jorge Luis Borges
Ficciones (short stories) 1944
The Aleph (short stories) 1949
Other Inquisitions (essays) 1952
William S. Burroughs
Naked Lunch (novel) 1959
Nova Express (novel) 1964
Italo Calvino
The Castle of Crossed Destinies (novel) 1979
If on a Winter's Night a Traveler (novel) 1982
Invisible Cities (novel) 1986
Truman Capote
In Cold Blood (nonfiction) 1966
Alejo Carpentier
Explosion in a Cathedral (novel) 1963
Robert Coover
The Public Burning (novel) 1977
Julio Cortázar
A Manual for Manuel (novel) 1978
Gilles Deleuze and Félix Guattari
Anti-Oedipus (criticism) 1977
Paul de Man
Blindness and Insight (criticism) 1971
Allegories of Reading (criticism) 1979
Jacques Derrida
Of Grammatology (criticism) 1967
Writing and Difference (criticism) 1967

OVERVIEWS

Robert Alter

SOURCE: "The Self-Conscious Moment: Reflections on the Aftermath of Modernism," in *TriQuarterly*, No. 33, Spring, 1975, pp. 209-30.

[*In the following essay, Alter presents an overview of postmodern fiction, including works by Cervantes, Borges, Flann O'Brien, Nabokov, and John Barth.*]

> Our literature has been for a hundred years a dangerous game with its own death, in other words a way of experiencing, of living that death: our literature is like that Racinean heroine who dies upon learning who she is but lives by seeking her identity.
>
> —Roland Barthes, "Literature and Metalanguage"

> A book is more than a verbal structure or series of verbal structures; it is the dialogue it establishes with its reader and the intonation it imposes upon his voice and the changing and durable images it leaves in his memory. . . . Literature is not exhaustible for the simple and sufficient reason that no single book is. A book is not an isolated entity: it is a relationship, an axis of innumerable relationships.
>
> —J. L. Borges, "A Note on (Toward) Bernard Shaw"

Over the past two decades, as the high tide of modernism ebbed and its masters died off, the baring of literary artifice has come to be more and more a basic procedure—at times, almost an obsession—of serious fiction in the West. The creators of self-conscious fiction in our time do not constitute a school or a movement, and the lines of influence among them, or to them from their common predecessors, often tend to waver and blur when closely examined. Some of these writers have tried their hand at shorter fictional forms, which, after the Borgesian model, one now calls "fictions" rather than "short stories"; but most of them, perhaps inevitably, have turned back to, or stayed with, the novel, attracted by its large and various capacity to convey a whole imaginatively constituted world. Scattered over three continents, they are an odd mixture of stubbornly private eccentrics, on the one hand, and promulgators of manifestoes, on the other; of powerfully evocative novelists or conductors of ingenious laboratory experiments in fiction; of exuberant comic artists and knowing guides to bleak dead ends of despair.

This mode of fiction is variously practiced by such diverse figures as Raymond Queneau, Samuel Beckett, Alain Robbe-Grillet, Michel Butor, Claude Mauriac in France; John Fowles in England; Robert Coover, John Barth, Thomas Pynchon, Donald Barthelme, Kurt Vonnegut in this country; J. L. Borges and Julio Cortázar in Latin America; and, of course, Vladimir Nabokov, perched on his height in Switzerland, working out of three literary cultures. The whole reflexive tendency in contemporary fiction has been reinforced by the prominence of self-conscious cinema since the early sixties in the work of directors like Fellini, Antonioni, Resnais, and Godard. Film, because it is a collaborative artistic enterprise involving a complicated chain of technical procedures, almost invites attention to its constitutive processes; and there is a clear logic in the involvement in filmmaking of several of the French New Novelists, or in the repeated recourse to cinematic composition by *montage* in a writer like Robert Coover. The close parallels between what is happening now in the two media suggest that the self-consciousness of both may reflect a heightened new stage of modern culture's general commitment to knowing all that can be known about its own components and dynamics. Our culture, a kind of Faust at the mirror of Narcissus, is more and more driven to uncover the roots of what it lives with most basically—language and its origins, human sexuality, the workings of the psyche, the inherited structures of the mind, the underlying patterns of social organization, the sources of value and belief, and, of course, the nature of art.

If this is the moment of the self-conscious novel, that is decidedly a mixed blessing, as the spectacular unevenness of innovative fiction today would indicate. The growing insistence of self-awareness in our culture at large has been both a liberating and a paralyzing force, and that is equally true of its recent developments in artistic expression. In this regard, criticism must be especially wary. The kind of criticism that often has to be invoked in discussing a traditional realistic novel is in the indicative mode: yes, we know that a woman like Rosamund Vincy would act in just that way, with just such a gesture, toward her husband at a given moment in *Middlemarch* because it *seems* right, because it corresponds to some subtle, gradually acquired sense of human nature in our extraliterary experience, and to this we can only point, signaling an act of recognition we hope others will share. Most self-conscious novels, on the other hand, lend themselves splendidly to analytic criticism because they operate by the constant redeployment of fiction's formal categories. Is the critic interested in the narrative manipulation of time, the arbitrariness of narrative beginnings, the writer's awareness of literary conventions, the maneuvering of language to produce multiple meanings, the expressive possibilities of punctuation, paragraphing, typography? It is all laid out for him across the printed pages of *Tristram Shandy,* ready to be analytically described, with no apparent need for recourse to a touchstone of "rightness" outside this and other literary texts. For this reason an astute critic, impelled by his own professional concern with formal experiment, can easily make a piece of self-conscious fiction sound more profound, more finely resonant with implication, than it is in fact. None of Robbe-Grillet's novels really equals in fascination Roland Barthes' brilliant descriptions of them. Queneau's *Exercices de style* (1947) is an intriguing and at times immensely amusing book, but it is just what its title implies, a set of exercises; and to suggest, as George

Steiner has done, that it constitutes a major landmark in twentieth-century literature, is to mislead readers in the interest of promoting literary "future shock."

The instance of *Exercices de style* is worth pausing over briefly because it represents one ultimate limit of the whole self-conscious mode. Queneau begins his book by reporting a banal anecdote of a young man with a long neck and a missing button on his coat who is jostled in a crowded bus. He tells this anecdote ninety-nine times, constantly changing the narrative viewpoint, the style, the literary conventions; going as far as the use of mathematical notation and anagrammatic scrambling of letters in one direction, and the resort to heavy dialect and badly anglicized French in the other; even rendering the incident in alexandrines, in free verse, as a sonnet, as a playlet. All this is extremely ingenious, and, I would admit, more than ingenious, because as one reads the same simple episode over and over through all these acrobatic variations, one is forced to recognize both the stunning arbitrariness of any decision to tell a story in a particular way and the endless possibilities for creating fictional "facts" by telling a story differently.

The controlling perception, however, of *Exercices* is one that goes back to the generic beginnings of the novel; and to see how much more richly that insight can be extended into fictional space, one has only to think of Sterne, where a "Queneauesque" passage like the deliberately schematic "Tale of Two Lovers" is woven into a thick texture of amorous anecdotes that critically juxtapose literary convention with a sense of the erotic as a cogent fact of human experience. Precisely what is missing from *Exercices de style* is any sense—and playfulness need not exclude seriousness—of human experience, which is largely kept out of the book in order to preserve the technical purity of the experiment. I don't mean to take Queneau to task for what he clearly did not intend; I mean only to emphasize that criticism need not make excessive claims for this kind of writing. Queneau, of course, has written full-scale novels of flaunted artifice, both before and after *Exercices de style,* that do involve a more complex sense of experience. One of the great temptations of the self-conscious novelist, however, is to content himself with technical experiment, trusting that in these difficult times (but then the times are always difficult) the only honesty, perhaps the only real profundity, lies in technical experiment. This is the chief limiting factor in most of Robbe-Grillet as well as in Coover's collection of fictions, *Pricksongs & Descants.* In both, one can admire the virtuosity with which narrative materials are ingeniously shuffled and reshuffled yet feel a certain aridness; for the partial magic of the novelist's art, however self-conscious, is considerably more than a set of card tricks.

The other, complementary fault of the self-conscious novel, also much in evidence among its contemporary practitioners, is to give free rein to every impulse of invention or fictional contrivance without distinguishing what may serve some artistic function in the novel and what is merely silly or self-indulgent. After all, if in an old-fashioned novel you have to describe a petulant, spoiled young woman like Rosamund Vincy, you are obliged to make her as close a likeness as you can to observed examples of the type, and so some commonly perceived human reality provides a constant check on your inventiveness. If, on the other hand, you are writing a novel about a novelist who invents still another novelist who is the author of bizarrely farfetched books, there is scarcely any piece of fabrication, however foolish or improbable, that you couldn't put into your novel if you set your mind to it. The Irish writer Flann O'Brien, in one of the earliest postmodern novels of flaunted artifice, *At Swim-Two-Birds* (1939), has devised just such a book. The second-remove novelist invented by the first-person narrator-novelist gives birth to a full-grown man (that is, a new character); but while this writer, fatigued with parturition, is asleep, his characters rebel against him, resenting the roles he has assigned them. In the end, they subject him to the most hideous torture and maiming, recounted in detail page after page—by writing chapters of a novel (within the novel-within-the-novel) in which he suffers these horrors. This scheme of recessed narratives also involves an amalgam of different kinds of fiction, starting with domestic realism in the frame story and running through the gunslinging western and the novel of erotic sensationalism to fairy tales and Irish myth.

"A satisfactory novel," the young writer who is the narrator tries to explain to a friend at the outset, "should be a self-evident sham to which the reader could regulate at will the degree of his credulity."[1] At first glance, this might seem a perfect capsule definition of the self-conscious novel, but upon consideration the formulation makes it too easy for both the writer and the reader. If one thinks of the history of the self-conscious novel from its early masters down to Gide, to the parodistic or overtly contrived sections in Joyce and the Nabokov of *Lolita* and *Pale Fire*, "sham" becomes far too crude and demeaning as a synonym for artifice or imaginative contrivance. The artifice, moreover, should not be flatly "self-evident" but cunningly revealed, a hide-and-seek presence in the novel, a stubbornly ambiguous substratum of the whole fictional world. To imagine, then, the reader regulating his credulity at will is to reverse the whole process of the self-conscious novel, in which it is the writer who tries to regulate the reader's credulity, challenging him to active participation in pondering the status of fictional things, forcing him as he reads on to examine again and again the validity of his ordinary discriminations between art and life and how they interact.

Flann O'Brien, however, following the formula he attributes to his own protagonist, in fact produces a hodgepodge of fictions in which nothing seems particularly credible and everything finally becomes tedious through the sheer proliferation of directionless narrative invention. *At Swim-Two-Birds* is a celebration of fabulation in which novelistic self-consciousness has gone slack because fiction is everywhere and there is no longer any quixotic tension between what is fictional and what is real. I am not aware that it has influenced later books, but it has certainly proved to be a novel ahead of its time, for its faults of conception and execution provide a perfect paradigm for those of much contemporary fiction, especially in this country, where a new literary ideology of fabulation has too often turned out to mean license, not liberty, for the novelist. In reading many of the voguish new writers, one is frequently tempted to invoke the words of the narrator at the end of John Barth's story "Title": "Oh God comma I abhor self-consciousness."

Those inclined to argue that the novel today is in a grave state of decay often draw evidence from the current popularity of self-conscious fiction, which they tend to see as a dwarfed offspring of the modernist giants, turned away from life, dedicated to the onanistic gratifications of the artist pleasured by his own art. It would of course be foolish to claim that we are now in anything like that extraordinary period of innovative literary creativity of the 1920s when modernism was in flower, but the opposite inference, that narrative literature has reached some terminal stage of sterility, is by no means necessary from the facts of contemporary writing. I have dwelt upon the two chief temptations of the self-conscious novelist— arid exercise and indiscriminate invention—precisely because they should be recognized as dangers, not taken as the inevitable results whenever a writer determines artfully to expose the fictiveness of his fiction. In fact, the prominent flaunting of artifice has led to some of the most impressive successes in the contemporary novel as well as to some of its most evident lapses, and the successes are by no means restricted to elder statesmen like Beckett and Nabokov. (In America, one might mention Barth, who in different books has been both an impressively original writer and an embarrassingly puerile one; or Coover, who has gone beyond manipulations of technique to a vividly imagined satire where fantasy and reality enrich one another.) The old question of the death of the novel, which seems as doggedly persistent as the novel itself, is in the air again, and I believe an understanding of the self-conscious tradition in the novel which stands behind many contemporary novelists may help set that hazy issue in clearer perspective.

One of the newly prominent American novelists, John Barth, has himself given a new twist to the death-of-the-novel argument in a widely read essay first published in 1967, "The Literature of Exhaustion."[2] Barth settles on Borges, Beckett, and Nabokov as his exemplary figures to expose the condition of narrative literature now, and that condition as he describes it proves to be thoroughly contradictory—apocalyptic and elegiac, at the end of an ultimate cultural cul-de-sac yet somehow reaching toward exciting new possibilities. The "exhaustion" of the title is defined as "the used-upness of certain forms or exhaustion of certain possibilities," and the work of Borges is taken to be the clearest model of this contemporary literature of exhaustion. The Argentine writer "suggests the view," according to Barth, "that intellectual and literary history . . . has pretty well exhausted the possibilities of novelty. His *ficciones* are not only footnotes to imaginary texts, but postscripts to the real corpus of literature." The characterization of Borges' fiction is memorable, and not without cogency, but Barth has worked himself into a corner by following Borges in this fashion, and he is constrained to use the last two paragraphs of his essay in a rapid maneuver to get out of the trap. For even if reality has come to resemble for the writer the library of a Borgesian fable where all the books that can ever be written already exist, even if Borges' Pierre Menard is an emblem of the modern writer's wry destiny, "creating" the *Quixote* by laboriously reconstituting it word for word in a version identical verbatim with Cervantes'—Barth himself nevertheless writes novels which he hopes have some novelty, and he is not willing to dismiss the literature of our age as a mere postscript to a completed corpus.

Now, two paragraphs are not much space to get out of such a quandary, so Barth resorts to a kind of literary intervention of divine grace: confronted with a labyrinthine reality of exhausted possibilities, the writer of genius finally can rely on his genius to achieve the impossible, to create a new literature when there is nothing left to create. "It's the chosen remnant, the virtuoso, the Thesean *hero,* who . . . with the aid of *very special* gifts . . . [can] go straight through the maze to the accomplishment of his work." (The italics are Barth's.) This strikes me as a peculiarly elitist and miraculist notion of literary continuity and renewal. Good writing has of course always required gifted writers. Now, however, Barth seems to be saying, we have come to such a pass that it is virtually impossible to write anything at all. Nevertheless a few geniuses, having recognized that difficult fact, will somehow manage to create.

Borges himself, as we shall see, is far from agreeing with this idea, but in any case the choice of Borges as the paradigmatic postmodernist is in one respect misleading, precisely because Borges the prose writer is an inventor of parables and paradoxes, not a novelist. That is, Borges of the *ficciones* is concerned with a series of metaphysical enigmas about identity, recurrence, and cyclicality, time, thought, and extension, and so it is a little dangerous to translate his haunting fables into allegories of the postmodern literary situation. Books, real and imaginary, and books about books, of course figure very prominently in Borges' fictions; but he is after all a remarkably bookish man, and the contents of a library are the aptest vehicle he could have chosen for writing about knowledge and its limits, the ambiguous relation between idea and existence, language and reality, and many of his other favorite philosophical puzzles. The fact that Borges is a fabulist, not a novelist, hardly suggests that the fable is all there remains for fiction to work with now. Were he a novelist, his prototypical protagonist would not be a meditative wraith wandering through the hexagonal mazes of the infinite Library of Babel, but a man or woman—one glimpses the possibility in his most recent stories—with a distinctive psychology living among other men and women, acting against a background of social values, personal and national history. Such a figure, it seems safe to assume, would have a rather different relationship to

the written word, past and present, than does the inhabitant of the great Library or the assiduous Pierre Menard.

Borges, it should be noted, has argued trenchantly against the whole idea of exhausting artistic possibilities in a brief essay, "A Note on (Toward) Bernard Shaw"[3]—which, not surprisingly, is hardly at all about Shaw. He begins with a list of fanciful notions, from the thirteenth century to the twentieth, of combinational reservoirs that would encompass all books, systems of ideas, or art works. One of these, "the staggering fantasy" spun out by the nineteenth-century popularizer of science Kurd Lasswitz "of a universal library which would register all the variations of the twenty-odd orthographical symbols, in other words, all that is given to express in all languages," is nothing less than the scheme of Borges' "The Library of Babel." But, he immediately goes on to say, such writers, by reducing art and philosophy to "a kind of play with combinations," forget that a book is not a flat, fixed entity composed of combined letters making an unchanging design in language. Every book exists through a collaborative effort with the imagination of each of its readers—the controlling idea of *Pale Fire* is not a trivial one—and so it changes with its readers, with their life experience and their accrued reading experience. Literary tradition, in other words, does not and cannot exist as a mass of determined data in the memory-bank of a computer. "Literature is not exhaustible, for the sufficient and simple reason that no single book is." The more books that are written, the more complicated with meaning are the books that exist before them, and the more possibilities there are for creating new works out of old books and new experience.

Nothing could demonstrate this more forcefully than the inherently allusive structure of the novel as a genre. *Don Quixote* becomes more than it initially was after its transmutation into the "Cervantick" *Tom Jones* and *Tristram Shandy,* after *The Red and the Black, Madame Bovary, Moby-Dick, Ulysses,* and *The Castle.* Each successive creation—to follow the implicit logic of Borges' plausible notion about a book's existence—does not foreclose future possibilities but rather opens up new vistas for creation out of the common literary tradition. A book is not an integer but "a relationship, an axis of innumerable relationships," which of course grow with the passage of historical time and literary history; and so "The Library of Babel" must be, after all, a metaphysician's nightmare, not a novelist's.

But let us return to the relation Barth proposes between Borges' own practice in his *ficciones* and the foreseeable possibilities of imaginative writing. Without begrudging Borges the general acclaim he has recently received, both in America and in France, I think one may resist the implication of Barth and others that he represents the future of fiction. Robert Coover, although he does not mention Borges by name, seems to have an idea of this sort in mind when he takes up where Barth's essay leaves off in his *Dedicatoria y Prólogo a don Miguel de Cervantes Saavedra,* the bilingual preface to his "Seven

Exemplary Fictions."[4] Unlike Barth, Coover applies the notion of exhaustion not to literary forms but to a general contemporary sense of reality and to the whole legacy of cultural values today: "But *don* Miguel, the optimism, the innocence, the aura of possibility you have experienced have been largely drained away, and the universe is closing in on us again. Like you, we, too, seem to be standing at the end of one age and on the threshold of another. . . . We, too, suffer from a 'literature of exhaustion.'" A quiet version of apocalyptic thinking is very much in evidence here. We love to think we are on the threshold of a radically new era, but in fact the continuity of much of contemporary fiction with its literary antecedents is too substantive to be dismissed as mere vestigial reflex. Contemporary novelists resemble Cervantes (as Coover recognizes further on) because of the underlying operations of their imaginative enterprise, not because our historical moment parallels his in marking the beginning of a new age. And the proposed contrast between Cervantes and the contemporaries seems overdrawn. The least innocent of writers, Cervantes ironically undercuts the innocence and optimism of his hero, and through the strategies he devises for doing that he invents the novel. In any event, Coover goes on to argue from the supposed draining away of optimism in our age the conversion of the novelist to fabulist:

> We seem to have moved from an open-ended, anthropocentric, humanistic, naturalistic, even—to the extent that man may be thought of as making his own universe—optimistic starting point, to one that is closed, cosmic, eternal, supernatural (in its soberest sense), and pessimistic. The return to Being has returned us to Design, to microcosmic images of the macrocosm, to the creation of Beauty within the confines of cosmic or human necessity, to the use of the fabulous to probe beyond the phenomenological, beyond appearances, beyond randomly perceived events, beyond mere history.

Some judgments it may be wise on principle to decline making at all, and I see no way of knowing at this point in history whether we are in fact witnessing the death of the humanistic world view. To base an argument for a new form of fiction on such a sweepingly prophetic historical assertion must in the end compromise the persuasiveness of the literary argument. In any case, of Barth's three exemplars of the literature of exhaustion, only one, Borges, really corresponds to this description of Coover's. In regard to Beckett, all that strictly applies is the pessimism and the sense of a closed universe, and it is Nabokov who once tartly observed that "cosmic" is but a slippery "s" away from "comic." Both Beckett and Nabokov are by intention, in their radically different ways, comic rather than cosmic writers; both are novelists rather than fabulists in their concern with the naturalistic textures of experience, whatever various structures they make of them. Both resemble Cervantes in deriving Design not from an image of eternal Being but, on the contrary, from a sense of the contradictions between traditional literary practice and their immediate perception of human reality.

The most questionable of Coover's claims, however, is that the writer of fiction is now moving "beyond mere history." Borges the fabulist does just that, but unless the novel is really dead, the one thing it ultimately cannot dispense with is history. The pressing actuality of historical time, or of an individual lifetime, or of both, is the stuff of all good novels, including self-conscious ones, the perennial subject that the medium of the novel—a sequential narrative use of unmetrical language extended at length in time—seems almost to require. Cervantes initiates the genre by using parody and the translation of literary criticism into narrative invention to juxtapose a literary dream of a Golden Age with real historical time. On the plane of individual experience, Sterne in his ultimate self-conscious novel makes time so much his subject that the printed text becomes a maze of intersecting, mutually modifying times—the time of writing and the time of reading, the actual duration of an event, time as a literary construct, time as an ambiguous artifact of memory or consciousness.

Perhaps the most reliable index to whether a piece of self-conscious fiction is closed off from life is whether it tends to diminish the actuality of personal and historical time. Queneau's *exercices* are only exercises because time doesn't really exist in them; it is only a necessary hypothesis to move the skinny young man from the beginning of the anecdote to the end. Robbe-Grillet's cinematic use of the present indicative, together with his constant shuffling of versions of each narrative incident in order to destroy all sense of causal sequence and of time, is a technical *tour de force* precisely because it goes so strenuously against the grain of the medium, which is, after all, prose fiction, not film. As a result the virtuosity of his achievement is inseparable from its marked limitations. The same could be said of the composition by *montage* in Coover's shorter fiction or, on a cruder level of technical skill and imagination, of Barthelme's satirical collages. It is instructive, however, that Coover is now working on a novel involved with public events in the Eisenhower years, a book he describes as "an historical romance." And, to judge by a published section, his reentry into history, cannily seen through the revealing distortions of fantasy, can produce energetically engaging fiction.

In the case of Robbe-Grillet, the one really striking success among his novels is the book in which his ubiquitous technique of suppressing temporal progression has a powerful psychological justification. *Jealousy* is a compelling novel because its imprisonment in a present indicative that circles back on itself again and again is the perfect narrative mode for a man whose consuming obsession has robbed him of any time in which things can unfold. The jealous husband, always the excluded observer peering at his wife and her supposed lover from oblique angles through a hatchwork of screens and obstacles, can only go over and over the same scanty data, reordering them and surrounding them with conjecture, describing them with a seemingly scientific objectivity that is actually quite maniacal. Consequently what is often felt elsewhere in Robbe-Grillet as an anomalous mannerism is here firmly grounded in the novel's peculiar facts of character and fictional situation.

Queneau's *Exercices de style,* as I intimated earlier, is a limited experiment that explores the most extreme possibilities of an underlying practice of his novels while deliberately omitting what is ultimately most essential to them—the potent force of time, analogous to the time of real experience, that sweeps along the imaginary personages and events. Over against *Exercices* one might usefully set a novel like *Le Chiendent* (1933), Queneau's remarkable fictional farce in the self-conscious mode. At the center of this grand display of verbal highjinks, parodistic ploys, hilarious stylizations, and satiric illuminations, stands a death—that of Ernestine the serving-girl, which, for all its abruptness, improbability, and absurdity, has large reverberations in the novel. "When a tree burns," says Ernestine, dying on her wedding night, "nothin's left but smoke and ashes. No more tree. That's like me. Nothin left but rot, while the li'l voice that talks in your head when you're all alone, nothin's left of it. When mine stops, it ain't gonna talk again nowhere else."[5]

The last section of *Le Chiendent* takes off on a zanily fantastic extrapolation from destructive modern history. At the very end, three of the protagonists, among the handful of survivors of a long bitter war between the French and the Etruscans (!), meet again and openly share the awareness that all their actions have been relentlessly tracked down and recorded by a book—the one we have been reading and are about to finish. Not pleased with all they have done, they wonder whether it might be possible to erase—*raturer*—or, rather, "literase"—*littératurer*—certain episodes. But no, the thing cannot be done: as one of them observes, even in these literary circumstances "time is time, the past is the past." Then, in a final paragraph, Queneau dissolves his joined characters into separate and unconnected entities, concluding with a single silhouette, not yet a realized character, one among thousands of possible alternatives—which was precisely the image of the novelist-artificer's arbitrary choice in the making of fictions that began the whole novel. And yet the arbitrary invention is one that has been elaborated in order to reveal something about the real world. The whole farce is in fact a sustained metaphysical meditation on the dizzying paradoxes of being and nonbeing, in life and in fiction; and that meditation culminates in these last two pages, where the characters are finally shuffled back into the shadowy pre-world of fictional beginnings but are not allowed the more-than-human luxury of reversing, altering, or erasing the particular experiences they have lived out in the time allotted to them.

It may seem a bit odd to insist on a connection with historical or personal time in a kind of novel devised to mirror its own operations, but the contradiction, I think, disappears upon close consideration. Language is of all art media the one most thoroughly and subtly steeped in memory, both public and private. It is not easy to use language for the length of a novel, out of a self-conscious awareness of its function as the medium of the fictional artifice, without in some way confronting the burden of a collective or individual past that language carries. Language through its layer upon layer of associations opens up complex vistas of time, and these tend to reveal—ultimately for cultures, imminently for individuals—loss, decline, and extinction. The continuous acrobatic display of artifice in a self-conscious novel is an enlivening demonstration of human order against a background of chaos and darkness, and it is the tension between artifice and that which annihilates artifice that gives the finest self-conscious novels their urgency in the midst of play. Tristram Shandy's wild flight from death across the pages of Volume VII in Sterne's novel provides the clearest paradigm for this general situation. In the two major novelists of our own century who magisterially combine the realist and self-conscious traditions of the novel, Joyce and Proust, it is again death and the decline of culture into ultimate incoherence that powerfully impel the writers to the supreme affirmation of art. The void looms beyond Bloom's Dublin and Marcel's Paris, as it does beyond Biely's St. Petersburg, Virginia Woolf's London, and the invented lost realms of Nabokov; and that is why art is indispensable.

Perhaps this may make every novel with self-conscious aspects sound like a version of Sartre's *Nausea,* but that is only because Sartre provides an emphatically defined, programmatic formulation of the general pattern. What I would like to stress is that even a novel worlds away from any intimation of existentialist views may tap this tension between the coherence of the artifice and the death and disorder implicit in real time outside the artifice. The tension is present even in Fielding, with his fine old eighteenth-century confidence in the possibilities of coherent order and his meticulous preservation of the purity of the comic world. An example may be helpful here. In Book V, Chapter XII, of *Tom Jones,* after a bloody brawl in which Tom has laid Blifil low only to be vigorously battered by the redoubtable Thwackum, the narrator, surveying the bruised combatants, takes off on one of his so-called essayistic excursuses:

> Here we cannot suppress a pious wish, that all quarrels were to be decided by those weapons only with which Nature, knowing what is proper for us, hath supplied us; and that cold iron was to be used in digging no bowels but those of the earth. Then would war, the pastime of monarchs, be almost inoffensive, and battles between great armies might be fought at the particular desire of several ladies of quality; who, together with the kings themselves, might be actual spectators of the conflict. Then might the field be this moment well strewed with human carcasses, and the next, the dead men, or infinitely the greatest part of them, might get up, like Mr. Bayes's troops, and march off either at the sound of a drum or fiddle, as should be previously agreed on.

The narrator spins out this fanciful hypothesis for another paragraph, then brings himself up short: "But such reformations are rather to be wished than hoped for: I shall content myself, therefore, with this short hint, and return to my narrative." What is all this doing in the middle of *Tom Jones?* To dismiss it as mere casual banter or extraneous digression is to ignore the integrity of Fielding's art and of his vision of life. The passage is a virtuoso aria set in the optative mode. It turns from *The History of Tom Jones* to history proper, but with a series of careful indications of a condition contrary to fact. It begins and ends with an explicit stress on "wish," and all the verbs are subjunctive or conditional. The emphasis through anaphora on "then" ("Then would war . . .";"Then might the field be . . .") points to an era that exists not now or soon but in the imagination alone. This condition is underlined by likening the weaponless battles to those of a popular Restoration farce, *The Rehearsal* ("Mr. Bayes's troops"), and by proposing that war should be conducted like theatrical convention, by previously agreed-upon signals.

Within the comic frame of Tom Jones's fictional world, we know very well that no fate much worse than a bloodied nose will be allowed to befall any of the personages who matter. Fielding, by proposing for the space of two paragraphs that this frame be extended into real historical time, is doing something more than make a suggestion for "reformation," as he pretends, or a satirical comment on historical man's irrationality, as is evident. What the excursion into optative history points up is that the whole comic world of the fiction is beautifully arranged, sanely humane in its essential playfulness—and ultimately unreal. The age-old impulse of the storyteller bespeaks a basic human need to imagine out of history a fictional order of fulfillment, but when the narrative is a novel and not a fairy tale, one is also made aware of the terrible persistence of history as a murderous realm of chaos constantly challenging or violating the wholeness that art can imagine. By the time we arrive at the narrator's explicit signal for the end of the excursus, "I shall content myself . . . with this short hint, and return to my narrative," we see with renewed clarity all that stands outside the artful narrative, inimical to it.

I have chosen from many possible texts, old and new, an example from Fielding in order to emphasize certain underlying continuities of concern between the novelists of our own age and the early masters. A clearer recognition of such continuities, which more often than one would suspect manifest themselves even on the level of fictional technique, might make us less inclined to see ourselves at the decisive end of an era, our writers footnoting with fables a literary corpus that has used up all the possibilities of primary creation. Looking over the actual production of living novelists in both hemispheres, I find it hard to believe that it is inherently more difficult to write a good novel now than in earlier periods. The realist mode of fiction that attained such splendid achievements in the nineteenth century may by now largely have run its course (though that, too, might be a presumptuous conclusion), but the self-conscious novelistic dialectic between art and reality initiated by Cervantes seems abundantly alive with new possibilities of expression, perhaps even more than ever before as the self-consciousness of our whole culture becomes progressively more pronounced. To write a good self-conscious novel today one does not have to be a unique "Thesean hero" finding a way out of some impossible labyrinth, but simply an intelligent writer with a serious sense both of the integrity of his craft and of the inevitably problematic relationship between fiction and life.

A case in point is Claude Mauriac's *The Marquise Went Out at Five* (1961), one of the most interesting novels to come out of the fervor of fictional experiment in France during the past fifteen or so years. Mauriac's book might be especially instructive as a concluding example because in both its design and its execution it ties up many of the major themes we have been considering, and because Mauriac, a gifted writer but surely no Borgesian wonder-worker defying the limits of nature, achieves what he does, not through impossible genius, but simply by an imaginative and keenly critical management of the self-conscious mode.

The Marquise Went Out is the third of four interlocking novels aptly called *Le Dialogue intérieur*. The title of the novel is taken from Breton's "First Surrealist Manifesto," the relevant passage appearing as the epigraph. Breton quotes Valéry on the imbecilic beginnings of most novels. Valéry would never permit himself, he once told Breton, to write a sentence like, "The Marquise went out at five." We then turn the page of Mauriac's novel and of course find it begins, *"La Marquise sortit à cinq heures.* The Marquise went out at five." At first, in the kaleidoscope shifting of interior monologues—perhaps a hundred different characters become posts of observation—with no indication of transitions, the reader has difficulty orienting himself; but gradually a fictional novelist, Bertrand Carnéjoux, emerges distinctly as the principal point of reference. As Carnéjoux stands at his window looking down over the Carrefour de Bucis, where all the events of the novel take place, one begins to suspect that all the interior lives exposed in the book are finally what he, the writer as distanced observer, projects onto the figures he sees. He is the fictional writer acting out his author's own literary impulse, in a contemporary version of the old quixotic pattern, by making a novel out of the world he inhabits:

> . . . Express the double brilliance, orangeish red bright yellow, of the bouquets, no, they're potted plants. Add to these two patches of bright color the movement transporting them, not fast but jolting, and the black mass of that old lady carrying her nasturtiums—they are nasturtiums, I think. I'm no different as an author from all the authors who ever existed since men first began to write. Using other devices, but analogous ones. Making use just as fallaciously, as arbitrarily, of the world I claim—quite insanely—to possess. At best I've tried to explain and justify the increasing presence, considered ridiculous by some people, of writer-heroes in the works of writers. . . . [6]

The sense of the writer's predicament as a perennial, not peculiarly modern, difficulty is notable: all serious novelists must confront the arbitrariness, the necessary falsification, of the worlds they invent through words. In his critical writings, Mauriac has coined the term *alittérature* to describe this intrinsic problematic of literature. All literary creation worthy of the name, now and in previous ages, is seen as a reaction against the inevitable falsity of antecedent literature, a restless devising of strategies to escape being "just" literature. I think the idea is more historically accurate than the notion of a contemporary literature of exhaustion, and *The Marquise Went Out at Five* is a persuasive demonstration of its efficacy as a rationale for the continual renewal of literature.

By the conclusion of the novel, Carnéjoux, the novelist as self-observing observer, imperceptibly gives way to the author of *The Marquise Went Out at Five.* The evoked world of fiction, revealed as fiction, shrivels up, and, as at the end of many of Nabokov's novels, the fabricator of the fiction himself stands in its place. Mauriac now describes precisely what he has given us: "A novelist animated by a novelist whom I (myself a novelist) have put into a novel in which, however, nothing was invented, a labyrinth of mirrors capturing some of life's sensations, feelings and thoughts" (p. 310). Cervantes' emblematic image of the mirror—it is of course also Nabokov's favorite—is complicated in Borgesian fashion by a labyrinth not because the old quixotic probing of reality through fiction has changed in nature, but only because our sense of the complexity of the enterprise has been many times multiplied by both historical and literary experience. (One might observe that as early as 1913 Andrey Biely was using the image of the labyrinth of mirrors in his *St. Petersburg.*) Mauriac, it should be noted, does not in the end make the facile gesture of some contemporary novelists who simply shrug off their own fictions as, after all, mere fictions: he avows the artifice but affirms it as a means of mirroring "life's sensations, feelings and thoughts," fiction seen as perhaps the only way to get at a whole range of real human experience.

After a paragraph of reflections on the Parisian square that has been the scene of the novel, Mauriac goes on to summarize and make even more explicit this baring of artifice as the basic procedure of his book: "Thus the novel has in its penultimate pages gradually faded away, and disappeared, without masks or make-believe, giving way to the novelist who, if he has put himself directly into his book, has at the end purified it of its last traces of fiction by granting it a truth in which literal exactitude was preferred to literature" (p. 311). The literal exactitude is of course necessarily a pretense, still another novelistic gesture (as Cervantes first shrewdly saw in his play with supposed documents), literature passing itself off as *alittérature* in order not to seem "literature" in the pejorative sense. In any case, the edifice of fiction that engaged our thoughts and emotions for a good many hours has been swept away, and the novel can conclude in the very next sentence by setting on its head that beginning borrowed from Valéry by way of Breton: "The Marquise did not go out at five . . . ." Much earlier, we learned that the Marquise of the initial sentence was no marquise at

all, and now the predicate as well as the subject is torn from its apparent exactitude and cast into the shadowy realm of fabrications.

All this might be mere cleverness if the novel did not have the impelling sense it does of the urgency, the philosophical seriousness, of its enterprise. What drives Bertrand Carnéjoux, and behind him Claude Mauriac, is an acute perception of two concentric abysses beneath the artifice of the novel—history and death. *The Marquise Went Out,* set between five and six on one warm afternoon in a few thousand square feet of the Carrefour de Bucis, attempts to exhaust the human experience intersecting that carefully delimited time and place. But as Carnéjoux and his inventor realize, such an undertaking is "doomed to failure" because "the unity of actual time . . . [is] surrounded, penetrated, absorbed . . . by the infinite pullulation of innumerable past moments" (p. 270). Though Mauriac explicitly compares the achronological method of composition here through a long series of separate "takes" with the methods of a film-maker, the effect is precisely the opposite of cinematic composition in Robbe-Grillet because Mauriac accepts and works with the essentially time-soaked nature of language as a medium of art.

Each of the interior monologues gives us glimpses of a deep tunnel into a private past, while Carnéjoux, overviewing the scene, weaves into the texture of the novel substantial quotations from actual historical documents of life in the Carrefour de Bucis from the middle of the thirteenth century to the post-World-War-II era. The documents reveal what in the poesy of a blurb one might call a "vivid panorama" of Parisian existence from medieval artisans to activists of the Revolution to the literary dinners of the Goncourt brothers. What is actually revealed, though, is the raw realm of chaos on the other side of Fielding's ironic observations about history—a long catalogue of rape, murder, torture, theft, perversion, brutality. Contemplating these documents, Carnéjoux is simultaneously aware of the senselessness of history and of the incomprehensible brevity of all human life. As he writes, he is rapidly, irrevocably, rushing toward the point where he will be no more than a few scratches on the historical record, like Mestre Giles the tile-maker and Richart the baker, listed as residents of the Rue de Bussy in the *Tax-Book of Paris for the Year 1292.* At the end, the author draws particular attention to this perception: "Bertrand Carnéjoux records in his novel, and I record in the novel in which I have given life and speech to Bertrand Carnéjoux, that impossibility of conceiving what seems so natural in others, what one has spent one's life fearing, knowing oneself ineluctably threatened by it in the beings one loves and in oneself: death" (p. 309).

Some readers may feel that Mauriac is too explicitly direct in the way he reveals these fundamental matters of motive and design in the making of his novel, but the fiction itself bears out in concrete detail what otherwise might seem portentous assertion. A writer, about to vanish like every human being born, has only words to grasp with at some sort of tenuous, dubious permanence. Words console, words are the most wonderful of human evasions; but the writer, using them as truly as a writer of fiction can—which is to say, with a consciousness of how their enchantment transmutes reality into fiction—comes to perceive profoundly what words help us to evade. The seriousness and the ultimate realism of the novel that mirrors itself could have no more vivid demonstration.

Perhaps the most basic paradox of this mode of fiction, which functions through the display of paradoxes, is that as a kind of novel concentrating on art and the artist it should prove to be, even in many of its characteristically comic embodiments, a long meditation on death. Myth, folktale, fable, and romance, all the archaic forms of storytelling from which the novel was a radical historical break, overleap or sidestep death as an immediate presence in the timeless cyclicality of divine lives or in the teleological arc from "once upon a time" to "lived happily ever after." The great realist novels of the nineteenth century, though they may be filled with scenes of disease and dying, are in another sense also an implicit evasion of death because, as the paradigmatic instance of Balzac makes clear, behind the vast effort to represent in fiction a whole society, the spawning of novel after novel with crowds of personages overflowing from one book to the next, was a dream of omnipotence, the novelist creating a fantasy-world so solid-seeming that he could rule over it like a god.

When the writer, on the other hand, places himself or some consciously perceived surrogate within the fiction's field of probing consideration, his own mortality is more likely to be an implicit or even explicit subject of the novel. It was Diderot who observed that one should tell stories because then time passes swiftly and the story of life comes to an end unnoticed. The novel as a genre begins when Don Quixote, approaching the grand climacteric or fiftieth year, which was old age in his time, realizes that his existence has amounted to nothing and proceeds before it is too late to make his life correspond to a book. The knight's peculiarly literary quest is a revealing functional analogue to that of the novelist, the literary man who invented him, and so Cervantes is not merely mocking chivalric romances through the don's adventures but contemplating, in the most oblique and searching way, the unthinkable prospect posed by his own imminent end.

I suspect that death in the novel might be a more useful focus for serious discussion of the genre than the death of the novel. What I have in mind is of course not the novelistic rendering of deathbed scenes but how the novel manages to put us in touch with the imponderable implications of human mortality through the very celebration of life implicit in the building of vivid and various fictions. This is the ultimate turn of the Copernican revolution in the making of fictions that Cervantes effected. The impulse of fabulation, which men had typically used to create an imaginary time beautifully insulated from the impinging presence of their own individual deaths, was turned back on itself, held up to a mirror of criticism as

it reflected reality in its inevitably distortive glass. As a result it became possible, if not for the first time then surely for the first time on this scale of narrative amplitude and richness, to delight in the lifelike excitements of invented personages and adventures, and simultaneously to be reminded of that other world of ours, ruled by chance and given over to death. The mirror held to the mirror of art held to nature, in Cervantes and in his countless progeny, proved to be not merely an ingenious trick but a necessary operation for a skeptical culture nevertheless addicted, as all cultures have been, to the pleasures and discoveries of fabulation. Ongoing literary history is always modifying our vision of earlier stages of literary development, and the course of the novel from Joyce to Nabokov and beyond may to some degree require a shift in perspective upon what happened in the novel during the three centuries before our own. Today, as varieties of novelistic self-consciousness proliferate, the mode of fiction first defined when a certain aging hidalgo set out to imitate his books appears far from exhausted. On the contrary, in the hands of gifted writers it comes to seem increasingly our most precisely fashioned instrument for joining imagined acts and figures with real things.

NOTES

[1] Flann O'Brien, *At Swim-Two-Birds* (New York: Pantheon, 1939), p. 33.

[2] *The Atlantic Monthly,* 220 (August 1967), pp. 29-34.

[3] J. L. Borges, *Labyrinths,* ed. Yates and Irby (New York: New Directions, 1964), pp. 213-216.

[4] Robert Coover, *Pricksongs & Descants* (New York: Dutton, 1969), pp. 76-79.

[5] Raymond Queneau, *Le Chiendent* (Paris: Gallimard, 1933), p. 206.

[6] Claude Mauriac, *The Marquise Went Out at Five,* tr. Richard Howard (New York: George Braziller, 1962), p. 69.

Gerald Graff

SOURCE: "The Myth of the Postmodern Breakthrough," in *Literature Against Itself: Literary Ideas in Modern Society,* The University of Chicago Press, 1979.

[*In the following essay, which was first published in slightly different form in 1973, Graff identifies postmodernism as both visionary and apocalyptic, and asserts that despite claims to the contrary, postmodernism derives from Romantic and modernist literary theory.*]

The postmodern tendency in literature and literary criticism has been characterized as a "breakthrough," a significant reversal of the dominant literary and sociocultural directions of the last two centuries. Literary critics such as Leslie Fiedler, Susan Sontag, George Steiner, Richard Poirier, and Ihab Hassan have written about this reversal, differing in their assessments of its implications but generally agreeing in their descriptions of what is taking place. What is taking place, these critics suggest, is the death of our traditional Western concept of art and literature, a concept which defined "high culture" as our most valuable repository of moral and spiritual wisdom. George Steiner draws attention to the disturbing implications of the fact that, in the Nazi regime, dedication to the highest "humanistic" interests was compatible with the acceptance of systematic murder.[1] Sontag and Fiedler suggest that the entire artistic tradition of the West has been exposed as a kind of hyperrational imperialism akin to the aggression and lust for conquest of bourgeois capitalism. Not only have the older social, moral, and epistemological claims for art seemingly been discredited, but art has come to be seen as a form of complicity, another manifestation of the lies and hypocrisy through which the ruling class has maintained its power.

But concurrent with this loss of confidence in the older claims of the moral and interpretive authority of art is the advent of a new sensibility, bringing a fresh definition of the role of art and culture. This new sensibility manifests itself in a variety of ways: in the refusal to take art "seriously" in the old sense; in the use of art itself as a vehicle for exploding its traditional pretensions and for showing the vulnerability and tenuousness of art and language; in the rejection of the dominant academic tradition of analytic, interpretive criticism, which by reducing art to abstractions tends to neutralize or domesticate its potentially liberating energies; in a less soberly rationalistic mode of consciousness, one that is more congenial to myth, tribal ritual, and visionary experience, grounded in a "protean," fluid, and undifferentiated concept of the self as opposed to the repressed Western ego.

I want here to raise some critical questions about the postmodern breakthrough in the arts and about the larger implications claimed for it in culture and society. I want in particular to challenge the standard description of postmodernism as an overturning of romantic and modernist traditions. To characterize postmodernism as a "breakthrough"—a cant term of our day—is to place a greater distance between current writers and their predecessors than is, I think, justified. There are distinctions to be drawn, of course, and both here and in the final chapter of this book I shall try to draw them. But this [essay] argues that postmodernism should be seen not as a break with romantic and modernist assumptions but rather as a logical culmination of the premises of these earlier movements, premises not always clearly defined in discussions of these issues. In the next chapter I question the utopian social claims of the postmodernist sensibility by questioning the parallelism they assume between social and esthetic revolution.

In its literary sense, postmodernism may be defined as the movement within contemporary literature and criticism that calls into question the traditional claims of literature

and art to truth and human value. As Richard Poirier has observed, "contemporary literature has come to register the dissolution of the ideas often evoked to justify its existence: the cultural, moral, psychological premises that for many people still define the essence of literature as a humanistic enterprise. Literature is now in the process of telling us how little it means."[2] This is an apt description of the contemporary mood, but what it neglects to mention is that literature has been in the process of telling us how little it means for a long time, as far back as the beginnings of romanticism.

It is clear why we are tempted to feel that the contemporary popularity of anti-art and artistic self-parody represents a sharp break with the modernist past. It does not seem so long ago that writers like Rilke, Valéry, Joyce, Yeats, and others sought a kind of salvation through art. For Rilke, as earlier for Shelley and other romantics, poetry was "a mouth which else Nature would lack," the great agency for the restitution of values in an inherently valueless world. Romantic and modernist writing expressed a faith in the constitutive power of the imagination, a confidence in the ability of literature to impose order, value, and meaning on the chaos and fragmentation of industrial society. This faith seemed to have lapsed after World War II. Literature increasingly adopted an ironic view of its traditional pretensions to truth, high seriousness, and the profundity of "meaning." Furthermore, literature of the postwar period has seemed to have a different relation to criticism than that of the classic modernists. Eliot, Faulkner, Joyce, and their imitators sometimes seemed to be deliberately providing occasions for the complex critical explications of the New Critics. In contrast, much of the literature of the last several decades has been marked by the desire to remain invulnerable to critical analysis.

In an essay that asks the question, "What Was Modernism?" Harry Levin identifies the "ultimate quality" pervading the work of the moderns as "its uncompromising intellectuality."[3] The conventions of postmodern art systematically invert this modernist intellectuality by parodying its respect for truth and significance. In Donald Barthelme's anti-novel, *Snow White,* a questionnaire poses for the reader such mock questions as, "9. Has the work, for you, a metaphysical dimension? Yes ( ) No ( ) 10. What is it (twenty-five words or less)?"[4] Alain Robbe-Grillet produces and campaigns for a type of fiction in which "obviousness, transparency preclude the existence of *higher worlds,* of any transcendence."[5] Susan Sontag denounces the interpretation of works of art on the grounds that "to interpret is to impoverish, to deplete the world—in order to set up a shadow world of 'meanings.'"[6] Leslie Fiedler, writing on modern poetry, characterizes one of its chief tendencies as a "flight from the platitude of meaning."[7] As Jacob Brackman describes this attitude in *The Put-On,* "we are supposed to have learned by now that one does not ask what art means."[8] And, as Brackman shows, this deliberate avoidance of interpretability has moved from the arts into styles of personal behavior. It appears that the term "meaning" itself, as applied not only to art but to more general experience, has joined "truth" and "reality" in the class of words which can no longer be written unless apologized for by inverted commas.

Thus it is tempting to agree with Leslie Fiedler's conclusion that "the Culture Religion of Modernism" is now dead.[9] The most advanced art and criticism of the last twenty years seem to have abandoned the modernist respect for artistic meaning. The religion of art has been "demythologized." A number of considerations, however, render this statement of the case misleading. Examined more closely, both the modernist faith in literary meanings and the postmodern repudiation of these meanings prove to be highly ambivalent attitudes, much closer to one another than may at first appear. The equation of modernism with "uncompromising intellectuality" overlooks how much of this intellectuality devoted itself to calling its own authority into question.

THE RELIGION OF ART

The nineteenth century's elevation of art to the status of a surrogate religion had rested on paradoxical foundations. Though in one sense the religion of art increased enormously the cultural prestige and importance of art, there was self-denigration implicit in the terms in which art was deified. Consider the following statement by Ortega y Gasset, contrasting the attitude of the avant-garde art of the mid-twenties, that art is "a thing of no consequence" and "of no transcendent importance," with the veneration art had compelled in the previous century:

> Poetry and music then were activities of an enormous caliber. In view of the downfall of religion and the inevitable relativism of science, art was expected to take upon itself nothing less than the salvation of mankind. Art was important for two reasons: on account of its subjects which dealt with the profoundest problems of humanity, and on account of its own significance as a human pursuit from which the species derived its justification and dignity.[10]

Ortega attributes the prestige of art in the nineteenth century to the fact that art was expected to provide compensation for the "downfall of religion and the inevitable relativism of science." But the downfall of religion and the relativism of science were developments which could not help undermining the moral and epistemological foundations of art. Once these foundations had been shaken—and the sense of their precariousness was a condition of the romantic glorification of the creative imagination—art could scarcely lay claim to any firm authority for dealing with "the profoundest problems of humanity" and for endowing the species with "justification and dignity." It is only fair to add that Ortega's own philosophical writings are profound commentaries on this crisis of authority in modern experience.

From its beginnings, the romantic religion of art manifested that self-conflict with its own impulses which

Renato Poggioli, in *The Theory of the Avant-Garde,* identifies as a defining characteristic of avant-garde thought.[11] The ultimate futility and impotence of art was implicit in the very terms with which romantic and subsequently modernist writers attempted to deify art as a substitute for religion. The concept of an autonomous creative imagination, which fabricates the forms of order, meaning, and value which men no longer thought they could find in external nature, implicitly—if not necessarily intentionally—concedes that artistic meaning is a fiction, without any corresponding object in the extra-artistic world. In this respect the doctrine of the creative imagination contained within itself the premises of its refutation.

Recent literature forces us to recognize the precariousness of the earlier religion of art, to see that the very concept of a *creative* imagination on which it depended contains an unavoidable difficulty. For an order or pattern of meaning which must be invented by human consciousness out of its inner structure—whether it is thought to derive from the private subjectivity of the individual, from some intersubjective *Geist* that is assumed to be common to all minds, or from the humanly created forms of custom and convention—is necessarily uncertain of its authority. Old-fashioned textbook descriptions of romanticism stressing the affirmative flights of the romantic priests of art ignored the ambivalence pervading romantic writing. Wordsworth, for example, celebrating the spirit in nature which "rolls through all things," pauses self-consciously to consider that this celebration may rest on "a vain belief," justifiable only on pragmatic grounds. And his affirmation of this spirit is haunted by his difficulty in determining whether man actually perceives it as an external reality or creates it out of his own mind. The Shelleyan stereotype of the poet as the "unacknowledged legislator of the world," a godlike creator who brings forth a new cosmos *ex nihilo* and soars beyond the range of commonsense reality, is, from another perspective, only an honorific reformulation of the alternate stereotype of the poet as a marginal person, a hapless trifler or eccentric who inhabits a world of autistic fantasy and turns his back on objective reality. The secret and unacknowledged collaboration between rebellious literati and their philistine detractors remains an unwritten chapter in the social history of art. Both poetolatry's glorification of the artist as a demigod and philistinism's denigration of him as an irresponsible social deviant share a common definition of the artist as a special kind of person, one who perceives the world in a fashion different from that of ordinary objective judgment. An inner connection links the doctrine of imaginative autonomy and the philosophical and social alienation of art.[12]

For the romantic belief in the power of the autonomous imagination was chastened by the recognition that the order and truth generated by this imagination are no more than arbitrary and subjective constructions. If imaginative truth is determined from within rather than without, how can a poet know whether one myth prompted by his imagination is truer than any other? And what basis has he for claiming that his particular myth is or should be shared by others? In the very assertion that poetry endows the universe with meaning—the proposition of Shelley's *Defence*—there lay an implied confession of the arbitrary nature of that meaning. Romantic esthetics typifies the more general crisis of modern thought, which pursues a desperate quest for meaning in experience while refusing to accept the validity of any meaning proposed. The paradox of the sophisticated modern mind is that it is unable to believe in the objective validity of meanings yet is unable to do without meanings. The ambiguous status of the concept of meaning in modern esthetic theory is one outcome of this paradox. For the last two centuries, theorists have engaged in a tightrope act in which the significance which must be ascribed to art in order to justify its importance has had to be eliminated from art in order to guarantee its innocence and authenticity. Thus we have the numerous self-contradictory attempts in the twentieth century to define art as a discourse somehow both referential and nonreferential, closed off from the external world yet embodying profound knowledge of the external world.[13]

THE APPEAL TO CONSENSUS

The equation of romanticism with "subjectivism" is, of course, a misunderstanding of the intentions of the major romantic thinkers, who glorified not the idiosyncratic subjectivity of the private ego but transcendental subjectivity of universal man, sometimes identified with the Absolute itself. Thus for Shelley, "a poem is the very image of life expressed in its eternal truth" according to "the unchangeable forms of human nature, as existing in the mind of the creator, which is itself the image of all other minds."[14] By assuming the unity and universality of "all other minds," this view makes it possible to do without an external ground of order and value. Henry David Aiken notes that nineteenth-century thinkers came "increasingly to recognize that objectivity is not so much a fact about the universe as it is a matter of common standards of judgment and criticism." Objectivity, in other words, was redefined as intersubjectivity: "Intersubjective norms are not agreed to by the members of a society because they are objective, but, in effect, become objective because they are jointly accepted."[15]

In other words, societies do not abide by certain rules because these rules are, by some preestablished standard, normative. Rather, societies *choose* to regard certain rules as normative, and these rules then become established as such. This reasoning refers normative judgments to what we now call an "existential" act of choice. In doing so, however, it begs the question of *how* this choice is made. On what basis does society choose? To take a provocative but nevertheless pertinent example, suppose one faction of society prefers a policy of genocide against certain minorities while another prefers a policy of democratic freedom. Is there no standard of *good reasons* that can be invoked to show that democratic freedom constitutes a wiser choice than genocidal extinction? (I have translated the problem into one of values, but the case is not altered when the question is

one of what to regard as objectively true.) The notion that choices *determine* norms rather than *obey* them does away with the idea that there are certain norms that *ought* to be chosen by societies and thus precipitates a radical cultural relativism. It is true, of course, that force, not good reasons, *has* governed most societies. Yet if we give up the notion that such reasons can exist prior to choice, we deny the legitimacy of resisting force.

To argue that the nature of a concept is whatever people *believe* it to be may be an adequate strategy as long as everybody in the relevant group believes the same things. It becomes a nonanswer when the nature of the concept has become a contested issue. The appeal to what people believe breaks down as soon as the question arises of whether they *ought* to believe it. The appeal to intersubjective consensus begs the question at hand; it was the breakdown of such consensus, when the literary and the commercial-utilitarian factions of society began to inhabit opposed mental worlds, that in large degree occasioned the cultural problem. It is this dilemma that may have induced Kant himself, in at least one passage, to swerve from his customary position and assert that our mental acts of constituting reality must be controlled by an external object. In the *Prolegomena to Any Future Metaphysics*, Kant poses the question of how we can assure ourselves that our judgments are shared by others. His answer is surprising: "there would be no reason for the judgments of other men necessarily agreeing with mine," Kant says, "if it were not for the unity of the object to which they all refer and with which they accord; hence they must all agree with one another."[16] This answer is surprising because elsewhere Kant insists that it makes no sense to speak of a "unity of the object" as if it were prior to our thinking, because unity inheres not in the object but in the conditions of our common understanding, specifically in the *category* of unity by which our minds constitute the object. Here Kant seems to undo his Copernican revolution by making our ability to constitute the object as a unity depend on the unity of the object in itself prior to our apprehension. In order to account for the universality of our perceptions, Kant is forced to lapse into the sort of "correspondence" theory of truth that his philosophy has presumably done away with.

But of course the great influence of Kant's thought—whether Kant intended it or not—was precisely to discredit this correspondence theory of truth, and to rule out any talk about the way reality *coerces* our judgments. And in the absence of any appeal to such a coercive reality to which the plurality of subjectivities can be referred, all perspectives become equally valid. The romantic Absolute degenerates into a myth or, as we now say, a fiction. The logic of romantic transcendental philosophy led to a relativism that was certainly antithetical to what most romantic thinkers intended, yet which furthered the loss of community they were seeking to redress.

This distinction between the intent of romantic argument and its consequences makes it possible to resolve some recent scholarly controversies over whether the

romantics were humanists or nihilists. In a sense, both
sides are right. The opposing theories of romanticism do
not really conflict, since they are not talking about the
same aspects of the subject. Those who see romanticism
as positive and optimistic (notably, M. H. Abrams in
Natural Supernaturalism and René Wellek in "Romanticism Reconsidered") base their view largely on what the
romantics themselves consciously intended—to respect
common truth and the artist's responsibility to his community. Those who by contrast see romanticism as nihilistic (critics such as J. Hillis Miller, Morse Peckham, and
Harold Bloom), base their views on the logical consequences of romantic ideas, independent of intentions.
Certainly neither Kant nor any of the thinkers and poets
who were influenced by his ideas thought they were
proposing a radical relativism that would reduce all values
and all reality to a set of fictions. In this sense, Wellek
is right when he objects to Peckham's statement that
"Romanticism learns from Kant that it can do entirely
without constitutive metaphysics and can use any
metaphysic or world hypothesis as supreme fiction."
Wellek replies, rightly, that one "learns" nothing of the
kind from Kant: "I am not aware of a single writer in the
late eighteenth or early nineteenth century to whom this
description would apply. Who then rejected the possibility of metaphysics or treated it as supreme fiction?"[17]
Nevertheless, in fairness to Peckham's view, there is
warrant for arguing that the effect of the romantic argument was to do just this.

THE DEHUMANIZATION OF REASON: $0 = 0$

The developments we have been discussing have their
origins in the social and philosophical crises of modern
culture. The critical and scientific philosophies of the
seventeenth and eighteenth centuries severed the ancient
connection between rational, objective thought and value
judgments. Not only values, but all ideas of order which
went beyond factual sense-data became increasingly
viewed as inherently subjective, a fate which would
overtake objective fact itself at a later date. There set
in the condition which Erich Heller has described as
"the loss of significant external reality," the sense that
the objective world and the realm of meanings and
values are irreparably divided.[18] Regarded by most
thoughtful men up to the end of the Renaissance as a
support for the eternal ethical, metaphysical, religious,
and esthetic absolutes, "reason," in its empiricist and
Cartesian forms, appeared as a threat to the survival of
absolutes. As soon became clear, this new reason undermined not only received certainties and traditions but
eventually the axioms of rationalism as well. Left to
progress without check, reason threatened to yield up
a universe in which the result of ethical inquiry, as
William James would put it, "could only be one of
those indeterminate equations in mathematics which
end with $0 = 0$," since "this is as far as the reasoning
intellect by itself can go. . . . "[19] This was the "universe
of death" encountered by many romantic writers and
their protagonists—Goethe's Faust, Coleridge's Ancient Mariner, and Carlyle's Teufelsdröckh among them.

In such a universe, choice and action were paralyzed, and
literature was deprived of its moral function.

A number of social developments immensely deepened
this skepticism toward reason. Industrialism intensified
the separation of fact and value by institutionalizing
objective thought in the form of technology, commerce,
and, later, bureaucracy, administration, and social engineering. "Reason" thus became equated with amoral
mechanism, with the commercial calculus of profit and the
laissez-faire economy, with *means* and instrumental efficiency over ends, with a regimented, overorganized society which destroys ritual, folk customs, and the heroic
dimension of life. In this kind of society, reason appears
commonly as a cause of alienation rather than a potential
cure: a value-free, depersonalized, finally aimless and *irrational* mode of calculation that serves the goals both
of arbitrary terror and dull commercialism.

At the same time, the fragmentation of the emerging
democratic and urbanized society generated an awareness of the private interests and prejudices motivating
the use of reason. The recognition that thought serves
"ideological" purposes gradually gave rise to the view—
at first a suspicion, later a programmatic theory—that all
thinking is ideological, that there is no disinterested basis
on which the competing claims of different nations,
classes, and individuals can be compared and judged. As
shared forms of social experience disappeared, the belief
in the possibility of shared experience weakened. Reason,
which from one point of view was inhumanly neutral, was
from another as relativistic, partial, and "human" as passion. And as the growth of class consciousness threatened the stability of established order, reason was associated with blind fanaticism, with a demented overconfi-
dence in the ability of theory alone to reform reality. As
advances in knowledge became more spectacular, society
was plagued by a sense of the discrepancy between the
pervasiveness of intellectual analysis and the poverty of
its results, between the avidity with which knowledge
was pursued and its inability to answer questions of
pressing human importance. With the proliferation of
scientific knowledge, men felt oppressed, rather than
enlightened, by "explanations."

All these developments helped shape an outlook which
sees modern history as a kind of fall from organic unity
into the original sin of rationality and which thus longs
to escape or "transcend" the burden of reflective consciousness. By his fall into reason, man had apparently
lost the harmony of subject and object, self and nature,
senses and reason, individual and society, play and
work—all this for the sake of the questionable benefits of
progress. As Schiller put it in a moving statement, "we
see in irrational nature only a happier sister who remained
in our mother's house, out of which we impetuously fled
abroad in the arrogance of our freedom. With painful
nostalgia we yearn to return as soon as we have begun
to experience the pressure of civilization and hear in the
remote lands of art our mother's tender voice. As long as
we were children of nature merely, we enjoyed happiness

and perfection; we became free, and lost both."[20] Schiller believed that the compensations of freedom and progress were ultimately sufficient to justify the loss, and that at any rate there could be no going back: "That nature which you envy in the irrational is worthy of no respect, no longing. It lies behind you, and must lie eternally behind you."[21] Nevertheless, he cannot help conveying the implication that the advent of rational consciousness and the critical spirit represents a great fall from grace.

One consequence of these developments was to weaken further the classical ideal of an integrated unity of man based on the hierarchical subordination of the "lower" to the "higher" faculties. Even in those German thinkers who glorified Greek culture, this hierarchical view of man, which it was natural enough to associate with tyrannical monarchy, gave way to an "organic" ideal of unity. Reason was not necessarily excluded from this organic unity, but its primacy was usurped by another faculty—sometimes called "Reason" but actually closer to imagination, myth, and fantasy, since it does not conform to "conceptual" or "theoretical" reality, but dictates its laws to reality through an autonomous human consciousness. Mere passive understanding was associated with conformity to traditional authoritarian political systems. Again, this rethinking was necessitated by the fact that understanding had been dehumanized through a kind of guilt-by-association: with soulless technology, with hierarchical social authority, with amoral political economy, with ideological fanaticism, and with a useless and oppressive machinery of explanation.

Given the circumstances, it was inevitable that the crisis of the industrial order would be diagnosed as a case of excess of reason at the expense of the inner life, or in Shelley's phrasing, "an excess of the selfish and calculating principle" and "the materials of external life" over "the power of assimilating them to the internal laws of human nature."[22] It would have to follow that the "human" goals of personal fulfillment, feeling, values, and creativity are arrived at only by overcoming objective consciousness. As Northrop Frye points out, in a statement on Shelley that reveals Frye's own guiding philosophy, "Shelley puts all the discursive disciplines into an inferior group of 'analytic' operations of reason. They are aggressive; they think of ideas as weapons; they seek the irrefutable argument, which keeps eluding them because all arguments are theses, and theses are half-truths implying their own opposites."[23] In other words, reason cannot take us beyond 0 = 0. Worse still, it is arrogant, aggressive, and divisive. With objective reason thus dehumanized, the autonomous creative imagination becomes the only hope for cultural salvation.

From this era dates one of the commonplaces of modern social criticism. This is the view that progress in objective knowledge and its practical applications has far outstripped progress in the moral and human sphere. Though this complaint seems correct to the point of obviousness, the way it is stated unobtrusively insinuates that moral and human concerns are fundamentally independent of the search for objective knowledge. From this it is a mere step to the idea that objective understanding of the world and human values (including the values expressed through the arts) are inimical, or that the best one can hope to do is to combine these opposing impulses in an uneasy alliance. In this alliance, objective thinking is to be controlled, directed, and humanized by a morality which is implicitly understood to be nonobjective and thus of dubious status right from the beginning. Even when romantic thinkers such as Shelley, Wordsworth, and Carlyle view science as potentially beneficial and capable of harmonizing with literature, the division of labor they adopt equates literature with the "internal," science and objectivity with the "external" phases of existence. This paves the way for the sharp separation of function that we find in so much subsequent literary and cultural criticism, and finally for the outright assault on objective reason that characterizes the recent cultural left.

THE FORTUNATE FALL INTO ESTHETIC AUTONOMY

In their very reaction against the scientific reduction of experience, the humanists conceded certain premises of science. W. H. Auden describes this underlying agreement between science and romantic humanists as follows:

> Modern science has destroyed our faith in the naïve observation of our senses: we cannot, it tells us, ever know what the physical universe is *really* like; we can only hold whatever subjective notion is appropriate to the particular human purpose we have in view.
>
> This destroys the traditional conception of *art* as *mimesis*, for there is no longer a nature "out there" to be truly or falsely imitated; all an artist can be *true* to are his subjective sensations and feelings. The change in attitude is already to be seen in Blake's remark that some people see the sun as a round golden disc the size of a guinea but that he sees it as a host crying Holy, Holy, Holy. What is significant about this is that Blake, like the Newtonians he hated, accepts a division between the physical and the spiritual but, in opposition to them, regards the material universe as the abode of Satan, and so attaches no value to what his physical eye sees.[24]

As described here by Auden, Blake's position converts a seeming disaster into a victory for the spirit: the spirit has lost its basis in objective nature and reason; but this is no misfortune, since it is better that the spirit not be "enslaved" to nature and reason anyway. What looks at first like the alienation of literature from its source of philosophical (and social) authority is actually a liberation. In this fashion, the new esthetics of romanticism made a virtue of necessity, or what was perceived as a necessity, by construing literature's dispossession of an objective world view as a fortunate fall into "autonomy." Humanists, from this point on, freely and happily choose to embrace a conception of art's station which has been forced upon them by the constraints of the historical situation. From the perception enforced by science that literature has no objective truth, one moves to the conclusion that this is for the best, since objective truth is merely factual, boring, and middle-class.

This strategy of redeeming a bad situation by redescribing it is seen in the various theories of "disinterestedness" that arose in eighteenth-century esthetics and were perfected by Kant in the *Critique of Judgment*. For Kant the judgments of taste peculiar to art constitute a "pure disinterested satisfaction," as opposed to judgments that are "bound up with an interest." The judgment of taste is "merely *contemplative*," that is, it is "indifferent as regards the existence of an object." It is "not a cognitive judgment (either theoretical or practical), and thus is not *based* on concepts, nor has it concepts as its *purpose*." Art embodies "the mere form of purposiveness" without aiming at a practical purpose, just as art incorporates the raw material of the concepts of the understanding without being itself conceptual.[25] It can hardly be accidental that this insistence on separating art from practical interests began to gain popularity at the very moment when the concept of "interest" was losing its metaphysical authority on the one hand, and acquiring derogatory commercial connotations on the other. Nor can it be accidental that art began to be defined as "purposeless" at the very moment when it was in fact losing its traditional social purpose as a means of understanding experience. A new class was arising that did not look to art for an explanation of things as they are and saw no useful purpose in art. How better to answer this class (while accepting its assumption) than to deride the concept of "useful purpose" and to excuse art from any responsibility to it? Thus art came to be celebrated for a freedom from purpose that had been thrust upon it by default.

Over and over, we find that modern esthetic concepts come about as rationalizations of states of affairs that art had little to do with bringing about. From the perception that "poetry makes nothing happen," as Auden in our century has said,[26] we move to the imperative that poetry *ought* to make nothing happen, and finally to the axiom that it is not real poetry if it aims at practical effect. By this logical route, the alienated position of literature ceases to be an aspect of a particular historical condition and becomes part of literature's very *definition*. Of course this pose of withdrawal from practical effect continues to be highly ambiguous. In its very adoption of a "purposeless" stance, literature performs the practical purpose of combatting philistinism. The very retreat of literature into formalism constitutes an assault on the utilitarians and an attempt to counteract their social and personal influence.

Yet the conditions which had brought about the need to conceive the antidote in these terms made its success unlikely. The strategy of promoting art to the status of universal legislator rested on an implicitly defeatist acceptance of art's disinheritance from its philosophical and social authority. The high claims made for art by writers like Shelley and Kant made the attenuated social and

philosophical authority of art seem like a form of power rather than of weakness. These claims rationalized art's already marginal social position. The terms in which the literary imagination was praised converted it into a sentimental compensation while imperceptibly conceding literature's loss of explanatory power. The way in which art was supposed to overcome the division between the rational or the practical and the creative—through a projection of "the internal laws of human nature"—only tended to deepen this division and to make it seem part of the very nature of things. Enemies of the fragmentation, specialization, and dissociation of modern society, the romantics themselves dissociated art from practicality and objective reason and paved the way for later theorists who would regard it as a specialized mode of discourse. These arguments reinforced the division of labor which made "imagination" the province of the artist and abstract thought, logic, and common sense the monopoly of other people.

FROM DEIFICATION TO DEMYSTIFICATION

Having been dispossessed of a rational world view, literature must be conceived as an "organism" that somehow, in a fashion infinitely described but never successfully explained by several generations of literary theorists, "contains" its meaning immanently within its concrete symbols or processes. Esthetic theory embarks on the attempt to explain how the concrete artistic structure can *mean* even though the structure does not rely on the now-discredited discursive, conceptual, referential forms of thought and expression. Though this appeal to nonconceptual models is supposed to help heal the divisions within culture, its actual tendency is to reinforce the isolation of art and its withdrawal from public accessibility.

The definition of literature as a nondiscursive, nonconceptual mode of communication has been proposed in a great variety of forms, closed, open, and mixed. It is a continuous impulse from the beginnings of romanticism to the latest postmodernisms. From Coleridge and his German predecessors to recent formalists, there runs a common theory of art as a *symbol* that contains or "presents" its meanings intransitively, by contrast with discursive *signs* or concepts, which make statements "about" external states of affairs. Despite mounting attacks, the theory shows no sign of losing confidence even today. Thus a recent critic, Leonard B. Meyer, can write with assurance: "There is a profound and basic difference between scientific theories, which are *propositional,* and works of art, which are *presentational*"[27]—as if it were necessary to choose between the propositional and the presentational, as if a work of art could not be both at the same time.

The denial of the propositional nature of literature makes it difficult for literary theory to make a place—as most theorists still wish to do—for a defensible notion of artistic *significance*. Rejecting the idea that literature is propositional, the critic is forced into a dilemma: on the one hand, he tries to elaborate a description of literary meaning that does not appeal to propositions, and plunges into obscurity and mystification; on the other hand, he tries to clarify that description by bringing it into line with our familiar notions of meaning and contradicts himself, since those notions are propositional. Furthermore, every time the critic tries to speak of the meaning or "theme" or "vision" of a particular, concrete work, he can hardly help sliding into a propositional conception of literature. Despite these difficulties, the critical refusal to see literature as propositional remains strong. In the main tradition of modern esthetics—which includes such figures as Croce, Richards, Dewey, Cassirer, Langer, Eliot, Jung, Frye, Jakobson, and Ingarden—literature and art deal with experience only as myth, psychology, or language, not as an object of conceptual understanding. A number of these theorists define art as the experiential complement of understanding without its content—as does Langer in her theory of art as "virtual experience" or Eliot in his view that poetry does not assert beliefs but dramatizes "what it feels like" to have them—again as if experience and ideas "about" experience were incompatible.[28] The intention of these theorists is not to make art irrelevant to life; art in its own ways allegedly gives order and form to life. But this artistic ordering is not supposed to offer itself as understanding, and it does not solicit verification by anything external to the work or to the autonomous consciousness out of which the work arose.

It often follows that the *content* of a literary work, assuming it is even valid to attribute content to literary works, has no interest in itself but serves merely as a pretext, the "bit of nice meat," according to Eliot, that the burglar holds out to the house dog while going about his real work.[29] Consequently, the reader need "believe" only provisionally, if at all, in the truth of the picture of reality presented by the work. Behind this thesis that belief is an inappropriate frame of mind in which to approach literature is the feeling that either there are no beliefs one can legitimately risk affirming, or that the belief-affirming modes of thought and expression have been hopelessly discredited. Often these theorists claim that art is a higher form of "knowledge," but since this knowledge is not conceptual knowledge "about" the world, since it does not invite belief, its credentials are not clear. The various theories of art as nonconceptual knowledge fail to provide art with any stronger cognitive function than was provided by I. A. Richards's logical positivist theory of art as pseudo-statement.[30]

From the position that the literary symbol means no more than itself (autotelic art), it is only a step to the position that literature has *no* meaning (anti-teleological art), or that its meaning is totally indeterminate and "open" to interpretation. The theory of the nondiscursive symbol, though capable of supporting Coleridge's affirmation of literature's transcendent truth, is equally capable of supporting the bleakest, most naturalistic denial of transcendence. Consider a brief illustration. Emerson, in a famous passage in "Self-Reliance," says that "these roses under my window make no reference to former roses or to better ones; they are for what they are; they

exist with God to-day. There is no time to them. There is simply the rose."[31] Emerson's rose is a Coleridgean symbol—self-sufficient, complete in itself, untranslatable, yet an embodiment of the immanence of God in nature. Though the feeling-tone of Emerson's statement is far different, the underlying logic is the same as that of the following statement by Robbe-Grillet: "the world is neither significant nor absurd. It *is* quite simply."[32] Both Emerson and Robbe-Grillet are concerned with the intransitivity of natural objects, but the analogy with artistic objects is obvious. Neither nature nor art means anything apart from itself—they simply *are*. Behind Emerson's rose there is the Over-Soul, whereas behind Robbe-Grillet's inexpressive objects there are only hysteria and paranoia—the demystified postmodern equivalent of the Over-Soul. Emerson's object is intransitive because it means everything, Robbe-Grillet's because it means nothing. But whether it is affirmatively or negatively expressed, the esthetic of self-contained meaning is symptomatic of an intellectual situation in which intelligibility is being emptied from the world, so that objects and artworks appear only in their simple presence. The logic underlying the romantic glorification of literature as an autonomous lawgiver is identical to that underlying the post-modern repudiation of literature and its pretensions to interpret life.

The theorists who have adopted these positions rarely suppose that they are draining literature of meaning or cutting it off from life. Charged with doing so, they offer disclaimers: "We are not draining literature of meaning but trying to get at the special character of that meaning; we don't mean to sever literature from life, only to redefine this extremely complex relation." Such disclaimers are largely rhetorical, however, since the critics do not make clear how it is possible to avoid the apparent implications of what they say. The fact that we do not *want* a certain implication to follow from our statements does not in itself prevent it from following. If a critic asserts that literature is an autonomous creation that is not obliged to conform to any preestablished laws, he does not disarm the charge of irresponsibility by adding, "of course I do not mean to suggest that 'anything goes' in literature and that writers are totally free to violate fundamental dictates of common sense." For one has to answer, "Why *shouldn't* anything go, if your original proposition is taken seriously?"

Having overthrown the mimetic theory of art, romantic and postromantic theories soon became the targets of the skepticism they had helped popularize. Their inability to define the cognitive function of art in any but the most equivocal terms has made earlier twentieth-century theorists vulnerable to the kind of attack from more recent critics which they themselves once levelled against traditional mimetic theory. This vulnerability emerges in current attacks on the New Criticism, a subject treated at length in my fifth chapter. With a kind of poetic justice, the New Criticism has been dethroned from its position of preeminence by arguments perfected by itself. The New Critics engaged in quixotic endeavor to defend poetic meanings by arguing that "a poem should not mean but be." In this effort they manifested the ambivalence about meaning and representation that is endemic to modern thinking about art. It demands only a moderate amount of historical sense to see that when Susan Sontag or Roland Barthes indicts the reductive nature of New Critical interpretation they revive the very charge which the New Critics had levelled against their own opponents, namely, "the heresy of paraphrase." We now see the same kind of accusation levelled against "organic" concepts of literature that the New Critical organicists levelled against mimetic concepts—the accusation of reducing the work to a determinate formula. Adepts of interpretation with a profound skepticism toward interpretation, the New Critics proposed a theory of literature that conflicted with their analytical method. While their close readings of texts called attention to the importance of meaning in literature, their theories aroused suspicion of the idea that a literary work can be said to have anything so discursive as a meaning, or that that meaning can be formulated by criticism. That the New Critics in the seventies are routinely disparaged as meaning-mongers and hyper-intellectualizers testifies to the continuing power of the skepticism they themselves helped to popularize. Here we see an example of the way the terms of the modern critical heritage inform the postmodern denigration of this heritage.

A logical evolution, then, connects the romantic and post-romantic cult of the creative self to the cult of the disintegrated, disseminated, dispersed self and of the decentered, undecidable, indeterminate text. Today's cultural battlefield is polarized between traditional humanists on one side and nihilistic "schismatics," in Frank Kermode's term, on the other.[2] Yet the humanists who celebrate the arts as the sovereign orderer of experience often seem nihilistic in their view of life. This nihilism is particularly overt in a critic like Northrop Frye, who praises Oscar Wilde for the view that "as life has no shape and literature has, literature is throwing away its one distinctive quality when it tries to imitate life."[33] How Frye came to know with such assurance that "life has no shape" is not clear, but if he is right one wonders what difference it should make if literature throws away its distinctive quality, or how literature—or anything—can have a distinctive quality. But those like Frye and Kermode, who defend humanism as a necessary fiction that somehow permits us to make sense of a reality known in advance to be senseless, share the same presuppositions as schismatics such as Artaud, Foucault, Derrida, Barthes, and Robbe-Grillet. The schismatics conclude, with better logic, that, if humanism is indeed a fiction, we ought to quit this pretense that it can be taken seriously.[34]

FROM MODERN TO POSTMODERN

If postmodern literature extends rather than overturns the premises of romanticism and modernism, we should expect this relation to be visible not only in the themes of literature but in its forms. Consider as an example the following passage from Barthelme's *Snow White*:

"Try to be a man about whom nothing is known," our father said, when we were young. Our father said several other interesting things, but we have forgotten what they were. . . . Our father was a man about whom nothing was known. Nothing is known about him still. He gave us the recipes. He was not very interesting. A tree is more interesting. A suitcase is more interesting. A canned good is more interesting.[35]

Barthelme here parodies Henry James's advice to the aspiring fiction writer: "Try to be one of the people on whom nothing is lost."[36] Barthelme inverts the assumptions about character, psychology, and the authority of the artist upon which James, the father of the modernist "recipe" for the novel, had depended. In postmodern fiction, character, like external reality, is something "about which nothing is known," lacking in plausible motive or discoverable depth. Whereas James had stressed the importance of artistic selection, defining the chief obligation of the novelist as the obligation to be "interesting," Barthelme operates by a law of equivalence according to which nothing is intrinsically more interesting than anything else.[37] Such a law destroys the determinacy of artistic selection and elevates canned goods to equal status with human moral choice as artistic subject matter. In place of Jamesian dedication to the craft of fiction, Barthelme adopts an irreverent stance toward his work, conceding the arbitrary and artificial nature of his creation. Retracting any Jamesian claim to deal seriously with the world, Barthelme's work offers—for wholly different reasons—the sort of confession of the merely "make-believe" status of fiction to which James objected in Thackeray and Trollope. The novel's inability to transcend the solipsism of subjectivity and language becomes the novel's chief subject and the principle of its form.

It would seem that the Jamesian esthetic could not be stood on its head more completely. But only a surface consideration of the comparison can be content to leave it at that. James himself, in both his fiction and his criticism, contributed to the skepticism which Barthelme turns against him. T. S. Eliot wrote that Paul Valéry was "much too sceptical to believe even in art."[38] The remark applies, in greater or lesser degree, to all the great modernist worshippers at the shrine of high art, not excluding James. Consider James's view of the infinite elusiveness of experience, which is "never limited, and . . . never complete,"[39] an elusiveness he dramatized in the interminable ambiguities of his later fiction. James combined an intense dedication to unraveling the secrets of motive and action with an acutely developed sense of the ultimate impossibility of such an enterprise.

Conflicting with James's insistence on the importance of artistic selection and shaping is the curiously subjectivistic justification James came to accord to this process. He frequently asserts, in his later reflections, that the orderings of the artist cannot derive from or be determined by the raw material of life itself. As he observes in *The American Scene*:

To be at all critically, or as we have been fond of calling it, analytically minded . . . is to be subject to the superstition that objects and places, coherently grouped, disposed for human use and addressed to it, must have a sense of their own, a mystic meaning proper to themselves to give out: to give out, that is, to the participant at once so interested and so detached as to be moved to a report of the matter. That perverse person is obliged to take it for a working theory that the essence of almost any settled aspect of anything may be extracted by the chemistry of criticism, and may give us its right name, its formula, for convenient use. From the moment the critic finds himself sighing, to save trouble in a difficult case, that the cluster of appearances can *have* no sense, from that moment he begins, and quite consciously, to go to pieces; it being the prime business and the high honour of the painter of life always to *make* a sense—and to make it most in proportion as the immediate aspects are loose or confused.[40]

James seems to be saying there are no objective determinants guiding the act of "making a sense" of experience. The "mystic meaning" of events is not in the events themselves, or controlled by them, but in the observer. James perceives that in these circumstances there is danger that the observer may "go to pieces" unless he is adequate to the artist's task of fabricating his own sense. But though James assigns "high honour" to the fabricator and shame to the person who surrenders to confusion, one might question his valuations. Could one not say that the artist who saves himself by inventing fictions of order he knows to be arbitrary is engaging in a deception of which the confused observer is innocent? Is it less honorable to "go to pieces" in honest confusion than to create forms of coherence whose truth is admitted to be mythical? James rests his claims of honor for the artistic process on the damaging admission that artistic order is not grounded on anything outside itself.

Perceiving that the modernist's seriousness rests on admittedly arbitrary foundations, the postmodern writer treats this seriousness as an object of parody. Whereas modernists turned to art, defined as the imposition of human order upon inhuman chaos—as an antidote for what Eliot called the "immense panorama of futility and anarchy which is contemporary history"—postmodernists conclude that, under such conceptions of art and history, art provides no more consolation than any other discredited cultural institution. Postmodernism signifies that the nightmare of history, as modernist esthetic and philosophical traditions have defined history, has overtaken modernism itself.[41] If history lacks value, pattern, and rationally intelligible meaning, then no exertions of the shaping, ordering imagination can be anything but a refuge from truth. Alienation from significant external reality, from *all* reality, becomes an inescapable condition.

THE TWO POSTMODERNISMS

In carrying the logic of modernism to its extreme limits, postmodern literature poses in an especially acute fashion the critical problem raised by all experimental art: does this art represent a criticism of the distorted aspects of modern life or a mere addition to it? Georg Lukács has argued persuasively that the successful presentation of distortion as such presupposes the existence of an undistorted norm. "Literature," he writes, "must have a concept of the normal if it is to 'place' distortion correctly, that is to say, to see it *as* distortion."[42] If life were really a solipsistic madness, we should have no means of knowing this fact or representing it. But once the concept of the normal is rejected as a vestige of an outmoded metaphysics or patronized as a myth, the concepts of "distortion" and "madness" lose their meanings. This observation provides a basis for some necessary distinctions between tendencies in postmodern writing.

In Jorge Luis Borges's stories, for example, techniques of reflexiveness and self-parody suggest a universe in which human consciousness is incapable of transcending its own mythologies. This condition of imprisonment, however, though seen from the "inside," is presented from a tragic or tragicomic point of view that forces us to see it *as* a problem. The stories generate a pathos at the absence of a transcendent order of meanings. As Borges's narrator in "The Library of Babel" declares, "Let heaven exist, though my place be in hell. Let me be outraged and annihilated, but for one instant, in one being, let Your enormous Library be justified."[43] The library contains all possible books and all possible interpretations of experience but none which can claim authority over the others; therefore, it cannot be "justified." Nevertheless, Borges affirms the indispensable nature of justification. As in such earlier writers as Kafka and Céline, the memory of a significant external reality that would justify human experience persists in the writer's consciousness and serves as his measure of the distorted, indeterminate world he depicts. Borges's kind of postmodern writing, even in presenting solipsistic distortion as the only possible perspective, nevertheless presents this distortion *as* distortion—that is, it implicitly affirms a concept of the normal, if only as a concept which has been tragically lost. The comic force of characters like "Funes the Memorious" and of solipsistic worlds such as those of "Tlön, Uqbar, Orbis Tertius" lies in the crucial fact that Borges, for all his imaginative sympathy, is *not* Funes, is not an inhabitant of Tlön, and is thus able to view the unreality of their worlds as a predicament. His work retains a link with traditional classical humanism by virtue of its sense of the pathos of this humanism's demise. The critical power of absence remains intact, giving Borges a perspective for judging the unreality of the present. His work affirms the sense of reality in a negative way by dramatizing its absence as a deprivation.

Whatever tendency toward subjectivism these Borges works may contain is further counteracted by their ability to suggest the historical and social causes of this loss of objective reality. Borges invites us to see the solipsistic plight of his characters as a consequence of the relativistic thrust of modern philosophy and modern politics. If reality has yielded to the myth-making of Tlön, as he suggests it has, "the truth is that it longed to yield." The mythologies of "dialectical materialism, anti-Semitism, Nazism" were sufficient "to entrance the minds of men."[44] The loss of reality is made intelligible to the reader as an aspect of a social and historical evolution. At its best, the contemporary wave of self-reflexive fiction is not quite so totally self-reflexive as it is taken to be, since its very reflexivity implies a "realistic" comment on the historical crisis which brought it about. Where such a comment is made, the conventions of anti-realism subserve a higher realism. Often, however, this fiction fails to make its reflexivity intelligible as a consequence of any recognizable cause. Estrangement from reality and meaning becomes detached from the consciousness of its causes—as in the more tediously claustrophobic and mannered experiments of Barthelme and the later Barth.[45] Even in these works, however, the loss of reality and meaning is seen as a distortion of the human condition.

Far different is the attitude expressed in the more celebratory forms of postmodernism. Here there is scarcely any memory of an objective order of values in the past and no regret over its disappearance in the present. Concepts like "significant external reality" and "the human condition" figure only as symbols of the arbitrary authority and predetermination of a repressive past, and their disappearance is viewed as liberation. Dissolution of ego boundaries, seen in tragic postmodern works like *Invitation to a Beheading* as a terrifying disintegration of identity, is viewed as a bracing form of consciousness-expansion and a prelude to growth. Both art and the world, according to Susan Sontag, simply *are*. "Both need no justification; nor could they possibly have any."[46] The obsessive quest for justification which characterizes Borges's protagonists is thus regarded, if it is noticed at all, as a mere survival of outmoded thinking.

It is symptomatic of the critical climate that Borges has been widely read as a celebrant of apocalyptic unreality. Borges's current celebrity is predicated to a large degree on a view that sees him as a pure fabulator revelling in the happy indistinguishability of truth and fiction. Richard Poirier, for example, urges us in reading Borges to get rid of "irrelevant distinctions between art and life fiction and reality."[47] But if distinctions between fiction and reality were really irrelevant, Borges's work would be pointless.

But then, in a world which simply *is,* pointlessness is truth. There is no ground for posing the question of justification as a question. We can no longer even speak of "alienation" or "loss" of perspective, for there never was anything to be alienated from, never any normative perspective to be lost. The realistic perspective that gives shape and point to works of tragicomic postmodernism, permitting them to present distortion *as* distortion, gives way to a celebration of *energy*—the vitalism of a world that cannot be understood or controlled. We find this celebration of energy in the poetry of the Beats, the "Projective" poets, and other poetic continuators of the nativist line of Whitman, Williams, and Pound, in the short-lived vogue of the Living Theater, happenings, and pop art, and in a variety of artistic and musical experiments with randomness and dissonance. It is also an aspect of the writing of Mailer, Burroughs, and Pynchon, where despite the suggestion of a critical or satiric point of view, the style expresses a facile excitement with the dynamisms of technological process.[48] Richard Poirier states the rationale for this worship of energy, making energy and literature synonymous: "Writing is a form of energy not accountable to the orderings anyone makes of it and specifically not accountable to the liberal humanitarian values most readers want to find there."[49] Literature, in short, is closer to a physical force than to an understanding or "criticism of life," both of which are tame and bourgeois. This celebration of energy frequently seems to hover somewhere between revolutionary politics and sophisticated acquiescence to the agreeably meaningless surfaces of mass culture.

The acquiescence seems to have the upper hand over the politics in the esthetics of John Cage. Susan Sontag says that "Cage proposes for our experience a world in which it's never preferable to do other than we are doing or be elsewhere than we are. 'It is only irritating,' he says, 'to think one would like to be somewhere else. Here we are now.'"[3] Cage, she writes, "envisages a totally democratic world of the spirit, a world of 'natural activity' in which 'it is understood that everything is clean: there is no dirt.' . . . Cage proposes the perennial possibility of errorless behavior, if only we will allow it to be so. 'Error is a fiction, has no reality in fact.'"[50] Elsewhere Cage puts it this way: "We are intimate in advance with whatever will happen."[51] Both nostalgia and hope are impossible because history has disappeared, replaced by an immanent present which is always, at every changing moment, the best of possible worlds. We are "intimate" with this present, not because it has any meaning or potential direction, but precisely because it is so pointless that to *expect* any meaning or direction would be out of the question. If one feels estrangement in contemplating this pointless world, it is because one has not yet abandoned the anthropocentric expectations that are the real source of our problem.

Alienation is thus "overcome" by the strategy of redescribing it as the normal state of affairs and then enjoying its gratifications. Political intransigence, from this point of view, is but a symptom of inadequate adjustment—the inability to get beyond old-fashioned alienation and immerse oneself in the unitary stream of things. Calvin Tomkins, admiring Robert Rauschenberg for his "cheerful and nearly total acceptance" of the materials of urban life, quotes the artist as follows: "I really feel sorry for people who think things like soap dishes or mirrors or Coke bottles are ugly, because they're surrounded by things like that all day long, and it must make them miserable."[52] What is interesting in Rauschenberg's statement is the way it endows urban commercial ugliness with the permanence and unchangeability of nature—one might as soon do something about it as do something about rain or wind. Whatever one may think about the urban anti-culture, the thing is *real* and is not going to go away because a few intellectuals happen not to like it, so therefore one had better learn to love it. One does not try to change the world but rather alters one's perspective (or "consciousness") so as to *see* the world in a new way.

THE NORMALIZATION OF ALIENATION

The assumption that alienation is the normal and unalterable condition of human beings has gained strength from structuralist theories of language described in my introduction: since meaning arises wholly from the play of differences within artificial sign systems, it follows that meanings are arbitrary and that everything we say in language is a fiction. Sometimes this assertion that everything is a fiction immunizes itself from criticism by claiming *itself* to be no more than a fiction. Thus Sontag tells us that "one can't object" to Roland Barthes's exposition of structuralist ideas "simply because its leading concepts are intellectual myths or fictions."[53] Robert Scholes summarizes this post-structuralist outlook as follows:

> Once we knew that fiction was about life and criticism was about fiction—and everything was simple. Now we know that fiction is about other fiction, is criticism in fact, or metafiction. And we know that criticism is about the impossibility of anything being about life, really, or even about fiction, or, finally, about anything. Criticism has taken the very idea of "aboutness" away from us. It has taught us that language is tautological, if it is not nonsense, and to the extent that it is about anything it is about itself. Mathematics is about mathematics, poetry is about poetry and criticism is about the impossibility of its own existence.[54]

The doctrine is particularly widespread in discussions of recent fiction. Raymond Federman, a theorist of "surfiction," informs us that the authentic fiction writers of our day "believe that reality as such does not exist, or rather exists only in its fictionalized version."[55] As William Gass puts it, "the novelist, if he is any good, will keep us kindly imprisoned in his language—there is literally nothing beyond."[56]

No doubt structuralism, properly understood, is only a method of analysis and need not carry the dismal ontological conclusions which such critics have derived from it. But one of its exponents, Perry Meisel, after reassuring us that "structuralism is a method, not a program or an ideology," goes on to say that "structuralism realizes that alienation is the timeless and normative condition of humanity rather than its special modern affliction."[57] For, according to Meisel, "semiotics is in a position to claim that no phenomenon has any ontological status outside its place in the particular information system(s) from which it draws its meaning(s)." From the proposition, unexceptionable in itself, that no signifier can mean anything apart from the code or sign system which gives it significance, one infers the conclusion that no signifier can *refer* to a nonlinguistic reality—that, as Meisel puts it, "all language is finally groundless." There is, then, no

such thing as a "real" object outside language, no "nature" or "real life" outside the literary text, no real text behind the critical interpretation, and no real persons or institutions behind the multiplicity of messages human beings produce. Everything is swallowed up in an infinite regress of textuality.

Meisel does not hesitate to draw the social moral of all this: "the only assumption possible in a post-Watergate era," he writes, is "that the artifice is the only reality available."[58] Since artifice is the only reality, the old-fashioned distinctions between "intrinsic" and "extrinsic," literature and life, are abolished. Literature and life are thus reconciled, but only by the strategy of enclosing "life" itself in an autonomous process of textuality which cannot refer beyond its structuring activity. The gulf imposed by romantic esthetics between literary and practical discourse is closed, not by ascribing objective truth to literature, but by withdrawing it from all discourse. Fact and value are reconciled by converting fact along with value into fiction. These reconciliations are dictated not only by philosophical and linguistic theory but by "the post-Watergate era." One wonders whether the moral of the Watergate episode might not actually be that some degree of penetration of artifice, some detection of the hidden facts *is* after all possible. But structuralist skepticism does not wait to be questioned on such points. Its method of demythologizing thinking ends up teaching that no escape from mythmaking is possible.[59]

The position of structuralism and poststructuralism, however, on the postmodern spectrum of attitudes is equivocal. On the one hand there is Derrida's influential invocation of "the joyful Nietzschean affirmation of the play of the world and the innocence of becoming, the affirmation of a world of signs which has no truth, no origin, no nostalgic guilt, and is proffered for active interpretation."[60] On the other hand, there is the insistence on the *risk* involved in the enterprise of doing without a truth and an origin as anchoring points outside the infinite play of linguistic differences. As Derrida puts it, "*this affirmation then determines the non-center otherwise than as a loss of the center. And it plays the game without security.*"[61] As he does often, Derrida here seems to be echoing Nietzsche, who stated that "the genuine philosopher . . . risks *himself* constantly. He plays the dangerous game."[62] However, neither the joy nor the risk invoked by this view seems fully convincing. The joy of affirmation is a diluted joy, since it comes about as a consequence of the absence of any reality or meaning in life to which effort might be directed. And the element of risk in the "dangerous game" becomes minimal when (a) relativistic philosophy has eroded the concept of error, and (b) the culture of pluralism and publicity has endowed deviation and eccentricity with "charisma."

The postmodern temper has carried the skepticism and anti-realism of modern literary culture to an extreme beyond which it would be difficult to go. Though it looks back mockingly on the modernist tradition and professes to have got beyond it, post-modern literature remains tied to that tradition and unable to break with it. The very concepts through which modernism is demystified derive from modernism itself. The loss of significant external reality, its displacement by myth-making, the domestication and normalization of alienation—these conditions constitute a common point of departure for the writing of our period. Though for some of this writing they remain conditions to be somehow resisted, a great deal of it finds them an occasion for acquiescence and even celebration. Unable to imagine an alternative to a world that has for so long seemed unreal, we have begun to resign ourselves to this kind of world and to learn how to redescribe this resignation as a form of heroism. And for some observers, to whom I turn in the next chapter, this loss of a reality principle is not a loss at all but a condition of political revolution.

NOTES

[1] George Steiner, *Language and Silence: Essays on Language, Literature, and the Inhuman* (New York: Atheneum, 1967), 162.

[2] Richard Poirier, *The Performing Self: Compositions and Decompositions in the Languages of Contemporary Life* (New York: Oxford University Press, 1971), xii.

[3] Harry Levin, "What Was Modernism?" *Refractions: Essays in Comparative Literature* (New York: Oxford University Press, 1966), 292.

[4] Donald Barthelme, *Snow White* (New York: Bantam Books, 1968), 82.

[5] Alain Robbe-Grillet, *For a New Novel: Essays on Fiction,* trans. R. Howard (New York: Grove Press, 1965), 87. Unless indicated, italics in quotations are not added.

[6] Susan Sontag, *Against Interpretation* (New York: Delta Books, 1967), 7.

[7] Leslie Fiedler, *Waiting for the End* (New York: Stein and Day, 1964), 227.

[8] Jacob Brackman, *The Put-On: Modern Fooling and Modern Mistrust* (Chicago: Regnery, 1971), 68.

[9] Fiedler, *Cross the Border—Close the Gap* (New York: Stein and Day, 1972), 64.

[10] Ortega y Gasset, *The Dehumanization of Art,* 46.

[11] Poggioli, *The Theory of the Avant-Garde,* 66.

[12] On this ambiguity of the romantic theory of autonomy, probably the most helpful analysis is still that of Raymond Williams, *Culture and Society, 1780-1950* (New York: Harper Torchbooks, 1966), 30-48.

[13] Murray Krieger analyzes this antinomy in the New Criticism and other literary theories in *The New Apologists for Poetry* (Minneapolis: University of Minnesota Press, 1956) and other works.

[14] P. B. Shelley, "A Defence of Poetry," in Adams, *Critical Theory Since Plato,* 502.

[15] Henry David Aiken, ed., *The Age of Ideology* (New York: Mentor Books, 1956), 23.

[16] Immanuel Kant, *Prolegomena to Any Future Metaphysics,* trans. Mahaffy, revised L. W. Beck (New York: Bobbs-Merrill, 1950), 46.

[17] René Wellek, "Romanticism Reconsidered," *Concepts of Criticism* (New Haven: Yale University Press, 1963), 201-2.

[18] Erich Heller, *The Disinherited Mind: Essays in Modern German Literature and Thought* (New York: Meridian Books, 1959), 172.

[19] William James, *The Varieties of Religious Experience* (New York: New American Library, 1958), 153.

[20] Friedrich von Schiller, *Naive and Sentimental Poetry,* trans. J. A. Elias (New York: Frederick Ungar, 1966), 100.

[21] Ibid., 101.

[22] Shelley, *Defence,* 511.

[23] Northrop Frye, *The Critical Path: An Essay in the Social Context of Literature* (Bloomington: Indiana University Press, 1971), 94.

[24] W. H. Auden, *The Dyer's Hand and Other Essays* (New York: Vintage Books, 1968), 78-79.

[25] Kant, *Critique of Judgment,* in Adams, *Critical Theory Since Plato,* 383, 384.

[26] Auden, "In Memory of W. B. Yeats," *The Norton Anthology of Modern Poetry,* ed. Richard Ellmann and Robert O'Clair (New York: Norton, 1973), 742.

[27] Leonard B. Meyer, "Concerning the Sciences, the Arts, AND the Humanities," *Critical Inquiry,* 1, no. 1 (September 1974), 166.

[28] T. S. Eliot, "The Social Function of Poetry," in *Critiques and Essays in Criticism, 1920-1948,* ed. R. W. B. Stallman (New York: Ronald Press Co., 1949), 107; Susanne K. Langer, *Feeling and Form* (New York: Charles Scribner's Sons, 1953), 234.

[29] Eliot, *The Use of Poetry and the Use of Criticism* (London: Faber and Faber, 1933), 151.

[30] Once again, further documentation can be found in my *Poetic Statement and Critical Dogma.*

[31] R. W. Emerson, "Self-Reliance," *Selected Writings* (New York: Modern Library, 1950), 157.

[32] Robbe-Grillet, *For a New Novel,* 19.

[33] Northrop Frye, *The Secular Scripture: A Study in the Structure of Romance* (Cambridge: Harvard University Press, 1976), 45-46.

[34] This point is elaborated above, 181ff.

[35] Barthelme, *Snow White,* 18-19.

[36] Henry James, "The Art of Fiction," in *Criticism: The Foundation of Modern Literary Judgment,* revised edition, ed. Schorer et al. (New York: Harcourt Brace and World, 1958), 49.

[37] Ibid., 47.

[38] Eliot, "From Poe to Valéry," *To Criticize the Critic* (New York: Farrar, Straus and Giroux, 1965), 39.

[39] James, "The Art of Fiction," in Schorer, *Criticism: the Foundation of Modern Literary Judgment,* 48.

[40] James, *The American Scene* (Bloomington: Indiana University Press, 1968), 273.

[41] Eliot, "'Ulysses,' Order, and Myth," in *Selected Prose,* ed. Frank Kermode (New York: Harcourt Brace Jovanovich, 1975), 177.

[42] Georg Lukács, *The Meaning of Contemporary Realism,* trans. J. and N. Mander (London: Merlin Press, 1963), 33.

[43] Jorge Luis Borges, *Labyrinths: Selected Stories and Other Writings,* trans. J. Irby (New York: New Directions, 1964), 57.

[44] Ibid., 17.

[45] See above, 220-21.

[46] Sontag, *Against Interpretation,* 27.

[47] Poirier, *The Performing Self,* 40.

[48] On Mailer, see above, 216-20.

[49] Poirier, *The Performing Self,* 40.

[50] Ibid., 93.

[51] John Cage, "Diary: How to Improve the World (You Will Only Make Matters Worse) Continued," *TriQuarterly,* 18 (Spring 1970), 101.

[52] Calvin Tomkins, *The Bride and the Bachelors: Five Masters of the Avant-Garde* (New York: Viking, 1965), 194.

[53] Sontag, Introduction to Roland Barthes, *Writing Degree Zero* (New York: Hill and Wang, 1953), xx.

[54] Robert Scholes, "The Fictional Criticism of the Future," *TriQuarterly,* 34 (Fall 1975), 233. Scholes's last sentence echoes a remark of T. S. Eliot's: "The poet makes poetry, the metaphysician makes metaphysics, the bee makes honey, the spider secretes a filament; you can hardly say that any of these agents believes: he merely does" ("Shakespeare and the Stoicism of Seneca," *Selected Essays* [New York: Harcourt Brace and World, 1960], 118).

[55] Raymond Federman, ed. *Surfiction: Fiction Now and Tomorrow* (Chicago: Swallow Press, 1975), 7.

[56] William Gass, *Fiction and the Figures of Life,* 8.

[57] Perry Meisel, "Everything You Always Wanted to Know About Structuralism but Were Afraid to Ask," *National Village Voice* (September 30, 1976), 43-45.

[58] Ibid.

[59] Jonathan Culler argues in this vein against the *Tel Quel* critics in *Structuralist Poetics: Structuralism, Linguistics, and the Study of Literature* (Ithaca: Cornell University Press, 1975), 247-50.

[60] Derrida, "Structure, Sign, and Play in the Discourse of the Human Sciences," quoted and translated by Jonathan Culler, *Structuralist Poetics,* 247. I have used Culler's translation of this passage, which is more accurate than the standard English translation by Macksey and Donato in *The Structuralist Controversy: The Languages of Criticism and the Sciences of Man,* ed. Richard Macksey and Eugenio Donato (Baltimore: Johns Hopkins University Press, 1972), 264.

[61] Derrida, "Structure, Sign, and Play," in Macksey and Donato, *The Structuralist Controversy,* 264.

[62] Nietzsche, as quoted by Gayatri C. Spivak, Translator's Preface to Derrida, *Of Grammatology* (Baltimore: Johns Hopkins University Press, 1976), xxx.

Ihab Hassan

SOURCE: "Pluralism in Postmodern Perspective," in *The Postmodern Turn: Essays in Postmodern Theory and Culture,* Ohio State University Press, 1987, pp. 167-90.

[*In the following essay, which was first published in 1986, Hassan discusses the historical aspects of postmodernism, concluding that the postmodern approach is the most appropriate to depict the wide-ranging aspects of human life in the twentieth-century.*]

I

Postmodernism once more—that breach has begun to yawn! I return to it by way of pluralism, which itself has become the irritable condition of postmodern discourse, consuming many pages of both critical and uncritical inquiry. Why? Why pluralism now? This question recalls another that Kant raised two centuries ago—*"Was heisst Aufklärung?"*—meaning, "Who are we now?" The answer was a signal meditation on historical presence, as Michel Foucault saw.[1] But to meditate on that topic today—and *this* is my central claim—is really to inquire *"Was heisst Postmodernismus?"*

Pluralism in our time finds (if not founds) itself in the social, aesthetic, and intellectual assumptions of postmodernism—finds its ordeal, its rightness, there. I submit, further, that the critical intentions of diverse American pluralists—M. H. Abrams, Wayne Booth, Kenneth Burke, Matei Calinescu, R. S. Crane, Nelson Goodman, Richard McKeon, Stephen Pepper, not to mention countless other artists and thinkers of our moment—engage that overweening query, "What is postmodernism?" engage and even answer it tacitly. In short, like a latterday M. Jourdain, they have been speaking postmodernism all their lives without knowing it.

But what *is* postmodernism? I can still propose no rigorous definition of it, any more than I could define modernism itself. The time to theorize it, though, to historicize it, is nearly at hand, without muting its errancies, vexations. These bear on problems of cultural modeling, literary periodization, cultural change—the problems of critical discourse itself in an antinomian phase.[2] Still, the exhaustions of modernism, or at least its self-revisions, have prompted incongruous thinkers to moot its supervention. Thus Daniel Bell, a "conservative" sociologist, testifies to "the end of the creative impulse and ideological sway of modernism, which, as a cultural movement, has dominated all the arts, and shaped our symbolic expressions, for the past 125 years."[3] And thus, too, a "radical" philosopher, Jürgen Habermas, tries to distinguish—vainly, as I see it—between the "premodernism of old conservatives," the "antimodernism of the young conservatives," and the "postmodernism of the neoconservatives."[4]

All "superventions" aside, let me offer a catena of postmodern features, a paratactic list, staking out a cultural field. My examples will be selective; my traits may overlap, conflict, or antecede themselves. Still, together they limn a region of postmodern "indetermanences" (indeterminacy lodged in immanence) in which critical pluralism takes shape.[5]

II

Here, then, is my catena:

1. *Indeterminacy,* or rather, indeterminacies. These include all manner of ambiguities, ruptures, and displacements affecting knowledge and society. We think of Werner Karl Heisenberg's principle of uncertainty, Kurt Gödel's proof of incompleteness, Thomas Kuhn's paradigms, and Paul Feyerabend's dadaism of science. Or we may think of Harold Rosenberg's anxious art objects, de-

defined. And in literary theory? From Mikhail Bakhtin's dialogic imagination, Roland Barthes' *textes scriptibles,* Wolfgang Iser's literary *Unbestimmtheiten,* Harold Bloom's misprisions, Paul de Man's allegorical readings, Stanley Fish's affective stylistics, Norman Holland's transactive analysis, and David Bleich's subjective criticism, to the last fashionable *aporia* of unrecorded time, we undecide, relativize. Indeterminacies pervade our actions, ideas, interpretations; they constitute our world.

2. *Fragmentation.* Indeterminacy often follows from fragmentation. The postmodernist only disconnects; fragments are all he pretends to trust. His ultimate opprobrium is "totalization"—any synthesis whatever, social, epistemic, even poetic. Hence his preference for montage, collage, the found or cut-up literary object, for paratactic over hypotactic forms, metonymy over metaphor, schizophrenia over paranoia. Hence, too, his recourse to paradox, paralogy, parabasis, paracriticism, the openness of brokenness, unjustified margins. Thus Jean-François Lyotard exhorts, "Let us wage a war on totality; let us be witnesses to the unpresentable; let us activate the differences and save the honor of the name."[6] The age demands differences, shifting signifiers, and even atoms dissolve into elusive subparticles, a mere mathematical whisper.

3. *Decanonization.* In the largest sense, this applies to all canons, all conventions of authority. We are witnessing, Lyotard argues again, a massive "delegitimation" of the mastercodes in society, a desuetude of the metanarratives, favoring instead *"les petites histoires,"* which preserve the heterogeneity of language games.[7] Thus, from the "death of god" to the "death of the author" and "death of the father," from the derision of authority to revision of the curriculum, we decanonize culture, demystify knowledge, deconstruct the languages of power, desire, deceit. Derision and revision are versions of subversion, of which the most baleful example is the rampant terrorism of our time. But "subversion" may take other, more benevolent, forms such as minority movements or the feminization of culture, which also require decanonization.

4. *Self-less-ness, Depth-less-ness.* Postmodernism vacates the traditional self, simulating self-effacement—a fake flatness, without inside/outside—or its opposite, self-multiplication, self-reflection. Critics have noted the "loss of self" in modern literature, but it was originally Nietzsche who declared the "subject" "only a fiction": "the ego of which one speaks when one censures egoism does not exist at all."[8] Thus postmodernism suppresses or disperses and sometimes tries to recover the "deep" romantic ego, which remains under dire suspicion in poststructuralist circles as a "totalizing principle." Losing itself in the play of language, in the differences from which reality is plurally made, the self impersonates its absence even as death stalks its games. It diffuses itself in depthless styles, refusing, eluding, interpretation.[9]

5. *The Unpresentable, Unrepresentable.* Like its predecessor, postmodern art is irrealist, aniconic. Even its

"magic realism" dissolves in ethereal states; its hard, flat surfaces repel mimesis. Postmodern literature, particularly, often seeks its limits, entertains its "exhaustion," subverts itself in forms of articulate "silence." It becomes liminary, contesting the modes of its own representation. Like the Kantian Sublime, which thrives on the formlessness, the emptiness, of the Absolute—"Thou shalt not make graven images"—"the postmodern would be," in Lyotard's audacious analogue, "that which, in the modern, puts forward the unpresentable in presentation itself."[10] But the challenge to representation may also lead a writer to other liminal states: the Abject, for instance, rather than the Sublime, or Death itself—more precisely, "the exchange between signs and death," as Julia Kristeva put it. "What is unrepresentability?" Kristeva asks. "That which, through language, is part of no particular language. . . . That which, through meaning, is intolerable, unthinkable: the horrible, the abject."[11]

Here, I think we reach a peripety of negations. For with my next "definien," Irony, we begin to move from the deconstructive to the coexisting reconstructive tendency of postmodernism.

6. *Irony.* This could also be called, after Kenneth Burke, perspectivism. In absence of a cardinal principle or paradigm, we turn to play, interplay, dialogue, polylogue, allegory, self-reflection—in short, to irony. This irony assumes indeterminacy, multivalence; it aspires to clarity, the clarity of demystification, the pure light of absence. We meet variants of it in Bakhtin, Burke, de Man, Jacques Derrida, and Hayden White. And in Alan Wilde we see an effort to discriminate its modes: "mediate irony," "disjunctive irony," and "postmodern" or "suspensive irony" "with its yet more radical vision of multiplicity, randomness, contingency, and even absurdity."[12] Irony, perspectivism, reflexiveness: these express the ineluctable recreations of mind in search of a truth that continually eludes it, leaving it with only an ironic access or excess of self-consciousness.

7. *Hybridization,* or the mutant replication of genres, including parody, travesty, pastiche. The "de-definition," deformation, of cultural genres engenders equivocal modes: "paracriticism," "fictual discourse," the "new journalism," the "nonfiction novel," and a promiscuous category of "para-literature" or "threshold literature," at once young and very old.[13] Cliché and plagiarism ("playgiarism," Raymond Federman punned), parody and pastiche, pop and kitsch enrich *re*-presentation. In this view image or replica may be as valid as its model (the *Quixote* of Borges' Pierre Menard), may even bring an *"augment d'être."* This makes for a different concept of tradition, one in which continuity and discontinuity, high and low culture, mingle not to imitate but to expand the past in the present. In that plural present, all styles are dialectically available in an interplay between the Now and the Not Now, the Same and the Other. Thus, in postmodernism, Heidegger's concept of "equitemporality" becomes really a dialectic of equitemporality, an intertemporality, a new relation between historical elements, without any suppression of the past in favor of the present—a point that Fredric Jameson misses when he criticizes postmodern literature, film, and architecture for their ahistorical character, their "presentifications."[14]

8. *Carnivalization.* The term, of course, is Bakhtin's, and it riotously embraces indeterminacy, fragmentation, decanonization, selflessness, irony, hybridization, all of which I have already adduced. But the term also conveys the comic or absurdist ethos of postmodernism, anticipated in the "heteroglossia" of Rabelais and Sterne, jocose prepostmodernists. Carnivalization further means "polyphony," the centrifugal power of language, the "gay relativity" of things, perspectivism and performance, participation in the wild disorder of life, the immanence of laughter.[15] Indeed, what Bakhtin calls novel or carnival—that is, antisystem—might stand for postmodernism itself, or at least for its ludic and subversive elements that promise renewal. For in carnival "the true feast of time, the feast of becoming, change, and renewal," human beings, then as now, discover "the peculiar logic of the 'inside out' (*à l'envers*), of the 'turnabout,' . . . of numerous parodies and travesties, humiliations, profanations, comic crownings and uncrownings. A second life."[16]

9. *Performance, Participation.* Indeterminacy elicits participation; gaps must be filled. The postmodern text, verbal or nonverbal, invites performance: it wants to be written, revised, answered, acted out. Indeed, so much of postmodern art calls itself performance, as it transgresses genres. As performance, art (or theory for that matter) declares its vulnerability to time, to death, to audience, to the Other.[17] "Theatre" becomes—to the edge of terrorism—the active principle of a paratactic society, decanonized if not really carnivalized. At its best, as Richard Poirier contends, the performing self expresses "an energy in motion, an energy with its own shape"; yet in its "self-discovering, self-watching, finally self-pleasuring response to . . . pressures and difficulties," that self may also veer toward solipsism, lapse into narcissism.[18]

10. *Constructionism.* Since postmodernism is radically tropic, figurative, irrealist—"what can be thought of must certainly be a fiction," Nietzsche thought[19]—it "constructs" reality in post-Kantian, indeed post-Nietzschean, "fictions."[20] Scientists seem now more at ease with heuristic fictions than many humanists, last realists of the West. (Some literary critics even kick language, thinking thus to stub their toes on a stone.) Such effective fictions suggest the growing intervention of mind in nature and culture, an aspect of what I have called the "new gnosticism" evident in science and art, in social relations and high technologies.[21] But constructionism appears also in Burke's "dramatistic criticism," Pepper's "world hypothesis," Goodman's "ways of world-making," White's "prefigurative moves," not to mention current hermeneutic or poststructuralist theory. Thus postmodernism sustains the movement "from unique truth and a world fixed and found," as Goodman remarked, "to a diversity of right and even conflicting versions or worlds in the making."[22]

11. *Immanence.* This refers, without religious echo, to the growing capacity of mind to generalize itself through symbols. Everywhere now we witness problematic diffusions, dispersals, dissemination; we experience the extension of our senses, as Marshall McLuhan crankily presaged, through new media and technologies. Languages, apt or mendacious, reconstitute the universe—from quasars to quarks and back, from the lettered unconscious to black holes in space—reconstitute it into signs of their own making, turning nature into culture, and culture into an immanent semiotic system. The language animal has emerged, his/her measure the intertextuality of all life. A patina of thought, of signifiers, of "connections," now lies on everything the mind touches in its gnostic (noö)sphere, which physicists, biologists, and semioticians, no less than mystic theologians like Teilhard de Chardin, explore. The pervasive irony of their explorations is also the reflexive irony of mind meeting itself at every dark turn.[23] Yet in a consuming society such immanences can become more vacuous than fatidic. They become, as Jean Baudrillard says, pervasively "ob-scene," a "collective vertigo of neutralization, a forward escape into the obscenity of pure and empty form."[24]

These eleven "definiens" add up to a surd, perhaps absurd. I should be much surprised if they amounted to a definition of postmodernism, which remains, at best, an equivocal concept, a disjunctive category, doubly modified by the impetus of the phenomenon itself and by the shifting perceptions of its critics. (At worst, postmodernism appears to be a mysterious, if ubiquitous, ingredient—like raspberry vinegar, which instantly turns any recipe into *nouvelle cuisine*.)

Nor do I believe that my eleven "definiens" serve to distinguish postmodernism from modernism; for the latter itself abides as a fierce evasion in our literary histories.[25] But I do suggest that the foregoing points—elliptic, cryptic, partial, provisional—argue twin conclusions: *(a) critical pluralism is deeply implicated in the cultural field of postmodernism; and (b) a limited critical pluralism is in some measure a reaction against the radical relativism, the ironic indetermanences, of the postmodern condition; it is an attempt to contain them.*

III

So far, my argument has been prelusive. I must now attend to those efforts that seek to limit—quite rightly, I believe—the potential anarchy of our postmodern condition with cognitive, political, or affective constraints. That is, I must briefly consider criticism as genre, power, and desire—as Kenneth Burke did, long ago, in his vast synoptics of motives.

Is criticism a genre? Critical pluralists often suppose that it may be so.[26] Yet even that most understanding of pluralists, Wayne Booth, is forced finally to admit that a full "methodological pluralism," which must aspire to a perspective on perspectives, only "seems to duplicate the problem with which we began"; so he concludes, "I cannot promise a finally satisfactory encounter with these staggering questions, produced by my simple effort to be a good citizen in the republic of criticism."[27] Booth's conclusion is modest but also alert. He knows that the epistemic foundations of critical pluralism themselves rest on moral, if not spiritual, grounds. "Methodological perspectivism" (as he sometimes calls his version of pluralism) depends on "shared tenancies" which in turn depend on a constitutive act of rational, just, and vitally sympathetic understanding. In the end Booth stands on a kind of Kantian—or is it Christian?—categorical imperative of criticism, with all that it must ethically and metaphysically imply.

Could it have been otherwise? Throughout history, critics have disagreed, pretending to make systems out of their discord and epistemic structures out of their beliefs. The shared tenancies of literary theory may make for hermeneutical communities of provisional trust, enclaves of genial critical authority. But can any of these define criticism both as a historical and cognitive genre? That may depend on what we intend by genre. Traditionally, genre assumed recognizable features within a context of both persistence and change; it was a useful assumption of identity upon which critics (somewhat like Stanley and Livingstone) often presumed. But that assumption, in our heteroclitic age, seems ever harder to maintain. Even genre theorists invite us, nowadays, to go beyond genre—"the finest generic classifications of our time," Paul Hernadi says, "make us look beyond their immediate concern and focus on the *order of literature,* not on *borders between literary genres.*"[28] Yet the "order of literature" itself has become moot.

In boundary genres particularly—and certain kinds of criticism may have become precisely that—the ambiguities attain new heights of febrile intensity. For as Gary Saul Morson notes, "it is not meanings but appropriate procedures for discovering meaning" that become disputable—"not particular readings, but how to read."[29] Since genres find their definition, *when* they find any, not only in their formal features but also in labile interpretive conventions, they seldom offer a stable, epistemic norm. This makes for certain paradoxes in the "law of genre," as Derrida lays it, a "mad law," though even madness fails to define it. As one might expect from the magus of our deconstructions, Derrida insists on undoing genre, undoing its gender, nature, and potency, on exposing the enigma of its "exemplarity." The mad "law of genre" yields only to the "law of the law of genre"—"a principle of contamination, a law of impurity, a parasitical economy."[30]

One is inclined to believe that even without the decreations of certain kinds of writing, like my own paracriticism, the configurations we call literature, literary theory, criticism, have now become (quite like postmodernism itself) "essentially contested concepts," horizons of eristic discourse.[31] Thus, for instance, the latest disconfirmation of critical theory, the latest "revisionary madness" is Steven Knapp and Walter Benn Michaels's statement against theory.[32] Drawing on the pragmatism of Richard Rorty and the stylistics of Stanley Fish, the authors brilliantly, berserkly contend that "true belief" and "knowledge" are epistemologically identical, that critical theory has no methodological consequences whatever. "If our arguments are true, they can have only one consequence . . . ; theory should stop," the authors conclude.[33] In fact it is their own conclusion that will have little consequence, as Knapp and Michaels themselves admit. So much, then, for the case of the self-consuming theorist.

My own conclusion about the theory and practice of criticism is securely unoriginal: like all discourse, criticism obeys human imperatives, which continually redefine it. It is a function of language, power, and desire, of history and accident, of purpose and interest, of value. Above all, it is a function of *belief,* which reason articulates and consensus, or authority, both enables and constrains.[34] (This statement itself expresses a reasoned belief.) If, then, as Kuhn claims, "competing schools, *each of which constantly questions the very foundations of the others*" reign in the humanities; if, as Victor Turner thinks, the "culture of any society at any moment is more like the debris, or 'fall out' of past ideological systems, rather than itself a system"; if also, as Jonathan Culler contends, "'interpretive conventions' . . . should be seen as part of . . . [a] boundless context"; again, if as Jeffrey Stout maintains, "theoretical terms should serve interests and purposes, not the other way around"; and if, as I submit, the principles of literary criticism are historical (that is, at once arbitrary, pragmatic, conventional, and contextual, in any case not axiomatic, apodictic, apophantic), then how can a generic conception of criticism limit critical pluralism or govern the endless deferrals of language, particularly in our indetermanent, our postmodern period?[35]

IV

To exchange a largely cognitive view of our discipline for another that more freely admits politics, desires, beliefs is not necessarily to plunge into Hades or ascend Babel. It is, I think, an act of partial lucidity, responsive to our ideological, our human needs. The act, I stress, remains partial, as I hope will eventually become clear. For the moment, though, I must approach power as a constraint on postmodern relativism and, thus, as a factor in delimiting critical pluralism.

No doubt, the perception that power profoundly engages knowledge reverts to Plato and Aristotle, if not to the *I Ching* and the Egyptian *Book of the Dead.* In the last century, Marx theorized the relation of culture to class; his terms persist in a variety of movements, from totemic Marxism to Marxism with a deconstructionist mask or receptionist face. But it is Foucault, of course, who has given us the most cunning speculations on the topic.[36] The whole burden of his work, since *Folie et déraison* (1961), has been to expose the power of discourse and the discourse of power, to discover the politics of knowledge. More recently, though, his ideology had become antic, to the chagrin of his orthodox critics.

Foucault still maintained that discursive practices "are embodied in technical processes, in institutions, in patterns for general behavior, in forms of transmission and diffusion."[37] But he also accepted the Nietzschean premise that a selfish interest precedes all power and knowledge, shaping them to its own volition, pleasure, excess. Increasingly, Foucault saw power itself as an elusive relation, an immanence of discourse, a conundrum of desire: "It may be that Marx and Freud cannot satisfy our desire for understanding this enigmatic thing which we call power, which is at once visible and invisible, present and hidden, ubiquitous," he remarks.[38] That is why, in his late essay "The Subject and Power," Foucault seemed more concerned with promoting "new kinds of subjectivity" (based on a refusal of those individual identities which states force upon their citizens) than with censuring traditional modes of exploitation.[39]

In a Foucauldian perspective, then, criticism appears as much a discourse of desire as of power, a discourse, anyway, both conative and affective in its personal origins. A neo-Marxist like Jameson, however, would found criticism on collective reality. He would distinguish and "spell out the priority, within the Marxist tradition, of a 'positive hermeneutic' based on social class from those ['negative hermeneutics'] still limited by anarchist categories of the individual subject and individual experience."[40] Again, a leftist critic like Edward Said would insist that the "realities of power and authority . . . are the realities that make texts possible, that deliver them to their readers, that solicit the attention of critics."[41]

Other critics, less partisan and less strenuously political, might concur. Indeed, the "institutional view" of both literature and criticism now prevails among critics as incongruous in their ideologies as Bleich, Booth, Donald Davie, Fish, E. D. Hirsch, Frank Kermode, and Richard Ohmann. Here, bravely, is Bleich:

> Literary theory should contribute to the changing of social and professional institutions such as the public lecture, the convention presentation, the classroom, and the processes of tenure and promotion. Theoretical work ought to show how and why no one class of scholars, and no one subject (including theory) is self-justifying, self-explanatory, and self-sustaining.[42]

The ideological concern declares itself everywhere. A bristling issue of *Critical Inquiry* explores the "politics of interpretation," and the facile correlation of ideology with criticism drives a critic even so disputatious as Gerald Graff to protest the "pseudo-politics of interpretation" in a subsequent number.[43] At the same time, a critic as exquisitely reticent as Geoffrey Hartman acknowledges the intrusions of politics in his recent work.[44] The activities of GRIP (acronym for the Group for Research on the Institutionalization and Professionalization of Literary Study) seem as ubiquitous as those of the KGB or the CIA, though far more benign. And the number of conferences on "Marxism and Criticism," "Feminism and Criticism," "Ethnicity and Criticism," "Technology and Criticism," "Mass Culture and Criticism," keeps American airports snarled and air carriers in the black.

All these, of course, refract the shifts in our "myths of concern" (Northrop Frey's term) since the fifties. But they reflect, too, the changes in our idea of criticism itself, from a Kantian to a Nietzschean, Freudian, or Marxist conception (to name but three), from an ontological to a historical apprehension, from a synchronous or generic discourse to a diachronic or conative activity. The recession of the neo-Kantian idea, which extends through Ernst Cassirer, Suzanne Langer, and the old New Critics, ambiguously to Murray Krieger, implies another loss—that of the imagination as an autochthonous, autotelic, possibly redemptive power of mind. It is also the loss, or at least dilapidation, of the "imaginary library," a total order of art, analogous to André Malraux's *musée imaginaire,* which triumphs over time and brute destiny.[45] That ideal has now vanished; the library itself may end in rubble. Yet in our eagerness to appropriate art to our own circumstances and exercise our will on texts, we risk denying those capacities—not only literary—which have most richly fulfilled our historical existence.

I confess to some distate for ideological rage (the worst are now full of passionate intensity *and* lack all conviction) and for the hectoring of both religious and secular dogmatists.[46] I admit to a certain ambivalence toward politics, which can overcrowd our responses to both art and life. For what is politics? Simply, the right action when ripeness calls. But what is politics again? An excuse to bully or shout in public, vengeance vindicating itself as justice and might pretending to be right, a passion for self-avoidance, immanent mendacity, the rule of habit, the place where history rehearses its nightmares, the *dur désir de durer,* a deadly banality of being. Yet we must all heed politics because it structures our theoretical consents, literary evasions, critical recusancies—shapes our ideas of pluralism even as I write here, now.

v

Politics, we know, becomes tyrannical. It can dominate other modes of discourse, reduce all facts of the human universe—error, epiphany, chance, boredom, pain, dream—to its own terms. Hence the need, as Kristeva says, for a "psychoanalytic intervention . . . a counterweight, an antidote, to political discourse which, without it, is free to become our modern religion: the final explanation."[47] Yet the psychoanalytic explanation can also become as reductive as any other, unless desire itself qualifies its knowledge, its words.

I mean desire in the largest sense—personal and collective, biological and ontological, a force that writers from Hesiod and Homer to Nietzsche, William James, and Freud have reckoned with. It includes the Eros of the Universe that Alfred North Whitehead conceived as "the active entertainment of all ideals, with the urge to their finite realization, each in its due season."[48] But I mean desire also in its more particular sense, which Paul Valéry

understood when he wryly confessed that every theory is a fragment of an autobiography. (Lately, the fragments have grown larger, as anyone who follows the oedipal *psychomachia* of critics must agree.) And I mean desire, too, as an aspect of the pleasure principle, that principle so freely invoked and seldom evident in criticism.

Here Barthes comes elegantly to mind. For him, the pleasure of the text is perverse, polymorph, created by intermittences of the body even more than of the heart. Rupture, tear, suture, scission enhance that pleasure; so does erotic displacement. "The text is a fetish object, and *this fetish desires me,"* he confides.[49] Such a text eludes judgment by anterior or exterior norms. In its presence we can only cry, "That's it for me!" This is the Dionysiac cry par excellence—Dionysiac, that is, in that peculiarly Gallic timbre. Thus, for Barthes, the pleasure of the text derives both from the body's freedom to "pursue its own ideas" and from "value shifted to the sumptuous rank of the signifier."[50]

We need not debate here the celebrated, if dubious, distinctions Barthes makes in that talismanic text; we need only note that pleasure becomes a constitutive critical principle in his later work. Thus in *Leçon,* his inaugural lecture at the Collège de France, Barthes insists on the "truth of desire" which discovers itself in the multiplicity of discourse: *"autant de langages qu'il y a de désirs."*[51] The highest role of the professor is to make himself "fantasmic," to renew his body so that it becomes contemporaneous with his students, to unlearn (*désapprendre*). Perhaps then he can realize true *sapientia: "nul pouvoir, un peu de savoir, un peu de sagesse, et le plus saveur possible."*[52] And in *A Lover's Discourse,* which shows a darker side of desire, Barthes excludes the possibility of explication, of hermeneutics; he would rather stroke language in erotic foreplay: *"Je frotte mon langage contre l'autre. C'est comme si j'avais des mots en guise de doigts."*[53]

Other versions of this critical suasion come easily to mind.[54] But my point is not only that critical theory is a function of our desires, nor simply that criticism often takes pleasure or desire as its concern, its theme. My point is rather more fundamental: much current criticism conceives language and literature themselves as organs of desire, to which criticism tries to adhere erotically (*"se coller,"* Barthes says), stylistically, even epistemically. "Desire and the desire to know are not strangers to each other," Kristeva notes; and "interpretation is infinite because Meaning is made infinite by desire."[55] Happily, this last remark leads into my inconclusion.

Let me recover, though, the stark lineaments of my argument. Critical pluralism finds itself implicated in our postmodern condition, in its relativisms and indetermanences, which it attempts to restrain. But cognitive, political, and affective restraints remain only partial. They all finally fail to delimit critical pluralism, to create consensual theory or practice—witness the debates of this conference. Is there anything, in our era, that *can* found a wide consensus of discourse?

VI

Clearly, the imagination of postmodern criticism is a disestablished imagination. Yet clearly, too, it is an intellectual imagination of enormous vibrancy and scope. I share in its excitement, my own excitement mixed with unease. That unease touches more than our critical theories; it engages the nature of authority and belief in the world. It is the old Nietzschean cry of nihilism: "the desert grows!" God, King, Father, Reason, History, Humanism have all come and gone their way, though their power may still flare up in some circles of faith. We have killed our gods—in spite or lucidity, I hardly know—yet we remain ourselves creatures of will, desire, hope, belief. And now we have nothing—nothing that is not partial, provisional, self-created—upon which to found our discourse.

Sometimes I imagine a new Kant, come out of Königsberg, spirited through the Iron Curtain. In his hand he holds the "fourth critique," which he calls *The Critique of Practical Judgment*. It is a masterwork, resolving all the contradictions of theory and praxis, ethics and aesthetics, metaphysical reason and historical life. I reach for the sublime treatise; the illustrious ghost disappears. Sadly, I turn to my bookshelf and pick out William James's *The Will to Believe.*

Here, it seems, is friendly lucidity, and an imagination that keeps reason on the stretch. James speaks crucially to our condition in a "pluralistic universe." I let him speak:

> He who takes for his hypothesis the notion that it [pluralism] is the permanent form of the world is what I call a radical empiricist. For him the crudity of experience remains an eternal element thereof. There is no possible point of view from which the world can appear an absolutely single fact.[56]

This leaves the field open to "willing nature":

> When I say "willing nature," I do not mean only such deliberate volitions as may have set up habits of belief that we cannot now escape from,—I mean all such factors of belief as fear and hope, prejudice and passion, imitation and partisanship, the circumpressure of our caste and set. As a matter of fact we find ourselves believing, we hardly know how or why. [*W*, 9]

This was written nearly a century ago and remains—so I *believe*—impeccable, unimpugnable. It proposes a different kind of "authority" (lower case), pragmatic, empirical, permitting pluralist beliefs. Between these beliefs there can be only continual negotiations of reason and interest, mediations of desire, transactions of power or hope. But all these still rest on, rest in, beliefs, which James knew to be the most interesting, most valuable, part of man. In the end our "passional nature," he says, decides *an option between propositions, whenever it is a genuine option that cannot by its nature be decided on intellectual grounds"* (*W*, 11). James even suggests that, biologically

considered, "our minds are as ready to grind out falsehood as veracity, and he who says, 'Better go without belief forever than believe a lie!' merely shows his own preponderant private horror of becoming a dupe" (*W*, 18).

Contemporary pragmatists, like Rorty, Fish, or Michaels, may not follow James so far. Certainly they would balk, as do most of us now, when James's language turns spiritual:

> Is it not sheer dogmatic folly to say that our inner interests can have no real connection with the forces that the hidden world may contain? . . . And if needs of ours outrun the visible universe, why *may* not that be a sign that an invisible universe is there? . . . God himself, in short, may draw vital strength and increase of very being from our fidelity. [*W*, 55, 56, 61]

I do not quote this passage to press the claims of metaphysics or religion. I do so only to hint that the *ultimate* issues of critical pluralism, in our postmodern epoch, point that way. And why, particularly, in our postmodern epoch? Precisely because of its countervailing forces, its indetermanences. Everywhere now we observe societies riven by the double and coeval process of planetization and retribalization, totalitarianism and terror, fanatic faith and radical disbelief. Everywhere we meet, in mutant or displaced forms, that conjunctive/disjunctive technological rage which affects postmodern discourse.

It may be that some rough beast will slouch again toward Bethlehem, its haunches bloody, its name echoing in our ears with the din of history. It may be that some natural cataclysm, world calamity, or extra terrestrial intelligence will shock the earth into some sane planetary awareness of its destiny. It may be that we shall simply bungle through, muddle through, wandering in the "desert" from oasis to oasis, as we have done for decades, perhaps centuries. I have no prophecy in me, only some slight foreboding, which I express now to remind myself that all the evasions of our knowledge and actions thrive on the absence of consensual beliefs, an absence that also energizes our tempers, our wills. This is our postmodern condition.

As to things nearer at hand, I openly admit: I do not know how to prevent critical pluralism from slipping into monism or relativism, except to call for pragmatic constituencies of knowledge that would share values, traditions, expectancies, goals. I do not know how to make our "desert" a little greener, except to invoke enclaves of genial authority where the central task is to restore civil commitments, tolerant beliefs, critical sympathies.[57] I do not know how to give literature or theory or criticism a new hold on the world, except to remythify the imagination, at least locally, and bring back the reign of wonder into our lives. In this, my own elective affinities remain with Emerson: "Orpheus is no fable: you have only to sing, and the rocks will crystallize; sing, and the plant will organize; sing, and the animal will be born."[58]

But who nowadays believes it?

NOTES

[1] "Maybe the most certain of all philosophical problems is the problem of the present time, of what we are, in this very moment," writes Michael Foucault in "The Subject and Power," reprinted as "Afterword" in *Michel Foucault: Beyond Structuralism and Hermeneutics,* ed. Hubert L. Dreyfus and Paul Rabinow (Chicago, 1982), 210. The essay also appeared in *Critical Inquiry* 8 (Summer 1982): 777-96.

[2] I have discussed some of these problems in *The Dismemberment of Orpheus: Toward a Postmodern Literature,* 2d ed. (Madison, Wis., 1982), 262-68. See also Claus Uhlig, "Toward a Chronology of Change," Dominick LaCapra, "Intellectual History and Defining the Present as 'Postmodern,'" and Matei Calinescu, "From the One to the Many: Pluralism in Today's Thought," in *Innovation/Renovation: New Perspectives on the Humanities,* ed. Ihab Hassan and Sally Hassan (Madison, Wis., 1983).

[3] Daniel Bell, *The Cultural Contradictions of Capitalism* (New York, 1976), 7.

[4] Jürgen Habermas, "Modernity versus Postmodernity," *New German Critique* 22 (Winter 1981): 13.

[5] For homologies in scientific culture, see my *The Right Promethean Fire: Imagination, Science, and Cultural Change* (Urbana, Ill., 1980), 139-71.

[6] Jean-François Lyotard, "Answering the Question: What is Postmodernism?" trans. Régis Durand, in *Innovation/Renovation,* 341. On the paratactic style in art and society, see also Hayden White, "The Culture of Criticism," in *Liberations: New Essays on the Humanities in Revolution,* ed. Ihab Hassan (Middletown, Conn., 1971), 66-69; and see William James on the affinities between parataxis and pluralism: "It *may* be that some parts of the world are connected so loosely with some other parts as to be strung along by nothing but the copula *and. . . .* This pluralistic view, of a world of *additive* constitution, is one that pragmatism is unable to rule out from serious consideration" (*"Pragmatism," and Four Essays from "The Meaning of Truth"* [New York, 1955], 112).

[7] See Jean-François Lyotard, *La Condition postmoderne: rapport sur le savoir* (Paris, 1979). For other views of decanonization, see *English Literature: Opening Up the Canon,* ed. Leslie Fiedler and Houston A. Baker, Jr., Selected Papers from the English Institute, 1979, n.s. 4 (Baltimore, 1981), and *Critical Inquiry* 10 (September 1983).

[8] Friedrich Nietzsche, *The Will to Power,* ed. Walter Kaufmann, trans. Walter Kaufmann and R. J. Hollingdale (New York, 1967), 199; see Wylie Sypher, *Loss of Self in Modern Literature and Art* (New York, 1962); see also the discussion of the postmodern self in Charles Caramello, *Silverless Mirrors: Book, Self, and Postmodern American Fiction* (Tallahassee, Fla., 1983).

[9] The refusal of depth is, in the widest sense, a refusal of hermeneutics, the "penetration" of nature or culture. It manifests itself in the white philosophies of post-structuralism as well as in various contemporary arts. See, for instance, Alain Robbe-Grillet, *For a New Novel: Essays on Fiction,* trans. Richard Howard (New York, 1965), 49-76, and Susan Sontag, *Against Interpretation* (New York, 1966), 3-14.

[10] Lyotard, "Answering the Question," 340. See also the perceptive discussion of the politics of the sublime by Hayden White, "The Politics of Historical Interpretation: Discipline and De-Sublimation," *Critical Inquiry* 9 (September 1982): 124-28.

[11] Julia Kristeva, "Postmodernism?" in *Romanticism, Modernism, Postmodernism,* ed. Harry R. Garvin (Lewisburg, Pa., 1980), 141. See also her *Powers of Horror: An Essay on Abjection,* trans. Leon S. Roudiez (New York, 1982), and her most recent discussion of "the unnameable" in "Psychoanalysis and the Polis," trans. Margaret Waller, *Critical Inquiry* 9 (September 1982): 84-85, 91.

[12] Alan Wilde, *Horizons of Assent: Modernism, Postmodernism, and the Ironic Imagination* (Baltimore, 1981), 10. Wayne Booth makes a larger claim for the currency of irony in postmodern times, a "cosmic irony," deflating the claims of man's centrality, and evincing a striking parallel with traditional religious languages. See his "The Empire of Irony," *Georgia Review* 37 (Winter 1983): 719-37.

[13] The last term is Gary Saul Morson's. Morson provides an excellent discussion of threshold literature, parody, and hybridization in his *The Boundaries of Genre: Dostoyevsky's "Diary of a Writer" and the Traditions of Literary Utopia* (Austin, Tex., 1981), esp. 48-50, 107-8, and 142-43.

[14] See Fredric Jameson, "Postmodernism and Consumer Society," in *The Anti-Aesthetic: Essays on Postmodern Culture,* ed. Hal Foster (Port Townsend, Wash., 1983). For a counterstatement, see Paolo Portoghesi, *After Modern Architecture,* trans. Meg Shore (New York, 1982), p. 11, and Calinescu, "From the One to the Many," 286.

[15] See M. M. Bakhtin, *Rabealis and His World,* trans. Helena Iswolsky (Cambridge, Mass., 1968), and *The Dialogic Imagination: Four Essays by M. M. Bakhtin,* ed. Michael Holquist, trans. Caryl Emerson and Michael Holquist, University of Texas Press Slavic Series, no. 1 (Austin, Tex., 1981). See also the forum on Bakhtin, *Critical Inquiry* 10 (December 1983).

[16] Bakhtin, *Rabelais,* 10-11.

[17] See Régis Durand's defense, against Michael Fried, of the performing principle in postmodern art ("Theatre/SIGNS/Performance: On Some Transformations of the Theatrical and the Theoretical," in *Innovation/Renovation,* 213-17). See also Richard Schechner, "News, Sex, and Performance Theory," *Innovation/Renovation,* 189-210.

[18] Richard Poirier, *The Performing Self: Compositions and Decompositions in the Languages of Contemporary Life* (New York, 1971), xv, xiii. See also Christopher Lasch, *The Culture of Narcissism: American Life in an Age of Diminishing Expectations* (New York, 1978).

[19] Nietzsche, *The Will to Power,* 291.

[20] James understood this when he said: "You can't weed out the human contribution . . . altho the stubborn fact remains that there *is* a sensible flux, what is *true of it* seems from first to last to be largely a matter of our own creation" (*Pragmatism,* 166).

[21] See Ihab Hassan, *Paracriticisms: Seven Speculations of the Times* (Urbana, Ill., 1975), 121-50; and Hassan, *The Right Promethean Fire,* 139-72. It was José Ortega y Gasset, however, who made a prescient, gnostic statement (see p. 96, above). And before Ortega, James wrote: "The world is One just so far as its parts hang together by any definite connexion. It is many just so far as any definite connexion fails to obtain. And finally it is growing more and more unified by those systems of connexion at least which human energy keeps framing as time goes on" (*Pragmatism,* 105). But see also Jean Baudrillard's version of a senseless immanence, "The Ecstacy of Communication," in *The Anti-Aesthetic,* 126-34.

[22] Nelson Goodman, *Ways of Worldmaking* (Indianapolis, 1978), x.

[23] Active, creative, self-reflexive patterns seem also essential to advanced theories of artifical intelligence. See the article on Douglas R. Hofstadter's latest work by James Gleick, "Exploring the Labyrinth of the Mind," *The New York Times Magazine,* 21 August 1983:23-100.

[24] Jean Baudrillard, "What Are You Doing After the Orgy?" *Artforum* (October 1983):43.

[25] See, for instance, Paul de Man, "Literary History and Literary Modernity," *Blindness and Insight: Essays in the Rhetoric of Contemporary Criticism* (New York, 1971), and Octavio Paz, *Children of the Mire: Modern Poetry from Romanticism to the Avant-Garde* (Cambridge, Mass., 1974).

[26] See, for instance, the persuasive article of Ralph Cohen, "Literary Theory as Genre," *Centrum* 3 (Spring 1975): 45-64. Cohen also sees literary change itself as a genre. See his essay, "A Propadeutic for Literary Change," and the responses of White and Michael Riffaterre to it, in *Critical Exchange* 13. (Spring 1983): 1-17, 18-26, and 27-38.

[27] Wayne Booth, *Critical Understanding: The Powers and Limits of Pluralism* (Chicago, (1979), 33-34.

[28] Paul Hernadi, *Beyond Genres: New Directions in Literary Classification* (Ithaca, N.Y., 1972), 184. See, further, the two issues on convention and genre of *New Literary History* 13 (Autumn 1981) and 14 (Winter 1983).

[29] Morson, *The Boundaries of Genre,* 49.

[30] Jacques Derrida, "La Loi du genre/The Law of Genre," *Glyph* 7 (1980): 206. This entire issue concerns genre.

[31] The term "essentially contested concept" is developed by W.B. Gallie in his *Philosophy and the Historical Understanding* (New York, 1968). See also Booth's lucid discussion of it, *Critical Understanding,* 211-15 and 366.

[32] See Steven Knapp and Walter Benn Michaels, "Against Theory," *Critical Inquiry* 8 (Summer 1982): 723-42, and the subsequent responses in *Critical Inquiry* 9 (June 1983). "Revisionary Madness: The Prospects of American Literary Theory at the Present Time" is the title of Daniel T. O'Hara's response (pp. 726-42).

[33] Steven Knapp and Walter Benn Michaels, "A Reply to Our Critics," *Critical Inquiry* 9 (June 1983): 800.

[34] The relevance of belief to knowledge in general and conventions in particular is acknowledged by thinkers of different persuasions, even when they disagree on the nature of truth, realism, and genre. Thus, for instance, Nelson Goodman and Menachem Brinker agree that belief is "an accepted version" of the world; and E. D. Hirsch concurs with both. See Goodman, "Realism, Relativism, and Reality," Brinker, "On Realism's Relativism: A Reply to Nelson Goodman," and Hirsch, "Beyond Convention?" All appear in *New Literary History* 14 (Winter 1983).

[35] Thomas S. Kuhn, *The Structure of Scientific Revolutions,* 2d ed. (Chicago, 1970), 163, my emphasis; Victor Turner, *Dramas, Fields, and Metaphors: Symbolic Action in Human Society* (Ithaca, N.Y., 1974), 14; Jonathan Culler, "Convention and Meaning: Derrida and Austin," *New Literary History* 13 (Autumn 1981): 30; Jeffrey Stout, "What Is the Meaning of a Text?" *New Literary History* 14 (Autumn 1982): 5. I am aware that other thinkers distinguish between "variety" and "subjectivity" of understanding in an effort to limit radical perspectivism; see, for instance, Stephen C. Pepper, *World Hypotheses: A Study in Evidence* (Berkeley and Los Angeles, 1942); Stephen Toulmin, *Human Understanding: The Collective Use and Evolution of Concepts* (Princeton, N.J., 1972); and George Bealer, *Quality and Concept* (Oxford, 1982). But I wonder why their arguments have failed to eliminate, or at least reduce, their differences with relativists; or why, again, Richard Rorty and Hirsch find it possible to disagree about the "question of objectivity," which became the theme of a *conference* at the University of Virginia in April 1984.

[36] Jürgen Habermas, in *Knowledge and Human Interests,* trans. Jeremy J. Shapiro (Boston, 1971), and *Technik und Wissenschaft als "Ideologie"* (Frankfurt am Main, 1968), also offers vigorous neo-Marxist critiques of knowledge and society. Kenneth Burke, in *A Grammar of Motives* (New York, 1945), preceded both Foucault and Habermas in this large political and logological enterprise.

[37] Michel Foucault, *Language, Counter-Memory, Practice: Selected Essays and Interviews,* ed. Donald F. Bouchard, trans. Bouchard and Sherry Simon (Ithaca, N.Y., 1977), 200.

[38] Ibid., 213

[39] See *Michel Foucault: Beyond Structuralism,* 216-20.

[40] Fredric Jameson, *The Political Unconscious: Narrative as a Socially Symbolic Act* (Ithaca, N.Y., 1981), 286.

[41] Edward Said, *The World, the Text, and the Critic* (Cambridge, Mass., 1983), 5.

[42] David Bleich, "Literary Theory in the University: A Survey," *New Literary History* 14 (Winter 1983): 411. See also *What Is Literature?* ed. Hernadi (Bloomington, Ind., 1978), 49-112.

[43] See *Critical Inquiry* 9 (September 1982); and see Gerald Graff, "The Pseudo-Politics of Interpretation," *Critical Inquiry* 9 (March 1983): 597-610.

[44] See Geoffrey Hartman, "The New Wilderness: Critics as Connoissuers of Chaos," in *Innovation/Renovation,* 87-110.

[45] "If social circumstances . . . contradict too powerfully the [Romantic] world-view of literature, then the Imaginary Library, first its enabling beliefs and eventually its institutional manifestations, can no longer exist," remarks Alvin B. Kernan, *The Imaginary Library: An Essay on Literature and Society* (Princeton, N.J., 1982), 166.

[46] Though "everything is ideological," as we nowadays like to say, we need still to distinguish between ideologies—fascism, feminism, monetarism, vegetarianism, etc.—between their overt claims, their hidden exactions. Even postmodernism, as a political ideology, requires discriminations. Lyotard, for instance, believes that "the postmodern condition is a stranger to disenchantment as to the blind positivity of delegitimation" (*La Condition postmoderne,* 8; my translation); while Foster claims a "postmodernism of resistance," a "counterpractice not only to the official culture of modernism but also to the 'false normativity' of a reactionary postmodernism" (*The Anti-Aesthetic,* xii). Interestingly enough, French thinkers of the Left—Foucault, Lyotard, Baudrillard, Gilles Deleuze—seem more subtle in their ideas of "resistance" than their American counterparts. This is curious, perhaps paradoxical, since the procedures of "mass," "consumer," or "postindustrial" society are more advanced in America than in France. But see also, as a counterstatement, Said's critique of Foucault, "Travelling Theory," *Raritan* 1 (Winter 1982): 41-67.

[47] Kristeva, "Psychoanalysis and the Polis," 78. In our therapeutic culture, the language of politics and the discourse of desire constantly seek one another, as if the utopian marriage of Marx and Freud could find consummation, at last, in our words. Hence the political use of such erotic or analytic concepts as "libidinal economy" (Jean-François Lyotard, *Economie libidinale* [Paris, 1974]), "seduction" (Jean Baudrillard, *De la séduction* [Paris, 1979]), "delirium" or "abjection" (Julia Kristeva, *Powers of Horror*) "anti-Oedipus" (Gilles Deleuze and Félix Guattari, *Anti-Oedipus: Capitalism and Schizophrenia,* trans. Robert Hurley, Mark Seem, and Helen R. Lane [New York, 1977]), "bliss" (Roland Barthes, *The Pleasure of the Text,* trans. Richard Miller [New York, 1975]), and "the political unconscious" (Jameson, *The Political Unconscious*). See also Ihab Hassan, "Desire and Dissent in the Postmodern Age," *Kenyon Review,* n.s. 5 (Winter 1983): 1-18.

[48] Alfred North Whitehead, *Adventures of Ideas* (New York, 1955), 276.

[49] Barthes, *The Pleasure of the Text,* 27.

[50] Ibid., 17, 65.

[51] Roland Barthes, *Leçon inaugurale faite le vendredi 7 janvier 1977* (Paris, 1978), 25.

[52] Ibid, 46.

[53] Roland Barthes, *Fragments d'un discours amoureux* (Paris, 1977), 87. A few sentences in the paragraph which this sentence concludes have appeared in my earlier essay, "Parabiography: The Varieties of Critical Experience," *Georgia Review* 34 (Fall 1980):600.

[54] In America, the work of Leo Bersani has addressed such questions as "Can a psychology of fragmentary and *dis*continuous desires be reinstated? What are the strategies by which the self might be once again theatricalized? How might desire recover its original capacity for projecting nonstructurable *scenes?*" And it answers them by suggesting that *the* "desiring self might even disappear as we learn to multiply our discontinuous and partial desiring selves" in language. See *A Future for Astyanax: Character and Desire in Literature* (Boston, 1976), 6-7.

[55] Kristeva, "Psychoanalysis and the Polis," 82, 86.

[56] William James, *"The Will to Believe" and Other Essays in Popular Philosophy* (New York, 1956), ix. All further references to this work, abbreviated *W,* will be included in the text.

[57] James once more: "No one of us ought to issue vetoes to the other, nor should we bandy words of abuse. We ought, on the contrary, delicately and profoundly to respect one another's mental freedom: then only shall we bring about the intellectual republic; then only shall we have that spirit of inner tolerance without which all our outer tolerance is soulless, and which is empiricism's glory; then only shall we live and let live, in speculative as well as in practical things" (*W,* 30). How far, beyond this, does any postmodern pluralist go?

[58] *Journals of Ralph Waldo Emerson,* 1820-1872, ed. Edward Waldo Emerson and Waldo Emerson Forbes, 10 vols. (Boston, 1909-14), 8:79.

C. Barry Chabot

SOURCE: "The Problem of the Postmodern," in *Zeitgeist in Babel: The Postmodernist Controversy,* edited by Ingeborg Hoesterey, Indiana University Press, 1991, pp. 22-39.

[In the following essay, originally published in 1988, Chabot argues that postmodernism eshibits more continuity with traditional literary methods than most critics admit.]

During the past fifteen years we have increasingly heard and read about something variously termed "fabulism" (Scholes), "metafiction" (McCaffery), "surfiction" (Federman), and, with growing unanimity, "postmodernism." The former terms were typically developed in efforts to account for apparent changes of direction and emphasis within recent fiction. "Postmodernism," on the other hand, is a broader term and has been pressed into service to describe developments throughout the arts; it is even said that we live in a postmodern society. Any number of people obviously believe that a cultural rupture of some moment has occurred, and that its mark is discernible across the range of our cultural activities. There seems to be little agreement, however, about the precise nature and timing of the supposed break, and even less about how we can most adequately characterize its effects upon our cultural products.

I remain doubtful that a rupture of such magnitude has occurred and want here to register a minority report. Our lack of an adequate and widely accepted understanding of literary modernism makes many arguments for the postmodern initially plausible, but much of what has been termed postmodern derives quite directly from the work of earlier writers. In order to demonstrate the hesitancies, confusions, and contradictions within and between various characterizations of the postmodern, I want to investigate the work of several representative critics. For the sake of focus, I shall concentrate initially upon characterizations of our recent novel; if my conclusions are valid, they should apply as well to comparable accounts of our recent poetry and drama.

I

When Ihab Hassan writes in *Paracriticisms* that the "change in Modernism may be called Postmodernism," he emphasizes the continuity between these literary movements (43). He locates the origins of the latter in 1938, with the publication of Sartre's *La Nausée* and Beckett's *Murphy,* but he is not primarily attempting to define the sensibilities of entire eras. "Modernism," he writes, "does not suddenly cease so that Postmodernism may begin: they now coexist" (47). Modernism and postmodernism for Hassan thus provide competing visions of the contemporary predicament, and it is as likely that a particular work will be informed by the one as by the other. Hassan does not completely neglect the temporal dimension implied by the terms themselves. He understands both as responses to the character of life and thought in the twentieth century. If individuals earlier in the century had reason to be apprehensive about the possibilities then available for perpetuating viable forms of life, there has subsequently been even more reason for disquiet. Modernism and postmodernism, respectively, represent the literary equivalents of such more pervasive concerns. "Postmodernism," writes Hassan, "may be a response, direct or oblique, to the Unimaginable which Modernism glimpsed only in its most prophetic moments" (53). Such sentences award the primacy of vision to postmodernism, but its perceptiveness is largely the product of its times, which have made the awful possibilities we face only too clear.

Hassan defines neither modernism nor postmodernism. Instead he offers a catalogue of characteristic modernist concerns—urbanism, technologism, dehumanization, primitivism, eroticism, antinomianism, and experimentalism; he then glosses each, providing instances of the forms it takes within postmodernism. In regard to primitivism, for instance, Hassan writes that its modernist forms represented a use of ritual and myth to structure contemporary experience, whereas its postmodernist forms move away "from the mythic, toward the existential," initially in the work of the Beats and later "the post-existential ethos, psychedelics (Leary), the Dionysian ego (Brown), Pranksters (Kesey), madness (Laing), animism and magic (Castaneda)" (56). As his examples make clear, for Hassan postmodernism is not exclusively a literary phenomenon; rather, it represents a broad cultural response to pressing contemporary issues, and is as likely to emerge within social practices as within artistic products.

Despite the potential importance of the postmodernist program, and despite his own desire to stay in sympathy with whatever is most current, Hassan's assessment of postmodernism is finally ambiguous. He concedes that modernists frequently resorted to questionable means in shoring up such artistic authority as they could muster, citing Hemingway's code as an example, but observes that postmodernism "has tended toward artistic Anarchy, in deeper complicity with things falling apart—or has tended toward Pop" (59). The choice between authoritarianism and anarchy seems a devil's choice, and it is not altogether clear, to Hassan at least, that the latter is unmistakably the course of wisdom. Finally, however, Hassan's reservations about a postmodern aesthetic go much deeper. It releases new imaginative energies, but Hassan worries that we might now have entered a time when no art "can help to engender the motives we must now acquire; or if we can long continue to value an art that fails us" (59). I am not sure how to take this reservation—does it imply that our needs are too pressing for us to fiddle with art, or that our art already fails to provide us with the necessary direction? In the end, Hassan suggests that postmodernism is in danger of being overwhelmed by the very cultural crisis that originally called it into existence.

Jerome Klinkowitz accepts Hassan's designation of postmodernism, and thus needs another term to designate work manifesting what he takes to be an independent and more recent impulse. He offers several—"Post-Contemporary," "disruptivist," "Superfiction," and most recently "self-apparent"—but there are reasons to assimilate Klinkowitz's efforts within the broader attempt to define postmodernism.[1] Klinkowitz has assumed the role of apologist for a relatively small group of recent fiction writers; he is, accordingly, eager to differentiate their particular virtues from those of other writers. Among readers of contemporary fiction, Klinkowitz is almost alone in believing that his writers form an identifiable school distinct from postmodernism. Hassan, for instance, cites several writers Klinkowitz would term disruptivists when developing his own understanding of postmodernism. I shall return to this question later, and shall assume for the present that, despite his intentions, Klinkowitz is struggling to define a version of postmodernism.

Klinkowitz locates the emergence of disruptivist fiction "with the publishing season of 1967-68, when for the first time in a long time a clear trend in literary history became apparent" (ix). Disruptivist fiction is particularly adamant about the need to abandon the mimetic aspirations of the traditional novel. "If the world is absurd," writes Klinkowitz, "if what passes for reality is distressingly unreal, why spend time representing it" (32). Such statements suggest that the disruptivists believe the world is not now worth representing, whereas others suggest that representation is not possible and has always been a misplaced aspiration. Whatever the rationale, on Klinkowitz's account disruptivists are concerned with "not just the reporting of the world, but [with] the imaginative transformation of it" (32). The transformative power of the imagination enters this fiction in two ways. First, at the thematic level, it figures in the plot, as in Vonnegut's use of time-travel in *Slaughterhouse-Five*. More importantly, however, it appears in the self-reflexiveness of its characters (who frequently know that they are fictive constructs) and narrators (who frequently comment on the difficulties they are having in constructing the piece at hand). Such narrative shifts frustrate whatever tendencies readers might have to suspend disbelief and take the work at hand as a representation of some common world; in the same way, they perform the instructive function of demonstrating the ways and means by which readers too make their worlds.

Hassan's postmodern always hovers on the edge of despair and enervation, but Klinkowitz's disruptivist fiction is almost programmatically playful and energetic. "The writers we're discussing are out to create a good time," writes Klinkowitz in the prologue to *The Life of Fiction* (4). These qualities are not ancillary to disruptivist fiction, and their absence is sufficient reason to read writers out of the disruptivist camp. Thus Klinkowitz

terms Barth and Pynchon "regressive parodists," and apparently believes that the former's influential essay, "The Literature of Exhaustion," has retarded appreciation of the disruptivists (ix). Barth's self-reflexive characters typically feel caught in and by their self-consciousness. It is a condition they would escape, whereas in disruptivist fiction it is perceived precisely as the condition of imaginative freedom. Exuberance is also what obviously differentiates disruptivist fiction from the French New Novel. In each of his books Klinkowitz approvingly quotes Barthelme's observation that the French New Novel "'seems leaden, selfconscious in the wrong way. Painfully slow-paced, with no leaps of the imagination, concentrating on the minutiae of consciousness, these novels scrupulously, in deadly earnest, parse out what can safely be said'" (174). Barthelme's description of the New Novel seems a catalogue of characteristics that disruptivist fiction on Klinkowitz's account is at pains to avoid.

Hassan's postmodernism and Klinkowitz's disruptivist fiction are similar in the emphasis each places on the transformative potential of the imagination. This similarity might account for Hassan's running together of writers from Beckett to Sukenick into a pervasive postmodernism; Klinkowitz, on the other hand, believes that to "the newer writers, Beckett is as traditional as Joyce" (LF 2), and accordingly would differentiate sharply among modern, postmodern, and disruptivist fiction. Hassan locates postmodernism within a general sense of cultural crisis and potential calamity; although he has written a cultural history, *The American 1960s*, Klinkowitz concentrates on the writers in question and rarely alludes to larger cultural issues. This difference in the ways they situate their work might account for a corresponding difference in tone: Hassan is prophetic, edgy, uncertain that the imagination will prove equal to the tasks at hand; Klinkowitz can be as bouncy as the authors he values, and since he sets the imagination no particular problems to solve he need not doubt its adequacy.

Alan Wilde also finds an affirmation at the core of what he terms postmodernism, but its character is far less exuberant and has quite different sources. *Horizons of Assent: Modernism, Postmodernism, and the Ironic Imagination* is a closely reasoned study of the shift in the novel during this century from modernism, through what Wilde terms "late modernism," to postmodernism. Wilde pays particular attention to the characteristic uses and meanings of irony; he argues that these shift as the century progresses and that each of his three phases corresponds to a characteristic form of irony.

For Wilde modernism is characterized by what he terms disjunctive or absolute irony, "the conception of equal and opposed possibilities held in a state of total poise, or, more briefly still, the shape of an indestructible, unresolvable paradox" (21). Wilde distinguishes absolute irony from an earlier and more pervasive form, which he terms "mediate irony." It "imagines a world lapsed from a recoverable . . . norm" (9) and has as its goal the recovery of that earlier wholeness. The modern ironist, by way of contrast, confronts a world apparently in such fundamental disarray that no recovery of previous states seems possible. The modern ironist nonetheless attempts to impose a shape or order, and for his efforts achieves "not resolution but closure—an aesthetic closure that substitutes for the notion of paradise regained an image . . . of a paradise fashioned by man himself" (10). Since the order achieved by the modern writer is exclusively aesthetic, he ends at a remove from the world he would make cohere. With no course of action clearly preferable to any other, in the end the modern ironist is finally inactive as well as detached, unable to commit himself to the world without thereby destroying the order he has struggled to create.

Wilde illustrates his definition of the modernist program primarily through references to the novels of E. M. Forster and Virginia Woolf. In the work of other and generally younger writers, especially those who come to attention during the thirties, he sees a subtle shift indicative of what he terms the "late modern" sensibility. His chief examples of the late-modern are Christopher Isherwood and Ivy Compton-Burnett. These writers are typically less concerned with depth than with surfaces; as a result, the relations between language and world are thought to be less problematic than among the modernists, and appearances are again held to be valuable in understanding people and events. The obvious pleasure that Isherwood and his narrators take in some aspects of their worlds not only contrasts with the discomfort typical of the modernists, it also implies that they have partially overcome the detachment characteristic of the latter.

In their participation in their worlds, the late-modernists anticipate what Wilde terms postmodernism. Although he calls Woolf's *Between the Acts* "still the most impressive of *postmodern* novels" (48), Wilde argues that postmodernism "is essentially an American affair" (12).[2] On Wilde's account, postmodernists typically deploy "suspensive irony." It involves the perception of "experience as random and contingent . . . rather than—the modernist view—simply fragmented" (27). Nonetheless, postmodernism does not press for or impose order, even one limited to the aesthetic realm; instead, the contingent world is simply accepted. Modernist paradox thereby gives way "to quandary, to a low-keyed engagement with a world of perplexities and uncertainties, in which one can hope, at best, to achieve what Forster calls 'the smaller pleasures of life' and Stanley Elkin, its 'small satisfactions'" (10).

Wilde isolates two strands within postmodernism. The first consists roughly of Klinkowitz's disruptivists, especially Ronald Sukenick and Raymond Federman, but Wilde attends less to their statements of intention than the effects of their practice. On Wilde's reading, Sukenick and Federman, for all their overt hostility to modernism, end by unintentionally reproducing, in an attenuated form, many modernist dilemmas; "they are," he writes, "Modernism's lineal descendants (or perhaps its illegitimate

sons), patricides manqués" (144). Wilde's other strand of postmodernism employs "generative irony: the attempt, inspired by the negotiations of self and world, to create tentatively and provisionally, anironic enclaves of value in the face of—but not in place of—a meaningless universe" (148). The world envisioned in these works is even more contingent than that found in modernist fiction, but its narrators and characters accede to that condition, recognizing that it cannot be redressed. Instead, they recognize that their worlds contain pleasures as well as pains, and therefore choose not to distance themselves, in the manner of their predecessors, from the phenomenal world. Elkin's *The Living End,* Apple's "The Oranging of America" and "Disneyad," and several of Barthelme's later stories serve as Wilde's primary examples of this postmodernism. It embodies "a vision that lacks the heroism of the modernist enterprise but that, for a later and more disillusioned age, recovers its humanity" (165).

Wilde's characterization of postmodernism does not, like those by Hassan and Klinkowitz, place a premium upon the imagination. For Hassan, the postmodern imagination must redeem a world on the brink of calamity, and its prospects for success are at best problematic; for Klinkowitz, the world similarly requires redemption, but he apparently has no doubt that the postmodern imagination is equal to the task. On Wilde's account, postmodern writers find the world fully as contingent, but he finds in them a willingness to endure the random and a capacity to identify sources of gratification within it. Both Klinkowitz and Wilde believe that an affirmative moment defines postmodern fiction, but they identify its sources differently. For Klinkowitz, what is affirmed is finally the supposedly transformative power of the imagination; for Wilde, on the other hand, it is the phenomenal world itself, which, amidst its various turnings, upon occasion throws up gratifying possibilities.

II

The efforts by Hassan, Klinkowitz, and Wilde to define postmodernism are representative of many others, and display many of the same strengths and weaknesses. They bring contemporary writers to our attention, provide insights into their particular ambitions, and begin to place them within the strands of literary and cultural history. Each defines postmodernism, however, in ways that are not only distinct but in the end mutually exclusive. Wilde's late-modern, for instance, is not the same as Hassan's postmodern, even though both are located in the thirties; and Hassan links the fiction of Beckett and Sukenick, whereas Klinkowitz sees the latter as being in rebellion against the former. The primary difficulties in the way of the very concept of postmodernism, in other words, involve its definition and inclusiveness.

As the term suggests, postmodernism is invariably defined vis-à-vis modernism—postmodernism is what comes after and in opposition to modernism. But there is little agreement about the nature of modernism, many characterizations of it enjoying some degree of currency within the profession. In Wilde's account, for instance, modernism is equivalent to the use of a particular form of irony, what he terms absolute irony. I have no quarrel with his readings of Forster and Woolf, but I find it difficult to extend the term so defined to cover the work of other writers typically termed modernists, such as Fitzgerald and Hemingway, or Stevens and Hart Crane. One wonders, in other words, if Wilde's postmoderns would seem equally distinct from modernism if they were read within the context of earlier American instead of British writers. Perhaps the differences that Wilde finds derive as much from differences between the national literary traditions, differences obscured by his framework, as from any supposed change in the literary sensibility that has occurred over time. Although I frequently find Wilde's readings of individual works compelling, such doubts leave me with questions about the history he constructs from them.

Unlike Wilde, Klinkowitz does not venture detailed accounts of the succession of literary sensibilities during the century. His conception of disruptivist or self-apparent fiction is the most narrow of the three surveyed. It identifies writers of a particular school, but then claims that it represents an entire generation of writers come of age during 1967-68. In *Literary Disruptions* he writes of a "generational gap" between Barth and Barthelme, which "has obstructed the critical understanding of new fiction" (175). When he reduces the relations between disruptivist and other fiction to the terms of generational conflict, Klinkowitz introduces several difficulties. One of his disruptivists, Kurt Vonnegut, is in fact eight years older than John Barth, and his first novel was published in 1952, four years before Barth's *The Floating Opera;* Klinkowitz is thus in the anomalous position of having a rebellious son who in fact arrives on the scene earlier than the figurative father. Such local anomalies, however, are the least of Klinkowitz's conceptual difficulties. I want to discuss three that particularly disable his argument.

First, Klinkowitz is concerned largely with younger or at least recently arrived writers who clearly feel a need to make a space for themselves on the literary scene. They do so in part by issuing manifestos and granting interviews in which they attempt to differentiate their own efforts from those of earlier and already established writers. As an apologist for these writers, Klinkowitz takes them at their word, rarely questioning either their announced goals, the measure of their success in meeting them, or their statements concerning the position of their own work in regard to that of other writers. A curiously naive species of literary history is the result, especially when one considers that Klinkowitz writes at the same time that Harold Bloom and others have been demonstrating how complicated the relations among writers can be. Klinkowitz's literary sons (and they are all sons) overcome their literary fathers with little difficulty, and the latter never survive to disfigure the former's efforts. We now know to be suspicious of such characterizations of literary succession, where literary influence is conceived purely as a negative affair and breaks between literary generations appear absolute.

Second, Klinkowitz, like the writers he admires, is so intent upon celebrating this generation that he fails to recognize the ways in which it simply continues or modifies the literary heritage. Wilde, for instance, observes that "the Surfictionists recall ('in attenuated form') nothing so much as the aesthetic manifestos of the earlier decades of the century" (144). When Sukenick and Federman engage in polemics against the novel as currently practiced and invent neologisms to identify themselves, they continue the tradition and rhetoric of Pound, Breton, and other poets earlier in the century. Indeed, one way of understanding these writers involves recognizing the extent to which they have adapted to the writing of fiction many of the practices common to poets during the teens and twenties. Fitzgerald, Hemingway, and Faulkner did not issue manifestos, nor did they devote much energy to berating other novelists to their own advantage. Poets of that time, especially those who self-consciously considered themselves part of the avant-garde, did engage in such activities, and the Surfictionists seemingly follow their example, simply adapting it to the conditions of another time and genre. This adaptation is particularly clear in the case of Sukenick, who wrote a dissertation and first book on the poetics of Wallace Stevens. In his own subsequent fiction Sukenick adapts Stevens's poetics to the condition of the contemporary novel, but large portions of the poet's work survive the adaptation virtually unaltered. Klinkowitz simply passes over such borrowings, either because he does not notice them, because they weaken his case, or because he believes the transportation of poetic doctrines and practices to fiction in itself constitutes a significant innovation. Whatever the reason, the neglect of such continuities with writers earlier in the century casts doubt upon Klinkowitz's account of the disruptivists.

Although Wilde does not use the language of generations and is characteristically more cautious in suggesting the kinds of departures that constitute postmodernism, his own account of the phenomenon encounters similar problems. Stanley Elkin is one of Wilde's exemplary postmoderns. Elkin wrote a dissertation on Faulkner and has said in an interview that Saul Bellow is probably the writer who has influenced him most strongly. "To the extent that I imitate anyone," he continued, "I think I may—in dialogue—imitate Saul Bellow" (140). Few people, including Bellow himself, would consider Bellow a postmodern writer, and Faulkner is certainly one of the foremost American modernists. Like Faulkner and Bellow, Elkin writes an extremely rhetorical prose. Although each possesses a distinctive voice and puts it to distinctive ends (consider, for instance, the differences between Faulkner's Flem Snopes and Elkin's Ben Flesh in *The Franchiser*), it seems excessive to posit an additional difference between them of the kind usually associated with the transition between modern and postmodern.

Modernism, in its usual usage, is a fairly capacious term, one covering a range of literary practices. A final difficulty in the way Klinkowitz and others typically propose definitions of the postmodern involves their violation of modernism in this larger sense. "Modernism" is not a term equivalent to "Imagism," "Futurism," "Surrealism," "Vorticism" and the like, which refer to specific literary schools or movements; instead, it is the term invoked to suggest what such particular and divergent programs have in common. It is a *period* concept; and its use involves the claim that in the end, and whatever their obvious differences, the individual energies of the time possess enough family resemblances that it makes sense to refer to them collectively. Modernism refers to whatever Ezra Pound and Wallace Stevens, Ernest Hemingway and William Faulkner, to name only American writers whose credentials as modernists seem beyond question, have in common. By its very nature, then, modernism is a second-order concept.

Since modernism is a period concept, one encompassing many divergent specific movements, it is likely to be surpassed or replaced only by a concept of the same kind and with comparable reach. The emergence of Surrealism, for instance, did not represent the overcoming of modernism so much as the emergence of another dimension within it. When we consider the various claims being made for the emergence of what is being called "postmodernism," we must ask whether the tendencies in question resemble in kind Surrealism or modernism. Klinkowitz, as we have seen, believes that the disruptivists form an identifiable "school" (x); we have also seen that they are unmistakably indebted to modernist poets for their means of self-promotion and their aesthetic. There are thus reasons to believe that these writers represent, like the Surrealists, a late development within modernism rather than its replacement. The rhetoric used in clearing themselves a place, of course, makes larger claims; but I understand the rhetorical intensity as itself in part a legacy from modernism, and in part as deriving from the felt urgency, at this late date, of claiming some necessarily marginal territory as its own.

Unlike Klinkowitz, Hassan recognizes that modernism is a period concept. He acknowledges the diversity of literary modernism when he catalogues its various schools and movements. His lists, however, fall short of providing definitions for either modernism or its supposed successor, because he does not indicate what the items on either list have in common, or what differentiates them from other contemporary cultural phenomena. He provides something of an anatomy without a conception of the whole the various organs and limbs finally compose. His attention is on the immediate future, or better on the question of whether we shall have one, and does not pause over what might be considered academic questions.

The situation in regard to Wilde's characterization of recent literary history and the emergence of the postmodern is somewhat more complicated. Wilde defines modernism narrowly, as the consequences that follow from the use of what he terms absolute irony. The emergence more recently of what Wilde terms suspensive or generative irony provides the grounds for claiming that it constitutes a new or postmodern sensibility. The narrow conception of modernism, in other words, is what lends credence to the claims for postmodernism; but, as mentioned earlier, I doubt the adequacy of Wilde's characterizations of modernism. My doubts take two forms. First, I doubt that it is possible to say that the entire range of modern novelists employ absolute irony. It seems that Wilde has mistaken a form of modernism for modernism itself, much as if he had identified it with, say, Pound's Imagism. Second, even if Wilde could make a reasonable case for the pervasiveness of absolute irony in this body of fiction, I do not believe he would thereby be identifying its most distinctive feature. I do not believe, in other words, that one can define modernism formally, despite its own obvious formal intensities; as a period concept, modernism must be approached more broadly and its distinctive features sought in the relationships it establishes with both the literary tradition and the immediate cultural context.

Horizons of Assent is in most respects the best book now available on our recent fiction, and Wilde's failure to develop a satisfactory account of postmodernism is therefore especially instructive. By its nature the postmodern is conceived in contrast to the modern—the era, sensibility, or set of literary strategies it would supplant. The initial plausibility of Wilde's description of postmodernism turns out to depend upon his prior conception of modernism. When that conception is found wanting, the claims for an emergent postmodernism are simultaneously thrown into doubt. In the absence of an adequate and widely accepted conception of modernism, we shall probably continue to be presented with claims in behalf of an emergent postmodern; but at least for the near term I doubt that upon inspection any will prove any more substantial than those already proposed by Hassan, Klinkowitz, and Wilde.[3]

III

In a series of recent essays, Fredric Jameson has been developing his own conception of postmodernism. It is explicitly a period concept, and thus does not fall prey to the difficulties enumerated above. Jameson believes that postmodernism has become the cultural dominant for the entire social order; accordingly, its force is to be found as much in the economy, the cinema, philosophy, and architecture as in literature itself. Indeed, Jameson says that his own formulation of postmodernism initially took shape in response to the continuing debates concerning the nature of contemporary architecture.[4] Since Jameson's use of the term is so distinctive among literary critics, it will be instructive to see if it proves more adequate to its appointed task.

At crucial points in these essays, after lengthy discussions of various cultural manifestations of what he terms postmodernism, Jameson alludes to its characteristic economic forms. His conception of economic postmodernism clearly derives from Ernest Mandel's *Late Capitalism.* Mandel argues that Western capitalism has evolved through three distinct stages: market capitalism, monopoly capitalism, and since the 1940s, what Jameson calls multinational capitalism. This latest form simultaneously clarifies the logic of capitalism and, to an unprecedented degree, expands its reach, drawing the entire globe within its ambit. In his contribution to *The Sixties without Apology,* Jameson suggests that the upheavals of that period parallel the culminating moments of the transition from monopoly to multinational capitalism, a shift that was largely completed by the early seventies. The postmodern, or so Jameson argues, is the culture appropriate to this last phase of capitalism, just as realism and modernism, respectively, had been appropriate to its earlier forms (78).

Jameson enumerates a number of constitutive features of this postmodern culture—among them, "a new depthlessness," "a consequent weakening of historicity," "a whole new type of emotional ground tone" (58), and the dissolution of the individual subject—but a new sense of space seems to hold a privileged position. The preoccupation of modernism with "the elegiac mysteries of *durée* and of memory" (64) have been replaced within the postmodern by a comparably intense concern with spatial questions. This apparent shift makes Jameson's interest in contemporary architecture especially relevant. He analyzes John Portman's Bonaventura Hotel in Los Angeles as postmodern, and suggests that the building aspires less to be a part of its environment than to be "a total space, a complete world, a kind of miniature city" (81), capable of replacing the city itself. Its interior is a stage for continual movement via escalators and exposed elevators; but what most distinguishes the building is the way it deprives patrons of spatial coordinates so that they are often unable to relocate shops on its balconies. Jameson believes that the confusion felt by the visitor to the Bonaventura Hotel is the architectural equivalent of a more fundamental confusion felt by inhabitants of the postmodern era; namely, our inability "to map the great global multinational and decentered communicational network in which we find ourselves caught as individual subjects" (84). Postmodern architecture, in Jameson's eyes, reproduces the experiential conditions of multinational capitalism.

In a review of two recent novels, Don Delillo's *The Names* and Sol Yurick's *Richard A.,* Jameson illustrates how this difficulty manifests itself within fiction. The latter is a version of the common conspiracy novel (the postmodern, says Jameson, effects a new relation with the forms of popular culture [PC 54-55]); it uses the image of the telephone system to suggest the ways in which people's lives have become interconnected. That image represents Yurick's attempt to conceptualize or map the locations of his characters within a world as disorienting as Portman's hotel. Delillo's narrator is an American abroad, an employee of a risk insurance firm, who is increasingly unable to assess the risks in an increasingly dangerous world. He picks up pieces of information, fragments of puzzling knowledge, but cannot make them cohere into anything resembling a map of his surroundings. Each of these

novels, according to Jameson, struggles with the special spatial dilemma of contemporary life: "That dilemma can be schematically described as the increasing incompatibility—or incommensurability—between individual experience, existential experience, as we go on looking for it in individual biological bodies, and structural meaning, which can now ultimately derive only from the world system of multinational capitalism" (116). The solutions found in these works differ markedly: Yurick constructs an image that evokes the interconnections that cannot be directly experienced, whereas Delillo renders the experience of living amidst fragments that, however suggestive of some larger order, resist our effort to piece them together.

Jameson's account of the postmodern is immensely suggestive. He seems to be a person unable to forget or ignore anything; his work, accordingly, invariably contains striking analogies and connections among the most disparate phenomena. I have only sketched a portion of his argument, but it should be clear that his conception of the postmodern differs strikingly from those discussed earlier. In particular, Jameson's postmodern is systematically a period concept, one that reaches not only across various movements and genres, but as well across the various arts and other social institutions in the contemporary world. Its very reach, however, produces an order of difficulties distinct from those discussed in regard to Hassan, Klinkowitz, and Wilde.

As we have seen, Jameson coordinates an apparent preoccupation with space with the establishment of a genuinely multinational economic system. He recognizes, of course, that the economic system became increasingly international throughout the earlier period of monopoly capitalism, as previously isolated cultures were penetrated and opened as markets. Jameson believes, however, that the effects upon local cultures of these earlier penetrations were comparably benign and that they are now being dramatically transformed as the logic of multinational capitalism takes hold on a global scale. I am not in a position to judge the adequacy of such sweeping claims; I do question, however, some of the cultural consequences Jameson would derive from them. In particular, I question his claim that contemporary arts are uniquely concerned with locating the individual within some "postmodern hyperspace" (83). Jameson himself makes substantial use of Kevin Lynch's *The Image of the City,* which argues that the "alienated city is above all a space in which people are unable to map (in their minds) either their own positions or the urban totality in which they find themselves" (89). Such cities and the confusions to which they give rise predate postmodernism, but Jameson nowhere differentiates specifically postmodern forms. Similarly, since at least the early years of this century Western culture has been exploring the implications of an increasingly interconnected world; such explorations have taken various forms, such as the use of artist resources drawn from other cultures, and the depiction of travel through distant and disorienting lands. The culminating achievement of Jameson's most recent book, *The Political Unconscious,* is his reading of Conrad's

Lord Jim, one of many exemplary works concerned with such issues. Neither experiences of spatial dislocation nor the existence of a multinational world, in other words, are unique to the last decade. The manifestations of both might have changed and become more pronounced, but Jameson would then have to demonstrate how differences in intensity have become differences in kind, such that one can speak of a distinctly postmodern disorientation. I suspect that Jameson's reliance upon Mandel's economic stages compels him to make claims for corresponding cultural transformations that he has not as yet adequately supported.

As we have seen, architecture holds a special place within Jameson's conception of postmodern culture. Not only is it the art primarily concerned with the spaces we inhabit; the recent debates within architecture have also informed Jameson's own formulations in important ways. Within architecture, the claims for postmodernism have developed in an especially clear way, and Jameson has largely appropriated these claims for more sweeping purposes. I believe that the reason postmodernism has emerged with special clarity within architecture has to do largely with the remarkable agreement within that field about the nature of modernism, the aesthetic it would replace. Architectural modernism consists largely of the so-called International Style. The increasingly strident reaction against the main tenets of this style is carried out in the name of postmodernism. The comparative uniformity of architectural modernism lends credibility to the claims of its new rivals that they constitute a genuinely postmodern alternative.

The situation within architecture, in other words, is quite different from that within the other arts, particularly literature. Literary modernism, as we have seen, has been characterized by a great diversity of separate movements and styles. It possesses nothing comparable to the Seagram Building. Since many different and competing aesthetic programs collectively constitute literary modernism, the claims of any particular program to supercede literary modernism per se must be scrutinized with some care; upon inspection, as we have seen, such programs are likely to represent new alternatives within modernism, not alternatives to it. The claims for the emergence of a genuine architectural postmodernism, on the other hand, possess a greater initial credibility due to the more monolithic quality of its predecessor.

Different cultural spheres, then, seemingly require different conceptualizations in terms of periods. By way of explanation, it might be said that different spheres evolve at different paces, depending upon a welter of factors, including both internal dynamics and their locations within the culture as a whole. In the case at hand, however, it is probably more to the point that the parallel between literary and architectural modernism was never more than an analogy. That is, roughly contemporary movements within architecture and literature were both termed modernism, but their contemporaneity and designations were all that they had in common. The mere fact

that both have been termed modernism has clearly tempted many to claim more substantial similarities between them, or to see both as manifestations of an overarching cultural shift; but such findings have invariably been metaphoric or analogic: architectural and literary modernism have about as much in common as any two contemporaries named John Smith.

Jameson, in brief, errs in attempting to apply the debate within contemporary architectural circles to contemporary culture generally. What might be true of one art need not be true of others. In particular, a genuine postmodern alternative might be emerging within architecture; but we have less reason to believe that a corresponding phenomenon is occurring within literature, due to the different nature of what is called literary modernism. A rhetoric of postmodernism might be common to both fields, but in the latter it is misplaced, at most a sign of impatience. Since Jameson is attempting to develop a period concept that encompasses all of social life, he presumes that changes occur across a broad front and thus discounts the conditions specific to discrete cultural spheres. As a Marxist, Jameson knows that contending energies are likely to be operative at any particular time, and that resolutions among them achieved in one sphere need not have occurred elsewhere. Social life changes unevenly. In his work on postmodernism, however, Jameson's awareness of these facts remains theoretical; whenever he gets to actual cases, postmodernism seems to be progressing apace in every cultural sphere.

If Jameson sometimes argues that significant changes are occurring within all cultural spheres, at other times his argument for an emergent postmodern culture takes a different form:

> The first point to be made about the conception of periodization in dominance, therefore, is that even if all the constitutive features of postmodernism were identical and continuous with those of an older modernism—a position I feel to be demonstrably erroneous but which only an even lengthier analysis of modernism proper could dispel—the two phenomena would still remain utterly distinct in their meaning and social function, owing to the very different positioning of postmodernism in the economic system of late capital, and beyond that, to the transformation of the very sphere of culture in contemporary society. (PC 57)

Jameson here argues that the conditions under which cultural production and reception take place have so changed that culture itself has been thoroughly transformed. I in fact agree with this assessment, but would not go on to say that we therefore now have a postmodern literary culture. American literary modernism was crucially shaped by its relations with the whole of contemporary social life; but it is best *defined* by the set of strategies it developed in response, and thus by the relations it establishes with the contemporary social order. Consistency would seem to demand that a proper literary postmodernism be defined in the same manner; that is, not alone by the social conditions in which it reaches us, but as well by the strategies it deploys for existing within those conditions.

Jameson is currently embarked upon an anatomy of contemporary culture; literary matters obviously figure in this undertaking, but only in a subsidiary manner. The entire undertaking is prone to the kind of error we have already seen in regard to his generalization of architectural debates. It is instructive to compare the difficulties encountered by Jameson in developing a conception of postmodernism with those encountered by Klinkowitz and Wilde. The latter, as we saw, generated initially plausible definitions of the postmodern by countering it with an impoverished sense of modernism. In particular, they failed to acknowledge that modernism is a second-order, period concept, and thus proposed definitions of postmodernism that could as well or better be conceived as developments within modernism itself. Jameson, on the other hand, knows that modernism is a period concept. His generalization of the situation within architecture, however, provides him with a fairly monolithic modernism against which he can conceive a postmodern alternative. Architectural modernism, in brief, serves the same function in Jameson's formulations that absolute irony serves in Wilde's. Since he conceives postmodernism as a period concept, Jameson then wants to locate parallel developments in other cultural spheres. In the process, however, he typically minimizes crucial differences among the spheres, thereby creating the erroneous appearance of a culture undergoing change in a fairly uniform manner. Jameson knows that cultural change is an uneven affair, but the ambition to describe an entire cultural transformation apparently leads him to pay more attention to claims for cultural change, and then to lend his voice to them, than the available evidence seems to warrant.

IV

Our survey of difficulties encountered in proposing definitions of some emergent postmodernism leads to several proposals. First, before we can speak meaningfully of the postmodern we require an adequate conception of modernism. That conception, at least in regard to literary modernism, must guard against mistaking one of its constitutive movements (Surrealism, for example) for modernism itself; it must, that is, be a period concept, able to clarify what its different and competing movements have in common. That definition, too, should be specific to literature. The existence of something termed modernism in other cultural realms does not mean that these various artistic modernisms have much in common. Different cultural realms have different histories, needs, and opportunities; and these differences combine to assure that "modernism" will mean different things in each. Finally, we should profit from the example of Wilde and at least initially confine our investigations of literary modernism to individual national traditions. Otherwise we too are likely to mistake differences between national literatures for developments within literature itself. Different national literatures differ in the same ways that literature differs

from architecture; since at any given time a national literature represents a specific disposition of cultural forces, each reacts uniquely to any attempt to introduce new and necessarily competing aesthetic programs. The distinctive colorations achieved by literary modernism within the British and American traditions are largely due to the native traditions, with their existing relations among competing interests.[5] It seems only prudent, therefore, that we attend to the configuration achieved by literary modernism within single national literatures before venturing more expansive characterizations of it. This research strategy was recently pursued successfully by June Howard, whose *Form and Function in American Literary Naturalism* conceives the work of Jack London and others as responses to the particular disposition of social and literary forces in the United States at the turn of the century. I am suggesting, in short, that we pursue a comparable program in regard to American literary modernism, for until we have an adequate conception of literary modernism, all claims for anything called postmodernism, like those addressed here, are likely to be premature.

It might be argued that these difficulties in establishing the canon and shape of a nascent postmodernism are only to be expected. The argument might invoke the authority of Thomas Kuhn, and claim that such critics are attempting to describe a shift between prevailing paradigms, and that such confusions are characteristic of transitional periods, times that lack the securities provided by stable intellectual coordinates. The tools of the old order are not appropriate to the new, assuring that those who use them will fail; the intellectual tools of the new order, on the other hand, are either unfamiliar or not yet to hand, with the result that their use is uncertain. Such arguments beg the question. They assume that we are in fact witnessing the emergence of some genuinely postmodern culture, whereas I want to question that assumption. It seems to me at least equally plausible that what some are calling postmodernism is actually a late development or mutation within modernism itself. I have presented several arguments to support my contention: (1) that no satisfactory and widely accepted account of postmodernism now exists; (2) that much of what is called postmodern in fact derives directly from modernism; and (3) that most arguments for its existence achieve their initial plausibility largely through impovershed characterizations of modernism, especially characterizations that neglect its nature as a second-order concept.

I suspect that the term's currency has more to do with impatience than with actual conceptual shifts. Modernism has been with us for the better part of the century. Its own restless search for innovation in part informs efforts to move beyond it. Some contemporary writers want to claim for their own efforts as radical a departure from now established strategies as that achieved earlier in the century. All honor seems to belong to the founders, and these writers want to avoid thinking of themselves as like Kuhn's normal scientists, working out the residual problems left them by the true innovators. Comparable motives inspire their academic apologists. In the end, as Frank Kermode has shown, there is considerable satisfaction in believing that one inhabits a cusp between eras, not the least of which is the belief that one is replicating the heroic phase of modernism. We might sympathize with such desires, but it seems to me that we should receive announcements of postmodernism's arrival as skeptically as we do commercials for other new products in the marketplace.

Whatever the merits of my arguments, the term "postmodern" has entered our lexicon and will doubtless continue to be used. Too many factors conspire to keep it in circulation, not least of which is inertia, the tendency for anything once set in motion to continue on its way. At the moment, however, the term is an empty marker. It holds a place in our language for a concept that might one day prove necessary; in the meantime, it is the recipient of the ambitions and apprehensions that our prospects for the future evoke.

NOTES

[1] The first two terms appear in *Literary Disruptions,* the third in *The Life of Fiction,* and the last in *The Self-Apparent Word.* Unless otherwise indicated, all quotations of Klinkowitz are from *Literary Disruptions.*

[2] This claim obviously puts Wilde's conception of postmodernism at odds with Hassan's and in line with Klinkowitz's and Rother's.

[3] The tendency to reduce modernism to some caricature of itself in order to get a definition of postmodernism off the ground is especially strong when critics define both terms simply against each other and in isolation from the implicit series of period concepts; see, for example, Lodge.

[4] "Postmodernism" 54. Unless otherwise indicated, all quotations of Jameson are from this essay.

[5] Compare the opening sentences of Jeffrey Herf's *Reactionary Modernism:* "There is no such thing as modernity in general. There are only national societies, each of which becomes modern in its own fashion" (1). Herf studies a phenomenon much wider than literary, architectural, or any other specific cultural modernism, but his research strategy resembles my proposals.

WORKS CITED

Barthelme, Donald. "After Joyce." *Location* 1 (1964): 13-16.

Elkin, Stanley. Interview, *Contemporary Literature* 16 (1975): 131-45.

Federman, Raymond. "Surfiction—Four Propositions in Form of an Introduction." In *Surfiction: Fiction Now and Tomorrow.* Ed. Raymond Federman, 5-15. Chicago: Swallow, 1975.

Hassan, Ihab. *Paracriticisms: Seven Speculations of the Times.* Urbana: U. of Illinois Press, 1975.

Herf, Jeffrey. *Reactionary Modernism: Technology, Culture, and Politics in Weimar and the Third Reich.* New York: Cambridge University Press, 1984.

Howard, June. *Form and Function in American Literary Naturalism.* Chapel Hill: U. of North Carolina Press, 1985.

Jameson, Fredric. "Periodizing the Sixties." In *The Sixties without Apologies.* Ed. Sohnya Sayres et al., 178-209. Minneapolis: U. of Minnesota Press, 1984.

————"The Politics of Theory: Ideological Positions in the Postmodernism Debate." *New German Critique* 33 (1984): 53-65.

————"Postmodernism, or the Cultural Logic of Late Capitalism." *New Left Review* 146 (1984): 53-92.

————Review of *The Names,* by Don Delillo, and *Richard A.,* by Sol Yurick. *Minnesota Review* 22 (1984): 116-22.

————"Wallace Stevens." *New Orleans Review* 11 (1984): 10-19.

Kermode, Frank. *The Sense of an Ending: Studies in the Theory of Fiction.* New York: Oxford University Press, 1967.

Klinkowitz, Jerome. *The Life of Fiction.* Urbana: U. of Illinois Press, 1977.

————*Literary Disruptions: The Making of a Post-Contemporary American Fiction.* Urbana: U. of Illinois Press, 1975.

————*The Self-Apparent Word: Fiction As Language / Language As Fiction.* Carbondale: Southern Illinois University Press, 1984.

Lodge, David. *The Modes of Modern Writing: Metaphor, Metonymy, and the Typology of Modern Literature.* Ithaca: Cornell University Press, 1977.

McCaffery, Larry. *The Metafictional Muse: The Work of Robert Coover, Donald Barthelme, and William Gass.* Pittsburgh: U. of Pittsburgh Press, 1982.

Rother, James. "Parafiction: The Adjacent Universe of Barth, Barthelme, Pynchon, and Nabokov." *Boundary* 25 (1976): 21-43.

Scholes, Robert. *Fabulation and Metafiction.* Urbana: U. of Illinois Press, 1979.

Wilde, Alan. *Horizons of Assent: Modernism, Postmodernism, and the Ironic Imagination.* Baltimore: Johns Hopkins University Press, 1981.

CRITICISM

Richard E. Palmer

SOURCE: "Postmodernity and Hermeneutics," in *boundary 2,* Vol. V, No. 2, 1977, pp. 363-93.

[*In the following essay, Palmer defends his postulation that postmodernism is an aesthetic movement of limited duration, and that modernity indicates the era beginning with the Renaissance and continuing into the present.*]

I. BEYOND POSTMODERNISM TO POSTMODERNITY

"These are apocalyptic times, Doctor," says Strelnikov in *Doctor Zhivago,* and the same might be said today. Andrew Hacker has said that we stand at "the end of the American era,"[1] but the more sobering thought is that we stand at the end of the modern era, an era stretching back not just two hundred but five hundred years. The "storming of the mind" to which Robert Hunter refers[2] is the storming of the modern mind: not the mind of modernism, the *modern mind.*

Something like a general effort to break out of the limits of "modern" thinking is becoming evident today on many fronts. There is the practical gesture of deserting urban life to join an alternative community. In fact "alternatives" are springing up around us: alternative education, alternative agriculture, alternative medicine, alternative nutrition. In the academy, the revolt against positivism is gaining ground in psychology, sociology, political science, philosophy, and other disciplines. In literature there is the rejection of tradition, of coherence and rationality, of nameability. (Beckett: "In the silence, you don't know, you must go on, I can't go on, you must go on, I can't go on, I'll go on"—*The Unnamable.*) In literary interpretation, one finds efforts to move beyond formalism and merely rhetorical criticism—speech act theory as the basis for a new criticism, new literary history, and more recently "deconstructionist" theories of language and text. The aestheticism inherent in formalist poetics becomes increasingly inadequate to the kinds of literature that are appearing and to the kinds of experience with a text which the reader may be seeking.

In literature and literary theory, the revolt against modernism—however one may choose to define the term—should be seen within the context of a whole constellation of rebellions. This means much more than recognizing that modernism is a phenomenon in music, representational arts, theater, painting, and so on; it means sensing something of the larger significance of these rebellions as part of the winding down of modernity itself. This winding-down is taking place in many different forms and levels of human endeavor; it involves a major change in worldview. I am suggesting that we should see postmodernism in the context of this larger transformation to which I have given the name postmodernity.

Postmodernism and postmodernity differ, then, profoundly. Postmodernism is something like a movement or current of thought, whereas the term postmodernity points to a diverse range of activities—indeed to a coming era of time. Postmodernism might last a decade or two, postmodernity some five hundred years; or perhaps all the time after the end of the "modern era," which I take to occupy the period from about 1480 to the present, perhaps to 1987. (This is the date the Aztec calendar predicts as the end of the age, and also the end of a sequence of five ages.[3]) *The New Yorker* can announce that "postmodernism is dead" and suggest that "post-postmodernism" is now the thing;[4] on the other hand, postmodernity is not a movement and its death cannot be announced. Moreover, the modernism to which postmodernism is "post" was a literary-artistic movement in France, then Spain, then England and the Americas.[5] Modernity, however, does not refer to "modernism" at all but to the five-hundred year cultural epoch in Europe extending from the Renaissance to the present. This epoch, I believe, is drawing to an end as we prepare for the transition to a "postmodern" consciousness and a "postmodern" era.

The vast difference in meaning between postmodernism and postmodernity has consequences for postmodern literary theory. As radical as postmodernism may seem to its exponents in the arts and in critical theory, it barely hints at the kind of epochal change implied in the term postmodernity. For instance, the postmodern literary theorist may be quite ready to reject the aesthetics (and aestheticism) of modernism as static and logocentric and to make a new start in terms of literary form, but he may balk at rejecting the heritage of humanism. The place of man at the center of things, of reason as man's best hope against the powers of irrationality, of nature as essentially separate from and alien to the being of man—these must remain axiomatic even while great changes in style and value take place. To call into question the heritage of humanistic rationality, the humanistic view of the world, the humanistic conception of the status of man in the cosmos—that would be going too far. So the postmodern artist and literary theorist may be ready for postmodernism but not for postmodernity.

To turn against modernity itself means to call the modern epoch, with all its artistic, scientific, and cultural grandeur, all its huge successes, into question. It involves the need for radical thinking—that is, thinking that goes to the roots. It means examining the foundations of modern thinking that took shape in the Renaissance: the secular self-assertion, the frenzy to measure everything—Galileo's famous maxim was "To measure everything measurable and to make measurable what is not yet measurable!"—and the effect of dichotomization between a monadic, observing subjectivity and a world of (essentially material) objects. It means calling into question the Enlightenment's faith in endless progress through scientific rationality. And it means exploring the impact of the rise of perspective on the structure of modern consciousness: the tendency to "see" in terms of extension and the situated observing eye, the spatializing of objects and of time—and ultimately the dominance of spatializing modes of thought. William Ivins has called this process "the rationalization of sight."[6] In Heideggerian terms, the turn against modernity involves calling the "subjectism" (*Subjektität*) and "will to power" at the heart of technology into question and realizing the extent to which they shape modern thought.[7]

It is one thing for the urban intellectual in New York or Paris to join the avant-garde theoretical critique of modernism; it is quite another matter to call liberal humanism and the beauties of traditional humanistic rationality into question. Alternative definitions of the nature of the real—such as Zen Buddhism, the reality experienced by primitives and shamans, the egolessness of schizophrenia—would shake the foundations of rationality and must be rejected. That would be "getting irrational." To talk about "epochal transformations of culture" (William Irwin Thompson), or the "rhapsodic intellect" (Theodore Roszak), or the "separate reality" of the shaman (Carlos Castaneda), or religious transcendence in relation to schizophrenia (R.D. Laing), would be to turn away from the only realistic response to the hard problems of today—technological rationality. It would be taking interplanetary refuge from the reality of stinking rivers.[8] the hard realities of unemployment, pollution, inflation, overpopulation, energy shortage, and so on, cannot—say the humanists—be solved by retreat into orientalism, romanticism, or schizophrenia. One can, as a liberal, academic, humanistic intellectual, protest against metaphysical thinking without going off the deep end.

Clearly, then, it is one thing to call modernism into question and quite another to try to venture beyond modernity itself. To be a "postmodern literary theorist" may not change anything about the way one is doing business as a liberal, urban, academic intellectual. To take the turn toward postmodernity, on the other hand, calls the benefits of *modernization* itself into question.[9] It calls the academic system, with all its sophisticated testing, into question.[10] It calls the liberal solutions to social problems into question. The "postmodern literary theorist" may be ready for sophisticated talk about language, philosophy, and social evils, but not for a real revolution—in either academia or society at large.

Whether or not we stand "at the edge of history," as William Irwin Thompson believes,[11] or at a transitional point on the way to a new epoch and a "new consciousness" which will be as different from the modern as it was from the pre-modern (as Jean Gebser argues[12]), certainly a broad spectrum of thinking today is attempting to venture "beyond modernity."[13] The thinkers in this spectrum do not represent a single, unified standpoint, nor even the cohesiveness of a movement that could be labelled an "ism." The term "postmodern" is not generally associated with them. Yet they provide a more encompassing context of rebellious thinking within which to place the more distinct phenomenon of postmodernism. Furthermore, many of their views have profound implications for hermeneutics, affecting the basic terms of the hermeneutical situation. Accordingly, the next section will review

ten distinct versions of postmodernity which have a direct significance for hermeneutics.

II. BEYOND MODERNITY (OR: SOME VERSIONS OF POSTMODERN[14])

1. *Outgrowing the epistemological self-portrait of modernity*

In his important work *Human Understanding*, Stephen Toulmin argues that the epistemological self-image of modern man inherited from the seventeenth century does not cohere with recent thinking in the sciences.[15] Scientists on the growing edge of thought today simply do not make use of the presuppositions of rationalist thought, yet these presuppositions persist because no one has come forward to articulate a clear "epistemological self-portrait" of man as viewed in contemporary models of thought. Consequently, present-day lay views of man tend to make assumptions about time, substance, mind and body, causality, and so on, that have been left behind in contemporary scientific theory. Toulmin's project is to bring epistemology up to date.

This version of postmodernity is perhaps the least radical of the ten we will discuss, since Toulmin does not venture to question scientific rationality as such but rather tries to bring contemporary epistemology (especially analytic philosophy) into harmony with advanced scientific theory. (At the end of his first chapter, Toulmin pays homage to Descartes' quest for firm, verifiable knowledge, and he claims only to be trying to bring Descartes up to date—one might say to "demythologize" him.) Yet Toulmin is important to the quest for a postmodern view of man because he is able, from within contemporary philosophy of science, to demonstrate the untenability of basic axioms of modern thought rooted in Descartes.

It is important and only fair to recognize that within contemporary science itself are modes of thought totally out of harmony with our inherited spatialized, perspectival awareness.[16] For example, I see Jürgen Habermas' *Logik der Sozialwissenschaften* and his more recent *Knowledge and Human Interests* (trans. 1971) as offering a valuable articulation of the ways in which the goals of scientific knowledge dictate in advance the shape of that knowledge. Habermas follows Nietzsche in seeing all knowledge as shaped by certain overriding "interests," and insists that it is the task of philosophy to explore the connection between the shape of knowledge and the goals of knowledge.[17] The case against the illusions of a one-dimensional, objectivist view of knowledge (and of man) can thus arise from *within* scientific thinking itself.

2. *Postmodernity and the project of going beyond metaphysics*

In philosophy since Descartes and Bacon, and especially since Locke and Hume, the underlying goal has been to extricate thought from metaphysics—or, to use a more loaded term, "superstition." The dream of Descartes one November night in 1619 was the achievement of a single body of verified knowledge in every area of human endeavor. And the obvious way to such a body of knowledge was to be a method that set up criteria for achieving it. Hume, then Kant, then Nietzsche took up the fight against "metaphysics." Kant, as Foucault has noted, preserved the autonomy and freedom of man only by making him an "empirical-transcendental doublet,"[18] thus escaping the depressing metaphysical consequences of Hume's radical empiricism. Yet this solution only substituted the metaphysical presuppositions of German idealism for the metaphysics of the great rationalists—Descartes, Spinoza, Leibniz, and Wolff.

It is Nietzsche, the relentless iconoclast, who goes to the roots of modern thought and who, in my opinion, is philosophically the door to postmodernity a door entered by Heidegger with results more radical than Nietzsche himself would have dreamed.[19] Nietzsche attacked Descartes, Kant, Schopenhauer, Christianity (as a life-denying form of Platonism-for-the-masses), scientific objectivity, romanticism, Wagner, morality, contemporary art, Germans, and so on. When Nietzsche was through "philosophizing with a hammer," the thought-forms on which the nineteenth century lived were in pieces. Nietzsche's thought was a conflagration, a purification of modern thought, and a careful study of his work is radical therapy for many illusions in twentieth-century thought.

Nietzsche passionately hated his own time, which he identified with the untragic this-worldliness of the Greek Alexandrian age. The modern age, he argued, lives on the lethal legacy of Socratic thinking—grounded in abstractions and theories, and willing to die for truths produced by rational deduction. Modernity, as Nietzsche saw it, is a combination of Alexandrian this-worldly triviality and Socratic absurd logocentrism. Nietzsche attacked the metaphysical view that man is a "thinking thing" or some kind of mental substance lodged in inert matter. This Cartesian dualism creates the "mind-body problem" and a view of man as a "ghost in a machine" (to use Gilbert Ryle's famous phrase from *Concept of Mind*). Nietzsche questioned whether what we call "consciousness" is truly the seat and core of subjectivity; rather, he suggested that in each human being a plurality of interpretative principles or centers (*Herrschaftszentren*)), like medieval fiefdoms, are in tension and competition with each other. Waking consciousness is only one of these centers, and perhaps a monitor of things rather than king of them all. He resolutely denied every metaphysical order of reality—that is, any order of reality above and outside the phenomenal world in which we have our experience. Such a belief, he held, was merely a form of Platonism. No firm and enduring "reality" lies behind the phenomenal world—no *Hinterwelt*.

For Nietzsche, human knowledge does not represent a contact with a "truth" behind phenomena; rather, it is a function of our life-goals. As Habermas has articulated it in the present decade, knowledge is "interest-guided."

Objective, scientific knowledge does not give us the form of the "way things are"; it is fabricated by the artistry of understanding in conformity with the purpose of gaining control over nature. If our interest or aim were different, our knowledge would take another form. Habermas, for instance, distinguishes the knowledge-guiding interests of the empirical-analytic sciences (a technical-cognitive interest) from the historical-hermeneutic sciences (a practical and action-orienting interest), both of which differ from the "critical sciences," which are neither technical nor pragmatic but emancipatory. Psychoanalysis is an example of the latter and is for Habermas the model of emancipatory reflection. Habermas attaches a special importance to emancipatory reflection for through its reflexivity man liberates himself from illusions. The knowledge gained from emancipatory reflection, unlike the other forms of knowledge, is worthless unless the subject himself is liberated through it. In its philosophical form, "critical theory" has the function of turning reflection back on the agent. Habermas holds that for this reason it goes beyond merely "hermeneutical" reflection to a form of thought that frees man from the internal and external chains of ideology.[20]

We could say, then, that Nietzsche, and after him, Habermas (as well as Marx and Freud) show the *ideological* character of human knowledge, shattering the firm underpinnings for knowledge as something grounded in immutable principles or transcendental categories. Thus, Nietzsche went beyond an attack on metaphysics to argue that knowledge itself, as the artistry of an interest-guided understanding, cannot be "truth" in the old rationalist sense. There are only different forms of "fiction." What we call "truths," said Nietzsche, are merely the useful "fictions" by which we live.[21]

3. Transcending objectivism and technological rationality

Perhaps nothing is more characteristic of modernity than the growth of science and technology. In premodern times (say, before 1480), human calculative reason was rated as only one among the several capacities of man, and it was always kept "in its place." With the rise of perspective (for with perspective came the spatializing and mathematizing of human reason), the powers of mind to control nature technologically were multiplied many fold. Perspective also separated the viewer of the world from what surrounded him, and by defining objects in terms of extension, of mass, perspective laid the foundations for the familiar Cartesian (and modern) dualism between a nonmaterial consciousness and a world of material objects. Galileo's maxim, "To measure everything measurable and to make what is unmeasurable measurable." may be called the slogan of the modern era. Time, too, came to be conceived in spatial terms, as the visual faculty began subtly to dictate the forms of modern thought. Being became "being-in-space" and time became a measured, linear continuum. An abstract, mental world of measurements, formulae, and conceptual thinking increasingly enabled modern man to take charge of his world.

Perspective, then, is more important than one might at first think. It furnishes the foundation for the spatialized thinking of modernity and the rise of mathematical geometry, which is the prerequisite for building modern machinery, as well as the natural basis for the metaphysics of objectivity. To it can be traced the problems that have dominated modern philosophy—the mind-body problem, the subject-object dichotomy, and the epistemological foundations for both rationalist and empiricist thought.[22] The quest for verifiable knowledge rests on the assumption of a central, verifying subject, with a method or set of definitions that gives sense to the world. The ego-centric, humanistic, and reason-centered cast of modern thought is rooted in the perspectivist model epitomized in Dürer's famous woodcut of a man looking through a grid as he draws a human body. The abstractness, the reduction of the model to spatial squares, the separation of the observer from the object, so that it appears to him only in terms of extension—these are all reflected in the famous woodcut. The saying of Protagoras that "man is the measure of all things" depends for its meaning on the dimensions of man. A definition of man emphasizing his spiritual nature will provide a different measure, however, than a merely humanistic definition. One might say in general that with the rise of perspective, *measurement*—that is, extension—becomes the measure of all things.

William Blake and the great romantic poets, especially Wordsworth, were among the first really effective voices of protest against modernity, and they were among the first to perceive the inner relationship of modernity to objectivizing and technological thought. Blake attacks the "single vision" of Newton's sleep which manacles the mind. The visionary gleam whose loss Wordsworth laments with the passing of childhood is the light of a way of seeing before reason and morality separated man from nature.[23] Yet pleas on behalf of nature, imagination, and the life of the senses could not halt the movement of invention, exploration, annexation, and exploitation spreading itself across the modern scene. In fact, the romantic protest seemed to point away from the central thrust of social development and invention to aesthetic escapes that belong after business hours. Romantic and postromantic literature and art became the compensation for an increasingly machine-dominated economic system.

Among the most trenchant critics of contemporary technology is Theodore Roszak, who consciously goes back to romanticist thought and visionary reality. His first major work, *The Making of a Counter Culture,* attempted to articulate a critique of technological rationality and scientific objectivity. Although probably more an attempt to supply after the fact a theoretical background for the counterculture than a description of the beliefs and motives of the quotidian cultural dropout, Roszak's work offers a sharp critique of prevailing cultural assumptions and reveals some of the seamy side of the modern idolatry of objectivity. *Where the Wasteland Ends* and, most recently, his *Unfinished Animal* continue and expand the critique, with explicit philosophical dependence on romantic and visionary realities.[24]

The case against technological rationality is stated with trenchancy on quite different philosophical foundations by Philip Slater and by Herbert Marcuse. Slater attacks the ideals on which American capitalist individualism is based, especially the pursuit of lonely success through competition. Technology is the perfect instrument for these ideals, yet it is self-defeating. "Technology," says Slater, "is an extension of the scarcity-oriented, security-minded, control-oriented side of man's nature, expressed vis-a-vis a world perceived as unloving, ungiving, and unsatisfying."[25] For Slater the solution is to turn away from the masculine virtues toward the feminine. Yet "Western culture is *founded* on the oppression of women and of the values associated with them: wholeness, continuity, communion, humanism, feelings, the body, connectedness, harmony."[26] No less penetrating in his criticisms of a technologized rationality that leads to modern "one-dimensional man," Herbert Marcuse bases his case on assumptions derived from Hegel, Marx, and Freud.[27] Marcuse argues for a transcendence that is able to overshoot and comprehend the prevailing structures of thought and the culturally created needs generated by them. We should be seeking not just more and better ways of meeting our "needs" as presently conceived, but a "redefinition of needs." In arguing for such a transcendence, Marcuse offers a postmodern global critique of the prevailing culture.

But unlike Slater and Roszak, Marcuse takes a basically Freudian attitude toward "irrationality" and civilization; he argues that only Reason (*Vernunft*)—some kind of post-technological rationality—will meet man's present crisis. Man frees himself from Nature and creates civilization through Reason, and it is only through Reason that man can realize himself as an historical being. "Civilization produces the means of freeing Nature from its own brutality . . . by virtue of the cognitive and transforming power of Reason. And Reason can fulfill this function only as post-technological rationality, in which technic is itself the instrumentality of pacification."[28] Marcuse obviously defines reason as much more than the mere calculative faculty in man. It is something like "mind" or "spirit." By following the Freudian analysis of desire and of cultural repression, Marcuse can define liberation in terms of a social order free of repression of desire and free of the artificial needs created by the present one-dimensional rationality—without having recourse to romantic terms like a "rhapsodized intellect" (Roszak), post-humanistic "visionary reality" (Roszak and others), or Slater's "feminine values." For Marcuse, irrationality and mysticism are not the way beyond technological rationality; what is needed is a new rationality that can control technique in behalf of liberation instead of repression, the satisfaction of eros without the abandonment of civilization.

Critiques of technology and technological objectivity are also found in Nietzsche, Heidegger, and Hans-Georg Gadamer. Indeed, it is not too much to say that the thinking of all three overshoots the basic horizons of modern technologized thought.[29] Nietzsche saw through modern objectivity as a disguised form of the will to power over nature: the heart of technology, therefore, is the will to power. Heidegger took the definitively postmodern step, however, in negating the will to power, subject-centeredness, and humanism itself. Heidegger argued that man must take a "step back" from *das vorstellende Denken*—representational thought. He must, in other words, take the step back from everything that has been constituted by the structure of modern thought. He must call subject-centeredness and humanism into question. He must call into question the presupposition that we must continue indefinitely in a time from which the gods and all divinity have fled. We must redefine what it means to "be" in the world and in the matrix of time; we must reask the most fundamental question of all—the meaning of being. Gadamer, as a follower of Heidegger, criticizes the modern conception of consciousness as inherited from Descartes and Kant, and even the "transcendental subjectivity" of Husserl. Aesthetics has been "subjectivized" since Kant, he argues, and needs to be put on a whole new footing.[30] The subject-centeredness of modern thinking gives us a distorted view of language and of dialogue. Ultimately, it gives us a false view of understanding as unhistorical and undialectical. Although he does not philosophize with a hammer, like Nietzsche, nor urge us to leap back from all representational thought, like the later Heidegger, Gadamer does so alter the fundamental notions on which modern interpretation operates that one has the feeling of transcending the general horizons of modern thought.

4. A. "New Gnosticism": Ihab Hassan

The technophobia—if one may call it that—found in Heidegger, Slater, and Roszak is by no means the definitive characteristic of postmodernity—a consoling fact, since we seem fated to live in an electronic and technological world for the forseeable future. Is it possible to articulate a perspective that does not uncritically surrender to either technophiles or technophobes? Ihab Hassan, an important literary theorist of postmodernism, believes that it is—that thought today is, under the influence of instantaneous electronic communication and other factors, moving toward a kind of gnosticism; but a "new gnosticism" appropriate to the postmodern age.[31]

Hassan notes "the growing insistence of Mind to apprehend reality im-mediately; to gather more and more mind in itself: thus to become its own reality. Consciousness becomes all, and as in a gnostic dream, matter dissolves before Light" (P, 122-23). The world in its solidity is dematerializing before our eyes. It is becoming all interpretation. "The syntropic force of consciousness is remaking our world in every way" (P, 124). In the wholeness of consciousness the extremes of arcadia, as dreamed by the technophobes, and utopia, as dreamed by the technophiles, come together. The two sides of reality—earth and sky, myth and technology, female and male, Eden and Utopia, first and last—form a unity in consciousness. For Hassan, the new technology is not some *bête noire* but a kind of magic that, in its instantaneity,

images an overcoming of all mediation. "Technology, like myth, suggests that man is creating a universal consciousness which renders mediated actions and speech gradually obsolete. A measure of radical American innocence is required to hold this view." (P, 138).

For Hassan, then, contemporary philosophical and scientific thinking at its best has messianic and mystical tendencies. It is not leading us into a jungle of materialistic barbarism or an abyss of triviality and shallowness, but upward into a mystical participation in universal consciousness—what Tielhard called the noösphere. It is the beginning and end of consciousness, the realm of dream and of creativity. "The dreaming animal, floating between his inner and outer worlds, began to weave the web of consciousness, of his language, culture and technics. Creativity began in the deep."[32] Thus the following formulation: "Ideology, Utopia, and Fantasy: agents of change, quests for a new reality, memories of a Dream" (P, 157).

Hassan's "new gnosticism" introduces a quite different form of postmodernity from the first three we have considered. It is unashamedly mystical and visionary, willing to tap the creativity of the depths as it wells up in dream and fantasy. It forms a radical contrast to prevailing modes of modern reflection. Filled with luminous insights, Hassan's position brings forward the possibility of a less hostile relationship between postmodern thinking and technology. This is not to say that gnosticism itself does not carry with it inherent liabilities for any philosophy of consciousness and any viable view of time and being; however, this is not the forum to unfold these problems but rather to indicate the fruitful, distinctive character of Hassan's contribution to postmodernity.

5. The movement beyond Western forms of reality

For some, the way beyond modernity is the way *outside* Western forms of thought: the orient, the Plains Indians, and Africa all offer radically nonmodern forms of reality. In the modern era, these have all been in part subjected to "modernization" (the movement toward centralized government, urbanization, secularization, the breakdown of kinship ties—a process well described by C. E. Black in relation to the "modernization" of Japan and other Asian countries[33]). But nonwestern viewpoints have penetrated the West as well. This is probably most notable in the vogue of Zen Buddhism and various forms of spiritual discipline from the East, such as yoga, transcendental meditation, and *t'ai chi chuan*. Nontheistic religions, such as Zen, offer depth in spiritual discipline to Westerners for whom the general credibility of theistic religion has been subtly undermined by the secularity and rationalism of the modern worldview. The use of koans to break the hold of logic on the mind serves as a powerful antidote to the Western rational orientation to the world.

But perhaps no single onslaught on the obvious ultimacy of Western definitions of reality and rationality has been more colorful, provocative, and effective than the four works by Carlos Castaneda describing his apprenticeship to a Yaqui sorcerer and "man of knowledge."[34] These works trace an odyssey in which a young, scientifically and analytically oriented Western investigator of hallucinogenic drugs slowly begins to suspect that his "hallucinations" and the other experiences to which don Juan Matus introduces him are not figments of his imagination but a "separate reality." His experience of the world, his definitions of what is real and imaginary, are but the products of a life-long set of interpretive habits that he has woven around himself like an invisible net. His reality is not the one "universal" reality, with only primitives and madmen outside it; it is "a" reality with definite limits. Furthermore, the warrior code by which don Juan lives is stronger and more viable—even for Carlos—than that of his own Western upbringing. Not only the Western view of reality is called into question but also the Western way of life in its spiritual emptiness and weakness. That is to say, it calls the lessons of modernity into question.

Nonwestern languages have always beckoned the Westerner outside the forms of thought structured by Greek and other Indo-European languages. Yet the modern strategy is to retain a detached and objective distance from other languages as merely "other structures of organizing experience" (the experiences being assumed to be universal) and thus as no threat to the Western view of reality. As the Europeanization of humanity proceeded, Edmund Husserl, for instance, could look forward to universal structures based on European models, just as European science and technology were being exported throughout the world. The next step would be a universal language in which all these universal (Western, modern, secularized) experiences could be articulated. Yet this approach betrays a European definition of language, of man, of reality. But if one looks, for instance, at the African philosophy of language (e.g., of the Bantu languages), the issue is not merely that of comparative structures of language but the African view of words as living and creative.[35] A word brings a thing into being, for the Bantu, which contrasts with the Western-modern view of words as conveyors of information and human "experience." This indicates something else very important: one's anthropology—that is, one's philosophy of man and his place in the world—stands behind one's philosophy of language, and ultimately one's philosophy of reality is reflected in one's use of language.

Thus, a study of Hopi language, or other American Indian languages, brings one into contact not just with a quite different perceptual field and mode of understanding "the world." It is not just another set of words for (pre-given) Western (read "universal") "realities." The study of Indian or of Oriental languages makes us vividly aware that the mindset of "modernity" as we experience it is in part a phenomenon of Western linguistic reality. Linear logic, for instance, has a connection with the structure of Western languages. Thus, a preliminary step for a "perspicuous view"[36] of modernity is the transcending of Europe—both spiritually and linguistically.

Finally, the rehabilitation of myth and the recent intense study of the mythic view of the world leads one outside Western and modern modes of reality. One becomes vividly aware that the fading of earlier mythical connectedness to the earth and of the sense of one's place in relation to it is directly related to the phenomenon of modernization and the rise of scientific modes of thought. The massive urban centers of culture which have been found most efficient for the scientific and technical mastery of the natural world through industrialization also tend to insulate modern man from relatedness to the cycle of the changing seasons and from a direct sense of relatedness to his natural habitat. Ernst Cassirer sees the scientific and mythic views of the world as antithetical.[37] What is involved is more than the loss of relatedness to the earth, however; the mythic and the scientific are two ways of sensing and defining what is "real." What is lost is a whole set of realities: the old sense of nature as holy (now it is a tool for man's use); the humility of man in the face of nature (nature must obey man); a sense of the sacred (modern man lives in a secular world). Nature no longer "speaks" to man; its gods have fled. Modern man lives in a *dürftiger Zeit*—a time of need—as Hölderlin and after him Heidegger and William Barrett note.[38]

Revived interest in spiritualism, astrology, alchemy, shamanism, and the occult all register the fact that the Western rational-humanistic view of reality is no longer so self-evident as it was even ten years ago. Furthermore, the feeling is growing that there may be alternatives to the unsatisfying shallowness of the modern sense of reality. Whatever the merits of spiritualism, occultism, and astrology, the study of myth makes us aware of modes of life which link up with cosmic forces.[39] One can, of course, study myth in a detached, objective way that does not call the modern worldview into question; but one can also try to reclaim what has been lost. The latter is the only way that transcends the modern view of things without recourse to gnosticism. For myth does not imply gnostic immediacy but living within history, although that history may be cyclic.

6. Beyond naturalism

A way of thought is indicated by what it regards as axiomatic, and naturalism is axiomatic for the contemporary scientific view of the world. Naturalism refers to the belief that the natural, material world, including the organic world of nature and our bodies, is an autonomous domain basically unaffected by consciousness—either one's own or that of higher or lower beings. In harmony with this naturalism is the modern view that diseases like cancer or arthritis have nothing to do with the mental state of their possessors. The mind is merely a monitor for pain and other messages from the body, and a receptor of stimuli from the external world. Its powers do not extend to overcoming diseases directly nor to telepathic communication with nature or other human minds.

While the presuppositions of naturalism are of great methodological value in searching for the natural causes of natural events, they have important negative consequences if taken into social relations, religion, or one's general view of things. For naturalism represents a prior judgment that no nonphysical agencies can be at work in our world. It opens the way to reducing reality to what can be observed and verified and then to what can be stated in terms of causal relation. Instances of telepathy or faith healing are incomprehensible within the framework of naturalist assumptions, and it is almost comical to see the absurd lengths to which the empirically minded will go to deny them.

Yet if one is not blind or pathologically closed off from the clear evidence of one's senses, there are firm indications that the mind is not nearly so limited as modern naturalism would have us assume. While it is not feasible here to enter into cases, one may mention a few recent works that raise the most interesting challenges to the naturalistic standpoint: Lyall Watson's *Supernature*[40] and Joseph Chilton Pearce's *The Crack in the Cosmic Egg* and *Exploring the Crack in the Cosmic Egg*[41] give a veritable catalog of instances that suggest agencies beyond the ken of naturalism. Dr. Irving Oyle, in *The Healing Mind*,[42] shows remarkable medical cases from his own practice where the action of mind on the healing process was evident. These were not just cases of "psychosomatic illness" but of clinically serious diseases. The career of Edgar Cayce, the remarkable psychic, raises many questions about telepathy, perception of illness at great distances, the intuitive prescription of treatment, and so on.[43] In his autobiography, *The Center of the Cyclone*, John Lilly raises interesting possibilities of realities quite beyond the level of naturalism.[44]

Of course, Martin Buber in *I and Thou*[45] submits a powerful critique of the limits of naturalistic seeing—without recourse to psychic phenomena, myth, mystical unions, or universal noospheres. Naturalism, in Buber's terms, locks itself into the I-it relationship. This walls one off in advance from the kinds of experience—the kinds of "reality"—that only *come into being* when one says the "you" of genuine relationship. Buber makes us aware that "relationship" is a prime condition of meaning; from the I-you relationship arises a different and deeper meaning forever closed to the person who does not say "you." The naturalistic stance does not say "you," thus prescribing limits on the meaning that will arise for it. The first step beyond the metaphysics of modernity, then, is to break the bewitchment of naturalism.

7. The apostles of "new consciousness"

The most extreme form of transcending modernity is probably that of proposing a whole "new consciousness." Into this category fall many efforts that have little claim to serious attention, efforts that venture off into fantasies and questionable extrapolation from puzzling bits of evidence. The works of von Däniken offer an interesting challenge to the prevailing evolutionary concepts,[46] as do the theories on myth as early astronomy suggested in Giorgio de Santillana's *Hamlet's Mill.*[47] Among the

striking points von Däniken makes is not only the possibility of human life having been initiated by interstellar visitors but also the idea that human subsolar time may not be the measure for interstellar travel; time may stretch or shrink for beings who venture outside the horizon of the solar system itself. Thus, interstellar travel may not be a human impossibility after all, although it would be anybody's guess who and what would be on earth if and when the interstellar traveller returned.

Perhaps the most interesting ideas about new consciousness revolve around the question of whether a "mutation" of consciousness is about to take place. The French duo of Louis Pauwels and Jacques Bergier, in *The Morning of the Magicians* and other works, argue that already in our historical past there have been mutations of consciousness—that is, beings whose mental powers were as far above the normal as the human is above the apes.[48] Colin Wilson's novel *The Philosopher's Stone*[49] fantasizes on the implications of a qualitatively higher consciousness able to travel back in time and plumb the origins of life on the planet.

But the most serious and systematic effort to articulate a "new consciousness" is that by Jean Gebser, the late Swiss historian of art and culture. In his 700-page masterwork, *Origin and Present,* Gebser argues that a "new consciousness" is already emerging which stands in radical contrast to that which has dominated the West since the Renaissance. The "new consciousness" is non-perspectival and holistic and has found a post-perspectival conception of time. José Argüelles, in his *Mandala* and *The Transformative Vision,*[50] argues for 1987 as the end of our era. The rise of a new consciousness will follow, along with the beginning of a new age. Gebser's argument does not rest on Hindu or Aztec myth, nor on a cyclic view of history, but on the evidence from many disciplines collected over two decades, indicating movement toward a consciousness in which the basic ego-centeredness and single-dimensionality of modern thought is overcome in the "logic of fields" and in the dissolution of perspective in modern art. Among many examples he alludes, for instance, to a 1926 Picasso drawing which shows several sides of a woman's figure at once.[51] The artist tries to overcome one-dimensional time by an intuitive articulation of the object from many sides.

One might say that the formalism of Picasso's cubistic seeing leads into (1) the desire to perceive the interior form, and (2) the desire to see the form from all sides at once in a new kind of unity. In this post-perspectival holism Gebser sees anticipations of a "new consciousness" that overcomes mensural time and space, a consciousness that differs radically from the single-perspective orientation of modern consciousness. He finds parallel anticipation in diverse realms of human activity—in mathematics, in the natural and social sciences, in literature, and in the arts. While one may find Gebser's analyses stretched and in details unsatisfactory, the issue remains: are we today undergoing a *mutation*[52] (as he calls it) in consciousness as fundamental as that which gave rise to the modern age? Is a qualitatively higher consciousness on the horizon?

. . . . .

In the spectrum of seven versions of "postmodernity" just discussed, the last is closest to fantasy. Many might see it as a construction influenced by apocalyptic anxiety or wishful thinking. The seven have run the gamut from Stephen Toulmin's sober, methodical project of constructing a new epistemological self-portrait to fantasies of "higher consciousness." The spectrum does not present disciplines but merely suggests dimensions or approaches to the transcendence of modernity. To it I would like to add a very cursory discussion of three areas of study where one can find significant impulses toward transcending the thought-forms and presuppositions of modernity: psychology, philosophy of language, and literary theory.

These three disciplines have in common a concern with man as an interpreting being, and with the linguistic forms in which the interpreting process takes place. In all three, standpoints informed by positivism, naturalism, and narrowly objectivistic thinking have moved—often under the influence of phenomenology—toward existential, phenomenological, or "hermeneutical" views of language and interpretation. These developments, if not necessarily postmodern, do point in that direction.

8. New foundations in psychology

The rebellion against the heritage of modernity in psychology has taken the form of an increasingly critical attitude toward the illusions of positivism. Greater methodological reflexivity in the discipline has suggested to psychologists (in some quarters) that the "objectively described" data have become objective only through an act of renouncing large blocks of subjective or otherwise nonobjectifiable reality. Empirical seeing can be a form of empirical blindness to the nonobjectifiable sides of phenomena. Especially in counselling, psychologists have keenly felt the gap between data from the laboratory or from objective studies and, on the other hand, the kinds of inner struggle in which their patients are engaged. We shall single out only a half-dozen or so developments with significance for our theme.

First, there is the rise of phenomenological psychology. Herbert Spiegelberg has devoted a lengthy book to this topic,[53] and other books have arisen out of the Lexington conferences on applied phenomenology, published by Duquesne University Press. We shall not attempt to describe this movement. A recent book—*Three Worlds of Therapy,*[54] by Anthony Barton—characterizes the psychotherapeutic approaches of Freud, Rogers, and Jung by imagining the same patient interacting with three different therapists. Three quite different analyses arise. The contrasts are almost caricatures and often are humorous: the hundreds of sessions with the detached Freudian, the mystical and far-away look of the Jungian, and the Rogerian endlessly repeating the client's statements and adding nothing of his own. None of the three therapies is precisely phenomenological, but Barton argues that phenomenology gives the best standpoint for understanding that the differences arise in the encounter-relationship with the therapist; as Buber says, meaning arises in relation.

Second, the complex of developments generally referred to as "third-force psychology" has found its articulation especially in the work of Abraham Maslow, who has been studying healthy and heightened states of being.[55] Of interest is the strongly humanistic education of most "third-force" psychologists. The writings of Maslow, Eriksen, Rogers, and Rollo May are rich in the influence of literature, art, and philosophy. In this regard, for instance, Rollo May, classically educated, is not afraid to draw on concepts like "eros" or the demonic and to trace these to their Greek roots.[56]

Third, R. D. Laing significantly emphasizes situation—a debt to Sartre and Goffman—and appreciates the metaphysical and religious dimensions of schizophrenia. His trenchant analyses of "mystification" in the family in *The Politics of Experience*[57] make it clear that Laing has in mind a critique of the modern way of being-in-the-world, with its relentless competitiveness, exploitation, and terrorism within the family. Jules Henry (*Pathways to Madness*[58]) and Thomas Szasz (*The Myth of Mental Illness*[59]) are willing to raise global questions about the legitimacy of the modern definitions of sanity. (Of course, Foucault in *Madness and Civilization*[60] has shown the social-political function of mental asylums.)

Fourth, some recent post-"third-force psychology" is moving toward a "transpersonal psychology" open to mystical experience and to states and concepts totally alien to the empirical tradition: bliss, awe, the "higher self," spirit, the sacralization of daily life, synergy, compassion.[61] Transpersonal psychology is open to dimensions of the psyche that have been systematically bypassed in modernity: for instance, "nonordinary reality" and states of heightened consciousness. The character of these concerns stands in the starkest contrast to that of traditional psychology and reveals the negative consequences of a perspective that is philosophically defined by naturalism.

Fifth, one can mention the recent interest in hermeneutics on the part of psychologists, especially in response to the works of Paul Ricoeur, such as *Freud and Philosophy.*[62] In a recent issue of *Journal of Religion* centered on the theme of hermeneutics,[63] Peter Homans contributed an article on hermeneutics and psychology. Under the influence of phenomenology and hermeneutics, Robert Sardello at the University of Dallas is developing a new program and with it a redefinition of psychology itself.[64]

Sixth, the contribution of Jacques Lacan pushes psychology toward a new stage.[65] Influenced by Hegel, Heidegger, and Sartre, as well as by Saussure and

Jakobson, and by structural anthropologists like Mauss and Lévi-Strauss, Lacan brings to his analysis of the hermeneutics of the analytic situation a background in philosophy, phenomenology, structural linguistics, and anthropology, not just his training in Freudian analysis. Lacan brings to Freudian psychoanalysis a vision of the deeply linguistic character of the psychoanalytic situation. Every utterance in the psychoanalytic situation, even the most meaningless word or phrase, is addressed to someone. As the analyst listens, he gives by his very presence a situation and meaning to the discourse—a theater for its performance.

Finally, one might note the emergence of James Hillman's "polytheistic" psychology. More explicitly and systematically than any of the psychologists we have mentioned, Hillman calls modernity into question. Monotheism, ego-psychology, male-domination (Apollonianism), and nominalism all go together to mark modernity with their repressive, materialistic, and desacralized vision of life. Reformation theology, says Hillman, represents the resurgence of a monotheistic, anti-feminine orientation. Not accidentally, we can date the rise of modernity from the Reformation. Hillman is a Jungian, and his view is that we must rehabilitate the gods and rediscover the "soul" which has become enigmatic or so hidden as to be virtually undiscoverable. Hillman's recent *Re-Visioning Psychology* is both a program for the future and a comprehensive frontal attack on the foundations of modernity.[66] Whatever the validity of his overall program, his analysis of the psychological bases of modern thought is unaccustomed illumination of the modern psyche.

9. Radical philosophy of language

Paul Ricoeur observed at the beginning of his book on hermeneutics and Freud (1964) that the problem of language has become the corssroads of contemporary European thought. No one concerned with the problem of language can ignore the tremendous ferment in French thought in the period since 1960, in which perhaps the most colorful development was the vogue of structuralism. The offspring of linguistics and anthropology, more a method than a philosophical position, structuralism intoxicated contemporary intellectual circles like a new and heady wine. Roland Barthes is perhaps the figure who most fruitfully responded to the impetus of structuralist thought. Yet structuralism in France was only one of several currents of thought in a milieu of Marxist literary theory, the continuing legacy of phenomenology and existentialism, and such unclassifiable thinkers as Foucault and Derrida. With Foucault and Derrida French thought takes conscious direction toward the transcendence of modern forms of thought. Foucault asserts that the sciences of man are dead because "man" as a conception is dead. The "study of man" must give way to the more interesting and definitive matter: shifts in forms of representation. Applying the concept of underlying forms of thought (*epistemê*), which would seem to derive from structuralism, Foucault in *The Order of Things* attempts an archeology of knowledge that charts fundamental

shifts in constellations of forms of representation and communication—say, in language, economics, and biology.[67] Depth shifts in these structures are what count, Foucault says, not the political-historical decisions of the living characters that seem to move on history's stage.

Lévi-Strauss and other anthropologists looked for underlying structures with structuralist techniques that could reduce data to certain atomic units, but this did not lead to the conclusion that "man is dead." Rather, their structuralism offered a clever set of tools, a method of analyzing bodies of material by reducing them to a few definitive signs, a fairly simple, scientific attitude. For all its penetration of hidden codes and "mythologies," for all its exciting methodological fruitfulness, structuralism did not turn away from modern presuppositions but was a rarified extension of the quantifying, analytical, and reductionist modes of modern thought. Only in the hands of a thinker like Foucault, who transcends the method with a comprehensive theory of his own, does it take on the power to encompass and transcend the development of modern thought.

French thought takes the postmodern turn in the work of Jacques Derrida. Derrida, having the hermeneutical capacity to enter into the center of a philosopher's thought and to think it from the inside, understood the issue of modernity from his first critique of Husserl's treatise on geometry.[68] He deconstructs both Husserl and Heidegger and moves toward a view of language and of being that ventures radically beyond the presuppositions of modern ontology and philosophy of language,[69] beyond both phenomenology and structuralism.

It is beyond our scope here to enter into the many facets of French contemporary thinking about language, such as that found in the works of the *Tel Quel* group—Sollers, Kristeva, Greimas, Genette, and others. It is enough to say that radical thinking about language leads to a fundamental questioning of modern views of language, time, and being.

10. Postmodern literary theory

One could define postmodern literary theory very loosely as theory that rebels against formalism—especially the New Criticism, with its roots in the aesthetics of Modernism and French Symbolism. One might see, then, already with Northrop Frye's *Anatomy of Criticism,* a movement away from the aestheticism of the New Critics.[70] Yet Frye is frankly Aristotelian (as he states in his Preface) and his theoretical self-understanding certainly does not take a "postmodern" turn. Nor are social criticism and eclecticism, as alternatives to New Criticism, radical alternatives that venture beyond modernity. They only modify the extremes of formalist-rhetorical criticism.

The Geneva critics, however, do find in phenomenology the philosophical basis for a standpoint that is not formalist, nor simply eclectic, but genuinely moves beyond the objectivist assumptions of most modern criticism.

Sarah Lawall's excellent survey *Critics of Consciousness* gives an account of these critics and of a single American critic, J. Hillis Miller.[71] Miller is now at Yale with Geoffrey Hartmann, Paul de Man, and others, in a group which well may prove a seminal source of postmodern literary criticism and theory. The influence of Derrida is strong in this group, and has been felt already in *Diacritics and New Literary History,* as well as in Hillis Miller's review of Joseph Riddel's *The Inverted Bell.*[72] Riddel himself should be mentioned in this context, for his book, devoted principally to the "counterpoetics" of William Carlos Williams, is a major effort in postmodern theory of literature. Riddel attempts to apply premises from Derrida and Heidegger to *Paterson,* which Williams' rebellion against literary and critical Modernism makes an ideal case study in postmodern aesthetics.

An independent and brilliant literary theorist of "postmodern literature" is Ihab Hassan, whose *Dismemberment of Orpheus*[73] and *Paracriticisms* are major documents in articulating the theory of postmodernism. Hassan's Orpheus book finds the breakdown of the muse as seen in the literature of silence, absurdity, ambiguity, the void, and determined non-literariness as central to postmodernism. He devotes chapters to de Sade, Hemingway, Kafka, Genet, and Beckett. In *Paracriticisms,* Hassan seeks a gnostic reconciliation of scientific utopian thinking with technophobic clinging to arcadia, bringing into the realm of "postmodernism" the literature of vision and the literature of imaginative science fiction. Hassan's openness to paraliterary forms should force the "English teachers" of America to stretch their categories—and it exerts the same pressure on postmodern theorists who might prefer to stick with Williams.

Three journals in particular take a special interest in exploring literary postmodernism: *Diacritics, New Literary History,* and *boundary 2.* Among the major contributions of these magazines has been an opening of American thinking to European modes of criticism. In particular, several valuable articles on the literary postmodern appeared in Volume 1 of *boundary 2* (1972-73): David Antin's "Modernism and Postmodernism"; Charles Altieri's "From Symbolist Thought to Immanence: The Ground of Postmodern Poetics"; and William V. Spanos' "The Detective and the Boundary: Some Notes on the Postmodern Literary Imagination." A special issue of *New Literary History* was also devoted to postmodernism.[74] A recent review of Nathan Scott's *Three Modern Moralists* takes up the problem of a postmodern ethics.[75] This is simply a random listing with many omissions.

William V. Spanos has taken up the project of developing a "postmodern hermeneutics" based on Heidegger's *Being and Time.* As the title of his forthcoming book, *Icon and Time,*[76] indicates, Spanos sees a basic dichotomy between the spatialization of being as represented in icons and images (in modernism) and the temporalization of being-in-the-world (in *Being and Time*). According to Spanos, the New Critics took their formalist aesthetics from the spatialized thinking of French Symbolism, and its

English versions in Eliot, Yeats, and Pound. On the other hand, Heidegger's *Being and Time* introduces a new and radically temporal ontology, a new definition of being in terms of time, care, anxiety, and guilt, which both defines the horizon of postmodern literature and conditions postmodern literary theory. The ramifications of this position are considerable, for they challenge the basic logocentrism and spatialized character of modernity and not just of modernism. Although *Icon and Time* has not yet appeared, major portions of it may be found in previous issues of *boundary 2,* as well as in this present issue.

Finally, Edward W. Said's major recent work, *Beginnings,* represents an impressive articulation of French poststructuralist thought in Said's own formulation and application to literary works and literary history.[77] To the image of a center or an "origin" Said opposes the image of a beginning that has no "origin" but represents a combination of historical situation and human intention. Whereas the implicit ontology of structuralist thinking assumed a balanced and static structure, Said follows Foucault, Deleuze, and Derrida in denying the center, the logos. Centers are finite and temporal—nomadic centers of meaning which will eventually change; they were not made eternally at some point of origin in creation. Thus, a text is "produced," is begun, in the intention of a human agent; its origin is a "beginning" by a person in a situation. Again the radically temporal and finite character of a beginning contrasts with the idea of a fixed, metaphysical origin-point, a logos. Said specifically contrasts his position with that of Northrop Frye in *Anatomy of Criticism,* where Platonism and tonality-centeredness contrast with his, Said's, decentered emphasis on the constructed and finite character of human knowledge and especially human fictions. In doing so, he suggests a standpoint beyond the metaphysics and the poetics of modernism.

Said's book has important hermeneutical implications. He suggests an image of the interpreter of the text that makes him not the knower of an "origin"-truth but a constructor, like the original writer of the text, of a meaning. Meaning is constructed, not given to man. Interpretation has analogies in the performance of an actor on the stage, who has a humanly created text and also a theater in which he must again bring that meaning into being. Enter man the interpreter, constructor, performer, the being with intentions and methods of bringing those intentions to fulfillment.

This survey has been necessarily impressionistic rather than systematic, but it may give some idea of the variety of thought that goes under the heading of postmodern literary theory. Much has been left out—for instance, the contemporary German theorists, like Wolfgang Iser, Hans-Robert Jauß, and Rainer Warning, and many contemporary American theorists, such as Fish and Holland, who make a frontal attack on the tradition of formalism and philological objectivity in the name of reader response or speech act theory. But these few citations outline at least some dimensions of postmodern literary theory.

III. POSTMODERNITY AND HERMENEUTICS

Postmodernity affects hermeneutics in many ways. It suggests that a one-dimensional definition of interpretation built around a perspectival model will not do. It suggests that a definition of hermeneutics in terms of establishing the "correct" interpretation of texts is unduly narrow and one-dimensional in setting a single interpretive standard and reference-point. It opens up new models of the interpreter's mediation. And most important, postmodernity raises the question of a transition and transformation so radical as to change the fundamental views of language, history, truth, time, and matter—so radical that "understanding" become a quite different process. It raises the possibility, in other words, of a "new hermeneutics."

1. Hermes: God of the gaps

If we want a hermeneutics that survives the transition to postmodernity, I think we need to renew our sense of the mythic meaning of Hermes. Hermes was a boundary-crosser, the god of exchanges of all kinds, as well as messenger-mediator between the realm of the gods and that of man. In ancient Greece, altars to Hermes stood at crossroads and at borders, where exchanges most often took place. Persons of different languages and different countries often made their exchanges at the border. So it is not strange that the term *hermeneuein* means to translate, to explain. The interpreters of Homer were "hermeneuts" even though their interpretation was not a translation or an explanation but a performance that brought the text to effective presence. The term hermeneutics is rich in associations and meaning; only in modern times does the term become a more specialized process of commentary on texts or validation of texts. When Hans-Georg Gadamer attempted a "philosophical hermeneutics" that approached interpretation in broader terms, he was restoring something of the breadth of meaning the term had in Greek usage.[78]

Just as the term "postmodern" may be broadened by relating it to postmodernity and not just postmodernism, the term hermeneutics may be broadened by considering it in the context of different forms of mediation and what they entail. For the essential thrust of the term hermeneutics is to involve a kind of *mediation*—a bridging the gap between languages, times, and even different levels and realms of existence. Hermes is the original "god of the gaps," one might say. For, historically, hermeneutics has arisen out of gaps: the gap created when the text is in another language and one must mediate between language-worlds, or the gap between historical present and a time long ago. These gaps have helped to define "the hermeneutical problem." Yet the problem of "making oneself understood" by a person of another life-style is also a form of the hermeneutical problem, as would be any form of "communication" with non-human being. Hermes has many gaps to preside over today, and a careful study of them would yield important insights, I believe, into the nature of communication between beings. I would like

simply to list a dozen or so such gaps that are worthy of study and take up one of them for further examination—the gap between modern and "postmodern" consciousness: God and man, language and language, past and present, man and woman, parent and child, ordinary and nonordinary reality, Eastern mind and Western mind, mountaintop and everyday experiences, man and dolphin, Black and White, Native American and Immigrant American (first-, second-, or seventh-generation), doctor and patient, expert and layman, man and superman, and of course modern and postmodern consciousness.

The hermeneutical problem of bridging the gap between modern and postmodern sets-of-mind goes in both directions: the problem of understanding a postmodern way of thinking when the assumptions and furniture of our thinking are themselves given by modernity, and the problem of a person who, having achieved a postmodern, post-spatialized, postperspectival, or holistic framework, must then communicate it to someone who has not reached it. One strategy is to study carefully the emergence of the modern from premodern ways of thinking so as to be able to specify the contrasts and as much as possible the generative factors in modernity. It then becomes possible to show that modernity is an historically created form of consciousness and can be changed again in history. This places subject-object metaphysics, modern objectivity, the exploitive, manipulative, mechanistic stance of modernity, the visualizing-spatializing modes of thought, and so on, in the context in which they arise—a context which can then be surpassed. Although premodern consciousness is obviously not a goal, it can be an aid in the identification and then transcendence of modernity.

2. Toward a broader conception of hermeneutics

Hermeneutics, then, is not an "ism." It is not the property of Heidegger and Gadamer, although I find that they are very helpful in grasping the relation between interpretation and the philosophical movement away from objectivity. Hermeneutics is the discipline of bridging gaps and of theorizing about what is involved in this process. For this reason it is open to the kinds of "reality" that come into view in Castaneda, or R. D. Laing, or James Hillman.

Hermeneutics must go deeper than all merely methodological reflection about interpretation. In fact, it asks about the effects on interpretation caused by the methodological stance itself. It comprises a new reflexivity about interpretation—what happens when interpretation takes place within the context of modern, premodern, and postmodern assumptions about reality. It functions as a critique of methodology, ideology, and epistemology; thus it is already a critique of modernity.

Hermeneutics as philosophical reflection about interpretation takes as its subject the conditions under which understanding takes place. It studies misunderstanding and breakdowns in interpretation because they reveal the absence of conditions necessary for understanding. The focus of hermeneutical reflection is not methodology but the hermeneutical situation. Hermeneutical reflection asks: What happens when one operates on the basis of one view of language rather than another, one view of history rather than another, one view of truth rather than another, one view of art rather than another? It asks what modernity has done to these views and what would be the effect of a quite different set of views. And it asks what might happen to our conception of *understanding* if it is not taken as a mere computer-like mechanical operation of the mind but rather—the site of ontological disclosure? deeply rooted in lifeworld and "form of life"? able to found a world and hold it in being?

3. Toward a new interpretive self-awareness for teachers

What do these considerations mean for the teacher-interpreter of literature? They mean that if a change in the conceptions of language, history, truth, myth, art, and understanding is involved, this is not a matter of changing a method of interpreting but the rules of the game; or perhaps, *making it a new game.* If postmodernity brings this kind of fundamental change the hermeneutical task must take on a new shape.

Obviously this new shape cannot be described in detail, and even my own image of it is but an interpretation, a construction. But I would look forward to a greater dignity for the teacher of literature. I find pale and thin the job-descriptions teachers carry in their minds. Interpreting texts is an important matter. It is not just a dialogical matter, although it must be this: it is an ontological matter, a matter of existing fully. To interpret (should I say perform) a text can be an act as meaningful as any external action one might take. An act of understanding a text can alter one's consciousness, redirect one's life, seal one's fate. Teachers are not hucksters of "aesthetic experiences," they are helpers and builders in the business of "soul-making"— to use a phrase of James Hillman. As the name hermeneutics suggests, one may be the agent of the gods, and one must be able to interact with the "gods." Not the monotheistic God but the gods that shape our lives.

Teaching literature is creative and delightful, for we are in the fictive, ontological, playful business of "creating a world." To read Homer, Dostoevsky, or Joyce is not a mere amusement with no implications for the soul; it is learning what soul is about. When a teacher of literature plays his game according to objectivistic rules, he loses. He yields to a self-understanding and sense of task that technologizes understanding and renders his work irrelevant to his audience. As teachers of literature, we are closest to the visionary and auditory imagination of man. The imagination and its doors of perception must be cleansed of the effects of modern thinking and modern education.

Teachers of literature are not scientists or librarians, and these should not function as models for our interpretive task. We need a clearer understanding of our roles as mediators, of what mediation does, and of the status of mediation (as ontological event). To be seen in terms of being an "expert on styles" or an encyclopedia of information on cultural history or an aesthetician of the "pleasures of poetry" cheapens our function as interpreters— and this cheapening is precisely the consequence of modern objectivizing modes of thinking and valuing. The modern world views teachers of literature as in love with the past, not in touch with the present. This is in part because we ourselves do not have a hermeneutically adequate view of the interpretive present. To interpret a text in a way that restores its power, the interpreter is dialectically engaged both with the present and with the past—at a depth not attained by moderns. It is not through mere analytical dexterity or imaginative sympathy that a mediator is able to bring a text to life. Because he is grounded in the present world and in the present dimensions of his own existing, he can catch the resonances of the text more fully. Without the engagement with the present the past would be meaningless.

So I argue that a more adequate hermeneutics, and a critical sense of the limits of modernity, will give a new dignity to the teaching of literature and, to the teacher himself, a deepened interpretive self-awareness.

NOTES

[1] See Andrew Hacker, *The End of the American Era* (New York: Atheneum, 1971).

[2] Robert Hunter, *The Storming of the Mind: Inside the Consciousness Revolution* (Garden City: Doubleday, 1972). Hunter is only one of many who are "storming" the modern mind. However, I personally am out of sympathy with his view that electronic media, especially television and rock music, are the true transformers of consciousness, and that one can thus dispense with such old-fashioned pursuits as philosophical reflection. Hunter is heavily influenced by the media-determinism of Marshall McLuhan and the gestalt psychology of Fritz Perls.

[3] See José A. Argüelles, *The Transformative Vision: Reflections on the Nature and History of Human Expression* (Berkeley: Shambhala, 1975), p. 248.

[4] "The Talk of the Town," *The New Yorker,* August 11, 1975, p. 19.

[5] In his history of postmodernism in Spanish-American literature, Octavio Corvalan has in mind the general period between the two world wars, in which major Spanish writers reacted against the aesthetics of modernism that had come into Spanish literature under the influence of French Symbolism. See *El postmodernismo* (New York: Las Americas Publishing Company, 1961): "La denominación *postmodernismo* abarca el período cuyos límites históricos son las dos guerras mundiales. Claro está que las primeras manifestaciones de una estética nueva aparecen algunos años antes de 1914 . . ." (p. 7).

[6] William M. Ivins, Jr., *On the Rationalization of Sight: With an Examination of Three Renaissance Texts on*

Perspective (New York: Da Capo Press, 1973). For a full treatment of modern consciousness as based on perspectival consciousness arising in the Renaissance, see Jean Gebser, *Ursprung und Gegenwart,* 3 vols. (Munich: DTV, 1973), forthcoming in translation through Ohio University Press, Athens, Ohio. Gebser emphasizes the way in which perspective spatializes thought and mechanizes time.

[7] See such works as Heidegger's *The End of Philosophy or Identity and Difference* (New York: Harper & Row, 1973 and 1969).

[8] I am indebted to John Romano, Columbia University, for this delightfully pungent phrasing in his critique of my paper. I wish to thank Professor Romano and also Professor Leon Goldstein of SUNY-Binghamton for their frank criticisms as respondents at the Symposium. In the light of these, I have made important deletions and attempted to sharpen the distinction between postmodernism and postmodernity.

[9] See C. E. Black, *Dynamics of Modernization* (New York: Harper & Row, 1968).

[10] See Richard Ohmann, *English in America: A Radical View of the Profession* (New York: Oxford University Press, 1976).

[11] See William Irwin Thompson, *At the Edge of History: Speculations on the Transformation of Culture* (New York: Harper & Row, 1971), and *Passages about Earth: An Exploration of the New Planetary Culture* (New York: Harper & Row, 1974).

[12] See Gebser's *Ursprung und Gegenwart,* cited above.

[13] I devoted a series of public lectures in the spring of 1976 to thinking beyond modernity, at the University of Minnesota, Minneapolis, and may publish them under the title *Beyond Modernity.* In a book that appeared in the fall of 1976, Frederick Ferré approaches the problem of transcending modernity in a way parallel to my own. See his *Shaping the Future: Resources for the Post-Modern World* (New York: Harper & Row, 1976). Ferré uses the term "post-modern" (with a hyphen) in the broader historical sense I am suggesting.

[14] It may be of interest to note that the first draft of this paper was entitled "Some Versions of Postmodern" (echoing *Some Versions of Pastoral*) and was intended as a lengthy preface to a discussion of the "postmodernity" of Heidegger. (The latter was contributed to the special issue of *boundary 2,* "Martin Heidegger and Literature," Winter 1976.) Its purpose was to stretch the meaning of the term "postmodern" in the direction of Heidegger's postmodernity by showing a spectrum of efforts to transcend the increasingly manifest limitations of modern culture. I have here added to it a short section before and a short section after, but the central purpose has remained the same.

[15] Stephen Toulmin, *Human Understanding,* 2 vols. (Princeton: Princeton University Press, 1972).

[16] See Gebser, *Ursprung und Gegenwart,* vol. 2, *Die Manifestation der aperspektivischen Welt,* for examples from the natural and social sciences as well as the arts.

[17] Jürgen Habermas, *Knowledge and Human Interests* (Boston: Beacon Press, 1972), especially pp. 301-17. See also his postscript to a collection of Nietzsche's epistemological writings: Friedrich Nietzsche, *Erkenntnistheoretische Schriften,* Nachwort von Jürgen Habermas (Frankfurt: Suhrkamp, 1968).

[18] See Foucault, *The Order of Things: An Archaeology of the Human Sciences* (New York: Pantheon, 1970), p. 318.

[19] For a little fuller account of Nietzsche as door to a postmodern interpretive self-awareness, see my article "Toward a Postmodern Interpretive Self-Awareness," *Journal of Religion,* 55 (July 1975), esp. 322-26 (special issue on the theme of hermeneutics), and also my paper for the Heidegger Circle, "The Contribution of Heidegger to a Postmodern Interpretive Self-Awareness," forthcoming in the published proceedings of the 1975 meeting, through Ohio University Press.

[20] See Habermas, *Knowledge and Human Interests,* cited above.

[21] "Metaphysics, morality, religion, science—in this book these things merit consideration only as various forms of lies: with their help one can have *faith* in life." *The Will to Power,* ed. Walter Kaufmann (New York: Vintage, 1968), 853, p. 451.

[22] See Gebser's much fuller account of this argument in *Ursprung und Gegenwart,* cited above. I devote a lecture to Gebser in my series of Minnesota lectures, mentioned above, note 13.

[23] Wordsworth, "Ode: Intimations of Immortality from Recollections of Earliest Childhood."

[24] Theodore Roszak, *The Making of a Counter Culture* (Garden City: Doubleday, 1969); *Where the Wasteland Ends* (Garden City: Doubleday, 1972); *Unfinished Animal* (New York: Harper & Row, 1975).

[25] Philip Slater, *Earthwalk* (Garden City: Doubleday, 1974), p. 19.

[26] Slater, *Earthwalk,* p. 129.

[27] See especially Marcuse, *Reason and Revolution* (Boston: Beacon, 1960), which gives an excellent introduction to Hegel; *Eros and Civilization: A Philosophical Inquiry into Freud* (Boston: Beacon, 1955); and *One-Dimensional Man* (Boston: Beacon, 1965).

[28] Marcuse, *One-Dimensional Man,* p. 238.

29 See Heidegger, *The End of Philosophy* and *Identity and Difference,* cited above, as well as the valuable new collection of Heidegger's later major essays, *Basic Writings* (New York: Harper, 1977). Three volumes by Gadamer have appeared recently: his masterwork, *Truth and Method* (New York: Seabury, 1975); a selection of his major articles, *Philosophical Hermeneutics,* ed. David Linge (Berkeley: University of California Press, 1976); and *Hegelian Dialectic,* trans. Christopher Smith (New Haven: Yale University Press, 1976). In Nietzsche, see principally *The Will to Power,* cited above, especially Book III.

30 See the opening part of Gadamer, *Truth and Method,* esp. pp. 39-73.

31 See Ihab Hassan, "The New Gnosticism: Speculations on an Aspect of the Postmodern Mind," *boundary 2,* I (Spring 1973), 547-69, later included in *Paracriticisms* (Urbana: University of Illinois, 1975), pp. 121-47. Subsequent references to *Paracriticisms* in text, abbreviated P.

32 Hassan, "Models of Transformation: Ideology, Utopia, and Fantasy in America," *Paracriticisms,* pp. 151-76; citation is to p. 151.

33 See C. E. Black et al., *The Modernization of Japan and Russia* (New York: Free Press, 1975).

34 Carlos Castaneda, *The Teachings of Don Juan* (Berkeley: University of California Press, 1968); *A Separate Reality* (New York: Simon and Schuster, 1971); *Journey to Ixtlan* (New York: Simon and Schuster, 1972); *Tales of Power* (New York: Simon and Schuster, 1974).

35 See Janheinz Jahn, *Muntu* (New York: Grove, 1961), especially Chapter 5.

36 I allude here to Wittgenstein's remark on the difficulties of gaining a perspicuous representation of our language. *Philosophical Investigations,* 122.

37 Ernst Cassirer, *An Essay on Man* (New Haven: Yale University Press, 1944), and in his larger *Philosophy of Symbolic Forms,* 3 vols. (New Haven: Yale University Press, 1953, 1955, 1957).

38 " . . . und wozu Dichter in dürftiger Zeit?" says Hölderlin in "Brot und Wein," to which Heidegger has reference in the famous essay "Wozu Dichter?" in *Holzwege* (Frankfurt: Klostermann, 1950), pp. 248-96; *Poetry, Language, Thought,* pp. 91-142. Karl Löwith took the phrase for the title of his book on Heidegger, *Heidegger: Denker in dürftiger Zeit* (Frankfurt: Fischer, 1953), and after him William Barrett used it more generally in his recent *Time of Need: Forms of Imagination in the Twentieth Century* (New York: Harper & Row, 1973).

39 This is one of the bases of the *I Ching,* as well as the individual-centered astrology of Dane Rudhyar.

40 Lyall Watson, *Supernature* (New York: Bantam, 1974).

41 Joseph Chilton Pearce, *The Crack in the Cosmic Egg,* (New York: Pocket Books, 1973), and *Exploring the Crack in the Cosmic Egg* (New York: Pocket Books, 1975); originally published by Julian Press.

42 Irving Oyle, *The Healing Mind* (Millbrae, Calif.: Celestial Arts, 1975).

43 See the biographies by Thomas Sugrue or Jesse Stearn, or the many publications of the Association for Research and Enlightenment in Virginia Beach, Virginia.

44 John Lilly, *The Center of the Cyclone* (New York: Bantam, 1973); originally Julian Press, 1972.

45 Martin Buber, *I and Thou,* newly translated by Walter Kaufmann (New York: Simon and Schuster, 1970).

46 Von Däniken, *Chariot of the Gods* (New York: Bantam, 1971), and others. Von Däniken assumes the intervention of beings from outer space in the initiation of "human" life on the earth.

47 De Santillana, *Hamlet's Mill* (Boston: Gambit, 1969).

48 Louis Pauwels and Jacques Bergier, *The Morning of the Magicians* (New York: Avon Books, 1968).

49 Colin Wilson, *The Philosopher's Stone* (New York: Warner Books, 1974).

50 José Argüelles, *Mandala* and *The Transformative Vision* (Berkeley: Shambhala, 1972 and 1975, respectively).

51 Gebser, *Ursprung und Gegenwart,* I, 61.

52 See "Bewußtseinsmutationen," Gebser, I, 24-26.

53 Herbert Spiegelberg, *Phenomenology in Psychology and Psychiatry* (Evanston: Northwestern University Press, 1972).

54 Anthony Barton, *Three Worlds of Therapy* (Palo Alto, Calif.: Mayfield, 1974).

55 See Abraham Maslow, *Toward a Psychology of Being,* 2nd ed. (Princeton: Van Nostrand, 1968), and *The Farther Reaches of Human Nature* (New York: Viking Press, 1971).

56 Rollo May, *Love and Will* (New York: Norton, 1969).

57 R. D. Laing, *The Politics of Experience* (New York: Ballantine, 1967).

58 Jules Henry, *Pathways to Madness* (New York: Vintage, 1973).

59 Thomas Szasz, *The Myth of Mental Illness* (New York: Harper & Row, 1974).

[60] Foucault, *Madness and Civilization* (New York: Random, 1973).

[61] See the *Journal of Transpersonal Psychology.*

[62] Paul Ricoeur, *Freud and Philosophy* (New Haven: Yale University Press, 1971).

[63] Vol. 55 (July 1975).

[64] I was recently asked to lecture on the relevance of hermeneutics. The text, "Hermeneutics and Postmodern View of the Psyche," is to be published in a collection edited by Robert Romanyshyn and Robert Sardello.

[65] See Jacques Lacan, *Écrits* (Paris: du Seuil, 1966).

[66] James Hillman, *Re-visioning Psychology* (New York: Harper & Row, 1975). See also his earlier work, *The Myth of Analysis* (Evanston: Northwestern University Press, 1972).

[67] The English title of *Les Mots et les choses* is *The Order of Things,* cited in footnote 18 above.

[68] See Derrida's *La voix et le phénomène* (Paris: PUF, 1967), available in translation through Northwestern University Press.

[69] See Derrida, *De la grammatologie* (Paris: de Minuit, 1967), translation by Gayatri Spivak forthcoming from Johns Hopkins.

[70] Northrop Frye, *The Anatomy of Criticism* (Princeton: Princeton University Press, 1957).

[71] Sarah Lawall, *Critics of Consciousness* (Cambridge: Harvard University Press, 1968).

[72] Joseph Riddel, *The Inverted Bell* (Baton Rouge: Louisiana State University Press, 1974). Miller's review appeared in *Diacritics,* "Deconstructing the Deconstructors," 5 (Summer 1975), 24-31. Riddel replied in a subsequent issue.

[73] Hassan, *The Dismemberment of Orpheus: Toward a Postmodern Literature* (New York: Oxford University Press, 1971).

[74] "Modernism and Postmodernism," 3, No. 1 (Autumn 1971).

[75] See J. W. Cullum, "Nathan Scott and the Problem of a Postmodern Ethics," *boundary 2,* 4 (Spring 1976), 965-72. Cullum rightly distinguishes postmodernism from postmodernity: "The Anglo-American literary quirk called Modernism lasted scarcely fifty years; the age called modern has endured for some four hundred and fifty. The passing of our cultural modernity into postmodernity is therefore a far more significant event than the passing of Modernism into Postmodernism" (p. 965).

[76] Forthcoming from Berkeley: University of California Press.

[77] Edward Said, *Beginnings: Intention and Method* (New York: Basic Books, 1975).

[78] See Norman O. Brown, *Hermes the Thief* (New York: Vintage, 1969), and Karl Kerényi, *Hermes: Guide of Souls* (Zurich: Spring, 1976).

Brian McHale

SOURCE: "Writing about Postmodern Writing," in *Poetics Today,* Vol. 3, No. 3, Summer, 1982, pp. 211-27.

[*In the following omnibus review of several critical works on postmodernist literature, McHale finds similarities and differences among the conclusions drawn by Christine Brooke-Rose, Christopher Butler, Anne Jefferson, and Alan Wilde.*]

"Postmodern"? No such word appears in the index of Ann Jefferson's book on the *nouveau roman,*[1] nor does it occur in the chapters that Christine Brooke-Rose devotes to contemporary French writing. Yet Brooke-Rose's index[2] does give a number of page-references under "postmodern (postmodernism, postmodernist)," including two entire chapters. All these contexts turn out to be discussions of contemporary *American* writing: for Brooke-Rose, "postmodernism" is the name of an exclusively American school or movement. But even having restricted it in this way, she is not much satisfied with this equivocal term: "postmodernism," she writes,

> is a sort of English equivalent to *nouveau nouveau,* for it merely means moderner modern (most-modernism?), although it could in itself (and sometimes does) imply a reaction against "modernism" (p. 345).

Christopher Butler,[3] who seems to share none of Brooke-Rose's dissatisfaction, uses the term more or less in her second sense of "a reaction against 'modernism'," certainly not in her first sense—"most-modernism," more of the same new thing—since for him it indicates a "quite distinct phase of historical development" requiring a "quite distinct reorientation of our critical and psychological responses" (pp. x-xi). But Butler's "postmodernism" is not, like Brooke-Rose's, restricted to American writing, about which he has little to say, as a matter of fact. For him the *nouveau roman* is also "postmodern," as indeed are contemporary avant-garde movements in the other arts—painting, music. Finally, Alan Wilde[4] is the only one of the four to take the term completely for granted, to the point of putting it on his title page. It is perhaps no coincidence that he is also the only American of the four, for, as he himself says—and here Brooke-Rose would probably agree with him—"postmodernism is essentially an American affair" (p. 12). But not *so* American as to preclude his drawing a number of analogies with the *nouveau roman.*

"Postmodern"? Obviously there is not much consensus here about whether the term ought to be used at all, let alone where or when. Just as obviously, however, all four of these new books are concerned with more or less the same phenomena, and, what is more to the point—for it justifies herding them together here in this review—all four are concerned with them in much the same *way*. Other differences aside, these books are all essays in descriptive poetics, a new kind of writing about what I would call postmodern writing. Most writing about post-modern writing to date has been polemical or apologetic. This includes, naturally, the postmodern writers them-selves in their roles as critics and self-explicators, as well as their popularizers and advocates—see, for example, Sarraute 1956, Robbe-Grillet 1963, Sontag 1966 and 1969, Ricardou 1967, 1971, and 1978 (see Ann Jefferson's re-view in *Poetics Today* 2:1b), Barth 1967 and 1980, Gass 1971, 1975, and 1978, Sukenick 1974-1975, 1975, 1976, and 1977, Federman 1975, Hassan 1975. But it also includes a number of critics who have claimed to be describing and explicating when they have actually been engaging in veiled (and not-so-veiled) polemic, among them Heath 1972, Alter 1975, Klinkowitz 1975, and Zavarzadeh 1976 (see Ria Vanderauwera's review in *Poetics Today* 1:3). Only very recently have genuinely descriptive accounts of postmodern writing begun to appear—for example, Dällenbach 1977, Lodge 1977.

All four of these new books contribute to this more descriptive, more "scientific" perspective on postmod-ernism. Not that they do not occasionally lapse into the older polemical manner. Butler, indeed, devotes two full chapters to a polemic on the value and prospects of postmodern art. But at least he gives us fair warning, frankly titling these chapters "Polemic"—which is more than can be said for some of the earlier postmodern crit-ics. In general, however, the polemical and apologetic impulse in these books is very much subordinated to the descriptive one.

If the underlying impulse is uniformly descriptive, the specific descriptive approaches vary considerably from book to book. Jefferson's poetics is very much in the mainstream of French structuralism, so long as we allow "French" to embrace also the recently "rediscovered" Russian protosemiotician Mikhail Bakhtin. Brooke-Rose, by contrast, positively flaunts her eclecticism—"plural ltd" is how she describes her approach (p. 51)—and cer-tainly there is in her book a wider range of reference to post- and non-structuralist theory, not least of all psy-choanalytic approaches, than in Jefferson's. This ought not to obscure the fact that basically she too is, after all, classically structuralist in orientation, and like Jefferson receptive to Bakhtinian ideas, which loom large in her final chapter. Wilde's approach is avowedly phenom-enological—Merleau-Ponty is the authority most often cited—although he cautions us, quite rightly, not to ex-pect "an orthodox phenomenological study" (p. 14). But-ler is the least systematic and theory-conscious of the four, the most "common-sensical."

All four books, I should hasten to say, are more or less successful at what they set out to do. Jefferson's is perhaps, in its own terms, the most successful, although

it is also the most limited in scope—the most successful *because* the most limited? By contrast, Brooke-Rose's book seems somewhat diffuse, unfocused, even rambling, casting its net too wide (metatheory, genre theory, the reader, Lacan, realism, science fiction, Henry James, Tolkien, Robbe-Grillet, parody and stylization . . .), yet it is also prodigal of insights and alternatives, a constant provocation to response and debate (as this review will demonstrate).[5] Wilde is the subtlest interpreter of the four, sometimes perhaps too subtle for his own, and *our* own, good. Butler's book, though somewhat thinner than the others, is nevertheless of great interest because of its comparisons among artistic media.

This brings us to a further point of similarity and differ-ence. None of these books, except Jefferson's, could be described wholly adequately as "writing about post-modern writing," even under the broadest definition. Butler, Wilde, and Brooke-Rose all exceed the limits of this topic in one direction or another. Butler, as I have just said, is interested above all in comparisons among media; that is, he is as much concerned with postmodern music and painting as he is with writing. Wilde sticks with writing, but not with postmodernism: better than two-thirds of his book is devoted to modernism and what he calls "late modernism." Brooke-Rose, as I have al-ready indicated, ranges the most widely of all. Indeed, the heart of her book lies not in the material on the *nouveau roman* or American postmodernism at all, but in her three impressive chapters on *The Turn of the Screw* (originally published in *PTL* 1:2, 1:3, and 2:3, 1976-1977). None of these "extras," however impressive, fall within my purview here. I shall have my hands quite full enough with trying to identify the common themes in these four authors' approaches to postmodern writing, reflecting at the same time on the state of the art of descriptive poetics of postmodernism.

I. THEORIES AND PRACTICES

Is there a conflict of interests when a practicing artist knows too much about the theory of his or her art? For instance, Christine Brooke-Rose herself, author of, among other things, the four postmodern novels (or so at least I would call them) *Out* (1964), *Such* (1966), *Between* (1968), and *Thru* (1975): does her novelistic art suffer because she also theorizes *about* postmodern writing? Personally, I think not; but there are many who would say that too much theory is detrimental to practice. Christo-pher Butler reexamines the all-too-familiar complaint that postmodern writers merely illustrate their a priori theories of writing, but from a neutrally descriptive standpoint, rather than the usual normative one. All postmodern art, he argues, gravitates either toward the pole of deliber-ately disorganized, even aleatory, art (e.g., Cage's alea-tory music, Burroughs's cut-up technique), or the pole of theory-dominated art, where the work of art tends to become simply "the demonstration of its own methods" (p. 52). At the theoretically overdetermined extreme he places "integral serialism" in music, conceptualism in the visual arts (but also Abstract Expressionism, because of the way it was made a hostage to the criticism written about it), and some aspects, at least, of the *nouveau roman*. When it succeeds—as it does, says Butler, in Claude Simon's *Triptyque* (1973)—theoretically over-determined writing has the capacity to "aestheticize" areas that had previously lain outside the bounds of art:

> The theory of literature [. . .] becomes aesthetically interesting. Its [literature's] medium and formal procedures become part of its content, as abstraction did of painting (p. 153).

At their worst, both postmodern tendencies, under- and overdetermined alike, are apt to produce the same kind of perceptually complex, "all-over" art which simply frustrates and defeats the perceiver (pp. 147-148).

Alan Wilde in some respects corroborates Butler's analysis. He warns of "the danger on the one hand of a too flaccid acceptance of disorder" in postmodern writing—Butler's underdetermined, aleatory art—"and, on the other, of a too easy retreat into a reductive, minimalist aestheticism"—Butler's theoretically overdetermined art (p. 47). And like Butler he also finds, as we shall see in a moment, that what from one perspective look like opposite poles, from another appear as extremes that meet.

Nevertheless, Wilde's general emphasis tends to be rather different from Butler's, falling not on the theme of the domination of practice by theory, but, on the contrary, on the *gap* between theory and practice. Wilde introduces this theme first in the context of modernist writing. "Modernist literature is by now virtually inextricable from the shape modernist criticism has impressed upon it" (p. 20), and nowhere is this truer than in the case of modernist irony. The modernists' practice of irony (or ambiguity, tension, paradox, or whatever cognate one prefers) is normally seen through the filter of modernist criticism like that of Cleanth Brooke; but Wilde finds here "two different models, superficially kin but, in the final analysis, subtly and determinedly at odds" (p. 25). Irony for Brooks reconciles irreconcilables and guarantees resolution and organic unity, while for the modernist writers themselves it is far less reassuring, the mark, rather, of alienation, willful imposition of aesthetic control, mere closure in the absence of any true resolution (pp. 22-27).

Wilde returns to his theme of the noncoincidence of theory and practice in the postmodern context. Here he discerns it among the self-proclaimed "Surfictionists"—Raymond Federman, Ronald Sukenick, and others—who practice an aggressively self-reflexive and antimimetic mode of writing. "Connoisseurs of chaos," the Surfictionists exalt messiness, randomness, disruptive energy—in theory, at least. In practice, a curious thing happens:

> The apparently free-wheeling form [. . .] in fact conceals—and without too much prying reveals—a more fundamental principle of abstraction [. . .] the supposedly aleatory, shapeless, self-destroying story [. . .] exists within the inhibiting grip of

the idea to which it relentlessly refers, just as we, as readers, are finally locked into the confines of a still more limiting structure: the structure of the narrator's consciousness (p. 140).

Whatever they may claim in theory about the openness of their art to disorderly reality, in practice the Surfictionists manifest "a need for order that outreaches that of the most chaos-ridden of the modernists" (p. 144). In short, Butler's extreme of underdetermined writing here collapses into its supposed opposite, overdetermined writing that is completely beholden to an a priori theory—in this case, the theory of underdetermined art!

Wilde relates this reductive strain in postmodern writing to the modernist tendency toward aestheticism, art for art's sake (p. 144), a connection which Butler, too, had made (p. 132). The Surfictionist Ronald Sukenick may reject in theory the explicit aestheticism of his fellow postmodernist William Gass, but Sukenick's own practice of writing exhibits the same art-for-art's-sake tendency as Gass's (Wilde, p. 145).

Wilde also compares the reductive aestheticism of the Surfictionists to aspects of the *nouveau roman* (pp. 177, 185), thus returning us to the question, already raised by Butler, of the relation between theory and practice in contemporary French avant-garde writing. It is a question which divides Jefferson and Brooke-Rose. If Butler's view of the *nouveau roman* is that it approaches the theory-dominated pole, while Wilde emphasizes the gap between certain postmodern theories and the corresponding practice, then Brooke-Rose can be said to align with Butler, Jefferson with Wilde.

Ann Jefferson cautions us against reading the *nouveau roman* through the filter of its practitioners' theoretical pronouncements (p. 56). Often, she observes, their theories lag well behind the theoretical implications of the novels themselves in sophistication (pp. 112-117). It is not to Sarraute's or Robbe-Grillet's or Butor's critical essays that one should turn for theoretical insights, but to their novels, for "fiction articulates theory more interestingly and exhaustively than any explicitly theoretical writing. [. . .] It is the novels which produce the theory and not the theory which produces the novels" (p. 7). She is above all suspicious of the rhetoric of advocates of the *nouveau roman,* such as Jean Ricardou, who proclaim its "subversion, violation or infraction of some supposed fictional norm" (p. 164). In the face of such rhetoric she emphasizes instead the way in which the New Novelists' practice of writing continues and indeed illuminates the conventions of traditional narrative. If these fictions are subversive of the norms of fiction, this is only because fiction, even the most conventional "Balzacian" realism, is always subversive of its own norms. The virtue of the *nouveau roman* is to make us aware of how "*All* novels can be read as the laboratory of narrative" (p. 17), of how *all* fiction is "a laboratory of mimesis [. . .] character and language" (p. 197).

Subversion, violation, infraction, transgression of fictional norms: this sort of rhetoric, of which Jefferson is so skeptical, is exactly the language Christine Brooke-Rose adopts in describing the *nouveau roman*. Indeed, "Transgressions" is the title of her chapter on the *nouveau* (and *nouveau nouveau*) *roman*, a chapter in which she measures the new fiction against the "classical structures" of narrative, using Gérard Genette's "Discours du récit" as a convenient statement of the norm.

Thus, for Brooke-Rose the *nouveau roman* is norm-violating art, while for Jefferson it is norm-displaying art. Or, to put it differently, Brooke-Rose proffers an account in which explicit theory and actual practice converge and the work of art "demonstrates its own method," while in Jefferson's account theory and actual practice diverge, revealing the presence of "two different models, superficially kin but, in the final analysis, subtly and determinedly at odds." What exactly is at stake here can be seen if we examine an area of specific disagreement between Jefferson and Brooke-Rose. One "transgression" which Brooke-Rose describes involves free indirect discourse (FID). "A stereotype of the realistic novel" (p. 323), FID is conspicuous by its absence from the *nouveau roman*, according to Brooke-Rose (cf. Pascal 1977: 140). Yet Jefferson claims that FID does occur in the novels of the *nouveau romancier* Nathalie Sarraute; indeed, she follows A.S. Newman (1976) in asserting that "free indirect speech amounts to a fundamental principle of writing" in Sarraute's fiction (Jefferson, p. 147). This ought to be an empirical matter, easily resolved; so, who is right, Jefferson or Brooke-Rose?

The dispute proves not so easy to adjudicate after all. In one sense, Brooke-Rose is obviously right, and Jefferson implicitly acknowledges this when she admits that "the primary grammatical markers of free indirect speech are not present" in her examples from Sarraute's *Vous les entendez?* (p. 149). No surprise there, for *Vous les entendez?*, like the rest of Sarraute's novels and most other *nouveaux romans*, uses the present tense for narrative purposes rather than the "epic preterite" of conventional fiction; therefore backshifted tense (past tense where the present tense of direct speech would be expected), which identifies FID, simply cannot occur. This is why Jefferson, apparently hedging, is forced to speak of "cognate forms" which are "similar to free indirect discourse" or "variants of free indirect speech" (pp. 150-152).

But is she really hedging? After all, Brooke-Rose also shows herself to be willing to extend the notion of FID to include instances where the background norms of the text preclude one or other of the primary grammatical markers—in Joseph McElroy's *Plus* (p. 269), or Ronald Sukenick's *98.6* (p. 382). She even goes so far as to commend McElroy for his "highly original use of free indirect discourse" (p. 269). In short, Brooke-Rose herself recognizes the existence of "cognate forms" of FID. But, in the absence of grammatical markers, what makes them "cognate"? Here Jefferson supplies the

answer, and it is an answer which proves her to be right after all, and Brooke-Rose wrong, about the place of FID in the *nouveau roman.*

Jefferson's point about FID is that even in conventional realistic fiction it is subversive of the mimetic intentions that presumably motivated its introduction there in the first place. As "language on the loose" (p. 143), FID is irreducibly ambiguous both in respect of its origin (who speaks?) and in respect of its object of representation (speech or thought?) (p. 146). Thus, though in conventional fiction it is no doubt used with a view to heightening psychological immediacy and realism, in fact it only makes mimesis that much more obscure and problematic. The "cognate forms" devised by Sarraute in *Vous les entendez?*—or by Sukenick in *98.6*, or McElroy in *Plus*—are wholly analogous to "classic" FID from the point of view of function and effect, but must differ formally because the background norms of these texts happen to preclude FID as such. Thus, Jefferson, and Newman before her, are right that we must "differentiate between free indirect speech as a syntactic form"—a syntactic form which, Brooke-Rose is perfectly right to point out, does not happen to occur in Sarraute's fiction—"and as a principle of writing" (Jefferson, p. 152).

The moral of the story? Brooke-Rose, committed to the New Novelists' own theoretical projections of their practice of writing, treats the presence or absence of FID as a distinguishing mark, a measure of the absolute discontinuity between the new writing and older, mimetic forms. Jefferson, emphasizing instead the noncoincidence of theory and practice, sees how an essential continuity, the same "principle of writing," joins conventional novelists' use of FID with the New Novelists'. practice of "language on the loose," despite the New Novelists' claims to subvert conventional fiction. Continuity or discontinuity with the past: clearly we have here another of the leitmotifs of the new approaches to postmodernism.

II. CONTINUITIES AND DISCONTINUITIES

Ann Jefferson, as we have just seen, makes the strongest case for viewing postmodern writing—or at least French postmodern writing—as continuous with traditional modes of fiction. More than continuous, it is actually, paradoxically, *conservative,* by her account. The *nouveau roman,* she tells us, "restores to us a new past [. . . .] it has thrown new light on the literature with which we have always lived" (p. 208). She evokes Harold Bloom's notion of poets' "anxiety of influence" to describe the relationship between the *nouveaux romanciers* and the powerful precursor-figure of Balzac—the bogeyman of all French postmodernist polemic—a relationship of creative misreading which affirms the strength of the realist tradition at the same time that it struggles against it (pp. 208-209). This simultaneous affirmation of and resistance to realism manifests itself in all aspects of the poetics of the new fiction: in story, where plot disappears as a medium of representation and principle of narrative ordering, only to be replaced by narrative ordering itself as the *object* of representation (pp. 56-57); in character, where individual psychology, a powerful means of conferring intelligibility and articulating theme, is supplanted by the thematic *problem* of character and intelligibility (p. 88); in the language of fiction, where, as in the case of FID and its surrogates, the problematic nature of traditional narrative discourse is brought into sharper focus through the very displacement of traditional linguistic forms. Finally, even the New Novelists' notorious rejection of the principle of mimesis, the kingpin of all traditional realist aesthetics, can be seen as after all an affirmation of the tradition, for the antimimetic self-reflexiveness of the *nouveau roman* lays bare the essential self-reflexiveness of all fiction:

> The nouveau roman deserves the title *anti-novel* only in so far as all fiction does. [. . .] The reflexivity of the nouveau roman, its concern with itself as fiction [. . .] derives from its very structure as fiction (pp. 174, 175).

In short, the *nouveau roman* manifests neither an absolute break with the past, nor, as some of its advocates have claimed, the triumph of a hitherto excluded counter-tradition (De Sade, Poe, Lautréamont, Kafka, Roussel, Bataille, Artaud . . .). Rather, it belongs to the mainstream, and its relevance to the poetics of classic realist fiction is as great as, or greater than, its relevance to the poetics of the new or the marginal.

Christopher Butler takes a position almost diametrically opposed to Jefferson's, championing the newness of the new writing (although not unequivocally, as it turns out). It was Butler, we recall, who spoke of a "quite distinct phase of historical development," and it is he who voices the doubt that treating the contemporary avant-garde as simply more modernism (or "most-modernism," as Brooke-Rose says) can be of much use:[6]

> The attempt to prove that everything has been done before can indeed advertise a scholarly ingenuity in digging out similarities, but it would do little to display the unique overall shape of contemporary culture (p. 132; cf. also p. xi).

Postmodern aesthetics represents for Butler a revolutionary break with the past, which can conveniently be dated from Pound's later *Cantos,* Sartre's *La Nau ee* (1938), and, inevitably, Joyce's *Finnegans Wake* (1939) (pp. 4-5). Yet even Butler has his moments of misgiving, when postmodern writing seems not so absolutely a new thing, a clean break with the past, but integrally related to the tradition—parasitic upon it, even. This is so insofar as the new writing relies upon its readers' awareness of the norms of realistic fiction from which it deviates: "its revolutionary techniques are parasitical upon earlier ones and will remain so, just as analytical cubism will always retain its relationship to representation" (p. 153; cf. Lodge 1977:245). Perhaps we ought to see this as just a restatement of Jefferson's theme of the essential continuity between the classic poetics of fiction and the new poetics, merely recast in negative terms—a small difference, yet all the difference in the world from Jefferson's point

of view, since it is her purpose "to outline a theory of fiction which includes the nouveau roman and does not give it a purely negative role" (p. 174).

Alan Wilde offers a more complex picture of continuity and discontinuity than either Jefferson's solidarity of past and present or Butler's (somewhat equivocal) revolutionary break. It is *his* purpose to do justice to the "jagged course of literary history" (p. 120). Like Butler, he insists on the difference between modernism and post-modernism, which is epitomized for him by the difference between their typical forms of irony: on the one hand, the disjunctive irony of modernism, which seeks to control disconnectedness from a superior vantage-point "above" the world, shaping irreconcilable opposites into an unresolvable paradox; on the other hand, the suspensive irony of postmodernism, which takes for granted "the ironists' immanence in the world he describes" (p. 166), and, far from claiming to master disconnectedness, simply ("or not so simply," Wilde interjects) accepts it as such (p. 10 et passim). These different forms of irony mirror and implement different modes of consciousness. Disjunctive irony is the form of a crisis of consciousness, the modernists' sense of the irreducible gap between their need for order and the disorderliness of reality (p. 49). Suspensive irony, by contrast, mirrors the postmodernists' acceptance of the world as "manageably chaotic" (p. 44), their ability, as Donald Bartheleme puts it, to "tolerate the anxiety" (quoted by Wilde, p. 45).

But if Wilde distinguishes fairly sharply between the modernist and postmodernist sensibilities, he is at the same time skeptical of simplistic "refutations" of modernism in postmodernist polemical writings (pp. 19-20, 43-44). For his map of discontinuity leaves room for a large measure of continuity as well. Like Butler, Wilde locates the "crisis point" of the shift of sensibility before the Second World War (p. 87), but his choice of "break-through" texts and writers differs strikingly from Butler's. *Finnegans Wake* is included, of course, but, surprisingly, so are Virginia Woolf's *Between the Acts* (1941), which Wilde calls "the most impressive of *postmodern* novels" (p. 48; Wilde's emphasis), and the stories in E.M. Forster's posthumous *The Life to Come* (1972). Forster's stories, projecting "a world in which the unexamined life is the only one worth living" (p. 88), are "no longer modernist" (p. 87), Wilde tells us, but anticipatory of Beckett, the Surfictionists, the *nouveau roman,* and even of Andy Warhol and photorealism (pp. 70, 88). In short, "high" modernists such as Woolf and Forster actually traverse in the course of their careers the entire distance from premodernist modes through modernist disjunctiveness all the way to postmodernist suspensiveness. The fact that texts like *Between the Acts* and *The Life to Come,* conventional enough in form though not in vision, were written by the modernist masters themselves "runs counter to the notion of a sharp break between modernism and postmodernism" (p. 87).

So too does Wilde's concept of "late modernism" as a "space of transition, a necessary bridge between more spacious and self-conscious experimental movements" (p. 120). This "space," occupied by such writers as Christopher Isherwood and Ivy Compton-Burnett, is characterized by a shift from the modernist thematics of depth to the postmodernists' horizontal orientation, from "the epistemology of the hidden" (p. 107) to the "epistemology of surfaces" (p. 109; cf. Ann Jefferson on the New Novelists' rejection of the "hidden life" and its revelation as an organizing principle of fiction, pp. 88-97). One ought to avoid, however, simply conflating the practice of a late-modernist writer like Compton-Burnett with postmodernist aesthetics (p. 113). For one thing, Compton-Burnett continues to exercise "the Flaubertian-Joycean privileges of the godlike observer" (p. 121): she is still *above* the world she describes, not, like the postmodernists to come, *of* it. The most that can be said of her and the other transitional figures Wilde discusses is that they are "hybrids" of older and newer tendencies (p. 113)—but hybrids which, whatever postmodern theorists of the "school of apocalyptic leaps and irrational flights" (p. 103) may say to the contrary, bridge the gap between modernist and postmodernist writing.

If Wilde's account of continuity and discontinuity in postmodernism is more nuanced than either Jefferson's or Bulter's, then Brooke-Rose's is, potentially at least, even more so. But something seems to have gone wrong with the organization of her book, so that it is almost impossible to make out Brooke-Rose's version of literary history.

Brooke-Rose's approach to the *nouveau roman,* as we have already seen, emphasizes discontinuity, the transgression of obsolete ideas of narrative order. But earlier chapters of her book had seemed to emphasize continuity rather than discontinuity. Some two-thirds of *A Rhetoric of the Unreal* is devoted, as its subtitle says, to "narrative and structure, especially of the fantastic"—that is, the classic fantastic of Poe's "The Black Cat" and Henry James's *The Turn of the Screw,* together with its neighboring genres, the "marvelous" and the "uncanny." Criticizing Tzvetan Todorov's classic analysis of the fantastic, Brooke-Rose suggests in these early chapters that the "pure fantastic," characterized by absolute ambiguity between natural and supernatural explanations, might be seen to belong to a more general category embracing not only medieval allegory (which Todorov had explicitly excluded from his fantastic genre) but also "many modern (non-fantastic) texts which can be read on several and often paradoxical levels" (p. 71). This seems to promise a connection between the classic fantastic of Poe and James and postmodern writing, and indeed several times in her discussion of the *nouveau roman* Brooke-Rose hints at just such a connection. Robbe-Grillet's novels, she writes, "produce *an* effect of the uncanny if not the same effect" (p. 310), "an eerie effect," she writes in another place, "close to the fantastic, or, in Todorov's terms, to the uncanny [the explicable fantastic]" (p. 336). *An* effect, not *the* effect; close to the fantastic *or* to the uncanny: what are we to make of such thoroughly unhelpful formulations? If they do not leave us with a very

clear idea of Robbe-Grillet's novels, neither do they go very far toward making the promised connection with Poe's and James's fantastic.

Nor does Brooke-Rose reclaim this loose thread in her concluding chapter on American postmodernism. Indeed, she makes it all but impossible for herself to do so, for here she abandons the formal description painstakingly developed in earlier chapters from Todorov's theory of the fantastic and Philippe Hamon's analysis of realism, in favor of an analysis based instead on the work of Mikhail Bakhtin. This analysis, she says, "cut[s] across all the philosophic, semiotic, psychoanalytical, thematic and formal considerations we have had so far" (p. 364); she means the considerations of other postmodern critics cited in the preceding chapter (Sontag, Hassan, Zavarzadeh, Lodge), but she might as well have meant *her own* earlier considerations. For this abrupt shift of theoretical models leaves us no way to join up her readings of the American postmodernists with her earlier discussions of the varieties of the fantastic. Hers, in short, is a highly discontinuous rhetoric of the unreal.

This is ironic, in that Brooke-Rose's reading of the American postmodernists, based on Bakhtinian notions of parody and stylization, stresses the *excessive* continuity of postmodern writing with earlier modes. Parody and stylization depend upon the maintenance of a distance between the parodying or stylizing text and the original model being parodied or stylized. If this distance dwindles, as Brooke-Rose insists it does in many postmodern parodies and stylizations, then the parody or stylization becomes indistinguishable from its model, becomes, in short, an imitation, "simply the model in its fatigued aspect" (p. 369). Brooke-Rose's special villain is Thomas Pynchon, whose fictions set out, she says, to parody the modes of intelligibility of classic realistic fiction but end up by simply reenacting those modes, "tipping over into realism" (p. 371). Discontinuity, the distance these texts ought to be maintaining from realistic fiction, collapses into continuity, even identity, with it.

The postmodern parodists seem, on the whole, worse offenders than the stylizers. Brooke-Rose finds less fault with the stylizations of William Gass, Richard Brautigan, Donald Barthelme, Ishmael Reed, and Ronald Sukenick, than she does with the parodies of Pynchon, Robert Coover, and John Barth. Perhaps, she suggests, the stylizations succeed better because they are generally *shorter* than Barth's or Pynchon's loose and baggy monsters (p. 373). Now this is a suspiciously *ad hoc* explanation, so much so that one begins to wonder whether it might be not the parodies but the theory of parody that is at fault here.

In the first place, what is the difference between parody and stylization anyway? Brooke-Rose is vague (pp. 370-371), but then so was Bakhtin before her (which no doubt is one reason why he is so often cited these days, in such a variety of contexts). Parody, for Bakhtin, reverses the evaluative "direction" or "orientation" of the parodied model, while stylization retains the original "orientation," taking care, however, to keep the original and its stylization distinct (see Bakhtin 1973:157-161). Even if this formulation were perfectly transparent and unproblematic, which it certainly is not, Brooke-Rose's application of it here is frustratingly inexplicit. On what grounds, for instance, is Barthelme classified as a stylizer rather than a parodist? or Pynchon as a (failed) parodist rather than a stylizer? Brooke-Rose never explains. In Pynchon's case in particular, even if we grant that his texts are globally parodic, there are still many local effects of what I would certainly call stylization, some of which Brooke-Rose dismisses as feeble parody (pp. 368-369).[7]

In any case, all this signally fails to clarify the relation between postmodern writing and the classic fantastic, which Brooke-Rose had led us to hope she would clarify. The key to this relation is in her possession, if only she had gone ahead and used it—namely, the principle of *hesitation,* central to Todorov's theory of the fantastic and, consequently, to her own (p. 63 et passim). In a fantastic story such as *The Turn of the Screw,* the text (and the reader) hesitate between a natural explanation of events—the governess is undergoing a nervous breakdown—and a supernatural one—the ghosts are really there. An uncanny text resolves the hesitation in the natural direction, a marvelous one in the supernatural direction; a "pure fantastic" text never resolves it at all. No doubt it is the extension of the principle of hesitation to the *nouveau roman* that underlies her description of Robbe-Grillet's novels as "close to the fantastic, or [. . .] to the uncanny." *La Jalousie,* Brooke-Rose writes, "can be read either in the objectivist way (complete absence of jealous man) or as the interior monologue of a husband obsessively spying on his wife" (p. 331)—that is, the reader hesitates between a naturalization in terms of psychological realism, and one in terms of the "practice of writing" itself (cf. Heath 1972). This account converges with that of Ann Jefferson, who castigates Bruce Morrissette (French postmodernism's favorite whipping-boy) for his overeager psychologizing of Robbe-Grillet's texts (pp. 67-71, 113-114), herself proffering a reading in which "hesitation itself becomes finally more interesting than either of [the] mutually exclusive alternatives" (p. 71; cf. also p. 136).

But Brooke-Rose fails to sustain this reading of the *nouveau roman* in terms of hesitation, performing psychological naturalizations which are distinctly Morrissettian in tone: the abrupt shifts from image to image in *La Jalousie* reflect the jealous husband's evasions (pp. 294-295), the confused representation of the world in *Dans le Labyrinth* is a projection of the soldier's mental confusion (pp. 307, 309), etc.[4]

By the time she reaches American postmodernism, Brooke-Rose seems utterly to have forgotten the principle of hesitation. Postmodern fiction, we are told, is about the uninterpretability of the world, a parody of the world's interpretability in classic realist fiction. Novels such as Barth's *Sot-Weed Factor* (1960) and *Giles Goat-Boy*

(1966), Pynchon's *V.* (1963) and *Gravity's Rainbow* (1973), or Coover's *Public Burning* (1977), "dramatise the *theme* of the world's non-interpretability" (p. 364; cf. p. 373). *Over*-interpretability, which would seem to characterize the worlds of Barth, Pynchon and Coover even better than uninterpretability, is, according to Brooke-Rose, really the same, not the opposite, theme: the world is equally unintelligible whether it means nothing or means too much for anyone to be able to absorb and master it all (pp. 367, 371).

But is this the only possible reading of these texts? Might not uninterpretability and over-interpretability, far from being merely variations on a theme, actually be "mutually exclusive alternatives" between which we hesitate? This possibility is explicit in *Gravity's Rainbow.* Here paranoia is defined as "nothing less than the onset, the leading edge, of the discovery that *everything is connected*" (Pynchon 1973:703), while "there is also anti-paranoia":

> If there is something comforting—religious, if you want—about paranoia, there is also anti-paranoia, where nothing is connected to anything, a condition not many of us can bear for long (p. 434).

Paranoia and anti-paranoia, the world as over-interpretable and as uninterpretable: these are the poles between which Pynchon's characters, plots, represented world, and narrative voice oscillate, and it is not at all clear where Pynchon himself or his text as a whole come to rest. The reader, faced with two mutually exclusive world views and compositional principles ("everything is connected," "nothing is connected to anything") hesitates, and hesitates, and hesitates some more. Unless, becoming impatient, he opts for one of the two alternatives— as Brooke-Rose does for anti-paranoia, the position reached toward the close of *Gravity's Rainbow* by characters such as Slothrop and Tchitcherine who, abandoning their paranoid quests for order, lapse into passivity and dis-integration, "not a thing in [their] heads[s], just feeling natural" (Pynchon 1973:626). Now this is a curious thing for Brooke-Rose to be doing—identifying with the phenomenological perspective of a character (or characters)—since earlier in *A Rhetoric of the Unreal* she herself had demonstrated with great ingenuity how the critics of *The Turn of the Screw* inadvertently identified with the perspective of James's protagonist-narrator, reproducing the neurotic governess's errors, omissions and distortions in their own criticism (p. 132). Neurosis, she observed, is contagious: "the structure of a neurosis involves the attempt (often irresistible) to drag the 'Other' down into itself, into the neurosis, the Other being here the reader" (p. 156). Anti-paranoia is contagious too, it appears, so irresistible that it drags down even Brooke-Rose, who was forewarned.

What I am arguing here is that hesitation continues to be the ruling principle of the postmodern "unreal" as it was of the classic fantastic, except that now it operates at a "higher" level. In the classic fantastic, we hesitate between two competing explanations, one bearing on the world "out there" (the supernatural explanation), one bearing on the observer's limited and distorted perspective (the natural one); it is, in short, an *epistemological* hesitation. In postmodern writing, we hesitate between competing structures of reality, alternative worlds—an *ontological* hesitation. Thus, in the case of *Gravity's Rainbow,* there is one structure of reality in which *"everything* is some kind of plot" (Pynchon 1973:603), where vast international cartels stage-manage the lives of individuals and of nations alike (see p. 566), and are themselves in turn determined by the inner dynamics of their own technologies (see p. 521). And there is a second world in which "nothing is connected to anything" and things fall apart, not least of all characters:

> There is also the story about Tyrone Slothrop [the story is called *Gravity's Rainbow*] who was sent into the Zone to be present at his own assembly—perhaps, heavily paranoid voices have whispered, *his time's assembly*—and there ought to be a punch line to it, but there isn't. The plan went wrong. He is being broken down instead, and scattered (p. 738).

Pynchon's two worlds are mutually exclusive and irreconcilable, and no final choice is possible between them.

This analysis of postmodern writing in terms of hesitation between competing ontologies has been anticipated in part by Alan Wilde. He writes of Donald Barthelme:

> Like the pop artists, Barthelme puts aside the central modernist preoccupation with epistemology, and it may be the absence of questions about how we know that has operated most strongly to "defamiliarize" his (and their) work. Barthelme's concerns are, rather, ontological in their acceptance of a world that is, willy-nilly, a given of experience (p. 173).

I agree with Wilde when he makes the *absence* of the characteristically modernist epistemological questions a distinguishing mark of postmodernism, but disagree with his suggestion that postmodernist ontology is unproblematic. On the contrary, what epistemology was for the modernists, ontology is for the postmodernists: not "willy-nilly" given, but richly problematic, the source of the tensions that structure their fictions.

What is finally most surprising about *A Rhetoric of the Unreal* is that Brooke-Rose, herself a writer of fictions of ontological hesitation, should turn a blind eye to the principle of ontological hesitation and instability in postmodernism. "I draw the line as a rule," says the protagonist of her novel *Such,* "between one solar system and another" (Brooke-Rose 1966:128), but of course that is the last thing that he does. He and his author everywhere confuse the "solar system" of his earthly life with that of his equivocal afterlife. Brooke-Rose similarly confronts and conflates our contemporary reality and the speculative future in her postmodern science-fiction novel *Out,* or ontological levels in her Escher-like fiction *Thru* (see Shlomith Rimmon-Kenan,

"Ambiguity and Narrative Levels: Christine Brooke-Rose's *Thru,*" *Poetics Today* 3:1, Winter 1982).[9] "Fiction articulates theory more interestingly and exhaustively than any explicitly theoretical writing," Ann Jefferson has told us, and it is certainly true of Christine Brooke-Rose's practice and theory.

III. MIMESIS AND THE MOTIVE FOR FICTION

We have just seen how Alan Wilde characterizes Barthelme's concerns as "ontological in their acceptance of [the] world," which brings me to my final theme, the fate of mimesis in postmodern writing. Wilde, it will be recalled, compares Barthelme's writings to Pop Art. Both phenomena manifest, he says, the more generative strain of postmodernism which, unlike the reductive, art-for-art's-sake strain of Gass and the Surfictionists, refuses to withdraw into the "heterocosm" of the autonomous artwork, but continues to engage with the world of experience (pp. 147-148 et passim). Wilde quotes Robert Indiana: "Pop is a re-enlistment in the world" (p. 149). Barthelme's fictions, too, are a re-enlistment in the world, for, although they may lack "an easily paraphrasable theme or an extractable moral," they still possess "human reference of one kind or another" (pp. 168-169). The "kind" varies. Some of Barthelme's fictions project recognizable human emotions—*small* emotions, however, "not anomie or accidie or dread but a muted series of irritations, frustrations, and bafflements" (p. 170). Others are more purely ludic, playing with the world's *objects trouvées;* but, says Wilde, "whether even play is without meaning is another matter" (p. 172).

Christopher Butler concurs. He, too, sees in Pop Art a continued engagement with the world (pp. 90, 93), and, like Wilde, connects Barthelme's writing with Pop, at the same time distinguishing it from purist and elitist trends in postmodernism (pp. 118-119). But Butler goes a step further, making explicit the conclusion that Wilde had left implicit: namely, that postmodernism (at least some varieties of it) is mimetic art after all. Just as modernist innovation seemed antirepresentational in its time, but with hindsight can be seen to have been mimetic, so the "mimetic commitments" of postmodernism may become more apparent with the passage of time (p. 159).

Now this ought to be a surprising conclusion, at least to critics and viewers-with-alarm like Robert Alter (from whom I have stolen the title of this section; see Alter 1978) and Gerald Graff (1979), who reject postmodern writing for its supposed abandonment of "mimetic commitments." Yet, if postmodernism has given up on mimesis, as Alter and Graff allege, how is it that all four of the books under review here ultimately affirm the mimeticism of postmodern writing, one way or another? "One way or another"—there's the rub. For what these authors mean by "mimesis" would, one suspects, scarcely satisfy realists as severe as Alter and Graff.

"The logic of criticism has come full circle," Gerald Graff writes.

From the ancient view that literary fictions illustrate general truths, we moved to the view that literary fictions illustrate fictions. But having in the meantime discovered that reality is itself a fiction, we reassert that, in illustrating fictions, literary fictions reveal truth. In a paradoxical and fugitive way, mimetic theory remains alive. Literature holds the mirror up to unreality (1979:179).

This is a travesty, of course, but not so gross a travesty that it does not bear a good deal of resemblance to Ann Jefferson's maneuvers in her account of *nouveau romanesque* mimesis. The *nouveau roman,* by her account, is ultimately "realistic" in its laying bare of the systems through which we construct reality, not only in fictions but also in everyday life. Robbe-Grillet's *La Maison de rendez-vous,* for instance, represents "the nature of the discourse which we use to talk about the world, particularly the language derived from popular fiction (trash)[. . .]"(p. 192; cf. Butler pp. 46-7). "The shape of the narrative lens through which we view so much of our experience," Jefferson writes, "is itself brought into focus by these novels" (p. 166). So there *is* a mimetic commitment here, but it is a commitment to the imitation of discourse *about* the world, not the direct representation of reality that Graff and Alter have in mind.

Brooke-Rose generally seems to share Jefferson's structuralist approach to mimesis. Realism, for her, is not so much a correspondence to reality "out there" as a relation to other discourse. Every new "advance" in realism has been achieved not through a closer approximation to the real, but through violating the norms of the last "realism": "the 'real' merely gets displaced whenever an earlier exploitation becomes exhausted" (p. 411, fn. 14; cf. Jakobson 1971). Yet there is also another impulse in Brooke-Rose's book, somewhat at odds with this one. The new "unrealism" may be the most recent in a series of displacements of the "real," but it is also in part directly mimetic, reflecting an "unreal reality" (cf. Zavarzadeh 1976). "That this century is undergoing a reality crisis," Brooke-Rose writes in her opening sentence, "has become a banality, easily and pragmatically shrugged off" (p. 3); but she does not herself shrug it off easily, nor, evidently, does she find it banal, since she returns to it again and again. She concludes that

> ultimately all fiction is realistic, whether it mimes a mythic idea of heroic deeds or a progressive idea of society, or inner psychology or, as now, the non-interpretability of the world, which is our reality as its interpretability once was [. . .](p. 388).

Thus Christine Brooke-Rose, for all her credentials as structuralist theoretician and postmodernist practitioner, is in certain respects surprisingly in accord with Gerald Graff, antistructuralist and anti-postmodernist:

> The representation of objective reality cannot be restricted to a single literary method. Fantastic or nonrealistic methods may serve the end of illustrating aspects of reality as well as conventionally realistic methods, and even radically anti-realistic

methods are sometimes defensible as legitimate means of representing an unreal reality. [. . .] The critical problem—not always attended to by contemporary critics—is to discriminate between anti-realistic works that provide some true understanding of non-reality and those which are merely symptoms of it (1979:12).

The only difference between Graff's position and Brooke-Rose's is the degree of dogmatism and *parti pris* with which this "critical problem" is formulated and resolved—but it is a crucial difference, precisely the difference between the practice of traditional literary criticism and the practice of descriptive poetics.

So, despite everything that has been written by apologists both for and against postmodernism about its abandonment of mimesis, the mimetic commitment apparently still persists, albeit transformed. Or at least so we must conclude on the strength of these four new essays on the descriptive poetics of postmodern writing. The question is, is it even possible to write fiction that has no mimetic commitment whatsoever? or to write *about* fiction in such a way that no mimetic commitment emerges? I raise this question not in the interest of any polemic, whether for or against postmodernism and its apologists, but in the interests of poetics.

NOTES

[1] Ann Jefferson, *The Nouveau Roman and the Poetics of Fiction.* Cambridge: Cambridge University Press, 1980. 209 pp.

[2] Christine Brooke-Rose, *A Rhetoric of the Unreal: Studies in Narrative and Structure, Especially of the Fantastic.* Cambridge: Cambridge University Press, 1981. 416 pp.

[3] Christopher Butler, *After the Wake: An Essay on the Contemporary Avant-Garde.* Oxford: Oxford University Press, 1980. 173 pp.

[4] Alan Wilde, *Horizons of Assent: Modernism, Postmodernism, and the Ironic Imagination.* Baltimore and London: The Johns Hopkins University Press, 1981. 200 pp.

[5] This is a convenient place to register a protest against the slipshod editing of *A Rhetoric of the Unreal.* There is a serious misprint on its very first page, and on nearly every page thereafter. Even Cambridge University Press sometimes nods, apparently.

[6] The case for viewing postmodernism as simply more of the same new thing has been put most uncompromisingly by Frank Kermode in a book appropriately titled *Continuities.* "There has been only one Modernist Revolution," Kermode writes, "and [. . .] it happened a long time ago. So far as I can see there has been little radical change in modernist thinking since then" (1968:24).

[7] Brooke-Rose gives several examples from Pynchon's *V.* (1963) of the "realistic machinery" of "constant shifts of

viewpoint," signalled by opening gambits of the form "new place/new person + explanatory description," e.g.:

> As the afternoon progressed, yellow clouds began to gather over Place Mohammed Ali, from the direction of the Libyan desert [. . .] For one P. Aïeul, café waiter and amateur libertine, the clouds signalled rain (Pynchon 1963:52).

This hackneyed device of transition, she claims, parodies realism, but so clumsily and repetitiously that the parody collapses into imitation. But is this really parody? Two of her three examples come from Chapter 3, in which a complicated spy-story is rendered through the successive perspectives of no fewer than eight uncomprehending minor characters, concluding with the "camera eye"—a deliberate tour-de-force, in short, an elaborate *stylization* of modernist multiple-viewpoint conventions, just as Chapter 9 is a stylization of Conrad, and Chapter 11 of Proust.

[8] Christopher Butler very sensibly observes that Robbe-Grillet's *oeuvre* is not a monolithic whole, and that the earlier novels from *Les Gommes* (1953) through *Dans le labyrinth* (1959) really *do* lay themselves more open to psychological naturalization than the later "ludic" novels from *La Maison de rendezvous* (1965) on (pp. 51-52).

[9] Brooke-Rose's *Between* (1968) is, it seems to me, the odd man out, a "regression" to epistemologically oriented fiction. Of course, *Out* too is rich in epistemological issues, but here it becomes a question of how far epistemological hesitation can go before it turns into ontological hesitation. How many times must a sequence be exposed as the protagonist's fantasy before the stability of this novel's represented world is fatally compromised? *Out,* in short, is a boundary-text, in this respect resembling Pynchon's *The Crying of Lot 49* (1966), which also teeters on the line between epistemological and ontological orientations, between modernism and postmodernism.

REFERENCES

Alter, Robert, 1975, *Partial Magic: The Novel as a Self-Conscious Genre* (Berkeley, Los Angeles: Univ. of California Press), 218-245.

———, 1975 "Mimesis and the Motive for Fiction," *TriQuarterly* 42 (Spring), 228-249.

Barth, John, 1967. "The Literature of Exhaustion," *Atlantic* (August), 29-34.

———, 1980 "The Literature of Replenishment: Postmodernist Fiction," *Atlantic* (Jan.), 65-71.

Bakhtin, Mikhail, 1973 [1929]. *Problems of Dostoevsky's Poetics,* trans. R.W. Rotsel (Ann Arbor: Ardis).

Brooke-Rose, Christine, 1966. *Such* (London: Michael Joseph).

Dällenbach, Lucien, 1977. *Le récit spéculaire: essai sur la mise en abyme* (Paris: Seuil).

Federman, Raymond, 1975. "Surfiction—Four Propositions in Form of an Introduction," in: *Surfiction: Fiction Now . . . and Tomorrow,* ed. Raymond Federman. (Chicago: Swallow Press), 5-15.

Gass, William, 1971. *Fiction and the Figures of Life* (New York: Vintage Books).

———, 1975 *On Being Blue* (Boston: David R. Godine).

———, 1978 *The World Within the Word* (New York: Knopf).

Graff, Gerald, 1979. *Literature Against Itself: Literary Ideas in Modern Society,* (Chicago and London: Univ. of Chicago Press).

Hassan, Ihab, 1975. *Paracriticism: Seven Speculations of the Times* (Urbana, Ill: Univ. of Illinois Press).

Heath, Stephen, 1972. *The Nouveau Roman: A Study in the Practice of Writing* (London: Elek).

Jakobson, Roman, 1971 (1921). "On Realism in Art," in: *Readings in Russian Poetics,* ed. Ladislav Matejka and Krystyna Pomorska (Cambridge, Mass.: M.I.T. Press), 38-46.

Kermode, Frank, 1968. *Continuities* (London: Routledge and Kegan Paul).

Klinkowitz, Jerome, 1975. *Literary Disruptions: The Making of a Post-Contemporary American Fiction* (Urbana, Ill: Univ. of Illinois Press).

Lodge, David, 1977. *The Modes of Modern Writing: Metaphor, Metonymy, and the Typology of Modern Literature* (London: Edward Arnold).

Newman, A.S., 1976. *Une poésie des discours: essai sur les romans de Nathalie Sarraute* (Geneva: Droz).

Pascal, Roy, 1977. *The Dual Voice: Free Indirect Speech and its Functioning in the Nineteenth-Century English Novel* (Manchester: Manchester UP).

Pynchon, Thomas, 1963. *V.* (New York: Bantam).

———, 1973 *Gravity's Rainbow* (New York: Viking).

Ricardou, Jean, 1967. *Problèmes du nouveau roman* (Paris: Seuil).

———, 1971 *Pour une théorie du nouveau roman* (Paris: Seuil).

———, 1978 *Nouveaux problèmes du nouveau roman* (Paris: Seuil).

Robbe-Grillet, Alain, 1963. *Pour un nouveau roman* (Paris: Minuit).

Sarraute, Nathalie, 1956. *L'ère du soupçon* (Paris: Gallimard).

Sontag, Susan, 1966. *Against Interpretation* (New York: Farrar, Straus, and Giroux).

————, 1969 *Styles of Radical Will* (New York: Farrar, Straus, and Giroux).

Sukenick, Ronald, 1974-1975. "Twelve Digressions Toward a Theory of Composition," *New Literary History* 6, 429-37.

————, 1975 "The New Tradition in Fiction," in Federman 1975: 35-45.

————, 1976 "Thirteen Digressions," *Partisan Review* 43, 99-101.

————, 1977 "Fiction in the Seventies: Ten Digressions on Ten Digressions," *Studies in American Fiction* 5, 99-108.

Zavarzadeh, Mas'ud, 1976. *The Mythopoeic Reality: The Postwar American Nonfiction Novel* (Urbana, Ill.: Univ. of Illinois Press).

John Johnstone

SOURCE: "Postmodern Theory/ Postmodern Fiction," in *Clio*, Vol. 16, No. 2, Winter, 1987, pp. 139-58.

[*In the following essay, Johnston surveys the theories of several postmodernist literary critics, including Brian McHale, Frederic Jameson, Patricia Waugh, and Michel Foucault.*]

In recent years the term "postmodernism" has acquired considerable currency, but without there being much consensus as to its meaning or even its legitimacy. For the sake of convenience, I would like to propose three categories for dealing with different versions of postmodernism: literary/aesthetic postmodernism, historical (or cultural) postmodernism, and theoretical postmodernism. In my critical remarks, however, I shall be less concerned with the periodization or the modern/postmodern break *per se* than with the extent to which these different approaches remain conceptually bound within a modernist domain which some contemporary works of fiction seem to have exceeded.

Probably the most familiar version of postmodernism is the literary or aesthetic one, of which I'll single out only two strands. The first is advanced by people like Patricia Waugh and Brian McHale in England, and Jerome Klinowitz and Ihab Hassan in the United States. What is important for them—what signals the presence of the postmodern—is the foregrounding of literary artifice, the presentation of the work as metafiction or fabulation, and above all the writer's self-conscious awareness of the

fictionality of literature and its status as a construction of language. The writers working according to these assumptions who are most often cited are Borges and Nabokov (especially the latter's *Pale Fire*), Barth, Barthelme, Coover, Calvino, Cortázar, Butor, Robbe-Grillet, Sollers, Fowles, and Handke. While the advocates of this strand tend to focus on fiction, those of the second, who are associated with the periodical *Boundary 2* and would include such critics as William Spanos, Paul Bové and Joseph Riddel, concentrate their attention on poetry. Since this second group will not be of direct concern here, let me characterize them very briefly. First of all, drawing particularly on the work of Heidegger and Derrida, they oppose T. S. Eliot's modernism with the postmodernism of Pound's *Cantos,* W. C. Williams' *Paterson,* and Charles Olson's Projective verse. Joseph Riddel, the most Derridean of this group, argues for example that these poets must be understood in terms of a "double deconstruction," both of their immediate predecessors and themselves, undertaken in order to problematize a poetry of the Word (as *logos*) and such notions as "tradition," "origin," and "citation."[1] Following the Derrida of "Structure, Sign, and Play," Riddel argues that the Moderns are haunted by a "nostalgia for origins," whereas the Postmoderns make what Derrida describes as "the Nietzschean *affirmation*—the joyous affirmation of the freeplay of the world and without truth, without origin, offered to an active interpretation."[2] The problem with this approach, as J. Hillis Miller points out in a review of Riddel's book on Williams, is that it is too easily *reversible,* and fails to account for the heterogeneity within a text or body of texts. Both Williams' poems "Asphodel" and "Patterson Five," Miller asserts, are "modernist and Post-Modernist at once, and can be shown to be so."[3] The problem is to show, Miller continues, that "periods differ from one another because there are different forms of heterogeneity, not because each period held a single coherent 'view of the world'" (31). And something similar could be said, *mutatis mutandis,* about Spanos' claim that modernist poetics privileges spatialization whereas postmodern poetics privileges temporalization.[4]

Because it does not appear to involve the problems of periodization, the current practice of what is called "metafiction" may provide a more convenient example of aesthetic postmodernism. In a recent book, Patricia Waugh argues that metafiction, broadly defined as "fictional writing which self-consciously and systematically draws attention to its status as an artifact in order to pose questions about the relationship between fiction and reality," exhibits a literary self-consciousness different in kind from that of typically modernist work.[5] The latter valorize consciousness by asserting a purely aesthetic order (like "spatial form" or the "epiphanies" of Joyce and Woolf) which compensates for the breakdown of traditional values and order in the "objective" historical world. The postmodernists, in contrast, are apt to regard such orderings of an aesthetic consciousness with satirical skepticism (as in Beckett's *Watt*), or to take them to an extreme by openly flaunting and manipulating the work's artifice and conventionality (the double ending of Fowles' fake "Victorian" novel *The French Lieutenant's Woman,* Calvino's dramatization of the reader in *If on a Winter's Night a Traveller,* or Nabokov's use of chess, mirrors, and acrostics throughout his fiction).

In the aesthetic version of postmodernism, consciousness is no longer a privileged source of order or an aestheticizing instrument, and has been pre-empted by a more direct concern with language as a field of endless re-articulations. Hence the conventions, assumptions and strategies of *writing* as such are much more important for the postmodernist, for whom language is no longer the idealistic and expressive medium of a pre-existing consciousness or ego, but a material part of the world, "always already" there. In various ways, therefore, postmodernist writers treat language "semiotically," restoring its opacity and immanent objecthood, sometimes even employing its arbitrary orderings and rules to generate new structures. This shift in ground or conceptual basis (from consciousness to language) also explains why modernist symbolism gives way to postmodernist allegory (which stresses the gap between signifier and signified), and the unified subject of modernism to the dispersion of the subject in the multiple signifying systems of postmodernism. In short, for the postmodernist, structure replaces interiority (or the subject's consciousness and intentionality) as the locus of meaning.

Within this general problematic, Waugh focuses mainly on how metafiction avoids the charge of self-indulgent aestheticism. In laying bare the conventions of realism and then playing with them, she argues, metafiction illustrates how imaginary worlds are created, and thereby helps us "to understand how the reality we live day by day is similarly constructed, similarly 'written'" (18). Yet this asserted analogy remains too undeveloped in Waugh's argument to have much analytic value, and is symptomatic of a problem to which we'll return. Of more pressing concern to her is the difference between metafiction and another kind of postmodern fiction that breaks down or dissolves this "meta" dimension. Citing a surrealistic story by Leonard Michaels called "Mildred" which deliberately confuses literal and metaphorical assertion (one character starts to eat another after the phrase "eating one's heart out" is uttered), Waugh notes its proximity to a "schizophrenic construction of reality" (38). Unlike metafiction, where the "real" and the "fantasy" world are held apart in a state of tension, in Michaels' story there is no "metalingual" means to distinguish between them.

The distinction Waugh draws here recalls the one Brian McHale makes between the epistemological uncertainties of modernism (how can we know a reality whose existence is not in doubt but which is rendered only through the limited perspectives of the characters—Henry James' *The Turn of the Screw* being a kind of *locus classicus*) and what he sees as postmodernism's refusal to distinguish between ontologically different realities.[6] In this view, if a work of fiction deliberately confuses ontological levels by incorporating visions, dreams, hallucinations, and pictorial representations in a way that makes them indistinguishable from what is depicted as apparently "real," then it is postmodern. Pynchon's *Gravity's Rainbow,* where it is often difficult to tell whether a scene is actually happening or is only a character's dream, hallucination, or fantasy, provides one clear example; Alain Robbe-Grillet's *In the Labyrinth,* where a description of a painting or photograph on the wall will suddenly become a scene we have entered, another. Similar blurrings of ontologically distinct levels of representation, we may see, occur in Robert Coover's story "The Babysitter," Gabriel Garcia Marquez's *100 Years of Solitude,* Doris Lessing's *Briefing for a Descent Into Hell,* J. G. Ballard's *The Atrocity Exhibition,* and most of the novels of William Burroughs. About the latter novels, Waugh remarks that "contexts shift so continuously and unsystematically that the metalingual commentary is not adequate to 'place' or to interpret such shifts" (37). And of course, as she observes, other kinds of postmodern fiction also refuse to provide "explanatory metalingual commentary" on their disorienting fictional strategies. Like *Gravity's Rainbow,* Joseph McElroy's *Lookout Cartridge* and *A Smuggler's Bible* threaten intelligibility through the sheer proliferation of codes and patterns of meaning which produce an overdetermination of meaning sometimes difficult to distinguish from meaninglessness, a situation allegorized in Barthelme's cryptic story "The Explanation" in *City Life.*

But in drawing a distinction between "schizophrenic" and "meta-" fiction, what is really at stake? Is it only a classification scheme for difficult kinds of postmodern fiction? To explain the function of metafiction, Waugh has recourse to theories of culture-as-play such as we find in the work of J. Huizinga and Roger Caillois. In contrast to the examples cited above, "metafiction functions through the problematization rather than the destruction of the concept of 'reality.' It depends on the regular construction and subversion of rules and systems. Such novels usually set up an internally consistent 'play' world which ensures the reader's absorption, and then lays bare its rules in order to investigate the relation of 'fiction' to 'reality' . . ." (40-41). In Waugh's examples the relationship usually turns out to be simple analogy, as in Muriel Spark's novel *Not to Disturb* (1971), where the machinations of a group of enterprising servants to film the imminent deaths of their aristocratic employers—in order to capitalize on the sensationalism of the event—mirror the novelist's efforts to construct a fictional world. Yet one only has to compare this novel with something like J. G. Ballard's *The Atrocity Exhibition* (1970) to sense a strong critique of such self-reflexive fiction. Ballard's text is presented as a series of tableaux in which gestures, geometric landscapes, and various public images—of movie stars, the Kennedy assassination, the Vietnam War, astronauts—are obsessively rearranged. Although no coherent narrative emerges, allusions to the mental breakdown of the central figure, whose name changes slightly from chapter to chapter, and to the fatal car crash of his wife, provide the reader with some orientation. But what at first seems to be a deliberate assault on fictional coherence gradually achieves an intense (although abstract) consistency as we come to realize that the novel does not so much *represent* the breakdown of the individual's interior world as demonstrate that these images of contemporary culture—patricularly images of atrocity—can be charged with meaning only in relation to the detached (even de-cathected) intentionality of a pathological subject. That is, pathology becomes a condition of the novel's formalism, as we see in its repeated assertion of the car crash as a "conceptual event" linking together its various geometries of violence and sexual perversion.

Faced with such an example, and others could be cited as well, "metafiction" begins to look like a containment strategy or a stabilizing function serving a modernist critical perspective. Nor is it clear that the mechanisms in Waugh's examples of metafiction are essentially different from the self-reflexive strategies of modernist works, where the process of their creation or self-begetting becomes their overt subject. I would further suggest that what metafiction preserves and what this other kind of postmodernist fiction threatens is the status of the author as the subject of a unified and coherent intentionality. One can play games only with such a subject, even if that subject is but a formal fiction. The analogy Waugh asserts between fiction as an authorial construction and reality as a social construction fails to hold, since the latter can in no way be said to have a "unified" author or subject. More generally, in Waugh's concern to separate overtly "schizophrenic" fiction from "metafiction"—and thus retain a unified and controlling authorial subject, we can see the limitations and difficulties that befall a formalist attempt to define postmodernism. For it is not only in "schizophrenic" fiction that the subject and representation become problematic, since metafiction itself also raises the problem of representation. As already indicated, the analogy between the construction of the social fabric in its various aspects and that of an artistic illusion in fiction is far too general to explain the specifically late modern or postmodern concern with autorepresentation, and its tendency to represent the processes of the fictional work's construction or even self-generation. Formalism can describe how this concern is manifest in a given fictional text, but seems unable to provide a convincing account of *why* it takes place.

Fredric Jameson confronts the problem of representation and the schizophrenic subject more directly.[7] Taking a clearly historical approach, Jameson proposes to understand postmodernism as the mode of cultural production that typifies a third evolutionary stage in the development of capitalism. In this scheme, which is based on Ernst Mandel's analysis of late capitalism, the first moment of emergent modernism corresponds to the first stage of market capitalism, and is represented directly in the ninteenth-century realist novel. The second or monopoly stage, the stage of imperialism, corresponds to the era of High Modernism, and finds its fullest "expression" in the "totalizing"aesthetic structures of Schoenberg and Joyce, and in the proliferation of numerous personal writing styles as so many "strategies of inwardness" elaborated in recoil against the ever more reified surfaces and impersonal forces of modern life. In this essay Jameson argues that we have arrived at a third moment in this scheme, "postmodernism," which is dominant or hegemonic in current cultural production in a way that modernism proper never was, and that it corresponds to the new de-centered networks and operations—to what Jameson calls the new world space or "hyperspace"—of multinational and global capitalism.

While admitting that many of postmodernism's various features can be read back into key works of modernism, Jameson insists that in postmodernism they are not only dominant (in Roman Jakobson's sense of stylistically foregrounded) but also assume a different social and even structural function in contemporary society. For whereas the great works of modernism articulated a critical distance from or positioned themselves in opposition to the social status quo (whether from the political Left or Right), and thus maintained a dialectical or critically negative relationship to bourgeois culture (empirically, modernist works were perceived as ugly, dissonant, obscure, scandalous, immoral, subversive and anti-social), postmodernist works have not only been absorbed and to some extent institutionalized without resistance, but have become an important source of novelty—as fresh images and stylistic devices—for the fashion changes of current commodity production. For Jameson this means that high culture no longer constitutes, as it did for modernism, a utopian realm of freedom which can stand above the brutal determinisms and degradations of everyday life. And yet, unlike his predecessor Georg Lukács, who denounced modernism as the pathological product of a disintegrating bourgeois individualism and exhorted socially responsible artists to return to critical realism, Jameson does not condemn postmodernism for merging with its culture in a collapse of critical distance. Instead, he urges, we must eschew a moral or aesthetic response for a more dialectical understanding that can think this latest cultural development positively and negatively all at once, that can see it as both progress and catastrophe. We must, like the Marx of the *Manifesto,* look at the latest workings of capitalism as both the best and the worst that has befallen humanity.

Jameson is most compelling, however, when he summarizes the stylistic features, surface attributes, and affects of postmodern works. First and foremost, he sees a flatness or depthlessness, a new kind of superficiality and an attendant waning of affect, which suggest that the "depth model"—as in phenomenology, existential hermeneutics, psychoanalysis, and historical thinking in general—has been displaced by a new textuality of the surface or intertextuality of multiple surfaces. Moreover, the anxiety and alienation typically expressive of the modernist sense of crisis have now been superseded by the emergence of new "intensities"—free-floating and impersonal feelings that are at once, in Jameson's words, "euphoric" and "hysterically sublime" (76)—a shift that he illustrates in passing from Edvard Munch's "The Scream" to Andy

Warhol's "Diamond Dust Shoes." These general features—the new textual surface and the feeling-tone most often associated with it—are correlated in turn with the fragmentation and dissolution of the subject, with, in other words, the "death" of the autonomous bourgeois individual. The loss of the individual subject (as author and character, representing and represented subject, or, in philosophical terms, of Husserl's transcendental ego) marks a dramatic distance from modernism, and for Jameson nowhere is this more evident that in the eclipse of style by pastiche.

If one of the most significant traits of modernism was the emergence of a number of distinctively recognizable personal or individual styles (Conrad, Lawrence, Woolf, Hemingway, Faulkner, etc.) which, more than just being a different wording of the world, constituted a different "phenomenology," then modernism in effect plunged us into a radical Nietzschean perspectivism: each modernist masterpiece represents not a different view of the same world, as would be true for say Dickens, George Eliot, and Thackeray, but an entirely different world, for which the author's style alone holds the key to its deciphering. For Jameson this situation can only be comprehended in turn by means of a larger, more encompassing narrative, for he sees modernism's host of distinct personal styles and mannerisms as so many attempts to "recode" the recognizable norms, beliefs, and practices widely held in Victorian society. In other words, the various styles or "recodings" of modernism become historically intelligible only when seen against the background of Victorian norms. Thus Jameson refers elsewhere to modernist work as "cancelled realism."[8] Now it is precisely these background norms which no longer exist in contemporary society. Even the older national language has been reduced to neutral and reified media speech, which itself becomes one more idiolect among many. The proliferation of "social codes, professional and disciplinary jargons, as well as the badges of ethnic, gender, race, religious, and class affiliation or identification," Jameson finds, only reveal the extent to which we now live in a "field of stylistic and discursive heterogeneity without a norm," and mask the fact that "faceless masters continue to inflect the economic strategies which constrain our existence, but no longer need to impose their speech [on us] (or are henceforth unable to)" ("Postmodernism" 65).

In this situation, parody and satire are unable to operate; instead, such impulses give rise to pastiche, now understood as a kind of blank parody or imitation without ulterior motive and a particular object of derision. And here we might observe that others have made a similar argument for "black humor" and "unstable irony," devices which also arise in the absence of ostensible social norms, or where the "norm" only indicates a statistical generality and may even indicate a symptomatic failure to register the overwhelming newness of the historical situation. In any case, what disturbs Jameson is the way pastiche now tends to eclipse more "genuine representations of history," and the way various "historicisms" randomly cannibalize the styles of the past, which

thereby becomes merely a vast storehouse of images. For Jameson this is the real meaning of contemporary nostalgia films and various "remakes" like *Body Heat,* in which glossy images "connote" the past while emptying it of its real historic substance, as well as the context in which to consider the novels of E. L. Doctorow ("Postmodernism" 67-68). *Ragtime* (1975), for example, is a

> historical novel [that] can no longer set out to represent the historical past; it can only "represent" our ideas and stereotypes about that past (which thereby at once becomes "pop history"). Cultural production is thereby driven back inside a mental space which is no longer that of the old monadic subject, but rather that of some degraded collective "objective spirit": it can no longer gaze directly on some putative real world, at some reconstruction of a past history which was once itself a present; rather, as in Plato's cave, it must trace our mental images of that past upon its confining walls. If there is any realism left here, therefore, it is a "realism" which is meant to derive from the shock of grasping that confinement, and of slowly becoming aware of a new and original historical situation in which we are condemned to seek History by way of our own pop images and simulacra of that history, which itself remains forever out of reach. ("Postmodernism" 71).

The representation of the past in pastiche and simulacra thus entails a loss of historical perspective, which indeed may be indicative of the culture's loss of the narrative function.[9] In *The Political Unconscious* Jameson argues for the necessary resurrection of narrative as the last horizon of meaning, but in the essay "Postmodernism" he attempts to characterize the postmodern breakdown of temporal organizations of experience by invoking Jacques Lacan's account of schizophrenia as a structural malfunction of language caused by the failure of the subject to enter fully into the symbolic order and thus to acknowledge "the Other." In Lacan's terms, this "forclusion of the Other" disrupts the subject's capacity to link signifiers together in a temporally coherent fashion. In the resulting breakdown of the signifying chain, signifiers are freed from their conceptual signifieds, thus allowing them to "float" in a present free of intentionality and praxis, where they are then experienced with a heightened intensity and even hallucinatory charge. Such, at any rate, is how Jameson would have us consider contemporary valorizations of "difference," for him emblematized in the disjunctive experiences of Nam June Paik's stacked television screens, John Cage's music, the discontinuities of collage, textuality, and the "schizophrenic" writing of Beckett, Philip Sollers, Ishmael Reed, Thomas Pynchon, John Ashbery, and others.

Yet for Jameson it is the new worldspace of contemporary global, multinational capitalism that finally poses the greatest problem to representation. What characterizes capital in this third stage is its prodigious expansion and penetration into areas—nature, the Third World, the Unconscious—never so totally commodified. And while we can know *how* it works, as Mandel's book attests, it cannot be directly *represented* in the totality of its disorienting effects. Hence what most distinguishes and makes possible our consumer society, our society of the spectacle and the mass-media image, is a new unrepresentable space that Jameson calls "postmodern hyperspace." This new space, embodied in the dizzying confusions of John Portman's Bonaventure Hotel in Los Angeles, goes beyond the "capacities of the individual human body to locate itself, to organize its immediate surroundings perceptually, and cognitively to map its position in a mappable external world" ("Postmodernism" 83). In conclusion, therefore, Jameson calls for a new aesthetic of cognitive mapping, but one that will have to be "representational" and "dialectical" so as to enable the individual subject to locate himself meaningfully in this new cultural space.

While Jameson's idea that late capitalism has shaped a new "hyperspace" holds out the possibility (or promise) of a coherent and unifying perspective on a wide range of contemporary works and practices, his call for a representational and dialectical map suggests to me a collapse or fall back into a modernist space. In fact, the very model he proposes—Kevin Lynch's *The Image of the City,* with its notions of "urban totality" and traditional markers (monuments, natural boundaries, built perspectives)—has been seriously questioned recently by urbanists like Paul Virilio, who has shown that the speed of advanced technology has dissolved the spatial coordinates of the city into a complex regime of different temporalities exceeding conventional representation and which demand to be analyzed in terms of interface, flow, and dissolving or unstable frame images.[10] In these terms, it is difficult to see how a form of "cognitive mapping" that remains primarily representational could resolve the theoretical problems posed by what we might call, adopting Freud's terminology, late capitalism's *representability*. The difficulties of such a project are well attested to by Jameson's essay as a whole. On the one hand, postmodernist works, in yielding to a new sense of schizophrenic temporality, fail to provide adequate (i.e., historically perspectived) representations of postmodern experience; on the other hand, the period itself is characterized, following Mandel's scheme, by the unrepresentability of the new "space" produced by the latest technology—nuclear power, the computer, mass media—which is geared toward *re*production rather than production, and only intensifies the tendency of modern culture toward autoreferentiality. Yet it is from within this aporia that Jameson will assert that "our faulty representations of some immense communicational and computer network are themselves but a distorted figuration of something even deeper, namely the whole world system of presentday multinational capitalism" ("Postmodernism" 79).

But suppose this overriding need for representational schemes and depth model hermeneutics is itself what produces the "distorted figurations" of which it speaks. Such indeed would be the assumption of what I am calling theoretical postmodernism, which abandons this representational framework and seeks to formulate the relationships between literature (and art) and the social context on a new conceptual basis, one that uses the fundamental concepts of modernism but at the same time attempts to go beyond them. It is in this sense that the immense theoretical work undertaken by Gilles Deleuze and Félix Guattari in their two-volume study of "Capitalism et Schizophrénia" may be called "postmodern," even though they themselves never employ the term.[11] Such a shift in perspective does not entail that we consider a new body of work as "postmodern," but rather that we "read" what is already all around us—including those hallowed modernist classics—in a new and completely different way.

Thus in *Kafka: Toward a Minor Literature,* Deleuze and Guattari explode the symbolist (and inevitably psychoanalytic) view, according to which Kafka's works are to be seen as so many different stagings and sublimations of Oedipal conflicts with his father, and argue to the contrary that

> [t]he question posed by the father is not how to become free in relation to him (the Oedipal question), but how to find a path where he did not find one . . . [T]he father appears as the man who had to renounce his own desire and faith (if only to get out of the rural ghetto where he was born) and who calls upon his son to submit—but only because the father himself has submitted to a dominant order in a situation which appears to have no escape . . . In short it is not Oedipus that produces neurosis; it is neurosis, *the desire that submits and tries to communicate its submission, that produces Oedipus.*[12]

In this reversal of Freud, Oedipus is made into a political issue, one that allows us, as they indicate, "to see over [the] father's shoulder what was in question all along: a whole micropolitics of desire, of impasses and exits, of submissions and rectifications" (19). In Kafka's fiction, therefore, the judges, commissioners and bureaucrats are not to be seen as father substitutes; the father, rather, is their representative, "a condensation of all the forces to which he submits and invites his son to submit" (22). Rather than reducing the drama of Kafka's works to the dynamics of the familial or Oedipal triangle, Deleuze and Guattari show that this triangle is not only connected to but defined by commercial, economic, bureaucratic, and judiciary triangles which indicate force-relationships in the social field.

By specifying these forces, moreover, the possibility of evading them along a "line of flight" also emerges. In Kafka's fiction this first occurs in the stories concerned with some kind of "becoming-animal." If the father—especially the Jewish father—having been uprooted from the country, is immediately caught up in a process of "deterritorialization," he never ceases to re-orient or "reterritorialize" himself in relation to his family, business, and spiritual authorities. But acts of becoming-animal involve the exact opposite process: they constitute attempts to follow a line or movement across thresholds of intensity toward "absolute deterritorializations" where forms and signifier-signified relationships dissolve into the unformed matter of uncoded fluxes and non-signifying signs. Thus for Deleuze and Guattari

> Kafka's animals never refer to mythology or to archetypes but correspond only to new gradients, zones of liberated intensities where contents free themselves from their forms as well as from their expressions, and from the signifier that formalized them. There is nothing any longer but movements, vibrations, thresholds in a deserted matter: animals, mice, dogs, apes, cockroaches are distinguished only by this or that threshold, this or that vibration, by a specific underground passage in the rhizome or burrow. For these passages are underground intensities. In the becoming-mouse, it is a whistling that pulls the music and the meaning from the words. In the becoming-ape, it is a coughing that "seems disturbing but that has no meaning" (becoming a tuberculoid ape). In the becoming-insect, it is a mournful whining that carries the voice and blurs the resonance of the words. Gregor becomes a cockroach not just to flee from his father, but rather to find an escape where his father couldn't find one, to flee from the director, the businessman and the bureaucrats, to reach that realm where the voice no longer does anything but hum: "Did you hear him speak? It was an animal's voice," said the director. (24-25)

It is important to understand that a "becoming-animal" is in no way a "becoming-like-an-animal"; it is not a copying or imitation but rather a metamorphosis brought about through the conjunction of two deterritorializations: the becoming-human of the animal and the becoming-animal of the human. Nor is it to be seen as a kind of metaphor, as symbolic or allegorical figuration. In the various examples cited by Deleuze and Guattari—the becoming-whale of Melville's Ahab, Lawrence's becoming-turtle, the various becomings of dog, bear or woman in Kleist's plays, the becoming-horse of Little Hans in Freud's case study, the becoming-rat in the Hollywood film *Willard,* the becoming-Jewish in Joseph Losey's film *Mr. Klein,* the various metamorphoses like those of the were-wolf or sorcerer in mythology and folklore, as well as the more general instances of becoming-woman or becoming-child—it is always a question of a process that must be understood in non-signifying terms, as sketching a movement of escape from dominant significations and regimes of control.[13]

All too often in Kafka's stories, however, this movement of deterritorialization through a "becoming-animal" fails. In "The Metamorphosis" Gregor's "becoming-cockroach" is finally blocked, and the story depicts his sad re-Oedipalization. The problem, Deleuze and Guattari suggest, may be that animals are too formed, too territorialized, too significative to go all the way along a line of flight. In the novels, consequently, Kafka tries another solution, involving the proliferation of characters and a new fictional topography, in what Deleuze and Guattari call a "socio-political investigation" of the new machinic arrangements" (88-89) that fascism, Stalinism, capitalism, and twentieth-century bureaucracy will usher in.

The key concept in their analysis is the notion of *agencement* (somewhat feebly translated into English as "arrangement"), by which they mean a multiplicity of heterogeneous parts that somehow function together in a kind of symbiosis. More specifically, an *agencement* always comprises two sides or faces, one involving *states of things* (bodies that mix or join in various ways and pass on effects), the other involving *statements,* or different regimes of signs (new formulations, styles and gestures). In the novels (*Amerika, The Trial, The Castle*) Kafka presents these two complementary sides of the *agencement* by creating situations where an extreme juridical formalization of statements (questions and answers, objections, pleas, reasons for a judgment, presentation of conclusions, verdicts, etc.) operates conjointly with things and bodies as so many machines (the boat-machine, the hotel-machine, the circus-machine, the trial-machine, the castle-machine). In asserting that the novels take "machinic arrangements" as their objects, Deleuze and Guattari draw attention to the fact that in Kafka's works human beings exist only as parts of or along side various kinds of social machines. (They use the term "machinic"—in opposition to the term "mechanical"—to indicate a functioning of parts which are independent of one other yet somehow function together.) And the terminology of their critical apparatus also allows them to avoid two misinterpretations which have plagued Kafka criticism, to wit, that the desire animating the major characters of the novels is accountable either in terms of a lack (the psychoanalytic reading) or an ungraspable, transcendent law (the negative theological reading).

Instead, they read the novels as the "dismantling of all transcendental justifications" (93). In *The Trial* the operations of justice and the law are relocated in a field of immanence defined by desire: "where one believed there was the law, there is in fact desire and desire alone. Justice is desire and not law" (90). Because justice is only a form for the working out of desire, it operates along a continuum, but a continuum made up of contiguities, since in Kafka "the contiguity of offices, the segmentalization of power, replaces the hierarchy of instances and the eminence of the sovereign" (92). Because of the immanence of desire, everyone in the novel, including the priest and the little girls, is caught up in the process of justice—if only as "auxiliaries" (91). Thus K finally realizes, despite his Uncle's advice, that he needs no legal representative, that no one should come between himself and his own desire, that he will find justice only by moving from room to room, following his desire, a process that is virtually interminable.[14]

Yet desire always proves to be a mixture or blend of what are really two co-existent movements of desire, each caught up in the other, and corresponding to two different kinds of "law": "One captures desire with great diabolical arrangements, sweeping along servants and victims, chiefs and subalterns in almost the same movement, and only bringing about a massive deterritorialization of man by also reterritorializing him, whether in an office, a prison, a cemetery (the paranoic law). The other movement makes desire take flight through all the arrangements, brushing up against all the segments without being caught in any of them, and always carries further along the innocence of a power of deterritorialization indistinguishable from escape (the schizo-law)."[15] Not surprisingly, then, in Kafka we also find two corresponding kinds of architecture and bureaucracy, actually opposed but often blending with and penetrating into each other: an archaic or mythic form with contemporary functions, and a "neo-formation" that is today becoming our own. Such mixtures explain Kafka's strange fictional topographies, especially evident in *The Trial* and *The Castle,* where we constantly encounter offices behind offices, long passages and corridors with separate entrances at one end and contiguous entrances at another. By analyzing this topography, together with the proliferating series of doubles and connectors, blocks of "becoming" and thresholds of intensity, Deleuze and Guattari show how Kafka's fiction maps the flows, encodings and decodings of desire as an immanent process in the social field.

Finally, every machinic arrangement of desire is, in their words, also a "collective arrangement of enunciation" (33) in the sense that the former always gives rise to certain kinds of statements. The first chapter of *Amerika* is filled with protestations by the stoker against his superior officer (a Rumanian) and complaints about the oppression which Germans aboard ship must undergo; and of course *The Trial* constitutes a complete anatomy of juridical statements, the rules of which adumbrate "the real instructions for the machine." As author of the novels, Kafka accedes to the various "collective arrangements of enunciation" through the invention of what Deleuze and Guattari call "the K-function" (157), the letter suggesting that "K" is not so much a character as a collective subject through which the individual in his solitude responds to the "diabolic powers knocking at the door," as Kafka himself described the new powers looming on the historical horizon.[16] It is through this invention that Kafka makes one arrangement—the one that invented him—pass into another, his own highly political "writing machine."

Deleuze and Guattari trace the evolution of Kafka's "writing machine" from the letters he wrote to Felice (which constituted a kind of "diabolical pact") to the animal stories and finally to the novels. Its condition of possibility stems ultimately from Kafka's employment in the office of an insurance company, with its secretaries and bosses, its social, political and administrative distributions, and the various technical devices and machines both utilized there and that Kafka had to deal with in accident claims. This set-up promoted an entire "erotic distribution . . . not because desire is desire of the machine but because desire never stops making a machine in the machine and creates a new gear alongside the preceding gear indefinitely" (146). Kafka's "writing machine" operates in a similar fashion," as the off-shoot of a vast bureaucratic machine located within a field of external relationships. As a German-speaking Jew in Prague and therefore a minority figure in a double sense, he made of his own peculiarly inflected and

somewhat impoverished German a new kind of expressive medium. Rather than choosing to be an author in the classical sense, like Goethe, whom he so admired, Kafka deliberately invented a form of what Deleuze and Guattari call a deterritorializing "minor literature" (29ff). That is, as a writer living in a cultural and linguistic ghetto, Kafka refused to inflate his language artificially by using symbolism, oneirism, or the Kabbala, as did Gustav Meyrink, Max Brod, and others of the Prague school. Instead, he went the other way—toward a new spareness and sobriety. Pushing further along points of deterritorialization already within his language, he created a strange form of "stuttering," a "minority" language, as Deleuze and Guattari say (41-42), within a major language that exerts a subversive pull toward regions beyond representation and signification, and that vibrates with new intensities. And contrary to a major literature of "masters," which always transforms social questions into individual problems, a "minor" literature functions outside of or exterior to hegemonic cultural formations, and always opens out onto socio-political networks. Thus Kafka's writing machine produces not only a different kind of language, but also announces a different function for literature: as Deleuze and Guattari show, in a "minor literature" there is no "subject," but a tracing of desire in the social field, a diagramming of how different machinic arrangements operate in conjunction with different "arrangements of enunciation."

At this point let us pause and take note of an emerging contrast of some consequence. First, as different as they are, both Jameson's and Waugh's versions of postmodernism derive from and maintain a transcendent perspective: in Jameson, through Marxism and the assumption of history as a dialectic process; in Waugh, through a formalism that privileges the authorial function or author as intentional subject. Secondly—and this is a major point—what troubles both critics, albeit in different ways, is precisely the fact that postmodernist works seem to throw into question this transcendent perspective, whether we call it the critical stance or the meta-dimensionality of the work, as if to suggest that there is no longer any Archimedean point "above" from which contemporary cultural production can be surveyed in a nonreductive way. Deleuze and Guattari, on the other hand, bring us to the very threshold of the postmodern, not by lamenting the loss of a transcendent or privileged point of view, but by theorizing its basis in particular social and cultural arrangements. Through their eyes, perhaps, we can envisage postmodernism as an attempt to think through as a specific *positivity* what modernism could only think negatively (through terms like alienation, cultural crisis, loss of God and tradition, chaos and disorder). In this perspective, at least in the theoretical formulations provided by Deleuze and Guattari, postmodernism constitutes a renewed attempt to link the philosophical problem of radical *immanence* or multiplicity to a theory of culture conceived as the conjoining of different "semiotic regimes" with various material arrangements, but without recourse to any transcendent unity or expressive function that would stand outside the historical field or domain as their cause or ground. A similar perspective emerges in the work of Michel Foucault, as the many parallels and exchanges between Deleuze and Foucault might suggest. In *Les Mots et Les Choses* Foucault tried to move beyond the modernist conceptual domain by thinking through the conditions of possibility of the *sciences humaines,* but it was only with his theory of power, linked with his theory of the production of statements, which thus joins non-discursive and discursive practices, with both conceived as immanent to the field of their distribution and not emanating from some transcendent instance like the subject or the State, that he advanced into a postmodern domain. In his recent book on Foucault, Deleuze demonstrates that Foucault was always centrally concerned with the historically changing forms of *le visible* and *l'énoncable,* and with how their different combinations are in turn "stratified"—given historical coherence and stability—through different arrangements of *pouvoir* and *savoir.* On the one hand the resulting "strata" (55 ff) are historical formations determinant of what can be seen and said at a given time; but on the other they are always and at the same time enveloped by a multiplicity or "becoming of forces that double history" (91) and are seen as arriving from an indeterminant "outside."[17]

It may seem evident that what I am calling theoretical postmodernism overlaps in many ways with the theoretical enterprise generally subsumed under the rubric of "poststructuralism." But here we must proceed case by case, and not treat "poststructuralism" as monolithic. The questioning of the unity and formation of the subject, of the expressionist and representational functions of language are, it seems to me, clearly postmodernist concerns, whereas the theorization of writing as a privileged form of textuality such as one finds in much of Roland Barthes and Paul de Man still operates within the conceptual domain of late modernism, as an often valuable refinement of modernist formalism and aestheticism. In these terms, Jacques Derrida could be seen as a kind of hinge or transitional figure, as a detailed comparison of Derrida's notion of the "scene of writing" with Deleuze and Guattari's notion of the "writing machine" (which cannot be undertaken here) would, I think, substantiate. But whatever the case, there can be no doubt that Deleuze and Guattari's conceptualization represents a theoretical advance beyond Jameson's, for the "mapping" that it makes possible is no longer tied to the modernist (or industrialist era) model of cultural production, nor constrained by the conceptual limits of dialectical and representational thinking.[18]

Finally, something like Deleuze and Guattari's version of theoretical postmodernism also seems urged upon us by the most ambitious recent American fiction as well. In Thomas Pynchon's *Gravity's Rainbow* and William Gaddis's *JR,* everything is connected to everything, yet also proliferating madly into divergent series of items, events and structures—as in what James Joyce perhaps meant by a "chaosmos." The only meta-dimension available is provided by what Pynchon calls the "meta-cartel"—an interlocking conglomerate of industries,

technologies and institutions which seek to render every subject and substance (human and otherwise) controllable, serviceable, and exchangeable, whether as labor, raw material, or links in a communication chain: "How alphabetic is the nature of molecules . . . These are our letters, our words: they too can be modulated, broken, recoupled, redefined, co-polymerized one to the other in world wide chains that will surface now and then over long molecular silences, like the seen part of a tapestry."[19] Pynchon thus describes what Deleuze and Guattari call a binary coding machine or abstract machine, which operates even at a molecular level. In the novel, this machine (generally referred to as the "They-system") is opposed by a "Counterforce," which must rely on hardly legitimized semiotic systems: "Those like Slothrop, with the greatest interest in discovering the truth, were thrown back on dreams, psychic flashes, omens, cryptographies, drug epistemologies, all dancing on a ground of terror, contradiction, absurdity" (582). And by the end of the novel, the German V-2 rocket has become a "text," Slothrop can read mandalas, trout guts, graffiti, paper scraps; Eddie Pensiero reads shivers, Saure Bummer reads reefers, Thanatz reads whip scars, and the narrator reads Tarot cards. Has the world become a text, or is it rather that all rational signifying systems can only deliver us into the hands of power? Perhaps they amount to the same thing. *Gravity's Rainbow* makes it clear how World War II was primarily the "site" of an immense technological transformation of the world. Everything that impeded the installation of a kind of cybernetic instrumentality—old territories, languages and social forms, ancient filiations and habits of mind—had to be dissolved so that this new form of rationality could be implemented. Cybernetics and feedback systems, Pynchon's narrator says (238-39), must be seen first as new means of control, and thus the necessary prelude to the commodification of all information by the giant "meta-cartel."[20]

According to Deleuze and Guattari, we have passed from a semiotics of the signifier to a semiotics of flow. Gaddis's portrayal of Wall Street and the machinations of corporate finance in *JR* renders the fluxes and flows of contemporary life in the medium of recorded speech, without narrative summary or connection. In this vast "acoustic collage" transcribed out of the discourses of advertising, big business, politics, and public relations, the slang of school kids and street people, the delirious ruminations of drunken intellectuals and failed artists, the bitter dialogues of breakdown and lovers' turmoils—intelligible "sounds" threaten to become barely distinguishable from the general background noise of our multi-media environment. All is flow—money, finance capital, video images, water, conversation, a radio playing, one scene or character impinging on another. As we are whirled from one epicenter of connection to another—from an old family home in Long Island to the local school, the local bank, then to a Wall Street investment firm, and finally to an impossibly crowded upper East Side apartment—it becomes clear that no overriding, stabilizing speech will be heard, indeed *could* be heard, no identifiable consciousness could be in control, even take it all in. Yet we cannot fail to notice that in this ceaseless break-up and movement which threaten not only production but intelligibility at least two machines appear to be functioning: the corporate finance institutions that generate gigantic "paper empires" and the novel we are reading that is their off-shoot.

If Gaddis's novel is thus a writing machine which operates by recording the breakdowns in the signifying chains of the characters' speech and in the lifelines of their movements, Deleuze and Guattari allow us to see how these breakdowns are part of the larger "deterritorializations" of contemporary capitalism, which requires new modes of individuation and yet at the same time must continue to assign and reinforce older kinds of identities and social investments. In the vocabulary of Deleuze and Guattari, Gaddis' novel may be said to articulate "a line of flight" along the borders of these two opposing movements, thereby tracing the break-up of the dominant systems of signification and meaning that will result in the characters being swept up in a "molecular becoming." Similarly, *Gravity's Rainbow* charts the breakdown of the main character Slothrop in relation to a vast reconfiguring of contemporary technology, politics, and big business, but in his gradual disappearance and final anonymity we can also see a molecular "devenir-imperceptible." In both cases the theoretical postmodernism of Deleuze and Guattari allows us to see how these novels push beyond the conceptual limits of modernism and make the new informational arrangements that perhaps define our present visible as part of the same movement in which the older ones are being dissolved.

NOTES

[1] Joseph Riddel, *The Inverted Bell: Modernism and the Counter Poetics of William Carlos Williams* (Baton Rouge: Louisiana State UP, 1974), esecially 257 ff, where he argues that Williams "wants to strike through the Modernist deconstruction of the classical with another effort at deconstruction."

[2] Derrida's often cited essay first appeared in English in *The Structuralist Controversy,* eds. Richard Macksey and Eugenio Donato (Baltimore: Johns Hopkins UP, 1972); Derrida's words, translated by the editors (264). Riddel discusses Derrida's statement (250-53 and passim).

[3] J. Hillis Miller, "Deconstructing the Deconstructors," *Diacritics* 5 (Summer 1975):31. But see Riddel's response, "A Miller's Tale," *Diacritics* 5 (Fall 1975):56-65.

[4] William V. Spanos, "The Detective and the Boundary: Some Notes on the Postmodern Literary Imagination," *Boundary 2* 1 (Fall 1972):147-68. In a later essay, "Repetition in *The Waste Land:* A Phenomenological Destruction," *Boundary 2* 7 (Spring 1979):225-85, Spanos argues against the spatialized reading of Eliot's poem and asserts that the poem "points toward . . . the demystifying 'anti-literature' of the postmodern period" by retrieving the "historical sense" (265).

[5] Patricia Waugh, *Metafiction: The Theory and Practice of Self-Conscious Fiction* (London: Methuen, 1984), 2.

[6] Brian McHale, "Modernist Reading, Post-Modern Text: The Case of *Gravity's Rainbow,*" *Poetics Today* 1 (Autumn, 1979):85-109.

[7] Fredric Jameson, "Postmodernism, or the Cultural Logic of Late Capitalism," *New Left Review* 146 (July-August, 1985):53-92.

[8] Fredric Jameson, "The Ideology of the Text," *Salmagundi* 31-32 (Fall 1975/Winter 1976):243.

[9] Jameson also takes up the problem of narrative in relation to postmodernism in his "Foreword" to Jean Francois Lyotard's *The Postmodern Condition: A Report on Knowledge* (Minneapolis: U of Minnesota P, 1984), trans. Geoff Bennington and Brian Massumi. Lyotard, who sees a dispersion of the narrative function into its different linguistic elements now taking place, defines "postmodernism" as a loss of belief in the great meta-narratives that sustain and legitimate our culture. But Jameson notes, correctly I think, that for Lytoard postmodernism is not a radically new historical stage but only heralds a new turn or cycle in the perpetual "revolution" of modernism.

[10] Kevin Lynch, *The Image of the City* (Cambridge, MA: M.I.T. Press, 1960), and Paul Virilio, *L'espace critique* (Paris: Christian Bourgois, 1984).

[11] Gilles Deleuze and Félix Guattari's *L'anti-oedipe* (Paris: Minuit, 1972) and *Mille Plateaux* (Paris: Minuit, 1980) constitute the two-volume study "Capitalism et Schizophrénie." Only *Anti-Oedipus* (New York: Viking Press, 1977), trans. Robert Hurley, Mark Seem, and Helen R. Lane, is currently available in English. A translation of *Mille Plateaux* is forthcoming from the University of Minnesota Press.

[12] Gilles Deleuze and Félix Guattari, *Kafka: pour une littérature mineure* (Paris: Minuit, 1975), 19 (my translation).

[13] See *Mille Plateaux,* chapter 10, entitled "1730-Devenir-intense, devenir-animal, devenir-imperceptible . . ." for Deleuze and Guattari's most extended treatment of "becoming."

[14] Deleuze and Guattari in fact argue that the novel *is* interminable, and contest the legitimacy of the final chapter depicting K's execution on both textual and interpretive grounds. See *Kafka* (80-81).

[15] *Kafka,* 110. These two kinds of "law" are explored in detail in *Anti-Oedipus;* see especially 273-83.

[16] In a letter to Max Brod, quoted by Deleuze and Guattari in *Kafka* (22); no date for letter given.

[17] Gilles Deleuze, *Foucault* (Paris: Minuit, 1986). See especially "Les Strates ou Formations Historiques: Le Vis-

ible et L'énoncable (Savoir)," 55-76, and "Les strategies ou le non-stratifié: La Pensée du dehors (Pouvoir)," 77-99.

[18] Jean Baudrillard's theory of "simulation" also moves beyond "dialectics" and "representation," and thus would appear to offer another version of theoretical postmodernism. Baudrillard deserves extended treatment, but here it must suffice to point out that his theory, although worked out in semiotic and poststructural terms, is actually historicist (like Jameson's) and proposes a succession of neo-Hegelian self-contained semiotic stages or orders. See "La fin de la production" and "Les trois orders de simulacres" in *L'échange symbolique et la mort* (Paris: Editions Gallimard, 1976), 17-77.

[19] Thomas Pynchon, *Gravity's Rainbow* (New York: Viking Press, 1973), 355.

[20] For a more extended treatment of this theme in relation to the new technologies of communication, see Jonathan Crary's "Eclipse of the Spectacle," in *Art after Modernism: Rethinking Representation* (New York: New Museum of Contemporary Art, 1984), 283-94.

David H. Hirsch

SOURCE: "Postmodernism and American Literary History," in *The Sewanee Review,* Vol. XCIX, No. 1, Winter, 1991, pp. 40-60.

[In the following essay, Hirsch defends New Criticism practices against what he perceives as the failed philosophical underpinnings of postmodern criticism.]

Anglo-American New Criticism had nearly run its course by the end of the 1960s. What had started as an innovative method of reading literary works creatively had, in all too many instances, declined into a robotic and repetitious exercise in counting images and demonstrating paradoxes for their own sake. A clear signal that the end was at hand for the New Criticism was the proliferation of essays that seemed to have as their goal nothing more than adding up various kinds of imagery without regard to their importance or to how the images functioned in the semantic system of the work. In a liberal society founded on an ideology of revolution and progress, change is always at hand; and in the late sixties one could sense that changes in the practice of literary criticism had become not only desirable but inevitable. Unfortunately the forerunners of change that came in the form of attacks on the New Criticism were directed not against particular essays of practical criticism but against such slogans as "the autotelic poem," "the intentional fallacy," and "the affective fallacy"—slogans derived from two theoretical essays that appeared after the innovative and most creative practical criticism had been done. In effect the great essays of the first generation of New Critics remained unchallenged, and indeed remain unchallenged to this day.

In their most important work the first generation of New Critics was not bound by the theories or the slogans that later developed around their essays. For example, in what turned out to be a seminal essay on "The Ancient Mariner," Robert Penn Warren, far from limiting himself to an analysis of what he considered an autotelic poem, took as the starting point of his essay a historical-biographical bit of information: Mrs. Barbauld's comment, reported in *Table Talk,* to the effect that the poem had two defects— "it was improbable and it had no moral." This bit of context then becomes the seed out of which the monograph grows, for Warren goes on to state that one of the purposes of his essay is to "establish that *The Ancient Mariner* does embody a statement"—namely "that the statement which the poem does ultimately embody is thoroughly consistent with Coleridge's basic theological and philosophical views as given to us in sober prose, and that . . . the theme is therefore 'intended.'" Warren's statement is clear enough to stand without comment, but the misinformation about an alleged New Critical denial of context, intention, and statement has been repeated so often that Warren's explicitly stated position is worth summarizing. He allows that the poem makes a statement, that it is generated out of an authorial intention, and that this intention can be confirmed by recourse to Coleridge's other writings—that is by recourse to statements that Coleridge made outside the poem.

Neither is it precisely accurate to say, as has often been alleged, that the New Critics eliminated the reader. Consider this passage by Robert Penn Warren, who is often regarded, along with Cleanth Brooks, as the ultimate New Critic: "The perfect intuitive and immediate grasp of a poem in the totality of its meaning and structure—the thing we desire—may come late rather than early—on the fiftieth reading rather than on the first. Perhaps we must be able to look forward as well as back as we move through the poem—be able to sense the complex of relationships and implications—before we can truly have that immediate grasp." This assertion, describing interpretation as a "back-and-forth process" taking place between the reader and the poem, in this case poetry by Robert Frost, anticipates what later became one of the fundamental tenets of both hermeneutics (the "hermeneutic circle," as it was called) and reader-response theory. In 1967 a three-pronged attack was launched on the New Criticism, two prongs coming from American critics and the third from a European. In Anglo-American theory the attack came on one front from a "reader-response critic," and on the other from an "intentionalist" critic. The first claimed to restore the reader and the latter to restore the author to critical practice. My contention was, and remains, that the attacks were for the most part directed against straw men, since a careful reader of the work of the original New Critics would have perceived that neither reader nor author had actually been removed from the reading process. Nor were the New Critics unaware that reading was indeed a process. The new theories did not greatly advance our understanding of literature in particular or of the ways in which we arrive at an understanding of written utterances in general. In discussing the work of Stanley

Fish, who spearheaded the effort to restore the reader, I tried to demonstrate that not only was such a restoration unnecessary, but that Fish himself had not managed to rid himself of the shackles of New Critical methods of reading, except that in his New Critical readings he adopts a slightly different rhetorical posture. That is, what Fish actually did in his criticism was to seek out image patterns, ironies, and paradoxes, just as the New Critics had instructed him, but instead of attributing "meanings" to an author or a text, he attributed meanings to the mind in the act of reading, thus institutionalizing the process described by Warren in the Frost essay. As his theory of reader response evolved, Fish eventually concluded that image patterns, irony, paradoxes, the unity of the text were all in the mind of the reader, not in the text itself, and this ultimately led him to claim that the text did not exist at all.

At the antipodes from American reader-response theory is intentionalist theory. As propounded by E. D. Hirsch, Jr., the theory developed the position that every text has a single fixed meaning, and that this fixed meaning is the "author's intention." In the course of developing his theory, Hirsch demolished the "hermeneutic" theories of Hans Georg Gadamer, a student of Martin Heidegger. He pinpointed the contradictions and inconsistencies in Gadamer's attempt to establish that the meaning of a text is the reader's interpretation of that text, and yet to affirm, at the same time, that there are limits to the possible number of readings. The debate between reader-responsists and intentionalists was intense, but when the dust had settled, it became clear that the rage for theory itself presented some serious difficulties, because the theorists were all too often inclined to paint themselves into a corner. The methods of the reader-responsists, for example, led them to the dead-end position that there was no text at all, only interpretations. Intentionalism, on the other hand, led to the position that there could be only one valid interpretation of any given text. If both these claims could be established by clever arguing, both were nevertheless counterintuitive, inconsistent with experience, and abhorrent to reason. What these extreme claims did was to raise unresolvable epistemological problems that had long been standard philosophers' dilemmas: Did meaning, if indeed there was such a thing at all, reside in the mind of the author, in the text, or in the perceiving mind? What the intentionalists wove by day, reader-responsists unraveled at night.

One other aspect of the attacks on the New Criticism was surprising. One would have expected that the restoration of either author or reader to the autotelic work of art would constitute a humanizing gesture—that is, one would have expected to see the "autonomous poem" of the New Criticism replaced with a more "human" poem. One would have thought that the two positions taken together might have represented a return to the human-centered poetics of Wordsworth, who wrote, in his preface to *The Lyrical Ballads* (1800): "Who is the poet? To whom does he address himself? And what language is to be expected of him?—He is a man speaking to men: a man, it is true, endowed with more lively sensibility, more enthusiasm and tenderness, . . . who rejoices more than other men in the spirit of life that is in him." But reader-response and intentionalist theories of reading, even taken together, did not return literature to a more human dimension, to a condition in which the literary work would once again become an act of passional thinking in which one human being addresses another. If anything, the attacks on New Criticism were more inimical to what was "human" in literature than the New Criticism was accused of being. Hence, in an essay taking issue with Wimsatt and Beardsley on "the affective fallacy," Stanley Fish concluded about his own reader-oriented approach: "Becoming good at the method [of Fishian reading] means asking the question "what does that . . . do?" with more and more awareness of the probable (and hidden) complexity of the answer; that is, with a mind more and more sensitized to the workings of language. In a peculiar and unsettling (to theorists) way, it is a method which processes its own user, who is also its only instrument."

Fish replaces what he takes to be a depersonalized method of reading with a robotic reader who is conceived as an "instrument . . . processed by the method." This seems to constitute a change without gain. I have seen no evidence (nor does Fish himself attempt to provide any) that Fish or his followers have established their credentials as commentators who are "more sensitized to language" than such critics as T. S. Eliot, Cleanth Brooks, Robert Penn Warren, Allen Tate, Kenneth Burke, John Crowe Ransom, G. Wilson Knight—to name only some of the New Critics Fish is trying to persuade us to "erase," yet whose essays on particular literary works still set a standard of linguistic sensitivity difficult to attain. In fact one may argue that "a method which processes its own user, who is also its only instrument" is antithetical to the development of a "more . . . sensitized . . . mind."

E. D. Hirsch, presumably at the opposite end of the spectrum from Fish, presents us with a robotized author instead of a robotized reader: "The discipline of interpretation is founded, then, not on a methodology of construction but on a logic of validation. . . . In the earlier chapters of this book, I showed that only one interpretive problem can be answered with objectivity: 'What, in all probability, did the author mean to convey?' In this final chapter, I have tried to show more particularly wherein that objectivity lies. It lies in our capacity to say on firm principles, 'Yes, that answer is valid' or 'No, it is not.'" As I have argued in earlier discussions of reader-response criticism, from a practical standpoint it does not seem to matter greatly whether we put the question as "What, in all probability, did the author mean to convey? or "What, in all probability, does the text mean to convey?" As in reader-response criticism we have a change without a gain.

Though both of the American attacks on the New Criticism were regressive, neither was as regressive as the third prong of the 1967 attacks, which was more totalistic and more destructive; but to show how and why these particular attacks on the New Criticism were reactionary, I must take my narrative both forward and backward at the same time. We must go forward from 1967, when *Validity in Interpretation* appeared to a book published in 1980, Frank Lentricchia's *After the New Criticism,* that was intended to announce the passing of the New Criticism and celebrate the development and eventual ascendancy, during the fifties and sixties, of continental (i.e., French and German) thinking (or, to be more precise, of French cultural criticism, a critical mode of analysis heavily influenced by the thinking of Karl Marx and Martin Heidegger, the latter having boasted, that "when the French want to think they have to think in German"). The ascendancy of the Franco-German school was characterized by a swift series of transitions, from structuralism, to semiotics, to hermeneutics, to poststructuralism, deconstruction, and postmodernism.

The scenario envisaged by Lentricchia leaves no doubt who are the good guys and who the bad. The sophisticated continental theorists are the former, while the black hats are made up of naive Americans who do not welcome continental developments wholeheartedly, partly because they do not understand them and partly because these American critics are hopelessly opposed to progress. American academics who were not thrilled by the Modern Language Association's having awarded the James Russell Lowell Prize for 1975 to Jonathan Culler's *Structuralist Poetics* are characterized by Lentricchia as having uttered "repeated cries of outrage and disbelief directed at the news of the latest French barbarism," though no evidence is ever given to support such a characterization. We are advised only that the cries could not help being overheard by "anyone working in a literary department (and particularly in an English department) in the late sixties and early seventies." In my own department the event passed without notice.

As it happens, Lentricchia himself was not entirely happy with the award, because in his view, Culler's book was a betrayal of structuralism: "Culler's book has made structuralism safe for us." Furthermore, according to Lentricchia, "Culler's book . . . performs the intellectually useful act of telling English-speaking critics what they need to know about formidable Continental sources of structuralist thinking, while at the same time providing the comforting reassurance that the governing conceptual framework of structuralism may be safely ignored." Lentricchia is troubled because Culler seems to him to be helping the forces of reaction to co-opt the revolution. I am little concerned with whether or not Lentricchia is right in his description of Culler's book and its presumed effects. What I want to stress is that though Lentricchia differs with Culler on certain details of the structuralist enterprise, he is, nevertheless, committed to the notion that in poststructuralism (mainly, for Lentricchia, poststructuralism of the Foucauldian, and, to some extent, of the Barthesian, variety) lies salvation. J. G. Merquior noted, in 1985, that "the literature on structuralism and poststructuralism continues to grow, though there are signs (nowhere more visible than in France) of

their decline as intellectual fashions. Yet most discussions are written in a vein of uncritical acceptance, the experts here tending to act as votaries." While it would not be accurate to say that Lentricchia writes about poststructuralist theory "in a vein of uncritical acceptance," it is nonetheless the case that he is a votary who celebrates poststructuralism and ultimately Foucauldian "genealogical" historicism for its bitter hostility to the liberal-democratic concepts of the integrity of the individual self and the inviolability of inalienable human rights.

As one of the "votaries" of poststructuralism, Lentricchia constructed a distorted version of literary and cultural history by performing what the deconstructionists themselves would call a mammoth "erasure." While devoting three hefty chapters to developments of the fifties and sixties in Europe—the triumph of structuralism, poststructuralism, deconstruction, and of Heideggerian and Marxist ideology—Lentricchia passes over the New Criticism in a single chapter devoted mainly to Northrop Frye's *The Anatomy of Criticism.* Perhaps he felt that the story of the eclipse of the New Criticism had already been told, but the result of the imbalance in Lentricchia's narrative is to create the impression that the New Criticism was productive only of "readings," and that the literary-cultural condition in the United States in the fifties and sixties was moribund. In fact this was not at all the case. During the postwar years American literature and culture experienced an efflorescence fueled by New Critical readings of nineteenth-century writers who had initially been given a new life by F. O. Matthiessen's *American Renaissance* (1941). Returning GIs, who went to college and then into PhD programs on the GI Bill, participated in a rediscovery of American literature. These returning GIs brought with them a renewed sense of optimism. They believed, and not without reason, that they had contributed to saving a large part of the world not only from tyranny but from Nazism with its culture of death and genocide implemented by means of bureaucracy and advanced technology.

Let us consider some seminal American books that appeared in the mid-fifties. Some of these books, such as Richard Chase's *The American Novel and its Tradition* (1957) and Charles Feidelson, Jr.'s *Symbolism and American Literature* (1953), attempted to define the contours of the American identity as embodied in its literature. But equally important were seminal studies of such individual American writers as Emerson, Hawthorne, and Poe by Stephen E. Whicher, Hyatt H. Waggoner, and Edward Davidson. Richly informed by a knowledge of philosophy and the American cultural context, these studies, which provided brilliant close readings of particular works, have yet to be surpassed. So while New Criticism was primarily a literary-critical movement that presumably advanced the cause of the autonomous poem, nevertheless the rediscovery of American literature through New Critical readings inspired the introduction and development of American Studies programs intended to encourage the study of American literature in a cultural and historical context.

The postwar analyses of the literary works of American writers, building on Matthiessen's enabling study, tended to reaffirm enlightenment values of freedom, human rights, and the sanctity of the individual human being embodied in the Declaration of Independence and the Bill of Rights, and in some instances sought to reconcile American optimism and the American belief in progress and human perfectibility with a postwar knowledge of darkness and of human tragedy. These studies of the fifties, though not necessarily written by New Critics, all tended to make use of New Critical methods of textual analysis to revalue American literature. Even as broadly based and as sociologically oriented a cultural critique as Leo Marx's *The Machine in the Garden: Technology and the Pastoral Ideal in America* (1967) would not have been conceivable without the New Criticism, and indeed much of the book consists of close readings of the New Critical kind.

Those engaged in the study of American literature and culture responded to the limitations of the New Criticism by expanding and moving forward, rather than by retrenching, as was the case with European oriented reader-responsists and intentionalists. American criticism in the sixties rediscovered a quintessentially liberating American dual source: Ralph Waldo Emerson, and the poet Emerson seemed to be calling for in his essays, Walt Whitman. Emerson's contribution to the American experiment in democracy was to Americanize the aesthetics of the British romantics and to romanticize (or perhaps spiritualize is a better word) American political theory. As an aesthetic thinker Emerson extended the Coleridgean metaphor of the organic poem. According to Coleridge, the poem was organic because, like a living thing, its unity and wholeness were both dependent on and inseparable from the perfect cohesion of its parts. But for Emerson the organic metaphor meant that a poem was the penultimate efflorescence of a tree whose roots were the "oversoul," and whose trunk was the mind of the poet: "For it is not meters but a meter-making argument that makes a poem,— a thought so passionate and alive that like the spirit of a plant or an animal it has an architecture of its own, and adorns nature with a new thing." For Emerson the poet was the conduit through whom the oversoul, or incessant inspiration, flowed.

Emerson's contribution to democratic ideology, like his contribution to aesthetics, was "expansive." He transformed the more or less precise enlightenment juridical notions of human freedom expressed in the Declaration of Independence, the Constitution, and the Bill of Rights into the optative mode. While the Declaration stated the principles of human equality and the right to "life, liberty and the pursuit of happiness," and while the Bill of Rights was intended to restrain the state's power over the individual, Emerson proclaimed "transcendental" freedom, and asserted that every individual contained within himself or herself a potential for unlimited development. For Emerson humanity was still an ongoing experiment: "Man," he declared, "is the dwarf of himself." Emerson's governing metaphor was the medieval image of God as a circle whose center was everywhere and whose circumference nowhere. He opened his essay "Circles" with the ringing annunciation: "The eye is the first circle; the horizon which it forms is the second; and throughout nature this primary figure is repeated without end. It is the highest emblem in the cipher of the world. . . . Every action admits of being outdone. Our life is an apprenticeship to the truth that around every circle another can be drawn; that there is no end in nature, but every end is a beginning; that there is always another dawn risen on mid-noon, and under ever deep a lower deep opens."

As an academic phenomenon the revalorization of Emerson and Whitman culminated in Hyatt H. Waggoner's *American Poets* (1968), a rendering of the centrality of the Emerson-Whitman tradition of American poetry that was visionary in its own right. The Emerson-Whitman revival was a cultural as well as an academic phenomenon. Allen Ginsberg's *Howl* (1956) constituted a turn away from modernist formalism and pessimism to reassert the Whitmanian "barbaric yawp." Everywhere the old "puritanism" was under attack, nowhere more trenchantly, perhaps, than in Norman O. Brown's *Life Against Death: The Psychoanalytical Meaning of History* (1959). Brown sought to transform a culture of death into a culture of love through an act of psychological liberation, converting the Western mind from an Apollonian into a Dionysian ego. Though Brown drew heavily on insights he found in Freud and Nietzsche, his point of view was distinctly Emersonian. As the epigraph to his chapter on "The Resurrection of the Body," Brown cited a passage from Henry Miller's *Sunday After the War* (1944): "The cultural era is past. The new civilization, which may take centuries or a few thousand years to usher in, will not be another civilization—it will be the open stretch of realization which all the past civilizations have pointed to. The city, which was the birth-place of civilization, such as we know it to be, will exist no more. . . . The peoples of the earth will no longer be shut off from one another within states but will flow freely over the surface of the earth and intermingle. The worship, investigation and subjugation of the machine will give way to the lure of all that is truly occult. This problem is bound up with the larger one of power—and possession. Man will be forced to realize that power must be kept open, fluid and free. His aim will be not to possess power but to radiate it."

It is perhaps no accident that the diction of Miller's last sentence ("power must be kept open, fluid and free") echoes Whitman's "When Lilacs Last in the Dooryard Bloom'd," where the speaker apostrophizes the consoling song of the bird: "O liquid and free and tender! / O wild and loose to my soul." Brown's argument for the dionysian ego, which had its real-world culmination in 1969, in the Woodstock "event," anticipated Michel Foucault's dionysian manifesto, *Histoire de la folie a l'age classique* (1961) by two years. One reason, perhaps, for the belatedness of the French in discovering dionysianism is that the United States had an indigenous dionysian tradition going back to Emerson and Whitman, whereas the French had to borrow their dionysianism from Nietzsche (who some believe took his own dionysianism from Emerson). In discussing the bizarre marriage of an apollonian structuralism with a dionysian irrationalism, J. G. Merquior notes that "the best-known instance of Foucault's Dionysian allegiance is his comment on Descartes's first *Philosophical Meditation* in *Histoire de la Folie*. Foucault strives to demonstrate that Descartes's famous 'evil genius' hypothesis actually amounts to an arbitrary expulsion of madness from thinking. . . . Foucault's discussion quickly became a locus classicus of the indictment of rationalism as sheer epistemological 'arrogance.'" Merquior then goes on to discuss Derrida's agreement/disagreement with Foucault in *Writing and Difference:* "Reason, according to Derrida, cannot be evaded; all we can do is deconstruct it, undermining its pretence of clear, stable meanings."

But in a twentieth-century historical context that includes the death camps and Nazi genocide, both the "apollonian" and the "dionysian" present a troubled reality, for Nazism and the Nazi genocide took place against a background which discredits both the dionysian and the apollonian. Nazi Germany itself was a culture gone mad, and we know from Hermann Rauschning's record of Hitler's table talk (*The Voice of Destruction*) that Hitler deliberately exploited dionysian tendencies in the German "Volk" to rouse them to subbestial violence. At the same time Reason was put to use in organizing a brilliant bureaucratic structure designed to exterminate human beings. The death camp itself is the ultimate example of Rationalism gone mad, and madness rationalized. As Foucault, who lived under the Nazi occupation, should have known, any talk of rationalism and madness that does not attempt to encompass the Nazi years can only be idle chatter.

By 1968 Theodore Roszak was publishing *The Making of a Counter Culture,* and in 1970 Charles A. Reich was anticipating *The Greening of America.* For Waggoner the centrality of Emerson and Whitman to the tradition of American poetry and culture lay in their conception of themselves as eternal soul voyagers:

> Focusing on Emerson [Waggoner wrote in 1968] seemed to me originally, and still seems, to throw more light on the question of what's American about American poetry than any other approach could have. . . . Our poetry has been, and continues to be, more concerned with nature than with society or culture, and more concerned with the eternal than with the temporal. . . . Deprived of the security offered by place, position, class, creed, and the illusion of a stable, an unchanging society, our poets, like our religious seekers, have had to discover meaning where none is given and test its validity personally. . . . The greatest of [American poets] have turned from society toward theology and metaphysics for their answers to the question [Edward] Taylor was the first to ask, "Lord, Who am I?"

Waggoner went on in *American Poets* to indicate how Whitman fulfilled the model of the poet called for by

Emerson: "Whitman is our greatest exponent of the individual conceived as containing the possibility of self-transcendence, or growth beyond the determined and known. Like Emerson before him, he refuses to place a limit on the self's possibilities." It is widely accepted that the flowering of the counter culture, with its mixture of religious and secular transcendences, experienced its zenith at Woodstock in 1969. Then history and human limitation started to reassert themselves.

I have outlined the dynamics of American literary and cultural criticism in the context of the fifties and sixties to give some sense of the magnitude of the "erasure" that has been enacted by recent "theorists" and historians of literary and poststructuralist theory. What is clear, I believe, is that American cultural criticism did not need Heidegger and the French antihumanist Heideggerians and Marxists to alert them to the evils and dangers of a postindustrial technological society, and to the threat against democracy and the integrity of the individual constituted by a technocratic culture. In fact, the dominance of the cluster of ideas constituted by Marxism-Heideggerism-deconstruction imported from France constituted a serious step backward.

To make this point more strongly, I should like to consider some sentences written by Horace Kallen, an American of the Jewish faith, who came to this country from Germany. Kallen was a progressive humanist whose style of life was certainly very unlike that called for by the counterculturists. In 1969, at the age of eighty-seven, he published "Of Love, Death, and Walt Whitman," a tribute to Whitman as the great poet of democracy. Kallen was one of the few, at that time, perhaps the only one, who would dare connect Whitman's attitudes toward death to those of the twentieth-century existentialists. For Whitman, Kallen wrote, the years of "the modern" turned out to be the tragic years of the Civil War, but nonetheless, conscious of the fearful death toll taken by that war, "Whitman chanted . . . a paean and prophecy of human progress *en masse,* [of individuals] in equal liberty to form a free society of free men." Those who had lived through the twentieth century, however,

> the talliers of these years of the modern, lived and suffered, still live and suffer . . . evil times. These years are years of the greatest, the bloodiest wars that mankind ever waged; years when cruelty and killing became articles of faith. . . .
>
> Some who became existentialists bet their own lives on resisting this evil; the most celebrated is French Jean Paul Sartre; others saw in the evil purpose of an ultimate good; the most celebrated of these is German Martin Heidegger; others rejected it and fled it; the most celebrated of these is Karl Jaspers. All became aware that death was the ultimate issue of their lives.

Kallen then continues:

> For Whitman, his role in the war was as momentous as Sartre's in the war against the

form of ultimate evil we call Hitlerism. The commander-in-chief of freedom's army became for Whitman, beyond anything a flag could be, the precious symbol of the American Idea, ever thrusting forward to establish as living fact the equal freedom and fellowship of all mankind. "Here," Whitman had written long before, "here is not merely a nation but a teeming nation of nations." America is the race of races. Its poet must be the voice and oracle of their diversity: "The genius of the United States is not best or at most, save always in the common people—their deathless attachment to freedom—the air they have of persons who never knew how it felt to stand in the presence of superiors." Elsewhere our Good Gray Poet had written, "The noble soul rejects any liberty or privilege or wealth that is not open to every other man on the face of the earth." On the battlefields and in the hospitals of the Civil War, Whitman had come face to face with this nobility; he had suffered with its champions and victims the costs of it, and he had grown into a reverent love of Abraham Lincoln as their incarnation, their sacrificial avatar.

It is unlikely that Kallen could have read Waggoner's book before he wrote his own tribute to Whitman. Yet Waggoner the antinomian Christian and Kallen the secular Jew were primarily children of the Enlightenment, and therefore humanists. Waggoner found in Whitman the poet of self-transcendence, the ultimate promulgator of the American ideology of what we may call "possibilism" (that is, of the ideology that each human being is a separate and integral individual protected by a Bill of Rights, and yet, is, at the same time, a set of infinite and always unfulfilled possibilities). Kallen, ever mindful of the Holocaust and genocide (and as a Jew, how could he not be?) focuses on Whitman's painful discovery of human limitation. After his traumatic encounter with death in his ministering to the Civil War wounded, and in the wake of his grief on hearing of the assassination of Lincoln, Whitman could no longer recapture the pure unrestrained joy in living of "Song of Myself." After citing the "Come lovely and soothing Death" passage of "When Lilacs Last in the Dooryard Bloom'd," Kallen comments that "Such now, was to Walt Whitman, the living inwardness of death. Whenever and however death happens, it is self-consummation, it is climax. It is life living itself out, using itself up, converting to joy of life all the fears, the dread and anxiety over loss, defeat, tragedy that so largely flow together in our awareness of death. . . . There is no cure for birth or death, George Santayana advises, save to enjoy the interval of existing. To enjoy it, Walt Whitman declares, is to die living and live dying, by loving."

What Waggoner and Kallen each discovered in Whitman independently, almost at the same time, was similar. The believing Christian and the secular Jew both found in Whitman a rare poet with the courage to face death and human mortality directly; both found consolation in the great bard of democracy, one in a message of love and transcendence, the other in a message of joy and love.

(Let us not forget that Whitman became a consoling and enabling figure for homosexual poets. See Robert K. Martin, *The Homosexual Tradition in American Poety* [1979].) What bound them together as enlightened humanists (Christian or secular) surely was stronger than what separated them, and may we not imagine them, now, as Melville once imagined himself and Hawthorne: "If ever, my dear Hawthorne, in the eternal times that are to come, you and I shall sit down in Paradise, in some little shady corner by ourselves; and if we shall by any means be able to smuggle a basket of champagne there (I won't believe in a Temperance Heaven), and if we shall then cross our celestial legs in the celestial grass that is forever tropical, and strike our glasses and our heads together, till both musically ring in concert,—then O my dear fellow-mortal, how shall we pleasantly discourse of all the things manifold which now so distress us,—when all the earth shall be but a reminiscence, yea, its final dissolution an antiquity."

Whether from the viewpoint of the counterculture, or that of Christianity, or of progressive secular humanism, American thinkers of the fifties and sixties who read and loved American literature and American writers were re-affirming the integrity of the individual, and were, at the same time, moving toward greater intellectual openness, and toward an expansion of American democracy that would result in a greater tolerance for a greater diversity of persons. By ignoring the writings of American humanists in the fifties and sixties, it was possible for Frank Lentricchia to present the influx of literary theory from France during the mid sixties through the seventies as a great leap forward. To hear Lentricchia tell it, a new world came to term and was born in the period from 1966 to the early seventies: "When in late October of 1966 over one hundred humanists and social scientists from the United States and eight other countries gathered at the Johns Hopkins Humanities Center to participate in a symposium called 'The Languages of Criticism and the Sciences of Man,' the reigning avant-garde theoretical presences for literary critics in this country were Georges Poulet, . . . and, in the distant background, in uncertain relationship to the critics of consciousness, the forbidding philosophical analyses of Heidegger (*Being and Time*), Sartre (*Being and Nothingness*), and Merleau-Ponty (*The Phenomenology of Perception*)." After explaining why structuralism did not establish itself in this country, Lentricchia then continued: "Sometime in the early 1970s we awoke from the dogmatic slumber of our phenomenological sleep to find that a new presence had taken absolute hold over our avant-garde critical imagination: Jacques Derrida. Somewhat startlingly, we learned that, despite a number of loose characterizations to the contrary, he brought not structuralism but something that would be called 'poststructuralism.'"

This view of poststructuralism (and deconstruction) as a leap forward, expressed by Lentricchia in 1980, was to become, if it was not already, the orthodox position among left-leaning literary historians. But was the advent of poststructuralism really a move forward or was it a step backward? Owing to recent critical studies by J. G. Merquior, and Luc Ferry and Alain Renaut (*French Philosophy of the Sixties: An Essay on Antihumanism,* 1990; and *Heidegger and Modernity,* 1990), we can now understand the thrust of French theory of the sixties from a more authentic and less partisan perspective. Both Merquior and Ferry-Renaut focus on the antihumanist bias of the French deconstructionists and of the thinkers (principally Nietzsche, Marx, Freud, and Heidegger) who stand in one way or another behind them. It is not surprising, given their common ideational origins, that in spite of superficial differences and petty family quarrels, the French deconstructionists cluster together to disseminate variations on a narrow set of ideas. Among these are the notion of "the dissolution of the self"; the claim that the individual is a "fiction," or that the individual is the creation of bourgeois ideology, or that the "subject" must be deconstructed; the denial of transcendence (or of the transcendent subject); and the belief, derived from Nietzsche and filtered through Heidegger, that there are no facts, only interpretations.

In the last two years, however, it has become increasingly difficult to maintain the hegemony of poststructuralist-deconstructionist ideology. Freud's authority has been seriously undermined by a growing scientific understanding of the physiology of the brain, and Marxism as an economic system lies everywhere in ruins. At the same time the authority of Heidegger has been seriously damaged by revelations about his personal life and political activities. The meticulous detective work of Victor Farias reveals that Heidegger was a dedicated and unrepentant Nazi. As a result we can no longer dodge the issue of what the implications are of taking a thinker seriously whose thinking reveals to him no difference between mechanized agriculture and the extermination of women and children in gas chambers to achieve an ideal of racial and national purity. In a speech delivered in Bremen in 1949, Heidegger said: "Agriculture is now a motorized food industry, in essence the same as the manufacturing of corpses in the gas chambers and extermination camps, the same as the blockade and starvation of the countryside, the same as the production of the hydrogen bombs."

Deconstructionist ideology, that bizarre fusion of Heidegger's pagan spiritualism with Marx's dialectical materialism, is beginning to fall apart. As Ferry and Renaut point out in *French Philosophy of the Sixties,* "that the two major critiques of modern humanism have proven to be linked with totalitarian adventures is most significant." Heidegger was part of the ideational context (call it a mass psychosis if you will) that led to Auschwitz, and he was encouraged to support Hitler's National Socialism (especially the populist version espoused by Ernst Roehm) by his philosophical belief in the spirit of the German Folk and in pan-Germanic and ultra-nationalistic ideas of blood and soil. In *To Mend the World* the theologian Emil Fackenheim asserts that "What the Fuhrer Adolf Hitler did in 1934 and 1935, respectively, to Germans and Jews, was no more than what the *Denker*

Martin Heidegger had endorsed in advance when, on November 3, 1933, as rector of Freiburg University, he addressed his students as follows: 'The Fuhrer himself and he alone is German reality and its law, today and henceforth.' . . . The indisputable and undisputed fact is, however, that when he endorsed in advance the Fuhrer's actions as German 'reality' and 'law,' he did so not, like countless others impelled by personal fear, opportunism, or the hysteria of the time, but rather deliberately and *with the weight of his philosophy behind it.*" The French intellectuals who think in Heidegger's shadow have yet to come to terms with the thinker's moral density, which did not improve after 1933, and persisted even after the fact of the death camps became widely known.

Heidegger's total obtuseness on the issue of Nazism as a culture of death, genocide, and enslavement, even after the war, is not only damaging to his reputation as a philosopher but should prevent us from accepting theories of literature and culture that are derived from his thinking. When Herbert Marcuse wrote to Heidegger, on August 28, 1947, asking him to take an unequivocal "stand against . . . the identification of you and your work with Nazism . . . ," Heidegger answered, in part, that "your letter just shows how difficult a dialogue is with people who have not been in Germany since 1933 and who evaluate the beginning of the National Socialist movement from the perspective of the end." To which Marcuse responded: "We knew, and I myself have seen, that the beginning already harbored the end; it was the end. Nothing has been added that was not already there in the beginning." Is it possible that in 1948 Heidegger was still unaware that, for some people, staying in Germany after 1933 meant a free ticket to Auschwitz?

The New Criticism was not without its limitations and weaknesses. Those who wrote New Critical essays worked with the world they inherited, though the essays they wrote helped to change that world and enlarge it. Perhaps it is an oversimplification to say that their greatest strength was their belief in a meritocracy of literature that was open to all, but it is nonetheless true. Though the cultural critics among the New York Intellectuals were quite distant from the New Critics not only in geography but in religion, politics, and ideology, they and the New Critics could still agree on the ideal of a meritocracy of literature. In a tribute to the retiring Supreme Court justice, William Brennan, that appeared in the *New York Times* for July 29, 1990, Anna Quindlen wrote: "The only thing I know about the framers [of the Constitution] is that they were general kinds of guys. They did not go on about the right to put fences around your farmland, or the right to pull your children out of school if the teacher taught sedition. They used broad terms. Life. Property. Liberty. They designed a document that wouldn't go out of fashion. Written by men whose wives couldn't vote and whose country permitted slavery, it has transcended their time." Of the New Critics, as well, it may be said that they designed a set of principles and a methodology that transcended their time. And it is ungenerous not to acknowledge their contribution to the many democratic and

expansive tendencies that broke out in American literature and culture during the seventies and eighties.

In neither methodology nor ideology did deconstruction
and postmodernism constitute a leap forward. Indeed the
ideologies on which these European movements are
based, in contrast to American New Criticism, represent
a return to a very unpleasant reactionary past that has
not yet been faced by the Europeans and is still essentially unknown to Americans. American literature, at its
best, has been a literature of progress, speaking out for
the integrity of the individual, and celebrating individual
human rights. American writers and literary critics have
invariably been the severest critics of American culture.
Should we bury that heritage under a literary history
written out of an antihumanist theory founded on two
failed philosophies, one of which led to the Soviet gulag,
and the other to Auschwitz?

Peter L. McLaren and Colin Lankshear

SOURCE: "Critical Literacy and the Postmodern Turn,"
and "Postscript to 'Critical Literary and the Pstmodern
Turn'," in *Critical Literacy: Politics, Praxis, and the
Postmodern,* edited by Colin Lankshear and Peter L.
McLaren, State University of New York Press, 1993, pp.
379-420; 421-25.

[*In the following essay, McLaren and Lankshear examine the impact of postmodernist literary thought on education and society.*]

Educators have become increasingly aware that, far from
being a sure means to attaining an accurate and "deep"
understanding of the world and one's place within it, the
ability to read and write may expose individuals and entire
social groups to forms of domination and control by
which their interests are subverted. During the past two
decades important advances have been made in understanding the ideological role of literacy within the production and "allocation" of economic, political, and cultural power. The "two-sided" character of literacy has
been revealed. Developments in the "new" sociology of
knowledge and the wider application of Marxist theory to
education during the 1970s and 80s greatly enhanced our
knowledge of how literacy in particular, and education in
general, can serve to domesticate populations and reproduce hierarchies of inequality and injustice. At much the
same time, such educational events as the dramatically
successful Cuban and Nicaraguan literacy campaigns,
and other initiatives throughout the world inspired by
Paulo Freire's approach to literacy, showed what can be
contributed to social transformation when educators revise their conceptions and practices of literacy and consciously turn reading and writing toward expansive and
emancipatory ends.

Critical literacy is grounded in these insights as well as
in the ethical and political commitment to democratic and
emancipatory forms of education. As evident from earlier

chapters, two main perspectives can be identified within
the critical literacy project at present. One is a radical
tradition, influenced particularly by Freirean and neo-
Marxist currents, with strong links to modernist social
theory. The other is an emerging Anglo-American theory
development drawing on a variety of contributions from
continental philosophy, poststructuralist currents, social
semiotics, reception theory, neopragmatism, deconstruction,
critical hermeneutics, and other postmodern positions.

This chapter deals with recent theoretical advances and
research approaches from this latter perspective, especially developments in poststructuralist theory, and asks
how they might contribute to the ongoing theory and
practice of critical literacy. Our discussion ranges over
several questions: What *is* the postmodern turn in social
theory? What are the points of strength and disputation
in postmodern theoretical developments as viewed from a
critical perspective? What can postmodern insights contribute to emancipatory projects, specifically critical literacy? In what ways does postmodern social theory enhance our *conception* of critical literacy and point to
important elements of a critical literacy *research* agenda?

To stake out more firmly the theoretical position of research practices which lead to a poststructuralist view of
critical literacy, let us describe briefly some of the most
basic theoretical conceptions of critical research in its
various manifestations (participatory research, critical
ethnography, action research, and so on). Operating
within a theoretical subterrain outside of the policing
structure of sovereign research discourses, the tradition
of critical research continues to make unconventional
alliances between descriptions and meanings.

From a critical standpoint, knowledge is never self-au-
thenticating, self-legitimating, or self-ratifying. Critical
research is not a process which can determine its own
effects or speak its own truth in a manner which transcends its relations to the sociopolitical context in which
learning takes place. It is always a creature of cultural
limits and theoretical borders, and as such is necessarily
implicated in particular economies of truth, value, and
power. Consequently, critical researchers need to remind
themselves of the following: Whose interests are being
served in social acts of doing research? Where is this
process situated ethically and politically in matters of
social justice? What principles should we choose in
structuring our pedagogical efforts?

To not ask these questions is to risk being reduced to
custodians of sameness and system-stabilizing functions
which serve the collective interests and regimes of truth
of the prevailing power elite(s). Similarly, to seek a neutral
balance of perspectives by refusing to capitulate to the
discourses of either left or right is to support those
whose interests prevail within the status quo.

Critical research works from a view of culture that focuses
on *disjuncture, rupture, and contradiction.* Culture is
best understood as a *terrain of contestation* that serves

as a locus of multivalent practical and discursive structures and powers. Knowledge is construed as *a form of discursive production.* As understood here, discourses are modalities which to a significant extent govern what can be said, by what kinds of speakers, and for what types of imagined audiences.[1] The rules of discourse are normative and derive their meaning from the power relations in which they are embedded. Discourses organize a way of thinking into a way of doing. Unlike language, they have both a subject and an object, and actively shape the social practices of which they are mutually constitutive.

At the level of research, discourses are always indexical to the context of researchers and their interpretations. All research discourses are conflictual and competitive. As such they embody particular interests, "establish paradigms, set limits, and construct human subjects."[2] Discourse "constitutes the guarantee and limit of our understanding of *otherness*."[3] Moreover, *discourse* refers to the conditions of any social practice.[4] The process of constructing knowledge takes place within an unevenly occupied terrain of struggle in which the dominative discourses of mainstream research approaches frequently parallel the discursive economies of the larger society, and are reinforced by the asymmetrical relations of power and privilege which accompany them.

A critical approach to analysis and research makes it clear that all knowledge consists of rhetorical tropes. These both reflect and shape the way that we engage and are transformed by the manner in which we consciously and unconsciously identify ourselves with our roles as researchers, and with the subjects we study. This process has been detailed in the work of Paulo Freire, Henry Giroux, Linda Brodkey, Patricia Bizzell, Donaldo Macedo, Jim Berlin, Jim Gee, and others. They have advanced the notion that reality does not possess a presignifying nature but is an interactive, cultural, social, and historical process. They have also described the relationship between discourses of literacy, research practices, and the workings of power, and revealed the various ways in which power operates as a regulating force which conforms to its dominant ideologies and their institutionalized supports as well as centralizes and unifies often conflicting and competing discourses in the interests of capitalist social relations.

The idea here is that discourses are not single-minded positivities but are invariably mutable, contingent, and partial. Their authority is always provisional as distinct from transcendental. The real is not transparent to the world; the real and the concept are insurmountably asymmetrical.[5] Truth has no real name other than the meanings rhetorically or discursively assigned to it. Discourses may in fact *possess* the power of truth, but in reality they are historically contingent rather than inscribed by natural law; they emerge out of social conventions. In this view, any discourse of conducting is bounded by historical, cultural, and political conditions and the epistemological resources available to articulate its meaning. Educators

involved in critical research remind us that people do not possess power but produce it and are produced by it in their relational constitution through discourse.

Critical research is not limited to any one methodology and can incorporate both qualitative and quantitative approaches. What characterizes research as "critical" is an attempt to recognize its own status as discourse and to understand its role as a servant of power. Critical researchers try to understand how the research design and process are themselves implicated in social and institutional structures of domination. They must also recognize what conflicts might exist within their subjective formation without sacrificing or hiding the political or ethical center of gravity that guides the overall research project. Research undertaken in a critical mode requires recognizing the complexity of social relations and the researcher's own socially determined position within the reality he or she is attempting to describe. Critical research must be undertaken in such a way as to narrate its own contingency, its own situatedness in power/knowledge relations. Critical researchers attempt to become aware of the controlling cultural mode of their research and the ways, often varied and unwitting, in which their research subjects and their relationship to them become artifacts of the *epistemes* that shape the direction of their research by fixing the conceptual world in a particular way and by selecting particular discourses from a range of possibilities.

POSTMODERNISM AND POSTMODERN SOCIAL THEORY

The term *postmodernism* straddles several definitional boundaries. It refers at once to a sensibility, a political perspective, a state of mind, and a mode of social analysis. Taking these as an amalgam, we may speak of the postmodern *age:* an era wherein democratic imperatives have become subverted, originary values simulated, and emancipatory symbols and their affective power commodified. It is an age in which the modernist quest for certainty and meaning and the liberal humanist notion of the individual as a unified and coherent essence and agency are being forcefully challenged.

Much of the discourse of postmodernism has been criticized for betraying a dry cynicism in which irony and pastiche become politics' last recourse at social change. It often reveals an uncompromising distaste for the masses, adopts a form of high-brow, antibourgeois posing, and occasionally assumes the role of a self-congratulatory vanguardism which resonates dutifully with the "high seriousness" of the academy, at times appearing as dressed-up restatements of Nietzsche and Heidegger.

In the postmodern age, breaks and disjunctures in contemporary social reality have led to the retreat of democratic forms of social life. MacCannell speaks of the "implosive reduction of all previously generative oppositions: male/female, rich/poor, black/white . . . into a single master pattern of dominance and submission . . . with . . . no semiotic or institutional way of breaking the patterns of advantaging one class, ethnic group or gender over another." The result is a proliferation of gender and racial inequality, all within the framework of apparently progressive legislation and administration which, in reality, seems to be doing the opposite.[6]

The turmoil of late capitalism is perhaps best displayed by the surging impulses of media images—from which the postmodern subject can hardly escape the cruel insistence of their ever-presentness—and the tragic liaison between the media industry and the viewing public, the former arrogating the right to legislate, produce, and serve up the latter's daily reality. Increasing youth alienation is evident, brought about by what Voss and Schutze refer to as "a world blanketed with signs and texts, image and media of all kinds . . . which has brought forth a culture . . . based on an overproduction of sensations that dulls our sensory faculties."[7]

Attendant characteristics of the postmodern condition also include the rejection of truth claims that have a grounding in a transcendent reality independent of collective human struggle, an abandonment of the teleology of science, the construction of lifestyles out of consumer products and cultural bricolage, and cultural forms of communication and social relations that have evolved from the disorganization of capitalism.[8] The postmodern condition signals the undecidability, plurality, or "thrownness" of culture rather than its homogeneity or consensual nature. Indeed, some characteristics of postmodernity seem to affirm Benjamin's equation of fascism and the aestheticization of politics, which includes the demise of a public democratic sphere of rational debate "replaced by a consumerist culture of manipulation and acclamatory politics."[9] From this standpoint, postmodernism represents a "'cultural' logic that correlates political-economic and social-psychological changes in late capitalism."[10]

As social theory, postmodernist perspectives attempt to advance an oppositional stance against the policing structures of modernist discourse. Of particular importance here are appropriations by postmodernist social theory of various currents of poststructuralist social theory. From these emerge numerous issues that have an important bearing on critical literacy and the development of critical research on literacy. Two central issues are especially noteworthy: the new social theories have radicalized the conception of the subject as social agent by relativizing the authority of the text-in-itself; and they have deterritorialized and deauthorized the task of conducting research as it is generally understood. We will try to draw out some implications of these shifts in terms of how they affect our theoretical approaches to the study of critical literacy.

Poststructuralism can be distinguished from its structuralist predecessor as follows. Structuralists typically conceive of language as an arbitrary system of differences in which meaning is *guaranteed* by the linguistic system itself and the values given to signifying practices within particular linguistic communities. In other words, given the signs and linguistic practices, meanings follow. For structuralists, meaning is *uncovered* by "cracking" the code that explains how elements of a social text function together. Often, these codes are granted a transcendental status, serving as privileged referents around which other meanings are positioned.

Poststructuralism is less deterministic. Much more emphasis is placed on meaning as *a contested event,* a terrain of struggle in which individuals take up often conflicting subject positions in relation to signifying practices. Poststructuralists acknowledge explicitly that meaning consists of more than signs operating and being operated in a context. Rather, there is struggle over signifying practices. This struggle is eminently *political* and must include the relationship among discourse, power, and difference. Poststructuralists put much more emphasis on discourse and the contradictions involved in subjective formation. They regard transcendental signifieds as discursive fictions.

In addition, poststructuralism draws attention to the significant danger of assuming that concepts can exist independently of signifying systems or language itself, or that meaning can exist as a pure idea, independently of its contextual embeddedness in the materiality of speech, gesture, writing, and so on. Poststructuralism does not locate the human subject within the structure of language, that is, within the rules of signification. Rather, the subject is an effect of the structure of language and the signifying system. Just as there exists no unified, monolithic, and homogeneous sign community which produces and interprets signs, so too there exists no self that precedes its social construction through the agency of representation. As Judith Butler explains,

> The subject is a consequence of certain rule-governed discourses that govern the intelligible invocation of identity. The subject is not *determined* by the rules through which it is generated because signification is *not a founding act, but rather a regulated process of repetition* that both conceals itself and enforces its rules precisely through the production of substantializing effects . . . There is no self that is prior to the convergence or who maintains "integrity" prior to its entrance into this conflicted cultural field. There is only a taking up of the tools where they lie, where the very "taking up" is enabled by the tool lying there.[11]

According to poststructuralists, we construct our future selves, our identities, through the availability and character of signs of possible futures. The parameters of the human subject vary according to the discursive practices, economies of signs, and subjectivities (experiences) engaged by individuals and groups at any historical moment. We must abandon the outmoded and dangerous idea that we possess as social agents a timeless essence or a consciousness that places us beyond historical and political practices. Rather, we should understand our "working identities" as an effect of such practices. Our identities as subjects are not tied to or dependent upon some transcendental regime of truth beyond the territory of the profane and the mundane. Rather, they are constitutive of the literacies we have at our disposal through which we make sense of our day-to-day politics of living.

From the postmodernist position, discourses are always saturated in power. Jane Flax says, "Postmodern discourses are all 'deconstructive' in that they seek to distance us from and make us sceptical about beliefs concerning truth, knowledge, power, the self, and language that are often taken for granted within and serve as legitimation for contemporary Western culture."[12] Postmodern thinking takes as its object of investigation issues such as "how to understand and (re)constitute the self, gender, knowledge, social relations, and culture without resorting to linear, teleological, hierarchical, holistic, or binary ways of thinking and being."[13]

A key feature of postmodern discourse has been its ability to effect a decentering of the authority of the text, and also a decentering of the reader. Readers are revealed to be restricted by the tropes and conventions of their reading practices just like, for instance, historians are constrained by the discourses available in the act of writing history.

Postmodernist social theory has much to offer the critique of colonial discourses within literacy research because it assumes the position that the age of modernism was characterized by the geopolitical construction of the center and the margins within the expansive hegemony of the conqueror. It was, in other words, marked by the construction through European conquest of the foundational "I."[14] Postmodern criticism has significantly revealed how even the language of critical theory, which has its roots in European history and philosophy, carries with it a debilitating Eurocentric bias that continues to privilege the discourse of the white male colonizer. All discourses, even those of freedom and liberation, carry with them ideological traces and selective interests which must be understood and transformed in the interests of greater justice and equality.

Moreover, from a postmodernist perspective, knowledge does not constitute decoded transcriptions of "reality" separable into the grand postulates of Western thought and what is left over: the lesser, vulgar, popular, and massified knowledges of the "barbarians." Rather, all knowledge is considered to be framed by interpretation and controlled by rhetorical devices and discursive apparatuses. It is an approach to knowledge that is perturbing and unsettling, especially to those who hold "objectivist" perspectives on reality. Derrida, for example, reveals the metaphorical character of knowledge and attacks the objectivism in our understanding of social relations inherited from the tradition of sociology: the notion that society can be reduced to a "metaphysics of presence," or an objective and coherent ensemble of conceptually formulated laws. He has uncovered the discrepancy between meaning and the author's assertion by rupturing the "logocentric" logic of identity,[15] and has highlighted the status of philosophy as writing which, following Nietzsche, entails a deconstruction of the history of metaphysics.

The postmodern turn in the study of English has moved beyond late modernist attempts to rupture realist narrative conventions. It now faces the chalenge of historiographic metafiction and interactive fiction. Mainstream literary theorists and English educators are witnessing serious attacks on dominant forms of literary discourse such as modernist notions of the original and originating author. They are further facing postmodernist critical practices which consist of a dethroning of totalized thought; the problemization of forms of autorepresentation; the transparency of historical referentiality; and an emphasis on the enunciative situation—text, producer, receiver, historical, and social context—and double-voicing or implied readers.[16] The ideological situatedness of all literary practices is now being highlighted, with a recognition of the impossibility of the disinterestedness of any discursive claim or cultural practice.

POSTMODERN SOCIAL THEORY: OBSTACLES FROM WITHIN

Although our aim in this chapter is to seek the contribution of postmodern social theory for the ongoing development and practice of critical literacy, it must be conceded that poststructuralism has met with trenchant criticism on several grounds and from several directions. To appreciate the potential inherent in the postmodern turn for further progress toward developing critical literacy as a mainstream rather than a marginalized educational engagement, it is necessary to rehearse some of these criticisms, most of which have an overtly *political* emphasis. These critiques identify limitations within postmodern theory which need to be overcome and, at the same time, help us clarify further the criteria and requirements of critical literacy in theory and practice.

Several of the criticisms which follow pertain to two of the central advances made by postmodern theory: the decentering of the subject and the decentering of the text. These ideas will be elaborated in our account of those objections which seem to us most important.

Of course, the criticisms of poststructuralism which follow do *not* preclude the development of a critical project in educational research and practice that can accommodate poststructuralism. Indeed, the contemporary world is largely *unintelligible* without a poststructuralist perspective. Here we share Jameson's view that although poststructuralism represents "the ideology of a new multinational stage of capitalism" and therefore shares certain counterrevolutionary tendencies, it nevertheless "contains some of the elements for the beginning of a critical analysis of the present."[17] Post-structuralism does, however, pose some difficult challenges for those committed to a critical emancipatory project: How can we construct narratives of cultural difference that affirm and empower and that do not undercut the efforts of other social groups to win self-definition? In what way are our own discourses as literacy researchers disguised by self-interest and defined by the exclusion of the voices of others? In what ways must we rewrite the stories which guide our research and our interpretations of these stories in relation to shifting cultural boundaries and new political configurations? How can we redefine research practices so that they no longer describe the discourses and practices of white, Western males who are charged to speak on behalf of everyone else? How do we position the "other" in the semantic field of our research so that he or she does not become a "silent predicate" that gives birth to Western patriarchal asumptions of what constitutes truth and justice?

Decentering the subject

Poststructuralist theorists, among others (notably, feminists), have criticized educators for working within a discourse of critical rationalism which reifies the humanist subject—the rational, self-motivating, autonomous agent—as a subject of history, change, and resistance. They maintain that what separates being an individual from being a subject is a linguistic membrane known as discourse. Discourses provide individuals with identifications which convert them into subjects. By contrast, the rationalist position associated with the modern Enlightenment rests on a "metaphysics of presence" which constitutes the individual as a noncontradictory, rational, self-fashioning, autonomous being: Descartes' fully conscious "I" immediately transparent to itself. There is a logic of identity here in which the self defines itself in opposition to the "other." The forced unity of this position and the unilinearity of its progressive rationality work to deny the specificity of difference and heterogeneity. The subject is projected as a unity, but this disguises and falsifies the complex disunity of experience.[18]

The debate over postmodernity is largely related to the advent of multi-national or late capitalism, which has formed, from its "centerless ubiquity,"[19] a new postmodern subject out of the pathological jumble of consumer myths and images fed by the global dispersal of capital and its constant promises of fulfillment through an ever-expanding market economy which structures the shape and direction of our desire. The debate, moreover, is about the construction of our identities as raced, classed, and gendered beings which have been decentered irrevocably, thereby giving ominous weight to Brenkman's observation that "the obligation to critize and transform outer reality wanes as authentic meanings and values are granted a purely inner reality."[20]

Postmodernist efforts to decenter the subject have met with criticisms and cautions. Hartsock sounds a note of deep suspicion that just at a time when many groups are engaged in "nationalisms" which involve redefining them as marginalized Others, the academy begins to legitimize a critical theory of the "subject" which holds its agency in doubt and which casts a general scepticism on the possibilities of a general theory which can describe the world and institute a quest for historical progress.[21] Henry Louis Gates, Jr., echoes a similar concern. He argues that in rejecting the existence of a subject, poststructuralist theorists are denying those who have been subjugated and made voiceless and invisible by the high canon of Western literature the chance to reclaim their subjectivity before they critique it.

> To deny us the process of exploring and reclaiming our subjectivity before we critique it is the critical version of the grandfather clause, the double privileging of categories that happen to be *preconstituted.* Such a position leaves us nowhere, invisible and voiceless in the republic of Western letters. Consider the irony: precisely when we (and other third world peoples) obtain the complex wherewithal to define our black subjectivity in the republic of Western letters, our theoretical colleagues declare that there ain't no such thing as a subject, so why should we be bothered with that? In this way, those of us in feminist criticism or African-American criticism who are engaged in the necessary work of canon deformation and reformation, confront the skepticism even of those who are allies on other fronts, over the matter of the death of the subject and our own discursive subjectivity.[22]

Elsewhere, postmodernist discourse has met the charge that its over-determination of the subject through discourse renders the social agent as politically innocuous as the liberal humanist. The obsession of both poststructuralists and the new historicists to formulate the self as an effect of discourse rather than as its origin necessarily submits human subjects to determinations over which they have little control. Frank Lentricchia targets "a literary politics of freedom whose echoes of Nietzsche and his joyful deconstructionist progeny do not disguise its affiliation with the mainline tradition of aesthetic humanism, a politics much favored by many of our colleagues in literary study, who take not a little pleasure from describing themselves as powerless. This is a literary politics that does not . . . [answer] . . . the question: So what?"[23]

Decentering the text

Another major contribution of poststructuralist theory has been its revelation that texts need to be understood in their historical, political, and cultural specificity. There are no texts which are meant in the same way by readers because readers occupy different subjective positions of articulation. The rhetorical claims of the text are integrated or transformed through the parallel rhetorics of common sense and the everyday against which they are read.

Poststructuralism has provided a necessary shift from a critical focus on text alone to the dynamics of culture and consumption reflected in the reader. Bennett[24] cuts across the notion of the unitary experience of reading in suggesting how subjects approach a text with already coded perceptions of "reading formations." These consist of a set of discursive and textual determinations which organize and animate the practice of reading. Reading formations, says Bennett, may be shaped by social positionality (such as the role of class and gender relations in organizing reading practices), intertextual determinations (readers' experience of other texts), and culturally determined genre expectations (the dominant codes that govern the popular text, or subcultural codes such as feminism, trade unionism, Marxism, moral majority thinking, and so forth). Readers are thus placed in a position in which they can potentially refuse the subject position which the text "coaxes" them to adopt. In this theoretical move, which sees the determinant text supplanted by the recipient of the text, no text can be so penetrative and pervasive in its authority as to eliminate all grounds for contestation or resistance.

Eagleton, however, urges moderation here, rejecting a swing from the all-powerful authority of the text to a total decentering of text. He satirizes the Readers' Liberation Movement and its fetishistic concern with consumer rights in reading, and describes the dominant strategy of this movement as an "all-out *putsch* to topple the text altogether and install the victorious reading class in its place." He argues that reader power cannot answer the question of what one has power over. For this reason he ridicules the ascendancy of reader reception theory, which transforms the act of reading into "creative enclaves, equivalent in some sense to workers' cooperatives within capitalism [in which] readers may hallucinate that they are actually writers, reshaping government handouts on the legitimacy of nuclear war into symbolist poems."[25]

There is much to commend this bold move to decenter the authorial discretion of the writer and the projection of the reader as a passive, actedupon object. Yet the very act of desituating and dehistoricizing the reader actually brings it into line with the humanist position. As Scully puts it, in each position "the work's specious authority will derive from the illusion that it is not value-bound, not historically conditioned, not responsible . . . its authoritativeness will depend not on the making of its particular human source but on the implicit denial that it comes from anywhere at all, or that it is class couched."[26]

What gets lost unavoidably in preoccupation with the construction of meaning at the point of reception is sufficient acknowledgment of the ways in which privileged forms of representing experience come to serve as regimes of truth. Reception theory permits us to disattend the various forms of competing interpellations which are at play simultaneously within a given text or social formation.

Collins reveals the self-legitimating aspects of interpellations which compete for our identification and involvement within any text or cultural form. He argues that within the fragmentary cultures of the postmodern condition, "competing discourses must differentiate themselves according to style and function."[27] He points out how, for instance, literary style may serve as an aesthetic ideology which valorizes certain ideologies competing in a cultural text as a means of converting individuals into subjects. Even though we are not free to choose as independent autonomous readers which discourses we wish to identify with,

we still participate in a process of *selection.* This is an important truth. Because of the vast array of competing discourses which offer themselves as a means of completing the subject, by giving it a temporarily fixed identity, it is necessary for the subject to hierarchize and arrange them.

The process of selecting the most politically transformative discourses in endless competition for "completing" the subject has never been more urgent, since we are presently in times when culture's unifying characteristics seem irrevocably decentered. Disparate discourses may be managed through multiple aesthetics and multiple styles: by a means of *bricolage* by which ideologies and representations may be selected and combined in new, transformative ways.[28] This has an important implication for developing a critical literacy, since it raises the following questions: *To what extent do conventional literacy practices duplicate the ideologies embedded in literary texts and the already constructed reading formations of teachers and students? If reading formations are not always already fixed, how can educators help their students develop reading formations which will enable them to resist the authority of the dominative ideologies produced within required texts?*

To reduce reading to the subjective act of the reader has dangerous consequences. It can blind us to the means by which power works on and through subjects and ignores the way in which textual authority is constructed as a form of production linked to larger economies of power and privilege in the wider social order. If the meaning of a text is reduced to individual interpretation, then the act of reading itself can be reduced to a textual palliative in which the material conditions of existence, the suffering of certain select groups in our society, can be turned into a fantasy of personal resolution. Furthermore, it enables us to engage in self-recuperation in a move that smoothly sidesteps collective participation in social transformation. It produces a mode of subjectivity that can participate gleefully in troubling the hegemony of social silence while avoiding the task of reconstructing the social practices which produce such silence. It can create an optimism that is strictly personal, removed from historical context. In this way the dominant culture can achieve both the individualism and poverty of theory necessary for it to escape the threat of resistance.

Left social and political theorists within the academy vary greatly in their opinion and appropriation of postmodern strategies of critique. Jameson warns against a simplistic, reductionistic view of the political,[29] and Merod regrets that much academic work falling into the category of "postmodernism" decidedly fails to move the reader "from the academic world of texts and interpretations to the vaster world of surveillance, technology, and material forces."[30] Harsher antagonists claim that the deconstructive enterprise often operates as a kind of left mandarin terrorism, displacing "political activism into a textual world where anarchy can *become* the establishment without threatening the actual seats of political and economic power," and sublimating political radicalism "into a textual radicalism that can happily theorize its own disconnection from unpleasant realities."[31]

Feminist theorists have identified a range of concerns associated with extreme versions of decentering text and/or subject. Mascia-Lees, Sharpe, and Cohen, for example, pose a crucial issue for social theory:

> Once one articulates an epistemology of free play in which there is no inevitable relationship between signifier and signified, how is it possible to write an ethnography that has descriptive force? . . . Once one has no metanarratives into which the experience of difference can be translated, how is it possible to write any ethnography?[32]

Feminists, among others, have also noted how in its assault on the classic figure of Western humanism—the rational, unified, noncontradictory, and self-determining individual—poststructuralist discourse has erased the suffering, bleeding, breathing subject of history. Poststructuralism's infatuation with the dancing signifier whose meaning is always ephemeral, elusive, disperse, and mutable, and the emphasis which it places on textualizing the reader as an intricate composition of an infinite number of codes or texts,[33] can be subversive of its potentially empowering and transformative agenda. Knowledge can be depotentiated and stripped of its emancipatory possibilities if it is acknowledged only as a form of textualization. Moreover, such a facile treatment of discourse can lead to the subject's encapsulation in the membranes of his or her rationalizations, leading to a soporific escape from the pain and sensations of living, breathing, human subjects. As Alan Megill warns:

> All too easy is the neglect or even the dismissal of a natural and historical reality that ought not to be neglected or dismissed . . . For if one adopts, in a cavalier and single-minded fashion, the view that everything is discourse or text or fiction, the realia are trivialized. Real people who really died in the gas chambers at Auschwitz or Treblinka become so much discourse.[34]

Clearly there is danger in assuming a literal interpretation of Derrida's "there is nothing outside of the text." We are faced with the postmodern "loss of affect" which occurs when language attempts to "capture the 'ineffable' experience of the Other."[35] We risk textualizing gender, denying sexual specificity, or treating difference as merely a formal category with no empirical and historical existence.[36]

Further criticisms

Various other obstacles to a political agenda of justice and emancipation have been discerned within postmodern social theory. Barbara Christian's critique of postmodern discourse takes aim at the *language* of literary critical theory. She condemns this language on the grounds that it "mystifies rather than clarifies our condition, making it possible for a few people who know that particular language to control the critical scene—that language surfaced, interestingly enough, just when the literatures of

peoples of color, of black women, of Latin Americans, of Africans, began to move to 'the center.'"[37]

Still further problems are seen to arise from postmodern attacks on the unified, transcendental ego and the rejection of theoretical procedures for arriving at ontologically and metaphysically secure truth claims. In particular, postmodern theorists are seen as at risk of lapsing into an ethical relativism and a burgeoning nihilism. French versions of postmodernism have been seen as reflecting "a disturbing kinship with facism," and Jürgen Habermas has actually accused Bataille, Foucault, and Derrida of being "young conservatives."[38]

Peter Dews has taken up this latter line, revealing its ethical and political implications. He targets post-structuralism, with its "Nietzsche-inspired assault on any putatively universal truth" and its tendency to implicitly equate the rational principle of modernity with cognitive instrumental thought. Poststructuralist invocations of the radical other of Enlightenment reason and social modernization produce a radical other which takes the form of an expressive subjectivity—"the untamed energies of mind and body—of madness, intensity, desire." This is a subjectivity freed from the demands of utility and morality and economic and administrative rationality. In this way, says Dews, poststructuralism "curiously coincides with neo-conservatism, although the polarity of values is reversed from one position to another."[39] He rejects the one-sidedness of poststructuralism's "cult of immediacy, the deflation of noble forms, anarchism of the soul," in favor of a stress on human and civil rights.

A WAY AHEAD: BEYOND THE OBSTACLES OF POSTMODERN THEORY

Feminist contributions

If feminists have advanced some of the more strident critiques of postmodern social theory on behalf of a politics of material engagement in the cause of freedom and justice, they have also given clear pointers to a way ahead. In resisting "the dangers inherent in a complete decentering of the historical and material" and in their task of "changing the power relationships that underlie women's oppression," feminists offer postmodernist discourse a way of dealing with contradictions which do not decenter their own categories of analysis in such a way that political reform is immobilized. Feminist discourse can move analysis away from the word and toward the world, since, according to Mary Hawkesworth, "feminist accounts derive their justificatory force from their capacity to illuminate existing social relations, to demonstrate the deficiencies of alternative interpretations, to debunk opposing views." It is "precisely because feminists move beyond texts to confront the world" that they are able to give "concrete reasons in specific contexts for the superiority of their accounts." From the perspective of feminist theory, postmodern anthropology may actually "erase difference, implying that all stories are really about one experience: the decentering and fragmentation

that is the current experience of Western white males."[40]
The dangers are obvious:

> If the postmodernist emphasis on multivocality
> leads to denial of the continued existence of a
> hierarchy of discourse, the material and historical
> links between cultures can be ignored, with all voices
> becoming equal, each telling only an individualized
> story. The history of the colonial, for example, can
> be read as independent of that of the colonizer. Such
> readings ignore or obscure exploitation and power
> differentials and therefore offer no ground to fight
> oppression and effect change.[41]

By revealing how women are constituted as voiceless
and powerless through dominant conceptions of the
subject, feminist theorists challenge us to recuperate a
non-Western, nonmale subject-agent likewise removed
from modernist philosophy's essentializing search for
origins and a universal sovereign consciousness. In
heeding this challenge, Giroux argues that modernism,
postmodernism, and feminism can be articulated in
terms of the interconnections between their differences
and the common ground they share for being mutually
corrective. All three discourses can and should be
used to mutually inform ways of advancing a new
politics of literacy research.[42]

Subjectivity and subjects/agency and agenthood: Problems with identity politics in emancipatory research

Recent work by Larry Grossberg on the relationship between
structure and agency offers valuable insights for
further developing a critical poststructuralist agenda in
literacy research and practice. The structure-agency debate
has haunted critical social theory for decades: initially
in its modernist "moment," but later within
poststructuralist theorizing as well.

Grossberg detects the carryover of an Althusserian
view of subject formation into dominant strands of
poststructuralism, resulting in an unwanted determinism.
The subject becomes essentially a passive occupant
of a particular discursive construction, although
individuals are not all constructed equally. Social
groups are positioned differentially within domains of
subjectivity—that is, places from which one experiences
the world—and according to discursively constituted
systems of social differences (black/white, gay/
hetero, poor/rich, female/male, and so on). Different
discourses (economic, educational, legal, medical) enable
or constrain the power that allows subjects to give
voice to their experiences within specific systems of
language and knowledge. The process of ideology
constructs sets of "cultural identities" which determine
the meaning and experience of social relations within
fields of difference such as race, gender, class, and
sexual preference.

Grossberg is critical of the determinism in such
poststructuralist conceptions of the formation of the historical
subject. Within them

the individual appears to be weightless, thrown
about by the weighty fullness of cultural texts. In
the end, history is guaranteed in advance. Ideology
(and history) seem to hold the winning hand,
determining as it were, in its own spaces and
structures, the subject-ion of the individual, hailing
them into places it has already identified for them
within its maps of meaning. It appears to guarantee
that history will constantly reproduce the same
experiences over and over, constantly replaying
the same psychic or social history that is always
already in place.[43]

Such a view denies the possibility of resistance to ideological
hegemony, since agency is structured into the
very reproduction of history. Finding little solace in the
concept of the fractured or decentered subject, Grossberg
sees no solution to the paradox of subjectivity because
it derives from a conceptual model that identifies individuals
with both the subjects and agents of history. He
attempts to escape the paradox by distinguishing subjectivity,
agency, and agenthood.

By *subjectivity* Grossberg means "the site of experience
and of the attribution of responsibility." *Agency* refers to
"the active forces struggling within and over history."
Agenthood signifies "actors operating, whether knowingly
or unknowingly, on behalf of particular agencies."[44]
Grossberg's account of agency is large. It refers to *historical*
agency as well as to the location of individuals in
systems of discourse and difference. Historical agency
has less to do with social identity than with historical
effectivity, or what Gramsci called "tendential forces"—
such as capitalism, industrialism, technology, democracy,
nationalism, and religion. Tendential forces "map
out the long-term directions and investments which
have already been so deeply inscribed upon the shape of
history that they seem to play themselves out in a constantly
indeterminate future."[45]

Agency, however, calls for historical and cultural agents
to accomplish specific activities. In other words, it presupposes
agenthood. Agents may be individuals or nominal
groups such as organizations and political parties. Although
these may have their own political agendas, such
agendas depend ultimately on the apparatuses of agency.

For Grossberg, the important question concerns the link
connecting ideological subjects to agents. What kinds of
investments of subjectivity occur in the formation of
nominal groups and social organizations? Grossberg
speaks here of "the domain of affective individuality."
This is the individual of "affective states" rather than the
individual of "identities."

> The affective individual exists within its nomadic
> wandering through the ever-changing places and
> spaces, vectors and apparatuses of daily life. Its
> shape and force are never guaranteed; its empowerment
> (i.e., its possibilities for action—in
> this case, for investment) depends in part on where
> it is located, how it occupies its places within
> specific apparatuses, and how it moves within and

between them. The affective individual always moves along different vectors, always changing its shape. But it always has an affective shape as a result of its struggles to win a temporary space for itself within the places that have been prepared for it. Such nomadic travels are not random or subjective; the nomad often carries not only its maps but its places with it, through a course determined by social, cultural and historical knowledges. The affective individual is both an articulated site and a site of ongoing articulation within its own history . . . The nomadic individual is the subject and the agent of daily life, existing within an affective economy of investment which makes daily life the link between private experiences and public struggles.[46]

This account of the affective or nomadic subject has important implications for political struggle. In particular, it suggests the limitation of identity politics based on gender, race, class, religion, or nationality for large-scale social transformation. Identity politics are grounded in the direct experience of particular groups. Strategies of alliance within identity politics face serious problems. Specifically, Grossberg argues that

the various strategies of alliance are all attempts to construct a "We" which can represent and speak for different individuals and groups, a collective identity which transcends differences and speaks for them as well. "We" speaks as a unity from the position which the other has already constructed for it (i.e., the essentialist view). "We" speaks from an imaginary place (the site of alliance) located in the midst of the differences (i.e., the postmodern view). The discourse of representation involves the circulation of a sign which articulates specific effects (e.g., it often activates a discourse of guilt or authenticity) in specific contexts (e.g., anti-abortion ads).[47]

Grossberg suggests that in creating a politics of transformation it is more important to mobilize affective subjects than to create a politics of identity or discourse of representation. Grossberg calls for the strategic and provisional deployment of a "We" that does not purport to represent anyone but rather is used as a "floating sign," not of unity or identity, "but of common authority and commitment to speak and act." This involves the ability to "structure the commitments which fashion everyday life and its relations to the social formation." A transformative politics needs to mobilize individuals through their affective investments in certain issues rather than through essentialist claims around the authenticity of identity through direct experience. This is not to claim that identity struggles are not important, since people invest in what they identify with, be it race, creed, or political party. The problem is that the building of coalitions based on multiple sites of identity collapses under the weight of calls for authenticity and "linguistic self-righteousness" and "political purity."

Grossberg's concern is distinctively postmodern. Fred Pfeil gets to the heart of it in recognizing that "the problem to be worked through and, ultimately, strategized" is that of "the *dis*unified and *de*-centered subject": "a vast array of ideological apparatuses, from advertizing to education, politics to MTV . . . work as much to *dis*-articulate the subject as to interpellate it, [offering] not the old pleasures of 'self-understanding,' of knowing and accepting our place, but the new delights of ever-shifting bricolage and blur."[48]

Ernesto Laclau speaks to a position that affirms Grossberg's unease with the Althusserian residue in poststructuralism and the importance of subjectivity as a hegemonic-articulatory process. Laclau writes that

the Althusserian theory of interpellation . . . leaves out the fact that interpellation is the terrain for the production of discourse, and that in order to "produce" subjects successfully, the latter must identify with it. The Althusserian emphasis on interpellation as a functional mechanism in social reproduction does not leave enough space to study the construction of subjects from the point of view of the individuals receiving those interpellations.[49]

Laclau, like Grossberg, attempts to eliminate the dualism between agent and structure by noting that social agents are always partially internal to institutions. However, since institutions never constitute closed systems but are always riven with antagonisms, social agents are always constituted within the gaps of institutional structures. The institutionalization of the social is always partial and contingent, and only to a relative degree does this constitute the subjectivity of the agents themselves.

The prespective advanced by Grossberg has much to offer transformative research agendas, especially as it concerns the role of the literacy teacher as an agent of transformative social change. Clearly, the perspective itself requires considerable further refinement and critical appraisal. Enough has been said, however, to demonstrate the fruitfulness of further research in this area on the part of those concerned with the theory and practice of critical literacy in the postmodern age.

Pedagogy in the postmodern age

The United States as global educator; constructing the "other". The United States is fast becoming the global educator par excellence. This is of growing concern for those interested in developing critical research practices for the study of literacy. Through its ideologies of individualism and free enterprise, it is fostering tutelary democracies among the "barbaric" and "uncivilized." This raises the following questions: How can we avoid reconstituting the "Other" in the language of a universal, global discourse (in this case an uncritical acceptance of liberal humanism)? How can we refrain from keeping the "Other" mute before the ideals of our own discourse? What research practices must exist in order to restore the marginalized and disenfranchised to history?

Inden argues that U.S. pedagogy is underpinned by a commonsense theory of the mind which assumes that most students are converted to the American way of life before entering school. Except in the most stubborn cases, the teacher need merely convey to the students' reasoning faculties through books (which mirror the world rather than deal with physical objects situated in the world) information needed to live in a natural, rational universe of commonsense enlightenment whose social analogue is U.S. civic culture.[50] Here educators confront the legacy left by the colonizer, especially in relation to minority populations in U.S. schools, where there are concealed attempts to integrate the oppressed into the moral imperatives of the ruling elite.[51]

We have inherited a legacy in which blacks, Latinos, and other groups are essentialized as either biologically or culturally deficient and treated as a species of outsiders. Yet the postmodernist perspective, while addressing the contingent, contradictory, and conflictual characteristics of subject formations, sometimes itself falls prey to a neocolonizing logic by dictating the terms by which we are to speak of the marginal and subaltern.

Although modernity has been haunted by the bourgeois historical subject which remains oblivious to its roots in oppression, the solution should not simply be to embrace the demise of the contemporary subject, reduced to "a dispersed, decentered network of libidinal attachments, emptied of ethical substance and psychical interiority, the ephemeral function of this and that act of consumption, media experience, sexual relationship, trend or fashion."[52] This strips the subject of authorship of its own will, yet leaves nothing in its place but a passive subject *always already determined* by discourse. Here again we must acknowledge the feminist critique, which raises the issue of whether or not women "can afford a sense of decentered self and a humbleness regarding the coherence and truth of their claims."[53] As Di Stefano points out, postmodernism depends on a notion of a decentered subjectivity, whereas feminism depends on a relatively unified notion of the social subject as "woman."[54] We should follow Eagleton and agree that "the subject of late capitalism . . . is neither simply the self-regulating synthetic agent posited by classical humanist ideology, nor merely a decentered network of desire, but a contradictory amalgam of the two."[55] This points once more to the importance of critical poststructuralist, neo-Marxist, and postmodern feminist discourses working together as self-correcting theoretical enterprises.[56]

Poststructuralist pedagogy versus political pedagogy

Eagleton argues that the discourse of modernism in the teaching of English constitutes both a moral technology and a particular mode of subjectivity. Dominant forms of teaching English serve to create a bourgeois body/subject that values subjectivity *in itself.* This occurs through "particular set[s] of techniques and practices for the instilling of specific kinds of value, discipline, behaviour and response in human subjects."[57] Within liberal capitalist society the lived experience of "grasping literature" occurs within a particular form of subjectivity which

values freedom and creativity as ends in themselves, whereas the more important issue should be: freedom and creativity *for what?* It would seem that one alternative to the modernist pedagogy decried by Eagleton would be a poststructuralist approach to teaching. But poststructuralist pedagogy, although an improvement on modernist approaches, can *appear* politically progressive while still serving the interests of the dominant culture.

Mas'ud Zavarzadeh[58] has recently attacked poststructuralist theory and pedagogy, arguing that the dominant humanist and poststructuralist pedagogies used in the academy are similar in that both reflect *a resistance to theory.* Whereas humanist pedagogy constructs a subject that is capable of creating meaning, poststructuralist pedagogy offers textuality as a panhistorical truth that exists beyond ideology. According to Zavarzadeh, humanist and poststructuralist pedagogies are both united against what he calls "political pedagogy," which is based on theory as the critique of intelligibility.

The effect of humanist and poststructuralist pedagogy is to recover and protect the subject of patriarchal capitalism. This is achieved by privileging individual experience over theory through a "pedagogy of pleasure." Pleasure becomes an experience for containing and subverting the political, yielding a politics of liberation underwritten by "playfulness" and "fancy" which is at odds with bourgeois norms and social practices, but without really *challenging* the social logic of those norms. Liberation becomes a "relief" from the fixity of the social rather than a form of emancipation that comes with seriously challenging existing social relations. The dominant logic is temporarily displaced in an *illusion of freedom.*

According to Zavarzadeh, poststructuralist pedagogy concerns itself with the "how" or "manner" of knowing, whereas humanist pedagogy generally concerns itself with the "what" of knowing (such as the canon, great books). Neither approach deals with the "why" or the "politics" of representation. At their best, poststructuralist and humanist pedagogies address how a given discourse is *legitimated* but avoid asking about its *legitimacy* and how this is embedded in the prevailing economies of power. The pedagogy of poststructuralism is about using "laughter," "parody," "pastiche," and "play" as strategies of subversion which, although they decenter bourgeois relations, do not fundamentally transform them. Such strategies serve merely as a fanciful way of recruiting students into subject positions which maintain existing social relations.

By contrast, radical pedagogy does not simply bracket reality, but radically restructures it, dismantling secured beliefs and interrogating social practices and the constituents of experience while foregrounding and rendering visible the power/knowledge relation between the teacher and the student. In the radical classroom, students are "made aware of how they are the sites through which structures of social conflict produce meanings."[59] Theory becomes posited as a form of resistance, a means of understanding how cultural practices transform the actual into the real. Theory is used as a means to situate tropes socially and historically according to specific practices of intelligibility through which they can be read. The subject of knowledge in this case is always theoretically positioned in the context of class, race, and gender relations.

Zavarzadeh uncovers various ways in which the discourses of poststructuralism and humanism actually work to *enforce* the larger economies of power, even though they profess to assisting social emancipation. His critique of poststructuralist pedagogy shows why we seek a "*critical* postmodernism" or "*critical* poststructuralism" which appropriates the socially emancipatory potential of postmodern social theory but refuses its tendency to reproduce forms of liberal humanism.

CRITICAL LITERACY IN THE AGE OF POSTMODERNISM

In this section we outline some of the theoretical advantages of the critical postmodernist postition.[60] Developing a critical literacy which can appropriate important insights from critical postmodernism means recognizing the limitations of this perspective while building on its strengths. We try to bring together here some summary positions on critical literacy research, while considering some of the advances that postmodern social theory might bring to this research.

(1) Research on critical literacy carries with it an important historical function: namely, to discover the various complex ways in which ideological production occurs, especially the way in which subjective formations are produced on a level which is often referred to as "common sense." Common sense, or "practical consciousness," is most commonly manufactured at the level of language production and language use, and a critical literacy must be able to account for the "mutual intelligibility of acts and of discourse, achieved in and through language."[61] Furthermore, critical literacy research needs to be able to identify the characteristics of an individual's "ethnomethods"—the routine actions, unconsciousness knowledge, and cultural memory from which community members draw in order to engage in a politics of daily living. This means developing participatory field approaches that can engage, interpret, and appropriate such knowledge.

(2) Critical literacy research needs to approach the process of becoming literate as something more than simply becoming rational. It must understand literacy as the means by which reality is constructed as being morality, truth, beauty, justice, and virtue, given the *social habitus* of society and the means by which society is able to reproduce and manage its symbolic and emotional economies. In this way, the literacy researcher needs to disrupt unconscious routines rather than simply report them, and bring into relief the politics which inhere in the dialectics of daily life and struggle.

(3) Literacy researchers must take an oppositional stance toward privileged groups within the dominant culture who have attained a disproportionately large share of resources, who are ceaselessly driven by self-perpetuatng ideologies, and who are able to incapacitate opposition by marginalizing and defaming counterdiscourses while legitimating their own. To accomplish this means understanding the production of subjectivity as something more than simply an ensemble of sliding, shifting signifiers constructed against a hyperrealistic backdrop of simulated meanings devoid of origins. Rather, it means grappling with the complex relationship between power and knowledge and how this works to affirm the interests of certain privileged groups against others.

(4) Critical literacy researchers need to seek means toward the political empowerment of oppressed groups, while at the same time avoiding discursive practices that are compatible with dominant social, economic, and political formations or congenial to the market order. They must assist groups and individuals seeking empowerment in clarifying their historical experience of oppression and subjugationa nd connect individual narratives of specific instances of oppression to an ever larger historical framework in order to recover social memory and an awareness of the struggle of other groups. Histories of survival and resistance must be recalled and efforts made to clarify "how the structural interaction among dynamics of oppression have differently affected the lives and perceptions of our own group and others."[62] A liberation ethics must be developed which includes solidarity with the marginal and oppressed and, in some instances, our co-suffering with them.[63]

In establishing the groundwork for a critical literacy, however, the tendency within poststructuralism to privilege the experience of the particular over the theoretical should be avoided. It must be remembered that experience is not something that speaks for itself, but is an understanding which is constructed as a particular interpretation over time of a specific concrete engagement with the world of symbols, social practices, and cultural forms. How we think and talk about our world through the particular language of theory largely shapes our understanding of experience. All our experiences are held accountable within a particular system of interpretation; they are not free of political, economic, social, and linguistic constraints.[64] Individual and group experiences should be taken seriously because these constitute the voices students bring with them into the classroom. They should not, however, be celebrated unqualifiedly. Rather, it is important to understand how the voices (experiences) of both the students and the teacher have been subject to historical and cultural constraints which help to shape their identities.

We believe the primary referent for the empowerment of dispossessed groups should not be their moral, ethnic, gender, or political strangeness or displacement outside the boundaries of the dominant and familiar, but rather the location of criteria which can distinguish claims of moral, ethnic, gender, or political superiority which we exercise as outsiders. 'Others' have a hermeneutical privilege in naming the issues before them and in developing an analysis of their situation appropriate to their context. How our research subjects name experience and place labels on their sense of reality should be the primary elements which inform our research. The marginalized have the first right to name reality, to articulate how social reality functions, and to decide how the issues are to be organized and defined.[65] Welch claims that "it is oppressive to free people if their own history and culture do not serve as the primary sources of the definition of their freedom." She warns that "the temptation to define others' hopes for liberation must be avoided." Furthermore, "a concept of freedom is most effective as it is rooted in the imagination of the people to be freed, if it does indeed speak to something in their experience and their history."[66]

Since the experiences of those with whom we study can never be regarded as self-evident—experience always being the seat of ideology and never a state of unmediated innocence—researchers need to help students understand the literalness of their reality, the context in which such a reality is articulated, and how their experiences are imbricated in contradictory, complex, and changing vectors of power.

(5) Literacy researchers need to explore seriously the idea that there is not just one way to become literate, but that there are multiple literacies. This idea comes from poststructuralism and feminist theory, as well as from certain modernist studies.[67] It suggests that literacy can be articulated in more than one form, depending on the cultural, historical, and ideological ways in which it unfolds within particular social formations and settings. To be a literate Latino living in a community in eastern Los Angeles may reflect qualitatively different interactions and skills than to be a Chicano living in upscale Manhattan. In a related sense, to be a minority woman in a minority culture or a woman in the dominant culture also carries profound implications for what counts as literacy.

The notion of being literate must also take into account the poststructuralist insight that every individual consists of an ensemble of multiple, shifting positions within discourses and social practices. This means that individuals can acquire knowledge from a variety of subject positions *and* a number of theoretical perspectives. Many of these positions, of course, can be articulated as positions of resistance to the dominant discourse on literacy, which labels them as illiterate or semiliterate.[68]

All this has implications for our understanding of critical literacy. Within critical literacy the personal is always understood as social, and the social is always historicized to reveal how the subject has been produced in particular. Subjectivity is understood, therefore, as a field of relations forged within a grid of power and ethics, knowledge and power. Literacy research provides a context for research subjects to analyze their identity as a product of larger social and historical struggles.

(6) Critical literacy research must counter the essentialization of difference reflected in the liberal humanist (and some postmodernist) positions, which consist of little more than a facile celebration or tolerance of the multiplicity of voices of the marginalized. It is worth emphasizing that celebrating difference without investigating the ways in which difference becomes constituted in oppressive asymmetrical relations of power often betrays a simpleminded romanticism and "exoticization" of the Other.[69]

The serious issue ahead for literacy researchers struggling to work through the pluralistic implications of postmodernist social theory is to elaborate a position for the human subject which acknowledges its embeddedness and contingency in the present political and historical juncture without, however, relinquishing the struggle against domination and oppression and the fight for social justice and emancipation. In the context of postmodernism, literacy researchers must ask "how . . . the discourse of theory [may] intervene in practice without bolstering domination."[70]

To further avoid falling into a laissez-faire pluralism, literacy researchers must develop a more detailed account of what Fraser calls "interpretive justification" of people's needs.[71] This means examing the inclusivity and exclusivity of rival interpretations and analyzing the hierarchy and egalitarianism of the relations among the rivals who are engaged in debating such needs. Fraser maintains that consequences should also be taken into consideration by comparing alternative distributive outcomes of rival interpretations. This should take the form of procedural considerations concerning the social processes by which various competing interpretations are generated. Fraser asks:

> Would widespread acceptance of some given interpretation of a social need disadvantage some groups of people vis-a-vis others? Does the interpretation conform to, rather than challenge, societal patterns of dominance and subordination? Are rival chains of in-order-to relations to which competing need interpretations belong more or less respectful, as opposed to transgressive, of ideological boundaries that delimit "separate spheres" and thereby rationalize inequality?[72]

Two autobiographical sources help enhance our theoretical understanding of subjectivity while helping us avoid the trap of a poststructuralist or liberal relativism: the idea of expansive otherness developed by Rigoberta Menchú, and Gloria Anzaldúa's concept of borderlands.[73]

Menchú's struggle as a Guatemalan Indian sees her participating in the regeneration of her culture by learning Spanish, but also by identifying with poor *ladinos,* incorporating two ethnicities in her struggle against oppression and exploitation. This resonates with perspectives contained in Anzaldúa's work, *Borderlands/La Frontera,* written from a Chicana lesbian stance. Anzaldua rejects the classic "authenticity" of cultural purity in favor of the "many-stranded possibilities of the borderlands."[74] She is able to transform herself into a complex persona which "incorporates Mexican, Indian, and Anglo elements at the same time that she discards the homophobia and patriarchy of Chicano culture." Anzaldúa writes that the new *mestiza* (person of mixed ancestry) "copes by developing a tolerance for ambiguity. She learns to be Indian in Mexican culture, to be Mexican from an Anglo point of view. She learns to juggle cultures. She has a plural personality, she operates in a pluralistic mode—nothing is thrust out, the good the bad and the ugly, nothing rejected, nothing abandoned. Not only does she sustain contradictions, she turns the ambivalence into something else."[75]

Undertaking critical research on literacy means being able to rupture effectively the charmed circle of exchange among cultural forms, historical consciousness, and the construction of subjectivity which coincide in the authorized version of the humanistic subject. It must, moreover, be an approach to critical literacy which does more than simply celebrate the infinite play of textual inscription or discover "double readings" in literary texts.

TOWARD CRITICAL POSTSTRUCTURALIST LITERACY RESEARCH

To address the antecedents and implications of new social theory in connection with formulating new advances in critical literacy research will mean a searching reevaluation of the Western metaphysical tradition, not a spurious rejection of it. The truths which modernity struggled so hard to justify, either with an objectivist world or upon transcendental grounds, should certainly be granted a provisional status, but it is incautious and politically imprudent to abandon them outright. The development of critical analyses of literacy will mean a continuing interchange with a wide variety of contemporary currents in social theory. Theorists will have to become discursive cross-dressers, always probing their own "secret heart" that undercuts the politics they are attempting to construct.

We are arguing, then, for the development of a *critical* poststructuralist research. This recognizes that the space between the actual and the real, between consciousness and identity, between the word and the world, is the space of experience: the space of giving voice to one's world. It is a space for restaging the ordinary and the mundane by giving it a name. A critical literacy must recognize that this space is always already occupied: a space in which the colonizer always owns a share. This colonizer, of course, is often the conquering white male of Western history.

In its critique of mainstream research, critical post-structuralist research does not argue that empirical verifiability or evidential supports are unimportant. Rather, it stresses the contingency of the social rather than "higher" forms of objectivity, the primacy of the discursive rather than the search for epistemological foundations, the transgression of the social as distinct from its positivity, and the splintering of the self-mirroring aspects of the social mundane rather than the scrutinizing of the adequacy of evidential claims.

Literacy researchers need to rethink and extend the notion of literacy to include "forms of linguistic experience that are peculiar to the twentieth century, and in particular the structures of domination they contain."[76] This means greater awareness of the development of new modes of information which "designates the way symbols are used to communicate meanings and to constitute subjects."[77] Literacy educators must address the following questions raised recently by Poster:

> What happens in society when the boundaries of linguistic experience are drastically transformed? How are social relations altered when language is no longer limited to face to face speech or to writing? What assumptions about the nature of society need to be revised when the already complex and ambiguous aspects of language are supplemented by electronic mediation?[78]

In our pursuit of a literacy that is truly critical, we need to understand that we are living in an epochal transition to an era of multiple feminisms, liberalisms, and Marxisms. These, on the one hand, hold the enabling promise of liberation from sexist subjugation and a loosening of the bonds of cultural and sociopolitical white supremacy, misogyny, and class privilege. On the other hand, they threaten to splinter the left irrevocably in a maze of often mutually antagonistic micropolitics.

This risk of splintering calls for some kind of totalizing vision—what McLaren has referred to as "an arch of social dreaming"—that spans the current divisiveness we are witnessing within the field.[79] An arch of social dreaming gives shape, coherence, and protection to the unity of our collective struggles. It means attaining a vision of what the total transformation of society might mean. When we refer to a totalizing vision, however, it must be clear that we intend what Laclau[80] calls "the search for the universal in the contingent" as well as the "contingency of all universality." The arch of social dreaming attempts to make "ambiguous connections" rather than foster "underlying systematicities." As Jameson remarks, "Without some notion of a *total* transformation of society and without the sense that the immediate project is a figure for that total transformation, so that everybody has a stake in a particular struggle, the success of any local struggle is doomed, limited to reform."[81] Jameson makes clear that in our research efforts *we cannot dismiss the search for totality.*

We must continue to seek multiple discourses (African-American pedagogy, Marxist pedagogy, feminist pedagogy) which mutually enhance the political project of each. But such nontotalizing alternatives to liberal humanist discourse must not reject the dream of totality outright. Although there may be a number of public spheres from which to wage an oppositional politics, and although the micropolitical interests of groups that fleck the horizon of the postmodern scene may have overwhelmingly separate and distinct agendas, we should—*all of us*—work together toward a provisional, perhaps evanescent or even *ephemeral, totality* to which we can all aspire, as paradoxical as this may seem.

The real challenge of postmodernity is to steer an ethical and political course in times of shifting theoretical borders and unstable systems of meaning and representation. We must heed Hartsock's challenge to build "an account of the world as seen from the margins, an account which can expose the falseness of the view from the top and can transform the margins as well as the center." This is not a theory of power in which one can afford to retreat from all that is oppressive and inhuman. It is "an engaged vision . . . a call for change and participation in alterning power relations."[82]

The proper response to the challenge of postmodernism is not to wish ourselves back to the halcyon days of the male subject's quest for total control of his subjectivity, but rather to return to a renewed sense of our own obligation to the other. Before we raise the epistemological question "Who are you?" we must first raise the ethical question "Where are you?" We cannot forget our commitment to the other. For, as Kearney notes, "When a naked face cries 'Where are you?,' we do not ask for identity papers. We reply, first and foremost, 'Here I am.'"[83]

It is important to remember that literacies are always brittle and that through the cracks seeps the stuff of possibility. Confronting the wall of subjective determination is Derrida's "gap"—*dehiscence*—the gap that allows and necessitates the further construction of subjectivity through language, even in the face of an always and already disappearing present.

It is in this sense that a poststructuralist approach to literacy can help students develop narratives of identity that do not abandon the reality of human suffering and struggle in a world rife with pain and suffering. It is a process that can help them develop *phronesis*—the competence to choose among seemingly incompatible values in situations where no a priori standard can be invoked.[84] A poststructuralist approach to literacy can assist us in answering the question: How do essentially arbitrarily organized codes, products of historical struggle among not only regimes of signs but regimes of material production, come to represent the "real" and the "natural" and the "necessary"? Part of the answer is that our "practical consciousness" masks the materiality of socially contested social relations by presenting norms to explain reality that purport to be self-referential, that appear to refer to immanent laws of signification, that are reflected away from being considered as the effects of social struggle. A critical poststructuralism recognizes that signs do not correspond to an already determined metaphysical reality, nor are they transhistorically indeterminable or undecidable. Rather, their meaning-making possibilities and their meaningfulness are legitimized through the specificity of discursive and material struggles, and the political linkages between them.

A poststructuralist perspective on literacy can help us understand the danger that arises when literacy is seen as a private or individual competency or set of competencies rather than a complex circulation of economic, political, and ideological practices that inform daily life—competencies that invite or solicit students to acquiesce in their social and gendered positions within a highly stratified society and accept the agenthood assigned to them along the axes of race, class, and gender.

Critical literacy, as we are using the term, becomes the interpretation of the social present for the purpose of transforming the cultural life of certain groups, for questioning tacit assumptions and unarticulated presuppositions of current cultural and social formations and the subjectivities and capacities for agenthood that they foster. It aims at understanding the ongoing social struggles over the signs of culture and over the definition of social reality—over what is considered legitimate and preferred meaning at any given historical moment. Of course, aesthetic concerns mediate such struggles, but their outcomes are largely ideological and economic. Through such struggles historically and ideologically contested class and social relations are naturalized. In this way, critical literacy can be described as investigating those communicational devices that reinscribe the human subject into prevailing social relations so that these relations are seen as conventional and uncontested. That is, critical literacy asks: How is cultural reality encoded within familiar grids or frames of intelligibility so that literacy practices that unwittingly affirm racism, sexism, and heterosexism, for example, are rendered natural and commonsensical?

Teachers and students engaged in the process of critical literacy recognize that dominant social arrangements are dominant not because they are the only possible arrangements but because those arrangements exist for the advantage of certain privileged groups. Critical literacy is not satisfied that students should know the 4,700 items that all Americans need to know according to E.D. Hirsch, Jr., or that they can reflect the cultural capital of an Allan Bloom or Roger Kimball. Critical literacy doesn't lament the dearth of bourgeois salons for cultivating allegiances to Western culture but rather asks: Creativity, culture, and literacy for what?

Critical literacy as a pedagogy of empowerment does not seek a universal truth, or a truth whose ideological effects permit some groups to survive at the expense of others. Critical literacy rather seeks to produce partial, contingent, but necessary historical truths that will enable the many public spheres that make up our social and institutional life to be emancipated—truths which are acknowledged for their social constructedness and historicity and the institutional and social arrangements and practices they legitimate.

For educators, this means constructing a place of hybrid pedagogical space where students do not feel that they need any longer the colonizer's permission or approval to narrate their own identities, a space where individual identities are not essentialized on the basis of race, gender, or nationality, but where these expressions of identity can find meaning in collective engagement with conditions which threaten to undermine the authority and power of individuals to speak and to live with dignity and under conditions of equality and social justice.[85]

Critical literacy enables us to rearticulate the role of the social agent so that he or she is able to make affective alliances with forms of agency that will provide new grounds of popular authority from which to speak the neverending narratives of human freedom. Poststructuralist educators must not abandon their rootedness in the struggles of the popular classes in favor of joining a patrician priesthood of left mandarin metropolitan intellectuals. They must never abandon Volosinov's recognition of the materiality of the sign as a product of social forces and relations of power, as a lived embodiment of both oppression and possibility, subordination and emancipation.

In the final analysis, we must reject any notion of the human subject which seals itself off from its own history, its own link to the community of multiple selves which surrounds it, its narratives of freedom. To construct a truly critical literacy, we need to make despair less salutory and economic, social, racial, and gender equality politically conceivable and pedagogically possible.

NOTES

* This is a reworked and greatly expanded version of Peter McLaren, "Literacy Research and the Postmodern Turn: Cautions from the Margins," In Richard Beach *et al.* (eds.) *Multidisciplinary Perspectives on Literacy Research,* Urbana, Illinois: National Conference on Research in English and the National Council of Teachers of English, 1992, pp. 319-339.

[1] Weedon, C., *Feminist Practice and Poststructuralist Theory* (Oxford and New York: Basil Blackwell, 1987).

[2] Collins, J., *Uncommon Cultures* (London: Routledge, 1990).

[3] Frow, J. *Marxism and Literary History* (Cambridge, Mass: Harvard University Press, 1986).

[4] Laclau, E., and Mouffe, C., *Hegemony and Socialist Strategy* (London: Verso, 1985).

[5] Laclau, E., "Building a New Left: Interview with Ernesto Laclau," *Strategies,* 1, pp. 10-28.

[6] MacCannell, D., "Baltimore in the Morning . . . After: On the Forms of Post-Nuclear Leadership," *Diacritics,* 1984, pp. 33-46.

[7] Voss, D., and Schutze, J., "Postmodernism in Context: Perspectives of a Structural Change in Society, Literature and Literacy Criticism," *New German Critique,* 47, 1989, pp. 119-142.

[8] Lash, S., and Urry, J., *The End of Organized Capitalism* (Madison: University of Wisconsin Press, 1987); McLaren, P., "Postmodernity and the Death of Politics: A Brazilian Reprieve," *Educational Theory,* 36, 4, 1986, pp. 389-401, and "Schooling the Postmodern Body: Critical Literacy and the Politics of Enfleshment," *Journal of Education,* 170, 3, 1988, pp. 53-83; McLaren, P., and Hammer, R., "Critical Pedagogy and the Postmodern Challenge: Towards a Critical Postmodernist Pedagogy of Liberation," *Educational Foundations,* 3, 3, 1989, pp. 29-62; Giroux, H., "Postmodernism and the Discourse of Educational Criticism," and "Border Pedagogy in the Age of Postmodernism," *Journal of Education,* 170, 3, 1988, pp. 5-30 and 162-181.

[9] Berman, R., *Modern Culture and Critical Theory* (Madison: University of Wisconsin Press, 1989), p. 41.

[10] Voss and Schutze, *op. cit.,* p. 120.

[11] Butler, J., *Gender Trouble* (London and New York: Routledge, 1987), p. 145.

[12] Flax, J., "Postmodernism and Gender Relations in Feminist Theory," *Signs,* 12, 4, 1987, p. 624.

[13] Flax, J., "Postmodernism and Gender Relations in Feminist Theory," in Nicholson, L.J. (ed), *Feminism/Postmodernism* (New York and London: Routledge, 1990), p. 39.

[14] Cf. Dussel, E., *Philosophy of Liberation* (Maryknoll, N.Y.: Orbis Books, 1980).

[15] Cf. Sarup, M., *Poststructuralism and Postmodernism* (Athens, Ga.: University of Georgia Press, 1989), p. 57.

[16] Cf. Hutcheon, L., *A Poetics of Postmodernism* (London and New York: Routledge, 1988).

[17] See Poster, M., *Critical Theory and Poststructuralism* (Ithaca, N.Y.: Cornell University Press, 1989), pp. 28-29.

[18] Cf. Butler, J., *Subjects of Desire: Hegelian Reflections in Twentieth Century France* (New York: Columbia University Press, 1987).

[19] Connor, S., *Postmodernist Culture* (Oxford and New York: Basil Blackwell, 1989), p. 48.

[20] Brenkman, J., "Theses on Cultural Marxism," *Social Text,* 7, 1983, p. 27.

[21] Hartsock, N., "Rethinking Modernism: Minority vs. Majority Theories," *Cultural Critique* 7: p. 106.

[22] Gates, H. L., Jr., "The Master's Pieces: On Canon Formation and the African-American Tradition," *The South Atlantic Quarterly,* 89, 1, 1990, pp. 89-111.

[23] Lentricchia, F., *Ariel and the Police* (Madison: University of Wisconsin Press, 1988), p. 100.

[24] Bennett, T., "Texts in History: The Determinations of Readings and Their Texts," in Attridge, D., and Bennington, G. (eds.), *Post-structuralism and the Question of History* (Cambridge: Cambridge University Press, 1986).

[25] Eagleton, T., *Against the Grain* (London: Verso, 1989), p. 184.

[26] Scully, J., *Line Break* (Seattle: Bay Press, 1988), p. 66.

[27] Collins, *op. cit.,* p. 89.

[28] *Ibid.*

[29] Jameson, F., "Interview," *Diacritics,* 12, 3, 1982, p. 75.

[30] Merod, J., *The Political Responsibility of the Critic* (Ithaca and London: Cornell University Press, 1987), p. 284.

[31] Scholes, R., "Deconstruction and Communication," *Critical Inquiry,* 14, Winter 1988, p. 284. Compare also Cornell West's position: Stephanson, A., "Interview with Cornell West" in Ross, A. (ed.), *Universal Abandon?* (Minneapolis: University of Minnesota Press, 1989), p. 274.

[32] Mascia-Lees, F., Sharpe, P., and Cohen, C.B., "The Postmodern Turn in Anthropology: Cautions from a Feminist Perspective," *Signs,* 15, 1, 1989, p. 27.

[33] Barthes, R., *S/Z* (London: Cape, 1975).

[34] Megill, A., *Prophets of Extremity* (Berkeley: University of California Press, 1985), p. 345.

[35] Yudice, G., "Marginality and the Ethics of Survival," in Ross, A. (ed.), *Universal Abandon?* (Minneapolis: University of Minnesota Press, 1989), p. 225.

[36] deLauretis, T., *Technologies of Gender* (Bloomington: Indiana University Press, 1987), p. 25.

[37] Christian, B., "The Race for Theory," *Cultural Critique,* 6, 1987, p. 55.

[38] Kellner, D., "Postmodernism as Social Theory: Some Challenges and Problems," *Theory, Culture and Society,* 5, 2-3, 1988, p. 263.

[39] Dews, P., "From Post-Structuralism to Postmodernity: Habermas' Counter-Perspective," *ICA Documents,* 4, published by Institute for Contemporary Arts, London, 1986, p. 15.

[40] Hawkesworth, M., "Knowers, Knowing, Known: Feminist Theory and Claims of Truth," *Signs,* 14, 3, 1989.

[41] Mascia-Lees et al., *op. cit.,* p. 29.

[42] Giroux, H., "Modernism, Postmodernism and Feminism: Rethinking the Boundaries of Educational Discourse," in his (ed.), *Postmodernism, Feminism, and Cultural Politics* (Albany: SUNY Press, 1991), pp. 1-59.

[43] Grossberg, L., *We Gotta Get Out of This Place,* working manuscript, forthcoming.

[44] *Ibid.*

[45] *Ibid.*

[46] *Ibid.*

[47] *Ibid.* The quotations in the following paragraph are from the same source.

[48] Pfeil, F., *Another Tale to Tell* (London and New York: Verso, 1990), p. 256.

[49] Laclau, E., *New Reflections on the Revolution of Our Time* (London and New York: Verso, 1990), p. 210.

[50] Inden, R., "America Teaches the World Order," paper delivered at the seminar "Intellectuals and Social Action," University of North Carolina, 1989.

[51] McLaren, P., *Life in Schools* (New York: Longman, 1989); Giroux, H., and McLaren, P., "Schooling, Cultural Politics, and the Struggle for Democracy: Introduction,: in Giroux, H., and McLaren, P. (eds.), *Critical Pedagogy, the State, and Cultural Struggle* (Albany: SUNY Press, 1989).

[52] Eagleton, T., *Against the Grain* (London: Verso, 1986), p. 145.

[53] Nicholson, L., "Introduction," in her (ed.), *Feminism/Postmodernism* (London and New York: Routledge, 1990), p. 6.

[54] Di Stephano, C., "Dilemmas of Difference: Feminism, Modernity, and Postmodernism," in Nicholson, L. (ed.), *ibid.,* pp. 63-82.

[55] Eagleton (1986), *op. cit.,* p. 145.

[56] Giroux (1991), *op. cit.*

[57] Eagleton (1986), *op. cit.,* pp. 96-97.

[58] Zavarzadeh, M., "Theory as Resistance," *Rethinking Marxism,* 2, 1, 1989.

[59] *Ibid.,* p. 66.

[60] McLaren (1987) and McLaren and Hammer (1989), both *op. cit.*

[61] Thompson, K., *Beliefs and Ideology* (New York and London: Tavistock and Ellis Horwood, 1986), p. 116.

[62] See Harrison, B. W., *Making the Connections,* ed. Carol S. Robb) (Boston: Beacon Press, 1985).

[63] Giroux (1988), *op. cit.*

[64] Morton, D., and Zavarzadeh, M., "The Cultural Politics of the Fiction Workshop," *Cultural Critique,* 11, 1988, pp. 155-173.

[65] Milhevc, J., "Interpreting the Debt Crisis," *The Economist,* 28, 1, 1989, pp. 5-10.

[66] Welch, S., *Communities of Resistance and Solidarity* Maryknoll, N.Y.: Orbis Books, 1985), p. 83.

[67] See, for example, Graff, H., *The Literacy Myth* (New York: Academic Press, 1979); Street, B., *Literacy in Theory and Practice* (Cambridge: Cambridge University Press, 1984); Lankshear, C., with Lawler, M., *Literacy, Schooling and Revolution* (London and New York: Falmer Press, 1987).

[68] Cf. Giroux (1988), both *op. cit.* (see note 8).

[69] *Ibid.*

[70] Poster, *op. cit.,* p. 27.

[71] Fraser, *op. cit.,* p. 182.

[72] *Ibid.*

[73] Menchú, R. *I, Rigoberta Menchú: An Indian Woman in Guatemala,* ed. and Introduction by Burgos-Debray, trans. Ann Wright (London: Verso, 1984); Anzaldúa, G., *Borderlands/La Frontera: The New Mestiza* (San Francisco: Spinsters/Aunt Lute, 1987).

[74] Rosaldo, R., *Culture and Truth: The Remaking of Social Analysis* (Boston: Beacon Press, 1989), p. 216.

[75] Anzaldúa, cited in *ibid.,* p. 216.

[76] Poster, *op. cit.,* p. 132.

[77] *Ibid.,* p. 131.

[78] *Ibid.,* p. 129.

[79] McLaren (1988), *op. cit.*

[80] Laclau (1988), *op. cit.,* p. 23.

[81] Jameson, F., "Cognitive Mapping," in Nelson, C., and Grossberg, L. (eds.), *Marxism and the Interpretation of Culture* (Urbana: University of Illinois Press, 1988), p. 360.

[82] Hartsock, *op. cit.,* p. 172.

[83] Kearney, R., *The Wake of Imagination* (Minneapolis: University of Minnesota Press, 1988), p. 362.

[84] Fererra, A., "On Phronesis," *Praxis International,* 7, 3-4, 1987, pp. 246-267.

[85] One of the difficulties that radical educators who work from a postmodern perspective have to face is a specious attack on their work as mere "textualism" or "aestheticism." Many of these attacks are launched by Marxist educators who seek the moral high ground by claiming that only they are really interested in the suffering and emanicipation of oppressed groups.

Many of these attacks are inadequately theorized and researched and carefully select out those works that specifically run counter to their claims. For a prime example, see London E. Beyer and Daniel P. Liston, "Discourse or Moral Action? A critique of Postmodernism." *Educational Theory,* Vol. 42, No. 4, pp. 371-393. Criticism such as this, which fails to adequately distinguish between ludie and resistance strands of postmodernism, cannot hope to appreciate the emancipatory possibilities of postmodern discourse. For works that not only address similar criticisms of postmodernism, but seek to establish a postmodernism of resistance—especially with respect to the development of a moral imagination—see Peter McLaren, "Multiculturalism and the Postmodern Critique: Towards a Pedagogy of Resistance and Transformation," *Cultural Studies,* in press; Peter McLaren and Rhonda Hammer, "Critical Pedagogy and the Postmodern Challenge: Towards a Critical Postmodernist Pedagogy of Liberation," *Educational Foundations,* Vol 3, No. 3 (1989), pp. 29-62; Peter McLaren, "Postmodernity, Postcolonialism and Pedagogy," *Education and Society,* Vol. 9, No. 2 (1991), pp. 136-158; and Henry Giroux, *Border Crossings,* (London and New York: Routledge, 1992). To acknowledge pedagogies informed by resistance or critical postmodernism would undercut Beyer and Liston's arguments so this strand of postmodernism remains absent in their critique.

POSTSCRIPT TO "CRITICAL LITERACY
AND THE POSTMODERN TURN"

In his recent book, *Common Culture,*[1] Paul Willis argues that we live in an era in which high culture or official culture has lost its dominance. Official culture—the best efforts of Allan Bloom and E.D. Hirsch, Jr., notwithstanding—cannot hope to colonize, dominate, or contain the everyday and the mundane aspects of life. Formal aesthetics have been replaced by a grounded aesthetics. The main seeds of cultural development are to be found in the commercial provision of cultural commodities.

Indeed, as Scott Lash points out,[2] postmodern culture permits us to see the economy itself as a kind of culture, a regime of signification. On the "demand side" of a post-Fordist economy we have specialist consumption and "sign value" rather than "use value"—and there are, seemingly, virtually no limits to sign value. We have an era of mass advertising with an oversupply of cultural significations in what is basically a self-service economy. The shift from producer capitalism to consumer capitalism, and the privileging of distributing over production, has created new restrictions and possibilities alike for identity formation and social change. Willis says,

We must start from unpalatable truths or no truths at all. The time for lies is gone. We need worse truths, not better lies. The "arts" are a dead letter for the majority of young people. Politics bore them. Institutions are too often associated with coercion or exclusion and seem, by and large, irrelevant to what really energizes them. "Official culture" has hardly recognized informal everyday culture, still less has it provided usable materials for its dialectical development. Worse, the "holiness" of "art" has made the rest of life profane.[3]

According to Willis, one way to work for the "best side" of this trend is to give everyday culture "back to its owners" and letting them develop it. "Let them control the conditions, production, and consumption of their own symbolic resources."[4] This, however, is no easy task, and there are no guarantees, especially since symbolic resources "are lodged in their own historical patterns of power and logics of production." But if the grounded aesthetics of everyday cultural life for youth are concretely embedded in the sensuous human activities of meaning making, there are implications for a critical approach to literacy. Literacy must help students "to increase the range, complexity, elegance, self-consciousness and purposefulness of this involvement" in symbolic work.[5] It must provide them with the symbolic resources for creative self and social formation so that they can more critically re-enter the broader plains of common culture.

Symbolic work within informal culture is unlike the symbolic work of school in fundamental ways.

> Where everyday symbolic work differs from what is normally thought of as "education" is that it "culturally produces" from its own chosen cultural resources. Psychologically, at least, the informal symbolic workers of common cultures feel they really "own" and can therefore manipulate their resources as materials and tools—unlike the books at school which are "owned" by the teachers.[6]

For these reasons, creative symbolic work within informal culture offers important possibilities for "oppositional, independent or alternative symbolizations of the self." Moreover, human beings must not be regarded merely as human capital or labor power, but as "creative *citizens,* full of their own sensuous symbolic capacities and activities and taking a hand in the construction of their own identities." The pursuit of emancipation and equality, therefore, requires more than being made equal as workers. It calls for all to be fully developed as *cultural producers.*[7]

Critical literacy is essential to this struggle in several ways. We need to be literate enough to deny the injunctions by which identities are constructed through official culture, in whatever form it appears. This presupposes that we create what Judith Butler calls "alternative domains of cultural intelligibility . . . new possibilities . . . that contest the rigid codes of hierarchical binarisms."[8] Within such hybrid pedagogical spaces educators can give greater attention to the everyday artifacts of popular culture and forms of knowledge that avoid the elitist

tyranny of the center. Critical literacy enables us to rearticulate the role of the social agent so that she or he can make affective alliances with forms of agency that provide new grounds of popular authority, ground to stand on from which to give voice to narratives of human freedom.

What educators like Hirsch and Bloom seemingly fail to understand is that schools are failing large numbers of minority and otherwise marginalized students precisely because too much emphasis is already placed on trading in the status of one's cultural capital. Ironically, students who populate urban settings in places like New York's Howard Beach, Ozone Park, and El Barrio are likely to learn more about the culture of Eastern Europe in settings designed by metropolitan intellectuals than they are about the Harlem Renaissance, Mexico, Africa, the Caribbean, or Aztec or Zulu culture. The sad irony is that test scores based on information decanted from the vessel of Western values and bourgeois cultural capital are used to justify school district and state funding initiatives.

Critical literacy helps us identify and answer the question: How do essentially arbitrarily organized cultural codes, products of historical struggle among not only regimes of signs but regimes of material production, also come to represent the "real," the "natural," and the "necessary"? A critical literacy reveals that signs do not correspond to an already determined metaphysical reality, nor are they transhistorically indeterminable or undecidable. Rather, their meaning-making possibilities and their meaningfulness are legitimized through the specificity of discursive and material struggles, and the political linkages between them. A critical perspective on reading and writing also enables teachers and students to understand the dangers in considering literacy to be a private or individual competency—or set of competencies—rather than a complex circulation of economic, political, and ideological practices that inform daily life, that invite or solicit students to acquiesce in their social and gendered positions within a highly stratified society and accept the agenthood assigned to them along the axes of race, class, and gender.

To this extent critical literacy becomes the interpretation of the social present for the purpose of transforming the cultural life of particular groups, for questioning the tacit assumptions and unarticulated presuppositions of our current cultural and social formations and the subjectivities and capacities for agenthood that they foster. Critical literacy is directed at understanding the ongoing social struggles over the signs of culture and over the definition of social reality, over what is considered legitimate and preferred meaning at any given historical moment.

The critical literacy we envisage does not suggest that diversity in and of itself is necessarily progressive; but it does suggest that curricula should be organized in ways that encourage and enable students to make judgments about how society is historically and socially constructed, both within and outside of a politics of diversity, how existing social practices are implicated in relations of equality and justice as well as how they structure inequalities around racism, sexism, economic exploitation, and other forms of oppression.

Students need to be able to cross over into different zones of cultural diversity for rethinking the relationship of self and society, self and other, and for deepening the moral vision of society. Moreover, the question arises: How are the categories of race, class, and gender shaped within the margins and center of society, and how can students engage history as a way of reclaiming power and identity?

Trinh T. Min-ha talks about constructing hybrid and hyphen-ated identities, identities which simultaneously affirm difference and unsettle every definition of otherness.

> The moment the insider steps out from the inside she's no longer a mere insider. She necessarily looks in from the outside while she's looking out from the inside. Not quite the same, not quite the other, she stands in that undermined threshold place where she constantly drifts in and out. Undercutting the inside/outside opposition, her intervention is necessarily that of both not-quite an insider and not-quite an outsider. She is, in other words, this inappropriate other or same who moves about with always at least two gestures: that of affirming "I am like you" while persisting in her difference and that of reminding "I am different" while unsettling every definition of otherness arrived at.[9]

Critical literacy is built on the notion of border identities and a politics of location as border crossers[10]. It is also grounded in the ethical imperative of examining the contradictions in society between the meaning of freedom, the demands of social justice, and the obligations of citizenship, on the one hand, and the structured silence that permeates incidences of suffering in everyday life. The politics of difference that undergirds critical literacy is one in which differences rearticulate and reshape identity so that identities are transformed and in some instances broken down, but never lost. That is, they are identities immersed not in the effete objections of a centrist politics which leaves individuals to function as obeisant servants of the power brokers, but identities which affirm them as reshapers of their own histories.

NOTES

[1] Willis, P., *Common Culture* (Boulder, Colo.: Westview Press, 1990).

[2] Lash, S. *Sociology of Postmodernism* (London and New York: Routledge, 1990).

[3] Willis, *op. cit.*, p. 129.

[4] *Ibid.*

[5] *Ibid.*, pp. 130-131.

[6] *Ibid.*, p. 136.

[7] *Ibid.*, p. 150.

[8] Butler, J. *Gender Trouble* (New York and London: Routledge, 1990), p. 145.

[9] Min-ha, Trinh T., "Not You/Like You: Post-Colonial Women and the Interlocking Questions of Identity and Difference," *Inscriptions*, 3-4, 1988, p. 76.

[10] Giroux, H. *Border Crossings*. (New York and London, 1992).

FICTION

Charles Russell

SOURCE: "Individual Voice in the Collective Discourse: Literary Innovation in Postmodern American Fiction," in *Sub-stance*, Vol. 27, 1980, pp. 29-39.

[*In the following essay, Russell surveys the fiction of several contemporary American authors, including Thomas Pynchon, to convey his belief that postmodernism reflects the ambiguity and self-consciousness of life in the latter half of the twentieth-century.*]

Since World War II, a new aesthetic and social configuration—the postmodern—has appeared in Europe and the Americas. Studied, but only imprecisely defined, by scholars, artists and writers alike, the postmodern signals a significant change in the nature of the individual's relationship to society. Like the dominant aesthetic traditions of the past 150 years, modernism and the avant-garde, postmodernism displays an alienated, if not antagonistic, response to the aesthetic, ethical and spiritual concerns of bourgeois culture. But with few exceptions, contemporary writing is much less anguished and is narrower in scope than its predecessors. Rare are the heroic modernist efforts to conceive metaphoric or mythic systems to both encompass and transcend the social referent. At the same time, the bravado of the avant-garde assault on culture is curiously lacking. At the heart of recent innovative writing is a troubled and problematic creative sensibility. The writer's analytic stance still fosters a critical response to culture, but there is clearly less faith in one's assumptions of self-knowledge and mastery, in one's perception and knowledge of the external world, and even more importantly, in the writer's very means of expression.

Gone are the modernist and avant-garde premises of the privileged nature of the writer's perspective and language. No longer does the feeling of alienation suggest a compensating critical and totalizing vantage point from which the writer can declare his independence from his culture. Instead, the essential dynamics of postmodernism indicate a major re-evaluation of the individual's response to his society, and in particular to society's semiotic codes of behavior, value and discourse. The postmodern individual, the writer, and the text now experience and articulate themselves self-consciously from within the social context—from which, nevertheless, they may still feel alienated and of which they may still be critical. Postmodern literature recognizes that all perception, cognition, action and articulation are shaped, if not determined, by the social domain. There can be no simple opposition to culture, no privileged perspective or language, no secure singular self-definition, for all find their meaning only within the social context.

This problematic situation is, of course, only one manifestation of a more general change in the social life of contemporary culture. Most sociological discussions of postmodern culture locate the origin of the confusion between personal and social domains in the dissolution of bourgeois hegemony and the development of mass culture, in which class lines are blurred and class antagonisms are unresolved but submerged in a late capitalist, state modulated economic system of consumption.[1] Inherent in this stage of capitalism is the increasing totalization of culture, the movement toward an internally consistent and all-encompassing social structure in which all institutions and patterns of human behavior are mutually regulated. But this culture also exhibits a series of internal oppositions and contradictions which become evident in postmodern literature. For example, with the growth of mass, pluralistic culture, we both encounter a heightened sense of individual freedom, even anarchic tendencies, and at the same time observe signs of a pervasive totalizing social uniformity and control. Individual innovation, style and desire are accented, but lose their distinctiveness and multi-dimensionality in a homogenizing pluralism that obscures originality. Constant change, either the product of personal effort or corporate plan, is experienced, but the society as a whole seems oppressively static. A central focus of postmodern literature is consequently the merging of personal and collective domains. Postmodern writing explores the patterns of mediation, control and opposition among individuals and mass culture, a culture experienced primarily through society's codes of discourse and behavior, its collective structures of order and articulation.

These concerns are especially evident in contemporary American fiction—in the works of writers such as Pynchon, Coover, Burroughs, Kosinski, Sukenick, Barthelme, Reed, Barth, Federman, Gass, Major, Vonnegut, Brautigan, Katz, Demby, and Sorrentino. All develop self-reflexive innovative literary strategies to illuminate the conflicts and paradoxes inherent in the individual's discovery of the nature and limits of identity and expression. The subject matter of these works is at once the complex interactions of individual and culture, of personal speech and collective discourse, of specific text and literary tradition, and of literature and society's semiotic codes. Each pairing reveals the ambiguous status of individual

creator or creation in a society which seems alternately to control or prefigure individual expression and yet to allow substantial personal freedom.

At the heart of this ambiguity, then, on both the formal and thematic levels, is the problematic nature of subjective presence—whether conceived in terms of character, writer or the speaking voice of the text—a subjectivity which rarely achieves clear definition or stable identity. Personal presence discovers itself as fundamentally in flux, as a process or transitory locus of shifting, disparate and incompletely known events, forces, concepts and systems, over which it has little control and which it can at most investigate and strive to pattern by a constant self-reflexive critique and creation.

Thematically, the most frequent expression of the ambiguity between personal and collective domains is paranoia. It is both a primary psychological state and literary motif. Both writer and character realize that successful selfdefinition depends on developing techniques of constant testing and interpreting of self and the encroaching world. They devise strategies of retreat or antagonism, of formalism or disruption. But since the integrity of personal identity is ever in doubt and the nature of the threatening environment is rarely revealed, these figures are never sure whether such disruption and creation prove to be adequate responses. Self-reflexive creative freedom may be but an expression of social encapsulation; disruption of the environment or text may result in a debilitating fragmentation of self or voice; and instead of providing an understanding of the social context, individual liberation may only unveil the visionary dreams and destructive reality of anarchism.

For example, William Burroughs' novels provide the most graphic and extreme expression of anarchic idealism and rage in contemporary literature. His characters are incessantly beset by forces of exploitation which push them into lives of addiction, self-destruction and progressive dehumanization. Rarely do they perceive either what is happening to them or their own participation in their degradation. Most accept uncritically the propaganda broadcast by the media, the institutions of social control, the "Time, Life, Fortune Monopoly," the "reality studios," or the political groups of *Naked Lunch*—the Liquifactionists, Divisionists and Senders, all of whom are intent on replicating themselves through their victims or dominating people's thoughts by instilling a single pattern of cognition and expression in society.

But Burroughs also suggests that to struggle against social control means to battle against one's prior identification with it—and, even more distressing, that to actively oppose the enemy insures that one remains defined by them; for as long as one is obsessed with fighting the opposition, one is not free of it. In Burroughs' novels, the greatest danger is thus to allow oneself to become rigidly defined by something external to oneself, for then one's identity is restricted and vulnerable. Consequently, the individual must not only disrupt the reality studios, but continuously disorient himself and his language to prevent his life from being controlled by anything except immediate, personal will. Against the institutions of control, Burroughs sends his anarchists, terrorists and the "Nova Police" who expose what is taken for reality for the grotesque horror it is. Against the three political parties of *Naked Lunch,* he pits a fourth, the Factualists, whose job it is to reveal in the most brutal—and often pornographic—terms the truth of our normal lives. The Factualists, however, cannot substitute an alternative vision, for Burroughs trusts no codified message or program, which might then be co-opted or become an authoritarian voice in others' lives. All the Factualists can do is disrupt and expose reality to force people to recognize themselves for what they are both before and after they accept a version of the "reality film"—"dying animals on a doomed planet."[2] Paradoxically then, precisely what sends people into addiction—their fear of chaos and pain, their sense of personal fragmentation and insignificance—becomes the means and the basis of their cure. Disruption, chaos, violence and exposure are what one must learn to live in. Only those strong enough to exist without external support, without a rigid identity, will survive.

In many ways, the world of Jerzy Kosinski's novels is similarly exploitative, and correspondingly, his characters' responses are as willful and antagonistic as are Burroughs'. Social and personal relationships in his novels are barely disguised forms of aggression. Political and collective social systems attempt to mold individuals' behavior. In turn, individuals depend on the exploitation of others for their own self-assurance and protection, since each person represents a threat to every other person. Kosinski's protagonists construct series of masks, offensive and defensive disguises, which enable them to manipulate others before they themselves are manipulated. But behind these masks the individual has no identity as such. He is only a predilection for control or self-defense. We never know a character except as fictive masks attempting to act upon others, or as he realizes he is the product of external forces acting upon him, or occasionally as he ponders the insubstantiality of his subjective presence. Furthermore, Kosinski's characters' lives have no apparent continuity. We perceive them only in series of discrete events, tests of self, and theaters of combat.

In Ronald Sukenick's novels, again, neither the social environment nor the characters' identities are stable, though they are not nearly as violent as are Burroughs' and Kosinski's. Everything in Sukenick's books is in a state of flux and fission. The half-lives of characters or their surroundings often last no longer than a few pages, at times a few sentences. Both reality and identity are perceived to be fictions, subject to revision as the shifting situation warrants. As in so many postmodern novels, the causes of these revisions are unclear. At times, changes in the characters' identities seem to be unconscious effects of alterations in the environment; at others, they appear to be creative or defensive responses to environmental changes; and at still others, their surroundings

modulate in tune with the characters' willed mutations; and finally, at times all these possibilities seem to occur at once. The result is a vision of complex and ill-defined connections between individuals and their world, leading alternately to conditions of extreme paranoia and exhilarating creative freedom. Characters are able to synthesize alternate versions of themselves out of their dreams, memories, subconscious, social roles and fantasies, while at the same time remaining almost totally dependent upon the vagaries of experience. The only adequate response, Sukenick suggests, is to accept identity as only a transitory locus of consciousness and experience. One must embrace and live within the flow of events, creating one's identity and insuring one's freedom from external control by improvising with the fragments of self and the stimuli thrust at one from the environment.

By counseling improvisation, the creation of personal reality in the absence of acceptable social totalities, Sukenick identifies one of the main aesthetic principles of postmodern literature, as well as of the visual arts, dance, music, theater and performance art. A character named Cloud in Sukenick's novel *98.6* refers to the improvisatory mode as Psychosynthesis: "Psychosynthesis is the opposite of psychoanalysis but apart from that Cloud refuses to define it. Cloud feels that life is a lot like a novel you have to make it up. That's the point of psychosynthesis in his opinion to pick up the pieces and make something of them. Psychosynthesis is based on the Mosaic Law. The Mosaic Law is the law of mosaics a way of dealing with parts in the absence of wholes."[3] However, even though the characters of Burroughs and Kosinski also participate in the synthesis of temporary identities, their authors recognize, as do many contemporary writers, that the "whole" may not be absent; it may just be obscure. In fact, the main justification of literary fragmentation and improvisation, they would argue, is to free oneself from a threatening external totality, whether it be literary or social, evident or hidden. Demystification of one's entanglement in the forces of totalization is thus the first stage of creation.

Significantly, the environment that postmodern characters confront is described as a fictive construct, as systems of social discourse. These characters, positioned self-consciously within the social framework, encounter no *natural* world, but rather a *cultural* reality, a reality structured by the patterns of social desire, discourse and ideology which manifest themselves throughout the environment and the characters' lives. Specifically, in the works of Pynchon, Coover, Barthelme, Brautigan, Gass, Reed, Wurlitzer, Vonnegut, Federman and those already mentioned, the environment the characters struggle with is often only a series of patent fictions, sign systems, hidden messages, obscure codes, familiar myths, pop images, and most frequently what Barthelme calls *dreck,* the detritus of popular culture, deracinated images of mass media in a pluralistic society. Barthelme's ironic and witty collages of high and popular culture rituals, Reed's adaptation of folk and popular narratives, Coover's grand orchestration of myths, cartoon images and historical facts, Brautigan's and Vonnegut's wry explorations of American myths and popular and minor literary genres all testify to the individual writer's and character's entanglement in the web of meaning systems that make up mass culture.

But the meaning of these meaning systems is rarely very clear; the environment is never neutral, and is frequently threatening. Interpretation of the environment—even before its demystification—is thus the initial step of self-definition. But in a chaotic, ambiguous and perhaps antagonistic environment, the problematic interpreter—the vulnerable, fragmented, paranoid character—can rarely achieve a coherent interpretation. The interpreter is never detached enough from his subject to master either himself or his surroundings.

The characters of Pynchon's novels, especially Stencil and Profane of *V.*, Oedipa Maas of *The Crying of Lot 49,* and Slothrop, Enzian and Tchitcherine of *Gravity's Rainbow* are emblematic of this dilemma. They continuously find themselves caught between the apparent chaos of a world of "so much replication, so much waste,"[4] and suggestions of an omnipresent malevolent order, hidden behind but determining the chaos and their lives. Most end as do Stencil and Oedipa, at the point of realizing that no answer is forthcoming, no coherent interpretation possible, and that their only hope is the small space of personal freedom and vitality found in sustaining their private searches, quests which will keep them from falling back into the rigid and ultimately self-destructive lifestyles so endemic to their culture. But even this search may become a mystifying system, another version of entropy. Similarly, the Counterforce in *Gravity's Rainbow,* though it adopts a politically aggressive posture against the totalizing System, quickly reveals its limitations. Their self-consciously alogical, disorganized anarchism turns willed fragmentation against the established order in an effort to disrupt and demystify it. But as Roger Mexico realizes, to define themselves as a "We-system" against the "They-system" the Counterforce must play "Their" game and remain a subsidiary system within the larger one, a subversive ideology living under the hegemony of a dominant, exploitative ideology. And even though they sing "It isn't resistance, it's a war," Mexico foresees that they have no hope of dismantling the System. At most, they will only be able to carve out relatively small areas of personal satisfaction, and, being no significant threat, will be condemned to "living on as their pet."[5]

This judgment can apply equally well to most contemporary literary characters, and is a succinct expression of the paradoxes confronting the self-conscious individual in mass culture. Of particular importance to postmodern fiction, however, is that this problem of subjective integrity is not limited to the characters created by writers, but is also manifested in the self-reflexive text's relationship to the established codes of literary and social language. Burroughs once wrote: "To speak is to lie—To live is to collaborate,"[6] and while he later qualified the extremism of this statement, such a sentiment ultimately indicates the limits of contemporary innovative writing. The postmodern literary sensibility must confront, as does the Counterforce, the ambiguous placement of the writer and text in society and its discourse. Indeed, the characteristic strategies of postmodern innovative fiction—the aggressive disruption of language and of the literary text through fragmentation, aleatory structures, strained metaphors, collage, "cut-ups," self-reflexively arbitrary formal structuration—adopt avant-garde techniques to alter both the reader's literary expectations and his habitual acceptance of social discourse. The constant linguistic and stylistic innovation of recent writing displays a critical response not only to society, but to the very medium of literature which is a product of society. But just as the fragmentation of the literary characters suggests both a diminishment of individual possibility and an anarchic freedom, the obverse side of the aggressive demystification of language and its concurrent search for a more personal and vital expression is a disheartening or resigned sense of linguistic restriction and individual creative inconsequence.

The self-reflexive text's focus on language reflects the analysis of the individual's relationship to society's semiotic codes that is the subject of contemporary semiological criticism. Both the literature and criticism conclude that: 1) there are no privileged codes of discourse, that literature is not qualitatively different from other modes of signification; 2) no particular code exists independently of all other linguistic formulations in its culture; 3) the terms of the individual work, no matter how innovative, are always determined by the conventions of the established literary tradition; 4) the writer, working inevitably from within a specific tradition—and its parent culture—cannot be considered the sole author or origin of the particular text.

The latter two lessons dominate self-reflexive literary investigations because they refer most directly to the possibilities inherent in literary innovation. For if, as the semioticians inform us, meaning is the product of the interactions among linguistic elements of a specific discourse and, consequently, any statement or work has meaning only in reference to the particular linguistic framework, in which it is placed, then any innovative text, though struggling to transform that framework, is necessarily dependent upon it, and at the same time legitimizes it. The literary work can never claim complete originality, but utilizes, or plagiarizes ("playgiarizes," in Federman's words), prior discourse, thus receiving life and meaning from that which it defines itself against. Like the fictional character who realizes that personality is only the locus of individual and social determinants, the author and text discover that they are spoken by the language which they give speech to. And even though the writer gives speech its reality by speaking, he, in turn, only exists as a speaker because of the patterns of existent discourse.

The two other lessons of postmodern criticism—the loss of the privileged status of literature, and its relation to other social codes of discourse—are important foci of those writers who most represent the avant-garde spirit in postmodern American fiction: Pynchon, Burroughs, Reed, Sukenick, Brautigan, Federman, Major, Katz and Barthelme. Their vanguard sensibility is displayed by an insistence on literary innovation, which both points to the deadening and generally oppressive workings of the social organization, here described in terms of its semiotic codes—functionalism, bureaucratic cant, cybernetics, political jargon, sexual and racial innuendo, ideological formulations—and offers by its self-reflexive formal disruption a paradigm for the analysis and demystification of, and a potential liberation from, those codes. These postmodern writers, rather than being obsessed with silence and an apparently meaningless world which troubled the modernists, recognize that the world they inhabit is surfeited with meaning systems from which they must wrest their own language. For just as their characters sense the mutually supportive operation of the various systems which shape their lives, the writers realize that literature is embraced by other social languages and has a role in legitimizing the ways people perceive, think and speak in this culture. If, furthermore, the characters never achieve a precise delineation of identity or external phenomena, and if the writer is never totally responsible for the discourse used, then neither is the writer ever sure of the ideological components and extensions of the work. Consequently, many contemporary avant-garde writers devise strategies of distrust and disruption, not only of society's semiotic codes, but of literature and their own texts.

Exemplifying the writer's paranoia, Burroughs states: "The writer sees himself reading to the mirror as always. . . . He must check now and again to reassure himself that The Crime Of Separate Action has not, is not, cannot occur. . . . Anyone who has ever looked into a mirror knows what this crime is and what it means in terms of lost control when the reflection no longer obeys."[7] His response, however, reveals one of the paradoxes confronting the postmodern writer, for ultimately, he must accept the necessity of this "crime." Burroughs radically disrupts the text's continuity and constructs collage novels made up of fragmentary moments of original creation and of cut-up and rearranged pieces of works by other writers and himself, in order to force the writer and reader to experience language and the literary text in a new manner, to be concerned not with narrative unity or with conventional grammatical sequence, hence predictable meaning, but rather to think in "association blocks," groups of random images which by their juxtaposition to each other suggest meanings beyond the writer's and traditional language's control. But here, Burroughs, distrustful of language, realizes there is no escaping it, so he allows himself to be governed by the random images and unpredictable workings of the idiosyncratic discourse he set in motion, since unavoidably, to speak *is* to lie and to live *is* to collaborate. The writer must willfully immerse himself in the collective language in order to speak, for it is a greater delusion to assume that his ego is integral or that it is in absolute control of its articulation. The only option is to admit the ambiguity of subjective placement in language and to highlight the struggle between individual expression and cultural meaning system, thus testifying to one's dependence on established discourse, yet hoping to purify it nonetheless by stressing the moment of surprise at the new creation.

The valuing of the surprising and the new is, of course, one of the primary tenets of the avant-garde, for the experience of the new thrusts one free of the fetters of the past and presages an unknown but anticipated future. However, in postmodernism there is no strong invocation of the future, but instead a preference for immediacy, for the intensity of experience found in the flow of constantly changing present moments. The focus of postmodern fiction is thus on the self-reflexive process of meaning-making which highlights the continuous deconstruction of established meaning and the projection of the new. Sukenick's character, who in *Out* says, "I want to write a book like a cloud that changes as it goes,"[8] is exemplary. And though few writers follow this desire to the extent he does, the sense of the mutability of meaning, of the writer's freedom to create new images through literary disruption and innovation, is the basis of many postmodern texts.

Pynchon's response to the interactions of individual voice in collective discourse is not to dismantle his own text, as does Burroughs, but to excessively parody the rage for order in society to the point that his metaphors become grossly exggerated and strained. Making ridiculous and grotesque the complex of social, political, sexual, cinematic, technological and popcultural meaning systems that envelop us, Pynchon's metaphors proliferate freely to reveal both how meaning systems *do* interpenetrate and tend toward aggressive totalization, and yet how no system can bear too much input before it starts to fall apart under its own weight. His novels, especially *Gravity's Rainbow,* work by a principle of comic and surreal overdetermination, themselves nearly falling apart as their many narrative lines dissipate or their characters are either left in a state of unresolvable inertia or disappear into the complex of conflicting subplots. Like the surreal antics of the Counterforce, they limn the process of meaning-making and its demystification without privileging any particular hierarchy of meaning. His works recall a statement from *Out:* "Connection develops meaning falls away."[9]

Such a pattern of the absence or ambiguity of meaning in the midst of surreal connections of images is common to the work of many postmodernists, such as Reed, Barthelme, Wurlitzer, Katz, Coover, Sorrentino, Charles Wright, Brautigan and Vonnegut. But this neo-surrealism does not represent a search for a primal super-reality which resolves contradictions; rather, it adapts the surrealists' love of absurd juxtaposition and the free play of the imagination. This new surrealism suggests both the fragmenting madness of the System and at the same time the liberating imaginative vision one may find within the

System by increasing the fragmentation. But here, again, we encounter the paradox of disruption which both describes a problematic situation for the individual and the text and is itself a means of achieving a degree of anarchic freedom. Such a freedom, as Pynchon has shown, is both attractive and perhaps delusive. For the improvisation of personal identity and meaning within the strictures of collective discourse can be seen as both an antagonistic response to an oppressive collectivity and an expression of it. Personal strategies of deconstruction are dependent on a semiological perspective which itself needs to be cast in doubt as a subordinate ideology of the culture in question. In particular, we need to inquire into four related tendencies of postmodern criticism and literature: the confusing multiplicity of meaning systems and the apparent devaluation of any specific meaning; the focusing on the structure of discourse as opposed to its operative function; the loss of subjective definition in culture and discourse; and the denial of historicity in social and linguistic change.

The totalization of meaning systems is described by many postmodern writers, but primarily as a confusing growth of competing and entwining sign systems in which no clear hierarchy is discernible, no infrastructure suggested, nor any undisputed meaning achieved. Literature recognizes its involvement in this web of meaning, but beyond its epistemological questioning is unsure of its social function and meaning.

The reduction of all experience and phenomena to elements of sign systems which can be "demystified" as arbitrary, fictive constructs, implies a political response to culture; but the strategies of demystification, disruption and improvisation are techniques played out solely within the formal dynamics of the semiotic system, and are consequently of questionable efficacy. The essential formalism—or idealism—of postmodern thought, its belief that meaning is primarily a function of the diacritical workings of discourse, not that the structure of the code is a response to material conditions, gives more significance to the mechanics of the semiotic system than to its function, as if the latter were entirely a product of the former. Furthermore, the presumed personal ability to play with and alter the system formally suggests that significant changes are not the result of alterations in the world to which it attempts to give meaning.

The goal of individual action on the code from within is twofold: to find those areas of free play that suggest self-creation and freedom, and to disrupt if not change the totalizing impetus of the system. But, as we have seen, the very notion of individual freedom is problematic precisely because each action within collective discourse reveals the unsure status of individuality. Defined in terms of the system of discourse, the individual can find freedom only by submitting to it, even as he tries to disrupt it, and consequently himself too.

The resulting changes of self and system may, therefore, be no more than formal dislocations of the system in which nothing substantial is altered. If the agent of change, self-reflexive innovation, is seen only as one element in a set of possible operations inherent in the discourse, what is the nature of the change that is desired? And can postmodern innovation be an avant-garde expression of historical development? To be in advance of change would merely place one in a state of premature semiological shift. And finally, can an historical perspective be easily sustained in a society which seems both to inspire constant formal change yet remains singularly static?

The literary innovation that characterizes postmodern American fiction provides no easy answer to these concerns for it is the expression of a troubled exploration of the relation of ill-defined individuals to an ambiguous social framework. The postmodern focus on the mediation of self and others through literary language and society's semiotic systems reveals a constant doubt about the nature of the collectivity of which the writer is a member. Writing self-consciously from within the social context and the "social text," the contemporary writer can offer no modernist or avant-garde privileged or idealist perspective. He can only ask himself and his audience whether social discourse, behavior and ideology are manifestations of a growing collective consciousness, or are they, as so many postmodernist novelists seem to fear, signs of the increasing corporate bureaucratic and cybernetic control of collective experience and thought?

The innovative sensibility in postmodern fiction suggests a guarded but avant-garde response nonetheless. It sustains the avant-garde's activist faith that discourse, become self-conscious and self-reflexive, can raise the writer's and reader's awareness of the properties and operations of language and social discourse and of their own problematic placement within them. But unable to locate within this society signs of imminent and significant change not compromised by the culture in general, innovative writing remains primarily personal and idealistic, as are the immediate, if limited and perhaps compromised, rewards—free play, improvisation and temporary self-creation. Perhaps more cannot be expected, at least not until the material conditions of the culture postmodern fiction responds to and is an expression of change. As much as postmodern avant-gardism is antagonistic to the given terms of social reality, it is implicated in the society it rebels against. Instead of being *in advance* of its time, it is a direct expression of this era.

NOTES

[1] See the discussions of postmodernism by Matei Calinescu, *Faces of Modernity* (Bloomington: Indiana University Press, 1977), pp. 132-148; Henri Lefebvre, *La Vie quotidienne dans le monde moderne* (Paris: Gallimard, Collection Idées, 1968), pp. 55-207; Lucien Goldmann, *Pour une sociologie du roman* (Paris: Gallimard, Collection Idées, 1964), pp. 21-57, 284-302; Donald D. Egbert, *Social Radicalism and the Arts* (New York: Knopf, 1970), pp. 741-745; and Herbert Marcuse, *Counter-revolution and Revolt* (Boston: Beacon, 1972).

[2] William Burroughs, *The Ticket That Exploded* (New York: Grove Press, 1967), p. 151.

[3] Ronald Sukenick, *98.6* (New York: Fiction Collective, 1975), p. 122.

[4] Thomas Pynchon, *Gravity's Rainbow* (New York: Viking, 1973), p. 590.

[5] *Ibid.*, pp. 712-713.

[6] William Burroughs, *Nova Express* (New York: Grove Press, 1964), p. 15.

[7] William Burroughs, *Naked Lunch* (New York: Grove Press, 1959), p. 223.

[8] Ronald Sukenick, *Out* (Chicago: Swallow Press, 1973), p. 136.

[9] *Ibid.*, p. 128.

Mark Parker

SOURCE: "'The Name of the Rose' as a Postmodern Novel," in *Naming the Rose: Essays on Eco's 'The Name of Rose,'* edited by M. Thomas Inge, University Press of Mississippi, 1988, pp. 48-61.

[*In the following essay, Parker examines the postmodernist tendencies of Umberto Eco's* The Name of the Rose *in light of Eco's own literary criticism.*]

We live in a decade of "post's": poststructuralism, postmodernism, and the teasingly paradoxical postcontemporary. Almost no one, however, seems happy with the term *postmodern.* It is most often used, as one critic puts it, "pis aller," as if it were a tool designed obsolete or a category always empty.[1] In his *Postscript to "The Name of the Rose,"* Eco slips by its insufficiencies with characteristic good humor, noting its ever-widening range and variety of application, and ultimately presenting it as "an ideal category—or better still, a Kunstwollen, a way of operating."[2] This tendency toward a functional, not a descriptive, definition is characteristic of his humor: Eco moves at once from the ambiguities of *what* to the palpabilities of *how,* treating the postmodern as an ironic "reply to the modern" (67). Despite some deprecating preliminaries, Eco takes pains to recast this term, redefining it with some of the irony he holds so central to a postmodern attitude. By the end of this section of the *Postscript,* perhaps the reader can say "postmodern" with the success that Eco's post-Cartland lovers can say "I love you."

To accept this "challenge of the past, of the already said, which cannot be eliminated" (67), one must, of course, know something about it. The term *postmodern* itself has a short but significant history; to see how Eco has inserted himself into the critical discussion of this movement or period or Kunstwollen, it is first necessary to take a short tour through some of the better-known discussions of it.

The term gets off to an inauspicious start in two early articles, Irving Howe's "Mass Society and Postmodern Fiction" and Alfred Kazin's "Psychoanalysis and Literary Criticism Today." Both articles fix upon a consistent problem for postmodern fiction: the lack of an authoritative system of values or tradition to criticize or rebel against. Kazin sees desperation in the attempts of Britain's "angry young men" to find suitable objects for their emotions and in Norman Mailer's celebration of the murderous assaults of two eighteen-year-olds on a candy-store keeper as a daring, revolutionary act. Howe sees "a world increasingly shapeless and an experience increasingly fluid," a world and an experience that resist the attempts of novelists to embody through them values and moral judgments.[3] Criticism of bourgeois values and society forms the backbone of modernist writing. Even the less analytic of modernists could easily snatch up and successfully employ the systematic, radical criticisms of nineteenth-century society provided by Marx, Freud, Nietzsche, and others. Novelists could count on this stable core of assumptions to provide them with "symbolic economies and dramatic conveniences."[4] There was a live consensus to which modernists had access, which they exploited by employing characters in conscious rebellion against society (perhaps given clearest expression in the youthful protagonists of Joyce and Lawrence). The postmoderns, however, lacking this coherent value system or authoritative moral tradition to rebel against, face a problem of self-definition. One can hardly criticize a social order so chaotic and elusive; it is necessary instead to project a moral order. According to Alfred Kazin, what is required "is no longer the rebel" but "the stranger—who seeks not to destroy the moral order, but to create one that will give back to him the idea of humanity."[5] Howe—and, by implication, Kazin—blame this sad situation on "mass society." Howe registers his objections in the form of a jeremiad:

> By the mass society we mean a relatively comfortable, half welfare and half-garrison society in which the population grows passive, indifferent, and atomized; in which traditional loyalties, ties, and associations become lax or dissolve entirely; in which coherent publics based on definite interests and opinions gradually fall apart; and in which man becomes a consumer, himself mass-produced like the products, diversions, and values he absorbs.

For Kazin and Howe, postmodern fiction is full of "distinctive failures" and should be accorded "patience and charity."[6]

These early assessments of the postmodern, made before the bulk of the novels deemed postmodern were written, seem cannily prophetic when considered in the light of Gerald Graff's later investigation of contemporary fiction, "Babbitt at the Abyss." Graff, through an extensive survey of recent fiction, reaffirms and extends their conclusions. To his mind, postmodernist fiction "has often been weakened by its inability or refusal to retain any moorings in social reality."[7] The modernist attack on bourgeois values has become an empty gesture in the hands of many postmoderns; since this culture no longer exists, "such demolition is needless."[8] It is as though the moderns had sunk all the ships, leaving to the postmoderns the barren joy of shelling the wreckage. Like Howe and Kazin, Graff attributes the failures of postmodern fiction to mass society:

> If this deficiency exists, then one reason for it may be that in the kind of mass society which has grown up in the last three decades, our personal relationships, public values, and the connections between the two have become so disoriented, scrambled, and confused that writers, as well as everyone else, have found it peculiarly difficult to arrive at clear, coherent, and convincing generalizations.[9]

Such pessimism features strongly in this strain of postmodern criticism, a strain that Graff, in another article, brands as "apocalyptic."[10]

Against this gloomy assessment stands a strain of postmodern criticism far more optimistic, at times even celebratory, one practiced by a determined Susan Sontag, by a puckish Leslie Fiedler, and in a "visionary" (Graff's term) mode by Ihab Hassan.[11] This strain tends to embrace mass culture, or at least portions of it, as a kind of revolutionary gesture toward liberation. According to Sontag, faced with a technique of interpretation and a corresponding set of interpretations so encrusted, so deadening, and so repressive, "What is important now is to recover our senses. We must learn to *see* more, to *hear* more, to *feel* more."[12] Fiedler, noting that an element of science fiction has passed into postmodern fiction, welcomes "the prospect of radical transformation" of man into "something else" and hails the coming of "the new mutants" who will disengage utterly from the humanist, bourgeois, Marxist, "cult of reason" traditions.[13] Hassan sees postmodernism as a reaction to "the unimaginable . . . extermination and totalitarianism," as a response that has "tended toward artistic Anarchy in deeper complicity with things falling apart— or has tended toward Pop," and as an open embrace of radical transformation: "Who knows but that our only alternative may be to our 'human' consciousness."[14] In their discussions of critical values and strategies, these critics lean toward a more popular aesthetic and an embrace of the mass society Kazin, Howe, and Graff by turns find so disturbing and depressing.

Eco inserts himself deftly into this critical debate in his 1964 analysis of mass culture, *Apocalittici e integrati* (Apocalyptic and Integrated Intellectuals).[15] Building on Dwight MacDonald's categories of mass-cult and mid-cult and on Clement Greenberg's insistence on the economic and political bases for mass culture, Eco locates part of the problem of defining and describing mass culture in the critics themselves. According to Eco, they tend to ask the wrong question. Implicitly or explicitly, these critics ask, "Is mass culture good or bad?" when the real question is somewhat different. As Eco himself puts it, "When the present situation of an industrial society makes mass communication a fact, what can be done to render these means of communication capable of transmitting cultural values?"[16] In other words, mass culture is controlled by economics. It moves to the logic of profit, and it is prepared without the benefit of intellectuals, Intellectuals, in fact, tend to adopt an attitude of protest and reservation toward mass culture. To withdraw, however, is to say that this system is so extensive and pervasive an order that no isolated act of modification would be able to affect it, in fact, that such acts are futile gestures. Although reform in politics or economics often suggests complicity between opposed groups (wages are raised, strikers appeased; but the fundamental relation between the two groups is unchanged, and basic inequalities are not addressed), in culture it has no such ramifications. (Put another way, culture is part of the superstructure of society, not the socioeconomic base. The same caution does not apply in this realm.) Slight reforms in these other spheres may attenuate contradictions and avoid violent change for a long time, ultimately becoming complicity, but this never happens in the realm of ideas. Ideas never become an unequivocal point of reference that brings about pacification; the level of discourse is always raised. If you raise the pay of striking workers, you may keep the same system; nothing changes. If you teach illiterates to read—even if only to stuff them with propaganda—you have changed things fundamentally: they may read other books tomorrow. Thus, the proper attitude for the intellectual toward mass culture is one of acceptance and intervention. Mass culture is a fact, a certainty; its ramifications require that the intellectual steer between the disgust and withdrawal displayed by those Eco calls "the apocalyptic" and the flaccid, unqualified acceptance of those he calls "the integrated." Mass culture deserves serious attention because of its apparent dangers and its often forgotten benefits. We need forget neither its atrocities of taste nor its facilitation of cultural access. According to Eco, the intellectual must analyze carefully the nature of these means of communication, their effects on people as well as the reciprocal effects of people on mass culture. To do this, a thoroughgoing investigation must be directed at such phenomena as comic strips, popular songs, and television programs. What Eco, after doing some exemplary investigations in the book, suggests is that these media all have the tendency to promote complacency in the spectator. Their messages tend to be consoling ones, promoting the sense that the world present to the spectator is a good one, or at least the best one possible, even that it is justified and permanent. Media often provide this consolation by omission; Superman comic strips exclude politics by concentrating on the righting of private wrongs. The virtues promulgated and issues examined by the comics are civic, not political; they never suggest that the system itself is capable of improvement, much less that it may be culpable. The great defect of mass culture is "to convey a standardized, oversimplified, static and complacent vision that masks the real complexity of things and implicitly denies the possibility of change." Eco suggests that what mass culture needs is instructions for use. According to him, nothing is wrong with the distraction and diversion it affords. The difficulty lies in the fact that, for most people, such offerings alone constitute culture and exert a strongly reactionary force in society. Eco is not, however, like those liberals whom Dwight MacDonald criticizes; he does not suggest that mass culture be raised wholesale to High Culture. Instead, Eco argues for what he calls "honest" works, works that do not belie the complexity of society, that admit to the historical circumstances in which we find ourselves, that promote thought instead of predigested opinion, that do not have artistic pretensions like those of kitsch.[17]

This kind of analysis emphasizes the instrumental nature of mass media and mass culture. By shifting the discussion from the dead-end dichotomy of "Is mass culture good or bad?" Eco has managed to avoid both the pointless jeremiads against and the mindless celebrations of mass culture, which only muddy the issue. Eco suggests that we examine mass media and mass culture as we would any other system, focusing on the way it functions. We might do well to think of it as if it were a perceptual tool, a way of knowing the world. Mass culture, according to Eco, is a fact; it can neither be eradicated nor ignored; it is necessary to engage it.

At the end of his theoretical treatment of mass culture, Eco makes what in retrospect is a wryly proleptic comment: "I believe that there can be a novel intended at once as a work of entertainment, a consumer item, and an aesthetically valid work capable of providing original, not kitsch, values."[18] This double intention fits well *The Name of the Rose.* Couched as a mystery in a fourteenth-century monastery replete with grisly (or witty) murders, sprinkled with a generous dose of latinate obscurity, offering historical accuracy for the plausibility-hounds in the audience, hinting at less than celestial relations among the monks, and providing a steamy sexual encounter for the narrator—the novel features many of the tricks of the potboiler trade. Alongside these devices, however, Eco places William of Baskerville, whose views, though carefully attuned to the historical moment in the novel, are much akin to Eco's own. William offers us the spectacle of the intellectual in confrontation with the mass culture of his own day. William's remarks on the people, whom he calls with a wonderfully bifurcated attitude "the simple," serve to remind us of the importance of this confrontation and the difficulties involved in it.

The gist of Eco's attitude is clearly seen in a conversation William has with Adso, his young naive assistant, who plays a kind of medieval, youthful Watson to William's Holmes. Adso, confused about the distinctions among heretical sects, asks William to clarify them. William responds by offering up several analogies—first, a comparison of the body of the church to a river which, over the centuries, has begun to meander and form a crisscrossing delta because of its sheer size. Characteris-

tically, as he pursues this analogy, William becomes dissatisfied with it, finally urging Adso: "Forget this story of the river."[19] For William, analogizing is simply one intellectual tool among others; when its efficacy becomes questionable, he discards it. William then serves up another analogy, which, to Adso's bewilderment, he subsequently discards as well. Then he begins to analyze the situation of the masses (the simple). It is at this point that we can see Eco's own appraisal of mass culture and mass media, for he moves from doctrinal matters, which tend to change according to the desires of those in power, to social theory. The simple have "no subtlety of doctrine" (234). They "cannot choose their personal heresy" (235); they are caught up in current movements which happen to include some of what they recall from other movements already abandoned. William then begins to speculate on the meaning of the simple; he concludes that the condition of being simple, of being in the masses, is of greater moment than the particular heresy—that, in fact, the heresy is (in Aristotle's terms) accidental rather than essential. What creates social unrest is the tendency on the part of those in power to leave part of the flock outside, to push some people to the margins of society—without land, guild, or corporation. The sign of this exclusion is leprosy, not on the physical but on the semiotic level. As William says, "All heresies are the banner of a reality, an exclusion. Scratch the heresy and you will find the leper. Every battle against heresy wants only this: to keep the leper as he is" (239). Adso, confused by William's refusal to assign blame to the heretics, the lepers, or the overseers, presses him to take a stand: "But who was right, who is right, who was wrong?" (240). William answers in Eco's own instrumental terms; what his explanation provides is not truth but a closer look at the situation. It is like looking at a tool closely and then more closely. What comes of the two examinations is not some ultimate, final certainty but skill in manipulating the conceptual tools one employs. This, despite William's insistence that he is saying more than Adso is willing to recognize, isn't enough for Adso. William then looks more closely at the concept and category of the simple. He proposes, in an axiomatic way, that the simple, both in themselves and as a sign, have something to tell the intellectual. Their message goes beyond the traditional belief that God often chooses to speak through them. According to William,

> The simple have something more than do learned doctors, who often become lost in their search for broad, general laws. The simple have a sense of the individual, but this sense, by itself, is not enough. The simple grasp a truth of their own, perhaps truer than that of the doctors of the church, but then they destroy it in unthinking actions. What must be done? Give learning to the simple? Too easy, or too difficult. The Franciscan teachers considered this problem. The great Bonaventure said that the wise must enhance conceptual clarity with the truth implicit in the action of the simple. . . . (241)

Eco's own theory of mass culture is sufficiently evident in this passage. In *Apocalittici e integrati,* Eco calls for a dialectic between the intellectuals who insert them-selves into the machinery of mass media and the consum-ers of mass culture. He insists that the situation change from the present one, in which the technicians of mass culture situate themselves in and exploit a paternalistic, self-serving relation to the masses. There must be a dia-lectical relation between the engaged intellectual—who has the benefits of the compression provided by broad, general laws and conceptual categories—and the masses, with their sense of the individual. William continues in this vein: "How are we to remain close to the experience of the simple, maintaining, so to speak, their operative virtue, the capacity [for] working toward the transforma-tion and betterment of their world?" (242). Eco's picture of William confronting the new world of mass culture dramatizes the predicament of the intellectual, consciously hindered by the exasperating limits to the tools of his inves-tigation, the broad, general laws and conceptual catego-ries which by their very nature, their own truth, obscure the truth of the experience of the simple. For Eco, the simple have a less mediated—perhaps, in some cases, relatively unmediated—view of the world which the intel-lectual, because of the conceptual apparatus that makes him an intellectual, cannot see. The only possibility of bridging this gap lies in cultivating a dialectical relation between the two groups, for each is, fundamentally and possibly irrevocably, outside the other's truth.

The *Postscript* reaffirms this activist stance toward mass society in its division of novels into two kinds: "the text that seeks to produce a new reader and the text that tries to fulfill the wishes of the readers already to be found in the street."[20] Clearly, Eco prefers the former, describing the kind of novelist who "wants to reveal to his public what it *should* want, even if it does not know it" and even going so far as to suggest that the "text is meant to be an experience of transformation for its reader."[21] Despite the withdrawal from social action described by the fictive transcriber of Adso's manuscript, who, in the preface to *The Name of the Rose,* claims to write "out of pure love of writing" and "for sheer narrative pleasure," the *Post-script* takes on a limited "commitment to the present, in order to change the world."[22]

As vexed as the question of mass society in postmodern critical discussion may be, it pales by comparison with the question of the relation of postmodernism to modern-ism. Periodization is a dubious activity under the best of circumstances, and these are, critically speaking, most unpropitious times. In an article written in 1971, Michael Holquist proposes a view of postmodernism as a re-sponse to a vivid split between high and low in modern-ism itself. What myth and depth psychology are to the modern period, the detective story—"radically anti-mythi-cal" and "militantly anti-psychological"—is to postmod-ernism.[23] Holquist provides a picture of modernism's caste of professional exegetes devoted to unraveling the unsettling complexities of Joyce, Pound, and Woolf by day and soothing their troubled minds with a bit of reas-suring detective fiction by night. The two realms of modernism are linked by intellectuals who not only read

both high and low but in many cases (Michael Innes, C. Day Lewis, Dorothy Sayers) wrote detective novels. In postmodernism, high modernism's world, one in which "dangerous questions are raised . . . a threatening, unfa-miliar place, inimical more often than not to reason" is expressed through the medium of detective fiction, pro-ducing variants of the old form which, instead of reassur-ing the reader, give "a strangeness which is more often than not the result of jumbling the well-known patterns of classical detective stories." Postmodern narratives defeat the "syllogistic order" of their detective progenitors and in doing so, "dramatize the void."[24]

Eco's participation in this aspect of the postmodern ven-ture is clear; his remarks in the *Postscript,* if anything, abruptly deflate any argument celebrating the reassuring nature of the use of the detective story in his novel: "this is a mystery in which very little is discovered and the detective is defeated."[25] Yet he differs from Holquist in describing the aims of this technique. Rather than dis-cussing the novel as yet another performance of the abyss-story, Eco stresses the fundamental element of conjecture, of structuring, in the detective genre and its consequent connection to many other stories. Holquist's interpretation of the postmodern use of the detective story, which implies many routes to the sight of the void, ulti-mately is reductive; Eco's displays a centrifugal tendency.

Hassan, in his essay "POST modernISM," views the re-lation between modern and postmodern somewhat differ-ently. He cites such critics as Richard Poirier who, per-haps unwittingly, "revalue Modernism in terms of Postmodernism"; that is, they tend not simply to revise modernism but to read it through a postmodern aes-thetic.[26] Although Hassan's gnomic, "paracritical" style omits specific instances, they are not difficult to find. For instance, in a review of a collection of articles on Eliot, Richard Poirier stresses Eliot's tendency "to devalue lit-erature in the interests of the preeminent values of lan-guage," a position that echoes Barthes' insistence in *Writing Degree Zero* that "the whole of literature" since Flaubert has become "the problematics of language."[27] For Poirier, Eliot is at his most impressive when he is "de-creative," when he de-authorizes part of his past, "when his language challenges the conceptual and poetic schemas on which he seems to depend."[28] At his best, Eliot refuses to "pacify" experience. He stubbornly refuses to give final significance to or to totalize what is given. Poirier's critical practice is Hassan's point: "Mod-ernism does not suddenly cease so that Postmodernism may begin: they now coexist."[30]

In his "Myth of the Postmodernist Breakthrough," Gerald Graff arrives at a similar conclusion to that of Hassan and Poirier but adopts a decidedly more pessimistic attitude.[31] Graff, in response to celebrations of a postmodern "break-through," argues that the movement is, rather, "the logi-cal culmination of the premises of these earlier move-ments," namely, romantic and modernist.[32] He defines postmodernism as "that movement within contemporary literature and criticism which calls into question the claims of literature and art to truth and human value," then argues that this is precisely what earlier authors did: Wordsworth's doubts about whether the "significant external reality" of nature was perceived or created are carried over in modernism's obsession with ritual, myth, provisional order, and frames of reference. Romanticism included a strong component of doubt of the authority of their productions, and the moderns have continued this ambiguous attitude. The New Critics, according to Graff, have a part in this sequence of doubt; they were "masters of interpretation who had a profound skepticism of interpretation," and their postmodern successors simply turn their own skepticism upon them.[33] Like Hassan, Graff suggests a certain coexistence between modernism and postmodernism; but his coexistence is far less benign. In a sharp critique of social and critical pluralism, Graff provides a picture of postmodernism as a "reactionary" ideology, one that "is the reigning philosophy of the establishment."[34] Far from being a breakthrough, postmodernism offers an avant-garde that is merely a weak copy of the status quo: "Advanced industrial society has outstripped the avant-garde by incorporating in its own form the avant-garde's main values—the worship of change, dynamic energy, and autonomous process, the contempt for tradition and critical norms."[35] He advocates a careful reassessment of humanist values, one that recognizes their foundation in a particular social class but that does not banish them simply for that reason.

Eco's solution to the nature of the modern-postmodern relationship is to leave out history altogether, at least for the time being. Characteristically, he defines postmodernism in terms of a "way of operating," a position that allows him to posit a relation between the two based on function, not some elusive essence: "We could say that every period has its own postmodernism, just as every period would have its own mannerism." This scheme helps explain the puzzling heterogeneity of the literary scene: "in the same artist the modern moment and the postmodern moment can coexist, or alternate, or follow each other closely."[36] By choosing the term *coexist* ("convivere," in the original), Eco shows affinities for the assessments worked out by Hassan and Graff; but Eco wears his term with a difference.[37]

Much closer to Eco's remarks in the *Postscript* are the ideas of postmodern novelist and critic William Gass, in his essay "Tropes of the Text."[38] Gass traces the tendency of English novelists to think of their work in terms of some trope. The early choices were made based on an innocent pragmatism, a desire to relax the reader's (and perhaps even the author's) strictures against the frivolity of novel-reading. Richardson, for example, chose the letter as a trope for his novels not because he had some deep interest in the letter as a form but because "it offered itself as the only way his tale could be told."[39] Postmodern novelists show a far deeper commitment to their tropes, even to difficult burdensome ones. Such tropes are fundamental to the moment, despite the fact that they bring "nothing but confusion, nothing but postmodernism, nothing but grief."[40]

Stripped of its agon, this version of postmodernism as a deepening, even self-conscious, commitment to the trope of the text has vivid parallels in the *Postscript*. Eco's discussion of labyrinths reveals how deeply this trope structures *The Name of the Rose*. The novel seems to be controlled not by the genre of detective fiction (an example of "conjecture") but the trope of the labyrinth, "an abstract model of conjecturality."[41] Both the genre and the trope have a built-in metaphysical dimension, but the trope offers added possibilities. Eco goes into some detail on these, positing three types of labyrinths: the Greek or classical, the mannerist, and the rhizome. It is through the possibilities of the trope that Eco can describe William's world, "a rhizome structure" that "can be structured but is never structured definitively."[42] This goes far beyond the idea of postmodernism as a failed detective metaphysic, or what Holquist suggested was a dramatization of the void. In this discussion of labyrinths, Eco hints at another view of the postmodern phenomenon. Later in the *Postscript*, Eco suggests that "we could say that every period has its own postmodernism, just as every period has its own mannerism (and, in fact, I wonder if postmodernism is not the modern name for mannerism as a metahistorical category)."[43] If we apply this bit of conjecture to the three types of labyrinths Eco posits, we find a slight bit of slippage between definitions. The labyrinths are presented so as to invite interpretation along the lines of literary movements. First, there is the Thesean or Greek version, with a definite center and no possibility for losing oneself. The mannerist maze follows, with its blind alleys which provide for losing oneself. Last comes the rhizome, with its decentered space. Given that Eco comments explicitly on the parallel between mannerism and postmodernism as metahistorical categories, it is not hard to see the Greek labyrinth as figuring modernism, that movement so intensely given to the search for authoritative centers in the deep structures of myth or psychology. Where, then, does that leave William—not lost, since being lost implies at least the possibility of finding one's way—but simply existing in his decentered rhizome space?

All of these aspects of the *Postscript*—its stand on the issue of mass society, its participation in the critical debate on the relation of postmodern to modern, and its self-conscious discussion of tropes—mark *The Name of the Rose* as postmodern. It is in the debts that Eco consciously pays, in those tips of the hat to Borges and, perhaps even more obviously, to John Barth that the postmodern quality of revisiting the past "with irony, not innocently" is most visible.[44] In the *Postscript*, Eco sends the reader to two of Barth's articles on postmodern fiction, mentioning the titles of both and quoting a long passage from one of them.

A quick look at the earlier of these two articles shows the nature and depth of Eco's obligation. Barth's "The Literature of Exhaustion" contains two foci that are relevant here. It introduces Borges as an exemplary contemporary writer, and it explores what Barth terms "the literature of exhausted possibility."[45] Not surprisingly, the two are related. Exhaustion, in Barth's sense, has to do not with "physical, moral or intellectual decadence" but "with the used-upness of certain forms or exhaustion of certain possibilities."[46] This burden of the past—more specifically, the past successes of writers—poses great difficulty for writers of the present. Rather than bewail the impossibility of the situation, however, Barth, much as Eco does in the *Postscript* and in *Apocalittici e integrati*, rephrases the question along functional lines: "What it comes to is that an artist doesn't merely exemplify an ultimacy; he employs it."[47] The "technically up-to-date artist" can use exhausted forms without embarrassment "if done with ironic intent by a composer quite aware of where we've been and where we are." As far as form is concerned, a writer can't put his foot in the same form twice, because, as time goes by, the same form isn't the same form—the context changes. As with Eco's post-Cartland lovers, recognition of "used-upness" provides an unexpected, almost paradoxical range of possibilities. Barth then introduces a definition of the Baroque by Borges: "that style which deliberately exhausts (or tries to exhaust) its possibilities and borders on its own caricature."[48] He then discusses images favored by Borges, ending with his most favored image, that of the labyrinth. For Barth, this "is a place in which, ideally, all the possibilities of choice (of direction, in this case) are embodied, and—barring special dispensation like Theseus'—must be exhausted before one reaches the heart."[49] Waiting at the heart is the Minotaur, representing "defeat and death, or victory and freedom." Barth, however, is not content to simply serve up Borges, no matter how apt or, in 1967 terms, new. He rejects the labyrinth, at least the Theseus version of it, as "non-Baroque," because here the hero has access to the "shortcut" of Ariadne's thread, and he offers the image of Menelaus holding fast to Proteus on the beach at Pharos as "genuinely Baroque in the Borgesian spirit."[50] Barth visits the past of Borges, with irony, and puts it to his own use, teasing out from this visit an allegory of "the positive artistic morality in the literature of exhaustion." Menelaus is truly in the labyrinth, for he

> is lost, in the larger labyrinth of the world, and has got to hold fast while the Old Man of the Sea exhausts reality's frightening guises so that he may extort direction from him when Proteus returns to his "true" self.[51]

From Borges' success, Barth plucks his own victory, turning the burden of Borges' achievement to an opportunity of his own. He closes by celebrating the heroic nature of this move, how it requires virtuosity, not simply competence, and how it requires "the aid of very special gifts." Barth structures the encounter with the strong writer by his successor as a quest, including all the basic Proppian elements of hero, donor, villain, and agon.

The presence of Barth, even of his terminology, throughout the pages of the *Postscript* is unmistakable. The question is, of course, an obvious one: With what ironic intent has Eco echoed Barth echoing Borges? Truly, as Eco notes at the end of his remarks, "there exist obsessive

ideas, they are never personal; books talk among themselves, and any detection should prove that we are the guilty party."[52] Criticism, as Eco's own story ramifies into other stories, ramifies into other criticism.

NOTES

[1] David Perkins, *A History of Modern Poetry: Modernism and After* (Cambridge: Harvard University Press, 1987), p. 393.

[2] Umberto Eco, *Postscript to "The Name of the Rose,"* trans. William Weaver (San Diego: Harcourt Brace Jovanovich, 1984), 66. Future references are followed by page numbers in parentheses.

[3] Howe, "Mass Society and Postmodern Fiction," in *Decline of the New* (New York: Harcourt Brace, 1970), p. 198.

[4] Howe, "Mass Society," 196.

[5] Kazin, "Psychoanalysis and Literary Culture Today," in *Contemporaries* (Boston: Atlantic Monthly Press, 1962), 373.

[6] Howe, "Mass Society," 196, 192.

[7] Graff, "Babbitt at the Abyss: The Social Context of Postmodern American Fiction," *Tri-Quarterly* 33 (1975): 307.

[8] Graff, "Babbitt," 308.

[9] Graff, "Babbitt," 307.

[10] Gerald Graff, "The Myth of the Postmodern Breakthrough," *Tri-Quarterly* 26 (1975): 384. Graff's terms for the two strains of postmodernism he perceives are almost identical to those Eco chooses in his 1964 *Apocalittici e integrati*, which translate roughly as "apocalyptic" and "integrated" (that is, happily ensconced in the mass culture) intellectuals.

[11] Susan Sontag, *Against Interpretation* (New York: Farrar, Strauss & Giroux, 1966). Leslie Fiedler, "The New Mutants," *Partisan Review* 32 (1965): 502-25. Ihab Hassan, "POSTmodernISM: A Paracritical Bibliography," in *Paracriticisms* (Urbana: University of Illinois Press, 1975).

[12] Sontag, *Against Interpretation,* 14.

[13] Fiedler, "New Mutants," 508.

[14] Hassan, "POSTmodernISM," 59.

[15] Umberto Eco, *Apocalittici e integrati* (Milano: Gruppo Editoriale Fabbri-Bompiani, 1985). To my knowledge, there is no English translation; the translations here are my own.

[16] Eco, *Apocalittici,* 47.

[17] David Robey, "Umberto Eco," in *Writers and Society in Contemporary Italy,* ed. Michael Caesar and Peter Hainsworth (New York: St. Martin's Press, 1984), 71.

[18] Eco, *Apocalittici,* 53-54.

[19] Eco, *The Name of the Rose,* trans. William Weaver (New York: Warner Books, 1983). Further references are followed by page numbers in parentheses.

[20] Eco, *Postscript,* 48-49.

[21] Eco, *Postscript,* 49, 53.

[22] Eco, *Postscript,* xviii.

[23] Holquist, "Whodunit and Other Questions: Metaphysical Detective Stories in Post-War Fiction," *New Literary History* 3 (1971): 135-56.

[24] Holquist, "Whodunit," 147, 155.

[25] Eco, *Postscript,* 54.

[26] Hassan, POSTmodernISM," 47.

[27] Poirier, "T. S. Eliot and the Literature of Waste," *New Republic* 156 (1967): 20. Roland Barthes, *Writing Degree Zero,* trans. Annette Lavers and Colin Smith (London: Jonathan Cape, 1967), 9.

[28] Poirier, "T. S. Eliot," 20.

[29] Poirier, "T. S. Eliot," 25.

[30] Hassan, "POSTmodernISM," 47.

[31] Graff, "Myth."

[32] Graff, "Myth," 385.

[33] Graff, "Myth," 400.

[34] Graff, "Myth," 410.

[35] Graff, "Myth," 415.

[36] Eco, *Postscript,* 66, 68.

[37] Umberto Eco, "Postillo a *Il nome della rosa,* in appendice a *Il nome della rosa*" (Milano: Gruppo Editoriale Fabbri, Bomiani, Sonzogno, 1986), 530.

[38] Gass, "Tropes of the Text," in *Habitations of the Word* (New York: Simon and Schuster, 1985).

[39] Gass, "Tropes," 145.

[40] Gass, "Tropes," 159.

[41] Eco, *Postscript,* 57.

[42] Eco, *Postscript,* 58.

[43] Eco, *Postscript,* 66.

[44] Eco, *Postscript,* 67.

[45] John Barth, "The Literature of Exhaustion," *Atlantic Monthly* 220 (1967): 29.

[46] Barth, "Literature of Exhaustion," 29.

[47] Barth, "Literature of Exhaustion," 31.

[48] Barth, "Literature of Exhaustion," 34.

[49] Barth, "Literature of Exhaustion," 34.

[50] Barth, "Literature of Exhaustion," 34.

[51] Barth, "Literature of Exhaustion," 34.

[52] Eco, *Postscript,* p. 81.

Richard Bradbury

SOURCE: "Postmdernism and Barth and the Present State of Fiction," in *Critical Quarterly,* Vol. 32, No. 1, Spring, 1990, pp. 60-72.

[In the following essay, Bradbury discusses the fiction of John Barth, finding that the author uses self-reflexive techniques to comment on American culture.]

It is a commonplace of postmodernist fiction that it contains within itself a degree of self-reflection and self-reference. Indeed, the absence of these elements from more recent departures within the development of, particularly, American fiction has led to claims for the rise of a new realism within the genre. The irony of this change is that it has been contemporaneous with the development of a poststructuralist criticism which has as one of its major projects the disassembly of classic realist texts into their component writerly parts.

In the manner of his writing, if in no other, John Barth has resisted the tides of 'conservative realism' as they have swept back towards presenting the 'good old' values of straight-talking fiction as the new avant-grade. The postmodernists, the game-players, the questioners of the ontological and epistemological status of fiction, have been supplanted by Raymond Carver and friends; those describers of a world with which 'we are all familiar'—and the ideological ramifications of this phrase for an increasing conservatism do not need to be spelled out by me.

John Barth's position within this set-up is ambiguous in several ways. Whilst he is a long-term success in the field of producing postmodernist fiction of all kinds, he also teaches within one of the more prestigious US universities, and one of his most regular classes is in creative writing. He is also a regular contributor to the scholarly and intellectual debate which has revolved around postmodernist fiction since the late sixties. Indeed, in 1967 he gave one of *the* definitions of the subject in the essay, 'The Literature of Exhaustion', and then refined that definition and estimate some fifteen years later with the self-directed reply 'The Literature of Replenishment'.

I have argued elsewhere that Barth's version of postmodernism is not the jagged, fragmented and montage philosophical form lauded and employed by the likes of Ihab Hassan, but rather a kind of postmodernism which is fundamentally synthetic in its approach. It demonstrates its eclecticism and absence of tradition by gathering up disparate elements from the past and present and then displays them alongside each other in an often disturbing but equally frequently satisfying mosaic. It is not part of the self-styled radical wing of postmodernism but rather stands four-square within the traditions of American liberalism and its commitment to synthesise and absorb conflict within the greater good—*I pluribus unum* could easily be the motto for this school of fiction!

Within the narrative structures this creates a tension between the desire to eliminate the omniscient narrator as a symptom of a unitary voice and the reinstatement of that omniscient narrator as the only presence capable of achieving the synthesis towards which the text is geared.

The structure of the rest of this essay will be an analysis of the narrative effects of *LETTERS, Sabbatical* and *The Tidewater Tales,* and a discussion of how well the techniques of postmodernism carry the burden of political debate. I am well aware that this is hardly a new topic of discussion, but by confining myself to three specific examples I hope to develop a more precise and detailed version of the debate.

THE PARTICULAR THEMES OF BARTH'S FICTION

Since the late sixties Barth's work has involved the recurrent strategy of reworking and thus redefining thematic and narratological structures. In the earlier work this appeared as a conscious adoption, and exuberant parody, of older (or even 'obsolete') forms into which distinctively twentieth-century content was poured. Hence the eighteenth-century novel form became the vehicle for the content of *The Sot-Weed Factor* and the hero-myths became the structural device of *Giles Goat-Boy.* But after the examination of the possibilities of contemporary forms of communication in *Lost in the Funhouse* and the questioning of the accepted relationships between form and content which took place in *Chimera,* there was a shift towards the integration of thematic content into the surface of the plot and story. Explication of the 'deeper levels' of the text took place overtly and at the surface of the fiction in a writing which developed into a characteristically auto-critical mode. Perhaps the best example of this is the inclusion of Freitag's diagram of the rising curve of action towards dramatic climax at the dramatic climax of *Lost in the Funhouse.* The general autocritical, self-deconstructive

qualities of postmodern fiction became interwoven with Barth's particular concern with narrative and the difficulties of finding a mechanism of expression.

The reasons for the particular form this development took in *Lost in the Funhouse* and *Chimera* becoming a cul-de-sac need not concern us here. Suffice to say that the recognition of this block led to a turn in a new direction; to the writing of *LETTERS.* Here, Barth returned to the idea that the way forward in narrative was to go backwards in search of an 'old' form which could be rejuvenated. Thus, the epistolary novel becomes the means by which a group of interconnecting stories set at the end of the 1960s are told. But it is not the 'simple' epistolary form of the eighteenth century, for Barth has synthesised this 'pre-realist' manner with a decidedly modernist sense of design. The letters which make up the text are not in chronological order but appear according to a pattern derived from writing the subtitle of the novel—*An old time epistolary novel by seven fictitious drolls & dreamers, each of which imagines himself actual*—onto the calendar for 1969; this also eliminates from the text certain letters which must logically exist. The effect produced by this pattern is the combination of the textual polyphonic qualities of the epistolary novel with the indeterminacies of the modernist temperament, not least of which is the destruction of temporal casuality. This synthesis, Barth argues, opens new possibilities for written narrative fiction in a period when the continuing 'felt ultimacies' are apocalyptic as far as the continuation of the written word (at the very least) is concerned.

This 'going backwards in order to go forwards' also includes re-introducing characters from earlier works into this new fiction and then adding to that ensemble a new character who draws the threads of the plot together. Indeed, this was the source of some of the most negative reviews of the book at the time of its publication and led to complaints from reviewers that, in order to understand this work, one had to have read the rest of Barth's oeuvre—a charge both untrue and revealing of many reviewers' reading habits and attitudes towards those for whom they think they are writing.

The most productive aspect of the text, as far as Barth's development is concerned, is the polyphonic quality which the epistolary form lends to the text. Always a good parodist, Barth here writes in a fashion designed to demonstrate his stylistic virtuosity. At the same time, the design of the novel permits an interrogation of the ontological premises upon which realist (post-epistolary?) fiction stands; most particularly, the place of the author as a structuring mechanism within the text. For here the 'author' is displaced from omniscience to the position of one of the correspondents, he is deprived of his place on the first page. When he does appear, on page 42, he writes:

> Gentles all: *LETTERS* is now begun, its correspondents introduced and their stories commencing to entwine. Like those films whose credits appear after the action has started, it will now pause.

But this self-confident opening is undermined by a long speculation on the meaning of the word 'now' and concludes with an uncertainty as to the existence of an audience, which casts an ironic glance towards one of the fears of many of the nineteenth-century writers. This is followed by a letter addressed to 'Whom it may concern' in which he describes the course of his work so far and the structure of the present text through the distorting lens of a concentric dream. His third letter, written as a character in the fiction, replies to the opening letter of the work. His fourth is a counter-invitation to Germaine Pitt to become a character in the fiction he is at present writing and involves him in another speculation, this time on 'a muddling of the distinction between Art and Life'. As the text continues, the author continues to make requests to the correspondents to appear as characters in his ongoing fiction and also fulfils his role as a corresponding character in the novel. At the end of the work it falls to him to write the last letter, entitled 'LETTERS is "now" ended. Envoi', which replays the doubts about the word 'now' from the perspective of the completed novel. But according to the chronological order of the letters this is not the last letter—that honour rests with Todd Andrews's draft codicil to his last will and testament which concludes (presumably) with the explosive destruction of the Tower of Truth. In these ways the author's position as omniscient presence within the text is called into question; an interrogation which allows the voices of the text to speak.

This development of a technique of productive synthesis gave rise to the various forms of the two novels which follow *LETTERS*. In *Sabbatical,* the combination produced a complex form in which chronological clarity is sacrificed in order to produce a polyphonic text in which the two central characters and the author speak/write in a complex of voices and styles designed to displace authority from any single position within the text. At the same time, a battery of footnotes, and references to both real and spurious texts, are employed to extend the text beyond the 'normal' textual boundaries. Indeed, this constant employment of footnotes in order to clarify words, names and sources, and to provide the interested reader with further reading on the subjects under discussion within the text itself is the most foregrounded element of the narrative construction because of its constant visual intrusion upon the reading eye. That these footnotes are a mixture of the accurate and the specious is completely in accord with one of the keynotes in Barth's postmodernism: the ontological blurring of the boundary between fiction and reality, in which reality often only becomes a meaningful reality when it is constructed by the authorial imagination out of the mass of inchoate events.

The issue presented, then, by this structure and by numerous of the discussions within the text itself is precisely this issue of the gap between fiction and reality, between the actual existence of a plot (in all senses of the word) and its generation by overactive paranoid imaginations. The machinations of the CIA provide the ideal version of this, with its information and disinformation, its agents and double-agents, its codes and super-codes, which tangle together until the possibility of an 'innocent' event recedes under the ballast of interpretation.

This situation will be familiar to all readers of Pynchon's work, with one proviso. Namely, that whilst Pynchon consciously avoids adopting a 'political' stance by his blurring together of both left and right—exemplified by his two versions of the CIA (Central Intelligence Agency and Conjuracion de los Insurgentes Anarquistas)—Barth has by this point in his career taken up a consistently liberal stance and has no doubts about the identity of those behind the initials. Both however are characteristic of the postmodernist novelist's response to the collapse of previously-existing systems of order.

The internal design of *Sabbatical* is contained within an overall form rooted in the traditions of the romance and the heroic sea journey, and this is, of course, made clear by constant references within the text to precisely this material. However, the key to the thematic, narratological, chronological and geographical movements of the two central characters is the idea of going backwards in order to go forward. The text moves forward chronologically in leaps, only to return to an earlier point in order to tell what has happened so far. The two central characters, Fenwick and Susan revisit the geographical sites of earlier moments in their relationship and the history of their entangled families in an attempt to discover the way forward from the impasse in which they find themselves—in the end, however, their decision is to stay put at the point of decision, at the island at the mouth of the two channels. The Y which appears as a graphical epigraph to the novel acquires a new meaning when Fenwick sees the fourth possibility it contains. That this has a metalaptical connection to their/Susan's decision not to reproduce is clear. For narrative technique, the metalaptic and metaphorical connections of this choice are a continuation of Barth's synthetic approach now ironically recast as an inability to make a definite decision. The crucial difference between this and his earlier version of the same crisis, presented as cosmopsis in the first three novels, is that here the choice is productive; it leads to fiction and not silence.

The narrative time of *Sabbatical* begins on Tuesday, 27 May 1980 and concludes on Sunday, 15 June, containing in itself a movement from the Big Bang to the present with several extended flashbacks to explain the ground-situation of the novel. Within this structure, an almost encyclopaedic demonstration of narrative techniques takes place, from explicatory reported dialogues, to extracts from newspaper articles, to revelatory dream-visitations to leading figures in the tale.

In *The Tidewater Tales* Barth reworks this ground again, by writing a second novel which has the same geographical area (the Chesapeake Bay) as the site of its action and begins at the temporal point at which its predecessor concluded. Indeed, scenes from the previous novel are revisited from another perspective, characters from the previous novel reappear (only this time under their 'real' names: Fenwick Scott Key Turner becomes Franklin Key Talbott and his book *KUDOVE* becomes his book *KUBARK*, Susan Rachel Allen Seckler becomes Leah Talbott, Carmen B. Seckler becomes Carla B. Silver, etc.) and several of the same narrative questions are played over again. One in particular: the question of reproduction. If the earlier novel ended with the decision not to physically reproduce, this work revolves around the characters' coming to terms with the prospect of parenthood. This novel goes over the same literal and thematic ground as its predecessor, only this time it works towards a fundamentally different conclusion. It follows the same geographical circuit—the favoured ground of the Chesapeake Bay—but works in a different narratological key. Whilst retaining the same tripartite authorial voice of two central characters—this time Peter and Katherine—and the author, this fiction has the familiarity of a novel with interpolated stories which spill over into the main narrative. It replays events from its immediate predecessor from different points of view; Doug/Dugald's memorial service is but one of these. It goes back to previous ground in order to go forward into new thematic fields. The textual key to this is the way in which it both overlaps with its predecessor's narrative time and then advances beyond it.

This is clearest in the recurrent appearance of the phrase *Blam! Blooey!* close to the start of both texts. In the first, it is several versions of the Big Bang and also the marker of the recognition that staying in place, maintaining the present state of (childless) affairs, is the solution to the problems of the way forward. In the latter, it is a double catalyst which precedes the birth of, first, the novel *The Tidewater Tales,* and, secondly, the twins. In *Sabbatical, Blam! Blooey!* is one occasion, albeit that happens twice, whereas in *The Tidewater Tales, Blam! Blooey!* is two separate events which parenthesise the action of the novel. This is but one example of the way in which *The Tidewater Tales* re-interrogates narratological and thematic positions established in *Sabbatical.*

One other significant way this process takes place is the shift from an overtly liberal political examination of the machinations of the CIA as pollutant of American idealism to the more generally 'political' question of environmental pollution by corrupt businessmen. This is a clear sign of shifts in the terms of the content of liberal concern in the USA between 1982 and 1987 and is, thus, an indication of the ways in which the specific moment of production affects the contours of the narrative of a text.

The final aspect of *The Tidewater Tales* I wish to comment on is the nature of its self-reflexivity. The text is, after all, the account and product of Peter Sagamore's move from acute and limiting consciousness of his position as a writer's writer (the paradigmatic postmodernist?) to the rediscovery of the delights of narrative, as demonstrated both by the stories he tells within the text of *The Tidewater Tales* and by the text itself. In that sense the novel is also autobiographical of its author's trajectory over the previous twenty years. It goes back over the course of the previous years in order to demonstrate what

has happened to the manner of his writing and also stands as an indication of what that development has meant in terms of his writing. It is, in relation to Barth's earlier work, *the* autocritical work. Which is in no sense an argument suggesting that this will be the last statement he makes on the subject!

SUMMARY

All these three recent works have retained Barth's affection for tumbling self-reflexivity and return to previous terrains in order to play variations of the song, 'what is happening to American society and culture, and do I like those developments I see?'.

LETTERS, with its central image and metaphor of the Tower of Truth rising over a university campus but inexorably sinking into the marshland even as it was built, was an extended and general discussion of the state and status of American culture and literature which, of necessity, concluded inconclusively. Even its one (apparently) definite death, that of Todd Andrews as he stood atop the tower at the moment of its explosive destruction, has been withdrawn and he is to be found sailing through the pages of *The Tidewater Tales.*

Sabbatical, taking its start from the final page of *LETTERS,* is a study of a retired CIA operative writing his memoirs as a revenge on the Company's more heinous deeds. Along the way, the Vietnam war, abortion, the role of the US secret service in South America, the pollution of the James river, the state of contemporary fiction and criticism are all discussed within the frame of a perambulatory narrative. All these discussions contribute obliquely to the central question of the book: whether, in the face of the present direction the world is taking, the two central characters of the novel should reproduce themselves biologically as well as literarily.

The Tidewater Tales replays and reworks that ground situation, with numerous references and sub-references to Barth's earlier works and concerns—many of his previous characters appear, some of them now under their 'real' names—and works towards the opposite conclusion of its predecessor. Along the way, again, this work addresses questions of environmental and sexual politics via a sub-plot about a character who pollutes the Chesapeake with toxic waste and numerous women with venereal disease of one form or another, and pays homage to the fictional character whom Barth sees as the goddess of the art of narrative by introducing her into the text as a player in the game.

Whilst it is easy to level the charge of over-self-reflexivity at Barth's more recent work, relying as it does for a great deal of its savour on a working knowledge of his previous fiction, it is an accusation which too quickly condemns his work. After writing *Chimera* he was accused of being incapable of writing about the world around him and had therefore opted to write about ways of writing about the world. These more recent works reject that position on both counts. First, he does write about the world—as is most obviously shown by the discussion of the dooms-day factor and Peter's politicisation of the apocalyptic state of fiction in the four chapters of *The Tidewater Tales* entitled 'The Doomsday Factor'. Secondly, he refuses to be drawn into writing about those issues in a style and manner which he would regard as simplistic.

For example, we need only look at the way in which the story of J. Arthur Paisley's death threads its way through three of his novels to see the ways in which the relations between fiction and reality are investigated as different perspectives are opened on the incident. On the final page of *LETTERS* there is the first reference:

> Sloop *Brillig* found abandoned in Chesapeake Bay off mouth of Patuxent River, all sails set, C.I.A. documents in attaché case aboard. Body of owner, former C.I.A. agent, recovered from Bay one week later, 40 pounds of scuba-diving weights attached, bullet hole in head. C.I.A. and F.B.I. monitoring investigation by local authorities. Nature of documents not disclosed.

(p. 772)

Paisley's body floats, as it were, in the background throughout *Sabbatical* as the tale of the Agency's dirty tricks unfolds and focuses on the incidents surrounding the discovery of his body, but he at no time becomes an integral part of the thematic devices and concerns of the text. In *The Tidewater Tales,* the discovery of Paisley's body by Peter Sagamore is the visceral moment which focuses his general disquiet at the state of the world onto his relationship with the CIA which has come via a course on fiction-writing. The result of this is the 'final reason for Peter Sagamore's late increasing silence'. The incident moves from being one of the catalogue of events at the end of *LETTERS,* to part of the plot of *Sabbatical,* to a thematic metaphor and device in *The Tidewater Tales.* As it becomes more 'real' by virtue of the revelation of more detail about the incident, it becomes less 'real' because it acquires a resonance in a debate about the techniques of producing fiction.

Of course, in order to see how this development takes place it is necessary to have knowledge of all three works and that, of course, lays Barth open to the weary old charge of self-indulgence. And yet, at the same time, lacking knowledge of the previous texts in no way defuses the reader's engagement with any one of the texts, because the reader is as much producer of sense and meaning in these texts as the author, and this is another of the ways in which Barth's work adheres to a set of general tenets about the techniques of postmodernism. Whilst this is generally true of all fiction, it is encoded into the structures of postmodernism as part of its programme for the future of writing.

LIBERALISM

The difficulty of critical engagement with the work of a living writer is that s/he continues to produce novels which seem to defy any neatly established conclusions about their fictional strategies. So, too, with John Barth. Since the final chapter of his career appeared to have been written out in *LETTERS,* he has produced two new works which have continued and extended the trajectory of both his narrative techniques and his American liberalism.

The particular shape of that liberalism has changed from a detached intellectual disenchantment with the conformities of Eisenhower's fifties to a flight from any sense of engagement with the world of the late sixties, through the silence of the seventies to the discovery of a 'socio-political' engagement in the eighties. The fate of this liberalism has been always to find itself at odds: at one moment finding itself to the left and the next to the right of dominating attitudes. Thus, Barth satirises fifties American attitudes towards extra-marital sex, the Communist party and other bugbears of the Eisenhower years in his first two novels but makes no contemporary (or even near-contemporary) reference to the Vietnam war. Indeed, at precisely the point at which a considerable number of American writers were dusting off (or inventing) their liberal credentials, Barth was concealing his beneath the argument that he remained true only to his artistic responsibilities. Equally, as the liberals of the late sixties now rediscover their conservative commitments, Barth is hard at work presenting his outrage at the activities of the darker side of US domestic and foreign policy.

In *Sabbatical* and *The Tidewater Tales,* Barth takes on in particular two questions which have plagued American liberalism since, at the very least, the mid-seventies. First, the role of the CIA as a force for (what Barth would describe as) evil. Secondly, the growing awareness of the impact of pollution on the environment. Not only this, but he has also developed a wider social awareness and sensitivity in his more recent works, which I found, as an eighties reader of his fiction, strangely absent or disguised by layers of parody in the earlier novels and collections for which he is, even now I suspect, remembered.

In these two novels then, and in their large predecessor *LETTERS,* Barth has confirmed himself as one of the voices in literary resistance to the tide of conservative know-nothingness which characterised the mainstream of cultural production during the Reagan years.

WOMEN

This is most clearly marked in his portrayal of women and sexuality, in the shift from the almost entirely passive female figures of the earlier fiction to a developing awareness of what can be called 'women's issues'. From Rennie, the site upon which Jake and Joe play out their philosophical contest and which ends in her physical death, and Anastasia, whom George pursues and 'looks through' in a moment which now seems almost written to demonstrate Rosalind Coward's argument about voyeurism as the male possession of the female body, to Germaine (not an idle choice of name surely!), who speaks for herself, and Susan, who makes decisions about her life and thereby acquires a feature missing from so many of his earlier female characters—a private life. From 'Night Sea Journey', a short story in which the active component in procreation is the sperm searching for She (who compounds the inherent sexism of this piece by becoming the maw which swallows our brave male swimmer at the end of the story), to *Sex Education,* in which the active speaking voices are, first, the ova who are then joined by atypical, 'unmacho', sperms and the act of procreation becomes seen as fusion rather than conquest. This shift of ground is clearly the product of the more generalised changes produced by the Women's Liberation Movement and then the Women's Movement, but they are kept firmly within the realm of the liberal consciousness by a consistent substitution of narratology for politics. The political questions raised by the women's movement and feminist scholarship about the construction of literature become, in Barth's novels, issues of technique. Indeed, the crucial question of abortion rights becomes the occasion for a bad joke in *Sabbatical* and is then evaded as the two sisters, Susan and Mimi, are reunited by their sorority despite the fact that one is an anti-abortion activist whilst the other has just had an abortion. The issue has been stripped of its social significance and reduced to a narrative device.

CENTRAL INTELLIGENCE AGENCY

'I write this as George Bush's candidacy for President is threatened by revelations about his involvement with the "dirty tricks brigade", as the after-effects of Iran/Contragate still reverberate at the end of a year which has seen the appearance of but the latest in a series of exposés of the behaviour and performance of CIA operatives both at home and abroad.' This sentence now appears as wishful thinking because, as we all now know, George Bush romped home in the 1988 presidential election despite (or perhaps because of) these revelations. He is, we should remind ourselves the first ex-director of the CIA to be elected president since the Agency was set up by Truman's administration in 1947.

In many ways, the CIA represents for the liberal not only all that is wrong with the conservative bastions of the American establishment but also a convenient scapegoat for those ills. All we need do, the argument appears to go, is excise the cancerous tissue from the essentially healthy body and all will be well. It is an argument which rests upon belief in the finally benevolent nature of the American state and as such has among its many antecedents Whitman's support of the US intervention in Mexico in 1856 and Steinbeck's decision to turn government propagandist during the Second World War.

Barth's version of it appears in *Sabbatical* as Fenn and Susan sail under the Chesapeake Bay bridge and greet America with mixed feelings, but feelings in which the drift is that the present operations of the state are some sort of deviation from the norm even as they recognise from their mutual sense of history that this is not the case and that the American state has operated since its

inception upon a basis of secret servitude. Susan's outburst pulls these threads together as it expresses the confusion generated by the collision between an awareness of the activities of the American secret state and her beloved's relationship therewith. In this case, the state's activities are in some sense ameliorated by the personal connection. Dugald Taylor is a pleasant and sophisticated friend, and it is the excesses of the Agency which have driven Fenn to write his exposure rather than its existence. The liberal's dilemma is the inability to imagine anything other than the prevailing situation; it may be complained about, campaigned against, but it cannot be changed in a fundamental fashion.

GREEN POLITICS

The development of 'eco-fiction' from the 1970s on has been away from the utopian novel containing elements of ecological, of 'green' thought—works such as Callenbach's *Ecotopia* and Piercy's *Woman on the edge of time*—towards a fiction which has confronted the prospect of ecological disaster in a contemporary context. The increase in popularity of this latter form is in part due to the rising number of publicised disasters and the development of an indigenous movement of protest against a wide range of abuses. In part it is also, it seems to me, a product of narrowing imaginative horizons in the years of crisis. A move away from imagining possibilities to a defence of a bad existing situation against a potentially worse future in the world of social activity has filtered through into the fiction of the eighties.

Barth approached this topic in an initially oblique fashion in *LETTERS,* where he initiated a discussion about the 'ecology' of the novel and of written literature in general; a discussion in which the continued existence of the endangered species of written fiction is defended as a cultural necessity. Indeed, in truly ecological fashion, the prospect of its disappearance is registered in its impact on the whole cultural field and the effect is seen as productive of cultural imbecility. In the next two novels the subject is moved towards the surface of the fiction, first with characters in *Sabbatical* prepared to voice the opinion that industrial pollution was disturbing the balance of nature in the Chesapeake Bay and then, in *The Tidewater Tales,* as the material is built into the narrative of the work. The movement, then, is from metaphor, via exposition, to integration. Of these, the move from exposition to integration is the more crucial because it indicates the absorption of the material into the texture of the work.

Even so, for Barth—never a committed 'social' novelist— the question has always also been employed metaphorically and narratologically. Metaphorically, it is another aspect of the apocalyptic climate Barth long ago identified as existing in the realm of narrative fiction. Narratologically, it is part of a series of images and incidents of pollutive behaviour which create the situation against which his most recent central characters assert themselves. The CIA pollute the democratic traditions of the USA, the USAF pollute the peace of the Chesapeake Bay, while Poonie sexually pollutes women and is involved in the Kepone pollution of the Bay.

CONCLUSION

Plots spin outwards in the 'real world' and in the world of postmodernist fiction, describing the mechanisms by which both operate. In that sense postmodernism can be seen as the realism of the contemporary period, because its formal techniques correspond to a perception of the social reality of state capitalism as an international phenomenon. The bureaucratic organisation of an increasingly crisis-ridden world system has generated apparent irrationalities, the explanation of which all too easily rests in a theory of conspiracy and plot.

Both senses of the word apply, because the elision of fiction and reality, the incapacity of the imagination to produce tales more unlikely than that which actually happens, the unsettling of previous systems of explanation by ever-faster dance of fashion, and the continuous employment of parodic self-reference is a description both of the resources of postmodernism and of the means by which information is conveyed in the 'realistic' forms of the dominant cultural modes.

Grasping the parody and reference becomes a way of situating oneself in this whirl of images because it provides a handle by which one can hold onto a sense of understanding. What disappears is a sense of history, by which I mean a sense of the temporal space between the various cultural patterns to which reference is being made. It is, perhaps, satisfying to recognise that an aria from Catalani's *La Wally* is used in a vacuum cleaner advertisement but it is also, in the strict sense of the word, meaningless because it has been stripped of its context. The same could be said of postmodernism generally, that in being all too familiar with the procedures of contemporary 'information technology', it has nothing critical to say of those procedures. It lives within them, unable to find a way into a different and thoroughly critical mode of expression.

John A. McClure

SOURCE: "Postmodern Romance: Don DeLillo and the Age of Conspiracy," in *The South Atlantic Quarterly*, Vol. 89, No. 2, Spring, 1990, pp. 337-53.

[*In the following essay, McClure examines novelist Don DeLillo's adaptation of popular novels of different genres, including science fiction, espionage, and occult adventures.*]

Don DeLillo crafts his fictions out of the forms of popular romance: out of the espionage thriller, the imperial adventure novel, the western, science fiction, even the genre of occult adventure. He may conduct us, in one novel, across several genres: *Running Dog* begins as a spy story, turns, as one of the characters remarks, into a western, and ends on a note of New Age adventure, with the introduction of a figure out of Castañeda's Don Juan books. Contemporary literary theory invites us to see in such minglings the project of pastiche: a play across forms uninflected with any impulse to criticism or reanimation. But DeLillo is not simply playful; there's a logic to the transitions he orchestrates, an urgency to the shiftings and sortings, a critical edge to his appropriations. He is engaged in tracing a kind of history of romance: challenging the modernist notion that global secularization and "rationalization" would make its production impossible; showing how these very processes produce new sources for romance. And he is interested in exploring the power of the new formulas, the nature of their appeal. But in the end he insists, against the manifest fact of his own fascination, that the deepest rewards of romance are not to be found in the roles and regions where the white male culture of America now locates them: in espionage and conspiracy. And he gestures, albeit tentatively, beyond these realms into regions where romance might yet find the resources it needs to be reborn in something like adequate form.

. . . . .

DeLillo portrays romance as a rich and protean mode that constantly adapts itself to changing historical conditions, returning again and again to the drama of the historical moment for the "raw materials"—the human models and settings and ideologies—it requires to construct its stories of quest and contest, radical alterity, divine or demonic otherness. One requirement of romance is a world plausibly permeated with mysterious forces, with magical or sacred or occult powers. But as Western society became increasingly secularized and rationalized, romance tended increasingly to locate this world on the great imperial frontiers: Africa, Asia, Latin America, and the American West. These "marginal" zones were imaginatively exploited both by writers of popular adventure fiction and by writers of high romance, novelists like Joseph Conrad, E. M. Forster, Malcolm Lowry, and Graham Greene. They were represented as places where the conditions of romance still obtained, where one could enjoy adventures unavailable in a world of law and order, achieve goals out of reach in a class-bound society, experience emotional and sensual intensities prohibited in a world of carefully regulated responses, and enjoy experiences of the sacred, the demonic, and the sublime unavailable in a utilitarian, scientific, and secular world.

The search for raw materials that preoccupies DeLillo is made necessary by the global elimination of such premodern places, the penetration of capitalism into all the enclaves once available for imaginative exploitation in romance. The moderns anticipated this moment with dread, and their relation to the imperialism that made its coming inevitable was a vexed one. On the one hand, they drew on the records and experiences of actual imperial adventurers to create their tales of exotic adventure, lend plausibility to their representations of magical and miraculous events; on the other, they recognized that the existence of these reports and reporters spelled doom for the exotic lives and exotic places they depicted. Even as they exploited the materials of romance made available by imperial penetration of premodern cultures, they projected a Weberian future in which the rationalizing spirit of the West would produce a universal disenchantment of the world. Conrad's Marlow reminisces wistfully, at the beginning of *Heart of Darkness,* over the time not so long ago when the map of Africa, now filled in, was "a blank space of delightful mystery—a white patch for a boy to dream gloriously over." In a similar vein, a character in Virginia Woolf's *The Voyage Out* condemns British imperialism, not for exploiting and impoverishing the peoples of Latin America, but for "robbing a whole continent of mystery." And in Conan Doyle's *The Lost World,* a character declares regretfully that "the big blank spaces in the map are being filled in, and there's no room for romance anywhere."

A passage deleted from the final version of *Heart of Darkness* provides a somewhat more detailed version of this narrative of disenchantment. At the beginning of the novel, as Marlow and his friends sit on their sailboat waiting for the tide to turn, a "big steamer," undeterred by such natural forces, comes down the channel. She is, we are told,

> bound to the uttermost ends of the earth and timed to the day, to the very hour with nothing unknown in her path [,] no mystery on her way, nothing but a few coaling stations. She went full-speed, noisily . . . timed from port to port, to the very hour. And the earth suddenly seemed shrunk to the size of a pea spinning in the heart of an immense darkness.

The steamboat, a symbol of triumphant technology, shrinks the world, displacing a terrestrial darkness which is at once threatening and satisfying, and rendering experience all too predictable. Its disenchanting passage might even be said to sponsor, emblematically anyway, Marlow's countervoyage up the Congo, a voyage which seems designed to reconstitute the world, put the darkness back where it belongs, at its heart. And Marlow's journey is but one of many by which modernists typically orchestrate a temporary escape from disenchantment into the so-called "dark places of the world."

The postmodern period begins, according to Fredric Jameson, at the moment when these places are abolished: The "prodigious expansion of capital into hitherto uncommodified areas," Jameson writes in *New Left Review* (1984), "eliminates the enclaves of precapitalist organization it had hitherto tolerated and exploited in a tributary way." The result is the "purer capitalism of our own times" and the eradication of those cultures and professions from which the modernists extracted romance. To hear a modernist's response to this act of foreclosure, we need only turn to John Berger, who declares, in *The Look of Things,* that the eradication of the precapitalist sanctuaries of the Western imagination has made the world

uninhabitable. "The intolerability of the world," he writes, "is, in a certain sense, an historical achievement. The world was not intolerable so long as God existed, so long as there was the ghost of a pre-existent order, so long as large tracts of the world were unknown."

DeLillo refuses to make this modernist judgment his point of departure. Instead, while modernists such as Berger continue to seek out remnants of the premodern among vestigial communities, DeLillo focuses his attention on sites within capitalism, and discovers there the materials of new forms of romance. It's true, he suggests, that capitalism has penetrated everywhere, but its globalization has not resulted in global rationalization and Weber's iron cage. It seems instead to have sponsored a profound reversal: the emergence of zones and forces like those that imperial expansion has erased: jungle-like techno-tangles; dangerous, unknown "tribes"; secret cults with their own codes and ceremonies, vast conspiracies. "This is the age of conspiracy," says a character in *Running Dog,* with the mixture of wonder and revulsion that is everywhere in DeLillo's work. This is "the age of connections, links, secret relationships." These zones and forces—the various computer circuits, multinational business networks, espionage agencies, private armies, and unconventional political players—make a mockery of collective desires for democracy and social justice. But at the same time they assuage collective fears of a totally domesticated and transparent world, and become substitutes, in the popular imagination, for earlier sources of mystery, adventure, and empowerment. Thus the espionage thriller, with its vision of a world riven by clashes between vast conspiratorial forces, replaces the imperial adventure story and its American subform, the western, as the most popular mode of (masculine) romance. And conspiracy theory, on which the thriller is based, replaces religion as a means of mapping the world without disenchanting it, robbing it of its mystery. For conspiracy theory explains the world, as religion does, without elucidating it, by positing the existence of hidden forces which permeate and transcend the realm of ordinary life. It offers us satisfactions similar to those offered by religions and religiously inflected romance: both the satisfaction of living among secrets, in a mysterious world, and the satisfaction of gaining access to secrets, being "in the know," a member of some esoteric order of magicians or warriors.

In *Players,* DeLillo's early venture in the conspiracy thriller, espionage networks provide certain satisfactions which used to be found only in the non-Western world. Now, it's "everywhere, isn't it?"

> Mazes. . . . Intricate techniques. Our big problem in the past, as a nation, was that we didn't give our government credit for being the totally entangling force that it was. They were even more evil than we'd imagined. More evil and much more interesting. Assassination, blackmail, torture, enormous improbable intrigues. All these convolutions and relationships. . . . Behind every stark fact we encounter layers of ambiguity . . . multiple interpretations.

The secret government has replaced Conrad's labyrinthine Congo and satanic Congolese, who taught Marlow "the fascination of the abomination," as the site of evil and interest, the darkly enchanted Elsewhere of our dreams. Indeed, DeLillo suggests, it is now "the secret dream of the white collar" to escape into that world,

> to place a call from a public booth in the middle of the night. Calling some government bureau, some official department, right, of the government. "I have information about so-and-so." Or, even better, to be visited, to have them come to you. "You might be able to deliver a microdot letter, sir, on your visit to wherever," if that's how they do things. "You might be willing to provide a recruiter with cover on your payroll, sir." Imagine how sexy that can be for the true-blue businessman or professor. What an incredible nighttime thrill. The appeal of mazes and intricate techniques. The suggestion of a double life. "Fantastic, sign me up, I'll do it."

The familiar has become fantastic, the public institutions of a rationalizing age have metastasized into sinister but alluring webs of mystery.

In another novel about Americans drawn into the secret world of espionage, *Running Dog,* DeLillo shows even more explicitly that in spite of modernist fears, the social world has not been rendered totally "readable" by science and technology. Max Weber equated rationalization not with "an increased and general knowledge of the condition under which one lives," but with the "belief that if one but wished one *could* learn [about] it at any time," that "there are no mysterious incalculable forces that come into play." But in DeLillo's America this process has been suspended, even reversed: "it's the presence alone, the very fact, the superabundance of technology. . . . Just the fact that these things exist at this widespread level. The process machines, the scanners, the sorters. . . . What enormous weight. What complex programs. And there's no one to explain it to us." We have been cast back into mystery by the very forces—scientific, rationalizing— that threatened or promised enlightenment.

DeLillo relates this reversal to the history of romance in *The Names,* his novel about an American based in Athens who does "risk analysis" of Asian and African nations for an American corporation. James Axton and his friends like to see themselves as playing out roles in an old-fashioned colonial romance: "It is like the Empire," says one character. "Opportunity, adventure, sunsets, dusty death." But their self-consciousness betrays an awareness that the roles they imagine themselves playing are no longer available in a world divided into nations and crisscrossed with air routes, telecommunications networks, and shipping lanes. Has the world become the "withered pea" of Conrad's nightmare? This view of things is emphatically denied:

> "They keep telling us it's getting smaller all the time. But it's not, is it? Whatever we learn about it makes it bigger. Whatever we do to complicate things makes it bigger. It's all a complication. It's

one big tangled thing. . . . Modern communications don't shrink the world, they make it bigger. Faster planes make it bigger. They give us more, they connect more things. . . . The world is so big and complicated."

In other words, the instruments that many modernists saw as adversaries of sublimity and enchantment turn out to be producing them: the great steamer which threatens to rob Conard's world of its satisfying strangeness is in effect celebrated by DeLillo—and not just in *The Names* but throughout his work—as the unwitting agent of a fascinating new intricacy.

In *The Names,* James Axton goes looking for mystery where the modernists found it, in the exotic countries he studies as a risk analyst for his employer, and in the mysterious cult of assassins he studies as a sideline. He likes to see himself as a colonial adventurer. But in the end he discovers that the most dramatic mysteries are *behind* him, in the corporate world he takes for granted, and in Athens, the seat of Western civilization. He has been working all along, it seems, not for a private company but for the CIA; he has been pursued not by exotic cultists but by Greek nationalists. Caught up in his nostalgia for outmoded forms of romance, he has failed to recognize that he is playing a leading part in a contemporary adventure story, a tale of conspiracy and terrorism. The drama of rationalization ends—or at least can be seen as ending—with a literal deus ex machina in which a zone of enchantment emerges out of the machinery of the modern. "Elsewhere," which was mapped geographically in the popular imagination of the modernist era, is now mapped geologically, as the subterranean segment of a global political and economic circuitry, the world of conspiracy. And romance, which once had to depend on distant premodern places for its raw materials, now finds them at the heart of the postmodern metropolis.

. . . . .

The age of conspiracy offers us, by way of satisfactions, new forms of intricacy, entanglement, and complication, a new jungle with its own "fibrous beauty." It offers us the opportunity to be thrilled by the power, the impenetrability, and the almost demonic malevolence of new systems. It even offers, to the lover of sacred and esoteric language, a new "poetry," the "technical idiom" of new systems of communication and control, "number-words and coinages [that] had the inviolate grace of a strict meter of chant." To the more daring, it offers the possibility of actual participation in the new cults and combat units, the "nighttime thrill" of a double life. To the rest of us, the readers of the fictitious *Running Dog* magazine or the real *Running Dog,* it offers the pleasure of vicarious participation in these adventures, momentary escape from our all-too-predictable lives. It rescues us, in other words, from the modernist nightmare of an entire world reduced to quotidian compromises and routines, an utterly disenchanted world.

So much for what is offered. But DeLillo's novels are no simple celebrations of the new Elsewhere. Indeed they seem designed, like the works of modernists such as Conrad, both to reproduce the excitements of popular romance and to reject them as unworthy: unfounded in reality and inferior to the effects produced by truer mysteries, more realistic romances. When we romanticize conspiracy, DeLillo suggests, we misrepresent it, invest it with powers and possibilities it does not possess. The great romance narratives posit a world alive with demonic and divine forces, and an inner world similarly profound and intense. They posit institutions—the faith, the court, the community—capable of satisfying individual and collective needs for transcendence: for testing, tempering, and triumph (courtly romance) or renunciation, purification, and illumination (spiritual romance). And they imply that human beings are up to these challenges. But the new intricacies are ultimately soulless, the new institutions debased. Even our capacity for trial is sadly diminished. The jungle of technical and human systems possesses only a spurious and superficial sublimity: it's the stuff of perverse fascinations and cheap thrills rather than awe and wonder. And the new orders of quest and contest, the secret agencies dedicated ostensibly to the protection of sacred cultural values, are actually no more than subsystems of a vast criminal enterprise that encompasses capitalist corporations, criminal entrepreneurs, and corrupt governments. As a character in *Running Dog* puts it, "[l]oyalties are so interwoven, the thing's a game. The Senator and PAC/ORD [a maverick intelligence unit] aren't nearly the antagonists the public believes them to be. They talk all the time. They make deals, they buy people, they sell favors. . . . That's the nature of the times." To be entangled in these systems is to be diminished—we all are. To be actively engaged is to be morally destroyed.

Within the world of conspiracy, one simply does not find the great ethical confrontations between good and evil that are at the heart of romance, nor the institutions—the secular or religious orders, legions of angels and demons, good guys and bad—that gave specific form to the struggle. Under such conditions, potential adepts drawn to conspiracy by the will to romance and by illusions fostered by popular romance find themselves "warriors without masters," their only roundtable an intelligence agency that operates by the corrupt codes of the very culture they would escape: "They didn't call it the Company for nothing. It was set up to obscure the deeper responsibilities, the calls of blood trust that have to be answered." We may mock the idea of such "calls," and see them as little more than the effects of an ideology that has long used the fictions of romance to enlist shock troops for the sordid business of conquest. But we continue to look for institutions that can satisfy such needs, and, when such institutions are absent, to settle for substitutes.

Running Dog is DeLillo's most sustained study of a single "warrior without a master." Fast-paced, scary, exciting, and grimly funny, it traces the attempts of one would-be knight, Glen Selvy, to find a channel for his aspirations. The novel invites us to be "suspicious of quests," to find "some vital deficiency on the part of the individual in pursuit, a meagerness of spirit." But it also reminds us that we are, as a culture, addicted to fantasies of quest, conspiracy, and illumination. And it appeals to us in these very terms, offering itself, at the outset anyway, as a supersophisticated version of the familiar story. Selvy, like so many recent adventure heroes—Rambo; the Robert De Niro character in *The Deer Hunter;* Hicks, the Vietnam vet of Stone's *Dog Soldiers*—wants to be a kind of knight: to practice ascetic disciplines, purify and perfect his body, join an order, serve a cause. His girlfriend casts him repeatedly as a hero of romance, "an English lancer on the eve of Balaclava," an adept trained by "some master of the wilderness." And the novel seems ready to confirm him in a contemporary version of that role: he is given a position in a secret security force, a boss named Percival, and a quest. But these possibilities are advanced only to be dashed. Both Selvy and the reader learn that in this America, in these times, there is no way to play out such dreams. The secret community Selvy joins (PAC/ORD) turns out to be every bit as corrupt and manipulative as the terror organizations it is ostensibly dedicated to destroying. Percival turns out to be a collector of pornography, and the quest that preoccupies all the major players—the Senator, the secret service, the Mafia, and Richie Armbrister, America's king of smut—is for a pornographic film shot in Hitler's bunker: "the century's ultimate piece of decadence."

Selvy, who is drawn to the ascetic life without any sense of concrete mission, at first doesn't feel "tainted by the dirt of his profession." He simply enjoys "the empty meditations, the routine, the tradecraft, the fine edge to be maintained in preparation for—he didn't know what." But ultimately, embittered and betrayed, he comes to see himself not as a modern knight, but as just another lackey of an utterly corrupt capitalist order, a servant of the god of our times, "The God of Body. The God of Lipstick and Silk. The God of Nylon, Scent and Shadow." "What's your real name?" his girlfriend asks. "Running Dog," he replies.

With this recognition, Selvy's second quest begins, and *Running Dog* turns into something of a metaromance, a quest narrative in which the aim of the quest is to find a viable romance form, a script that will enable Selvy, and perhaps the reader, to begin pursuing redemption. No longer looking for the pornographic grail of a perverse society, fleeing assassins set on him by his own employers, Selvy breaks out of the Northeastern Corridor world of the espionage thriller and out of the genre itself: "This is turning into a Western," remarks his girlfriend. But there's no longer room in the West into which Selvy flees to stage the old western romance, and besides, the players have been scrambled beyond recognition. Thus Selvy, the WASP, is pursued by two Vietnamese in cowboy hats and sunglasses through a Texas town slowly filling up with tourists, "mostly older people and eight or nine Japanese." When he retreats even further, back to the abandoned desert training camp where he once studied covert warfare, his flight takes him across yet another generic boundary, into the world of sixties shamanistic romance, the Don Juan stories. Levi Blackwater, a "gringo mystic" whose name evokes both the priestly tribe of his forebears and the Indian tribes of the land he wanders, appears at this point to warn Selvy that his final stab at living by the rules of romance, an attempt to orchestrate a spiritually meaningful death, will also fail. "There's no way out," says Blackwater.

> "No clear light for you in this direction. You can't find release from experience so simply."
>
> "Dying is an art in the East."
>
> "Yes, heroic, a spiritual victory."
>
> "You set me on to that, Levi."
>
> "But this is part, only part, of a longer, longer, process. We were just beginning to understand."

Selvy's attempt to write himself into Eastern rituals is hopelessly oversimplified, and he dies, ironically, thinking not about spiritual victory but about spirits—"What he needed right now was a drink." Levi's plans for Selvy—he wants to enact a burial ritual passed along to him by the "masters of the snowy range"—are similarly shipwrecked. The ceremony requires taking a few locks of the deceased's hair, but Selvy's Vietnamese assassin, who is also versed in the lore of the spirits, has decapitated his victim and carried the head away.

There are no adequate patterns for romance in the American culture to which Selvy belongs and from which he gets his bearings. The West of the western no longer exists; the new Orientalisms of the sixties celebrate disciplines Westerners cannot master; and espionage, the freshest region of romance, is a realm of all-too-familiar corruptions. Its secrets are sordid, its quests salacious, its contests little more than internecine battles between competitors who share the same mean aims. DeLillo suggests, in other words, that we have avoided rationalization without rescuing enchantment, have entered an era of aimless intensities, pornographic passions, cheap thrills, and warriors without wisdom.

. . . . .

DeLillo has continued to be fascinated with conspiracy, even as he warns against its fascinations. *The Names* and *Libra,* two of the three novels he has published since *Running Dog,* focus on conspiracies. They succeed, like *Running Dog,* both in conveying the excitements associated with conspiracy and in making these excitements seem spurious, disabling. They do this, in part, by working with and against the conventions of the espionage thriller, offering some of the satisfactions of the genre, denying others. They catch us up in sensational stories of conspiracy and assassination, but deny us the pleasures of compression and pacing we associate with such

stories. *The Names* is a tangle of loosely integrated plot lines, unresolved conflicts, and suspended actions. And in *Libra,* DeLillo refuses to shape his subject, the first Kennedy assassination, to the forms of the conventional thriller. "If we are on the outside,"

> we assume a conspiracy is the perfect working of a scheme. Silent nameless men with unadorned hearts. A conspiracy is everything that ordinary life is not. It's the inside game, cold, sure, undistracted, forever closed off to us. We are the flawed ones, the innocents, trying to make some rough sense of the daily jostle. Conspirators have a logic and a daring beyond our reach. All conspiracies are the same taut story of men who find coherence in some criminal act.

> But maybe not.

Certainly not in *Libra,* which challenges the conventional "taut story" about conspiracy not only by what it depicts—a rambling, confused, and incoherent series of events, but also by its method of depiction, through a capacious and frequently meditative narrative which is anything but "taut." DeLillo structures both works in a way that challenges the romance of conspiracy, the "stories" we tell ourselves about the way things work in that mysterious domain. But he is not content, in *The Names* and *Libra,* merely to challenge the romantic representation of conspiracy. He is also searching, as Selvy does in *Running Dog,* for alternatives to conspiracy, social sites and ideologies that provide more adequate raw materials of romance. *The Names* explores "the world of corporate transients," expatriate employees of the great multinational business and government interests James Axton at first finds romantic: "I don't mind working for Rowser at all," he says, speaking of his superior in the risk analysis firm.

> This is where I want to be. History. . . . We're important suddenly. . . . We're right in the middle. We're the handlers of huge sums of delicate money. Recyclers of petrodollars. Builders of refineries. Analysts of risk. . . . The world is here. Don't you feel that? In some of these places, things have enormous power. They have impact, they're mysterious.

Axton is especially fascinated with the speech of his corporate knights-errant. He likes their habit of turning places into "one-sentence stories," a manner of speaking which suggests at once the speakers' amazing mobility (they've been everywhere), their worldliness, and their power to define and dismiss. He likes, too, their command of specialized jargons, "the technical cant" of security specialists, bankers, businessmen, and spies, which resonates with the power of the institutions that employ them. And he likes, finally, the protocols of conspiratorial exchange:

> He asked a few questions about my trips to countries in the region. He approached the subject of the Northeast Group several times but never mentioned the name itself, never asked a direct

question. I let the vague references go by, volunteered nothing, paused often. . . . It was a strange conversation, full of hedged remarks and obscure undercurrents, perfect in its way.

By the end of the novel, though, Axton has had more than enough of conspiracy and, it would seem, its idioms. Before he leaves Athens, he makes a long-postponed visit to the Acropolis, and finds there examples of a strikingly different politics of discourse, resources for a different kind of romance. Axton's Acropolis is a place of congregation, free exchange, and "open expression," a language community antithetical in its purposes and principles of exchange to the conspiratorial community he is fleeing. "Everyone is talking," and the impression conveyed is one of rich heteroglossia, constructive dialogue, and catharsis. Even the stones seem to speak, and to instruct those who come to them in the purposes and powers of speech:

> I hadn't expected a human feeling to emerge from the stones but this is what I found, deeper than the art and mathematics embodied in the structure, the optical exactitudes. I found a cry for pity . . . this open cry, this voice we know as our own.

Here are the resources for a very different kind of romance, one in which people come together to share knowledge, pain, and longing on a site resonate with history and with absence. This terrain—the half-empty temple, denuded of its divinities but still filled with suppliants, still ringing, albeit silently, with a "cry for pity" addressed to absent redeemers—resembles the space that Jameson designated in *The Political Unconscious* as the terrain of authentic romance in our time. It is one of the "abandoned clearings across which higher and lower worlds once passed," and which we still visit to remember older dreams of fulfillment and to confront our impoverishment. *The Names,* like *Running Dog,* depicts a kind of transgeneric quest, but one that ends more promisingly than Selvy's. And it repudiates, as *Running Dog* does, that version of history which would offer the intricate systems and conspiracies of postmodernity as adequate sources of wonder and transcendence. If romance has a home in the present, it is not within the machinery of capitalism, but in archaic and marginal places, like the Acropolis, where memory and desire bring people together to speak openly about what they have lost and what they want.

But the episode at the Acropolis is not the end of *The Names.* It is followed by a brief fragment from a novel, being written by James Axton's son, in which the young protagonist is attending a Pentecostal revival meeting somewhere on the American plains. Here again there is a play of voices: the boy's parents and other worshipers are speaking in tongues, recreating that moment from biblical history when the spirit descended on the disciples and they began miraculously to speak in the different languages of the ancient world. But for the boy at least, this cacophony of voices is terrifying: he cannot understand, and, even worse, he cannot join them: "The

gift was not his, the whole language of the spirit which was greater than Latin or French was not to be seized in his pityfull mouth." Fleeing the church, he finds himself in a bleak world without "familiar signs and safe places," but not without wonder. The last words of the fragment, and of *The Names,* describe the boy's reaction to this world: "This was worse than a retched nightmare. It was the nightmare of real things, the fallen wonder of the world."

I read this fragment as a second parabolic retort to the postmodern narrative that discovers romance in conspiracy, a counterhistory in which wonder survives the crisis of desacralization not by investing the mechanisms of multinational capitalism with all the power and mystery once ascribed to the forces of magicians and gods, but by facing the fact of our disinheritance, the emptiness of a world without God. And I imagine, even if DeLillo does not, the youngster fleeing toward the Acropolis, on his way to an encounter that will provide him with company and prepare him for the longer struggle, that of casting, in merely human speech, an image of the future as rich or richer than that which died with the gods.

Libra, DeLillo's most recent novel of conspiracy, ends on a similar note, with an extended cry for pity, and call for justice, from Marguerite, Lee Oswald's mother. Marguerite's monologue is addressed, like Job's, to an invisible judge. Of course she lacks the rich man's eloquence: she speaks in the only languages she knows, the debased languages of popular culture, the world of women's magazines and television: "Judge, I have lived in many places but never filthy dirty, never not neat, never without the personal loving touch, the decorator item. We have moved to be a family. This is the theme of my research." In her desperation she remakes and recombines the clichés she uses, fusing the fragments borrowed from so many debased utterances into an utterance which is not debasing but profoundly moving. Her voice, unlike the voices of the conspirators, is raw with emotion, resonant with memory and disappointment and confusion. "I have suffered," she proclaims, and suddenly we are back in the realm of the "open cry," the homeland of romance. "I stand here on this brokenhearted earth," she declares, and we recall that, in the genre of romance, passions are not contained in individual characters but seem to circulate through them and the world they inhabit. "You have to wonder," she says, and her words have the force of a command. Listening to her cries as she mourns her son under a wild and urgent sky, we are reminded of the young boy imagined by another young boy at the end of *The Names,* in that other country of romance where wonder is not a matter of human secrets, human institutions, machinery, but of tragic vision and open expression.

The unfashionably passionate and awkward language of the "open cry" exposes the emptiness of all the carefully closed and polished language that has preceded it, reminds us that the language of DeLillo's tough guys, so strikingly frank and transgressive in some respects, has its own decorums, effects its own suppressions. What it renders unspeakable are precisely those protests and prayers (for a Day of Judgment, a Day of Reconciliation, a salvational future) on which the great traditions of romance, sacred and secular, are founded. In giving voice to these protests and prayers, the visitors to the Acropolis, the prairie Pentecostals, the boy who flees their chapel, and Marguerite Oswald invite us to get in touch with them as well, to remember the historic vocation of romance, and to reject all romance formulas that do not reflect that vocation.

But Marguerite's monologues are not the only passages in *Libra* which point the reader toward alternatives to popular postmodern romance. Character after character in the novel comments on the role played by coincidence in the unfolding of the plot against Kennedy. "We were all linked," thinks one, "in a vast and rhythmic coincidence, a daisy chain of rumor, suspicion and secret wish." Nicholas Branch, the CIA employee assigned to write the secret history of the assassination, resists the temptation to look beyond the amazing play of coincidence for some "grand and masterful scheme," although he does come to think that "someone is trying to sway him toward superstition" by feeding him instance after instance "of cheap coincidence." But David Ferrie, the unofficial "spiritual adviser" to the conspiracy, is bolder. He insists that "there's a pattern in things. Something in us has an effect on independent events. We make things happen. The conscious mind gives one side only. We're deeper than that. We extend into time." Finally, then, "There's no such *thing* as coincidence. We don't know what to call it, so we say coincidence."

Ferrie's speculations gain credibility from their context: events in this novel (which takes its title from Ferrie's favorite science, astrology) are shaped in remarkable ways by what most characters think of as coincidence. Someone, it would seem, is trying to *sway* us toward superstition, trying to get us to see something like a grand psychic conspiracy at work in what we call coincidence. DeLillo presses us toward that familiar and academically unsavory resource of romance, the discourse of the occult. While the romance of conspiracy is rejected in *Libra,* the whole trope of conspiracy undergoes what might be called a respiritualization: we are asked to envision a world in which dark, unnameable psychic forces are in play, forces which, like those of magic and divinity, are not subject to the physical laws we think we are bound to obey.

. . . . .

DeLillo repudiates the romance of conspiracy and promotes certain alternatives. But while each of the novels I've discussed ends by dismissing conspiracy—the activity, the mode of speech it sponsors, the genre—in each novel DeLillo also returns to the topic. It might be argued that he has been unable to extricate himself from the spell of conspiracy, to write for long in the very different registers of romance he arrives at in the final moments of *The*

Names and *Libra.* Is he trapped, then, like so many of his protagonists, outside that world of "deep wondering" and "ordinary mysteries" toward which he gestures at the end of these works? And is he driven, like many of his main characters, by a desire for the chilly disciplines, intricacies, and entanglements of the new multinational order? These are, of course, unanswerable questions. But they lead to other questions, which may be answerable. What about us—the avid readers of DeLillo's work? Does our readiness to return with him, again and again, to his chosen terrain, suggest that, like it or not, we too are enthralled by those networks of power and manipulation which we also—most of us—claim to abhor? Writing from within the enchantments of the new Elsewhere, but also against them, DeLillo helps us place ourselves, recognize our own unsavory enthrallments, acknowledge, even if we cannot embrace, some of the alternatives to this particular, historically determined enchantment.

John M. Unsworth

SOURCE: "Practicing Post-Modernism: The Example of John Hawkes," in *Contemporary Literature,* Vol. 32, No. 1, Spring, 1991, pp. 38-57.

[*In the following essay, Unsworth defends Jerome Klinkowitz's assertion that contemporary artists and writers influence each other by examining the relationship between John Hawkes and Albert Guerard.*]

"The excitement of contemporary studies is that all of its critical practitioners and most of their subjects are alive and working at the same time. One work influences another, bringing to the field a spirit of competition and cooperation that reaches an intensity rarely found in other disciplines" (x). In these remarks on "contemporary studies," Jerome Klinkowitz takes for granted that contemporary writers and their critics belong to one "discipline," the academic discipline of literary study. This affiliation of criticism and creative writing within a single institutional framework does indeed compound the influence that critic and author have on one another's work, as it multiplies the opportunities and the incentives for cooperation; but rather than simply celebrating this fact, as Klinkowitz does, we ought to inquire into the consequences of the professional interaction and practical interdependence of author and critic, particularly as it affects the creativity of the former and the judgment of the latter.

John Hawkes provides an excellent opportunity for such an inquiry, for several reasons. Discovered by Albert Guerard in 1947 and vigorously promoted by him in the years that followed, Hawkes was the first American "post-modern" author to gain notoriety.[1] Writers of Hawkes's generation were, in turn, the first in this country to spend their entire creative lives in the academy: they have used that position with unprecedented success to shape and control critical reception, especially through the mechanism of the interview. At the same time, as

Guerard's influence on Hawkes demonstrates, criticism can shape a writer's understanding of what is important in his or her creative work.

There are two places to look for evidence of the kind of influence I am discussing: in the author's work and in representations of that work, either by the author or by the critics. In what follows, I will look at a short story by Hawkes which encodes a drama of authorial influence on critical reading, and along with it I will consider a critical essay on the story which enacts the part scripted for the reader in that drama. Thereafter, I will take a broader sampling of Hawkes's critical fortunes, with an eye not only to the migration of descriptive language from author to critic, via the interview,[2] but also to the genesis of that language in the writing of Hawkes's earliest and most influential critic, Albert Guerard.

The story and the critical reading I start with were both published in a 1988 anthology called *Facing Texts: Encounters Between Contemporary Writers and Critics,* edited by Heide Ziegler. This volume deserves comment in its own right, as an emblem of post-modern literary practice. The title of the anthology refers to the fact that it pairs creative texts by prominent first-generation postmodern authors with critical essays on those texts; what makes the volume emblematic is that the critics were in most cases hand-picked by the authors themselves. In fact, as her preface informs us, Ziegler herself was picked by one of those authors: *Facing Texts* originated in a suggestion made by William Gass to an editor at Duke University Press, that Ziegler should edit a collection of contemporary American fiction. Ziegler says that, when the project was proposed to her,

> I immediately recognized that in effect I was being offered the opportunity to realize one of my pet ideas: to bring together . . . unpublished pieces by authors as well as critics that would, in a sense, defy the chronological secondariness of critical interpretation. Such a book would make the relationship between author and critic an unmediated encounter, with authors and critics becoming one another's ideal readers.
>
> . . . if possible, the pieces offered by the authors should indeed be hitherto unpublished so as to give the critics a sense of the exclusiveness, even privacy of their work and thus convey to them the impression of a close encounter with the respective author. . . . [and] the authors should choose their own critics in order to ensure that the close encounter I had in mind would not, unintentionally, be hostile, and thus destroy the possibility of mutual ideal readership. (ix)[3]

In Hawkes's case, Ziegler's solicitude is unnecessary: his contribution to this volume was designed to foster the kind of reading that she desired for it.

"The Equestrienne" is a portion of Hawkes's 1985 novella *Innocence in Extremis,* which is, in turn, an outtake from a novel, *Adventures in the Alaskan Skin Trade.* A large part of the novel is devoted to relating the misadventures of "Uncle Jake," as recalled by his daughter; relative to that story, *Innocence in Extremis* is an extended flashback, to a time when Uncle Jake, as a boy, visited his ancestral home in France with *his* father and family. "The Equestrienne" is one of the three set pieces that make up the novella, but it has been published here without introduction or reference to the context in which it was developed, and it can be read as a free-standing, very short story.[4]

In "The Equestrienne," Uncle Jake's French grandfather (referred to exclusively as "the Old Gentleman") stages an exhibition of dressage, on what we are told is one of several "occasions deemed by the Old Gentleman to be specially enjoyable to his assembly of delighted guests" (216). In this, the first of those (three) occasions and the only one presented here, a young cousin of Uncle Jake's performs for an audience consisting of the visitors (including Uncle Jake), members of the household, and some neighbors, all seated in rows of plush Empire chairs arranged in a courtyard of the family chateau. The girl and her horse are the center of attention, but the performance itself is the medium for an interaction between the audience and the Old Gentleman.

In this case, the audience *in* the tale clearly stands for the audience *of* the tale, and almost from its opening lines the text signals the effect it wants to achieve—most notably in the modifiers that cluster around descriptions of the represented audience. As an example, take the passage just quoted: "the days of harmony and pleasure were further enhanced by certain occasions deemed by the Old Gentleman to be specially enjoyable to his assembly of delighted guests." It is the narrator who tells us that days already harmonious and pleasurable were "enhanced" by what is about to be related; and while we might be privy to some delusion in the Old Gentleman when we are told that he "deemed" his entertainment "to be specially enjoyable" to his guests, any distance between his objective and their reaction is collapsed in the very same sentence, when we learn that they are in fact "delighted." Each detail of the performance is similarly described and received. "The gilded frames and red plush cushions of the chairs shone in the agreeable light and . . . moved everyone to exclamations of surprise and keen anticipation." In the world of the text as we are given it, the light *is* "agreeable," and the audience is unanimous in its expression of "surprise and keen anticipation." Throughout the tale, the reactions of the audience consistently confirm what the narration announces. "Through the gateway rode a young girl on a small and shapely dappled gray horse. Here was a sight to win them all and audibly they sighed and visibly they leaned forward. . . . [an] already grateful audience" (216).

There is no point in piling up further examples; suffice it to say that this high pitch of appreciation is insistently sustained, the only two discordant notes resolving into it almost immediately. In the first of these, contemplating his cousin, Uncle Jake thinks "with shame . . . of himself and his shaggy and dumpy pony" (218). In the second, shortly thereafter, his mother whispers to him: "mark my words, dear boy. That child is dangerous." These are important moments, but their importance lies not so much in any pall they cast over the performance as in the evidence they give of its irresistible charm. Uncle Jake's insecurity and his mother's mistrust soon give way to the universal sentiment: Uncle Jake realizes that "he wanted to become [his cousin] and take her splendid place on the gray horse," and even his mother admits, "'she is a beautiful little rider, Jake. You might try to ride as well as she does. It would please your father'" (219).

In her essay on the story, Christine Laniel remarks that "The Equestrienne" "focuses on one of the most pervasive metaphors in Hawkes's works, which he analyzes as essential to his fiction writing when he refers to 'horsemanship as an art'" (221-22). Specifically, Laniel is suggesting that Hawkes offers dressage as a metaphor for the artistic use of language. That much can easily be read between the lines from which she quotes, but taken in full these lines also suggest that the same metaphor might be extended to include an association of other kinds of horsemanship with other ways of using language—after all, the audience is composed of equestrians:

> Nearly everyone in that audience rode horseback. Most of them were fox hunters. Their lives depended on horses. . . . Yet for all of them their mares and geldings and fillies and stallions were a matter of course like stones in a brook or birds in the boughs. Most of the horses they bred and rode were large, rugged, unruly, brutish beasts of great stamina. The horses raced and hunted, pulled their carriages, carried them ambling through sylvan woods and took them cantering great distances. But little more. So here in the Old Gentleman's courtyard the spectacle of the young equestrienne and her gray horse schooled only in dressage appealed directly to what they knew and to their own relationships to horse and stable yet gave them all a taste of equestrian refinement that stirred them to surprise and pleasure. They had never thought of horsemanship as an art, but here indeed in the dancing horse they could see full well the refinement of an artist's mind. (218)

The thrust of this passage, it seems to me, is first to suggest horsemanship as a figure for the use of language in general, and then to distinguish between the nonutilitarian "refinement" of its use in fiction and the practicality of more quotidian language used with an end in mind, as for example to convey information (in "rugged, unruly, brutish" words "of great stamina" but no elegance). In this scene "artist" and audience share what might be called a professional interest in horses, not unlike the professional interest in language Hawkes shares with his readers; and while it may be the general reader and not the critical one who takes language as "a matter of course," even the most perspicacious fox hunters among us are obviously supposed to be "stirred" to "surprise and pleasure" at Hawkes's demonstration of verbal dressage.

In fact, at the conclusion of the performance the story explicitly announces the lesson we are to draw from it: "the audience rose to its feet, still clapping. They exclaimed aloud to each other, while clapping, and smiles vied with smiles and no one had praise enough for the exhibition which had taught them all that artificiality not only enhances natural life but defines it" (220). Hawkes's instruction of the reader is too deliberate to be unintended and too obvious to ignore, so it must be explained. In Laniel's analysis, the author at these moments is "forestalling interpretation by anticipating it. As a consequence, the critic is thwarted in efforts to unveil supposedly hidden significations, which are obtrusively exposed by the writer himself" (222). She regards this aspect of the story as a problem only for a criticism which needs "to unveil supposedly hidden significations"; as we have seen, though, "The Equestrienne" does more than interpret itself: it so relentlessly superintends response that it is likely to frustrate any reader, and not merely a certain sort of critic.

But for Laniel at least, the "alluring fascination" (222) of "The Equestrienne" survives in its strategy of "seduction, which implies the obliteration of reality and its transfiguration into pure appearance" (226). That is, although she acknowledges that the story reads its own moral, she still finds Hawkes's presentation of "the artificial" fascinating, because it undertakes "the willful deterioration of language as the vehicle of meaning."

This deterioration is said to take place in a series of puns and paradoxes (*sister-sinister,* mastery-fragility, innocence-corruption, and so forth) and in sentences like the following (which explains the effect of the Old Gentleman's having positioned the girl sidesaddle on her horse, with her legs away from the audience): "The fact that she appeared to have no legs was to the entire ensemble as was the white ribbon affixed to her hat: the incongruity without which the congruous whole could not have achieved such perfection" (217). In this sentence, Laniel says,

> we are made to experience both frustration and supreme satisfaction, since the expected word is missing and yet is virtually present, enhanced by the strange, incongruous connections that implicitly suggest it. By establishing the curious relationship of the logically unrelated, by uniting the like with the unlike in sudden and unexpected juxtapositions, the poetic text produces a jarring effect, so that we are left with the notion of a fundamental vacancy, of a basic lack that is the very essence of aesthetic pleasure. (228)

Yet the sentence Laniel has chosen not only contains the "missing" word—"perfection"—but emphasizes it by placing it in the ultimate position. And in any case, Hawkes's notion of an "incongruity without which the congruous whole could not have achieved such perfection" is more plausible as a model than as an occasion for Laniel's observation that the "jarring effect" brought about by "the curious relationship of the logically unrelated" results in "a fundamental vacancy . . . that is the very essence of aesthetic pleasure."

Laniel also tries to restore some ambiguity to the story by arguing that Hawkes's "rhetoric of seduction" is always "reversed into derision, as an insidious vein of self-parody gradually penetrates the text" (222). As she sees it,

> Hawkes's writing cannot function without initiating its own ironical debunking. The "morality of excess" [*Innocence in Extremis* 55] that guides the artist in his work also guides Hawkes in his writing, as exemplified by the profusion of superlatives and comparatives in the novella and in all his fiction. But this very excessiveness entails a crescendo, an escalation into more and more incongruous associations, so that his texts are relentlessly undermined by their own grotesque redoubling. (235)

Self-parody is indeed an abiding characteristic of Hawkes's writing—and often its saving grace—but though the language we have already quoted from "The Equestrienne" does suggest an excessiveness that might easily escalate into self-parody, Laniel herself admits that "during the performance of the equestrienne the burlesque element is extremely slight" (233). Consequently, when she makes the argument that this text undermines itself she is forced to rely entirely on evidence collected from other, later sections of the novella and from the originary novel. Still, even if there is no parody in "The Equestrienne," its absence makes it worth discussing.

In general, the significant gap in Hawkes's work is not between appearance and reality but between the serious and the parodic elements that constitute his fiction: the uneasiness of his texts is that while his self-parody seems deliberate, it doesn't ground or control the seriousness with which he presents his primary material. Since the critic is bound to make statements about the text, and since making those statements usually involves taking a position relative to the text by offering a reading, critics have often resolved this conflict in the text by going too far in one direction or the other—either affirming the response offered by the text (the more common tactic) or overstating the control exercised by the parodic element. Laniel's piece is unusual in that it does the latter, but in order to make this case she has to read beyond the immediate text. By so doing, she is in effect submitting "The Equestrienne" to the control of a self-parody which develops across other, broader contexts. This move begs the question of whether the parodic strain controls the larger contexts from which she abstracts it. In fact, I would argue, it does not—the uneasiness simply reasserts itself when we look at *Innocence in Extremis* or *Adventures in the Alaskan Skin Trade* as texts in their own right.

The significance of Hawkes's unstable self-parody, both with regard to its presence in his other fiction and its absence in the present case, is bound up with the problem of the audience and its response. In order to avoid the problem Laniel has with contextualization, let us look briefly at a discrete work, *Travesty,* written by Hawkes in the early 1970s.

Travesty is the monologue of a man who intends to crash the car in which he, his daughter, and an existentialist poet (the lover of both his wife and daughter) are traveling. Papa, the driver, denies being jealous or having any murderous motive; instead, he tells Henri (the poet) that his plan is to create an "accident" so inexplicable that their deaths will have to be understood as the deliberate execution of an abstract design. Henri is apparently nonplused, since Papa reproaches him for his failure to appreciate the beauty of the thing: "Tonight of all nights why can't you give me one moment of genuine response? Without it, as I have said, our expedition is as wasteful as everything else" (82). The response Papa wants from Henri is specifically an aesthetic one, and he sees it as a mark of Henri's artistic insincerity that he is not able to provide it. But, as the reader well understands, the detachment from self-interest which such a response would require is too much to expect, even from an existentialist.

As a monologist, Papa necessarily speaks for Henri, and in a similar way Hawkes, as a writer, speaks for the reader. His conceit is auto-destructive, but self-parody—a preemptive mode of discourse—is by definition both exclusive of and also highly attentive to the audience. The element of self-parody in *Travesty* asserts itself as the difference between the supposed reality of death within the fiction and the reality of death supposed which is the fiction—Hawkes, in other words, is Henri if he is anyone in this story. But as this equation suggests, the parody does not extend to Papa, and much of what he says is seriously intended, not least his confessed need for a response:

> Let me admit that it was precisely the fear of committing a final and irrevocable act that plagued my childhood, my youth, my early manhood. . . . And in those years and as a corollary to my preoccupation with the cut string I could not repair, the step I could not retrieve, I was also plagued by what I defined as the fear of no response. . . . If the world did not respond to me totally, immediately, in leaf, street sign, the expression of strangers, then I did not exist. . . . But to be recognized in any way was to be given your selfhood on a plate and to be loved, loved, which is what I most demanded. (84-85)

Self-parody, this suggests, is more than an attempt to forestall a feared lack of response (or an undesirable response); it may also become a way to avoid "committing a final and irrevocable [speech] act." On one level, Hawkes is deadly serious about everything that Papa says; on another, he implicitly denies responsibility for the ideas Papa expresses. At both levels, he precludes response—within the narrative through the technique of monologue, without it through the technique of self-parody. The effect on the reader is, as Laniel says, often baffling: the proffered position is clearly untenable, and yet the parody does not enable an alternate response because it equally clearly does not control the text.

The instability I have been describing might also be regarded as a side effect of characterization. Hawkes is fond of creating figures of the artist, but these figures never completely fill the role in which they are cast; most often they are people who have the sensibility of the artist but who do not actually create art. Cyril in *The Blood Oranges,* Papa in *Travesty,* Uncle Jake in *Adventures in the Alaskan Skin Trade* are all men whose medium is action, not language, and who do not pretend to present the fiction in which their artistry is conveyed to the reader. In *Travesty,* the distinction would seem to be mooted when narration is placed entirely in the hands of "the man who disciplines the child, carves the roast" (44)—but in fact it persists, since Papa's "creation," the actual crash, cannot be presented within the narrative structure Hawkes has set up and so is not presented at all. In other words, although Hawkes's novella develops in the space between the disclosure and the enactment of Papa's intentions, the aesthetic Hawkes has embodied in those intentions can be expressed only in words, never in action— hence the equation of Hawkes with Henri. Seeking to evade both the irrevocable commitment of unfeigned statement and the fear of no response, Hawkes has adopted a narrative perspective that results in a fiction which implies but does not constitute the realization of an aesthetic.

If the conflict between a desire to present this aesthetic and the fear that it will be rejected is settled in *Travesty* by giving the narrative over entirely to statement, in "The Equestrienne" Hawkes experiments with the opposite solution, usurping the response of his audience. Rather than seducing the reader, this makes her superfluous: hence Laniel's frustration at trying to present a reading of the story as given—something that her recourse to other texts demonstrates she is ultimately unable to do. And like response, the absence of a controlling intelligence is dislocated in "The Equestrienne" from a metatextual position to a thematic one: "All at once and above the dainty clatter of the hooves, they heard the loud and charming tinkling of a music box. Heads turned, a new and livelier surprise possessed the audience, the fact that they could not discover the source of the music, which was the essence of artificiality, added greatly to the effect" (219). But even within the story, this absence proves to be more apparent than real: at the end of the girl's exhibition,

> the Old Gentleman appeared and as one the audience realized that though they had all seen him act the impresario and with his raised hand start the performance, still he had not taken one of the red plush chairs for himself, had not remained with them in the courtyard, had not been a passive witness to his granddaughter's exhibition. He was smiling broadly; he was perspiring; clearly he expected thanks. In all this the truth was evident: that not only had he himself orchestrated the day, but that it was he who had taught the girl dressage, and he who had from a little balcony conducted her performance and determined her every move, and he who had turned the handle of the music box. Never had the old patrician looked younger or more pleased with himself. (220)

The Old Gentleman is not "a passive witness" to the presentation; he is its conductor, and his curtain call

might be compared to Hawkes's persistent assertion of the authorial self in his interviews: in both cases, the creator remains behind the scenes during the actual performance but reappears afterward to make sure that its significance is properly understood.

The nature of Hawkes's dilemma and the variety of his attempts to resolve it are characteristically post-modern, in that they demonstrate a very real need to assert critical control over the text, combined with a desire that the reader should be persuaded to a particular aesthetic position. Such desires are not peculiar to post-modern authors, of course: Henry James once admitted to dreaming, "in wanton moods, . . . of some Paradise (for art) where the direct appeal to the intelligence might be legalised" (296). Late in his life, James made that appeal to future readers in his prefaces to the New York edition of his works, but he might well have envied the post-modern author, who can address the contemporary reader through the mechanism of the interview.

Hawkes's inclination to avail himself of opportunities to discuss his work has resulted in quite a substantial body of interviews.[5] In these interviews, Hawkes propounds his aesthetic program, characterizes his fiction, and explains his intentions in specific novels; the images and analogies he uses migrate visibly from the interviews to the criticism and reappear in the questions posed by subsequent interviewers. In this way, the language of Hawkes's self-descriptions comes to dominate the critical reception of his work, functioning—to borrow an idea from Kenneth Burke—as a "terministic screen."[6] Hawkes's career also demonstrates, however, the influence of critics on authors: although the authority of this particular terministic screen is derived from Hawkes via the interview, Hawkes himself seems to have derived many of its component terms from Albert Guerard's early analyses of his work.

Hawkes has often acknowledged his debt to Guerard, but to fully understand the nature of that debt we need to know something about the history of the relationship between these two men. Hawkes was not much of a student when he came to Harvard: the semester before he left for the war, he had flunked out.[7] His career as a writer started in Guerard's fiction writing class at Harvard, which he took after returning from service in the Ambulance Corps during World War II. At that time, he had just started working on his first piece of fiction, the novella *Charivari,* and though manifestly talented, he lacked experience both as a writer and as a reader of modern fiction. Prior to 1947, he had written only some juvenile verse, which he submitted to qualify for Guerard's class; during that class (for which he wrote *The Cannibal*), Hawkes's "reading of modern experimental literature was largely confined to poetry," according to Guerard (Introduction xn). In a recent interview, Hawkes recalled that when they first met, "Guerard . . . was probably in his early thirties, but to me he was an awesome figure. He was quite formidable, quite authoritarian, extremely knowledgeable, a novelist himself, and he had so suddenly and abruptly praised my fiction at the outset in such a way as to give me real confidence" ("Life" 112). Obviously, in the course of this long friendship Hawkes has had many occasions to express his ideas about fiction, and it is likely that Guerard's published criticism of Hawkes reflects those ideas to some extent. We may even grant that, as Guerard has faded from the forefront of contemporary criticism, and as Hawkes has become firmly established as one of the major talents of his generation, the balance of power in the relationship may have shifted somewhat in recent years. But it is nonetheless clear that Guerard played an influential role in molding Hawkes's understanding of the value of his own fiction. The nature and extent of that influence is clear if we compare a few passages from Guerard's early criticism to Hawkes's subsequent self-evaluations.

It was Guerard who brought Hawkes and James Laughlin together, and when, in 1949, New Directions published Hawkes's first novel (*The Cannibal*), Guerard provided the introduction. This introduction is the earliest critical analysis of Hawkes's work, and its influence on later Hawkes criticism, including the author's own, is inestimable. In it, Guerard says that "Terror . . . can create its own geography" (xiii) and announces, in terms that persist to this day, that "John Hawkes clearly belongs . . . with the cold immoralists and pure creators who enter sympathetically into all their characters, the saved and the damned alike. . . . even the most contaminate have their dreams of purity which shockingly resemble our own" (xii). Not long thereafter, the *Radcliffe News* published Hawkes's first interview, entitled "John Hawkes, Author, Calls Guerard's Preface Most Helpful Criticism" (March 17, 1950)—and so it would seem to have been. Guerard's remarks about sympathy for "the saved and the damned alike" are reflected in Hawkes's earliest published critical writing (1960), in which he talks about the experimental novel as displaying "an attitude that rejects sympathy for the ruined members of our lot, revealing thus the deepest sympathy of all" ("Notes on Violence").[8] As late as 1979, Hawkes still describes himself as being "interested in the truest kind of fictive sympathy, as Albert Guerard, my former teacher and lifelong friend, has put it. To him the purpose of imaginative fiction is to generate sympathy for the saved and damned alike" ("Novelist" 27).[9]

In his 1949 introduction, Guerard confidently compares Hawkes to William Faulkner, Franz Kafka, and Djuna Barnes (although he predicts that Hawkes "will move . . . toward realism"), and he concludes—on a disciplinary note—that "How far John Hawkes will go as a writer must obviously depend on how far he consents to impose some page-by-page and chapter-by-chapter consecutive understanding on his astonishing creative energy; on how richly he exploits his ability to achieve truth through distortion; on how well he continues to uncover and use childhood images and fears" (xv). In an addendum to the introduction, written for *The Cannibal*'s reissue in 1962, Guerard notes that "the predicted movement toward realism has occurred" but reiterates the importance of nightmare and "vivifying distortion" in Hawkes's fiction (xviii). The concepts of distortion and terror, and the paradoxical

linkage of purity and contamination, have since become staples in the discussion of Hawkes's work: the Hryciw-Wing bibliography lists at least twenty-one essays with the words "nightmare" or "terror" in the title (beginning with a review by Guerard in 1961), and countless others have incorporated the same idea into their arguments.[10]

Guerard's addendum also praises Hawkes for being able "to summon pre-conscious anxieties and longings, to symbolize oral fantasies and castration fears—to shadow forth, in a word, our underground selves" (xviii). In his first essay in self-explanation, presented at a symposium on fiction at Wesleyan University in 1962 and published in *Massachusetts Review,* Hawkes himself states:

> The constructed vision, the excitement of the undersea life of the inner man, a language appropriate to the delicate malicious knowledge of us all as poor, forked, corruptible, the feeling of pleasure and pain that comes when something pure and contemptible lodges in the imagination—I believe in the "singular and terrible attraction" of all this.
>
> For me the writer should always serve as his own angleworm—and the sharper the barb with which he fishes himself out of the blackness, the better. ("Notes on *The Wild Goose Chase*" 788)[11]

The image of the fishhook is a more memorable formulation of Guerard's claim that Hawkes's fiction has the ability to "shadow forth our underground selves"; certainly it seems, in keeping with the metaphor of which it is a part, to have set itself deep in Hawkes's vision of his own work.

In a 1964 interview, one which has remained among the most often cited, Hawkes told John Enck: "my aim has always been . . . never to let the reader (or myself) off the hook, so to speak, never to let him think that the picture is any less black than it is or that there is any easy way out of the nightmare of human existence" ("John Hawkes" 145). In 1971, the piece in which the metaphor originally appeared was reprinted along with Enck's interview in John Graham's *Studies in Second Skin* (the dedication to which reads: "For Albert Guerard, who led the way"—Graham is another of Guerard's former students), and in 1975 the image returns in the following exchange with John Kuehl:

> *Kuehl:* You once referred to fishing for yourself.
>
> *Hawkes:* I said that "the author is his own best angleworm and the sharper the barb with which he fishes himself out of the darkness the better." . . . I mean that the writer who exploits his own psychic life reveals the inner lives of us all, the inner chaos, the negative aspects of the personality in general . . . our deepest inner lives are largely organized around such impulses, which need to be exposed and understood and used. (Kuehl 164-65)

It is perhaps significant that a few pages later, Hawkes remarks: "For me evil was once a power. Now it's a powerful metaphor" (166).[12]

The "powerful metaphor" of authorship as auto-piscation was also used by Hawkes the year before to open an influential essay called "Notes on Writing a Novel," which was first printed in 1973 in the *Brown Alumni Monthly,* reprinted the next year in *TriQuarterly,* and finally revised and collected in a 1983 volume fittingly entitled *In Praise of What Persists*. In that piece, Hawkes relates the following anecdote:

> A scholarly, gifted, deeply good-natured friend once remarked that "Notes on Writing a Novel" is a deplorably condescending title. . . . At that moment . . . I thought of a metaphor with which I'd ended a talk on fiction ten years ago at Boston College, when I said that "for me, the writer of fiction should always serve as his own angleworm, and the sharper the barb with which he fishes himself out of the darkness, the better." But when I proposed "The Writer as Angleworm" as an alternative, my friend pointed out that preciousness is worse than condescension. (109)

The "friend" remains unnamed, but it is somehow appropriate that Hawkes has trouble remembering the genesis of his image, mistaking the Wesleyan venue for a Boston College one; in an interview given in 1979 and published in 1983, he makes a similar mistake when Patrick O'Donnell remarks on "the fetus fished out of the flood in *The Beetle Leg*." Hawkes responds: "Yes. Thinking of that image reminds me of an interview with John Graham where I said that 'the writer should be his own angleworm [etc.].'" By this point Hawkes is not remembering the occasion on which he originally formulated the idea but misremembering one on which he quoted it—the interview with Enck, published in Graham. Hawkes goes on to dwell on the image at some length, demonstrating that it still informs his understanding of his own work, however vague its origins:

> It's an interesting paradox: separating the artist from the human personality, the artistic self from the human self, then thinking of the artist's job as one of catching, capturing, snaring, using a very dangerous and unpleasant weapon, a hook, knowing that his subject matter is himself or his own imagination, which he has to find himself and which he catches ruthlessly. It's a very schizophrenic image, full of dangerous, archetypal maneuvers in the deepest darkness within us. ("Life" 123)

Hawkes's choice of words is revealing, in that schizophrenia is often linked to the presence of an overpowering authority figure; we have already seen that Hawkes initially regarded Guerard as "an awesome figure . . . quite formidable, quite authoritarian." In a 1971 encounter called "John Hawkes and Albert Guerard in Dialogue," Hawkes jokes about that "awesome" authority, but with an insistence and intensity that belie his tone:

> *Hawkes:* . . . I have long suspected that I'm a fiction created by Albert Guerard. I think I knew from the very first moment we met. (14)

> when I met him, and for years afterwards, he was, as a teacher, a ruthless authoritarian, a tremendous

disciplinarian. About fifteen years ago, I had thought that I had achieved some kind of equality with Albert, at least on a personal level, and had escaped this terrible awe, and the awesome business of father/teacher, but now I've been plunged right back into it. (15)

> My writing has been filled with awkwardness. . . . It's always been Albert who has pointed out where the distorting glasses have been taken off, or where the writing was flabby. . . .

> *Guerard:* That's fantasy. It's not true at all . . . (25-26)

Despite Hawkes's bantering manner (and Guerard's denial), it is obvious that this relationship was an extremely important one for Hawkes, and his gratitude seems more than slightly tinged with the anxiety of influence. This is understandable, in light of the fact that for more than a decade after leaving Guerard's class, Hawkes submitted each of his novels to Guerard before publishing it; and in at least one instance, Guerard seems to have exercised his authority in the form of a veto. As Hawkes tells it, when Guerard read the manuscript for *The Lime Twig*, "he sent it back saying 'Jack, this is deplorable; it's a good idea, but poorly conceived and written, and you'll have to start over again'" ("Life" 112). After that, it took Hawkes four years to revise the book, and although Guerard continued to exert a shaping influence on Hawkes's career, this was the last time he was given a manuscript for preapproval.

Elsewhere in his dialogue with Guerard, Hawkes says, "just as you controlled everything else, you are, as a matter of fact, responsible for my fiction becoming increasingly so-called 'realistic'" (23), but after *The Lime Twig* this realism coincided with a new emphasis on the comic and a marked uneasiness on the part of Hawkes:

> Beginning with *Second Skin,* I was reluctant and partly afraid to ask my mentor for his approval of my work. That was the first manuscript I published without Guerard's pre-reading. I know he likes *Second Skin* a great deal. . . . [but] I don't think he likes the next two novels all that much; my feeling is that he thinks *The Blood Oranges* is, in some ways, a falling off. But he liked *Travesty* a great deal. . . . The reason that we first went to France was because Guerard, himself, is partly French. . . . So France was the world that Guerard represented. ("Life" 113)

If Hawkes was conscious of his comic novels as a departure from the kind of writing approved of by his mentor, *Travesty* (a "French" novel) would seem to have been his gesture of reconciliation. His next book, *The Passion Artist,* returned to the earlier style and setting and was very favorably reviewed by Guerard.

With regard not only to Hawkes's stylistic oscillations but also to the genealogy of his self-understanding, the central issue is the relation of the artist to the contents of his unconscious mind. In exactly this connection, Frederick Busch—one of John Hawkes's earliest and friendliest critics—recently wondered whether

> John Hawkes, studying his life, perhaps studies his art as well. . . . [he] now faces the danger he has faced throughout a distinguished career—of tapping his usual psychic resources, of using his usual dreams, of relying upon his usual metaphors, and therefore of risking the loss of new language, new fictive worlds.
>
> . . . I go so far as to sorrow over his considerable praise from academics . . . because I fear that they seek to encourage Hawkes to write what is "teachable" and teachably "post-Modern."
>
> . . . like every writer who taps his inner imagery, [Hawkes] must determine when he is to avoid his own urgings and the temptation to use what becomes a habitual vocabulary of images. (*When People Publish* 110)

It is interesting that, in an earlier version of the same essay, Busch's pessimism was decidedly less pronounced:

> In *Death, Sleep & The Traveler,* Hawkes may be thinking about who he is as a writer, what he has done, and what he ought to do. He may, at times, seem to be writing out of a sense of *Hawkes.* . . . When Hemingway became a student of Hemingway—*To Have and Have Not,* as compared to its point of origin, "After the Storm," is a good example—he failed to measure up to his teacher. While I do not see signs of such a failure in *Death, Sleep & The Traveler,* I do see Hawkes as engaged in the most profound examination of his own writings; and he is daring to risk being influenced by that seductive writer, John Hawkes. ("Icebergs" 62-63)

Busch's change in tone between 1977 and 1986 suggests that he does feel Hawkes, with the aid of his academic critics, has seduced himself. I would want to add only that Hawkes's "sense of *Hawkes*" has, from the beginning, been shaped and developed by his most important reader, Guerard. And although influence here reverses the direction it followed in the case of "The Equestrienne," in each case the academic context shared by reader and writer has fostered an extraordinary symbiosis, one which ultimately enervates both criticism and creativity.

In *The Romantic Ideology,* Jerome McGann says that there is "[an] essential difference which separates the journalistic and polemical criticism whose focus is the present from the scholarly and historical criticism which operates in the present only by facing (and defining) the past" (2-3). To date, much of the criticism of post-modern fiction has indeed been polemical and journalistic and has aimed at reproducing the ideology of the fiction it discusses. But even though no one at present can claim to have the same distance from post-modernism as we have from romanticism, it is still possible to submit post-modern fiction to a criticism that scrutinizes its cultural and institutional determinants. Indeed, as McGann points out, there are good reasons for doing so:

> When critics perpetuate and maintain older ideas and attitudes in continuities and processive traditions they typically serve only the most reactionary purposes of their societies, though they may not be aware of this; for the cooptive powers of a vigorous culture like our own are very great. If such powers and their results are not always to be deplored, cooperation must always be a process intolerable to critical consciousness, whose first obligation is to resist incorporation, and whose weapon is analysis. (2)

What was new in 1947 has begun to age, and it is now time to ask what purposes are served by perpetuating the ideas and attitudes identified with it. The problem McGann describes is only exacerbated when author and critic are contemporaries cohabiting in one institution. Under these circumstances, the material inducements to cooperation may well subvert the independence of both parties: each is in the position to augment the prestige of the other, but neither is really in control. As McGann predicts, having been incorporated, each is controlled by the ideology of the institution that creates and confers their prestige, and both end up serving the most reactionary purposes of that institution. Where post-modernism is concerned, the institution is the academy and the ideology is that of professionalism. Others have pointed out before now that academic professionalism is itself at the service of larger cultural mechanisms, and that its most reactionary purpose is to co-opt and sequester intellectual energies—whether critical or creative—so that they do not disrupt the smooth operation of those mechanisms.[13]

Earlier I asserted that the post-modernism of Hawkes and his generation is continuous with modernism, but here that assertion needs to be qualified. First-generation post-modernism differs from its predecessor in one crucial way, namely in being institutionalized. Modernism, for the most part, rejected the security of the academy *in order* to take liberties with the culture; by contrast, post-modernism stands at the embarrassing conjunction of that modernist heritage of alienation and a practical condition of institutional respectability and security. The aesthetic similarities between modernism and post-modernism pale into insignificance next to this situational difference—and since the aesthetic features of post-modernism serve purposes different from those they served under modernism, our advocacy of those features serves different purposes as well. It may be too late for authors such as Hawkes to alter their course, but it is by no means too soon for the criticism of post-modern fiction to put aside polemic in favor of analysis and begin resisting the urge to cooperate.

NOTES

[1] According to Michael Koehler, the term "post-modern" was introduced (in English) in the 1940s by Arnold Toynbee, who used it to denominate the entire period from 1875 to the present. Koehler says that Irving Howe

may have been the first person to call the literature after modernism "post-modern," in his 1959 essay "Mass Society and Post-Modern Fiction." A good deal of the confusion that has accompanied the use of this term in recent years might be attributed to the failure to acknowledge that there have already been two generations of the postmodern and that, in many ways, the two have little in common. For the sake of clarity, I use the original form of the word (in which the hyphen privileges the modern) to refer to the first of these two generations, which sees itself as extending the project of modernism. In "postmodernism," on the other hand, the hyphen has dropped out and the agglutinated form, in which "post" gets top billing, implies the emergence of a new entity. This form of the word is increasingly common, but I would suggest that rather than being applied indiscriminately it ought to denote specifically that rising generation which conceives of itself as distinct from and often opposed to modernism.

[2] Kenneth Burke's idea of the migration of metaphor is relevant here: "In general, primitive magic tended to transfer an animistic perspective to the charting of physical events. And positivistic science, by antithesis, leads to an opposite ideal, the transferring of physicalist perspective to human events. Each is the migration of a metaphor" (*Philosophy* 147). In the present case, the migration consists in a transfer of an authorial perspective to the criticism of fiction.

[3] The other authors in Ziegler's anthology are Robert Coover, Guy Davenport, John Barth, Donald Barthelme, Stanley Elkin, Susan Sontag, Walter Abish, and Joseph McElroy.

[4] "The Equestrienne" appears in *Facing Texts; Innocence in Extremis* was published by Burning Deck in 1985; *Adventures in the Alaskan Skin Trade* was published in hardcover by Simon and Schuster in 1985 and then, as part of the Contemporary American Fiction series, in paperback by Penguin in 1986.

[5] According to Carol A. Hryciw-Wing's recent bibliography, forty-four interviews with Hawkes were published between 1950 and 1985.

[6] See Kenneth Burke, "Terministic Screens," chapter 3 of *Language as Symbolic Action*. Burke says that "even if any given terminology is a *reflection* of reality, by its very nature as a terminology it must be a *selection* of reality; and to this extent it must function also as a *deflection* of reality" (45). He goes on to elaborate the point as follows: "Not only does the nature of our terms affect the nature of our observations, in the sense that the terms direct the attention to one field rather than to another. Also, *many of the 'observations' are but implications of the particular terminology in terms of which the observations are made.* In brief, much that we take as observations about 'reality' may be but the spinning out of possibilities implicit in our particular choice of terms" (46).

[7] To my knowledge, the only personal nightmare ever related by Hawkes (for whom the nightmare has become a trademark) is a recurrent dream "about not passing courses and not graduating from Harvard, in which case I would not have been a teacher, *et cetera*" (Hawkes and Guerard 21).

[8] This brief essay and a story are accompanied by Guerard's "Introduction to the Cambridge Anti-Realists," among which Guerard includes Hawkes.

[9] This interview is accompanied by Guerard's review of *The Passion Artist.*

[10] Guerard himself, through all four revisions of his entry on Hawkes in the reference work *Contemporary Novelists* (1972, 1976, 1982, 1986), has continued to praise Hawkes for his use of "childhood terror, oral fantasies and castration fears, fears of regression and violence, profound sexual disturbances" (395). Not surprisingly, in the 1986 entry Guerard seems somewhat dissatisfied with *Adventures in the Alaskan Skin Trade,* because it contains so "few archetypal dreams [which] echo powerful dreams in the earlier books"; for Guerard, it is only in these echoes that "the author's true voice is dominant" (397).

[11] This piece has not only been reprinted in Graham but also in Klein and in volume 29 of *Contemporary Literary Criticism.*

[12] Kuehl publishes this interview as a chapter in his book on Hawkes—not an uncommon practice in book-length studies of contemporary authors.

[13] For a full-length discussion of professionalism as an ideological tool in the administration of culture, see Larson.

WORKS CITED

Burke, Kenneth. *Language as Symbolic Action: Essays on Life, Literature, and Method.* Berkeley: U of California P, 1966.

———. *The Philosophy of Literary Form: Studies in Symbolic Action.* 3rd ed. Berkeley: U of California P, 1973.

Busch, Frederick. "Icebergs, Islands, Ships Beneath the Sea." *A John Hawkes Symposium: Design and Debris.* Ed. Anthony C. Santore and Michael Pocalyko. New York: New Directions, 1977. 50-63.

———. *When People Publish: Essays on Writers and Writing.* Iowa City: U of Iowa P, 1986.

Contemporary Literary Criticism. Detroit: Gale, 1984.

Contemporary Novelists. Ed. D. L. Kirkpatrick. 4th ed. New York: St. Martin's, 1986.

———. Ed. James Vinson, 1st-3rd eds. New York: St. Martin's, 1972, 1976, 1982.

Graham, John, ed. *Studies in Second Skin.* The Charles E. Merrill Studies. Columbus, OH: Merrill, 1971.

Guerard, Albert. Introduction. *The Cannibal.* By John Hawkes. 1949. New York: New Directions, 1962. ix-xx.

————. "The Passion Artist: John Hawkes." Rev. of *The Passion Artist,* by John Hawkes. *New Republic* 10 Nov. 1979: 29-30.

Hawkes, John. "The Equestrienne." *Facing Texts: Encounters Between Contemporary Writers and Critics.* Ed. Heide Ziegler. Durham: Duke UP, 1988. 215-20.

————. "John Hawkes: An Interview." With John Enck. *Wisconsin Studies in Contemporary Literature* 6 (1965): 141-55.

————. "Life and Art: An Interview with John Hawkes." With Patrick O'Donnell. *Review of Contemporary Fiction* 3.3 (1983): 107-26.

————. "Notes on *The Wild Goose Chase.*" *Massachusetts Review* 3 (1962): 784-88.

————. "Notes on Violence." *Audience* 7 (1960): 60.

————. "Notes on Writing a Novel." *TriQuarterly* 30 (1974): 109-26. Rpt. from *Brown Alumni Monthly* Jan. 1973: 9-16. Rpt. as "Dark Landscapes." *In Praise of What Persists.* Ed. Stephen Berg. New York: Harper, 1983. 135-47.

————. "The Novelist: John Hawkes." With Thomas LeClair. *New Republic* 10 Nov. 1979: 26-29.

————. *Travesty.* New York: New Directions, 1976.

Hawkes, John, and Albert Guerard. "John Hawkes and Albert Guerard in Dialogue." *A John Hawkes Symposium: Design and Debris.* Ed. Anthony C. Santore and Michael Pocalyko. New York: New Directions, 1977. 14-26.

Hryciw-Wing, Carol A. *John Hawkes: A Research Guide.* New York: Garland, 1986.

James, Henry. Preface to the New York edition of *The Portrait of a Lady. The Art of Criticism: Henry James on the Theory and the Practice of Fiction.* Ed. William Veeder and Susan M. Griffin. Chicago: U of Chicago P, 1986. 286-99.

Klein, Marcus, ed. *The American Novel Since World War II.* Greenwich, CT: Fawcett, 1969.

Klinkowitz, Jerome. "Cross-Currents/Modern Critiques/ Third Series." *The Fiction of William Gass: The Consolation of Language.* By Arthur M. Saltzman. Cross-Currents/Modern Critiques. Carbondale: U of Southern Illinois P, 1986. ix-x.

Koehler, Michael. "'Postmodernismus': Ein begriffsgeschichtlicher Uberblick." *Amerikastudien* 22.1 (1977): 8-18. Unpublished translation by Tom Austenfeld, held in Bowers Library, Wilson Hall, U of Virginia, Charlottesville, VA.

Kuehl, John. *John Hawkes and the Craft of Conflict.* New Brunswick: Rutgers UP, 1975.

Laniel, Christine. "John Hawkes's Return to the Origin: A Genealogy of the Creative Process." *Facing Texts: Encounters Between Contemporary Writers and Critics.* Ed. Heide Ziegler. Durham: Duke UP, 1988. 221-46.

Larson, Magali Sarfatti. *The Rise of Professionalism: A Sociological Analysis.* Berkeley: U of California P, 1977.

McGann, Jerome J. *The Romantic Ideology: A Critical Investigation.* Chicago: U of Chicago P, 1983.

Ziegler, Heide. Preface and Introduction. *Facing Texts: Encounters Between Contemporary Writers and Critics.* Durham: Duke UP, 1988. ix-x, 3-13.

Raymond J. Wilson III

SOURCE: "The Postmodern Novel: The Example of John Irving's 'The World According to Garp'," in *Critique: Studies in Modern Fiction,* Vol. XXXIV, No. 1, Fall, 1992, pp. 49-62.

[*In the following essay, Wilson claims John Irving's* The World According to Garp *as an example of postmodern literature precisely because it borrows stylistically from such diverse writers as James Joyce, John Cheever, and John Barth.*]

As a novel that recapitulates within itself a history of twentieth-century fiction, John Irving's *The World According to Garp* illustrates a key aspect of postmodernism, that of formal replenishment. The earlier segments of *Garp* exhibit strong elements of modernism whereas in its final third, Irving's book is a postmodern novel of bizarre violence and black humor, flat characters, and metafiction—a mode of writing one might expect from the pen of John Barth, Robert Coover, or Thomas Pynchon. Specifically, in its first segment, *Garp* is the artist's *bildingsroman* like James Joyce's *A Portrait of the Artist as a Young Man.* Then *Garp* becomes a mid-century novel of manners dealing with the surface tone, the daily rituals, and the social patterns of American couples, its chief drama being found in adultery and sexual interaction—a novel such as one might have expected from John Updike or John Cheever. However, in John Barth's concept of a literature of exhaustion, imitation of earlier modes is a basic strategy of the postmodern novel. Thus, despite *Garp*'s shifts of mode, as a contemporary fiction operating in three modes, it must be intrinsically postmodern throughout.[1] My analysis proceeds in two stages: first, a theoretical overview of postmodernism, followed by the specific example of *The World According to Garp*.

POSTMODERN FICTION

The term *postmodern* requires careful investigation. Since the 1960s, readers have noticed a difference in some of our fiction; attempting to discuss this new fiction without long circumlocutions, critics invented a term: *postmodern fiction*. Attempts to define this expression followed its use but led to a problem. As John Barth points out, no agreement has been reached on a definition; and because widespread agreement has not yet been reached even for a definition of modernism, we cannot expect a rapid agreement on a definition of postmodernism (Klein 272).[2] In this situation we might find it effective not to attempt a strict logical definition but simply to list those characteristics that first made us notice a difference. In this essay, I suggest a noninclusive list: (1) a propensity to contain and reuse all previous forms in a literature of exhaustion and replenishment; (2) a zone of the bizarre, where fantasy best expresses our sense of reality; (3) a turning away from penetration into the psychological depth of character as the primary goal of fiction; and (4) a propensity for metafiction, in which writing draws attention to the techniques and processes of its own creation.

A literature of exhaustion and replenishment

The postmodern novel contains all the earlier modes of the novel, contains them intrinsically within the process by which a literature of exhausted possibilities replenishes itself. Such commentators as Albert J. La Valley, Herman Kahn, and Christopher Lasch may see causes of change in recent literature in deep cultural contexts. La Valley says that the new literature reflects a new consciousness that has been "inspired in part by the breakdown of our culture, its traditions, and its justifications of the American social structure," (1); Kahn and Wiener refer to our culture as being in the "Late Sensate" stage, our art, including literature, reflecting a culture in the state of decline (40-41); and Lasch argues that "Bourgeois society seems everywhere to have used up its store of constructive ideas" and that there is "a pervasive despair of understanding the course of modern history or of subjecting it to rational direction" (xii). However, the originator of the expression "literature of exhaustion," John Barth, referred to it as "the literature of exhausted possibilities" and says that by "'exhaustion' I don't mean anything so tired as the subject of physical, moral or intellectual decadence, only the usedupness of certain forms or exhaustion of certain possibilities" (Klein 267). Despair might be the reaction of a contemporary writer of fiction when he or she faces the realization that the limited number of possible variations in the form of fiction may have already been explored, but Barth has an answer. While today's author may panic at the idea of being condemned to merely repeat what a Flaubert, a James, a Fitzgerald, or a Joyce has discovered and what countless others have already repeated, Barth finds the situation "by no means necessarily a cause for despair" (Klein 267).

The escape from panic, Barth finds, comes in a story by Borges. In the story "Pierre Menard, Author of *Quixote*," Borges described his character Menard's astonishing effort of will in producing—composing, not copying—several chapters of Cervantes' *Don Quixote*. Borges's narrator points out that despite being verbally identical the recomposition is a new, fresh work: what for Cervantes was merely an everyday, workmanlike style of prose is for Menard a clever, playful use of quaint, semi-antiquated diction; what for Cervantes were mere commonplaces of conventional rhetoric can be for Menard a series of radical, exciting departures from the accepted wisdom of his day. Barth points out that it would have "been sufficient for Menard to have *attributed* the novel to himself in order to have a new work of art, from the intellectual point of view" (Klein 267). However, Barth feels that "the important thing to observe is that Borges *doesn't* attribute the *Quixote* to himself, much less recompose it like Pierre Menard; instead, he writes a remarkable and original work of literature, the implicit theme of which is the difficulty, perhaps the unnecessity, of writing original works of literature. Barth believes that Borges's "artistic victory," emerges from confronting "an intellectual dead end," and employing it "against itself to accomplish new human work" (Klein 272).

In its reuse of earlier forms, we can see how *The World According to Garp* is related to postmodern works by John Barth and Robert Coover. In "Menelaiad," a story in *Lost in the Funhouse*, John Barth parodies the Greek epic form; and in *The Sot-Weed Factor*, Barth contorts the genre of the eighteenth-century novel. It would be a mistake to think that Barth is writing an epic or an eighteenth-century novel. Nor is Barth really writing a Richardsonian epistolary novel in *Letters*. Instead, Barth writes a postmodern novel that plays with the form. Similarly, Coover is not writing a mystery in *Gerald's Party;* instead, this novel, as William Gass is quoted as saying on the dust jacket, "sends up the salon mystery so far it will never come down. What comes down is a terrible indictment of our desires." Just so, *The World According to Garp* plays with the modernist forms of the artist's *bildingsroman* and the mid-century American comedy of manners and necessarily makes an implicit comment upon them, as I shall argue later. *Garp,* by its reuse of modernist forms, stands in the same territory as these works by Barth and Coover.

By reusing existing forms this new fiction opens for itself doors to endless opportunities for freshness. Borges's story, for example, is itself a parody of the critical article. The postmodern novel's parody reveals a literary form returning to its point of origin to renew itself. Barth points out that the *Quixote* is itself a parody of an earlier form—the poetic romance. One thinks immediately of Defoe's stories parodying news articles and his novels in the form of personal reminiscences. Richardson is said to have begun *Pamela* as a model set of letters for young ladies and to have thus invented the English epistolary novel almost by accident.

The zone of the bizarre

Because the term *zone* comes from *Gravity's Rainbow,* this category highlights the relationship between *Garp* and Thomas Pynchon's great novel. Speaking of the zone of occupation in defeated Germany, Brian McHale says that as *Gravity's Rainbow* unfolds, "hallucinations and fantasies become real, metaphors become literal, the fictional worlds of the mass media—the movies, comic-books—thrust themselves into the midst of historical reality." As such, "Pynchon's zone is paradigmatic for the heterotopain space of postmodernist writing" (45). *The World According to Garp* has a zone, as I shall argue, that fits *Gravity's Rainbow*'s paradigm. Brian McHale suggests that behind all the postmodernist fictional construction of zones "lies Apollinaire's poem, 'Zone' (from *Alcools,* 1913), whose speaker, strolling through the immigrant and red-light districts of Paris, finds in them an objective correlative for modern Europe and his own marginal, heterogeneous, and outlaw experience" (44). However, an even better explanation might be found in Philip Roth's observation that "the toughest problem for the American writer was that the substance of the American experience itself was so abnormally and fantastically strange, it had become an 'embarrassment to one's own meager imagination'" (Bellamy 3). "If reality becomes surrealistic," Joe David Bellamy asks, "what must fiction do to be realistic?" (5). It must become bizarre, goes one answer.

The bizarre connects realistic fiction to fantasy and myth. Fantasy is an old form that takes on new implications when used consciously by the contemporary writer, not as an alternative or escape from reality but as the best method available for catching the emotional essence of our era. The distinction between fantasy and myth is not always easy to maintain when one looks at individual stories, although theoretically a mythically structured story may maintain a surface sense of realism the way a fantasy story cannot.

Also connected to the bizarre characteristic of these zones is the postmodern novel's black humor. In *The Fabulators,* Robert Scholes says that black humorists, in a century of historical horror, deal with the absurdity of "the human situation" by seeing it "as a cosmic joke" (45). He suggests that in contrast to the existentialist, the black humorist offers an alternative: "The best response is neither acquiescence nor bitterness"; rather one must play "one's role in the joke in such a way as to turn the humor back on the joker or cause it to diffuse itself harmlessly on the whole group which has participated in the process of the joke" (44).

As the extreme epitome of the atmosphere of much postmodern fiction, the zone of the bizarre compensates for its retreat from the strict tenets of realism by evoking echoes of no-less-real feelings from our personas pasts, feelings that today we can experience only in dreams or in moments of great stress—of terror, perhaps—when our "normal" functioning breaks down. Although we repress these feelings, we react with a mixture of anxiety and secret welcoming when the television news reports events that cannot be grasped without reference to such emotions. Through the bizarre, postmodern fiction taps and reflects this source of emotional power and does so, not despite, but because of its departure from the formal tenets of "realism," which center on an attempt to penetrate into the depths of character.

The turn away from psychological depth in character

Umberto Eco notes the shift in contemporary novels, where an author "renounces all psychology as the motive of narrative and decides to transfer characters and situations to the level of an objective structural strategy." Eco sees this "choice familiar to many contemporary disciplines" as one in which an author passes "from the psychological method to the formalistic one" (146). Eco's words fit with Robert Scholes's prediction that the key element in the coming new fiction would be a new dimension of the "care for form" (41). This noncharacter orientation provides a point of reference between *The World According to Garp* and Robert Coover's *The Universal Baseball Association,* which is organized neither by plot nor by revelation of its intentionally flat characters but by the structural relationship of game and ritual and the progressive transformation of the one into the other.

Metafiction

Metafiction is another instance where fiction turns away from outside reality and seeks a subject intrinsically suited to the written word. In this method, the technique of composition becomes to some extent the subject of fiction itself.[3] If television and movies are vastly better adapted to creating an illusion of reality—the depiction of objects—then fiction must find other subjects for its own surivival, just as painting turned to the nonrepresentational when painters recognized the photograph's power to recreate a scene accurately. In the metafictional dimension, we see the connection of *The World According to Garp* to other postmodern fiction, for example to the stories John Barth's *Lost in the Funhouse,* especially the title story, in which the implied author presents himself as trying—and failing—to write a conventional story by the cookbook-recipe method but actually writing a postmodern story. Of another story in the volume, "Autobiography," Barth says in his author's note, that it is "the story, speaking of itself" (x).

THE WORLD ACCORDING TO GARP AS POSTMODERN FICTION

Reuse of earlier forms

As a novel that shifts from mode to mode, *The World According to Garp* illustrates the postmodern as a literature of replenishment: *Garp* recapitulates within itself a history of the twentieth-century novel, performing a tacit critique of the earlier forms. Irving starts in an early twentieth-century mode. Reviewing the fiction of this era, Irving Howe (Klein 124-41) says that whereas nineteenth-century realism studied social classes, early twentieth-century fiction studied the rebellion of the Stephen Dedaluses against behavior patterns imposed by social classes in a particular country. In this conception, the modern novel came into being when James Joyce reconstructed the existing form of the *bildingsroman* to create *A Portrait*.[4] More than merely recasting the autobiographical novel into the "individuating rhythm" of *Dubliners,* Joyce helped form the modern consciousness itself. D. H. Lawrence's *Sons and Lovers* shares this feature with Joyce's *A Portrait;* and although Lawrence's novel retains more of the trappings of nineteenth-century realism than Joyce's book, both create characters that do not fit into their own world but who express an aesthetic that is familiar in our intellectual climate.[5] John Irving achieves similar effects in his *bildingsroman.*

The *bildingsroman* form is suited to linearity of narrative flow, reflecting the linear growth of a boy's life. In the McCaffery interview, John Irving claimed that he was "very conscious of attempting to make my narrative as absolutely linear as possible. . . . With my first four novels I was always troubled," says Irving, "particularly with *Garp,* about the convoluted flow of my narrative. . . . *Garp* was, in fact, a kind of minor breakthrough for me just in the sense that it was the first novel I managed to order chronologically" (11). Irving rejects the unreadable masterpieces of high modernist literature and implies that he is returning to the simpler forms of earlier days; however, no nineteenth-century author could have written *The World According to Garp.* John Irving is moving on into postmodernism, as the three-segment analysis of the novel can demonstrate.

As in the early works of Joyce and Lawrence, the opening section of *Garp* fits the genre's depiction of parents and childhood surroundings. In the chapter entitled "Blood and Blue," Garp's near fall from a roof and his being bitten by a dog parallel Stephen Dedalus's being shouldered into a playground puddle and having his hands smacked by his teacher. And similarly, the succeeding chapters fulfill other criteria for the genre, combining Garp's sexual initiation with an encounter with pain and death in the demise of a prostitute named Charlotte.

Garp's involvement with the death of this "whore," whom he had come to know better than Joyce's Stephen knew the prostitutes he visited, precipitates Garp's forming his working aesthetic as a writer. Combined with the play of Garp's imagination on the war damage at the Vienna zoo, the death of Charlotte ties Garp's emergence as an adult to his emergence as a writer: a creator and reflector of modern consciousness like Stephen Dedalus. Garp had been unable to finish the story that would make him a "real writer." "The Pension Grillparzer," as the story was called, consisted of two major elements that Garp was having trouble reconciling: a continuous line of hilarious, almost farcical action, low comedy, approaching slapstick that coexisted with a somber theme generated by a dream-omen of death. After Charlotte's death, Garp fell under "a writer's long-sought trance, wherein the world falls under

one embracing tone of voice" (118). Here, Irving's narrator emphasizes the importance of what Gerard Genette, following Tzvetan Todorov, has called "aspect," or "the way in which the story is perceived by the narrator" (29).

Visiting the zoo that still bore the signs of war damage, "Garp discovered that when you are writing something, everything seems related to everything else" (119). In the evidences of war Garp saw the connection between larger human history and each person's individual history and so was able to finish the story. His notion of modern, consciousness is that "the history of a city was like the history of a family—there is a closeness, and even affection, but death eventually separates everyone from each other" (119). It may be that this is an aesthetic as appropriate for the post-Hiroshima era as Stephen Dedalus's aesthetic was for the era he heralded. Finishing the story after having formed his guiding aesthetic, Garp met Helen's standard for a "real" writer and thus "earned" a wife for himself. Thus, Irving completed the segment of the novel with the forecast that "in their stubborn, deliberate ways," Helen and Garp would fall in love with each other "sometime after they had married" (130).

Irving's implicit comment on the Joycean *bildingsroman* is ironic. By writing in the form, Irving is affirming the value of the early modernist mode, despite his rejection of excessively complicated modernist literature in the McCaffery interview (11). However, even an affirmation is a comment, and a comment on modernism is not modernism; by its nature, a comment on modernism must be something standing outside of modernism, viewing it, and implicitly judging it. The existence of bizarre violence and the associated vein of black humor, even in the first section of the book, contributes to irony. The novel opens to the backdrop of a war, and Jenny Field's brusque categorizing of the wounded into classes of Externals, Vital Organs, Absentees, and Goners certainly contains an element of the blackly humorous. In its vividness, Jenny's slashing of a persistent masher verges on the gothic. Garp's being bitten by a dog is merely an element of *bildingsroman,* but Garp's biting off the ear of the dog verges on the bizarre. With their hint of anti-realist absurdism, these elements provide a counterpoint to the modernist mode, repeatedly rupturing it, threatening to radicalize the novel into the postmodern, and foreshadowing the third section where the transformation does occur. Implict in these reptures is the notion that the early modernist mode has difficulty expressing a contemporary reality that itself has become postmodern.

A similar point and counterpoint arises in the second section of the novel. Here, John Irving introduces a mid-century novel of manners, a section of *Garp* that approximates the aura of an Updike novel or a Cheever story.[6] The central characteristic of the cultural attitude found in mid-century can be illuminated by an insight Stanley Kaufmann drew from the words of a contemporary Italian filmmaker: "When Vittorio de Sica was asked why so many of his films deal with adultery, he is said to have replied, 'But if you take adultery out of the lives of the bourgeoisie, what drama is left?'"[7] The middle segment of Irving's novel, which culminates with Garp's discovery of Helen's affair with Michael Milton, contains the tale of a suburban marriage, its fidelities and infidelities: Garp's sexual encounter with a babysitter, his resisting an attempted seduction by "Mrs. Ralph," and a temporary swap of sexual partners between the Garps and a couple named Harry and Alice—a situation like that with which Updike dealt in his novel *Couples.*

The suburban domestic tale fits Howe's belief that mid-century fiction, having abandoned the rebellious stance of a Stephen Dedalus, studied the search for values (looking for them, to some degree, in marriage) by a people who live in a world where social class may still exist but where it no longer dominates every detail of daily existence or predestines one to as limited a range of expectations as did the earlier class system (136). Fitting with Howe's analysis, the point of reference in the middle of *Garp,* as in the mainstream American novel in the middle of the century, is sociological; the question asked is whether monogamous marriage, as it is found in suburbia, can sustain or bring happiness to people of any sensitivity. What Garp said about his second novel might describe both the midsection of *Garp* and the American novel at mid-century: it was "a serious comedy about marriage," Garp said, "but a sexual farce" (160).

The central section is made ironic by isolated outcroppings of the bizarre, which implicitly undermine our belief in the fruitfulness of this modernist form. The marriage-comedy/sex-farce enclosed an episode in which Garp helps in the capture of a man who habitually rapes little girls, a sequence that takes on ominous implications when Garp happens to meet the rapist who has been released on a legal technicality, collecting tickets at a basketball game. Implicit in the counterpoint created by the intrusion of public and epochal violence into the private and personal is the conclusion that a mode, such as mid-century modernist realism, the Updike/Cheever comedy of manners, which exists to reveal the private and personal, loses its force.

The reader can guess at the historical moment recreated in Irving's implicit irony from a comment Saul Bellow made about novelists of the early 1960s who sought to "examine the private life." Bellow says that some "cannot find the [private] life they are going to examine. The power of public life has become so vast and threatening that private life cannot maintain a pretense of its importance" (25). Unhappy with the situation in which modernist fiction found itself, some authors began turning away, as Irving Howe has noted, from "realistic portraiture" to express their spirit in "fable, picaresque, prophecy, and nostalgia." Novels by these writers, Howe says, "constitute what I would class 'post-modern fiction.'" (137). Howe was identifying a trend that came to be designated, much more inclusively, by the term he used in 1959.

We are deeply involved in the serio-comic complications of Garp's marriage-comedy/sex-farce when an auto accident wrenches us into the postmodern mode—the accident that killed one of Garp's little boys and maimed the other. The transfer between modes comes from a shattering experience—the accident and its physical and emotional consequences. An analogy (with an important difference) can be seen in the work of Saul Bellow. Irving Howe says that when Bellow writes in *Henderson the Rain King,* "that men need a shattering experience to 'wake the spirit's sleep,' we soon realize that his ultimate reference is to America, where many spirits sleep." (Klein 22-29). Bellow, though he keeps his mode in the realistic mainstream, takes his character to Africa for the shattering experience; Irving keeps the scene in America, but this America has become a postmodern "zone" and is no longer the familiar scene of an Updike novel.

The zone of the bizarre

The nearly gothic episodes of the first two sections prepare us for the novel's final section. The salient events in the third section are intrusions of public life into the private: assassinations, mob violence, and highway mayhem, much of it not accidental. The public/private dichotomy presents itself most clearly in Garp's refusal to accept the fact that a strictly women's memorial service for his mother, Jenny Fields, is not a private funeral but a public, political event. It would be unthinkable to bar a son from the one, but unthinkable to welcome a man to the other.

As for the bizarre, not only is the setting moved to Jenny Field's madcap home for "injured women" at Don's Head Harbor; but even more significantly, we suddenly find ourselves in a world as strange as the fictional zones of a Thomas Pynchon or a John Hawkes, if not one reaching the extremes of a William Burroughs. In the final section of Irving's novel, T. S. Garp expresses the dominant feeling: "*Life* is an X-rated soap opera" (338). Akin to both fantasy and myth, this feeling becomes progressively objectified when the horrible "Under Toad" first grows from a family joke, introduced analeptically, into a code word for speaking about a hovering fear. Then, although the reader's mind tries to reject overt supernaturalism, the Under Toad becomes a veritable character, a vengeful beast who at times becomes as real as Grendel in the Old English poem. The myth-fantasy dimension of Irving's novel would thus partake of what Tzvetan Todorov calls "the fantastic"; in the book of that name, Todorov defines the state as a hovering between "the uncanny," in which apparently supernatural events receive some ultimate explanation, and "the marvelous," in which the supernatural becomes the norm. McHale finds such "hesitation" to be characteristic of postmodernist fiction (74-76).

Significantly, the Under Toad is mentioned only in the third section of the book, although its origin—in a little boy's misunderstanding of his father's warning about the "undertow" on the beach—occurs in the chronological middle of the book. There may be technical reasons why Irving decided to develop the Under Toad only in retrospect, after the reader knows of little Walt's death. Even so, it is clear that the fantasy and myth aspects of the Under Toad contribute to a mode of postmodernism in the novel's concluding section, reminding us for example of Pynchon's notion that the modern world can only be fathomed through the agency of paranoia. The Under Toad's myth and fantasy elements would have been less appropriate in the more realistic, comic-farce mode of *Garp*'s center section, but they provide an ideal backdrop for black humor.

Garp's death itself typifies black humor "in its random, stupid, and unnecessary qualities—comic and ugly and bizarre" in the words of the novel itself (414). "In the world according to Garp," the novel says, "an evening could be hilarious and the next morning could be murderous" (406). These elements of the bizarre, myth/fantasy, and black humor distract the reader from a feature that arouses curiosity when first noticed, that the characters have flattened out.

Flatness of character

The third section, more than the first two, bears out the postmodern ethic by which to declare a character psychologically flat need not be to denigrate the author's skill. Irving's mistrust of over psychologizing may have led to his statement that "the phrase 'psychologically deep' is a contradiction of terms." Irving feels that such a view "is a terribly simplistic and unimaginative approach. Ultimately it is destructive of all the breadth and complexity in literature" (McCaffery interview 11). Complexity in the final third of *Garp* arises from structure, from ironic genre manipulation, from the problematic nature of the text's relationship to the world, and not from any probing of psychological motive that might lead to internal character revelation. The third section of the text is marked by a lack of interest in motive: of assassins, of the Ellen Jamesians, of Garp when he insists on performing actions that he knows draw destruction down upon himself, even though he desires safety. While reflecting the postmodern distrust of "the subject" as a useful category, the flattening of character in the third section of *Garp* may, even more, express a sense of the individual's powerlessness within an absurd situation.

The novel draws its unity, not from continuity of plot, as in the premodernist novel, nor from analysis of character, a feature of modernist fiction, but partially from the operation of motif: a repetition of impaired speech that interacts with a counter-motif of "writing." Garp's father had a speech impediment stemming from profound brain damage suffered in war. From then on, the novel contains numerous other instances of impaired speech, depicted either as a temporary or a permanent condition. Apparently permanently afflicted are Alice Hindman, whose speech problem is a psychological outgrowth of her marriage problems; Ellen James, who was raped and left tongueless by men who did not have the sense to realize that she was old enough to implicate them by writing; the Ellen Jamesians, women who have their tongues removed in sympathy with Ellen; and Garp's high school English teacher Tinch and Tinch's eventual replacement, Donald Whitcomb who was to become Garp's biographer. Temporarily

"struck dumb" were the young girl whose rapist Garp had helped capture, and Garp himself—for a long while after his auto accident and for the few moments he lived after being shot by Pooh Percy. Pooh's rage, her inarticulate curses from a gaping self-wounded mouth, forms a near-tableau at the end of Garp's life to match the one at its beginning when his future father's decreasing level of articulation from "Garp" to "Arp" to "Ar" led Jenny to realize that he was soon to die and spurred her to get on with the business of Garp's conception. In between, Garp was to wonder "Why is my life so full of people with impaired speech?" He then asks, "Or is it only because I'm a writer that I notice all the damaged voices around me?" (364).

Compensating for the flatness of character, providing coherence within the zone of the bizarre, these repeated elements are the motor oil for the postmodern fictional machine. Their theme of speech brings us to the author's means of speaking to us, his fiction. Having made ironic modernist realism's implicit claim to tell us about the world, the postmodern fictionist has questioned the writer's own instrument, and he or she thus often turns to examine it in the reader's presence. Irving is not exempt from this tendency toward metafiction.

Metafiction

Irving's novel alludes to the phenomenon of metafiction when discussing the rejection note that Garp received for "The Pension Grillparzer": *"The story is only mildly interesting, and it does nothing new with language or with form"* (129). Tinch, Garp's former instructor, said he really did not understand the "newer fiction" except that it was supposed to be "about it-it-itself. . . . It's sort of fiction about fi-fi-*fiction*," Tinch told Garp. Garp did not understand either and, in truth, cared mainly about the fact that Helen liked the story. But although Garp was not interested in metafiction at this stage of his career, we can see that Irving is to some degree practicing this aspect of the new fiction in the third section of *Garp*. While the accounts of Garp's earlier novels may bear a certain resemblance to Irving's own earlier works, these need not be considered metafictional manifestations; one merely suspects Irving of a certain wry humor of self parody, while he remains in the traditional mode of autobiographical fiction or even within the mere technique of an author drawing on his own experience for his fiction.[8] In contrast, when we enter the third section we encounter Garp's novel *The World According to Bensenhaver,* with its obvious similarity in title to *The World According to Garp*. Although there are significant differences between the novel we are reading and the one we are reading about, the parallels and even the comedy of the differences cannot help but act as implicit comments upon the technique and compositional process of *Garp*.

"'Life,' Garp wrote," according to the novel, "'is sadly *not* structured like a good old-fashioned novel. Instead, an ending occurs where those who are meant to peter out have petered out'" (418). Such a metafictional comment in the third section does not surprise us. Indeed, we see this mode occurring repeatedly. When Garp's publisher, John Wolf, was dying he asked Garp's son Duncan "What would your father say to this? . . . Wouldn't it suit one of *his* death scenes? Isn't it properly grotesque?" (423). To the extent that we could ask this question equally of Irving as of Garp, the question has metafictional implications, as does what Wolf said about Garp's own grotesque mode of dying: "It was a death scene, John Wolf told Jillsy Sloper, that only Garp could have written" (414). When a character in a novel says that a death scene in that novel occurred in a way which "only" the dying character could have written, we are involved with metafiction.

The structure of the final chapter, which opens with a comment on Garp's fictional technique, has further metafictional implications: "He loved epilogues, as he showed us in 'The Pension Grillparzer.' 'An epilogue,' Garp wrote, 'is more than a body count. An epilogue, in the disguise of wrapping up the past, is really a way of warning us about the future'" (407). And the final chapter—the nineteenth, identical to the number of chapters in *The World According to Bensenhaver*—ends with just such an epilogue. Irving's narrator makes the metafictional element nearly explicit: "He would have liked the idea of an epilogue, too," says the narrator after Garp's death, "—so here it is: an epilogue 'warning us about the future,' as T. S. Garp might have imagined it" (414). Thus the final twenty pages of the novel present us the interesting metafictional situation of an author writing the epilogue to his character's death as the narrator says the character would himself have imagined it. Metafiction, combined with the zone of the bizarre and the turn away from psychological depth makes the third section of the novel postmodern. While the first two thirds exhibit far less of these characteristics and more of those of earlier modes, these sections exhibit the postmodern reuse of earlier forms; thus, *Garp* is postmodern throughout.

In writing this novel, Irving stays true to his rejecting the spirit of the unreadable masterpieces of high modernism, but he is not returning to the mode of the nineteenth century; he is moving forward into postmodernism. In his desire to avoid the esoteric, Irving might find an ally in John Barth, who in "The Literature of Replenishment: Postmodernist Fiction" offers his "worthy program" in hopes that the postmodern mode may become a fiction "more democratic in its appeal" than the marvels of late modernism, reaching beyond the "professional devotees of high art" but perhaps not hoping to reach the "lobotomized mass-media illiterates" (Klein 70). In its best-seller popularity, *The World According to Garp* has at least fulfilled that aspect of Barth's program for postmodern fiction. This success may be described by the proposition that the postmodern novel, besides its special characteristics, also contains all earlier fictional forms, and John Irving's use of two of them opens his novel to a fruitful variety of combination and interaction.

NOTES

[1] Linda Hutcheon explores the specifically postmodern implications of genre manipulation in *A Theory of Parody*.

[2] Barth discusses the arguments of Gerald Graff, Robert Alter, and Ihab Hassan in "The Literature of Replenishment: Postmodernist Fiction." Events have proved Barth correct: writing in 1989 of the debate over a definition for the postmodern, Dietmar Voss and Jochen C. Schutze say that the participants "seem to agree on one thing: that there is the greatest possible disagreement as to what postmodernism is." The term "resists comprehensive definition," they say, and it "appears, at the same time, to accept content so arbitrarily that some commentators are deluded into regarding this arbitrariness itself as an essential characteristic of postmodernism" (119).

[3] Linda Hutcheon examines the technique in her *Narcissistic Narrative*.

[4] For a definition of *bildingsroman*, see Cuddon (78); Cuddon also defines *kunstlerroman* (246), an artist's *bildingsroman*, but Joyce was doing more than writing a *kunstlerroman*.

[5] The expression "individuating rhythm" comes from Joyce (65) in an essay discussed by Litz (61). Among authors seeing the artist's *bildingsroman* as a specifically modern form are Scholes (18) and Sukenick (42).

[6] Irving admires Cheever and feels "a great affinity with the class of people" that Cheever "writes about": upper-class people in trouble or pain, Irving (McCaffery interview 17).

[7] The insight is attributed to Stanley Kaufmann by Howe in Klein (136).

[8] In the McCaffery interview, Irving says that "there is a lot of self-parody" in *Garp*, "spoofs of my earlier works, games I'm having fun with" (7). Irving considers "autobiography as being merely a stepping-off point in fiction" (3).

WORKS CITED

Barth, John. "The Literature of Exhaustion." *The Atlantic,* CCXX (August 1967): 29-34; rpt. in Klein, *The American Novel.* 267-279.

————. *Lost in the Funhouse.* 1968. New York: Bantam, 1978.

————. "The Literature of Replenishment: Postmodernist Fiction," *Atlantic Monthly,* (Jan. 1980): 56-71; rpt. in Klein, *The American Novel.*

Bellamy, Joe David. *Superfiction or the American Story Transformed: An Anthology.* New York: Vintage, 1975. 3-28.

Bellow, Saul. "Some Notes on Recent American Fiction." *Encounter* (November 1963): 22-29; rpt. Klein, *The American Novel.* 159-74.

Coover, Robert. *Gerald's Party.* New York: Simon and Schuster, 1986.

Cuddon, J. A. *A Dictionary of Literary Terms.* Garden City, NY: Doubleday, 1979.

Eco, Umberto. *Role of the Reader: Explorations in the Semiotics of Texts.* Bloomington: Indiana UP, 1979.

Genette, Gerard. *Narrative Discourse: An Essay in Method.* Trans. Jane E. Lewin. Ithaca: Cornell, 1980.

Howe, Irving. "Mass Society and Post-Modern Fiction." *Partisan Review* (Summer 1959): 420-36; rpt. Klein, *The American Novel.* 124-141.

Hutcheon, Linda. *A Theory of Parody: The Teachings of Twentieth-Century Art Forms.* London: Methuen, 1985.

———. *Narcissistic Narrative: The Metafictional Paradox.* Waterloo, Ontario: Wilfred Laurier UP, 1980.

———. *A Poetics of Postmodernism: History, Theory, Fiction.* New York: Routledge, 1988.

Irving, John. "An Interview with John Irving." With Larry McCaffery. *Contemporary Literature,* 23, 1 (Winter 1982): 3-15.

———. *The World According to Garp.* New York: Dutton, 1978.

Joyce, James. "A Portrait of the Artist," in *The Workshop of Daedalus,* ed. Robert Scholes and Richard M. Kain. Evanston: Indiana UP, 1965, 55-69.

Kahn, Herman and Anthony J. Wiener. *The Year 2000.* New York: Macmillan, 1967.

Klein, Marcus. *The American Novel Since World War Two.* New York: Fawcett, 1969.

Lasch, Christopher. *The Culture of Narcissism.* New York: Norton, 1979.

La Valley, Albert J. "Introduction," *The New Consciousness.* Cambridge, Massachusetts: Winthrop, 1972.

Litz, A. Walton. *James Joyce.* New York: Twayne, 1966.

McHale, Brian. *Postmodernist Fiction.* New York: Methuen, 1987.

Scholes, Robert. *The Fabulators.* New York: Oxford, 1967.

Sukenick, Ronald. "The New Tradition in Fiction," *Surfiction,* ed. Raymond Federman. Chicago: Swallow, 1981. Second edition, enlarged.

Todorov, Tzvetan (1970). *The Fantastic: A Structural Approach to a Literary Genre,* Trans. Richard Howard. Ithaca: Cornell UP, 1975.

———. "Les Categories du recit litteraire." *Communications,* 8 (1966).

Voss, Dietmar and Jochen C. Schutze. "Postmodernism in Context: Perspectives of a Structural Change in Society, Literature, and Literary Criticism," *New German Critique* 47 (Spring/Summer 1989): 119-42.

Raymond Federman

SOURCE: "Surfiction: A Postmodern Position," in *Critifiction: Postmodern Essays,* State University of New York Press, 1993, pp. 35-47.

[*In the following essay, Federman proposes that surfiction is the only contemporary literature that revels in humankind's intellect, imagination, and irrationality because it recognizes life itself as fiction.*]

> *Now some people might say that the situation of fiction today is not very encouraging, but one must reply that it is not meant to encourage those who say that!*

> —Raymond Federman

Writing about fiction today, one could begin with the usual clichés: the novel is dead; writing fiction is no longer possible nor necessary because **real** fiction happens, everyday, in the streets of our cities, in the spectacular hijacking of planes, in space, on the Moon, in the Middle-East, in China, in Eastern Europe, and of course on television (especially during the news broadcasts); fiction has become obsolete and irrelevant because life has become much more interesting, much more dramatic, much more intriguing and incredible than what the dying novel can possibly offer.

And one could go on saying that writing fiction is now impossible (as many theoreticians and practitioners of fiction have demonstrated lately) because all the possibilities of fiction have been used up, abused, exhausted, and therefore all that is left, to the one who still insists on writing fiction, is to repeat (page after page, *ad nauseam*) that there is nothing to write about, nothing with which to write, and thus simply continue to write that there is nothing to write (as for instance the so-called *Nouveau Roman* in France has been doing for the past forty years).

Indeed, such works of non-fiction as Truman Capote's *In Cold Blood,* or Norman Mailer's *The Day Kennedy Was Shot* and *Armies of the Night,* or Hunter Thompson's *Fear and Loathing in Las Vegas,* and all those books written recently about terrorism, drug trafficking, violence, financial success or financial disaster, political scandals, and all those autobiographies written by people who supposedly have experienced **real life** in the streets of our cities, in the ghettos, in the jails, in the political arena, on the stock-markets of the world, are possibly better fictions thant the foolish and vacuous stories (love stories, murder stories, spy stories, adventure stories, sexual deviate stories, the rich and the famous stories, and so on) the novel—the commercial novel that is—is still trying to peddle and make us believe.

Yes, one could start this way, and simply give upon fiction, abandon the novel forever. For as Samuel Beckett once said: "It is easy to talk about being unable, whereas in reality nothing is more difficult."

Well, I propose that the novel is far from being dead (and I mean now the traditional novel—that moribund novel that became moribund the day it was conceived, some four hundred years ago when Cervantes wrote *Don Quixote*). I propose that, in fact, this type of novel is still very much alive—very **healthy** and very **wealthy** too. I know many novelists who can brag that their latest book has brought them one million dollars, two million dollars, or more. James Michener, Harold Robbins, Judith Krantz are only three of the many second-rate rich novelists who should be mentioned. No, the commercial novel is not dead; it is quite prosperous in some parts of the world.

But if we are to talk seriously about fiction—**serious** fiction—this is not the kind of writers and the kind of fiction I am interested in. The kind of fiction I am interested in is that fiction that those who control the literary establishment (publishers, editors, agents, reviewers, booksellers, etc.) brush aside because it does not conform to their notions of what fiction should be, or how it should be written, and consequently has no value (commercial that is) for the common reader. And the easiest way for these people to brush aside that kind of fiction is to label it, quickly and bluntly, as **experimental.**

Everything that does not fall into the category of successful fiction (commercially that is), or what Jean-Paul Sartre once called *"la littérature alimentaire"* (nutritious literature), everything that is found "unreadable for our readers" (that's the way publishers and editors speak—but who gave them the right to decide what is **readable** or **valuable** for the readers?) is immediately relegated to the domain of experimentation—a safe and useless place.

Personally I do not believe that a fiction writer with the least amount of self-respect and integrity, and who believes in what he is doing, ever says to himself: "I am now going to write an experimental novel." Others say that about his work. It is the middleman, the procurer of literature (the failed novelist turned editor or journalist) who gives that label **EXPERIMENTAL** to what is unusual, difficult, innovative, provocative, intellectually challenging, and even original. In fact, true experiments (as in the sciences) never reach, or at least should never reach the printed page. A novel is always a form of experiment, and therefore becomes an experience. After all the two terms were synonymous at one time. Fiction is called experimental out of incomprehension and despair. it is those who are unwilling to give to a novel what it demands intellectually that declares that novel experimental. Samuel Backett's novels are not experimental—no!—it is the only

way he could write them; Jorge Luis Borges' stories are not experimental; Italo Calvino's fiction is not experimental; or going back in time to James Joyce or Franz Kafka, their fiction is not experimental (even though it was called that when it first appeared and is still called that by those who cannot accept what departs from the norm or refuses to submit to simple-mindedness). All these writers created successful and accomplished works of art that function on their own terms rather than on a set of predetermined rules.

And so, for me, the only fiction that still means something today is the kind of fiction that tries to explore the possibilities of fiction beyond its own limitations; the kind of fiction that challenges the tradition that governs it; the kind of fiction that constantly renews our faith in man's intelligence and imagination rather than man's distorted view of reality; the kind of fiction that reveals man's playful irrationality rather than his righteous rationality.

This I call **SURFICTION.** However, not because it imitates reality, but because it exposes the ictionality of reality. Just as the Surrealists called that level of man's experience that functions in the subconscious **SURREALITY,** I call that level of man's activity that reveals life as a fiction **SURFICTION.** In this sense there is some truth in the cliché that claims that "life imitates fiction," or that "life is like fiction," but not because of what is happening in the streets of our cities, but because reality as such does not exist, or rather exists only in its fictionalized version, that is to say in the language that describes it.

The experiences of life gain meaning only in their recounted form, in their verbalized versions, or as Louis-Ferdinand Céline stated, some years ago, in answer to those who claimed that his novels were barely disguised autobiographies: "Life, also, is fiction . . . and a biography is something one invents afterwards."

But in what sense is life fiction? To live is to understand that one lives, and fiction is above all an effort to apprehend and comprehend human existence played on the level of words, and only on the level of words. Or as Roland Barthes once put it: "The book creates meaning, and meaning creates life." In other words, fiction is made of understanding which for most of us means primarily words—only words (spoken or written). Therefore, if one admits from the start (at least to oneself) that no meaning precedes language, but that language creates meaning as it goes along, that is to say as it is used (spoken or written), as it progresses, then writing (fiction especially) will be a mere process of letting language do its tricks.

To write, then, is to **PRODUCE** meaning, and not **REPRODUCE** a pre-existing meaning. To write is to **PROGRESS,** and not **REMAIN** subjected (by habit or reflexes) to the meaning that supposedly precedes language. As such fiction can no longer be reality, or an imitation of reality, or a representation of reality, or even a re-creation of reality; it can only be itself a reality—an autonomous reality whose only relation to the real world is to improve that world. To create fiction today is, in fact, to transform reality, and to some extent even abolish reality, and especially abolish the notion that reality is truth.

Therefore, rather than serving as a mirror or redoubling on itself, fiction adds itself to the world thus creating a meaningful relation that did not previously exist. Though fiction is often viewed as an artifice, it is not artificial. To write fiction today is before all an effort to create a **DIF-FERENCE,** and not to pretend that fiction is the same thing as reality. The traditional realistic novel was a representation of the **SAME.** Surfiction will be a presentation of difference—a liberation of what is different.

Defining the contemporary discourse, Michel Foucault wrote some twenty years ago: "In order to liberate difference we must have a contradictory thought, free of dialectic, free of negation. A thought that says yes to divergence; an affirmative thought, whose instrument is disjunction; a thought of the multiple; a thought that does not obey a scholarly model, but that addresses insoluble problems within a play of repetition."

Though Michel Foucault was only trying to define how the contemporary historical or philosophical discourse ought to function, his definition seems applicable to the surfictional discourse as well. Far from being the incomplete and blurred image of an **IDEA** which, from time immemorial, held some absolute answer, the problem of fiction today is to affirm an **IDEA** in which the question never ceases to be displaced toward another question. What is the answer to this question? The problem itself. How to solve this problem? By constantly displacing the question. That, in effect, is how Surfiction functions.

Displacement, difference, and repetition, these are the givens of Surfiction, and no longer faithful imitation and truthful representation. Consequently, in the fiction of today and tomorrow, all distinctions between the real and the imaginary, between the conscious and the subconscious, between the past and the present, between truth and untruth will be abolished. All forms of duplicity will disappear. And above all, all forms of duality will be negated—yes, especially duality: that double-headed monster which for centuries subjected us to a system of ethical and aesthetical values based on the principles of good and bad, true and false, beautiful and ugly.

Surfiction will not be judged on such principles. It will neither be good nor bad, true nor false, beautiful nor ugly. It will simply **BE,** and its primary purpose will be to unmask its own fictionality, to expose the metaphor of its own fraudulence and simulacrum, and not pretend any longer to pass for reality, for truth, or for beauty.

As a result, Surfiction will no longer be regarded as a mirror of life, as a pseudorealistic document that informs us about life, nor will it be judged on the basis of its social, moral, psychological, metaphysical, or commercial value, but only on the basis of what it is and what it does

as an autonomous art form in its own right—just as poetry, music or the plastic arts are autonomous.

These preliminary remarks serve as an introduction to four propositions I would now like to make for the present-future of fiction. These are but an arbitrary starting point for the possibilities of a New Fiction. Other positions and other propositions are possible. My propositions will be dogmatic, but that's how it should be, because this text is in fact a manifesto for Surfiction, and as such it can only be dogmatic. One accepts or rejects a manifesto in its entirety, but one cannot argue with it. That is the ironic idea inscribed in the epigraph to this text (quoted from one of my surfictional novels) which I want to reaffirm in order to discourage those who will disagree with me: "Now some people might say that the situation of fiction today is not very encouraging but one must reply that it is not meant to encourage those who say that!"

PROPOSITION ONE—THE READING OF FICTION

The very act of reading a book, starting at the top of the first page, and moving from left to right, top to bottom, page after page to the end in a consecutive prearranged manner has become *restrictive and boring.* Indeed, any intelligent reader should feel frustrated and restricted within that preordained system of reading.

Therefore, the whole traditional, conventional, fixed, and boring method of reading a book must be questioned, challenged, and demolished. And it is the writer (and not modern printing technology alone) who must, through innovations in the writing itself—in the typography of the text and the topography of the book—renew our system of reading.

All the rules and principles of printing and bookmaking must be forced to change as a result of the changes in the writing (or the telling) of a story in order to give the reader a sense of free participation in the writing/reading process, in order to give the reader an element of choice (active choice) in the ordering of the discourse and the discovery of its meaning.

Thus the very concept of syntax must be transformed. Syntax, traditionally, is the unity, the continuity of words, the law that dominates them. Syntax reduces the multiplicity of words and controls their energy and their violence. It fixes words into a place, a space, and prescribes an order to them. It prevents words from wandering. Even if it is hidden, syntax always reigns on the horizon of words which buckle under its mute exigency.

Therefore, words, sentences, paragraphs (and of course the punctuation) and their position on the page and in the book must be rethought and rewritten so that new ways (multiple and simultaneous ways) of reading these can be created. And even the typographical design of the pages and the numbering of these pages must be reinvented. The space itself in which writing takes place must be transformed. That space—the page, but also the book made of pages—must acquire new dimensions, new shapes, new relations in order to accommodate the new writing. Pages no longer need to be the same uniform rectangular size, and books no longer need to be rectangular boxes. It is within this transformed topography of writing, from this new **paginal syntax** rather than **grammatical syntax** that the reader will discover his freedom in relation to the process of reading a book, in relation to language.

In all other art forms there are always three essential elements at play: the creator who fabricates the work of art, the medium through which the work of art is transmitted, and the receiver (listener or viewer) to whom the work of art is transmitted. It seems that in the writing of fiction only the first and the third elements are at work: the writer and the reader. Me and you. And the medium—and by medium I do not mean the story or the mental cinema one plays while reading fiction, but the language itself—is forgotten. It becomes absent, or rather it is absented, negated by the process of reading, as if it were transparent, as if it were there only to carry the reader into the realm of illusions. Is it because while reading fiction one does not think of the language as being auditory or visual (as in music, painting, and even poetry) that it merely serves as a means of transportation from the author to the reader? From me to you, from what I supposedly meant to what you supposedly understand of my meaning? This obsolete form of reading devaluates the medium of fiction, reduces language to a mere function.

If we are to make of the novel an art form, we must raise the printed word as the medium, and therefore **where** and **how** it is placed on the page makes a difference in what the fiction will be for the reader. In other words, we as fiction writers must render language concrete and visible so that it will be more than just a functional thing that supposedly reflects reality. Thus, not only the writer will create the fiction, but all those involved in the producing and ordering of that fiction; the typist, the editor, the typesetter, the printer, the proofreader, and of course the reader will all partake of the fiction. The real medium will be the printed words as they are presented on the page, as they are perceived, heard, visualized (not abstractly but concretely), as they are read by all those involved in the making of the book.

PROPOSITION TWO—THE SHAPE OF FICTION

If life and fiction are no longer distinguishable one from the other, nor complementary to one another, and if we agree that life is never linear, that in fact life is always discontinuous and chaotic because it is never experienced in a straight line or an orderly fashion, then similarly linear, chronological, and sequential narration is no longer possible.

The pseudorealistic novel sought to give a semblance of order to the chaos of life, and did so by relying on the well-made plot (the story line as it was called) which, as we now realize, has become quite inessential to fiction. The plot having disappeared, it is no longer necessary to

have the events of fiction follow a linear, sequential pattern in time and space. Nor is it necessary for the narrative to obey logical transitions, or be controlled by a system of cause and effect.

Therefore, the elements of the surfictional discourse (words, phrases, sequences, scenes, spaces, word-designs, sections, chapters, etc.) must become digressive from one another—digressive from the element that precedes and the element that follows. In fact, these elements will not only wander freely in the book and even be repeated, but in some places they will occur simultaneously. This will offer multiple possibilities of rearrangement in the process of reading.

No longer progressing from left to right, top to bottom, in a straight line, and along the design of an imposed plot, the surfictional discourse will follow the contours of the writing itself as it takes shape (unpredictable shape) within the space of the page. In other words, as it improvises itself, the surfictional discourse will circle around itself, create new and unexpected movements and figures in the unfolding of the narration, repeating itself, projecting itself backward and forward along the curves of the writing—(much here can be learned from the cinema, or experiments in the visual arts).

As a result of the improvisational quality of language in this process, the events related in the narration will also unfold along unexpected and unpredictable lines. The shape and order of the story will not result from an imitation of the artificial shape and order of life, but from the formal circumvolutions of language as it wells up from the unconscious.

No longer acting as a mirror being dragged along the path of reality, Surfiction will now reproduce the effects of the mirror acting upon itself. It will not be a representation of something exterior to it, it will be a self-representation. Surfiction will be self-reflexive. That is to say, rather than being the stable image of daily life, Surfiction will be in a perpetual state of redoubling upon itself in order to disclose its own life—**THE LIFE OF FICTION.** It will be from itself, from its own substance that Surfiction will proliferate—imitating, repeating, echoing, parodying, mocking, re-tracing what it will say. Thus fiction will become the metaphor of its own narrative progress, and will establish and generate itself as it writes itself.

This does not mean, however, that the future novel will only be a *novel of the novel,* but rather it will create a kind of writing, a kind of discourse whose shape will be an interrogation, an endless interrogation of what it is doing while doing it, but also a relentless denunciation of its own fraudulence, of what **IT** really **IS:** an illusion (a fiction), just as life is an illusion (a fiction).

PROPOSITION THREE—THE MATERIAL OF FICTION

If the experiences of a human being (in this case those of the writer) occur only as fiction, gain meaning only as they are recalled or recounted, afterwards, and always in a distorted, glorified, sublimated manner, then these experiences become inventions. And if most fiction is based (more or less) on the experiences of the one who writes (experiences that are not necessarily anterior to, but simultaneous with, the writing process), there cannot be any truth nor any reality exterior to fiction. In other words, if the material of fiction is invention (lies, simulations, affectations, distortions, exaggerations, illusions), then writing fiction will be a process of fabricating or improvising on the spot the material of fiction.

The writer will simply materialize (render concrete) experiences into words. As such there will be no limits to the material of fiction—no limits beyond the writer's power of imagination, and beyond the possibilities of language.

Everything can be said and must be said in any possible way. While pretending to be telling the story of his life, or the life story of some imaginary being, the surfictionist can at the same time tell the story of the story he is in the process of inventing, he can tell the story of the language he is using, he can tell the story of the pencil or the typewriter or whatever instrument or machine he is using to write the story he is making up as he goes along, and he can also tell the story of the anguish or joy, disgust or exhilaration he is feeling while writing his story.

Since writing means filling a space (blackening pages), in those spaces where there is nothing to write, the writer can, at any time, introduce material (quotations, pictures, charts, diagrams, designs, illustrations, doodles, lists, pieces of other discourses, etc.) totally unrelated to the story he is in the process of inventing. Or else he can simply leave those spaces blank, because fiction is as much what is said as what is not said, since what is said is not necessarily true, and since what is said can always be said another way. There is no constriction in the writing of fiction, only arbitrariness and freedom.

As a result, the people of fiction, the fictitious beings will no longer be called characters, well-made characters who carry with them a fixed personality, a stable set of social and psychological attributes (a name, a gender, a condition, a profession, a situation, a civic identity). These surfictional creatures will be as changeable, as volatile, as irrational, as nameless, as *unnamable,* as playful, as unpredictable, as fraudulent and frivolous as the discourse that makes them. This does not mean, however, that they will be mere puppets. On the contrary, their being will be more complex, more genuine, more authentic, more true to life in fact, because (since life and fiction are no longer distinguishable) they will not appear to be what they are: imitations of real people; they will be what they are: word-beings.

What will replace the well-made personage (the hero, the protagonist) of traditional fiction who carried with him the burden of a name, an age, parental ties, a social role, a nationality, a past, and sometimes a physical appearance and even an interior psyche, will be a creation, or better

yet a creature that will function outside any predetermined conditions of society, outside any precise moment of history. That creature will be, in a sense, present to its own making, present also to its own unmaking. The surfictional being will not be a man or a woman of a certain moment, it will be the language of humanity. Totally free, arbitrary, and disengaged, uncommitted to the affairs of the outside world to the same extent as the fictitious discourse in which it will exist, this creature will participate in the fiction only as a grammatical being (in some cases devoid of a pronominal referent). Made of linguistic fragments often disassociated from one another, this word-being will be irrepressive, amoral, irrational and irresponsible in the sense that it will be detached from the real world, but entirely committed to the fiction in which it will find itself, aware only of the role it has to play as a fictional element.

Since Surfiction will no longer offer itself as a social or historical document that informs the reader about **real life** and **real people,** but as a work of art that functions on its own terms, the reader will no longer be tempted to identify with the characters. Instead the reader will participate in the creation of the fiction in the same degree as the creator or the narrator or the creature of that fiction. All of them will be part of the fictional discourse, all of them will be responsible for it. The writer (just as fictitious as his creation) will only be the point of junction (the source and the recipient) of all the elements of fiction. The story that he will be writing will also write him, just as it will write the reader who gives meaning to the story as he reads it.

PROPOSITION FOUR—THE MEANING OF FICTION

It is evident from the preceding propositions that the most striking and most radical aspects of Surfiction will be its semblance of disorder and its deliberate incoherency. Since, as stated earlier, no meaning preexists language, but meaning is produced in the process of writing and reading, Surfiction will not attempt to be meaningful, truthful, or realistic, *a priori;* nor will it serve as the vehicle of a ready-made sense. On the contrary, Surfiction will be seemingly devoid of meaning, it will be deliberately illogical, irrational, irrealistic, non sequitur, digressive, and incoherent. And of course, since the surfictional story will not have a beginning, middle, and end, it will not lend itself to a continuous and totalizing form of reading. It will refuse resolution and closure. It will always remain an open discourse—a discourse open to multiple interpretations. Surfiction will not only be the product of imagination, it will also activate imagination. For it will be through the collective efforts of all those who participate in the fiction (author, narrator, fictitious being, reader) that a meaning will be formulated. Surfiction will not create a semblance of order, it will offer itself for order and ordering. Thus the reader will not be able to identify with the people or the situations, nor will he be able to purify or purge himself in relation to the actions of the people in the story. In other words, no longer manipulated by an authorial (and authoritarian) point of view, no longer entrapped into the suspension of credibility, the reader will be the one who extracts, invents, creates an order and a meaning for the creatures and the material of fiction. It is this total and free participation in the fiction that will give the reader the sense of having invented a meaning, and not simply having passively received a neatly prearranged meaning.

As for the writer, he will no longer be considered a seer, a prophet, a theologian, a philosopher, or even a sociologist who predicts, preaches, teaches, or reveals absolute truths. Nor will he be looked upon (admiringly and romantically) as an omnipresent, omniscient, omnipotent creator. He will simply stand on equal footing with the reader in their efforts **to make sense** out of a language common to both of them—their collective efforts **to give sense** to the fiction of life. In other words, as it has been said of poetry, fiction will also **BE** and no only **MEAN**.

CONCLUSION

One should, I suppose, in conclusion to such a presentation, attempt to justify, or at least illustrate with examples, the propositions I just made for the present-future of fiction. But justifications and illustrations are readily available, and to a great extent many contemporary writers have already forged their way into Surfiction, or what has also been called postmodern fiction.

For I must admit, I am not alone in this wild undertaking. Many writers in many parts of the world (each in his or her own personal **mad** and **unique** way) have already successfully created the kind of fiction I have attempted to define here. The names of these writers appear in the pages of this volume. However, I am certain that none of them would pretend to have solved all the problems of contemporary fiction. And I do not pretend myself to have done so, nor to have presented the only possible **way of fiction** for the future. I am sure there are other ways, easier, less radical, and more accessible than the one I am proposing, but like most of my fellow-surfictionists, I think this is the path that must be followed and explored if fiction is to have a chance to survive as a serious genre in our complex postmodern world.

It is a fiction writer, as a surfictionist that I follow this path myself, but not in order to succeed (commercially or socially or in any other way), but in order to transform "the fiasco of reality into a howling success," as the great Samuel Beckett once put it.

Miriam Marty Clark

SOURCE: "Contemporary Short Fiction and the Postmodern Condition," in *Studies in Short Fiction,* Vol. 32, No. 2, Spring, 1995, pp. 147-59.

[*In the following essay, Clark examines the viability of the short story in the age of postmodernist literature.*]

Entangled on one side with the tribe, on another with the marketplace, the short story inhabits postmodernity differently from the novel. It moves differently, and in ways still unarticulated, on the force field of contemporary culture, participating in what Fredric Jameson has called a "revival of storytelling knowledge" in the postmodern world and giving voice to the increased "vitality of small narrative units" (Foreword xi) but inadequately explained with respect both to its modernist precursors in Chekhov, Joyce, and Welty and to its raw materials, life at the end of the twentieth century.

While a few story writers (Donald Barthelme, Robert Coover, William Gass, and Max Apple, among them) have advanced under the sign of the postmodern, producing in sometimes-brilliant miniature the kinds of metafictional, anti-mimetic, ontologically indeterminate narration writ large in the postmodern novel, many recent stories appear to have no significant share in those ironies and indeterminacies. The working class passivity of Raymond Carver's characters, the middle-class anomie of Ann Beattie's seem no more than life-like, minutely reflective of individual alienation and disarray in America but unaffected by postmodern disruptions of discursive practice and the dislodging of referentiality. I want to argue here, however, that beneath the finely drawn neo-realist surfaces of their stories writers like Carver and Beattie, Grace Paley, Mary Robison, Jayne Anne Phillips and others mark out the radical troubling of realist claims; beyond their modernist inheritance they surrender in small ways and little narratives the expectation of epiphany, the hope for metaphysical consolation in a fragmenting world, a lingering commitment to a transcendental subject.

The end of epiphany and the exhaustion of familiar reading strategies and genre definitions call for new ways of reading and for a redefinition of both the narrative and the cultural logic of short fiction. Unlike the unified, complex modernist short story, grounded in image or metaphor and moving toward revelation, many stories of the last decade and a half are marked by depthlessness, incoherence, and ephemerality. In a bitter attack on American fiction, particularly short fiction, in the 1980s, John W. Aldridge gives voice to the disappointment of readers in search of insight:

> Memory is given nothing to retain, nor form in which the harmonious relation of part to part creates a pattern on which the mind is able to construct a memory . . . There is no evidence that these experiences are meant to coalesce into drama or so arrange themselves as to produce some climactic insight into a truth about the human condition. (35)

Both Aldridge's complaint and his diagnosis (too many writer's workshops, too little of silence, exile and cunning) are echoed in other reviews and commentaries on the state of the story, most recently by Madison Smartt Bell, who remarks on the temporal depthlessness and "weird foreshortening" of contemporary stories (58-59).

Still, contemporary stories have readers, perhaps more readers than ever before. From the late 1970s to the present, the genre has seen a revived or at least a sustained popularity among American book buyers. Although mass-circulation magazine outlets for the story dwindled,[1] little magazines (some of them underwritten by commercial houses, as *Quarterly* was by Random House) and writing workshops flourished. Story annuals and anthologies multiplied. Between January 1988 and December 1992 American trade book publishers brought out nearly twice as many single-author volumes of short stories as during a comparable period between 1973 and 1977.[2] By most accounts the story's fate in the American book market improved dramatically during the 1980s.

"Has there ever been a time like the present for short story writers? I don't think so," Raymond Carver mused in a late piece on contemporary fiction, "An author who publishes a collection of stories can expect to sell, generally speaking, roughly the same number of copies as his or her novelist counterpart. And, besides, as anyone can tell you, it's mainly the short story writers who are being talked about these days" (*No Heroics* 152). Susan Mernit makes a similar point in her 1986 review essay. "In 1980," she writes, "it would have been difficult even to publish a book of short stories. Popular publishing wisdom stated that the short story collection had no commercial value. . . . [Now] it is as though the short story, like Rip Van Winkle, suddenly awoke from a long, refreshing sleep. Publication has boomed, interest is at an all-time high, and short stories are now financially successful" (302-03).[3]

The viability and vitality of the genre undoubtedly owe something to what John Barth calls "the sharp-eyed, relaxless muse of the short story, who, unlike good longwinded Homer, *never* dozes off, even for a second" (37). But in our time even the relaxless muse must be historicized. A great deal remains to be said about the short story, its production and consumption in the postmodern age: from its long occupation of the boundary, now largely effaced, between high culture and mass culture to its particular forms of expression after the decentering of the individual subject. For the present, however, I want to think in fairly specific terms about the logic of the story's currency in the professional-managerial class and the baby boom generation during the last decade and a half, proposing that for this "numerically large and privileged generation" (Pfeil 98)—those who choose and market and consume books—the genre in its contemporary form serves as an ideal site for the displacement and negotiation of postmodern concerns.

The story is neither unprecedented nor unparalleled in this situation. Richard Ohmann has written persuasively about the canonization or pre-canonization of "illness narratives," novels of the mid-twentieth century that function as displacements of American anxieties about autonomy and individualism under monopoly capitalism. More recently, Fred Pfeil identifies a wide range of contemporary forms—from "low mediation" mass culture

enterprises like *Saturday Night Live* to "limited access," high culture ventures including Laurie Anderson's performance art and the Glass/Wilson opera *Einstein on the Beach*—which "reproduce the social experience and constitution of present day [Professional Managerial Class]" (98). Among these forms, in ways particular to the genre, the story registers and mediates the loss both of "truth" and "insight" and of those coalescences that constitute selfhood, character, and history.

It is a great reckoning, of sorts, in little rooms. If the modern story is situated at the fringes of society—the locale of human loneliness, as Frank O'Connor puts it— the stories of our time are founded not on the margins but in the ruins of the public sphere. In the doomed conversation, the harassing phone call, the dead letter, the retreat into suburban rental houses and furnished apartments, Carver's characters negotiate the wreckage of social discourse, of community and institution. Beattie's stories, like those of Richard Ford, Jayne Anne Phillips and many other contemporary writers, understand the common life as irretrievable, its institutions collapsed, its conventions unraveling, its terms no longer tenable. Joyce Carol Oates's recent, characteristically dark story "Is Laughter Contagious?" is set in Franklin Village, a suburban tract where people don't have "neighbors" or "'friends' in the old sense of that word . . . the majority of us make no claims to have (or to be) 'friends'" (72). All that remains of community and all that displaces it is contagion—of violence, of sexual exploitation, of derisive laughter, of AIDS and the fear of AIDS.

As stories represent and reproduce the disintegration of public life they also represent the colonization of private life by consumer capitalism. The term "Kmart realism" is commonly used to denote a fiction of brand names and contemporary cultural references, work that achieves texture without substance and that invokes an array of material practices it fails to investigate or challenge. But if the importing of names and slogans is sometimes no more than that—a technical device, a papering over of the generic with the brand name—it is sometimes considerably more. The short story addresses, as directly as any contemporary genre and more pervasively, the insinuation of mass culture into psychic and discursive landscapes, the transformation of brand names into signifiers of self and world. "The only light in the room is from outside," remarks the narrator of Frederick Barthelme's "Chroma," "a mercury vapor street lamp that leaves the shadow of the Levelors stretched along one wall . . . The shadow has a flicker to it. I get a fresh drink and sit there watching this shadow and feeling like somebody in an Obsession ad, sitting there" (85). In Amy Hempel's "Celia Is Back," mental breakdown is signified in a jumble of slogans. In it, a father—recently released from a hospital and headed for an unspecified weekly appointment—tries to help his children compose a winning sentence for the Jell-O Pudding contest.

> The father looked confused. "This is the Jell-O pudding contest, isn't that what you said?" he

said. "Well, okay then," he said. "I like Jell-O pudding because it has a tough satin finish that resists chipping and peeling." "No, no," he said, "I mean, I like Jell-O pudding because it has a fruitier taste. Because it's garden fresh," he said. "Because it goes on dry to protect me from wetness longer. Oh, Jell-O pudding," the father said. "I like it because it's more absorbent than those other brands. Won't chafe or ride up."

He opened his eyes and saw his son leave the room. The sound that had made the father open his eyes was the pen that the boy had thrown to the floor.

"You may already be a winner," the father said. (19)

Hempel's story and others like it register not so much, in Raymond Williams's terms, the "bourgeois evacuation of the sites of social power" (86)—the founding impulse of realist fiction—as the dispersal (paradoxically, by merger and conglomeration) of social power under late capitalism and its penetration into the private sphere. While a few writers like Bobbie Ann Mason record with equanimity the effacement of the local and the refiguring of the self in a world of commercials and commodities, Hempel and Barthelme reckon with it more darkly, peering into an abyss of postmodern selfhood.

Thus the individual consciousness remains, in Ohmann's phrase, the "locus of significant happening" (80); its illness and malaise are predominant concerns in contemporary short fiction as they were in the mid-century texts Ohmann examines. But in the generation between the novels Ohmann writes about—*Franny and Zooey, The Bell Jar, Portnoy's Complaint*—and recent story collections like Carver's *Where I'm Calling From,* both the character of social relations and the symptoms of the illness narrative are altered. The social contradictions Ohmann sees displaced into narrative arise under monopoly capitalism; the advent of late capitalism or postmodernism, as it is delineated by Ernest Mandel and later by Fredric Jameson, brings significant though not absolute changes in the nature of those relations and contradictions.

Jameson's account of the changes takes, like others before it, the terms of illness, marking a shift from modern paranoia and alienation to postmodern schizophrenia and disorientation. Late or multinational corporate capitalism is characterized, the suggests, by "a new depthlessness"—expressed in a "whole new culture of the image or the simulacrum"—and a consequent "weakening of historicity, both in our relationship to public History and in the new forms of our private temporality" (6). These changes issue in the situation that Jameson calls, after Lacan, "schizophrenia," a linguistic malfunction, a detachment of signifier from signified, a disruption of personal identity as it is constituted in a temporal unification of past, present, and future. The "active temporal unification" at stake, Jameson points out, "is itself a function of language"; it is what enables both selfhood as we know it and storytelling:

If we are unable to unify the past, present, and future of the sentence, then we are similarly unable to unify the past, present, and future of our own biographical experience or psychic life. With the breakdown of the signifying chain, therefore, the schizophrenic is reduced to an experience of pure material signifiers, or, in other words, a series of pure and unrelated presents in time. (27)

David Harvey makes a cogent association between these symptoms and two decades of rapid compression in our experience of time and space. Harvey argues that the past century and a half have been marked by a series of dramatic compressions, produced by technological (radio, television, air travel, computer, etc.), political, and economic forces. These lead, he contends, to "crises of representation" and to significant changes in our understanding of narrative, its functions and its possibilities. One such crisis, beginning in the middle of the nineteenth century, precipitated modernism and the dismantling of realist practices and presuppositions that assumed, Harvey points out, "that a story could be told as if it was unfolding coherently, event after event, in time" (265).

The postmodern condition ensues from another dramatic compression, Harvey argues, a "general speed up in the turnover times of capital," which leads to a further acceleration in the rate of exchange and consumption and an increase in the "volatility and ephemerality of fashions, products, production techniques . . . ideas and ideologies, values and established practices" (285), as well as to a sense of the temporariness and diversity of value systems in a fragmenting society (286). The result as Harvey describes it is schizophrenia: a failure of continuity, the compression of the past into an overwhelming present, and "a loss of a sense of the future except insofar as the future can be discounted into the present" (291).

The force of schizophrenia, so defined, is, as I have already suggested, anti-narrative; its implications for narrative are considered in a wide variety of experimental and metafictional texts. The stories I am interested in here, however, thematize *within* narrative the weakening of historicity and the reconfiguration of private temporality. They are—in a sense, paradoxically—narratives of psychosis; they reflect the circumstances of late capitalism, displace them, drive them into frail narratives. They have to do with coherence rather than autonomy, with language and narrativity rather than integrated personhood. Addressing anxieties of a purely postmodern kind, driven by forms of nostalgia, they are stories of selves, highly provisional: voices, moments.

The temporal logic of the story has long been understood to differ from that of the novel—and to matter less. The modernist story has been widely described as more vertical than horizontal in orientation and operation, more mythic than social, more spiritual than public (May 329), more inclined to moral revelation than to moral evolution (Schorer 7). It is seen as more epigrammatic than progressive, showing an affinity for the "essential truth or idea or image which rises above time" (Pasco

420); it originates in folklore and anecdote rather than in history and travel (Eikhenbaum 4). "If the novel creates the illusion of reality by presenting a literal authenticity to the material facts of the external world," May suggests, "the short story attempts to be authentic to the immaterial reality of the inner world of the self in its relations to eternal rather than temporal reality" (328-29). Elsewhere I have suggested some of the ways in which those "relations to the eternal" are disrupted in the postmodern story as metanarratives of self-knowledge and insight are called into question. But with the breakdown of its metaphysical logic and the restructuring of subjectivity, the short story emerges as site for consideration of the postmodern. Generic qualities of brevity, compression, and ephemerality along with the story's minimal temporality make it a logical vehicle for the displacement of postmodern loss and the thematization of diminished, even failing historicity.

Recent stories encode these instabilities and failures, particularly what Jameson calls the "waning of the centered subject," in several distinct ways. The first is, ironically, by means of metaphor. In Ann Beattie's "Shifting," a story about a young woman in a stifling marriage, pictures signify both the depthlessness and unreality of the protagonist's world and her disrupted sense of self. During her long days alone, Natalie sometimes goes to the art museum. There she does not look at the works of art but rather buys museum postcards and sits on a bench with them. Later in the story, instructed by her husband to take pictures of their furniture and other possessions for insurance purposes, Natalie photographs parts of her own body. After the pictures have been developed, Beattie writes, Natalie

> sat on the sofa and laid them out, the twelve of them, in three rows on the cushion next to her. The picture of the piano was between the picture of her feet and the picture of herself that she had shot by aiming into the mirror. She picked up the four pictures of their furniture and put them on the table. She picked up the others and examined them closely. She began to understand why she had taken them. She had photographed parts of her body, fragments of it, to study the pieces. (68)

In Stephanie Vaughn's recent story, "The Architecture of California," the metaphor is linguistic. Her protagonist Megan writes sentences for Comp Currics, Inc., which sells computerized educational programs to large school systems. "The sentences she writes," Vaughn says,

> do not add up to little communities of paragraphs. They are fed randomly into a computer, which, through telephone hookups, feeds them to terminals in New York, St. Louis, Dallas, and Detroit, where students with low grades practice reading the English language. It is hard to write thousands of sentences that have nothing to do with each other and that must be very short, use a limited vocabulary and make no references to forests, farms, streams, wildflowers, nuclear families, or anything else associated with country life or middle-class values. Megan is good at her job. (149-50)

Another Vaughn character, the narrator of "Other Women," describes her work for an architectural firm in terms of simulacra: "I make small houses, office buildings, even airports. I also make streets, trees, shrubs, flower beds, ponds, streams, and miniature people . . . I create a stationary world, ageless and colorful, a shopping center or school no bigger than the top of a desk, and completely manageable" (96-97).

Beattie's early stories often operate metonymically, undermining teleology, resisting epiphany, refusing metaphoric revelations and moments of insight. But for all that it has to say about Natalie's experience in the postmodern world, Beattie's metaphor of the pictures has the paradoxical and perhaps reassuring effect of pulling her story forcefully back into an epiphanic mode, a more traditional kind of storytelling and meaning making. By means of the photographs, the reader and Natalie alike come to understand the nature of the problem and the meaning of the story: she is, like the furniture, a possession of her husband's; moreover she is flattened, immobilized, without depth or vitality. Randomness and depthlessness are more insistent in the two Vaughn stories, where they are also evident at the level of events and relationships; but in these stories, as in Beattie's, the metaphors serve to contain and give meaning to the very meaninglessness they inscribe; the rubble of signifiers is made to signify at last.

Amy Hempel's story "Going," first published in Vanity Fair in the early 1980s, also figures the moment, the postmodern condition, the extreme compression of time and space metaphorically. Hempel's metaphor is less static, though, and suggests not only a set of circumstances but an array of narrative possibilities. In it she overlays and undermines a story about memory and selfhood—a story in which the young narrator's loss of his parents explains his self-destructiveness and depression—with an image of temporal and spatial categories briefly, and perilously, merged. From the hospital bed where he is laid up with a concussion and a two-day memory loss, her narrator explains the accident in this way:

> I did not spin out on a stretch of highway called Blood Alley or Hospital Curve. I lost it on flat dry road—with no other car in sight. Here's why: in the desert I like to drive through binoculars. What I like about it is that things are two ways at once. Things are far away and close with you still in the same place. (73)

The telescoping of time, the collapse of temporal planes, is here weirdly, brilliantly reconfigured in the image of the binoculars. "I can't even remember all I've forgotten," Hempel's narrator quips. "I do remember the accident, though. I remember it was like the binoculars. You know—two ways? It was fast and it was slow. It was both" (73).

In many stories like this one, the breakdown of narrative and the narration of breakdown are inextricably linked as past and future, time and space, are drawn into a multiple, disorienting, and overwhelming present. "Although the city was still unfathomable," says the narrator of Deborah Eisenberg's story "Transactions in a Foreign Currency," "I could recall no other place, and the rudiments of a past seemed to be hidden here for me somewhere, beyond my memory" (162). Her past hidden or lost, her future uncertain, Eisenberg's nameless character is adrift in a strange country and a disorienting present:

> I entered a door and was plunged into noise and activity. I was in a supermarket arranged like a hallucination, with aisles shooting out in unexpected directions and familiar and unfamiliar items perched side by side. If only I had made a list! I held my cart tightly, trusting the bright packages to draw me along correctly and guide me in my selections. (162)

She pushes her disorientation further, experimentally, thinking about what it means to call a life her own. After chatting with a butcher about her children, she allows that she has no children and then suggests that "it just doesn't ultimately matter—to the universe, for instance— whether [the person with children] happens to be me or whether that person happens to be someone else. And I was thinking," she goes on, "does it actually matter to you whether that person is me or that person is someone else!"

"To me . . . does it matter to me . . ." the butcher responds amiably, "Well, to me, sweetheart, you are someone else" (164).

Bharati Mukherjee's characters, moving between cultures and languages, often experience similar varieties of detachment and hallucination. "Wife's Story," for example, ends with a woman—her Indian past discarded, her American present unintelligible, and her future unknowable—looking into a mirror: "The Body's beauty amazes me," she says, "I stand here shameless. . . . I am free, afloat, watching somebody else" (41). The narrator of Elizabeth Spencer's "I, Maureen" also experiences her life, her self, as unstable, multiple, illusory, finally reducible to a photographic image that her former lover sells to a US distributor. "The world over," she remarks, "copies of it will eventually stick up out of garbage cans, or will be left in vacated apartments. Held to the wall by one thumb tack, it will hang above junk not thought to be worth moving" (362).

In other stories the disorder is more specifically one of telling, of language and narration, and is marked by the attenuation of cause and effect, a slippage between event and narration, the detachment of image from meaning. Ann Beattie's early and widely imitated use of non sequitur is one signal of this disorder; "Many of the flat statements that I bring together," Beattie says, "are usually non sequiturs or bordering on being non sequiturs— which reinforces the chaos" (qtd. in McQuade et al. 2704).

The truncated quality of many short stories and the predominance of the very short story in the 1970s and 80s is another indication of this disorder. Unlike early and modern stories, in which compression is achieved by artful omission and by suppression of exposition, many

contemporary short stories abandon exposition altogether, particularly exposition rooted in personal history, essential identity, or ultimate truth; the chains of signification are short and fragile and not much depends on them. Sixteen of the 27 stories in Jayne Anne Phillips's first collection, *Black Tickets,* for example, are very brief, fewer than 500 words each. They are not distilled forms, or mythologized ones, of long stories; they are less elliptical than momentary, provisional. They seem to be disintegrating even as they are uttered. "I keep dropping how things went, which story goes where" the narrator of "Accidents" says,

> This week and next week and next week. Somewhere out there's a winner but I'm losing track. I try to stay home and turn the pages in my books. But the words are a dark crusted black that cracks. Black as wine or water. I keep wading out and the deep part is over my head. I wanna dance I wanna just wrap my legs around you like those rings are round the moon. Lemme press my mouth against you like the rain against the glass it's see-through. I can see clear out there to the end and I'm alone I'm burning like a fire fuel. I'm hot. I'm hot I'm a streak across the sky. You watch me, now bring me down hard and hold on. It doesn't matter if I tell one truth or another. (250)

The small stories in Mary Robison's early volume *Days* operate in a similar way; Robison's stories end without respect to episode but rather, it appears, as soon as they have exhausted a brief, barely won moment of narrative coherence.

Other stories, generally longer ones, call attention to a break in the connection between event and narrative, story and discourse. Alice Munro's "Friend of My Youth" begins straightforwardly with a novelist's reconstruction, from letters and her mother's stories, of a friendship from many years before. But where the documents and recollections leave off, midway through, Munro's story exfoliates into a multiplicity of stories, of possible lives: what the mother says she would have made of her friend Flora's life, "If I could have been a writer"; the endless, pious tale her daughter *thinks* her mother would have made of Flora's life; the novelist's "own ideas about Flora's story." These stories, all of them present in the text, constitute not multiple perspectives on a unitary and knowable (if, within the limits of the story, unknowable) reality but rather separate stories, overlaid, competing, at odds, told in a single voice. Kent Nelson's "A Country of My Own Making" moves in a different direction, defoliating toward a single story: a spare one, not mythic in its propositions. "She recounted her life," the narrator says of an old high school friend as they sit together at the kitchen table, "hours in a motel room in Moab, Utah, days and nights in the Wagon Wheel, arguments with lovers. It was a life not unusual, a slow dissimulation not unlike my own, but with different details" (111).

I raise these turns of event and changes of symptom not only as a way of explaining why the short story is, increasingly it seems, a favored genre in the American book market and not only as an occasion to look again at the hegemonic processes Ohmann describes. I want also to consider in them, as I have said, some of the ways stories reckon with the disruption of selfhood and temporality, which have historically been the story's domain, as well as with the depthlessness, the more general weakening of historicity that undermines narrative and realism in every genre in the twentieth century.

Such a reading puts into context not only the relative commercial and critical success of many contemporary short fiction writers but also the dismay of some critics at the failure of recent stories to provide reading experiences of the modernist variety. "It is a kind of writing," Aldridge complains of recent American fiction,

> particularly in the shorter form, that bears a very close resemblance to the scenic blips of television. . . . Television projects glimpses of experience as if seen from a train that is moving so fast that the connection of one glimpse to another is often impossible to perceive. The glimpses may follow one another in temporal sequence, but it is not a sequence in which meaning is normally accrued or progress is made toward a definitive conclusion. (35)

Read as reflections or displacements of the postmodern condition, these impossibilities of perception, these failures of coherence and accrual, have a different effect altogether. In their brevity, their instantanaeity, the stories I am concerned with hold out not revelation, not a durable or ultimate knowledge, but narrativity itself. The forces that disrupt narrative are met by and converge for a moment with the need to tell, the power of telling. That power is provisional, sometimes merely pronominal—the telling "I," the "he" or "she." It is, again and again, endangered, waning, decentered. It is only, ever, briefly sustained.

"We have a growing appetite / For littleness," Mark Strand observes in a recent poem, "a piece of ourselves, a bit of the world / An understanding that remains unfinished, unentire, / Largely imperfect so long as it lasts."[4] These stories do not show the world in a grain of sand, as good stories have long been thought to; nor do they offer a slice of life. But they hold out selves in a moment of dispersal: voices before the overwhelmed, beneath the overwhelming.

NOTES

[1] *Mademoiselle,* for example, stopped publishing fiction in March 1992 after more than 50 years. In the 1940s and 50s the magazine offered as many as six short stories and novel excerpts per issue; the fiction of those years was uneven at best, but included work by Mark Schorer, John Cheever, Dylan Thomas, Shirley Jackson, Carson McCullers, and Elizabeth Hardwick. During the sixties and seventies the number of stories dwindled to one per issue.

[2] The total number of short fiction titles for the period from January 1973 to December 1977 was 730; between January 1978 and December 1982 the number dropped to 689. From January 1983 to December 1988 a total of 1,078 volumes appeared; from January 1988 to December 1992, 1,207 short fiction titles were published.

These data were provided by Celia Wagner of Blackwell's North America.

[3] Many other commentators have remarked on the efflorescence of the American story in the 1980s; among them David Slavitt in "The Year in Short Stories" and Shannon Ravenel in her introduction to *Best American Stories of the Eighties.*

[4] Mark Strand, "From the Academy of Revelations" (35).

WORKS CITED

Aldridge, John. "The New Assembly-Line Fiction." *American Scholar* 59 (1990): 17-38. [See also John W. Aldridge, *Talents and Technicians: The New Assembly-Line Fiction.* New York: Macmillan, 1992]

Barth, John. "It's a Short Story." *Mississippi Review* 21 (1993): 25-40.

Barthelme, Frederick. *Chroma.* New York: Penguin, 1987.

Beattie, Ann. *Secrets and Surprises.* New York: Random, 1991.

Bell, Madison Smartt. "The Short Story Revival (or Whatever it Was)." *Mississippi Review* 21 (1993): 55-66.

Carver, Raymond. "On Contemporary Fiction." *No Heroics, Please.* New York: Vintage, 1992.

———. *Where I'm Calling From.* New York: Atlantic Monthly Press, 1988.

Eikhenbaum, Boris. *O. Henry and the Theory of the Short Story.* Trans. I. R. Titunik. Ann Arbor: U of Michigan P, 1968. [Also cited in Pratt 181]

Eisenberg, Deborah. *Transactions in a Foreign Currency.* New York: Knopf, 1986.

Harvey, David. *The Condition of Postmodernity.* London: Blackwell, 1989.

Hempel, Amy. *Reasons to Live.* New York: Knopf, 1985.

Jameson, Fredric. Foreword. *The Postmodern Condition: A Report on Knowledge.* By Jean François Lyotard. Minneapolis: U of Minnesota P, 1984.

———. *Postmodernism, Or, The Cultural Logic of Late Capitalism.* Durham: Duke UP, 1991.

Mandel, Ernest. *Late Capitalism.* London: NLB, 1975.

May, Charles E. "On the Nature of Knowledge in Short Fiction." *Studies in Short Fiction* 21 (1984): 327-38.

McQuade, Donald et al. "Ann Beattie." *The Harper American Literature.* 2 vols. New York: Harper, 1987. 2: 2704-05.

Mernit, Susan. "The State of the Short Story." *Virginia Quarterly Review* 62 (1986): 302-11.

Mukherjee, Bharati. *The Middleman and Other Stories.* New York: Ballantine, 1988.

Munro, Alice. *Friend of My Youth.* New York: Knopf, 1990.

Nelson, Kent. *The Middle of Nowhere.* Salt Lake City: Gibbs-Smith, 1991.

Oates, Joyce Carol. "Is Laughter Contagious?" *Harper's* Sept. 1991: 72-74.

O'Connor, Frank. *The Lonely Voice: A Study of the Short Story.* Cleveland: World, 1963.

Ohmann, Richard. *The Politics of Letters.* Middletown: Wesleyan UP, 1987.

Pasco, Allen H. "On Defining Short Stories." *New Literary History* 22 (1991): 407-22.

Pfeil, Fred. *Another Tale to Tell.* London: Verso, 1990.

Phillips, Jayne Anne. *Black Tickets.* New York: Dell, 1979.

Pratt, Mary Louise. "The Short Story: The Long and the Short of It." *Poetics* 10 (1981): 175-94.

Ravenel, Shannon. Introduction. *The Best American Stories of the Eighties.* Boston: Houghton, 1990. ix-xvii.

Robison, Mary. *Days.* New York: Knopf, 1979.

Salinger, J. D. *Franny and Zooey.* Boston: Little, 1961.

Slavitt, David. "The Year in Short Stories." *Dictionary of Literary Biography Yearbook: 1988.* Ed. J. M. Brook. Detroit: Gale, 1988. 39-48.

Spencer Elizabeth. *The Stories of Elizabeth Spencer.* New York: Penguin, 1983.

Strand, Mark. "From the Academy of Revelations." *The New Republic* 3 Aug. 1992: 35.

Vaughn, Stephanie. *Sweet Talk.* New York: Random, 1990.

Williams, Raymond. *The Politics of Modernism.* London: Verso, 1989.

John Barth

SOURCE: "Postmodernism Visited: A Professional Novelist's Amateur Review," in *Further Fridays: Essays, Lectures, and Other Nonfiction: 1984-94,* Little, Brown and Company, 1995, pp. 291-310.

[*In the following essay, Barth distinguishes between definitions of postmodernist as a literary aesthetic practice and postmodern as a description of contemporary culture, and declares that practitioners of the literary art influence their chosen style more than the critics who theorize about it.*]

Let's sidle up to the grand topic of Postmodernism by way of two nit-picking questions: whether the term should be hyphenated and whether it should be capitalized. The latter question doesn't come up *auf Deutsch,* but it does in English, for example, with certain consequences.

In a recent issue of the *New York Times Book Review* (June 23, 1991), Professor Bernard Williams, a philosopher at Oxford and Berkeley, reminds his readers that the adjective "postmodern" has come to have at least two quite different primary meanings: In the arts, says Professor Williams, especially in architecture and music, "a postmodern style represents a rejection of the formal austerities of the modern movement[1] in favor, roughly, of eclecticism, historical reference and greater jollity."

> In other connections, however, and above all in relation to politics, post-modernism hopes to overcome *modernity,* which is a phenomenon, and a spirit, identified with such things as the Enlightenment and the ambitions of 19th-century political theory. Since modernity set in not later than the 18th century, and [since] modernism, flourishing in the first half of this century, rejected many of [modernity's] most typical products, such as naturalism and romanticism, [the] conflation of the two conceptions produces an epical degree of historical confusion.

That strikes me as well said indeed—except that if Modernism rejects Romanticism, I would say that it does so in the way that some children reject their parents, while still carrying their genes. There is much more Romanticism in the Modernist program, it seems to me, than there is in Postmodernism. Anyhow, inasmuch as Postmodernist artists ineluctably live in a climate of cultural postmodernity, I'm not optimistic about keeping the distinction clear. It's hard enough to come to an understanding in the matter of whether the terms should be capitalized or lowercased, and whether the prefix "post" ought to be hyphenated from or run into what follows it. There is no way of knowing what Professor Williams's preferences are in these weighty matters, inasmuch as he is writing for the *New York Times,* which (as I know from sore experience) insists on its own house style—in this instance, lowercase initial letters for such terms as "Modernism," "Postmodernism," and "Romanticism," and hyphenation for the term "Postmodern."[2] Looking around the critical landscape, I see that whoever wrote the copy for the brochure of our Stuttgart Seminars—"The End of Postmodernism: New Directions"—also prefers the lowercase initial (except in titles), but drops the hyphen. Likewise the notable French theorist Jean-François Lyotard, in his 1979 book *La Condition postmoderne*—but of course, the French language is as averse to uppercase letters as the German language is fond of them; French book titles are all lowercase after the first noun. Likewise too Professors G. R. Thompson and N. Katherine Hayles, on whom I shall be relying heavily in these lectures: lowercase, no hyphen. I have not yet personally consulted the pope of the church of Postmodernism, our colleague Professor Hassan, as to his preference; his bibliographical credits in our seminar brochure follow the style of that brochure: no hyphen, uppercase in the titles but lowercase in the text.[3] That seems to be the rough consensus in languages other than German, although British English inclines, *New York Times* like, to the hyphen (I don't know how it goes in Japanese, although I can attest from firsthand, on-site experience that the Japanese are keenly interested in whatever it is that we *gaijin* mean by the term "Postmodern").

As for myself: You will be excited to hear that I shrug my shoulders at the question of hyphenation, but am inclined to prefer the uppercase initial, and not merely out of respect for the German side of my ancestry. There is a difference, and not only in quality, between the lowercase-romantic novels of Barbara Cartland and the uppercase-Romantic novels of Goethe and Schlegel, between the lowercase-romantic aspects of candlelight and wine and the uppercase-Romantic aspects of a hike through the Bavarian Alps. Just as I find the adjective "Modernist" more precise than "Modern" when speaking of the dominant aesthetic movement of the first half of the twentieth century in Europe, the United States, and elsewhere, and the adjective "Postmodernist" more precise than "Postmodern" when speaking of an aesthetic movement that follows Modernism in one spirit or another, so also I find it useful to employ the uppercase when referring to contemporary aesthetic Postmodernism, because doing so leaves us a lowercase postmodernism to describe analogous phenomena in other times and places: Tom McEvilly's Middle Kingdom Egyptian postmodernism and Silver Age Roman postmodernism;[4] perhaps Friedrich von Schlegel's uppercase-Romantic lowercase postmodernism of the late-eighteenth/early-nineteenth centuries.

You get the idea: It is the difference between Burgundy from the Burgundy region of France and burgundy from the Napa Valley of California (in this instance, not necessarily a difference in quality). Thus I shall try to use the adjective "Postmodernist" when speaking of contemporary aesthetics, and the adjective "Postmodern" when speaking of other aspects of our contemporary culture, on the grounds that we need every possible aid to clarification when we're snorkeling such muddy waters. And I shall use the uppercase noun "Postmodernism" when speaking of the latter-twentieth-century aesthetic

phenomenon, and to hell with the rest, for the inarguable reason that postmodernism as a condition, like post-industrialism, looks queer to me in the upper case.

In this matter of usage I seem to have the eminent Octavio Paz on my side (at least in the English translation of his recent volume of essays called *Convergences: Essays on Art and Literature*[5])—though inasmuch as Paz has published (in the Mexican literary journal *La Jornada Semanal*) an attack on my essay "The Literature of Replenishment" wherein he denominates me *un bobo* for writing that essay, I imagine that he wouldn't enjoy being on my team any more than I enjoy being on his. In any case, we are in sweet agreement only on the question of uppercase initial letters, for Paz reserves the term "Modernist" exclusively for Hispanic *Modernismo*—he prefers such terms as "Avant-Gardism" or "Expressionism," or the more particular terms "Dadaism" and "Surrealism" and so forth, to describe what was going on in the rest of Europe and in North America—and by "Postmodernist" he means Hispanic *Postmodernismo,* of which more presently. (Among Spanish-language copyeditors, by the way, there seems to be at least as much inconsistency in the typesetting of these terms as there is in other languages.)

Here is Paz on Hispanic *Postmodernismo,* in any essay called "A Literature of Convergences," undated, from the aforementioned collection. After asserting that the literatures of both North and South America are marked by alternating impulses, even periods, of "Cosmopolitanism" ("the sallying forth of ourselves and our reality") and "Americanism" ("the return to what we are and to our origin"), Paz writes:

> An example of the first was the initial phase of Hispano-American Modernism, between 1890 and 1905, characterized in poetry by the influence of European Symbolism and in prose by that of Naturalism. This phase was followed around 1915 by so-called Postmodernism, which represented a return to our hemisphere and to colloquial speech.

It is quite clear that Paz in Mexico City is not talking about what we're talking about here in Stuttgart.[6]

In other instances, his usage is less clear. For example, in (interestingly enough) a 1970 essay called "The Tradition of the Haiku," speaking of a 1918 volume by the Mexican poet José Juan Tablada, Paz writes,

> The . . . book was still Modernist; its relative novelty lay in the appearance of those ironic and colloquial elements which historians of our literature have seen as the hallmarks of a movement that, with notorious inexactitude, they label Postmodernism. This movement is a textbook invention: Postmodernism is simply the criticism that, within Modernism and not venturing beyond its aesthetic horizon, certain Modernist poets level against Modernism. It is the line of descent, via [the aforementioned poets] Darío and Lugones, of the anti-Symbolist Symbolist Laforgue.

The context does not make it altogether clear whether, in this case, Paz is extending the term to include non-Hispanic Postmodernism (his phrase "the line of descent" suggests that possibility). Given the date of the essay—1970, when Ihab Hassan was just bringing the term "postmodern" to our gringo attention—I suspect that Paz added this remark by way of an update when he was putting together the collection *Convergences*. But perhaps not; he is a knowledgeable and sophisticated *hombre*. Despite the dismissive tone of his remark, I think it does in fact describe one kind of literary Postmodernism: an essentially Modernist criticism of Modernism; one that (rather like my own) not only declines to throw out the baby with the bathwater, but maintains a high regard for that bathwater as well. I daresay that something of that sort is what William Gass has in mind when he describes such writers as Samuel Beckett and Italo Calvino (and himself and me and Donald Barthelme and Robert Coover and John Hawkes) as late-Modernists, and reserves the term "Postmodernist" for the likes of Raymond Carver, Frederick Barthelme, and Ann Beattie: the "Diet Pepsi minimalists."

One more quotation in this vein from Señor Paz before we bid him *hasta la vista:* this one from an excellent 1970 essay called "Blank Thought." The essay deals with Tantric art (Paz was once the Mexican ambassador to India), but its opening paragraph sounds to me like a call for a kind of Postmodernism more substantial than the "mere textbook phenomenon" that he earlier dismissed:

"We are living at the end of linear time," he writes, "the time of succession: history, progress, modernity" (note the appropriate lower case):

> In art the most virulent form of the crisis of modernity has been the criticism of the object; begun by Dada, it is now ending in the destruction (or self-destruction) of the "artistic thing," painting or sculpture, in celebration of the act, the ceremony, the happening [remember that Paz is writing in 1970], the gesture. The crisis of the object is little more than a (negative) manifestation of the end of time; what is undergoing crisis is not art but time, our idea of time. The idea of "modern art" is a consequence of the idea of a "history of art"; both were inventions of modernity and both are dying with it. . . . Is another art dawning? In certain parts of the world, particularly in the United States, we are witnessing different attempts to resurrect Fiesta (the "happening," for example).[7] . . . I recognize [in these attempts] the old Romantic dream, taken up and transmitted to today's younger generation by the Surrealists: that of erasing the boundaries between life and poetry. An art embodying images that satisfy our world's needs for collective rites. At the same time, how can we not imagine another art satisfying a no less imperative need: solitary meditation and contemplation? This art would not be a relapse into the idolatry of the "art object" of the last two hundred years, nor would it be an art of the destruction of the object; rather, it would regard the painting, sculpture, or poem as a point of departure. Heading where?

> Toward presence, toward absence, and beyond. Not the restoration of the object of art but the instauration of the poem or the painting as an inaugural sign opening up a new path.

"My reflections on Tantric art," Paz concludes, "are situated within the framework of such concerns." And very astute reflections they are. But Paz's call, or wish, for "another art" besides defunct Romanticism/Modernism on the one hand and the destruction of the art object or erasure of "the boundaries between life and poetry" on the other hand sounds to me very much like a call for Postmodernism—though not for the Hispanic *Postmodernismo* at which he has already sniffed, and not for *my* kind of gringo Postmodernism, which has no grand quarrel with the art object, at least in its manifestation as the Postmodernist novel.[8]

I conclude my consideration of Paz the Potential Postmodernist with two reflections and a more recent quotation. The first reflection is that, as a novelist, I am uneasy with the notion of the art object regarded *mainly* as a point of departure "toward presence, toward absence, and beyond" (whatever that language means) rather than as a wonderful thing in itself, while at the same time I protest that artistic *Meisterstücken,* even less-than-*Meisterstücken,* have always also been points of departure for "solitary meditation and contemplation," to a degree depending, I suppose, on the particular *Meisterstück,* the particular reader, viewer, or auditor, and the particular circumstances of their encounter. The second reflection is that I do not see how this "other art" that he imagines "dawning," even if it has prefigurations in Tantric art, for example, can be regarded otherwise than as something new in the ongoing history of Western art—a prospect that does not bother *me* in the least, but that seems to contradict Paz's original thesis concerning the end of time, succession, history, and all that. I'll return to this "end of" business presently, with respect to "The End of Postmodernism." But I cannot resist a final quotation from Mr. Paz—this from his speech accepting the 1990 Nobel Prize for literature—to demonstrate how seriously (though eloquently) he equivocates his terminology while attempting to clarify it (the speech is reprinted by Harvest/HBJ in the volume *In Search of the Present*):

> What is modernity? It is, first of all, an ambiguous term: there are as many types of modernity as there are societies. Each society has its own. The word's meaning is as uncertain and arbitrary as the name of the period that precedes it, the Middle Ages. If we are modern when compared to medieval times, are we perhaps the Middle Ages of a future modernity? Is a name that changes with time a real name? Modernity is a word in search of its meaning. Is it an idea, a mirage or a moment of history? Are we the children of modernity or are we its creators? Nobody knows for sure. . . . Since 1850 [modernity] has been our goddess and our demoness. In recent years there has been an attempt to exorcise her, and there has been much talk of "postmodernism." But what is postmodernism if not an even more modern modernity?

In my judgment, Mr. Paz is simply playing in a not very interesting way with that conflation of meanings that Bernard Williams remarked upon earlier. "Modern" and "postmodern" are ambiguous adjectives; "Modernist" and "Postmodernist," while certainly arguable, are much less ambiguous (especially with uppercase initials and outside their particular Hispanic literary-historical reference); the nouns "modernity" and "postmodernity" (especially with lowercase initials) unfortunately include both sets of adjectives. We must endeavor steadfastly to keep our terminology clear, but we need not throw up our hands. It may be valid, though it is not especially clever, to say that a Postmodernist writer like Italo Calvino and a Postmodernist architect like Philip Johnson are "more modern Modernists"; but it is not valid to say that they are more Modernist Modernists than, for example, Wallace Stevens and Ludwig Mies van der Rohe. No: They are better described by the term "Postmodernist"—a term that does, after all, have meaning.

Let's turn now briefly to the subject of postmodernity, or the postmodern condition, before coming back to Postmodernist art in general and PM fiction in particular. In preparation for these Stuttgart seminars, I duly took a look at some major studies of Postmodernism that have appeared or come to prominence since the last time I did such homework (i.e., since 1979, when I wrote the essay "The Literature of Replenishment" in preparation for my visit to the Tübingen meeting of the *Deutsche Gesellschaft für Amerikastudien*)—in particular, at reflections on the subject by the British architect Charles Jencks, the Italian semiotician/novelist Umberto Eco, the French philosopher-critics Jean-François Lyotard and Jean Baudrillard, their German counterpart Jürgen Habermas, and the American critical theorist N. Katherine Hayles. Some of these—the ones that I believe I understand, like Jencks and Eco—I have quoted already in my essay "Postmodernism Revisited." Eco's parable of the postmodern condition I find particularly "in synch" with my own position on the subject, in part no doubt because his example involves the problem of *getting something said,* which obviously speaks to my condition, but also because he avoids extended abstractions. I cannot say the same for Lyotard and Habermas, whom I do not understand very well at all, although I don't doubt that each knows not only what he himself is talking about but equally what the other is talking about. Reading them, alas, I find myself back in the eminent philologist Leo Spitzer's doctoral seminar at Johns Hopkins in the 1950s, when I realized that the classmates on my right and my left were going to be among the scholar-critics of their generation, and that I was going to have to make it as a fictionist, if at all. In the face of extended theoretical argument, unless it is laced with splendid concrete examples and dynamite one-liners, my eyes glaze over; my attention wanders to the nominalist world outside the classroom windows; I am obliged to push my head back and down with my hand to the next line of text, like the carriage of an old manual typewriter, until presently I close the book and go take a swim, or pick up a novel. There, back in my student days, went Hegel (but not Nietzsche or Schopenhauer); there in later years went Lacan and Derrida and other seminal figures, to my loss; and there, alas, went much of Lyotard and Baudrillard and more of Habermas this past spring. I apologize.

On the other hand, I don't want to cast myself as the Huckleberry Finn of Johns Hopkins University. Do I understand, for example, Lyotard's preliminary definition of postmodernism (the postmodern condition, I presume he means, not Postmodernist art) as "incredulity toward metanarratives"—by which he means, e.g., the "legitimating narrative" of science as the search for objective truth? I believe that I do understand that proposition; I would even second it if he substituted the word "skepticism" for "incredulity"—but M. Lyotard has the Gallic taste for hyperbole that used to give me trouble with Roland Barthes.[9] I quite agree with Lytoard that the postmodern condition involves (not *is*) skepticism (not necessarily *incredulity*) toward "metanarratives." So far, so good. And I like his remark (in the essay "Answering the Question: What Is Postmodernism?") that "eclecticism is the degree zero of contemporary general culture: one listens to reggae, watches a western, eats McDonald's food for lunch and local cuisine for dinner, wears Paris perfume in Tokyo and 'retro' clothes in Hong Kong. . . . " That pervasive eclecticism is an aspect of what N. Katherine Hayles calls "the denaturing of context" and what G. W. S. Trow (speaking of contemporary Americans) describes as living one's life "within the context of no context." I like also Lyotard's observation that "the essay (Montaigne) is postmodern, while the fragment ([Schlegel's] *The Athenaeum*) is modern"—an observation that echoes McEvilly's characterization of postmodernism as rational-skeptical as opposed to mystical-romantic—although I would have preferred Lyotard to say that Montaigne is postmodern*ist,* like the Middle Kingdom scribe Khakheperresenb, while the fragment is modern*ist.*

I like even better, because I understand it better, Fredric Jameson's observation (in his introduction to the American edition of Lyotard's book) that "Postmodern architecture . . . comes before us as a peculiar analogue to neoclassicism, a play of ('historicist') allusion and quotation that has renounced the older high modernist rigor and that itself seems to recapitulate a whole range of Western aesthetic strategies. . . . " Jameson goes on to cite architectural instances of

> a mannerist postmodernism (Michael Graves), a baroque postmodernism (the Japanese), a rococo postmodernism (Charles Moore), a neoclassical postmodernism (the French, particularly Christian de Portzamparc), and probably even a "high modernist" postmodernism in which modernism is itself the object of the postmodernist pastiche. This is a rich and creative [architectural] movement, of the greatest aesthetic play and delight, that can perhaps be most rapidly characterized as a whole by two important features: first, the falling away of the protopolitical vocation and the terrorist stance of the older modernism and, second, the eclipse of all the affect (depth, anxiety, terror, the

emotions of the monumental) that marked high modernism and its replacement by what Coleridge would have called fancy or Schiller aesthetic play, a commitment to surface and to the *superficial* in all the senses of the word.

Despite the inappropriate lowercase initial letters, that seems to me well said, perhaps even transferable to Postmodernist fiction, although I suspect that these aesthetic movements seem clearer to us fiction writers when the illustrations are from architecture or painting. In any case, I begin to hear Roland-Barthesian hyperbolical paradox and Octavio-Pazian equivocation in such passages as this (from the same essay by Lyotard, to which we now return):

> What, then, is the postmodern? . . . It is undoubtedly a part of the modern. All that has been received, if only yesterday . . . must be suspected. . . . A work can become modern only if it is first postmodern. Postmodernism thus understood is not modernism at its end but in the nascent state, and this state is constant.

I believe that I understand what Lyotard is saying here, but I disapprove of his saying it because he is unnecessarily muddying the waters that had seemed so clear when he and Jameson were talking architecture. He is stretching the terminology like Paz until it becomes all but meaningless.

And then we come to those passages of theoretical abstraction that make my eyes glaze over with incomprehension: passages like this one, that have the sonority of sense but that defy my comprehension:

> The postmodern would be that which, in the modern, puts forward the unpresentable in presentation itself; that which denies itself the solace of good forms, the consensus of a taste which would make it possible to share collectively the nostalgia for the unattainable; that which searches for new presentations, not in order to enjoy them but in order to impart a stronger sense of the unpresentable. A postmodern artist or writer is in the position of a philosopher: the text he writes, the work he produces are not in principle governed by preestablished rules, and they cannot be judged according to a determining judgment, by applying familiar categories to the text or to the work. Those rules and categories are what the work of art itself is looking for. The artist and the writer, then, are working without rules in order to formulate the rules of what *will have been done.* Hence the fact that work and text have the characters of an *event;* hence also, they always come too late for their author, or, what amounts to the same thing, their being put into work, their realization (*mise en oeuvre*) always begin too soon. *Post modern* would have to be understood according to the paradox of the future (*post*) anterior (*modo*).

To the extent that I comprehend this paradoxical passage, it sounds to me like a banality, as much a manifesto of the

Romantics and the Modernists as of the Postmodernists. Every "innovative" work of art is a leap into the unknown, an exploration of aesthetic possibilities, a quest; Friedrich von Schlegel understood that as well as Fredric Jameson and Jean-François Lyotard do. But I'm not at all sure that I *do* comprehend the passage just quoted, and in any case it does not seem to me to go very far toward distinguishing between the spirit of García Márquez's *Cien años de soledad* and the spirit of James Joyce's *Finnegans Wake:* the homely practical task that I addressed in my essay "The Literature of Replenishment."

Finally (with respect to Lyotard), there are aspects of the contemporary situation of artists and writers in late-capitalist societies of which Lyotard disapproves, but which Umberto Eco and I, for example, do not find to be self-evident disvalues: "Artistic and literary research [in postmodern society]," Lyotard writes (I believe he means "research" here in the sense of artistic experimentation), "is doubly threatened":

> . . . once by the "cultural policy" and once by the art and book market. What is advised, sometimes through one channel, sometimes through the other, is to offer works which, first, are relative to subjects which exist in the eyes of the public they address, and second, works so made ("well made") that the public will recognize what they are about, will understand what is signified, will be able to give or refuse its approval knowingly, and if possible, even to derive from such work a certain amount of comfort.

To this I would reply, Why on earth not, if the thing can be done with proper artistic responsibility? The situation Lyotard describes is that of Umberto Eco's postmodern lovers (aforecited in "Postmodernism Revisited") trying to give voice to their love—passionately but uninnocently, in full awareness of and responsibility to "the already said." It exemplifies the difference between a magnificent Postmodernist writer like García Márquez and a merely interesting one like, say, Georges Perec.

One could go on comparing and contrasting the prominent theorists of Postmodernism, I suppose, until the phenomenon really does come to an end: Jürgen Habermas ("Modernity versus Postmodernity"), Andreas Huyssen ("Mapping the Postmodern"), Craig Owens ("The Allegorical Impulse: Toward a Theory of Postmodernism"), Hal Foster ("Postmodernism, a Preface"), and of course Ihab Hassan, a charter member of the club. I myself have not yet read every one of these theorists; I begin to suspect that I never shall. But before I restate my own position on Postmodernist aesthetics, I want briefly to consider one more theorist—the earlier-cited N. Katherine Hayles of the University of Iowa—because I will be depending on her assistance when the time comes to relate chaos theory to Postmodernism.

In her most recent book, *Chaos Bound,* while acknowledging Lyotard's definition of cultural postmodernism as "an incredulity toward metanarratives," Hayles constructs her own narrative of the evolution of postmodernism and then speculates intelligently on the aesthetics of high-tech Postmodernist literary narration. Her definition of cultural postmodernism is somewhat different from Lyotard's; its root, she declares, is "the realization that what has always been thought of as the essential, un-varying components of human experience are not natural facts of life but social constructions." These essential life-components—whose "denaturing" in our century has, in her view, led to cultural postmodernism—include language, context, time, and "the human" itself, for in Hayles's opinion "The postmodern anticipates and im-plies the posthuman" (she is, remember, speaking of postmodern culture, not necessarily Postmodernist art). She proceeds to examine in some detail the denaturing of these erstwhile natural facts into social constructions. Radically summarized, her argument goes like this:

First, as to language: Its denaturing consists of its com-ing to be seen "not as a mimetic representation of the world of objects but as a sign system generating sig-nificance internally through a series of relational differ-ences. . . . Denatured language," says Hayles, "is language regarded as ground painted under our feet while we hang suspended in a void. We cannot dis-pense with the illusion of ground, because we need a place from which to speak. But [that illusion] is bracketed by our knowledge that it is only a painting, not natural ground." This vertiginous state of affairs, Hayles main-tains, is the historical consequence of two main currents of thought: in mathematics, physics, and philosophy, the undermining of Whitehead and Russell's *Principia Mathematica* by Gödel's theorem, of Einstein's special theory of relativity by quantum mechanics, and of logical positivism by such philosophers of science as Kuhn, Hanson, and Feyerabend, "who argued convincingly that observational statements are always theory-laden." And in linguistics, the Saussurean view that "language is in-herently self-referential and ungrounded . . . an interac-tive field in which the meaning of any one element de-pends upon the interactions present in the field as a whole." The resultant denaturing of language, in Hayles's narrative, constitutes the first wave of cultural postmod-ernism, a wave cresting in the period between the two world wars—although, to be sure, we can hear clear an-ticipations of it at least as early as Flaubert.[10]

The second wave, says Hayles—the denaturing of con-text—crested after the denaturing of language and is, in her view, an effect of the postwar explosion of interest in information theory and technology. "Initially," she writes, "messages were separated from contexts because such a move was necessary to make information quantifiable. Once this assumption was used to formulate a theory of information, information technology developed very rap-idly. And once this technology was in place, the disjunc-tion between message and context which began as a theoretical premise became a cultural condition." Hayles proceeds to illustrate this blurring of the distinction be-tween text and context with persuasive examples—from advanced weapons systems, from biogenetics (test-tube

babies), from MTV, from satellite image-enhancement, and even from literature (citing, e.g., Borges's stories "Pierre Menard, Author of the *Quixote*" and "Tlön, Uqbar, Orbis Tertius").

She then turns her attention to the denaturing of time, declaring that the "cutting loose of time from sequence, and consequently from human identity, constitutes the third wave of postmodernism. Time still exists in cultural postmodernism, but it no longer functions as a continuum along which human action can be plotted." She cites Heidegger and Derrida and then asks the question "How did we come to believe that the future, like the past, has already happened?" Her engaging answer is that "The rhythm of our century [had come to seem] predictable. World War I at the second decade; World War II at the fourth decade; World War III at the sixth decade, during which the world as we know it comes to an end. But somehow it did not happen when it was supposed to. By the ninth decade, we cannot help suspecting that maybe it happened after all and we failed to notice. Conse-quently time splits into a false future in which we all live and a true future that by virtue of being true does not have us in it." She illustrates this interesting state of affairs as manifested in Nabokov's *Ada,* Walker Percy's *Love Among the Ruins,* and a number of movies, and then applies it to Postmodernist aesthetics, citing for example the critic Michel Serres's view that the temporal aes-thetic of nineteenth-century realism gives way in our century to "a spatial aesthetic focusing on deformations, local turbulence, and continuous but nondifferentiable curves"—a hint of chaos theory already, and reminiscent of William Gass's recent lectures on "spatial form" in literature. And Hayles concludes her discussion of the denaturing of time by pointing out that it makes paradoxi-cal the writing of a *history* of postmodernism. The vari-ous theorists whose names we keep mentioning are all "concerned to locate postmodernism in a sequence that began with modernism."

> They vary in their estimations of how successful, and even what, modernism was; they disagree about whether it is continued or refuted by postmodernism. Whatever their stance, however, they concur that postmodernism *has a history,* and thus that it has roots in such intellectual issues as the self-referentiality of symbol systems, the Kantian sublime, the cultural logic of late capitalism, and so forth.

The case is very different, she declares, for those who *live* postmodernism rather than theorize about its history:

> For them, the denaturing of time means that they have no history. To live postmodernism is to live as schizophrenics are said to do, in a world of disconnected present moments that jostle one another but never form a continuous (much less logical) progression. The prior experiences of older people [such as all those theorists] act as anchors that keep them from fully entering the postmodern stream of spliced contexts and discontinuous time. Young people, lacking these anchors and immersed

in TV, are in a better position to know from direct experience what it is to have no sense of history, to live in a world of simulacra, to see [even] the human form as provisional. The case could be made that the people in this country [the USA] who know the most about how postmodernism *feels* (as distinct from how to envision or analyze it) are all under the age of sixteen.

I want to return to this distinction presently: not between the young and the old, but between those who theorize about postmodernism and those who live it (some of that latter group, I know for a fact, are older than sixteen, and not all of them lack a sense of history or live like schizophrenics). But there remains to be considered the prospective fourth wave of Professor Hayles's narrative of cultural postmodernism: the denaturing of the human, by which she means something considerably more ominous than the famous "dehumanization of art" that the Spanish philosopher José Ortega y Gasset was applauding back in the 1940s. I'll surf down this fourth wave quickly, first because it happily has yet to break fully upon us, and second because Hayles's discussion of it has mainly to do with such things as cyborgs and the new "cyberpunk" fiction of William Gibson and his confreres, which I resist as I resist most science fiction, as being artistically thin, as a rule, however occasionally ingenious. But Hayles is surely correct when she writes that "the denaturing process arouses intense ambivalence, especially as it spreads to envelop the human."

> Language, context, and time are essential components of human experience . . . [whereas] the human is a construction logically prior to all three, for it defines the grounds of experience itself.[11] If denaturing the human can sweep away more of the detritus of the past than any of the other postmodern deconstructions, it can also remove taboos and safeguards that are stays, however fragile, against the destruction of the human race. What will happen to the movement for human rights when the human is regarded as a construction like any other? Such concerns illustrate why, at the heart of virtually all postmodernisms, one finds a divided impulse.

That said, Hayles concludes her study by applying Lyotard's postmodern "incredulity toward metanarratives" to her own narrative of denaturing and to narrative itself, asking rhetorically,

> What are the essential components of narrative construction, if not language, context, time, and the human? The denaturing of experience, in other words, constitutes a cultural metanarrative; and its peculiar property is to imply incredulity not just toward other metanarratives but toward narrative as a form of representation. It thus implies its own deconstruction.

That seems to me to be reasonably said, particularly if we follow my advice and substitute "skepticism" for "incredulity." What sort of narrative fiction, for example, might one write out of a fundamental postmodern skepticism

toward narrative itself? "In a fully denatured narrative," Hayles argues, "one would expect the language to be self-referential; the context to be self-consciously created, perhaps by the splicing together of disparate contexts; the narrative progression to be advanced through the evolution of underlying structures rather than through chronological time; and the characters to be constructed so as to expose their nature as constructions." As a working Postmodernist literary aesthetic, that certainly sounds close to the mark, although it leaves out a few things that I regard as essential. It also sounds a lot like Rabelais, Sterne, Diderot, and company, and Hayles (unlike Lyotard) wisely acknowledges that Postmodernist texts have no monopoly on these literary strategies. "What could be more self-referential than the end of *A Midsummer Night's Dream*," she asks, "or more effective at representing the denatured human than *Frankenstein?*" What makes a text postmodern (and, I would add, what makes it Postmodernist as well) is not the above-mentioned literary strategies in isolation, but rather "their connection through complex feedback loops with postmodernism as a cultural dominant. Other times have had glimpses of what it would mean to live in a denatured world. But never before have such strong feedback loops among culture, theory, and technology brought it so close to being a reality."

To this I say Brava, Professor Hayles—even before we examine (somewhere down the road) how she fits chaos theory into her postmodern Weltanschauung and how the Romantic arabesque can be said to bear upon both.

. . . . .

I now return briefly to the overall subject of these Stuttgart seminars, "the end of postmodernism," and to my own position on these matters as a working writer.

As to the former: Whether or not Hayles's apocalyptical "denaturing of the human" comes to pass—and I for one profoundly hope and almost believe that it will not—there is no reason to doubt that the experience of being human will continue to be *refigured* by changes in technology, as it has been being refigured dramatically ever since the industrial revolution, and that this refiguration will be reflected in—even anticipated by—whatever passes for art in the next century (to look no farther). Even the "denaturing of time" will not prevent our artistic successors from doing things rather differently from the way we've done them, and therefore what we call Postmodernist literature, for example, will by no means prove to be the last word. On the subject of the future of literature as a medium of art and entertainment I'll have my say another time[12]—but I do not doubt that by the year 2030, let's say, when I turn one hundred, we won't be calling what we do Postmodernist. The ending of this century and of the millenium has already prompted so many "endgames"— the end of history, the end of nature, the end of Western linear time that we heard Octavio Paz speak of earlier— that 2000 seems an appropriate target date for winding up Postmodernism as a cultural and aesthetic dominant, just as 1950 or thereabouts was a historically tidy date for bidding auf Wiedersehen to High Modernism.

What's more, for writers "like myself" and of my approximate age, whose product has been classified over the decades as existentialist, black humorist, fabulist, and now Postmodernist, it wouldn't surprise me if that last term turns out to be the one we're stuck with in the history books, if there continue to be such things as history and history books. I here report that that prospect is quite okay by me. I have never resisted the term "Postmodernist"; indeed, QED, I have, if not quite embraced it, at least accepted it and attempted to understand how it applies to what I've done and what I'm doing in my daily practice. I have never written anything because it was the Postmodernist thing to write; I've written what I've written because I have seen fit to do so, whereafter others (myself more or less included) have seen fit to classify the product as Postmodernist. In many respects, I think, that adjective describes my output better than those earlier classifications did, and so if it turns out that I am too far along in my curriculum vitae to get to be called a post-Postmodernist or whatever in my old age, I am quite prepared to shrug my shoulders and get on with the story.

Because (to conclude) while I know that there is a feedback loop between my thinking about postmodern culture and Postmodernist aesthetics and my practice of writing fiction—a "coaxial esemplasy," each shaping the other—I continue to affirm the primacy of the work. Following Professor Hayles's Postmodernist literary aesthetic might well make a work Postmodernist, but it won't ipso facto make it wonderful, and for me, as you have heard,[13] the important thing is that it be wonderful. Can it be wonderful (Donald Barthelme once asked[14]) even if it drags along after it "the burnt-out boxcars of a dead aesthetic"? Maybe so, maybe not. But I am convinced that blockbustingly wonderful novels, for instance, can influence literary fashion at least as much as literary fashion influences more routine specimens of the genre. I would contend that James Joyce affected literary Modernism at least as much as Modernism affected Joyce, and that the Postmodernist novel has been influenced more by the example of Gabriel García Márquez than he has been influenced by Postmodernist literary theory. Rousseau and Goethe don't owe nearly as much to Romanticism as Romanticism owes to them. The individual terrific writer, the individual terrific work, is the main thing. The labels are neither meaningless nor unnecessary; but by whatever name we label it, on with the story.

NOTES

[1] For reasons presently to be set forth, I wish he would say "Modernist" instead of "modern."

[2] Also the omission of commas before conjunctions in serial items ("electicism, historical reference and greater jollity") and the digitalization of century-names (18th, 19th), both practices frowned upon by the present author's house style and by his publishers' as well.

[3] Likewise Hassan's seminal *Dismemberment of Orpheus,* aforecited.

[4] Cited in "Postmodernism Revisited."

[5] San Diego: Harcourt Brace Jovanovich, 1987.

[6] I should add that he does not, at least in this essay, go on to describe any subsequent phase of Hispano-American Modernism after that "initial" phase of 1890-1905.

[7] A charming idea: The Fiesta as a prototype of the Happening!

[8] In general, Paz has little to say about novels, even the exemplary Postmodernist novels of his fellow Mexico Cityman Gabriel García Márquez.

[9] Barthes's proposition in *Writing Degree Zero,* for example, that "the whole of literature, from Flaubert to the present day, becomes the problematics of language." If only he had been content to say that "the problematics of language"—indeed, the problematics of every aspect of the medium of literature, not language alone—becomes one of several prominent field-identification marks of our literature after "Flaubert." But that kind of reasonable modification, I suppose, de-zings such zingers.

[10] E.g., in *Madame Bovary:* "Language is a cracked kettle that we beat on for bears to dance, when all the while we wished to move the stars."

[11] Which, we might recall here, is the Aristotelian "subject of literature."

[*] See this collection's concluding Friday-piece: "Inconclusion: The Novel in the Next Century."

[13] E.g., in "Postmodernism Revisited."

[14] In his 1985 *Georgia Review* essay, "Not-Knowing."

POETRY

Michael Davidson

SOURCE: "Languages of Post-Modernism," in *Chicago Review,* Vol. 27, No. 1, Summer, 1975, pp. 11-22.

[In the following essay, Davidson examines some defining characteristics of postmodernism that have appeared in American poetry and art.]

Aristotle tells the story of C ratylus, who became so infatuated with Heraclitean notions of flux and change that he proceeded to amend the famous statement, "No man steps into the same river twice," to the effect that 'no man can do it once.' His reasoning, apparently, was based on the fact that in the interval between the time that man touches the surface of the river and when his foot touches the bottom, the river has already changed. So committed was Cratylus to this view that he finally gave up speaking altogether (since to form words was to give a false image of permanence) and could be seen about the public square only waggling his finger.

The crisis of Cratylus is the crisis of all modernisms, since the act of taking up a new reality involves a reevaluation of the terms in which it is embodied. Cratylus' silence might be seen as the recognition of Heraclitus' failure and his finger waggling as the attempt to "do" philosophy in a manner coincident with its ideas. The contemporary poet is in the same situation: how is it possible to "do" poetry authentically without resorting to the rhetorics and dictions of the previous period?

The artist in the period since World War II has, for the most part, been involved in a critique of language which has reverberations in the history of mimetic and representational forms.

The confluence of artists, dancers, poets and musicians at Black Mountain brought a wide variety of realizations of this "field" together. I am interested in possible ramifications of Olson's concerns with the physiological basis of the poem and his adherence to a personalized, "everyday" language in the painting and poetry of the post-abstract expressionist generation in New York. And I am interested in such extensions ("the languages of post-modernism") in terms of their use of the work of art structured *as* a language and as part of an ongoing critique of language itself.

The writing of the poets associated with the New York School extends notions of "everyday" speech in a direction which would seem the opposite of Black Mountain formalistic concerns. And yet, the work of Frank O'Hara, John Ashbery, James Schuyler, Kenneth Koch and others is certainly a "field" proposition in that what happens during a given moment structures the shape of the poem. The emphasis is less, however, on complex systems of notion, spacing, punctuation, etc., and more on the overall "feel" of a day's events.

Frank O'Hara's "Personist" manifesto puts it in a nutshell:

> You just go on your nerve. If someone's chasing you down the street with a knife you just run, you don't turn around and shout, "Give it up! I was a track star for Mineola Prep."

> *(The Collected Poems of Frank O'Hara, p. 498.)*

And later he describes the origins of "personism": "I was realizing that if I wanted to I could use the telephone instead of writing the poem." And this reevaluation should be seen in the context of developments in current philosophy of language which locates at the level of

ordinary discourse a problematic of the sign with pertinence for contemporary art in general. To "do" one's art means to solve problems in a language which the art establishes as it is being created. Its grammar and lexicon emerge less as a result of a commitment to prior forms and more as a response to immediate necessity.

It is some such possibility which is opened up by notions of "field" verse as formulated by Charles Olson and other poets of the Black Mountain group during the early fifties. "Field" verse contains a conception of the poem as a place where things happen, an open area of possibility or, as Robert Duncan calls it, "a place of first permission." Olson derived the idea from his work in topology, quantum mechanics, his interest in the philosophy of Whitehead, and the linguistics of Sapir and Whorf. For these concerns, the field is a nexus, a convergence of separate points which, like beams in a holograph, come together to make an event. Perhaps the most useful statement of "field" in terms of writing is made by Robert Duncan:

> The poem is not a stream of consciousness, but an area of composition in which I work with whatever comes into it. Only words come into it. Sounds and ideas. The tone leading of vowels, the various percussions of consonants. The play of numbers in stresses and syllables. In which meanings and ideas, themes and things seen, arise. So that there is not only a melody of sounds but of images. Rimes, the reiteration of formulations in the design, even puns, lead into complexities of the field. But now the poet works with a sense of parts fitting in relation to a design that is larger than the poem.

> *(Bending The Bow, p. vi.)*

And perhaps the best commentary on New York poetry comes from O'Hara's art criticism and his introductions to the work of Pollock, Motherwell and others. In discussing the term "action painting" in relation to Jackson Pollock, he speaks as well for his own purposes as a poet:

> So difficult is the attainment that, when the state has finally been reached, it seems that a maximum of decisions has already been made in the process, that the artist has reached a limitless space of air and light in which the spirit can act freely and with unpremeditated knowledge. His action is immediately art, not through will, not through esthetic posture, but through a singleness of purpose which is the result of all the rejected qualifications and found convictions forced upon him by his strange ascent.

> *(Jackson Pollock, p. 21)*

Like Stein's attempt to approximate the activity of cubism, O'Hara's connection with the first generation abstract expressionists is significant for a view of his poetry. The blank canvas is a field of action and would be the record of a painter's activity much as Olson wanted to include the physical breath and metabolic ratios of the poet in his poem.

O'Hara's long poems have a kind of innocent aimlessness to them—like letters to friends or conversations with oneself. "In Memory of My Feelings," to take a great example, is a meditation on the problem of one's masks, but O'Hara does not step outside of those masks and describe them. He adopts one after another, moving from scenes at a race track to a discourse on his family to an Arabian desert to the deck of the Prinz Eugen among German prisoners. The theme, if the poem has one, is stated towards the end:

> Grace
> to be born and live as variously as possible. The
>   conception
> of the masque barely suggests the sordid
>   identifications.
>   (*The Collected Poems,* p. 256)

This variousness occurs in the poem as a series of images which change direction almost from line to line. If it is frustrating to read, it is because O'Hara so totally occupies the terms of the poem:

> My quietness has a man in it, he is transparent
> and he carries me quietly, like a gondola, through
>   the streets.
> He has several likenesses, like stars and years, like
>   numerals.
>
> My quietness has a number of naked selves,
> so many pistols I have borrowed to protect
>   myselves
> from creatures who too readily recognize my
>   weapons
>   and have murder in their heart!

The poem's opening, quoted here, moves out gently like the gondola but quickly changes pace when the revery is seen to be mediated by self-protecting masks. We see the problem firsthand; the paranoia which demands "pistols" to "protect myselves" creates forms of itself and speaks from those centers of uncertainty.

As tempting as it might be to read a development of "personae," O'Hara speaks confidently in his own voice. The images which pass before us as we read through the poem do not reduce themselves to any given pattern. And despite the darkness of the opening lines, the poem is at turns playful, at times reflective. What he captures is the "scene" of his masks which, paradoxically, is the one aspect of his life that he cannot have:

> I could not change it into history
> and so remember it,
>   and I have lost what is always and
>   everywhere
> present, the scene of my selves, the occasion of
>   these ruses,
> which I myself and singly must now kill
>   and save the serpent in their midst.

The "scene" in which each mask is adopted is what the poem may contain, despite his denial. O'Hara wants to "bend the ear of the outer world" and tell us about the situation of masks and about the frustration of living after them. As a meditation on the failure of art in the face of personal despair, it is a powerful dialogue with the creating self as it throws off disguises.

Although the long, rambling poetry, of "In Memory of My Feelings" is a customary mode, much of the New York writing is programmatically formal, at least in the sense that it investigates the limits of form. Attempts at writing sestinas, villanelles, epistolary novels, sonnets, collaborations, etc., are not uncommon. The basic form of the proposition "it is possible that . . ." leads to a multiplicity of variations on the theme of classical forms. Most significant is a challenge to the idea that there are discrete differences between prose and poetry. The influence of the French prose poem and of Stein's attempt to create an "extended present" in prose are some of the sources for such experimentation.

John Ashbery's work is a case in point. In a recent book, *Three Poems* (Viking, 1972), the title is challenged by the appearance of justified margins on each page of text. If one assumes that prose is simply a sub-set of poetry (as David Antin and others have) along with question-asking, narration, lyric, conversation, drama, then some of the confusion is removed. But there is more to it than a simple reclassification of modes. What characterizes the three poems in *Three Poems* is the lack of seriality to the prose, the absence of an end toward which each sentence strives. The language is maddeningly nonspecific; antecedents are lost, pronouns come to refer to a variety of persons, what look to be paragraph breaks are actually arbitrary spacings between certain lines which may or may not generate from a period. The absence of paragraph indentations, the arbitrariness of the caesurae, the density of the language (and its occasional banality) all point away from conventional prose and the traditional prose poem.

One might enter *Three Poems* anywhere, though the opening lines of "The New Spirit" suggest a kind of program of reading:

> I thought that if I could put it all down, that
>   would be
> one way. And next the thought came to me that to
>   leave all out
> would be another, and truer way.

Three Poems enacts the absence of those distinguishing marks by which a story might be recognized, the "leaving-out" of the usual bridges which, like Cratylus' view of words, give a false impression of permanence. Instead, the language is elusive, continually intimating things to come—as the title of the first section, "The New Spirit," suggests.

Behind the elusiveness exists a love relationship whose existence and complexities are as unspecific as the prose:

> It is not easy at first. There are dark vacancies the
> light of the hunter's moon does little to attenuate.
> Ever thought about the moon, how well it fits
> what it has to light? And those lacquer blobs and
> rivers of daylight, shaked out of a canister—so

unmanageable, so indigestible . . . Well isn't that the point? No, but there comes a time when what is to be revealed actually conceals itself in casting off the mask of its identity, when the identity itself is revealed as another mask and a lesser one antecedent to that we had come to know and accept.

(p. 8)

The prose "style" imitates its content; the relationship which emerges from time to time throughout the section is given concrete presence by the masking and foiling of the prose—a creation by absence. "It is not easy at first," Ashbery says, and there is little resolution at the end either. Later on, however, we find what seems to be a congruent section:

Such particulars you mouthed, all leading back into the underlying question; was it you? Do these things between people partake of themselves or are they a subtler kind of translucent matter carrying each to a compromise distance, painfully outside the rings of authority? For we never knew, never knew what joined us together. Perhaps only a congealing of closeness, directing out, living into their material and in that way somehow making more substance before, and yet the outward languid motion, like girls hanging out of windows . . . Is this something to be guessed at, though? Can it be identified with some area in someone's mind?

(p. 39)

This last sentence is precisely the question which the poet's prose uncovers: the inability of the art to contain "some area in someone's mind," the failure of ratios which exist between mind and matter, signs and referent, "outward languid motion" and the image which prompts it, "girls hanging out of windows." If, as the poet says, "we never knew what joined us together," he is going a long way to indicate that this strange bond remains obscure well into the writing of the present poem.

As if explaining this same process, Ashbery has remarked of his poetry:

When it is commenting on itself it's only doing so in such a way as to point out that living, creating is a process which tends to take itself very much into account and it's not doing so with any attempt to explain the poetry or what poetry ought to do.

("Craft Interview with John Ashbery," *The Craft of Poetry,* ed. William Packard, p. 128.)

Much of Ashbery's poetry seem to comment on itself or at least move in a realm between self-reflection and a world of images. A crucial poem of this sort is "The Skaters" (*Rivers and Mountains,* p. 39) whose title suggests the very process of its composition: a skating, desultorily, over a broad flat surface. At first, the actual image of a "warm February day" and a brief snapshot present what seems to be a conventional winter landscape: "Here a scarf flies, there an excited call is heard."

But Ashbery is interested in novelty (as he says in the poem) and such glimpses merely establish a mood, draw attention to the fragmentary nature of perception in such a scene. As in "The New Spirit," self-conjecture and questioning enter the poem:

But this is an important aspect of the question
Which I am not ready to discuss, am not at all
      ready to,
This leaving-out business. On it hinges the very
      importance
                    of what's novel
Or autocratic, or dense or silly. It is as well to call
      attention
To it by exaggeration, perhaps. But calling
      attention
Isn't the same thing as explaining, and as I said I
      am not ready
To line phrases with the costly stuff of
      explanation, and shall not,
Will not do so for the moment. Except to say that
      the carnivorous
Way of these lines is to devour their own nature,
      leaving
Nothing but a bitter impression of absence, which
      as we know
                    involves presence, but still.
Nevertheless these are fundamental absences,
      struggling to get up and
be off themselves.

Here, Ashbery seems to mock his own measure. The intrusion of a polemical tone is hardly that suggested by a day in February, the skaters ranging themselves near and far over a white surface. It is difficult to know which is more important, the analytical tone or the landscape. In the poet's mind, they are part of the same thing, and this poem is an attempt to understand the relationship between the creation of atmosphere (the poetic depiction of place and person) and the act of making art; they are inclusive and must speak from the same source.

What is the matter with plain old-fashioned cause-
      and-effect?
Leaving one alone with romantic impressions of
      the trees, the sky?
Who, actually, is going to be fooled one instant by
      these phony
            explanations,

There is a delight in the poet's discovery of himself in the role of poet manqué and a recognition that both the delight and the "romantic impressions" must be kept intact:

      I am fascinated
Though by the urge to get out of it all, by going
Further in and correcting the whole mismanaged
      mess.
      But am afraid I'll
Be of no help to you. Good-bye.

Perhaps it is in this role of poet that we hear Ashbery's debt to another creator of supreme fictions—Wallace Stevens.

Another example of a "language" of post-modernism concerns the world of painting during the early sixties. It has been characteristic to refer to the abstract expressionist generation which preceded pop art in terms of its flattening of the picture plane and its emphasis upon the materials of painting rather than upon illusionist perspective. Clement Greenberg, in his famous essay "Modernist Painting," emphasized the development of a self-critical art which used the medium of the painting—the support, the physical properties of paint, the flat surface of the stretched canvas—to "eliminate from the effects of each art any and every effect that might conceivably be borrowed from or by the medium of any other art" [*Art and Literature,* 4 (Spring, 1965), p. 194]. Presumably Mr. Greenberg was not thinking of Pollock's early interest in surrealism or in the wall murals of Diego Rivera and Siquieros as models for his own psychological paintings and wall-sized canvases. Nor was he thinking of the use of heavily washed canvases of someone like Helen Frankenthaler to develop textural density, or the use of heavily layered oil in DeKooning to create areas of underpainting and depth.

With the emergence of pop art, critics tended to overlook the continuation of certain aspects of abstract expressionism, and although the criterion of flatness is certainly an aspect of Warhol's or Rosenquist's style, the "depth" is still there in a complex series of oppositions which occur at the semiotic level: the transformation of photograph to paint, the illumination of figure-ground problems in enlarged comic-strip sections, the confusion of size ratios in billboard art, the doubling of reproduced market items in a language of duplication (print, silkscreen, stencil, etc.), the confusion of word as object versus word as sign, the opposition between sign and "subject matter," etc.

The waves of criticism which followed the appearance of pop art in showings during the early sixties tended to center around certain criteria: 1) vulgarity of the subject matter—the idea that an accurate representation of banal existence is sheerly banal (cf. Max Kozloff, "Pop Culture, Metaphysical Disgust, and the New Vulgarians" in *Renderings,* pp. 216-23); 2) the dissociation of the artist from his medium, the intrusion of technological materials (print-making, plastics, sprayguns, etc.) into the creation of art; 3) the idea that the "new realism" was a poor imitation of the great realist masters or an attempt to find in billboard-perfect advertising copy an equivalent for Van Gogh's shoes; 4) the essential conservatism, the rigidity of line, color, texture, etc. Most criticism was based upon iconographical criteria. Clement Greenberg had provided a critical vocabulary for viewing abstract painting in its heyday, and no one was going to be fooled by this new intrusion.

But the criteria of abstract expressionism, the overall technique, its painterliness, its emphasis of the medium of paint and stretched canvas, is precisely what distinguishes pop art and pop artists. The language of surfaces in a Jasper Johns distinctly refers back to the earlier 'muscular' brushstroke of Kline, Pollock, etc. while the smooth surface and primary colors of a Warhol Campbell's Soup Can refer to the very process of duplication by

which both Campbell's soup and its advertising copy are produced. Warhol's background in fashion advertising, Rosenquist's past as a billboard painter and Lichtenstein's work as a cartoonist are no small features in their languages of representation.

As Robert Rosenblum has said,

> If Pop Art is to mean anything at all, it must have something to do not only with *what* is painted but also with the *way* it is painted; . . . The authentic Pop artist offers a coincidence of style and subject, that is, he represents mass-produced images and objects by using a style which is also based upon the visual vocabulary of mass production.
>
> ["Pop Art and Non-Pop Art," *Art and Literature,* 5 (Summer, 1965), p. 89.]

This coincidence is graphically illustrated in Jasper Johns's "subjects" which are taken not from the world of mass-produced market items but from the world of signals, numbers, direction signs and maps. Is a target or a flag a "representation" of a target or flag? Or is it by definition what it is? If a number is painted onto a canvas, does it then become a picture of a number, or is it always a number in any form? These targets, flags and numbers rest in the interstitial realm in which signs refer only to themselves as signs.

Johns presents a series of conflicting problems concerning flatness versus illusion, natural object versus represented object, painterly surface versus flat object. The "visual language" which Rosenblum mentions is carefully coordinated to coincide with the ambiguity of the icons. Numbers and words are stencilled onto the canvas as if to give directions for future placement of paint. In his "Field Painting" of 1963-64, one realizes that although Johns has painted words for primary colors along a vertical axis, their relationship to the actual colors in which they are painted is nowhere to be seen. The ambiguity between the outline of RED and the fact that it is painted variously in blue, orange, purple, etc., is the tension which informs much of Johns's work as well as that of Larry Rivers (and Robert Rauschenberg, whose work has at times been associated with developments in pop art).

It is a different world with James Rosenquist, Roy Lichtenstein and Andy Warhol, in whose Marilyn Monroes, Campbell Soup cans, billboard-sized collages, blown-up comic strips complete with Ben-Day dots, America in general saw a camp satire on modern-day life and in specific saw a renovation of earlier realist aesthetics in a new setting. But pop art initiated a romance of the reproduced object. The print became a major medium and the smooth textures made possible by silkscreen and spraygun replaced the mottled surface of the pallet knife and paintbrush. Rosenquist's and Lichtenstein's evocation of commercial design and advertising copy refers back to the hard-edged industrial landscapes of Charles Sheeler and Charles Demuth and the mechanical constructivism of Léger.

Whatever the subject, whether Jackie Kennedy or a giant slice of pie, the reference is flattened by the medium and so emphasis returns to the idea of a reproduced or represented object. In this crucial sense, pop art detaches itself from "realism." What is striking about a billboard-sized comic strip section is its size; the amplification of the black outline and dots which are transparent on a smaller scale creates ambiguities of figure and ground. Its dissociation from the comic's narrative sequence equally heightens the strangeness, creating weird new twists to the customary "zap" and "pow" by which sounds translate themselves into a two-dimensional world. In a Wayne Thiebaud slice of pie, what is being represented is not a piece of pie but a world of ideal pie slices painted in powder blues and muted yellows more reminiscent of plaster of paris copies than food on a cafeteria tray.

Despite the references to worlds of primary shapes and colors, the contexts in which such patterns occur are distorted or heightened, giving new dimension to so-called objects of daily life. In Claes Oldenburg's soft sculpture, ordinary objects such as wall plugs and icepacks and toasters assume heroic proportions. (A giant soft icepack seems to breathe and sigh with an identity all its own.) George Segal's environments of the modern urban street develop existential realms of dry cleaners and theater marquees. Robert Indiana's hard-edged arrangements of circles, triangles and squares present a world of gigantic words and numbers advertising LOVE, NINE, EAT, and DIE. Their geometrical arrangements and bold colors suggest altars or monuments to words themselves. The designs of Nicolas Krushenick suggest a world of details from mammoth comic-book paintings.

In the work of pop art, the terms of its criticism are contained within the work itself. No amount of appeal to its "subject matter" will suffice to explain what occurs in each work. It recognizes a return not merely to figurative painting but to a problematic of representation no less critical than that experienced by the impressionists or the abstract expressionists. The self-critical stance of much of the art which I've discussed is characterized succinctly by Harold Rosenberg:

> In sum, there is no greater esthetic value in copying the design on a beer can. If you do either, you are talking to the audience about itself, not engaging in creation. In dramatizing this principle, Pop Art has been a contribution to art criticism.

(The Anxious Object, p. 75.)

The work of the Black Mountain poets and their concern for the poem as an energized "field," the New York School and post-abstract expressionist painting is only a small segment of the total scene. A thorough investigation of language and ordering-systems in contemporary art would have to cover the music of indeterminacy and chance operations (Cage, Tudor, Feldman, Young), the dance of Merce Cunningham and the Judson group, developments in minimalist and conceptual art, the poetries of deep image and concrete poetry, happenings, theater

events, and so forth. What links these areas is a fundamental concern with art as process. The "finished" work is often a record of the steps taken in formulating a problem, stating a crisis, or becoming happy.

My use of the word "language" serves to relate art to its role as an expressive totality. The work of language philosophy during the last few decades, while in no strict sense interacting with art movements, has been aware of the role of internal cohesiveness of systems and has attempted to broaden the frame of language to cover the field of signs in general. The work of art *as* a language begins with the moment of conjecture and extends to find what it will become.

Charles Altieri

SOURCE: "What Is Living and What Is Dead in American Postmodernism: Establishing the Contemporaneity of Some American Poetry," in *Critical Inquiry,* Vol. 22, No. 4, Summer, 1996, pp. 764-89.

[In the following essay, Altieri finds that contemporary American poetry has to a significant extent divested itself from the stylistic and thematic traits of postmodern critical theory.]

I think postmodernism is now dead as a theoretical concept and, more important, as a way of developing cultural frameworks influencing how we shape theoretical concepts. With its basic enabling arguments now sloganized and its efforts to escape binaries binarized, it is unlikely to generate much significant new work.[1] On this I suspect most critics would agree. But that then raises the more troubling question of whether the notion of postmodernism has any more vitality as a rubric capable of sponsoring significant new work in the arts. Perhaps now that the theory has lost much of its power it may be possible to recognize how much it appropriated from the arts and to focus on differences between the two orientations. It may even be possible to regain for the arts some of the cultural authority they at least thought they possessed before "theory" took over the role of shaping how imaginations might cultivate alternatives to the ideologies dominating "official culture."

I propose to show how some contemporary American poetry makes good on these possibilities. But to make that case I have to turn first to two preliminary tasks. I have to illustrate the pressures put on several contemporary arts by recent emphases within postmodernist theory, so that we understand the serious split that has been emerging between the current state of that theory and the experimental artists and writers who had been its allies. And then I have to spell out in some detail how a good deal of this pressure derives from deeper, structural problems fundamental to these theoretical orientations. I will argue that as theorists tried to elaborate the turn against modernism that had developed first in the arts and then in poststructural philosophy, they worked themselves into several paralyzing contradictions that only now have become fully manifest.[2] Recognizing these contradictions is not simply a matter of critical lucidity. By attending to them, criticism may be able to gain a position from which it can offer much fuller appreciations of the intelligence and flexibility that various artists and writers bring to the same sets of concerns, and hence may develop less problematic conceptual models for contemporary social conditions. In part because of the different demands of their media, these artists not only manage to finesse the most severe aspects of the contradictions but they also develop imaginative stances projecting alternatives to modernism that are far more plausible and liveable than those current theory has managed to formulate. And, if I am right, these arguments then help support the further claim that there are important ways these arts directly engage what is deeply disturbing in contemporary life even though they refuse to take direct political stances.

For my first example of the way "radical" contemporary writing has grown uncomfortable with "radical" postmodernist theory, I will turn to a statement by Charles Bernstein, a poet deeply committed to finding alternatives both to modernism and to marketplace values:

> Within the emerging official cultural space of diversity, figures of difference are often selected because they narrate in a way that can readily be assimilated—not to say absorbed—into the conventional forms of dominant culture. Difference is confined to subject matter and thematic material, a.k.a. local color, excluding the formal innovations that challenge those dominant paradigms of representations.

Because "works that challenge these models of representation run the risk of becoming more inaudible than ever within mainstream culture," poems "selected to represent cultural diversity" tend towards the same fundamental, quite conventional structure:

> "I see grandpa on the hill / next to the memories I can never recapture" is the base line against which other versions play: "I see my yiddishe mama on Hester street / next to the pushcarts I can no longer peddle" or "I see my grandmother on the hill / next to all the mothers whose lives can never be recaptured" or "I can't touch my Iron Father / who never canoed with me / on the prairies of my masculine epiphany."[3]

Bernstein's complaints make all too clear the consequences of a pervasive uneasiness in postmodernism's relations to the modernist values it tries both to extend and to transform. At one pole postmodernist artists and writers have claimed to continue the experimental ambitions fundamental to modernism—at least insofar as modernism fostered ways of resisting structures of expectation that developed around realist ideals. Countering realism entailed treating art less as a mode of referring directly to the world than as an emphasis on the capacity of the artistic syntax to exemplify ways of feeling, thinking, and imaginatively projecting investments not bound to dominant social structures. But how does one keep the

resistance to realism from becoming a modernist formalism, blind to historical forces and refusing to take responsibility for the political conditions created by those forces? This is postmodernism's problem. Both antagonism towards modernism and a need to respond to those political conditions has created a situation in which it becomes increasingly difficult to trust to the play of signification. The more urgent the art world's sense of political pressures, the more imposing the case to return to some kind of representational aesthetics, if only to find ways of providing representatives for the diverse social units now seeking political voices.

Those pressures are exacerbated by the fact that postmodern theory has not managed to develop its own analogue to the distinction between modernism and modernity that enables us clearly to set the art of the early twentieth century in opposition to mainstream culture.[4] In contrast, as I will argue more fully below, the dominant recent theorizing about the relation between the arts and their cultural context seems to wobble between strong claims about how the arts participate in their culture and equally insistent arguments that they provide critical alternatives to it. So increasing demands are put on the one position that may afford a workable compromise—a position in which art is seen as participating in its culture by virtue of its representing the sufferings and powers of specific communities and hence as offering at least a politics of testimony. But then, as Bernstein acutely points out, the very need to be heard as a representative imposes conventional, overall formal methods and blocks large-scale changes in our overall approaches towards our needs, powers, and responsibilities.

We get a richer sense of the stakes involved in this set of tensions if we turn briefly to the visual arts. Exhibitions like the Whitney Biennial take on such public significance that it becomes necessary to spell out the social interests served by the various positions. Take for example two conflicting stances articulated in an *October* roundtable on the 1993 Biennial, the show where theoretical postmodernism seemed finally to set an agenda for artistic practice.[5] I use Hal Foster to represent the first stance, since he has been the most influential figure over the past decade in holding out the possibility that emphases on formal experiment could provide a means of addressing the artist's political responsibilities. But the 1993 Biennial presented a very different artistic politics. Foster found himself allied with Rosalind Krauss in his dismay at the degree to which the art represented by that show seemed eager to dispense with the intricacies of the signifier in order to honor urgent political commitments. In his view, much of the art in this show relied on "applied" theory as a substitute for any concern for the work that signifiers qua signifiers can do, so that art seemed little more than the illustration of ideas gesturing towards a reality external to the work.[6] Bound to an essential pictorialism stressing the signified content, such work is drawn to an identity politics, even if it uses a rhetoric of multiple identities, because personal agency tends to be defined in terms of how one represents specific social groups.

Consequently, the very factors that allow the art its cultural currency also considerably weaken its capacity to make substantial modifications in received ideas.

Benjamin Buchloh's response to Foster and Krauss begins by pointing out how their appeal to the work of the signifier repeats from modernism certain unexamined assumptions about universal values in art and about art critics as the idealized representatives of society, whose task is to assess the ways in which these universals are and are not honored.[7] These assumptions blind the critics to the very different commitments governing most of the work in the Biennial, commitments based primarily on models of audience most fully articulated in Habermas's work on communicative competence. For this art, the work's primary responsibility is to quite specific audiences, organized by shared needs and shareable hopes. So if a stress on the signified can do the appropriate political work, which may be simply mobilizing underprivileged groups, then there is no reason to heed the traditional art critic's demand for complexly worked surfaces. Art empowers different audiences differently; beyond that there simply is no more general abstract criterion for value.[8]

From Buchloh's perspective, Foster is shying away from the very conditions that his own call for an oppositional postmodernism helped to produce. To Buchloh, younger artists seem no longer satisfied by an art they see as bound to complex strategies whose political significance is evident only to a specialist audience, an audience that is schooled in art history and always already in abstract agreement with the political values involved. The Biennial artists insisted that an effective political art must also be at least a relatively popular art, capable of rallying interests if not changing minds. Therefore, this art has to have the courage to resist modernist shame at pictorialism, discursiveness, and even borrowed social theory, since fear of that shame has served too long to block the possibility of a direct "communicative action" concerned with practical results.[9]

Buchloh's logic seems to me impeccable—as politics. But his reasoning will dispel neither the widespread dissatisfaction with the art he defends nor the cogency of Bernstein's and Foster's critiques of how thoroughly such art embodies its political content in formal frameworks that reinforce the conventional models of feeling, thinking, and interrelating socially and that are at least complicit in the oppressions being resisted. So what options do we have? We will not get much help from criticism in any of the arts, since critics seem either to ignore the problem or to muddle along, vacillating between political and aesthetic rhetorics while congratulating themselves for both identifications. And while such muddling has its postmodern proponents—recall John Ashbery's praise of "fence-sitting / Raised to the level of an esthetic ideal"—I think that stance exacts substantial costs.[10] It may be too melodramatic and politically naive to blame the current mood in Congress towards the arts on the limitations of our theorizing, but being trapped in the dilemma Buchloh helps define certainly does not improve the situation.

One could of course simply accept Buchloh's powerful argument for subordinating what had been aesthetic priorities to more direct political criteria based simply on how effectively art manages to work its desired effects on its chosen audiences. This path has considerable affinities with traditional rhetorical views of the arts. But my commitment to the modernist understanding of art's cultural powers leads me to take another tack. I think one can historicize Buchloh's position by understanding the degree to which it at once reacts against and is subject to a range of contradictory assertions fundamental to postmodernist theory. And if that is so, then I can argue that a richer case can be made for the social powers of art by tracing the ways in which various works try to negotiate that same set of contradictions. That route allows us to establish cultural relevance without renouncing emphasis on the signifier and without having to choose among highly segmented audience groups. It may even be possible at this late moment of postmodern cultural theorizing to reverse the structure of appropriation by which this theorizing has prospered. The abstractions characterizing postmodernism as a fundamentally social phenomenon may now be so trapped in contradictions and so much a symptomatic feature of what they hoped to clarify that we now need the arts to face up to such contradictions and to offer alternative imaginative models for engaging contemporaneity.[11]

Let me then set the stage for addressing contemporary poetry by turning directly to what I take to be the five fundamental contradictions now pervading postmodernist theory and strongly influencing Buchloh's sense of the available options.

1) Postmodern cultural theory can, most directly, clarify the social task of the arts by articulating both the postmodern conditions within which the arts operate and the changes it tries to produce. But in attempting this the theory faces what I think are insuperable problems because it has simultaneously to expose the symptomatic features of the artworks that reflect postmodernity and to establish imaginative strategies for helping the culture "resist" what entraps it. Making it new cannot suffice. Instead the theory also makes demands on this novelty, insisting that it share defining characteristics of a culture while redeploying them. And the art must do this without having recourse to any humanistic rhetoric that posits as an ideal the possibility of bearing witness for others.

Perhaps the best way to appreciate the force of this contradiction is to recognize how thoroughly theory's reliance on a language of symptoms seems to force us to make victimhood our means of locating possibilities for change, even though we then have to ignore the danger that the values driving the resistance might themselves be distorted by the injustices that were suffered. Otherwise there seem to be only two unsatisfying options. We can, with Lacan, redefine resistance as learning to embrace one's own symptoms, but that solution is oddly too utopian to suffice in dealing with what in those symptoms might have changeable external causes. Or we can, with

Jameson, try a dialectical stance, maintaining more than one perspective so that as we participate actively within the pastiche and schizophrenia symptomatic of late monopoly capitalism we also seek a totalizing mapping that unifies the entire scene "with an eye to power and control."[12] But then one falls right into Baudrillard's hands. For if we ask how "power and control" can be envisioned on any terms but those realized within the postmodern condition (where Jameson's own notion of transcoding replaces any more qualitative measure for control), we must wonder how the Jamesonian dialectic can reconfigure its own negative forces. If we then become somewhat suspicious, this call for dialectic may seem not merely a nostalgic desire for some grounding reality but also a paradigmatic simulacral gesture appropriating a bankrupt intellectual tradition that survives only as a bid for status. Therefore the call for dialectic is on the verge of turning into an absolutely antidialectical social spectacle in which ideas are recycled as self-promotion by intellectuals who think that only they can avoid a world in which marketing is the only reality.

If I am right about what we might call the Baudrillardian effect of failed leftist gestures, we have to face the disturbing consequence that within postmodernity attitudes like those of Jeff Koons come to appear as our only cogent way to carry out the Lacanian project of learning to live our symptoms. Koons can embrace contradiction, but only by bringing Bataille from the study to the marketplace. Then, by suggesting that Bataille has always already belonged there, Koons can empty even excess of the possibilities for romantic vision that might sustain a rhetoric of resistance.

2) Theorists need not ground political resistance so completely in how agents take on the specific burdens of postmodernity. They can focus directly on what has become of the ideals on which democratic social life is based. At one pole this entails exposing how the rhetorics of democracy are used to cover over indifference and injustice; at the other it warrants exploring how these ideals might be brought into closer conjunction with social realities. But here too postmodernist theory finds itself pursuing incompatible paths that nonetheless seem necessary complements. On the theoretical level it makes sense to derive contemporary injustice from Enlightenment habits of universalizing; these are blind to specific interests sustained by different local social organizations. Then the obvious response is to call on intellectuals to help cultivate differences, even incompatible ones, by idealizing participatory democracy and hence emphasizing the importance of extending participation to what seems heterogeneous and marginal. But because social power in the United States depends on having large identifiable groups with claims on social resources, there have to be ways of locating specific representatives for that heterogeneity. However, then it seems impossible to avoid translating the need for such representatives into the terms provided by some version of identity politics, since the representative has to stand for a collective, even if the collective has its origin in the very process of resisting received ideas of identity.

Put bluntly, postmodernism needs ideals of heterogeneity to save it from universals, from ideals of coherent selfhood, and from reliance on commonsense judgment; but it then also needs an identity politics so that it has a basis for negotiating among those differences within an Enlightenment heritage. However, that identity politics is very difficult to correlate with the constructivist and performative ideals required to make that heritage sufficiently sensitive to the differences that in theory should proliferate. So at times it seems as if the only conceptually plausible alternative is Thomas Docherty's celebration of irresponsibility as the heroic mode of social theory.[13]

3) These political tensions have significant analogues in the contradictory stances on personal agency that characterize postmodernist claims. On the most general level, we might say that postmodern theory manages simultaneously to be entirely dismissive of traditional "bourgeois" notions of subjectivity and ideals of subjective agency and also to rely heavily on a closely related ideal of singularity that exceeds or negates the categories produced by conventions and stable practical concepts. These competing pulls need not be contradictory, since the negative force of dismantling old assumptions about the self may be necessary for any powerful sense of singularity to emerge (whether that occur along Derrida's Nietzschean lines or in accord with Stanley Cavell's more therapeutic sense of owning oneself within conversation). Yet the entire domain that opens up is very difficult to explore without having to opt for concepts that narrow our options and lead quickly into contradictions, thereby also making clear how much room there is here for artistic experiments in reconciling these competing pulls.

Take first the simple range of tensions that emerges within the now-standard calls for breaking down the ego's armor (or loosening the hold of the male imaginary). Which of the many possibilities for dissolving fixed identity will one then pursue, and how will one hold off the more extreme possibilities that now emerge as we hover between ideals of sublimity and of renewed sociality? Clearly, deemphasizing the need for single, coherent selves will help us accept fragmentation and come to better terms with vulnerabilities in ourselves and in others. But then why stop with a psychology that still cultivates traditional caring intimacy with others? Why not explore the more radical opportunities of self-dissolution that fully shatter any sense of individual ego and open onto radical, subline states of self-dispossession (such as those Alphonso Lingis explores in his 1983 book *Excesses: Eros and Culture*)?

Similarly, numerous problematic options open up for determining how these various negations of the ego still allow ethically significant forms of self-consciousness or shareable grammars by which to develop social relationships. There arise thrilling ways to imagine self-consciousness compressed into fine, elemental forces attuned to the urgencies of one's own bodily impulses, capable of startling intimacies with other people, and intricately woven into the play of cultural features taking form in a variety of contexts. And because of those linkages it becomes possible to imagine various collective or transsubjective versions of agency. But each version of subtle attunement leads in opposing directions—a focus on one's own body is ultimately in tension with most forms of intimacy with other people, while the networks that bind us within collective versions of agency all too easily subsume both the body and other individuals. The more collective the model of subjectivity and the more strident the replacing of slogans about history (the buzz word of the eighties) with slogans about community (our new pet notion), the more the pressure of the seductions, conventions, and collectivities returns—pressure that modern and postmodern critiques of rhetoric and representation had initially needed to undo in order to get to the intricate interfaces between self and world where all the theoretical ladders start.

4) Whereas postmodern psychology details ways of coming to terms with the otherness within what had been the unified and unifying self, postmodern ethics has to develop responsible ways of adapting that psychology to a full range of social situations. It ought not to be surprising that these projections encounter quite similar contradictions that have perhaps even greater implications for the arts, since these contradictions affect how audiences are imagined and engaged. Again we can state the problem in blunt terms, but it becomes more interesting as we work out the subtleties. At one pole postmodernism is perhaps the first large-scale cultural movement in the West since Augustinian Christianity to base ethical ideals on overthrowing the masculine performing and ordering ego. If we look at Mike Kelley's dolls, or read popular theorists like Kaja Silverman who idealize castration, or reflect on Levinasian ethics, we see that decentering seems inseparable from demasculinizing. From these ethical perspectives it is crucial not merely to respect the other but to understand, in Levinasian fashion, that in some deep way the call from the other that positions the self is more primary, logically and temporally, than any impulse towards self-fulfillment. And then the deepest ethical adventure involves getting far enough away from the ego's demands to enter into proximity with what can be said to call to us in that other. Yet as we try to move in that direction we are haunted by the contrary pull, in the form of languages of empowerment or of coming to "own the self," which shifts the focus from how we listen to others to how we actively resist their seductions, especially those seductions that restore old power hierarchies under the guise of fostering community. We find ourselves confronted with both a good other, whose call we must hear, and a bad Other, who reduces us to imposed categories and hence must be denied. But we cannot at once yield to castration and assert ourselves, nor can we quite specify any particular other to help us tell the difference between these alternatives. Our only possible escape from this dilemma, within postmodernism, may be to treat castration and dispossession as entrances into some version of Jean-Luc Nancy's sublime. But under such pressure the sublime begins to take on some of the features that we saw accruing to Jamesonian dialectic. Trusting its power seems at

once a mark of pathos and an evasion of responsibility for the actual role the concept plays in manipulating the power struggles it promises to evade.

5) The final contradiction to be discussed is the most abstract and perhaps the most fundamental. Its point of departure is the one theme on which all postmodern thinkers seem to agree, namely, that theirs is a fundamentally antifoundationalist position that derives all criteria from within practices or discourses and hence needs no ontological loyalties. But serious problems emerge as these thinkers work out the implications of this constructivism because the general case warrants both deconstruction and Richard Rorty's new pragmatism, yet these stances are incompatible with each other.

For pragmatism, poststructural critiques of Enlightenment values seem unnecessarily caught up in the metaphysical tradition they are trying to deconstruct. All their talk of transgression—of decentering what had grounded rationality, of problematizing the relations between inside and outside, and of undoing the very presuppositions about self-knowledge and judgment fostered by humanism—seems to do little more than reassert philosophy's position as master discourse and hence fails to adapt to the actual social heterogeneity fundamental to postmodernity. What matters is simply adapting ways of talking that are justified in terms of the emotional and practical needs that beset specific communities. On that basis we can preserve individual freedom as the capacity to detach and explore ways of representing oneself, while the mechanisms of the liberal state are adequately explained by our feelings for solidarity and our need to protect the range of possible discourses that comprise the public sphere. However, for deconstruction this minimalist confidence stems from problematic assumptions about our powers of judgment, our capacities to discern and follow the appropriate social emotions, and our willingness to accept the authority of specific communities. Moreover, as we analyze such assertions we see that deconstruction is not a statement of principle but a process of endless self-questioning to keep us wary of just such restorations of easy faith in our "regular" practices. So it seems that the very quasi-foundational dream of escaping the Enlightenment founders on this dream's inability to establish just how much it can give up or how much to risk in the quest for change.

It is tempting to use my own abstractness in formulating these contradictions as a vehicle for sharpening the contrast I now will draw to the arts. One could say that they provide a better means than hegemonic theory for negotiating a postmodern world because they embrace a concreteness and mobility not so easy to fix in terms of structural oppositions and much easier to manipulate when one confronts such oppositions. And indeed I will say that. But the concreteness is not the most important point. What matters is how the concreteness helps develop specific stances by which we can explore alternative ways of disposing our investments and understanding our needs and powers. So I will turn directly to discussing how some contemporary poetry sets itself to these tasks.

1) There is no way to claim that significant contemporary art can at once establish what can be considered symptomatic about postmodernity and also provide some plausible notion of cure. It is not even reasonable to claim that art offers cogent general models for escaping the play of simulacra or the alienations that stem from the collapse of scene into screen and mirror into network. However, one can show how specific writers develop imaginative energies that do not fit easily into these binaries. And one can hope to build on those examples by showing that there are feasible imaginative strategies for finessing the entire model of judgment that invites predicates like symptom and cure.

Robert Creeley and Frank O'Hara initiated what I take to be the most suggestive of these strategies. Despite their very different emotional agendas, both poets refused to give their texts the look and feel of well-made poems and turned instead to what we might call an anti-artefactual aesthetics. They did this in part to resist the New Criticism, but in larger part to develop an alternative way of realizing New Critical ideals of casting poetry as a form of knowledge. For O'Hara and for Creeley, knowledge based on abstract meditation, however committed to concrete ambivalence, left the poet trapped in a culture of vague idealizations and insufficiently examined psychological constructs. So they turned instead to a poetry that presented itself as testing at every moment its own formal and existential choices simply in terms of the qualities of life that the poetic thinking made available for the poet. Poetry becomes direct habitation, a directly instrumental rather than contemplative use of language. And its test of value becomes the mobility and intensity immediately made available to the poet, so that he or she need not rely on any of the abstract versions of those values or even on any of the formulated social ideals that establish the markets in which cultural capital is traded.

Now these values become even more important, or so it seems, if one notices how this resistance to artefactuality has become fundamental to poets as diverse as Ashbery, C. K. Williams, Robert Hass, and Adrienne Rich. Each writer refuses to separate the person from the poem but does not collapse the poem into the person, as confessional work tends to do. And each refuses to be content with an aesthetics of sincerity, since ideals like sincerity are as abstract and media driven as more traditional ideals calling for a mature, tragic wisdom. What matters is not sincerity per se but becoming articulate about the conditions within which the process of imagining enriches the possibilities of fully investing in the specific life one is leading. For by adapting these values poets can respond to a contemporary cultural theater where the old artefactuality, the old achievement of order out of chaos, has become inseparable from the new trade in commodities, and poetry has now become little more than cultural capital effective primarily in allowing us to luxuriate in convictions about our own sensitivity and "insight." Even contemporary poetry's effort to extend the romantic psychology that sanctions new visions of imaginative power now seems to offer little more than floating signifiers that

circulate only within a very small social world and that even there have very little effect on how people actually live their lives.

There may be no escaping that small social world. And we may have to do without the belief that poetry somehow gives us access to a reality inaccessible to other discourses. It may be task enough to show people how poetry is capable of giving civilized pleasure. But the very terms of such pleasure do have their own potential cultural force. This is especially true when the poets develop imaginative investments adapting postmodern critiques of idealization to models of value that are not reducible to the rhetorics of the simulacral and the schizophrenic that emerge from those critiques.

The best single contemporary example I know of this anti-artefactuality is the last stanza of Ashbery's "As We Know"—simply because of how Ashbery transforms the problematic term *real* into an example of the values that the adverb *really* is capable of bringing to bear:

> The light that was shadowed then
> Was seen to be our lives,
> Everything about us that love might wish to
>   examine,
> Then put away for a certain length of time, until
> The whole is to be reviewed, and we turned
> Toward each other, to each other.
> The way we had come was all we could see
> And it crept up on us, embarrassed
> That there is so much to tell now, really now.[14]

On one level this poem is remarkable primarily for what it refuses to do. The lyric climax takes place as a moment of embarrassment, not as any sudden understanding of forces or specific memories that bind the lovers, and not as any promise to change their lives. This kind of poetry cannot hope to provide any overt imaginative order for the particulars it engages; nor can it build capacious structures. Its attention must be focussed on some immediate situation or flow of mind. But that compression of space allows the writer to concentrate on how, within time, intricate folds and passages open among materials. Even though reflexive consciousness can do no more than trace the ways we have come to and through those situations, it can focus close attention on the contours of its own engagements, and it can locate an affirmative will simply in what thereby becomes visible and shareable, without any need for or hope in more comprehensive allegorical structures.

"Now, really now" carries the full force of that willing, in a way that brilliantly evades the self-congratulatory self-representation almost inescapable in love poetry. That phrase becomes a simple instrument for engaging a present whose configurations can be willed and whose intensities can be shared. And the minimalism here, the capacity simply to mine the resources of grammar without having to pose more ambitious and abstract interpretive structures, also allows the poem a way of responding to the quasi-metaphysics of theorizing about simulacra, or about the symptomatic as our only access to the real. Ashbery refuses to allow consciousness the thematizing distance necessary if one is even to dream of distinguishing symptom from cure. What matters is the present—not as some metaphysical absolute but as the locus of minute processes of judgment that simply go into neutral if they are forced to deal with large questions. This does not at all entail' any relativism on that same large scale. Rather, it invites us to base our thinking about values and about the paths our lives take simply on our capacity to appreciate the difference between "now" as a descriptive specification of time and "really now" as an assertion of something like a will able to envision itself stabilized by the world it sees itself sharing. "Really now" so fully inhabits the simulacral that all questions about reality seem only marks of an alienation that cannot find its way to lyric expression.

2) It is comparatively easy to recognize the tensions between ideals of identity politics and efforts to create a heterogeneous, multicultural stage on which competing versions of identity can coexist. The challenge is figuring out how alternatives might be possible, so that writers can articulate imaginative interests that are basic for minorities without relying on the autobiographical forms that pervade postmodern thinking on this subject. Commitment to autobiography forces writers to either serve as a representative for some community, which imposes the categorical on the personal, or to develop a bitter distance from all general fealties and hence becomes indistinguishable from mainstream celebrations of personal differences (as in V. S. Naipaul). Moreover in both cases the autobiographical mode itself constantly risks making theatrical and personal what may be better seen as structural and shareable features of the lives represented.[15] Or, probably worse, the effort to construct identity gets transformed into a celebration of participating in multiple identities, and sophisticated theory provides a self-congratulatory alternative to the kind of cultural work that requires aligning the self with specific roles and fealties.

Against this backdrop I think it becomes important to turn to the work of recent self-consciously ethnic poetry that attempts to reconfigure how the lyric imagination can engage the memories and desires binding agents to specific communal filiations. Aware of the traps that occur when one moves directly to the levels of psychology involved in postulating identities, this poetry turns to aspects of ethnic life in America too opaque and diffuse to be thematized by memory and too embedded in complex pressures and demands to be represented in terms of dramatic scenes and narrative structures. Ethnicity, then, cannot be effectively represented through a directly introspective psychology that enables agents to stage for themselves what makes them different and to decide who they will be in the future. Instead, these poets explore lyrical states where the conditions of agency are best understood by adapting Hegel's notion of substance. *Substance* can help designate a sense of historicity resistant to any of the predicates we have available for talking about personal identity.

The notion of substance plays two basic roles in our assessment of this work. It enables us to shift our attention from the agents per se to the dense cultural networks within which agents feel at once interpellated and alienated, at once too much and too little involved in mainstream life. And it makes sense of the ways that experimental ethnic writing resists the temptation to offer clear, positive concepts by which we might describe adequately what is involved in these engagements. Hegel's own awareness of such limitations is of course complemented by his insistence that spirit comes to full self-consciousness by developing within substance its own sense of purposive direction, so that one can transform what had been alien being-in-itself or being-for-others into the kind of awareness that constitutes being-for-oneself. But the two poets I will look at here, Alfred Arteaga and Myung Mi Kim, are much more wary of the romantic tendency to postulate within substance precisely those attributes that can then be affirmed as the signs of spirit. They have seen far too many efforts to treat the substance of minority experience as if it could be adequately handled within discursive and autobiographical modes. For them the most spirit can do is respond to the difficulties involved in developing images registering the tensions that give resonance and intensity to the artist's work.

This commitment makes both poets difficult to read, at least initially. And because Arteaga's richest effects depend on familiarity with the overlapping strands of his *Cantos,* I can here only indicate what I find most exciting in his work. Poetry for Arteaga is not quite dramatic or scenic. It is better conceived of as letting desires enter echo chambers provided by the linguistic resources available to a bilingual community. In reading this work we are constantly poised between feeling lost, feeling that this multiplicity is an impediment to desire, and finding the overlap of languages opening new and surprising emotional resonances. We enter a site of transformations where a moment that seems only a "lacuna" for English speakers actually functions as *la cuna,* or the cradle, of possibilities for one willing or able to set the two languages in relation to each other.[16] Then one finds within the languages, and within the complex cultural grammars brought into conjunction, a dynamic cultural field where personal power lies not in the construction of personal identities but in elaborating what the languages afford, as if they composed a home so rich and intricate that autobiography comes to seem an indulgent and thin way to deploy one's imagination. Concerns for personal identity—whether representative or deconstructively multiple—require both scenes and narrative sequences that dramatize aspects of cultural life not compatible with the versions of power and need offered by standard narrative patterns of selfhood.[17]

Myung Mi Kim's *Under Flag* provides a more overt thematic focus on the density of substance because she reverses Arteaga's situation. For her the underlying drama consists of the pressures that one feels as one tries to learn English. At one pole one's sense of self as a dense assembly of substances emerges in negative form—as awareness of all that her new English language does not contain but forces into a complex of memory and repression. At the other pole the new language appears laden with more demands than permissions, as if one could feel within it all those mutual understandings and prejudices that have emerged within a dominant history the immigrant does not easily share. Identity poetics responds to such pressures, but the language of autobiography will not quite register the intricate phenomenology involved. And no political rhetoric will capture the range of emotions evoked by the interplay of language contexts—from rage to self-hatred to fear to hope, to registering numerous partial identifications with other people.

This is the opening of "And Sing We," the first poem of *Under Flag:*

> Must it ring so true
> So we must sing it
>
> To spawn even yawning distance
> And would we be near then
>
> What would the sea be, if we were near it
>
>   Voice
>
> It catches its underside and drags it back
>
> What sound do we make, "n", "h", "g"
>
> Speak and it is sound in time
>
>
> Depletion replete with barraging
>
> Slurred and taken over
>
> Diaspora. "It is not the picture
>
> That will save us."
>
> All the fields fallow
>
> The slide carousel's near burn-out and yet
>
> Flash and one more picture of how we were to be[18]

I love the opening oscillation between question and command and the corollary play of forces generated by repeating the same term with different grammatical functions. We cannot know the referent of "it." But we can understand that whatever "it" is, it puts in motion the dual senses of "so"—one an intensifier, the other a logical connective. Both senses of "so" then provide the combination of intensity and logical force that helps flesh out the full implications of "must."

But why is all this density so abstracted from any concrete scene? Perhaps we have to question our usual assumptions about what empirical concreteness can actually tell us in such situations. Can we usually specify and represent what counts as an imperative for us, especially

when the imperative involves song? The "it" seems irreducibly part of the situation, part of what it means to be coming to terms with what a language affords. And this "it" also seems inseparable from a need to worry about the limitations of what the person is learning to sing, whatever the immediate context. Can the new language give form to old memories? Can what becomes "sound" in time sufficiently resound to bring other times to bear?

Any more direct answers to such questions would make us risk deceiving ourselves by letting our needs project more certainty than the situation warrants. Probably all we can do is circulate through and around the conditions that this learning situation entails. That is why the second section of my quotation (beginning with "depletion") puts such emphasis on the independent phrase units, most of which seem to fix the agent within certain attributions that then must be worked through by exploring what associations follow. Here the entire process of barraging culminates in the trope of feeling the self bound to something like a slide projector, with each picture imposing on the present an oppressive future. Indeed, the sense of oppression is bound less to any given content than it is to the force of that future as pure form and hence as a chilling abstract reminder of the designs that language has upon us.

As the poem goes on through four more sections we witness the feeling of being bound to the "ponderous" phrase ("AS," p. 14), relieved only by sudden and unsummoned memories of Kim's life in Korea. These memories help relieve the task of learning a foreign language by embedding in that process strangely liberating material qualities of specific voices that enter the poem as both torment and hope. That tension then drives the poem to the following resolution: "Mostly, we cross bridges we did not see being built" ("AS," p. 15). Thematically, the bridges go back to a rural past while also indicating how important it is to adapt to what one can neither control nor psychologize. The bridges do not depend on our witnessing their being built; they simply make possible the range of transitions enabling us to live with loss. As evidence of that capacity we need look no further than "mostly," which deliberately imposes a note of awkward qualification on the speaker's knowledge. This "mostly" involves an act of wary trust—the only attitude that will allow one to negotiate this poem's melange of external demands and haunting memories, each all too eager to trap the speaker in an autobiographical obsession. Here, instead of seeking any one identity, the poet has to accept a range of possible identifications to be explored—"each drop strewn into such assembly."[19]

3) Postmodern psychology creates the problem of having to dissolve fixed identity while preserving a range of values like intimacy that derive from now-outmoded versions of selfhood. Moreover, a psychology adequate to postmodernity has to recognize the sublimity possible in pure self-dissolution (or related "cyborgian" experiments) while offering possible routes for reintegrating this sublimity within something resembling social life. One might argue

that the contemporary arts have responded to these demands in two fundamental ways: one involves the refigurations of surrealist versions of how we inhabit our bodies that Foster has analyzed, and the other involves the various experiments in deictic agency that I have explored. These experiments, I have argued, appear quintessentially in assertions like "now, really now" that allow us to reflect on investments that neither depend on nor lead to the practices of self-representation fundamental to modern culture. Rather than accepting either romantic inwardness or versions of subjective agency as entirely constituted by social practices, this perspective emphasizes the range of expressive registers that agents bring into focus simply by manipulating and elaborating deictics. Here I want to explore another, differently gendered variant of this deictic model of agency that foregrounds issues of intimacy and responsiveness to the world while also refusing to invoke any traditional deep psychology. So I will turn to the remarkably elemental decomposition and reorientation of subjectivity explored in Lyn Hejinian's *The Cell*.

This volume brilliantly foregrounds a personal agency so vital in its silences, in its ways of repeating itself, and in its shifting attentions that it convincingly inhabits the form of a lyric diary while refusing the dramatic confrontations between represented and representing selves fundamental to that form. Traditionally, such a focus on the subject's experiences tempts authors to have each entry build to a climatic dramatic moment, as in Robert Lowell's *Notebook 1967-1968*. But to Hejinian such climaxes lead away from what she is most interested in. The dramatic organization blinds the author to the most intimate features of repetition and change as life unfolds and greatly oversimplifies the play of voices that constitutes self-consciousness within that unfolding. As Hejinian memorably puts it, "personality is a worn egress / to somewhere in particular."[20] Personality confines consciousness to preestablished ends and, ironically, tells introspection what it is bound to find. So she proposes instead exploring those imaginative paths where poetry can take up the "chance / of enhancement," as if simply hearing the puns within the master term provides reason enough to align oneself with more mobile versions of subjective agency (*C*, p. 42).

Once one grows suspicious of "personality," lyric self-reflection becomes a very different enterprise:

> A person decomposing the unity
> of the subjective mind by
> dint of its own introspection
>
> [*C*, p. 157]

Introspection sets the mind against its own images, not simply to maintain ironic distance but also to dramatize the resonant forces that circulate around the desire for self-representation. As an example of this interplay between decomposition and redeployment of imaginative investments, consider the volume's penultimate poem. Its opening lines invite us to recognize how many senses come into play around the act of seeing, or better,

around the way sight is poised between what disappears and what appears:

> All sentences about the sense
> of seeing, the sense of
> embarrassment
> It could all disappear—instead
> it appeared
> My language
> My language is a genital—
> let's say that
>
> [*C*, p. 214]

Seeing involves a sense of embarrassment because it leaves one open to and dependent on the supplementary processes that sentences bring into play. Even the syntax is ambiguous because seeing cannot be given one stable position as it vacillates between serving as an element within an extended clause (which, in its concern for sense, never achieves its verb) and serving as the focal unit that everything "sentences about," as if the seeing were the wellspring of possible meanings. No wonder that the "it" could all disappear: it depends on the vagaries of these sentences and the difficult interplay between the time of pure seeing and the work of sentencing. But "it" also can seem to come into focus, making language itself seem inseparable from the person's hold on the scene. And that satisfaction, framed by the fear of disappearance, invites the sexual analogies that Hejinian's reference to genitals brings to bear.

"Let's say that" breaks the enchantment. If we can achieve the distance to treat these sayings as provisional, we have to wonder whether we have lost touch with the immediate impulses that have been shaping our investments in this "sense" of seeing. Language can sustain a thinking at one with "the composition / of things / distinctions steering sunlight," but such intensified self-consciousness can also get caught up in its own overdetermined sequences, which now take over the poem (*C*, p. 214). However, rather than take the time to track these movements, I will go directly to the moment when the poem develops its conclusion:

> It could all disappear
> Streets
> With remorse for individualism, provoking
> scale
> Dimension sinks
> It's the event of seeing
> what I speak of with
> someone's eyes
> The event of a carnality
> covered by eye
> The light proceeding along the
> yellow sides of night
> A word is a panorama
> of a thing
> It's the eye's duty to
> tell
> It's relevant—though a person
> is implicated in the process
> it keeps in sight
>
> [*C*, pp. 214-15]

These lines are not easy to interpret. They demand a good deal of guesswork. But in responding to that demand we find ourselves embodying a cardinal principle of Hejinian's poetics: it foregrounds processes of "conjecture" that force us to recognize the apparently arbitrary or uncaused leap of proprioceptive activity fundamental to a person's making any part of the world her own. Conjecture, in other words, is inseparable from our sense of the ego taking up residence in a world that exceeds it but that also provides a ground for its sense of its own free contingency. And because of its fluidity, conjecture does not demand that the "I" build a melodramatic stage on which to interpret its independence (such staging only confirms the version of the self one initially postulates). So for Hejinian even sex is best figured as "the pleasure of / inexactitude" (*C*, p. 140), because the alternative is sex by the book, sex blind to the arbitrariness and playfulness by which we come to appreciate how our lives might remain open to, even hungry for, what we cannot control in other people. Why should poetry be different, since it seeks the same correlation of intimacy and pleasure playing through the same absorbing interest in seeing exact attention create indefinable edges?

My conjectures project Hejinian's using this fear of disappearance to highlight what Heidegger might call "a worldliness of the world" constantly at risk of collapsing into public pieties and private psychodramas. The passage from the poem begins with a fear that landscape will turn into mapped streets that in their turn can instantly be made into allegories of "remorse for individualism." What else can the demand for individuation produce except endless repetition feeding on anxieties that agency may be unrepresentable? Since these are not the fears that admit of heroic confrontations, all one can do is let the earlier querying within the poem generate a syntactic form around which some resisting energies can be gathered. As dimension sinks, and hence as the specific image collapses, the poem replaces "it could all disappear" with another "it" construction leading beyond the eager scrutiny to a more general sense of how persons inhabit the "eye." If the "I" must give up the hope of somehow establishing private access to the real, it can instead treat embodiment as simply accepting the carnality of its bodily functions. This enables one to identify with the eye without making demands that vision be tied closely to the demands of any specific ego. Instead, this abstracting of the eye leads back to the panorama of words, as if words, too, open into vision as long as we maintain enough distance from specific imaginary demands to explore the access language gives us to the ways that our unconscious beings are deployed in particular moments.

This intricate balancing of "eye," "I," and "word" finally takes on its full emotional and sexual implications in the last three lines:

> It's relevant—though a person
>   is implicated in the process
>   it keeps in sight

We arrive at this sense of implication by recognizing that language is part of the eye's imperative, even when one brackets individual sensibility, because language allows vision its "sentences," in every sense of that term. Then once that process is grasped in its independence, one can return to the issue of how particular persons make investments in what they see. Rather than being the source of the seeing, the person is literally folded into that which appears, so that one in effect learns about one's own desires in the very processes that allow vision to unfold a world.

Everything the poem implies about the force of language as bearer of investments comes into the foreground in the brilliant final pun on keeping materials in sight. For it seems as if the plenitude of the pun arises out of nowhere, a grace within language attuned to the situation it tries to articulate. The eye not only keeps objects in its sight; it also has stakes in those objects, so that it matters how over time the person treasures what is seen. Decomposing the ego into its carnal functioning, then, does not repress feeling but allows us to encounter its most elemental forms—forms that depend on a syntax that works with an "it" in the subject position rather than a projected self-image. And this sense of forms then helps temper the fear with which the poem began that thought will make sight overdetermined. For the poem helps us to see how merely holding objects before the eye can modulate into actively *keeping in* sight, as if the eye expressed a version of the containing force that can be associated with female genitals. And this active keeping then becomes a full willing of what the eye sees, even though there has been no introspection by which to organize that will. Here the power of commitment does not depend on some inner state but on a specific way of engaging in events that prevents our isolating that personal dimension as a unique and representable center. The only workable mirror for the self seems to consist in folding consciousness within its own embodied activities. Anything more speculative may entail self-divisive idealism.

I have to be this abstract if I am to keep Hejinian in sight. But it is crucial that readers not confuse the speculation required to orient ourselves within the poem with the very different mode of expression by which the poetry itself engages the world. Hejinian can be as minimalist as she is about emotions because she relegates much of the work of feeling to a remarkably fluid and intricate play of tones. Tone makes it possible to keep a mode of conjecture within experience, a mode that we easily lose if we push too hard to capture the entire process as someone's possession and hence as an extension of personality. So I think it fair to say that Hejinian's poetry offers a dynamic alternative to the modes of self-reflection generated by both analytic philosophy and the therapeutic practices postulated to save us from the self-division such thinking creates. In her work, what makes us persons is not how we compose self-images but how the degrees and modalities of concern that that tone embodies compose a world for our keeping. As Hejinian's final poem in *The Cell* puts it, rather than worrying about a gulf between word and world, we might think of how we can orient ourselves towards a "consciousness of unconsciousness" attuned to the ways we are always already part of the sentences that our grammars afford us. Then she adds, in order to close with her characteristic twinkle, "It is good to know / so" (*C*, p. 217). That is, we may need only this playful cross of rhyme and pun in order to correlate the "so" of method with the "so" of alignment and adjustment and, hence, to demonstrate what consciousness of unconsciousness can afford us. And then it becomes possible to have poetry speak what we might call the legislative "let it be so" rarely achieved in postromantic poetry. Such a blessing depends only on managing to keep lyrical intelligence responsive to the delights embedded in the panoramas language affords, as if in this alternative to specular self-reflection, in this gentle and mobile distance, may lie our peace.

4) I still have the last two sets of contradictions to face and I have almost no space. This will not seem much of a loss since I also have almost nothing to say about them that I have not said elsewhere. The fourth set of contradictions takes place in postmodernist moral theory's desire to undo the sense of demand basic to the masculine ego while also cultivating versions of self-empowerment that help agents respond to their social situations. While poetry cannot be very helpful in developing specific moral arguments that might address these contradictions, it can explore versions of agency that we then call upon for our representations of moral powers and moral responsibilities. In particular I have argued that contemporary poetry is keenly responsive to the Levinasian and Lacanian concern to replace the dream of autonomy with an insistence on how deeply otherness pervades any experience of our own possible identities. Two basic features of moral agency then come to the fore: at one pole poets ranging from Hejinian to Hass ask us to shift from an emphasis on the ideals we pursue to an emphasis on the concrete texture of needs and cares that bind us to other people and invite various kinds of reciprocity; while at the other pole poets like Bernstein make that reciprocity fundamentally structural by exploring the degree to which the very conditions of self-reflection bind us to grammars we share with other people.[21] Both modes of writing then make the work of reading inseparable from exploring what these bonds with other people afford us.

5) I can say even less on the last set of contradictions because I cannot think of any conceptual or imaginative way to reconcile the pragmatist and deconstructive poles of antifoundational thinking. It is no accident that Rorty remains a radical dualist in espousing deconstructive irony as fundamental for individual subjectivity while basing public thinking entirely on pragmatist principles. But that very impossibility may afford the strongest possible argument for aligning postmodernism in the arts with basic modernist imperatives, despite the many differences between them. For both orientations share a commitment to resisting empiricism and to exploring plural worlds, where particulars prove inseparable from the local frameworks that make them intelligible, whether these frameworks be modernist constructivist wills or postmodernist

conjectures. And much of the best postmodern art shares modernism's refusal to bestow on social practices what it denies to metaphysics; such art will not yield authority to those versions of will and judgment that rely on social negotiations and idealized rhetorics of community. Instead it foregrounds a tangential relation between the artist's work and any specific social agenda, and hence it reminds us how unstable and self-divided all our idealizations must be. Yet instability is not sufficient reason for renouncing idealization entirely in favor of the satiric mode that comes far too easily within twentieth-century life. Postmodern art like the poetry we have been examining articulates one domain where it makes sense to bring modernist intensity to the postmodern thematics of thriving on contradiction.

Appendix

When I use the term *postmodernist theory,* I refer to conceptual work conforming to the parameters of one or more of five basic discursive frameworks that provide partial, overlapping arguments devoted at least in part to characterizing postmodern culture and its consequences. The first, and now least current, of these orientations has been devoted to clarifying how the arts see themselves as reacting critically to the formal and cultural values basic to late modernism—for example, by undoing the primacy of optical experience; by shattering formal purity so as to let through the "noise of the world" with all its historical density; by challenging the idealization of poetry as an engagement with universal tragic realities demanding mature, self-reflexive, balanced contemplative attitudes; by letting form play with the imperatives of function; and by cultivating those event-qualities within art that create the mysterious openness that Ihab Hassan calls "indetermanency."

Traces of these themes remain in the other four discourses, but their basic concern is with transforming predicates about art into those that apply to the overall cultural theater: the emphasis on surfaces culminating in Warhol now takes the form of a general claim about the simulacral texture of contemporary life; Robert Rauschenberg's flat-bed principle becomes a generalized openness to heterogeneity and contradiction; Jasper Johns's duplicities become Jameson's schizophrenia, and architecture's playful decorativeness his pastiche. The most elaborate transformations take place in the overall discourse committed to isolating and assessing those specific social traits that can be characterized as creating a distinctive postmodern condition. Here we find Lyotard's replacing grand narratives with an insistence on local phrase regimes and the eruption of irreducibly unrepresentable factors; Jameson's argument that pastiche and schizophrenia can be mapped onto late commodity capitalism; and Baudrillardian accounts of simulacral culture and the externalizing of the internal—accounts created with very little concern for how these traits mesh with residues of older cultural formations or with the needs that agents might bring to the social order.

A third discourse shifts the emphasis from social conditions to the intellectual frameworks responsible for contemporary crises. It tries to expose and counter limitations inherent in modernity's reliance on Enlightenment universals by showing the extent to which inherited ideals of truth must be recast in terms of power and context; ideals of judgment as matters of interest, fantasy, and identification; and ideals of rights and social bonds as dangerous abstractions unresponsive to the particular needs and genius of concrete communities. And then it elaborates ways of developing similar values without having to rely on any foundational speculations.

The last two discourses focus more closely on specific features of postmodernity's anti-Enlightenment orientation. One is fundamentally political, epitomized in the efforts of postcolonial theory to provide a rallying point for elaborating how we can accommodate ourselves to heterogeneity, adapt to an irreducibly agonistic political theater, redefine ethical values in accord with principles of truthfulness rather than relying on abstract obligations, and foster participatory democratic structures. Finally there is now emerging a fifth discourse, driven mostly by Lacanian concepts, that is devoted to conditions of personal agency that become central as modernist faith in self-reflexive lucidity crumbles and as we become aware of unconscious factors inseparable from the necessary yet doomed effort to produce clear and distinct conceptual and optical disciplines.

Were one then to put these frameworks within some larger social condition called postmodernity, I think one would have to point to the consequences of an intensified shift from an industrial economy to one based on producing and exchanging information, of a corollary internationalization of capital, and of an almost total erosion of the complex of values put in place by Christianity.

NOTES

[1] For examples of the sloganizing, see the charts produced by Ihab Habib Hassan, Robert Venturi, and David Harvey. Hassan's and Venturi's charts are available in *Postmodernism: A Reader,* ed. Thomas Docherty (New York, 1993), and Harvey's is in David Harvey, *The Condition of Postmodernity: An Enquiry into the Origins of Cultural Change* (Oxford, 1989). And for examples of the tendency to displace the versions of postmodernist imaginative strategies developed within the arts in favor of more general and activist political theorizing one need only turn to Baudrillard and Lyotard, as well as to a host of political theorists such as Anthony Woodiwiss, *Postmodernity USA: The Crisis of Social Modernism in Postwar America* (London, 1993), who explicitly dismiss the aesthetic aspects of postmodernism. See the appendix for a discussion of what I mean by postmodernism.

[2] It may seem odd to accuse postmodern theories, which claim to embrace contradiction, of suffering because of it. But I do not see how one can celebrate a level of contradiction that logically precludes deriving any positive claims from the theory. For example, if a theory calls for both identity politics and cultivating heterogeneity, it cannot help us decide among competing claims that privilege one or the other; nor can it determine what within the identity politics provides the interest in—or powers of judgment for—acting in relation to that heterogeneity. For good analyses of contradictions within postmodern theory, see John McGowan, *Postmodernism and Its Critics* (Ithaca, N.Y., 1991), and Christopher Norris, *The Truth about Postmodernism* (Oxford, 1993). But it is also crucial to realize that neither of these critics grants any value at all to postmodernism, in large part because they too are tempted to take it now entirely as a set of philosophical and political claims. McGowan relies on Habermasian models of judgment that are not easy to correlate with the psychology developed by much recent art, and Norris invokes epistemic ideals that I think are legitimate for the sciences and for many practical questions but that cannot be easily applied to questions about value or commitment. For example, Norris claims that postmodernism has no place for the subject (p. 254), but while this may be true of some theory, it certainly does not hold for the arts. In fact the arts develop a version of subjectivity that insists on sharp differences between domains governed by specific personal desires and those employing the modes of reflection and judgment that function in third-person epistemic frameworks.

It might also seem odd now to concentrate on ideas proposed by postmodernist theory rather than its shifts in styles of self-presentation and packaging that make it seem anachronistic to worry about justifying oneself in conceptual terms. Here I can only hope that some of us will continue to seek an intellectual life that makes demands on us to develop frameworks clarifying and synthesizing our values and commitments, even if we doubt that the intellect is the locus for forming those commitments. If the reflective mind is no longer the legislature that matters for our deepest commitments, it might continue to function as the judiciary, since the alternative seems to be pure banality.

[3] Charles Bernstein, *A Poetics* (Cambridge, Mass., 1992), p. 6. For critical arguments based on observations like Bernstein's, see Marjorie Perloff, *Radical Artifice: Writing Poetry in the Age of Media* (Chicago, 1991), pp. 18-23.

[4] I cannot here take up at any length the question of how to describe either postmodernism or postmodernity. But I can indicate why a distinction between postmodernity and postmodernism is necessary simply by directing the reader to Evan Watkins's account of the speech "Post-Modern Politics: The Search for a New Paradigm" given to the Washington, D.C. Rotary Club by James Pinkerton, then President Bush's assistant for policy planning; see Evan Watkins, *Throwaways: Work Culture and Consumer Education* (Stanford, Calif., 1993), pp. 10-12. Watkins uses this speech to show how postmodernity as consumer culture can swallow and transform almost any purportedly revolutionary

rhetoric. Therefore one has to have a model for what remains forceful inside that rhetoric that cannot be thus subsumed without obvious reductionism. Reasons like this have also led Simon During, in his "Postmodernism: Or, Post-Colonialism Today," in *Postmodernism: A Reader,* pp. 448-62, to propose an opposition between postmodernism and postmodernity. But where his goal is to mobilize postmodernist versions of history as a critical force, mine is to emphasize how the arts offer their own versions of engaging that history.

[5] The roundtable takes place in "The Politics of the Signifier: A conversation on the Whitney Biennial," *October,* no. 66 (Fall 1993): 3-27. The passages I paraphrase from Hal Foster appear on pp. 3, 10, and 15 and, below, those from Benjamin Buchloh appear on pp. 9, 11, 14, and 25. When I go on to criticize Buchloh's position I am aware that he is less interested in arguing its truth than in demonstrating a possible way to take seriously the political ambitions driving the 1993 Biennial and hence forcing us to question the ease with which we turn to aesthetic universals.

[6] Ibid., p. 4.

[7] Bernstein makes exactly the same claims against universalized audiences and against critics trying to become their representatives in *A Poetics,* pp. 4-5, but in the service of a very different aesthetic politics.

[8] To see what is ultimately at stake in Buchloh's analysis I think we have to set this Biennial against the Salon des Refusés of 1863, where a nascent modernist spirit first produced a public institution defining two major changes from the traditions it had inherited: (1) art could not simply continue the work of the dominant high culture but had to be able to stage itself as pursuing contemporary realities not available to that culture's preferred modes of attention, investment, and reflection; and (2) even to test such ambitions, this new art required the fiction of an advanced audience authorized by its capacity to criticize dominant high-art taste and to provide discursive frameworks for specifying the value claims involved in the new art. This context then enables us to say that for Foster the Biennial fails because for the most part the work does not satisfy this modernist spirit, while for Buchloh the show raises the almost unthinkable possibility that even postmodern variations on that spirit have run their course, so it may now be time to try alternative overall models of how art relates to social life.

[9] "The Politics of the Signifier," p. 9.

[10] John Ashbery, "Soonest Mended," *The Double Dream of Spring* (New York, 1970), p. 18.

[11] I have tried to clarify the specific terms of such appropriations in my "John Ashbery and the Challenge of Postmodernism in the Visual Arts," *Critical Inquiry* 14 (Summer 1988): 805-30.

[12] Fredric Jameson, *Postmodernism, or the Cultural Logic of Late Capitalism* (Durham, N.C., 1991), p. 332.

[13] See Docherty, *After Theory: Postmodernism/Postmarxism* (London, 1990).

[14] Ashbery, "As We Know," *As We Know* (New York, 1979), p. 74. I have developed a more thorough reading of this poem in my "Contemporary Poetry as Philosophy: Subjective Agency in John Ashbery and C. K. Williams," *Contemporary Literature* 33 (Summer 1992): 214-42.

[15] Consider the dilemma that pervades Homi K. Bhabha's *The Location of Culture* (London, 1994). He makes a forceful pragmatist case that there are no fixed identities but only a constant weaving of partial identifications and filiations. Yet he also has to distinguish ethnic identity-construction from anything sanctioned by pragmatism in order to insist on the agonistic nature of public space and in order to keep in the foreground a constant focus on the repressive force of Enlightenment universals. But the agon depends on quite fixed identities, at least in principle, and the refusal to forget the past seems an anachronistic demand for authenticity. There is in fact nothing in his accounts of identity that applies specifically to postcolonial or ethnic situations because the entire story fits so neatly into a pragmatist psychology.

[16] The relevant lines from Arteaga's poem are "[cctbc, Frida, / y ccsa letra tdg a / kiss, a lacuna" (Alfred Arteaga, "Respuesta a Frida," *Cantos* [Berkeley, 1991], p. 48). Literally, the lacuna here is the *e* that Frida Kahlo dropped from her name in order to separate herself from Nazi Germany. I take the concept of language as impediment from my colleague Gwen Kirkpatrick.

[17] Notice the important difference from Pound's use of foreign languages. Pound justified this practice in terms of capturing the exact character of certain exalted expressions. He was not interested in the qualities of the languages per se but in the truths that became available within them for those who could appreciate the precision. Arteaga, on the other hand, is less interested in the specific moments captured by Spanish than in the very fact of what it means to be a user of Spanish. He is absorbed by life in the language, not by vision through the language.

[18] Myung Mi Kim, "And Sing We," *Under Flag* (Berkeley, 1991), p. 13; hereafter abbreviated "AS."

[19] Kim, "Into Such Assembly," *Under Flag,* p. 31. This quotation is from the end of her most accessible poem.

[20] Lyn Hejinian, *The Cell* (Los Angeles, 1992), p. 42; hereafter abbreviated C.

[21] I develop these alternatives at length in my "What Differences Can Contemporary Poetry Make in Our Moral Thinking?" in *Ethical Inquiry in the Nineties,* ed. Richard Freadman, Vane Adamson, and David Parker (forthcoming).

DRAMA

Erika Fischer-Lichte

SOURCE: "Postmodernism: Extension or End of Modernism? Theater between Cultural Crisis and Cultural Change," in *Zeitgeist in Babel: The Postmodernist Controversy,* edited by Ingeborg Hoesterey, Indiana University Press, 1991, pp. 216-28.

[*In the following essay, Fischer-Lichte distinguishes between Modernism and Postmodernism in the theater.*]

The controversy surrounding postmodernism which has currently aroused fierce debate in various fields on different levels culminates in the persistent question of whether postmodernism has effected a complete break with modernist traditions, or whether it has, on the contrary, only radicalized the trends first formulated and pronounced by modernism and extended its conclusions. Both viewpoints are vigorously upheld. This is all the more extraordinary since the ground on which the controversy should be discussed is not yet clearly plotted: Does the modernism dealt with here begin with the *Querelle des anciens et des modernes* or with the Enlightenment? With the industrialization of Western Europe or with Nietzsche? Should one see the historical avant-garde movement as an integral component of modernism (as most European critics seem to do), or should modernism be defined by the exclusion of the avant-garde movement (as many American critics would argue)? In attempting to examine the question of whether the "true" *Epochenschwelle* [threshold of an epoch] is to be termed modern or postmodern, one must first secure agreement on these issues.

The most important arguments so far exchanged in the controversy have been collated in a most informative research report entitled "The Postmodern *Weltanschauung* and Its Relation with Modernism" by Hans Bertens. Rather than repeating those arguments here, which in the meantime have become sufficiently well known, I shall take as starting point those elements which refer to postmodernism in literature and examine them from a semiotic point of view.

There is a wealth of argument which concerns literary device. Distinctive characteristics are formulated whose opposites are held to be representative of modernism: indeterminancy, fragmentation, montage, collage, intertextuality, hybridization, the carnivalesque (in the sense of Bakhtin), constructivism, randomness, openness of the form, discontinuity, etc. This catalog which concentrates on the syntactic level of a work, has yet to be completed.

On the semantic level, the presentation of possible worlds, the redefinition of the relationship between time and space, and the dissolution of the self and its boundaries are most frequently referred to. The pragmatic level is conspicuously absent from the argumentation. Here the only discussion is concentrated on the shift of the focus away from the work itself and onto the reader, so that one can only speak of a literary object in the strictest sense as the interaction between the reader and the text.

In addition to this, a string of metasemiotic notions are appealed to, such as the shift of the dominant as epistemological question to the dominant as ontological one (McHale, 1987); from monism to pluralism; from representation to performance; from referentiality to nonreferentiality; or, yet again, the firmly held belief in the self-reflexivity of a literary text and its production. Still largely unclarified remains the status of the various arguments and the interconnections between them: Must all distinctive characteristics be listed in order to be able to speak of a postmodern work, or would it suffice to specify certain chosen ones, and, if so, which? Do they create a structure with one another, within which each fulfills a function, or does one simply enumerate them ad libitum? How can one relate the distinctive characteristics found on the different semiotic levels to one another? Does it make sense simply to list specific literary devices without having analyzed and differentiated their relation to the semantic, pragmatic, or metasemiotic levels?

Apart from these more systematic questions, others arise which stem from the actual methods of procedure. Thus as verification that it is indeed the distinctive characteristics given that differentiate postmodern works from the modern, a literary corpus is created which, despite all its differences in detail, is nonetheless homogeneous in two significant aspects: the examples are predominantly drawn from the narrative genres (short stories and novels) and exclude texts from the historical avant-garde almost entirely. Hence I should like to elucidate the systematic problem of the distinction between postmodernism and modernism by recourse to a body of literature which principally consists of texts of dramatic literature and which will include those of the historical avant-garde movement as it has recently been foregrounded by Peter Bürger (1984). Texts such as *Sphinx and Strohmann* (Kokoschka), *Les mamelles de Tiresias* (Apollinaire), *Le coeur à gaz* (Tzara), *Methusalem* (Yvan Goll), *Le serin muet* (G. Ribemont Dessaignes), and Hugo Ball's texts for the Dada soirées will therefore be referred to as examples of modernist literature. Since Dada was in existence at that time, one must also take it into account. The same of course applies to dramas such as *Mysterium buffo* (Mayakovsky), or *Pobedr nrd solncem (Victory Over The Sun)* (Kru enych), as well as to texts of futurist and constructivist performances.

As a starting point, I have selected a problem which has arisen on the semantic level, and through it, the relation to the syntactic, pragmatic, and metasemiotic levels can easily be established: the area to be examined is the presentation of the individual, the self in modern and postmodern drama.

By way of introduction, I shall cite a somewhat lengthy passage from Bertens's *Forschungsbericht:*

For Gerald Graff the celebratory mode of Post-modernism is characterized by a "dissolution of ego boundaries"; for Daniel Bell "the various kinds of postmodernism . . . are simply the decomposition of the self in an effort to erase the individual ego," and Ihab Hassan notes that "the Self . . . is really an empty 'place' where many selves come to mingle and depart." For Hoffmann this movement in the direction of a less defined, less stable identity is even a shift of epistemic proportions: "The perceivable signs of a tendency toward the disappearance of a subjectivity in modern literature become a fact in postmodern works. Thus a radical gap between modern and postmodern literature is reflected in the opposition of two *epistemes:* subjectivity versus loss of subjectivity." The postmodern self is no longer a coherent entity that has the power to impose (admittedly subjective) order upon its environment. It has become decentered, to repeat Holland's phrase. The radical indeterminacy of postmodernism has entered the individual ego and has drastically affected its former (supposed) stability. Identity has become as uncertain as everything else. (Fokkema/Bertens 1986, 46f.)

Aside from the fact that the boundaries of the individual ego were dissolved as early as Strindberg's first dream play *Till Damascus* (1889), it is true to say that modern drama in the early twentieth century was constituted out of the negation of the individual, as the theory here proposes. Pirandello's *Six Characters in Search of an Author,* written and premiered in 1921, for example, can immediately be described as the "Spiel von der Unmöglichkeit des Dramas" (Szondi), since here the possibility of drama is called into question by dramatic characters who no longer have a definable individual ego at their disposal. The "Father" summarizes the problem in the following way:

> My drama lies entirely in this one thing. . . . In my being conscious that each one of us believes himself to be a single person. But it's not true. . . . Each one of us is many persons. . . . Many persons . . . according to all the possibilities of being that there are within us. . . . With some people we are one person. . . . With others we are somebody quite different. . . . And all the time we are under the illusion of always being one and the same person for everybody. . . . We believe that we are always this one person in whatever it is we may be doing. But it's not true! It's not true!

Here we are faced quite clearly with self-reflexion as well as the shift of the dominant from an epistemological question to an ontological one: Since the 'being' (*Sein*) cannot be known or defined by the individual, the question arises how it can then be represented in drama?

Pirandello took recourse in the Baroque topos of role-play and the immanent problem of the *Sein-Schein* which he recast in special ways: Each individual does not only act but also *is* the different roles without the possibility of being defined either by the set role itself or even as a persona beyond the role. His being *(Sein)* is the "life that ceaselessly flows and changes" and thus one which knows no boundaries. His appearances *(Schein)* are the different roles which in each case function as the "form" which seeks to "detain it, keep it unchanging."

The literary devices which Pirandello employs to represent dramatically his concept of the self are, among others, intertextuality, irony, and hybridization. Similarly, another so-called classic author of modern drama, Eugene O'Neill, also denies a bound individual ego. In *Mourning Becomes Electra* (1929-31), the characters are introduced almost as replicas of replicas of replicas in a basically unendable stream back to the source. Individuality no longer exists. This characteristic is true on the psychical level and in the physical development of the action.

All the men in the Mannon family, Abe, David, Ezra, Adam, and Orin, share the same facial characteristics: "an aquiline nose, heavy eyebrows, swarthy complexion, thick, straight black hair, light hazel eyes" (*Homecoming,* act 1; *The Hunted,* act 1). The women who marry into the family like Marie Brantome and Christine, or those from the family itself like Lavinia, also share a number of similar physical features: they all have "thick, curly hair, partly a copper brown, partly a gold, each shade distinct and yet blending with the other," "deep-set eyes of a dark violet-blue," "black eyebrows, which meet in a pronounced straight line above her strong nose," "a heavy chin," and "a large sensual mouth" (*Homecoming,* act 1). Furthermore, the male and female members of the Mannon family seem so intertwined that their faces at rest give the impression of a "life-like mask." To these physical similarities, O'Neill ties psychical ones: all the members of the family are driven by incestuous desire. The men all suffer from an Oedipus complex, the women from an Electra or Jocasta complex.

O'Neill uses this system of psychical and physical similarities and equivalents to divest the characters of any individuality: each duplicates the other who is himself a duplication of yet another. There is no "original" and therefore no individual ego. Each repeats one who is repeating another who is repeating another and so on ad infinitum. In fact, not only do they appear as not individual selves, but also rather as seeming substitutes for someone who is absent—as Orin discovered in the war: "Before I'd gotten back I had to kill another in the same way. It was like murdering the same man twice. I had a queer feeling that war meant murdering the same man over and over, and that in the end I would discover the man was myself! Their faces keep coming back in dreams—and they change to Father's face—or to mine" (*The Hunted,* act 3, 304.). Equally, the characters act as if they are driven by an "other," or are recalling an action initiated by an "other" in the past. In this way, an earlier action is exactly recalled by others, as for example the small gesture used by Ezra, Adam, and Orin on many occasions to try and smooth Marie, Christine, and Lavinia's hair; or alternatively a whole action sequence is repeated as in the case of Orin and Lavinia in the third part of the trilogy (*The Hunted,* act 2, 355f.). In their nature, their desires, their words and deeds, the characters recall others who came before them; they are neither identical among themselves, nor to others—they have no individual self, no definable identity. The self is indeed an "empty place where many selves come to mingle and depart." The most important literary device that O'Neill uses is that of consistently setting the text in its relation to the intertext (Aeschylus's *Oresteia*) and thereby building up a meaning-generating system of differences.

The outstanding feature in both Pirandello and O'Neill of presenting the self as an "empty place" in which widely divergent "roles" (Pirandello) or "others" (O'Neill) can meet, is further radicalized in the Dada movement. Whilst Pirandello and O'Neill in part—principally in terms of language and dramaturgy—employ thoroughly "traditional" literary devices, the Dadaists turn the play into an antiplay, the theater performance into an antitheater; all the traditional devices are parodied, negated, thrown overboard.

In Tristan Tzara's *Le coeur à gaz*, which was premiered in 1921 in the "Salon Dada" in Paris, the dramatic characters are Oreille, Bouche, Oeil, Cou, Nez, Sourcil, a dancer and other characters, who "entrent et sortent ad libitum."

Whilst Strindberg questioned the idea of psychical wholeness in a character by introducing the Doppelgänger, and O'Neill by stressing physical similarities, Tzara on the other hand fragments the human body and defines these isolated parts as the characters of the action. The self becomes literally the "empty space" between the characters of the action. The dialogue between them proceeds as follows:

> *Oreille:* C'est le printemps, le printemps
>
> *Nez:* Je vous dis qu'il a 2 mètres
>
> *Cou:* Je vous dis qu'il a 3 mètres
>
> *Nez:* Je vous dis qu'il a 4 mètres
>
> *Cou:* Je vous dis qu'il a 5 mètres
>
> *Nez:* Je vous dis qu'il a 6 mètres

and so on up to 16 meters.

Alternatively, they confront each other with maxims and proverbs which follow senselessly on from each other:

> *Oreille:* . . . Les hommes simples se manifestent par un maison, les hommes importants par un monument.
>
> *Bouche:* Non je veux rien dire. J'ai mis depuis longtemps dans la boîte à chapeau ce que j'avais dire. (171)
>
> *Soucil:* "ou", "combien", "pourquoi" sont des monuments. Par exemple la Justice. Quel beau fonctionnement régulier, presque un tuic nerveux ou une religion. (159)

> *Cou:* Mandarine et blanc d'Espagne, je me tue Madeleine, Madeleine. (158)

The literary devices employed here can be described as indeterminacy, disconnectedness, randomness, fragmentation, montage, carnivalesque, hybridization; in short, the whole arsenal of distinctive characteristics belonging to postmodernism finds its realization on a syntactic level.

Similar findings can be confirmed on the metasemiotic level. Indeed, here it is more a question of approaching pluralism—to the point where "anything goes." The trend toward loss of referentiality is also clearly to be seen. In Tzara's *La première aventure céleste de Mr. Antipyrine* we find, for example, the following dialogue:

> *La femme enceinte:* Toundi-a-voua Soco Bgai Affahou
>
> *Mr. Bleubleu:* Farafamgama Soco Bgai Affahou
>
> *Pipi:* amerture sans église allons charbon chameau synthétisé amerture sur l'église isisise les rideaux dodododo
>
> *Mr. Antipyrine:* Soco Bgai Affahou zoumbai, zoumbai, zoumbai, zoum.
>
> *Mr. Cricri:* il y a pas d'humanité—il y a les réverbères et les chiens dzinaha dzin aha bobobo Tyaco oahiii hii hii héboum iéha iého
>
> *Mr. Bleubleu:* incontestablement. (77)

Here it is clear that the trend toward performance outweights that toward representation. This is of course also the case to a certain extent of the Dada soireés and activities which took place rather like happenings. Hausmann, among others, has recorded:

> On Sunday, 17th November 1918, Baader attended the morning service at the cathedral in Berlin. As the court chaplain, Dryander, was about to begin the sermon, Baader called out in a loud voice, "Wait! What does Jesus Christ mean to you? Nothing . . ." He wasn't able to go on, there was a terrible tumult, Baader was arrested and a charge of blasphemy held against him. Nothing could be done with him in the end, however, since he was carrying the whole text of his outburst with him in which it continues, "for they do not heed his commands etc." Naturally, all the papers were full of this incident. (Huelsenbeck 1984, 226)

In conjunction with the performative character of the Dada productions and soirées, the concept of the audience as an integral component of the performance was deliberately planned. The Dada chronicler, Walter Mehring, who had himself participated in the sixth performance of the Dada soirée in November 1919, describes how the audience uprising stage-managed by the Dadaists was provoked. Mehring was reciting Goethe's poem *Wanderers Sturmlied* in Dadaist style,

> up to a pre-arranged cue when the whole Dada tribe burst onto the podium and bellowed "Stop!"

"Stop that rubbish!" they roared, and "Walt" snarled Böff, his monocle jammed in place, "Walt, you're not going to throw these—ah—pearls to such swine?" and "Stop!" yelled the Dada chorus simultaneously: "Get out! Ladies and Gentlemen, you are kindly requested to go to hell . . . if you really want amusement, go to the whorehouse, or (said Huelsenbeck) to a Monas Thann lecture!" and they stepped down from the podium arm in arm in a chain to face the enraged stalls. (52, German)

From here to Handke's *Offending the Audience* no longer seems such a giant step.

The literary devices which constitute the syntactic level and the trends realized on the semantic and metasemiotic levels stand in clear relation to the pragmatic level which decides and fixes their respective functions: the intended effect on the reader/spectator is the underlying structural moment. All the Dadaist activities were directed at an audience. Since the founding of the Cabaret Voltaire in 1916 in Zürich, they utilized newspaper advertisements and leaflets as an important instrument of self-publicity, to draw public attention. While at first they only aimed to "épater le bourgeois," these ventures occurred increasingly in the form of an organized assault on the audience, a "strategy of revolt." The devices shown above were directly aimed at challenging and re-examining the purely passive attitude of expectation and customary practices of reception in the audience. In this way, they attempted to dissolve the discrepancies between art and society for the duration of the performance. Theatrical conventions and habits of audience perception were deliberately abused, indeed utterly destroyed. In the end, it was left to the audience to decide how to react to the Dadaist activities and happenings, how to arrive at a new understanding of "art" and how to create a different kind of receptive attitude: the Dadaist performance "work" only existed in the (mostly aggressive) reaction of the audience; it was the product and result of a process of interaction between the agents of the action and the audience.

The Dadaist devices not only operated in the pragmatic dimension, but also in the semantic dimension. These devices enabled the presentation of the concept of the world, which they saw as disordered, as chaos.

Reality seemed incalculable, and thus nonrepresentable. Even if one could admit a fundamental ordering principle to reality, this was in essence beyond human perception. Life was interpreted as a "vital chaos," and man a clown hopelessly trapped within it. Only a work which is random, incoherent, hybrid, indeterminant, and nonsequential can function as an adequate reaction to, or possible way of representing the condition of the world. The Dadaist activities and the techniques and devices employed to achieve them should thus be seen in relation to the so-called "culture crisis" (*Kulturkrise*) which, at the beginning of this century, principally after the First World War, shook the middle classes in Europe. While the majority of the audience which participated in the Dada soirées, as members of the educated middle class,

still firmly held to the idea of the world and works of art as ordered wholes, the Dadaists attempted to "decondition" them by leading them to specific reactions through their actions and thus to force new attitudes on them.

The fundamental perception of a far-reaching crisis in Western culture is also characteristic of the "classic" authors of modern theater such as Pirandello or O'Neill as well as for the members of the avant-garde theater before and after the First World War such as Craig, Meyerhold, or Artaud. Artaud thus writes in his third letter "On Language" (9 November 1932):

> Nous vivons une èpoque probablement unique dans l'histoire du monde, où le monde passé au crible voit ses vieilles valeurs s'effondrer. La vie calcinée se dissout par la base. Et cela sur le plan moral ou social se traduit par un monstrueux déchainement d'appétits, une libération des plus bas instincts, un crépitement de vies brûlées et qui s'exposent prématurément à la flamme. (112)

Our thoughts and argumentation so far have led us to three general conclusions:

> 1) The factors that can be called the distinctive characteristics of a postmodern literary work can partly (e.g., Pirandello, O'Neill) or wholly (Dada) be found in works dating from the early twentieth century.
>
> 2) These factors, which can be related to very different semiotic dimensions, are not separate from each other, but rather create such relations with one another that a structure is formed.
>
> 3) This structure is in its turn related to the circumstances of the culture crisis, and most particularly to the immanent consciousness of standing at the "threshold of an era" which will either lead to the birth of a new mankind and a new world, or which will lead to catastrophe.

If, therefore, postmodernism cannot be sufficiently distinguished from modernism by the criteria evidence/absence of certain distinctive characteristics, other criteria must be sought. The conclusions of our examination open at least two possibilities. Postmodernism can be differentiated from modernism on the basis of:

> a) the relations made by the distinctive characteristics situated on the different levels, i.e., on the basis of the structure they form,
>
> b) the historical, social Zeitgeist of the age to which the structure of relations corresponds.

In this way, Beckett's later dramas (*Play, Not I, That Time, Ends and Odds*), Heiner Müller's plays since *Germania Tod in Berlin,* and the dramas of Peter Handke and Thomas Bernhard can actually be identified through the very distinctive characteristic (which describes postmodern literature in general) that they are open to the reader/spectator: the disintegration of the dramatic characters on a semantic level, for example, or incoherence, randomness, fragmentation, hybridization on the syntactic level, are leveled at the reader/spectator who must himself decide how he will deal with the components offered to him. This can be observed in a very acute way in Robert Wilson's postmodern theatre. In Wilson's mammoth project *CIVIL warS* (1983/84), separate parts of which were produced and premiered in Rotterdam, Marseille, Lyon, Nice, Rome, Cologne, Tokyo, and Milwaukee, different ways of treating language were realized and performed. The texts of the characters' speech, for example, might consist of ready-made phrases from everyday life, ("are you alright," "just leave me alone," "oh come on"), phrases which are on the one hand presented as set scenes in the process of which the text is disconnected and there is no meaning in the dialogue, or on the other hand they are broken up into separate words and phonetic sounds ("are," "you," "alright," "a") and spoken alternately by the dramatic characters often many times over (*CIVIL warS* act 1, scene A).

Here, the manifest refusal to employ language in such a way that the sequence of sounds, words, or sentences yields a cohesive dialogue that will thus make sense, is based on yet another device. In act 4 of *CIVIL warS,* for which Heiner Müller was responsible, literary ready-mades, quotes from world literature are compiled together, (e.g., from *Hamlet, Phaedra, Empedocles*). Single parts of text are broken away from their original contexts and placed nonsequentially next to one another. In fact, the isolated fragments do yield meaning, but not, however, the sequence as a whole.

Another device used to the same effect is that in which the text spoken by the actor is employed as an element of a collage of recorded sound which is as much composed of different but simultaneously spoken text as it is of shreds of music, sound, and speech. Now, in this context, even the single words and speeches are no longer understandable, but instead solely identifiable as elements of language. To a large extent they are reduced to the distinctive quality of a sound perceived as noise. In this way, the linguistic sign is more or less wholly deconstructed as sign. At first this seems to be a comparable kind of device to that which we have identified in the constructivist, dadaist, and futurist theater experiments: language is almost wholly desemanticized and no longer acts and functions as a sign within the context of the performance. However, while there the desemanticization of language creates a concentration on the quality of sound, in Wilson's case, language is allowed to decay into noise, which because of its multiple and simultaneously transmitted phonetic phenomena can no longer be perceived as a meaningful sign. The desemanticization of language which all three devices considered here effect—even in different ways—is even further advanced through the dissolution of the spoken language on the one hand from a "character" and on the other from the actor's body. The sounds, words, or texts are spoken by the actor at the same time as they are transmitted on tape through a loudspeaker. In this way, they are disengaged from the body of the actor—the language creates its own acoustic space. In so doing, however, language becomes incapable of functioning as the sign of character: speech is deconstructed not only as part of a meaningful dialogue but also as the sign of character. Speech is presented as phonetic phenomena and fragments of text which can neither be linked to one another nor to the body of the actor in a meaning-generating semiosis.

Alongside the desemanticization of language, Wilson presents the desemioticization of the body. Here again he has developed different devices to achieve it. The most important, and one which is especially typical of Wilson, is that he directs the actors to move so slowly that the impression of a slow-motion picture is created. Through this extremely slow motion the spectator's attention is drawn to the process of the movement itself. The spectator perceives gesture as movement, that is, as part of a moving body, and there is no possibility of perceiving it as or interpreting it as the sign for something else (as for example the expression of a role type). The slow-motion technique puts the actor's body on the same level as the objects presented on stage. The actor's body no longer represents or means anything, and finds satisfaction in being presented next to its co-objects. Another device shows the particular use of costume and make-up. In so far as the actor's body can suggest a specific character—as in the German part of *CIVIL warS,* for example, the character Frederick the Great, his mother Sophie Dorothée, an angel, a soldier, the tinman, and Lincoln, or in the American part, Admiral Perry, or a Japanese basket-peddler—it is employed as a quotation, so that characters are barely suggested and do not even begin to be built up dramatically. The separate elements presented by the actor's body such as costume, make-up, gesture, movement in space, and voice do not relate to one another, and thus cannot be integrated by the spectator with one another to provide internal relations that will produce any meaning. On the contrary, they create the potential of many random associative external relations which are almost wholly dependent on the spectator's own universe of discourse. A further device consists of simply employing the actor's body on the stage as bearer or prop of an object being presented, as for example, the bird in *Knee Plays*. Although Wilson has adopted this device from the Japanese theater, where the stagehands dressed in black hold ready the necessary props for the actor, or a glass of water should the actor grow hoarse, or stand ready to light the actor's face when the mime is particularly important, Wilson, in contrast, uses this device to show the unity between the object presented by the actor and the actor's body, thus demonstratively underlining its nonmeaning. The actor's body becomes part of a dream-like image floating by, in that it contains no semantic cohesion.

The single image can now be received on two levels: 1) on the syntagmatic level of the process on stage, which through the lack of internal relations is received as an incoherent sequence of ready-made linguistic and bodily quotations, or meaningless sounds and movements, or at best as a chain of information transmitted in bits; to discover a coherent meaning in the sequence of which is utterly impossible, or 2) on the paradigmatic level of the subjectively triggered chain of associations which integrates the single elements into subjectively asserted and structured areas of meaning and thus allows it to change back into subjective carriers of meaning.

The first level of reception can be linked to the flood of communication brought about by the mass media in that it allows the words to decay into noise and breaks up the succession of events into incoherent pictures so that they can only be perceived as information in bits whose sequence is meaningless. The second level of reception, on the contrary, opens the spectator to the possibility of perceiving the process on the stage as he would his own dream images—as a wonderful, unique, at first foreign world, the single elements of which seem wholly familiar without, however, admitting the possibility of being tied to one another into a superior unit of meaning. If the spectator admits the idea of the concreteness of this world, without needing to bring instant interpretation to it, the associative connections which he can now make release him to new experiences and unlock new possibilities of meaning. This level of reception thus initiates new kinds of perception and constitution of meaning, and is diametrically opposed to the "consumer habit" promoted by the mass media. Similar to the Dada soirées, the work can only be constituted in the interaction between text and spectator.

In the case of Dada, the interaction was aimed at a predominantly educated middle-class audience which was used to tracing specific, if not eternal then at least fixed, meanings in works of art, with the intention of upsetting this expectation and attitude of reception: The audience must be shocked, attacked, and provoked into aggression to get it to engage in any activity at all.

Interestingly, the Dada performances did not even achieve the desired effect in an audience composed mostly of workers who did not bring such expectations with them, and it was for this reason that experiments of this kind were discontinued. The audience at which postmodern drama/theater aims has, on the contrary, long since departed from the expectations and attitudes of reception characterized and fixed by the educated middle classes. It is—as a metropolitan audience—not easily shocked, or made aggressive. Consequently the interaction between text and spectator is realized quite differently: Either the spectator overlays the single elements and their incoherent sequence with meanings which stem from his own historical, social and private, autobiographical experience (he knows in this case that meanings have no fixed, intersubjectively valid values to be conveyed, but that they rather consist of the products of his own imaginative and associative activity); or he refuses to constitute any meanings at all and perceives the bodies, objects, words, and lighting in their concreteness as bodies, words, and lighting without interpreting them as signs of something else, so that, free of the need to bring any meaning to them, he finds satisfaction in the very concreteness of the items presented.

On the basis of these changed attitudes of reception in an audience (as opposed to those brought about by Dada) the distinctive characteristics found on the syntactic, semantic, and metasemiotic levels also take on another function. Fragmentation and collage should not, for example, shock the spectator into perceiving the world which he assumes is interconnected and causal as in fact ruled by incoherence and randomness. Rather, the device should encourage the spectator already oriented toward the principle of randomness to apply his own meaning to the randomly presented single object, without looking to possible links to the meaning he brings it, or to perceive it simply as an object in its concrete fact.

The dissolution of the boundaries of the self on the semantic level should not shock the spectator who believes he has an individual personality by demonstrating the fact that such a supposition of the individual personality is a middle-class fiction, but should rather expose the spectator who is already conscious of the instability of the self to different possibilities of its projection.

The shift of the dominant as epistemological question to the dominant as ontological one does not pursue the goal of sensitizing an essentially rational spectator to the view of the imbalance between the self and the consciousness, but rather confirms to the spectator who has already begun to question his rational consciousness, his rather more concretely directed perceptions.

Thus although we can observe the same distinctive characteristics in modern theater of the early twentieth century as we find in the postmodern, and although in both instances the distinctive characteristics on the syntactic, semantic, and metasemiotic levels only fulfill their function in their relation to the pragmatic dimension, the phenomena we are dealing with are clearly dissimilar. The Zeitgeist to which they belong is fundamentally different.

Whether these differences, however, constitute another *Epochenschwelle* in transition toward postmodernism has yet to be answered. Personally, I believe that the underlying changes on which postmodernism was built had already been fully executed by the end of the nineteenth and beginning of the twentieth centuries: the new perception of time and space, the dissolution of the boundaries of the individual ego, the relativism of rational, logic, causal thinking which in its entirety as *conditio sine qua non* are all evident in postmodern writing and suggest the point of transition into the twentieth century and with it the beginning of modernism.

The essential difference between modernism/avant-gardism and postmodernism seems to lie far more in the fact that the postulate formulated at the beginning of the century as an expression and consequence of a far-reaching culture crisis has in the eighties long been a reality: since the sixties, cultural change has occurred de facto. Thus I would suggest on the one hand to date the *Epochenschwelle* at the outbreak of the culture crisis in art, and on the other hand, plead not to equalize the vast differences between modernism and postmodernism with reference to their very real similarities. Instead, considering that cultural change has long since been effected, it will prove illuminating to define and judge these differences through a kind of functional examination that has been neglected heretofore.

BIBLIOGRAPHY

Artaud, Antonin. *Oeuvres Complètes IV.* Paris: Gallimard, 1978.

Bürger, Peter. *The Theory of the Avant-Garde.* Transl. Michael Shaw. Minneapolis: University of Minnesota Press, 1984.

Calinescu, Matei. *Five Faces of Modernity.* Durham: University of North Carolina Press, 1987.

———, and Douwe Fokkema, eds. *Exploring Postmodernism.* Amsterdam: John Benjamins, 1987.

Fischer-Lichte, Erika. "Jenseits der Interpretation." *Kontroversen, alte und neue.* Proceedings of the 7th International Congress of Germanists. Tübingen: Niemeyer, 1986.

———, "Postmoderne Performance: Rückkehr zum rituellen Theater?" *Arcadia* 22, 1 (1987): 191-201.

Fokkema, Douwe, and Hans Bertens, eds. *Approaching Postmodernism.* Utrecht Publications in General and Comparative Literature, vol. 21. Amsterdam: John Benjamins, 1986.

Huelsenbeck, Richard, ed. *Dada—eine literarische Dokumentation.* Reinbek bei Hamburg: Rowohlt, 1984.

Huyssen, Andreas, and Klaus R. Scherpe, eds. *Postmoderne: Zeichen eines kulturellen Wandels.* Reinbek bei Hamburg: Rowohlt, 1986.

Kamper, Dietmar, and Willem van Reijen. eds. *Die unvollendete Vernunft: Moderne versus Postmoderne.* Frankfurt am Main: Suhrkamp, 1987.

McHale, Brian. *Postmodernist Fiction.* New York and London: Methuen, 1987.

Mehring, Walter. *Berlin Dada: Eine Chronik mit Photos und Dokumenten.* Zürich: Arche, 1959.

O'Neill, Eugene. *Three Plays of Eugene O'Neill.* New York: Random House, 1959.

Pirandello, Luigi. *Six Characters in Search of an Author.* Trans. Frederick May. London: Heinemann, 1966.

Tzara, Tristan. *Oeuvres Complètes.* 4 vols. Texte établie, présenté et annoté par Henri Behar. Paris: Flammarion, 1975-1982.

FURTHER READING

Secondary Sources

Calinescu, Matei and David Fokkema, eds. *Exploring Postmodernism: Selected Papers Presented at the XIth International Comparative Literature Congress, Paris, 20-24 August 1985.* Amsterdam and Philadelphia: John Benjamins Publishing Company, 1987, 269 p.
　　Includes essays by Ihab Hassan, Marjorie Perloff and Stefano Rosso.

Caramello, Charles. *Silverless Mirrors: Book, Self & Postmodern American Fiction.* Tallahassee: University Presses of Florida, 1983, 250 p.
　　Traces the development of the authorial self throughout American fiction.

Docherty, Thomas, ed. *Postmodernism: A Reader.* New York: Columbia University Press, 528 p.
　　Includes a wide range of essays by major postmodernist thinkers, including Frederic Jameson, Ihad Hassan, Jean Baudrillard, and Umberto Eco.

Hutcheon, Linda. *A Poetics of Postmodernism: History, Theory, Fiction.* New York: Routledge, 1988, 268 p.
　　Maintains that postmodernism embraces history while challenging its assumptions, and that postmodernism is deliberately contradictory.

Journal of Modern Literature 3, No. 5 (July 1985): 1065-1268.
　　Presents essays from Timothy Materer, Charles Baxter, and others that trace the development of literature from such modernists as Ezra Pound and Gertrude Stein to such later writers as Theodore Roethke and Samuel Beckett.

Mazzaro, Jerome. *Postmodern American Poetry.* Urbana: University of Illinois Press, 1980, 203 p.
　　Argues that the roots of postmodern poetry are found in the works of W. H. Auden, Randall Jarrell, Theodore Roethke, David Ignatow, John Berryman, Sylvia Plath, and Elizabeth Bishop.

McCaffery, Larry, editor. *Postmodern Fiction: A Bio-Bibliographic Guide.* New York: Greenwood Press, 1986, 604 p.
　　Collection of essays on such topics as metafiction, experimental realism, science fiction, and postmodern journalism.

McGowan, John. *Postmodernism and Its Critics.* Ithaca, N.Y.: Cornell University Press, 1991, 296 p.
　　Examines Marxism, neopragmatism, and poststructuralism as represented by Jacques Derrida and Michel Foucault.

Newman, Charles Hamilton. *The Post-Modern Aura: The Act of Fiction in an Age of Inflation.* Evanston, Ill.: Northwestern University Press, 1985, 203 p.

Finds that there is little distinction between the the avant-garde and modernism in contemporary art.

Putz, Manfred and Peter Freese, editors. *Postmodernism in American Literature: A Critical Anthology.* Darmstadt: Thesen-Verlag, 1984, 238 p.
 Includes essays by such critics as Ihab Hassan, Raymond Federman, and Leslie A. Fiedler.

Russell, Charles, editor. *The Avant-Garde Today: An International Anthology.* Urbana: University of Illinois Press, 1986, 269 p.
 Contains essays by American, European, and Japanese critics on the nature of avant-garde literature in the era of postmodern practice.

Tani, Stefano. *The Doomed Detective: The Contribution of the Detective Novel to Postmodern American and Italian Fiction.* Carbondale: Southern Illinois University Press, 1984, 183 p.

Examines the influence of such detective novelists as Raymond Chandler and Dashiell Hammett on the anti-detective postmodern works of Umberto Eco, John Gardner, Leonardo Sciasicia.

Thiher, Allen. *Words in Reflection: Modern Language Theory and Postmodern Fiction.* Chicago: University of Chicago Press. 1984, 247 p.
 Uses predominant critical definitions of writing from David Hume, John Locke, and Goethe to examine the nature of postmodern writing since the publication of works by Ludwig Wittgenstein, Martin Heidegger, and Jacques Derrida.

Trachtenberg, Stanley, editor. *The Postmodernism Moment: A Handbook of Contemporary Innovation in the Arts.* Westport, Conn.: Greenwood Press, 1985, 323 p.
 Includes essays on architecture, art, dance, film, literature, music, photography, theater, and appendices on postmodern German and Latin American literature.

Science and Modern Literature

INTRODUCTION

The modern era has witnessed rapid advancements in science and technology that rival, if not displace, traditional knowledge systems represented by the fields of literature, art, philosophy, and religion. Despite the traditional gulf between scientific and literary discourse, however, writers and critics of imaginative literature in the nineteenth and twentieth centuries have consistently looked to science as a source of knowledge and valuable insight into the human condition. Discoveries such as relativity, chaos theory, evolution, cybernetics, and quantum theory have provided writers with considerable inspiration and new modes of thought that have become an integral part of literature in the postmodern age.

By the nineteenth century the hegemony of scientific thought as the paradigm of modern knowledge had begun to increasingly exert itself in the imaginations of writers. Advances in the field of biology in particular played a role in the intellectual and artistic currents of the Victorian era, especially by Charles Darwin's theory of biological evolution through natural selection. Darwin's publication of *On the Origin of Species* in 1859 and the later application of his deterministic theories to social rather than purely biological systems by Herbert Spencer exercised considerable influence on writers of naturalist fiction such as George Eliot, Thomas Hardy, Emile Zola, and many others. Another discovery of the period, the Second Law of Thermodynamics, also had an enduring effect on literature that followed, although it appears most conspicuously in the works of postmodern writers of the twentieth century. The Second Law defines the concept of entropy—a measure of homogeneity or lack of differentiation in a system—and is typically associated in literature with a tendency toward depicting increasing chaos in the universe.

Accelerated scientific advancements in the twentieth century have contributed to the decline of belief in the mechanistic, rational, and supremely-ordered Newtonian universe and have inspired themes of discontinuity and unpredictability that are common tropes of postmodern literature. Twentieth-century discoveries in science and logic, including Albert Einstein's Theory of Relativity, Werner Heisenberg's Uncertainty Principle, Kurt Gödel's Incompleteness Theorem, and the complexities of quantum physics have contributed to a particular view of reality apparent in the works of John Updike, Thomas Pynchon, John Barth, and Kurt Vonnegut, Jr., and others. Taking cues from such theories, which realize natural barriers to scientific knowledge even while opening hitherto unexplored areas of study, these and many other writers and critics of the twentieth century have tended to apply the concepts of randomness, uncertainty, and the breakdown of traditional causality in their works. Other developments in science from the latter half of the twentieth century have also contributed to the literary atmosphere of postmodernism. Notable among these are the study of chaos theory, which establishes the complex order of disorderly systems while positing their long-term unpredictability, and cybernetics, which views both humans and machines as complex systems of information—ideas analogous to those of such writers as Italo Calvino, Don DeLillo, Stanislaw Lem, and Jacques Derrida.

Related areas of critical interest in the subject of science and literature include the perception that science is a social construct like other forms of human inquiry, and therefore subject to certain cultural limitations. Commentators have outlined the important differences between poetic and scientific discourse while observing that scientific language, though exacting and verifiable, as yet has failed to duplicate the language of feeling and beauty found in poetic utterances. Finally, several commentators have observed the importance of science fiction as a subgenre. First exhibited in the imaginative writings of Edgar Allan Poe, Mary Shelley, Jules Verne, and H. G. Wells, science fiction focuses on the place of science in contemporary and future life and is concerned with the possible impacts of rapidly-accelerating technological discoveries on society and on human perceptions of reality. As such, science fiction continues to provide a viable medium of speculation and communication in a technological world.

REPRESENTATIVE WORKS

Isaac Asimov
    I, Robot (novel) 1967
John Banville
    Doctor Copernicus (novel) 1976
John Barth
    Giles Goat-Boy (novel) 1966
Samuel Beckett
    Comment c'est [*How It Is*] (novel) 1964
    Imagination morte imaginez [*Imagination Dead Imagine*] (drama) 1965
Edward Bellamy
    Dr. Heidenhoff's Process (novel) 1880
Saul Bellow
    Mr. Sammler's Planet (novel) 1969
Bertold Brecht
    Leben des Galilei [*The Life of Galileo*] (drama) 1938

Hermann Broch
  Die unbekannte Grösse [*The Unknown Quantity*] (novel) 1933
Robert Browning
  "Paracelsus" (poetry) 1835
Pearl S. Buck
  A Desert Incident (novel) 1959
Samuel Butler
  Erewhon (poetry) 1872
Italo Calvino
  Le cosmicomiche [*Cosmicomics*] (short stories) 1965
  Ti con zero [*t zero*] (short stories) 1967
G. K. Chesterton
  The Man Who Was Thursday (novel) 1908
Arthur C. Clarke
  2001: A Space Odyssey (novel) 1968
Wilkie Collins
  Heart and Science (novel) 1893
Joseph Conrad
  The Secret Agent (novel) 1907
Don DeLillo
  White Noise (novel) 1986
Philip K. Dick
  Do Androids Dream of Electric Sheep? (novel) 1968
Friedrich Dürrenmatt
  Die Physiker [*The Physicists*] (drama) 1962
Gabriel García Márquez
  Cien años de soledad [*One Hundred Years of Solitude*] (novel) 1970
William Gibson and Bruce Sterling
  The Difference Engine (novel) 1991
Nathaniel Hawthorne
  "The Birthmark" (short story) 1845
E. T. A. Hoffman
  "The Sandman" (short story) 1816
Aldous Huxley
  Brave New World (novel) 1932
Franz Kafka
  "Ein Landarzt" ["A Country Doctor"] (short story) 1919
D. H. Lawrence
  The Rainbow (novel) 1915
Stanislaw Lem
  Cyberiada [*Cyberiad: Fables for a Cybernetic Age*] (short stories) 1965
Primo Levi
  The Periodic Table (novel) 1984
Clarice Lispector
  A paixão segundo G. H. [*The Passion According to G. H.*] (novel) 1964
Thomas Mann
  Doktor Faustus [*Doctor Faustus*] (novel) 1947
Mark Twain
  Some Learned Fables for Good Old Boys and Girls (short stories) 1875
James Merrill
  The Changing Light at Sandover (poetry) 1982
Walter Miller
  A Canticle for Leibowitz (novel) 1959
Howard Nemerov
  The Collected Poems of Howard Nemerov (poetry) 1977

Edgar Allan Poe
  "Von Kempelen and His Discovery" (short story) 1849
Thomas Pynchon
  Gravity's Rainbow (novel) 1973
Hans Rehberg
  Johannes Kepler: Schauspiel in drei Akten (drama) 1933
Michel Serres
  Le cinq sens (nonfiction) 1985
Mary Shelley
  Frankenstein; Or, the Modern Prometheus (novel) 1818
Charles Percy Snow
  The Sleep of Reason (novel) 1968
Olaf Stapledon
  Odd John: A Story between Jest and Earnest (novel) 1954
Robert Louis Stevenson
  "The Strange Case of Dr. Jekyll and Mr. Hyde" (short story) 1886
Thomas Stoppard
  Rosencrantz and Guildenstern Are Dead (drama) 1966
Jules Verne
  Voyage au centre de la terra [*Journey to the Centre of the Earth*] (novel) 1864
  Vingt mille lieues sous les mers [*Twenty Thousand Leagues under the Sea*] (novel) 1870
Kurt Vonnegut, Jr.
  Cat's Cradle (novel) 1963
  Slaughterhouse Five; Or, The Children's Crusade (novel) 1969
H. G. Wells
  "The Time Machine" (short story) 1895
  The War of the Worlds (novel) 1898

OVERVIEWS

David J. Gordon

SOURCE: "The Dilemma of Literature in an Age of Science," in the *Sewanee Review*, Vol. LXXXVI, No. 2, Spring, 1978, pp. 245-60.

[*In the following essay, Gordon examines tensions between modern literature and science.*]

The French scientist Jacques Monod, using the evidence of modern biology, has brought up to date the hypothesis formulated by Democritus—that all natural processes are governed by the impersonal forces of chance and necessity. Monod thus questions, as science, animistic or idealistic positions which sanction the projection of will, reason, or feeling onto nature in order to establish a humanly significant conception of natural power and destiny. But he respects an independent realm of values and the experience of freedom from which values are derived. Acknowledging a world of mind separate from a world of matter or brain, he aligns himself with a tradition of philosophic dualism extending from Descartes to Chomsky.

Where does his persuasive argument leave the arts, particularly the art of poetry, which is unimaginable without the license of animistic projection? Monod apparently seeks only to undermine certain philosophies with scientific pretensions rather than poetry itself, but readers of *Chance & Necessity* who are students of literature may be prompted to reconsider the difficulties faced by humanistic study in an era when the freedom and power of the mind are brought into question with each advance of science, especially the difficulties encountered by ambitious artists and critics who attempt to overcome the split between mind and matter, choice and chance, freedom and necessity.

Logically there is no split at all between scientific materialism and poetic idealism. What a scientist means by necessity is not the same thing as what a poet presents as such. The two ideas are not on the same scale. Poetic necessity—an experiential fact—is a synonym for compulsion, constraint, inexorability, fate. Its true opposite is freedom or choice. The true opposite of scientific necessity, on the other hand, is chance. These two senses of necessity, like the Yeatsian terms *Choice* and *Chance,* are incommensurable. Thus the familiar antithesis between free will and determinism is, logically, a confusion. For determinism, in science, is simply the assumption that all effects have causes, and it has nothing to do with the experience of freedom and unfreedom.

The basis of science is, to be sure, similar to that of art. We have known with increasing clearness since Kant made the point that the framing of theories and hypotheses is as imaginative an activity as the conceiving of poems, both of them grounded in undemonstrable assumption, in metaphysics or "myth." But an essential characteristic of scientific method, aimed practically at permitting a measure of control over the processes of nature, is the deliberate withdrawal of attention from metaphysical speculation. As Whitehead observed in *Science and the Modern World,* it is inaccurate to think of science as the triumph of rationalism. Instead the seventeenth-century founders of modern science turned away from the unbridled rationalism of medieval metaphysics, and they claimed an allegiance to the facts derived from observation and experimentation. And Monod asserts with some emphasis that the decision to restrict one's vision in this manner must be initially an ethical decision, for scientific work cannot be substituted for values.

One might say that the scientific view of things is partial, whereas the poetic view (in this respect like the religious view) is total. When Milton and Pope prescribe knowledge within bounds, they are not at all recommending the scientific partial view; they simply want to make clear the idea that a total view is to be identified with divine knowledge rather than human knowledge. But theirs is not a less modest view—simply a different way of looking at the world. Whatever the underlying similarities between scientific and literary knowing, the procedures of the two activities are quite different. Scientific "myths"—theories and hypotheses—must be reasoned

out, refined, and corrected; whereas literary "myths"—fictions—seek their justification immediately by a direct appeal to the reader's empathetic sense, winning or failing to win his participation.

Clearly it would be naive to say that the relation between science and literature in the modern era has been innocent or that the suspicion apparent on either side is superficial. Any demonstration that chance and necessity rule in yet another area of the natural world is bound to vitiate some prevailing and supportive view, to loosen some binding ideal and create anxiety. Theories do not replace fictions—the scale being different—but a new theory is likely to make certain fictions seem less adequate to contemporary need.

Moreover new poets must make their poems out of currently available material, which since the seventeenth century has increasingly come to include the latest scientific or pseudoscientific theories. And here a particular problem arises. Theories are tentative, more or less useful constructs for organizing facts and connecting them to laws presumed to operate beyond our perceptions. Their poetic potentialities—which they have by virtue of the fact that all theories are fundamentally a species of mythology—must remain undeveloped. But a poet who attempts to absorb a theory will inevitably animize and humanize it, will seek to make it responsive in some way to human need. And this process involves a transference of scale which must result in some measure of logical confusion. For example the physicist's concept of entropy, when assimilated to literature by someone like Thomas Pynchon, no longer refers to a material loss of energy but to our *experience* of diminishment. Or Heisenberg's Uncertainty Principle, sometimes invoked by literary critics with a semiological bias, is made to mean that the interpreter of texts lacks standards of reliability rather than that there is a margin of error in our perceptions. Again the psychoanalytic terms *id-ego-superego,* when we find them in criticism, refer seldom to chiefly unconscious processes but rather to preconscious ones or even to the pre-Freudian concepts of passion, reason, and conscience.

Wordsworth was quite right when he eloquently predicted that poetry will supplement rather than be replaced by science:

> Poetry is the first and last of all knowledge—it is as immortal as the heart of man. If the labours of men of science should ever create any material revolution, direct or indirect, in our condition, and in the impressions which we habitually receive, the poet will sleep then no more than at present, but he will be ready to follow the steps of the man of science, not only in those general indirect effects, but he will be at his side, carrying sensation into the midst of the objects of science itself.

But he might have added that the poet who would "lend his divine spirit to this transfiguration" is compelled to change theory into fiction and that this change, particularly when it is rationalized, tends to create a logical (hence also an aesthetic) problem.

Certainly scientists themselves, or those who appeal to their authority, are not an innocent party in this relationship. Because their subject is esteemed highly in the modern era, spokesmen for science have, however unwittingly, condescended to the arts. Even so generous a man as J. Bronowski, who would never have scorned art directly, can say, in his very popular *Ascent of Man:* "The intellectual leadership of the twentieth century rests with scientists. . . . It is not the business of science to inherit the earth, but to inherit the moral imagination." And this human error (and error it is if Bronowski means science itself rather than simply the scientist as one man among others) is greatly compounded by the fear and intellectual laziness of the general public. Every person of adult years has seen a number of medical theories come and go, for example, the newest one embraced as if no one will ever learn either how limited is our knowledge or how unlimited our need to rely blindly on authority. Furthermore we confer a quasi-mystical authority on technical vocabularies, and school ourselves thereby in a habit of literalism that makes it more difficult for us to experience the charms of plastic language and more difficult, of course, for artists to create such language.

One of the first literary works to register this dilemma was *Paradise Lost.* Milton did not, it is true, respond directly to the new scientific spirit of his day (his allusion to Galileo in a poem whose conception is based on a pre-Copernican cosmology is only casual), but his strenuous effort to justify the ways of God by discursive as well as poetic logic may reflect that spirit. There were comparable earlier attempts by philosophers—most notably by St. Augustine in book 5 of *The City of God*—but there is nothing in the theism of Shakespeare or Dante that suggests, as Milton's does, underlying doubts being suppressed. If we do not share Hamlet's belief in "a divinity that shapes our ends, / Rough-hew them how we will," we can readily believe in *his* believing, and however remote we may be from Dante's world view we can, as T. S. Eliot observed, respond to his showing us what it feels like to believe it. Of course Milton's poem works in similar ways. The poet's evocations of God's creative power or even His severity usually win our imaginative assent. But His speeches sometimes solicit also the approval of the critical intelligence, and they give the impression of overriding resistance by the mere force of sonorous assertion.

The most questionable element of these speeches—which cannot be ignored because it bears directly on a central theme of *Paradise Lost,* human responsibility for the fall—is the Augustinian argument that God's omniscient will contains no tincture of necessity that in the least compromises Adam's freedom of choice: "Necessity and Chance / Approach not me, and what I will is Fate." Milton categorically excludes from divine will the principles underlying scientific knowledge, but the exclusion creates a certain awkwardness. The poet wants us to imagine God's will as identified with Fate, which, if it is

not to mean a blindly impersonal necessity, is bound to associate itself in our minds with experiential necessity, with compulsion, a connection not intended. He cannot escape a logical dilemma.

The problem is more evident, though less disruptive, in the eighteenth-century didactic poem "Essay on Man," in which Pope attempted directly to reconcile a belief in a providential deity with the achievement of Newton. The poet's attitude toward the scientist is positive, even enthusiastic; but Newton is transformed into an ironic instance enabling Pope to make a moral point—the chastening of pride—with wit and force:

> Superior beings, when of late they saw
> A mortal man unfold all Nature's law,
> Admired such wisdom in an earthly shape,
> And showed a NEWTON as we show an ape.

Pope still thinks of nature as the creation of God, a moral order responsive to human need (though not, of course, to human pride), and so Newton's achievement, which must have required a withdrawal of attention from that order, is not very precisely appreciated. (It is not to the point that Newton himself believed in God since he evidently could put aside theology while doing physics.) The "Essay on Man" asserts man's limitations and the wisdom of not presuming to examine God, but it must itself examine God in order to provide a rationale for human limitation. Overtly, however, Pope seems as untroubled by this difficulty as by the general difficulty of reconciling physics and theology.

With the rise of romanticism and a new sensibility disposed toward revolution, the problem takes on another aspect. Shelley's wrestlings with the concept of Necessity are illustrative. The great charm for Shelley of this idea as he found it in Godwin was that it effectively replaced the orthodox belief in an anthropomorphic deity or supernatural intelligence without surrendering the solace contained in that belief, for it conceived a moral force (a force not ourselves yet making for righteousness) at work as an inexorable pressure within the human creation of civilization. Shelley admitted a passion for reforming the world, yet he loathed brute power and assertions of dictatorial will. His poems suggest an elusive compromise between an inclination to adopt a scientifically credible view of nature (we know that he was attracted to the experimental science of his day) and the need of a poet for a myth of human freedom or enslavement. Fascinated by a hidden power, Shelley sometimes writes of it as virtually unrelated to human will, for example in "Mont Blanc": "Power dwells apart in its tranquillity, / Remote, serene, and inaccessible." But he is a poet, and cannot imagine the power inhumanly. In "Hymn to Intellectual Beauty" it is pictured supportively as "a grace dearer for its mystery," a presence to whom he can dedicate his powers, a force he can hope will free the world from its "dark slavery," and, in the Wordsworthian manner, a power which can "to my onward life supply / Its calm." The inconsistency here is apparent in much visionary politics, certainly in Marx's where, on the one hand, capitalism is shown to be necessarily doomed and, on the other, the workers of the world are enjoined to active rebellion.

After Darwin the efforts of speculative fictionists "to follow the steps of the man of science" led inevitably to a moralizing of the theory of natural selection. In English literature we could trace this tendency in Tennyson (in whom, however, the sense of having lost a cherished myth is compensated by a reaffirmation of that myth rather than by any bolder, more interesting strategy), in Butler, in Shaw (who absorbed Butler), or even in Yeats and Lawrence. Shaw's *Back to Methuselah,* Yeats's *A Vision,* and Lawrence's *Fantasia of the Unconscious* are similar documents in this new phase of literary response to science. What is essentially alike in the three works (written within a few years of one another) is their fundamental ambiguity as to how literally they are intended. They represent, compared to our earlier examples, a distinct shift from poetic toward discursive logic, yet all retain in one way or another a protective diffidence about their scientific pretensions. All three assert, for example, that man has created death, but how are we to read this? Surely not as we read *Beyond the Pleasure Principle* in which an inquiry into the possible nonexistence of natural death is frankly speculative yet not mythic, Freud making a point of saying that such speculation need not correspond to any emotional disposition on our part. Nor, just as surely, as we read a doctrinal tract on man's fall asserting that it was disobedience that brought death into the world. The literary artists are now grappling with scientific theory at close range and by a similar, more discursive use of language.

Back to Methuselah, usually dismissed as a bore, takes on a special fascination in this context. The premise of the play is that a life expectancy of only seventy years does not enable us to develop moral maturity. The Brothers Barnabas, a clergyman and a biologist, formulate a "gospel" that presumes to be at the same time a scientific prediction based on a clue offered by the story of Adam and Eve. Natural death, it occurs to them, did not exist in the beginning but was chosen by man in order to escape the burden of immortality. And if this is true, then with sufficient courage the choice can be remade; and immortality or an approximation thereof (they would begin with a life expectancy of three hundred years) is possible. The play concedes to science—i.e. to the impersonal operation of chance and necessity—that the characters in whom this crucial biological variation occurs are not those who have consciously willed or imagined it, and it even alludes to the Darwinian idea that accidental variations do sometimes occur and are thereafter replicated consistently by genetic necessity except for subsequent variations. But the concession is hedged. The play does not really surrender the idea that mind governs matter. It denies the effectiveness of conscious will only to enforce a deeper idea of will. And the two characters whose life expectancies are first actually extended had exhibited distinct signs of repudiating the moral conditions of their lives. What Shaw is seeking is a kind of heroic fusion of

mechanistic and vital theory, as when Franklyn Barnabas speaks of "the tremendous, miracle-working force of will nerved to creation by a conviction of Necessity." The whole action of the play, moreover, is eventually shown to be an emanation of the life force embodied in Lilith, who pronounces final judgment on the human experiment.

In the preface Shaw mixes intelligent appreciation of the scientific point of view with a defiant distortion of it that would simply be perverse if it were not, on its face, counteracting popular extensions of Darwinian theory to the moral sphere. He understands that Darwin's distinctive contribution was the discovery not of evolution itself but of one particular mode of it—circumstantial selection—and that Darwin himself, as a good scientist, had no intention of extending this idea into the realm of values. Nevertheless he resents hearing the theory called *natural selection.* For him accidents are *unnatural:* natural selection must mean something more humanly assuring, like creative evolution. And this becomes more than an argument against misunderstandings of Darwin, for Shaw insists that creative evolution itself is scientific: "it is deductive biology *if* there is such a thing as biology" (italics mine).

During the last sixty years the unresolvable tension between scientific and literary ways of seeing has been most observable in connection with Freud's contribution to psychological science. For what psychoanalysis investigates are the phenomena of consciousness itself, and its demonstrations of chance and necessity operating *within* the mind have shaken our confidence in those old heroes of our myths of freedom, who were sung from Milton to Shaw: will, reason, and conscience.

Therefore it must be emphasized that psychoanalysis, like any other science, may only prompt us to discard or revise certain myths: it cannot threaten the grounds of belief. Indeed, as a therapy, it cooperates with our beliefs in a unique way, enabling the patient to extend his moral freedom, although morality itself is independent of science as such. But it is not surprising that the psychological novel or play—by which I mean the novel which roots the motives of its characters in individual and social history—enjoyed a richer life before Freud's work came to be known than it has since. Although there have been some more or less successful efforts in contemporary literature to dramatize insights associated with Freud (e.g. Bellow's *Seize the Day,* Miller's *A View from the Bridge*), a number of fictionists have turned away from the conventions of the psychological novel or play and have attempted to present the irrational philosophically, in the spirit of Ionesco's injunction: "Avoid psychology, or rather, give it a metaphysical dimension." But the more they deemphasize unconscious motives—that is to say, the inner experience of chance and necessity—the more they are obliged at the same time to deemphasize the mind's freedom to guide them in thought and conduct. They will therefore be drawn to the idea of presenting human experience in terms of blind chance and blind necessity, of accident and repetition.

Blind chance and necessity are indeed conspicuous thematic emphases in the fictions of our day. And the writers who handle them most successfully are those who least suggest that they are competing for credence with scientific hypotheses, either, like Pynchon, by robustly assimilating hypotheses into their own myths or, like Beckett, by cunningly obscuring from the backgrounds of their characters whatever might prompt us to think of their natures and destinies deterministically.

Pynchon is remarkable for the degree to which he has knowledgeably and unselfconsciously coopted scientific hypotheses for an artistic purpose: to render the experience of total cognitive entrapment. As Richard Poirier has astutely commented, he goes beyond "the dream of Wordsworth that poetry or a radical esthetics derived from poetry provides a basis for understanding and resisting any of the other systematic exertions of power over human consciousness." He makes us believe that "science, the analytical method, technology—all of these are not merely impositions upon consciousness. They are also a corporate expression of consciousness: they express us all as much as do the lyrical ballads. They express us more than does our late and befuddled resistance to them." Hence the term *paranoia,* regularly associated with Pynchon and used even by his own characters, takes on a special nonpsychoanalytic meaning: it is not a delusion of unconscious origins that is in question in the novels but an extensively, though ambiguously, authenticated picture of reality. One might fairly object to the excess of detail in *Gravity's Rainbow* or to the narrowness of the sensibility that it reflects, but it largely avoids the logical difficulty which greater writers have encountered when they tried to adapt scientific ideas to artistic ends.

Beckett and his disciple Pinter, employing an alternative strategy, have proven wonderfully adept at conveying pathos and menace, even sexual pathos and sexual menace, without letting their characters assume the shape of individual histories. Their wit and irony either obscure motivation or deflect any inference of irrationality from a psychological and social to a logical and philosophical plane. Tom Stoppard, who has learned some of their tricks, plays them with less certain success, partly because he competes with psychological explanations of irrationality by ridiculing them. In *Rosencrantz and Guildenstern Are Dead,* for example, one of his title characters simply mocks the Freudian explanation of Hamlet's melancholy as absurd; and the effect, though superficially witty, is unsatisfying, for Stoppard is not subduing a propositional statement to an artistic vision so much as challenging it on its own terms, and thus provoking us, whether we accept the statement or not, to resolve the matter on our ground rather than on his.

French modernist fiction seems to me especially problematic in this regard because it is characteristically theoretical and seems to argue against psychological explanations. Camus's *The Stranger* is certainly a dazzling performance, but the notion of a gratuitous crime presented so literally (without the humor we find in Gide) takes on a contrapsychological rather than simply a metapsychological aspect. Compare Beckett's elliptical glimpse of the past life of Vladimir and Estragon ("a million years ago, in the nineties") with the sober if sketchy picture of Meursault's earlier life when he used to care, when he was someone like ourselves—a picture that makes us want to know more, or less, about how his consciousness came to be estranged. And in the novels of Robbe-Grillet and Sarraute, where accident and repetition dominate, the chief interest lies in the thoroughness with which reference is avoided and hence moral and psychological implications are nullified. These writers are more interesting, because more candid, in theory than in practice. Or, one can say, the interest of their fiction is primarily a theoretical interest.

Modern lyrical poetry too, having drawn nearer to the form of discursive argument, illustrates this general difficulty. I would say, for example, that W. H. Auden's poetic use of psychoanalysis, because it is a frank exploitation of colloquial tags without pretense of strictly accurate reference, works better than do those few poems of Wallace Stevens in which Freud is soberly discountenanced as an unsound moralist.

In view of the diffusion of this theoretic sensibility, it is not surprising that the literary reaction to psychoanalysis is markedly evident in criticism itself. The conceptual defense of art against science (and I am concerned only with this tendency in criticism, not with the objections to inferior criticism's making use of psychoanalysis) goes back to the time of Wordsworth and Hegel, if not to the time of Vico: but today, under the strong influence of structuralism, it is directed against one particular kind of hypothesis with astonishing intensity.

Starting with a denial of the premise that Freud considered basic—that consciousness was not the whole of mind—these revisionists (and Freudian revisionist is a better linking term than structuralist for critics as diverse as those I will refer to) have reinvigorated the romantic rejection of Cartesian dualism, distrust of the meddling analytic intellect, and fondness for imaginative metaphysics. But there is a new twist to the modern argument. The key word now is not consciousness but language. "All that *I* know (& that you know)," writes Harold Bloom, "is *rhetoric.* Poetry *is* rhetoric, and criticism is the rhetoric *of* rhetoric."

Perhaps the key figure in this revisionist enterprise is the psychologist Jacques Lacan, who dismisses the Freudian idea of repressed sexuality because, after all, sexuality has been a major literary subject throughout the ages; and then, with this triumphant naiveté, he asserts that the unconscious itself is linguistic in structure: "It is neither primordial or instinctual; what it knows about the elementary is no more than the elements of the signifier." On the basis of this premise Lacan translates those unconscious processes named by Freud *condensation* and *displacement* into the rhetorical terms *metaphor* and *metonymy.* Without this very questionable premise, however, these substitutions are only analogies, striking and suggestive, but no more persuasive as argument than analogy can be.

It seems essential to the revisionist enterprise that all of the key psychoanalytic terms be modified to accord with a concept of the repressed unconscious that does not denote any reality beyond language, writing, poetry. Thus, for Jacques Derrida, "writing is unthinkable without repression." A Freudian would find the survival of childhood (let alone writing) unthinkable without repression, though by repression Derrida apparently means something as un-Freudian as the secondariness of writing to speech and the implicit protest within texts against this secondariness. Bloom alters Freud in a peculiarly clever way. Exploiting the important axiom of criticism that we should not judge art as we judge states of mind, he takes Freudian concepts designed to be applied to the operation of the mind—anxiety, repression, oedipal relationship—and restricts their use to the relations of artists as artists. Roland Barthes, in the opening pages of *The Pleasure of the Text,* frostily disparages "neurosis," "inconsistency," "self-contradiction," and then, having, as it were, disarmed any would-be mundane sexualist, launches into a highly erotic yet absolutely complacent meditation on the act of reading. Geoffrey Hartman, in a way the subtlest of revisionists because he attempts to draw an improved theory out of undeveloped implications in Freud himself, postulates a compulsion to communicate of equal importance to libido, although libido was for Freud the whole of our instinctual inheritance.

Linguistics is the science that the structuralists consider most congenial, but in their hands it can hardly be said to remain a science at all—that is, a branch of cognitive psychology, as Noam Chomsky has repeatedly said it is. They would combine the arts and sciences and call them all myths or *les sciences humaines,* fulfilling Nietzsche's vision of a total aestheticization of knowledge. Superficially, of course, the structuralists are not hostile to science at all, but they have changed its meaning. For them science entails no dualism of subject and object, no distinction between instrumental and aesthetic uses of language. The underlying hostility in this seemingly benign accommodation comes out sharply in an essay by Barthes called "Science versus Literature," in which we read: "The destruction of the instrumental use of language must be at the center of the structuralist program."

There is, as I have earlier indicated, some truth—and not unimportant truth—in the idea that theories and myths are alike. They are created alike, and philosophers of science as well as aestheticians have, in our century, not been at all reluctant to stress this common denominator, the underlying similarity of structure uniting all products of mind and language. (Freud himself acknowledged this in a letter to Einstein: "It may perhaps seem to you as though our theories are a kind of mythology . . . but does not every science come in the end to a kind of mythology?") But it is not only the common basis that the structuralists want to remind us of. They want to erase all trace of the distinction Monod put forth between scientific

materialism and poetic idealism and to establish, in the words of their sympathetic student Robert Scholes, "a methodology which seeks nothing less than the unification of all the sciences into a new system of belief." A new system of belief might well provoke some question, for it would certainly destroy the nature if not the name of science. There is an important difference, I think, between such a view and the purely analytic thrust of Wittgenstein's claim that psychoanalysis is only a powerful mythology; Wittgenstein is inquiring into the radical limits of our thinking on any subject, without a desire to make psychoanalysis over into a system of belief.

For all my distrust of the covert imperialism of structuralist aesthetics—its fondness for the idea of plurisignificance in texts but fundamental distaste for pluralism in intellectual viewpoints—it is unquestionably a serious response to the dilemma of literature in an age of science. It *is* difficult to compose fictions without becoming theoretical or to write about literature without getting embroiled in theory.

One of the most honorable attempts to erect an aesthetic theory that would distinguish fiction both from hypothesis and from myth was carried out by Frank Kermode in *The Sense of an Ending,* and the difficulty of his exemplary effort is worth notice. Fictions are distinct from hypotheses, writes Kermode, because "they are not subject . . . to proof or disconfirmation, only, if they come to lose their operational effectiveness, to neglect." So far so good. Yet "we have to distinguish between myths and fictions. Fictions can degenerate into myths whenever they are not consciously held to be fictive." Therefore "my suggestion is that literary fictions belong to Vaihinger's category of 'the consciously false.'" This is an attractive distinction, since, as Kermode points out, myths understood as unconscious fictions would have to include all kinds of deplorable political ideologies. But it is hard to accept as a general rule the idea that the artist conceives his vision as "the consciously false," that as a rule he lives up to the severe ideal of Wallace Stevens's dictum: "The final belief is to believe in a fiction, which you know to be a fiction, there being nothing else." Surely the artist, as he composes, is likely to be thinking also in the spirit of Beckett's title *Comment c'est.* I daresay that Stevens himself, an exceptionally theoretical poet, must have often, in his earnest desire to set down his vision of how it is, lost sight of this distinction. But my point is sufficiently taken if we simply note that Stevens *is* a highly theoretical poet and that his example, in our day, is perceived by critics and poets alike as paradigmatic.

In the strong opening paragraph of *Mr. Sammler's Planet* Saul Bellow laments that "intellectual man has become an explaining creature." I think that this statement is true and that it helps to explain why critics to such an extent have taken over the job that Wordsworth thought of as a poet's and why artists themselves find it more difficult to create compelling *un*theoretic fictions. Much of the materia poetica today is explanation.

I do not think, however, that we need be depressed about this situation. Human happiness depends fundamentally on the existence of creative opportunities, and these are as abundant as ever, whether or not, by comparative estimate, the modern achievement in a certain genre ranks below the achievement of a past age. The imaginative activity that we call the conceiving of scientific theories shifts the ground of the imaginative activity that we call the conceiving of works of art. But this leads to changes of form, and does not signify an attenuation of intellectual vitality.

Criticism by its nature contains elements of both the arts and the sciences. It has always been required to mediate *l'esprit de finesse* and *l'esprit de géometrie,* intuitive recreation and methodical analysis. Today, when the difficulties of this mediation have become explicit and stimulate controversy, the work of criticism has become particularly complex and interesting. This may explain the paradoxical fact that, since the time of Spengler, many pronouncements of the decline of the West based on the perception of art's increasing self-consciousness are charged with a current of energy that belies their thesis, and they are not nearly so lugubrious as we might expect them to be.

N. Katherine Hayles

SOURCE: "Chaos as Orderly Disorder: Shifting Ground in Contemporary Literature and Science," in *New Literary History,* Vol. 20, No. 2, Winter, 1989, pp. 305-22.

[*In the following essay, Hayles explores contemporary chaos theory as it relates to postmodern literary analysis.*]

Imagine that you are in the bowels of a computer, and a sequence of ones and zeros floats by. Without knowing anything about the program, you have no way of knowing whether you have just seen a portion of the Manhattan telephone directory, the number 1,456, or "To be or not to be." At this level all information, whether Gödel's Theorem or Hamlet's soliloquy, exists in the same form. Carry the fantasy a step further and imagine that the computer itself, along with you, could also be specified by sequences of ones and zeros. We are now close to the world of Edward Fredkin, who asserts "the basic stuff that everything is made of is information."[1] A professor at MIT who works at the intersection of physics and computer science, Fredkin believes that the fundamental structure of both matter and energy can be reduced to flows of information. To Fredkin the world is quite literally a text, a physical embodiment of informational markers. There was a time when Fredkin's views would have seemed extreme. But no longer. Across a wide spectrum of disciplines, information is emerging as a synthesizing concept that changes how we see the world.

Technological developments have undoubtedly played crucial roles in bringing an information perspective into being, as have the social and economic interdependencies that have made instantaneous communication around the globe a necessity.[2] In keeping with my focus on chaos, I should like to concentrate on a transformation within the information perspective itself. It occurred when information ceased to be thought of as inherently structured and became associated with randomness. Given the forces already at work within the culture that privileged information, this shift authorized a reevaluation of chaos. From this revisioning of chaos derive implications not yet fully understood, although it is already clear that they will be important in literary study and in many other fields.

The identification of information with randomness can be dated precisely. It occurred in 1948, when Claude Shannon published a theory of information in two articles that have since become classics. Shannon defined information through an equation that looked very much like Boltzmann's equation for entropy.[3] In contrast to Leon Brillouin, who used Maxwell's Demon to argue that information and entropy are opposites, Shannon used information and entropy as interchangeable terms. As early as 1877, Boltzmann had interpreted entropy as a statistical measure of disorder. By equating information with entropy, Shannon intimated that disorder could be seen in positive terms as the presence of information, rather than simply as the absence of order.

Ironically, having raised this possibility, Shannon refused to explore its implications. He regarded such larger philosophical concerns as a waste of time. In fact, when other scientists began to see in his work possibilities for applications to other disciplines, he went into print to caution them that information theory properly applied only to a very restricted, technical domain.[4] With thirty years' hindsight it is possible to see that Shannon's view of information *was* revolutionary, because it enabled a new view of chaos to emerge. Shannon's theory was appropriated by chaos theorists to redefine chaos as maximum information. From this appropriation has emerged a perspective that sees chaos not as an absence or a lack, but as the source of all that is new in the world.

As with many ideas that seem new, this one is very old. In *Paradise Lost,* for example, God creates the world not from nothing but from primordial chaos. For Milton as for Shannon, chaos is not order's opposite but its precursor. What is new is the idea's rigorous quantitative expression and its centrality to research programs in nonlinear dynamics, irreversible thermodynamics, meteorology, epidemiology, and fractal geometry, among others. Known as the science of chaos, this interdisciplinary research has revealed a terrain between order and disorder. Chaos in the sense it is used in this research denotes complex systems that operate according to deterministic laws, and yet that behave unpredictably. Complex systems are configured so as to bring minute uncertainties in initial conditions quickly up to macroscopic expression: in the parlance of chaos theory, this is known as "extreme sensitivity to initial conditions." Although their behavior quickly becomes unpredictable, complex systems nevertheless become chaotic in predictable ways. Combining qualities that classical mechanics considered antithetical, chaos can be assimilated neither into order nor disorder. It names a new territory, designates previously unrecognized interactions, and relies upon different assumptions.

Conditioned by classical modes of thought, we may wonder if any but the rarest of systems fulfills these criteria. In fact the orderly disorder of chaos is all around us, from cream swirling in coffee to the rise and fall of the Nile River, from global weather patterns to outbreaks of measles epidemics. In fact, so extensive are chaotic systems that they dwarf the ordered systems which science has traditionally regarded as norms for the universe. James Gleick, in his recent book on chaos, recalls Stanislaw Ulam's comment that to characterize chaos theory as "nonlinear science" is like calling zoology "the study of nonelephant animals."[5]

To see how chaos theory embodies new kinds of assumptions about complex systems, consider the work of Mitchell Feigenbaum, a physicist at Cornell University. In a review article in *Los Alamos Science,* Feigenbaum approaches chaos through the closely-related concept of randomness.[6] He asks us to consider in what way a number generated by a computer can be random. He points out that a computer-based random number generator can easily be constructed by creating a program that does "nothing more than shift the decimal point in a rational number whose repeating block is suitably long"(4). Numbers generated by this method are so lacking in pattern that they satisfy the most rigorous tests for randomness, yet the method that produces them is perfectly simple and deterministic. Technically, these numbers are called pseudorandom to indicate that they have been generated by a deterministic computer program. Feigenbaum's inspiration was to wonder whether other phenomena considered to be chaotic might also be pseudorandom, obeying deterministic programs just as pseudorandom numbers do. This astonishing premise amounts to saying that chaos possesses a deep structure of order.

One of the first indications that such a deep structure might in fact exist was Feigenbaum's discovery that systems which go from ordered to chaotic states follow a characteristic pattern of period doubling. Let us say, for example, that we are looking for a pattern in the behavior of an electrical oscillator. We notice the oscillator repeats its behavior after some time interval T. When the temperature is raised, the behavior of the oscillator becomes more erratic, and we now have to extend the time period to $2T$ to have a repeating pattern. When the temperature is raised yet again, the time required to observe a repeating pattern jumps to $4T$, and so on. Eventually the time period will become so great that the oscillator has no repetitions in the time scale available for observation. At this point it is said to be chaotic. Period doubling is now recognized as a powerful generalization, describing the onset of chaos in everything from dripping faucets to Niagara Falls.[7] At the time of his discovery, however, Feigenbaum was not thinking about physical systems. He was looking at the behavior of mathematical functions when they are iterated.

To iterate a function means to use the output of one calculation as input for the next, each time performing the operation called for by the function. It is analogous to beginning at a certain place and doing a dance step; then starting from the new location each time, doing the dance step again and again. Iterating strongly nonlinear functions produces paths that have folds in them. So intricate are these folds that although the trajectories remain within a defined area, no two paths intersect or coincide. "This general mechanism," Feigenbaum comments, "gives a system highly sensitive upon its initial conditions and a truly statistical character: since very small differences in initial conditions are magnified quickly, unless the initial conditions are known to *infinite precision,* all known knowledge is eroded rapidly to future ignorance" (21).

The startling aspect of Feigenbaum's work was his discovery that despite the different operations performed by different nonlinear functions—despite the different dance steps they used—their iterated paths approached chaos at the same rate and showed the same characteristic patterns of period doubling. All that mattered was that the paths had folds of sufficient steepness. It may be hard for a nonscientist to appreciate the enormity of this discovery, but to a mathematician, sine waves are as different from quadratic equations as pirouettes are from bows to a ballet dancer. To find out that there is a way of looking at these functions that makes their operations seem not just similar but *identical* is analogous to discovering that there is a way of looking at Nureyev dancing and Donald Duck waddling that makes their performances into a universal constant applicable to anyone moving on that stage.

What was this new way of looking? At the same time that the iterative process had the effect of overwhelming individual differences between functions, it also revealed a universality in how large-scale features related to small details. The shift in focus is from the particularities of a given function to the relation between different recursive levels in the iterative process. Imagine two paintings, each showing an open door through which is revealed another open door, through which is revealed another and another. . . . One way to think about the doors in these two paintings is to focus on the particularities of the repeated forms. Suppose the doors of the first painting are ornately carved rectangles, whereas the second painting shows doors that are unadorned arches. If we attend only to these shapes, the paintings might seem very different. But suppose we focus instead on the recursive repetition of doors in each painting and discover that in both paintings, the doors become smaller at a constant rate. Through this shift in focus, we have found a way of looking at the paintings that reveals their similarity to each other and to any other painting constructed in this way. The key is recursive symmetry.

In physical systems, recursive symmetries permit fluctuations at the smallest level to be rapidly transmitted through the system. The symmetrical relationships between levels act like coupling mechanisms that allow tiny uncertainties to ripple through the system until they become macroscopic disturbances. Say, for example, that we are standing on a river bank, watching the water flow by. Most of the time small disturbances in the fluid path cancel each other out, so that the river flows smoothly between its banks. But when the right kind of symmetries are present, small disturbances are amplified until eddies and backwaters form. At these points turbulence sets in, and the flow patterns become extremely complex. Nevertheless, these complexities very often express themselves through recursive symmetries; large swirls of water have small swirls inside them, within which are smaller swirls. . . . The complex symmetries that are repeated across different levels of a complex system are crucial in understanding how the onset of chaos occurs. Chaos theory recognizes the importance of scale in a way that classical paradigms do not. In sharp contrast to the scale independence of Newtonian and Euclidean paradigms, chaos models are *intrinsically and inevitably scale dependent.*

Fractal geometry is closely related to chaos theory, and it too emphasizes scaling symmetries across different levels. Benoit Mandelbrot, the inventor of this new geometry, coined the word *fractal* from the Latin adjective *fractus* (meaning "breakable") and fractional; it connotes both fractional dimensions and extreme complexity of form.[8] The mathematics of fractional dimensions is complex, but the general idea is not hard to grasp. Whereas the familiar integer dimensions of Cartesian space are entirely adequate to represent Euclidean shapes such as circles, triangles, and squares, they do not do justice to highly complex and irregular forms. The corrugations that mark the surfaces of these forms give them, in effect, an added fraction of a dimension.

To show the importance of scale for fractal figures, Mandelbrot asks a question that looks as if it should have a straightforward, factual answer: How long is the coastline of Britain? (25-33). The question is more devious than it appears, because the answer is scale dependent. If we measure the coastline using a mile-long rule, we get a shorter answer than if we use a yardstick, for the mile rule cuts across irregularities that the yardstick measures around. If we use an inch rule the answer is still longer, because small pebbles are measured around; and if a micrometer is used, even irregularities within a single pebble count. In fact, Britain's coastline *continues to grow without limit* as the ruler scale decreases, at least down to molecular scales. Without specifying a ruler length, the question cannot be accurately answered.

The example demonstrates why questions of scale are foregrounded in the new paradigms. In Euclidean geometry and Newtonian mechanics, the idea that one could get different answers when using different scales does not appear. It is not quite correct to say these older paradigms make global statements which are considered true for every level, because their globalizing approaches are so complete that the system is not conceived as having levels in any meaningful sense. In Euclidean geometry it does not matter whether an isoceles triangle is twice as large or two hundred times as large as another

triangle of the same shape; whatever the scale, Euclidean geometry states that the three sides of similar triangles will be in the same proportion to each other. Fractal geometry does not challenge this assertion as such. Rather, it shifts the focus to complex irregular forms, for which scale appears as an important consideration, and movement between length scales becomes highly nontrivial.

Similarly, Newtonian mechanics applies the same partial differential equations whether the object is a golf ball or a planet; in either case the masses move through time according to uniform laws of motion. But when the object has a complex internal structure consisting of distinct local levels, as is the case for a fluid in turbulent flow, length scale is critical because different portions of the fluid move at different speeds and with different kinds of motions. Under these conditions, Newtonian-based calculations are unmanageable for even a few points, and unthinkable for the thousands or millions it would take to model the system.

The movement from scale-invariant models to scale-dependent paradigms has an obvious correspondence to the movement in critical theory away from totalizing theories. We must, however, be cautious in drawing inferences about what this correspondence means. What the new scientific paradigms cannot do, I think, is give us a transcendent perspective from which we can say other cultural developments are good or bad, true or false. In *The Postmodern Condition,* Lyotard argues that "paralogy" (an umbrella term under which he groups such diverse theories as fractal geometry, quantum mechanics, and Gödel's Theorem) provides corroborating evidence from within the physical sciences that will let us "wage a war on totality."[9] This interpretation of the new scientific paradigms ignores the fact that they have not renounced globalization. Chaos theory, for example, simply achieves totalization in a different way, by focusing on recursive symmetries between levels rather than by following the motions of individual molecules. Chaos theory would not have attracted the attention it has if it had simply confirmed what everyone already knew, that chaotic systems are disordered. No, what makes it noteworthy is the discovery that *despite* this disorder, universal structures can still be discerned. The thrust toward globalization is apparent in the name Feigenbaum chose for his discovery that chaotic systems can be described through universal constants: he calls it "Universality Theory." The belief that the science of chaos opposes globalizing theories is, then, a misapprehension about how these theories work.

More fundamentally, Lyotard's claim that these paradigms can be used to wage a war against totality is wrongheaded because it confuses scientific theories with social programs. His apparent conviction that fractal geometry can combat totalitarianism is a modern version of social Darwinism. Such a belief ignores the ways in which scientific theories, like literary and cultural theories, are themselves social constructions.[10] Scientific paradigms do not exist in some ideal space above or beyond culture. They are part of their culture, which they both replicate and reinforce. In my view, the more productive ways to think about the relation of these paradigms to literary theory and literature start with the premise that they are social constructions and ask how their assumptions reinforce other assumptions in the culture.

To begin probing these correspondences, consider how the new paradigms treat time.[11] In Newtonian mechanics, objects moving through time are modeled as trajectories that can be broken into arbitrarily small intervals (this is essentially the basis for calculus). As the intervals approach zero, they are added together to get the trajectory as a whole. Underlying this method is the commonsense perception that movement through time can be equated with an object moving along some predictable path—for example, the parabolic arc of a baseball as it comes off the bat. However, if the moving shape is complex in the sense of being composed of multiple levels acting in different ways, the calculations very quickly become unmanageable because they involve many coupled degrees of freedom.

In the new paradigms, a shape is no longer conceived as a mass of points, but as the formulae used to generate and randomize the self-similar forms that compose it. The new paradigms do not attempt to describe how each point within a shape moves. Rather, they focus on the transformation rules that govern the evolution of the shape's recursive symmetries through time. The advantage of this approach derives from the fact that in complex systems, very small changes in the initial conditions lead to very large changes in the final forms. By changing the iterative formulae only a little, complex forms can be made to move in very different ways.[12] Hence large-scale changes can be encoded with many fewer bits of information than would be required if each point within a complex form had to be advanced through time individually.

Now consider how these views of time correlate with other kinds of cultural and social theories. Newton's conception of objects as masses of points is matched by Hobbes's conception of society as a group of autonomous individuals and by Adam Smith's conception of the economy as a collection of competing customers. Different as these theories are, they each assume that systems are constituted as groups of individual units which act in accord with general laws. They make the transition from the local site to the global system by applying general laws to masses of individual units. To make the system move through time, they add together the motions of individual units to arrive at a resultant.

In contrast to these classical assumptions are those Foucault uses in his archaeologies. Foucault considers the individual not as an autonomous actor, but rather as a microcosm constituted by the tropes and organizing figures characteristic of the episteme. For Foucault, individuals do not constitute culture; culture constitutes individuals. Moreover, at least in his early work, Foucault sees different cultural sites as manifesting the same principles of organization. Thus he argues that during the neoclassical period in Europe, the same organizing tropes

appear in grammar, biology, political theory, and psychology.[13] My point here is not to validate Foucault's theory, but to show how the assumptions underlying his view of culture are isomorphic with the assumptions embodied in chaos theory. Both theories, although they are very different in many respects, embody a shift in focus away from the individual unit to structures that are replicated across many levels of a system. The correspondence suggests that the contemporary episteme is characterized by deep assumptions that have made the concept of an episteme thinkable.

One criticism frequently made of Foucault's early approach is that it does not explain how changes take place through time (for purposes of this argument, assume that Foucault has characterized the periods accurately). How and why, Foucault's critics ask, did people stop believing in similitude as an organizing trope and start believing in representation? The objection is not as straightforward as it appears, for what counts as a temporal explanation is fundamentally different in the new paradigms than it was in the old. The objection implies that a temporal explanation should place groups of autonomous actors along a time line and advance them according to laws or generalizations that explain why the actors behaved as they did. In the new paradigms, however, temporal explanation means something different. It implies understanding the structural principles that relate different sites by self-similarity, along with rules that state how these principles evolve over time. Foucault has achieved the first step in this kind of explanation by anatomizing the structural principles that underlie self-similar cultural forms. Although he has not given a full temporal explanation, he has nevertheless come much closer to it than his critics acknowledge, because they discount comparison of different kinds of self-similarities as the foundation on which temporal explanations are built.

The correlation between the new scientific paradigms and Foucault's archaeologies suggests that an extremely wide-ranging cultural shift is in progress. It can perhaps best be characterized through the dialectics that the new paradigms have energized. The most important is the destabilization of the order/disorder opposition and the subsequent reevaluation of chaos as a presence rather than an absence—a presence, moreover, that is seen as more rewarding and fecund in its complexity than classical order. Closely related to the transvaluation of chaos is the energizing of the local/global dialectic. With the passages from one scale to another rendered problematic, the relation of local sites to global configurations becomes an important nexus for inquiry. Both the order/disorder and local/global dialectics are underlaid by a shift in focus from the individual unit to self-similar replication across the different levels of a system.

When an opposition as central to Western thought as order/disorder is destabilized, it is no exaggeration to say that a major fault line has developed in the foundations of the culture. It would be strange indeed if there were not other theoretical enterprises that also work the fault line. Some of the most visible are within critical theory. Just as new concepts of chaos are changing how scientists think about informational systems, they are also affecting how literary critics write about texts. The major impetus for this revision has come from deconstruction, which Paul de Man sees as warning us that "nothing, whether deed, word, thought or text, ever happens in relation, positive or negative, to anything that precedes, follows or exists elsewhere, but only as a random event whose power . . . is due to the randomness of its occurrence."[14] As the text is opened to an infinitude of readings and as meaning becomes indeterminate or disappears altogether, chaos apparently reigns supreme. In this extreme form, deconstruction seems to have gone beyond the premises that make science possible.

Yet Geoffrey Hartman, confronted with the "tangled, contaminated, displaced, deceptive" text of Derrida's *Glas,* speculates that deconstruction is opposed to more traditional, humanistic readings because it is more *scientific.* "The result for our time [of deconstruction in general and *Glas* in particular] may be a factional split between simplifying types of reading that call themselves humanistic and indefinitizing kinds that call themselves scientific," Hartman writes.[15] He is correct, perhaps in a sense he did not intend, in linking deconstruction's "indefinitizing" strategies with science. Deconstruction shares with chaos theory the desire to breach the boundaries of classical systems by opening them to a new kind of analysis in which information is created rather than conserved. Delighting in the increased complexity that results from this "scientific" process, both discourses invert traditional priorities: chaos is deemed more fecund than order, uncertainty is privileged above predictability, and fragmentation is seen as the reality that arbitrary definitions of closure would deny.

The vertigo characteristic of deconstruction appears when we realize that texts, far from being ordered sets of words bounded by book covers, are reservoirs of chaos. Derrida initiates us into this moment through his concept of iteration. Any word, he argues, acquires a slightly different meaning each time it appears in a new context. Moreover, the boundary between text and context is not fixed. Infinite contexts invade and permeate the text, regardless of chronology or authorial intention. For example, *Hamlet* influences how we read *Rosencrantz and Guildenstern Are Dead;* but *Rosencrantz and Guildenstern Are Dead* also influences how we read *Hamlet.* The permeation of any text by an indefinite and potentially infinite number of intertexts implies that meaning is always already indeterminate. Because all texts are necessarily constructed through iteration (that is, through the incremental repetition of words in slightly displaced contexts), indeterminacy inheres in writing's very essence.

We can see iteration at work in the dense, highly repetitive analysis of Rousseau that occupies the last half of Derrida's *Of Grammatology.* Rousseau is well suited to Derrida's deconstructive project because his thought is expressed through a series of hierarchical dualities: nature/culture,

animal/human, speech/writing. For Rousseau, the first term of each of these dualities is privileged. The second term is belated, contaminated, a fall from the "pure" first term. His announced aim is to correct modern decadence by returning to the originary first term, rejecting culture for nature, writing for speech, and so on.

Through a rigorous reading of Rousseau's texts, Derrida shows that this attempt at purification is fundamentally misguided because the idea of origin is an illusion. The demonstration concentrates on the *supplement,* a word that Rousseau uses in the *Confessions* as a euphemism for masturbation.[16] Sex is natural, good, healthy; but since he is tormented by fear of women and venereal disease, Rousseau continually finds it necessary to resort to the supplement. Derrida shows that a similar dialectic emerges with each set of Rousseau's dualities. Rousseau denounces writing but does so by writing texts; he embraces nature but finds that its deficiencies necessitate the education he advocates in *Emile,* and so forth. To supplement something implies that the original is already full and self-sufficient, in contrast to the supplementary material, which comes after and is superfluous. Yet in each case the first term, nature for example, is "naturally" deficient, making the supplement indispensable. In what sense then is the supplement more "unnatural" than nature? Through this implicit contradiction, Derrida shows that the supplement is in fact *what allows the privileged term to be constituted.* The originary precedence of the privileged term is revealed as an illusion, a myth or longing for origin rather than an origin as such.

According to Derrida, every text will have a concept that functions as the supplement does in Rousseau. The supplement (or its analogue) is, Derrida argues, a kind of fold in the text whose indeterminacy is revealed through repetition. In his view such a fold is *necessarily* present, because there must always be some means by which the text can constitute the differences that enable it to postulate meaning. The fold can be thought of as a way to create the illusion of origin. Once in place, all subsequent differences are declared to derive from the originary difference marked by the fold. When the text is "unfolded," this stratagem is revealed and the regulated exchanges between the alleged origin and subsequent differences that enable the text to operate will appear.

It is precisely this "unfolding" that iteration accomplishes. In Derrida's hands, repeating Rousseau's language with incremental differences becomes a way to unfold and make visible the inherent contradictions upon which the text's dialectic is based. This iterative procedure produces the undecidables that radically destabilize meaning. "It [is] certainly a production," Derrida writes, "because I do not simply repeat what Rousseau thought of [the supplement]. The concept of the supplement is a sort of blind spot in Rousseau's text . . . [The production of undecidables] is contained in the transformation of the language [that the text] designates, in the regulated exchanges between Rousseau and history. We know that these exchanges only take place by way of the language and the text" (163-64). The goal of iteration is thus to make visible the lack of ground for the alleged originary difference, thus rendering all subsequent distinctions indeterminate.

Derrida's deconstructive methodology is strikingly similar to the mathematical techniques of chaos theory. Recall that Feigenbaum attributed the universal element in chaotic systems to the fact that they were generated from iterative functions. He showed that for certain functions, individual differences in the equations are overwhelmed as iteration proceeds, so that even though the systems become chaotic, they do so in predictable or *regulated* ways. Derrida claims that his iterative methodology is similarly regulated, in the sense that its production of undecidables is not a capricious exercise but a rigorous exposition of the text's inherent indeterminacies.

For both Derrida and Feigenbaum, iterative methodology is closely tied in with the concept of the fold. Feigenbaum showed that systems which make orderly transitions to chaos always have folds in their iterative paths. Within the complex regions created by these folds, orbits wander in unpredictable ways. Where does this unpredictability come from? Since the iterative formulae and computer programs that enact them are perfectly deterministic, it could *only* come from the initial conditions. Iteration produces chaos because it magnifies and brings into view these initial uncertainties. Similarly, Derrida attributes textual indeterminacy to the inherent inability of linguistic systems to create an origin. In Derrida, the fold marks the absence of an origin, just as the inability to specify initial conditions with infinite accuracy marks the onset of chaos for Feigenbaum. Thus nonlinear dynamics and deconstruction share not just a general attitude toward chaos, but specific methodologies and assumptions.

There are, of course, also significant differences between them. Feigenbaum works with the exact definitions of mathematical formulae; Derrida is concerned with language, which is notoriously resistant to formalization. One measure of these differences is disagreement among deconstructionists and scientists on how extensive chaos is. For Derrida, textual chaos is always already in Rousseau and in every other text. By contrast, scientists acknowledge that ordered, predictable systems do exist, although they are not nearly as widespread as classical science had supposed. Feigenbaum, for example, takes as granted that only certain classes of iterative functions become chaotic. Moreover, he acknowledges that until very recently, virtually all scientific knowledge derived from the study of ordered systems (14-15). Where deconstructionists see an apocalyptic break with logocentrism, scientists are likely to think of their work as a continuation of what went before. To a deconstructionist, to say someone is a recuperator is a damning comment; for most scientists recuperation is not an issue, because they see their work as enhancing rather than discrediting traditional scientific paradigms. These differences are symptomatic of the different values the two disciplines place on chaos. For deconstructionists, chaos repudiates order; for scientists, chaos makes order possible.

These differences notwithstanding, Derridean deconstruction and nonlinear dynamics parallel each other in a number of ways. The new scientific paradigms challenge the primacy traditionally accorded to ordered systems; deconstructive theories expose the interrelation between traditional ideas of order and oppressive ideologies. The scientific theories show how deterministic physical systems become chaotic because initial conditions cannot be specified with infinite accuracy; deconstructive readings operate upon texts to reveal the indeterminacy that remarks an absent origin. The scientific paradigms embody a shift of perspective away from the individual unit to recursive symmetries; deconstruction writes about the death of the subject and the replicating, self-similar processes that constitute individuals. The science of chaos reveals a territory that cannot be assimilated to either order or disorder; deconstruction detects a trace that cannot be assimilated to the binary oppositions it deconstructs.

These correspondences are not accidental. They reflect what Christine Froula, in comparing deconstruction with quantum mechanics, has identified as a deepening crisis of representation in Western thought.[17] Froula suggests that common sources for quantum physics and Derridean deconstruction do exist. It may be that common sources also exist for chaos theory and deconstruction, most probably in information theory. However, I have chosen *not* to make an influence argument, because I believe that such arguments obscure the larger significance of the parallels outlined above.

Let us suppose, for example, that I could identify a definitive source that would connect Derrida with chaos theory. This still would not explain why that source, among many possible ones, caught his attention. To explain this, I would have to postulate some prior source, for it must have sensitized him to the issues he found in the later source. But this prior source must also have had an earlier source to explain why it seemed significant. . . . If I attempt to trace an entire network of sources, then I have in effect moved from an influence to an argument about culture.

In addition to the problem of infinite regress, influence arguments also suffer from a tendency to flatten the complexities of scientific inquiry. In practice, identifying an influence almost always means finding a scientific work that has influenced a literary text. The premise that influence flows from science to literature implicitly valorizes science as the source of truth to which literature responds. Such an approach ignores the ways in which scientific theories, no less than literary theories and literature, are social constructions that reflect the prevailing concerns of the culture. Science is not a monolithic "source," but a complex field of discursive and experimental activities that has its own dissonances, fault lines, and convergences.

Let us agree, then, to leave the question of influence aside, and turn instead to the implications these isomorphisms have for literary study. In my view, the parallels between chaos theory and deconstruction signal more than the emergence of new paradigms. They point to a shift in the ground of representation itself, which is bound to have profound implications for literature.[18] In the space remaining, I sketch very quickly a few of the many possibilities for literary study by speculating on the significance of this shifting ground for reading individual texts, developing critical strategies, and postulating cultural theories.

READING INDIVIDUAL TEXTS

The emergence of similar concerns across a wide variety of disciplines suggests that they run very deeply through the cultural matrix. There are many sites within the culture where one can read the inscription of these isomorphisms, including contemporary literature. For example, in Doris Lessing's *The Golden Notebook,* the concern with chaos is at once thematic, social, psychological, and specifically literary.[19] The fragmented form of the novel reflects the psychic fragmentation of the central character, Anna Wulf. Anna attempts to cope with her life by relegating its complexities to different notebooks: a red notebook for her political experiences, black for her African experiences, blue for her personal life, yellow for the present. As each narrative becomes more unsettled—the British Communist party fragments over Stalin's atrocities, her lover abandons her, her best friend's child attempts suicide—Anna seeks desperately for some way to integrate the proliferating disorder into some kind of intelligible system. The crisis comes when she papers her apartment walls, as high as she can reach, with newspaper clippings about horrific events, rapes, murders, genocide, riots. Spending her days reading the clippings and putting up more, Anna is surrounded by chaos inside and out. From this nadir, she tries to rediscover herself as a writer, and the golden notebook—the narrative the novel turns into—comes into being.

Central to Anna's emerging reorganization is her ability to recognize recursive symmetries among and between her different notebook narratives, while still validating their local variations. After she becomes involved in a destructive relationship with a psychotic lover (Saul Green), she replays some of the scenes in another narrative with a different lover and is able to break out of the cycle because she can recognize the futility of her self-replicating assumptions. The final chapter repeats the text's opening lines but then develops in different directions. These almost-but-not-quite reflections suggest that chaos and order have come together in a union delicately balanced between schizophrenic disorder and sterile repetition. *The Golden Notebook,* then, is playing out in narrative form some of the same dialectical tensions that are embodied in the new paradigms. Of course I do not mean to imply by this that Lessing was influenced by chaos theory. Rather I am suggesting that the same forces within the culture that authorized chaos theory are inscribed within Lessing's narrative. Although I will not have time to discuss them here, other contemporary fictions where these inscriptions may be read include (to mention only a few) Calvino's *If on a winter's night a*

traveler, DeLillo's *White Noise,* Robbe-Grillet's *Jealousy,* Coover's *Pricksongs and Descants,* Lem's *Fiasco,* and Robinson's *Housekeeping.*

DEVELOPING CRITICAL STRATEGIES

The emphasis on scale in the new paradigms speaks to a familiar phenomenon in literary studies—the way a text may be perfectly coherent on one level, and yet on another level chaotic. For example, consider the scale-dependence of Derrida's deconstruction of Rousseau. Before Derrida there was widespread consensus about what Rousseau meant; yet the inversions that Derrida effects within Rousseau's text are virtually irrefutable. The new paradigms suggest these different views may be a function of the reader's critical distance from the text. From a certain distance the *Confessions* appears coherent; closer up (and Derrida's readings are typically very close), the ungrounded nature of the discourse appears. Closer still and the text becomes regulated again, as the systematic nature of the ungrounded oppositions appears; closer still, and it dissolves into the undecidability of the trace.

The lingering assumption that propositions, if they are to be valid, must hold true for all critical distances from the text is challenged by the new paradigms. By revealing scale invariance as an assumption rather than a given, they help to bring into view similar assumptions within literary discourse. I can imagine a time when any statement about a text would have to be prefaced by an indication of the critical distances for which it holds true. Already under suspicion within the literary community, globalizing statements which purported to hold true for every level would be subjected to even more severe scrutiny than they now are. (The exception, of course, would be globalizing statements which took scale dependence as their subject.) One possibility for developing new critical strategies, then, is to attend to questions of scale and use them to think about how local sites are incorporated into textual systems.

A second set of possibilities emerges from the redefined relation between order and chaos in the new paradigms. Here I shall mention the work of just one theorist to indicate very briefly how these ideas are being incorporated into literary discourse. William Paulson, in his study of information theory and literature, *The Noise of Culture,* argues that texts can be seen as self-organizing systems in Prigogine's sense.[20] Paulson asks us to consider how we read a difficult poem. On a first reading there will be parts of the poem that do not seem to make sense—parts that we perceive as noise rather than information, disorder rather than order. Because we accept the poem as a functioning entity (that is, as a system), we reread it. Now our perceptions are different, for they have been slightly reorganized by the first reading. On the second reading, more elements are fit into what we begin to perceive as an emerging design. The point Paulson makes about this process is that it is *because* the system is initially perceived as disordered that a more complex kind of order can emerge. As the transvaluation of chaos becomes more extensive within the culture, there may well emerge still other kinds of theories that reenact this transvaluation in terms of reading and writing texts.

POSTULATING CULTURAL THEORIES

The new paradigms suggest that culture itself might be constituted as a complex system. Following this clue, we can think of the local as designating a site within a culture where the self-similarities characteristic of the system are reproduced. Conceived as images of each other, local and global are related as microcosm is to macrocosm, although each level also contains areas so complex that they are effectively chaotic. Movement between levels is easy or possible only when the symmetries align. At this point cultures are ripe for change, because they become extremely sensitive to microscopic perturbations. Such a view of the systemic behavior of a culture does not require that all configurations within it be self-similar. But when significant convergence does occur, the model predicts that small fluctuations will have large-scale effects.

From the viewpoint of the cultural analyst, this model is attractive because it foregrounds self-similar replications, which are obviously easier to find and document than isolated instances. Moreover, because the system at this point is susceptible to dramatic and sudden changes, an exploration of the deep assumptions embodied in these configurations is likely to have significant explanatory power for epistemic shifts. The model gives us a way to understand how Foucault could be right in postulating a self-similar episteme for a given period, and still not commit us to saying that knowledge everywhere in this period was organized according to these tropes (because there are always random variations), nor to saying that culture always works like this. In other words, it gives us a way to say that the local and global sometimes reproduce each other so that universals appear to run through the system, and sometimes not.

The model should be of especial interest to theorists working in the area of literature and science. One of the most problematic issues in the field at present—one that I have wrestled with repeatedly—is how to talk about isomorphic concepts between disciplines and yet do full justice to the distinct tonalities and values that these concepts have when they are embedded in different sites. The double gesture of recognizing global structures and yet valorizing local sites is in my view both necessary and inevitable. It speaks to postmodern culture; but beyond this, in a very real sense, it *is* postmodern culture.

In conclusion, I wish to emphasize that I do not see the shifting ground explored in this essay as a uniform change throughout the culture. The accommodations, resistances, and convergences that occur between the scientific and literary paradigms indicate how fissured and multilayered the cultural response is to the transvaluation of chaos. Change arrives not as a monolithic unity, but as complex vortices of local turbulence. Not to see that the agitation is general is to miss the fact that there

are significant changes in the underlying cultural currents; not to notice that the turbulence follows different dynamics at different sites is to miss the complexities that the new views of chaos both initiate and signify.

NOTES

[1] Edward Fredkin, quoted in Richard Wright, "The On-Off Universe," *The Sciences* (January-February 1985), 7.

[2] The literature on these aspects of the information perspective is too extensive to cite here. Representative texts are Daniel Bell, *The Coming of the Post-Industrial Society* (New York, 1973), and *Communication and Control in Society,* ed. Klaus Drippendorff (New York, 1979).

[3] Claude E. Shannon, "A Mathematical Theory of Communication," *Bell System Technical Journal,* 27 (1948), 379-423, 623-56. The papers are reprinted along with an interpretive commentary in Claude E. Shannon and Warren Weaver, *The Mathematical Theory of Communication* (Urbana, Ill., 1949).

[4] Claude E. Shannon, "The Bandwagon," *IEEE Transactions on Information Theory,* IT-2 (1956), 3.

[5] James Gleick, *Chaos: Making a New Science* (New York, 1987), p. 68.

[6] Mitchell Feigenbaum, "Universal Behavior in Nonlinear Systems," *Los Alamos Science,* 1 (1980), 4-27; hereafter cited in text.

[7] Robert Shaw, *The Dripping Faucet as a Model Chaotic System* (Santa Cruz, Calif., 1984). Niagara Falls would of course be an instance of turbulent flow; see, e.g., Kenneth Wilson, "The Renormalization Group and Critical Phenomena," *Reviews of Modern Physics,* 55 (1983), 583-600.

[8] Benoit Mandelbrot, *The Fractal Geometry of Nature* (New York, 1983); hereafter cited in text.

[9] Jean-François Lyotard, *The Postmodern Condition: A Report on Knowledge,* tr. Geoff Bennington and Brian Massumi (Minneapolis, 1984), p. 82.

[10] In other sections of *The Postmodern Condition* Lyotard shows a keen awareness and sensitivity to the interrelations between culture and science. I suspect that Lyotard's valorization of these scientific paradigms as enemies of totalitarianism derived from his desire to find a counterbalance to his foregoing argument (which in my view leads to quite other conclusions) and to close his book on an optimistic note.

[11] In this discussion I am indebted to lectures by Mitchell Feigenbaum and Benoit Mandelbrot at the Cornell University conference on "Analyzing the Inchoate," Ithaca, N.Y., April 1987.

[12] This procedure is discussed in M. F. Barnsley et al., "Solutions of an Inverse Problem for Fractals and Other

Sets," *Proceedings of the National Academy of Sciences,* 83 (1986), 1975-77.

[13] Michel Foucault, *The Order of Things: An Archaeology of the Human Sciences* (New York, 1970).

[14] Paul de Man, "Shelley Disfigured," in Harold Bloom et al., *Deconstruction and Criticism* (New York, 1979), p. 69.

[15] Geoffrey Hartman, "Monsieur Texte II: Epiphony in Echoland," *Georgia Review,* 30 (1976), 183.

[16] Jacques Derrida, *Of Grammatology,* tr. Gayatri Chakravorty Spivak (Baltimore, 1976), pp. 141-64; hereafter cited in text.

[17] Christine Froula, "Quantum Physics/Postmodern Metaphysics: The Nature of Jacques Derrida," *Western Humanities Review,* 39 (1985), pp. 287-313.

[18] These implications are explored in depth in my book-in-progress, *Chaos Bound: Orderly Disorder in Contemporary Literature and Science* (forthcoming, 1989).

[19] Doris Lessing, *The Golden Notebook* (New York, 1962).

[20] William Paulson, *The Noise of Culture: Literary Texts in a World of Information* (Ithaca, 1988).

Paul Konrad Kurz

SOURCE: "Literature and Science," in *On Modern German Literature,* Vol. I, translated by Sister Mary Frances McCarthy, The University of Alabama Press, 1967, pp. 56-79.

[*In the following essay, Kurz discusses the place of literature in a world increasingly dominated by science and technology.*]

THE DISCUSSION IN ENGLAND

The last essay of the late Aldous Huxley[1] deals with the tension between literature and science. It was written against the background of the controversy in England between Charles P. Snow and Frank R. Leavis. In the Rede Lecture of 1959, Snow, who was first a physicist, then a novelist, and in the last war Director of Technical Personnel in the Ministry of Labor, advanced the thesis of the two separate cultures: the intellectual and literary as opposed to the strictly scholarly, or more exactly scientific, culture. This thesis was certainly not new, but it became a theme of primary importance in England, where it aroused wide discussion, in which the literary critic Lionel Trilling and the atomic physicist Robert Oppenheimer took part. Snow, the initiator of the controversy, placed the responsibility for the gulf, which had been clearly recognizable since the turn of the century, on those educated in the humanistic tradition and gifted with literary creativity, who, on the one hand, were scarcely aware of developments in the natural sciences and, on the other, accorded no recognition to scientists or those engaged in laboratory work. For this accusation, Snow was attacked by Frank R. Leavis, a respected professor of literature at Cambridge, in the Richmond Lecture of 1962. Snow, said Leavis, imagines that he possesses both cultures, but he possesses neither the true scientific nor the true literary mentality. In presenting his thesis, he is comparing things that are not comparable. Ignorance, for instance, of the Second Law of Thermodynamics is not on the same plane as ignorance of the works of Shakespeare. But neither Snow nor Leavis attempted to say what the relationship between the two cultures actually is, or what it could become with some thought and mutual tolerance. Aldous Huxley was a cultivated, many-sided author and a keen critic of the cultural scene. Obviously he had both the background and the training to ask the right questions and to establish the proper perspective in the struggle between the two views. He was a grandson of Thomas Henry Huxley (1825-1895), the naturalist and staunch defender of the theory of evolution, and a grandnephew of Matthew Arnold (1822-1888), the writer, critic, and school inspector. Moreover, he was a brother of the biologist Julian Huxley.

Huxley's questions read: "What is the function of literature, what its psychology, what the nature of literary language? And how do its function, psychology, and language differ from the function, psychology and language of science? What, in the past, has been the relationship between literature and science? What is it now? What might it be in the future? What would it be profitable, artistically speaking, for a twentieth-century man of letters to do about twentieth-century science?"[2]

OBJECT, METHOD, AND GOAL OF SCIENCE AND LITERATURE

Every intellectual discipline can be described in terms of its object, of the viewpoint from which that object is considered, and of the method by which it is presented. "In the present context, science may be defined as a device for investigating, ordering and communicating the more public of human experiences. Less systematically, literature also deals with such public experiences. Its main concern, however, is with man's more private experiences, and with the interactions between the private worlds of sentient, self-conscious individuals and the public universes of 'objective reality,' logic, social conventions, and the accumulated information currently available."[3]

The object of the natural sciences is nature circumscribed by natural laws—concrete, objective, logical, general, calculable nature; that of literature, on the other hand, is the specifically human individual person, composed of body and soul, limited by his social milieu, and gifted with freedom, and the personal world of the society in which he lives. Over all literature, as over all the other arts, stands the sentence from Alexander Pope's *Essay on Man* (1773): "The proper study of mankind is man." Both natural scientists and literary artists observe their object and present their observations. But they do it in different ways, from different vantage points and viewpoints, with different eyes and different perspectives, and for a different end. The scientist is interested, above all, in explaining a single property according to theoretical principles. He prepares the object of his investigation, introduces it into the constellation of his experiment, establishes the most ideal conditions possible for observing a particular behavioral pattern, a possible reaction, or a measurable, and therefore demonstrable, property. He abstracts and dissects his object, repeats his experiment under conditions that are as similar as possible. The literary artist, on the contrary, looks at the concrete and complex whole, at the multiplicity and involvement of its properties, its milieu, its historical development, and its personal decisions; at the intractable and often antagonistic nature of man with its rationalism and irrationalism, its matter and spirit. He knows about the uniqueness of the person, the irretrievability of the situation. He wants neither to reduce his object to a single level of meaning nor to isolate it from its surroundings, but to observe the play and counterplay of behavioral patterns and decisions in a world of multifarious and unlimitable tensions. "The world with which literature deals is the world in which human beings are born and live and finally die; the world in which they love and hate, in which they experience triumph and humiliation, hope, and despair; the world of sufferings and enjoyments, of madness and common sense, of silliness, cunning, and wisdom; the world of social pressures and individual impulses, of reason against passion, of instincts and conventions, of shared language and unsharable feeling and sensation; of innate differences and the rules, the roles, the solemn or absurd rituals imposed by the prevailing culture. Every human being is aware of this multifarious world and . . . by analogy with himself, he can guess where other people stand, what they feel and how they are likely to behave."[4]

The literary artist has to interpret rather than analyze his object, look at it rather than dissect it experimentally part by part, present it rather than explain it. His mental vision is not enlightened by *ratio* alone. He is capable of figurative and structural perception, of emphatic, intuitive, often mythical and mystic vision. His interpretation is frequently based on a preconceived (which does not mean unfounded) estimation of the world. Every artistic presentation of one part of the world contains a certain view of the whole world. The individual scientist investigates and observes only parts of nature. The more exact his individual observations have been, the greater is the danger that he will lose sight of the whole, in fact, must lose sight of it in order to concentrate wholly on his individual observation. The literary artist is always, in one way or another, engaged with the whole of mankind.

Huxley designates the method and goal of the natural sciences as "nomothetic," that is, "they seek to establish explanatory laws" that are as universally valid and as unequivocal as possible. "Literature is . . . 'ideographic'; its concern is not with regularities and explanatory laws, but with descriptions of appearances and the discerned qualities of objects perceived as wholes, with judgments,

comparisons and discriminations, with 'inscapes'. . . ."[5] A science seeks to erect a system of knowledge, to coordinate a series of concepts in such a way that, with their help, an aspect or a part of the world will be explained according to regular laws. Thus every science wants to have "its own frame of reference." "For Science in its totality, the ultimate goal is the creation of a monistic system in which—on the symbolic level and in terms of the inferred components of invisibility and intangibly fine structure—the world's enormous multiplicity is reduced to something like unity . . . and simplified into a single rational order. . . . The man of letters [on the contrary] . . . accepts the uniqueness of events, accepts the diversity and manifoldness of the world, . . . the radical incomprehensibility . . . of . . . unconceptualized existence . . ."[6] He gives form to that which cannot be grasped either mechanically, electrically, or optically; to that which cannot be established conceptually; to the vacillating, the undetermined, the only partially determined, the too quickly determined; to the valid and the invalid; the grotesque and the absurd; to the claims of truth and of masked deceit. He wants neither to create a system of knowledge nor to force the world through the retort. Yet he does want to discover and to reveal. He wants, for example, to reveal the spirit of the age, the forms of society, the relationship of individual and society; of tradition, convention, and freedom; of reason and passion; of appearance and actuality in the life of the individual and of society. He wants to reveal the conditions of progress, of freedom, of human dignity; to show profit and loss in the *condition humaine,* the perils of being human. He wants to make the claims of truth visible; to expose the forms of deceit; to diagnose the sicknesses of the age, of the nation, of social groups; to denounce the unjust strongholds of might; to call attention to contradictions;[7] to remind man repeatedly that he is man. Huxley includes within the scope of the writer an area of observation and inquiry which certain literary groups, in Germany and elsewhere, would gladly dispense with: the area concerned with the metaphysical nature and transcendental potentiality of man. "Who are we? What is our destiny? How can the often frightful ways of God be justified?"[8] A theodicy, then, in a modern anthropodicy. Huxley's psychologically colored transcendence and predilection for myth seem to us just as questionable as his so-called "infused contemplation,"[9] with its shades of the Orient, of Buddhism, of Gnosticism—and even of drugs! He fails to recognize the authenticity of Christianity and the historical structure of Christian existence. But he sees correctly that the man of letters must burst the seams of the scientific horizontality of the modern world, that he must reveal to civilized man, entangled in the horizontal planes of life, the verticality of religion.

THE DIFFERENCE OF LANGUAGE

Science and literature are distinct, then, even in their objects, but above all in their formal viewpoints, in their methods of searching for truth, and in their goals. They are also distinct in their methods of presentation and in their language. Literature does not present its findings conceptually, or graphically, or photographically. Its presentation is through the plastic structure of the word. The literary artist tries to present an animated reflection of man's world in dialogue and plot, in narrative, evocation, and image, in simile and suggestive metaphor. All this reflection and visualization can take place only through the medium of speech. Even the scientist, despite "electron microscopes, cyclotrons, and electronic brains," despite all his mathematical, physical, and chemical symbols and formulas, must use human speech when he wishes to formulate his observations and findings. But he will use a technical language, an unambiguous jargon, freed as far as possible from human subjectivity and emotion. Word and sentence will be simplified, exactly defined, and unequivocal to the point of allowing only a "single interpretation." Speech is not presented here for its own sake, but merely as a means for the presentation of something else. It is used in a purely functional manner. Comprehension is already present before the process of verbal presentation begins.

It is different with literary language. In it, meaning appears for the first time in word and image, in linguistic form. Comprehension and presentation—what is presented and the medium through which it is presented—are here much more closely connected; they affect each other and penetrate one another mutually. What is comprehended is identical with the poetic word by which it is expressed, and the poetic word is identical with that which is comprehended, with that which is nowhere present except in the poetic word. "The purified language of literary art is not the means to something else; it is an end in itself," insofar as "significance and beauty" are in it, and insofar as it makes human existence real and gives form, content, and meaning to intellectual being.[10] The literary artist puts the rough and worn common language of men through a creative process of purification and renewal. He takes the overused, misused, and abused words and sentences, which the world around him has hardened into clichés and filled with poison, and breaks them up, melts them down, re-forms them, and coins them anew. One might compare this literary processing of language to the melting down of old metals or to the purifying of healthful, natural water. "Donner un sens plus pur aux mots de la tribu"[11]—this is the linguistic task of the man of letters. Just as healthful, natural water absorbs a certain amount of waste water, decomposes it, removes the poison, purifies it, and restores it to the household of nature, so can the language of literature capture the worn and abused language of every day, the jargon, the clichés, the slogans, the hyperboles, filter them, break them up, form the words anew from their linguistic elements, and restore them with new life to the world of man. Since literary language presents the world of man, it cannot be broken into horizontal segments and anchored in concepts. It must present its complete object in all his diversity, with all his wealth of relationships, and in his concrete, dynamic, and living individuality. That is why the literary word has many levels and often many meanings. It has bearings in depth and space that the conceptual word does not have. Its exactness often consists in

the fact that it has no sharp delimitations, but is open on all sides, just as man himself has no sharp delimitations but is open on all sides to historical, social, and cosmic relationships. The literary word neither can nor may have the clearcut distinctions of conceptual language, because, like concrete and individual man, it is incommensurable and almost infinitely related to the universe around it. For that reason, it can almost never claim the unambiguousness of chemical formulas or of metropolitan traffic regulations. If even the paragraphs of a law book, despite all efforts at exactitude, cannot be sharply defined but still remain open to a multiplicity of interpretations, how much more true is this of man himself. Added to this is the fact that literary language must express both the finite and the infinite, the fixed and the variable. If, in its own way, it repeatedly abstracts, reduces, and simplifies, it must, nonetheless, depict everflowing life with its complicatedly conscious and unconscious imaginings, rational and irrational impulses, associations, thoughts and images, drives and decisions, influences from within and without—and the interrelationships and interpenetrations of all of these. What is unthinkable in scientific language is necessary in literary language. That is why undertones and overtones, even dissonances and static, and an almost endless chain of reminiscences and images vibrate in it, as they do in the language and deeds of man himself. "Even if logic is the prerequisite for scientific language, in which singleness of meaning and precision of inference are essential," said Werner Heisenberg, "it is no adequate description of living speech, which has at its disposal so many richer means of expression. Not only does the spoken word evoke in our minds a particular movement, which is fully known to us and which we might designate as the meaning of the word, but it causes to emerge from the half-darkness of our consciousness those many secondary meanings and associations that, though we are hardly aware of them, may be essential to the meaning of the sentence we have heard. . . . Therefore poets, especially, have often protested against exaggerated emphasis on the logical structure of language and have pointed with justice to these other structures"—to the logic of literature as opposed to the horizontal and one-sided logic of science—"which form the basis of the specifically artistic use of language. . . . If, in the sciences, we must make the logical structure of language the basis of our thinking, at least we should not be oblivious to its other, richer, possibilities."[12]

A HISTORY OF THE ENCOUNTER BETWEEN SCIENCE AND LITERATURE

As yet, no one has written the definitive history of the segregation and integration of science and literature. Huxley himself did not do so even for English literature. When knowledge about nature had not yet been separated from verbal imagery and from a personally constructed myth, as, for instance, in Hesiod's *Works and Days,* there was no opposition between science and literature. Yet even Socrates, by his ethical questioning, expressed his dissatisfaction with knowledge about nature alone and opposed to it the idea of knowledge about man. "Now nature is on one side, man with his culture on the other. The problem of whether it is more important to know nature or the nature of man stands, therefore, at the very beginning of Western thought."[13] As their heritage from Aristotle, Stoics and Epicureans retained the division of the world into nature and spirit and, with it, the gulf between "physics" on the one side and "ethics" on the other. In Neoplatonism, nature was degraded as "physics." The Christian Middle Ages raised the status of nature, which they regarded as being as much God's creation as was spirit, and thus gave rise to a new wholeness. But the new and really decisive step toward modern science occurred during the Renaissance (Leonardo da Vinci, Copernicus, Giordano Bruno, Galileo), when man turned away from Aristotelian cosmology and medieval Scholastic philosophy and toward experiment and exact observation of nature. The modern dichotomy between science and the arts has existed since that time. It was intensified and rendered acute in the course of the nineteenth century.[14]

Once, in the sixteenth and seventeenth centuries, a lyric poet like John Donne could, without undue difficulty, incorporate his increased knowledge of the natural history of the world (not the impact of the cosmic system) into his lyrics. As long as man's new discoveries and his broadened understanding of the world were met with entities that could be seen or at least imagined, which could be understood without any special prerequisites, the poet, like every other man, was able to appropriate them to himself. He could also transfer them to his poetry. Thus Goethe, with his great interest in new ideas, appropriated the scientific title *De attractionibus electivis* from the Swede Torbern Bergman and used it creatively as the title of his novel *Die Wahlverwandtschaften* [Elective Affinities] in 1809. The observation that certain chemical substances are attracted to one another by a kind of natural necessity and that they strive toward union offered him both a simile and an explanation for that compulsive "choice" [*Wahl*] in human beings that takes precedence over freedom. He attempted to encompass in lyric verses, in which he even anticipated the concept of evolution, his new scientific findings about the metamorphosis of plants and animals. Some decades later in England, while composing the poem "In Memoriam" (published 1850), the lyric poet Alfred Tennyson became interested in Charles Lyell's *Principles of Geology* (1830-1833) and his exciting ideas about the evolution of the earth. By the middle of the century, in fact, "even a poet could understand the Darwinian hypothesis in its primitive form—could understand and rejoice, if he were a freethinker, over its antitheological implications or, if he were an orthodox Christian, react indignantly or with nostalgic tears to what *The Origin of Species* had done to Noah's ark and the first chapter of Genesis. Today the picture, once so beautifully clear, has had to incorporate into itself all the complexities of modern genetics, modern biochemistry, even modern biosociology. Science has become an affair of specialists. Incapable any longer of understanding what it is all about, the man of letters, we are told, has no choice but to ignore contemporary science altogether."[15]

In Germany, Arno Holz and other naturalistic writers toward the end of the century were extreme Darwinists. The young Franz Kafka was not only a Darwinist but also a follower of Ernst Haeckel. The general scientific tendencies of the age were, so to speak, in the air.

For English-speaking countries, Huxley made the comment: "Of the better poems written since 1921, the great majority do not so much as hint at the most important fact of contemporary history—the accelerating progress of science and technology. Insofar as they affect the social, economic and political situation in which individuals find themselves, some of the consequences of progressive science receive attention from the poets; but science as a growing corpus of information, science as a system of concepts operationally defined, even science as a necessary element in the formulation of a tenable philosophy of nature and man, science, in a word, as science, is hardly ever mentioned."[16] The question is whether "science as a system of operationally defined concepts," as it is currently understood, has any place at all in poetry, and whether it can produce anything more than a few didactic poems. The presentation of science as such, that is, in its own sphere, to a broader public is certainly not the task of literature but of modern technical manuals and other means of communication. It is my opinion that science and literature can have a common meeting place only insofar as science comes into contact with man and with human society; insofar as it influences, revolutionizes, and imperils human consciousness—*total* human consciousness; insofar as it decisively reshapes the world of man, his thinking, feeling, and willing. In the sphere of the novel, Huxley might have pointed to his own disillusioned anti-utopias—*Brave New World* (1932) and *Ape and Essence* (1948)—for the presentation of the unsalutary changes in human consciousness and the disastrous influences wrought on men by the findings of science. Signs of a change in consciousness and awareness as well as in the interpretation of facts are discernible almost everywhere in the modern novel. In German-speaking countries, for instance, Robert Musil described, in the first chapter of his novel *Der Mann ohne Eigenschaften* [The Man without Qualities], a "beautiful August day of the year 1913" in technical phrases drawn from meteorology: "barometric minimum" and "maximum," "isotheres" and "isotherms." Readers were repelled by this deviation from the usual concept of the beautiful and by the loss of feeling. At the same time, from the beginning of the thirties, Hermann Broch had been steadily asking himself what consequences the "theory of relativity" might have for the narrator of a modern novel.[17] In general, it can be said that the theory of relativity can be expected to alter the consciousness of the narrator, the narration itself, and the events narrated, only to the extent that human consciousness itself has been altered by the theory of relativity and its consequences—whether rightly or wrongly understood. As was to be expected, writers and authors manifested the greatest interest in the observations, findings, and hypotheses of the psychoanalysts. It is well known to what an extent young Franz Kafka was influenced by the scientifically oriented findings of psychoanalysis.

The "stream-of-consciousness" novel, with its juxtaposition of many currents of thought, belongs, since the time of James Joyce and Virginia Woolf, among the narrative forms possible at the present time; the ability to manipulate the stream of consciousness is one of the prerequisites of modern narration.

Huxley is of the opinion that lyric and tragedy offer little scope for the inclusion of science. The lyric poets seem, in fact, to have had the strongest disinclination for the rising sciences. Blake and Keats, two prominent lyricists of English romanticism, shunned Isaac Newton. Wordsworth, on the contrary, held him in high esteem, though his lyrical penchant for nature had almost nothing in common with the Newtonian observations of nature. For Rilke, the greatest of the German lyric poets of the twentieth century, science played no role. Even before World War I, however, young Gottfried Benn was incorporating medical vocabulary and ideas into his early poems. Oddly enough, they are almost completely absent from the poems of his middle and late years. The literary genre of tragedy has been rendered well-nigh impossible by the scientifically causal determination of events and by the psychological dismemberment of consciousness. The modern trend toward demythologizing and strict inquiry into the historical course of a personal or social "catastrophe" has likewise contributed to this situation. Where man is confronted only by himself, a "tragedy" may still be possible, though all comedy seems to become "tragicomedy." Drama cannot, and in the natural order of things need not, treat of scientific themes. It presents human conflicts. They arise when scientific results enter the realm of human society, whether the scientific findings contradict the traditional views of society (as in Brecht's *Leben des Galilei,* 1943) or are misused for political purposes (as in Dürrenmatt's *Die Physiker,* 1961) or are politically "betrayed" (as in the recent play by R. Kipphardt, *In der Sache J. R. Oppenheimer,* 1964). Many social and human conflicts are conceivable in these areas. They occur wherever an attempt is made to segregate or integrate the scientifically known and the merely human.

The stricter form of the essay, if one includes it among the literary genres, affords a direct possibility for the encounter of scientific content and literary form. The essay appeared as an independent literary form at about the same time that science was beginning to separate itself from the humanities, that is, during the Renaissance (Montaigne, Francis Bacon). It plays an important role within the modern novel, as, for instance, in the works of Hermann Broch, Robert Musil, and even Thomas Mann. The narrator reveals himself as thinker, knower, observer; as the expert, who expresses himself about an area in which he is competent or about his scientifically determined personal observations.

Huxley felt that there was far too little incorporation of scientific findings and content into modern literature. From the point of view of content and theme, that may be so. But the literary man's way of thinking and seeing, the temper of his mental outlook does, nonetheless, show

that he is coming closer to the scientist's attitude toward the object of his investigation. It is no accident that the very title of Franz Kafka's earliest work, *"Beschreibung eines Kampfes"* [Description of a Struggle] (1904-1905), reveals it as the attempt to describe methodically the inner and outer condition of a complicated and immature man. The concept of "description" became significant for Kafka under the influence of the teachings of Ernst Mach and the experimental and inductive psychology of Franz Brentano. The second part of the above-mentioned story is, against all tradition, labeled "proof": "a proof that it is impossible to live." That is a new narrative attitude for an author to adopt toward the world that he is to observe and portray. Since the fifties, the efforts of the authors of the *nouveau roman* have been going much further. Uwe Johnson's novels, *Mutmassungen über Jakob* [Speculations about Jacob] and *Das dritte Buch über Achim* [The Third Book about Achim], show clearly this critical, scientifically influenced awareness on the part of the younger writers. Men of letters are becoming increasingly concerned about preserving a critical distance from the object to be observed and described, about the avoidance of all possible subjectivity, about conscious knowledge, about their own position within the sphere of reality that is under observation. They illuminate their object from all sides, show critically to what distortion a one-sided contemplation may lead, prescribe cold observation instead of a feeling of identification with the object, change the position and perspective of observation, force what is factual, psychic, and emotional through the filter of reflection, analysis, and criticism, and thus prevent our direct concurrence with what has been presented.

In contrast to the English romanticists, the early romantic writers in Germany had introduced the concept of "experiment" into literary work. "A good physical experiment can serve as the model of an inner experiment and is itself, besides, a good inner, subjective experiment." "To experiment with images and concepts and with the possibilities of presenting them in a way analogous to that of physical experimentation."[18] These fragments from Novalis refer to the cognitive experiment with the object and the formal experiment of linguistic presentation. Emile Zola's programmatic work of 1880, *Le Roman expérimental,* did not refer to an experiment with a new form of novel, but with a new method of evolving the action of the novel from the premises of experience and philosophy. "For Zola, the consciousness of the writer was a kind of test tube in which a chain reaction was set in motion according to strict scientific laws. The protocol of this reaction yielded the action of the novel. These two married persons with this particular heredity, united at this particular time, must in the end kill one another in this particular way as determined by the teachings of heredity and the theory of environment."[19] In the chapter *"Symposion oder Gespräch über die Erlösung"* [Symposium or a Conversation about Redemption] in his trilogy *Die Schlafwandler* [The Sleepwalkers] (1929-1932), Hermann Broch transfers some of his main characters into an experimental situation. His purpose is not to demonstrate, as Zola did, the naturalistic principle of determinism; he wants, in the shortest way possible and in a model situation erected by himself, to demonstrate and allow free play to the thoughts, trials, and struggles of his characters. Beda Allemann has shown "that experimental traits and the will to artistic experiment are recognizable in all spheres of modern literature, that, in fact, the reference to this experimental character of modern literature has for some time now belonged among the commonplaces of literary criticism."[20] That an unsuccessful linguistic experiment is not a work of art is self-evident. That an author like Alfred Andersch should resist the thoughtless transference of the concept of experiment into the realm of literature is a healthy reaction against the vague and the merely modish. In the present context, there has been an effort to point out not merely the points of contact in the content of literary and scientific works, but also the increasing proximity of the two disciplines in method, in the observation of their object, and in the preparation of their product.

THE DE-POETIZING OF THE WORLD
AND THE SELF-KNOWLEDGE OF THE MODERN AUTHOR

"Science sometimes builds new bridges between universes of discourse and experience hitherto regarded as separate and heterogeneous. But science also breaks down old bridges and opens gulfs between universes that, traditionally, had been connected. Blake and Keats, as we have seen, detested Sir Isaac Newton because he had cut the old connection between the stars and the heavenly host, between rainbows and Iris, and even between rainbows and Noah's Ark, rainbows and Jehovah—had cut the connections and thereby de-poetized man's world and robbed it of meaning."[21] Scientific thinking and mythically interpreted experience, science and the humanities, science and supernatural faith, immanence and transcendence, world and God—all these have been separated. The world that appears to man's senses has been put more and more often under the microscope, dissected, analyzed, measured, objectified, planned, rebuilt, and misbuilt. The world as nature—as the natural, created, and hereditary living space of man—is being driven further and further into the background. The world projected by the scientist, the artificially reconstructed, technically produced world, is looming larger and larger, this world of tracks and wires, glass and cement, pills, formulas, aggregates, traffic lights, and windshields. Closely linked to this reconstruction of the world are the processes of demythologizing, deanthropomorphizing, denaturalizing. Typical of the development of this world is the substitution of city-lyrics for nature-lyrics by the German Expressionists and, in more recent times, the substitution of test-tube-lyrics for city-lyrics.

We can illustrate the loss of the old natural and mythical world by two examples. The moon, having become the goal and already the landing place of rockets, no longer serves as the subject of tender lyrics. Goethe's immortal lyric to the moon is not even conceivable today:

> Füllest wieder Busch und Tal
> Still mit Nebelglanz,

> Lösest endlich auch einmal
> Meine Seele ganz;
> Breitest über mein Gefild
> Lindernd deinen Blick,
> Wie des Freundes Auge mild
> Über mein Geschick.[22]

This free transferral of mood and sentiment to the friendly moon, the awakening of a spiritual and poetic mood by reference to earth's companion, her great and friendly neighbor, no longer even occurs to a poet, to an "enlightened" man. Such a sentiment and awakening are no longer possible. The moon is no longer the trusted, mysteriously silent friend of man. It is a satellite that rotates around the earth on a constantly narrowing elliptical course at a mean distance of about 238,857 miles and about whose climatic conditions, mountains, and reflection of the sun man is somewhat informed. But human feelings? At the best, feelings of inquiry and conquest, that is, modern scientific feelings of the objective, "matter of fact" kind, not poetic and personal feelings.

From time immemorial, another favorite subject of lyric poetry has been the nightingale. In England there are at least as many lyrics about nightingales as there are in Germany about the moon. But the nightingale, too, has lost its tender lyric nature since the animal psychologists have discovered that the cock nightingale (not Philomel) sings "not in pain, not in passion, not in ecstasy, but simply in order to proclaim to other cock nightingales that he has staked out a territory and is prepared to defend it against all comers." Nothing remains of love's nightly longing and lament since man has discovered through scientific observation that the cock sings "because, like all the other members of his species, he has the kind of digestive system that makes him want to feed every four or five hours throughout the twenty-four. Between caterpillars, during these feeding times, he warns his rivals . . . to keep off his private property."[23] Like the philosopher and the man in the street, the poet must learn today that things signify themselves first. Inappropriate transferrals of feeling, unconsidered hyperboles of thought, naïve anthropomorphizing of the world are no longer permissible. "In an age of science the world can no longer be looked at as a set of symbols, standing for things outside the world. *Alles Vergaengliche ist NICHT ein Gleichnis,*"[24] at least not in the idealistic *a priori* sense of a Plato. Unconsidered allegorizing and exaggeration create today the impression of a flight from the harder realities of the uncompromisingly real. Such a flight makes everything that was previously believed about reality no longer quite believable.

In the preface to the second edition of the "Lyrical Ballads" in 1801, Wordsworth describes poetry as the "spontaneous overflow of powerful feelings." It would be difficult to find a definition less suited to the greater part of contemporary poetry. Feelings, especially the feelings that affirm the world, have been, in almost every case, skeptically and critically withdrawn. The intellect is sent ahead to reconnoiter, take soundings, spy. Feelings are suspect, are consciously subdued. This world can no longer evoke a spontaneous affirmation. The withdrawal of feeling is at the same time the protection of a self whose deductions about the world have given it a different orientation. A spontaneously experienced unity between poet and world no longer exists. For the poet and artist, there remains almost no other reaction to the world than a gradual and partial affirmation, brought about by the painful process of observation and reflection, criticism and abstraction. It is doubtful whether the new synthesis, which Huxley proposes as the ideal—a synthesis, for example, of the ornithological truth about the nightingale and a mythologically constructed human projection—is possible for the literature of our generation. A generation that has experienced the shock of emotional disillusionment, the results of an inappropriate projection of the emotions, and the rejection of their own, naïvely spontaneous trustfulness can scarcely be expected to produce, in the next breath, a new "yes" to the world, a sympathy now critically filtered, a sentiment—consciously differentiated by scientific means—of new trust and psychic contact, a sense of inclusion in the inner, meaningful world of men. Perhaps a relationship on a scientific basis will be possible between man and nature in the next generation, for man will no longer experience the shock, but will have accepted science as a matter of course, and will know the limits of the scientific viewpoint and the extent to which science can be conquered. The process of demythologizing nature will, at first, proceed as before. For the rest, Kafka has already shown that the secondary, administered, bureaucratic world is susceptible of both myth and poetry.

Poets do not speak today of a "divine instinct" that guides them, of "inspiration," of "enthusiasm," of the "spontaneous overflow of powerful feelings." Poetry is, for the most part, no longer "inspired"—at least no one speaks of it as such. It no longer "originates"; it is "made." For that reason, the German classical idea of the "organism" is seldom used in the interpretation of or as a norm for the modern literary work. The modern artistic entity no longer aspires to imitate an organic entity. It is no longer to be understood simply as "mimesis." The *poiesis,* the *making,* has become more important. The literary work of art is a "piece," a "piece of work," an entity made as technical products are made. Modern writers think of themselves as "chemists," who mix poems out of linguistic elements (W. H. Auden), or as "literary engineers" (Valéry, Enzensberger). Louis MacNeice wrote in 1948: "Literature is a precision instrument for showing how man reacts to life."[25] The writer no longer wants to act as guide to the rarefied heights of a harmonious life that has no existence in reality and is radically misunderstood by a sleepy and uninterested bourgeoisie. He lays no claim to an authority that transcends his own observation, the world of characters that he has presented, the word he has formulated. Even he is engaged, although he must keep the scope of the whole work in mind, with partial questions, which, admittedly, are not so much quantitative in nature as humanly, historically, and socially qualitative. It never occurs to him to present a

whole—the road to maturity, for example, as portrayed in the "classical" German psychological novel [*Bildungsroman*]. In intensive preliminary inquiry, he concerns himself not only with the formal side of presentation but with the processes of observing and approaching the object to be presented—processes that are at once presupposed by the linguistic form and contained in it. The recently deceased T. S. Eliot has given us Valéry's concept of the poet: "He is no longer the disheveled madman who writes a whole poem in the course of one feverish night; he is a cool scientist, almost an algebraist . . . comparable to the mathematical physicist, or else to the biologist or chemist . . . , the austere, bespectacled man in a white coat. . . . The ivory tower has been fitted up as a laboratory—a solitary laboratory."[26] These and similar comparisons are not intended to degrade the poet of times past or to deny that new problems in regard to both his profession and his task confront the laboratory-poet of today. When, for example, society as a whole recognizes no generally binding truth, then the writer in such a society cannot be guided by a generally binding "norm" of truth. Truth is for him—and in this, too, he is like the scientist—only that understanding of reality which he himself has discovered, or can discover, through "experience." "Tradition" is for him a word as meaningful and problematical as it is for the man in a chemical laboratory. It may be taken for granted here that a concept of reality whose sole criterion is the "experiment" is a great loss to humanity. It seems important for our understanding of the relationship between modern literature and science that we realize how much the self-understanding of modern writers is expressed in scientific and technical language. The modern author is no longer primarily a man imbued with feelings of oneness with the "gods" or the cosmos or nature. On the contrary, he must discipline himself to approach his "object," to observe it critically, to present his findings both objectively and poetically. Occasional extreme outbursts of phantasy merely show the effect of such strong discipline, the swing of the pendulum into an area that is less demanding and not so predetermined by the object to be presented—an area of primitive and self-determining creative freedom.

PRESERVATION AND RECOVERY OF THE HUMAN ELEMENT IN A SCIENTIFICALLY UNDERSTOOD AND TECHNICALLY CONSTRUCTED WORLD

Enthusiastically, though not without reservations, Wordsworth, in 1801, anticipated the future covenant between poet and scientist. "If the labours of Men of science," he wrote, "should ever create any material revolution, direct or indirect, in our condition, and in the impressions which we habitually receive, the Poet will sleep then no more than at present; he will be ready to follow the steps of the Men of science, not only in those general indirect effects, but he will be at his side, carrying sensations into the midst of the objects of science itself. The remotest discoveries of the Chemist, the Botanist, or Mineralogist, will be as proper objects of the Poet's art as any upon which it can be employed, if the time should ever come when these things shall be familiar to us, and the relations under which they are contemplated by the followers of these respective sciences shall be manifestly and palpably material to us as enjoying and suffering beings. If the time should ever come when what is now called science, thus familiarized to men, shall be ready to put on, as it were, a form of flesh and blood, the Poet will lend his divine spirit to aid the transfiguration, and will welcome the Being thus produced as a dear and genuine inmate of the household of man."[27] Wordsworth's ability to envisage the developments of science was obviously limited. Some of the most important discoveries of the newer physics, for instance the structure of the atom or the nature of electromagnetic waves, are simply not apprehensible by the senses. They cannot "put on a form of flesh and blood." When the realms of representation, of what can be described in words or at least conceived by the imagination, have been left behind, literature and art can no longer function representationally.[28] To this must be added the fact that the "divine spirit" of the poet is not even needed for the scientific and, in its wake, the technical transformation of the world. Science and technology can change the world without any help from the poet.

Wordsworth was totally unaware of the threatening and rapidly advancing banishment of man from the "paradise" of nature, of the increasingly spiritual homelessness of modern man, of the attempt to reconstruct the world of man as scientifically as possible—and, certainly, of the steadily increasing political threat to nations from the instruments of superpower, the so-called ABC weapons, that science has made possible.[29] He was unaware of the increasing inner estrangement from the world that accompanies man's increasing scientific familiarity with it. Convinced that the poet "is the rock of defence for human nature, an upholder and preserver,"[30] one who sympathizes with all that exists, Wordsworth did not know to what extent man is at the disposal of the world he has conquered by science, how it directs him as if he were an objective potential, disregards his last possession, his freedom, and regards him as a small functioning part of an immense scientific, technical, and economic piece of equipment. To the scientific belief in progress, in a unilateral process that reduces everything to the realm of science and makes no distinction between theory and practice, the man of letters cannot but refuse his unreserved assent, his uncritical acceptance, because this process encroaches upon man's rights, because this paradoxically practical utopian belief imperils man, however many pain-killing drugs and work-lightening gadgets he may invent.

Nevertheless, the man of letters must be as conversant as possible with the scientific mind and attitude. "Literature cannot be spared the necessity of adapting itself to the scientific world view, and a part of its present irrelevance is due to the fact that it is so slow in doing so," wrote Robert Musil in 1927.[31] Henceforth only pseudopoets can cling to their ancestral emotions, their dim idylls, their allegedly unimpaired fortress. For the most part, it is their language that betrays their lack of alertness toward reality. They do not live in the real world that oppresses man

from all sides. Modern man, unless he wants to withdraw to the last recesses of bush, island, or dream, can no longer accept or reject the scientifically and technically altered world. It is simply there. He is born into it. And just as the individual person, the family, the religious community, and the nation live in this world and must prove themselves precisely as person, family, religious community, and nation, so must the literary artist prove himself according to the demands of this world, its criteria, its conditions, its elimination of free time, its media of communication, its language. Science will influence him not only by its attitude toward the world, but also by its consciously objectifying and critically observant way of thinking and of seeing everything from its own standpoint. The omniscient author, for example, whose ideal view of persons, things, and events was so much taken for granted in the traditional novel, is no longer conceivable today. Such a way of narrating would no longer be acceptable. It is based on presuppositions about knowledge that science and the scientifically limited, partial, object-bound way of regarding the world—both long since absorbed into the general consciousness—can no longer recognize as being in accord with reality and hence true. The idealistic concept of "omniscience" and the idealistic subjection of the world to its dominion no longer correspond to the structure of our knowledge or to the true demands of the world.

If the contemporary writer should be conversant with the scientific attitude toward the world and the scientific way of viewing the world, this does not mean that science as such, its conceptuality, its formulas, its specialized areas of compartmentalized knowledge, its systems, is to become the object of literature so that literature may prove its relevance to reality, its up-to-dateness. From the literary point of view, that would be poetic materialism; from the scientific point of view, an education of the masses. But this latter—certainly, a necessity—is, as we have already said, being carried out by the so-called technical manuals and mass media of communication. The man of letters does not have to become the handyman and aide of science. In the first place, he cannot, "because the advance information that readers have gained from instruction through other media makes direct instruction through novels, lyrics, or dramas automatically unnecessary."[32] In the second place, he should not be permitted to attempt it. If he does, his words will "settle" on the level of information and instruction, of the merely useful and objective. That would, perhaps, excuse him, but it would also disarm him; he would be rendered *a priori* harmless to society, degraded to the state of "fellow traveler" and "yes man."

The real theme of literature and literary culture is man. But, in 1970, that does not mean the man of 1770. Even the manner of looking at things is different now (which does not mean that it is better or worse, though to demand, even implicitly, the retention of the vision of 1770 would be to demand that it be worse, for it would mean the inability to grasp the phenomena, and therefore the reality, of the modern world as it is.) To the writer and poet "it is a question of showing the substance of man in a world that has sacrificed all poetic charm and has, in consequence, until now eluded the grasp of literature; that is, the world of science. The Russian Revolution may have been assimilated into the poetic consciousness, but the second industrial revolution has not been; in fact, poetry has as yet scarcely crossed the threshold beyond which the modern age begins; that hazardous enterprise lies before it."[33] It would be difficult to conceive of a more intensive and pressing theme for the conflict that is present in a thousand variations in modern life than that of the struggle of man with his scientifically and technically changed and changing world. Just as a preacher, for instance, by becoming acquainted with the method and content of modern Biblical exegesis, can bring considerable clarity to the understanding of the Bible that he had, perhaps, earlier learned and accepted, so must the poet be as open as possible to changes in the method and content of modern consciousness, especially as it is fostered by science. It is hardly necessary to prove that he must, in the process, observe certain definite professional limits, that he cannot himself become a scientific research scholar.

The real theme and the real scope of the poet is man and man's world in the here and now. But the man of today is also that man whom the factual and partial findings of science have left unnoticed; that man who is more than a number of molecules, chromosomes, cells, electric charges, circulatory and digestive organs; more than a sum of attitudes, expectations, and reactions; that "citizen of the republic" who does not simply wear a production and consumer code on his back; that man who, it is true, needs science, but to whom science can give only the surface facts and no information at all about his total orientation as man, about his spiritual horizon, which surpasses and penetrates the material world. Werner Heisenberg gives a summary description of the multitude with its unreserved confidence in the scientific bid for power: "With the apparently limitless extension of its material power, mankind is in the position of a captain whose ship is so strongly constructed of steel and iron that the magnetic needle of his compass points only to the iron mass of his ship, not to the north. With such a ship, he can reach no goal, but merely ride around in circles, exposed to the wind and the current."[34] In a world predominantly guided by its scientific and material *credo,* the writer, as the guardian of human values, will stress the importance of the intellect and the person, perhaps even help to rediscover and reconquer them. In this scientific and technical world, which is almost always preoccupied with isolated questions and partial systems, he is responsible for the larger horizon of man and its relation to the whole. The problem of the poet's responsibility for knowing the whole scheme of things is one that Hermann Broch saw very clearly. In his essay, *Geschichtsgesetz und Willensfreiheit* [Free Will and the Law of History], which belongs among his studies of mass psychology, he wrote: "The talent for arousing participation, a gift and talent which is proper in the highest degree to the religious intelligence, is almost totally lacking in the purely rational [we might interpolate "the purely scientific"] intelligence.

Above all, it is not, in contrast to religious intelligence, a centralized intelligence, that is, it is not ordered around a central truth from which the organon of knowledge and hence of culture is to be grasped as a unit, at least in its essential unifying principles; rather it is a web, which possesses in each of its points an unchanging significance and importance, so that the appearance of unity, without which there is no participation, no illumination of the dusk . . . , and finally even no wisdom, is rendered utterly impossible."[35]

The responsible writer, who is both aware of the scientific mind and attitude and cognizant of the value of the person and the basic orientation of personal life, will always be man's defender, guardian, and admonisher. Wherever the scientifically oriented world draws man objectively and superficially into its material world of observation and schedule, wherever shortsighted utilization of scientific claims imperils man and his society, the writer will rise up as the critic and corrector of public consciousness. Whence he derives his better knowledge, his more critical experience, his more comprehensive and structured truth, in what manner he is, as citizen and critic of this world, at the same time immersed in the scientific superficiality and imperiled consciousness of the world that he is to portray—these problems of the search for truth and its discovery cannot be touched upon here. The inquiry about the larger horizon will be formulated differently by the philosophically, theologically, and historically educated writer than by one who merely calls upon his own experience, whether present or buried in memory; it will be formulated differently, too, by the Christian writer than by the expressly non-Christian one. For their part, leading men of science have already declared: "Even in science, the object of research is no longer nature as such, but nature as delivered over to human questioning; thus here, too, man once more confronts himself."[36]

NOTES

[1] Aldous Huxley, *Literature and Science* (New York, 1963). Kurz uses H. E. Herlitschka's German version of this work, *Literatur und Wissenschaft.* All quotations in the present English translation are, however, from Huxley's own text. [Translator's note.]

[2] Huxley, *Literature and Science,* p. 3.

[3] Ibid., p. 5.

[4] Ibid., p. 8.

[5] Ibid., pp. 7-8. Cf. also A. Brunner, *Erkenntnistheorie* (Cologne, 1948), p. 287ff.: "Die Naturwissenschaften."

[6] Huxley, *Literature and Science,* pp. 9-10.

[7] Huxley mentions, for instance, the scholarly findings of science and their antischolarly use for the organized manipulation of man into so-called mass murder.

[8] Huxley, *Literature and Science,* p. 82.

[9] Ibid., p. 77.

[10] Ibid., pp. 38-39. Literature as "a magical object endowed . . . with mysterious powers" (p. 38) must be understood correctly. It seems preferable not to seek its mystery and fascination in the realms of magic, fairy tale, or myth. Its fascination lies, in good measure, in the literary presentation and form itself.

[11] The famous line originates in Mallarmé's sonnet "On the Grave of E. A. Poe." The French word "tribu" is derived from the Latin "tribus." Its first reference is to a group of persons speaking the same language, then to the "plebs," the "masses." In the present context, not only the common language in general use but also the much-used language of daily life is meant.

[12] Werner Heisenberg, "Sprache und Wirklichkeit in der modernen Physik," in the lecture series *Wort und Wirklichkeit* (Munich, 1960), p. 37f.

[13] E. Grassi, "Das Naturbild der heutigen Physik," in *Rowohlts deutsche Enzyklopädie,* no. 8 (Hamburg, 1955), p. 133. Cf. also E. Grassi, *Von Ursprung und Grenzen der Geisteswissenschaften und Naturwissenschaften* (Munich, 1950).

[14] Since Heidegger, we have been aware that the question that must precede any attempt to distinguish between "nature" and "spirit," i.e., the question as to what supports and governs both, viz., being, has not been sufficiently discussed in Western philosophy. See W. Strolz, "Die Frage nach der ursprünglichen Einheit der Wissenschaften," in *Experiment und Erfahrung in Wissenschaft und Kunst,* ed. W. Strolz (Freiburg and Munich, 1963).

[15] Huxley, *Literature and Science,* p. 62.

[16] Ibid., pp. 60-61.

[17] H. Broch, *Gesammelte Werke* (Zürich, 1953ff.), vol. 2, p. 597 and vol. 6, pp. 69, 197. "For thirty years I have been tormented by the question of the 'observer in the field of observation,' a question that the theory of relativity aroused in me" (letter of Dec. 20, 1949 in vol. 8, p. 369).

[18] Novalis, *Werke, Briefe, Dokumente,* ed. E. Wasmuth (Heidelberg, 1953-1957), Fragmente 1442 and 1444.

[19] Beda Allemann, "Experiment und Erfahrung in der Gegenwartsliteratur," in *Experiment und Erfahrung in Wissenschaft und Kunst,* p. 271.

[20] Ibid., p. 268.

[21] Huxley, *Literature and Science,* p. 111.

[22] E. A. Bowring's translation of this poem appears in *The German Classics,* ed. Kuno Francke et al. (New York, 1913), vol. 1, pp. 27-28. The two stanzas quoted in the text read as follows:

> Bush and vale thou fill'st again
>   With thy misty ray,
> And my spirit's heavy chain
>   Casteth far away.
>
> Thou dost o'er my fields extend
>   Thy sweet soothing eye,
> Watching like a gentle friend,
>   O'er my destiny.

[23] Huxley, *Literature and Science,* p. 116.

[24] Ibid., p. 111. Cf. also L. Scheffczyk, "Der Sonnenuntergang des heiligen Franz von Assisi und die Hymne an die Materie des Teilhard de Chardin," in *Geist und Leben* (1962), p. 226.

[25] Quoted by W. Clemens, *Das Wesen der Dichtung in der Sicht moderner englischer und amerikanischer Dichter* (Munich, 1961), p. 4.

[26] Ibid., p. 5. Eliot's original statement in English, as it appears in this translation, has been quoted from Paul Valéry, *The Art of Poetry,* trans. from the French by Denise Folliot with an introduction by T. S. Eliot (New York, 1958), Introduction, pp. xviii-xx and passim [translator's note].

[27] From Wordsworth's preface to the second edition of the *Lyrical Ballads,* quoted in Huxley, pp. 42-43.

[28] Even in modern physics, the possibility of a verbal description of certain procedures and experiments has become a problem. See Heisenberg, *Wort und Wirklichkeit,* p. 40f.

[29] See also A. Einstein, "Zur Erniedrigung des wissenschaftlichen Menschen," in *Mein Weltbild* (Berlin, 1964), p. 172f.

[30] Quoted in Huxley, *Literature and Science,* p. 42.

[31] Robert Musil, *Tagebücher, Aphorismen, Essays und Reden* (Hamburg, 1955), p. 755.

[32] W. Jens in *Schwierigkeiten, heute die Wahrheit zu schreiben,* ed. H. Friedrich (Munich, 1964), p. 74.

[33] Ibid., p. 75f.

[34] Werner Heisenberg, *Das Naturbild der heutigen Physik* (Hamburg, 1955), p. 18.

[35] H. Broch, *Gesammelte Werke,* vol. 9, p. 291.

[36] Heisenberg, *Das Naturbild der heutigen Physik,* p. 18.

FICTION

Harry Levin

SOURCE: "Science and Fiction," in *Bridges to Science Fiction,* George E. Slusser, George R. Guffey, Mark Rose, eds., Southern Illinois University Press, 1980, pp. 3-21.

[*In the following essay, Levin offers his view of the affinities between modern fiction and science.*]

Since my three-word title echoes those two nouns which denote the subject of this symposium, it should be self-evident that my own key-word is the conjunction between them. Not that I would wish to put asunder what has clearly been compounded with so much imagination, industry, and ingenuity. The copula is merely my confession that I have little right to expatiate on the compound. Though I have had frequent opportunity to read and write and talk about various forms of fiction, my encounters with the genre that we have been invited to discuss—enjoyable and instructive as they may have been—have been somewhat casual and slight. As for science, I can only confide that in my case the ordinary layman's interest has been enhanced; if not solidified, by a number of happy associations with professional scientists through academies, common rooms, and personal circumstances. Yet I realize, as I begin to fill in the pages that follow, that I am adopting the simple-minded tactic of the journalist in *Pickwick Papers.* Having been assigned an article on Chinese Metaphysics, it will be remembered, he looked up both China and Metaphysics in the encyclopedia and thereupon combined the information. As a bug-eyed alien among a galaxy of experts, I feel something of the thrill that must alert the interplanetary voyager. Since the rhythms of my thought are conventionally measured by academic semesters rather than light-years, we may have some degree of mental synchronization to work out among us. Such considerations do not make the adventure less exciting for me; but, not wanting to travel under false colors, it should be clear from the very outset that I view myself as rather a tourist or passenger than a pilot or guide.

Perhaps we may take our chronological bearings by noticing that we now stand within five years of 1984. Reading the newspapers, we may even wish to congratulate ourselves on having come so near to fulfilling George Orwell's projections for intercommunication and cognition: Newspeak and Doublethink. Orwell made his prognostication in 1949, thereby allowing us another lustrum for its fulfillment. One decade afterward, just exactly twenty years ago, C. P. Snow delivered his reverberating pronouncement on *The Two Cultures.* This, as the problematic formulation of an important issue, has weathered better than F. R. Leavis's virulent counterattack. There has meanwhile been some tendency, I suspect, for scientific and literary sensibilities to come closer together. What could be a better witness to that than science-fiction? Can there be a scholar-teacher or writer-critic here who could not respond correctly to Snow's elementary

shibboleth for scientific literacy: the Second Law of Thermodynamics? On the other hand, there must be some who put forth, or lend credence to, fictive postulates that have still to be acknowledged by Snow or Carnot or the canons of physics itself. One of my colleagues who was awarded a Nobel Prize in that field, and who reads extensively beyond it, has testified that Snow's early novel *The Search* is the only book that conveys what it feels like to be a practicing scientist today. Other scientists have written fiction, Kepler in elaborately phantasmagorical form. Still others, even closer to the Cavendish Laboratory than Lord Snow, have written autobiographical accounts of what has been going on there. But, though James Watson's *Double Helix* chronicles the discovery of DNA, his underlying themes are human competition and vanity.

Literature, taken in its broadest sense, has acted as an agent for the dissemination of science. Some of the most technical treatises, in the early days, were couched in poetic modes. The Greeks and Romans read Aratus and Lucretius for information about meteors and atoms. Indeed the evocation of Epicurus, at the beginning of *De Rerum Naturae,* "proceeding far beyond the flaming walls of the firmament," is a more eloquent tribute than any Nobel Prize winner has ever been paid. Dante, in transit through the celestial regions, listens to a lecture from Beatrice on gravity. Chaucer is transported to his House of Fame by an eagle who discourses upon the principles of acoustics. Scientific popularizers, like Fontenelle and Algarotti, wrote as if they were novelists addressing themselves to feminine readers. The scientist himself, when cast as a literary character, has played an equivocal role: a subspecies of the archetypal trickster, a man of many inventions like the elusive Odysseus, a fabulous artificer like Daedalus, who became Joyce's archetype for the artist. Faust was the prototype of the modern mage, though it was never wholly clear whether he had dedicated himself to a disinterested quest for wisdom or to an egoistic cult of experience. His case is shadowed by a primitive taboo against forbidden knowledge, like the parable of Frankenstein—or, for that matter, Adam or Prometheus. Unlike Faust's demonology, Prospero's white magic—what Shakespeare called his "art"—could be entertained as proto-science, a command over nature through an understanding of its inherent properties and hidden interrelations. This was, to be sure, the original purview of alchemy, from which we can trace surviving concepts of chemistry and physics, not to mention Jungian psychology. Yet its consistent failure to live up to its gilt-edged promises made it for several writers—Chaucer, Erasmus, Ben Jonson—a hoax to be exposed. For Balzac it was a characteristic obsession: *La Recherche de l'absolu.*

Since the techniques and objectives of empirical research are likely to seem arcane and hieratic to the uninitiated, these have become a target of philistine satire, to be caricatured by Aristophanes with his sophistical think-tank or by Swift in Gulliver's *reductio ad absurdum* of the Royal Society. The contraptions of the late Rube Goldberg, where unlikely concatenations of home-made machinery are circuitously arranged to bring about what might otherwise have been accomplished by a simple human gesture, may be viewed as a critique of our increasing dependence on push-button gadgetry. The clysters and phlebotomies and embrocations and faddish operations and bedside manners of physicians have made them popular butts on the comic stage from Molière to Shaw. Yet the worldly success of such charlatanism was grounded upon a quasi-religious awe, as Molière himself intimated: an acceptance of quacks as a priesthood conniving, for better or worse, in the powers of life and death. With contrasting reverence, Balzac apotheosized the doctor as humanitarian benefactor in his *Médecin de campagne*; and, though the husbands of Emma Bovary and Carol Kennicott were mediocre rural practitioners, they were men of bumbling good will; while Sinclair Lewis, with the cooperation of the bacteriologist Paul De Kruif, surveyed the heights and depths of the American medical establishment in his *Arrowsmith*. The physician, after all, is often the only person of scientific training that most other people ever get to see very much. When, instead of going on his clinical rounds, he isolates himself within a laboratory, his experimentation gets clouded in mystery, and he is perceived as a sinister figure, coldly or madly treating humans as guinea-pigs: Dr. Rappacini, Dr. Heidegger, Dr. Jekyll, Dr. Moreau.

Historically, we are well aware that the line of demarcation between science and pseudo-science is difficult to draw, not less so because accepted theories are continually being confuted and discarded. Rationalists have attempted to sharpen it by their satirical exposures. But we also know that science-fiction battens on pseudo-science: that alchemy, astrology, phrenology, mesmerism, and ESP adapt themselves much more aptly to fictitious narration than do the more quantifiable disciplines. Thus Brian Aldiss cites the inspiration of Gurdjieff and Ouspensky, whom he terms "the slav dreamers"—he might likewise have mentioned Velikovsky. Precisely because of their illusory assumptions, such mystagogues and gurus are more at ease in the realm of illusion than, let us say, Planck, Rutherford, or the Joliot-Curies would be. This distinction may help to explain why Milton, though he was fairly well abreast of contemporary astronomy, chose to locate the scenes for *Paradise Lost* in a Ptolemaic rather than a Copernican universe. Even so, he dared allude to Galileo's telescope, the "optic glass" of "the Tuscan artist," and he must have felt something of that tension between Christian dogma and the new cosmology which would be ironically dramatized by Brecht in his *Galileo*. Hamlet, in his brief metaphysical poem addressed to Ophelia, had made no secret of his own heliocentric skepticism: "Doubt that the sun doth move." The gradual consequence of such anti-geocentric reductionism was to shatter those chains of being which had related man, in his central position, to the correspondent influences of the zodiac and the universal harmony of the spheres—to relocate his earth as a lesser outpost in a plurality of worlds. A second and even more shattering reduction was to come, as we shall be

noting, with Darwin. But it was already enough of a shock to raise the question, which would pulsate back and forth from *King Lear* through Thomas Hardy, of nature's indifference to mankind.

The sense of chilling detachment and emotional deprivation, as it bore upon the novelist, might be brought home by this paragraph closing a chapter from an early story of George Eliot's:

> While this poor little heart was bruised with a weight too heavy for it, Nature was holding on her calm inexorable way, in unmoved and terrible beauty. The stars were rushing in their eternal courses; the tides welled to the level of the last expectant week; the sun was making brilliant day to busy nations on the other side of the swift earth. The stream of human thought and deed was hurrying and broadening onward. The astronomer was at his telescope; the great ships were laboring over the waves; the toiling eagerness of commerce, the fierce spirit of revolution, were only ebbing in brief rest; and sleepless statesmen were dreading the possible crisis of the morrow. What were our little Tina and her trouble in this mighty torrent, rushing from one awful unknown to another? Lighter than the smallest center of quivering life in the waterdrop, hidden and uncared for as the pulse of anguish in the breast of the tiniest bird that has fluttered down to its nest with the long-sought food, and has found the nest torn and empty.

Here the pathos is not of the sort that Ruskin would term the pathetic fallacy; for this would assume that nature really cared, that storms would sympathize with the heroine's grief and sunbeams smile upon her happiness. Nor is it to be compared with Pascal's shudder over the eternal silences of the infinite spaces, since a bustling world is going about its callous business around her. It does presume the disappearance of God, and consequently the individual feeling of complete psychological isolation. Little Tina seems farther away from the astronomer than from the lost nestlings. Tennyson would wrestle with the problem throughout *"In Memoriam"*: "Are God and Nature then at strife / That Nature lends such evil dreams?" Or are these ostensible cold facts, on the contrary, the material actualities that scientists would confirm? For the romantic poets, licensed dreamers, science had become the encroaching nightmare, the adversary to be warded off by conjuring up the enchantments of storied tradition once more. Blake's couplets had been incantations, if not auguries:

> The atoms of Democritus
> And Newton's particles of light
> Are sands upon the Red Sea shore,
> Where Israel's tents do shine so bright.

Blake was voicing a mystical reaction to Newtonian rationalism; for, as Marjorie Nicolson has demonstrated in her monograph *Newton Demands the Muse* (the title being a quotation from a minor poet, Richard Glover), Newton's *Opticks* had profoundly affected the treatment of light and color in eighteenth-century English poetry. The painter Benjamin Haydon, notwithstanding, recollects a convivial evening when Lamb and Keats agreed that Newton "had destroyed all the poetry of the rainbow by reducing it to the prismatic colors." Wordsworth, who was present, had played an ambivalent part in the ongoing argument between vitalistic beauty and analytical reason; both sides are forcefully stated in "Expostulation and Reply." He could lament, in the mood of George Eliot over her Tina, a heroine going young to her grave and being "Rolled round in earth's diurnal course, / With rocks, and stones, and trees." (A distinctive feature of Wordsworthian diction is this contrast between the distant and slightly pedantic *diurnal* and the down-to-earth monosyllables: *rocks, stones, trees.*)

Goethe had wrong-headedly devised a color-theory of his own, challenging optical instruments and mathematical physics as well as Newton in person. Yet Wordsworth, recollecting his Cambridge days in *The Prelude,* could pause respectfully before Newton's statue, "The marble index of a mind forever / Voyaging through strange seas of thought alone." And in his preface to *Lyrical Ballads* he pledged that the poet would follow the man of science, whenever the latter's investigations led to a further enlargement of man's consciousness:

> The remotest discoveries of the Chemist, the Botanist, or Mineralogist, will be as proper objects of the Poet's art as any upon which it can be employed, if the time should ever come when these things shall be familiar to us, and the relations under which they are contemplated by the followers of these respective sciences shall be manifestly and palpably material to us as enjoying and respecting beings.

Coleridge, in his retrospective account of the *Lyrical Ballads,* used the term *experiment,* possibly for the first time in literary criticism. He recounted the division of labor between the two poets by attributing to Wordsworth "the power of exciting the sympathy of the reader by a faithful adherence to the truth of nature," while relating his contributions to "the power of giving the interest of novelty by the modifying colors of imagination." At the prosaic extreme was "Goody Blake and Harry Gill," at the exotic "The Rime of the Ancient Mariner." Shakespeare had struck a happy medium, according to Dr. Johnson: "he approximates the remote and familiarizes the wonderful." Storytellers have always acknowledged the double need to contrive a tale that is interesting—which implies being novel, strange, surprising—and to tell it with credibility, so that it sounds like the truth. But the emphasis has tended to oscillate between romantic and realistic poles, between anomaly and familiarity. Aristotle had set the main direction for the West by stressing the importance of representation, the criterion of verisimilitude, the concept of *mímesis,* which Richardson would paraphrase as "copying Nature." The course of the modern European novel, as exemplified by Cervantes, was a repudiation of the medieval romance in the light of an advancing realism. In the longest of the essayistic chapters interspersed

through *Tom Jones,* Fielding discusses a topic often considered by his critical predecessors, the Marvellous. "I think," he declares, "that it may very reasonably be required of every writer that he keeps within the bounds of possibility; and still remembers that what is not possible for man to perform, it is scarce possible for man to believe he did perform." Fielding has been credited nonetheless with a work of proto-science-fiction, his facetious *Voyage to the Next World.*

"Nor is possibility alone sufficient to justify us," Fielding continues, "we must keep within the rules of probability." This Aristotelian approach was pressed harder and harder as belief in the supernatural receded or was displaced by an increasingly naturalistic worldview. The Spinozistic indentification of God with nature made it impossible to hold any further faith in miracles—that is, in events that could not be explained by natural causes. "This impulse to believe in the marvellous gradually becomes weaker," wrote the great romancer Scott, significantly while reviewing the tales of the German fantasist, E.T.A. Hoffmann. The Gothic novel had predicated a revival of wonder; and Horace Walpole's *Castle of Otranto* is haunted by spectral marvels which go unexplained with impunity; but Mrs. Radcliffe's *Mysteries of Udolpho* turn out to be all-too-human machinations which can be unmasked by detective-story disclosures. Similarly, the mystery-stories of Charles Brockden Brown beckon us toward pseudo-scientific resolutions; whereas the ironic Hawthorne liked to shade his transcendental enigmas with a penumbra of ambiguity, such as the question of Donatello's ears in *The Marble Faun.* Generally speaking, so long as western culture has been pervaded by the idea of progress, writers have done whatever they could to keep pace with the march of intellect. Professor Nicolson has shown that the animalcules of *Gulliver's Travels* would have been unthinkable without the microscope. When Dryden undertook to dramatize *Paradise Lost,* he began with Adam wakening to consciousness and pronouncing these first words: "Who am I? or from whence? For that I am / *(Rising)* I know because I think." The initial thought of this primordial man—the realization that he must now exist because he has discovered his identity through the process of thinking—marks him as a sophisticated thinker of Dryden's period, a Cartesian rationalist.

In his programmatic book, *L'Avenir de la science,* drafted during the revolutionary ardors of 1848 and published somewhat anticlimactically in 1890, the ex-priest Renan proclaimed that science had become a religion, which would be creating the symbols and solving the problems of the future through its *"sacerdoce rationaliste,"* its community of *savants.* Many influential men of letters proved willing to accept that secular credo. Just as life was being demystified by science, so it would be demythologized by literature. "In my opinion," remarked Flaubert, "the novel should be scientific—that is to say, should be based on probable generalities." Though the qualification may point back toward Aristotle, Flaubert's rigorous professionalism is reflected in his documentary research and stylistic precision. Sainte-Beuve, in his well known review of *Madame Bovary,* suggested that the novelist wielded his pen as his surgical father and brother had been handling their scalpels. But the real exemplar was Balzac, who had presented his *Comédie humaine* as a series of studies in natural history. He had eagerly followed the debate on the interrelationship of animal species between Cuvier and Geoffrey Saint-Hilaire, to whom *Le Père Goriot* is dedicated. In the foreward declaring his intentions for the whole series, Balzac proposed a social taxonomy similar to that of the naturalists. However, in addition to the male and female sexes, he introduced a third category, things. What had been mere background was advanced to the foreground; the function of material objects in men's and women's lives became a major component of Balzac's realism; and, as the nineteenth century developed its metropolitan habitats and technological industries, later novelists would more explicitly register the impact of reification.

Zola, roughly starting out where Balzac left off, and adhering to more radical views of both society and nature, made it his aim to show how men and women were being subordinated to things. A moment ago, when I spoke of *naturalists,* I took the word as an old-fashioned synonym for biological scientists, whether botanists or zoologists. Zola would not have us take it otherwise; *"Le naturalisme,"* he announced, *". . . c'est l'anatomie exacte."* Taking *naturalism* as his novelistic slogan was to intensify the rigor of his philosophical determinism. In the mean time the Darwinian theory had intervened, and its anti-anthropocentric reductionism went even farther to undermine the status of human dignity than the astronomical reductions of the Renaissance. Theodore Dreiser's rising tycoon, Frank Cowperwood, learns the lessons of social Darwinism by watching an aquarium and musing: "Things lived by each other—that was it. Lobsters lived on squid and other things. What lived on lobster? Men, of course! Sure, that was it! And what lived on men?" The answer, of course, is "men." Here in *The Financier* and in its sequel, *The Titan,* there is a struggle for existence at any rate, a Balzacian will to power. The outlook is more Zolaesque, more prone to concentrate upon more passive victims of the environment, in Dreiser's later masterwork, *An American Tragedy.* The downwardly mobile family is there envisaged as "one of the anomalies of psychic and social reflex and motivation such as would tax the skill of not only the psychologist but the chemist and the physicist as well, to unravel." The disaffection of the conditioning milieu serves to reinforce "those rearranging chemisms upon which all the morality and immorality of the world is based." Psychology, as well as ethics, is reduced under such conditions to the irredeemable pessimism of a cosmic shrug.

Zola's mentor had been the eminent physiologist Claude Bernard. "The novelist who studies habits complements the physiologist who studies organs," he commented when Bernard was succeeded by Renan at the Académie Française. Zola looked upon himself as such a novelist, and had found his guide in Bernard's *Introduction à l'étude de la médecine expérimentale.* His manifesto, *Le Roman expérimental,* consists mostly of quotations and paraphrases from that medical treatise, routinely and naïvely making the verbal substitution of *romancier* for *médecin.* Zola believed that he had been employing such exact procedures in his twenty-volume sequence, *Les Rougon-Macquart,* wherein he delineated the patterns of advancement and deterioration through the genealogy of two related families. Now experimentation is controlled observation, as Zola echoed Bernard; yet, in its application to fictional constructs, that notion can be no more than a metaphor. Zola surpassed all previous novelists in his reliance on carefully documented observation; but he had no control over what he observed, whereas his control over what he recorded could be subjective and arbitrary. His presentation of his material, as he elsewhere admitted, was "an aspect of nature viewed through the medium of a temperament." Part of the confusion may derive from the equivocal French noun *expérience,* which signifies both a laboratory test and an acquaintance with life. A novelist tends to be, in T. S. Eliot's phrasing, "expert beyond experience." He can play God with his characters, if he so wishes, determining their hereditary destinies by any set of doctrinaire presuppositions he chooses to espouse. Actually, Zola had no physiological data of any exactitude. He simply made his story-lines conform to certain genetic theories, currently under challenge and subsequently discredited. Hence his method rested not upon induction but on deduction, the very antithesis of scientific empiricism.

In its formal aspect, there is not very much that seems strikingly experimental in Zola's fiction—as contrasted, for instance, with the novelties of technique and style in *Tristram Shandy.* Furthermore, the history of ideas can teach us that Sterne's meandering and fragmented monologue parodied the epistemology of Locke, plus the associations and sensations of eighteenth-century psychology. Given the sensitivity of fiction to its cultural climate, it was bound to reflect the growing assimilation of conceptions shaped by and gathered from science. The reaction could be critical, as in Turgenev's *Fathers and Sons.* There the protagonist Bazarov is a chemist and medical student, a thoroughgoing materialist who despises Pushkin and venerates Bunsen, Liebig, and Büchner, who vivisects frogs and preaches nihilism. Inevitably a conflict between generations provokes a duel in which little is resolved. A parallel dialectic was being argued out across Europe on the educational plane. Matthew Arnold's essay, "Literature and Science," was delivered first as a Rede Lecture, seventy-seven years before C. P. Snow would avail himself of that Cambridge platform to propound his views on the two cultures. Arnold in his turn was replying to T. H. Huxley's "Science and Culture," a plea for introducing more of the sciences into the curriculum. Arnold conceded that educated persons ought to know something about their own bodies and about the corporeal world they inhabited. However, he contended that if they were acquainted with the factual results of scientific investigation, they could leave the experimental methods to specialists. It is evident, in retrospect, that Arnold and Huxley did not totally differ in their basic notions of science. Both of them thought of it as a stable body of solid knowledge, still incomplete and needing to be organized, having been accumulated slowly in the past but lately approaching a fruition of certainty.

"At the end of the nineteenth century," Stanislaw Lem has observed in *The Investigation,* "it was universally believed that we knew almost everything there was to know about the material world, that there was nothing left to do except keep our eyes open and establish priorities." No wonder that the simplistic disseminators of such messianic beliefs had expected and even planned a scientific take-over in all fields of human endeavor, as with the positivistic religion of Auguste Comte or the social statics of Herbert Spencer. The exploits of technology, particularly in the United States, urbanized and electrified the ubiquitous landscape. Mark Twain's Sir Boss could stage a confrontation between Yankee know-how and old-world legend; but Huck Finn has been fading into nostalgia, having lighted out from a civilization personified not so much by Aunt Polly as by the teen-age inventor, Tom Swift. The twentieth century seemed to herald a millennium, through its progress-marking expositions and lunar futuramas. It is no accident that the nineteen-twenties, whose lifestyle was shaped by such culture-heroes as Edison, Ford, Burbank, Marconi, and Lindbergh, witnessed the new wave of science-fiction magazines, or that *Amazing Stories* could flaunt the motto: "Extravagant Fiction Today . . . Cold Fact Tomorrow." When Jules Verne criticized H. G. Wells for unduly fantasizing, for not being plausible enough in backing his pseudo-inventions with corroborative detail, Verne was acknowledging the extent to which he and his followers had been working within the realistic conventions. Conrad evoked "the Realities of the Fantastic" in this very connection; Michel Butor would call for their counterpart, *"un fantastique encadré dans un réalisme."* Latterly, with cybernetic systems and nuclear bombs and rockets, reality has been outdoing fantasy and rapidly proceeding from the millennial toward the apocalyptic.

Aldous Huxley, as the literary scion of a scientific dynasty, has commented upon the comparative slowness and uninventiveness of the earlier futurological authors in transcending the undeveloped technologies of their day. To the several examples he has cited, we might add that of Poe in *"Mellonta Tauta,"* where balloons are still the primary means of aerial transportation in the year 2848—a thousand years after the story's date—and the railways have so expanded that they now utilize twelve tracks rather than two. (That, at least, was an optimistic projection.) "Rooted as they are in the facts of contemporary life," Huxley concluded, "the fantasies of even a second-rate writer of modern science-fiction are incomparably richer, bolder, and sharper than the utopias or millennial imaginings of the past." Those developments which we have chiefly been considering were related to an epoch of positivism in science, which bore a special relation to the epoch of realism in literature, as we have seen. This movement has continued, with due allowance for time-lag, well into the present. Yet, away from its

near-certitudes, there has been a quantum leap into the more restless epoch of Heisenberg's uncertainty, Gödel's indeterminacy, Einstein's relativity, and the apprehension of bright planets collapsing into black holes. The old and outmoded ideal was one of steady accumulation and continuous progression, filling in the gaps and rounding out the contours of a single, well-defined system, so that Einstein could affirm that nature had been an open book to Newton. But, as Thomas Kuhn has been demonstrating, science moves in intermittent cycles and in uncharted directions. Obviously the positivists of the nineteenth century were basing their presuppositions on paradigms differing from those envisaged by our twentieth-century relativists, and were therefore offering different models to be culturally absorbed or emulated. All that can be confidently predicted, in the face of another scientific revolution, is an utter change in implicit values and sustaining attitudes.

To revert to the novel again is to perceive an analogous shift. Its turning-point has been Joyce's *Ulysses,* which earned immediate notoriety as the *nec plus ultra* of naturalism, but has since been exercising leadership as an introjector of symbolism in fiction. Joyce's youthful surrogate, Stephen Dedalus in *A Portrait of the Artist as a Young Man,* had confessed himself an indifferent member of a college class in physics. Leopold Bloom, the latterday Ulysses, differs from Stephen so diametrically that, when they are finally brought together, they are visualized as respective examples of the artistic and the scientific temperaments. But Bloom, a self-educated common man blandly up-to-date in 1904, can invoke no more than the prevalent commonplaces of popular science. Two physical principles come and go in his mind throughout that crucial day. One is the law of falling bodies ("thirty-two feet per sec"); and the other "parallax," the apparent displacement caused by a change of vantage-point in astronomy. Both have their thematic significances for the symbolic interplay. The chapter that brings the two protagonists *tête-à-tête* over a belated cup of tea, "Ithaca," has been labelled a catechism; but it is much more like an examination paper in its worked-up factuality. Its questions and answers elicit detailed statistics about the flow of water from the reservoir to Bloom's kitchen tap, or the calorific effect of the stove upon the teapot. When the pair exchange their farewells on the doorstep, the starry night is specified in astronomical terminology. Bloom's final—if not uncontested—resting place, his wife's bed, is designated by longitude and latitude. The last line, inadvertently omitted from many editions, is a small black dot suggesting that the earth itself has been whirling off into "the cold of interstellar space."

Here the artistic, not the scientific, temperament, was the demiurge that created a fabulous artifact. If *Ulysses* carried the literal reproduction of daily routine about as far as it could be conveyed in serious prose, it simultaneously opened the way for a renewal of fantasy. Not that the naturalistic movement had ever completely succeeded in grounding the marvellous. Henry James lent his prestigious *cachet* to the composition of ghost stories. The devil makes an appearance in *The Brothers Karamazov,* as does an angel in André Gide's *Faux-monnayeurs,* and God reveals Himself in G. K. Chesterton's detective-story, *The Man Who Was Thursday.* The posthumous emergence of Kafka's fables contributed to the vein of anti-realism. That latitude for the imagination which Hawthorne had requested, and on which he based his distinction between the novel and the romance, is manifest in the writing of such contemporaries as J. L. Borges, Günter Grass, Italo Calvino, and Thomas Pynchon. To collate the three editions of I. A. Richards's *Science and Poetry* (1926, 1935, 1970) is to observe that this sensitive critic, moving from a quasi-positivistic analysis to a neo-romantic defense of poetry, has completely reversed his stand. It may not be impertinent to note that Professor Richards, who had his university training in logic and psychology, has himself become a poet during his elder years. The pace at which the hot facts of our century have outdistanced its anticipatory fictions, has led to suspensions of disbelief far deeper and more widespread than anything Coleridge could have prophesied, in his romantic recoil from the predispositions of eighteenth-century rationalism. A pivotal event was the crisis of 1938, when Orson Welles' broadcast dramatization of an invasion from Mars, as conceived by H. G. Wells, spread panic through whole suburbs of radio listeners.

Another case in the annals of our subject had a genuine cause and an opposite consequence. After the Sputnik entered its first trajectory, as you are doubtless aware, there was a marked—if temporary—decline in the circulation of science-fiction. Reality, on that rare occasion, had come nearer than usual to satisfying man's appetite for amazement. But, although the knowable is necessarily limited, there can be no limits to the unknown; and, for space-opera, the sky itself is not necessarily the limit. The surrounding "mystery of things," to borrow a Shakespearean phrase, is irregularly and sporadically penetrated by reason's lights. This is what makes it so much easier to believe than to doubt, though it is sometimes tempting to speculate or extrapolate; new beliefs are posited upon such speculations and extrapolations, to be either taken on faith or tested by experiment. Whenever institutions or ideologies formed around traditional beliefs are questioned or rejected, then a swarm of esoteric cults seems to creep forth from underground. The Enlightenment, for all its skeptical inclinations, harbored sects of Illuminists, Rosicrucians, and Swedenborgians. During the very years of the French Revolution, a minor playwright and advocate who was participating in it, C. G. T. Garnier, published at Amsterdam a collection of thirty-nine volumes: *Voyages imaginaires, romanesques, merveilleux, allégoriques, amusants, comiques, et critiques: suivis des songes et visions, et des romans cabalistiques.* These included translations of *Robinson Crusoe* first of all, *Gulliver's Travels* (with a French sequel), and *The Life and Adventures of Peter Wilkins* (their once-popular derivate), along with such other pioneering excursions as Voltaire's *Micromégas* and Holberg's *Nils Klim.* It is not without

significance that they were intermixed with "visions" and supernatural fantasies, and that Garnier also edited *Le Cabinet des fées,* a forty-one volume collection of fairy tales.

Every work of fiction, in a certain sense, constitutes an extraordinary voyage for its reader. So Tzvetan Todorov maintains in his *Introduction à la littérature fantastique,* and the sweep of the generalization is strengthened if we apply it *a fortiori* to Joyce's *Ulysses.* Travel has furnished a dynamic impetus for civilization itself, and it is their transmigrations which have logged the heterogeneous cultures into an intellectual continuum. It is not surprising when the imaginative curiosity of some self-dispatched voyagers has exceeded any viably geographical itinerary, or when historical explorations—adventurous enough on the surfaces of the earth—have been fancifully extended to subterranean or extraterrestrial regions. Travellers' tales have been proverbially heightened toward comic proportions, what with Lucian, Sir John Mandeville, Cyrano de Bergerac, Baron Münchausen, or Davy Crockett. More humanely, the interest in unexplored territories or in worlds elsewhere has converged with the utopian quest for better worlds. The retrospective outlook was elegiac and pastoral, centering upon a golden age or an earthly paradise. The future prospect, setting its sights from Bacon's *New Atlantis,* is postulated as urban and technocratic. The applications of science were largely seen, through the nineteenth century and somewhat beyond, as a means of ameliorating the quality of life, most optimistically in the utopias of Bellamy and Wells. But, with the accelerated automation of the twentieth century, utopias have been giving way to dystopias, like the bleak regimes described by Huxley and Orwell—or, more recently and worst of all, the "cacotopia" of Anthony Burgess, *1985.* The idealist, with Plato or More, embodies his ideals in another country, a lost fatherland, a heterocosm. The satirist, disillusioned by his homeland, especially when inhibited by Marxian censorship, can vent his satire on an unmapped domain, as Evgeni Zamyatin did in *We.* The Ukrainian dissenter, Mykola Rudenko, attests: "It was science-fiction that turned me into a 'renegade'."

Such Victorian prophets as Morris and Butler had sought guidelines for the future by turning back to the past. *News from Nowhere* supplanted factories with crafts and relocated townspeople in the countryside. *Erewhon* reverted to its antipodean pastoralism by staging a neo-Luddite revolt and sabotaging the oppressive machines. More currently *A Clockwork Orange,* if I read its Russo-English dialect correctly, has been protesting against the behavioral engineering of such a utopia as B. F. Skinner's *Walden Two.* Since the most violent delinquency may be regarded as an assertion of free will, Mr. Burgess seems to believe, it is morally preferable to a social rehabilitation programmed through conditioned reflexes. A comparable dialectic was provoking its counterstatements more than a hundred years before, when the Goncourt brothers jotted down their reactions to an American writer just translated:

After having read Poe. Something heretofore unnoted in criticism, a new literary world, portents of twentieth-century literature. Science as miracle, algebraic fiction, a lucid and morbid literature. More poetry, imagination with thrusts of analysis. Zadig as police investigator, Cyrano de Bergerac studying astronomy with Arago. Somewhat monomaniacal.— Things playing more roles than people; love yielding to deductions and to other sources of ideas, phrases, stories, and general interest; the basis of the novel displaced and transposed from the heart to the head and from passion to intellect; drama in liquefaction.

The fraternal diarists did not go so far as to prophesy the invention of the hydrogen bomb, but the faceless landscape they foresaw looks very much as if it had been dehumanized by one. Nor can we deny that their preview has, to some extent, come to pass. "Men and landscape interfuse," as Mr. Aldiss perceives so clairvoyantly: "Machines predominate." The Philosophes, though they did not dream of bionic androids, could conceive the human body as a mechanism: La Mettrie's *"L'homme machine."* The concentration on things, evinced by Balzac and intensified by Zola, has culminated among the authors of the *nouveau roman*: for example, in the *chosisme* of *La Jalousie,* where Robbe-Grillet's cinematic focus is less upon the men and women within a given room than on the spot left by a crushed centipede on the wall. Comparable to the impressions of the Goncourts were those of the French novelist who became the most successful of Poe's emulators. Jules Verne also sensed a certain coldness in "this positivist of a man," which he blamed on the regimented materialism of Poe's native American surroundings. Yet the latter characteristic, too, was a source of strength and originality, for it had enabled him to confront and dispel all vestiges of the supernatural: "He claims to explain everything by physical law, which he is even ready to invent, if need be."

When Verne went on to deplore Poe's alcoholic tendencies, he failed to recognize that Poe's overemphasis on "ratiocination" was like the heavy drinker's effort to convince his sober interlocutors that he is in a rational frame of mind. It is ironic—in view of such emotional Gallic responses—that, when Poe came to portray his past master of deduction and cerebration, he could not make him other than a Frenchman: M. Auguste Dupin. For the mysteries Poe conjured up there would invariably be *éclaircissements,* practical solutions to his riddles, enigmas, and parlor tricks. He enjoyed playing the self-appointed debunker of other people's hoaxes, as with "Maelzel's Chess-Player," where his exposure of an actual person concealed within the machinery of the spurious automaton constituted a Bergsonian victory of the living over the mechanical. (It is still not possible to program a computer for meeting the virtual infinitude of contingencies that could theoretically arise in a game of chess.) Poe's most ambitious undertaking, "Eureka," originally presented as a two-hour lecture on cosmogony, is nothing less than an attempt to solve the riddle of the universe. Prefacing the printed version, Poe offered it to the reader as a prose poem rather than a scientific treatise, for its beauty rather than its truth. There was not much Keatsian equivalence. On the one hand, the pseudo-professional patter borrowed from Alexander von Humboldt and the cosmographers was hardly the stuff of poetry. On the other, Poe was well advised in not pretending to be a scientist. A. H. Quinn, his loyal if pedestrian biographer, managed to extract a letter from Sir Arthur Eddington, making polite allowances for cranky amateurism and for contemporaneous misconception, while conceding some amount of credit to a romantic poet who was sufficiently interested to dabble in questions now under scrutiny by the astrophysicists.

The predominant intention of "Eureka," which could not be adjudged as either true or false, was to unify the concepts of spirit and matter, of time and space, through a single-minded commitment to the integrity of the imagination. Paul Valéry's oracular essay about it may tell us more about himself than Poe: how, on discovering it at the age of twenty, while vacillating between a career in letters and one in mathematics, it struck him with all the force of a cosmic vocation (*"voilà mon premier univers"*). And the testimonial concludes by rounding an interdisciplinary circle: "IN THE BEGINNING WAS THE FABLE!" It will always be there." The more we learn about intelligence, the more we respect its permutations and varieties, and the less we feel inclined to subdivide it crudely into two categorical opposites. "There is no science without fancy and no art without facts," as Vladimir Nabokov has written in *Ada,* that amorphous novel which includes—among so many other outlandish things—a burlesque of what the author (himself a part-time entomologist) preferred to label "physics-fiction." What we consider occult is by definition what we do not understand, and this may well expose our own ignorance in contradistinction to the expertise of the genuine professionals. But science, unsupported by direct conversance with the experimental evidence, has no more positive standing in our minds than magic; hobbits have much the same espistemological status as robots; and there is a philosophical inference to be drawn from the intermingling of science-fiction with fantasy, not excluding religious allegory and medievalized folklore, on our bookshelves and in our conference. Carlyle's formula, "natural supernaturalism," has been fruitfully revived by M. H. Abrams, and it might well be transferred from romanticism to a newer blend of pantheism, not so much a *mystique* as a resurrection of miracles without the intervention of an established God.

"Not everyone can be Lord God *tout court,* a creator of autonomous worlds, and a writer most certainly cannot," Stanislaw Lem has warned us, in a recent review of a nonexistent book. The more improbable the writer's world, the less explainable is its relation to ours—or rather, the Lord's. Science abhors transcendence, naturally enough, and transposes the supernatural to the paranormal. When the Brobdingnagian professors who examined Gulliver ended by classifying him as a freak of nature, *lusus naturae,* Swift's ironic conclusion was that they were "disdaining the old evasion of occult causes" and finding "a wonderful solution of all difficulties, to the unspeakable advancement of human knowledge." In other words, they were getting rid of the problem by sweeping it under the rug. The rigorous empiricist would take the stance of Newton: "*Hypotheses non fingo.* All that is not deduced from phenomena is hypothesis, and hypotheses—be they metaphysical, physical, mechanical, or occult—have no place in experimental philosophy." I cite the famous dictum in Newton's original Latin because the verb is suggestively linked to my subject-matter. *Fingo* here is best translated "fabricate." Thus it has the same ambiguous connotations as the Greek *poíesis,* which can mean either making something or making something up. Even more to the point, its participial substantive is the etymological precedent for our word *fiction.* Newton equated hypothesizing with fabrication or fiction: "I do not fabricate hypotheses." The Newtonian scholar, Alexandre Koyré, has pointed out that on inconsistent occasions Newton himself made use of hypothetical propositions, but that he consistently reserved the specific expression for pejorative comment on the researches of rival scientists. Modern scientific procedure, as formulated by Henri Poincaré in *La Science et l'hypothèse,* while concurring with Newton on the necessity for experimental verification, would concede that hypotheses could perform heuristic functions.

In that respect, the ultimate cosmos of science is not so far removed from the artificial microcosms of literature. "A fictive covering," Wallace Stevens has written, "Weaves always glistening from the heart and mind." And within the domain of fiction, as we have been taking notice, the fabrications of science are not so far removed from the fantasies of the literary—or, beyond the self-consciously literary, the traditional and popular—imagination. The Russian folklorist, Vladimir Propp, has worked out a *Morphology of the Folktale* which, since it breaks down narrative into its most elemental components and schematized relationships, need not vary much from one genre to another. It could be applied almost as readily to the sophistications of Proust as to the simplicities of the brothers Grimm. The dean of American folklorists, Stith Thompson, from a very different angle of observation, has compiled his *Motif-Index of Folk-Literature.* Since he has ordered his vast range of materials by a thematic scheme of classification, it is revealing to observe the principal themes: cosmogony, the creation of life, arcane knowledge, magical transactions, otherworldly journeys, ogres and ordeals, raising the dead, foreseeing and controlling the future. What are these folkloristic categories but the standard situations of science-fiction? Of course, we must allow for a certain amount of temporal adaptation. Pseudo-science may be counted upon to have modernized the technique of necromancy; but thaumaturgy continues to work its recurrent wonders, no more wonderful when manifested in witches' cauldrons than in physicists' cyclotrons. Personally, I remain enough of a skeptical rationalist to feel somewhat uneasy over the cultural currents that have been remystifying and remythologizing our precarious

century. Our technorevolutions seem to foster, not so much a rule of reason, as an efflorescence of credulity. Perhaps the last word should be left to P. T. Barnum.

John J. Brancato

SOURCE: "Kafka's 'A Country Doctor': A Tale For Our Time," in *Studies in Short Fiction,* Vol. 15, No. 2, Spring, 1978, pp. 173-76.

[*In the following essay, Brancato interprets Franz Kafka's "A Country Doctor" as a work concerned with the ultimate inadequacy of science.*]

Kafka's "A Country Doctor" is a surrealistic tale about the powerlessness of scientific man in confrontation with the brute force of nature. Although Kafka suggests the cyclical and interdependent aspects of all life, he makes it very clear that *only* man has the capacity to feel ultimately betrayed by life. This short story captures a profound sense of futility through its nightmarish quality. Coming to the end of "A Country Doctor" has the same effect as waking from a bad dream—the incubus has been lifted and we are relieved, but we also know that our anxieties, crystallized by the dream, are still very much with us.

Kafka uses a country doctor's experience, real or imagined, as a metaphor for the failure of scientific man to assuage the pain of dying. The doctor answers his alarm bell, which warns him of the death of one of his patients, but the alarm turns out to be a "false alarm," since he can do nothing to save his patient or himself from death. Equating the consciousness of the doctor with scientific knowledge, Kafka suggests that although modern man has tried to make science replace his ancient beliefs, it is unable to perform well in this sacred capacity. Modern man has worshipped science, and scientists have assumed the role of gods. Because of this apotheosis, when scientists find themselves impotent in the face of death, their self-condemnation is as great as the condemnation that they are subjected to by the general populace. In this story the country doctor becomes as helpless as the patients he is trying to cure. (An archaic meaning of the word "patient," by the way, is "to be acted upon rather than acting.")

Throughout the story we see evidence of the doctor's helplessness. When we first meet him he is in "great perplexity." He has answered his night bell but is "forlorn," "distressed," and "confused" about how to get to his "seriously ill patient." Although nature is working against him (the blizzard, the death of his own horse), he is willing to accept his role as country doctor if he can find a means of getting to the patient. When his servant Rose returns from seeking assistance, she confirms what he already knows—that no one has volunteered to help him. We see the doctor, however thwarted, accepting his role despite human selfishness and indifference. Up to this point in the story the reader can identify with the setting and the situation on a realistic level. It is then that the nightmarish quality of the plot begins.

In the dreamlike incidents that follow, Kafka gives us further objectification of the doctor's sense of futility and betrayal. There is a proliferation of those uncontrollable forces of nature that so often determine what we can and cannot do in life. On his own property the doctor discovers two horses and a groom in an abandoned pigsty. As he looks into the open door of the sty, he discovers, crouched on his hams, a groom who offers to yoke up two horses. The doctor and Rose laugh at what they unexpectedly find in their own backyard. In language that suggests the process of defecation (a basic, natural process), the doctor describes the emergence of the horses from the sty—horses who "by sheer strength of buttocking squeezed out through the door hole," and whose bodies "steam thickly." The doctor's momentary relief at finding a way to get to his patient is negated when the groom bites Rose's face. The doctor calls the groom a "brute" but at the same moment feels he cannot condemn one who is offering help when no one else has. Sensing this acceptance, the groom does not even respond to the doctor's threat. ("Do you want a whipping?") The entire sequence suggests man's dilemma in confrontation with the inexplicable forces of nature. From out of his "yearlong uninhabited pigsty" (his farm is effete) comes an opportunity to get where he wants to go. The condition is that he will have to lose Rose, his only human contact on the farm and a person whom he has taken for granted. Nature, benign or malignant, has offered help, but not without exacting a toll. The scientist must often abandon his own comforts and humane concerns if he wants to have any effect at all. He laments the loss of his Rose, but he justifies his complicity with the groom by telling himself that he is doing his official duty.

The groom may represent natural man—or the devil. (One meaning of the word groom—"a forked stick used by thatchers"—is reminiscent of representations of the devil.) The doctor's involvement with the groom is another source of his growing sense of powerlessness. The groom not only prepares the way for the doctor to fulfill his official business but also becomes Rose's "bridegroom." Although the doctor feebly protests, he can do nothing to keep the groom from this unwilling and frightened "bride." The scientist has lost control of himself, and in a "storming rush" that buffets all his senses, he arrives at his patient's house, which turns out to be uncannily close (suggesting a growing human bond). The implication is that the scientific man may submerge his own basic sexual impulses in order to answer a more altruistic call. His willingness to accept help that requires the sacrifice of Rose, however, may make him seem in league with the devil rather than God. Expediency, Kafka seems to be saying, is the rule for the modern scientist.

The veneration of his patient's family only makes the doctor feel greater powerlessness. After he is "almost lifted" out of his gig by the parents and sister, he finds himself in the "unbreathable" air of the sickroom. He wants to open a window, but duty calls him directly to his patient. The boy entreats the doctor to let him die (as though he could control life and death), while the doctor thinks "blasphemously" about the helpful gods who got him to his patient. He is reminded at this point that he cannot return to save Rose because the horses cannot be controlled. The horses, just at this moment, do what the doctor himself didn't do—they maneuver the windows open with their heads, and the parents, afraid of such unbridled forces, cry out. The horses, Brother and Sister, suggest the incubus and succubus that the family fear will take the boy's life.

Although the doctor would like to return home, he allows himself to be "cajoled" closer to the bed and "yields" to examine the boy. One of the horses whinnies loudly as the doctor puts his head to the boy's breast. (The succubus does not want the doctor to help the boy.) Oddly, the doctor finds nothing wrong with his patient. He has done his duty however, and he rationalizes his failure to find anything wrong by saying "the boy might have his way, and I wanted to die too." The doctor admits defeat: "to write prescriptions is easy," he says, "but to come to an understanding with people is hard."

Kafka has crystalized here the dilemma of the modern scientist: he can be honest or he can offer placebos. The country doctor would like to avoid the dilemma entirely, but the evidence of the "blood-soaked towel" finally gets him to admit "conditionally" that the boy is as seriously ill as he has told us at the beginning of the narrative. The horses' whinnying together at this point may be doing so not, as the doctor thinks, because the sound is "ordained in heaven" to assist his examination, but to protest his interference with the death process.

The doctor admits to the true enormity of the force he is fighting when he gives a "low whistle of surprise at the rose-red wound containing worms that "wriggle toward the light." Here the doctor suddenly uses the past tense, as if in an afterlife, to tell the boy he was past helping. The wound itself suggests cyclic regeneration. (The worms are feeding on the wound that is killing the boy.) The doctor calls the wound the "blossom" in the boy's side. Out of destruction, the scientist knows, new life will emerge.

Again the doctor is powerless—he cannot communicate what he has seen and what he knows to be the bitter truth. The boy's family won't let him. The doctor is forced to act the role of God. They are pleased that the doctor has acted by busying himself with the boy, but the doctor knows his service is futile. "They misuse me for 'sacred services'" he thinks, while the parson, who once might have offered the consolation they need, uselessly "unravels his vestments." The doctor knows he is not omnipotent, but the mystical choir is being taught nevertheless to sing "Only a doctor, only a doctor." Even after he is stripped and placed in bed with the boy, he must suffer the accusations of the dying patient. He tries to comfort the boy by telling him that his wound is not as bad as some—he even gives the boy the "word of honor of an official doctor" on this point. Here again we see the physician forced into a situation that he tries to make the best of. The doctor's being placed at the right side of the boy's wound does not position the boy at the right hand of God but on the left hand of Science, a false god. After the doctor has shared the deathbed with the boy for a little while and has attempted to mitigate his fears, he decides it is time to go home. He leaves without bothering to put on his clothes, since he hopes to be home as quickly as he came. This is not the case, and, still stripped of his clothes, recognizing a "new but faulty" song of the children that goes "O be joyful, all you patients, The doctor's laid in bed beside you!" he mounts a horse. The horses are no longer Brother and Sister but old men crawling through the "snowy wastes."

He will not reach home, for he is being led to his death by the "unearthly horses." His impotence is once again underlined when he cannot reach the fur coat hanging from a hook on the back of the gig. He knows and we know that "it [dying] cannot be made good, not ever." The inscrutable forces of nature move on, and although no one can ever take the doctor's place, his irreplaceability is no comfort to him. He is alone and alienated. No one will lift a finger to help him in the end. The alarm has indeed been false, for there is nothing he can do to keep the end from being hard. Once man tries to act by answering the night bell, he loses his innocence and feels disappointed when his presumptions about having power turn out to be incorrect. This age, for Kafka, seems the "most unhappy of ages," for science is no better than religion in assuaging pain—the pain of knowing that we must all die. "Betrayed! Betrayed!" is the country doctor's cry, and we know the reason.

Brian Conniff

SOURCE: "The Dark Side of Magical Realism: Science, Oppression, and Apocalypse in 'One Hundred Years of Solitude'," in *Modern Fiction Studies,* Vol. 36, No. 2, Summer, 1990, pp. 167-79.

[*In the following essay, Conniff views Gabriel García Marquez's* One Hundred Years of Solitude *as a critique of scientific progress.*]

In criticism of the Latin American novel, "magical realism" has typically been described as an impulse to create a fictive world that can somehow compete with the "insatiable fount of creation" that is Latin America's actual history.[1] This concept of magical realism received perhaps its most influential endorsement in the Nobel Prize acceptance speech of Gabriel García Márquez. The famous Colombian novelist began this speech, suggestively enough, with an account of the "meticulous log" kept by Magellan's navigator, Antonia Pigafetta. In the course of this fateful exploration of the "Southern American continent," the imaginative Florentine recorded such oddities as "a monstrosity of an animal with the head and ears of a mule, the body of a camel, the hooves of a deer, and the neigh of a horse" (207). In the course of his Nobel speech, García Márquez recorded many less imaginative

but equally improbable facts—"in the past eleven years twenty million Latin American children have died before their second birthday. Nearly one hundred and twenty thousand have disappeared as a consequence of repression. . . . A country created from all these Latin Americans in exile or enforced emigration would have a larger population than Norway" ("Solitude of Latin America" 208, 209)—on and on, as if he were trying to combat a plague of amnesia.

In such a "disorderly reality," Garíca Márquez explained, the "poets and beggars, musicians and prophets, soldiers and scoundrels" of Colombia had been forced to respond to one of the saddest and most productive challenges in modern literature: "the want of conventional resources to make our life credible" (208-209). Fortunately, conventional resources were not everything. So, according to conventional wisdom, "magical realism" was born, offering the type of hope that García Márquez tried to provide, in that famous speech, when he said that the writer can somehow "bring light to this very chamber with his words" (208). Perhaps magical realism might allow the writer to create in his work a "minor utopia," like the one inhabited by Amaranta Ursula and the next to last Aureliano at the end of *One Hundred Years of Solitude,* a fictive order that might somehow, like the birth of a child, affirm life in the face of the most brutal oppression. It was a novelistic act analogous to pulling a rabbit, or a child with the tail of a pig, out of a hat. It was magic.

Needless to say, critics have been quick to make use of such a powerful precept. "Magical realism" has typically been seen as the redemption of fiction in the face of a reality that is still becoming progressively more disorderly. But some critics have noted that the term, as it has most often been used, has always lent itself to certain simplifications. Most important, it has sometimes served as "an ideological stratagem to collapse many different kinds of writing, and many different political perspectives, into one single, usually escapist, concept" (Martin 102). Still, the overall optimism needs further qualification. In fact, there is another side of "magical realism," just as there is another side of magic. Not only can the conjuror make rabbits and flowers and crazed revolutionaries appear instantly, but he can also make them disappear, just as instantly. Although critics have not been quick to notice, García Márquez also sensed this darker side of magical realism. Unlike his "master" William Faulkner thirty-two years before, he could not "refuse to admit the end of mankind." Apocalypse, he was forced to admit, had become "for the first time in the history of humanity . . . simply a scientific possibility" ("Solitude of Latin America" 211). By the end of *One Hundred Years of Solitude,* apocalypse had become, perhaps for the first time in the history of the novel, just one more calamity on "this planet of misfortune" (211). When apocalypse does occur, García Márquez suggested, it will be pervaded, like so many events toward the end of *One Hundred Years of Solitude,* with a strange air of eternal repetition. It will only be the logical conclusion of the progress already brought by "advanced" ideas. In the disorderly modern world, magical realism is not merely an expression of hope; it is also a "resource" that can depict such a "scientific possibility." That is, it can depict events strange enough, and oppressive enough, to make apocalypse appear not only credible but inevitable.

On the first page of *One Hundred Years of Solitude* such a strange event occurs, an event that will recur, over and over, like the ceaseless repetition—of names and incest, solitude and nostalgia, madness and failed revolutions—that haunts the house of Buendia: the gypsies come to Macondo. For a long time, they will come every year, always "with an uproar of pipes and kettledrums," and always with new inventions, until the wars make such trips too dangerous, and the natives become too indifferent; but their first appearance is the most impressive, and the most ominous. They first appear in a distant past, "when the world was so recent that many things lacked names, and in order to indicate them it was necessary to point" (11). Into this "primitive world" the gypsies bring an omen of the future, an invention of great wonder and potential: the magnet.

Melquiades, the "heavy gypsy with the untamed beard," calls this invention "the eighth wonder of the learned alchemists of Macedonia." (11). He drags it around, from house to house, so that everyone can see pots and pans fly through the air, nails and screws pull out of the woodwork, long lost objects reappear. Like any great missionary of progress, Melquiades is concerned with enlightening the natives, so he also provides an explanation: "Things have a life of their own. . . . It's simply a matter of waking up their souls" (11).

But José Arcadio Buendia, the first citizen of Macondo, has an idea of his own. Prophet, patriarch, inventor, and murderer—José Arcadio is not a man to forsake progress. He is, in fact, "the most enterprising man ever to be seen in the village" (18). His "unbridled imagination" often takes him, along with anyone he can convince to follow, "beyond the genius of nature, and even beyond miracles and magic," just as he once led a handful of men and women on an "absurd journey" in search of the sea, the journey that resulted in the founding of their inland village (31-32). Confronted with the marvelous magnet, José Arcadio feels that it is necessary to discover a useful application. Whereas Melquiades is content to mystify the natives, José Arcadio must look, with a wonder of his own, toward the future. He comes up with an idea that is portentious, just as his technological imagination will be fatal. Through a process no one else seems to understand, he calculates that it must be possible to use this marvelous invention "to extract gold from the bowels of the earth" (12). A "brilliant idea," to a man like José Arcadio, should translate into a well-deserved profit.[2] Even though Melquiades is honest and tells him that this idea will not work, José Arcadio begins to search for "gold enough and more to pave the floors of the house." He trades in "his mule and a pair of goats for the two magnetized ingots" and explores "every inch of the region"; but he fails to find anything he considers valuable.

All he finds is "a suit of fifteenth-century armor which had all of its pieces soldered together with rust and inside of which there was the hollow resonance of an enormous stone-filled gourd" (12). Searching for gold, José Arcadio finds the remains of Spanish imperialism.

The following March, when the gypsies next appear in Macondo, they bring a telescope and a magnifying glass, "the latest discovery of the Jews of Amsterdam." Once again, Melquiades provides an explanation—"Science has eliminated distance"—and, not surprisingly, he once again mystifies the natives (12). His theory of the elimination of distance, like his theory of magnetic souls, is a fusion of chicanery and "advanced" science—and it is just as prophetic as José Arcadio's accidental discovery of the suit of armor. Even though the natives, José Arcadio in particular, are unable to understand the principles of Melquiades' discoveries, they are all too willing to assume that it is because they are not "worldly" or "advanced" enough. Melquiades' perspective, unlike theirs, is "global"; he has circled the world many times; he seems to know "what there was on the other side of things" (15). Perhaps he even believes he is being honest when he tries to comfort them by promising that such a perspective will soon be available to everyone, through the wonders of science, with no disruption of domestic tranquility, without the inconvenience of travel: "In a short time, man will be able to see what is happening in any place of the world without leaving his own house" (12).

But Melquiades' "theoretical" approach to science, just like José Arcadio's "practical" approach, suffers from a fatal blindness. Both of them are willing to assume that science is essentially democratizing. They do not undersand that José Arcadio's misdirected discovery of the rusted armor, and its "calcified skeleton," has already brought to Macondo a vision of "progress" that is both mystifying and applied—but not democratizing. Years later, after the prolonged senility and death of José Arcadio, after the innumerable deaths of Melquiades, Macondo will eventually see the outside world—which José Arcadio tried so hard to discover, which Melquiades leads them to believe he knows completely—and science will be responsible. But, by then, the chicanery of the gypsies will only be displaced by more sophisticated and more determined exploitation.

For the moment, however, José Arcadio is simply inspired by the magnifying glass, so he allows his fantasies to transport him, once again, closer to an "outside" reality that he badly misunderstands. After watching another of the gypsies' demonstrations, in which the magnifying glass is used to set a pile of hay on fire, he immediately decides that this invention has even greater potential than the magnet because it can prove useful as an "instrument of war." Ignoring the protests of Melquiades, and ignoring the legitimate fears of his wife, José Arcadio is compelled, once again, to invest in an invention. This time, he uses a more progressive currency, the two magnetized ingots and three "colonial coins." His enthusiasm prevents him from noticing that his currency is being debased. Many years later, gold, and even colonial coins, will be superseded by the banana company's scrip, which is "good only to buy Virginia ham in the company commissaries" (278); but José Arcadio will never be able to understand how the debasement of the currency helps support the domination of his people.[3] He is happy to dream of progress, to experiment, to burn himself, to almost set the house on fire, and to finally complete "a manual of startling instructional clarity and an irresistible power of conviction" (13)—thus linking, for the first time in the history of Macondo, and without noticing, scientific discovery and political rhetoric.

Then, in his zeal to improve his village, José Arcadio makes the greatest of his many misjudgments: he sends his manual to "the military authorities" (13). With it, he sends all the scientific evidence he considers appropriate, "numerous descriptions of his experiments and several pages of explanatory sketches" (13). He is determined to leave no doubt that he is ready to do his part for the perfection of military technology: if called upon, he will even "train them himself in the complicated art of solar war" (13). Nothing happens. At least, nothing happens in Macondo. But it is clearly not José Arcadio's fault that the government fails to respond. He has even anticipated Star Wars.

José Arcadio never quite recovers from his disappointment at having been denied the excitement of futuristic wars. Melquiades tries to console him with more "new" discoveries: an astrolabe, a compass, a sextant, and the alchemical equipment that Colonel Aureliano Buendía will later use to make the little gold fishes that will ultimately, and ironically, become the symbol of failed subversion.[4] José Arcadio does revive his spirits just long enough to prove that "The earth is round like an orange" (14). By this time, however, his dedication to science only convinces Ursula, and most everyone else, that he has lost what little was left of his mind. Later, when confronted with the marvel of ice, he will imagine an entire city constructed entirely of the fantastic substance; he will create a memory machine in an attempt to combat Macondo's plague of somnambulistic insomnia; he will spend sleepless nights trying to apply the principle of the pendulum to oxcarts, to harrows, "to everything that was useful when put into motion"; he will even try to execute a daguerreotype of God—but he will continue to lose faith in the reality of his fantasies. So his family must fight a losing battle, struggling to keep him from "being dragged by his imagination into a delirium from which he would not recover" (80). Finally, they all have to be content with his strange senility, interrupted only by prophecies in Latin.

The tragedy of José Arcadio Buendía is that his infatuation with science allows the government to exploit a passion that was, initially, a "spirit of social initiative." His first creations were the traps and cages he used to fill all the houses in the village with birds. He made sure that the houses were placed "in such a way that from all of them one could reach the river and draw water with the same effort" (18); he saw that no house received more

sun than another. He was, from the start, a type of "model citizen," useful to his people. It is the appearance of "advanced" science in Macondo that makes him, virtually overnight, useful to authority: "That spirit of social initiative disappeared in a short time, pulled away by the fever of magnets, the astronomical calculations, the dreams of transmutation, and the urge to discover the wonders of the world" (18). That is how his faith in progress, and the faith of his people, is betrayed.

But more important than José Arcadio's tragic disappointment, more important than his invested doubloons—which Melquiades returns in any case—even more important than his final senility, is the fact that he resolves his debate with the gypsy. Throughout the rest of the novel, scientific discoveries will continue to serve two purposes: science will mystify the citizens of Macondo and will lead to their exploitation. The novel's arresting first sentence suggests that these two purposes have always been inseparable: "Many years later, as he faced the firing squad, Colonel Aureliano Buendía was to remember that distant afternoon when his father took him to discover ice" (11). But, perhaps, if his father had avoided such discoveries, Aureliano Buendía might never have wound up before a firing squad of his own government.

The equally arresting ending of the novel is a full-scale denial of José Arcadio's ill-begotten dream. The novel's "apocalyptic closure" is a denial of progress, as conceived by either the scientist or the politician, and a momentary glimpse of the world that might have been, if the great patriarch had not been so carried away with his idea of the future—if he had tried, instead, to understand history. Only Amaranta Ursula and Aureliano, the last adults in the line of the Buendías, see "the uncertainty of the future" with enough demystified clarity to forsake progress, "to turn their hearts toward the past"; only they are not exploited (375). Their child, Aureliano, is "the only one in a century who had been engendered with love"—but by then it is too late (378). They cannot enjoy their primal, "dominant obsessions" for long; they cannot remain "floating in an empty universe where the only everyday and eternal reality was love" (374).[5] They are confronted, instead, with an end that is as ridiculous as their family's beginning: "The first of the line is tied to a tree and the last is being eaten by the ants" (381). The world has not progressed one bit. In fact, the key to understanding the present, and all of history, is not in the science so valued by José Arcadio, but in Melquiades' ancient manuscripts, written in Sanskrit. Macondo is finally devoured by the "prehistoric hunger" of the ants, then obliterated by "the wrath of the biblical hurricane" (383).

Because he is the man of technology, the man of science-as-progress, who brings together, more than anyone else, mystification and exploitation, José Arcadio is never able to forsee this end, just as he is never able to turn his obsessive nature toward love, just as he is never able to admit the kind of association that occurs to Colonel Aureliano Buendía when he faces the firing squad. He never understands, as Ursula does, that time is circular.

He never really pays any attention to the suit of armor from the past, so he never learns that the rusted coat of armor anticipates the soldiers and machine guns that will support the banana company, that the imperialism of the past prefigures the imperialism of the future. In this sense, Ursula is capable of learning; José Arcadio is not. Ursula learns, at least, that her schemes for prosperity have set her up to be betrayed. Ultimately, José Arcadio cannot understand any of these things because his view of the world shares too much with the oppressors who will take over his village in the delirium of banana fever; in other words, whether he realizes it or not, his horizon is determined by the interests he serves. As John Incladon has written, José Arcadio's fascination with scientific inventions—as sources of wealth, power, control—"reveals a frantic desire to grasp and manage his world" (53).

The difference between José Arcadio and the other residents of Macondo—who think he is crazy, when they are not following him—is merely that he is a useful citizen of the active type, whereas they are useful citizens of the passive type. The only exceptions are Colonel Aureliano Buendia and his men, but their revolutions always take place outside of Macondo. José Arcadio is doomed because he has convinced himself that "Right across the river there are all kinds of magical instruments while we keep on living like donkeys" (17). His greatest fear is that he might die "without receiving the benefits of science" (21). The village is doomed by the same belief that magic—in particular, advanced technology—is valuable in itself, uplifting, and the privileged possession of the outside world. Once the people believe that science, like all uplifting things, must come from elsewhere, that the outside world is better because it is more "advanced," then imperialism becomes much easier to justify. The gypsies' "discoveries" are always excessively foreign. Later, the residents of Macondo easily convince themselves of the innate superiority of Italian music and French sexual techniques. The Crespi brothers' business in mechanical toys, aided by their foreign looks and foreign manners, develops into a "hothouse of fantasy" (108).

If the government had only understood this inclination when they received José Arcadio's manual on solar war, they could have saved themselves a lot of time. But José Arcadio's plans did not convince them that Macondo was a regular hothouse of applied fantasy; in this sense, they did not fully appreciate their "natural resources" until they learned from Mr. Brown and the banana company.

For their part, the villagers never understand what all these foreign wonders do to them. Like José Arcadio when he bumps into the suit of armor, they let their infatuation with the promises of the future render them incapable of uncovering their past: "Dazzled by so many and such marvelous inventions, the people of Macondo did not know where their amazement began" (211). They merely enjoy, with more moderation than José Arcadio, the excitement of closing the "technical gap" that has separated them from the "outside world."[6] The bearers of science are always exoticized. At the same time, the villagers' "primitive" past is rendered so insignificant that it is not worth remembering. To them, the important things have always happened somewhere else—and their future will be determined by somebody else.

Many years later, when the government massacres thousands of civilians in order to crush a union strike, no one except José Arcadio Segundo, great-grandson of the first José Arcadio, will even be capable of remembering "the insatiable and methodical shears of the machine guns" (284). As for the rest, they will only remember what they have been taught to remember by the technocrats and by the government that supports them: "Nothing has happened in Macondo, nothing has ever happened, and nothing ever will happen. This is a happy town" (287). In this "modern" world, things always happen somewhere else. The banana company, with the help of the government, is raising the village's standard of living, so it must be benevolent. It cannot be responsible for a massacre. The irony that José Arcadio Segundo has the name of his great-grandfather is just one of the novel's, and history's, countless circles, one more indication that, despite their "progress"—or, in fact, because of their "progress"—the oppressed have been unable to learn what is really important.

The first José Arcadio has a quality of many characters in García Márquez' fiction: he is so strange, so absurd, that it seems he must be real. José Arcadio Segundo is, in this sense, his precise opposite. He sees the events of the government massacre with a clarity that suggests he is unreal. So when government troops enter the room where he has given up hiding, they cannot see him, even though they are looking right at the place where he believes he is sitting. Opposition, to such a government, must be invisible. It makes no difference that they did not actually kill him, that he jumped off the train on which the corpses had been "piled up in the same way in which they transported bunches of bananas" (284). He is merely left alone, once again, to decipher Melquiades' ancient manuscripts.

In the end, however, José Arcadio Segundo shares something important with the first José Arcadio. "The events that would deal Macondo its fatal blow"—the strike, the public unrest, the massacre, and its aftermath—take shape at the precise moment that the train begins to control the events of the novel (272). Transportation, in Colombia, has inescapable links to the desire for "progress." Auerliano Triste's initial sketch of Macondo's railroad "was a direct descendent of the plans with which José Arcadio Buendía had illustrated his project for solar warfare." Aureliano Triste believed that the railroad was necessary "not only for the modernization of his business but to link the town with the rest of the world" (209). Only Ursula, who had seen so much of the suffering that results from such schemes, understood that "time was going in a circle"; only she knew enough to fear modernization that came from "the rest of the world" (209).

The train also allows Fernanda to travel back to the dismal, distant city of her birth. She has never stopped thinking of the villagers of Macondo as barbarians; and she is so intent on her desire to sequester her daughter in a convent, away from the "savagery" of the Caribbean zone, that she does not even see "the shady, endless banana groves on both sides of the tracks," or "the oxcarts on the dusty roads loaded down with bunches of bananas," or "the skeleton of the Spanish galleon" (273). At this point it is clear that she has failed in her attempt to colonize Macondo with the manners and rituals of the inland cities; but her "internal colonialism" has been superseded, without her noticing it, by the brutal imperialism of the banana company. When Fernanda returns to Macondo, the train is protected by policemen with guns. Macondo's "fatal blow" is underway. José Arcadio Segundo has already organized the workers in a strike against the banana company, and he has already been "pointed out as the agent of an international conspiracy against public order" (276). Fernanda's two rides on the train are opposite in direction, but tell of a single effect: "civilization," modernization, and progress are finally assured, even in Macondo—if not with "proper" manners and gold chamberpots, then with guns.

The train is, if anything, even more symbolic of this "progress" in Colombia than it is in Macondo. Under the dictatorship of General Rafael Reyes (1904-1909), "British capital was, for the first time, invested in Colombian railways in substantial amounts" (Safford 232). Not surprisingly, this period saw the completion of the railway between Bogota and the Magdalena River; "Macondo" was irreversibly linked to the "outside world." But, of course, that was only the start: "As the transportation improvements of 1904 to 1940 began to knit together a national market, significant innovations occurred in other economic sectors," and it was the nationalization of Colombia's railways that made many such "innovations" possible (Safford 232-234). In the period of the strikes against the United Fruit Company, in particular, reorganization of the railroads was a central issue of American diplomacy in Colombia. The National City Bank and the First National Bank of Boston refused to extend short-term credits until a railroad bill was passed. By 1931, they demanded, in their negotiations with the Colombian government, an even greater control: "that the railroad system be taken out of the hands of the government and placed under the direction of professional management" (Randall 64). In his description of the banana strike, García Márquez makes the implications obvious: the same trains that send bananas and profits toward America transport the murdered bodies to the sea. There—both the government and the "professional management" hope—they will disappear, even from history.

The repeated follies of José Arcadio—like the name and hereditary stubbornness of his great-grandson, like Ursula's pronouncements, like the end of the novel—are attempts on the part of García Márquez to assert that history is, in some sense, circular. The "primitive" past of Latin America, like that of Macondo, might have provided countless omens of Colombia's future, if anyone would have paid attention—that is, if anyone would have

avoided the delirium of progress. From the first half of the nineteenth century, the combination of foreigners and trains was devastating, in Argentina, in Chile, in Guatemala, in Mexico, and in Uruguay. With their public services, especially the railroads, controlled by foreigners, or by governments serving foreigners—first from Paraguay, then principally from Britain, then principally from the United States—these countries faced extraordinary military expenditures, "a frenzied increase in imports," and growing debts, subject to inflationary manipulation. In Galleano's words, they "mortgaged their futures in advance, moving away from economic freedom and political sovereignty" (216-219). Later, in Colombia, the tendency to see railroads as "forerunners of progress" would be just one more failure to remember. For García Márquez, such an assertion of history's circularity is not merely a matter of philosophical speculation; it is a calculated attempt to make the outrages of oppression, ancient and recent, visible again; it is an attempt to make Colombian history credible.

After the massacre, when the train from which he has escaped slips off into the night, "with its nocturnal and stealthy velocity," on its way to dump more than three thousand murdered bodies into the ocean, José Arcadio Segundo cannot see it in the darkness; the last things he sees are "the dark shapes of the soldiers with their emplaced machine guns" (285).[7] Perhaps José Arcadio Segundo came to understand such progress as his great-grandfather could not, and perhaps that is why the government's search squad could not see *him*. For men indoctrinated by such a government, opposition must not exist.

For such men the past must disappear. That is why they seem so improbable, and so real. That is why a "resource" like "magical realism" is needed to depict them. And that is why the novel's famous "apocalyptic closure" is not only credible but also anticlimactic. Apocalypse is merely the darkest side of "magical realism," in which the "magic" and the "realism" are most completely fused, in which the most unimaginable event is the most inevitable. The "biblical hurricane" that "exiles" Macondo "from the memory of men" is "full of voices from the past, the murmurs of ancient geraniums, sighs of disenchantment that preceded the most tenacious nostalgia" (383). The ceaseless repetitions of the novel lead to this final conviction that apocalypse is only one more "scientific possibility," which the "primitive world" only understands after it is too late. Apocalypse is only the logical consequence of imperialist oppression, supported by science. The "events" that bring about the end of Macondo were actually determined much earlier, even before the trains came. The end began the first time the gypsies appeared with their foreign discoveries.

NOTES

[1] Gabriel García Márquez, in "The Solitude of Latin America: Nobel Address, 1982," describes Latin American history as such a fount (208). Gerald Martin provides a detailed and critical summary of this criticism in his essay.

[2] I have borrowed this idea from Ariel Dorfman's *The Empire's Old Clothes:* "having a 'brilliant idea' is not only what allows a contestant to win in the game of life. It is also a sign that such a victory is well deserved" (35). In the United States the belief in such radical insight is one component of our mystification of ideas, in particular our mystification of science. We want to believe that certain people have privileged access to the truth and that they have, therefore, a "natural" authority over those people who lack such insight. Dorfman explains how the government of the United States has tried to cultivate this ideology in Latin America—even through such apparently innocuous vehicles as Donald Duck, The Lone Ranger, and Babar the Elephant—as part of our effort at domination. In *How to Read Donald Duck,* referring to the United States' assistance in the overthrow of the Allende government, Dorfman and Armand Mattelart write: "There were, however, two items which were not blocked: planes, tanks, ships, and technical assistance for the Chilean armed forces; and magazines, TV serials, advertising, and public opinion polls for the Chilean mass media" (9).

[3] In his study of nineteenth-century European colonialism, Ralph Schnerb writes of Latin America: "These republics' histories may be said to be that of the economic obligations they incur to the all-absorbing world of European finance," obligations that were quickly exacerbated by "inflation, which produces depreciation of the currency." Eduardo Galeano adds, "The use of debt as an instrument of blackmail is not, as we can see, a recent American invention" (217-218).

[4] Perhaps it is no coincidence that Colonel Aureliano Buendia is both the revolutionary and the alchemist—that he is, like José Arcadio Segundo, the heir of both Ursula's indominability and Melquiades' manuscripts. For the Latin American who would resist domination, a knowledge of transformation, even alchemy, might be much more practical than it would at first appear. Galeano suggests such a connection, at least metaphorically, in his *Open Veins of Latin America,* a book that would be immensely popular in Colombia a few years after its initial publication in 1971: "Our defeat was always implicit in the victory of others; our wealth has always generated our poverty by nourishing the prosperity of others—the empires and their native overseers. In the colonial and neocolonial alchemy, gold changes into scrap metal and food into poison" (12).

[5] The final situation of Amaranta Ursula and Aureliano will become increasingly important as criticism begins to address García Márquez' recent novel, *Love in the Time of Cholera.* As Thomas Pynchon suggests, with some trepidation, in his review of that novel, critics will inevitably ask "how far" that novel, so dominated by love, has departed from the more "political" concerns of *One Hundred Years of Solitude* and *The Autumn of the Patriarch*: "we have come a meaningful distance from Macondo, the magical village in *One Hundred Years of Solitude.* . . . It would be presumptuous to speak of moving 'beyond'

One Hundred Years of Solitude, but clearly García Márquez has moved somewhere else, not least into deeper awareness of the ways in which, as Florentino comes to learn, "nobody teaches life anything" (49).

[6] I have borrowed the phrase "technical gap," as well as the basic idea of this passage, from Dorfman's reading of Babar the Elephant in *The Empire's Old Clothes.* Of course, there are systems—of ownership, of trade, of education—that keep the gap from actually closing, despite the useful illusion of progress. In this regard, see Galeano, especially the section appropriately entitled "The Goddess Technology Doesn't Speak Spanish" (265-268). Dorfman's explanation of the capitalist's equation of childhood and underdevelopment is also worth noting, especially in reference to José Arcadio's later senility. Once he abandons his hope of reaching the "outside world's" level of civilization, José Arcadio destroys his scientific equipment and allows himself to lapse into his "second childhood," to be spoonfed by Ursula.

[7] Later, José Arcadio Segundo would tell little Aureliano his "personal interpretation of what the banana company had meant to Macondo" (322). But no one would want to believe Aureliano, either: "one would have thought that he was telling a hallucinated version, because it was radically opposed to the false one that historians had created and consecrated in the schoolbooks" (322). In *Gabriel García Márquez: Writer of Colombia,* Stephen Minta provides a brief, useful summary of the surviving accounts of the 1928 strike against the United Fruit Company in Cienaga. Accounts differ, of course, in their estimates of the number murdered. Cortes Vargas, who signed the decree that "declared the strikers to be a bunch of hoodlums" and "authorized the army to shoot to kill," and whose name appears unchanged in *One Hundred Years of Solitude,* wrote his own account, in which he claims that only nine were killed. Officially sanctioned accounts typically mention "the menace of Bolshevism." But perhaps the most telling document is a telegram from the Head of the U.S. Legation in Colombia to the U.S. Secretary of State: "I have the honor to report that the Bogota representative of the United Fruit Company told me yesterday that the total number of strikers killed by the Colombian military exceed one thousand" (171).

WORKS CITED

Dorfman, Ariel. *The Empire's Old Clothes.* Trans. Clark Hansen. New York: Pantheon, 1983.

———, and Armand Mattelart. *How to Read Donald Duck.* Trans. David Kunzle. New York: International General, 1975.

Galeano, Eduardo. *Open Veins of Latin America.* Trans. Cedric Belfrage. New York: Monthly Review, 1973.

García Márquez, Gabriel. *Autumn of the Patriarch.* Trans. Gregory Rabassa. New York: Harper, 1976.

————. *Love in the Time of Cholera.* Trans. Edith Grossman. New York: Knopf, 1988.

————. *One Hundred Years of Solitude.* Trans. Gregory Rabassa. New York: Avon, 1970.

García Márquez, Gabriel. "The Solitude of Latin America: Nobel Address 1982." McGuirk and Cardwell. 207-211.

Incladon, John. "Writing and Incest in *One Hundred Years of Solitude.*" *Critical Perspectives on Gabriel García Márquez.* Ed. Bradley A. Shaw and Nora Vera-Godwin. Lincoln: Society of Spanish and Spanish-American Studies, 1986. 51-64.

Martin, Gerald. "On 'Magical' and Social Realism in García Márquez." McGuirk and Cardwell. 95-116.

McGuirk, Bernard, and Richard Cardwell, eds. *Gabriel García Márquez: New Readings.* Cambridge: Cambridge UP, 1987.

Minta, Stephen. *Gabriel García Márquez: Writer of Colombia:* London: Cape, 1987.

Pynchon, Thomas. "The Heart's Eternal Vow." Rev. of *Love in the Time of Cholera,* by Gabriel García Márquez. *The New York Times Book Review* 10 April 1988: 1, 47-49.

Randall, Stephen J. *The Diplomacy of Modernization: Colombian-American Relations, 1920-1940.* Toronto: U of Toronto P, 1976.

Safford, Frank. *The Ideal of the Practical: Colombia's Struggle to Form a Technical Elite.* Austin: U of Texas P, 1976.

Schnerb, Robert. *Le XIXe siècle: l'apogée de l'expansion européenne, 1815-1914.* Paris: Gallimard, 1968.

George Levine

SOURCE: "The Novel as Scientific Discourse: The Example of Conrad," in *Novel: A Forum on Fiction,* Vol. 21, Nos. 2 & 3, Winter-Spring, 1988, pp. 220-27.

[*In the following essay, Levine considers Joseph Conrad's fiction as a form of scientific discourse that subverts Victorian realism and Darwinian gradualism.*]

The word "discourse" in its traditional meaning implies rationality, thematic coherence, and sustained argument; it also obviously carries the suggestion of non-fiction. Discourses are about something (presumably). In modern theory, "discourse" implies something else again. With Foucault it implies a cultural and political context so that when, in a characteristic contemporary move of intellectual imperialism, we want to argue that science is only another form of discourse, we mean to be diminishing, or challenging its truth claims, and implicating it in the ideologies it has, by defining itself, excluded. Like other kinds of discourse, the argument implies, science is not exempt from epistemological limitations; it has no more claim on the real than biography, or history, or perhaps even fiction. As discourse, science is subject to the kinds of criticism to which we have been trained to subject any text. And as text, it ceases to be a transparent description of nature; it is rather a marker of difference, of absence rather than presence. It becomes a set of linguistic conventions, or of ideological predispositions. So non-fictional, even scientific discourse very rapidly becomes indistinguishable from fiction.

Important as recent concentration on "discourse" has been, differences remain after the assimilation of science to other discourses of power has been completed. There is, after all, more than a little fluttering after power, as well as much silliness, in the move to blur entirely the distinction between fiction and non-fiction. Certainly, science does need to be considered in contexts other than those professionally affirmed by scientists; and certainly, science from many perspectives can be seen as participating in the myths of power that dominate within the culture and as developing within the contexts of social and political and economic pressures (and theories). Recent studies by Adrian Desmond, Martin Rudwick, and Simon Schaffer and Steven Shapin provide superb case studies of the way this happened in different phases of English science.[1] Moreover, Malthus did, after all, provide the "Eureka" for Darwin's theory of natural selection; and Adam Smith had laid out in the world of Economics the kinds of mechanisms that Darwin was to find propelling evolution, so that Marx could argue that Darwinism simply extended laissez-faire economics into nature. Yet Darwinian theory requires different kinds of argument and different kinds of authorization than do political arguments or literature. The equation between a work of fiction and of what we might still call non-fiction must become trivial since the equation would be appropriate for *any* works. Short of universal homogenization, there are differences that remain to be accounted for and assimilations that need to be queried.

I don't, however, want to ask for an exemption for science, or to privilege it; I am only suggesting that science is obviously not simply a "fiction," whatever we might mean by that. Moreover, it needs special attention because it carries with it an authority within the culture that other forms of discourse have often attempted to imitate but have not achieved. Scientific discourse offers itself as non-fiction, as a transparent description, however tentative, of the real. It proposes to be a means to understand the workings of the world, or to the manipulation of that world beyond words. Moreover, it makes an argument, asks to be falsified, and provides quite elaborate procedures for testing; it insists on replication. Now while every aspect of this self-presentation has been importantly challenged by philosophers of science, it would be absurd not to recognize that scientific discourse is another kind of thing from the discourse of the novel. At the very least, we might allow Bas van Frassen's almost minimalist point that science asks acceptance of its propositions even if, as he says, "acceptance is not belief."[2]

The discourse of Newton's *Principia* obviously offers itself on terms very different, say, than *Tom Jones*. One gains nothing from treating them as equivalent, although something might well be gained by thinking of them as related, as expressing in alternative ways certain shared assumptions. Consider, first, how one might think about the relation between two less obviously disparate texts ostensibly from different worlds of discourse, say, Arnold's *Culture and Anarchy*—very much a cultural discourse in the most obvious senses—and *Jude the Obscure,* which found itself, willy-nilly, in the middle of social battles that Arnold would have recognized if not approved. The two books might be seen as alternative discourses, Arnold's constructing an argument by using materials drawn from social and historical worlds accepted as real by its readers, and Hardy's implying an argument by using fictional materials that are understood to "represent" a real world overlapping and contiguous with the "real" world of *Culture and Anarchy.*

But my interest in the question hasn't so much to do with the truth claims a novel might seem to be making. In the case of *Jude,* for example, what is interesting is not its obvious place in cultural battles—the marriage question, the woman question—that its first readers, like Mrs. Oliphant, recognized immediately. Hardy's novel evoked such antipathy and passion because it *felt* authentic, and it felt so because of its use of familiar terms of cultural discourse, many of which were borrowed from Arnold's analysis. The fiction oddly confirms Arnold's outrageous division of culture into the Hebraic and Hellenic, while wildly complicating it. In any case, *Jude* participates in a discourse already established as descriptive of the culture; and that we might, from another perspective, want to talk of that discourse itself as fictional in no way diminishes the point that the novel uses, participates in, even reshapes cultural discourse.

The case might be more difficult with Newton and Fielding, a connection which, as far as I know, hasn't been made; perhaps it shouldn't be made. And certainly, I don't know enough to make it. But I want to suggest the possibility that the formal structure of *Tom Jones* owes something to the way Newton's imagination of the world as a mathematically organized phenomenon reflecting intelligence, and accessible to the abstract intelligence of humanity had permeated the culture. The more obvious model is the Christian/providential one; but Fielding's book might be seen as bringing together various Christian and narrative traditions within the assumptions about order and the constitution of nature itself that Newton's work had fairly recently authorized.

Here as elsewhere, the assumptions and fundamental values of a culture, as they are formulated in the discourse taken generally to be its most authoritative, will almost certainly inform its art. In a way, that is a truism. But the play of assumptions within fiction is often no mere replication of ideas and attitudes already available elsewhere. While the novel will inevitably work with unarticulated cultural assumptions, its form can entail a rich exploration of their implications, sometimes a raising of them to consciousness and a demystifying of them, sometimes direct subversion. The symmetries and the polarities of *Tom Jones,* the solidity of characterization, the sharpness of definition and the precision of elaboration, the confidence in sequence of cause and effect in unrolling the narrative—all participate in an imagination of experience at least consonant with the Newtonian world, which was, after all, the eighteenth-century world, as well. Traditional narrative, in which cause and effect determine sequence, and in which intrusions implying design are conventional, is largely homologous with the scientific world view of early modern Western history.

However wildly unrealistic it often is, the novel as a genre speaks into (or defines itself against) a recognizable world, made recognizable because it works with the unself-conscious discourse of its own culture. The peculiar interest of science is that against the threats of various kinds of relativism and, indeed, the modern dominance of anti-foundationalist theory, it has seemed to provide one ultimate foundation. Since Newton, at least, it has become the most authoritative discourse, the one by which most people are likely to be intimidated, the one whose assertions are most likely to be accepted. Science clearly did replace religion as the definer of our faith in what the world is really like; and even the most fanatic of believers in the West are likely to seek the sanction of science for much of what they argue and believe. Creationist, anti-evolutionary arguments, note, are themselves full of scientism, insisting that Creationism is a science, and that it is more scientific than evolutionary theory, which is after all, they complain, only a "theory."

But to see it as having achieved the kind of authority hitherto belonging to religion is not to mistake its particular base in power. The very epistemological (and therefore, implicitly, social and even "spiritual") authority it has achieved makes it extremely valuable in social discourse. That is, ideology puts scientific discourse to use precisely because science, at least, seems disinterested, objective, concerned to tell the truth as in itself it really is; science is the most important discourse by which ideology is naturalized. It is the discourse that power needs to use, and the discourse that most needs to be demystified. Its pervasiveness in literature testifies to this double use.

Using scientific metaphor is as commonplace now as using Biblical metaphors would have been two hundred years ago. Most obviously, in contemporary writing, there is Pynchon's use of thermodynamics and entropy and his transformation of scientific ideas into something very like fantasy. It's worth recalling, as well, how Lawrence drops into scientific metaphor in his well-known argument against the traditional stable ego of character in *The Rainbow*: denying the individual, he talks of the ego passing through "allotropic states," of his interest being not in diamond, nor in coal, nor in soot, but in the underlying single element, "carbon." This is old stuff by now, of course, but Lawrence was importantly right in finding the conception of character linked to ostensibly unrelated aspects of science. Equally famous, if perhaps more discredited, is Zola's project described in "The Experimental Novel"—based on Claude Bernard's *Introduction to the Study of Experimental Medicine,* and realized in The Rougon-Marquart series. And although the differences are obvious, George Eliot in *Middlemarch* also self-consciously reflects on narrative as a scientific activity.

But the novelists who really know a lot about science and who self-consciously use it make a small minority. The power of science within our culture is reflected in the way it infiltrates consciousness that knows very little about it. Perhaps to put it more carefully, it shares, as Michel Serres has shown, in the dominant concerns of the culture, is in fact a powerful myth whose shape can be discerned well outside the realms of specifically scientific discourse.[3] Scientific ideas are absorbed, used, and created by a culture that is only partially aware of science as a professional practice.

While there has been much debate about how legitimate it is to transfer scientific ideas to other forms of discourse, literature makes the move frequently and easily through metaphor, sometimes to deny or satirize the transference, sometimes to accomplish it. "Social Darwinism" has often been attacked as an illegitimate metaphorizing of Darwin's biological theory; sociobiology insists that the move is not metaphorical. The constraints of biology determine the constraints of culture. In any case, literature is the place where, in the absorption, use, or rejection of science—consciously or not—the transference most frequently takes place. Criticism requires an alertness to the presence of scientific discourse, or its metaphors, not only because it helps clarify what the texts are doing, but because the texts themselves often constitute a fictional test of the science and of the transference. Participating equally but differently in the culture's myths and ideologies, science and literature support, reveal, and test each other.

To make my point, I will concentrate for the rest of this paper on a particular scientific idea, evolutionary gradualism, to suggest how it becomes a part of narrative discourse, is reflected in, reenforced, and ultimately subverted by English nineteenth-century realism and the developing modernism of Joseph Conrad.

The English nineteenth-century novel, reflecting and inspiring dominant assumptions about what reality and nature are really and naturally like, seemed to entail a gradualist reading of change. At the same time, those guiding assumptions about what is real, usually also implying an ethical imperative to behave "naturally," concealed their own incoherence. Darwin's argument stands behind both the gradualism and the incoherence. Geological and biological gradualism was so fundamental

an aspect of the way reality was understood that it helped determine the way novels were written and was almost automatically transferred from the realms of science to the realms of society and politics.[4]

Certainly, within Victorian realism, which in narrative method stresses continuity and connection, attempt at radical change is perceived as violent, a disruption of normal human and social relations: the disruption of the idea of the organic community or the natural human bond, as in Hetty Sorrel's murder of her illegitimate infant, or Sikes's murder of Nancy.

Victorian realism and Darwinian evolution tend to be mutually supporting imaginations of the real, whose structures are most obviously threatened by the possibility of catastrophic change. Darwin staked everything on the view that Nature does not take leaps. So did Victorian novelists. When Razumov, in *Under Western Eyes,* scrawls "evolution not revolution," he says no more—though more desperately—than George Eliot did: "what grows up historically can only die out historically."[5]

The language of *The Origin of Species* is the nineteenth century's most imaginative and powerful denial of catastrophic change, and became its most powerful text for the denial of revolutionary change as well. Here is some rather neutrally formulated language, but one can see how easily it could be adapted to political argument:

> *Why should all the parts and organs of independent beings, each supposed to have been separately created for its proper place in nature, be so invariably linked together by graduated steps? Why should not Nature have taken a leap from structure to structure? On the theory of natural selection, we can clearly understand why she should not; for natural selection can act only by taking advantage of slight successive variations; she can never take a leap, but must advance by the shortest and slowest steps.*[6]

For Darwin, this is not merely a description of Nature, but a defense of science; for science itself was at stake in this argument. Uniformitarianism, allowing no causes but such as are now in operation, was what Darwin learned from his mentor in geology, Charles Lyell. Once the possibility were allowed of intrusion beyond the explanatory power of natural law, natural law could not be relied upon either for inference or prediction. George Eliot, we remember, similarly depended heavily for her moral teaching on laws of necessary sequence, and the deterministic implications of her narratives issue from the same extension of scientific law to human activity.

But there is a gap in the Darwinian argument—as in realist narratives—through which chance and potential disruption emerge. We may understand why natural selection allows some variations to survive and others not, but the variation is a sudden and unexplained intrusion on the lawful processes of nature. The variation appears as "chance" (although Darwin wished to avoid the implication) and as sudden and unexplained as the intrusion of Haldin into Razumov's rooms at the beginning of *Under Western Eyes*. Into the law-bound system that Darwin was attempting to create, lawlessness immediately thrusts itself.

While the uniformitarian basis of Darwin's arguments, which parallel closely the methods and themes of realistic fiction, implicitly denies the possibility of successful revolution, the true generating power of Darwin's theory was what he could not reduce to law, nor account for by gradualism.[7] The great spokesman for gradualism, Darwin needed to disguise or downplay those aspects of his theory and argument that would not fit uniformitarian theory. And in its duality, Darwin's theory exposes by analogy fundamental contradictions in the Victorian realist project, which also entails an implicit commitment to gradualism but invariably must include in its resolution elements that resist gradualist interpretation. The determination to view all experience from the perspective of the ordinary closes out the possibility of real change and locks all characters into an organic-determinist system. But the conventions of coincidence by which even a novel like *Middlemarch* releases its protagonists from social or psychological imprisonment do not so much represent a retreat from the ideals of realism as a necessary element in any imagination of the possibility of real change and growth in the realist's world.

Conrad's fiction is at least as ideologically conservative as that of the realists who preceded him and whose techniques he was coming to reject. The use of science for such ideologically conservative purposes suggests again how the authoritative discourse of science is implicated in a broader cultural discourse. Science can be used spuriously to authorize political positions. What is interesting about Conrad in this respect is that while his narratives reflect the breakdown of belief in Darwinian gradualism, that very breakdown is taken for authority for an even more intense and irrational conservatism. That is, as he rejects the conventions of narrative that have traditionally been allied with antirevolutionary political attitudes, he explicitly commits himself even more ferociously to such attitudes while—as, say, with the famous figure of the sailor in *Heart of Darkness*—he invokes arbitrarily the discredited traditional realist and gradualist positions to reaffirm the necessity of political stability.

Most narratives turn on the convergence of at least two narrative lines, as when Haldin and Razumov meet. But such convergence almost always has the effect of surprise or even shock. We can even detect this in the way Darwin uses it, for in order to bring home to us the interdependence of all organisms he seeks for examples that emphasize the unlikeliness of convergences. There is a quality of wonder as Darwin explains how the enclosure acts helped "determine the existence of Scotch fir": careful study had shown him that where cattle graze the fir gets no chance to grow. Then he goes on to show that "in several parts of the world insects

determine the existence of cattle."[8] Clearly, the enclosure acts were not designed to affect the growth of Scotch fir, nor do the flies of Paraguay act in order to affect the life of cattle. Any "design" to be inferred from the intersection must be the consequence of omniscience. In fiction, novelists must devise plausible ways to bring narrative lines not ostensibly related to each other by design or intention into contact. Seen from this perspective, the device of omniscient narrator is not an accident of nineteenth-century realism, but a condition of it. Once allow not only that limitation of perspective is a condition of all actors, but that omniscience is impossible, and the realist project of discovering the paths of necessary sequence breaks down. It becomes conceivable not only that none has the power to discover the paths, but that the paths are not there in the first place.

The conservative Professor of *Under Western Eyes* radically subverts the gradualism of Darwinian evolution in the very way he tells his story. He becomes spokesman for other aspects of the Darwinian program—the element of chance, and the fundamentally irrational and inhuman energies of nature. The Professor's story implies—with the authority of Darwinian science behind it—the arbitrariness of the very civilization that Darwinian science had been used to authorize in the earlier tradition. "Words, as is well known," the Professor notoriously says, "are the great foes of reality."[9] Ironically, science lies behind this, the science that posits an irrational source and material explanation for life. In *Under Western Eyes*, narrative is a series of disruptions, and explanations are delayed as long as possible, in some cases never clearly made. The realist preoccupation with ordinary details becomes, in Conrad, phantasmagoric. Ironically, in every respect Conrad's world and Conrad's fiction announce the separation of language from its material base, the unnaturalness, then, of language, and of fiction itself.

The scientific discourse of Conrad's fiction leads to the positing of a reality beyond language, but a reality from which fictions protect him. That reality is, indeed, revolutionary, in the sense that it is governed not by regularities, but by irrationalities, by forces incomprehensible to human consciousness, and violently threatening. Aware of the artificiality of human constructs, Conrad does not move to a revolutionary displacement: instead he is committed to supporting them in their artificiality against the deep irrationality of phenomena.

Absorbing scientific ideas, Conrad writes narratives filled with the pain of living in a world governed by the assumptions of the scientific enterprise and the traditions by which science had come to assert its Huxleyan imperialism in relation to all knowledge. Conrad explores the difficulties of seeing the human within the context of the nature science was describing. Conrad's modernism is not an escape for scientific discourse but another selective use of it; and its profound authority shapes his world. It informs his critique of a realism which was itself based in a "scientific" discourse. His techniques of disruption, discontinuity, of elaborating a radical distrust of language, lead to a vision of the world that totally undercuts the gradualism in which Darwin and Victorian realism had invested so much. As he describes a revolutionary, chance-ridden, disruptive nature, he sees the anti-revolutionary stance of realism itself as a conventional and arbitrary construction of nineteenth-century bourgeois imagination, like the domestic dullness of Geneva presided over by a statue of Rousseau. He exposes the contradictions latent in that construction in the image of the revolutionary cabal developing in the heart of Geneva. Razumov, ironically, is saved by being thrust into the irrational truth of nature; he becomes a scientist in that by losing his capacity to hear words, he stops being a foe of reality.

Conrad finds sanction for his chancy world in the very Darwin whose gradualism was a scientific manifestation of realist ideology. He finds in Darwin's revelation of the irrational sources of human rationality evidence for the arbitrariness of civilization. He finds in the mechanical and mindless and anti-teleological structure of Darwin's world clues for the writing of a new kind of disruptive and fragmented narrative. And ironically, he seeks in the gradualist conventions of Darwin's narrative, his overt refusal of mystery and irrational disruption of law, the moral sanction for an anti-revolutionary position which he did *not* find endorsed in nature.

The relation between science and narrative here is characteristically complex. The two discourses provide a running commentary and critique of each other. And the critic gains immensely from learning how to hear the dialogue.

NOTES

[1] See Adrian Desmond, *Archetypes and Ancestors: Palaeontology in Victorian London* (London: Blond and Briggs, 1982); Steven Shapin and Simon Schaffer, *Leviathan and the Air Pump* (Princeton: Princeton University Press, 1985); and Martin Rudwick, *The Great Devonian Controversy: The Shaping of Scientific Knowledge Among Gentlemanly Specialists* (Chicago: University of Chicago Press, 1987). Rudwick, however, is concerned to demonstrate that the process of scientific thinking and argument, deeply rooted in social and biographical causes, is nevertheless epistemologically sound. In a fascinating final chapter, he considers the question of whether "consensual victory of one particular interpretation was due to its objective superiority in explanatory terms or to the superior rhetorical skill and firepower of those who advocated it" (p. 438).

[2] Bas C. van Frassen, "Empiricism in the Philosophy of Science," in *Images of Science,* ed. Paul M. Churchland and Clifford A. Hooker. Chicago: University of Chicago Press, 1985), p. 247. Van Frassen's theory of "Constructive Empiricism" is anti-realist, but attempts to account for the success of science by, among other things, demonstrating the irrelevance of truth claims to scientific argument, whose acceptance does not require belief.

[3] See *Hermes: Literature, Science, Philosophy,* ed. Yosué V. Harari and David F. Bell (Baltimore: Johns Hopkins University Press, 1982).

[4] Since this paper was completed, Stephen Jay Gould's impressive study of uniformitarian ideas in geology has appeared. Gould brilliantly demonstrates how the idea of deep time in geology and the idea of gradual, directional change were implicated in major ideological and religious attitudes. Neither Hutton nor Lyell, the two great British propagandists for gradualism, produced their theories out of empirical evidence, though both writers were persuasively "scientific." The crossing between "scientific" and cultural discourses was constant and powerful. See Stephen Jay Gould, *Time's Arrow, Time's Cycle* (Cambridge, Mass: Harvard University Press, 1987).

[5] Joseph Conrad, *Under Western Eyes* (Garden City, N.Y.: Anchor Books, 1963), p. 54. *Essays of George Eliot,* ed. Thomas Pinney (New York: Columbia University Press, 1963), p. 287.

[6] Charles Darwin, *The Origin of Species by Means of Natural Selection, or The Preservation of Favoured Races in the Struggle for Life,* first edition, ed. J. W. Burrow (Harmondsworth, Middlesex: Penguin Books, 1959), pp. 223-224.

[7] Although it was possible to derive from Darwin's arguments, stripped of their creative multivalence, a strictly determinist and rather bleak view of the workings of nature, his language and the structure of his argument left a wide space for creativity. Gillian Beer has analyzed his language in several works to show how important to Darwin's science was the unresolved excess of meaning in his language. "He gives room," she says, "for mystery, for exploration, and insists upon the dark space behind the summary formulation of 'the struggle for life.'" See "Darwin's Reading and the Fictions of Development," in David Kohn, ed., *The Darwinian Heritage* (Princeton: Princeton University Press, 1985), p. 572. Beer also argues that "it was the element of obscurity, of metaphor whose peripheries remain undescribed, that made the *Origin* so incendiary—and that allowed it to be appropriated by thinkers of so many diverse political persuasions" (p. 574). This is certainly partly the case; but I would want to argue that *any* scientific argument might be put to almost any political use because scientific argument allows metaphorical extension.

[8] *The Origin of Species,* p. 124.

[9] *Under Western Eyes,* p. 1.

Robert Crossley

SOURCE: "Olaf Stapledon and the Idea of Science Fiction," in *Modern Fiction Studies,* Vol. 32, No. 1, Spring, 1986, pp. 21-42.

[In the following essay, Crossley studies the writings and views on science fiction of Olaf Stapledon.]

Unlike his great predecessor H. G. Wells, Olaf Stapledon never wrote an essay on the genre of the scientific romance or about the influences on his own imagination. Wells's career endured long enough for him to see a collected edition of his works and numerous reissues of separate texts. Sometimes he contributed Forewords to such later editions, but one of them—a 1933 omnibus of his best-known scientific romances—prompted a retrospective Preface surveying his entire achievement in what he called "my fantastic stories" (240). Although there is some self-disparaging revisionism as Wells, approaching seventy, looks back over his shoulder at books written mostly in his thirties, the Preface to *The Scientific Romances* is important as a record of his thoughts about his literary genealogy, as an account of intentions and aspirations, and as a compact Wells's Rules of Order designed to help the reader of fantastic fiction "to play the game properly" (241).[1]

If Wells downplayed the artistic and social value of the "playful parables" of his younger days, he was still careful to outfit himself with a distinguished and selective pedigree. He claimed descent from Apuleius, Lucian, Swift, and Mary Shelley, but he disavowed kinship with his one rival for the title of the originator of modern science fiction. Contesting the reviewers who used to call him "the English Jules Verne," Wells insisted that "there is no literary resemblance whatever" between their two kinds of fiction (240).[2] Verne, he said, was an ingenious forecaster interested in "practical" applications of science, but the typical Wellsian fantasy had a human rather than a mechanical center, and it aspired to exercise the reader's moral imagination. In addition to locating himself within a tradition of ethically based fantasy, Wells emphasized three principles governing his scientific romancing: the author's need "to *domesticate* the impossible hypothesis" by yoking the beautiful lies of fiction to current scientific theory, or at least to enough scientific jargon to cover the tale decently; the critical and satirical function of exotic or extraterrestrial locales used "in order to look at mankind from a distance"; and Arnoldian and antiescapist commitments to be "critical of life" and "to make the stories reflect upon contemporary political and social discussions" (241-243). Despite Wells's disinclination to wrap himself in the mantle of "Art," the Preface to *The Scientific Romances* offers a strikingly serious defense of what he called "fantasy" and is one of the first coherent statements toward a definition of the aesthetic of science fiction.

It would be natural to expect Olaf Stapledon to continue Wells's effort to define and legitimize the form. Next to Wells, he was the most original practitioner of the scientific romance in the first half of this century. Professionally trained as a philosopher, much more patient with—and drawn to—abstraction than Wells, he ought to have been better equipped to formulate a theory of science fiction. Besides, he had a personal motive for stating a distinctive aesthetic of the literary forms he was pioneering. From the day Stapledon's first novel, *Last and First Men,* appeared in 1930, reviewers noticed, and overstated, his work's resemblance to Wells's. Just as Wells was irritated by being known as an English Verne, so Stapledon labored under the burden of having all his most innovative books tagged as "Wellsian romances" by critics unable to find a more accommodating pigeonhole for his disturbing visions of far futures and present oddities.[3]

But what did Stapledon think he was up to when at the age of forty-four he started publishing speculative fictions on a scale vaster and more inhuman than anything of Wells's? Scholars looking for wider frames of reference for naming Stapledon's literary ambitions and assessing their products have been confounded by his apparent reticence on the whole subject of the scientific romance. There are scattered clues to his sources of inspiration to be found in references tucked away in odd pockets of his books: the acknowledgement to Gerald Heard in the prefatory note to *Last Men in London* (vi), or the allusion made by the narrator of *Odd John* to J. D. Beresford's 1911 novel *The Hampdenshire Wonder* (6), or the homage to Edwin Abbott's Victorian mathematical fantasy *Flatland* in the description of dying stellar worlds in *Star Maker* (405). But even a diligent collector of such fugitive references would not emerge with a very coherent picture of Stapledon's reading. It is amusing, for instance, to come upon the intelligent, self-improving dog in *Sirius* making his way through Wells's *Outline of History* (217) and to have Stapledon tell us in the introductory note to that novel that he was influenced by a "delightful" book on sheep dogs (163), but what we really want to know is whether Stapledon was thinking about *Frankenstein* when he wrote *Sirius.* For more substantial critical perspectives we can go to Stapledon's *Scrutiny* essay on "Escapism in Literature," but it focuses almost exclusively on the political content and conduct of literary texts with little direct reflection on the kind of fiction he himself wrote.[4]

Until recently the closest things we have had to an exposition of the poetics and ideology of Stapledon's fiction have been the short Prefaces he attached to some of his books, notably *Last and First Men* and *Star Maker.* They are important for understanding his concern to write romances that are philosophically sound and socially responsible, but focused as they are on freshly composed single works, they lack the resonance and rich applicability of Wells's retrospective Preface. In introducing *Last and First Men* Stapledon outlines his central fictional principle that future-fiction is a medium for designing cultural myths. Because "the merely fantastic has only minor power," he writes, the mythic romance exercises "controlled imagination" in the service of a "serious attempt to envisage the future of our race" and "to mould our hearts to entertain new values" (9). The Preface to *Star Maker,* with the Spanish Civil War in the foreground and the prospect of a second Great War on the horizon, stresses the politics of fantasy and defends the exploration of imaginary worlds and distant times in a period of terrestrial crisis. The "attempt to see our turbulent world against a background of stars" may heighten awareness of human politics and "strengthen our charity toward one another" (250). Eloquent as they are, these two Prefaces remain tantalizingly vague on larger generic questions about science fiction. On Stapledon's reading and the processes of his imagination they are silent, save for brief testimonials to the physicist J. D. Bernal and several academic acquaintances at the University of Liverpool. Instead of revealing how Stapledon saw himself in the tradition of fantastic writing, the Prefaces reinforce the common perception of him as idiosyncratic.

In the absence of other evidence, recent critics have tended to fall back on the same expedient used by the early reviewers to explain Stapledon: the Wells connection. But even the most famous of Stapledon's comments on Wells's influence is ultimately cryptic and equivocal. It is now almost de rigueur to cite the closing of his first letter to Wells (16 October 1931) explaining why he didn't footnote Wells in *Last and First Men:* "A man does not record his debt to the air he breathes in common with everyone else." But the same letter specifies that the *only* scientific romances by Wells he had read were *The War of the Worlds* and "The Star" (Crossley, "Correspondence" 35). Either Stapledon was disingenuous or the Wellsian atmosphere he inhaled was remarkably thin. In fact, Wells replied to Stapledon with a good-humored dismissal of his supposed influence: "Thank you for a very pleasant letter but it is all balls to suggest *First and Last Men* [*sic*] (which I found a very exciting book) owes anything to my writings. I wish it did" (Crossley, "Wells to Stapledon" 38). The link with Wells is so attenuated that one is tempted to conclude that Stapledon worked mostly in ignorance of other experimenters in the scientific romance. A year before his death, when his career was in decline except among science fiction enthusiasts, Stapledon had to say: "I find myself in a hold about Science Fiction. I never was a fan of it, and I read very little of it. I recognise it as a legitimate medium of expression, and I think it has a future" ("Fandom" 14).[5] Stapledon's reluctance to associate his work with "science fiction" is not in itself surprising; Wells preferred other terminology as well. But the gingerly distancing of himself from the whole "medium of expression" makes the definition of Stapledon's idea of science fiction even more problematic. He does make himself sound like the great outsider in science fiction, stolidly composing books as aloof and inaccessible as the stars that kindled his imagination.[6]

There is now newly available evidence that Stapledon was not nearly so isolated from the tradition of the scientific romance as has been surmised. If he had no occasion to see into print his mature thoughts on the nature of the literary forms he worked with, he had another natural outlet for his accumulating reflections on the interplay of the literary and scientific imaginations. Long before his writing came to public attention, Stapledon had been a lecturer in the adult education movement in Britain, both formally as a tutor in the Workers' Educational Association and in ad hoc talks given to women's clubs, high schools, political societies, student organizations, soldiers' study circles, and a variety of philosophical, educational, and scientific conferences. The Stapledon Archive at the University of Liverpool contains 240 sets of detailed notes for lectures he gave between 1913 and 1950. Among them are several that bear on the ideas and aims of Stapledon's fiction and two that are central to his own theories and judgments about science fiction. On the basis of these notes some of Stapledon's silences can be filled in, and we can begin to learn how widely read and how thoughtful he was about science fiction.

In fall, 1937, a few months after *Star Maker* appeared and following critical successes in *Last and First Men, Last Men in London,* and *Odd John,* Stapledon prepared a talk called "Science and Literature."[7] Jottings at the top of the first sheet indicate that he made the presentation at least three times in 1937 and 1938; as with all his lecture notes there are many interpolations and revisions as he kept adapting it to successive occasions. In "Science and Literature" Stapledon takes a historical view of the impact of scientific knowledge on poetry and fiction. Interestingly for critics who have linked *Star Maker* to the *Divine Comedy,*[8] his analysis begins with Dante and itemizes a dozen writers from the Renaissance, the Enlightenment, and the nineteenth century whose works are shaped by incorporating or resisting scientific inquiry and experiment. Thus Dante's effort to envisage Ptolemaic astronomy and adjust it to Christian cosmography leads the way to Milton's struggle to reconcile mythology and Copernican astronomy, to Shelley's Prometheanism with its "medley of science and Greece," to Hardy's testing of humanist individualism against the cold and inhuman realities disclosed by modern astrophysics. "*Immensity*—fear—fascination," reads a telegraphic note on Hardy's *Two on a Tower*; not incidentally, this verbal configuration also contours the emotional situation of the narrator in the first chapter of *Star Maker.*

The roll call of scientifically venturesome poets and novelists in "Science and Literature" is the framework for Stapledon's construction of an iconoclastic tradition of writers who respond imaginatively both to words and numbers, to books and machines, and who try to unify the perspectives of the two cultures. The artists he names all seek, as he says of Dante, scientific "verisimilitude" according to the lights of their age. Even two writers whom Stapledon says display "no direct influence of science" are treated as examples not of pure fantasy but of scientific method applied to fictional procedure: Rabelais' Gargantua is not just a fantastic creature but an instance of "gigantism *realistically* worked out," and the worlds of Gulliver reveal how Swift "works out *consequences of novel ideas*—realism." Only the name of Wordsworth on the list represents literature's retreat from the scientific ethos. Citing a famous instance from "A Poet's Epitaph"—a scientist "botanizing on his mother's grave"—Stapledon characterizes Wordsworth's hostility to science: "alarmed, flies to perceived nature."

Stapledon's lecture finds ancestors for the modern scientific romancer in writers who combine fantasy with realism by logical extension and amplification of innovative ideas or imaginary hypotheses. They create not unreal worlds but imagined worlds "realistically worked out." In addition to the writers already mentioned Stapledon sees Bacon, Butler, Meredith, Rosny, Abbott, and Verne forming a line of prophet-critics who offer visions, fancies, and warnings in fictional speculations that are rooted in scientific discoveries and laboratory methods. The impact of all these writers on their audiences is what Stapledon, with a large X in his notes, attributes specifically to Swift: "Puts man in his place." Again, this note could serve to gloss Stapledon's own major fictions that, from premises different from those of the mostly Christian writers he cites, mount assaults on the limitations and pretensions of anthropocentrism.

The second part of "Science and Literature" moves from prototypes to "contemporary examples" of a dozen writers situated at the junction of the literary and scientific cultures. In addition to expected names such as Wells (identified as "the master") and Aldous Huxley, we find the then-little-known novelists M. P. Shiel and David Lindsay, the geneticist J. B. S. Haldane, the physicist Bernal, the pseudonymous Murray Constantine (Katharine Burdekin), and Régis Messac, whose futuristic fiction was at that time available only in French. Stapledon is more judgmental of his contemporaries than of his forebears, finding Shaw "hostile to science, medicine"; noting the antifascist myth developed in Joseph O'Neill's *Land under England* but regretting the narrative's "implausible mechanism"; approving James Hilton's combination of psychology, mysticism, and science in *Lost Horizon;* and condemning J. C. Powys's *Morwyn* for equating scientists with sadists and for its "faulty mechanism."[9] At the high end of Stapledon's critical scale Wells's work is admired for its narrative powers of "scientific melodrama," for the "sheer *mind-stretching*" it requires of readers, and for the prophecies of "scientific utopia" to be found "in all his work." At the bottom end Stapledon is characteristically standoffish about the "crude human factor" in what he labels "Scientification: Wonder Stories, Amazing Stories, etc."[10] There may be a few surprising absences from Stapledon's lists—notably *Frankenstein* from the earlier one and Zamyatin's *We* from the contemporary one—but the notion that Stapledon was insulated from other work in the fantastic mode should now be obsolete.

Perhaps most interestingly, "Science and Literature" ponders the cultural significance of the new hybrid of scientific literature. (Stapledon had not yet learned to call this hybrid "science fiction.") In 1937 the body of literature that was genuinely scientific seemed to him "v. small," but he was ready to name its distinctive virtues. He describes the new form functionally in terms now taken for granted in science fiction criticism but still fresh in the mid-1930s as "critical" and "speculative." Scientific literature provides a corrective to "the *specialist's fallacy*," a target he subdivides to include "abstraction, materialism, determinism, magnitude, myopic detail." He distinguishes it from the literature of escape and from literature that responds narrowly to the current moment and finds a place for it within what he calls "creative literature."[11] As science infiltrates the literary imagination, fiction's prophetic powers are enhanced, and Stapledon indicates the two extrapolative directions such fiction can take: toward the visionary splendor of utopianism and the celebration of human potentiality or toward the literature of disaster and "*revulsion* against science."

Stapledon's climactic arguments concern the epistemological and spiritual effects of science's influence on literature. The new fiction, he says, encourages a "*natural piety* toward the universe for its aloofness, for its potentiality," and it contributes to the "atrophy" of Alexander Pope's dictum that "the proper study of mankind is man." Because scientific literature tends philosophically to the "weakening of human interest," its "literary style" shifts in the direction of the "unemotional, unrhetorical, dry, concise, abstract." In this litany of stylistic markers that concludes the lecture notes we find a distinctively Stapledonian approach to the language of science fiction. The stylistic terms Stapledon uses do not at all fit either Wells's lively, colloquial storytelling or the unsophisticated purple prosiness of the fiction in American pulp magazines. But these terms describe accurately one side of Stapledon's style. His own fictions typically alternate between dispassionate and evocative language, between the clinical record and the startling metaphor, between the conceptual and the lyrical, between the numerical austerity of an astronomer's star catalogue and the sonorous grandeur of a Homeric catalogue. Stylistically his works behave in exactly the way one would expect of that symbiotic kind of text called science fiction.

Stapledon wrote his fictions and developed his ideas about science fiction at a time when the possibilities of interchange between the scientific and literary minds were especially fruitful. Researchers of the caliber of James Jeans and A. S. Eddington believed in writing plainly and vividly about difficult scientific topics for a general audience. Jeans illustrated *The Stars in Their Courses* with Tintoretto as well as star charts, and he used his own hybrid style to translate a technical problem into the language of the kitchen. The stellar components of a galaxy, he assured his readers, "proved to be rather like the arrangement of currants in an ordinary currant-bun; in other words they are fairly uniformly distributed through a space shaped like a bun, a space of circular cross-section whose thickness is less than its length and breadth" (105). J. B. S. Haldane once proudly noted: "In my last book on genetics, there are seven quotations from Dante's *Divine Comedy*" ("How to Write" 158). C. H. Waddington moved comfortably back and forth between embryology and twentieth-century art history, writing landmark books in both fields. In a 1941 Penguin for the general reader he described the scientific ethos in relation to the larger culture using terms much like those of Stapledon in 1937:

The scientific attitude to the world does not in the slightest deny the emotional effects produced on men by their experience; what it tries to do is to classify the mechanisms by which these effects were produced. . . . This attitude which I have called the scientific might be described in other ways. It is the matter-of-fact as against the romantic, the objective as against the subjective, the empirical, the unprejudiced, the *ad hoc* as against the *a priori*. The emotional tone which goes with it is quite definite and quite complex, although at first sight, and to those brought up in a different mode of thought, it may seem emotionless and banal. (46-47)

The striking combination of technically precise language with the articulate rendering of feeling and perception is a hallmark of Stapledon's fiction. Often the most moving episodes in his books are those in which the narration seems, to use a favorite Stapledon word, "disembodied." Haldane's sister Naomi Mitchison, who read several of Stapledon's novels in draft, regularly commented on the descriptive surprises and innovative rhythms of his fiction. About *Star Maker* she wrote to him: "The thing that I believe you are so immensely good at is convincing *detail*—almost mechanical detail—about something one knows nothing about and hasn't even imagined, but which yet you can make absolutely clear." When she read *Sirius* she told him: "It was like you always are, sometimes jogging along like a nice reasonable scientific paper, and sometimes suddenly becoming very moving."

Some readers with more narrowly "literary" expectations were disconcerted by Stapledon's peculiar style; L. P. Hartley's complaint about *Odd John* may be typical: "Mr. Stapledon's plain, straightforward style suggests the laboratory (or the lab., as he calls it) rather than the library." But the effort to bridge the two cultures won admiration from scientists such as Haldane and Freeman Dyson and from philosophers such as Bertrand Russell and C. E. M. Joad. And there were enthusiastic readers in some literary quarters. The Shakespearean scholar John Dover Wilson spent three exhilarating days reading *Last and First Men* straight through and then wrote Stapledon: "You have invented a new kind of book, & the world of Einstein & Jeans is ready for it." When Virginia Woolf read *Star Maker* she found its philosophical framework difficult but had no trouble with its imaginative aims: "I have understood enough to be greatly interested, & excited too, since sometimes it seems to me that you are grasping ideas that I have tried to express, much more fumblingly, in fiction. But you have gone much further, & I can't help envying you—as one does those who reach what one has aimed at."[12] The responses of his contemporaries in many fields suggest that Stapledon the lecturer was defining the intellectual groundwork on which Stapledon the romancer consciously built his most accomplished fictions.

"Science and Literature" is the only one of Stapledon's lectures from the 1930s to explore so extensively the literary history and scientific inquiry that facilitated his own contributions to science fiction. But several other talks from that period have at least a tangential bearing on his fiction. In "Living on Other Planets" (1933) he proposes an "exercise of imagination" for his audience: how would they react to a headline announcing the end of the world in 300 years? He then summarizes some conventional responses: the suicidal thrill in the idea of global annihilation; indifference bred of the assurance that the end will be deferred until after one is dead; the carpe diem impulse to self-indulgence and a last fling for the human race. But Stapledon fastens on the question that had preoccupied his first two romances: could the species preserve itself by seeking a new home for a remnant of homo sapiens on another world? The lecture considers the scientific, technological, political, and spiritual problems of building a vehicle, managing the "first ether voyage," and terraforming and colonizing a planet. The only specific attention to science fiction comes in a section on Mars as a possible human habitat. Stapledon observes that a resident Martian would need a physiology very different from ours, and he has penciled in a note to prompt himself to an illustrative digression: "Wells. WOS." The examples are the swollen-headed, tentacular Martians of *The War of the Worlds* and the submicroscopic Martians in his own (William Olaf Stapledon's) *Last and First Men*. Near the end of the lecture, asking his listeners whether they could imagine life on stars, Stapledon may have wanted to try out the idea of the stellar and nebular beings he would invent for *Star Maker*. Essentially, though, "Living on Other Planets" is a digest of his ideas about space exploration, and it foreshadows the subject of what would be his most famous lecture and one that did achieve a life in print: "Interplanetary Man," delivered at the invitation of Arthur C. Clarke to the annual meeting of the British Interplanetary Society in 1948.[13]

In a 1934 lecture, "Man's Prospects," Stapledon considers the uses of forecasting. Speculation about the future, he says, "stretches the mind," helps us "distinguish the ephemeral & the permanent in human aims [and] problems," "brings out the essentials of the human drama," "makes for clear *orientation* of world policy," assists social evolution by preparing "the way for *long-range* planning," and "teaches *detachment* from humanity." As a critical exercise, forecasting helps us "realize the future" so that the next century becomes as vital to us as the next day or next year. In fact, Stapledon is more interested in forecasting as a discipline of the mind than as a tool for predicting particular technological or social events. His analysis of the value of speculation bears on his own fictions about the future that aim to be prophetic in the widest sense: educative, cautionary, eye-opening, stirring.[14]

The notes for "Man's Prospects" are unusually full in analyzing seven "rules of the game of speculation." These principles offer some insight into the way Stapledon's mind works and into the kind of rigor he applies to his futuristic fiction. The game demands:

1) up-to-date knowledge from a wide variety of disciplines (sociology, astronomy, biochemistry, philosophy, and so forth);

2) imaginative freedom from the limitations of contemporary knowledge and the audacity to "peer beyond" those limits;

3) a comprehensive and balanced vision that avoids the one-dimensionality of a forecast that is merely economic, merely physical, merely psychological, and so on;

4) a "radical skepticism" on the part of the prophet who should acknowledge the unlikelihood of all specific anticipations of the future, including his own;

5) an ability to define the main questions about the future: questions of work, class, leisure, human interests, political organization, etc. (the usual utopian agenda);

6) a commitment to pursue "the fundamental question": "Will man be *more developed* mentally? or fallen into barbarism?";

7) working distinctions among the near future (measured in centuries), the middle future (thousands and hundreds of thousands of years), and the remote future (millions and billions of years).

Stapledon's rules are more comprehensive and even more intimidating than Wells's genial instructions to his readers on "how to play the game" of the scientific romance (though the first six of Stapledon's rules certainly fit Wells's practice in his utopian books). Where Wells emphasizes the tricks of the storytelling trade, Stapledon enumerates the philosophical requirements for a valid attempt at prophecy. Wells does not neglect the social and political issues of prophetic fiction—he was, after all, often pilloried for being too tendentious[15]—but his rules give greatest weight to the pleasures of imagination. Stapledon's principles stress the obligations of the speculative imagination—at least in this instance, where he is thinking less of fiction than of epistemology.

The last of Stapledon's talks I want to consider, "Science and Fiction," comes a full decade after "Science and Literature" and is his last formal presentation on his chosen literary genre. The circumstances of this talk were unusual for Stapledon. He delivered it in 1947 at a Book Exhibition in Manchester at the urging of his editor at Secker and Warburg. Because sales of his most recent fantasy, *The Flames,* were disappointing, the hope was that Stapledon might help himself by giving a public lecture on the genre to which it belonged (Sennhouse). The result is the unique case among his talks in which he offers an overview of his own fiction in relation to the history of the scientific romance. For the first time in his career we hear him using, a little awkwardly, the term "science fiction" to describe his work and that of other writers from Wells forward in whose fiction there are "scientific ideas *in the focus.*" Unlike the 1937 talk,

however, "Science and Fiction" emphasizes the art of science fiction rather than the science in scientific literature. His discussion here is often judicial, discriminating the "imaginative doodling" and "sheer marvels" found in "the science fiction mags" from what he calls "serious science fiction" that aims at "mind stretching" and giving "concrete life to abstract possibilities." Although careful to insist that "*orthodox novel standards* [are] *not applicable*" to science fiction, he does not hesitate to reject the standards of magazines that print stories "often scientifically poor & humanly atrocious."

Once more in "Science and Fiction" Stapledon sets up as legislator of the speculative imagination. The seven rules in "Man's Prospects" are replaced by three crisply stated "rules of the game of science fiction," all of which are directed especially to the demands of fictionmaking. Stapledon requires: 1) plausibility, achieved by the fiction's conformity to the best current scientific knowledge; 2) the imaginative creation of further possibilities developed by logical extension from current ideas; and 3) psychological and spiritual relevance to human readers in the present through the construction of "*Myths* for a scientific age." The first of Stapledon's rules is what separates science fiction decisively from tales of magic and the preternatural and other forms of fantasy. His second rule states what is now generally accepted as the extrapolative principle for writing science fiction. The last rule obviously addresses the particular aims of his own kind of fiction, though it works as a thumbnail description of the ambitions of a wide range of later authors from J. G. Ballard to John Brunner, from Ursula LeGuin to Octavia Butler, from Brian Aldiss to Doris Lessing, all of whom write what may be thought of as anthropological (if not anthropocentric) science fiction.

Stapledon divides his discussion of individual writers in "Science and Fiction" into four sections, concluding with himself. In Part One he takes up "science *in* early fiction." He avoids saying "early science fiction," and his careful choice of words anticipates much later critical debate over when science fiction became a recognizably distinct literary form.[16] In this first section Stapledon's preeminent examples are Dante and Milton, each of whom, he says, accepted current science and shaped religious vision to it. He contrasts them with fairy tale authors whose magic may enchant readers but who cannot achieve the plausibility of the scientific imagination: Sinbad in the *Arabian Nights* is "lifted by a *big* bird (too big to fly!)" and stories with angels in them were "plausible to Middle Ages but not to us" because of their "mechanically bad centre of gravity." Stapledon finds an ambiguous relationship to scientific knowledge in Swift's Lilliputians, a case he discusses as parallel to Orwell's recently published *Animal Farm*. Neither Swift nor Orwell ignores science; each suspends a scientific law purposefully.

The second part, *"notes on masters,"* discusses the scientific romances of Wells, Verne's *Voyage to the Moon* and *20,000 Leagues under the Sea,* Karel Čapek's *War with the Newts* and *Insect Play,* Shiel's *The Purple*

Cloud, and Messac's *La Cité des Asphyxiés* and *Quinzinzinzili.* Unfortunately, the outline does not indicate what Stapledon planned to say about these texts. He also pays attention to two writers not generally thought of as "masters" of scientific fantasy. One is Haldane, praised for his "stories for children" in *My Friend Mr. Leakey* and for his apocalyptic prophecy "The Last Judgment."[17] The second is the novelist and architectural historian John Gloag, who is cited for five works. The fairly lavish homage given Gloag may be explained by the fact that Gloag had quoted from a letter of Stapledon's in the Preface to his 1946 omnibus volume *The First One and Twenty.* There Stapledon makes a provocative comment on science fiction as a distinctively modern phenomenon and stresses its continuity with earlier non-scientific forms of fantasy:

> All this modish playing about with time and space, which you and I have so often indulged in, is of course symptomatic of our period. It opens up new worlds for the writer of fantastic fiction, or at any rate it gives him a new and exciting game to play. The rules of the game are imposed on him by the new attitude to time and space, but he can go beyond the accepted conditions as much as he likes so long as he does not actually or flagrantly violate them, and so become implausible or even positively incredible. (Gloag viii)

A third section of notes on writers works out the contrast between "science fiction & other fantasies, or fantasies not primarily scientific." Alongside fiction by Balzac, Anatole France, Morland Bishop, Samuel Butler, and Murray Constantine, Stapledon looks at several important modern works of fantasy: Lindsay's *Voyage to Arcturus* has "high *aesthetic* value & *spiritual* significance" despite its scientific absurdity; C. S. Lewis' interplanetary novels are "anti-science," and his *Screwtape Letters* is "witty" but its "fundamental assumptions [are] false"; and T. H. White's *The Sword in the Stone,* although "antimodern," makes "fine play with time." These notes suggest Stapledon's effort to judge scrupulously, often balancing his philosophical disagreements (particularly with doctrinaire Christians such as Lewis[18]) against admiration for narrative invention and risk-taking. Here, as in others of his talks, the Stapledon so often represented as cold and magisterial, "the great classical example" in science fiction (Aldiss 208), in fact celebrates the ludic imagination, fantasy as game and play rather than as a strictly cognitive vehicle. But the most unexpected feature of this part of "Science and Fiction" is the determination to draw a line between science fiction and other fantastic fictions—a distinction largely blurred in the 1940s and one that continues to attract and frustrate critics. The only lecture from this era that rivals Stapledon's for sophisticated subgeneric distinctions is one delivered eight years later at Oxford by his old antagonist C. S. Lewis, "On Science Fiction" (*Of Other Worlds* 59-73).[19]

For students of Stapledon's career the most teasing part of this lecture must be the concluding fragmentary notes intended to prompt the speaker to assess "my own aims" as writer. . . . Because the lecture was composed after publication of *The Flames,* which turned out to be his last science fiction, this self-study is interesting as a summing-up of Stapledon's entire eighteen-year production of scientific romances. He frames his review with two large critical observations on his fiction—one by "L. H. Myers on *Last and First Men,*" the other by Rebecca West comparing his work with Milton's. Myers corresponded frequently with Stapledon for thirteen years, and it is hard to be sure which comment Stapledon intended to cite. But because he kept a special file of letters about *Last and First Men* in his study—including Myers' first letter to him—and because the Rebecca West review with which Myers is paired concerns style, it is likely that Stapledon paraphrased this portion from Myers' letter of 6 June 1931:

> Lastly I must say something about your style & method. It is very difficult to make a strictly intellectualistic approach to beauty & grandeur with any effect, or rather without a poor effect. They have to be illustrated through Art with lyric or tragic fire rather than just talked about. Well, you have succeeded better than I shd have thought possible on intellectual lines as such, and this is a great achievement. What you have borrowed from Art, what recourse you have made to the emotions, has been strictly subordinated to the thinking mind and made a part of it, so that there is no violation of the mind's purity and austerity.

Myers extolled precisely the aspect of *Last and First Men*'s style that Stapledon would claim in his 1937 lecture as characteristic of scientifically inspired literature ("unemotional, unrhetorical, dry, concise, abstract"). Stapledon in 1947 epitomizes the alternative viewpoint with the note, "What *Rebecca West* said of Star Maker." Remembering clearly enough *what* she said, he forgot that her target was not *Star Maker* but the less successful novel *Darkness and the Light.* In her review of that book West applauded the splendor of its conception and the "apocalyptic power" of its closing vision, but she was devastating on its style:

> This book should be read, though it is unlikely to be read with any exhilaration, owing to a self-denying ordinance of the author. Mr. Stapledon has a Miltonic imagination. . . . But Mr. Stapledon has evidently a conscious abhorrence of the Miltonic phrase, and the effect is as if Milton had sent the completed manuscript of "Paradise Lost" to be rewritten by the author of Bradshaw's Railway Guide.[20]

Having offered competing perspectives on his art, Stapledon turns to his own evaluation. Predictably, he puts greatest emphasis on his desire *"to write modern myths,"* though he believes that to a more sophisticated age his fictions "will seem very crude." In a running gloss on his works he notes his recurrent concern "to relate science to religion," and he lists the thematic centers of each of his romances: "man's vicissitudes" in *Last and First Men,* "glimpse of a super human" in *Odd John,* "spirit & the other" in *Death into Life,* "wild biology" and "spirit again" in *The Flames,* and so forth. The thematic tags are self-evident, and there needs no ghost come from the grave to tell us this. But there is one intriguing question in the margin, addressed either to himself or to his audience, about *Sirius:* "My best sc. fictn?" The question may have been prompted by a letter from Haldane shortly after *Sirius* was published, saying: "I regard it as a far more plausible futuristic book than 1st and last men, last men in London, etc."[21] Whatever lies behind the question, it signals the kind of critical scrutiny of his work that he seems to have been ready to make.

One page of notes has been added to these minimal thematic comments, perhaps for a future expansion of the lecture. Here Stapledon limits himself to commentary on only four of his books—and they are the quartet that later critics almost unanimously agree are his essential body of work: *Last and First Men, Odd John, Star Maker,* and *Sirius.* The jottings on the first are fairly cryptic, but it is possible to reconstruct the substance of what he talked about. One note reads: "Anglesey vision; stout Cortes." He alludes to the moment when the idea for *Last and First Men* burst on him during a holiday with his wife on the Welsh coast when they observed seals sunning on the rocks.[22] The sight must have started a train of associations—life emerging from the ocean, the long pageant of evolution, the huge spectacle of time imprinted on rocks creased and polished by the ceaselessly moving waters, wonderment about the biological forms that intelligence might inhabit in future ages. From the cliffs of Anglesey he looked down on the ocean and forward into time, and the sestet from Keats's sonnet on Chapman's Homer came into his head:

> Then felt I like some watcher of the skies
>   When a new planet swims into his ken;
> Or like stout Cortez when with eagle eyes
>   He star'd at the Pacific—and all his men
>
> Look'd at each other with a wild surmise—
>   Silent, upon a peak in Darien. (ll. 9-14)

It is like Stapledon, however, not to stop with the glamour of a Pisgah view that would wrap in mystery the "wild surmise" that became *Last and First Men.* His notes move directly to the more mundane stage of composing fictions. After the flash of vision, he tells his audience, "'the artificer' gets to work." He consults "scientific friends" for technical advice and referees his imagination by the "rules of the game" so that his "successive species" of the human race from man to "super-man" to the "extravagances" of Great Brains, flying Venusians, and other evolutionary marvels in the next 2,000,000,000 years of history will have scientific and narrative credibility. Stapledon reflects on the paradox of creating fiction about, as the subtitle of *Last and First Men* reads, "the near and far future." Plausibility about events millions of years ahead is won through scientific homework and carefully plotted extrapolation, but the reader's assent to the narrative illusion can be jeopardized by failures of forecasting in the near future. By 1947 the early chapters of *Last and First Men* had become obsolete as prediction,

and Stapledon was in the position of having sheepishly to submit a scorecard to his audience. If in the aftermath of the death camps and a global war against fascism he had to confess that he had "missed Hitler," he could at least claim that he got "atomic power."[23] The desire for "transcendence of time" is, as the lecturer points out, basic to the structure of *Last and First Men,* but time and history have a way of sabotaging the merely human and transient narrative artist.

With *Star Maker* Stapledon worked on a "larger canvas" and adopted a "more philosophical perspective." His most interesting note here reads: "fiction of the Maker—artist." This is the climactic entry in a short list of topics for discussion on *Star Maker,* and it suggests that the author wanted to look at his masterpiece not primarily as a theological romance but as a self-reflective parable about the nature of creativity in which the visionary spectacle of the star maker's drafting and redrafting of the universe becomes a macrocosmic emblem of the human artist's repeated struggle to achieve satisfying forms.

Like later critics of his work, Stapledon evidently viewed *Odd John* and *Sirius* as a pair of exercises in plausible speculation on a deliberately narrower and more intimate scale than his large cosmic histories. In the case of *Odd John* the "aim" was to depict a superman whose powers are rendered credibly by a direct "extrapolation" (Stapledon uses the term here himself) from existing human capabilities and by a more delicate "hinting" at powers that are "qualitatively new."

Sirius, Stapledon reveals, originated in "Waddington's story of experiments on rats"[24] and is like *Odd John* in being problem-centered. The conceptual challenge, for which the novelist must "work out the consequences," is the hormonal inducement of brain growth in a nonhuman mammal. The lecture emphasizes the sequence of steps in the making of *Sirius.* Only *after* the problem in its abstract form ("the conflict of natures") has occurred to Stapledon does he turn to the specific "choice of beast & of environment." For the reader the unforgettable images of the macrocephalic sheepdog, oscillating sometimes comically, often painfully between his canine instincts and his human education, are in the foreground of the reading experience; for the author the question of what sort of mammal Sirius would be was secondary. Waddington's rats produce Stapledon's dog; the idea generates the fiction. On precisely this point Arthur Koestler registered a reservation about *Sirius.* In a letter to Stapledon he questioned an episode in which the dog sings sacred music of his own devising in a medley of canine sounds with "echoes of Bach and Beethoven, of Holst, Vaughan Williams, Stravinsky, and Bliss" (*Sirius* 260-261). Koestler thought the narrative credibility had been sacrificed to intellectual coherence: "I believe it is almost a great book, the 'almost' referring to those passages which I feel you wrote prompted by philosophical integrity against your own artistic taste—e.g. the dog singing Bach in the East End church."

However one judges the particular moment Koestler objects to in *Sirius,* the larger issue in his critique persists. Stapledon's lectures only confirm what many readers besides Koestler have intuited about his books: that it is the idea of science fiction that commands his imagination, and all the narrative apparatus exists in support of that idea. C. S. Lewis, a much more polemical fantasist than Stapledon, and Ursula LeGuin, who owns as rich an anthropological imagination as Stapledon's, have described the origins of their stories in mental pictures. Lewis envisioned the floating islands and then created the locale for *Perelandra* (*Of Other Worlds* 87); LeGuin saw the face of Shevek in her mind's eye, and the construction of *The Dispossessed* framed that face (100-103). But for Stapledon the idea antedates the image. Even the "vision" he claims as inspiration for his first novel did not beget an episode or a picture; he saw seals on the Welsh coast, but there is not a seal to be found in *Last and First Men.* In Stapledon's fiction the idea also determines the voice. The sheer number of narrators who are explicitly mediums for messages is telling: the amanuenses who record the telepathically dictated texts of *Last and First Men* and *Last Men in London*; the Boswellian anonym who is induced to tell Odd John's "biography" under the guise of fiction; the doubting Thomas who transmits the epistolary prophecy of a mad, male Cassandra possessed by solar creatures in *The Flames.* That such taletellers should be instrumental to some other being who manipulates them to serve a higher purpose suggests the degree to which Stapledon was inclined to fabricate and manipulate fictions in order to make a point or to explore a hypothesis or to unfold the layers of a problem.

To say all this, however, is not to imply that Stapledon neglected the art of his science fiction. Neither the sequence in which he assembled his artifice nor the demonstrable prominence of ideas in his narratives argues against his status as a scientific and philosophical *romancer.* Certainly he did not shun Art as Wells pretended to, nor did he share Wells's habit of polemical disjunction: either it is Literature or Journalism. The force of Stapledon's lectures is to consolidate rather than polarize, to argue for the uniting of literary and scientific perspectives, of moral designs and narrative play, of the inspiration of the visionary and the mechanisms of the artificer. The practice matches the theory. In his four most famous works, as well as the smaller triumphs of *Last Men in London, Death into Life,* and *The Flames,* Stapledon houses his ideas in powerful, innovative, and beautiful forms.[25]

Stapledon was a teacher long before he became a novelist, and he remained a teacher after his fiction declined in popularity in the late 1940s. The commitment to teaching shows in his fiction and points to his place in the line of English didactic romancers—the line of Thomas More, Bunyan, Swift, Godwin, Carlyle, Butler, and, of course, Wells. Stapledon is always a writer with a purpose, fitting words to ideas and images to intellectual strategies, outfitting his readers for citizenship in the world, in the universe, in the days and eons to come. Because people at the present stage of human civilization are provincials

in space and time, the task Stapledon marked out for himself as a writer required all the resources of art along with philosophical acuity and a breadth of scientific knowledge. In an undated lecture called "Ourselves and the Future" he speaks of the difficulty of teaching people to care about and prepare for the future. In the outline for that talk he jotted down what amounts to his artistic credo, the vital motivation of his writing career, the idea behind all the ideas in his science fiction: "The improvident are to be got at by appeal to imagination."

NOTES

[1] Wells's Preface has recently been reprinted in Parrinder and Philmus' collection of his *Literary Criticism.* Their commentary on the Preface (222-229) emphasizes the disillusionment and ambivalence of the older Wells and cautions against accepting his dismissal of the value of his earlier fictions.

[2] Wells was touchy about sharing his laurels. The Wells Archive contains an amusing exchange of letters between Wells and the very minor fantasist John Russell Fearn. When Fearn boasted that some American readers called him "H. G. Wells II," Wells replied drily that such a nickname did them both an injustice, and he urged Fearn to repudiate the title.

[3] For fuller discussions of Stapledon's Wellsianism see Crossley, "Famous Mythical Beasts," and Shelton. Fiedler's confident account of all that Stapledon learned from Wells's novels (43-45) is not founded on any evidence.

[4] The relevance of Stapledon's *Scrutiny* essays to his 1942 novel *Darkness and the Light* is discussed in Crossley, "Politics and the Artist."

[5] For this reference, in a letter Stapledon wrote to the editor of a science fiction fan magazine, I am indebted to Harvey J. Satty.

[6] This view of Stapledon has become a critical commonplace. McCarthy in *Olaf Stapledon* calls him "an anomalous figure within his own field" (30); Priest considers him "probably the most isolated" of the interwar trio of Stapledon-Huxley-Orwell (192); Fiedler sees his writing as a "lonely enterprise" (40); and Aldiss suggests that "reading his books is like standing on the top of a high mountain" (202).

[7] The manuscript notes for "Science and Literature" are in the Stapledon Archive at the Sydney Jones Library, University of Liverpool, as are all the other lecture notes and unpublished letters to Stapledon cited in this essay. I am grateful for permission from the Librarian and the Estate of Olaf Stapledon to quote from these materials. Unless otherwise noted, words in italics represent Stapledon's own underscorings.

[8] See, for instance, McCarthy, *Olaf Stapledon* (76-77) and Scholes (64-65).

[9] Stapledon had just published his *London Mercury* review of *Morwyn* under the title "Descent into Hell."

[10] Stapledon reported his dislike of pulp magazine science fiction in a 1937 interview with Walter Gillings (9). Twelve years later he remained disappointed with the standard of magazine fiction and argued that science fiction must be "much more than scientifically plausible. It must be humanly plausible also, and it must have some significant reference to the contemporary world" ("Fandom" 14).

[11] The terms here reflect the critical lexicon Stapledon developed, not wholly successfully, in his *Scrutiny* essay on "Escapism": creative literature, propaganda literature, literature of release, and literature of escape.

[12] In the final volume of Virginia Woolf's *Diary* (99, n. 21), Anne Olivier Bell quotes from Stapledon's reply to Woolf but believes Woolf's letter did not survive. In fact it was at Stapledon's house but did not come to public light until August, 1983, when the Stapledon papers were assembled for the Archive.

[13] "Interplanetary Man" was first published in the *Journal of the British Interplanetary Society* (Nov. 1948) and is reprinted in Moskowitz (209-252). It addresses the ethical and spiritual challenges the human species must face when it leaves the home planet to explore other worlds. Stapledon's speculations include rehearsals of ideas he had already tried out in fiction: the "wildest" possibility of discovering intelligent solar beings (*The Flames* 217); genetic engineering to enable people to adapt to alien environments (*Last and First Man* 224); and automatically powered planets leaving their orbits to make interstellar voyages (*Star Maker* 246). His only allusions to fiction other than his own are two nods toward Huxley's *Brave New World*, which he sees as a persuasive forecast of one likely future if human beings, motivated by lust for power, choose to use science to dominate the environment and each other (226, 229).

[14] See Huntington for the most thoughtful study of Stapledon as a writer about the future.

[15] There is a convenient and wide-ranging summary of the attack on Wells as ideologue in Parrinder's Introduction to *H. G. Wells: The Critical Heritage* (15-23). For similar complaints about Stapledon see, for example, Toynbee's review of *Sirius* and the concluding section of Fiedler's analysis of *Last and First Men* (64-72).

[16] My italics. In withholding the name "science fiction" from works by writers before Wells, Stapledon takes a position similar to Mark Rose's that science fiction as a discrete genre was determined by historical, intellectual, and literary pressures that did not coalesce until the last third of the nineteenth century (1-23).

[17] "The Last Judgment" is not mentioned by name in the notes, but Stapledon alludes to it when he mentions one speculation of Haldane's that impressed him: "the abolition of pain, & reversal." He recalls Haldane's imagined future in which by a "striking piece of artificial evolution" an advanced humanity eradicates its pain-sense, only to restore it still further in the future when adverse environmental conditions make pain useful for the species' survival ("Last Judgment" 52, 60). These passages bear directly on the kinds of eugenical alterations depicted in *Last and First Men*. In his biographical sketch of Stapledon, Moskowitz gives extended attention to the crucial influence of "The Last Judgment" on Stapledon's first novel (35-37).

[18] Lewis intended his series of fantasies—*Out of the Silent Planet, Perelandra,* and *That Hideous Strength*—as in part a counterblast to ideas he attributed to Stapledon and Haldane. Lewis was fair enough to acknowledge in his Preface to *That Hideous Strength* an imaginative debt to Stapledon (presumably to the Fourth Men or "Great Brains" of *Last and First Men*): "I admire his invention (though not his philosophy) so much that I should feel no shame to borrow" (7). Nevertheless, Stapledon resented Lewis' fictional attacks on him; when J. B. Coates published a book in 1949 with sections on both Stapledon and Lewis, Stapledon immediately drafted a response. The letter may never have been sent, but it is eloquent testimony of his anti-Lewisite feelings: "Why waste your time on Lewis? He is sometimes brilliant but always superficial, his arguing is revoltingly insincere, and he seems to have no genuine religious experience at all."

[19] At the time of Stapledon's lecture the first two scholarly books on science fiction were appearing. J. O. Bailey's *Pilgrims through Space and Time* offers rough-and-ready definitions of science fiction in its first chapter, but the book is essentially a feat of prodigious reading rather than subtle discriminations. Marjorie Hope Nicolson's *Voyages to the Moon* is a learned, shrewd, and entertaining study, but generic classification of the kind Stapledon and Lewis were attempting was not relevant to her narrow focus on cosmic voyages and fantasies of human flight.

[20] For further consideration of Stapledon's Miltonism see McCarthy, "*Last and First Men* as Miltonic Epic."

[21] The judgment that *Sirius* is Stapledon's best "conventional" novel and most "human" book is increasingly made. See Aldiss 107, Fiedler 184, Rabkin 238.

[22] Stapledon spoke often of this visionary moment. For one brief version of it, see his posthumous book *The Opening of the Eyes* (29).

[23] As early as 1942 Stapledon was feeling rueful about his inability to foresee the rise of fascism; in the Preface to *Darkness and the Light* he admitted, "Historical prediction is doomed always to fail" (v). When *Last and First Men* was reprinted in Davenport's 1953 American selection of his works *To the End of Time,* the editor severely abridged the book's topical first fifty pages—a clear illustration of the price of unsuccessful forecasting.

[24] Presumably Stapledon refers to an article Waddington wrote for *Nature,* reporting on recent experiments in which pregnant rats were injected with hormones that stimulated brain growth in the fetuses. It is an unproven "speculative possibility," says Waddington, that artificially enlarged craniums and brains could result in dramatically higher levels of intelligence in later generations of rats ("Some Biological Discoveries" 260). This is precisely the speculative premise, applied to sheepdogs, on which *Sirius* is based.

[25] An interpolated note on the last sheet of "Science and Fiction" to "the vital art" may suggest that chapter 10:4 of *Last and First Men* (titled "The Vital Art") is relevant to Stapledon's own fictional practice. One hundred million years from now the Third Men create new life forms through a combination of biochemical and surgical advances that exemplify, according to the narrator, one of the "original and precarious" triumphs of the human mind aspiring to divinity. Each time a new form is achieved the "vital art" contributes "a new type to fill a niche in the world, which had not yet been occupied" (153). Stapledon's linking of this chapter to his own methods as "artificer" is revealing; as his literary reputation began to dim he seems to have remained convinced of the originality of his formal experiments, his effort to invent "a new type" of fiction "to fill a niche in the world."

WORKS CITED

Aldiss, Brian. *Billion Year Spree: The True History of Science Fiction.* 1973. New York: Schocken, 1974.

Bailey, J. O. *Pilgrims through Space and Time: Trends and Patterns in Scientific and Utopian Fiction.* New York: Argus, 1947.

Crossley, Robert, ed. "The Correspondence of Olaf Stapledon and H. G. Wells, 1931-1942." *Science Fiction Dialogues.* Ed. Gary K. Wolfe. Chicago: Academy Chicago, 1982. 27-57.

———. "Famous Mythical Beasts: Olaf Stapledon and H. G. Wells." *Georgia Review* 36 (1982): 619-638.

———. "Politics and the Artist: The Aesthetic of *Darkness and the Light.*" *Science-Fiction Studies* 9 (1982): 294-305.

———. "Wells to Stapledon: A New Letter." *The Wellsian* ns 7 (1984): 38-39.

Davenport, Basil, ed. *To the End of Time: The Best of Olaf Stapledon:* New York: Funk, 1953.

Fearn, John Russell. Letter to H. G. Wells. 3 Sept. 1935. Wells Archive. U of Illinois Library, Urbana.

Fiedler, Leslie. *Olaf Stapledon: A Man Divided.* New York: Oxford UP, 1983.

Gillings, Walter. "The Philosopher of Fantasy." *British Scientifiction Fantasy Review* 1 (1937): 8-10.

Gloag, John. *The First One and Twenty.* London: Allen, 1946.

Haldane, J. B. S. "How to Write a Popular Scientific Article." *A Banned Broadcast and Other Essays.* London: Chatto, 1947. Rpt. in *On Being the Right Size and Other Essays.* Ed. John Maynard Smith. New York: Oxford UP, 1985. 154-160.

———. "The Last Judgment." *Possible Worlds and Other Essays.* London: Chatto, 1927. Rpt. in *On Being the Right Size.* 45-66.

———. Letter to Olaf Stapledon. Sept. 1944. Stapledon Collection. Sydney Jones Library, U. of Liverpool.

Hartley, L. P. "The Literary Lounger." Rev. of *Odd John. Sketch* (London) 16 Oct. 1935.

Huntington, John. "Olaf Stapledon and the Novel about the Future." *Contemporary Literature* 22 (1981): 349-365.

Jeans, Sir James. *The Stars in Their Courses.* Cambridge: Cambridge UP, 1931.

Keats, John. *Poetical Works.* Ed. H. W. Garrod. London: Oxford UP, 1956. 38.

Koestler, Arthur. Letter to Olaf Stapledon. 14 June 1944. Stapledon Collection. Sydney Jones Library, U of Liverpool.

LeGuin, Ursula K. "Science Fiction and Mrs. Brown." *The Language of the Night: Essays on Fantasy and Science Fiction.* Ed. Susan Wood. 1979. New York: Berkley, 1982. 91-109.

Lewis, C. S. *Of Other Worlds: Essays and Stories.* Ed. Walter Hooper. New York: Harcourt, 1966.

———. *That Hideous Strength: A Modern Fairy-Tale for Grown-Ups.* 1946. New York: Macmillan, 1965.

McCarthy, Patrick A. "*Last and First Men* as Miltonic Epic." *Science-Fiction Studies* 11 (1984): 244-251.

———. *Olaf Stapledon.* Boston: Twayne, 1982.

Mitchison, Naomi. Two Letters to Olaf Stapledon. Undated (c. 1936 and 1944). Stapledon Collection. Sydney Jones Library, U of Liverpool.

Moskowitz, Sam, ed. *Far Future Calling: Uncollected Fantasies and Science Fiction of Olaf Stapledon.* Philadelphia: Train, 1979.

Myers, Leo H. Letter to Olaf Stapledon. 6 June 1931. Stapledon Collection. Sidney Jones Library, U of Liverpool.

Nicolson, Marjorie Hope. *Voyages to the Moon.* New York: Macmillan, 1948.

Parrinder, Patrick, ed. *H. G. Wells: The Critical Heritage.* Boston: Routledge, 1972.

Priest, Christopher. "British Science Fiction." *Science Fiction: A Critical Guide.* Ed. Patrick Parrinder. London: Longman, 1979. 187-202.

Rabkin, Eric. "The Composite Fiction of Olaf Stapledon." *Science-Fiction Studies* 9 (1982): 238-248.

Rose, Mark. *Alien Encounters: Anatomy of Science Fiction.* Cambridge: Harvard UP, 1981.

Scholes, Robert. *Structural Fabulation: An Essay on Fiction of the Future.* Notre Dame: U of Notre Dame P, 1975.

Sennhouse, Roger. Letter to Olaf Stapledon. 30 Sept. 1947. Stapledon Collection. Sydney Jones Library, U of Liverpool.

Shelton, Robert. "The Mars-Begotten Men of Olaf Stapledon and H. G. Wells." *Science-Fiction Studies* 11 (1984): 1-13.

Stapledon, Olaf. *Darkness and the Light.* 1942. Westport: Hyperion, 1974.

————. "Descent into Hell." Rev. of *Morwyn,* by J. C. Powys. *London Mercury* 37 (1937): 78.

————. "Escapism in Literature." *Scrutiny* 8 (1939): 298-308.

————. "Fandom." *Operation Fantast* ns 1 (1949): 14.

————. *The Flames: A Fantasy.* London: Secker, 1947.

————. *Last and First Men: A Story of the Near and Far Future.* 1930. New York: Dover, 1968.

————. *Last Men in London.* London: Methuen, 1932.

————. Letter (draft) to J. B. Coates. Undated (written in back flyleaf of a copy of Coates's *Crisis of the Human Person*). Stapledon Collection. Sydney Jones Library, U of Liverpool.

————. "Living on Other Planets." Ms. notes for a lecture. Stapledon Collection. Sydney Jones Library, U of Liverpool.

————. "Man's Prospects." Ms. notes for a lecture. Stapledon Collection. Sydney Jones Library, U of Liverpool.

————. *Odd John: A Story between Jest and Earnest.* 1935. New York: Dover, 1972.

————. *The Opening of the Eyes.* Ed. Agnes Z. Stapledon. London: Methuen, 1954.

————. "Ourselves and the Future." Ms. notes for a lecture. Stapledon Collection. Sydney Jones Library, U of Liverpool.

————. "Science and Fiction." Ms. notes for a lecture. Stapledon Collection. Sydney Jones Library, U of Liverpool.

————. "Science and Literature." Ms. notes for a lecture. Stapledon Collection. Sydney Jones Library, U of Liverpool.

————. *Sirius: A Fantasy of Love and Discord.* 1944. New York: Dover, 1972.

————. *Star Maker.* 1937. New York: Dover, 1968.

Toynbee, Philip. Rev. of *Star Maker, New Statesman* 1 July 1944: 12-13.

Waddington, C. H. *The Scientific Attitude.* Harmondsworth: Penguin, 1941.

————. "Some Biological Discoveries of Practical Importance." *Nature* 150 (1942): 257-260.

Wells. H. G. Letter to John Russell Fearn. 4 Sept. 1935. Wells Archive. U of Illinois Library, Urbana.

————. Preface. *The Scientific Romances.* 1933. Rpt. in *H. G. Wells's Literary Criticism.* Ed. Patrick Parrinder and Robert Philmus. Sussex: Harvester, 1980. 240-245.

West, Rebecca. "The University Struggle." Rev. of *Darkness and the Light. Sunday Times* (London) 19 April 1942.

Wilson, John Dover. Letter to Olaf Stapledon. 6 Nov. 1930. Stapledon Collection. Sydney Jones Library, U of Liverpool.

Woolf, Virginia. Letter to Olaf Stapledon. 8 July 1937. Stapledon Collection. Sydney Jones Library, U of Liverpool.

————. *The Diary.* Vol. 5. Ed. Anne Olivier Bell. New York: Harcourt, 1984.

W. Warren Wagar

SOURCE: "H. G. Wells and the Scientific Imagination," in *Virginia Quarterly Review,* Vol. 65, No. 3, Summer, 1989, pp. 390-400.

[*In the following essay, Wagar estimates the influence of the writings of H. G. Wells on two great scientists of the twentieth century.*]

One of the rarest birds in the lands of literature is the scientist who writes novels. In mainstream fiction, such a creature is almost unknown. As C. P. Snow observed in *The Two Cultures and the Scientific Revolution* (1959), modern civilization is split in two. The scientists go one way, the humanists another, and those who would travel with both (like Snow himself, a novel-writing scientist) court the condemnation of both.

But one courageous band of writers straddles the two cultures ineluctably, no matter what the training or allegiance of its members. Their patron saint is H. G. Wells, and their craft is science fiction, the fiction of science.

Some few writers of science fiction are bona fide men or women of science, such as the biochemist Isaac Asimov, the astronomers Fred Hoyle and Carl Sagan, the physicists Gregory Benford and David Brin, or the experimental psychologist Alice B. Sheldon (better known by her pseudonym of James Tiptree, Jr.). Many others have no special competence in science at all, or, in curious deference to C. P. Snow's thesis, may even be hostile to the scientific world-view. But they share with their scientist-colleagues a fascination, almost an obsession, with the powers of science.

The prototypical writer of science fiction, H. G. Wells—Brian Aldiss calls him "the Shakespeare of science fiction"—started out in life not quite a scientist, but a teacher of science, educated at the Normal School of Science in South Kensington, London, now the Imperial Institute of Science and Technology. Among his teachers was T. H. Huxley, the chief apostle in late Victorian England of the theory of evolution put forward by Charles Darwin, and a tireless champion of science and scientific education. Huxley and evolutionary theory shaped decisively the impressionable intellect of the young Bertie Wells. In recent years, whole volumes have been devoted to the fierce grip of science, and evolutionary biology in particular, on Wells's imagination.

The grip is well illustrated by *The War of the Worlds* (1898), the novel that inspired Orson Welles's infamous Halloween broadcast 40 years later. *The War of the Worlds*—Wells's novel, not Welles's radio show—may be construed in various ways, as horror tale, apocalypse, political fantasia, or warning to a complacent England, basking in the warmth of Queen Victoria's 60th-anniversary Jubilee. Clearly, it owed something to the "tale of enemy invasion" popular in England from 1871 onward after the startling defeat of France by Prussia the year before. Bernard Bergonzi sees the novel as a typical product of the *fin-de-siecle* mentality, which doted on thoughts of the decadence and dissolution of modern society, and may have reflected Wells's guilty conscience, as an Englishman, about the crimes of British imperialism. There is also merit in Mark Hillegas's suggestion that *The War of the Worlds* was Wells's first experiment in forecasting the coming Great War of 1914-18, "a warning of the changes in human life to be brought by new science and technology."

But most of this is speculation and hindsight. All we can say with assurance from the available evidence is that what most forcefully engaged the mind of H. G. Wells in the early and middle 1890's was the theory of evolution and its bleak implications for the future of *Homo sapiens*. He seldom if ever referred, at the time, to the burdens of Empire or the menace to England of foreign aggressors or the prospects for global conflict in an age of soaring progress in science and technology.

The vision uppermost in the young novelist's eye was of evolution: the struggle for survival, the transformation of species resulting from environmental stimuli, the threat of extinction, and the intoxicating (yet also sinister) thought that humankind might one day become unrecognizably "advanced," all brain and no heart, like the Martians of *The War of the Worlds*. When he did ponder political matters, like most of his contemporaries, his thoughts turned to the warfare of the classes expounded by the socialists of his day and dramatized in two of his own novels of the period, *The Time Machine* (1895) and *When the Sleeper Wakes* (1899). But there is only a faint echo of such concerns in *The War of the Worlds*.

In Roslynn Haynes's recent study of Wells and the influence of the scientific world-view on his thinking, she goes to the heart of the matter.

> The Martians [in Wells's novel] are not 'evil', only amoral and highly efficient. Their fighting machines are simply their means of trapping or overrunning a more vulnerable species—a practice which Wells compares to the British colonisation of Tasmania. *The War of the Worlds* provides no answer.

Just so. There is no answer. Portrayed as coldly intelligent octopi whose only nourishment is mammalian blood, the Martians arrive in England with their overwhelming technology. They treat human beings as edible fauna, suitable (once subdued) only for rounding up and domesticating like wild cattle. One or two of the Martians are killed by their stampeding victims, but the human remnant is brought into line, and in the end the only thing that stops the invaders is yet another force of nature: the bacteria that infest the earth, to which Martians have no immunity. In Frank McConnell's phrase, *The War of the Worlds* is literally "a war of *worlds*," of competing ecologies, a Darwinian fight to the finish in which not the best but the strongest (the terrestrial bacteria) win the day. In this sense the "triumph" of mankind is wholly serendipitous, a by-product of the real triumph of earth's micro-organisms.

In most of his later work, Wells carried the logic of his biological obsessions a step further, and tried to recommend strategies for *Homo sapiens* that would spare the species from extinction without having to call in the *deus ex machina* of the bacterial microworld. Human beings, using their intelligence, their knowledge of nature, themselves, and their own possible futures, could evade destruction by fashioning a rational world state run by scientists and engineers.

But Wells had no doubt that it would be touch and go all the way. Drawing on his scientific training and his novelist's intuitions of human nature, he anticipated many of the horrors of the new century in the years before the outbreak of the First World War: the mobilization of economies for total war, tanks and bombing planes, nuclear weapons (which he was the first to call "atomic bombs"), poison gas and beam weapons (both of which appear in *The War of the Worlds* itself), and the harnessing of modern technology by totalitarian super-states to crush privacy and freedom. Nothing foreseen by the Zamyatins, Huxleys, and Orwells of later generations was missed by Wells in the science fiction and studies of the human future that he published before 1914.

II

His preoccupation in all this work was the impact on civilization of the dizzy progress of science and technology. Time and again, Wells was among the first to fathom the implications of a given advance, and the first to cheer its coming or foresee grim consequences that others, less acquainted with the human condition, failed to grasp.

Not surprisingly, he started early in his career to call for a science of the future, a disciplined inquiry into the shape of things to come, that would enable humankind to gain control of its own destiny. All contemporary futures inquiry traces its origins to Wells's *The Discovery of the Future,* a little book first published in 1902 and cited almost reverently in the work of various present-day futurists.

Much later, Wells even suggested the appointment of "Professors of Foresight," indeed "whole Faculties and Departments of Foresight," doing their best to anticipate and prepare for the consequences of the abolition of space and time made possible by modern technology. In the struggle to safeguard humankind from the dark dangers lurking in the unchecked growth of science, the only efficacious weapon available was science itself, the rational planning of the human future by scientifically trained experts. It was Wells's way—and he knew it—of bringing up to date Plato's ancient dream of philosopher-kings.

No one will be flabbergasted to learn that many of Wells's most devoted fans throughout his long literary career were scientists themselves. Quite a few were personal friends and occasionally colleagues, notably in the writing of *The Science of Life* (1930), a handsome survey of the biological sciences, which he produced in collaboration with the marine biologist, G. P. Wells (his own eldest son), and the great evolutionist Julian Huxley.

Among Wells's admirers in the scientific community, two stand out in particular. Both were physicists and both were directly inspired by the science fiction of Wells to make fateful contributions in their fields of expertise. Both men exhibit, as did Wells himself, the astonishing fertility of the scientific imagination. Both men were, like Wells, idealists with an abiding concern for human welfare and the arts of peace. Both men also uniquely share, with Wells, the distinction of having helped to usher in the nuclear age and make possible the swift annihilation of all life on earth.

The first is Leo Szilard, the Hungarian-born nuclear physicist who emigrated to the United States in the 1930's,

worked with Enrico Fermi to develop the first self-sustained fission reactor fueled by uranium, and persuaded Albert Einstein to take the initiative that led to the first atomic bombs of 1945.

The story has been told more than once, but bears repeating. Szilard was familiar with Wells's writings in his earlier years and met Wells briefly in 1929. He admired both the fiction and Wells's plans for world reconstruction. In 1932 while living in Berlin, he happened on a new German edition of one of Wells's least successful science-fiction novels, *The World Set Free.* Written in 1913 and published early the next year in book form, *The World Set Free* had taken as its central premise the speculation that radioactivity could provide a source of unlimited energy and also the means of destroying the human race. The novel was dedicated to a book by Frederick Soddy, in which the British chemist had recounted his research on radioactive isotopes, research that eventually earned him a Nobel Prize.

From the raw material supplied by Soddy's discussion of radioactivity, Wells spun an amazing tale of nuclear reactors generating vast stores of energy and the fashioning of atomic bombs from an artificial element known as Carolinum (analogous to the plutonium of later research). The bombs were dropped from airplanes in a great war that erupted in 1958 and destroyed most of the world's cities. The survivors came to their senses in the aftermath and forged a world state. But what sticks in the reader's imagination is the forceful description that Wells supplied of atomic ruin, not so very different from the devastation wreaked on London by the Martians in *The War of the Worlds.*

Not that *The World Set Free* compares even remotely as a work of art. Written in haste, it has none of the splendid shapeliness of *The War of the Worlds.* Nevertheless, Wells's grasp of the implications of scientific research was never stronger. And when Szilard read it in 1932, it made, he wrote in his memoirs, "a very great impression on me." In that same year, in a conversation with a German Wellsian named Otto Mandl, he even came to the conclusion that he should devote himself to nuclear physics and discover a source of power that would enable humankind to travel to other worlds. But for a year the seeds planted in Szilard's mind by *The World Set Free* lay dormant.

Then, in September 1933, in one of those protracted double takes that often result in great scientific discoveries, Szilard was walking down a street in London. When he stopped for a red light at an intersection,

> it suddenly occurred to me that if we could find an element which is split by neutrons and which would emit *two* neutrons when it absorbed *one* neutron, such an element, if assembled in sufficiently large mass, could sustain a nuclear chain reaction.

In no more time than is needed for a red light to turn green, atomic energy had been born.

And with it the atomic bomb. Unlike most scientists then doing research into radioactivity, Szilard perceived at once that a nuclear chain reaction could produce weapons as well as engines. After further research, he took his ideas for a chain reaction to the British War Office and later the Admiralty, assigning his patent to the Admiralty to keep the news from reaching the notice of the scientific community at large. "Knowing what this [a chain reaction] would mean," he wrote, "—and I knew it because I had read H. G. Wells—I did not want this patent to become public."

Also in 1934, Szilard tried to interest the founder of the British General Electric Company, Sir Hugo Hirst, in the possibility of the industrial application of nuclear energy. To support his case, he enclosed in his letter a few relevant pages from *The World Set Free,* admitting that Wells's story was all "moonshine" and yet likely to prove "more accurate than the forecasts of the scientists," most of whom, at this time, were adamantly denying the feasibility of wringing usable energy from atomic fission.

Szilard plunged deeply into nuclear research in the years that followed. As everyone knows, it was he who talked Einstein into signing his name to the letter to President Roosevelt that Szilard drafted in 1939 urging the U.S. government to develop an atomic bomb before the Nazis did. The work went slowly at first, but in due course, Szilard's initiative bore fruit, and the bomb intended to frustrate Adolf Hitler's plans for world conquest killed thousands of civilians on the other side of the globe.

The story does not end there. Szilard was the complete Wellsian, attracted not only to Wells's scientific prophecies but also to his vision of a new world order. As early as 1930, he had tried to organize a *Bund* or League of idealistic scientists and intellectuals from which would arise a quasi-religious, quasi-political Order capable of eventually replacing the parliamentary system of modern capitalism with something akin to technocracy. His ideas ran parallel to, and were probably influenced by, the notion of a new Order of Samurai in Wells's *A Modern Utopia* (1905) and the call for a worldwide "open conspiracy" of scientists and business leaders broached by Wells in his book *The Open Conspiracy: Blue Prints for a World Revolution* (1928), which Szilard knew and to which he sometimes referred in later years.

The *Bund* never materialized, except briefly as a small circle of German friends and followers of Szilard. But as his fame grew, Szilard continued his efforts in his adopted country, the United States. He led a group of physicists at the University of Chicago opposed to the use of the atomic bomb against Japan, drafting a petition to this effect, which was signed by 68 scientists and sent to President Truman in July 1945. He was active in launching the Pugwash movement. In 1962 he organized the Council for Abolishing War, which carries on today as the Council for a Livable World, a political action group headed by scientists that lobbies Congress and campaigns for candidates in the cause of arms control.

Szilard died in 1964, but his work continues. Scientists are still creating nuclear weapons. Other scientists, sometimes the same ones, warn humanity of their menace. This ghoulish paradox is more apparent than real: in both instances, men and women of science are acting rationally, applying their gifts of reason to the solution of problems, but in the context of a largely irrational world they do not fathom. As Einstein himself said of Szilard at the time he was forming his *Bund* in 1930, Szilard was a "fine, intelligent man," but "perhaps, like many such people, he is inclined to overestimate the significance of reason in human affairs."

III

The same pattern of inspiration, discovery, application to warfare, and humane idealism recurs in the life of Robert Hutchings Goddard. If Szilard was the father of the atomic bomb, Goddard is the father of the technology now used to deliver nuclear weapons to their targets, the rocket-propelled missile. And he, too, was a fervent Wellsian.

In 1898 the young Goddard, then 16 and living in Massachusetts, read *Fighters from Mars, or The War of the Worlds, in and near Boston,* an adaptation of Wells's novel serialized in the Boston *Post.* As Orson Welles later transferred the Martians from England to New Jersey, so the *Post* shifted them to the suburbs of Boston. Writing in 1932 to Wells, Goddard remarked that the novel "made a deep impression" on his fledgling imagination. Elsewhere he noted that his discovery of Wells's Martians and their spacecraft was

> an event . . . which was destined to provide me with all the scientific speculative material that I could desire. . . . [It] gripped my imagination tremendously. Wells's wonderfully true psychology made the thing very vivid, and possible ways and means of accomplishing the physical marvels set forth kept me busy thinking.

But not at first. Again, as with Szilard, Goddard did a long double take. The ideas borrowed from Wells fermented in his mind for more than a year before the moment of illumination came. When it did arrive, it was not on a crowded city street but in the boughs of a cherry tree in his own backyard. On Oct. 19, 1899, Goddard climbed the tree and had a vision of a whirling spaceship capable of flying to Mars. In later years he came to regard that moment as the one that transformed his life, and celebrated October 19 as "Anniversary Day," visiting the old tree from time to time to refresh his memory. He also evolved the ritual of rereading *The War of the Worlds,* usually during the Christmas season. His letters and papers teem with references to the novel, and to several other works of Wells, including *The First Men in the Moon, In the Days of the Comet,* and "A Story of the Stone Age."

Over the years Goddard toiled away at the development of liquid-fuel rockets, at first with little support or encouragement. He was granted two key patents in February 1914, which contained the essential features of all the rockets that followed. Later that same year he tried to interest the U.S. Navy in military applications of his inventions, and in 1918 the Army also became briefly involved in his research. The bazooka, not employed on the battlefield until World War II, was actually a Goddard invention of 1918. In 1926 he built and successfully test-fired the world's first liquid-fuel rocket. All modern rocket artillery, jet-propelled aircraft, and of course ballistic missiles, owe much to Goddard's studies.

But although Goddard worked for the military again during World War II, it is clear from his papers that the dream animating his research was not weaponry but space flight, the same vision that sparked the parallel labors in Germany of Hermann Oberth and Wernher von Braun, the vision instilled in Goddard by reading *The War of the Worlds* in 1898. In 1932, as already noted, he acknowledged his debt in a fan letter to Wells. He followed it four years later with another congratulating Wells on his 70th birthday and enclosing a report on his latest researches. Ironically, Wells had predicted the use of guided missiles in warfare in a radio talk delivered over the B.B.C. just a few months after receiving his first letter from Goddard, although there seems to have been no connection between the two events.

Goddard also shared Wells's humanism and his hopes for a brighter future made possible by science and scientists. In his 1932 letter to Wells he confessed to

> the greatest admiration for your later work, which you no doubt feel is much more important than your writings of the nineties. What I find most inspiring is your optimism. It is the best antidote I know for the feeling of depression that comes at times when one contemplates the remarkable capacity for bungling of both man and nature.

In 1941 he added, in a letter to a friend, "I agree with you, and also H. G. Wells, that we must hope to have the race ruled by science. To continue with our present hit-or-miss policies may be disastrous."

What conclusions should one draw from all this? Were Wells, Szilard, and Goddard fools or sages? Devils or angels? Destroyers or saviors?

Actually, a little of both. They were human beings, doing what they knew best, dreaming dreams of reason in an irrational world. They were also not indispensable. Science fiction, atomic reactors, nuclear bombs, and rockets would have happened with or without H. G. Wells, Leo Szilard, and Robert H. Goddard. Perhaps not quite as soon or in quite the same way. But we cannot hold them personally responsible for what came to pass.

Yet one valuable lesson may surely be learned from their exploits. The steadfast application of reason, science, and technology to the relief of human distress is no guarantee of anything. It can lead to ruin, just as the Martians ruined London and lost their own lives in the process, victims of the mindless genocidal hunger of terrestrial

bacteria. The Martians had, wrote Wells, "intellects vast and cool and unsympathetic," far in advance of those of *Homo sapiens*. But their great brains did not save them. The problems of modern civilization transcend the categories accessible to reason. In the final analysis science can assist in their solution only if guided at every step by the hearts and wills and spirits of all humankind.

Susan Strehle

SOURCE: "Thomas Pynchon: 'Gravity's Rainbow' and The Fiction of Quantum Continuity," in *Fiction in the Quantum Universe,* The University of North Carolina Press, 1992, 282 p.

[*In the following essay, Strehle sees Thomas Pynchon's* Gravity's Rainbow *as a novel that renders a non-Newtonian world full of discontinuity, instability, and quantum unpredictability.*]

Nowhere in contemporary fiction is modern historical reality more carefully presented, or recent science more prominently explored, than in Pynchon's *Gravity's Rainbow.* Pynchon shares with other actualists an understanding of the new physical reality and a delight in exploring it in his fiction; his third and most complex novel is an important, perhaps even quintessential actualistic text. While some critics read it as a late-modernist exploration of self-reflexivity, most of the voluminous critical writing about this novel recognizes . . . not only the worldliness of Pynchon's text but also its use of a metaphorics based on the new physics.[1]

Gravity's Rainbow constitutes a massive, detailed, and encyclopedic portrait set in the historical, scientific, economic, and political context of Europe during nine months of 1944-45. Like other actualists, Pynchon also sketches the rough beast our age has inherited from that tense gestation: the rockets rising near the end of World War II eventually fall on the Western theater in which we sit, suggesting, among other things, that our postwar technologies and bureaucracies somehow "rose" at the end of the war with a promise to return and crush us. Pynchon chooses his historical setting, moreover, for its scientific significance: like, [Robert Coover's] *Public Burning, Gravity's Rainbow* chronicles a period near the beginning of the atomic age, when scientific discoveries began to invalidate traditional assumptions about reality. The novel refers frequently to the new science, quantum leaps, cloud chambers, and Heisenberg's uncertainty principle. "Right now," says zootster-anarchist Blodgett Waxwing, "all the hepcats are going goofy over something called 'nuclear physics.'"[2]

The "un-hep," meanwhile, persist in imagining Newtonian levers beneath experience, in Pynchon's version of the clash between old and new realities. Like other actualists, Pynchon writes a large and public novel, with a huge cast of characters, many of whom are "public servants." Like, [William] Gaddis and Coover, he locates the most conservative dedication to Newton's principles in the public sector—in various governments and corporations, in the firm and the cartel. These institutions encourage and exploit popular beliefs in stability, continuity, causality, objectivity, and certainty, because Newtonian beliefs make citizens and soldiers more docile and more useful for institutional work. An assumption that phenomena are causally linked, for example, can be channeled into dutiful productivity for "the war effort" or "the nation," but a notion that things are accidental and mysterious creates an undependable worker. The very principle of linear, rational problem-solving, or "the scientific method" (Blicero will call it "the order of Analysis and Death" [722]), emerges from and depends on a Newtonian cosmos.

In private, Pynchon's men and women are confused, like those in Gaddis and Coover, as they experience the new reality and try to make sense of it with old concepts. Failing to discover lines of continuity or causality in their lives, they fall back on invention: paranoia, so prevalent among Pynchon's characters, constitutes their imagination of a traditional realistic plot focused on the heroic self. The paranoid plot occurs, in various forms, to Tyrone Slothrop, Edward Pointsman, Franz Pökler, Duane Marvy, Byron the Bulb, Richard M. Zhlubb, and dozens more. As these characters experience relativity, accident, and the radical uncertainty of the world, they understand all this opacity as a challenge to their sanity: they must "solve" apparent mysteries by constructing causal continuities.

While Pynchon explores various implications of the new physics in *GR,* he devotes special attention to its invention of non-Newtonian continuities. Discussing the shift from classical to quantum physics, historian of science Daniel Kevles writes:

> Classical physics assumed natural phenomena to be continuous, describable in space and time, causally predictable, and, as such, mathematically expressible in differential equations. Quantum theory could describe atomic behavior only as a series of discontinuous transitions between states, could not locate atomic electrons in space and time when they leaped from one orbit to another, and could not predict when such leaps would occur. To theorists who appreciated these divergences, a genuine quantum mechanics might possibly be a mechanics of discontinuity, mathematically expressed in equations of differences rather than in differential equations.[3]

Recent physics supposes that reality, at least at the subatomic level, has gaps which electrons leap in nonlinear fashion and for no evident cause. Phenomena remain "connected," in a sense: electrons do not leap out of the nuclear orbit. But the connections are looser and more discontinuous than a classical physicist could have imagined.

For a writer like Pynchon, the new mechanics suggests a vision of identity, history, and fictional plotting arranged in some nonlinear order that suspends causal

links. Episodes in *GR* cannot be said to "produce" or "cause" others, but rather to parallel each other, metaphorically. In a resonant passage, Leni Pökler tries to explain such a possibility to her husband, the "cause-and-effect man": "'Not produce,' she tried, 'not cause. It all goes along together. Parallel, not series. Metaphors. Signs and symptoms. Mapping onto different coordinate systems, I don't know'" (159). While serial connections imply the rigid and explicable orderings of Newton, parallels suggest the relative and mysterious form of the new physical world.[4] To inhabit this richer and more dangerous terrain, actualists like Fausto Maijstral will sell their souls to history. "It isn't so much to pay for eyes clear enough to see past the fiction of continuity, the fiction of cause and effect, the fiction of a humanized history endowed with 'reason.'"[5]

While most of his characters devote their lives to inventing paranoid continuities in their own and the world's history, Pynchon imagines their parallel efforts in a narrative form full of leaps, digressions, gaps, and anticlimaxes. This chapter begins with a thematic analysis of Newtonian expectations of end-ordered linearity preserved in the public understanding—in politics, business, family structures, science, and the arts—and, disastrously, in the private hopes of Westerners like Tyrone Slothrop. Slothrop, I argue in a second section, enacts the Western view of history as realistic narrative. Slothrop begins as a realist, chasing a deterministic version of the past, and ends as a surrealist, renouncing connections and forgetting the past: he never achieves an actualistic perception of the mysterious, metaphoric links between events. Others do, however; a third section of this chapter explores the open forms of continuity imagined by characters like Tchitcherine, Mexico, Geli Tripping, and Leni Pökler. These and other characters manage, without abandoning history, to imagine it as loose and accidental. Pynchon, too, invents open, energetic, random continuities, as the last section of this chapter explains. Setting chaotic disconnectedness against rigid, imposed, serial connections, Pynchon's novel occupies the middle ground between; *GR* maintains the temporal continuity without which narratives cannot reflect the external world but denies the linear, causal, and unbroken nature of time. Plots break off, characters disperse, suspense trails off into anticlimax, and allusions provide fragmentary glimpses of vast and dissimilar realms of knowledge. Connections do not disappear in the richness of Pynchon's text; rather, they proliferate to the point of resonant uncertainty. Unlike the narrative continuity of realism, Pynchon's continuity does not render multiplicity into graspable unity; rather, it reveals behind every seeming unity an intricate and endless tangle. *GR* introduces a new, actualistic fiction of quantum continuity.

ANTIQUATED CONTINUITIES

In the first of four epigraphs, all ironic, beginning the four sections of *GR,* Wernher von Braun voices the commitment to a Newtonian, linear, teleological continuity that pervades the novel. "Nature does not know extinction; all it knows is transformation. Everything science has taught me, and continues to teach me, strengthens my belief in the continuity of our spiritual existence after death" (1). Since life is ordered from the end, this transforming death, human beings should read experience in end-ordered lines, study the causal links between successive events, and impose a clearer, more useful order on the "messy" changes of nature. For the good public servant like Teddy Bloat or Pirate Prentice, such a view encourages submission to duty and dedication to higher causes—like Nazism, for example, which von Braun served during the war. The faith in causal continuity, which is inscribed in the public consciousness in scientific/Newtonian, religious/Calvinistic, and aesthetic/realistic forms, carries with it a sinister belief that the *dis*continuous, the arbitrary, the aberrant, and the preterite should be either assimilated to the meaningful series—colonized, as it were—or eradicated. A seemingly innocuous notion that the world obeys Newton's laws thus becomes, for Pynchon, a commitment to the imperialist politics through which the West has fought to control life.

Colonialist expansions of political and economic power preoccupy most public institutions and their servants in *GR*. Every Western nation characterized in the novel has a similar colonialist history. Each encloses its open, natural spaces, each attempts to assimilate other races, and each has exterminated some "unassimilable" populations: Hereros, Jews, American Indians, and Russian, Argentine, and Indian natives. The various forms of colonialistic conquest aim to establish global political continuities so that civilization—the government, religion, and cultural customs of the West—might be continuous worldwide, and so that Western technologies might profit from these links. Above all, Pynchon suggests, European colonizers teach their linear and teleological view of time, their rational systems of "death and repression," to tropical natives who have believed in natural cycles (317). In this way, Western history becomes a single "mission to propagate death" (722).

While colonialist policies make eco-political power continuous through space, the bureaucratic systems supporting every Western organization in the novel ensure the continuity of power through time. The war, Pynchon reminds us, "was never political at all, the politics was all theatre, all just to keep the people distracted" while various bureaucracies and technologies compete for funding (521). Individuals become bureaucrats to partake in the sheltered continuity of the firm. "We're all going to fail," says Sir Marcus, "but the Operation won't" (616). This illusion of temporal continuity serves death just as surely as imperialism does: like colonizers, bureaucrats eliminate what they can't use. In their bored, routine, and apparently insignificant service to organizations whose policies they often distrust, "a million bureaucrats are diligently plotting death and some of them even know it" (17).

At the domestic level, Pynchon's families enforce the continuation of social values (obedience, duty, work) supported by the teleological basis of Western culture. In

fact, the parents of *GR* become colonizers, regarding their children as recalcitrant natives to be conquered in the name of decency and submissiveness. At the same time, these parents also function as bureaucrats, serving authority in menial, routine gestures. "'Mother,' that's a civil-service category, Mothers work for them: They're the policemen of the soul," says Leni Pökler (219), and Otto identifies a "Mother conspiracy" to destroy children with guilt and casseroles (505). Two women, Katje and Greta, play "Mother Night" in the novel, destroying sons in the process; all mothers, including Nalline Slothrop, hope their sons will die heroically, so they may hang the Gold Star (134, 682).[6] Like their partners, fathers also perpetuate the joyless and deadly codes they have inherited. "The fathers have no power today and never did, but because 40 years ago we could not kill them, we are condemned now to the same passivity, the same masochist fantasies *they* cherished in secret, and worse, we are condemned in our weakness to impersonate men of power our own infant children must hate, and wish to usurp the place of, and fail. . . . So generation after generation of men in love with pain and passivity serve out their time in the Zone [. . .] willing to have life defined for them by men whose only talent is for death" (747). By accepting the continuity of "pain and passivity," fathers sacrifice their children to death or death-in-life, as surely as Abraham, passive before God the father, was ready to kill his son—followed in Pynchon's text by Blicero, Broderick Slothrop, and Franz Pökler, among many others.

Scientists, too, pursue dual roles as bureaucrats and colonizers in feeding the world's illusion of Newtonian continuity. As bureaucrats, they offer routine services to armies and nations, in exchange for funding that allows them only to go on providing the same dubious services. Like Pointsman and the scientists of PISCES, Franz Pökler and others of the VfR, founded to build interplanetary rockets, agree to serve the army in exchange for money (400-401). Worse, the scientists of *GR* also serve as colonizers: nature itself appears in the role of the undisciplined savage committed to superstitious organic cycles, and Western science comes to tame this native vitality. To the chaotic accidents of nature, Pointsman hopes to bring an absolute causality that will show "the stone determinacy of everything, of every soul" (86). Jamf exhorts students to "move beyond life, toward the inorganic. Here is no frailty, no mortality—here is Strength, and the Timeless" (580). Just as German colonizers exterminated the less "useful" or docile Hereros and converted the others to a Christian faith in death, scientists in *GR* attempt to eliminate the faces of nature they cannot control, while changing the teeming, time-bound world into enduring, synthetic forms of death.

The great lie of continuity has, in *GR,* its artistic form and medium as well: film, which Pynchon presents as the most Newtonian of arts. Popular films (Westerns, musicals, situation comedies, gothic horror and adventure movies) invariably rely on linear continuity in structuring experience. In the interest of plausibility, they use seemingly arbitrary details, but like other forms of realistic fiction, including the *Time* magazine story discussed in the chapter on Coover and the "tubal" clichés in *Vineland,* they begin from the end of the adventure and so exclude chance. Every detail can, by the end, be fit together by the detective-viewer, for apparent mysteries have underlying causes. The Argentine epic *Martín Fierro* might be filmed with this beginning: "A shadowed plain at sundown. An enormous flatness. Camera angle is kept low. People coming in, slowly, singly or in small groups, working their way across the plain, in to a settlement at the edge of a little river. Horses, cattle, fires against the growing darkness. Far away, at the horizon, a solitary figure on horseback appears, and rides in, all the way in, as the credits come on" (386). In this scene, dispersed elements slowly gather together into a single unity, as they are supposed to do in teleologically ordered narratives—and as, in the projected film, the Gaucho and Indian populations will be united by the "solitary" hero. The camera angle is low, of course, to encourage viewer identification with the "lowly" Indians, but behind that deceptive angle, cameraman and director really see the whole plot from high above.

That *GR* makes frequent references to film has been commonly noted; that these allusions indict popular movies for their dangerous ordering and false simplifying of reality has, however, not often been understood.[7] John Stark, for example, suggests that Pynchon presents film as an innocuous, often powerful art form that "reproduces bits of objective reality more accurately than any other artistic medium."[8] David Cowart goes further: "Pynchon uses film as a critique of life, insisting that the one is not more or less real than the other," so references to film challenge readers' conventional views of reality.[9] On the contrary, I believe that film seems to Pynchon to uphold precisely those conventional views, which, like any form of realistic narrative, it does by "finagling" so that reality appears coherent. Pynchon insists that we must distinguish reality from film. His own fiction does not at the end transform itself into the "show" for which we "old fans who've always been at the movies" clamor but rather resembles the "darkening and awful expanse of screen," the "film we have not learned to see" (760). *GR* does not pretend to be the entertaining film we came to watch, but rather the break in that film, when the darkness, the falling rocket, and the reality of death intrude.

Repeatedly, Pynchon emphasizes the disjunction between reality and film—or, more simply, the lying nature of popular film. Whatever Pynchon's views of artistic films (to which he seldom refers), he clearly regards the Hollywood/German/international "industry" as part of the cartel's effort to "colonize" film viewers and render them docile. Quite plainly, he finds popular films simplistic and sentimental, especially in their politics. They give us, for instance, the Irish, "those million virtuous and adjusted city poor you know from the movies—you've seen them dancing, singing, hanging out the washing on the lines, getting drunk at wakes, worrying about their children going bad [. . .] on through every wretched Hollywood lie" (641). Such films tend to glamorize war, like "the lads

in Hollywood telling us how grand it all is over here, how much fun"; on the other side, it "looks like German movies have warped other outlooks around here too" (135, 474). The movies also endorse colonialism, making tropical hierarchies seem jolly and predictable; in India in 1935 Pirate Prentice is surprised to find "no Cary Grant larking in and out slipping elephant medicine in the punchbowls out here" (13). In short, the film industry reaffirms all of the old assumptions about social and cosmic order that support conventional, repressive power structures.

By no accident, then, such powers (cartels, firms, and nations) not only influence but also directly employ filmmakers and thus buy into their falsifications of reality. The Germans hire Morituri to watch "Allied footage for what could be pulled and worked into newsreels to make the Axis look good" (473). The British hire von Göll, a German with "sinister connections" to the IG cartel, to fake a film sequence showing black rocket troops in Germany (387). As *GR*'s main filmmaker, von Göll deserves a closer look, for Pynchon locates in this egomaniacal character some reasons why film is so pliant to various political uses.[10] Like filmmaker-agent Hector Zuñiga of *Vineland,* von Göll finds film attractive for its glamour and for its "exorbitant profits" (386). From *Alpdrücken,* made for the prewar Germans, to *New Dope,* made for postwar drug fans, von Göll's films show a sensitivity to commercial interests that almost matches their insensitivity to art, morality, or taste. Politically neutral in a text where one's political stance is one's morality, von Göll betrays his friends for profit: he brings the police to close Säure Bummer's counterfeiting operation, turns Klaus Närrisch, who is ready to die for him, over to the Russians, fails in his promise to deliver Slothrop a discharge, and even, it seems, betrays Slothrop's location to Pointsman and his castration team. In von Göll, Pynchon shows that the director of popular films—and by extension the medium itself—has only the most tenuous commitment to reality and therefore accedes readily to a variety of uses.

Film's primary use in *GR* is to condition and manipulate. In our first glimpse of moviemaking, a cameraman shoots footage that Pointsman will use to train octopus Grigori to attack Katje on a Riviera beach. The secrecy of this conditioning process, from Katje, Slothrop, and the dumb beast Grigori; its results, creating a violence unknown in the nature of crab-eating Grigori; and the layers of illusion involved, as film, itself stills counterfeiting movement, serves the larger "filmic" pretense that Slothrop rescues Katje from danger—all these elements of the novel's first film introduce the sinister potential that characterizes later movies. Grigori, who watches the film uncritically and responds to it instinctively, figures all of Pynchon's subsequent film fans. Slothrop, for example, an ardent Western-watcher, not only quotes "Saturday-afternoon western movies dedicated to Property if anything is" (264) but also shows, in the narcosis episode at PISCES, that the Western's violence, racism, and simplistic continuities have formed his perception of reality. Greta Erdmann expects the world to conform to the "vaguely pornographic horror movies" in which she has acted (393); Pökler and, he implies, a generation of Nazis envisioned the world in the decadent romantic forms of German movies between the wars (577), and Osbie Feel thinks he lives amid the simple fantasies and fears of *White Zombie* and *Dumbo* (106). In these and other characters, Pynchon suggests that movie audiences happily consume bad movies and then, without reflection, behave like Western heroes, German supermen, or zombies, as if they lived in a film reality.

Eventually, devoted moviegoers lose their ability to see a reality unmediated by the standard scenes of popular film, and they expect to achieve the easy resolutions of the typical movie plot. Pynchon's readers are not exempt from this movie conditioning. He accuses us of being loners, "slouched alone in your own seat" watching *Alpdrücken* (472), and he describes us at the end as "old fans who've always been at the movies" (760). While Pynchon provides readers with standard filmic fare, he twists typical film elements into ironic and unfulfilled forms. So, for example, groups of extras break into the song and dance routines of musicals (12, 15, 22, 593, 657), suffer the physical gags of situation comedies—including the inevitable pie throwing (334)—and escape the near-brushes with tame death of adventure movies (186, 248). Above all, there are chase scenes (198, 308, 334, 637, etc.), every one of them peculiar in its mixture of comedy and terror (as when Slothrop, wearing only a purple bedsheet, chases the unknown thief of his American identity—which he never recovers), and every one, also, unsuccessful: no chaser ever catches what he or she pursues. Pynchon ridicules the set of expectations behind the chase scene, especially the assumption that chases, movies, and lives must always end in fulfillment. He scoffs at "aficionados of the chase scene, those who cannot look at the Taj Majal, the Uffizi, the Statue of Liberty without thinking chase scene, chase scene, wow yeah Douglas Fairbanks scampering across that moon minaret there" (637).[11]

In all of *GR,* no fan follows movies more ardently than Tyrone Slothrop—who is, by no accident, the most conditioned and conditionable of men. While characters who perceive the world as actualists rarely see movies—Enzian, Tchitcherine, and Geli never mention films, and Roger Mexico finds the popular *Going My Way* "awful" (38)—others couple enthusiasm for film with a belief that life shares the order shown on screen. "Slothrop's been to enough movies," the narrator comments (114); the American lieutenant has absorbed the moving picture of reality. As though his life were a series of plotted scenes, he imitates his favorite actors: Errol Flynn (248, 381), Cary Grant (292), Fred Astaire (561), and the fictitious Max Schlepzig, among others. He awaits the happy end, the "Shirley Temple smile" from a little girl trapped for hours in the rubble (24). When, much later, he finds that smile in Bianca's elaborate imitation of Shirley Temple, Slothrop responds enthusiastically—in the limited way film has taught: he acts a passionate scene with Bianca and then leaves her as nonchalantly as he might leave a theater.

SLOTHROP'S STORY

Slothrop embodies Pynchon's troubled assessment of modern Western man. Men control history in *GR:* they exert power in making the political and economic decisions that shape and express the West. To be sure, women may collude with the system that perpetuates men's control, and women characters are as manipulative and damaging in this novel as in *V.* Greta Erdmann, Nalline Slothrop, and Katje Borgesius are, for example, as vain, controlling, and emotionally dead as lady V. They lack her status as an organizing and powerful symbol, however, and the novel implies that the worst acts perpetrated by these women are invented and choreographed by hidden men. So Pointsman entirely controls Katje's degradation of Brigadier Pudding. Pynchon's protagonist is, by a logic important to the novel, a young man seeking to understand his relationship to the male configuration of power that Pynchon calls the elect. Tyrone Slothrop's earliest infancy was given over to men of power; in the virtual absence of his mother, he was traded and used by men. Slothrop's manhood, his penis, is Their object: it has made him first useful, then threatening, to various men. Ironically, even its heterosexual drive does not lead Slothrop to intimacy with women. His business is with men: Slothrop is the young man who must first read, and then choose a relationship to, the network of power termed, after Derrida, "phallogocentrism," and summed up in *GR*'s abiding image: the rocket.

Various critical approaches to Slothrop's character have yielded divergent readings of his fate and of the novel describing it; his dispersal has often, surprisingly, been regarded as an achievement of pre-Westernized natural peace. Mark Siegel, for example, writes that "Slothrop fails to fulfill his destiny but seems to succeed, through the loss of the self that causes man to be egocentrically irresponsible to nature, to find harmony with the world."[12] Similarly, Douglas Fowler believes "Slothrop's fate may not be *quite* as terrible as death, and although he has been lost as an 'integral creature,' as an identity with a service number and a personal history, Slothrop's scattering may have been a transformation into another, humbler form of life."[13] William Plater suggests that Slothrop achieves "Dionysian charisma" and "may have found the preterite's form of grace. . . . There is no evidence of Slothrop's death in the novel, only his disintegration. One of the last to see him is Pig Bodine when he gives Tyrone the symbol of grace."[14] My own understanding is closer to that of Edward Mendelson, who argues that Slothrop, a "mock-charismatic figure," "progressively forgets the particularity of his past, and replaces his memory of past events with garish and crude comic-book versions of them. His disintegration of memory is not the work of those who oppose or betray him, but is the consequence of his own betrayals, his own loss of interest in the world, his own failures to relate and connect."[15] The end of *GR* does not, in my view, constitute Slothrop's recovery of the pastoral garden, but rather his progressive loss of memory in the despoiled urban Zone, accomplished not by shedding the Western analytic ego but rather by succumbing to what Pynchon considers the quintessential Western disease, the failure of will (472). Slothrop is never more fully the modern American than when, playing his harmonica amid European natural beauty, he forgets the war, the rocket, and his own humanity.

Reading Slothrop at some length is necessary for several reasons, despite the connections sketched in *GR* between interpretation and the repressive, death-oriented face of modern culture. Molly Hite puts it well: "All such attempts to enclose Slothrop in an explanatory structure (which tacitly affirm Pointsman's working premises by making Slothrop an object of study) fail to comprehend him, 'even as a concept.' Slothrop's conceptual fragmentation becomes an emblem for the impossibility of explaining him."[16] More starkly, Katherine Hayles argues that, for Pynchon, inevitable destruction follows from structures of organization and control that are basic to consciousness: "As long as we remain cognitively conscious, the holocaust is inevitable."[17] Yet, at the same time, Pynchon's fiction *also* suggests that consciousness, rationality, and reading are inescapable for human beings—his characters constantly engage in acts of interpretation, and his readers can do nothing else.[18] Surely there are more (as well as less) valid, viable, open, nonlinear, acausal, noncontrolling modes of reading.

In reading Slothrop, we read Pynchon's text. As the novel's "central character" who moves to the periphery, he demonstrates Pynchon's egalitarian impulse to mingle the narrative elect and preterite. More important, he points both to the external world and to the realm of art—to Pynchon's meditations on culture, history, science, and technology and to his reflections on narrative and interpretation. Slothrop is, on the one hand, connected intimately with the rocket, and as Hite points out, this affinity "promises to make him a mirror of all the forces at work in the cosmos."[19] On the other hand, since so much of the text occupies itself with his own and others' readings of his story, he serves as a focal point for Pynchon's exploration of acts of interpretation. His story requires readers to choose a position reflecting on Slothrop's own hermeneutics, as Maureen Quilligan insists. "We must judge Slothrop's reading to have been at one point surely very trivial. But his persistent concern with texts, along with all the other characters' obsessions with reading, makes us judge his success or failure in terms of how well he reads the signs about him."[20]

Slothrop's story comments directly on my concerns in this book: he is, I believe, a realistic reader in an actualistic text. He brings Newtonian assumptions to his reading of reality until his experience forces him to abandon them; then, unable to imagine other alternatives, he simply turns Newton's cosmos on its head and envisions its binary opposite. He begins with expectations of linear continuity in his own and the world's history, with the realist's anticipation of causal connections. He pursues his identity as though self and world were simple and graspable. Gradually, however, after Tantivy's disappearance

and various frustrations of his pursuit of linear order, Slothrop abandons realism for surrealism.[21] He "flips" from causality and "flops" for chaos, in *V.*'s terms; like Herbert Stencil, he seeks to unravel a singularly determined past, and then, like Benny Profane, he obliterates all memory of the past. From paranoia, "the discovery that *everything is connected*" (703), he turns to "anti-paranoia, where nothing is connected to anything, a condition not many of us can bear for long" (434). Unlike Oedipa Maas, who "had heard all about excluded middles; they were bad shit, to be avoided,"[22] Slothrop unreflectively ignores a range of middle possibilities, that *some* things might be connected, loosely and mysteriously. Slothrop's story, or Pynchon's story of the modern West, thus resembles other actualistic texts in which the realistic/Newtonian heritage continues to baffle people's understanding of actuality.

The famous office scene in which Slothrop's goods provide a first glimpse of his character anticipates both the realist and the surrealist positions he will later take. His map of London constitutes a realist's effort to fix, sort out, and memorialize his experience; his desk, in contrast, displays a surrealist's capitulation to disorder, flux, and unconnectedness. On the map, Slothrop plots events; on the desk, he allows them to scatter and disperse. The same impulse that leads him to record his conquests on the map's grid makes him "a faithful reader" of *News of the World,* where events are detailed in realistic narrative, and a student of "Weekly Intelligence Summaries from G-2," and the "F. O. *Special Handbook* or *Town Plan*" (18). That commitment to ordering disparate phenomena also accounts for Slothrop's interest in jigsaw puzzles, for the puzzle solver, like the detective, uses careful observation of detail to recover the intended unity, or "big picture," beneath apparently discontinuous fragments. But Slothrop's desk contains "lost pieces to different jigsaw puzzles," which, like the "forgotten memoranda" and "busted corkscrewing ukulele string," serve as monuments to lost, even irrecoverable connections—to a Dali-like surrealism where the disembodied "amber left eye of a Weimaraner" floats above a wasteland.

The scene also introduces Pynchon's actualistic parody of realistic narrative conventions. Slothrop first appears through a catalog of his goods, a standard literary device in which the external, material objects a character collects manifest his internal nature. This device rests on the assumptions, implicit in realistic representation, that identity is material and materially expressible and that the life story of an individual may be invoked through a chain of physical symbols. But in parodying the realistic catalog, Pynchon rejects these assumptions.[23] He includes, first, several nonsignificant items that do not reveal character: "bits of tape, string, chalk," and other debris that challenges the realistic detective to make something of average bureaucratic waste. Second, he describes several items with multiple links and with indeterminate or polyvalent significance to the rest of the novel. These things do not solve Slothrop's identity for the reader, nor does the aggregate collection on his desk; rather, they provide a mysterious and disunified glimpse of some of his interests. And the realistic reader, determined to carry away a clear picture of Slothrop? Pynchon mocks this sneaking, voyeuristic detective in the figure of Teddy Bloat, who threads his linear way through the maze of office/ prose/life, who seizes the picture he wants from the welter of Slothropian detail, and who delivers Slothrop up to a mode of interpretation that will grasp and use him as an object.

Though the office scene indicates conflicting impulses in Slothrop, his principal role in part 1 of *GR* is that of realistic plotter. He acquires importance in the novel for his mapmaking: he pastes colored stars, labeled with the names of girls he has met, lusted after, conquered, or simply imagined, all over the map of London. The narrator suggests, "At its best, it does celebrate a flow, a passing from which—among the sudden demolitions from the sky [. . .]—he can save a moment here or there" (23). Slothrop's map attempts, in other words, to fix pleasant moments and to track in a series of times and places a multitude of girls. By plotting these conquests in a sequential order of dated stars on the grid of London, Slothrop reveals his Western, analytical understanding of the world, in which the map—the two-dimensional survey from a God's-eye view *above* experience—becomes an acceptable symbol for experience itself. If his map tries to counter his own tendency to lose and forget (girls, memories, paper clips) and to save meaning from the world's "sudden demolitions," it remains, perversely, a dead memorial and a mockery of meaning, precisely because it valorizes material quantity and external setting.

Slothrop's map attracts the attention of other cartographers, with their inevitable realistic expectations. Because Slothrop's map is identical to Roger Mexico's map of rocket strikes, "It's the map that spooks them all" (85). Those who study Slothrop misinterpret the correlation of the two maps when, unable to envision the two as *parallel,* the result of a purely mysterious coincidence, they try instead to imagine causal connections linking them in *series.* While Roger Mexico, alone, argues that the correlation is "a statistical oddity," "Rollo Groast thinks it's precognition," Edwin Treacle imagines "psychokinesis," and Pointsman believes Slothrop responds to a stimulus in the rocket (and in Jamf's early conditioning) which Slothrop somehow feels before the rocket strikes (85-87). These psychoscientists attempt, in short, to invent reasons, whether mechanical or extrasensory, determining the peculiar correlation; as arch-Newtonian Pointsman says, "No effect without cause, and a clear train of linkages" (89). But the curiously matching maps, whose mystery generates Pynchon's plot, derail causality and deconstruct the very notion of the map as a fixed and accurate representation of the world.[24]

In part because of the scientists' obsession to explain Slothrop's sexuality and its connection with the rocket, readers have also tried to solve what Pynchon intends as inexplicable mystery. Jamf's conditioning leads Slothrop to have erections in anticipation of the rockets, critics suggest;[25] perhaps "his penis has been replaced or grafted with Imipolex G."[26] But Pynchon provides no such reassuring cause, psychological or mechanical, for Slothrop's erections. In fact, he undermines the likelihood of any direct link—especially Imipolex G—between Jamf's experiments and Slothrop's later behavior. The plastic, Jamf's supposed stimulus, may not have been invented until well after the experiments (249, 286); moreover, the V-2 rockets fired at London did not contain Imipolex G, for Slothrop finds reference to it only in the materials list for the Schwarzgerät, the single rocket 00000 modified by Blicero (242). Furthermore, Slothrop receives, and carries in his pocket for several days, a white chess knight supposedly made of Imipolex G—to which he does not respond with an erection (436). Any connection between whatever Jamf used to cause the infant's erections and the rockets, which seem to arouse the adult, becomes impossible to forge from the evidence. And, to expand the ambiguities, Slothrop later reveals that his map and his stories were partly fictionalized (302). The perfect correlation of maps was based, then, on a mixture of real and invented data.

Other moments in Pynchon's text suggest that the correlation happens by purest chance. By chance, Tantivy proposes that Slothrop investigate bomb strikes: "It's the best chance we'll have to one-up that lot over in T.I." (234). By accident, then, Slothrop's job makes him follow the bombs, which strike in a Poisson distribution all over London; Slothrop meets girls in that same pattern. The episodes marked by stars on his map occur by chance and by the woman's desire: Slothrop is, if anything, a passive but willing follower in the meetings we see with Cynthia (26) and Darlene (114), both of which begin with coincidental contacts in accidental places. Instead of the realist's causal link between serial events, sought so desperately by Pointsman and his mad scientific crew, Pynchon rests his plot on the actualist's metaphoric parallel between various eruptions of chance.

True, Slothrop does respond to rocket falls with erections (26, 120), and to the study of rocket technology with lust for Katje (224); but his sexuality is neither simpler nor more determined than that of other characters. Does his sexual response to rocketry confirm analyst Mickey Wuxtry-Wuxtry's hypothesis that Slothrop is "in love, in sexual love, with his, and his race's, death" (738)? Or does it amount to a more life-affirming quest for pleasure and warmth in the face of a terrifying death-technology, as Darlene suspects (120)? We cannot be sure, and so the rocket-erection link remains ambiguous in nature as well as in cause and extent. Parallels with other characters stir the same muddy waters: Pudding's coprophilia, Pirate's fetishism, and Blicero's or Sir Marcus's sadomasochism all reveal Western society's death instinct, as Lawrence Wolfley observes,[27] but all, simultaneously, attempt to reject the deadened sexlessness the West encourages. "Just a neuter, just a recording eye" is what "They" want, according to Sir Stephen Dodson-Truck: "They aren't even sadists. . . . There's just *no passion at all*" (216). It is not, then, Slothrop's sexuality but rather his impulse to grid his conquests on a map that demonstrates his Western, realistic consciousness in part 1 of the novel.

These mental traits reach full bloom in part 2, where Slothrop's definitive role changes from plotter to reader: he becomes the realistic exegete. Sent to the Riviera to read, he spends most of his time studying voluminous documents on rocketry, plastics, propulsion, and marketing. When he is not reading printed words and figures, Slothrop occupies himself with compulsive interpretations of the minute details of his surroundings. On the first morning, he reads Katje's ID bracelet, then her face, and "the conniving around him now he feels instantly, in his heart" (188). He learns to interpret dialogue by the books: "He will learn to hear quote marks in the speech of others. It is a bookish kind of reflex" (241). He sees raindrops as asterisks, "inviting him to look down at the bottom of the text of the day, where footnotes will explain all" (204). Not only does Slothrop interpret everything, major or minor, plotted or accidental, as though it all bore directly on him, but he also applies a particularly paranoid mode of reading, in which everything connects to everything else in one grand design revealing the careful hand of the creator.

In part 2, Slothrop allows chance no role at all in his own or the world's affairs; for every effect, he posits a cause. Most of part 2 is set in the Casino Hermann Goering, whose ornate game room makes Slothrop prickle repeatedly with a sense of hidden design. Though Pynchon never provides any basis for Slothrop's hunches, Slothrop resolutely reads the game room as a sinister locus intended, like the realistic narrative, to invoke the appearance of chance while excluding the reality. "These are no longer quite outward and visible signs of a game of chance. There is another enterprise here, more real than that, less merciful, and systematically hidden from the likes of Slothrop" (202). His own pursuits at the casino are not, in his view, accidental: "Slothrop has been playing against the invisible House, perhaps after all for his soul, all day" (205). Finally, inevitably, the same logic extends backward to include his entire life story in one rigidly determined realistic plot. "All in his life of what has looked free or random, is discovered to've been under some Control, all the time, the same as a fixed roulette wheel" (209). Slothrop eventually interprets all phenomena—Tantivy's death, the bomb patterns destroying railroad tracks—as causally ordered results of hidden designs.

Slothrop's readings also rely on the realistic assumption that all phenomena, however apparently discontinuous, actually cohere in a single unified design: not only are all accidents linked by plots, but all plots are connected by an Overplot. Amassing information from various documents on rocketry at the beginning of part 2, and a history of Jamf and Imipolex G at the end, Slothrop assimilates all the data into a continuous story, all the corporations into a single cartel, and all the villains into one simple They. His own education at Harvard, the heterocyclic polymer, a Swiss chemical cartel, and the gathering of rocket intelligence in the office of Duncan Sandys—

these and other apparently disparate phenomena conceal an all-inclusive order, a continuous global conspiracy focused on Slothrop. Pynchon places Slothrop at Jamf's grave as part 2 ends and shows him that "Jamf is only dead," but Slothrop will not be deterred from his obsessive continuities. "The absence of Jamf surrounds him like an odor, one he knows but can't quite name, an aura that threatens to go epileptic any second" (268-69).

In part 3, Slothrop shifts from questing to drifting and from paranoia to anti-paranoia. He stops forging the linear continuities of realism and abandons detective rationality. "Rain drips, soaking into the floor, and Slothrop perceives that he is losing his mind. If there is something comforting—religious, if you want—about paranoia, there is still also anti-paranoia, where nothing is connected to anything, a condition not many of us can bear for long. Well right now Slothrop feels himself sliding onto the anti-paranoid part of his cycle, feels the whole city around him going back roofless, vulnerable, uncentered as he is [. . .] Either They have put him here for a reason, or he's just here. He isn't sure that he wouldn't, actually, rather have that *reason*" (434). In the anti-paranoid state he inhabits through the later episodes of part 3, mindless and antirationalistic pleasures, including sex, drugs, and food, gain the upper hand over Slothrop's urge to map or to read them. Indeed, Slothrop increasingly cultivates mindlessness, imagining himself in a surreal, disconnected environment where he can become a "glozing neuter." He forgets continuities of mind, will, and heart in the act of shedding rigid Western causality. Caught in the either/or, reason/reasonlessness, garden/glass binary logic that Pynchon presents as a central problem in Western thought, Slothrop stops being a Western man, but he also ceases to be human. This change, which occupies him throughout part 3, can be measured through Slothrop's encounters with other characters, especially as they increasingly supply his motivation.

Geli Tripping, Slothrop's first companion in part 3, displays mental powers different from the linear, rational, analytical ones synonymous with the West and thus suggests alternatives to Slothrop. Like other benign figures Slothrop meets near the end of part 2, Geli stimulates Slothrop's mind, providing him with information as well as food and safety. She awakens his memory and intelligence, and she challenges his habitual modes of perception: "Forget frontiers now. Forget subdivisions. There aren't any" (294). When she takes Slothrop to the Brocken to make God-shadows at dawn, she demonstrates a natural vitality that does not exclude mind, but rather draws on intuitive and alogical mental powers the West has suppressed, and these enable a united celebration of mind and body. Like the good witch in *The Wizard of Oz,* Tripping gives Slothrop magical shoes (Tchitcherine's boots), furthers his travels (in the Oz-like balloon), and liberates him from some misconceptions. Shortly after he leaves her, he comes to the realization that "the Schwarzgerät is no Grail, Ace, that's not what the G in Imipolex G stands for. And you are no knightly hero" (364).

Emil ("Säure") Bummer, Slothrop's next important companion, helps both to free Slothrop from social rules and linear logic and to strip him of mind and identity. A one-man sedition act, cat burglar, counterfeiter, doper, and "depraved old man" (365), Bummer provides a model of counterculture resistance to Western social norms and thus encourages Slothrop's readiness to drop out of that particular game. Bummer quickly drafts him for a different game, however; he projects superhuman powers onto Slothrop (now Rocketman) as surely as Pointsman and the Home Office did, reclothes him as they did, and sends him out into the Zone for his own purposes, as they did. Slothrop is willing enough to forget his own identity and quest, put on Rocketman's cape, and go to Potsdam for hashish. Under the influence of drugs, Slothrop suspends connections and loses contact with people and memories. Hence Bummer, suggestively named for a bad encounter with drugs, and the life-style of mindless pleasures he represents, actually hasten Slothrop's disintegration.

Dissolution guides Slothrop's alliance with Margherita (Greta Erdmann. Slothrop plays another temporary role with her, suspending pursuit of his own history in order to follow her quest for her daughter Bianca. Acting the part of Max Schlepzig, whip wielder, he becomes a meek appendage to Erdmann's masochism. Their couplings parody human connection, as do their conversations, all filmic, false, and self-absorbed. Since Slothrop feels his isolation more acutely in these mock contacts, he naturally slips into anti-paranoia, "where nothing is connected to anything," while lying in bed beside Greta (434). Worse, he also slides into a willingness to cause pain, to which Pynchon suggests all Western men are prone; "their" punishments become "his own cruelty," and Erdmann "his victim" (396-97).

The ease, then, with which Slothrop turns from whipping the mother to using eleven-year-old Bianca suggests that links of moral accountability remain operative in Pynchon's world, if not in Slothrop's. Bianca provides an alternative to disconnectedness in the possibility of a loving union. "He knows. Right here, right now, under the make-up and the fancy underwear, she *exists,* love, invisibility . . . for Slothrop this is some discovery" (470). Like Geli Tripping, who fulfills a similar promise with Slothrop's double, Tchitcherine, Bianca is very young, innocent despite her sexual precociousness, natural despite her affectations (Bianca tells time by the sun, not clocks [468]), vulnerable, and lonely. But Slothrop refuses to risk being transformed by union: "for this he is to be counted, after all, among the Zone's lost. The Pope's staff is always going to remain barren, like Slothrop's own unflowering cock" (470). He not only resists the magical connection of love, but he even rejects the links of memory: he forgets Bianca as his eyes turn away.

From the beginning, Slothrop uses Bianca as an object and thus repeats the sins of the fathers: his contact with her marks his transition from sinned-against-son to sinning father. On first sight of Bianca, he reacts with instant lust (463). He joins the decadent partiers on the *Anubis*

in a voyeuristic mass orgy, replete with couplings of every variety except those capable of producing life, as Greta spanks Bianca's naked bottom. When she comes to his bed, Slothrop explodes like the rocket that can only bring death. While the narrator emphasizes her childishness throughout this scene—her smallness, "presubdeb breasts," "little feet," "the little girl," "slender child," face "round with baby-fat," and while Bianca herself reminds him, "I'm a child," Slothrop treats her like any other adult female object (469-70). Though the narrator pleads, "she must be more than an image, a product, a promise to pay," Slothrop takes his mindless pleasure with her as though she were a futureless thing, which she soon becomes. Like Blicero, who uses his "children" Gottfried and Katje, or even more like his own father, who has sold him as a commodity for sexual use, Slothrop doubly betrays the child Bianca. Framed on the one side by the story of Achtfaden's betrayal of his friend Klaus Närrisch (456), and on the other side by the account of Greta Erdmann's murder of Jewish children (478), Slothrop's encounter with Bianca constitutes both a betrayal of friendship and a sacrifice of innocence.

Appropriately, then, Slothrop next takes up with Gerhardt von Göll (der Springer), manipulator, profiteer, father figure, and betrayer. Slothrop serves von Göll unquestioningly; after failing to rescue Bianca, he succeeds in saving von Göll from the Russians and then in recovering a package for him—one planted, ironically, beneath the dead Bianca's feet. Von Göll, meanwhile, virtually reenacts Broderick's original betrayal: he evidently sells Tyrone out to Pointsman, who, like Jamf, has evil designs on Slothrop's penis. His alliance with von Göll comments on Slothrop's assumption of the father-user's role. It also reveals his growing indifference to actuality, his diminishing awareness of a consequential world outside the one he "frames" in any instant. On the *Anubis,* the narrator has pointed out Slothrop's "general loss of emotion, a numbness he ought to be alarmed at, but can't quite" (490-91). Later, the narrator adds that Slothrop "has begun to thin, to scatter [. . .] the narrower your sense of Now, the more tenuous you are. It may get to where you're having trouble remembering what you were doing five minutes ago, or even, as Slothrop now— what you're doing *here.* [. . .] So here passes for him one more negligence . . . and likewise groweth his Preterition sure. . . . There is no good reason to hope for any turn, any surprise *I-see-it,* not from Slothrop" (509). Slothrop sheds the pernicious Western determination to forge linear, causal chains of time—only to explode time's continuity into small, unmemorable fragments of "now."

After von Göll, Slothrop's companions mean less to him and to his story as, increasingly isolated, he shuns close contacts and forgets the people he meets. He tries to become less visible and to see others as little as possible. He avoids involvement, learns few names, keeps moving, and becomes "intensely alert to trees," grass, and inanimate things (552). To evade the burden of his memory, he "won't interpret, not any more" (567). His associations during this period are brief, and he prefers the company of children. For a time Slothrop follows a "fat kid of eight or nine" named Ludwig, whose plumpness, doomed innocence, and unlikely quest (for a lost lemming) make him a young double for Slothrop. Soon, though, Slothrop leaves Ludwig in dangerous company and never thinks of him again (559). Slothrop plays games with groups of nameless children, one of which drafts him as Pig-Hero Plechazunga (567). He loses the "tiny girl" who clutches his leg in the riot; he leaves the girl of seventeen who helps him escape without asking her name (570-71).

Toward the end of part 3, Slothrop willingly sheds adulthood, reason, and human identity. He wears the pig suit for weeks, rather than changing to human attire. While he has previously fit into various borrowed suits, uniforms, and evening clothes, now, with his humanity become tenuous, the pig costume "seems to fit perfectly. Hmm" (568). Frieda the pig adopts him as kindred flesh, and even the narrator seems to forget Slothrop's name and race: he calls him "the pig" ten times as the sequence in Cuxhaven begins (595-96). Others have, of course, failed to recognize Slothrop in different clothes, as if only his inanimate and always borrowed apparel gave him identity at all. David Seed argues that Slothrop's disguises suggest a "ubiquitous stage-director choosing these costumes for him," and his resemblances to others "undermine his individuality."[28] As he renounces more and more of his adult humanity, Slothrop fittingly appears for the last time in part 3 naked, curled, asleep, his regression to mindless and irresponsible babyhood complete. He dreams of Zwölfkinder, the city of falsely preserved, illusory childhood, "and Bianca smiling, he and she riding on the wheel" (609).

Slothrop virtually disappears from part 4: he does little but think, and his mind becomes increasingly confused and chaotic. Having rid himself of the sense of continuity in his own and the world's history, he has lost any recognizable identity. "He has become one plucked albatross. Plucked, hell—*stripped*. Scattered all over the Zone. It's doubtful if he can ever be 'found' again, in the conventional sense of 'positively identified and detained'" (712). Invisible, then, to others, he has eventually no human contacts; even the narrator turns away from Slothrop, as he ceases to be involved in events in time, and focuses instead on other characters who still have stories.

In his last appearance as an active character, Slothrop appears to merge with nature. All his renunciations of mind and identity, begun in part 3, reach full expression here: he recalls less and less, eventually forgetting the rain by the time the rainbow appears (626); he lives naked and alone and does not speak to anyone (623). In his advanced anti-paranoia, even his past selves appear disconnected—all "ten thousand of them" (624). His last two gestures, however, suggest to some critics that Slothrop achieves grace, transcendence, or Rilkean salvation. First, Slothrop lies "spread-eagled at his ease in the sun . . . he becomes a cross himself, a crossroads, a living intersection where the judges have come to set up a gibbet" (625). Critics often quote from Rilke's *Sonnets to Orpheus*:

Be, in this immeasurable night,
magic power at your senses' crossroad,
be the meaning of their strange encounter.

Pynchon refers to Rilke here and elsewhere far more ironically than critics suppose.[29] Pynchon sees Rilke as part of a decadent Germanic romanticism which contributed to Nazi power. Like his references to Wagner, who is played on the Nazi toiletship (450), his allusions to Rilke actually parody the Austrian's mysticism. In the crossroads passage of *GR*, Slothrop does not attain magic power or feel his senses converge. Rather, he lies, oblivious, at an intersection *once* charged with magic power that has since dispersed: ages before, a hanged man ejaculates as his neck breaks, and one drop of his sperm changes to a mandrake root. This power is immediately exploited for profit by a magician who carries the root home to multiply his cash. The mandrake's magic is further routinized when a bureaucrat arrives to discuss the long-range fiscal implications of the uprooting, with a "fraternal business smile" (625). If the sexual response to death, as old as European civilization and still shared by Slothrop, as well as virtually every character in *GR*, once contained possibilities for magic, those were at once seized by bourgeois professionals and turned to profit. Does Slothrop become "the meaning of his strange encounter" with this resonant crossroads? Hardly. He lies "spread-eagled at his ease."

Once, the narrator reminds us, Slothrop had "days when in superstition and fright he could *make it all fit*," when he forcibly read all phenomena as entries "in a record, a history." Now, instead, he sees "a very thick rainbow here, a stout rainbow cock driven down out of public clouds into Earth, green wet valleyed Earth, and his chest fills and he stands crying, not a thing in his head, just feeling natural" (626). This gesture suggests that Slothrop achieves emotional and physical peace—and indeed he does, but at the cost of the mental qualities that have made him a human being as opposed to a rock or a tree. The "stout rainbow cock" promises fertility for Earth, but not for Slothrop, whose "unflowering cock" "is always going to remain barren" (470). That he must empty his head to feel natural suggests that Slothrop has defined his alternatives too narrowly—early on, when he was still able to define alternatives, he might have saved both head and heart, civilized reason and natural feeling.

The rest is anticlimax: later glimpses present Slothrop's inevitable fritterings away of self. Significantly, the last depictions of Slothrop seem intended deliberately to undermine whatever peace or transcendence he might have achieved in the rainbow vision. Rather than leaving Slothrop "feeling natural," we see him subsequently engaged in the same old Oedipal conflicts, the same movie and comic-book simplifications, and the same regressive nostalgia for childhood. In one episode, Slothrop inhabits a comic-book Raketen-Stadt where, as part of the Floundering Four, he battles the ever-murderous father (674). In another, he becomes the "Sentimental Surrealist," obsessed with paranoid plots like the vacuum of "sun-silence." This last picture emphasizes his isolation from external reality (he hears only his own heart), from humanity (he becomes "the stranger"), from the past (he does not remember "how he got to the white tiled room half an hour before hose-out time"), and especially from nature: he sits inside a greasy spoon, under "bulb-shine," at a "riveted table" (696-97). Later, he returns to the father theme he can neither resolve nor outgrow; young Tyrone instructs his father in the mechanical means to immortality: "*We* can live forever, in a clean, honest, purified Electro-world" (699). Speaking for this vision, as *un*natural and oversimplified as any in the novel, Slothrop's voice takes on the vocabulary and the stammer of the perennial ten-year-old, suggesting once again that he has regressed rather than transcended.

An understanding of the end of the novel depends, I believe, on an awareness that Weissmann/Blicero's sacrifice of Gottfried in the rocket not only bears on Slothrop's story but logically completes it. First, though, I want to examine an alternative approach, one advanced in rather extreme form by Douglas Fowler in *A Reader's Guide to GR.* Interpreting *GR* as "romantic art," the rocket as "a graceful piece of romantic death-machinery," and Gottfried as motivated by a "romantic impulse to *die beautifully,*" Fowler sees the ending as a satisfying culmination for the "acetylene intensity of Weissmann's and Gottfried's hopeless love."[30] This ending also provides a tragic catharsis for the reader, according to Fowler. "Life is obvious and tiresome; it is repetitious, inconclusive, utterly anticlimactic. We do our best not to admit to this fact, but our most impressive responses to it are fantasies of escape—of death. The confinement from which so much of our great artistic achievement releases us is probably nothing more glamorous than boredom with the continuity of instinctual life. Whatever its ethical claims, tragic literature is immensely satisfactory because our participation in it brings us to an *ending,* a way out, an escape from continuity."[31]

One must, I think, object: surely Blicero embodies romantic ideals in a perverse and decadent form; surely Pynchon suggests neither boredom with life, whose rich variety interests his narrator, nor longing for death; and surely no text can intend so climactic "an *ending*" when it has, as Fowler himself ably explains, continually withheld resolutions, suspended subplots, and celebrated a "pattern of inconclusiveness and anticlimax."[32] A better approach must allow the ending its continuity with the rest of Pynchon's text and Blicero his relationship to Slothrop.

These two have, first, a schematic relationship as antithetical doubles: they can be imagined as zero and one, where both points represent different forms of death, and life occupies the excluded middle ground. While Slothrop abandons connections, including those linking his various selves, and thus loses human identity, Blicero pursues linear connections to their inevitable end in death and thus loses human identity. Slothrop ceases to make fictions about his own role, and Blicero constructs a perfect, closed fiction; both thereby deny themselves living roles. Slothrop, the realist-turned-surrealist, abandons

the quest for coherence at the cost of life; Blicero, the romantic, pursues an exclusive, even monomaniacal coherence at the cost of life. Blicero, the anti-Slothrop, achieves prominence in *GR*'s last movement partly because his yearning for a climactic, ego-affirming end at once parallels and opposes—and both ways illuminates—Slothrop's own anticlimactic and ego-dissolving end.

Slothrop's scattering has, more importantly, a dynamic and enabling relationship to Blicero's rocket firing: Slothrop, the sacrificed son, fails to break out of the disastrous cycle of filial passivity and paternal ruthlessness, thus empowering Blicero's murder of his "beloved son," Gottfried. Slothrop never outgrows his adolescent resentment of the father, or his alternating wish for revenge on and atonement with this figure; Slothrop reenacts the sins for which he blames his father, especially in his use of Bianca. Slothrop thus legitimates Blicero, who "is the father you will never quite manage to kill," and helps to perpetuate the Oedipal cycle (747). Granted power by the son's meekness, Blicero fires the phallic rocket that signifies Western man's age-old lust for conquest, while Gottfried—a clear analogue for Slothrop—climbs inside the father's system and rides it passively to his death. Like Slothrop, Gottfried chooses his own annihilation at the father's hands. "He knows, somehow, incompletely, that he has a decision to make . . . that Blicero expects something from him . . . but Blicero has always made the decisions" (724). Like Slothrop, Gottfried simply fails to choose and thereby obeys the father's will, while the narrator ironically comments: "If there is still hope for Gottfried here in this wind-beat moment, then there is hope elsewhere. The scene itself must be read as a card: what is to come" (724)—which is, as we soon learn: the sons, Gottfrieds and Slothrops, betray their potential to create "God's peace."

Pynchon, meanwhile, has plucked the rocket firing out of its sequence (it supposedly occurred in the last days of the war, otherwise presented in part 2 of *GR*) and placed it at the very end: this disruption of chronology emphasizes the connection between these sons' submission to the father and the apocalypse descending on the Western world. In the final pages of Pynchon's text, Blicero takes on a larger meaning than the unkillable father. As his tarot unfolds, he becomes the intellectual authority sustaining political and corporate powers. "The King of Cups, crowning his hopes, is the fair intellectual-king. If you're wondering where he's gone, look among the successful academics, the Presidential advisers, the token intellectuals who sit on boards of directors. He is almost surely there. Look high, not low. His future card, the card of what will come, is The World" (740). Blicero stands behind "Richard M. Zhlubb" (Nixon), who manages the theater in which we sit, absorbing images of reality and waiting to be destroyed. Thus, in its fullest implication, Slothrop's capitulation to a past that he only imagines has conditioned his responses authorizes powers that promise to devastate the future. A victim of authority like all Western sons, Slothrop nonetheless spends his life affirming traditions—especially the realistic vision of linear continuity—whose inadequacy eventually shuffles him, and may explode the rest of us, into oblivion.

PARALLEL, NOT SERIES

Against Slothrop, the primary—though certainly not the only—realist of *GR,* Pynchon contrasts several secondary and inevitably preterite characters who see the world as actualists. These characters do not occupy elect roles in Pynchon's narrative, but rather minor ones commenting, through parallel and metaphoric resemblances, on Slothrop's problems and choices. Unlike the Mossmoons, the Pointsmans, or the Bliceros, they have little power within the various systems they serve and from which they are always partly alienated. Given the wartime setting, most of them work for a government and therefore come under the direct influence of the elect, with Their assertion that life is realistic; typically, then, the actualists only gradually trust their own intuitions of contingency. Although magic often follows when chance brings two of them together, they do not form a systematized group. They are not all members of the Counterforce, which becomes in its later days another colonizing elect. Who, then, are the actualists? They include Tchitcherine, Geli Tripping, Roger Mexico, Enzian, Leni Pökler, Pig Bodine—and among the yet more minor, Tantivy, Bianca, Darlene, Trudi, Webley Silvernail, Squalidozzi, Graciela Imago Portales, and Beláustegui.

The actualists envision a form of continuity that is, to return to Leni Pökler's formulation, "parallel, not series": links are neither obliterated nor imagined in rigid, causal lines. Events and phenomena remain connected, but by loose, conditional bonds like those metaphor sketches between entities whose difference it openly acknowledges. While stories of the past may be constructed (for events are not simply a chaotic jumble), the actualist genealogy posits an intricacy to the plot, grants accident a major role, and assumes that motives, origins, and causes are not solvable. Actualists neither forget the past, public or personal, nor dedicate their lives to perpetuating it. For this reason, they use drugs more sparingly than, say, Osbie Feel or Säure Bummer: actualists avoid the loss of memory as emphatically as they reject its overzealous reconstructions.

Very near the start of *GR,* two different images of continuity juxtapose linear against metaphoric links and, not coincidentally, deadliness against vitality. In the first, a train moves. "They pass in line, out of the main station, out of downtown, and being pushing into older and more desolate parts of the city. Is this the way out? [. . .] No, this is not a disentanglement from, but a progressive *knotting into* [. . .] much too soon, they are under the final arch: brakes grab and spring terribly. It is a judgment from which there is no appeal. [. . .] It is the end of the line" (3-4). Like the rocket's linear motion from point *A* to point *B,* the train's journey suggests the realist's conception of one-directional time, moving toward "the final arch," or last judgment, or death. The second image, appearing a few pages later, follows the nonlinear spread

of banana odor. "Now there grows among all the rooms [. . .] the fragile, musaceous odor of Breakfast: flowery, permeating, surprising [. . .] taking over not so much through any brute pungency or volume as by the high intricacy to the weaving of its molecules, sharing the conjuror's secret by which—though it is not often Death is told so clearly to fuck off—the living genetic chains prove even labyrinthine enough to preserve some human face down ten or twenty generations" (10). Woven, highly intricate, labyrinthine, and unpredictable, this molecular continuity serves the multiple needs of life, with its linked helical "chains" that preserve without imprisoning. Nonlinear as this meandering growth is, it constitutes a form of continuity for our organic lineage; the train, by contrast, can only follow its tracks to "the end of the line."

With linear continuity, actualists also reject the colonialistic conquest of the "out-of-line." They refuse to assimilate or convert the other but rather allow it to remain alien, accidental, and free. Politically, they oppose imperialism—whether they fight it in the streets, like Leni Pökler; or lead anti-imperialist groups, like Enzian; or subvert the power of imperialist systems, like Pig Bodine and Roger Mexico. Personally, they try to achieve relationships based not on dominance and submission but on equality. Typically, they do not fix, control, or keep the other but rather encourage change and freedom, as Geli Tripping permits Tchitcherine to roam. Pynchon's actualists do not passively efface themselves, like Katje, Gottfried, Franz Pökler, and the later Slothrop; they do not submit any more than they seek to dominate, but they manage to insist actively on their own voice and values without imposing any system forcefully on others. Rather than colonialist hierarchies, then, their relationships are characterized by fluidity, openness, and tolerance for eccentricity.

Pynchon's actualists resist teleologies; they do not allow life to be shaped by its end. For these actualists, time is not a causal chain directed at death, transcendence, or salvation but a succession of coincidental moments to be celebrated for their own sake. "There is the moment, and its possibilities," thinks Leni Pökler (159); the Argentinian Beláustegui "knows his odds, the shapes of risk are intimate to him as loved bodies. Each moment has its value, its probable success against other moments in other hands, and the shuffle for him is always moment-to-moment" (613). This metaphor of time as a game of chance suggests both the risks actualists perceive in momentary time and the playful attitude with which they accept the odds. Their perception of time liberates actualists from the debilitating earnestness of those like Jeremy, Pointsman, and Blicero; though they work, actualists always have time for play, jokes, song, dance, and fantasy. So Roger Mexico clowns during Pointsman's dog hunt, Webley Silvernail imagines a comic dance routine with the rats and mice from the lab, and Darlene plays her elaborate "English candy drill" on Slothrop; none sees their work, their company, or its products as ends worthy of their entire attention.

As actualists, these characters affirm accident and multiplicity in place of causality and unity; hence they understand even their own paranoid suspicions as possible metaphors, not certain truths. While others imagine a single, causally unified plot, Bodine and Leni/Solange envision many plots, and looser ones.

> "This is some kind of a plot, right?" Slothrop sucking saliva from velvet pile.
>
> "*Everything* is some kind of a plot, man," Bodine laughing. "And yes but, the arrows are pointing all different ways," Solange illustrating with a dance of hands, red-pointed finger-vectors. Which is Slothrop's first news, out loud, that the Zone can sustain many other plots besides those polarized upon himself. (603)

If actualists remain paranoid, in other words, they do not understand events as simply "caused" by other plotters, and they insist on a relative freedom to elude Their clumsy stratagems. The subject, envisioned by actualists as contingent rather than necessary, may not finally be so important in Their plans: Slothrop, for example, turns out to be a trivial tool in the eyes of Sir Marcus and the Home Office, while the blacks and their rocket are the real, short-term objective (615). Early on, Enzian tries to suggest to Slothrop such a statistical view; the Hereros, he says, have "a sense for the statistics of our being. One reason we grew so close to the Rocket, I think, was this sharp awareness of how contingent, like ourselves, the Aggregat 4 could be—how at the mercy of small things" (362). While actualists continue to invent coherent fictions about their experience, they do not forge the linear, necessary, and unified plots of realism: they tell themselves the plural and indeterminate stories of actualism.

As a final expression of their openness to chance, Pynchon's actualists are inveterate risk-takers and, therefore, lovers: of individuals, races, humanity, life. Where realists like Teddy Bloat and Pointsman try to minimize risk, establishing bureaucratic systems for self-preservation and avoiding the dangers of close contact with others, actualists like Geli Tripping accept their own vulnerability, "not holding a thing back," taking the world in "bare and open arms" (294-95). Unlike Slothrop, actualists refuse numbness; they risk losing those they love, but they remain emotionally vital. Slothrop's friend Bodine, for example, undergoes "a transvestism of caring, and the first time in his life it's happened" when he takes on Magda's mannerisms after her arrest (742). Long after he and Blicero part, Enzian "risks what former lovers risk whenever the Beloved is present" (659). By itself, caring is not enough in *GR;* no character says, with *V.*'s McClintic Sphere, "Keep cool but care." Indeed, as if in answer to Sphere's too-simple formula, several characters in *GR* care while remaining icy. Pirate Prentice cares for Roger and Jessica (35); Franz Pökler adores Leni (162); Pointsman cares about Gwenhidwy (170-71); and Dodson-Truck feels fond of Slothrop and Katje: "I care about you, both of you. I do care, believe me, Slothrop. . . . I *care!*" (216). In addition to caring, the actualists of *GR* also refuse to use, sacrifice, dominate, or control. Their caring does not constitute a passive yearning to escape the confines of self, but rather an active, responsible, and generous creation of continuities between subject and other.

While film is *GR*'s realistic art, with its emphasis on linear narrative, plausible detail, and causal continuity, actualistic art has its particular representative in music, especially song. Relying as it does on parallels, counterpoints, harmonies, and repeated motifs, as well as a series of notes and words, song is ideally suited to express the actualist's sense of multiplicity, accident, and quantum continuity. Song reflects the playful, momentary temporal faith of the preterite, as opposed to the end-ordered earnestness of the elect. "While nobles are crying in their nights' chains, the squires sing. The terrible politics of the Grail can never touch them. Song is the magic cape" (701). While film serves the colonialist ends of those in power, song—even the traditional religious lyrics of the compline service, and even sung by a choir of soldiers—retains a subversive, system-disrupting and life-affirming potential. Celebrating as it does the possibility that *"love occurs"* (440), song enables one's furthest reach beyond rationality, materialism, and causality, toward intangible and unpredictable magic. In the evensong, with "the tired men and their black bellwether reaching as far as they can, as far from their sheeps' clothing as the year will let them stray," listeners suddenly arrive in Bethlehem, "for the one night, leaving only the clear way home and the memory of the infant you saw" (134-35). Song does not dispel time or darkness or uncertainty; song frees people from the determinacy of their own rational systems. That *GR* ends by granting us time, despite the darkness and the falling rocket, to sing a hymn invoking alternatives to our imminent ruin ("there is a Hand to turn the time") surely signals Pynchon's hope that we might yet lift the repressive burden of Western linear reason.

Of those who come to actualistic perceptions of reality in *GR,* Tchitcherine particularly merits a closer look for the parallels between his and Slothrop's stories. The Russian bears a signal resemblance to his American counterpart: "When you came in I almost thought you were Tchitcherine," Geli says to Slothrop (290). Both men are pattern seekers and paranoids; both intuit a multinational cartel; and both chase the rocket through the Zone. Both go east in the service of their governments—Slothrop to Europe, Tchitcherine to Central Asia. Both encounter revelations at "Holy Centers" (the Kirghiz Light and Peenemünde), but both fail to recognize their meaning, doomed "always to be held at the edges of revelations" (566). Both enjoy drugs and costumes; both share an obsession with blackness; both feel betrayed by their fathers; both undertake personal quests in the Zone—quests for origins, for causality, and for their own lineage, which become perverse quests for annihilation. Quickly suspected by their governments, both men are isolated and exiled in the Zone. Such resemblances, central (as Molly Hite argues) to Pynchon's narrative strategy, function to multiply loose, parallel connections;[33] they also invite readers to explore questions of difference.

Tchitcherine's fate, unpredictably, differs sharply from Slothrop's. Near the end, Tchitcherine becomes a willing accomplice of Geli Tripping's benevolent magic. He abandons the pursuit of a closed and causal history—of his father, his brother, and his own past; but Tchitcherine does not, like Slothrop, give up continuity altogether. Rather, he chooses local and momentary continuities with Geli, whose important role in his recent past demonstrates that Tchitcherine has not simply forgotten or abolished history. His last appearance, camping by a stream with Geli in the open air, marks a departure from the linear pursuit of quests. Similarly, his attitude to the Enzian he meets in the middle of the bridge does not fulfill his previous anticipation that one or both would not survive the meeting. "The two men nod, not quite formally, not quite smiling, Enzian puts his bike in gear and returns to his journey. Tchitcherine lights a cigarette, watching them down the road, shivering in the dusk. Then he goes back to his young girl beside the stream" (734-35). This meeting occurs, not as the end of a line, but as the middle of various continuities: midbridge, midjourney, middusk, mid-Zone, and, above all, since he takes food rather than death from Enzian, midlife.

Given the similarities between Slothrop and Tchitcherine, we must wonder why they adopt such different positions as the novel ends. Predictably, Pynchon admits no one cause. In part, Tchitcherine is simply lucky, for by good chance he has won the love of a powerful and determined, as well as playful and open, young witch. A believer in nonrational magic, Geli enters the text singing about the continuity of love through memory. By no more predictable accident, Slothrop has not formed such an attachment. But Tchitcherine has consistently displayed an openness to magic and to love, especially in his repeated returns to Geli, while Slothrop habitually avoids returning to any woman. In one nightmare, he admits, "Jenny, I heard your block was hit [. . .] and I meant to go back and see if you were all right, but . . . I just *didn't*" (256). The two men diverge definitively in their willingness to return in memory: Tchitcherine recalls much more than Slothrop does. When in the Zone he sees a duel between black and white singers, he remembers the same structure signaling his approach to the Light a decade before (610-11). Later, Tchitcherine cultivates memories for company; he welcomes "an albatross with no curse attached: an amiable memory" (701). Unlike Slothrop, who plucks away the albatross of past selves, Tchitcherine remembers and thereby remains continuous: he can, at the end, return to Geli. This makes his story one of "magic. Sure—but not necessarily fantasy" (735).

QUANTUM CONTINUITY: THE FORM OF *GRAVITY'S RAINBOW*

Avoiding in its own larger motions the "zero" of discontinuity and the "one" of serial causality, Pynchon's story resembles neither the fragments into which Slothrop disperses nor the monomyth Blicero creates as he fires his rocket. *GR* occupies the actualistic space between, where narrative elements, like historical events or subatomic particles, remain loosely bonded but unsolvable. "It all

goes along together. Parallel, not series. Metaphors." The very density of Pynchon's novel, where Slothrop, Blicero, Tchitcherine, Enzian, and Mexico enact permutations of similar responses to reality, doubling and diverging in a Western "League of Nations," and where dozens of other characters reflect different facets of their overlapping struggles, enforces a parallel, not serial, mode of understanding. Phenomena as related as Pudding's coprophilia, Slothrop's rocket-erections, Greta Erdmann's sadomasochism, and Pirate Prentice's fetishism do not have one identical underlying cause, nor do they follow one another with any serial clarity in the text. Where serial order exists, as in Slothrop's story, the content of the story militates against the assumptions traditionally attached to its form: Slothrop's linear progress takes him out of line, off the Western time-line, away from a linear identity altogether. As if in answer to Forster's too-simple "only connect," *everything* connects in Pynchon's text, and the mysteries proliferate.

One feature of Pynchon's quantum continuity is an unpredictable motion from subject to subject: the narrative eye leaps surprising gaps, which the narrative voice does not fill in or justify through any retrospective reasoning. In a traditional realistic narrative, changes of temporal or spatial plane tend to follow the blocks of chapter divisions and to be "mapped" for the reader with clear transitions. After Isabel Archer's engagement, for example, James skips four years, beginning chapter 36 of *The Portrait of a Lady*: "One afternoon of the autumn of 1876, toward dusk, a young man of pleasing appearance rang at the door of a small apartment on the third floor of an old Roman house," and right away readers know where they are. Within the chapter, all the significant events of Isabel's experience during the temporal gap have been retrospectively extracted and summarized. The gap becomes, not a void, but a sketchy line: Isabel married, settled in Rome, had a son, who died six months later, and she learned to disagree with her husband.

Pynchon's quantum leaps differ in several ways. First, because he does not envision his narrative as embellishments around a single line, he does not supply missing segments but rather leaves narrative threads truly broken. What happens to Roger, Jessica, and Jeremy between II, 8, when Pointsman decides to send Jess away, and IV, 2, when she appears engaged to Jeremy? How does Katje come to leave Slothrop on the Riviera in II, 3, and why does she agree to act her sinister role with Pudding in II, 4? What does Franz Pökler do between leaving Dora in III, 1 and playing chess with Slothrop in Zwölfkinder in III, 28? Pynchon does not fill in the blanks. He does not place the reader securely or map relations between disconnected events. In three consecutive sections of part 1, Roger and Jessica spend a night together, Slothrop follows his harp down the toilet under narcosis, and Pirate receives a coded message: no narrative guide provides dates, locations, or transitions among these events. As his text progressively dissolves spatialized time-lines, Pynchon's leaps of focus occur more frequently within, as well as between, chapter units. No rationale appears for the ordering or the breaks in continuity between segments: Pynchon's narrative does not invoke causal reasoning to account for its fluctuations but rather makes of accident and uncertainty sufficient structural principles. Those empty squares between narrative sections, so frequently explicated as film-sprocket holes, also figure the gaps left by Pynchon's quantum leaps.

Pynchon similarly dismisses the stable, spatializing binary divisions on which many characters and institutions rely. Categories like war and peace disintegrate in a novel where the war's nominal end arrives unannounced, and where, as several characters perceive, the "real" wars have only begun. Distinctions like black and white, male and female, we and they, or hero and villain may indeed obsess Pynchon's characters, seeking a static order and a balanced clarity in experience; Pynchon undermines these flimsy constructions to demonstrate the fluidity and shapelessness of real time. For every opposition his characters imagine, he interjects contradictions, qualifications, confusing third and fourth terms, and webs of complication: black and white lose meaning when one central black character, named for a yellow and blue flower, is half white, and another is nicknamed "Red"; the white Russian is part silver and part gold—and there are "Norwegian mulattos." Force and counterforce, assumed to be viable alternatives by some characters, emerge as similar entities serving the same firms, especially after the Counterforce becomes, inevitably, routinized. Pynchon's narrative refuses to balance itself on these traditional pilings: it does not alternate between "hero" and "villain," it does not set dark lady against fair, it does not juxtapose civilized interiors against natural gardens. To balance pairs is to stabilize reality and to stop time; Pynchon disrupts his characters' binary assumptions and immerses them in an unbalanced, unpredictable temporal flow. His novel's four parts do not form pairs; in length, they do not balance; although numbered, titled, and provided with epigraphs, they do not impose or expose a meaningful order patterning events.

With binary oppositions, Pynchon rejects an insidious corollary: namely, the hierarchical categories erected to preserve systems in power. Not only does he interrogate colonialism in all its various guises, as it privileges "civilized" over "savage," Western over non-Western, elect over preterite; he also undermines the hierarchies of narrative form that tacitly support colonialism in traditional narratives. Divisions like "major" and "minor" characters, significant and insignificant information, or dominant and subordinate motifs appear in texts reaffirming ontological and political hierarchies, whether explicitly or implicitly. Even the structural paradigm calling, after Aristotle, for a crisis and denouement implies a hierarchical arrangement of experience in which narratives valorize one event over all others. Pynchon begins with a major character, convinced of his own major status in the plot, but as Slothrop's sense of living in a realistic novel wanes, he turns to a minor character in his own mind and in *GR*. When the category of "minor" characters broadens to include over two hundred figures, the novel has

not simply inverted, but exploded this hierarchy. Similarly, information—about the past, the rocket, the tribal customs of Hereros, or the migratory habits of lemmings—fills the novel, to such an extent that none of it can matter, but with such insistent connections that it *all* matters. The novel's "crisis" cannot be pinpointed, especially since so many of the figures who expected crises (Slothrop, Tchitcherine, Enzian, for example) do not encounter them, and those who arguably do (Blicero and Gottfried) do not experience them as epiphanic moments: rising in the rocket, Gottfried thinks of the red setter who bade him good-bye and of other minute phenomena, rather than of the meaning of life and death. No one event determines Slothrop's scattering; no single crisis precipitates the rocket hanging over the West at the novel's end. Since hierarchies such as these are necessarily retrospective and detached, selected from an exterior and final view of what mattered "in the end," an actualist like Pynchon must inevitably dismiss them in favor of the uncertain, inconclusive view of one involved in time.[34]

Like other actualists, Pynchon rejects a disciplined novelistic economy to produce in *GR* a large, sprawling, inclusive "baggy monster." Since the diffuse energies of an actualistic reality do not lend themselves readily to condensation or miniaturization, none of Pynchon's texts constitutes a synecdoche for the world it represents; even *Crying*, Pynchon's "smallest" novel, figures the artist's task not as reproducing the world in little but as "embroidering a kind of tapestry which spilled out the slit windows and into a void, seeking hopelessly to fill the void."[35] *GR*, too, spills out: without seeming edited from a foreknowledge of the end, it includes in its selected version of reality events that impend but do not fulfill their adventurous promise, acts that lead nowhere, things with no significance beyond themselves. In fact, it focuses squarely on the coincidental, the digressive, and the "finally" insignificant: Prentice picks bananas; Pointsman steps into a toilet bowl; Katje wanders around a house; Pökler plays chess. While events that would be highlighted in traditional narratives (Bianca's death, von Göll's betrayal of Slothrop, or Blicero's reaction to Gottfried's death) happen offstage in *GR*, so that their reality and import are never fully established, the events making up *GR* are comical, accidental, and, from a traditional perspective, unimportant. A novel celebrating the narrative preterite, as *GR* and other actualist texts do, commits itself to be all "middle," loose, prodigal, lengthy—anything but economical.

For related reasons, *GR* does not aspire to unity, as that has been understood and honored in the Western literary tradition. Pynchon's text emphasizes its plural focus, expanded beyond the main plot and subplot which still coalesce in a unified whole. *GR* ramifies subplots and characters past any possibility of fusion into oneness; while its multiple strands relate to each other in multiple ways, their density mocks any simple unity. Where traditional narratives devote their conclusions to a gathering together of loose ends and an integration of figures or events that have seemed (but never really been) eccentric, *GR* spins characters and actions off into more and more widely separated orbits. The novel is nowhere less single or more fractured than near its end, as Pynchon dissolves whatever illusory unity he has preserved to that point.

Allusive patterns, too, function in *GR* to suggest the dispersion of knowledge, rather than the essential unity of the world. David Cowart reads Pynchon as a traditional novelist when he asserts that "all of Pynchon's allusions—scientific and artistic—form patterns that lend unity not only to the individual stories and novels, but to the author's work as a whole."[36] On the contrary, Pynchon's allusions seem precisely intended to abolish the unities of traditional reference. As Cowart, Stark, Fowler, Ozier, and others have indicated, Pynchon alludes to worlds of information so diverse as to be unassimilable by any one reader or even—until the annotated edition, perhaps—by any one reader's guide: from calculus to King Kong, tarot to Tannhauser, Poisson to Pabst, fragments of data baffle the reader who pursues wholeness and harmony beneath this encyclopedic debris. The very nature of early criticism of *GR*, so much of which has "tracked down" references and allusive patterns without "solving" the novel's mysteries, attests the problematic disunity generated by Pynchon's allusions.

Pynchon rejects the various forms of closure through which conventional novels present reality as a stable and determined thing. From brief individual sequences to the novel at large, he substitutes anticlimax and irresolution for the cathartic end. On the last page of *V.*, "Nothing was settled"; on the last page of *GR*, the fate of the West hangs in midair, while the novel culminates, not in a definitive period, but in a dash: "Now everybody—" (760). In the meantime, Slothrop has never located the rocket or the cause of his own erections in response to it; Tchitcherine and Enzian have met without recognizing each other, and Pointsman has neither died from the "Book's curse" nor won the Nobel Prize. Peripheral sequences, too, come to nothing: Närrisch does not die, the torpedo misses the USS *Badass*, and Tantivy's death is never confirmed or explained. By refusing to bring these plots to a "satisfactory" conclusion and by repeatedly invoking readers' expectations of climactic outcomes that he suspends or denies, Pynchon makes of endlessness an epistemological strategy. With the "sense of an ending" conditioned in readers, he exposes the consequent assumptions that history itself has an end in which all loose threads will be knotted and all puzzling phenomena explained and that individuals' experience properly follows the same course of return after errancy to atonement with the Father and alignment with the past.

As closure vanquishes time by turning it to a spatial object, epiphany too constitutes a static, permanent illumination in which mind conquers time; Pynchon denies his characters that inward conclusiveness so favored by modernist writers. Unable to get out of time or to achieve a final perspective on temporal events, because

their reality *is* time-bound acts rather than spatial things, these characters cannot achieve revelation. Every time one of them credits a vision of truth, the vision explodes and the "truth" turns useless or wrong. Pointsman has a repeated vision of a face turning to meet his eyes and confirm his destiny; no face turns. Närrisch envisions his imminent end "about to burn through the last whispering veil" (518), but no end, burning, or vision beneath the veil occurs. Tchitcherine encounters the Kirghiz Light, "but not his birth" (359). Even Gottfried, the only character given accurate knowledge that he is about to die, does not thereby see conclusively. "Where did he—it's already *gone*, no . . . they're beginning to slide away now faster than he can hold, it's like falling to sleep—they begin to blur" (759). Like these characters, the novel itself does not move toward revelation; if it concludes by warning that Western civilization may be rushing toward a self-destructive end, it never pretends to forecast anything beyond the realm of time.

Because actualists can only see subjectively and from the uncertain midst, Pynchon avoids the favorite realistic illusion of authorial detachment. The narrative perspective in *GR* is neither objective nor omniscient; while the narrator adopts a personal stance within the novel, he does not try to seem unbiased or unlimited in his knowledge. He offers no smug hints at outcomes, at Jessica's eventual choice of Jeremy or Geli's success with Tchitcherine. Knowing no more of the future than the characters themselves, he cannot write from the end. He displays his biases openly, setting the "mean heart" of Pointsman against "rough love in the minor gestures" of Gwenhidwy (171, 170), the destructive "claw" of Greta against the vulnerable "baby rodent hands" of Bianca (478, 469). He chides readers who bring the wrong expectations to his text, in direct addresses emphasizing their personal origin. "You will want cause and effect. All right," he says, and proceeds with a farcical burlesque (663). "You used to know what these words [perception and will] mean," he complains, but now "somebody has to tell you" (472). Losing Jessica forever, Roger suffers: "Sure. You would too. You might even question the worth of your cause" (716). In these and other asides to the reader, Pynchon disbands the old narrative conspiracy allowing readers to share in an authorial wisdom superior to the characters' limited understanding. Pynchon's implied reader, by contrast, is as subjective, limited, and involved as characters and author, but even more liable to misjudgment because of the conditioning of earlier texts. For character, narrator, author, or reader, no vantage point remains but the actualistic one: involved, uncertain, personal and temporal.[37]

In various related ways, Pynchon rejects the teleological forms traditional among Western narratives. The four large sections of *GR* have mock-titles and ironic epigraphs, parodying the habit of labeling experience from the end, as Fielding and others did. The seventy-three smaller divisions have no titles, numbers, or epigraphs, showing that one cannot extract spatial form from temporal flow. The novel occupies the present tense: "A screaming comes across the sky," plunging readers and characters into time, rather than lifting them above or after events. The preterite, in which a screaming came across the sky once and for all, allows elect readers to see the past from its end and thus creates a class of blindly preterite characters; actualistic writers like Pynchon more often choose the present. Although *GR* does, like conventional novels, cycle back, repeat itself, and develop echoes among scenes, characters, and motifs, it creates an *open* cycle that never closes or stabilizes. The novel arches from one Western city to another, from a rocket ascent to a descent, from blackout to burnout, from a sense that "it's all theatre" to a seat in "this old theatre," from one nightmare of annihilation to another. *GR* does not, however, arrive back at its point of origin but rather celebrates change and difference in a network of similar phenomena. Its repetitions do not therefore nullify energy but, instead, increase it; its echoes do not result in stasis but in motion.

Given all these related commitments to a narrative form capable of reflecting actualistic reality, it must come as no surprise that *GR* occupies itself in large part with an intertextual response to *the* realistic novel form par excellence, the bildungsroman. Its very name designates a certain end-shaped plot, dependent on linear continuity, on causal stability in the world, on epiphanic insights in an educable hero, on hierarchy, unity, and objective certainty in the account of his progress. The one miniaturized man of his times, the bildungsroman's protagonist always reveals the properly traditional order in the world, whether by religious atonement with the father in *Robinson Crusoe* or by aesthetic alignment with the "old Artificer" in *Portrait of the Artist*. As the protagonist achieves an identity, he comes to oneness with himself and reality—to unity and certainty, not to multiplicity and indeterminacy. How inevitable, then, that Pynchon elects to invoke this narrative form for his story of Infant Tyrone's growth to manhood and then inverts and subverts its every premise. To be sure, Tyrone receives his education, so that he and his story and its underlying conventions scatter beyond retrieval. Slothrop's story brings one sort of education to its end.

And inaugurates a different sort: just as James's protagonists learn through their experience the "realistic" nature of reality, Pynchon's characters confront the less graspable, actualistic nature of theirs. This latter education is complicated, on the one hand, by the uncertainty of all knowledge in the new physical reality; at best, Pynchon's figures are liberated by knowing how little, and how subjectively, they know. On the other hand, education in the new reality is also constrained by the powerful conservative force of Newtonian assumptions; at worst, like Slothrop, characters either fall into old habits of thinking or fall out of the habit of coherent thought altogether. Actualistic texts attempt to dispel the outmoded and pernicious Newtonian/realistic system and to deconstruct the literary forms it has authorized; *GR* interrogates virtually every assumption underlying the Western traditions in science, philosophy, and narrative art. But it does so without being merely negative or simply revisionary.

Hence, *GR* also educates its readers: it teaches us a massive new song—"one They never taught anyone to sing"—for our actualistic occasion.

NOTES

[1] The definitive essay on Pynchon's self-reflexivity is Russell, "Pynchon's Language." . . .

[2] Pynchon, *Gravity's Rainbow,* 385. Citations of this novel, hereafter *GR,* appear in the text. All ellipses in quotations are Pynchon's, except those in brackets, which are mine.

[3] Kevles, *Physicists,* 162.

[4] Pynchon's unique strategy of narrative connection is discussed by many critics; I found especially important readings in Hite, *Ideas of Order*; T. Moore, *Style of Connectedness*; and Cooper, *Signs and Symptoms*. James Perrin Warren treats the narrative discontinuities of *GR* from a linguistic perspective in "Ritual Reluctance." Steven Weisenburger argues that episodes in *GR* "are composed according to a complex, circular motion," a "heterocyclic" looping together of cycles based on the Christian liturgical calendar (*"Gravity's Rainbow" Companion,* 9-10).

[5] Pynchon, *V.,* 286.

[6] On mothers and other women in *GR,* see Kaufman, "Brünnhilde and the Chemists."

[7] Notable exceptions include Mendelson, "Gravity's Encyclopedia," 182-83; Schaub, *Pynchon,* 46; Simmon, "Beyond the Theater of War," 127; these critics observe the falseness, control, or "spurious continuity" of films in *GR*. See also Clerc, "Film in *Gravity's Rainbow*."

[8] Stark, *Pynchon's Fictions,* 142.

[9] Cowart, *Thomas Pynchon,* 32.

[10] For a related assessment of von Göll, see Hayles, *Cosmic Web,* 183-84.

[11] Pynchon writes in the introduction to *Slow Learner* that he remains "a dedicated sucker" of chase scenes: "it is one piece of puerility I am unable to let go of" (19).

[12] Siegel, *Pynchon,* 70.

[13] Fowler, *Reader's Guide to "Gravity's Rainbow,"* 55. Similar positions are taken in Hayles, *Cosmic Web,* 183-88; and Hume, *Pynchon's Mythography,* 217-21.

[14] Plater, *Grim Phoenix,* 214-15.

[15] Mendelson, "Gravity's Encyclopedia," 176, 183. Similar readings appear in Slade, *Thomas Pynchon,* 200-210; and Weisenburger, "End of History?," 140-56.

[16] Hite, *Ideas of Order,* 119-20.

[17] Hayles, *Cosmic Web,* 188.

[18] See Hite, *Ideas of Order,* 18; Quilligan, "Thomas Pynchon," 195-97; on Pynchon's own active reading of historical sources, see Weisenburger, "End of History?"

[19] Hite, *Ideas of Order,* 127.

[20] Quilligan, "Thomas Pynchon," 209-10.

[21] Surrealism means as many different things as realism does to its various definers and practitioners. For my purposes here, what principally matters is the common agreement to see realism and surrealism as opposites and hence to define surrealism as an inversion of some aspects of realism. When Slothrop turns from the pursuit of linear order characteristic of realistic systems to the conviction that *no* order exists, he becomes what Pynchon will call a "sentimental surrealist": "There's nothing so loathsome as a sentimental surrealist" (696). See also *Slow Learner:* "I could also with an easy mind see axed much of the story's less responsible Surrealism" (22).

[22] Pynchon, *Crying of Lot 49,* 136.

[23] See George Levine's useful early discussion of Pynchon's catalogs in "V-2."

[24] William Plater argues that Slothrop evolves beyond his early "map-consciousness" toward a perception of interior space (*Grim Phoenix,* 60-61). In the resonant terms provided by John Vernon, Slothrop should be understood, according to Plater, as leaving the map, a locus of discrete spaces often structured as opposites, for the garden, a place uniting opposites and making all areas of experience accessible to each other; see Vernon, *Garden and the Map.* I see Slothrop's abandonment of mapmaking, not as a liberation, but as a capitulation to precisely the schizophrenia Vernon describes. "The either-or structure of isolation from the world and merging with it represents such a polarization that the two are the same; both represent an alienation and deadening of consciousness, a total surrender to objectivity" (28).

[25] This common assumption appears, for example, in Fowler, *Reader's Guide to "Gravity's Rainbow,"* 96; Mackey, *Rainbow Quest of Thomas Pynchon,* 37; and Simmon, "*Gravity's Rainbow* Described," 58.

[26] Wolfley, "Repression's Rainbow," 883.

[27] Wolfley argues convincingly that Pynchon presents "no totally healthy sex" in *GR,* but rather various sexual oddities, each "traceable to some peculiarly Western social perversion" (ibid., 882-83).

[28] Seed, *Fictional Labyrinths of Thomas Pynchon,* 163.

[29] Douglas Fowler, for example, believes that "Rilke's romanticism is always apropos in reading Pynchon" (*Reader's Guide to "Gravity's Rainbow,"* 284). See also Ozier, "Calculus of Transformation." Ozier argues that "the dissolution of Slothrop's persona is not a diminution but part of a transformation into the timeless Being of Rilke's angels" (197). Thomas Schaub reads the Rilkean references as more ambiguous (*Pynchon,* 72-73).

[30] Fowler, *Reader's Guide to "Gravity's Rainbow,"* 80-85.

[31] Ibid., 80-81.

[32] Ibid., 14-15.

[33] Hite, *Ideas of Order,* 40.

[34] Kathryn Hume proposes that the novel is unified by a recurrent image-complex involving "an aerial force of destruction, the targeted city, and the cowering creature awaiting annihilation. Significantly, the image-complex is not rendered from the sidelines, from the distanced perspective of bystander or artist," but rather from above and below ("Views from Above," 625).

[35] Pynchon, *Crying of Lot 49,* 10.

[36] Cowart, *Thomas Pynchon,* 8.

[37] Insightful discussions of Pynchon's subjective narrative voice appear in Schaub, *Pynchon,* 103-38; and Hite, *Ideas of Order,* 131-57.

David Porush

SOURCE: "Cybernetic Fiction and Postmodern Science," in *New Literary History,* Vol. 20, No. 2, Winter, 1989, pp. 373-96.

[*In the following essay, Porush analyzes the place of cybernetics—in which both humans and machines are viewed as systems of information—in postmodern fiction.*]

> The poem is a kind of machine for producing the poetic state of mind by means of words.
> Paul Valéry, *Literature*

> And so the author vanishes—that spoiled child of ignorance—to give place to a more thoughtful person, a person who will know that the author is a machine, and will know how this machine works.
> Italo Calvino, "Cybernetics and Ghosts"

> I can no longer accept any situation other than this transformation of ourselves into the messages of ourselves.
> Italo Calvino, *T-Zero*

For the first time in the long and fruitful relationship between literature and science, literature actually has the means to meet science on its own territory in a contest concerning which epistemological activity does a better job of telling the truth. Until quite recently, literature and science have been limited to an occasional polite exchange of metaphors, with the largest debt undoubtedly on literature's side. At the very least, literature was immersed in the same world view as science, and gave more poetic expression to verities found in mathematics. At the very best, literature could no more than act as an accomplice to the nature portrayed by science, or demonstrate nature at play in her own fields. But two related *scientific* developments have conspired to give literature the power to contest science's supremacy as an epistemological force, and on science's own terms.

The first of these intertwined developments is the rise of cybernetics, which quite simply has mathematized and scientized the very stuff of literature: that is, communication and information. The second development is the current emergence of a postmodern paradigm in science paralleling the well-documented literary one.

I. OUR CYBERNETIC AGE

Cybernetics offers one of the most broadly influential paradigms of our era. Consequently, cybernetic fiction (along with certain kinds of modern, hypertechnologized music such as punk rock), by effectively resisting the cybernetic paradigm *from within* qualifies as one of the more robust and relevant genres of contemporary literature.[1] The cybernetic view of the cosmos and everything in it as elaborate information machinery is a seductive one. Cybernetic fiction offers an equally tantalizing counternarrative.

If we must characterize our era with slogans, I suggest we ought to call it "The Cybernetic Age" rather than "The Information Age." Focusing on the whole cybernetic movement in science, rather than the phenomenon of information it embraces, adds a much needed cultural context to the discussion.[2] Where *information* is a neutral and abstract term, like *energy* or *matter* or *space* or *time,* the word *cybernetics* has more troubling implications. Since it treats both humans and machines as systems of control and communication, it explicitly suggests a collapse of distinctions between them. Since it assumes that the metaphor "The Brain is a Machine" is literally accurate, it has promoted this as a powerful model for research in cognition, artificial intelligence, and behavioral science. Indeed, cybernetics is, by Norbert Wiener's definition, the science that seeks those laws of communication that apply equally to living beings and machines.[3] Furthermore, this collapse of distinctions has successfully colored the way we work, speak, think, plan, and play in the culture at large. Finally, and most importantly for our purposes, the broader term *cybernetics* more accurately reflects the larger concerns of literary texts and theory, not by using the abstractions of science for their own sake, but by working with the assumptions about human knowing and telling tacit in those abstractions.

Cybernetics entails a powerful metaphysics. By suggesting that everything in the knowable universe can be modeled in a system of information, from the phase shifts of subatomic particles to the poet's selection of a word in a poem, to the rent in the fabric of spacetime created by a black hole, it returns science to a neoclassical position of certainty and mechanism.

The birth of cybernetics in the 1940s was fueled by certain advances in communications technology. But the primary impetus to the cybernetic view came from scientists who felt that troubling new discoveries in quantum physics, which originated twenty years earlier, called for a refutation. Specifically, quantum physics shoved the human observer's uncertainty into the center of the scientific stage, interposing human indeterminacy between the scientist's theory and reality. Cybernetics was framed as a response to what for many, including Einstein and Wiener, was an intolerable situation. It sprang from a neoclassical urge to banish probabilism or uncertainty from science, to co-opt the human role in favor of logic. Wiener reveals the depth to which a Manicheistic metaphysics motivated his theory (and also his leaden prose) when he writes about this struggle in *The Human Use of Human Beings*: "This random element, this organic incompleteness [proposed by Heisenbergian physics], is one which without too violent a figure of speech we may consider evil; the negative evil which St. Augustine characterizes as incompleteness."[4]

Cybernetics' tactic here ranks as one of the great philosophical tricks of the century. Acting on a suggestion made by Leo Szilard as early as 1922, Wiener and Claude Shannon in the 1940s took the formula for thermodynamic randomness (entropy) and used it to define the randomness which provides the necessary precursor for information, and then also called *it* entropy. From there, it was one small step to define information as negentropy. This little trick had powerful consequences. It appropriated the idea that the human introduced uncertainty into the system—which many phenomenologists, but especially Heidegger and Poincaré, have subsequently viewed as a refutation of determinism from within science's own method—and defined it as nothing more or less than a precondition for having a quantifiable amount of information. Cybernetics thereby managed to subsume the messiness of the human observer's role into a system of positive math.

Wiener aptly named the science after the Greek word for "governor" (or "pilot" or "steersman"), *kybernos.* A governor is a servo-mechanism, a controlling device that mediates the feedback loop of information between sender and receiver; a servo-mechanism could be a thermostat (mediating between room temperature and oil burner), or a cruise control on your auto (mediating between accelerator and engine speed), or a literary text (mediating between a reader and her own knowledge), or an observer of an electron (mediating between the electron's position and momentum and his knowledge about that electron). From the point of view of cybernetics, all of the above obey the same laws and therefore are metaphysically indistinguishable.[5]

However abstruse this struggle between cybernetics and quantum physics may be, however, its consequences have trickled down to us in powerful material forms. The success of the cybernetic metaphor has virtually altered the way we view the world and has created one of the most pervasive contemporary myths we have, one so powerful that we have taken it for granted, even as we inhabit it. The surface signs of the total operation of this myth are everywhere in the pop culture, however; for example, Max Headroom, a computer-generated character plagued by electrical tics, has become a cultural hero in Europe and on television commercials here. MTV's hypertechnologized music/dance videos blur the line, thematically, between humans and robots and, visually, between free-hand animation, computer-generated graphics, and simple videotape or mimetic film. The most common advertisements glorify and perfect the human body by mechanizing it. Our past decade's obsession with the computer is quickly evolving into the next decade's obsession with artificial intelligence devices and robots.

At the same time, cybernetics has spawned and aided a number of subdisciplines, including cryptography, behaviorism, robotics, prosthetic engineering, computational linguistics, neurochemistry, information science, brain science, general systems dynamics, game theory, computer modeling, and so on. We see its influence in the prevalence of "expert systems," software packages that supposedly are able to climb various professional decision trees (from medical diagnosis to legal brief writing to tax preparation, even to instruction in composition). It is apparent in the erosion of privacy as a result of the massive uploading and correlation of trivial information about us and our transactions, but it is equally apparent in a new kind of freedom of expression enabled by personal computers that give us desktop publishing and private access to huge libraries of information. Perhaps the surest sign of the radical energy of this myth is that it has displaced traditional children's imaginings, expressed in their toys and cartoons. To know an American seven-year-old today is to know Gobots and Transformers.[6]

II. POSTMODERN SCIENCE

As is true whenever a new paradigm is about to emerge, critics, historians, sociologists and other culture watchers struggle to give it a name and then, in a more protracted and bloody battle, to define it. In part this struggle reflects the predictable confusion over what to call whatever it is we're in at any given moment, but part of it stems from a desire to own the bragging rights to a new territory. No term has suffered from such a struggle more than *postmodernism.*

Even so, there *are* constants to most discussions of postmodernism, and these constants emerge in most of postmodernism's manifestations, whether literary or artistic or scientific. In fact, the unities of postmodern expression are so great, it is probably more accurate to talk of *literary* postmodernism and *scientific* postmodernism as two aspects of a single enterprise.

Postmodernism has two interconnected points of departure, both of which privilege literature. First, postmodernism places the self-conscious activities of the human observer/scientist/teller—and consequently the making of narratives—in the center of things.[7] Second, postmodernism stresses the paradoxical power of structures of information and codes. That is, while the postmodern position states that *codes create reality,* postmodernism does not trust codes to tell the whole truth. Indeed, from the postmodern perspective codes are cultural artifacts, cannot be both complete and consistent (as Goedel's Theorem suggests), and, in philosophical terms, are "glosses on silence"; they do a good job of delivering information, but they are less successful at capturing an underlying inexpressible, inchoate, silent realm where meaning resides. Consequently, from a postmodern view, all narratives, including scientific ones, contain their own deconstruction. If one looks hard enough, scientific discourse, like other postmodern narratives, plays on the tension between order and chaos, sense and nonsense, information and silence. And by postmodern standards, the most potent narratives are those that include the self-consciousness of the author, a calculation for the position of the observer, and an expression for the paradoxes and failures of the narrative code.

As a consequence of the popularity of postmodern deconstructions, the generic divisions of the sciences, the cultural neutrality of science, the nomenclatures and taxonomies of science, and even the very logic of the sciences have all been called into question. Unfortunately, these attacks have for the most part come from without the fortress of science, while scientists have largely ignored the claims laid upon their objectivity by humanists eager to diminish science's authority. However, there is another set of arguments—by far the most convincing—for the emergence of a postmodern paradigm, a set which has come from science itself. These pieces of evidence no longer rely solely on the shopworn clichés of Heisenbergianism. Though it is true that uncertainty over the position of the electron leads to an ineluctable connection between the observer and the observed,[8] Heisenberg's Theorem has been much abused by literary scholars and critics of science, many of whom have seized upon it as definitive proof of the collapse of scientific objectivity and certainty in general.[9]

But other developments in the sciences are even more convincingly postmodern. For instance, a number of works such as *Quantum Reality* by Nick Herbert and *Other Worlds* by Paul Davies portray an underlying fabric of forces and particles, revealed by physical experimentation, that undermines the fundamental structure of reality on which the rest of the sciences rely.[10] One of the most powerful of these deconstructions rests on Bell's Interconnectedness Theorem. Bell's Proof[11] has led physicists to conclude that local operations (such as measuring light quanta) have nonlocal effects (such as simultaneously altering the structure of "reality" elsewhere in the universe). In literal terms this implies that the stories we tell have reality-altering consequences, however minute, and that at some fundamental level, consciousness itself is "a nonlocal operator." In another view, words like *and, or, if, then,* and *nor* have different meanings on the quantum level.

Physics is not alone in its postmodernism. Because of the rise of genetic engineering, biology has shown an increasing concern with the structure of codes. Jeremy Campbell compares DNA explicitly to a "generative grammar," a view which not only reinforces our version of "nature as an information process," but collapses even further our sense of the unity between the language of humans and the code of the cosmos.[12] Genetic engineering will soon enable us to alter the code of life at will, and this in turn has placed emphasis both on the role of information and on narrativity. Now more than ever the sorts of stories we tell can be translated from human codes into genetic code (by computers programmed in machine language).

Contemporary mathematics is strikingly postmodern because of its persistent abstractness. While applied mathematics remains intensively practical, mathematical theory, in one mathematician's terms, is "unreasonably esoteric."[13] Some even suggest that mathematics is no more or no less than the study of the mind's power to abstract in and of itself. In this view, the mathematician is really studying the minute electrical tick-tocking of the brain, carried along on an electrochemical current of logic alone. Such mathematical mysteries as the *n-dimensional kissing problem* sometimes seem like apotheoses of thumb twiddling.

In physical chemistry, new versions of how order arises spontaneously in nature have influenced other disciplines to abandon the bleak portrait, offered by the Second Law of Thermodynamics, of a mechanical universe inexorably winding down. In its place, Ilya Prigogine's view of dissipative structures shows a universe of constant flux in which open systems of order emerge spontaneously out of chaos, feed from the universal entropic stream, and grow more orderly according to specific laws. This model has been applied with equal force to biology, traffic jams, social systems, economic models, and atmospheric disturbances. As is typical for postmodern narratives in science, rather than stressing objects, positions, order, and stability, it stresses processes, relations, chaos, and instability as the foundations of reality.

In sum, then, certain aspects of contemporary science seem more involved with their own codes, processes, and formalisms than with the stuff that this machinery has been assembled to describe. What is most striking about all these postmodern sciences is that they share an underlying concern with *information.* For Heisenberg, the problem was the relationship between what information we *ought* to be able to specify about an electron's position versus what we *are* indeed able to say. Bell's proof of the nonlocal nature of reality relies upon the instantaneous communication of information between two otherwise discrete phenomena. In biology, as Jeremy Rifkin has noted, the coming revolution in bioengineering would be absolutely impossible without the framing tools for manipulating information that cybernetics provides, and without the manipulating tool of the computer itself, which cybernetics also has provided.[14] And Ilya Prigogine's work is essentially a mathematical proof of how the cybernetic principles of positive feedback and organization work together in highly destabilized systems (systems far from equilibrium that vibrate in nonlinear fluctuations) to precipitate growing crystals of order.

Therefore, without exaggeration we can say that cybernetics is the paradigmatic postmodern science. It views the universe as a set of interconnected systems of energy, matter, space, and time all of which can be described in terms of (or reduced to) how much information those systems transmit or contain. To put it another way, *cybernetics is the quintessential science of narrativity,* if you accept that any exchange of information creates a narrative. Cyberneticists claim that mathematical algorithms describe the amount of information transferred in any system, including those that involve humans. It is no wonder, then, that certain postmodern novelists are engaged in a struggle with cybernetics over who or what will control the way we view human communication. Certain postmodern writers, in direct response to the cybernetic proposition, portray humans trapped in, metamorphosed into, or controlled by cybernetic systems and machines. In typical postmodern fashion, these fictions themselves pose as such cybernetic devices in their form and language, as "self-aware" mechanical communications links apparently operating according to algorithms for the organization of information. But far from celebrating mechanical descriptions of human communication—including their own hyperevolved formalisms—these fictions insist that authors, readers, and characters alike somehow elude cybernetic reduction.[15] This breed of postmodern fiction accomplishes a sort of literary sleight of hand. It defeats the powerful implications of the cybernetic paradigm by making readers feel that there is something left over—some irreducible, inexpressible, and unquantifiable substratum of meaningful silence beyond or beneath cybernetic analysis—in human communication, even when it occurs through so complex and controlled a "servo-mechanical system" as the literary text. Elsewhere, I have called this complex subgenre of postmodernism "cybernetic fiction."[16] The single most important point about cybernetic fiction is that it actually employs cybernetic principles to demonstrate its superiority over scientific narratives as an epistemological force.

III. CYBERNETIC FICTION

Like many myths that are this deeply rooted, the cybernetic myth—that human communication is no more than the cybernetic machinery of consciousness and can be described in mechanical terms—arises from an unnamed collision of images, a monstrous oxymoron that lacks a name. I call it The Myth of The Soft Machine, stealing William Burroughs's term. In Burroughs's wild mythography, humans are simply messages typed onto the jelly of flesh by a biological typewriter he calls the "soft machine," referring not only to that most cybernetic of biological concepts, the genetic code, but also to media and even language itself. He tells us to send the machine a self-dismantling feedback message in order to free ourselves from the dominion of The Word (communication) over our imaginations.[17] This complex image embodies the essentially postmodern version of human vulnerability, freedom, and uncertainty wedded to mechanical hardness, determinism, and order: we find its reflection not only in cybernetic fiction but at large in our culture.

Furthermore, this image signifies an inner condition common to many of us who feel that we are species of soft machines who embody two contrary instincts for freedom and determinism, for the inexpressible and the totally inscribable, for spontaneity confined by a grammar of motives. Texts—like the ones Burroughs has assembled—which embody this felt paradox about mechanisms and systems or order, control and language, are also soft machines and form the emergent subgenre of cybernetic fiction.

As a result of the metaphysical reconception of the human role in meaning making initiated in the 1940s by cybernetics, literature that concerned itself with philosophical questions could no longer comfortably embrace the machine metaphor.[18] Where modernism seemed to engage in a romance with machines and mechanisms, especially mechanisms of form and language,[19] by the early 1950s the emergent postmodern movement shows a definite hostility toward technology, perhaps as much in response to the cybernetic proposition as because (as is commonly assumed) of the unleashing of atomic weaponry. Ultimately, the former is more threatening than the latter: radioactivity may demolish your body, destroy whole cities, and threaten to make the human race extinct. But cybernetics challenges us where we live—in our heads. It threatens to deprive all humans of our authority as authors by replacing the mind with a brain, meaning with information, reading with information processing, the text with technique, uncertainty with closure, and love with feedback loops.[20]

Thus, the cybernetic position directly threatens literature, and it is not surprising that in the ensuing decades we suddenly see the emergence of a new countergenre, mixing apocalyptic imaginings with anti-mechanistic themes, deliberate use of cybernetic principles, and anti-formalistic experiments.[21] In addition to the works of William Burroughs (*Nova Express* [1964], *The Ticket that Exploded* [1967] and *The Soft Machine* [1966]), which prescribe a cure for our imminent cyberneticization in "demolishing the Word," we find a cooler but no less adamant demolition of the machinery of logic and language in Samuel Beckett's *Comment C'est* (*How It Is* [1958]) and Kurt Vonnegut, Jr.'s early satirical thrust against cybernetics in *Player Piano* (1952), which responded directly to Wiener's landmark popularization of cybernetics, a book with the chilling title *The Human Use of Human Beings* (1948).

The single unifying feature of cybernetic fictions is that they pose as cybernetic devices which ultimately—and this is the source of their power and postmodernism—do not work. In other words, they are *soft* (vulnerable and uncertain) *machines* (systems which strive for invulnerability and completeness). Their tacit twofold message is clear: the text-as-machine is both more and less than what it appears, it's an oxymoron. Furthermore, humans are not merely mechanisms, either, so that the communication between soft-machine human reader and soft-machine text cannot be reduced to cybernetic calculations, for in cybernetic terms, both continually add noise to the channel of transmission.

Yet, for all the threatening aspects of the cybernetic narrative, there is no denying its attractiveness to clever authors who seek some apt metaphor for the play between structure and silence that lies at the root of the postmodern imagination, and the play between mechanism and inspiration, order and chaos, "plot" and "rot," that lies at the heart of all literary method. For example, John Barth's *Giles Goat-Boy* (1966) tells us that it is written by a fabulous computer, WESCAC, and that JB is only an editor. Samuel Beckett's *The Lost Ones* (1973) is a text which asks the reader to participate in a *gedanken*, a thought experiment designed to "maintain the notion" of an enormous cylinder machine where two hundred humanlike beings are trapped. And of course it receives full-blown treatment in the novels of Thomas Pynchon (*V.* [1963], *The Crying of Lot 49* [1967], and *Gravity's Rainbow* [1973]). Pynchon explicitly traces the important theoretical development of cybernetics to World War II, and illustrates its connections to Pavlovian behaviorism, theories of communication, development of automata, and the new physics, all the while reflexively illustrating these themes in his narrative forms. Joseph McElroy's entire œuvre shows a growing concern for systems of communication and information (especially in *Hind's Kidnap* [1969] and *Lookout Cartridge* [1974]), but the theme achieves its full-blown expression in *PLUS* (1977). This text is narrated—in a strange automatized voice that grows its own de-automatized language as it proceeds—from inside a brain which has been cut out of its human body, linked to a weather-monitoring computer, inserted into a communications satellite, and launched into orbit around the earth. Similarly, William Gibson's *Neuromancer* (1983) places us inside the soaring, impressionistic space ("cyberspace") of a worldwide computer network which can link directly with an individual's nerve net, a not-too-far-flung fantasy that fulfills Marshall McLuhan's definition of technology as an extension of the human nerve net. Barthelme places us inside uncertainty itself—a communications black box—in his short story "The Explanation" from *City Life* (1973). We also find it in the postmodern, self-conscious science fiction of Philip K. Dick (for example, "Do Androids Dream of Electric Sheep?"), and Stanislaw Lem (especially *The Cyberiad: Fables for a Cybernetic Age* [1976]). Recent fiction by Don Delillo touches on the theme (*White Noise* [1986] and *Ratner's Star* [1978]). However, these texts adopt this cybernetic pose with at least some irony. Their purpose is not merely to further complicate the ancient metaphor "This text is a machine," but their texts explore, and even create or replicate in the reader, that gap where mechanism and human being differ, where cybernetics fails to account for human activity, or where mathematical principles strike at but do not reach the elements of the incalculable. In short, cybernetic fiction employs a hyperevolved technique of self-reflexiveness that makes the reader intensely aware of his or her own status as an information processing machine, too. This is a sort of inoculation: the text injects the patient with a dose of cybernetic techniques to get the host to resist future deployments.

That is, these text-machines play upon those talents in the reader that are precisely most mechanical, most compulsive, if you will, most cybernetic. But the virtue in this tactic is that somehow, by forcing the reader into a cybernetic fix, these texts succeed in pushing the reader out and beyond the point of his or her own "automatization." Even before cybernetics, theorists recognized this unique capability of natural languages (as opposed to strict codes) to alienate the reader. Viktor Shklovsky identified instances in which authors purposely decontextualized the familiar meanings of words expressly to communicate a sense of alienation. His word for it was *ostranenie,* commonly translated as "defamiliarization."[22] However, William Hendricks, interestingly, translates it as "deautomatization."[23] In fact, these fictions accomplish not merely a deautomatization of our sense of language but a formal deconstruction of the text's authority, in the sense Derrida intended. They exaggerate the "illusion of logocentrism"—building the illusion of complete, self-contained systematic mechanisms of information—in order to demolish it. They privilege the cybernetic version of human communication in order to de-privilege it, by exposing its insufficiency as a means of exchanging any essential meaning. They use, in Derrida's terms, a "positive science of writing" which exposes its own fallacy. Derrida calls this failure "incompetence—the *closure* of the *epistémè.*"[24] In order to support my claim that these works accomplish such feats of deconstruction, in what follows I examine an exemplary cybernetic fiction rather closely—Calvino's "Night Driver."

Of the many authors of cybernetic fiction, none has more explicitly addressed the attractions and power of cybernetics than Italo Calvino. All of Calvino's later works show both furtive and explicit uses of cybernetic themes and principles in their composition. *The Castle of Crossed Destinies* involves a series of narratives generated from the recombinations and permutations of a finite assortment of tarot cards, thereby illustrating the essential cybernetic principle of negentropy. *If on a winter's night a traveler* is thoroughly concerned with the feedback process between signal and noise out of which an author's inspiration may arise, and there are innumerable references to cybernetic ideas, tropes, themes, and principles. (For instance, the heroine visits "a representative of the OEPHLW of New York [Organization for the Electronic Production of Homogenized Literary Works].")

Among his *Invisible Cities,* Calvino erects several on cybernetic principles of assorted signs, redundancy, memory, and so on. And much of this concern can be traced back to Calvino's earliest explorations in *T-Zero.*

Calvino himself has left the best record of his purpose in dedicating most of his work to cybernetic fiction. His essay "Cybernetics and Ghosts" convincingly describes the seductions of cybernetics.[25] For Calvino, cybernetics offers the best possible explanation of what an author does. Rather than being a conduit for genius or insight, the author is merely a hyperevolved device for sorting through the language and seeking the combinations that strike to some deeper, unreachable realm. Stripped of his delusions of romantic "inspiration" and other obsolete and grandiose explanations of creativity, the author is now revealed as a cybernetic device, a machine. Does this mean for Calvino that the mystery of literature is somehow erased? That the mechanical process therefore implies some deterministic reduction of the "privileged place of literature"? No, Calvino says. "[T]hough entrusted to machines, literature will continue to be a 'place' of privilege within the human consciousness, a way of exercising the potentialities contained in the system of signs"(16).

Though later in the essay Calvino denies it, it is hard to believe that he isn't being slightly whimsical. Yet, even if we take him at face value as he asks us to, it is clear that Calvino's version of the author-machine is a very special sort of cybernetic device, one which at least has access to the unconscious and the mysterious. For in Calvino's terms, this new cybernetically generated literature will continue to "struggle to escape from the confines of language; it stretches out from the utmost limits of what can be said; what stirs literature is the call and attraction of what is not in the dictionary"(18).

T-ZERO

With this echo of the "call and attraction" of literature, we can begin to understand the quintessential aspects of cybernetic fiction. Certain moments in postmodern texts seize readers with an interpretive compulsion, sending them into ever-widening orbits of apparent organization and decipherment while leading only to irresolution. In certain especially well-wrought texts, this spiral absorbs, like a black hole, every other aspect of the text until readers are captivated by and left to confront their compulsion to interpret. Beckett, Pynchon, and McElroy are masters of this technique.[26]

In cybernetic fiction this textual event or verbal mechanism leading to "seizure" is invariably created by the author's deliberate use of cybernetic principles. Kathleen Woodward was one of the first to point to the cybernetic quality of these interpretive seizures in Pynchon's *The Crying of Lot 49.* Following Pynchon's own direct references to cybernetic principles and theory in his fiction, she describes this characteristic postmodern moment as "information processing out of control" and "positive feedback at its crazy work."[27] She explores how Oedipa

Maas, the heroine, uncovers a system of exfoliating clues in the will of Pierce Inverarity that sends her into circuits of wilder and more destabilizing oscillations. The more information Oedipa receives, the more helplessly puzzled she becomes. Far from helping her to achieve resolution, her interpretive acts only serve to expose the futility of her techniques of interpretation. Of course, as many critics have noted, Oedipa becomes an avatar of the reader. In the typical cybernetic fiction, the narrator becomes an avatar of the reader at the very moment that his or her situation is most indeterminate and yet most definitely aware of itself as an act of meaning making straining against the ineluctability of cybernetic laws.[28]

Such a moment occurs in *T-Zero,* Calvino's remarkable book which contains the short cybernetic fiction "Night Driver." But in order to understand that small moment, which occurs at the very end of the story, we first must take a brief look at the larger text of which it is a part.

T-Zero initially presents itself to the reader as a collection of short stories, linked thematically by a concern for scientific images and theories, and comic anthropomorphizations of different phenomena as scientists have described them. However, if we read these stories more closely, a novelistic coherence emerges. In short, an underlying unity grows and climaxes as surely as any novelistic plot, qualifying the text entire to be viewed as a larger, more coherent narrative. This narrative traces the evolution of epistemological (and consequently fictive) power of science itself. It follows a genealogical logic, exploring earlier modern sciences in Part I—taxonomies like astronomy, zoology, crystallography, and evolution; more sophisticated modern sciences in Part II—genetics and cell biology; and the most contemporary and embracing of sciences, general systems theory and cybernetics, in Part III. Furthermore, in each story there is a unique dichotomy playing back and forth across the desires of the characters.

In "Crystals," for instance, the male Qfwfq (a primordial disembodied intelligence who is incarnated in various ur-original situations throughout Calvino's earlier collection *Cosmicomics* and in the first part of *T-Zero*) represents a desire for order; he's an instinctive positivist: "A total crystal I dreamed, a topaz world that would leave out nothing." But his partner Vug, a female, is Qfwfq's foil. "What she liked—I quickly realized—was to discover in crystals some differences, even minimal ones, irregularities, flaws."[29]

In "Blood, Sea" the premise is that creatures evolved out of the sea by infolding exterior surfaces to create a ramification of cavities—the circulatory system and intestines—which enfolded the primordial sea (warm, saline, soupy) within, thus sustaining life even on land. In Calvino's hands, this elaborates into a dichotomy between inside (moist, warm, fecund, rich) and outside (arid, impoverished, sterile), which in turn becomes a play on narrative stances (first and third person point of view) and desire (as figure and ground of all human motivation). Qfwfq projects all this while alongside his lover in the

back seat of a car (which stops and goes, ebbs and flows) driven by his rival. At the end, the three players hurtle over the side of a cliff, spilling their blood back into the sea.

In "Mitosis," perhaps the most provocative story in *T-Zero* from an information perspective besides "Night Driver," Calvino's narrator is a cell on the verge of reproducing itself.[30] The narrative capitalizes on the tension between remembering—which corresponds to the recapitulation of the DNA code of the parent in the children—and forgetting, the paradoxical "discontinuity" of the parent cell in splitting into two offspring. Of course, the text also capitalizes completely upon the metaphorical-literal aspect of the genetic code as a generative grammar. In this scheme, the nucleus becomes "consciousness" and chromosomes "lines of expression." Jeremy Campbell, as I mentioned above, explores this literal metaphor characteristic of the postmodern mode: "There are certain basic resemblances between genes and language that are beyond dispute. . . . As it happens, this system is closer to Shannon's binary code, which consists of just the two digits 0 and 1, than to the alphabet of any human language, making it easier to apply the principles of information theory and to establish how much information is contained in a DNA molecule. . . . The message of DNA is intrinsic. If we speak in metaphor about the 'ideas' contained in it, then those ideas are innate."[31] Thinking along parallel lines, the narrator of "Mitosis" notes that "each line [of DNA] had a function, each being—to return to the language metaphor—a word, the fact that one word was to be found twice didn't change what I was, since I consisted of the assortment or the vocabulary of the different words or functions at my disposal"(68).

Best of all, Calvino accomplishes these syntheses of scientific and literary discourse with wit and humor, often at the expense of hapless heroes pursuing inaccessible mates, overly rational narrators pursuing order and logic in indeterminate situations, and contemporary men and women who seem to spend most of their time enacting crimes of passion in their automobiles. All this hints at a satirical disposition which his work shares with that of Pynchon, Vonnegut, Barth, Barthelme, Coover, and other postmodernists. Perhaps they take their cue from Henri Bergson's definition of humor as arising when people act like machines.

But the last story of the volume, "The Count of Monte Cristo," is a red herring. Unlike all the others, it doesn't use a scientific premise for its ruminations, but rather a literary one. This Borgesian story is narrated by Alexandre Dumas's character Edmond Dantés, prisoner of the Château D'If. Dantés relates his fruitless efforts to escape—or his even more futile and endlessly elaborating "hypotheses of escape." In its last section, this story trails off into circumlocutions about theories of narrative, and a labyrinthine series of self-reflections about authorial point of view.

However, as in much postmodern fiction, red herrings are also salmon we can follow upstream to a spawning ground. "The Count of Monte Cristo" signals to the reader (at first subtly and then more explicitly) that the Château D'If is the entire, massive, labyrinthine project of knowledge itself.[32] The walls of the fortress separate the prisoner from the sea, which in turn represents essential, primordial Truth, the goal of science. In short, the text is a little allegory about how Science not only fails to lead us to Nature, but becomes an obstacle to our embracing the truth. Edmond Dantés tells us

> I too have thought and still think about a method of escape; in fact, I have made so many surmises about the topography of the fortress, about the shortest and surest way to reach the outer bastion and dive into the sea, that I can no longer distinguish between my conjectures and the data based on experience. Working with hypotheses, I can at times construct for myself such a minute and convincing picture of the fortress that in my mind I can move through it completely at my ease; whereas the elements I derive from what I see and what I hear are confused, full of gaps, more and more contradictory. (139)

Edmund Dantés is the exemplary postmodern observer. As the story progresses, it becomes clear that the dichotomy here is between Dantés, the pure theoretician whose theories and models become (or construct) the very castle from which he is trying to escape, and the Abbé Faria, Dantés's other self, who is an empiricist, a pure experimentalist. Faria's "fortress-as-theory-of-fortress" comprises all the tunnels he's actually dug while trying to escape.

> The images of the fortress that Faria and I create are becoming more and more different: Faria, beginning with a simple figure, is complicating it extremely to include in it each of the single unforeseen elements he encounters in his path; I, setting out from the jumble of these data, see in each isolated obstacle the clue to a system of obstacles, I develop each segment into a regular figure, I fit these figures together as the sides of a solid, polyhedron or hyperpolyhedron, I inscribe these polyhedrons in spheres or hyperspheres, and so the more I enclose the form of the fortress the more I simplify it, defining it in a numerical relation or in an algebraic formula. (144)

"The Count of Monte Cristo" ends in a discussion of the relative positions of the narrator-authors Dantés/Faria/Dumas. Dantés imagines superimposing the theoretical (imaginary) map of the Château D'If onto the map that Dumas has had to construct of the different pieces and fragments of his narrative, *The Count of Monte Cristo*. Dantés concludes, "To plan a book—or an escape—the first thing to know is what to exclude . . . and this, then, is a sign that here an opportunity of escape exists: we have only to identify the point where the imagined fortress does not coincide with the real one and then find it" (151-52).

This short capstone text is a retroactive tutorial: it teaches us how to read all that has come before it in *T-Zero*. It hints strongly that Calvino's purpose is not so

much to express an interest in the sciences for their own sake, as to compare the relative potency of science and literature—their metaphors, their methods, their visions of order, their controlling paradigms, their manners of experimentation—as narratives of the world. "The Count of Monte Cristo," in this light, is about postmodern epistemology. And Calvino concludes, as inevitably he must, that postmodern fictive narratives are epistemologically more potent than postmodern scientific ones. Or rather, that the distinction between the two is erased by the postmodern mode: *science and fiction are two aspects of the same project—mapping the fortress.*

Given this collapse of distinctions, fiction has an advantage, as narrative, over the sciences. It makes room for the observer in its calculus, and includes a vision of the beauty not only of order but of disorder.

Armed with this understanding of the novelistic coherence of *T-Zero,* we can begin to read the short story (or chapter) about cybernetics, "Night Driver."

"NIGHT DRIVER"

X, a resident of City A, has just hung up the phone on his lover Y, of City B. They had an argument and decided to break up. But Y got in the last word by threatening X that she would now take up with X's rival, Z. Z also lives in X's city, A. So now X, frenzied with jealousy and regret, is furiously driving to B where he hopes to reconcile with Y, or at least forestall a tryst between Y and Z (whom he imagines also driving furiously along the same road between A and B to meet Y). It is nighttime. So the driving is at once more dangerous, but also simplified, because as X the narrator tells us, "[O]ur eyes . . . have to check a kind of black slate which requires a different method of reading, more precise but also simplified, since the darkness erases all the picture's details which might be distracting and underlines only the indispensable elements, the white stripes on the asphalt, the headlights' yellow glow, and the little red dots" (128-29). We've been forewarned: we're solidly inside a postmodern fiction, where the narrator's and characters' observations are tropes for our acts of reading, a situation we also find in Beckett, Pynchon, Barth, Coover, and others. As the story proceeds, the abstraction and simplification of X's position increases. It starts to rain, which further reduces the "visibility." Then, nearing the end, X (looking forward to Edmund Dantés) imagines what it would be like if the situation were reduced to its barest minimum, which is also its most abstract:

> Naturally, if I were absolutely alone on this superhighway, if I saw no other cars speeding in either direction, then everything would be much clearer, I would be certain that Z hasn't moved to supplant me, nor has Y moved to make peace with me, facts I might register as positive or negative in my accounting, but which would in any case leave no room for doubt. And yet if I had the power of exchanging my present state of uncertainty for such a negative certainty, I would refuse the

bargain without hesitation. The ideal condition for excluding every doubt would prevail if in this part of the world there existed only three automobiles: mine, Y's, and Z's; then no other car could proceed in my direction except Z's, and the only car heading in the opposite direction would surely be Y's. (134).

This direct appeal to the jargon of cybernetics sends us searching for other pieces of the Calvino puzzle: In which science's narrative has he trapped us this time? We retrace our steps along the path of the text. X has told us that he has "lost all sense of space and time." In cybernetic parlance, that leaves him operating only with *matter* and *information*: his car, the road, and the message he carries (or the message he *is!*). X sorts among those signs he receives from the road and his context, heeding the important and filtering out the noise ("the numbers of the miles on the signs and the numbers that click over on the dashboard are data that mean nothing to me"; "the information I receive from outside consists only of yellow and red flashes distorted by a tumult of drops" [130]). X tries to refine even further the message he wants to deliver to Y and the message he most wants to receive from her: "what I desire most is not to find Y at the end of my race: I want [rather] Y to be racing toward me, this is the answer I need" (131-32).

But in wishing this reciprocity (a normal enough desire for anyone in a relationship), X has wished himself into a paradox, one that leads us to the heart of cybernetics' fallibility as a narrative of human communication. Because it is dark and raining, if Y drives towards X as X drives towards Y, in the night and rain, they will be unrecognizable to each other! "Speeding along the superhighway is the only method we have left, she and I, to express what we have to say to each other, but we cannot communicate it or receive the communication as long as we are speeding" (132).

In part, Calvino has merely exaggerated the reduction that we all have felt when we have been forced to conduct our intimate relationships over the telephone. XYZ driving along channel of transmission AB is an oversimplification of (and satire on) experiences we've all encountered (and undoubtedly resisted): trying to resolve personal conflicts over the telephone. But on the other hand, the telephone is also a cybernetic medium: one of the direct motives for Shannon's work at Bell Labs was to refine the signal-to-noise ratio in telecommunications. Consequently, this reduction is also Calvino's ploy to expose the fallibility of viewing human relations as a cybernetic activity. In the next paragraph, then, Calvino cribs from Swift, who employed Gulliver to indict the literal-mindedness and over-technicalism of the natural philosophers of *his* age; Calvino launches an indictment of the cybernetic reduction of *our* age by having X, an overly technical or repressed character, express it in its pure form with utter conviction:

> Of course I took my place behind the wheel in order to reach her as fast as possible; but the more

I go forward the more I realize that the moment of arrival is not the real end of my race. Our meeting, with all the inessential details a meeting involves, the minute network of sensations and meanings and memories that would spread out before me— the room with the philodendron, the opaline lamp, the earrings—and the things I would say to her, some of which would surely be mistaken or mistakable, and the things she would say, to some extent surely jarring or in any case not what I expect, and all the succession of unpredictable consequences that each gesture and each word involved would raise around the things that we have to say to each other, or rather that we want to hear each other say, a storm of such noise that our communication already difficult over the telephone would become even more hazardous, stifled, buried as if under an avalanche of sand. This is why, rather than go on talking, I felt the need to transform the things to be said into a cone of light hurled at a hundred miles an hour, to transform myself into this cone of light moving over the superhighway, because it is certain that such a signal can be received and understood by her without being lost in the ambiguous disorder of secondary vibrations. . . . What counts is communicating the indispensable . . . reducing ourselves to essential communication, to a luminous signal that moves in a given direction, abolishing the complexity of our personalities and situations and facial expressions. (132-33)

The indictment comes ironically, of course. X, as is typical of males in Calvino's fictions, urges an overly scientized, rationalized version of things. He wants love reduced to algebra. But it is exactly what he discounts, "the ambiguous disorder of secondary vibrations," that most of his readers would seek to preserve as giving value and meaning to human communication over and above its information content. In short, as X himself realizes in one final futile clinging to his humanity, he finds himself in an unbearable paradox: "[I]f I want to receive a message I must give up being [only] a message myself, but the message I want to receive from Y—namely, that Y has made herself into a message—has value only if I in turn am a message [and vice versa]" (134-35).

Finally, though, X embraces his cybernetic conversion or translation in a seizure of what we can only call madness, a kind of flip-flop characteristic of our postmodern cybernetic age.

> I can no longer accept any situation other than this transformation of ourselves into the messages of ourselves. . . . Everything is more uncertain than ever but I feel I've now reached a state of inner serenity: . . . we will continue, all three of us, speeding back and forth along these white lines, with no points of departure or of arrival to threaten with their sensations and meanings the single-mindedness of our race, freed finally from the awkward thickness of our persons and voices and moods, reduced to luminous signals, the only appropriate way of being for those who wish to be identified with what they say, without the

distorting buzz our presence or the presence of others transmits to our messages. (135-36)

Here we are building to that postmodern moment: that point when the text sends us into a spiraling seizure of interpretations that fling us out and beyond our own acts of interpretation. In the passage above, three phrases hint at cybernetic self-reflection. The first, of course, is the expression by the narrator as he feels himself metamorphosing into the *message of himself.* The second is more elusive: when I read "speeding back and forth along these white lines," I construe it as a direct reference to the actual letters I see before me on the page, the voice of X-the-message embodied in yet another form of "cybernetic" communication—black marks on a white page. This phrase forces us into a kind of double vision, in which we conceive of X both as a luminous signal traveling down an abstract highway and at the same time as trapped in the letters we are reading in the printed text.

The second phrase erases any doubt we may have had about the overnicety of such self-reflexive interpretations: "the only appropriate way of being for those who wish to be identified with what they say." The avatar of those who "wish to be identified with what they say" is the author, who here is signaling to us that he has transformed himself into a pure signal, an act of communication.

However, this leaves two important turns of the text in order for it to qualify as a cybernetic fiction: first, it must demolish such a proposition—even as it posits it—through irony. At the same time, the text must gesture at (or better yet, convince us of) the existence of some alternative narrative of communication, a realm beyond the cybernetics of reading and deciphering. It ought to deliver us back into the embrace of our humanness and engender within us an awareness of those aspects which lie outside the mechanisms of communication. Otherwise, the text, for all its clever manipulation and allegorizing and satirizing of the cybernetic point-of-view, will have failed to offer a counterstatement that rises above mere philosophy into artistic demonstration.

Calvino accomplishes all this in the final paragraph of "Night Driver": X still ruminates about his conversion into a pure signal, unencumbered by the noisiness of "sensations and meanings": "To be sure, the price paid is high but we must accept it: to be indistinguishable from all the other signals that pass along this road, each with his meaning that remains hidden and undecipherable because outside of here there is no one capable of receiving us now and understanding us" (136). To be sure, X has it all wrong; the reader quickly realizes that X is still a Gulliver, a pawn of the author's irony. Calvino is signaling to us through X that he is engaged in an altogether different communications act than X's night drive. There *is,* Calvino insists, an "outside of here" (a world outside the text); there *are* those "capable of receiving us now and understanding us" (we

readers); and fortunately, there *are* means of deciphering hidden meanings that lie outside the mechanisms of language and signals, that rely on the "distorting buzz" of *presence* which X has disavowed.

In this postmodern moment, Calvino has wrested the "bragging rights"—epistemological control—over human communication away from cybernetics and placed it back in the hands of the reader and writer, for whom the text acts only as a channel of transmission, and who reside in a territory dominated by "the awkward thickness of bodies, voices and moods." Calvino has demonstrated the incompetence of the text when it operates solely according to cybernetic algorithms—as a luminous signal—and he has done so by using the very illusion of logocentrism ("outside of here there is no one") to demolish itself.

This feat and feats like it accomplished in other cybernetic fictions are especially important in an era when cybernetic methods, theories, metaphors, and models have come to exert influence over many of our important disciplines, and have conjured an image, which our culture seems to have already embraced, of humans subsumed in cybernetic mechanisms. We need a counternarrative, one forged from postmodern principles equally strong, to show that even as the cybernetic age progresses ineluctably, humans will manage to preserve their humanness, however metamorphosed, however wedded to cybernetic machinery, and however disguised, in the postmodern fashion—through irony, paradox, rich metaphor, and self-effacement.

NOTES

[1] Cybernetic fiction shares its explicit resistance to cybernetics with phenomenological philosophy. Heidegger, Polanyi, Merleau-Ponty, and others (see n. 12) all provide an alternative view of human communication as richer and involving more indeterminate mechanisms than cybernetics can account for. However, I would argue that cybernetic fiction shares with punk music an advantage over philosophy: the former can express the distinctions while the latter can only posit that those distinctions exist.

[2] Daniel Bell, among others, has called our era "The Information Age." See *The Coming of the Post-Industrial Society* (New York, 1973). But I suggest it is too abstruse to call our era an Information Age and leave it at that. But at the same time—perhaps paradoxically—I think of cybernetics as postmodern, following Stephen Toulmin's lead, because it also is forced to confront, self-consciously, the human role in information-gathering and communication.

[3] Norbert Wiener, *Cybernetics: Control and Communication in the Animal and in the Machine* (Cambridge, Mass., 1948).

[4] Norbert Wiener, *The Human Use of Human Beings* (New York, 1954), p. 11.

[5] In fairness to cybernetics, however, we must acknowledge that as a science, it has not been historically immune to questions regarding humanity's new epistemological status under its definitions. Norbert Wiener, in *The Human Use of Human Beings,* represents the hard-line when he boldly states (somewhat oxymoronically) that the "mechanism-vitalism duality can be banished to the limbo of badly posed questions." Warren Weaver and Claude Shannon, in popularizing Shannon's ideas about information theory, ask the question but slyly avoid answering it in their collection of essays and commentary, *The Mathematical Theory of Communication* (Urbana, Ill., 1949). Abraham Moles attempts to reconcile the humanistic position with the scientific one by proposing a cybernetic model for aesthetic activity in his work *Information Theory and Esthetic Perception* (1958; rpt. Urbana, 1966). More recently, however, cyberneticists have noted that the problem of self-consciousness becomes shorthand for the entire question about the distinction between how machines use information and how humans make meaning. Gordon Pask, for instance, notes that each cybernetic model contains two levels of analysis: one in which the observer attempts "to stipulate the system's purpose" and one in which the observer attempts "to stipulate his own purpose" ("The Meaning of Cybernetics in the Behavioral Sciences," in *Progress in Cybernetics,* ed. J. Rose, vol. 14 [New York, 1969], 15-44). Humberto Maturana, a Chilean neurophysicist, calls this second level of cybernetic modeling by a curiously literary name, "autopoiesis" (*Autopoiesis and Cognition* [Boston, 1980]). In turn, this leads Heinz von Foerster to call for a "cybernetics of cybernetics" ("Cybernetics of Cybernetics," in *Communication and Control in Society,* ed. Klaus Krippendorff [New York, 1979], p. 5). In this fashion, cybernetics finds itself to be in the same fix that the postmodern novel is in; at very least, it is grappling with the same questions.

A more phenomenological counterstatement is adopted in two volumes of essays edited by Frederick Crosson and K. Sayre, *The Modeling of Mind* and *The Philosophy of Cybernetics* (Notre Dame, 1963 and 1967 respectively). Similarly, Hubert Dreyfuss uses Maurice Merleau-Ponty's work as a philosophical point of departure to form a refutation of cybernetics and artificial intelligence in his work *What Computers Can't Do* (New York, 1972). All these discussions tend to focus on language as the battleground, as they have ever since Descartes. When asked by a student how he would know if an automaton were human or not, Descartes replied, "I will believe he is a man when he tells me so himself." I.e., the philosophical proof lies in the technological pudding: If computers can learn to speak with the spontaneity and inventiveness and richness of humans, then the cyberneticists have proved their point.

[6] We can gauge the myth's invisibleness by the extent to which its metaphors have become literal: *data, bytes, feedback, noise, sender, receiver, open and closed systems, organization, redundancy,* and *entropy*—all the mumbo jumbo of cybernetic mythology.

[7] Stephen Toulmin, *The Return to Cosmology: Postmodern Science and the Theology of Nature* (Berkeley, 1982), p. 210. Toulmin suggests that contemporary science in general is growing more and more postmodern because it calls for a new epistemology that reinserts the human perspective into the model of nature.

[8] Another way to view this shift is in terms of the experiment itself. In the classical model, the experimental apparatus is a neutral tool for measuring nature at work. Voyeuristic in the best Victorian tradition, it peers in on Mother Nature disrobing unselfconsciously for the (exclusively male) scientist's delectation. Or in even more concrete terms, the experiment is a weighing scale that doesn't weigh itself. Postmodernism has shucked the notion of any such weightless delivery of data. In its place it has erected a model in which the scale and weight alter each other in a mutual embrace of fields and forces—in this case, gravitation and information. However, Heisenberg's own philosophical claims for the implications of his Uncertainty principle were probably inflated, partly as the result of his association with Heidegger.

[9] As Nick Herbert has noted, in his *Quantum Reality: Beyond the New Physics* (New York, 1985), these discoveries do "not mean that the quantum world is subjective. . . . The quantum world is objective but objectless" (p. 162).

[10] Paul Davies, *Other Worlds* (London, 1980). This is conducted in much more authoritative ways and in much less hyperbolic and metaphorical terms than similar claims made by Gary Zukav in *The Dancing Wu Li Masters: An Overview of the New Physics* (New York, 1979) and Fritjof Capra in *The Tao of Physics: An Exploration of the Parallels between Modern Physics and Eastern Mysticism* (Toronto, 1977).

[11] Bell's Theorem has been proven by the Aspect experiments, conducted at the Institute of Theoretical and Applied Optics in Paris in 1982 by Alain Aspect, Jean Dalibard, and Gérard Roger.

[12] Jeremy Campbell, *Grammatical Man: Information, Entropy, Language and Life* (New York, 1982).

[13] Joe P. Buhler, "Of Primes and Pennies," *Science 85,* Nov. 1985, p. 86.

[14] Jeremy Rifkin, *Algeny* (New York, 1983), pp. 180-215.

[15] I use "cybernetic" and "mechanical" as equivalents, following William Barrett's suggestion that we think of machines not only as those gleaming instruments designed to accomplish work in the material world, but as incarnations of logic or algorithms. In his words, "A machine is an embodied decision procedure"; *The Illusion of Technique* (New York, 1979), p. 23.

[16] David Porush, *The Soft Machine: Cybernetic Fiction* (London, 1985).

[17] Tony Tanner's account of Burroughs's fiction elucidates his antimechanism rather thoroughly in *City of Words: American Fiction 1950-1970* (New York, 1971).

[18] As late as 1933, Raymond Roussel in his collection *Comment J'ai écrit certaine de mes livres* [How I Wrote Some of My Books] (Paris, 1963), constructed verbal mechanisms that aspired to a pure and total congruence between the machinery of language and the machinery described by that language.

[19] See Cecilia Tichi's recent *Shifting Gears* (Chapel Hill, N.C., 1987), which portrays the relations between American technology and literary modernism; Hugh Kenner's *The Counterfeiters* (New York, 1972), which meditates on a similar relation between European modernism and the machine; and *The Soft Machine,* ch. 2, in which I show the contrasting use of the machine as a model in the French modernist Raymond Roussel's work, and by extension, in Kafka and Joyce.

[20] Interestingly enough, the bomb and cybernetics are intimately linked. As Norbert Wiener documents in his work on cybernetics (see nn. 3, 4), one of his original motives for developing a mathematics of control and communication was to further refine the guidance systems and trajectory calculations for mortar and rocket technology during World War II. Thomas Pynchon makes literary hay out of this connection in *Gravity's Rainbow* (New York, 1973), in which the hero (Tyrone Slothrop) slowly discovers that there is a cybernetic-behaviorist-mystical connection between his sexual conquests in London and the *schwarzgerat*—the "dark" or "mysterious thing"—the black-box guidance governor in the nose cone of V-rockets falling on London.

[21] I would argue that even the highly formalistic experiments of Barth and Pynchon are "anti-formalistic" since they are designed expressly to defeat the purpose of formalism, which is to achieve a totalizing system. I further argue (below) that this is the distinguishing feature between modernism, which pretends that its system is effectively totalizing, and postmodernism, which drives at some phenomenological sense of the insufficiency of system.

[22] Viktor Shklovsky, "Art as Technique," in *Russian Formalist Criticism: Four Essays,* ed. and tr. Lee T. Lemon (Lincoln, Nebr., 1965), pp. 11-12.

[23] William Hendricks, "Style and the Structure of Literary Discourse," in *Style and Text,* ed. Hakan Ringbom (Stockholm, 1975), p. 72. Lemon uses the term "defamiliarization."

[24] Jacques Derrida, *Of Grammatology,* tr. Gayatri Chakravorty Spivak (Baltimore, 1976), p. 93.

[25] Italo Calvino, "Cybernetics and Ghosts," in *The Uses of Literature: Essays,* tr. Patrick Creagh (New York, 1986), pp. 3-27; hereafter cited in text.

[26] I would contrast this with modernist technique, where the text leaves a trail of clues—as in Nabokov's *Lolita* and Joyce's *Ulysses*—that leads to the uncovering of a map of reading, so that a correlation of clues ends with a completion of the puzzle that closes the door to further interpretation. Though this is not necessarily sterile (for the vision is delivered whole), it is "positivistic" in the sense that it strives for a complete and consistent system. I would argue that this is the distinguishing feature between the two modes of discourse, modernist and postmodernist.

[27] Kathleen Woodward, "Cybernetic Modelling in Recent American Fiction," *North Dakota Quarterly,* 51 (Winter 1983), 57-73.

[28] I characterize these laws as follows:

(1) *University creates a gap where fools and angels alike rush in.* Humans find it compulsory to interpret (disambiguate) uncertainty. If nothing else, homo sapiens is a superb disambiguating machine.

(2) *One man's noise is another man's signal.* Changing contexts or points of view, particularly those provided by variants in the human situation, can potentially make a code of static and nonsense of the message, since noise and signal exist in a figure/ground relationship to each other. The conflict caused by shifting frames of reference creates more ambiguity.

(3) See (1).

[29] Italo Calvino, *T-Zero,* tr. William Weaver (1967; rpt. New York, 1969), p. 33; hereafter cited in text.

[30] Reminiscent of Barth's story narrated by a spermatozoan on its way to consummation with an ovum, "Night-Sea Journey," in *Lost in the Funhouse: Fiction for Print, Tape, Live Voice* (New York, 1968).

[31] Campbell, *Grammatical Man,* pp. 92-93.

[32] I can't help but wonder if Calvino is employing a bilingual pun here: Science is the Castle of Ifs.

POETRY

Kelly Cherry

SOURCE: "The Two Cultures at the End of the Twentieth Century: An Essay on Poetry and Science," in *The Midwest Quarterly,* Vol. XXXV, No. 2, Winter, 1994, pp. 121-35.

[*In the following essay, Cherry emphasizes the importance of communication between poets and scientists.*]

In an essay first published in *The New Statesman* in 1956 and later included in a series of lectures delivered at Cambridge University, C. P. Snow said of himself, "By training I was a scientist; by vocation I was a writer. . . . It was a piece of luck, if you like, that arose through coming from a poor home." I, too, came from a poor home, though it was an educated home, and my parents, who were string quartet violinists, thought that economic salvation would lie in having one of their children turn out to be a scientist. I never got further than a hodgepodge of introductory science courses and rather more math, but even that superficial acquaintance with science has proved to be "a bit of luck." I have taken seriously what C. P. Snow called the problem of "The Two Cultures"—that "the intellectual life of the whole of western society is increasingly being split into two polar groups"—and tried to find ways in my writing to reunite what had been separated, to bring together what had been estranged, to fuse, as it were, what had been fissioned. If the results are essentially private, well, that is because those scientists and scholars over there on the other side of the chasm need to get busy and do *their* part, by, of course, reading some contemporary poetry.

C. P. Snow may seem an unfashionable figure by now; he's probably unknown to most younger people. Despite his many novels, none of my writing students has ever heard of him. But there was a time when, in the heat of the Cold War, in the Race to Space, his essay came as a call to arms. In October, 1957, Sputnik went up—and C. P. Snow's analysis of "The Two Cultures" was thought to have been prophetic. Thus it was that a little while later, at the age of seventeen, I found myself a sophomore at the New Mexico Institute of Mining and Technology. My being a student at a mining school, precisely because it *was* such a ridiculous thing for me to be, is a good indication of the values the country held at that time. I recall sitting in a classroom with mining students and young engineers, budding atmospheric physicists and possibly a future oil magnate or two, taking an I.Q. test for spatial perspective. Thousands of miles from my home in Virginia, wearing East Coast hemlines that were shockingly short in the fifties Southwest, I chewed on my pencil and tried to figure out how many hidden sides a two-dimensional object might possess. I believe I had the lowest I.Q. ever recorded at New Mexico Tech.

All the same, like loving a man the world has said you may not marry, I lived in a kind of constant scientific swoon, ravished by the beauty of mathematics, the complicated narrative of paleontology, the diagrams of vectors in our physics notebooks, Mondrian in their clarity.

If spatial configurations were not my forte, temporal ones may have been. Even before I read C. P. Snow, I liked almost nothing better, during high school, than to listen to the Beethoven quartets, which are the most beautiful explorations of time ever conducted in music, late at night while drawing up charts of geologic eras and periods at my desk. I had an attic room, with dormer windows. You could listen to music there without disturbing the rest of the house. And so, late at night, the whole house was sound asleep—sleeping sound; sound, sleeping—except for my room, which was wakeful with sublime music and the meditation of time, that long line next to which my own life, at fourteen, was not so much as a visible dot.

Some of the images of those nights that I spent lost in time returned to me as I was working on my most recent book of poetry, *Natural Theology*. I chose to open this book with a poem titled "Phylogenesis," and perhaps, as I wrote it, I was remembering the vivid intellectual fantasies of my youth:

> She cracks her skin
> like a shell, and goes in
>
> She camps in her womb
> She sucks the marrow from her bones
>
> and sips bison's blood
> in the afternoon; for years,
>
> snow piles outside the cave she burrows in
> She wakes to warm weather,
>
> fur on her four feet, grass
> rising and falling in waves like water
>
> She feeds on flowering plants,
> enjoys a cud of orchid and carrot
>
> In the Middle Permian, scales slippery as shale
>   appear
> on her back; her spine unfurls a sail broadside
>
> to the sun, filling with a light like wind, while
> *Sphenodon*
> turns its third eye on the sky, sensing
>
> rain, and rock salt washes into the ocean
> Silent as mist, she slides down a mud bank on her
>   underbelly
>
> Lobe-finned and fleshy,
> she pumps air through her gills
>
> She's soft as jelly
> Her skull is limestone
>
> She drifts, like a continent
> or a protozoan, on the planet's surface,
>
> and sinks into the past
> like a pebble into a brackish pool
>
> The seas catch fire
> The earth splits and gapes
>
> The earth cracks open like an egg
> and she goes in
>
> We begin

Whatever else may be said about that poem, I am pretty sure that it is the only poem ever to get into it a reference to *Sphenodon,* a predecessor of the modern lizard. I hope that this is a scientific enough reference to appease the spirit of C. P. Snow. After complaining that "it is bizarre how very little of twentieth-century science has been assimilated into twentieth-century art," he admitted wryly that, at least, "Now and then one used to find poets conscientiously using scientific expressions, and getting them wrong—there was a time when 'refraction' kept cropping up in verse in a mystifying fashion, and when 'polarised light' was used as though writers were under the illusion that it was a specially admirable kind of light." And I know that when black holes began to be talked about in *Time* and *Newsweek,* they were suddenly cropping up in poems everywhere (mine too), as if the mere importation of a scientific term into a poem were enough to freight the poem with new meaning. It isn't, of course.

No, the challenge of using science in poetry lies in using it in a way that results in stronger poetry, a poetry that incorporates as much as possible of the real world. One contemporary poet who has been much drawn to the bleak romance of astronomy as a way of training a telescope on the real world we live in is Robert Watson. In certain of his poems we come to know an astronomer's stubborn love for space itself, as if the distance between two objects were more seductive than any mere object could be. "This is a universe of luck and chance," Watson writes in "The Radio Astronomer," and continues, "Galaxies / Spin in flight like snow, rattle in space, are gone."

In another poem, "Riding in Space I Kiss My Wife," he allows us to view a more mundane romance through the lens of the speaker's romance with the "universe of luck and chance," so that we see our messy, mortal world as if from very far away, from as far away as cosmic unconcern:

> Over us in bed together kissing,
> The night rides,
> Dumps a splintered ice-boat, its shrouds,
> The universe in our bed, our children's beds.
> The arteries of heaven run bursting with cars.
> "There are billions of galaxies," I read,
> "And a galaxy contains countless billions of stars."

Robert Watson's use of astronomical imagery heightens, brilliantly, the sense of despair in his poems; it extends despair, the sense of overwhelming distance between actuality and ideal, into a lyricism of the first magnitude.

The poet and fiction writer R.H.W. Dillard, whose vocabularies of reference are astonishingly varied and knowledgeably detailed, encompassing, among others, science, cinema, literature, art, and linguistics, takes as an epigraph the philosopher of process A. N. Whitehead's pronunciamento, "The stable universe is slipping away from us," to enter a poem, "March Again," about the fixity of love.

> Christ could have swum away
> From the cross on air,
> But he chose to be nailed
> To the ground. You grow dizzy
> And each step is like walking
> On water. . . .

Reading Whitehead, the writer has recognized in an idea about the world something that can be employed not only as hypothesis or conclusion but as a way of thinking, an approach to *another* idea. This, after all, is central to what writers, I believe, want to do. They don't want just to embellish the world with images, decking the world's hall with bough after bough of ivy. They want to lead the reader through the hall into all the rooms that lie beyond. A way to get to those rooms is by using an *idea* as an image.

For instance, in my collection *Relativity: A Point of View,* I turned to the theory of relativity as a way of thinking about the Trinity, three-in-one, and especially about the Trinity as it might manifest itself—or its selves—to a woman's point of view. There is a phrase, "duets with Einstein," that might seem to the uninitiated to be the whole of my use of the theory of relativity in that poem but in fact the whole poem is predicated on the theory, presenting, as it does, a series of parallel triads through which the point of view slides in a very strange way, bending the time of the poem back on itself like reflected—or possibly refracted, and maybe even polarized—light.

Still, what the poet wants to make of science is not more science but more poetry. I have to admit that I am not always bothered by an excessive need to be factual (though I hope, always and forever, to be truthful). In a longish narrative poem I tried to imagine a scientific expedition in Siberia in 1913. I have no idea whether an expedition like the one in the poem ever actually took place, and yet an encounter with a prehistoric creature that has been frozen during an Ice Age to reemerge into life thousands of years later certainly recurs again and again as a kind of unarticulated myth, and so I decided to articulate it. I picked the year 1913 out of the historical air, to increase the tension: the First World War is about to begin; the Russian Revolution is waiting in the wings. Readers have asked me about the paleobotanist who appears in the poem and is named Szymanowski. There may well be a paleobotanist named Szymanowski, but I have never read of him. The only Szymanowski I know of was a Polish violinist, and I know of him only because, finding myself in need of a name that would provide a satisfying mouthful of syllables in my poem, I raced downstairs—I was visiting my parents at the time—and asked my father what he could suggest. My father, not having read C. P. Snow, seized upon what he knew best and came up with the name "Szymanowski." I believe that if I had just stayed downstairs he could have found me a violinist's name that would do for every occupation I might ever have literary occasion to refer to. I ran with "Szymanowski" back to my room and stuck it into my poem. What is important, sometimes, is the scheme of science rather than the science itself, although I suspect the scheme will not likely occur to writers who don't regularly include science as one of the things they think about. For example, in a poem about the rose, which I wanted to convey in all its traditional romantic, theological, and literary dimensions, I took a botanical lecture as my model for the poem's form. Each description that the poem gives of "the rose" is presented as a definition, as if something scientifically taxonomic were going on, which, of course, it is not:

THE ROSE

It's the cup of blood,
the dark drink lovers sip,
the secret food

It's the pulse and elation
of girls on their birthdays,
it's good-byes at the railroad station

It's the murmur of rain,
the blink of daylight
in a still garden, the clink
of crystal; later, the train

pulling out, the white cloth,
apples, pears, and champagne—
good-bye! good-bye!
We'll weep petals, and dry
our tears with thorns
A steep country springs up beyond
the window, with a sky like a pond,

a flood. It's a rush
of bright horror, a burning bush,
night's heart,
the living side of the holy rood

It's the whisper of grace in the martyr's wood

Writing that poem, I felt as though having access to the *idea,* at least, of a botanical lecture gave me a new route into an otherwise familiar place, arguably even an overtrafficked place, in the land of poetic symbolism. It gave me a new take on an old problem. It worries me that so many writing students confine themselves to the study of literature—and literature in English, at that. Obviously, writers need to know their own literatures as well as possible, but that is not all they need to know. I think it is unfortunate for students that so many of them are now able to earn college degrees without taking serious courses in science and math (and let's throw classical literature in there while we are at it). There is a world out there to be written about.

Because, the truth is, I am an empiricist at heart and I do believe that there is a world out there but that it is a world difficult to know. I believe we must bring every instrument at our disposal to bear on the knowing of it. And science is one of those instruments, but so is literature. Literature is not merely an ornament or a therapy; it is a way of knowing the world. This is what *scientists* need to understand about *literature.*

(I will go even further, all the way out on a theoretical limb, and state that different forms of literature are essentially different modes of perception, though each form partakes to some degree of the others. Fiction is the way we come to know the world of relation; the personal essay is the way we come to know—more than the subject of its discussion—the mind of the essayist, how

thinking occurs; poetry, for all the use it makes of emotion, is the way we come to know the thing itself, the simple undeniable fact of existence, of existence in all its manifold particularity. I won't try to defend these propositions. But I will say that I believe them to be truths, learned from my experience working in all three forms.)

If literature (and other art) is a kind of knowledge, it is equally clear that math and science are forms of beauty, to anyone who will recognize them as such. I will never forget that day in a classroom at the University of Virginia when Ian Hacking was attempting to explain to a group of graduate students Gödel's proof of the impossibility of establishing the presence of internal logical consistency in deductive systems. Some of the students were working on their doctorates in mathematics; others of us were philosophy students dazed by the entire mad enterprise of mathematical logic, and for weeks we had been wondering how we were ever going to get out of this class alive. Hacking went to the blackboard and proceeded to work his way around the room until all four walls were white with chalked equations constituting an abbreviated version of the proof. And suddenly, I went from being dazed to being dazzled, as everything revealed itself to me. It was a vision, surely, not unlike the moment of illumination I experienced when, at five, I finally, after great effort, learned how to tie my shoelaces—but that was a triumph too, a door opening onto a universe of pattern and intricacy and scope. It was like reading Shakespeare or listening to Beethoven. It was beauty, pure and simple, or not so simple, and if I no longer remember anything I ever knew of mathematical logic, I have never forgotten the sheer gorgeousness of it. This is what *writers* need to understand about *mathematics and science.*

Two books of poetry published in the seventies spoke directly to the writer's responsibility to understand what he can of mathematics and science. John Bricuth, in *The Heisenberg Variations,* an extremely interesting and often very funny collection, evokes a contemporary sense of uncertainty, our sense that we are probably, right now, the butt of a joke we don't quite get. Here is "Talking Big":

We are sitting here at dinner talking big.
I am between the two dullest men in the world
Across from the fattest woman I ever met.
We are talking big. Someone has just remarked
That energy equals the speed of light squared.
We nod, feeling that that is "pretty nearly correct."
I remark that the square on the hypotenuse can more
Than equal the squares on the two sides. The squares
On the two sides object. The hypotenuse over the way
Is gobbling the grits. We are talking big. The door
Opens suddenly revealing a vista that stretches
To infinity. Parenthetically, someone remarks
That a body always displaces its own weight.
I note at the end of the gallery stands a man
In a bowler and a black coat with an apple where
His head should be, with his back to me, and it is me.
I clear my throat and re (parenthetically) mark
That a body always falls of its own weight.
"whoosh-WHOOM!" sighs the hypotenuse across,
And (godknows) she means it with all her heart.

Who are the squares on the two sides, if not ourselves? And we are talking big, but no matter how big, "a body always displaces its own weight." Who is the man in the bowler and black coat? Traditionally Death, he is also, here, the speaker in the poem, who will displace his own weight. Does he also represent the death of the Newtonian universe, those reasonable laws displaced by the apple of relativity? And is the apple also the apple of the knowledge of good and evil? Oh, the poet *meant* it when he said, "We are talking big."

Al Zolynas, in *The New Physics,* takes an opposite tactic, turning to the unseen structures of subatomic physics to comment on our daily life in the middle range. His book is divided in three sections, "Color," "Charm," and "Strangeness," as if the most minuscule particles of the world, quarks, were also metaphors for it. In the title poem, a prose poem, he explains his method:

> And so, the closer he looks at things, the farther away they seem. At dinner, after a hard day at the universe, he finds himself slipping through his food. His own hands wave at him from beyond a mountain of peas. Stars and planets dance with molecules on his fingertips. After a hard day with the universe, he tumbles through himself, flies through the dream galaxies of his own heart. In the very presence of his family he feels he is descending through an infinite series of Chinese boxes.
>
> This morning, when he entered the little broom-closet of the electron looking for quarks and neutrinos, it opened into an immense hall, the hall into a plain—the Steppes of Mother Russia! He could see men hauling barges up the river, chanting faintly for their daily bread.
>
> It's not that he longs for the old Newtonian Days, although something of plain matter and simple gravity might be reassuring, something of the good old equal-but-opposite forces. And it's not that he hasn't learned to balance comfortably on the see-saw of paradox. It's what he sees in the eyes of his children—the infinite black holes, the ransomed light at the center.

What we want to know, what we crave to know, is, of course, the answer to the oldest questions: Why are we— even our children—made to die? Why must the good suffer? Can we be good? Why should we be good? Is there point or purpose to our existence? These are the questions both scientists and poets would like to know the answers to. If none has yet fathomed a single answer, we may acknowledge that the questions themselves compose a kind of Rosetta stone. Asking the same questions in our different languages of science and art, we learn to translate ourselves into one another, we see that we are different words for the same humanity. There is a vision of oneness here, amid the many voices in which the universe speaks its own being. In "The Study of Ecology," Dillard says that Thoreau, examining the veins of leaves against sunlight,

> Also looked at his hand—
> Branching, veined, barked,

> The fine black hairs
> That need sunlight to be seen,
> Lines, branches, the universal M,
> Cain's mark.
>
> Raise your hand, hold it,
> Know the stilling of winter,
> And when you grow tired, forget
> And let it fall, the flow
> Of new springs.
>
> You rub your eyes,
> Bone, skin on water,
> You see heavens, stars,
> Fires, fire.
>
> Leaves riddle with sunlight
> The ground, the grass,
> Your hand, holding sunlight,
> Leaves of shadow, of air.

This is to say that both kinds of knowing, literature and science, are vehicles that carry us out of our solipsistic selves and into the world. Both make it possible for us to recognize one another as real beings moving in a real world. I tried to say something like this in a poem in which I imagined the world as it might have been viewed by the first woman to orbit the earth, in 1963, Lt. Col. Valentina Vladimirovna Tereshkova. The poem itself makes an orbit, closing in a circle, and pulls lines from Genesis and Job into its scientific compass. (I should mention that the Daugava is a river in Latvia, one of the Baltic countries whose rightfully independent status has now been recognized. That the Daugava, in this poem, is "tangy," is an allusion to—what else?—Tang, fabled orange drink of space missions!)

> It looked like an apple
> or a Christmas orange:
> I wanted to eat it.
> I could taste the juice
> trickling down my throat,
> my tongue smarted,
> my teeth were chilled.
> How sweet those mountains seemed,
> how cool and tangy, the Daugava!
>
> What scrawl of history
> had sent me so far from home? . . .
>
> When I was a girl in school, comrades,
> seemingly lazy as a lizard
> sprawled on a rock in Tashkent,
> I dreamed of conquest.
> My hands tugged at my arms,
> I caught flies on my tongue.
>
> Now my soul's as hushed as the Steppes on a
>   winter night;
> snow drifts in my brain, something
> shifts, sinks, subsides inside,
>
> and some undying pulse hoists my body
> like a flag, and sends me up,
> like Nureyev.

From my samovar I fill my cup with air,
and it overflows.
Who knows who scatters the bright cloud?

Two days and almost twenty-three hours
I looked at light,
scanning its lines like a book.

My conclusions:

At last I saw the way
time turns,
like a key in a lock,
and night becomes day,
and sun burns away the primeval mist,
and day is, and is not.

Listen, earthmen,
comrades of the soil,
I saw the Black Sea shrink to a drop
of dew and disappear;
I could blot out Mother Russia with my thumb in
    thin air;
the whole world was nearly not there.

It looked like an apple
or a Christmas orange:
I wanted to eat it.
I thought, It is pleasant to the eyes,
good for food,
and eating it would make men and women wise.

I could taste the juice
trickling down my throat,
my tongue smarted,
my teeth were chilled.
How sweet those mountains seemed,
how cool and tangy, the Daugava!

The Scottish poet Hugh MacDiarmid, in "Poetry and Science," his own response to C. P. Snow's call for communication between scientists and artists, nicely quoted Chekhov, pledging allegiance to Chekhov's stated goal: "Familiarity with the natural sciences and with scientific methods has always kept me on my guard, and I have always tried, where it was possible, to be consistent with the facts of science." We do not want to fail to speak, or hear, any of those voices crying "I am" in the wilderness of our existence.

Many years have passed since C. P. Snow made his plea for communication between scientists and nonscientists. There were some things time has shown he was wrong about. He did not foresee the ways in which the literary canon would be stretched or revised. He did not foresee that the Soviet Union could ever be faced with economic calamity, with the result that what was left of it would wind up putting its space program up for sale to any and all buyers. He did not foresee that the "scientific revolution," which he said had followed on the industrial revolution, would be succeeded by what people are calling "the information revolution." I am sure he did not foresee that I would write this essay on a computer.

He did not foresee poets like Robert Watson and Al Zolynas, or many others, or numerous nonfiction writers who would pursue an understanding of the scientific world in creative prose.

But his thesis, that scientists and nonscientists need to try to understand each other's language, is as generally valid as ever. When cultures meet, the first order of business is translation. This is as true for cultures of knowledge as for cultures of race or gender or nationality. *If we cannot even speak to one another, what good does it do us to have something to say?*

And if we speak only to ourselves, how long will we have anything new to say? We must listen to one another, if we are not to grow old telling the same anecdotes over and over, mumbling our way into graves of habit.

It is rather like two cultures meeting, then, this interchange between scientist and poet. It is rather like conversation and friendship. It is rather like strolling hand-in-hand across a shining suspension bridge flung over the endless drop into our own unknowing. Finally, here at the end of the twentieth century, it must be, for all our sakes, rather like scientist and poet accompanying each other into the twenty-first.

Maura High

SOURCE: "The Poetry Lab: Science in Contemporary American Poetry," in *New England Review and Bread Loaf Quarterly,* Vol. XII, No. 4, Summer, 1990, p. 336-48.

[*In the following essay, High surveys various responses and approaches to science in modern American poetry.*]

> We have to return to some measure, but a measure
> consonant with our time and not a mode so rotten
> that it stinks.
>
>   —William Carlos Williams, "On Measure,"
>   *Selected Essays.*

In James Merrill's poem, "Mirabell's Books of Number," one of the spirits of the Ouija board tells "JM" that if he wants to achieve "a breakthru," he must write "poems of science." Merrill writes in response:

> Poems of Science? Ugh.
> The very thought. To squint through those steel-
>   rimmed
> Glasses of the congenitally slug-
> Pale boy at school, with his precipitates,
> His fruit-flies and his slide rule? Science meant
> Obfuscation, boredom—; which, once granted,
> Odd lights came and went inside my head.
> Not for nothing had the Impressionists
> Put subject matter in its place, a mere
> Pretext for iridescent atmosphere.
> Why couldn't Science, in the long run, serve . . . ?

The poem proceeds to address that question, trying repeatedly to articulate the narrative of the lives of the poet, his friends, and their relatives in terms of science, as it is traditionally conceived: that is, without figures of speech and rhetoric, without history, culture, doubt, or sympathy. Not surprisingly, the poem demonstrates that the task is impossible and that a poem of science is, in effect, an oxymoron.

Merrill explains why it is so hard to write such poems. To begin with, in response to the challenges to our imagination and intellect, we feel:

> Self-pity for the maze
> Of meaning to be stumbled through blindfolded.
> Dread of substances, forms and behavior
> So old, original, so radically
> Open yet impervious to change,
> That no art, however fantastic or concrete,
> More than dreams of imitating them.

Nor can we purify our language and bring it into line with the "scientific" ideal. How *can* one, for example, ever avoid metaphor?

> Putting it into words
> Means also that it puts words into me:
> *Shooting ringing ramify root green*
> Have overtones not wholly for the birds. . . .

And if one tries to splice science into traditional language of poetry, the effect is disorienting, to say the least:

> Proton and Neutron
> Under a plane tree by the stream repeat
> Their eclogue, orbited by twinkling flocks.
> And on the dimmest shore of consciousness
> Polypeptides—in primeval thrall
> To what new moon I wonder—rise and fall.

The music of elegy doesn't miss a beat, but what are these alien figures who have invaded the beloved, familiar landscape? The two worlds, it seems, are demonstrably incompatible.

The challenge that proves to be the hardest for Merrill's characters to accept is the Word of the God "Biology," for whom suffering and love—"the sacred bonds"—are merely "chemical":

> Friend, lover, parent, amphorae that took
> Eons to dream up, to throw and turn. . . .
> . . . Come, your lecture on the cell!
> Spread your tail, incubus,
> We're listening. Make the story good.

As DJ says, "I don't see how a formula / Can be made flesh."

If Merrill's poem is a source of traditional answers to the problem of science, it also provokes a good many questions. Is he right in his definition of science? Are there any poets who don't see poetry and science as incompatible discourses? How *has* science, in fact, been used in contemporary poetry?

In casting around for answers, I made an informal survey of books and individual poems that have come out recently. Books included those with titles like *Arts and Sciences* (Albert Goldbarth), *Palladium* (Alice Fulton), *The Weight of Numbers* (Judith Baumel), *A Curve Away from Stillness* (John Allman), *Elements* (James Galvin), *Sutured Words* (ed. John Mukand), *Orrery,* and *The Evolution of the Flightless Bird* (both by Richard Kenney), *Parallax* (Maureen Mulhern), *Laughing at Gravity* (Elizabeth Ann Socolow) *Einstein's Brain* (Richard Cecil), and Philip Appleman's *Darwin's Ark*; and there were others whose titles didn't declare themselves as scientific, but which contained many science poems: Pattiann Rogers's *The Tattooed Lady in the Garden,* for example, *Before It Vanishes* by Robert Pack, *Shores and Headlands* by Emily Grosholz, and Chase Twichell's *The Odds.* I counted all the poems that touched more or less directly on science in a year's issues of *NER/BLQ* and *Poetry,* and calculated that the poems I found represent about six percent of all the poems published in each magazine over the period. The figures don't suggest an obsessive interest in science by poets, but they do indicate quite a sizable one.

Reading these poems of science, one notices fairly quickly that poets are drawn to science precisely because its relation to poetry is problematical. To use science in your poetry is to do something unconventional: it has the flavor of conquest in it, of rebellion; it asserts your autonomy as an individual. It is an act rich in implications and parallels. One could think of poetry's use of science as a kind of literary cross-dressing; as a subversive act; as stealing; as colonization; as an act of transubstantiation from the world of fact to that of idea; as the son's wish to kill the father, or the daughter's to unite with him. It could be any or all of these things, and all of them assume some kind of opposition.

Even the poets who are most at ease with science—A. R. Ammons and Richard Kenney come to mind—seem to anticipate a response of surprise from the reader at their feats of observation, synthesis, and knowledge.

Some poets like to capitalize on the oddity of a scientific term in the context of poetry, if only for a startling image, or for opening and framing moments. It's a device that gets our attention and bypasses the assumptions which we conventionally bring to the reading of poetry and which might prevent us from experiencing it fully. The device wouldn't work if poetry and science shared the same language. Alicia Ostriker's poem "Helium" (*Poetry,* July 1989) is a case in point. The poem is not about that lightest of elements, helium, or at least, not directly. It's more about the fear of aging, and how the speaker and her companion get a small reprieve from it by releasing a balloon into the sky. The poet is well aware of the deceptions involved in the poem and in the act—part of the poem's pathos derives from this wise and brave little fiction. "Helium" is both a fact in the story, and a metaphor, and maybe, too, a private reference to the poet's husband, who is a physicist.

Pattiann Rogers's poems are, typically, celebrations of Creation—meaning both the natural world and our own acts of making and bonding. What makes them distinctive is her biological imagery. An example is her poem, "Elinor Frost's Marble-Topped Kneading Table" (*NER/BLQ*, 11.4), which links the act of kneading with cell division and other scientific processes:

> Imagine that motion
>   . . . that *first*
> motion, I mean, like the initial act
> of any ovum (falcon, leopard, crab) turning
> into itself, taking all of its outside surfaces
> inward; the same circular mixing and churning
> of thunderheads born above deserts; that
>   involution
> ritualized inside amaryllis bulbs
> and castor beans in May.

The disjunction between science and literature isn't always exploited so agreeably. Often, it seems more like a wall of misinformation and suspicion, grounded in conflicting ideologies, with the forces on either side at more or less open war with each other. The history of this conflict is very old and starts with Plato and Aristotle, with scholastic philosophy, schisms, heresies, and the Inquisition. Galileo and the Romantic Movement figure largely in it. (The attacks made by Blake and Keats against Newton and "reaching after fact and reason" are still revived from time to time.) Darwin was a victim in his day, though he mustered all his considerable rhetorical powers in an effort to persuade his contemporaries to accept his theory. Modern poets like Robert Bly, James Galvin, Robert Cording, and Gjertrud Schnackenberg use the figures of scientists (Descartes, Newton, Audubon, Darwin . . .) to define more clearly their own opposing visions of right thinking and the world.

It's common to see science represented as neurosis, even among poets sympathetic to science and well versed in it. Elizabeth Ann Socolow speculates in her book, *Laughing at Gravity,* that Newton was impelled into science because he had a wretched childhood. He needs rescuing from the incompleteness and loneliness of his life:

> The laws of life are these: when she left, after such
> a birth and you only three, death or some discovery
> of enormous magnitude was a necessity.
> To prove there is continuity across vast space
> became the burden of your vision.

The rescue she proposes is a union with herself. She is drawn to him as he was to his theory—by the same forces, by sympathy born of shared experience, and by awe of his achievement. It's a quirky, appealing notion, that this unlikely pair could be lovers across the divide of time; but this analysis of his motives and drive—not to mention hers—seems a little reductive.

James Galvin, in his recent book, *Elements,* is following a long poetic tradition of antipathy to analytical thinking when he writes in "Geometry is the Mind of God":

> And what regards the reeling firmament
> with sympathy? . . .
> If the point has no part,
> I'd say it's a green thorn in the heart.

In many poems, he implies that to reach human experience at all, he must reject any kind of thinking, and simply watch and feel:

> In regard to its own movement, the willow tree
> knows less and less.
> Now and then now and then
> I forget what I'm saying
> To myself, often
> when you touch me. . . .
>
>   ("Regard")

One short poem, "About," reads in its entirety:

> Facts about the iris
> Do not make the iris
> Open. Open your eyes.
> It's tomorrow. Call out for someone.

Galvin paradoxically often uses facts "about"—even quite technical facts—to open our eyes to people and landscapes. "Coming into His Shop from a Bright Afternoon," for example, takes the form of a beautifully lit and detailed camera sequence.

Most poets are, like Robert Pack, more ambivalent. His book, *Before It Vanishes,* consists of thiry-one poems addressed to Heinz Pagels, each one an attempt to relate Pagels's science to Pack's own modest and comfortable life in rural Vermont. He tries to demystify the subject and bring it under his control by being funny, making comic paraphrases of Pagels's statements and cracking raunchy, scatalogical jokes. The often mannered diction, the elbow-in-your-ribs allusions and jokes are a posture of humility: of the nervous schoolboy or apprentice, in the company of the magus and his arcane and terrifying knowledge.

In other poems, Pack is literally on his own turf, accepting the difference or separateness of science, its concerns, and points of view. In "Autumn Warmth" he tells how he stands "bare-armed in my garden," absorbing "the bleak, mild rays" of the morning sun:

> Hornets bore in the rotting pears
> clinging from loosened stems;
> wasps in the spider-threaded eaves
> deliriously thrum. . . .

He's commenting, of course, on Keats, but also, on his own individual existence: "I lived here, too, / with all my fellow fossils." Science, he feels, tells him he is fungible, but in this poem, he is so present in his garden, so sure of his autonomy, that he is not threatened. Another fine moment of equilibrium is in "The Red Shift," where he uses Hubble's theory as a metaphor, not just to decorate or prompt the poem, but to understand the process and structure of memory.

Pack sees the scientist as someone who possesses an equanimity and command that he desires, but cannot reach. There is, though, something unearthly and unlifelike about Pagels's vision; Pagels is, in a way, already dead, and his actual death, commemorated in the book's final poem, releases the poet from his fascination and allows him to return to his own life.

Robert Bly also obviously feels deeply divided, if not muddled, about science and its concerns. On the one hand, he can write, in his anthology *News of the Universe: Poems of Twofold Consciousness,*

> As people began to invest some of their trust in objects, handmade or wild, and physicists begin to suspect that objects, even down to the tiniest molecular particles, may have awareness of each other as well as "intention," *things* once more become interesting. . . .

and, a few sentences later, say "science rips the perceiver and the thing perceived apart."

Bly is trying to come up with a literary response to the precariousness of the earth's ecology, a response that could serve as a rallying point for others concerned by the same problems. He has campaigned for "ecologically responsible" rather than "egocentric" poetry, in much the same way that many poets have responded, either at the urging of people like Terrence Des-Pres, or Jonathan Schell in *The Fate of the Earth,* or to their own imperatives, to reject solipsistic poetry for one more concerned with the future of the planet. Bly's meditations on nature tend not to grow out of the phenomena he is describing, but to present an ideological position that precedes the facts. Consider, for example, "The Dead Seal near McLure's Beach":

> Goodbye brother, die in the sound of the waves, forgive us if we have killed you, long live your race, your inner-tube race, so uncomfortable on land, so comfortable in the ocean. Be comfortable in death, then when the sand will be out of your nostrils, and you can swim in long loops through pure death, ducking under as assassinations break above you. You don't want to be touched by me. I climb the cliff and go home the other way.

He doesn't discover the seal's feelings, nor his brotherhood with the seal, nor his equanimity towards death through this poem—they are brought in from elsewhere, from North American myth, possibly, or Zen practice.

Some poets address the same concerns less sentimentally in poetry. In his book *Darwin's Ark,* Philip Appleman is concerned with the development of technology, from the simple hand-ax to the atomic bomb, and lament the "descent of man" that it entails. His knowledge of science moves him to do something for the world—to rally support for environmental causes, condemn ignorance, and to evolve as a "decent animal" himself. The writing is not simply polemical—it is imaginative and graceful (he is one of the few poets who can paraphrase scientific

information well—John Updike is another). He plays with science, extending the meaning of technical terms like *phobia, euphoria,* and *evolution,* to cover such subjects as ten-year-olds, the Waldorf Astoria, and Studebaker cars: a kind of wise silliness; and assembles collages from present experience, memory, and fantasy. He can lace science and non-science together so that the science is not obtrusive, but works naturally into the rhythm and flow of information in the line:

> . . . the ache in our marrow dissolving
> to memories of mosses, ferns,
> protozoans in the soup
> of ancestral mud: all
> in our bones: out there in that little town
> that looks like a game of tic-tac-toe
> run wild.
>
>   ("Nostalgie de la Boue")

Science is assumed by many to use a uniquely transparent language of fact, free from historical and discursive presuppositions (though historians and philosophers of science like J. D. Bernal and Stanley Aronowitz make it clear that this is not the case). To some non-scientists, like Merrill, this constitutes poverty; to others, scientific terms have a seductive purity, denoting entities and processes in the world outside of one's mind. The Fact has, for our times, the status of a platonic idea, untainted by Man, which the poet merely imitates at three removes. Poets long for the authority of science. It's what makes language dangerous—as the Catholic Church knew when it forced Galileo to recant and reduce his cosmology to a mere formulation of words (to poetry, one might say).

Poets are often praised if they demonstrate a command of facts: precise observation and reporting of landscapes and events, both intimate and public is valued highly. This respect for facts has a complicated origin, but it is one that seems very much at home in America. The folk heroes of this country are practical people: Johnny Appleseed, Betsy Ross, Henry Martin, Paul Revere, Ben Franklin. We like our poetry to be useful and, indeed, most of it is documentary and didactic. Poetry about the land and about people and activities directly connected to it is popular and common, and, like our traditions of landscape painting and regional crafts and histories, both invents and perpetuates our myths of origin as a people. See for example Donald Hall, Sydney Lea, Robert Cording, Ed Hirsch, Gary Snyder, John Haines, and Wendell Berry—poets whose work, clearly, extends beyond this function, but also clearly fulfills it. Poets of cities and working people, notably Philip Levine, are as much part of this phenomenon as poets who specialize in more rural settings.

One can see something very like science in the scrupulous concern for clear sight and clear thinking in A. R. Ammons. His poetry achieves a purity that one could call photographic (as Osip Mandelstam called the writing of Charles Darwin, praising it for its lack of teleology). Consider a short sample from his poem "Corsons Inlet":

. . . in nature there are few sharp lines: there are
  areas of primrose
    more or less dispersed;
disorderly orders of bayberry; between the rows
of dunes,
irregular swamps of reeds,
though not reeds alone, but grass, bayberry, yarrow,
  all . . .

predominantly reeds:

I have reached no conclusions, have erected no
  boundaries,
shutting out and shutting in, separating inside
from outside: I have
drawn no lines:
  as

manifold events of sand
change the dune's shape. . . .

(The Selected Poems)

Ammons knows the value of precise, even technical, analysis, and does not feel that it amounts to Gradgrindism, devaluing and reducing a thing in nature to something less than itself. In "Mechanism," he lists and invites us to "honor" in the goldfinch those "billion operations / that stay its form"—facts which the bird is unconscious of, and which we reach after with our intellect, as much as with our imagination.

Ammons is not the only poet who seems quite at home with technicalities. Richard Kenney is another. His second book, *Orrery* (1985), is best read cover to cover, rather than dipped into, like an anthology. Its structure mimics that of an orrery, a working mechanical model of the universe, and the three sections of the book mesh intricately into each other to work as one whole. We are, I believe, supposed to be puzzled and dazzled by the cleverness of the machine. If we are not put off by artifice, if we are curious enough, and responsive to the surface beauty of the two framing sections and the frequently lucid and moving poems in between, we will be rewarded by the pleasures of discovery.

Kenney's subject is the lives of himself, his wife, their children and neighbors on a cider-milling farm in Vermont:

  A simple clockwork
world, this farm, where evening stars and drifting
  quarks
spin lazily across the dark according
to the Laws . . .

("Hours")

He uses not an Einsteinian model of the universe but a version of "Sir Isaac Newton's / world, all crankcase cogs and whirring gears" ("Hours"), because it is a more precise model for his purpose. It works, but not without recourse to metaphysics, since the mechanisms that make it possible for him to see time—his own time—as cyclical are the mechanisms of memory and something he calls "prescience." Both run "perpendicular to time," arcing across from one season to the next, and allow the kind of conflations, reversals and leaps that even Einsteinian theory denies. The heart

. . . keeps its own calculus,
all lock and freeze, free fall, light speed, all
  prescience
and memory *tic toc* on the same trick abacus
whose beads blink back and forth at will. There's
  no field theory
for these things.

("Hours")

The technical and cosmological imagery and the use to which it is put strongly recall the seventeenth-century Metaphysical poets. To take just one example, here is a poem that starts off as an account of himself following a snow-plow in a blizzard, which reveals itself as it develops, images of plow and line and bed intricately connected, into a love poem:

I etch this line across what curvature
of space and time still separates us, now,
and night dilates, all night, all night the plow
grinds the stone road bed—like my heart
grinding through this last bad month alone
  . . . without you. . . .

("Speed of Light")

What is it about love that draws metaphysics to it? One often finds contemporary poets—Emily Grosholz and Theodore Worozbyt are two other examples—who place the love expressed in the poems and their expression of it in the larger historical and literary context of Metaphysical love poetry, thereby guaranteeing both the poem and the love.

The most concentrated science imagery in Kenney's book occurs in the third and final section of the book, "Physics"—as, for example, in the following passage:

all life unreels
through black magnetic
stone-strewn fields
where pitch-blende blinks
its slow decay
tic-tic-tic
de-lightedly
by alpha, beta,
gamma, delta—
time dilates,
and starlight bends
in gravity
like roundelays.
All light, partic-
ulate, licks out
one-way, in waves . . .

Far from perplexing or disturbing him, the facts and methods of science for Kenney seem to be energizing, rich in implication and potential for his art. Richard Kenney's earlier book, *The Evolution of the Flightless Bird* was chosen by James Merrill for the Yale Younger Poets Prize in 1983. Kenney's work, therefore, can be seen in more ways than one to comment on the issues raised by Merrill in "Mirabell's Books of Number."

There are, of course, many other questions to be raised in this context. Why are there so few poems of science fiction?

Do writers like Jorie Graham and John Ashbery write as they do because of Heisenberg's Uncertainty Principle, non-Euclidean geometries, and Chaos Theory? Or did they arrive at their characteristic style more through developments in art and music, which in turn were a response to history? How does the use of computers or other technological artifacts in the composition and dissemination of poetry affect the form and content of a poem, and way we will read and evaluate it? Isn't most contemporary poetry being written in the literary equivalent of the Ptolemaic system?

One only has to begin to explore the relationship between science and poetry—and, by extension, science and all literature—and doors of enquiry and debate open up wherever one looks. Poems of science—using science and exploiting it, arguing for and against it—appear to be possible after all. Wordsworth, maybe, would have viewed all this activity with interest. In his Preface to the Second Edition of the Lyrical Ballads, he envisaged a time—far in the future, he thought—when poetry could carry "sensation into the midst of the objects of science itself," and when, in a nice converse flow, the sciences would be made "manifestly and palpably material to us as enjoying and suffering beings."

BOOKS DISCUSSED

A. R. Ammons. *The Selected Poems*: Expanded Edition. New York: W. W. Norton, 1986.

Philip Appleman. *Darwin's Ark.* Bloomington: Indiana University Press, 1984.

Robert Bly, ed. *News of the Universe.* San Francisco: Sierra Club Books, 1980.

James Galvin. *Elements.* Port Townsend: Copper Canyon Press, 1988.

Richard Kenney. *Orrery.* New York: Atheneum, 1985.

James Merrill. *The Changing Light at Sandover.* New York: Atheneum, 1982.

Robert Pack. *Before It Vanishes.* Boston: David Godine, 1989.

Elizabeth Ann Socolow. *Laughing at Gravity: Conversations with Isaac Newton.* Boston: Beacon Press, 1988.

DRAMA

Gordon Armstrong

SOURCE: "Cultural Politics and the Irish Theatre: Samuel Beckett and the New Biology," in *Theatre Research International,* Vol. 18, No. 3, Autumn, 1993, pp. 215-21.

[*In the following essay, Armstrong discusses the influence of Erwin Schrodinger's theory of quantum biology on the dramas of Samuel Beckett.*]

> Sweat and mirror notwithstanding they might well pass for inanimate but for the left eyes which at incalculable intervals suddenly open wide and gaze in unblinking exposure long beyond what is humanly possible.

> Samuel Beckett, *Imagination Dead Imagine,*
> (12-13)

Lawrence Stone, Princeton Professor Emeritus of History, has recently declared that 'every cultural enterprise, even science, is at least in part a social construction.'[1] Biologist Jay Gould vehemently agrees. 'Science', says Gould, 'is done by individuals, whose conclusions are influenced by the beliefs they bring with them.'[2] The contamination factor is unavoidable. On the other hand, Erwin Schrodinger, the renowned quantum physicist, brought to biology experimental truths that may take us to the edge of the universe. For him, the contamination factor was intentional. Beginning in the 1940s, his work had a direct effect on the writings of Samuel Beckett.

Criticized by Irish friends like Jack Yeats for being amoral in his writings, Samuel Beckett, in his refusal to cater to the modernist, absurdist, existential tides of his generation was, on the contrary, profoundly engaged in cultural politics. His affinity for pictorial artwork, and his friendship with painters and sculptors—Jack Yeats, Bram and Geer Van Velde, Avigdor Arikha, and Henry Hayden in particular—was matched by his enthusiasm for quantum science. Beckett obtained a copy of Schrodinger's quantum biology lectures, and gave it to his uncle, Dr Gerald Beckett, in June 1946.[3] Examining the deep structures of Beckett's works through Schrodinger's quantum biology lens clarifies a number of puzzling details. *Imagination Dead Imagine, How It Is, Endgame,* and *Play* are only a few of Beckett's works that are anchored in the bio-artistic framework that begins with *Waiting for Godot.*

Delivered in February 1943, under the auspices of the Institute at Trinity College, Dublin, Erwin Schrodinger's quantum biology lectures extended his elegant 1926 theory of quantum physics—describing the unfolding of quantum events not as the certainties of Newtonian mechanics, but as an undulating wave of possibilities—into the field of molecular biology. An edition of these lectures, entitled *What Is Life? The Physical Aspect of the Living Cell,* was published by Cambridge University Press in 1944. In 1992, Professor L. C. Lewontin of Harvard described this particular text as 'the ideological manifesto of the new biology.'[4] At the time, Samuel Beckett was in hiding from the Gestapo somewhere in the South of France (possibly at Roussillon in the Vaucluse). Where Beckett obtained the text is unknown, but he regarded it highly. As it turned out, Schrodinger's small text began a revolution in more than molecular biology. In a conversation with me in 1985,

Beckett acknowledged with a wry grin the importance of Schrodinger's small oracle to his own work.[5]

The question might then be asked: 'How does the new biology relate to theatre, specifically, to Beckett's theatre?' One response is that theatre is constituent to the species. Theatre *is* because we evolved as we did. In our unique genetic development as *homo sapiens sapiens,* neurobiological capacities developed that can objectively be described as 'theatrical.' The union of a sound image and a concept in the left temporal lobe made possible the development of language capacity and abstract verbal formulations. In the beginning there were no words. Language arose as a compressed formulation of abstract concepts. Writing arose as a means of exchanging goods and fostering trade. But the capacities themselves arose and persisted for the broad benefit of the species because, as Antonio and Hanna Damasio described it, 'humans and species before them had become adept at generalizing and categorizing actions and at creating and categorizing mental representations of objects, events and relations.'[6] As can no other species, we can plan the future; we can judge the past; we can contemplate the present.

Far from being pre-ordained even in a biological sense, we are a product of random evolutionary circumstances that Jay Gould has called, in an evolutionary context, 'punctuated equilibrium.' Five heads, for example, each with a different function, and three limbs, to propel us forward in circular motions (perhaps another version of Beckett's 'headlong tardigrade'), could have been options. As Gould explains: 'The contingency of evolution does not depend on the random nature of genetic mutation. It arises because mutations have qualitatively different effects, and because these effects can be amplified. . . . '[7] Only the remarkable intelligence of a tiny creature on a primeval forest floor sixty-five million years ago marked the potential for our species' survival. When we do theatre we are replaying a biological heritage that extends well back into pre-history. The *homo sapiens* story began 570 million years before the present with the appearance of shelled, carapace animals in the Cambrian Age. The punctuated mutations evolved into modern man's precursors, some two and a half million years ago. Looking again at the immediate and long past history of the earth, John Wheeler, quantum physicist at Princeton University suggests, 'The deepest lesson of quantum mechanics may be that reality is defined by the questions we put to it.'[8] This comes as no surprise to playwrights and performers who, similarly, have long framed the dramatic experience. There is no question that theatre, expressing the needs and conditions of human life, is any less indebted than our species to the track of photons as they approached a 'galactic beam splitter' some fifteen and a half billion years ago, waiting to be subjected to experimental forays conducted by unborn beings on a still nonexistent planet.

The emergence of *homo sapiens sapiens* across the evolutionary track of species is unique and fundamentally unpredictable. Surviving the disappearance of the dinosaurs, sixty-five million years ago, and the recent ice ages from one hundred thousand years ago down to ten or twelve thousand years ago, we are a prime example of successive quantum adaptations. The fact is that when one examines evolution, it is immediately apparent that the figure of an actor appearing onstage in a performance arena is only one tiny fragment of an epic story whose likelihood is manifestly unreasonable.

The opening citation from *Imagination Dead Imagine* indicates the same deep 'Schrodingerian' structure in Beckett's own creative works, and his profound interest in amplifying segments of *What Is Life?* in an artistic venue. In looking at the mechanisms of genetic development, 'on the average, only the 50th or 60th descendent of the egg that I was,' Schrodinger remarked on the marvels of 'the visible and manifest nature of the individual, which is reproduced without appreciable change for generations, permanent within centuries—though not within tens of thousands of years—' and carried forward by the species and within the species at a temperature that has not varied from the beginning. Beckett's text begins: 'No trace anywhere of life, you say, pah, no difficulty there, imagination not dead yet, yes, dead, good, imagination dead imagine' (7). Something is taking place beneath the level of intellectual conception, something in a place as deep as the strata of Schrodinger's analysis of the DNA molecule. Beckett's processes of temperature and of light are Schrodingerian, 'combining in countless rhythms, commonly attend the passage from white and heat to black and cold, and vice versa . . . until, in the space of some twenty seconds, pitch black is reached and at the same time say freezing-point. Same remark for the reverse movement, towards heat and whiteness.'[9] Even Beckett's pendulum swing of temperatures is Schrodingerian: a return to stasis, 'rediscovered miraculously after what absence in perfect voids' against the background of 'the *little fabric*' (emphasis added).[10]

In *What Is Life?,* with a nod to quantum mechanics, Schrodinger suggested not linear continuity in the species, but genetic molecular discontinuity. At a given moment across a span of many centuries, everything changed. For Schrodinger, 'The great revelation of quantum theory was that features of discreteness were discovered in the Book of Nature' that defied the continuity anticipated by classical physics. 'The transition from one of these configurations to another is a quantum jump. If the second one [had] the greater energy (a higher level), the system [had to be] supplied from outside with at least the difference of the two energies to make the difference possible.' Beckett obliged with his bio-artistic imagery: 'Piercing pale blue the effect is striking, in the beginning. Never the two gazes together except once, when the beginning of one overlapped the end of the other' (13).

Beckett's contribution to the revolution was to envision this overlapping span in a concrete, bio-artistic frame 'from the fraction of the second to what would have seemed, in other times, other places, an eternity' (9). How did Beckett acknowledge this leap? Returning to the figures, each lying within his and her semicircle, he described the circumstances of a multi-generational quantum leap: 'Sweat and mirror notwithstanding they might well pass for inanimate but for the left eyes which at incalculable intervals suddenly open wide and gaze in unblinking exposure long beyond what is humanly possible' (12-13).

When analyzing difficult works, one must always be concerned not to construct forced and tortured interpretation, especially for works of a playwright who deliberately 'vaguens' his texts. But there is some evidence to suggest that, at one level, Beckett intended the source of energy to be from the outside. That energy was, as might have been predicted, the eye of the observer: the 'unique inquisitor' in *Play,* 'E' in *Film,* Bom or Pim in *How It Is,* and a range of observers from Vladimir in Act Two of *Waiting for Godot*: 'At me too someone is looking' . . . , to *Imagination Dead Imagine:*' . . . and at the same instant for the eye of prey the infinitesimal shudder instantaneously suppressed' (14). But on the level of 'new biology', Beckett explored this possible effect in the gene pool of the species: 'to see if they still lie still in the stress of that storm, or of a worse storm, or in the black dark for good, or the great whiteness unchanging . . . ?' (14)

As Beckett so expressly indicated, one need only use one's imagination—not the dead imagination of classical physics but the living imagination of the Book of Nature that Erwin Schrodinger deciphered, and Beckett so eloquently described. By adding an adjective and a noun phrase to the opening lines of *Imagination Dead Imagine,* the meaning becomes clear: with '[Classical] Imagination Dead, Imagine [the Book of Life and quantum genetics].'

The last phrase of *Imagination Dead Imagine,* 'and if not what they are doing,' returns the inquiry to Schrodinger's text, and the wait for the next eon of time and the contingencies of evolution. In another ten thousand years, qualitatively different mutations may develop, born of quantum leaps in the diploid molecules of Samuel Beckett's imaginative formulations—a discontinuous change, perhaps once in ten millenia.[11]

A second thesis, and possibly of more interest than Schrodinger's brilliant adaptation of quantum physics to what has now become the new molecular biology, to Beckett and to us, is his description of positive and negative entropy—the basic behavioural principles of the living organism.[12] Described by Schrodinger as the characteristic feature of life, the state of maximum entropy is a dynamic equilibrium: 'Every process, event, happening—call it what you will: in a word, everything that is going on in Nature means an increase of the entropy of the part of the world where it is going on. Thus a living organism continually increases its entropy—or, as you may say, produces positive entropy—and thus tends to approach the dangerous state of maximum entropy, which is death.'[13] To avoid death, according to Schrodinger, a creature feeds upon

negative entropy, drawing sustenance from the environment. In so doing, every living organism succeeds in freeing itself from all the entropy it cannot help producing while alive.

Beckett put this principle to work in a typically striking visual way. The most dramatic exemplars of the unavoidable positive entropy of life, old folk in various states of decay, litter the landscape of Beckettian dramaticules. Two examples illustrate a partial range of Beckett's thinking on this topic: Winnie's mound in *Happy Days* is an expression of the build-up of positive entropy (in Act One, up to her waist; in Act Two, up to her neck) as is Clov's first speech in *Endgame,* 'Grain upon grain, one by one, and one day, suddenly, there's a heap, a little heap, the impossible heap.'[14] (The reference to Zeno's pile is only the more obvious basis of Beckett's thought processes.) The apparent contradiction of death growing stronger in the midst of life is the very foundation of Beckett's theatre.

The third thesis, directly related to Schrodinger's importance to Beckett's emergence as a playwright, came almost as a footnote to *What Is Life?* In a postscripted chapter—an Addendum on Free Will—Schrodinger described the self as 'not I' but 'the canvas' of life that we interpret as self.[15] That notion opened a world of possibilities for Beckett that culminated in the 1972 première of *Not I* at New York City's Lincoln Center. Our notions of self—of 'I'—are not a substance at all, according to Schrodinger, but an interpretation of experience that is promoted to the level of 'I' at any given moment. So where is the permanent trace of life? In our minds only, or in a succession of minds that we determine as substance: 'Not I—me'! is Mouth's third person summary of this situation in *Not I.* The new biology, and possibly the developing dramatic theory of chaos, insist on the analysis of this basic hermeneutic as a keystone of man's relations to his environment. This is particularly true in Beckett's theatre, in which stages of an image evolve before the spectator's eyes, a methodology that Beckett developed from the writings and paintings of Jack Yeats.

The coupling factors of DNA biology played a central role in the emergence of Beckett's own bio-artistic works. Described by Lewontin as the 'grail of molecular biology,' he updated the missing pieces of a forty-nine-year-old debate begun at Trinity College, by noting that DNA is a dead molecule: 'It is also not self-reproducing, and it makes nothing. And finally, organisms are not determined by it.'[16] What it does do is serve as a template. Lewontin explains:

> Reproduction of DNA is, ironically, an uncoupling of the material strands, followed by a building up of new complementary strands on each of the parental strings. . . . The role of DNA is that it bears information that is read by the cell machinery in the production process. Subtly, DNA as information bearer is transmogrified successively into DNA as blueprint, as plan, as master plan, as master molecule.[17]

In *How It Is,* Beckett stunningly anticipated this entire sequence. Positing the replicating double helix of the DNA molecule in many specifics, the invariable sequence of *How It Is* works as follows: in a simplified four-part series, narrator flees Bom, finds Pim, unites with Pim, is abandoned by Pim, unites with Bom, and beginning again, flees Bom. Lewontin described the *biological grail* process: 'By turning genes on and off in different parts of the developing organism at different times, the DNA creates "the living being" body and Mind.'[18] In Beckett's *biodramatic grail,* Pim and Bom know each other only by reputation: Pim as the victim, and Bom as the tormentor of the narrator. They never meet, but serve in their sequential uncouplings as 'blueprint'-victim, as 'master molecule'-tormentor to the narrator. United in the interests of torment, separated in the event of suffering, in Beckett's unrelenting biodramas these DNA-couples present the spectacle of life's most basic confrontations. In every case, the tormentor bears information of the persona of a prior tormentor, which he inflicts upon a new victim, to 'transmogrify' as a tormentor at the next stage. Speaking in the third person, in a text without punctuation, 'before Pim', the narrator carries a prior identity into Part Two, awaiting instructions for 'life the other above in the light said to have been mine . . . no one asking that of me never there a few images on and off' (8).

A series of images begins with, presumably, a young Samuel Beckett saying his prayers at his mother's knee: 'I steal a look at her lips / she stops her eyes burn down on me again I cast up mine in haste and repeat awry' (15-16); then that of a girl and a dog on a grassy mound, the 'girl too whom I hold who holds me by the hand the arse I have . . . again about turn introrse fleeting face to face transfer of things swinging of arms silent relishing of sea and isles' (30); the last of a youth 'pale staring hair red pudding face with pimples protruding belly gaping fly spindle legs sagging knocking at the knees wide astraddle for greater stability feet splayed one hundred and thirty degrees fatuous half-smile' (30). These images from scenes in the light above mix with an immediate reality of a tongue lolling in the mud, of the sack 'where saving your reverence I have all the suffering of all the ages' (38), and filled with sustenance—Pim's tins of 'miraculous sardines.' The narrator's means of locomotion by crawling in the mud, 'right leg left right arm push pull' (47), continues until at last, with the left hand 'clawing for the take instead of the familiar slime an arse two cries one mute' (48). Pim has been overtaken. The former tormentor becomes victim, the narrator as former victim, the new tormentor.

In part two of *How It Is,* the narrator replaces Pim's memories with his own datum of life, 'namely the canvas upon which [experiences] are collected.' Part Three, Pim's departure, corresponds to Schrodinger's 'youth that was I, [whom] you may come to speak of . . . in the third person.' The sequence of how it was before, with, and after Pim's arrival and departure is Beckett's artistic development of Schrodinger's metaphor for the evolving self: 'you may come to a distant country, lose sight of all

your friends, may all but forget them; you acquire new friends, . . . you still recollect the old one that used to be "I" but is now no loss at all.'[19]

Part Three of *How It Is* is life after Pim before Bom, with the voice of us all 'without quaqua . . . alone in the dark the mud end at last of part two' (99). A moment of reflection occurs before the sequence renews itself: Bem reaches for the narrator, to begin Part Three, as the narrator reached for Pim in Part One: 'Bem had come to cleave to me see later Pim and me I had come to cleave to Pim the same thing except that me Pim Bem me Bem left me south' (109). With Bom's arrival the narrator acquires Bem's name, and a borrowed life 'said to have been mine above in the light' (109), moving in procession like some medieval *tableau vivant*; a vast train of beings where 'at the same instant I leave Bem another leaves Pim and let us be at that instant one hundred thousand strong then fifty thousand departures fifty thousand abandoned no sun no earth nothing turning the same instant always everywhere' (112).

Outside time and space without extension, Beckett's characters have become quantum molecules in one dimension, failed habits of life in a more immediate sense, but inevitably depicted in real terms, in real life that transcends epistemological abstractions or Newtonian mathematical equations. Reproducing without appreciable change for generations—centuries if not for ten thousand years, 'and borne,' as Schrodinger noted, 'at each transmission by the material structure of the nuclei of the two cells which unite to form the fertilized egg cell,' the biology of *homo sapiens* is exposed at its quantum basis.[20] The marvel of that premise is the basis of *What Is Life?*, and of Beckett's *How It Is.* The template has been passed to the next generation.

A last commentary on Schrodinger's 'little canvas' of 'experience and memory': In *Endgame,* Hamm's bloodied handkerchief frames the action from the opening dialogue:

> *(Pause. Hamm stirs. He yawns under the handkerchief. He removes the handkerchief from his face. Very red face. Black glasses).* HAMM. ME—*(he yawns)*—to play . . . (2)

to the last scene:

> . . . speak no more.
> *(He holds handkerchief spread out before him).*
> Old stancher!
> *(Pause.)*
> You . . . remain.
> *(Pause. He covers his face with handkerchief. Lowers his arms to arm rests, remains motionless).*
> *(Brief tableau).*
>   *Curtain* (84)

In this strange play about 'zeros' in perspective, of creatures dying of darkness, the use of a bloodied handkerchief to conceal Hamm's face is, on the surface, equally enigmatic. There are no running sores, no cankers or ulcers, as in earlier pieces; no external bleeding, no hint of a physical calamity to 'staunch.' Metaphysics is not ignored. Hamm tells the story of an engraver who, having seen the rising corn fields and the sails of a herring fleet, saw only ashes. He was 'spared,' according to Hamm, the presumptive world of hope through transcendent beauty. Momentary salvation comes only in the recognition of 'the game'—an endgame to be sure—where one can freely recognize the necessity of weeping and weeping, 'for nothing, so as not to laugh, and little by little . . . you begin to grieve' (68). Occasionally Hamm falters, as in the moment when he asks Clov for certain words from the heart: 'Stop, raise your head and look at all that beauty . . . that order. . . . Come now, you're not a brute beast, think upon these things and you'll see how all becomes clear. . . ." (80). To which Clov replies, significantly addressing not Hamm but the spectators: 'what skilled attention they get, all these dying of their wounds' (81).

Those wounds of memory cover Hamm's face, bloodying him all over, as surely as they bloodied Pim in *How It Is.* To go on with life, Hamm staunches the wounds with his handkerchief, a manifestation of Beckett's deepest cry, of an earth 'extinguished though humankind never saw it lit' (81), and of Beckett's consolatory benediction to the dead from the living:

> One day you'll say to yourself, I'm tired, I'll sit down, and you'll go and sit down. Then you'll say, I'm hungry, I'll get up and get something to eat. But you won't get up. You'll say, I shouldn't have sat down, but since I have I'll sit on a little longer, then I'll get up and get something to eat, but you won't get up and you won't get anything to eat.
>
> *(Pause).*
>
> You'll look at the wall a while, then you'll say, I'll close my eyes, perhaps have a little sleep, after that I'll feel better, and you'll close them. And when you open them again there'll be no wall any more (36).

All of these speeches combine in the central image of identity, of self, of relations to others, of memory and of experiences of 'I' as a knowable bio-coupling. The maddening datum of recognition is precisely Schrodinger's neutral 'canvas,' upon which the data is collected. After long years of self-determination, Hamm's pathetic discovery that, 'what you really mean by "I" is merely that ground-stuff upon which [experience and memory] are collected.'[21] Hamm's agony of recognition that past lives are no longer germane, even while 'hamming it up onstage,' or on the stage that Beckett takes as exemplary of life itself, is the last phase of life's processes. The bloody handkerchief signifies the pain of giving over to other selves and facing the humiliation of amounting only to 'that groundstuff,' a canvas of possibilities that is successionally discounted. There are no options. Hamm's multiple images create *fractal* zones of non-linear series of successive 'I's', of DNA molecules outside of our immediate time-space continuum: 'Infinite emptiness will be all around you, and all the resurrected dead of all ages wouldn't fill it, and there you'll be like a little bit of grit in the middle of the steppe' (36).

In *Endgame,* the quantum biology of self, indicated by the *fractal* boundaries of communication—in particular, of what has been described as 'discontinuous neural mappings of the brain of *homo sapiens'*—is displayed with consummate artistic skill.[22] The disparate stories add up to a lifetime of successive 'I's. With the addition of the handkerchief, 'bloodied all over,' as an expression of Hamm's internal predicament in staving off the final build-up of positive entropy, the thrust of this memory play is clear. In a universe of chaos, composed primarily of discontinuous endgames, play is all we have. What better form of play do we have than theatre play? In Schrodinger's *What Is Life?,* the declaration of the canvas of the self, the exploration of positive and negative entropy was the characteristic feature of life. The first manifesto of quantum biology changed the entire course of Beckett's literary career.

It has taken us five hundred years to begin to understand the geography of earth, and now with the COBE satellite and new space explorations, the geography and primordial structure of the universe: it may take us another five hundred years to begin to understand the geography of civilization, the components of Samuel Beckett's theatre and of Schrodinger's quantum biology, more recently described as 'the selfish gene.'[23]

NOTES

[1] Lawrence Stone, 'The Revolution Over the Revolution,' *New York Review of Books,* Vol. XXXIX, No. 11, June 11, 1992, p. 47.

[2] John Maynard Smith, 'Taking a Chance on Evolution,' *New York Review of Books,* Vol. XXXIX, No. 9, May 14, 1992, p. 34.

[3] James Knowlson, catalogue: *Samuel Beckett: An Exhibition,* exhibition: Reading University Library, May-July 1971. London: Turret Books, 1971, p. 52.

[4] R. C. Lewontin, 'The Dream of the Human Genome,' *The New York Review of Books,* Vol. XXXIX, No. 10 (May 28, 1992), p. 31.

[5] Erwin Schrodinger, *What Is Life? The Physical Aspect of the Living Cell,* (Cambridge: Cambridge University Press, 1944, repr. 1955).

[6] Antonio R. Damasio and Hanna Damasio, 'Brain and Language,' *Mind and Brain, Scientific American,* September, 1992, p. 89.

[7] John Maynard Smith, 'Taking a Chance on Evolution,' *New York Review of Books,* Vol. XXXIX, No. 9, May 14, 1992, p. 34.

[8] John A. Wheeler, cited by John Horgan, 'Quantum Philosophy,' *Scientific American,* July 1992, p. 101.

[9] Samuel Beckett, *Imagination Dead Imagine,* London: Calder and Boyars, 1965, p. 10.

[10] Beckett, *Imagination,* p. 11.

[11] Schrodinger, *Life,* p. 51.

[12] Schrodinger, *Life,* pp. 69-70.

[13] Schrodinger, *Life,* p. 72.

[14] Samuel Beckett, *Endgame,* New York: Grove Press, 1958, p. 1.

[15] Schrodinger, *Life,* p. 91.

[16] Lewontin, 'Genome,' p. 33.

[17] Lewontin, 'Genome,' p. 32-33.

[18] Lewontin, 'Genome,' p. 32.

[19] Schrodinger, *Life,* pp. 91-2.

[20] Schrodinger, *Life,* p. 31.

[21] Schrodinger, *Life,* p. 92.

[22] Gordon Armstrong, 'Unintentional Fallacies,' *Journal of Dramatic Theory and Criticism,* Fall 1992, Vol. VII, No. 2, pp. 7-27.

[23] See the popular science development of this idea in Richard Dawkins, *The Selfish Gene.* Oxford University Press, 1976, 1989.

Matthew Martin

SOURCE: "Stephen Poliakoff's Drama for the Post-Scientific Age," in *Theatre Journal,* Vol. 45, No. 2, May, 1993, pp. 197-211.

[*In the following essay, Martin investigates Stephen Poliakoff's early plays as they dramatize life in the contemporary age of science and technology.*]

The year 1989 saw the appearance both of a new play by Stephen Poliakoff, *Playing with Trains,* and of the first volume of his collected plays, *Poliakoff Plays: One.*[1] An unfortunate side-effect of issuing separate volumes of his collected work is the reinforcement this practice will give to the commonplace notion that Poliakoff's early plays, before *Breaking the Silence* (1984), are stylistically and theoretically distinct from the later plays. In trying to escape the shadow of his "most promising," strikingly unique Urban Canyon plays of the 1970s, Poliakoff clearly did set out to do some things differently in *Breaking the*

Silence.[2] Its introduction of East European elements into his stage world, its sense of history as well as its historical setting, and its markedly mature handling of details, dialogue and stagecraft all combine for an effect calculated to be distinct from the quirky, volatile plays that preceded it. But upon closer inspection, we discover that Poliakoff's themes have changed little, and that perhaps the quirky, volatile Urban Canyon plays expressed them better, certainly with greater passion and energy. Like Brecht, Poliakoff has been interested in the functioning of individual characters as they interact with their physical and cultural environment. His is not primarily a social drama. Social relations in his work are consistently predicated by the physical, technological, and cultural realities that surround them. What Poliakoff produces after examining this interaction, unlike Brecht, is not epic theatre intended to motivate people of the Scientific Age to change their world. Rather, his plays inform us that the spirit of the scientific age has passed, and that we live among that age's decayed ruins, in the Urban Canyon.

Brecht's hope of motivating theatre audiences to change the structure of human relations was based on the natural inclination his early-to mid-twentieth century audiences had for scientifically altering their physical environment to make it more suitable for human existence.

> It was as if mankind for the first time now began a conscious and coordinated effort to make the planet that was its home fit to live on. . . . In all directions man looked about himself with a new vision, to see how he could adapt to his convenience familiar but as yet unexploited objects. His surroundings changed increasingly from decade to decade, then from year to year, then almost from day to day.[3]

Science had empowered and encouraged people to understand the alterability of their natural, physical surroundings; armed with technology, it seemed no obstacle was too great for man's ingenuity. Brecht wanted to translate this scientific excitement into a similar perspective on our social environment, just as Marx had done in developing the scientific laws of social history.

> Our own period, which is transforming nature in so many and different ways, takes pleasure in understanding things so that we can interfere. There is a great deal to man, we say; so a great deal can be made out of him. We must not start with him; we must start on him.[4]

But Brecht's assumption of his audience's scientific excitement and natural desire to investigate their surroundings has been rendered untenable by the generation with which Poliakoff grew up and about which he writes. Ironically, for the late twentieth century, it is the progress spawned of man's enthusiasm for changing his environment that has come full circle now to stamp that enthusiasm out. The physical environment of Poliakoff's world has been so altered by a decadent science run rampant, changing things for no apparent purpose or improvement, that it has become again bewilderingly oppressive, as monolithic and immutable as nature once seemed to be. Brecht may have sensed the qualitative shift taking place in our technological progress as his generation was passing ("It was together with my son that I first saw the moving pictures of the explosion at Hiroshima"),[5] but it would take Poliakoff's perspective throughout the 1960s, 1970s, and 1980s to document for the stage the social and cultural effects of technological progress in detail, and to analyse its historical roots.

Poliakoff's first major success, in the form of his West End debut, came after he shifted to the Urban Canyon style of drama, with the companion pieces *Hitting Town* and *City Sugar* (1975); *The Carnation Gang* (1974), *Strawberry Fields* (1977), *Summer Party* (1980) and the last stage play before *Breaking the Silence, Favourite Nights* (1981) can also be classified in this group. These works share one common, basic principle that helps to determine their thematic and dramaturgical style. Characters tend to define themselves not so much in terms of their own independent beliefs and attitudes, nor in terms of other characters, but in terms of their environment. The environment has become canyon-like—monolithic, encircling, immutable, inescapable—yet man-made, filled with TVs, radios, bizarre lighting, muzak, and more muzak. The people behind this artificial environment, however, are themselves rarely visible. (Leonard Brazil, as the man behind the pap-producing radio of *Hitting Town* and *City Sugar,* is a notable exception.) As Poliakoff manipulates this urban stage environment he brings various pressures to bear on his characters. Their reactions to these environmental forces reveal not so much how we should judge the individuals, but how we should understand the dynamics of their lives in connection with contemporary urban life.

What may strike the audience (and did strike the critics) as occasionally meandering dialogue or action, thematic indirection, or inconsistent character development in these plays, can usually be attributed to a difference of focus between audience and playwright. In fact, such critical dissatisfaction can be traced back to his early plays, *Clever Soldiers* (1974) and *Heroes* (1975). Irving Wardle could see no connection, for instance, between *Heroes*'s striking characters and the play's political themes.

> The life the two characters acquire runs in unrelated parallel to the ideological course the author has marked out for them.[6]

Similarly, Randall Craig praised *Clever Soldiers*'s "Richly evocative atmospheres and exciting tensions," but found it thematically inadequate.[7] With the Urban Canyon plays, Poliakoff learned to outflank his critics while continuing to avoid ideological didacticism. Atmospheres and tensions become central to his aesthetic, as, through them, he analyses and dissects the interrelationships between characters and environment.

Poliakoff aptly uses the metaphor of atomic structure to describe his characters' interactions in this post-scientific age, or atomic age drama.

> My characters don't stand for anything, they are atoms bumping against each other. Through their lives I hope I throw shafts of light on to something larger.[8]

It is not as if an understanding of these atoms bumping together will reveal for Poliakoff a Boyle's Law of dramatic action. Nonetheless, the principle of experimentation is not dissimilar. Recurring variables are introduced into these environments: electronic and mass media (including practically all forms of electronic communication from radios and telephones to video cameras, VCRs and public address systems), music (in a variety of forms, including muzak, characters' singing, and a huge outdoor rock concert), and occasional, rare, outbreaks of silence. These are the environmental terms in which all of Poliakoff's canyon-dwellers define themselves, from the most mercurially anarchic, to the most emotionally apathetic.

Though his handling of the urban environment in *Hitting Town* was unusual, a clear sign of a unique voice coming into the British theatre, much of the critical attention was directed at the disturbing incestuous relationship between the architecture student, Ralph, and his sister, Clare, which serves as the subject of the play. The two, style and subject, are of course intimately related, for the nature of human relationships is dependent on the character of the physical environment. And in a society in which the environment has become hopelessly and decadently oppressive, human relationships will happen haphazardly. Poliakoff recently made the social/environmental connection explicit by noting, in retrospect, that

> The incestuous relationship [in *Hitting Town*] seemed as fragile and impermanent as the architecture Clare and Ralph were passing through.[9]

The prototypical symbol of the Urban Canyon's pervasive, man-made oppression is muzak. Throughout many of Poliakoff's plays, and especially in *Hitting Town,* it serves as a reminder that this is an unnatural and inescapable landscape, exemplifying the manner in which society's inventions have taken on a life of their own. Ralph and Clare, the brother and sister who are just beginning to flirt with one another in a dirty, serviceless Wimpy bar, comment on this sign of their environment's impersonal and oppressive nature. Muzak is playing as they await any sign of a waiter or waitress.

> Ralph: There's no escape.... There's one woman, you know, one *single, anonymous,* lady, who arranges all this muzak, produces it by herself, she does, this is true! It just pours out of her, uncontrollably, tons and tons of it! A real madwoman. We ought to find her, quickly, she's contaminating the whole place.[10]

Obviously, there is no finding this imaginary, crazed arranger and producer. But in Poliakoff's world, there's no finding the real perpetrators either. Although Ralph has come to visit his sister in Leicester, his comments about the recent terrorist bombings in his university town of Birmingham suggest that anonymous powers of all sorts seem to be controlling all of Britain's urban environments.

Nicola, the blank-faced teeny-bopper of *Hitting Town* and *City Sugar* and Ralph reflect two generations' reactions to such environmental nightmares. Nicola is the prototype of her generation and those to come. She is one of millions of "kids lapping up pap" on the radio and TV, and Poliakoff wishes to explore "the sterility of their lives."[11] Ralph is slightly older and a college student, just old enough to recall the 1960s, and that decade's apparent near-miss in actually returning the power of the popular media to the hands of the populace. This is very much the historical position Poliakoff found himself in when he began his own short-lived academic career at Cambridge.

> I was there just as the smoke of student rebellion was clearing—I found it very claustrophobic, a finishing school for the upper middle classes.[12]

Ralph has not entirely submitted to his environment; he maintains a degree of mercurial, questioning energy which is a prerequisite for a Brechtian sort of scientific and social investigative fervor. But energy is all Ralph has, because he, like the 1960s generation before him, is controlled and oppressed by his environment sufficiently to limit any creative, productive or critical thinking that might translate into useful action at some point. Surrounded by noises, muzak, depressing buildings, all Ralph can do is make lame jokes and lash out violently. As a student of architecture, someone who clearly took an interest at some point in gaining control over his environment, he speaks to Nicola of his and his sister Clare's night of hitting the town.

> Ralph: Look at it! Totally unsafe, it'd burn like balsa wood. (*Aggressive*) And full of TV shops, it's just a morgue for them.
>
> . . . Whole centre has changed—me and my sister used to know a different place. You know most of the architects of this atrocity are probably in gaol or just about to be. But we're left with it! Something ought to be done.[13]

But this post-1960s generation is nearly defeated. Ralph will do nothing even though he is both a student of architecture and a (former) student activist. As their relationship continues to become more and more sexually tense, Clare suddenly confronts Ralph with his incapacity for useful action.

> Clare: . . . (*With a provocative smile, touching him*) You've given up all your rebellious activities . . . at college, haven't you.
>
> Why are students now all so grey and defeated, and miserable and can't do anything? All that energy and you just don't know what to do with it, all you can do is thrash about and *shout*.[14]

Without an active academic or social interest in the environmental problems this new age poses for his generation, Ralph's social relationships receive no analytical attention either. Poliakoff is here not simply demonstrating the thesis that the environment has gone to pot, so social relationships have become decadently perverted. The more striking aspect of Ralph and Clare's sexual attraction to one another, rather than its perversion, consists in Poliakoff's careful detailing of its psychological progression, particularly their own lack of self-questioning as they fall into it. They worry about getting caught, for they know incest is illegal, but never wonder about what is drawing them toward each other or what effects such a relationship might have. But Ralph is progressively failing to question anything, as he releases his energies haphazardly, often in obviously dangerous and immoral ways, such as phoning the newspaper with a fake I.R.A. bomb threat—a last-ditch effort to transform himself into one of the anonymous manipulators of his urban world. The investigative spirit of the scientific age, of which Ralph is a decaying remnant, is quite nearly dead.

Poliakoff highlights this controlling dynamic between the couple and their environment by including a brief dialogue focused on the possibility of feeling something, in this case guilt, during the first extended moment of environmental silence in the play. The couple are again in Clare's high-rise apartment.

> Ralph: It's terrifyingly quiet, isn't it, Clare.
>
> Clare: For once, yes.
>
> Ralph: Are you feeling guilty then?
>
> Clare: About what?
>
> Ralph: Don't start that. You know what I mean. . . . About us doing it—are you? . . .
>
> Clare: No, not really. Why should I.

This moment soon passes, as Ralph points out, "The noise is beginning to come up, hear it?"

> Clare: Yes.
>
> Ralph: . . . Can't have that happening, can we? Look at it Clare. . . . Great grey mess—starting up again, spilling out.[15]

Within minutes, Ralph is dialing in his bomb threat, and Clare is suggesting that she might see him again in the near future. As Leonard Brazil comes over the radio with *"some loud Muzak,"* Clare sums up the degree of its control over her physical and intellectual life in the play's last line: "When this music stops . . . I'm going to work."[16]

Nicola, who is examined in more detail in *City Sugar*, is quite a bit different from Ralph in ways that reflect the greater sterility of her generation. She has none of his rebellious tendencies, and is even more environmentally-dependent than Ralph or Clare. *City Sugar* is a well-balanced companion piece to *Hitting Town* because in it we get a rare glimpse of one of the men behind this inhuman, Muzak-filled environment—pop disc jockey Leonard Brazil. The play itself is not fascinated so much with the sterility of Nicola's pap-filled life—that was sufficiently established in *Hitting Town*. Rather it focuses on Brazil's fascination with her life's sterility. And because the play pinpoints Brazil as the man responsible for much of her environment (he is equivalent to the anonymous lady of Ralph's nightmarish Muzak anecdote), it becomes a contemporary version of Shelley's *Frankenstein* story. Brazil has very much *created* an alienated, nearly inhuman creature, and he tracks her down in a desperate attempt to establish some sort of human contact with her.

Brazil becomes fascinated with Nicola upon first hearing her voice during a call-in contest in which fans compete for a chance to meet members of their favorite pop group, The Yellow Jacks. (The band is appropriately named; a ship flies the Yellow Jack when disease is present on board.) Described in the stage directions as "extremely flat, unemotional," her voice signals to him that she is the prototype of his followers—deadened and controlled as far as the human spirit will allow.[17] And he immediately begins thinking of her in intimate, sexual ways.

> Leonard: (*suddenly interested*) And what are you wearing, Nicola?
>
> Nicola: Trousers . . . shoes.
>
> Leonard: That's an interesting picture, she's wearing just trousers and shoes. Only wish we had television phones, sexy Nicola. . . .[18]

Seen in comparison with Brazil's description of a contemporary open-air concert, his fascination with making some sort of human contact with the generation he has created appears to have virtually necrophilic overtones.

> Everybody was lying about in lifeless heaps. . . . I saw one girl. . . . Her face and also her lips were sort of swollen, and completely ashen, almost blue, in fact, as if she was actually physically dead. I almost wanted to go up and touch her. . . . In fact I haven't got that picture out of my mind yet.[19]

This last description is juxtaposed with Rex, his on-air sidekick, bringing in the "twenty-five dummies on a trolley, piled high," which Brazil has made his fans put together as part of the competition. Brazil's fascination with his own monster-making power has led him to demonstrate it by making his creations in turn create even more-obviously dead creatures. Nicola's dummy is a particularly poignant representation of her own condition, as she has filled it up, literally, with all the objects that have been filling up her environment—things she has "nicked" from the supermarket, and all the pop music "posters and ornaments—everything in her room."[20]

In her work-place, where she and her friend Susan do no work at all, Nicola is subjected to the environmental pressure of the video camera. If, she says, we're "seen talking . . . by the camera . . . we'll both get it, won't we?" And just as Ralph fantasized earlier who the maniacal individual might be who could take responsibility for Muzak, so these two girls speculate about who is on the other side of the lens.

> Nicola: Do you know what he looks like?
>
> Susan: Yes, I saw him through the door once. He's very fat. I've heard all about him, he sits there all day, with one of his socks off, picking his toes, and eating the stuff, while he watches. . . .
>
> Nicola: You're making all this up, like always.[21]

Although Nicola and Susan, and Ralph and Clare, are never depicted as utterly defeated, serious speculation into their environment or social relationships seems beyond them. Poliakoff directly contravenes Brecht's statement that in epic theatre "the 'historical conditions' must of course not be imagined . . . as mysterious powers (in the background); on the contrary, they are created and maintained by men (and will in due course be altered by them)."[22] Poliakoff's "historical conditions" are deliberately mysterious and oppressive to his characters. And the only man the audience sees maintaining them, Leonard Brazil, is so hidden away up in the sky in his broadcast booth, it seems he has become a mysterious, controlling deity. It is due only to Brazil's own whim that Nicola gets a chance to run the obstacle course, the Yellow Jacks' competition, necessary to meet and speak with him. *City Sugar* ends with no indication that Brazil will change, only move to London and hence gain an even greater audience. His sidekick/clone, Rex, will be prepared to take over his position in Leicester. The records will continue to play and, as Brazil puts it, continue to "spin another circle of happiness and pour a little more sugar over the city."[23] He signs off saying, insincerely, "Be seeing you"—the only more unlikely occurrence being that any of *us* might actually see *him,* the man behind the music.

The most powerful and memorable of Poliakoff's Urban Canyon plays is *Strawberry Fields* (1977), the story of Kevin and Charlotte, two confused political activists, who travel Britain in pursuit of their vague ideals. The continuing success of the play has come as a bit of a surprise to the author himself, who expected it to age less well than it has.

> The play clearly belongs to the mid-seventies in its depiction of the hippy dream turning sour. . . . But with all the incidents of European terrorism both from the left and the right since the play was written [it] has proved to have one of the busiest lives of any of my plays, being regularly performed all over the world.

Even the conservationist themes take on a particular resonance for us now, he notes, raising the possibility of some people reacting with savagery against the urban world they have grown up in, as they try to project themselves into a never-never land where the car can be de-invented and motorways no longer exist.[24]

The title appropriately alludes to the high priest of the hippy dream, one who never lost touch with that dream's fundamental confusion, or dark side, John Lennon, and that awareness as reflected in his song, "Strawberry Fields."

> Always know, sometimes think it's me,
> But you know I know when it's a dream.
> I think a "No" will be a "Yes," but it's all wrong,
> That is I think I disagree.

Whether or not the 1960s really offered any substantial hope "that things were going to get better and better, that there would be inevitable progress towards more freedom, love not war, all that sort of thing" does not seem to be the question in the drama. The environment is as unalterable as ever, the final, decadent, logical extension of the scientific spirit; and the characters are logical extensions of what Poliakoff calls "wishy-washy liberal attitudes."[25] Both the bad and the good aspects of the 1960s—the phenomenal growth and pervasiveness of pop culture, and the rise of spirited individualism, respectively—had decayed in the 1970s into most of that individualism being destroyed in turn by that pop culture. The few individuals remaining, Poliakoff fears, are "individuals" by virtue of their remaining energy and spark, but intellectually and emotionally they have been equally as vulnerable to environmental derangement as others of their generation. Their individuality, thus twisted, now seems more of a threat, morally dangerous and potentially fascistic.

The central image of *Strawberry Fields* is that of the B-grade film, as the play itself enacts a sort of degenerated version of a road movie, in the *Easy Rider* tradition. Kevin, who is apparently going blind to the world around him, physically and metaphorically, has visions of every horrible, blood-and-gore film he has ever seen running through his head—and he describes them in remarkable detail, even pretending for a moment that he could project them out of his eyes onto a wall. He wallows, as well, in the vapid memories he has of the sixties, leaving him little mental energy with which to question his political approach to the 1970s.

Charlotte, who is considerably younger than Kevin, is deceptively normal-looking, while being rather like Nicola of *City Sugar* insofar as she has been emotionally flattened by her world. She does not have Kevin's memories of the 1960s, but rather an even more vague nostalgia for an edenic past:

> (She gazes out across the landscape.) This sprawling mess, it's just degrading. It presses down on us all. (*Loud*) Do you know what used to be here . . . a valley and fields. . . . Somebody's got to do something.[26]

Like Ralph's in *Hitting Town,* Charlotte's angst seems to be as far as she has thought the issue through, and she is unsure exactly what that "something" is that needs doing. Nonetheless, her remaining energy will lead her to kill for it. When an outsider, Nick, asks questions about the details of her views, suspecting her of National Front membership, she is unable to articulate them.

> Charlotte: You know what they are. You read the leaflet.
>
> Nick: I want to hear you say them. . . . Explain them to me Charlotte.
>
> Charlotte: . . . No. You'd only mock, wouldn't you?[27]

Whereas Kevin's and Charlotte's reasoning has been addled by their environment, the play's moments of greatest dramatic tension occur as soon as the constant background noise disappears. For Ralph and Clare in *Hitting Town,* such a moment of silence in the morning was a fleeting opportunity to gain a fresh perspective on their situation. For Charlotte, moments of silence serve as a call to reason and to human contact, both of which Nick himself represents, and neither of which she finds herself able to respond to. Hence these moments provoke her most intense crises, driving her ultimately to murder.

Two shootings occur in the play, both taking place in quiet, deserted areas at particularly quiet moments, and both being followed by deliberately loud, jarring noises that accentuate the silence preceding them. At the end of act 1, after Charlotte empties her gun into a police officer on a deserted street, who seemed about to uncover the purpose of their journey, the lights fade quickly and the stage directions call for "a loud electric buzz lasting 50 seconds in the blackout." That buzz is what opens act 2 and draws us back into the heart of the Urban Canyon—a neon-lit motorway cafe. We are reminded that the previous scene was far from this electronic environment, in a place where Charlotte said she felt "a little exposed . . . out here." Symbolically, this first shooting is set outside a decaying, condemned movie theatre, leaving Kevin, for once, outside this contemporary equivalent of Plato's allegorical cave, a place shut out from reality with only flickering representations on the wall. But in this exposed area of town, which news reports tell us "is awaiting demolition," Kevin only persists in trying to project his own distorted mental images against the outside of the theatre, while Charlotte follows her own lights by pulling the trigger.

The second shooting, the murder of Nick at the end of act 2, takes place on a hillside also far outside the city. The stage directions call for lights up full to indicate the arrival of dawn, as the sirens that have been pursuing our fugitive trio have passed them by and faded into the distance.

> Nick: God, it's still, isn't it? Suddenly there's no wind at all . . . just quiet.
>
> Charlotte: Yes. Don't turn round, now, Nick.

With that she shoots him, and again the silence is overtaken by the soundtrack, which immediately produces "traffic news . . . blasting out fiercely. Then total silence."[28]

Charlotte is ill-equipped to deal with these moments of silence, moments of choice beyond the canyon walls. She vividly sums up the subjective experience and consciousness of individuals living in the various urban environments which Poliakoff has described for us in this phase of his career, when she recounts an experience she had swimming in a lake "thick with mud and oil and things." She expresses the overwhelming sense of helplessness Brecht wanted to eradicate in his theatre audiences.

> I couldn't see anything except a sort of horrid, muzzy darkness. It went all over me and in me. Over my mouth like a mud gag. (*Suddenly*) It feels like that now doesn't it, all the time. . . . Doesn't it? Put your hand over your mouth. . . . That's what it felt like—feels like—all the time for a lot of people.[29]

The most remarkable aspect of Poliakoff's very different "European" play, *Breaking the Silence,* is the degree to which it manages to explore the same themes of the Urban Canyon plays—albeit from a fresh, revealing perspective. Probing along the two new axes of history and geography, the playwright discovers in post-revolutionary Russia the rich sense of "possibility" that characterized the height of the scientific age, as well as the seeds of the scientific decadence which would eventually become the scourge of England. Verkoff is correct in noting the former when he says in this play, "What rich times these are, eh?" And so is Nikolai Semenovitch when he warns of the latter: "I can assure you my friend—the modern world is grinding around in this carriage, forcing its way out, coming into existence right here."[30]

Nikolai Semenovitch Pesiakoff is an inventor living obliviously through the social upheavals of post-revolutionary Russia. Verkoff, a government bureaucrat, orders Nikolai to become a telephone examiner, forcing him and his family to live in a rail car on a deserted north-eastern line. Nikolai ignores all his new duties in favor of pursuing his experiments; he is attempting to join sound to motion pictures. His family finds the tension in the car unbearable as their fear of government retaliation for Nikolai's truancy mounts, and as his own dictatorial behaviour towards others, especially the maid, Polya, increases with his passion for his designs. Eugenia, his wife, begins covering for Nikolai, falsifying his work-journal in hopes of pleasing the regime. Sasha, his son, eventually destroys his father's camera lenses, crucial to completing the virtually-finished and successful experiments.

Verkoff, it turns out, had landed Nikolai this ludicrously isolated post knowing full well that the inventor was too bullheaded to fulfill its duties, and that he would then continue to experiment in peace. (Nikolai had repeatedly applied to Verkoff and the Leninist government for official support, to no avail—but he had unknowingly gained Verkoff's admiration and sympathy.) As the

brief tolerance of the early Stalin period gives way, Verkoff does Nikolai a final favor by securing his family permission to emigrate. The play closes with them in another rail car, bound for England.

The same environmental pressures are at work on Nikolai's family in the railway carriage as those faced by Ralph, Clare and Nicola back in *Hitting Town*. The compressed atmosphere of the carriage, aggravated by the scientific dictatorship of the father, contains in embryo all the elemental dynamics of culture and science which will control Nicola, Nikolai Semenovitch's spiritual offspring, decades later in the contemporary England of *City Sugar*. Nikolai embodies the contradictions inherent in the decline of the scientific age. His obsession (for what will eventually become a form of mass-media entertainment) turns him away from the emotional realities of his family—it becomes development for development's sake. Nikolai speaks of the wonderful potential of his work for the field of communication; spin-off inventions might enable us to speak to the deaf, he tells us. And yet he is the man slowly going deaf to those around him, ignoring the stress he is placing on his family, and listening to none of them. All for sound movies, which should remind us of that film-victim, Kevin, for whom film had become a mass communicator with little of value to say.

Verkoff is the great, enabling character of the play, the creative force, with a sense for how personalities operate, that provides Nikolai with his opportunity to succeed. He is a controlling figure, a bureaucrat made visible again, like Leonard Brazil—except that he pulls the invisible strings of government to sponsor creative energy and individual initiative, rather than to stamp it out. It is the tragedy of the future Urban Canyon that the creative opportunity Verkoff provides is destroyed by Nikolai's own overwhelming creative drive, which runs rampant, squelching the initiatives of those he lives with, disturbing and warping them.

Nikolai's son Sasha is, like Nicola in *Hitting Town,* a hint of the spiritless, unimaginative generations to come. When travelling with his father on his first train trip to the Northern District, Sasha can only complain of his hunger, and must have Nikolai conjure up images of what wonderful food they might be eating, rather than the millet they have. Sasha is not one to have his eyes on the future or on imaginative developments. When required to do a report for school, he chooses as his topic the sewage system of Moscow, and memorizes a string of facts associated with it. He is keenly embarrassed by his father's eccentricities, keenly sensitive to the pressure of his peers, and wants only to conform. In miniature, Sasha's destruction of his father's lenses mirrors the same blind ignorance that leads someone like Kevin, who really is suffering from diseased retinas, to his destructive agenda in *Strawberry Fields*. In Sasha's case the violent act turned out momentarily for the best—abandoning the destroyed project allowed Nikolai to break his personal silence with his wife—but it was nonetheless an act of blind, ill-informed violence on the son's part.

The history of "the modern world" to which Nikolai refers is not presented in this play with the Brechtian intention of revealing the cracks—places where society might have done otherwise and so improved our present lot. Instead we are left at the end of this play with the sense that the constructive release of energies which takes place in the various interrelationships among the characters is a possibility linked inextricably with the time and place in which they occur. As the whole family moves from the desolation and silence of northern Russia, where Nikolai came close to breaking the silence of film, to the eastern-most border of the country on their way to England, the noises of modern technology in the background increase. Consequently, so does Nikolai's and Eugenia's horrified understanding of what the future in the West holds for them. Even though Nikolai was the telephone examiner, we haven't heard a single phone ring throughout the play—now it is one of many constant background noises.

> *An ear-splitting screech, the sound of a locomotive backs up towards them, a piercing sound of movement and violent braking that touches the pit of the stomach.*
>
> Eugenia: I wish something would happen to stop us going. . . . You did it, though. I know you did. We know we existed.
>
> *The crunch of a locomotive up close, the sounds are violent, wrenching.*
>
> Sasha: I will write it up here, Papa, . . . on the wall, a record, there must be a record, the date . . . and what happened here.[31]

Even the memory of this time, Poliakoff suggests, is destined to be lost to Sasha and future generations, for Nikolai's son cannot manage to write the record on the wall.

Here on the edge of Russia is Nikolai's and Eugenia's last chance to break their own personal silence, and to recognize their more human achievements despite their scientific failure. Eugenia overcomes the "enormous weight in the air" of Nikolai's scientific obsession to act on her own desires, and Nikolai overcomes his scientific obsession to recognize Eugenia's worth as a human being, not just as an ornamental wife.

> Nikolai: . . . the energy generated in here, felt at times, if you will allow the slight exaggeration, felt it could flatten city walls. A way was found of releasing our separate energies. . . . [32]

The exaggeration is deliberate, and falls into line with much of Poliakoff's thinking in his other plays. The basic release of meaningful energies between individuals is always intertwined with the flattening of the city walls of the Urban Canyon. It is as if the drama in this railway carriage came painfully close to fulfilling Brecht's hopes for an empowering theatre.

> We need a type of theatre which not only releases the feelings, insights, and impulses possible within

the particular historical field of human relations in which the action takes place, but employs and encourages those thoughts and feelings which help transform the field itself.[33]

But, as often in Poliakoff, this field remains untransformable by individuals; it is not changed, but merely left behind.

The field *is* undergoing the transformation from Leninism to Stalinism, but no individual we see has a powerful role to play in that process. As Nikolai says, "Large events, great events even, have happened just outside, and we've seen most of them—or heard most of them to be more accurate. Meanwhile in here, locked up in this, squashed into this matchbox."[34] The manner in which these characters' lives run simultaneously with the rise of Stalinism, never intersecting significantly with the political scene, is reminiscent of Irving Wardle's complaints about the early play, *Heroes. Breaking the Silence* makes clear the necessity of such a division to Poliakoff's aesthetic.

We know that none of the actions of these characters is going to change the course of history. Nonetheless, we can blame Nikolai for pursuing the idea of sound-on-film as a decadent pursuit of scientific "achievement" for its own sake, which demanded the insensitive distancing of human relationships. Just as most urban dwellers would never get a chance to make contact with the man behind the name "Leonard Brazil," or the people behind the video camera, so here Nikolai begins to disappear behind his own rudimentary technology. As Polya sings to him through the speaking tube at one point, she can't see out the window to determine whether or not he is really at the other end.

> Polya: I am sure the Master is no longer there. (*Calling down*) Are you? He's walked off and left me singing to an empty railway line.[35]

She might as well be calling out to a movie screen or a video camera, for their creators may just as well have walked away and we would never know the difference. But to blame Nikolai is to suggest in a Brechtian manner that he should have acted differently, and been more sensitive to those around him. Yet we know no matter what Nikolai does, *The Jazz Singer* is going to open in New York in 1927, and, further west, a million other sound movies are going to be produced for the likes of Kevin in *Strawberry Fields*. What happens among these Russian characters cannot do much to change that.

What little hope Poliakoff does see for counteracting the sterility of contemporary British society inevitably comes out of Europe, as it almost does here in *Breaking the Silence,* and as in the appearance of Halina in *Coming in to Land.* A Polish emigré seeking citizenship in England, she brings some earthy vitality into the stunted, self-satisfied existence of Neville, a London lawyer specializing in, predictably, the deadening world of the entertainment industry. Halina obstinately refuses Neville's offer of a mock-marriage for the purpose of 'landing' her at emigration, and instead mounts her own one-woman media campaign, complete with a fabricated story of the abuse she had suffered at the hands of the Polish police. Although her strategy fails in gaining her asylum, she is not only successful in transmitting her energies in an immediate, personal way to Neville, but she actually manages to make a dent in the pop techno-culture of London using only the sheer force of her personality. Neville is shocked to find her popping up "all over the media, handling it with alarming efficiency." So alarmed, in fact, is Neville, that he re-examines his media-centric existence, and now finds himself "peering at a world of dying video shops. . . . "[36]

It is unfortunately difficult to see in what way Poliakoff's most recent play, *Playing with Trains,* is much more than a rather predictable variation on the ideas (and images) introduced in *Breaking The Silence.* And the emphasis *is* on ideas in this play, as opposed to dramatic technique. Whereas *Breaking The Silence* continued to make effective stage use of the environmental pressures within the rail car, both visually and aurally (a key to the energy of his earlier plays), *Playing With Trains* is content more or less with putting ideas on trial before an audience. During Bill Galpin's libel suit, he is questioned about his philosophy as an industrial researcher and developer, and one observer on stage gives us our choices as to how we should consider responding to this character.

> There're two ways of looking at him I suppose. . . .
> An inspired innovator taking risks, evangelical, ahead
> of his time—or somebody who's just turned into a
> slightly careless property tycoon.[37]

There is something bloodless or enervated in this kind of schematizing of characters. Galpin becomes a Verkoff-like, impresario figure gone haywire, with none of Verkoff's texture as a person on stage, as well as none of the Russian character's understanding of the individual personalities which surround him. Galpin has an eye for spotting talent, but when it comes to promotion, he can promote nothing but his own ideas, if indeed they are his own. In addition to his insensitivity and failures on a personal level, some of his philosophical pronouncements begin to sound simply like Poliakoff's own, rather than the stuff of drama.

> We [are] over concentrating on high tech at the
> expense of low. . . . High tech products . . . are
> seducing us away from reality. . . . The ideal
> existence we are being offered to strive for is a
> house stuffed with home computers and video
> recorders and two ridiculously energy-wasteful cars
> in the drive.[38]

Until now, Poliakoff has always been concerned with allowing us to feel this high tech disease in the pit of our stomachs, by stuffing his stage with its presence—muzak, videos, radio pop. Why now choose to outline it in more abstract terms? Poliakoff might instead take the time to begin questioning his own terms or move on to new territory.[39] The paradox of the scientific age's having

provided the creative impulse which ultimately squelches similar initiative in ensuing generations gets played out again here. Galpin's vision, particularly that of the road-rail vehicle which he has high hopes for, and from which the play derives its title, like Nikolai's vision, nearly becomes his own undoing, as his projects flounder and his family leave him. People are always trying to speak to him over intercoms, unsuccessfully, just as Polya sang "to an empty railway line" through a speaking tube. Physical contact with the man is virtually non-existent, as he begins, in his daughter Roxanna's words, "inhabiting [his] vision." And yet this play never allows us to forget its allegorical nature, types never quite become characters, position speeches never quite entrance us as plot. Poliakoff himself has come to inhabit his own vision in a strangely detached way, refusing to allow his characters any of the anarchic energy which characterized his earlier creations. Both Roxanna, in *Playing With Trains,* and Clare, of *Hitting Town,* conclude their respective plays by declaring their intention to "get to work." But in Clare's case, we have been made to feel what incredible environmental odds she is up against in making good on her promise. (She declares she'll start as soon as "this music stops.") Roxanna and her father settle into a productive companionship at the end, which seems to have little to do with the environment itself that Galpin has been lecturing about all along.

Many of Poliakoff's thematic concerns seem, in this latest play, to have become uninterestingly schematized, and critics who complained in the 1970s that his plays were thematically vague (but atmospherically provocative) should now be no better pleased with a piece that is thematically deliberate (and atmospherically dull). For many, *Breaking The Silence* marks the high point of the playwright's achievement—an ambitious and skillful balancing of history and contemporary social critique, compelling drama and idiosyncratic staging, theme and atmosphere. Yet it is important to keep the success of early plays like *Hitting Town, City Sugar,* and *Strawberry Fields* in mind. A better understanding of how *Playing With Trains*'s themes underlie the volatile anti-Brechtian, post-scientific age workings of nearly all the early plays should lead critics to a better, more sympathetic appreciation of what they will be re-reading in *Poliakoff Plays: One.* The need to "flatten city walls" is ongoing, and the effort will not be helped by Poliakoff's disappearance behind the overt themes and more traditional staging of his recent, "well-made" plays.

NOTES

[1] Stephen Poliakoff, *Poliakoff Plays: One* (London: Methuen, 1989).

[2] Poliakoff won the *Evening Standard*'s "Most Promising Playwright" award in 1976 for *Hitting Town* and *City Sugar.*

[3] Bertolt Brecht, *Brecht on Theatre: The Development of an Aesthetic,* trans. John Willett (London: Methuen, 1964), 184.

[4] Ibid., 193.

[5] Ibid., 184.

[6] Irving Wardle, *"Heroes," The Times,* 3 July 1975, 37.

[7] Randall Craig, Rev. of *Clever Soldiers, Drama* 116 (1975): 69-71.

[8] From an interview with Lyn Gardner, "Coming of Age," *Drama: The Quarterly Theatre Review* 163 (1987): 20.

[9] *Poliakoff Plays: One,* xi.

[10] Stephen Poliakoff, *Hitting Town and City Sugar* (London: Eyre Methuen, 1976), 14.

[11] Gardner, "Coming of Age," 20.

[12] Ibid., 19.

[13] Poliakoff, *Hitting Town and City Sugar,* 22.

[14] Ibid., 38.

[15] Ibid., 44-46.

[16] Ibid., 51.

[17] Poliakoff is careful to point out that his "characters always refuse to be trampled on—even the girls in *City Sugar* are not totally destroyed or made into zombies"; in Oleg Kerensky, *The New British Drama: Fourteen British Playwrights since Osborne and Pinter* (New York: Taplinger, 1977), 262.

[18] Poliakoff, *Hitting Town and City Sugar,* 65.

[19] Ibid., 91.

[20] Ibid., 82, 84.

[21] Ibid., 69.

[22] Brecht, *Brecht on Theatre,* 190.

[23] Poliakoff, *Hitting Town and City Sugar,* 121.

[24] *Poliakoff Plays: One,* xiv.

[25] Kerensky, *The New British Drama,* 261, 262.

[26] Stephen Poliakoff, *Strawberry Fields* (London: Eyre Methuen, 1977), 44.

[27] Ibid., 19.

[28] Ibid., 51-52.

[29] Ibid., 42.

[30] Stephen Poliakoff, *Breaking The Silence* (London: Methuen, 1987), 27.

[31] Ibid., 51-52.

[32] Ibid., 49-50.

[33] Brecht, *Brecht on Theatre,* 190.

[34] Poliakoff, *Breaking the Silence,* 49.

[35] Ibid., 19.

[36] Stephen Poliakoff, *Coming Into Land* (London: Methuen, 1986), 100.

[37] Stephen Poliakoff, *Playing With Trains* (London: Methuen, 1989), 63.

[38] Ibid., 68-69.

[39] The uncomfortable parallels between Galpin's and Poliakoff's views were made more explicit in performance by the program's listing of British technical innovations that had gone overseas for development.

FURTHER READING

Secondary Sources

Cosslett, Tess. *The "Scientific Movement" and Victorian Literature.* New York: The Harvester Press, 1982, 188 p.
    Considers the "values of science" presented in the works of such writers as Alfred, Lord Tennyson, George Eliot, George Meredith, and Thomas Hardy.

Demastes, William W. "Re-Inspecting the Crack in the Chimney: Chaos Theory from Ibsen to Stoppard." *New Theatre Quarterly* X, No. 39 (August 1994): 242-54.
    Applies the scientific paradigm of chaos theory to an analysis of Henrik Ibsen's *The Master Builder* and to the works of later absurdist and postmodern dramatists.

Foster, John Wilson. "Against Nature? Science and Oscar Wilde." *University of Toronto Quarterly* 63, No. 2 (Winter 1993): 328-46.
    Examines the hostility toward science displayed in the writings of Oscar Wilde.

Hayles, N. Katherine, ed. *Chaos and Order: Complex Dynamics in Literature and Science.* Chicago: University of Chicago Press, 1991, 308 p.
    Collection of essays on the intersection of chaos theory and modern literature.

Haynes, Roslynn D. *From Faust to Strangelove: Representations of the Scientist in Western Literature*. Baltimore: Johns Hopkins University Press, 1994, 417 p.

> Historical survey of shifting literary perceptions of the scientist figure.

Knapp, Shoshana. "Herbert Spencer in Cexov's 'Skucnaja Istorija' and 'Duel': The Love of Science and the Science of Love." *Slavic and East European Journal* 29, No. 3 (Fall 1985): 279-96.

> Observes the ironic handling of Spencerian views on scientific progress in two stories by Anton Chekhov.

Levine, George. *Darwin and the Novelists: Patterns of Science in Victorian Fiction*. Cambridge, Mass.: Harvard University Press, 1988, 319 p.

> Analyzes the considerable impact of Darwinian theory on the writings of such novelists as George Eliot, Charles Dickens, Sir Walter Scott, Anthony Trollope, and Joseph Conrad.

Limon, John. *The Place of Fiction in the Time of Science: A Disciplinary History of American Writing*. Cambridge: Cambridge University Press, 1990, 216 p.

> Probes the intellectual influence of scientific thought on the writings of Charles Brockden Brown, Edgar Allan Poe, Nathaniel Hawthorne, Theodore Dreiser, Thomas Pynchon, and Norman Mailer.

MacDiarmid, Hugh. "Poetry and Science." In *The Poet's Work: 29 Masters of 20th Century Poetry on the Origins and Practice of Their Art*, edited by Reginald Gibbons, pp. 121-35. Boston: Houghton Mifflin Company, 1979.

> Comments on the pivotal importance of a true understanding of the languages of science and mathematics among poets.

Nadeau, Robert. *Readings from the New Book on Nature: Physics and Metaphysics in the Modern Novel*. Amherst: University of Massachusetts Press, 1981, 213 p.

> Studies the impact of advances in contemporary physics on such writers as John Barth, Kurt Vonnegut, Jr., Thomas Pynchon, John Updike, and Don DeLillo.

Ricoeur, Paul. "The Power of Speech: Science and Poetry." *Philosophy Today* 29, No. 1 (Spring 1985): 59-69.

> Contrasts poetry as a language of feeling with the exact and verifiable language of science.

Schatzberg, Walter, Ronald A. Waite, and Nathan K. Johnson, eds. *The Relations of Literature and Science: An Annotated Bibliography of Scholarship, 1880-1980*. New York: Modern Language Association of America, 1987, 458 p.

> Comprehensive bibliography of secondary sources on the subject of literature and science, arranged by historical time period.

Scholnick, Robert J., ed. *American Literature and Science*. Lexington: University of Kentucky Press, 1992, 287 p.

> Collection of diverse essays on the boundaries and intersections of literature and science in the American milieu.

Slade, Joseph W. and Judith Yaross Lee, eds. *Beyond the Two Cultures: Essays on Science, Technology, and Literature*. Ames: Iowa State University Press, 1990, 308 p.

> Includes essays on the scientific contexts of modern literature and on a range of literary responses to science and technology by various contributors.

Stark, Susanne. "Overcoming Butlerian Obstacles: May Sinclair and the Problem of Biological Determinism." *Women's Studies* 21, No. 3 (1992): 265-83.

> Views the work of the Victorian writer May Sinclair as a response to the overwhelmingly deterministic biological theories of her time.

Steinman, Lisa M. *Made in America: Science, Technology, and American Modernist Poets*. New Haven, Conn.: Yale University Press, 1987, 219 p.

> Concentrates on the role that William Carlos Williams, Marianne Moore, and Wallace Stevens played in defining the place of poetry in modern, technological society.

Taylor, John. "Scientific Thought in Fiction and in Fact." In *Science Fiction at Large: A Collection of Essays, by Various Hands, about the Interface between Science Fiction and Reality*, edited by Peter Nicholls, pp. 57-72. New York: Harper & Row, 1976.

> Contains a scientist's view of the importance of science fiction as a means of exploring the possibilities of current and future scientific discoveries.

Zlatic, Thomas D. "Mark Twain's View of the Universe." *Papers on Language and Literature* 27, No. 3 (Summer 1991): 338-55.

> Explores Mark Twain's appropriation of scientific thought in his late writings.

How to Use This Index

The main references

Calvino, Italo
1923–1985 .... **CLC 5, 8, 11, 22, 33, 39,**
73; SSC 3

list all author entries in the following Gale Literary Criticism series:

BLC = *Black Literature Criticism*
CLC = *Contemporary Literary Criticism*
CLR = *Children's Literature Review*
CMLC = *Classical and Medieval Literature Criticism*
DA = *DISCovering Authors*
DAB = *DISCovering Authors: British*
DAC = *DISCovering Authors: Canadian*
DAM = *DISCovering Authors: Modules*
      DRAM: Dramatists Module; MST: Most-Studied Authors Module;
      MULT: Multicultural Authors Module; NOV: Novelists Module;
      POET: Poets Module; POP: Popular Fiction and Genre Authors Module
DC = *Drama Criticism*
HLC = *Hispanic Literature Criticism*
LC = *Literature Criticism from 1400 to 1800*
NCLC = *Nineteenth-Century Literature Criticism*
PC = *Poetry Criticism*
SSC = *Short Story Criticism*
TCLC = *Twentieth-Century Literary Criticism*
WLC = *World Literature Criticism, 1500 to the Present*

The cross-references

See also CANR 23; CA 85-88;
   obituary CA116

list all author entries in the following Gale biographical and literary sources:

AAYA = *Authors & Artists for Young Adults*
AITN = *Authors in the News*
BEST = *Bestsellers*
BW = *Black Writers*
CA = *Contemporary Authors*
CAAS = *Contemporary Authors Autobiography Series*
CABS = *Contemporary Authors Bibliographical Series*
CANR = *Contemporary Authors New Revision Series*
CAP = *Contemporary Authors Permanent Series*
CDALB = *Concise Dictionary of American Literary Biography*
CDBLB = *Concise Dictionary of British Literary Biography*
DLB = *Dictionary of Literary Biography*
DLBD = *Dictionary of Literary Biography Documentary Series*
DLBY = *Dictionary of Literary Biography Yearbook*
HW = *Hispanic Writers*
JRDA = *Junior DISCovering Authors*
MAICYA = *Major Authors and Illustrators for Children and Young Adults*
MTCW = *Major 20th-Century Writers*
NNAL = *Native North American Literature*
SAAS = *Something about the Author Autobiography Series*
SATA = *Something about the Author*
YABC = *Yesterday's Authors of Books for Children*

Twentieth-Century Literary Criticism

Cumulative Indexes
Volumes 1-90

Alcott, Amos Bronson 1799-1888 .... NCLC 1
    See also DLB 1
Alcott, Louisa May 1832-1888 . NCLC 6, 58;
    DA; DAB; DAC; DAM MST, NOV; SSC
    27; WLC
    See also AAYA 20; CDALB 1865-1917; CLR
    1, 38; DLB 1, 42, 79; DLBD 14; JRDA;
    MAICYA; SATA 100; YABC 1
Aldanov, M. A.
    See Aldanov, Mark (Alexandrovich)
Aldanov, Mark (Alexandrovich) 1886(?)-1957
    TCLC 23
    See also CA 118
Aldington, Richard 1892-1962 .... CLC 49
    See also CA 85-88; CANR 45; DLB 20, 36, 100,
    149
Aldiss, Brian W(ilson) 1925- . CLC 5, 14, 40;
    DAM NOV
    See also CA 5-8R; CAAS 2; CANR 5, 28, 64;
    DLB 14; MTCW 1; SATA 34
Alegria, Claribel 1924-CLC 75; DAM MULT
    See also CA 131; CAAS 15; CANR 66; DLB
    145; HW
Alegria, Fernando 1918- .... CLC 57
    See also CA 9-12R; CANR 5, 32, 72; HW
Aleichem, Sholom .... TCLC 1, 35; SSC 33
    See also Rabinovitch, Sholem
Aleixandre, Vicente 1898-1984 ... CLC 9, 36;
    DAM POET; PC 15
    See also CA 85-88; 114; CANR 26; DLB 108;
    HW; MTCW 1
Alepoudelis, Odysseus
    See Elytis, Odysseus
Aleshkovsky, Joseph 1929-
    See Aleshkovsky, Yuz
    See also CA 121; 128
Aleshkovsky, Yuz .... CLC 44
    See also Aleshkovsky, Joseph
Alexander, Lloyd (Chudley) 1924- ... CLC 35
    See also AAYA 1, 27; CA 1-4R; CANR 1, 24,
    38, 55; CLR 1, 5, 48; DLB 52; JRDA;
    MAICYA; MTCW 1; SAAS 19; SATA 3, 49,
    81
Alexander, Samuel 1859-1938 .... TCLC 77
Alexie, Sherman (Joseph, Jr.) 1966- CLC 96;
    DAM MULT
    See also CA 138; CANR 65; DLB 175, 206;
    NNAL
Alfau, Felipe 1902- .... CLC 66
    See also CA 137
Alger, Horatio, Jr. 1832-1899 .... NCLC 8
    See also DLB 42; SATA 16
Algren, Nelson 1909-1981CLC 4, 10, 33; SSC
    33
    See also CA 13-16R; 103; CANR 20, 61;
    CDALB 1941-1968; DLB 9; DLBY 81, 82;
    MTCW 1
Ali, Ahmed 1910- .... CLC 69
    See also CA 25-28R; CANR 15, 34
Alighieri, Dante
    See Dante
Allan, John B.
    See Westlake, Donald E(dwin)
Allan, Sidney
    See Hartmann, Sadakichi
Allan, Sydney
    See Hartmann, Sadakichi
Allen, Edward 1948- .... CLC 59
Allen, Fred 1894-1956 .... TCLC 87
Allen, Paula Gunn 1939- .... CLC 84; DAM
    MULT
    See also CA 112; 143; CANR 63; DLB 175;
    NNAL
Allen, Roland
    See Ayckbourn, Alan
Allen, Sarah A.
    See Hopkins, Pauline Elizabeth

Allen, Sidney H.
    See Hartmann, Sadakichi
Allen, Woody 1935- CLC 16, 52; DAM POP
    See also AAYA 10; CA 33-36R; CANR 27, 38,
    63; DLB 44; MTCW 1
Allende, Isabel 1942- . CLC 39, 57, 97; DAM
    MULT, NOV; HLC; WLCS
    See also AAYA 18; CA 125; 130; CANR 51,
    74; DLB 145; HW; INT 130; MTCW 1
Alleyn, Ellen
    See Rossetti, Christina (Georgina)
Allingham, Margery (Louise) 1904-1966C L C
    19
    See also CA 5-8R; 25-28R; CANR 4, 58; DLB
    77; MTCW 1
Allingham, William 1824-1889 ...... NCLC 25
    See also DLB 35
Allison, Dorothy E. 1949- .... CLC 78
    See also CA 140; CANR 66
Allston, Washington 1779-1843 .... NCLC 2
    See also DLB 1
Almedingen, E. M. .... CLC 12
    See also Almedingen, Martha Edith von
    See also SATA 3
Almedingen, Martha Edith von 1898-1971
    See Almedingen, E. M.
    See also CA 1-4R; CANR 1
Almodovar, Pedro 1949(?)- .... CLC 114
    See also CA 133; CANR 72
Almqvist, Carl Jonas Love 1793-1866 N C L C
    42
Alonso, Damaso 1898-1990 .... CLC 14
    See also CA 110; 131; 130; CANR 72; DLB
    108; HW
Alov
    See Gogol, Nikolai (Vasilyevich)
Alta 1942- .... CLC 19
    See also CA 57-60
Alter, Robert B(ernard) 1935- .... CLC 34
    See also CA 49-52; CANR 1, 47
Alther, Lisa 1944- .... CLC 7, 41
    See also CA 65-68; CAAS 30; CANR 12, 30,
    51; MTCW 1
Althusser, L.
    See Althusser, Louis
Althusser, Louis 1918-1990 .... CLC 106
    See also CA 131; 132
Altman, Robert 1925- .... CLC 16, 116
    See also CA 73-76; CANR 43
Alvarez, A(lfred) 1929- .... CLC 5, 13
    See also CA 1-4R; CANR 3, 33, 63; DLB 14,
    40
Alvarez, Alejandro Rodriguez 1903-1965
    See Casona, Alejandro
    See also CA 131; 93-96; HW
Alvarez, Julia 1950- .... CLC 93
    See also AAYA 25; CA 147; CANR 69
Alvaro, Corrado 1896-1956 .... TCLC 60
    See also CA 163
Amado, Jorge 1912- CLC 13, 40, 106; DAM
    MULT, NOV; HLC
    See also CA 77-80; CANR 35, 74; DLB 113;
    MTCW 1
Ambler, Eric 1909-1998 .... CLC 4, 6, 9
    See also CA 9-12R; 171; CANR 7, 38, 74; DLB
    77; MTCW 1
Amichai, Yehuda 1924- ... CLC 9, 22, 57, 116
    See also CA 85-88; CANR 46, 60; MTCW 1
Amichai, Yehudah
    See Amichai, Yehuda
Amiel, Henri Frederic 1821-1881 .... NCLC 4
Amis, Kingsley (William) 1922-1995CLC 1, 2,
    3, 5, 8, 13, 40, 44; DA; DAB; DAC; DAM
    MST, NOV
    See also AITN 2; CA 9-12R; 150; CANR 8, 28,
    54; CDBLB 1945-1960; DLB 15, 27, 100,
    139; DLBY 96; INT CANR-8; MTCW 1

Amis, Martin (Louis) 1949-CLC 4, 9, 38, 62,
    101
    See also BEST 90:3; CA 65-68; CANR 8, 27,
    54, 73; DLB 14, 194; INT CANR-27
Ammons, A(rchie) R(andolph) 1926-CLC 2, 3,
    5, 8, 9, 25, 57, 108; DAM POET; PC 16
    See also AITN 1; CA 9-12R; CANR 6, 36, 51,
    73; DLB 5, 165; MTCW 1
Amo, Tauraatua i
    See Adams, Henry (Brooks)
Amory, Thomas 1691(?)-1788 .... LC 48
Anand, Mulk Raj 1905- .. CLC 23, 93; DAM
    NOV
    See also CA 65-68; CANR 32, 64; MTCW 1
Anatol
    See Schnitzler, Arthur
Anaximander c. 610B.C.-c. 546B.C.CMLC 22
Anaya, Rudolfo A(lfonso) 1937- ..... CLC 23;
    DAM MULT, NOV; HLC
    See also AAYA 20; CA 45-48; CAAS 4; CANR
    1, 32, 51; DLB 82, 206; HW 1; MTCW 1
Andersen, Hans Christian 1805-1875NCLC 7;
    DA; DAB; DAC; DAM MST, POP; SSC
    6; WLC
    See also CLR 6; MAICYA; SATA 100; YABC
    1
Anderson, C. Farley
    See Mencken, H(enry) L(ouis); Nathan, George
    Jean
Anderson, Jessica (Margaret) Queale 1916-
    CLC 37
    See also CA 9-12R; CANR 4, 62
Anderson, Jon (Victor) 1940- .. CLC 9; DAM
    POET
    See also CA 25-28R; CANR 20
Anderson, Lindsay (Gordon) 1923-1994C L C
    20
    See also CA 125; 128; 146
Anderson, Maxwell 1888-1959TCLC 2; DAM
    DRAM
    See also CA 105; 152; DLB 7
Anderson, Poul (William) 1926- .... CLC 15
    See also AAYA 5; CA 1-4R; CAAS 2; CANR
    2, 15, 34, 64; DLB 8; INT CANR-15; MTCW
    1; SATA 90; SATA-Brief 39
Anderson, Robert (Woodruff) 1917-CLC 23;
    DAM DRAM
    See also AITN 1; CA 21-24R; CANR 32; DLB
    7
Anderson, Sherwood 1876-1941 TCLC 1, 10,
    24; DA; DAB; DAC; DAM MST, NOV;
    SSC 1; WLC
    See also CA 104; 121; CANR 61; CDALB
    1917-1929; DLB 4, 9, 86; DLBD 1; MTCW
    1
Andier, Pierre
    See Desnos, Robert
Andouard
    See Giraudoux, (Hippolyte) Jean
Andrade, Carlos Drummond de .... CLC 18
    See also Drummond de Andrade, Carlos
Andrade, Mario de 1893-1945 .... TCLC 43
Andreae, Johann V(alentin) 1586-1654LC 32
    See also DLB 164
Andreas-Salome, Lou 1861-1937 ... TCLC 56
    See also DLB 66
Andress, Lesley
    See Sanders, Lawrence
Andrewes, Lancelot 1555-1626 .... LC 5
    See also DLB 151, 172
Andrews, Cicily Fairfield
    See West, Rebecca
Andrews, Elton V.
    See Pohl, Frederik
Andreyev, Leonid (Nikolaevich) 1871-1919
    TCLC 3
    See also CA 104

Andric, Ivo 1892-1975 .... **CLC 8**
See also CA 81-84; 57-60; CANR 43, 60; DLB 147; MTCW 1
Androvar
See Prado (Calvo), Pedro
Angelique, Pierre
See Bataille, Georges
Angell, Roger 1920- .... **CLC 26**
See also CA 57-60; CANR 13, 44, 70; DLB 171, 185
Angelou, Maya 1928-**CLC 12, 35, 64, 77; BLC 1; DA; DAB; DAC; DAM MST, MULT, POET, POP; WLCS**
See also AAYA 7, 20; BW 2; CA 65-68; CANR 19, 42, 65; CLR 53; DLB 38; MTCW 1; SATA 49
Anna Comnena 1083-1153 .... **CMLC 25**
Annensky, Innokenty (Fyodorovich) 1856-1909 **TCLC 14**
See also CA 110; 155
Annunzio, Gabriele d'
See D'Annunzio, Gabriele
Anodos
See Coleridge, Mary E(lizabeth)
Anon, Charles Robert
See Pessoa, Fernando (Antonio Nogueira)
Anouilh, Jean (Marie Lucien Pierre) 1910-1987 **CLC 1, 3, 8, 13, 40, 50; DAM DRAM; DC 8**
See also CA 17-20R; 123; CANR 32; MTCW 1
Anthony, Florence
See Ai
Anthony, John
See Ciardi, John (Anthony)
Anthony, Peter
See Shaffer, Anthony (Joshua); Shaffer, Peter (Levin)
Anthony, Piers 1934- .... **CLC 35; DAM POP**
See also AAYA 11; CA 21-24R; CANR 28, 56, 73; DLB 8; MTCW 1; SAAS 22; SATA 84
Anthony, Susan B(rownell) 1916-1991 **T C L C 84**
See also CA 89-92; 134
Antoine, Marc
See Proust, (Valentin-Louis-George-Eugene-) Marcel
Antoninus, Brother
See Everson, William (Oliver)
Antonioni, Michelangelo 1912- .... **CLC 20**
See also CA 73-76; CANR 45
Antschel, Paul 1920-1970
See Celan, Paul
See also CA 85-88; CANR 33, 61; MTCW 1
Anwar, Chairil 1922-1949 .... **TCLC 22**
See also CA 121
Apess, William 1798-1839(?)**NCLC 73; DAM MULT**
See also DLB 175; NNAL
Apollinaire, Guillaume 1880-1918**TCLC 3, 8, 51; DAM POET; PC 7**
See also Kostrowitzki, Wilhelm Apollinaris de
See also CA 152
Appelfeld, Aharon 1932- .... **CLC 23, 47**
See also CA 112; 133
Apple, Max (Isaac) 1941- .... **CLC 9, 33**
See also CA 81-84; CANR 19, 54; DLB 130
Appleman, Philip (Dean) 1926- .... **CLC 51**
See also CA 13-16R; CAAS 18; CANR 6, 29, 56
Appleton, Lawrence
See Lovecraft, H(oward) P(hillips)
Apteryx
See Eliot, T(homas) S(tearns)
Apuleius, (Lucius Madaurensis) 125(?)-175(?) **CMLC 1**
Aquin, Hubert 1929-1977 .... **CLC 15**
See also CA 105; DLB 53

Aquinas, Thomas 1224(?)-1274 ..... **CMLC 33**
See also DLB 115
Aragon, Louis 1897-1982 .. **CLC 3, 22; DAM NOV, POET**
See also CA 69-72; 108; CANR 28, 71; DLB 72; MTCW 1
Arany, Janos 1817-1882 .... **NCLC 34**
Aranyos, Kakay
See Mikszath, Kalman
Arbuthnot, John 1667-1735 .... **LC 1**
See also DLB 101
Archer, Herbert Winslow
See Mencken, H(enry) L(ouis)
Archer, Jeffrey (Howard) 1940- ..... **CLC 28; DAM POP**
See also AAYA 16; BEST 89:3; CA 77-80; CANR 22, 52; INT CANR-22
Archer, Jules 1915- .... **CLC 12**
See also CA 9-12R; CANR 6, 69; SAAS 5; SATA 4, 85
Archer, Lee
See Ellison, Harlan (Jay)
Arden, John 1930-**CLC 6, 13, 15; DAM DRAM**
See also CA 13-16R; CAAS 4; CANR 31, 65, 67; DLB 13; MTCW 1
Arenas, Reinaldo 1943-1990 . **CLC 41; DAM MULT; HLC**
See also CA 124; 128; 133; CANR 73; DLB 145; HW
Arendt, Hannah 1906-1975 .... **CLC 66, 98**
See also CA 17-20R; 61-64; CANR 26, 60; MTCW 1
Aretino, Pietro 1492-1556 .... **LC 12**
Arghezi, Tudor 1880-1967 .... **CLC 80**
See also Theodorescu, Ion N.
See also CA 167
Arguedas, Jose Maria 1911-1969 **CLC 10, 18**
See also CA 89-92; CANR 73; DLB 113; HW
Argueta, Manlio 1936- .... **CLC 31**
See also CA 131; CANR 73; DLB 145; HW
Ariosto, Ludovico 1474-1533 .... **LC 6**
Aristides
See Epstein, Joseph
Aristophanes 450B.C.-385B.C.**CMLC 4; DA; DAB; DAC; DAM DRAM, MST; DC 2; WLCS**
See also DLB 176
Aristotle 384B.C.-322B.C. ... **CMLC 31; DA; DAB; DAC; DAM MST; WLCS**
See also DLB 176
Arlt, Roberto (Godofredo Christophersen) 1900-1942 ....
TCLC 29; DAM MULT; HLC
See also CA 123; 131; CANR 67; HW
Armah, Ayi Kwei 1939- . **CLC 5, 33; BLC 1; DAM MULT, POET**
See also BW 1; CA 61-64; CANR 21, 64; DLB 117; MTCW 1
Armatrading, Joan 1950- .... **CLC 17**
See also CA 114
Arnette, Robert
See Silverberg, Robert
Arnim, Achim von (Ludwig Joachim von Arnim) 1781-1831 ...... **NCLC 5; SSC 29**
See also DLB 90
Arnim, Bettina von 1785-1859 .... **NCLC 38**
See also DLB 90
Arnold, Matthew 1822-1888**NCLC 6, 29; DA; DAB; DAC; DAM MST, POET; PC 5; WLC**
See also CDBLB 1832-1890; DLB 32, 57
Arnold, Thomas 1795-1842 .... **NCLC 18**
See also DLB 55
Arnow, Harriette (Louisa) Simpson 1908-1986 **CLC 2, 7, 18**
See also CA 9-12R; 118; CANR 14; DLB 6; MTCW 1; SATA 42; SATA-Obit 47

Arouet, Francois-Marie
See Voltaire
Arp, Hans
See Arp, Jean
Arp, Jean 1887-1966 .... **CLC 5**
See also CA 81-84; 25-28R; CANR 42
Arrabal
See Arrabal, Fernando
Arrabal, Fernando 1932- .... **CLC 2, 9, 18, 58**
See also CA 9-12R; CANR 15
Arrick, Fran .... **CLC 30**
See also Gaberman, Judie Angell
Artaud, Antonin (Marie Joseph) 1896-1948 **TCLC 3, 36; DAM DRAM**
See also CA 104; 149
Arthur, Ruth M(abel) 1905-1979 ...... **CLC 12**
See also CA 9-12R; 85-88; CANR 4; SATA 7, 26
Artsybashev, Mikhail (Petrovich) 1878-1927 **TCLC 31**
See also CA 170
Arundel, Honor (Morfydd) 1919-1973**CLC 17**
See also CA 21-22; 41-44R; CAP 2; CLR 35; SATA 4; SATA-Obit 24
Arzner, Dorothy 1897-1979 .... **CLC 98**
Asch, Sholem 1880-1957 .... **TCLC 3**
See also CA 105
Ash, Shalom
See Asch, Sholem
Ashbery, John (Lawrence) 1927-**CLC 2, 3, 4, 6, 9, 13, 15, 25, 41, 77; DAM POET**
See also CA 5-8R; CANR 9, 37, 66; DLB 5, 165; DLBY 81; INT CANR-9; MTCW 1
Ashdown, Clifford
See Freeman, R(ichard) Austin
Ashe, Gordon
See Creasey, John
Ashton-Warner, Sylvia (Constance) 1908-1984 **CLC 19**
See also CA 69-72; 112; CANR 29; MTCW 1
Asimov, Isaac 1920-1992 **CLC 1, 3, 9, 19, 26, 76, 92; DAM POP**
See also AAYA 13; BEST 90:2; CA 1-4R; 137; CANR 2, 19, 36, 60; CLR 12; DLB 8; DLBY 92; INT CANR-19; JRDA; MAICYA; MTCW 1; SATA 1, 26, 74
Assis, Joaquim Maria Machado de
See Machado de Assis, Joaquim Maria
Astley, Thea (Beatrice May) 1925- ... **CLC 41**
See also CA 65-68; CANR 11, 43
Aston, James
See White, T(erence) H(anbury)
Asturias, Miguel Angel 1899-1974 **CLC 3, 8, 13; DAM MULT, NOV; HLC**
See also CA 25-28; 49-52; CANR 32; CAP 2; DLB 113; HW; MTCW 1
Atares, Carlos Saura
See Saura (Atares), Carlos
Atheling, William
See Pound, Ezra (Weston Loomis)
Atheling, William, Jr.
See Blish, James (Benjamin)
Atherton, Gertrude (Franklin Horn) 1857-1948 **TCLC 2**
See also CA 104; 155; DLB 9, 78, 186
Atherton, Lucius
See Masters, Edgar Lee
Atkins, Jack
See Harris, Mark
Atkinson, Kate .... **CLC 99**
See also CA 166
Attaway, William (Alexander) 1911-1986 **CLC 92; BLC 1; DAM MULT**
See also BW 2; CA 143; DLB 76
Atticus
See Fleming, Ian (Lancaster); Wilson, (Thomas) Woodrow

See Moorcock, Michael (John)

Barea, Arturo 1897-1957 .... **TCLC 14**
See also CA 111

Barfoot, Joan 1946- .... **CLC 18**
See also CA 105

Baring, Maurice 1874-1945 .... **TCLC 8**
See also CA 105; 168; DLB 34

Baring-Gould, Sabine 1834-1924 .. **TCLC 88**
See also DLB 156, 190

Barker, Clive 1952- .... **CLC 52; DAM POP**
See also AAYA 10; BEST 90:3; CA 121; 129; CANR 71; INT 129; MTCW 1

Barker, George Granville 1913-1991 **CLC 8, 48; DAM POET**
See also CA 9-12R; 135; CANR 7, 38; DLB 20; MTCW 1

Barker, Harley Granville
See Granville-Barker, Harley
See also DLB 10

Barker, Howard 1946- .... **CLC 37**
See also CA 102; DLB 13

Barker, Jane 1652-1732 .... **LC 42**

Barker, Pat(ricia) 1943- .... **CLC 32, 94**
See also CA 117; 122; CANR 50; INT 122

Barlach, Ernst 1870-1938 .... **TCLC 84**
See also DLB 56, 118

Barlow, Joel 1754-1812 .... **NCLC 23**
See also DLB 37

Barnard, Mary (Ethel) 1909- .... **CLC 48**
See also CA 21-22; CAP 2

Barnes, Djuna 1892-1982 **CLC 3, 4, 8, 11, 29; SSC 3**
See also CA 9-12R; 107; CANR 16, 55; DLB 4, 9, 45; MTCW 1

Barnes, Julian (Patrick) 1946- **CLC 42; DAB**
See also CA 102; CANR 19, 54; DLB 194; DLBY 93

Barnes, Peter 1931- .... **CLC 5, 56**
See also CA 65-68; CAAS 12; CANR 33, 34, 64; DLB 13; MTCW 1

Barnes, William 1801-1886 .... **NCLC 75**
See also DLB 32

Baroja (y Nessi), Pio 1872-1956 **TCLC 8; HLC**
See also CA 104

Baron, David
See Pinter, Harold

Baron Corvo
See Rolfe, Frederick (William Serafino Austin Lewis Mary)

Barondess, Sue K(aufman) 1926-1977 **CLC 8**
See also Kaufman, Sue
See also CA 1-4R; 69-72; CANR 1

Baron de Teive
See Pessoa, Fernando (Antonio Nogueira)

Baroness Von S.
See Zangwill, Israel

Barres, (Auguste-) Maurice 1862-1923 **TCLC 47**
See also CA 164; DLB 123

Barreto, Afonso Henrique de Lima
See Lima Barreto, Afonso Henrique de

Barrett, (Roger) Syd 1946- .... **CLC 35**

Barrett, William (Christopher) 1913-1992 **CLC 27**
See also CA 13-16R; 139; CANR 11, 67; INT CANR-11

Barrie, J(ames) M(atthew) 1860-1937 **TCLC 2; DAB; DAM DRAM**
See also CA 104; 136; CDBLB 1890-1914; CLR 16; DLB 10, 141, 156; MAICYA; SATA 100; YABC 1

Barrington, Michael
See Moorcock, Michael (John)

Barrol, Grady
See Bograd, Larry

Barry, Mike
See Malzberg, Barry N(athaniel)

Barry, Philip 1896-1949 .... **TCLC 11**
See also CA 109; DLB 7

Bart, Andre Schwarz
See Schwarz-Bart, Andre

Barth, John (Simmons) 1930- **CLC 1, 2, 3, 5, 7, 9, 10, 14, 27, 51, 89; DAM NOV; SSC 10**
See also AITN 1, 2; CA 1-4R; CABS 1; CANR 5, 23, 49, 64; DLB 2; MTCW 1

Barthelme, Donald 1931-1989 **CLC 1, 2, 3, 5, 6, 8, 13, 23, 46, 59, 115; DAM NOV; SSC 2**
See also CA 21-24R; 129; CANR 20, 58; DLB 2; DLBY 80, 89; MTCW 1; SATA 7; SATA-Obit 62

Barthelme, Frederick 1943- ...... **CLC 36, 117**
See also CA 114; 122; DLBY 85; INT 122

Barthes, Roland (Gerard) 1915-1980 **CLC 24, 83**
See also CA 130; 97-100; CANR 66; MTCW 1

Barzun, Jacques (Martin) 1907- .... **CLC 51**
See also CA 61-64; CANR 22

Bashevis, Isaac
See Singer, Isaac Bashevis

Bashkirtseff, Marie 1859-1884 ...... **NCLC 27**

Basho
See Matsuo Basho

Bass, Kingsley B., Jr.
See Bullins, Ed

Bass, Rick 1958- .... **CLC 79**
See also CA 126; CANR 53

Bassani, Giorgio 1916- .... **CLC 9**
See also CA 65-68; CANR 33; DLB 128, 177; MTCW 1

Bastos, Augusto (Antonio) Roa
See Roa Bastos, Augusto (Antonio)

Bataille, Georges 1897-1962 .... **CLC 29**
See also CA 101; 89-92

Bates, H(erbert) E(rnest) 1905-1974 **CLC 46; DAB; DAM POP; SSC 10**
See also CA 93-96; 45-48; CANR 34; DLB 162, 191; MTCW 1

Bauchart
See Camus, Albert

Baudelaire, Charles 1821-1867 **NCLC 6, 29, 55; DA; DAB; DAC; DAM MST, POET; PC 1; SSC 18; WLC**

Baudrillard, Jean 1929- .... **CLC 60**

Baum, L(yman) Frank 1856-1919 ... **TCLC 7**
See also CA 108; 133; CLR 15; DLB 22; JRDA; MAICYA; MTCW 1; SATA 18, 100

Baum, Louis F.
See Baum, L(yman) Frank

Baumbach, Jonathan 1933- .... **CLC 6, 23**
See also CA 13-16R; CAAS 5; CANR 12, 66; DLBY 80; INT CANR-12; MTCW 1

Bausch, Richard (Carl) 1945- .... **CLC 51**
See also CA 101; CAAS 14; CANR 43, 61; DLB 130

Baxter, Charles (Morley) 1947- **CLC 45, 78; DAM POP**
See also CA 57-60; CANR 40, 64; DLB 130

Baxter, George Owen
See Faust, Frederick (Schiller)

Baxter, James K(eir) 1926-1972 .... **CLC 14**
See also CA 77-80

Baxter, John
See Hunt, E(verette) Howard, (Jr.)

Bayer, Sylvia
See Glassco, John

Baynton, Barbara 1857-1929 .... **TCLC 57**

Beagle, Peter S(oyer) 1939- .... **CLC 7, 104**
See also CA 9-12R; CANR 4, 51, 73; DLBY 80; INT CANR-4; SATA 60

Bean, Normal
See Burroughs, Edgar Rice

Beard, Charles A(ustin) 1874-1948 **TCLC 15**
See also CA 115; DLB 17; SATA 18

Beardsley, Aubrey 1872-1898 .... **NCLC 6**

Beattie, Ann 1947- **CLC 8, 13, 18, 40, 63; DAM NOV, POP; SSC 11**
See also BEST 90:2; CA 81-84; CANR 53, 73; DLBY 82; MTCW 1

Beattie, James 1735-1803 .... **NCLC 25**
See also DLB 109

Beauchamp, Kathleen Mansfield 1888-1923
See Mansfield, Katherine
See also CA 104; 134; DA; DAC; DAM MST

Beaumarchais, Pierre-Augustin Caron de 1732-1799 .... **DC 4**
See also DAM DRAM

Beaumont, Francis 1584(?)-1616 **LC 33; DC 6**
See also CDBLB Before 1660; DLB 58, 121

Beauvoir, Simone (Lucie Ernestine Marie Bertrand) de 1908-1986 **CLC 1, 2, 4, 8, 14, 31, 44, 50, 71; DA; DAB; DAC; DAM MST, NOV; WLC**
See also CA 9-12R; 118; CANR 28, 61; DLB 72; DLBY 86; MTCW 1

Becker, Carl (Lotus) 1873-1945 ..... **TCLC 63**
See also CA 157; DLB 17

Becker, Jurek 1937-1997 .... **CLC 7, 19**
See also CA 85-88; 157; CANR 60; DLB 75

Becker, Walter 1950- .... **CLC 26**

Beckett, Samuel (Barclay) 1906-1989 **CLC 1, 2, 3, 4, 6, 9, 10, 11, 14, 18, 29, 57, 59, 83; DA; DAB; DAC; DAM DRAM, MST, NOV; SSC 16; WLC**
See also CA 5-8R; 130; CANR 33, 61; CDBLB 1945-1960; DLB 13, 15; DLBY 90; MTCW 1

Beckford, William 1760-1844 .... **NCLC 16**
See also DLB 39

Beckman, Gunnel 1910- .... **CLC 26**
See also CA 33-36R; CANR 15; CLR 25; MAICYA; SAAS 9; SATA 6

Becque, Henri 1837-1899 .... **NCLC 3**
See also DLB 192

Beddoes, Thomas Lovell 1803-1849 **NCLC 3**
See also DLB 96

Bede c. 673-735 .... **CMLC 20**
See also DLB 146

Bedford, Donald F.
See Fearing, Kenneth (Flexner)

Beecher, Catharine Esther 1800-1878 **NCLC 30**
See also DLB 1

Beecher, John 1904-1980 .... **CLC 6**
See also AITN 1; CA 5-8R; 105; CANR 8

Beer, Johann 1655-1700 .... **LC 5**
See also DLB 168

Beer, Patricia 1924- .... **CLC 58**
See also CA 61-64; CANR 13, 46; DLB 40

Beerbohm, Max
See Beerbohm, (Henry) Max(imilian)

Beerbohm, (Henry) Max(imilian) 1872-1956 **TCLC 1, 24**
See also CA 104; 154; DLB 34, 100

Beer-Hofmann, Richard 1866-1945 **TCLC 60**
See also CA 160; DLB 81

Begiebing, Robert J(ohn) 1946- .... **CLC 70**
See also CA 122; CANR 40

Behan, Brendan 1923-1964 **CLC 1, 8, 11, 15, 79; DAM DRAM**
See also CA 73-76; CANR 33; CDBLB 1945-1960; DLB 13; MTCW 1

Behn, Aphra 1640(?)-1689 **LC 1, 30, 42; DA; DAB; DAC; DAM DRAM, MST, NOV, POET; DC 4; PC 13; WLC**
See also DLB 39, 80, 131

Behrman, S(amuel) N(athaniel) 1893-1973 **CLC 40**
See also CA 13-16; 45-48; CAP 1; DLB 7, 44

Belasco, David 1853-1931 .... **TCLC 3**
See also CA 104; 168; DLB 7

Belcheva, Elisaveta 1893- .... **CLC 10**

Bessie, Alvah 1904-1985 .... **CLC 23**
See also CA 5-8R; 116; CANR 2; DLB 26
Bethlen, T. D.
See Silverberg, Robert
Beti, Mongo ... **CLC 27; BLC 1; DAM MULT**
See also Biyidi, Alexandre
Betjeman, John 1906-1984 **CLC 2, 6, 10, 34, 43; DAB; DAM MST, POET**
See also CA 9-12R; 112; CANR 33, 56; CDBLB 1945-1960; DLB 20; DLBY 84; MTCW 1
Bettelheim, Bruno 1903-1990 .... **CLC 79**
See also CA 81-84; 131; CANR 23, 61; MTCW 1
Betti, Ugo 1892-1953 .... **TCLC 5**
See also CA 104; 155
Betts, Doris (Waugh) 1932- ...... **CLC 3, 6, 28**
See also CA 13-16R; CANR 9, 66; DLBY 82; INT CANR-9
Bevan, Alistair
See Roberts, Keith (John Kingston)
Bey, Pilaff
See Douglas, (George) Norman
Bialik, Chaim Nachman 1873-1934 **TCLC 25**
See also CA 170
Bickerstaff, Isaac
See Swift, Jonathan
Bidart, Frank 1939- .... **CLC 33**
See also CA 140
Bienek, Horst 1930- .... **CLC 7, 11**
See also CA 73-76; DLB 75
Bierce, Ambrose (Gwinett) 1842-1914(?) **TCLC 1, 7, 44; DA; DAC; DAM MST; SSC 9; WLC**
See also CA 104; 139; CDALB 1865-1917; DLB 11, 12, 23, 71, 74, 186
Biggers, Earl Derr 1884-1933 .... **TCLC 65**
See also CA 108; 153
Billings, Josh
See Shaw, Henry Wheeler
Billington, (Lady) Rachel (Mary) 1942- **C L C 43**
See also AITN 2; CA 33-36R; CANR 44
Binyon, T(imothy) J(ohn) 1936- .... **CLC 34**
See also CA 111; CANR 28
Bioy Casares, Adolfo 1914-1984 **CLC 4, 8, 13, 88; DAM MULT; HLC; SSC 17**
See also CA 29-32R; CANR 19, 43, 66; DLB 113; HW; MTCW 1
Bird, Cordwainer
See Ellison, Harlan (Jay)
Bird, Robert Montgomery 1806-1854 **NCLC 1**
See also DLB 202
Birkerts, Sven 1951- .... **CLC 116**
See also CA 128; 133; CAAS 29; INT 133
Birney, (Alfred) Earle 1904-1995 **CLC 1, 4, 6, 11; DAC; DAM MST, POET**
See also CA 1-4R; CANR 5, 20; DLB 88; MTCW 1
Biruni, al 973-1048(?) .... **CMLC 28**
Bishop, Elizabeth 1911-1979 **CLC 1, 4, 9, 13, 15, 32; DA; DAC; DAM MST, POET; PC 3**
See also CA 5-8R; 89-92; CABS 2; CANR 26, 61; CDALB 1968-1988; DLB 5, 169; MTCW 1; SATA-Obit 24
Bishop, John 1935- .... **CLC 10**
See also CA 105
Bissett, Bill 1939- .... **CLC 18; PC 14**
See also CA 69-72; CAAS 19; CANR 15; DLB 53; MTCW 1
Bitov, Andrei (Georgievich) 1937- ... **CLC 57**
See also CA 142
Biyidi, Alexandre 1932-
See Beti, Mongo
See also BW 1; CA 114; 124; MTCW 1
Bjarme, Brynjolf
See Ibsen, Henrik (Johan)

Bjoernson, Bjoernstjerne (Martinius) 1832-1910 .... **TCLC 7, 37**
See also CA 104
Black, Robert
See Holdstock, Robert P.
Blackburn, Paul 1926-1971 .... **CLC 9, 43**
See also CA 81-84; 33-36R; CANR 34; DLB 16; DLBY 81
Black Elk 1863-1950 **TCLC 33; DAM MULT**
See also CA 144; NNAL
Black Hobart
See Sanders, (James) Ed(ward)
Blacklin, Malcolm
See Chambers, Aidan
Blackmore, R(ichard) D(oddridge) 1825-1900 **TCLC 27**
See also CA 120; DLB 18
Blackmur, R(ichard) P(almer) 1904-1965 **CLC 2, 24**
See also CA 11-12; 25-28R; CANR 71; CAP 1; DLB 63
Black Tarantula
See Acker, Kathy
Blackwood, Algernon (Henry) 1869-1951 **TCLC 5**
See also CA 105; 150; DLB 153, 156, 178
Blackwood, Caroline 1931-1996 **CLC 6, 9, 100**
See also CA 85-88; 151; CANR 32, 61, 65; DLB 14, 207; MTCW 1
Blade, Alexander
See Hamilton, Edmond; Silverberg, Robert
Blaga, Lucian 1895-1961 .... **CLC 75**
See also CA 157
Blair, Eric (Arthur) 1903-1950
See Orwell, George
See also CA 104; 132; DA; DAB; DAC; DAM MST, NOV; MTCW 1; SATA 29
Blair, Hugh 1718-1800 .... **NCLC 75**
Blais, Marie-Claire 1939- **CLC 2, 4, 6, 13, 22; DAC; DAM MST**
See also CA 21-24R; CAAS 4; CANR 38, 75; DLB 53; MTCW 1
Blaise, Clark 1940- .... **CLC 29**
See also AITN 2; CA 53-56; CAAS 3; CANR 5, 66; DLB 53
Blake, Fairley
See De Voto, Bernard (Augustine)
Blake, Nicholas
See Day Lewis, C(ecil)
See also DLB 77
Blake, William 1757-1827 . **NCLC 13, 37, 57; DA; DAB; DAC; DAM MST, POET; PC 12; WLC**
See also CDBLB 1789-1832; CLR 52; DLB 93, 163; MAICYA; SATA 30
Blasco Ibanez, Vicente 1867-1928 **TCLC 12; DAM NOV**
See also CA 110; 131; HW; MTCW 1
Blatty, William Peter 1928- **CLC 2; DAM POP**
See also CA 5-8R; CANR 9
Bleeck, Oliver
See Thomas, Ross (Elmore)
Blessing, Lee 1949- .... **CLC 54**
Blish, James (Benjamin) 1921-1975 . **CLC 14**
See also CA 1-4R; 57-60; CANR 3; DLB 8; MTCW 1; SATA 66
Bliss, Reginald
See Wells, H(erbert) G(eorge)
Blixen, Karen (Christentze Dinesen) 1885-1962
See Dinesen, Isak
See also CA 25-28; CANR 22, 50; CAP 2; MTCW 1; SATA 44
Bloch, Robert (Albert) 1917-1994 .... **CLC 33**
See also CA 5-8R; 146; CAAS 20; CANR 5; DLB 44; INT CANR-5; SATA 12; SATA-Obit 82
Blok, Alexander (Alexandrovich) 1880-1921

TCLC 5; PC 21
See also CA 104
Blom, Jan
See Breytenbach, Breyten
Bloom, Harold 1930- .... **CLC 24, 103**
See also CA 13-16R; CANR 39, 75; DLB 67
Bloomfield, Aurelius
See Bourne, Randolph S(illiman)
Blount, Roy (Alton), Jr. 1941- .... **CLC 38**
See also CA 53-56; CANR 10, 28, 61; INT CANR-28; MTCW 1
Bloy, Leon 1846-1917 .... **TCLC 22**
See also CA 121; DLB 123
Blume, Judy (Sussman) 1938- ... **CLC 12, 30; DAM NOV, POP**
See also AAYA 3, 26; CA 29-32R; CANR 13, 37, 66; CLR 2, 15; DLB 52; JRDA; MAICYA; MTCW 1; SATA 2, 31, 79
Blunden, Edmund (Charles) 1896-1974 **C L C 2, 56**
See also CA 17-18; 45-48; CANR 54; CAP 2; DLB 20, 100, 155; MTCW 1
Bly, Robert (Elwood) 1926- **CLC 1, 2, 5, 10, 15, 38; DAM POET**
See also CA 5-8R; CANR 41, 73; DLB 5; MTCW 1
Boas, Franz 1858-1942 .... **TCLC 56**
See also CA 115
Bobette
See Simenon, Georges (Jacques Christian)
Boccaccio, Giovanni 1313-1375 ... **CMLC 13; SSC 10**
Bochco, Steven 1943- .... **CLC 35**
See also AAYA 11; CA 124; 138
Bodel, Jean 1167(?)-1210 .... **CMLC 28**
Bodenheim, Maxwell 1892-1954 .... **TCLC 44**
See also CA 110; DLB 9, 45
Bodker, Cecil 1927- .... **CLC 21**
See also CA 73-76; CANR 13, 44; CLR 23; MAICYA; SATA 14
Boell, Heinrich (Theodor) 1917-1985 **CLC 2, 3, 6, 9, 11, 15, 27, 32, 72; DA; DAB; DAC; DAM MST, NOV; SSC 23; WLC**
See also CA 21-24R; 116; CANR 24; DLB 69; DLBY 85; MTCW 1
Boerne, Alfred
See Doeblin, Alfred
Boethius 480(?)-524(?) .... **CMLC 15**
See also DLB 115
Bogan, Louise 1897-1970 . **CLC 4, 39, 46, 93; DAM POET; PC 12**
See also CA 73-76; 25-28R; CANR 33; DLB 45, 169; MTCW 1
Bogarde, Dirk .... **CLC 19**
See also Van Den Bogarde, Derek Jules Gaspard Ulric Niven
See also DLB 14
Bogosian, Eric 1953- .... **CLC 45**
See also CA 138
Bograd, Larry 1953- .... **CLC 35**
See also CA 93-96; CANR 57; SAAS 21; SATA 33, 89
Boiardo, Matteo Maria 1441-1494 .... **LC 6**
Boileau-Despreaux, Nicolas 1636-1711 . **LC 3**
Bojer, Johan 1872-1959 .... **TCLC 64**
Boland, Eavan (Aisling) 1944- .. **CLC 40, 67, 113; DAM POET**
See also CA 143; CANR 61; DLB 40
Boll, Heinrich
See Boell, Heinrich (Theodor)
Bolt, Lee
See Faust, Frederick (Schiller)
Bolt, Robert (Oxton) 1924-1995 ..... **CLC 14; DAM DRAM**
See also CA 17-20R; 147; CANR 35, 67; DLB 13; MTCW 1
Bombet, Louis-Alexandre-Cesar

See Stendhal
Bomkauf
  See Kaufman, Bob (Garnell)
Bonaventura .... **NCLC 35**
  See also DLB 90
Bond, Edward 1934- **CLC 4, 6, 13, 23; DAM DRAM**
  See also CA 25-28R; CANR 38, 67; DLB 13; MTCW 1
Bonham, Frank 1914-1989 .... **CLC 12**
  See also AAYA 1; CA 9-12R; CANR 4, 36; JRDA; MAICYA; SAAS 3; SATA 1, 49; SATA-Obit 62
Bonnefoy, Yves 1923- ... **CLC 9, 15, 58; DAM MST, POET**
  See also CA 85-88; CANR 33, 75; MTCW 1
Bontemps, Arna(ud Wendell) 1902-1973 **C L C 1, 18; BLC 1; DAM MULT, NOV, POET**
  See also BW 1; CA 1-4R; 41-44R; CANR 4, 35; CLR 6; DLB 48, 51; JRDA; MAICYA; MTCW 1; SATA 2, 44; SATA-Obit 24
Booth, Martin 1944- .... **CLC 13**
  See also CA 93-96; CAAS 2
Booth, Philip 1925- .... **CLC 23**
  See also CA 5-8R; CANR 5; DLBY 82
Booth, Wayne C(layson) 1921- .... **CLC 24**
  See also CA 1-4R; CAAS 5; CANR 3, 43; DLB 67
Borchert, Wolfgang 1921-1947 .... **TCLC 5**
  See also CA 104; DLB 69, 124
Borel, Petrus 1809-1859 .... **NCLC 41**
Borges, Jorge Luis 1899-1986 **CLC 1, 2, 3, 4, 6, 8, 9, 10, 13, 19, 44, 48, 83; DA; DAB; DAC; DAM MST, MULT; HLC; PC 22; SSC 4; WLC**
  See also AAYA 26; CA 21-24R; CANR 19, 33, 75; DLB 113; DLBY 86; HW; MTCW 1
Borowski, Tadeusz 1922-1951 .... **TCLC 9**
  See also CA 106; 154
Borrow, George (Henry) 1803-1881 **NCLC 9**
  See also DLB 21, 55, 166
Bosman, Herman Charles 1905-1951 **T C L C 49**
  See also Malan, Herman
  See also CA 160
Bosschere, Jean de 1878(?)-1953 ... **TCLC 19**
  See also CA 115
Boswell, James 1740-1795 . **LC 4; DA; DAB; DAC; DAM MST; WLC**
  See also CDBLB 1660-1789; DLB 104, 142
Bottoms, David 1949- .... **CLC 53**
  See also CA 105; CANR 22; DLB 120; DLBY 83
Boucicault, Dion 1820-1890 .... **NCLC 41**
Boucolon, Maryse 1937(?)-
  See Conde, Maryse
  See also CA 110; CANR 30, 53, 76
Bourget, Paul (Charles Joseph) 1852-1935 **TCLC 12**
  See also CA 107; DLB 123
Bourjaily, Vance (Nye) 1922- .... **CLC 8, 62**
  See also CA 1-4R; CAAS 1; CANR 2, 72; DLB 2, 143
Bourne, Randolph S(illiman) 1886-1918 **TCLC 16**
  See also CA 117; 155; DLB 63
Bova, Ben(jamin William) 1932- ...... **CLC 45**
  See also AAYA 16; CA 5-8R; CAAS 18; CANR 11, 56; CLR 3; DLBY 81; INT CANR-11; MAICYA; MTCW 1; SATA 6, 68
Bowen, Elizabeth (Dorothea Cole) 1899-1973 **CLC 1, 3, 6, 11, 15, 22, 118; DAM NOV; SSC 3, 28**
  See also CA 17-18; 41-44R; CANR 35; CAP 2; CDBLB 1945-1960; DLB 15, 162; MTCW 1
Bowering, George 1935- .... **CLC 15, 47**

See also CA 21-24R; CAAS 16; CANR 10; DLB 53
Bowering, Marilyn R(uthe) 1949- .... **CLC 32**
  See also CA 101; CANR 49
Bowers, Edgar 1924- .... **CLC 9**
  See also CA 5-8R; CANR 24; DLB 5
Bowie, David .... **CLC 17**
  See also Jones, David Robert
Bowles, Jane (Sydney) 1917-1973 **CLC 3, 68**
  See also CA 19-20; 41-44R; CAP 2
Bowles, Paul (Frederick) 1910- **CLC 1, 2, 19, 53; SSC 3**
  See also CA 1-4R; CAAS 1; CANR 1, 19, 50, 75; DLB 5, 6; MTCW 1
Box, Edgar
  See Vidal, Gore
Boyd, Nancy
  See Millay, Edna St. Vincent
Boyd, William 1952- .... **CLC 28, 53, 70**
  See also CA 114; 120; CANR 51, 71
Boyle, Kay 1902-1992 **CLC 1, 5, 19, 58; SSC 5**
  See also CA 13-16R; 140; CAAS 1; CANR 29, 61; DLB 4, 9, 48, 86; DLBY 93; MTCW 1
Boyle, Mark
  See Kienzle, William X(avier)
Boyle, Patrick 1905-1982 .... **CLC 19**
  See also CA 127
Boyle, T. C. 1948-
  See Boyle, T(homas) Coraghessan
Boyle, T(homas) Coraghessan 1948- **CLC 36, 55, 90; DAM POP; SSC 16**
  See also BEST 90:4; CA 120; CANR 44, 76; DLBY 86
Boz
  See Dickens, Charles (John Huffam)
Brackenridge, Hugh Henry 1748-1816 **N C L C 7**
  See also DLB 11, 37
Bradbury, Edward P.
  See Moorcock, Michael (John)
Bradbury, Malcolm (Stanley) 1932- **CLC 32, 61; DAM NOV**
  See also CA 1-4R; CANR 1, 33; DLB 14, 207; MTCW 1
Bradbury, Ray (Douglas) 1920- **CLC 1, 3, 10, 15, 42, 98; DA; DAB; DAC; DAM MST, NOV, POP; SSC 29; WLC**
  See also AAYA 15; AITN 1, 2; CA 1-4R; CANR 2, 30, 75; CDALB 1968-1988; DLB 2, 8; MTCW 1; SATA 11, 64
Bradford, Gamaliel 1863-1932 ...... **TCLC 36**
  See also CA 160; DLB 17
Bradley, David (Henry), Jr. 1950- ... **CLC 23, 118; BLC 1; DAM MULT**
  See also BW 1; CA 104; CANR 26; DLB 33
Bradley, John Ed(mund, Jr.) 1958- .. **CLC 55**
  See also CA 139
Bradley, Marion Zimmer 1930- **CLC 30; DAM POP**
  See also AAYA 9; CA 57-60; CAAS 10; CANR 7, 31, 51, 75; DLB 8; MTCW 1; SATA 90
Bradstreet, Anne 1612(?)-1672 **LC 4, 30; DA; DAC; DAM MST, POET; PC 10**
  See also CDALB 1640-1865; DLB 24
Brady, Joan 1939- .... **CLC 86**
  See also CA 141
Bragg, Melvyn 1939- .... **CLC 10**
  See also BEST 89:3; CA 57-60; CANR 10, 48; DLB 14
Brahe, Tycho 1546-1601 .... **LC 45**
Braine, John (Gerard) 1922-1986 **CLC 1, 3, 41**
  See also CA 1-4R; 120; CANR 1, 33; CDBLB 1945-1960; DLB 15; DLBY 86; MTCW 1
Bramah, Ernest 1868-1942 .... **TCLC 72**
  See also CA 156; DLB 70
Brammer, William 1930(?)-1978 .... **CLC 31**
  See also CA 77-80

Brancati, Vitaliano 1907-1954 .... **TCLC 12**
  See also CA 109
Brancato, Robin F(idler) 1936- .... **CLC 35**
  See also AAYA 9; CA 69-72; CANR 11, 45; CLR 32; JRDA; SAAS 9; SATA 97
Brand, Max
  See Faust, Frederick (Schiller)
Brand, Millen 1906-1980 .... **CLC 7**
  See also CA 21-24R; 97-100; CANR 72
Branden, Barbara .... **CLC 44**
  See also CA 148
Brandes, Georg (Morris Cohen) 1842-1927 **TCLC 10**
  See also CA 105
Brandys, Kazimierz 1916- .... **CLC 62**
Branley, Franklyn M(ansfield) 1915- **CLC 21**
  See also CA 33-36R; CANR 14, 39; CLR 13; MAICYA; SAAS 16; SATA 4, 68
Brathwaite, Edward Kamau 1930- . **CLC 11; BLCS; DAM POET**
  See also BW 2; CA 25-28R; CANR 11, 26, 47; DLB 125
Brautigan, Richard (Gary) 1935-1984 **CLC 1, 3, 5, 9, 12, 34, 42; DAM NOV**
  See also CA 53-56; 113; CANR 34; DLB 2, 5, 206; DLBY 80, 84; MTCW 1; SATA 56
Brave Bird, Mary 1953-
  See Crow Dog, Mary (Ellen)
  See also NNAL
Braverman, Kate 1950- .... **CLC 67**
  See also CA 89-92
Brecht, (Eugen) Bertolt (Friedrich) 1898-1956 **TCLC 1, 6, 13, 35; DA; DAB; DAC; DAM DRAM, MST; DC 3; WLC**
  See also CA 104; 133; CANR 62; DLB 56, 124; MTCW 1
Brecht, Eugen Berthold Friedrich
  See Brecht, (Eugen) Bertolt (Friedrich)
Bremer, Fredrika 1801-1865 .... **NCLC 11**
Brennan, Christopher John 1870-1932 **T C L C 17**
  See also CA 117
Brennan, Maeve 1917-1993 .... **CLC 5**
  See also CA 81-84; CANR 72
Brent, Linda
  See Jacobs, Harriet A(nn)
Brentano, Clemens (Maria) 1778-1842 **N C L C 1**
  See also DLB 90
Brent of Bin Bin
  See Franklin, (Stella Maria Sarah) Miles (Lampe)
Brenton, Howard 1942- .... **CLC 31**
  See also CA 69-72; CANR 33, 67; DLB 13; MTCW 1
Breslin, James 1930-1996
  See Breslin, Jimmy
  See also CA 73-76; CANR 31, 75; DAM NOV; MTCW 1
Breslin, Jimmy .... **CLC 4, 43**
  See also Breslin, James
  See also AITN 1; DLB 185
Bresson, Robert 1901- .... **CLC 16**
  See also CA 110; CANR 49
Breton, Andre 1896-1966 **CLC 2, 9, 15, 54; PC 15**
  See also CA 19-20; 25-28R; CANR 40, 60; CAP 2; DLB 65; MTCW 1
Breytenbach, Breyten 1939(?)- . **CLC 23, 37; DAM POET**
  See also CA 113; 129; CANR 61
Bridgers, Sue Ellen 1942- .... **CLC 26**
  See also AAYA 8; CA 65-68; CANR 11, 36; CLR 18; DLB 52; JRDA; MAICYA; SAAS 1; SATA 22, 90
Bridges, Robert (Seymour) 1844-1930 **T C L C 1; DAM POET**

See also CA 117; 155
Collins, Hunt
See Hunter, Evan
Collins, Linda 1931- .... **CLC 44**
See also CA 125
Collins, (William) Wilkie 1824-1889**NCLC 1, 18**
See also CDBLB 1832-1890; DLB 18, 70, 159
Collins, William 1721-1759 . **LC 4, 40; DAM POET**
See also DLB 109
Collodi, Carlo 1826-1890 .... **NCLC 54**
See also Lorenzini, Carlo
See also CLR 5
Colman, George 1732-1794
See Glassco, John
Colt, Winchester Remington
See Hubbard, L(afayette) Ron(ald)
Colter, Cyrus 1910- .... **CLC 58**
See also BW 1; CA 65-68; CANR 10, 66; DLB 33
Colton, James
See Hansen, Joseph
Colum, Padraic 1881-1972 .... **CLC 28**
See also CA 73-76; 33-36R; CANR 35; CLR 36; MAICYA; MTCW 1; SATA 15
Colvin, James
See Moorcock, Michael (John)
Colwin, Laurie (E.) 1944-1992**CLC 5, 13, 23, 84**
See also CA 89-92; 139; CANR 20, 46; DLBY 80; MTCW 1
Comfort, Alex(ander) 1920-**CLC 7; DAM POP**
See also CA 1-4R; CANR 1, 45
Comfort, Montgomery
See Campbell, (John) Ramsey
Compton-Burnett, I(vy) 1884(?)-1969**CLC 1, 3, 10, 15, 34; DAM NOV**
See also CA 1-4R; 25-28R; CANR 4; DLB 36; MTCW 1
Comstock, Anthony 1844-1915 ...... **TCLC 13**
See also CA 110; 169
Comte, Auguste 1798-1857 .... **NCLC 54**
Conan Doyle, Arthur
See Doyle, Arthur Conan
Conde, Maryse 1937- .... **CLC 52, 92; BLCS; DAM MULT**
See also Boucolon, Maryse
See also BW 2
Condillac, Etienne Bonnot de 1714-1780 **LC 26**
Condon, Richard (Thomas) 1915-1996**CLC 4, 6, 8, 10, 45, 100; DAM NOV**
See also BEST 90:3; CA 1-4R; 151; CAAS 1; CANR 2, 23; INT CANR-23; MTCW 1
Confucius 551B.C.-479B.C. . . **CMLC 19; DA; DAB; DAC; DAM MST; WLCS**
Congreve, William 1670-1729 **LC 5, 21; DA; DAB; DAC; DAM DRAM, MST, POET; DC 2; WLC**
See also CDBLB 1660-1789; DLB 39, 84
Connell, Evan S(helby), Jr. 1924-**CLC 4, 6, 45; DAM NOV**
See also AAYA 7; CA 1-4R; CAAS 2; CANR 2, 39, 76; DLB 2; DLBY 81; MTCW 1
Connelly, Marc(us Cook) 1890-1980 .. **CLC 7**
See also CA 85-88; 102; CANR 30; DLB 7; DLBY 80; SATA-Obit 25
Connor, Ralph .... **TCLC 31**
See also Gordon, Charles William
See also DLB 92
Conrad, Joseph 1857-1924**TCLC 1, 6, 13, 25, 43, 57; DA; DAB; DAC; DAM MST, NOV; SSC 9; WLC**
See also AAYA 26; CA 104; 131; CANR 60; CDBLB 1890-1914; DLB 10, 34, 98, 156; MTCW 1; SATA 27

Conrad, Robert Arnold
See Hart, Moss
Conroy, Pat
See Conroy, (Donald) Pat(rick)
Conroy, (Donald) Pat(rick) 1945-**CLC 30, 74; DAM NOV, POP**
See also AAYA 8; AITN 1; CA 85-88; CANR 24, 53; DLB 6; MTCW 1
Constant (de Rebecque), (Henri) Benjamin 1767-1830 ....
NCLC 6
See also DLB 119
Conybeare, Charles Augustus
See Eliot, T(homas) S(tearns)
Cook, Michael 1933- .... **CLC 58**
See also CA 93-96; CANR 68; DLB 53
Cook, Robin 1940- .... **CLC 14; DAM POP**
See also BEST 90:2; CA 108; 111; CANR 41; INT 111
Cook, Roy
See Silverberg, Robert
Cooke, Elizabeth 1948- .... **CLC 55**
See also CA 129
Cooke, John Esten 1830-1886 .... **NCLC 5**
See also DLB 3
Cooke, John Estes
See Baum, L(yman) Frank
Cooke, M. E.
See Creasey, John
Cooke, Margaret
See Creasey, John
Cook-Lynn, Elizabeth 1930-.. **CLC 93; DAM MULT**
See also CA 133; DLB 175; NNAL
Cooney, Ray .... **CLC 62**
Cooper, Douglas 1960- .... **CLC 86**
Cooper, Henry St. John
See Creasey, John
Cooper, J(oan) California .... **CLC 56; DAM MULT**
See also AAYA 12; BW 1; CA 125; CANR 55
Cooper, James Fenimore 1789-1851**NCLC 1, 27, 54**
See also AAYA 22; CDALB 1640-1865; DLB 3; SATA 19
Coover, Robert (Lowell) 1932- **CLC 3, 7, 15, 32, 46, 87; DAM NOV; SSC 15**
See also CA 45-48; CANR 3, 37, 58; DLB 2; DLBY 81; MTCW 1
Copeland, Stewart (Armstrong) 1952-**CLC 26**
Copernicus, Nicolaus 1473-1543 .... **LC 45**
Coppard, A(lfred) E(dgar) 1878-1957 **T C L C 5; SSC 21**
See also CA 114; 167; DLB 162; YABC 1
Coppee, Francois 1842-1908 .... **TCLC 25**
See also CA 170
Coppola, Francis Ford 1939- .... **CLC 16**
See also CA 77-80; CANR 40; DLB 44
Corbiere, Tristan 1845-1875 .... **NCLC 43**
Corcoran, Barbara 1911- .... **CLC 17**
See also AAYA 14; CA 21-24R; CAAS 2; CANR 11, 28, 48; CLR 50; DLB 52; JRDA; SAAS 20; SATA 3, 77
Cordelier, Maurice
See Giraudoux, (Hippolyte) Jean
Corelli, Marie 1855-1924 .... **TCLC 51**
See also Mackay, Mary
See also DLB 34, 156
Corman, Cid 1924- .... **CLC 9**
See also Corman, Sidney
See also CAAS 2; DLB 5, 193
Corman, Sidney 1924-
See Corman, Cid
See also CA 85-88; CANR 44; DAM POET
Cormier, Robert (Edmund) 1925-**CLC 12, 30; DA; DAB; DAC; DAM MST, NOV**
See also AAYA 3, 19; CA 1-4R; CANR 5, 23,

76; CDALB 1968-1988; CLR 12, 55; DLB 52; INT CANR-23; JRDA; MAICYA; MTCW 1; SATA 10, 45, 83
Corn, Alfred (DeWitt III) 1943- .... **CLC 33**
See also CA 104; CAAS 25; CANR 44; DLB 120; DLBY 80
Corneille, Pierre 1606-1684 .... **LC 28; DAB; DAM MST**
Cornwell, David (John Moore) 1931-**CLC 9, 15; DAM POP**
See also le Carre, John
See also CA 5-8R; CANR 13, 33, 59; MTCW 1
Corso, (Nunzio) Gregory 1930- .... **CLC 1, 11**
See also CA 5-8R; CANR 41, 76; DLB 5, 16; MTCW 1
Cortazar, Julio 1914-1984**CLC 2, 3, 5, 10, 13, 15, 33, 34, 92; DAM MULT, NOV; HLC; SSC 7**
See also CA 21-24R; CANR 12, 32; DLB 113; HW; MTCW 1
CORTES, HERNAN 1484-1547 .... **LC 31**
Corvinus, Jakob
See Raabe, Wilhelm (Karl)
Corwin, Cecil
See Kornbluth, C(yril) M.
Cosic, Dobrica 1921- .... **CLC 14**
See also CA 122; 138; DLB 181
Costain, Thomas B(ertram) 1885-1965 **C L C 30**
See also CA 5-8R; 25-28R; DLB 9
Costantini, Humberto 1924(?)-1987 . **CLC 49**
See also CA 131; 122; HW
Costello, Elvis 1955- .... **CLC 21**
Cotes, Cecil V.
See Duncan, Sara Jeannette
Cotter, Joseph Seamon Sr. 1861-1949 **T C L C 28; BLC 1; DAM MULT**
See also BW 1; CA 124; DLB 50
Couch, Arthur Thomas Quiller
See Quiller-Couch, SirArthur (Thomas)
Coulton, James
See Hansen, Joseph
Couperus, Louis (Marie Anne) 1863-1923 **TCLC 15**
See also CA 115
Coupland, Douglas 1961-**CLC 85; DAC; DAM POP**
See also CA 142; CANR 57
Court, Wesli
See Turco, Lewis (Putnam)
Courtenay, Bryce 1933- .... **CLC 59**
See also CA 138
Courtney, Robert
See Ellison, Harlan (Jay)
Cousteau, Jacques-Yves 1910-1997 .. **CLC 30**
See also CA 65-68; 159; CANR 15, 67; MTCW 1; SATA 38, 98
Coventry, Francis 1725-1754 .... **LC 46**
Cowan, Peter (Walkinshaw) 1914- .... **SSC 28**
See also CA 21-24R; CANR 9, 25, 50
Coward, Noel (Peirce) 1899-1973**CLC 1, 9, 29, 51; DAM DRAM**
See also AITN 1; CA 17-18; 41-44R; CANR 35; CAP 2; CDBLB 1914-1945; DLB 10; MTCW 1
Cowley, Abraham 1618-1667 .... **LC 43**
See also DLB 131, 151
Cowley, Malcolm 1898-1989 .... **CLC 39**
See also CA 5-8R; 128; CANR 3, 55; DLB 4, 48; DLBY 81, 89; MTCW 1
Cowper, William 1731-1800 . **NCLC 8; DAM POET**
See also DLB 104, 109
Cox, William Trevor 1928- .... **CLC 9, 14, 71; DAM NOV**
See also Trevor, William
See also CA 9-12R; CANR 4, 37, 55, 76; DLB

1878-1957
See Dunsany, Lord
See also CA 104; 148; DLB 10
Dunsany, Lord .... **TCLC 2, 59**
See also Dunsany, Edward John Moreton Drax
Plunkett
See also DLB 77, 153, 156
du Perry, Jean
See Simenon, Georges (Jacques Christian)
Durang, Christopher (Ferdinand) 1949-**C L C
27, 38**
See also CA 105; CANR 50, 76
Duras, Marguerite 1914-1996**CLC 3, 6, 11, 20,
34, 40, 68, 100**
See also CA 25-28R; 151; CANR 50; DLB 83;
MTCW 1
Durban, (Rosa) Pam 1947- .... **CLC 39**
See also CA 123
Durcan, Paul 1944-**CLC 43, 70; DAM POET**
See also CA 134
Durkheim, Emile 1858-1917 .... **TCLC 55**
Durrell, Lawrence (George) 1912-1990 **C L C
1, 4, 6, 8, 13, 27, 41; DAM NOV**
See also CA 9-12R; 132; CANR 40; CDBLB
1945-1960; DLB 15, 27, 204; DLBY 90;
MTCW 1
Durrenmatt, Friedrich
See Duerrenmatt, Friedrich
Dutt, Toru 1856-1877 .... **NCLC 29**
Dwight, Timothy 1752-1817 .... **NCLC 13**
See also DLB 37
Dworkin, Andrea 1946- .... **CLC 43**
See also CA 77-80; CAAS 21; CANR 16, 39,
76; INT CANR-16; MTCW 1
Dwyer, Deanna
See Koontz, Dean R(ay)
Dwyer, K. R.
See Koontz, Dean R(ay)
Dwyer, Thomas A. 1923- .... **CLC 114**
See also CA 115
Dye, Richard
See De Voto, Bernard (Augustine)
Dylan, Bob 1941- .... **CLC 3, 4, 6, 12, 77**
See also CA 41-44R; DLB 16
Eagleton, Terence (Francis) 1943-
See Eagleton, Terry
See also CA 57-60; CANR 7, 23, 68; MTCW 1
Eagleton, Terry .... **CLC 63**
See also Eagleton, Terence (Francis)
Early, Jack
See Scoppettone, Sandra
East, Michael
See West, Morris L(anglo)
Eastaway, Edward
See Thomas, (Philip) Edward
Eastlake, William (Derry) 1917-1997 **CLC 8**
See also CA 5-8R; 158; CAAS 1; CANR 5, 63;
DLB 6, 206; INT CANR-5
Eastman, Charles A(lexander) 1858-1939
TCLC 55; DAM MULT
See also DLB 175; NNAL; YABC 1
Eberhart, Richard (Ghormley) 1904-**CLC 3,
11, 19, 56; DAM POET**
See also CA 1-4R; CANR 2; CDALB 1941-
1968; DLB 48; MTCW 1
Eberstadt, Fernanda 1960-................ **CLC 39**
See also CA 136; CANR 69
Echegaray (y Eizaguirre), Jose (Maria Waldo)
1832-1916 .... **TCLC 4**
See also CA 104; CANR 32; HW; MTCW 1
Echeverria, (Jose) Esteban (Antonino) 1805-
1851 .... **NCLC 18**
Echo
See Proust, (Valentin-Louis-George-Eugene-)
Marcel
Eckert, Allan W. 1931- .... **CLC 17**
See also AAYA 18; CA 13-16R; CANR 14, 45;

INT CANR-14; SAAS 21; SATA 29, 91;
SATA-Brief 27
Eckhart, Meister 1260(?)-1328(?) ... **CMLC 9**
See also DLB 115
Eckmar, F. R.
See de Hartog, Jan
Eco, Umberto 1932-**CLC 28, 60; DAM NOV,
POP**
See also BEST 90:1; CA 77-80; CANR 12, 33,
55; DLB 196; MTCW 1
Eddison, E(ric) R(ucker) 1882-1945**TCLC 15**
See also CA 109; 156
Eddy, Mary (Morse) Baker 1821-1910**T C L C
71**
See also CA 113
Edel, (Joseph) Leon 1907-1997 .. **CLC 29, 34**
See also CA 1-4R; 161; CANR 1, 22; DLB 103;
INT CANR-22
Eden, Emily 1797-1869 .... **NCLC 10**
Edgar, David 1948- ... **CLC 42; DAM DRAM**
See also CA 57-60; CANR 12, 61; DLB 13;
MTCW 1
Edgerton, Clyde (Carlyle) 1944- ...... **CLC 39**
See also AAYA 17; CA 118; 134; CANR 64;
INT 134
Edgeworth, Maria 1768-1849 .... **NCLC 1, 51**
See also DLB 116, 159, 163; SATA 21
Edmonds, Paul
See Kuttner, Henry
Edmonds, Walter D(umaux) 1903-1998 **C L C
35**
See also CA 5-8R; CANR 2; DLB 9; MAICYA;
SAAS 4; SATA 1, 27; SATA-Obit 99
Edmondson, Wallace
See Ellison, Harlan (Jay)
Edson, Russell .... **CLC 13**
See also CA 33-36R
Edwards, Bronwen Elizabeth
See Rose, Wendy
Edwards, G(erald) B(asil) 1899-1976**CLC 25**
See also CA 110
Edwards, Gus 1939- .... **CLC 43**
See also CA 108; INT 108
Edwards, Jonathan 1703-1758 .... **LC 7; DA;
DAC; DAM MST**
See also DLB 24
Efron, Marina Ivanovna Tsvetaeva
See Tsvetaeva (Efron), Marina (Ivanovna)
Ehle, John (Marsden, Jr.) 1925- .... **CLC 27**
See also CA 9-12R
Ehrenburg, Ilya (Grigoryevich)
See Ehrenburg, Ilya (Grigoryevich)
Ehrenburg, Ilya (Grigoryevich) 1891-1967
CLC 18, 34, 62
See also CA 102; 25-28R
Ehrenburg, Ilyo (Grigoryevich)
See Ehrenburg, Ilya (Grigoryevich)
Ehrenreich, Barbara 1941- .... **CLC 110**
See also BEST 90:4; CA 73-76; CANR 16, 37,
62; MTCW 1
Eich, Guenter 1907-1972 .... **CLC 15**
See also CA 111; 93-96; DLB 69, 124
Eichendorff, Joseph Freiherr von 1788-1857
NCLC 8
See also DLB 90
Eigner, Larry .... **CLC 9**
See also Eigner, Laurence (Joel)
See also CAAS 23; DLB 5
Eigner, Laurence (Joel) 1927-1996
See Eigner, Larry
See also CA 9-12R; 151; CANR 6; DLB 193
Einstein, Albert 1879-1955 .... **TCLC 65**
See also CA 121; 133; MTCW 1
Eiseley, Loren Corey 1907-1977 .... **CLC 7**
See also AAYA 5; CA 1-4R; 73-76; CANR 6;
DLBD 17
Eisenstadt, Jill 1963- .... **CLC 50**

See also CA 140
Eisenstein, Sergei (Mikhailovich) 1898-1948
TCLC 57
See also CA 114; 149
Eisner, Simon
See Kornbluth, C(yril) M.
Ekeloef, (Bengt) Gunnar 1907-1968 **CLC 27;
DAM POET; PC 23**
See also CA 123; 25-28R
Ekelof, (Bengt) Gunnar
See Ekeloef, (Bengt) Gunnar
Ekelund, Vilhelm 1880-1949 .... **TCLC 75**
Ekwensi, C. O. D.
See Ekwensi, Cyprian (Odiatu Duaka)
Ekwensi, Cyprian (Odiatu Duaka) 1921-**CLC
4; BLC 1; DAM MULT**
See also BW 2; CA 29-32R; CANR 18, 42, 74;
DLB 117; MTCW 1; SATA 66
Elaine .... **TCLC 18**
See also Leverson, Ada
El Crummo
See Crumb, R(obert)
Elder, Lonne III 1931-1996 .... **DC 8**
See also BLC 1; BW 1; CA 81-84; 152; CANR
25; DAM MULT; DLB 7, 38, 44
Elia
See Lamb, Charles
Eliade, Mircea 1907-1986 .... **CLC 19**
See also CA 65-68; 119; CANR 30, 62; MTCW
1
Eliot, A. D.
See Jewett, (Theodora) Sarah Orne
Eliot, Alice
See Jewett, (Theodora) Sarah Orne
Eliot, Dan
See Silverberg, Robert
Eliot, George 1819-1880 **NCLC 4, 13, 23, 41,
49; DA; DAB; DAC; DAM MST, NOV; PC
20; WLC**
See also CDBLB 1832-1890; DLB 21, 35, 55
Eliot, John 1604-1690 .... **LC 5**
See also DLB 24
Eliot, T(homas) S(tearns) 1888-1965**CLC 1, 2,
3, 6, 9, 10, 13, 15, 24, 34, 41, 55, 57, 113;
DA; DAB; DAC; DAM DRAM, MST,
POET; PC 5; WLC**
See also CA 5-8R; 25-28R; CANR 41; CDALB
1929-1941; DLB 7, 10, 45, 63; DLBY 88;
MTCW 1
Elizabeth 1866-1941 .... **TCLC 41**
Elkin, Stanley L(awrence) 1930-1995 **CLC 4,
6, 9, 14, 27, 51, 91; DAM NOV, POP; SSC
12**
See also CA 9-12R; 148; CANR 8, 46; DLB 2,
28; DLBY 80; INT CANR-8; MTCW 1
Elledge, Scott .... **CLC 34**
Elliot, Don
See Silverberg, Robert
Elliott, Don
See Silverberg, Robert
Elliott, George P(aul) 1918-1980 .... **CLC 2**
See also CA 1-4R; 97-100; CANR 2
Elliott, Janice 1931-............................ **CLC 47**
See also CA 13-16R; CANR 8, 29; DLB 14
Elliott, Sumner Locke 1917-1991 ..... **CLC 38**
See also CA 5-8R; 134; CANR 2, 21
Elliott, William
See Bradbury, Ray (Douglas)
Ellis, A. E. .... **CLC 7**
Ellis, Alice Thomas .... **CLC 40**
See also Haycraft, Anna
See also DLB 194
Ellis, Bret Easton 1964-**CLC 39, 71, 117; DAM
POP**
See also AAYA 2; CA 118; 123; CANR 51, 74;
INT 123
Ellis, (Henry) Havelock 1859-1939 **TCLC 14**

Farrell, James T(homas) 1904-1979**CLC 1, 4, 8, 11, 66; SSC 28**
See also CA 5-8R; 89-92; CANR 9, 61; DLB 4, 9, 86; DLBD 2; MTCW 1
Farren, Richard J.
See Betjeman, John
Farren, Richard M.
See Betjeman, John
Fassbinder, Rainer Werner 1946-1982**CLC 20**
See also CA 93-96; 106; CANR 31
Fast, Howard (Melvin) 1914- **CLC 23; DAM NOV**
See also AAYA 16; CA 1-4R; CAAS 18; CANR 1, 33, 54, 75; DLB 9; INT CANR-33; SATA 7
Faulcon, Robert
See Holdstock, Robert P.
Faulkner, William (Cuthbert) 1897-1962**CLC 1, 3, 6, 8, 9, 11, 14, 18, 28, 52, 68; DA; DAB; DAC; DAM MST, NOV; SSC 1; WLC**
See also AAYA 7; CA 81-84; CANR 33; CDALB 1929-1941; DLB 9, 11, 44, 102; DLBD 2; DLBY 86, 97; MTCW 1
Fauset, Jessie Redmon 1884(?)-1961**CLC 19, 54; BLC 2; DAM MULT**
See also BW 1; CA 109; DLB 51
Faust, Frederick (Schiller) 1892-1944(?)
TCLC 49; DAM POP
See also CA 108; 152
Faust, Irvin 1924- .... **CLC 8**
See also CA 33-36R; CANR 28, 67; DLB 2, 28; DLBY 80
Fawkes, Guy
See Benchley, Robert (Charles)
Fearing, Kenneth (Flexner) 1902-1961 . **C L C 51**
See also CA 93-96; CANR 59; DLB 9
Fecamps, Elise
See Creasey, John
Federman, Raymond 1928- .... **CLC 6, 47**
See also CA 17-20R; CAAS 8; CANR 10, 43; DLBY 80
Federspiel, J(uerg) F. 1931- .... **CLC 42**
See also CA 146
Feiffer, Jules (Ralph) 1929- ..... **CLC 2, 8, 64; DAM DRAM**
See also AAYA 3; CA 17-20R; CANR 30, 59; DLB 7, 44; INT CANR-30; MTCW 1; SATA 8, 61
Feige, Hermann Albert Otto Maximilian
See Traven, B.
Feinberg, David B. 1956-1994 .... **CLC 59**
See also CA 135; 147
Feinstein, Elaine 1930- .... **CLC 36**
See also CA 69-72; CAAS 1; CANR 31, 68; DLB 14, 40; MTCW 1
Feldman, Irving (Mordecai) 1928- ..... **CLC 7**
See also CA 1-4R; CANR 1; DLB 169
Felix-Tchicaya, Gerald
See Tchicaya, Gerald Felix
Fellini, Federico 1920-1993 .... **CLC 16, 85**
See also CA 65-68; 143; CANR 33
Felsen, Henry Gregor 1916- .... **CLC 17**
See also CA 1-4R; CANR 1; SAAS 2; SATA 1
Fenno, Jack
See Calisher, Hortense
Fenollosa, Ernest (Francisco) 1853-1908
TCLC 91
Fenton, James Martin 1949- .... **CLC 32**
See also CA 102; DLB 40
Ferber, Edna 1887-1968 .... **CLC 18, 93**
See also AITN 1; CA 5-8R; 25-28R; CANR 68; DLB 9, 28, 86; MTCW 1; SATA 7
Ferguson, Helen
See Kavan, Anna
Ferguson, Samuel 1810-1886 .... **NCLC 33**
See also DLB 32

Fergusson, Robert 1750-1774 .... **LC 29**
See also DLB 109
Ferling, Lawrence
See Ferlinghetti, Lawrence (Monsanto)
Ferlinghetti, Lawrence (Monsanto) 1919(?)-
CLC 2, 6, 10, 27, 111; DAM POET; PC 1
See also CA 5-8R; CANR 3, 41, 73; CDALB 1941-1968; DLB 5, 16; MTCW 1
Fernandez, Vicente Garcia Huidobro
See Huidobro Fernandez, Vicente Garcia
Ferrer, Gabriel (Francisco Victor) Miro
See Miro (Ferrer), Gabriel (Francisco Victor)
Ferrier, Susan (Edmonstone) 1782-1854
NCLC 8
See also DLB 116
Ferrigno, Robert 1948(?)- .... **CLC 65**
See also CA 140
Ferron, Jacques 1921-1985 .... **CLC 94; DAC**
See also CA 117; 129; DLB 60
Feuchtwanger, Lion 1884-1958 .... **TCLC 3**
See also CA 104; DLB 66
Feuillet, Octave 1821-1890 .... **NCLC 45**
See also DLB 192
Feydeau, Georges (Leon Jules Marie) 1862-1921 .... **TCLC 22; DAM DRAM**
See also CA 113; 152; DLB 192
Fichte, Johann Gottlieb 1762-1814**NCLC 62**
See also DLB 90
Ficino, Marsilio 1433-1499 .... **LC 12**
Fiedeler, Hans
See Doeblin, Alfred
Fiedler, Leslie A(aron) 1917- . **CLC 4, 13, 24**
See also CA 9-12R; CANR 7, 63; DLB 28, 67; MTCW 1
Field, Andrew 1938- .... **CLC 44**
See also CA 97-100; CANR 25
Field, Eugene 1850-1895 .... **NCLC 3**
See also DLB 23, 42, 140; DLBD 13; MAICYA; SATA 16
Field, Gans T.
See Wellman, Manly Wade
Field, Michael 1915-1971 .... **TCLC 43**
See also CA 29-32R
Field, Peter
See Hobson, Laura Z(ametkin)
Fielding, Henry 1707-1754 ..... **LC 1, 46; DA; DAB; DAC; DAM DRAM, MST, NOV; WLC**
See also CDBLB 1660-1789; DLB 39, 84, 101
Fielding, Sarah 1710-1768 .... **LC 1, 44**
See also DLB 39
Fields, W. C. 1880-1946 .... **TCLC 80**
See also DLB 44
Fierstein, Harvey (Forbes) 1954- ... **CLC 33; DAM DRAM, POP**
See also CA 123; 129
Figes, Eva 1932- .... **CLC 31**
See also CA 53-56; CANR 4, 44; DLB 14
Finch, Anne 1661-1720 .... **LC 3; PC 21**
See also DLB 95
Finch, Robert (Duer Claydon) 1900- **CLC 18**
See also CA 57-60; CANR 9, 24, 49; DLB 88
Findley, Timothy 1930- . **CLC 27, 102; DAC; DAM MST**
See also CA 25-28R; CANR 12, 42, 69; DLB 53
Fink, William
See Mencken, H(enry) L(ouis)
Firbank, Louis 1942-
See Reed, Lou
See also CA 117
Firbank, (Arthur Annesley) Ronald 1886-1926
TCLC 1
See also CA 104; DLB 36
Fisher, Dorothy (Frances) Canfield 1879-1958
TCLC 87
See also CA 114; 136; DLB 9, 102; MAICYA;

YABC 1
Fisher, M(ary) F(rances) K(ennedy) 1908-1992
CLC 76, 87
See also CA 77-80; 138; CANR 44
Fisher, Roy 1930- .... **CLC 25**
See also CA 81-84; CAAS 10; CANR 16; DLB 40
Fisher, Rudolph 1897-1934**TCLC 11; BLC 2; DAM MULT; SSC 25**
See also BW 1; CA 107; 124; DLB 51, 102
Fisher, Vardis (Alvero) 1895-1968 ...... **CLC 7**
See also CA 5-8R; 25-28R; CANR 68; DLB 9, 206
Fiske, Tarleton
See Bloch, Robert (Albert)
Fitch, Clarke
See Sinclair, Upton (Beall)
Fitch, John IV
See Cormier, Robert (Edmund)
Fitzgerald, Captain Hugh
See Baum, L(yman) Frank
FitzGerald, Edward 1809-1883 .... **NCLC 9**
See also DLB 32
Fitzgerald, F(rancis) Scott (Key) 1896-1940
TCLC 1, 6, 14, 28, 55; DA; DAB; DAC; DAM MST, NOV; SSC 6, 31; WLC
See also AAYA 24; AITN 1; CA 110; 123; CDALB 1917-1929; DLB 4, 9, 86; DLBD 1, 15, 16; DLBY 81, 96; MTCW 1
Fitzgerald, Penelope 1916- ... **CLC 19, 51, 61**
See also CA 85-88; CAAS 10; CANR 56; DLB 14, 194
Fitzgerald, Robert (Stuart) 1910-1985**CLC 39**
See also CA 1-4R; 114; CANR 1; DLBY 80
FitzGerald, Robert D(avid) 1902-1987**CLC 19**
See also CA 17-20R
Fitzgerald, Zelda (Sayre) 1900-1948**TCLC 52**
See also CA 117; 126; DLBY 84
Flanagan, Thomas (James Bonner) 1923-
CLC 25, 52
See also CA 108; CANR 55; DLBY 80; INT 108; MTCW 1
Flaubert, Gustave 1821-1880**NCLC 2, 10, 19, 62, 66; DA; DAB; DAC; DAM MST, NOV; SSC 11; WLC**
See also DLB 119
Flecker, Herman Elroy
See Flecker, (Herman) James Elroy
Flecker, (Herman) James Elroy 1884-1915
TCLC 43
See also CA 109; 150; DLB 10, 19
Fleming, Ian (Lancaster) 1908-1964 . **CLC 3, 30; DAM POP**
See also AAYA 26; CA 5-8R; CANR 59; CDBLB 1945-1960; DLB 87, 201; MTCW 1; SATA 9
Fleming, Thomas (James) 1927- .... **CLC 37**
See also CA 5-8R; CANR 10; INT CANR-10; SATA 8
Fletcher, John 1579-1625 .... **LC 33; DC 6**
See also CDBLB Before 1660; DLB 58
Fletcher, John Gould 1886-1950 .... **TCLC 35**
See also CA 107; 167; DLB 4, 45
Fleur, Paul
See Pohl, Frederik
Flooglebuckle, Al
See Spiegelman, Art
Flying Officer X
See Bates, H(erbert) E(rnest)
Fo, Dario 1926- **CLC 32, 109; DAM DRAM; DC 10**
See also CA 116; 128; CANR 68; DLBY 97; MTCW 1
Fogarty, Jonathan Titulescu Esq.
See Farrell, James T(homas)
Folke, Will
See Bloch, Robert (Albert)

74; DLB 13; MTCW 1; SATA 66

Frye, (Herman) Northrop 1912-1991 **CLC 24, 70**
   See also CA 5-8R; 133; CANR 8, 37; DLB 67, 68; MTCW 1

Fuchs, Daniel 1909-1993 .... **CLC 8, 22**
   See also CA 81-84; 142; CAAS 5; CANR 40; DLB 9, 26, 28; DLBY 93

Fuchs, Daniel 1934- .... **CLC 34**
   See also CA 37-40R; CANR 14, 48

Fuentes, Carlos 1928- **CLC 3, 8, 10, 13, 22, 41, 60, 113; DA; DAB; DAC; DAM MST, MULT, NOV; HLC; SSC 24; WLC**
   See also AAYA 4; AITN 2; CA 69-72; CANR 10, 32, 68; DLB 113; HW; MTCW 1

Fuentes, Gregorio Lopez y
   See Lopez y Fuentes, Gregorio

Fugard, (Harold) Athol 1932- **CLC 5, 9, 14, 25, 40, 80; DAM DRAM; DC 3**
   See also AAYA 17; CA 85-88; CANR 32, 54; MTCW 1

Fugard, Sheila 1932- .... **CLC 48**
   See also CA 125

Fuller, Charles (H., Jr.) 1939- **CLC 25; BLC 2; DAM DRAM, MULT; DC 1**
   See also BW 2; CA 108; 112; DLB 38; INT 112; MTCW 1

Fuller, John (Leopold) 1937- .... **CLC 62**
   See also CA 21-24R; CANR 9, 44; DLB 40

Fuller, Margaret .... **NCLC 5, 50**
   See also Ossoli, Sarah Margaret (Fuller marchesa d')

Fuller, Roy (Broadbent) 1912-1991 **CLC 4, 28**
   See also CA 5-8R; 135; CAAS 10; CANR 53; DLB 15, 20; SATA 87

Fulton, Alice 1952- .... **CLC 52**
   See also CA 116; CANR 57; DLB 193

Furphy, Joseph 1843-1912 .... **TCLC 25**
   See also CA 163

Fussell, Paul 1924- .... **CLC 74**
   See also BEST 90:1; CA 17-20R; CANR 8, 21, 35, 69; INT CANR-21; MTCW 1

Futabatei, Shimei 1864-1909 .... **TCLC 44**
   See also CA 162; DLB 180

Futrelle, Jacques 1875-1912 .... **TCLC 19**
   See also CA 113; 155

Gaboriau, Emile 1835-1873 .... **NCLC 14**

Gadda, Carlo Emilio 1893-1973 .... **CLC 11**
   See also CA 89-92; DLB 177

Gaddis, William 1922-1998 **CLC 1, 3, 6, 8, 10, 19, 43, 86**
   See also CA 17-20R; 172; CANR 21, 48; DLB 2; MTCW 1

Gage, Walter
   See Inge, William (Motter)

Gaines, Ernest J(ames) 1933- **CLC 3, 11, 18, 86; BLC 2; DAM MULT**
   See also AAYA 18; AITN 1; BW 2; CA 9-12R; CANR 6, 24, 42, 75; CDALB 1968-1988; DLB 2, 33, 152; DLBY 80; MTCW 1; SATA 86

Gaitskill, Mary 1954- .... **CLC 69**
   See also CA 128; CANR 61

Galdos, Benito Perez
   See Perez Galdos, Benito

Gale, Zona 1874-1938 **TCLC 7; DAM DRAM**
   See also CA 105; 153; DLB 9, 78

Galeano, Eduardo (Hughes) 1940- ... **CLC 72**
   See also CA 29-32R; CANR 13, 32; HW

Galiano, Juan Valera y Alcala
   See Valera y Alcala-Galiano, Juan

Galilei, Galileo 1546-1642 .... **LC 45**

Gallagher, Tess 1943- ...... **CLC 18, 63; DAM POET; PC 9**
   See also CA 106; DLB 120

Gallant, Mavis 1922- ... **CLC 7, 18, 38; DAC; DAM MST; SSC 5**

See also CA 69-72; CANR 29, 69; DLB 53; MTCW 1

Gallant, Roy A(rthur) 1924- .... **CLC 17**
   See also CA 5-8R; CANR 4, 29, 54; CLR 30; MAICYA; SATA 4, 68

Gallico, Paul (William) 1897-1976 ..... **CLC 2**
   See also AITN 1; CA 5-8R; 69-72; CANR 23; DLB 9, 171; MAICYA; SATA 13

Gallo, Max Louis 1932- .... **CLC 95**
   See also CA 85-88

Gallois, Lucien
   See Desnos, Robert

Gallup, Ralph
   See Whitemore, Hugh (John)

Galsworthy, John 1867-1933 **TCLC 1, 45; DA; DAB; DAC; DAM DRAM, MST, NOV; SSC 22; WLC**
   See also CA 104; 141; CANR 75; CDBLB 1890-1914; DLB 10, 34, 98, 162; DLBD 16

Galt, John 1779-1839 .... **NCLC 1**
   See also DLB 99, 116, 159

Galvin, James 1951- .... **CLC 38**
   See also CA 108; CANR 26

Gamboa, Federico 1864-1939 .... **TCLC 36**
   See also CA 167

Gandhi, M. K.
   See Gandhi, Mohandas Karamchand

Gandhi, Mahatma
   See Gandhi, Mohandas Karamchand

Gandhi, Mohandas Karamchand 1869-1948 **TCLC 59; DAM MULT**
   See also CA 121; 132; MTCW 1

Gann, Ernest Kellogg 1910-1991 ...... **CLC 23**
   See also AITN 1; CA 1-4R; 136; CANR 1

Garcia, Cristina 1958- .... **CLC 76**
   See also CA 141; CANR 73

Garcia Lorca, Federico 1898-1936 **TCLC 1, 7, 49; DA; DAB; DAC; DAM DRAM, MST, MULT, POET; DC 2; HLC; PC 3; WLC**
   See also CA 104; 131; DLB 108; HW; MTCW 1

Garcia Marquez, Gabriel (Jose) 1928- **CLC 2, 3, 8, 10, 15, 27, 47, 55, 68; DA; DAB; DAC; DAM MST, MULT, NOV, POP; HLC; SSC 8; WLC**
   See also AAYA 3; BEST 89:1, 90:4; CA 33-36R; CANR 10, 28, 50, 75; DLB 113; HW; MTCW 1

Gard, Janice
   See Latham, Jean Lee

Gard, Roger Martin du
   See Martin du Gard, Roger

Gardam, Jane 1928- .... **CLC 43**
   See also CA 49-52; CANR 2, 18, 33, 54; CLR 12; DLB 14, 161; MAICYA; MTCW 1; SAAS 9; SATA 39, 76; SATA-Brief 28

Gardner, Herb(ert) 1934- .... **CLC 44**
   See also CA 149

Gardner, John (Champlin), Jr. 1933-1982 **CLC 2, 3, 5, 7, 8, 10, 18, 28, 34; DAM NOV, POP; SSC 7**
   See also AITN 1; CA 65-68; 107; CANR 33, 73; DLB 2; DLBY 82; MTCW 1; SATA 40; SATA-Obit 31

Gardner, John (Edmund) 1926- **CLC 30; DAM POP**
   See also CA 103; CANR 15, 69; MTCW 1

Gardner, Miriam
   See Bradley, Marion Zimmer

Gardner, Noel
   See Kuttner, Henry

Gardons, S. S.
   See Snodgrass, W(illiam) D(e Witt)

Garfield, Leon 1921-1996 .... **CLC 12**
   See also AAYA 8; CA 17-20R; 152; CANR 38, 41; CLR 21; DLB 161; JRDA; MAICYA; SATA 1, 32, 76; SATA-Obit 90

Garland, (Hannibal) Hamlin 1860-1940 **TCLC 3; SSC 18**
   See also CA 104; DLB 12, 71, 78, 186

Garneau, (Hector de) Saint-Denys 1912-1943 **TCLC 13**
   See also CA 111; DLB 88

Garner, Alan 1934- **CLC 17; DAB; DAM POP**
   See also AAYA 18; CA 73-76; CANR 15, 64; CLR 20; DLB 161; MAICYA; MTCW 1; SATA 18, 69

Garner, Hugh 1913-1979 .... **CLC 13**
   See also CA 69-72; CANR 31; DLB 68

Garnett, David 1892-1981 .... **CLC 3**
   See also CA 5-8R; 103; CANR 17; DLB 34

Garos, Stephanie
   See Katz, Steve

Garrett, George (Palmer) 1929- **CLC 3, 11, 51; SSC 30**
   See also CA 1-4R; CAAS 5; CANR 1, 42, 67; DLB 2, 5, 130, 152; DLBY 83

Garrick, David 1717-1779 .... **LC 15; DAM DRAM**
   See also DLB 84

Garrigue, Jean 1914-1972 .... **CLC 2, 8**
   See also CA 5-8R; 37-40R; CANR 20

Garrison, Frederick
   See Sinclair, Upton (Beall)

Garth, Will
   See Hamilton, Edmond; Kuttner, Henry

Garvey, Marcus (Moziah, Jr.) 1887-1940 **TCLC 41; BLC 2; DAM MULT**
   See also BW 1; CA 120; 124

Gary, Romain .... **CLC 25**
   See also Kacew, Romain
   See also DLB 83

Gascar, Pierre .... **CLC 11**
   See also Fournier, Pierre

Gascoyne, David (Emery) 1916- .... **CLC 45**
   See also CA 65-68; CANR 10, 28, 54; DLB 20; MTCW 1

Gaskell, Elizabeth Cleghorn 1810-1865 **NCLC 70; DAB; DAM MST; SSC 25**
   See also CDBLB 1832-1890; DLB 21, 144, 159

Gass, William H(oward) 1924- **CLC 1, 2, 8, 11, 15, 39; SSC 12**
   See also CA 17-20R; CANR 30, 71; DLB 2; MTCW 1

Gasset, Jose Ortega y
   See Ortega y Gasset, Jose

Gates, Henry Louis, Jr. 1950- **CLC 65; BLCS; DAM MULT**
   See also BW 2; CA 109; CANR 25, 53, 75; DLB 67

Gautier, Theophile 1811-1872 .. **NCLC 1, 59; DAM POET; PC 18; SSC 20**
   See also DLB 119

Gawsworth, John
   See Bates, H(erbert) E(rnest)

Gay, John 1685-1732 .... **LC 49**

Gay, Oliver
   See Gogarty, Oliver St. John

Gaye, Marvin (Penze) 1939-1984 ..... **CLC 26**
   See also CA 112

Gebler, Carlo (Ernest) 1954- .... **CLC 39**
   See also CA 119; 133

Gee, Maggie (Mary) 1948- .... **CLC 57**
   See also CA 130; DLB 207

Gee, Maurice (Gough) 1931- .... **CLC 29**
   See also CA 97-100; CANR 67; SATA 46, 101

Gelbart, Larry (Simon) 1923- .... **CLC 21, 61**
   See also CA 73-76; CANR 45

Gelber, Jack 1932- .... **CLC 1, 6, 14, 79**
   See also CA 1-4R; CANR 2; DLB 7

Gellhorn, Martha (Ellis) 1908-1998 **CLC 14, 60**
   See also CA 77-80; 164; CANR 44; DLBY 82

Genet, Jean 1910-1986 **CLC 1, 2, 5, 10, 14, 44,**

See Futabatei, Shimei

Hasek, Jaroslav (Matej Frantisek) 1883-1923 **TCLC 4**
See also CA 104; 129; MTCW 1

Hass, Robert 1941- ... **CLC 18, 39, 99; PC 16**
See also CA 111; CANR 30, 50, 71; DLB 105, 206; SATA 94

Hastings, Hudson
See Kuttner, Henry

Hastings, Selina .... **CLC 44**

Hathorne, John 1641-1717 .... **LC 38**

Hatteras, Amelia
See Mencken, H(enry) L(ouis)

Hatteras, Owen .... **TCLC 18**
See also Mencken, H(enry) L(ouis); Nathan, George Jean

Hauptmann, Gerhart (Johann Robert) 1862-1946 .... **TCLC 4; DAM DRAM**
See also CA 104; 153; DLB 66, 118

Havel, Vaclav 1936- ... **CLC 25, 58, 65; DAM DRAM; DC 6**
See also CA 104; CANR 36, 63; MTCW 1

Haviaras, Stratis .... **CLC 33**
See also Chaviaras, Strates

Hawes, Stephen 1475(?)-1523(?) .... **LC 17**
See also DLB 132

Hawkes, John (Clendennin Burne, Jr.) 1925-1998 .. **CLC 1, 2, 3, 4, 7, 9, 14, 15, 27, 49**
See also CA 1-4R; 167; CANR 2, 47, 64; DLB 2, 7; DLBY 80; MTCW 1

Hawking, S. W.
See Hawking, Stephen W(illiam)

Hawking, Stephen W(illiam) 1942- . **CLC 63, 105**
See also AAYA 13; BEST 89:1; CA 126; 129; CANR 48

Hawkins, Anthony Hope
See Hope, Anthony

Hawthorne, Julian 1846-1934 .... **TCLC 25**
See also CA 165

Hawthorne, Nathaniel 1804-1864 **NCLC 39; DA; DAB; DAC; DAM MST, NOV; SSC 3, 29; WLC**
See also AAYA 18; CDALB 1640-1865; DLB 1, 74; YABC 2

Haxton, Josephine Ayres 1921-
See Douglas, Ellen
See also CA 115; CANR 41

Hayaseca y Eizaguirre, Jorge
See Echegaray (y Eizaguirre), Jose (Maria Waldo)

Hayashi, Fumiko 1904-1951 .... **TCLC 27**
See also CA 161; DLB 180

Haycraft, Anna
See Ellis, Alice Thomas
See also CA 122

Hayden, Robert E(arl) 1913-1980 . **CLC 5, 9, 14, 37; BLC 2; DA; DAC; DAM MST, MULT, POET; PC 6**
See also BW 1; CA 69-72; 97-100; CABS 2; CANR 24, 75; CDALB 1941-1968; DLB 5, 76; MTCW 1; SATA 19; SATA-Obit 26

Hayford, J(oseph) E(phraim) Casely
See Casely-Hayford, J(oseph) E(phraim)

Hayman, Ronald 1932- .... **CLC 44**
See also CA 25-28R; CANR 18, 50; DLB 155

Haywood, Eliza (Fowler) 1693(?)-1756 **LC 1, 44**
See also DLB 39

Hazlitt, William 1778-1830 .... **NCLC 29**
See also DLB 110, 158

Hazzard, Shirley 1931- .... **CLC 18**
See also CA 9-12R; CANR 4, 70; DLBY 82; MTCW 1

Head, Bessie 1937-1986 **CLC 25, 67; BLC 2; DAM MULT**
See also BW 2; CA 29-32R; 119; CANR 25;

DLB 117; MTCW 1

Headon, (Nicky) Topper 1956(?)- ..... **CLC 30**

Heaney, Seamus (Justin) 1939- **CLC 5, 7, 14, 25, 37, 74, 91; DAB; DAM POET; PC 18; WLCS**
See also CA 85-88; CANR 25, 48, 75; CDBLB 1960 to Present; DLB 40; DLBY 95; MTCW 1

Hearn, (Patricio) Lafcadio (Tessima Carlos) 1850-1904 .... **TCLC 9**
See also CA 105; 166; DLB 12, 78, 189

Hearne, Vicki 1946- .... **CLC 56**
See also CA 139

Hearon, Shelby 1931- .... **CLC 63**
See also AITN 2; CA 25-28R; CANR 18, 48

Heat-Moon, William Least .... **CLC 29**
See also Trogdon, William (Lewis)
See also AAYA 9

Hebbel, Friedrich 1813-1863 **NCLC 43; DAM DRAM**
See also DLB 129

Hebert, Anne 1916- **CLC 4, 13, 29; DAC; DAM MST, POET**
See also CA 85-88; CANR 69; DLB 68; MTCW 1

Hecht, Anthony (Evan) 1923- **CLC 8, 13, 19; DAM POET**
See also CA 9-12R; CANR 6; DLB 5, 169

Hecht, Ben 1894-1964 .... **CLC 8**
See also CA 85-88; DLB 7, 9, 25, 26, 28, 86

Hedayat, Sadeq 1903-1951 .... **TCLC 21**
See also CA 120

Hegel, Georg Wilhelm Friedrich 1770-1831 **NCLC 46**
See also DLB 90

Heidegger, Martin 1889-1976 .... **CLC 24**
See also CA 81-84; 65-68; CANR 34; MTCW 1

Heidenstam, (Carl Gustaf) Verner von 1859-1940 .... **TCLC 5**
See also CA 104

Heifner, Jack 1946- .... **CLC 11**
See also CA 105; CANR 47

Heijermans, Herman 1864-1924 .... **TCLC 24**
See also CA 123

Heilbrun, Carolyn G(old) 1926- .... **CLC 25**
See also CA 45-48; CANR 1, 28, 58

Heine, Heinrich 1797-1856 **NCLC 4, 54; PC 25**
See also DLB 90

Heinemann, Larry (Curtiss) 1944- ... **CLC 50**
See also CA 110; CAAS 21; CANR 31; DLBD 9; INT CANR-31

Heiney, Donald (William) 1921-1993
See Harris, MacDonald
See also CA 1-4R; 142; CANR 3, 58

Heinlein, Robert A(nson) 1907-1988 **CLC 1, 3, 8, 14, 26, 55; DAM POP**
See also AAYA 17; CA 1-4R; 125; CANR 1, 20, 53; DLB 8; JRDA; MAICYA; MTCW 1; SATA 9, 69; SATA-Obit 56

Helforth, John
See Doolittle, Hilda

Hellenhofferu, Vojtech Kapristian z
See Hasek, Jaroslav (Matej Frantisek)

Heller, Joseph 1923- **CLC 1, 3, 5, 8, 11, 36, 63; DA; DAB; DAC; DAM MST, NOV, POP; WLC**
See also AAYA 24; AITN 1; CA 5-8R; CABS 1; CANR 8, 42, 66; DLB 2, 28; DLBY 80; INT CANR-8; MTCW 1

Hellman, Lillian (Florence) 1906-1984 **CLC 2, 4, 8, 14, 18, 34, 44, 52; DAM DRAM; DC 1**
See also AITN 1, 2; CA 13-16R; 112; CANR 33; DLB 7; DLBY 84; MTCW 1

Helprin, Mark 1947- **CLC 7, 10, 22, 32; DAM NOV, POP**
See also CA 81-84; CANR 47, 64; DLBY 85;

MTCW 1

Helvetius, Claude-Adrien 1715-1771 ..**LC 26**

Helyar, Jane Penelope Josephine 1933-
See Poole, Josephine
See also CA 21-24R; CANR 10, 26; SATA 82

Hemans, Felicia 1793-1835 .... **NCLC 71**
See also DLB 96

Hemingway, Ernest (Miller) 1899-1961 **C L C 1, 3, 6, 8, 10, 13, 19, 30, 34, 39, 41, 44, 50, 61, 80; DA; DAB; DAC; DAM MST, NOV; SSC 1, 25; WLC**
See also AAYA 19; CA 77-80; CANR 34; CDALB 1917-1929; DLB 4, 9, 102; DLBD 1, 15, 16; DLBY 81, 87, 96; MTCW 1

Hempel, Amy 1951- .... **CLC 39**
See also CA 118; 137; CANR 70

Henderson, F. C.
See Mencken, H(enry) L(ouis)

Henderson, Sylvia
See Ashton-Warner, Sylvia (Constance)

Henderson, Zenna (Chlarson) 1917-1983 **S S C 29**
See also CA 1-4R; 133; CANR 1; DLB 8; SATA 5

Henley, Beth .... **CLC 23; DC 6**
See also Henley, Elizabeth Becker
See also CABS 3; DLBY 86

Henley, Elizabeth Becker 1952-
See Henley, Beth
See also CA 107; CANR 32, 73; DAM DRAM, MST; MTCW 1

Henley, William Ernest 1849-1903 .. **TCLC 8**
See also CA 105; DLB 19

Hennissart, Martha
See Lathen, Emma
See also CA 85-88; CANR 64

Henry, O. .... **TCLC 1, 19; SSC 5; WLC**
See also Porter, William Sydney

Henry, Patrick 1736-1799 .... **LC 25**

Henryson, Robert 1430(?)-1506(?) ...... **LC 20**
See also DLB 146

Henry VIII 1491-1547 .... **LC 10**
See also DLB 132

Henschke, Alfred
See Klabund

Hentoff, Nat(han Irving) 1925- .... **CLC 26**
See also AAYA 4; CA 1-4R; CAAS 6; CANR 5, 25; CLR 1, 52; INT CANR-25; JRDA; MAICYA; SATA 42, 69; SATA-Brief 27

Heppenstall, (John) Rayner 1911-1981 **C L C 10**
See also CA 1-4R; 103; CANR 29

Heraclitus c. 540B.C.-c. 450B.C. .. **CMLC 22**
See also DLB 176

Herbert, Frank (Patrick) 1920-1986 **CLC 12, 23, 35, 44, 85; DAM POP**
See also AAYA 21; CA 53-56; 118; CANR 5, 43; DLB 8; INT CANR-5; MTCW 1; SATA 9, 37; SATA-Obit 47

Herbert, George 1593-1633 ..... **LC 24; DAB; DAM POET; PC 4**
See also CDBLB Before 1660; DLB 126

Herbert, Zbigniew 1924-1998 ..... **CLC 9, 43; DAM POET**
See also CA 89-92; 169; CANR 36, 74; MTCW 1

Herbst, Josephine (Frey) 1897-1969 **CLC 34**
See also CA 5-8R; 25-28R; DLB 9

Hergesheimer, Joseph 1880-1954 .. **TCLC 11**
See also CA 109; DLB 102, 9

Herlihy, James Leo 1927-1993 .... **CLC 6**
See also CA 1-4R; 143; CANR 2

Hermogenes fl. c. 175- .... **CMLC 6**

Hernandez, Jose 1834-1886 .... **NCLC 17**

Herodotus c. 484B.C.-429B.C. ...... **CMLC 17**
See also DLB 176

Herrick, Robert 1591-1674 **LC 13; DA; DAB;**

See also CA 114; DLB 207
Hollis, Jim
  See Summers, Hollis (Spurgeon, Jr.)
Holly, Buddy 1936-1959 .... **TCLC 65**
Holmes, Gordon
  See Shiel, M(atthew) P(hipps)
Holmes, John
  See Souster, (Holmes) Raymond
Holmes, John Clellon 1926-1988 ...... **CLC 56**
  See also CA 9-12R; 125; CANR 4; DLB 16
Holmes, Oliver Wendell, Jr. 1841-1935**TCLC 77**
  See also CA 114
Holmes, Oliver Wendell 1809-1894**NCLC 14**
  See also CDALB 1640-1865; DLB 1, 189;
  SATA 34
Holmes, Raymond
  See Souster, (Holmes) Raymond
Holt, Victoria
  See Hibbert, Eleanor Alice Burford
Holub, Miroslav 1923-1998 .... **CLC 4**
  See also CA 21-24R; 169; CANR 10
Homer c. 8th cent. B.C.- ... **CMLC 1, 16; DA;
  DAB; DAC; DAM MST, POET; PC 23;
  WLCS**
  See also DLB 176
Hongo, Garrett Kaoru 1951- .... **PC 23**
  See also CA 133; CAAS 22; DLB 120
Honig, Edwin 1919- .... **CLC 33**
  See also CA 5-8R; CAAS 8; CANR 4, 45; DLB
  5
Hood, Hugh (John Blagdon) 1928-**CLC 15, 28**
  See also CA 49-52; CAAS 17; CANR 1, 33;
  DLB 53
Hood, Thomas 1799-1845 .... **NCLC 16**
  See also DLB 96
Hooker, (Peter) Jeremy 1941- .... **CLC 43**
  See also CA 77-80; CANR 22; DLB 40
hooks, bell .... **CLC 94; BLCS**
  See also Watkins, Gloria
Hope, A(lec) D(erwent) 1907- .... **CLC 3, 51**
  See also CA 21-24R; CANR 33, 74; MTCW 1
Hope, Anthony 1863-1933 .... **TCLC 83**
  See also CA 157; DLB 153, 156
Hope, Brian
  See Creasey, John
Hope, Christopher (David Tully) 1944- **CLC 52**
  See also CA 106; CANR 47; SATA 62
Hopkins, Gerard Manley 1844-1889 .. **NCLC 17; DA; DAB; DAC; DAM MST, POET;
  PC 15; WLC**
  See also CDBLB 1890-1914; DLB 35, 57
Hopkins, John (Richard) 1931-1998 .. **CLC 4**
  See also CA 85-88; 169
Hopkins, Pauline Elizabeth 1859-1930**TCLC 28; BLC 2; DAM MULT**
  See also BW 2; CA 141; DLB 50
Hopkinson, Francis 1737-1791 .... **LC 25**
  See also DLB 31
Hopley-Woolrich, Cornell George 1903-1968
  See Woolrich, Cornell
  See also CA 13-14; CANR 58; CAP 1
Horatio
  See Proust, (Valentin-Louis-George-Eugene-)
  Marcel
Horgan, Paul (George Vincent O'Shaughnessy)
  1903-1995 .... **CLC 9, 53; DAM NOV**
  See also CA 13-16R; 147; CANR 9, 35; DLB
  102; DLBY 85; INT CANR-9; MTCW 1;
  SATA 13; SATA-Obit 84
Horn, Peter
  See Kuttner, Henry
Hornem, Horace Esq.
  See Byron, George Gordon (Noel)
**Horney, Karen (Clementine Theodore
  Danielsen)** 1885-1952 .... **TCLC 71**

See also CA 114; 165
Hornung, E(rnest) W(illiam) 1866-1921
  TCLC 59
  See also CA 108; 160; DLB 70
Horovitz, Israel (Arthur) 1939-**CLC 56; DAM DRAM**
  See also CA 33-36R; CANR 46, 59; DLB 7
Horvath, Odon von
  See Horvath, Oedoen von
  See also DLB 85, 124
Horvath, Oedoen von 1901-1938 ... **TCLC 45**
  See also Horvath, Odon von
  See also CA 118
Horwitz, Julius 1920-1986 .... **CLC 14**
  See also CA 9-12R; 119; CANR 12
Hospital, Janette Turner 1942- .... **CLC 42**
  See also CA 108; CANR 48
Hostos, E. M. de
  See Hostos (y Bonilla), Eugenio Maria de
Hostos, Eugenio M. de
  See Hostos (y Bonilla), Eugenio Maria de
Hostos, Eugenio Maria
  See Hostos (y Bonilla), Eugenio Maria de
Hostos (y Bonilla), Eugenio Maria de 1839-1903
  TCLC 24
  See also CA 123; 131; HW
Houdini
  See Lovecraft, H(oward) P(hillips)
Hougan, Carolyn 1943- .... **CLC 34**
  See also CA 139
Household, Geoffrey (Edward West) 1900-1988
  CLC 11
  See also CA 77-80; 126; CANR 58; DLB 87;
  SATA 14; SATA-Obit 59
Housman, A(lfred) E(dward) 1859-1936
  **TCLC 1, 10; DA; DAB; DAC; DAM MST,
  POET; PC 2; WLCS**
  See also CA 104; 125; DLB 19; MTCW 1
Housman, Laurence 1865-1959 .... **TCLC 7**
  See also CA 106; 155; DLB 10; SATA 25
Howard, Elizabeth Jane 1923- ..... **CLC 7, 29**
  See also CA 5-8R; CANR 8, 62
Howard, Maureen 1930- .... **CLC 5, 14, 46**
  See also CA 53-56; CANR 31, 75; DLBY 83;
  INT CANR-31; MTCW 1
Howard, Richard 1929- .... **CLC 7, 10, 47**
  See also AITN 1; CA 85-88; CANR 25; DLB 5;
  INT CANR-25
Howard, Robert E(rvin) 1906-1936 **TCLC 8**
  See also CA 105; 157
Howard, Warren F.
  See Pohl, Frederik
Howe, Fanny (Quincy) 1940- .... **CLC 47**
  See also CA 117; CAAS 27; CANR 70; SATA-
  Brief 52
Howe, Irving 1920-1993 .... **CLC 85**
  See also CA 9-12R; 141; CANR 21, 50; DLB
  67; MTCW 1
Howe, Julia Ward 1819-1910 .... **TCLC 21**
  See also CA 117; DLB 1, 189
Howe, Susan 1937- .... **CLC 72**
  See also CA 160; DLB 120
Howe, Tina 1937- .... **CLC 48**
  See also CA 109
Howell, James 1594(?)-1666 .... **LC 13**
  See also DLB 151
Howells, W. D.
  See Howells, William Dean
Howells, William D.
  See Howells, William Dean
Howells, William Dean 1837-1920**TCLC 7, 17,
  41**
  See also CA 104; 134; CDALB 1865-1917;
  DLB 12, 64, 74, 79, 189
Howes, Barbara 1914-1996 .... **CLC 15**
  See also CA 9-12R; 151; CAAS 3; CANR 53;
  SATA 5

Hrabal, Bohumil 1914-1997 .... **CLC 13, 67**
  See also CA 106; 156; CAAS 12; CANR 57
Hroswitha of Gandersheim c. 935-c. 1002
  CMLC 29
  See also DLB 148
Hsun, Lu
  See Lu Hsun
Hubbard, L(afayette) Ron(ald) 1911-1986
  CLC 43; DAM POP
  See also CA 77-80; 118; CANR 52
Huch, Ricarda (Octavia) 1864-1947**TCLC 13**
  See also CA 111; DLB 66
Huddle, David 1942- .... **CLC 49**
  See also CA 57-60; CAAS 20; DLB 130
Hudson, Jeffrey
  See Crichton, (John) Michael
Hudson, W(illiam) H(enry) 1841-1922**TCLC 29**
  See also CA 115; DLB 98, 153, 174; SATA 35
Hueffer, Ford Madox
  See Ford, Ford Madox
Hughart, Barry 1934- .... **CLC 39**
  See also CA 137
Hughes, Colin
  See Creasey, John
Hughes, David (John) 1930- .... **CLC 48**
  See also CA 116; 129; DLB 14
Hughes, Edward James
  See Hughes, Ted
  See also DAM MST, POET
Hughes, (James) Langston 1902-1967**CLC 1,
  5, 10, 15, 35, 44, 108; BLC 2; DA; DAB;
  DAC; DAM DRAM, MST, MULT, POET;
  DC 3; PC 1; SSC 6; WLC**
  See also AAYA 12; BW 1; CA 1-4R; 25-28R;
  CANR 1, 34; CDALB 1929-1941; CLR 17;
  DLB 4, 7, 48, 51, 86; JRDA; MAICYA;
  MTCW 1; SATA 4, 33
Hughes, Richard (Arthur Warren) 1900-1976
  CLC 1, 11; DAM NOV
  See also CA 5-8R; 65-68; CANR 4; DLB 15,
  161; MTCW 1; SATA 8; SATA-Obit 25
Hughes, Ted 1930-1998 . **CLC 2, 4, 9, 14, 37;
  DAB; DAC; PC 7**
  See also Hughes, Edward James
  See also CA 1-4R; 171; CANR 1, 33, 66; CLR
  3; DLB 40, 161; MAICYA; MTCW 1; SATA
  49; SATA-Brief 27
Hugo, Richard F(ranklin) 1923-1982 **CLC 6,
  18, 32; DAM POET**
  See also CA 49-52; 108; CANR 3; DLB 5, 206
Hugo, Victor (Marie) 1802-1885**NCLC 3, 10,
  21; DA; DAB; DAC; DAM DRAM, MST,
  NOV, POET; PC 17; WLC**
  See also DLB 119, 192; SATA 47
Huidobro, Vicente
  See Huidobro Fernandez, Vicente Garcia
Huidobro Fernandez, Vicente Garcia 1893-
  1948 .... **TCLC 31**
  See also CA 131; HW
Hulme, Keri 1947- .... **CLC 39**
  See also CA 125; CANR 69; INT 125
Hulme, T(homas) E(rnest) 1883-1917 **TCLC 21**
  See also CA 117; DLB 19
Hume, David 1711-1776 .... **LC 7**
  See also DLB 104
Humphrey, William 1924-1997 .... **CLC 45**
  See also CA 77-80; 160; CANR 68; DLB 6
Humphreys, Emyr Owen 1919- .... **CLC 47**
  See also CA 5-8R; CANR 3, 24; DLB 15
Humphreys, Josephine 1945- ..... **CLC 34, 57**
  See also CA 121; 127; INT 127
Huneker, James Gibbons 1857-1921**TCLC 65**
  See also DLB 71
Hungerford, Pixie
  See Brinsmead, H(esba) F(ay)

See also CA 144; CAAS 22; DLB 175; NNAL

Kent, Kelvin
See Kuttner, Henry

Kenton, Maxwell
See Southern, Terry

Kenyon, Robert O.
See Kuttner, Henry

Kepler, Johannes 1571-1630 .... **LC 45**

Kerouac, Jack .... **CLC 1, 2, 3, 5, 14, 29, 61**
See also Kerouac, Jean-Louis Lebris de
See also AAYA 25; CDALB 1941-1968; DLB 2, 16; DLBD 3; DLBY 95

Kerouac, Jean-Louis Lebris de 1922-1969
See Kerouac, Jack
See also AITN 1; CA 5-8R; 25-28R; CANR 26, 54; DA; DAB; DAC; DAM MST, NOV, POET, POP; MTCW 1; WLC

Kerr, Jean 1923- .... **CLC 22**
See also CA 5-8R; CANR 7; INT CANR-7

Kerr, M. E. .... **CLC 12, 35**
See also Meaker, Marijane (Agnes)
See also AAYA 2, 23; CLR 29; SAAS 1

Kerr, Robert .... **CLC 55**

Kerrigan, (Thomas) Anthony 1918-**CLC 4, 6**
See also CA 49-52; CAAS 11; CANR 4

Kerry, Lois
See Duncan, Lois

Kesey, Ken (Elton) 1935- **CLC 1, 3, 6, 11, 46, 64; DA; DAB; DAC; DAM MST, NOV, POP; WLC**
See also AAYA 25; CA 1-4R; CANR 22, 38, 66; CDALB 1968-1988; DLB 2, 16, 206; MTCW 1; SATA 66

Kesselring, Joseph (Otto) 1902-1967**CLC 45; DAM DRAM, MST**
See also CA 150

Kessler, Jascha (Frederick) 1929- ...... **CLC 4**
See also CA 17-20R; CANR 8, 48

Kettelkamp, Larry (Dale) 1933- .... **CLC 12**
See also CA 29-32R; CANR 16; SAAS 3; SATA 2

Key, Ellen 1849-1926 .... **TCLC 65**

Keyber, Conny
See Fielding, Henry

Keyes, Daniel 1927-**CLC 80; DA; DAC; DAM MST, NOV**
See also AAYA 23; CA 17-20R; CANR 10, 26, 54, 74; SATA 37

Keynes, John Maynard 1883-1946 **TCLC 64**
See also CA 114; 162, 163; DLBD 10

Khanshendel, Chiron
See Rose, Wendy

Khayyam, Omar 1048-1131**CMLC 11; DAM POET; PC 8**

Kherdian, David 1931- .... **CLC 6, 9**
See also CA 21-24R; CAAS 2; CANR 39; CLR 24; JRDA; MAICYA; SATA 16, 74

Khlebnikov, Velimir .... **TCLC 20**
See also Khlebnikov, Viktor Vladimirovich

Khlebnikov, Viktor Vladimirovich 1885-1922
See Khlebnikov, Velimir
See also CA 117

Khodasevich, Vladislav (Felitsianovich) 1886-1939 ....
TCLC 15
See also CA 115

Kielland, Alexander Lange 1849-1906**T C L C 5**
See also CA 104

Kiely, Benedict 1919- .... **CLC 23, 43**
See also CA 1-4R; CANR 2; DLB 15

Kienzle, William X(avier) 1928- ..... **CLC 25; DAM POP**
See also CA 93-96; CAAS 1; CANR 9, 31, 59; INT CANR-31; MTCW 1

Kierkegaard, Soren 1813-1855 ...... **NCLC 34**

Killens, John Oliver 1916-1987 .... **CLC 10**

See also BW 2; CA 77-80; 123; CAAS 2; CANR 26; DLB 33

Killigrew, Anne 1660-1685 .... **LC 4**
See also DLB 131

Kim
See Simenon, Georges (Jacques Christian)

Kincaid, Jamaica 1949- **CLC 43, 68; BLC 2; DAM MULT, NOV**
See also AAYA 13; BW 2; CA 125; CANR 47, 59; DLB 157

King, Francis (Henry) 1923-**CLC 8, 53; DAM NOV**
See also CA 1-4R; CANR 1, 33; DLB 15, 139; MTCW 1

King, Kennedy
See Brown, George Douglas

King, Martin Luther, Jr. 1929-1968 **CLC 83; BLC 2; DA; DAB; DAC; DAM MST, MULT; WLCS**
See also BW 2; CA 25-28; CANR 27, 44; CAP 2; MTCW 1; SATA 14

King, Stephen (Edwin) 1947-**CLC 12, 26, 37, 61, 113; DAM NOV, POP; SSC 17**
See also AAYA 1, 17; BEST 90:1; CA 61-64; CANR 1, 30, 52, 76; DLB 143; DLBY 80; JRDA; MTCW 1; SATA 9, 55

King, Steve
See King, Stephen (Edwin)

King, Thomas 1943- ... **CLC 89; DAC; DAM MULT**
See also CA 144; DLB 175; NNAL; SATA 96

Kingman, Lee .... **CLC 17**
See also Natti, (Mary) Lee
See also SAAS 3; SATA 1, 67

Kingsley, Charles 1819-1875 .... **NCLC 35**
See also DLB 21, 32, 163, 190; YABC 2

Kingsley, Sidney 1906-1995 .... **CLC 44**
See also CA 85-88; 147; DLB 7

Kingsolver, Barbara 1955-**CLC 55, 81; DAM POP**
See also AAYA 15; CA 129; 134; CANR 60; DLB 206; INT 134

Kingston, Maxine (Ting Ting) Hong 1940-
CLC 12, 19, 58; DAM MULT, NOV; WLCS
See also AAYA 8; CA 69-72; CANR 13, 38, 74; DLB 173; DLBY 80; INT CANR-13; MTCW 1; SATA 53

Kinnell, Galway 1927- **CLC 1, 2, 3, 5, 13, 29**
See also CA 9-12R; CANR 10, 34, 66; DLB 5; DLBY 87; INT CANR-34; MTCW 1

Kinsella, Thomas 1928- .... **CLC 4, 19**
See also CA 17-20R; CANR 15; DLB 27; MTCW 1

Kinsella, W(illiam) P(atrick) 1935- . **CLC 27, 43; DAC; DAM NOV, POP**
See also AAYA 7; CA 97-100; CAAS 7; CANR 21, 35, 66, 75; INT CANR-21; MTCW 1

Kinsey, Alfred C(harles) 1894-1956**TCLC 91**
See also CA 115; 170

Kipling, (Joseph) Rudyard 1865-1936 **T C L C 8, 17; DA; DAB; DAC; DAM MST, POET; PC 3; SSC 5; WLC**
See also CA 105; 120; CANR 33; CDBLB 1890-1914; CLR 39; DLB 19, 34, 141, 156; MAICYA; MTCW 1; SATA 100; YABC 2

Kirkup, James 1918- .... **CLC 1**
See also CA 1-4R; CAAS 4; CANR 2; DLB 27; SATA 12

Kirkwood, James 1930(?)-1989 .... **CLC 9**
See also AITN 2; CA 1-4R; 128; CANR 6, 40

Kirshner, Sidney
See Kingsley, Sidney

Kis, Danilo 1935-1989 .... **CLC 57**
See also CA 109; 118; 129; CANR 61; DLB 181; MTCW 1

Kivi, Aleksis 1834-1872 .... **NCLC 30**

Kizer, Carolyn (Ashley) 1925-**CLC 15, 39, 80; DAM POET**
See also CA 65-68; CAAS 5; CANR 24, 70; DLB 5, 169

Klabund 1890-1928 .... **TCLC 44**
See also CA 162; DLB 66

Klappert, Peter 1942- .... **CLC 57**
See also CA 33-36R; DLB 5

Klein, A(braham) M(oses) 1909-1972**CLC 19; DAB; DAC; DAM MST**
See also CA 101; 37-40R; DLB 68

Klein, Norma 1938-1989 .... **CLC 30**
See also AAYA 2; CA 41-44R; 128; CANR 15, 37; CLR 2, 19; INT CANR-15; JRDA; MAICYA; SAAS 1; SATA 7, 57

Klein, T(heodore) E(ibon) D(onald) 1947-
CLC 34
See also CA 119; CANR 44, 75

Kleist, Heinrich von 1777-1811 **NCLC 2, 37; DAM DRAM; SSC 22**
See also DLB 90

Klima, Ivan 1931- .... **CLC 56; DAM NOV**
See also CA 25-28R; CANR 17, 50

Klimentov, Andrei Platonovich 1899-1951
See Platonov, Andrei
See also CA 108

Klinger, Friedrich Maximilian von 1752-1831
NCLC 1
See also DLB 94

Klingsor the Magician
See Hartmann, Sadakichi

Klopstock, Friedrich Gottlieb 1724-1803
NCLC 11
See also DLB 97

Knapp, Caroline 1959- .... **CLC 99**
See also CA 154

Knebel, Fletcher 1911-1993 .... **CLC 14**
See also AITN 1; CA 1-4R; 140; CAAS 3; CANR 1, 36; SATA 36; SATA-Obit 75

Knickerbocker, Diedrich
See Irving, Washington

Knight, Etheridge 1931-1991**CLC 40; BLC 2; DAM POET; PC 14**
See also BW 1; CA 21-24R; 133; CANR 23; DLB 41

Knight, Sarah Kemble 1666-1727 .... **LC 7**
See also DLB 24, 200

Knister, Raymond 1899-1932 .... **TCLC 56**
See also DLB 68

Knowles, John 1926- . **CLC 1, 4, 10, 26; DA; DAC; DAM MST, NOV**
See also AAYA 10; CA 17-20R; CANR 40, 74, 76; CDALB 1968-1988; DLB 6; MTCW 1; SATA 8, 89

Knox, Calvin M.
See Silverberg, Robert

Knox, John c. 1505-1572 .... **LC 37**
See also DLB 132

Knye, Cassandra
See Disch, Thomas M(ichael)

Koch, C(hristopher) J(ohn) 1932- .... **CLC 42**
See also CA 127

Koch, Christopher
See Koch, C(hristopher) J(ohn)

Koch, Kenneth 1925- ..... **CLC 5, 8, 44; DAM POET**
See also CA 1-4R; CANR 6, 36, 57; DLB 5; INT CANR-36; SATA 65

Kochanowski, Jan 1530-1584 .... **LC 10**

Kock, Charles Paul de 1794-1871 . **NCLC 16**

Koda Shigeyuki 1867-1947
See Rohan, Koda
See also CA 121

Koestler, Arthur 1905-1983**CLC 1, 3, 6, 8, 15, 33**
See also CA 1-4R; 109; CANR 1, 33; CDBLB 1945-1960; DLBY 83; MTCW 1

Kogawa, Joy Nozomi 1935- .. **CLC 78; DAC; DAM MST, MULT**
See also CA 101; CANR 19, 62; SATA 99
Kohout, Pavel 1928- .... **CLC 13**
See also CA 45-48; CANR 3
Koizumi, Yakumo
See Hearn, (Patricio) Lafcadio (Tessima Carlos)
Kolmar, Gertrud 1894-1943 .... **TCLC 40**
See also CA 167
Komunyakaa, Yusef 1947-**CLC 86, 94; BLCS**
See also CA 147; DLB 120
Konrad, George
See Konrad, Gyoergy
Konrad, Gyoergy 1933- .... **CLC 4, 10, 73**
See also CA 85-88
Konwicki, Tadeusz 1926- **CLC 8, 28, 54, 117**
See also CA 101; CAAS 9; CANR 39, 59; MTCW 1
Koontz, Dean R(ay) 1945- ..... **CLC 78; DAM NOV, POP**
See also AAYA 9; BEST 89:3, 90:2; CA 108; CANR 19, 36, 52; MTCW 1; SATA 92
Kopernik, Mikolaj
See Copernicus, Nicolaus
Kopit, Arthur (Lee) 1937-**CLC 1, 18, 33; DAM DRAM**
See also AITN 1; CA 81-84; CABS 3; DLB 7; MTCW 1
Kops, Bernard 1926- .... **CLC 4**
See also CA 5-8R; DLB 13
Kornbluth, C(yril) M. 1923-1958 .... **TCLC 8**
See also CA 105; 160; DLB 8
Korolenko, V. G.
See Korolenko, Vladimir Galaktionovich
Korolenko, Vladimir
See Korolenko, Vladimir Galaktionovich
Korolenko, Vladimir G.
See Korolenko, Vladimir Galaktionovich
Korolenko, Vladimir Galaktionovich 1853-1921 .... **TCLC 22**
See also CA 121
Korzybski, Alfred (Habdank Skarbek) 1879-1950 .... **TCLC 61**
See also CA 123; 160
Kosinski, Jerzy (Nikodem) 1933-1991**CLC 1, 2, 3, 6, 10, 15, 53, 70; DAM NOV**
See also CA 17-20R; 134; CANR 9, 46; DLB 2; DLBY 82; MTCW 1
Kostelanetz, Richard (Cory) 1940- .. **CLC 28**
See also CA 13-16R; CAAS 8; CANR 38
Kostrowitzki, Wilhelm Apollinaris de 1880-1918
See Apollinaire, Guillaume
See also CA 104
Kotlowitz, Robert 1924- .... **CLC 4**
See also CA 33-36R; CANR 36
Kotzebue, August (Friedrich Ferdinand) von 1761-1819 ....
NCLC 25
See also DLB 94
Kotzwinkle, William 1938- ..... **CLC 5, 14, 35**
See also CA 45-48; CANR 3, 44; CLR 6; DLB 173; MAICYA; SATA 24, 70
Kowna, Stancy
See Szymborska, Wislawa
Kozol, Jonathan 1936- .... **CLC 17**
See also CA 61-64; CANR 16, 45
Kozoll, Michael 1940(?)- .... **CLC 35**
Kramer, Kathryn 19(?)- .... **CLC 34**
Kramer, Larry 1935-**CLC 42; DAM POP; DC 8**
See also CA 124; 126; CANR 60
Krasicki, Ignacy 1735-1801 .... **NCLC 8**
Krasinski, Zygmunt 1812-1859 .... **NCLC 4**
Kraus, Karl 1874-1936 .... **TCLC 5**
See also CA 104; DLB 118
Kreve (Mickevicius), Vincas 1882-1954**TCLC**

27
See also CA 170
Kristeva, Julia 1941- .... **CLC 77**
See also CA 154
Kristofferson, Kris 1936- .... **CLC 26**
See also CA 104
Krizanc, John 1956- .... **CLC 57**
Krleza, Miroslav 1893-1981 .... **CLC 8, 114**
See also CA 97-100; 105; CANR 50; DLB 147
Kroetsch, Robert 1927-**CLC 5, 23, 57; DAC; DAM POET**
See also CA 17-20R; CANR 8, 38; DLB 53; MTCW 1
Kroetz, Franz
See Kroetz, Franz Xaver
Kroetz, Franz Xaver 1946- .... **CLC 41**
See also CA 130
Kroker, Arthur (W.) 1945- .... **CLC 77**
See also CA 161
Kropotkin, Peter (Aleksieevich) 1842-1921
TCLC 36
See also CA 119
Krotkov, Yuri 1917- .... **CLC 19**
See also CA 102
Krumb
See Crumb, R(obert)
Krumgold, Joseph (Quincy) 1908-1980 **C L C 12**
See also CA 9-12R; 101; CANR 7; MAICYA; SATA 1, 48; SATA-Obit 23
Krumwitz
See Crumb, R(obert)
Krutch, Joseph Wood 1893-1970...... **CLC 24**
See also CA 1-4R; 25-28R; CANR 4; DLB 63, 206
Krutzch, Gus
See Eliot, T(homas) S(tearns)
Krylov, Ivan Andreevich 1768(?)-1844**N C L C 1**
See also DLB 150
Kubin, Alfred (Leopold Isidor) 1877-1959
TCLC 23
See also CA 112; 149; DLB 81
Kubrick, Stanley 1928- .... **CLC 16**
See also CA 81-84; CANR 33; DLB 26
Kumin, Maxine (Winokur) 1925- **CLC 5, 13, 28; DAM POET; PC 15**
See also AITN 2; CA 1-4R; CAAS 8; CANR 1, 21, 69; DLB 5; MTCW 1; SATA 12
Kundera, Milan 1929- ..**CLC 4, 9, 19, 32, 68, 115; DAM NOV; SSC 24**
See also AAYA 2; CA 85-88; CANR 19, 52, 74; MTCW 1
Kunene, Mazisi (Raymond) 1930- .... **CLC 85**
See also BW 1; CA 125; DLB 117
Kunitz, Stanley (Jasspon) 1905-**CLC 6, 11, 14; PC 19**
See also CA 41-44R; CANR 26, 57; DLB 48; INT CANR-26; MTCW 1
Kunze, Reiner 1933- .... **CLC 10**
See also CA 93-96; DLB 75
Kuprin, Aleksandr Ivanovich 1870-1938
TCLC 5
See also CA 104
Kureishi, Hanif 1954(?)- .... **CLC 64**
See also CA 139; DLB 194
Kurosawa, Akira 1910-1998 . **CLC 16; DAM MULT**
See also AAYA 11; CA 101; 170; CANR 46
Kushner, Tony 1957(?)-**CLC 81; DAM DRAM; DC 10**
See also CA 144; CANR 74
Kuttner, Henry 1915-1958 .... **TCLC 10**
See also Vance, Jack
See also CA 107; 157; DLB 8
Kuzma, Greg 1944- .... **CLC 7**
See also CA 33-36R; CANR 70

Kuzmin, Mikhail 1872(?)-1936 ...... **TCLC 40**
See also CA 170
Kyd, Thomas 1558-1594**LC 22; DAM DRAM; DC 3**
See also DLB 62
Kyprianos, Iossif
See Samarakis, Antonis
La Bruyere, Jean de 1645-1696 .... **LC 17**
Lacan, Jacques (Marie Emile) 1901-1981
CLC 75
See also CA 121; 104
Laclos, Pierre Ambroise Francois Choderlos de 1741-1803 .... **NCLC 4**
Lacolere, Francois
See Aragon, Louis
La Colere, Francois
See Aragon, Louis
La Deshabilleuse
See Simenon, Georges (Jacques Christian)
Lady Gregory
See Gregory, Isabella Augusta (Persse)
Lady of Quality, A
See Bagnold, Enid
La Fayette, Marie (Madelaine Pioche de la Vergne Comtes 1634-1693 .... **LC 2**
Lafayette, Rene
See Hubbard, L(afayette) Ron(ald)
Laforgue, Jules 1860-1887**NCLC 5, 53; PC 14; SSC 20**
Lagerkvist, Paer (Fabian) 1891-1974 **CLC 7, 10, 13, 54; DAM DRAM, NOV**
See also Lagerkvist, Par
See also CA 85-88; 49-52; MTCW 1
Lagerkvist, Par .... **SSC 12**
See also Lagerkvist, Paer (Fabian)
Lagerloef, Selma (Ottiliana Lovisa) 1858-1940
TCLC 4, 36
See also Lagerlof, Selma (Ottiliana Lovisa)
See also CA 108; SATA 15
Lagerlof, Selma (Ottiliana Lovisa)
See Lagerloef, Selma (Ottiliana Lovisa)
See also CLR 7; SATA 15
La Guma, (Justin) Alex(ander) 1925-1985
CLC 19; BLCS; DAM NOV
See also BW 1; CA 49-52; 118; CANR 25; DLB 117; MTCW 1
Laidlaw, A. K.
See Grieve, C(hristopher) M(urray)
Lainez, Manuel Mujica
See Mujica Lainez, Manuel
See also HW
Laing, R(onald) D(avid) 1927-1989 . **CLC 95**
See also CA 107; 129; CANR 34; MTCW 1
Lamartine, Alphonse (Marie Louis Prat) de 1790-1869 ....
NCLC 11; DAM POET; PC 16
Lamb, Charles 1775-1834 ..... **NCLC 10; DA; DAB; DAC; DAM MST; WLC**
See also CDBLB 1789-1832; DLB 93, 107, 163; SATA 17
Lamb, Lady Caroline 1785-1828 ... **NCLC 38**
See also DLB 116
Lamming, George (William) 1927- **CLC 2, 4, 66; BLC 2; DAM MULT**
See also BW 2; CA 85-88; CANR 26, 76; DLB 125; MTCW 1
L'Amour, Louis (Dearborn) 1908-1988 **C L C 25, 55; DAM NOV, POP**
See also AAYA 16; AITN 2; BEST 89:2; CA 1-4R; 125; CANR 3, 25, 40; DLB 207; DLBY 80; MTCW 1
Lampedusa, Giuseppe (Tomasi) di 1896-1957
TCLC 13
See also Tomasi di Lampedusa, Giuseppe
See also CA 164; DLB 177
Lampman, Archibald 1861-1899 ... **NCLC 25**
See also DLB 92

Lee, Shelton Jackson 1957(?)- .... **CLC 105;**
BLCS; DAM MULT
See also Lee, Spike
See also BW 2; CA 125; CANR 42
Lee, Spike
See Lee, Shelton Jackson
See also AAYA 4
Lee, Stan 1922- ....**CLC 17**
See also AAYA 5; CA 108; 111; INT 111
Lee, Tanith 1947- ....**CLC 46**
See also AAYA 15; CA 37-40R; CANR 53;
SATA 8, 88
Lee, Vernon .... **TCLC 5; SSC 33**
See also Paget, Violet
See also DLB 57, 153, 156, 174, 178
Lee, William
See Burroughs, William S(eward)
Lee, Willy
See Burroughs, William S(eward)
Lee-Hamilton, Eugene (Jacob) 1845-1907
TCLC 22
See also CA 117
Leet, Judith 1935- .... **CLC 11**
Le Fanu, Joseph Sheridan 1814-1873**NCLC 9,**
58; DAM POP; SSC 14
See also DLB 21, 70, 159, 178
Leffland, Ella 1931- .... **CLC 19**
See also CA 29-32R; CANR 35; DLBY 84; INT
CANR-35; SATA 65
Leger, Alexis
See Leger, (Marie-Rene Auguste) Alexis Saint-
Leger
Leger, (Marie-Rene Auguste) Alexis Saint-
Leger 1887-1975 . **CLC 4, 11, 46; DAM**
POET; PC 23
See also CA 13-16R; 61-64; CANR 43; MTCW
1
Leger, Saintleger
See Leger, (Marie-Rene Auguste) Alexis Saint-
Leger
Le Guin, Ursula K(roeber) 1929- **CLC 8, 13,**
22, 45, 71; DAB; DAC; DAM MST, POP;
SSC 12
See also AAYA 9, 27; AITN 1; CA 21-24R;
CANR 9, 32, 52, 74; CDALB 1968-1988;
CLR 3, 28; DLB 8, 52; INT CANR-32;
JRDA; MAICYA; MTCW 1; SATA 4, 52, 99
Lehmann, Rosamond (Nina) 1901-1990**CLC 5**
See also CA 77-80; 131; CANR 8, 73; DLB 15
Leiber, Fritz (Reuter, Jr.) 1910-1992 **CLC 25**
See also CA 45-48; 139; CANR 2, 40; DLB 8;
MTCW 1; SATA 45; SATA-Obit 73
Leibniz, Gottfried Wilhelm von 1646-1716**LC**
35
See also DLB 168
Leimbach, Martha 1963-
See Leimbach, Marti
See also CA 130
Leimbach, Marti .... **CLC 65**
See also Leimbach, Martha
Leino, Eino .... **TCLC 24**
See also Loennbohm, Armas Eino Leopold
Leiris, Michel (Julien) 1901-1990..... **CLC 61**
See also CA 119; 128; 132
Leithauser, Brad 1953- .... **CLC 27**
See also CA 107; CANR 27; DLB 120
Lelchuk, Alan 1938- .... **CLC 5**
See also CA 45-48; CAAS 20; CANR 1, 70
Lem, Stanislaw 1921- .... **CLC 8, 15, 40**
See also CA 105; CAAS 1; CANR 32; MTCW
1
Lemann, Nancy 1956- .... **CLC 39**
See also CA 118; 136
Lemonnier, (Antoine Louis) Camille 1844-1913
TCLC 22
See also CA 121
Lenau, Nikolaus 1802-1850 .... **NCLC 16**

L'Engle, Madeleine (Camp Franklin) 1918-
CLC 12; DAM POP
See also AAYA 1; AITN 2; CA 1-4R; CANR 3,
21, 39, 66; CLR 1, 14; DLB 52; JRDA;
MAICYA; MTCW 1; SAAS 15; SATA 1, 27,
75
Lengyel, Jozsef 1896-1975 .... **CLC 7**
See also CA 85-88; 57-60; CANR 71
Lenin 1870-1924
See Lenin, V. I.
See also CA 121; 168
Lenin, V. I. .... **TCLC 67**
See also Lenin
Lennon, John (Ono) 1940-1980 . **CLC 12, 35**
See also CA 102
Lennox, Charlotte Ramsay 1729(?)-1804
NCLC 23
See also DLB 39
Lentricchia, Frank (Jr.) 1940- .... **CLC 34**
See also CA 25-28R; CANR 19
Lenz, Siegfried 1926- .... **CLC 27; SSC 33**
See also CA 89-92; DLB 75
Leonard, Elmore (John, Jr.) 1925-**CLC 28, 34,**
71; DAM POP
See also AAYA 22; AITN 1; BEST 89:1, 90:4;
CA 81-84; CANR 12, 28, 53, 76; DLB 173;
INT CANR-28; MTCW 1
Leonard, Hugh .... **CLC 19**
See also Byrne, John Keyes
See also DLB 13
Leonov, Leonid (Maximovich) 1899-1994
CLC 92; DAM NOV
See also CA 129; CANR 74, 76; MTCW 1
Leopardi, (Conte) Giacomo 1798-1837**NCLC**
22
Le Reveler
See Artaud, Antonin (Marie Joseph)
Lerman, Eleanor 1952- .... **CLC 9**
See also CA 85-88; CANR 69
Lerman, Rhoda 1936- .... **CLC 56**
See also CA 49-52; CANR 70
Lermontov, Mikhail Yuryevich 1814-1841
NCLC 47; PC 18
See also DLB 205
Leroux, Gaston 1868-1927 .... **TCLC 25**
See also CA 108; 136; CANR 69; SATA 65
Lesage, Alain-Rene 1668-1747 .... **LC 2, 28**
Leskov, Nikolai (Semyonovich) 1831-1895
NCLC 25
Lessing, Doris (May) 1919-**CLC 1, 2, 3, 6, 10,**
15, 22, 40, 94; DA; DAB; DAC; DAM MST,
NOV; SSC 6; WLCS
See also CA 9-12R; CAAS 14; CANR 33, 54,
76; CDBLB 1960 to Present; DLB 15, 139;
DLBY 85; MTCW 1
Lessing, Gotthold Ephraim 1729-1781 **. LC 8**
See also DLB 97
Lester, Richard 1932- .... **CLC 20**
Lever, Charles (James) 1806-1872 **NCLC 23**
See also DLB 21
Leverson, Ada 1865(?)-1936(?) ...... **TCLC 18**
See also Elaine
See also CA 117; DLB 153
Levertov, Denise 1923-1997**CLC 1, 2, 3, 5, 8,**
15, 28, 66; DAM POET; PC 11
See also CA 1-4R; 163; CAAS 19; CANR 3,
29, 50; DLB 5, 165; INT CANR-29; MTCW
1
Levi, Jonathan .... **CLC 76**
Levi, Peter (Chad Tigar) 1931- .... **CLC 41**
See also CA 5-8R; CANR 34; DLB 40
Levi, Primo 1919-1987 . **CLC 37, 50; SSC 12**
See also CA 13-16R; 122; CANR 12, 33, 61,
70; DLB 177; MTCW 1
Levin, Ira 1929- .... **CLC 3, 6; DAM POP**
See also CA 21-24R; CANR 17, 44, 74; MTCW
1; SATA 66

Levin, Meyer 1905-1981 . **CLC 7; DAM POP**
See also AITN 1; CA 9-12R; 104; CANR 15;
DLB 9, 28; DLBY 81; SATA 21; SATA-Obit
27
Levine, Norman 1924- .... **CLC 54**
See also CA 73-76; CAAS 23; CANR 14, 70;
DLB 88
Levine, Philip 1928-**CLC 2, 4, 5, 9, 14, 33, 118;**
DAM POET; PC 22
See also CA 9-12R; CANR 9, 37, 52; DLB 5
Levinson, Deirdre 1931- .... **CLC 49**
See also CA 73-76; CANR 70
Levi-Strauss, Claude 1908- .... **CLC 38**
See also CA 1-4R; CANR 6, 32, 57; MTCW 1
Levitin, Sonia (Wolff) 1934- .... **CLC 17**
See also AAYA 13; CA 29-32R; CANR 14, 32;
CLR 53; JRDA; MAICYA; SAAS 2; SATA
4, 68
Levon, O. U.
See Kesey, Ken (Elton)
Levy, Amy 1861-1889 .... **NCLC 59**
See also DLB 156
Lewes, George Henry 1817-1878 ... **NCLC 25**
See also DLB 55, 144
Lewis, Alun 1915-1944 .... **TCLC 3**
See also CA 104; DLB 20, 162
Lewis, C. Day
See Day Lewis, C(ecil)
Lewis, C(live) S(taples) 1898-1963**CLC 1, 3, 6,**
14, 27; DA; DAB; DAC; DAM MST, NOV,
POP; WLC
See also AAYA 3; CA 81-84; CANR 33, 71;
CDBLB 1945-1960; CLR 3, 27; DLB 15,
100, 160; JRDA; MAICYA; MTCW 1; SATA
13, 100
Lewis, Janet 1899-1998 .... **CLC 41**
See also Winters, Janet Lewis
See also CA 9-12R; 172; CANR 29, 63; CAP
1; DLBY 87
Lewis, Matthew Gregory 1775-1818**NCLC 11,**
62
See also DLB 39, 158, 178
Lewis, (Harry) Sinclair 1885-1951 **. TCLC 4,**
13, 23, 39; DA; DAB; DAC; DAM MST,
NOV; WLC
See also CA 104; 133; CDALB 1917-1929;
DLB 9, 102; DLBD 1; MTCW 1
Lewis, (Percy) Wyndham 1882(?)-1957**TCLC**
2, 9
See also CA 104; 157; DLB 15
Lewisohn, Ludwig 1883-1955 .... **TCLC 19**
See also CA 107; DLB 4, 9, 28, 102
Lewton, Val 1904-1951 .... **TCLC 76**
Leyner, Mark 1956- .... **CLC 92**
See also CA 110; CANR 28, 53
Lezama Lima, Jose 1910-1976**CLC 4, 10, 101;**
DAM MULT
See also CA 77-80; CANR 71; DLB 113; HW
L'Heureux, John (Clarke) 1934- .... **CLC 52**
See also CA 13-16R; CANR 23, 45
Liddell, C. H.
See Kuttner, Henry
Lie, Jonas (Lauritz Idemil) 1833-1908(?)
TCLC 5
See also CA 115
Lieber, Joel 1937-1971 .... **CLC 6**
See also CA 73-76; 29-32R
Lieber, Stanley Martin
See Lee, Stan
Lieberman, Laurence (James) 1935- **CLC 4,**
36
See also CA 17-20R; CANR 8, 36
Lieh Tzu fl. 7th cent. B.C.-5th cent. B.C.
CMLC 27
Lieksman, Anders
See Haavikko, Paavo Juhani
Li Fei-kan 1904-

Lucas, Craig 1951- .... **CLC 64**
See also CA 137; CANR 71

Lucas, E(dward) V(errall) 1868-1938 **T C L C 73**
See also DLB 98, 149, 153; SATA 20

Lucas, George 1944- .... **CLC 16**
See also AAYA 1, 23; CA 77-80; CANR 30; SATA 56

Lucas, Hans
See Godard, Jean-Luc

Lucas, Victoria
See Plath, Sylvia

Lucian c. 120-c. 180 .... **CMLC 32**
See also DLB 176

Ludlam, Charles 1943-1987 .... **CLC 46, 50**
See also CA 85-88; 122; CANR 72

Ludlum, Robert 1927-**CLC 22, 43; DAM NOV, POP**
See also AAYA 10; BEST 89:1, 90:3; CA 33-36R; CANR 25, 41, 68; DLBY 82; MTCW 1

Ludwig, Ken .... **CLC 60**

Ludwig, Otto 1813-1865 .... **NCLC 4**
See also DLB 129

Lugones, Leopoldo 1874-1938 .... **TCLC 15**
See also CA 116; 131; HW

Lu Hsun 1881-1936 .... **TCLC 3; SSC 20**
See also Shu-Jen, Chou

Lukacs, George .... **CLC 24**
See also Lukacs, Gyorgy (Szegeny von)

Lukacs, Gyorgy (Szegeny von) 1885-1971
See Lukacs, George
See also CA 101; 29-32R; CANR 62

Luke, Peter (Ambrose Cyprian) 1919-1995
CLC 38
See also CA 81-84; 147; CANR 72; DLB 13

Lunar, Dennis
See Mungo, Raymond

Lurie, Alison 1926- .... **CLC 4, 5, 18, 39**
See also CA 1-4R; CANR 2, 17, 50; DLB 2; MTCW 1; SATA 46

Lustig, Arnost 1926- .... **CLC 56**
See also AAYA 3; CA 69-72; CANR 47; SATA 56

Luther, Martin 1483-1546 .... **LC 9, 37**
See also DLB 179

Luxemburg, Rosa 1870(?)-1919 ..... **TCLC 63**
See also CA 118

Luzi, Mario 1914- .... **CLC 13**
See also CA 61-64; CANR 9, 70; DLB 128

Lyly, John 1554(?)-1606**LC 41; DAM DRAM; DC 7**
See also DLB 62, 167

L'Ymagier
See Gourmont, Remy (-Marie-Charles) de

Lynch, B. Suarez
See Bioy Casares, Adolfo; Borges, Jorge Luis

Lynch, David (K.) 1946- .... **CLC 66**
See also CA 124; 129

Lynch, James
See Andreyev, Leonid (Nikolaevich)

Lynch Davis, B.
See Bioy Casares, Adolfo; Borges, Jorge Luis

Lyndsay, Sir David 1490-1555 .... **LC 20**

Lynn, Kenneth S(chuyler) 1923- .... **CLC 50**
See also CA 1-4R; CANR 3, 27, 65

Lynx
See West, Rebecca

Lyons, Marcus
See Blish, James (Benjamin)

Lyre, Pinchbeck
See Sassoon, Siegfried (Lorraine)

Lytle, Andrew (Nelson) 1902-1995 ... **CLC 22**
See also CA 9-12R; 150; CANR 70; DLB 6; DLBY 95

Lyttelton, George 1709-1773 .... **LC 10**

Maas, Peter 1929- .... **CLC 29**
See also CA 93-96; INT 93-96

Macaulay, Rose 1881-1958 .... **TCLC 7, 44**
See also CA 104; DLB 36

Macaulay, Thomas Babington 1800-1859
NCLC 42
See also CDBLB 1832-1890; DLB 32, 55

MacBeth, George (Mann) 1932-1992**CLC 2, 5, 9**
See also CA 25-28R; 136; CANR 61, 66; DLB 40; MTCW 1; SATA 4; SATA-Obit 70

MacCaig, Norman (Alexander) 1910-**CLC 36; DAB; DAM POET**
See also CA 9-12R; CANR 3, 34; DLB 27

MacCarthy, Sir(Charles Otto) Desmond 1877-1952 .... **TCLC 36**
See also CA 167

MacDiarmid, Hugh**CLC 2, 4, 11, 19, 63; PC 9**
See also Grieve, C(hristopher) M(urray)
See also CDBLB 1945-1960; DLB 20

MacDonald, Anson
See Heinlein, Robert A(nson)

Macdonald, Cynthia 1928- .... **CLC 13, 19**
See also CA 49-52; CANR 4, 44; DLB 105

MacDonald, George 1824-1905 .... **TCLC 9**
See also CA 106; 137; DLB 18, 163, 178; MAICYA; SATA 33, 100

Macdonald, John
See Millar, Kenneth

MacDonald, John D(ann) 1916-1986 **CLC 3, 27, 44; DAM NOV, POP**
See also CA 1-4R; 121; CANR 1, 19, 60; DLB 8; DLBY 86; MTCW 1

Macdonald, John Ross
See Millar, Kenneth

Macdonald, Ross .... **CLC 1, 2, 3, 14, 34, 41**
See also Millar, Kenneth
See also DLBD 6

MacDougal, John
See Blish, James (Benjamin)

MacEwen, Gwendolyn (Margaret) 1941-1987
CLC 13, 55
See also CA 9-12R; 124; CANR 7, 22; DLB 53; SATA 50; SATA-Obit 55

Macha, Karel Hynek 1810-1846 .... **NCLC 46**

Machado (y Ruiz), Antonio 1875-1939**T C L C 3**
See also CA 104; DLB 108

Machado de Assis, Joaquim Maria 1839-1908
TCLC 10; BLC 2; SSC 24
See also CA 107; 153

Machen, Arthur .... **TCLC 4; SSC 20**
See also Jones, Arthur Llewellyn
See also DLB 36, 156, 178

Machiavelli, Niccolo 1469-1527**LC 8, 36; DA; DAB; DAC; DAM MST; WLCS**

MacInnes, Colin 1914-1976 .... **CLC 4, 23**
See also CA 69-72; 65-68; CANR 21; DLB 14; MTCW 1

MacInnes, Helen (Clark) 1907-1985 **CLC 27, 39; DAM POP**
See also CA 1-4R; 117; CANR 1, 28, 58; DLB 87; MTCW 1; SATA 22; SATA-Obit 44

Mackay, Mary 1855-1924
See Corelli, Marie
See also CA 118

Mackenzie, Compton (Edward Montague) 1883-1972 .... **CLC 18**
See also CA 21-22; 37-40R; CAP 2; DLB 34, 100

Mackenzie, Henry 1745-1831 .... **NCLC 41**
See also DLB 39

Mackintosh, Elizabeth 1896(?)-1952
See Tey, Josephine
See also CA 110

MacLaren, James
See Grieve, C(hristopher) M(urray)

Mac Laverty, Bernard 1942- .... **CLC 31**

See also CA 116; 118; CANR 43; INT 118

MacLean, Alistair (Stuart) 1922(?)-1987**C L C 3, 13, 50, 63; DAM POP**
See also CA 57-60; 121; CANR 28, 61; MTCW 1; SATA 23; SATA-Obit 50

Maclean, Norman (Fitzroy) 1902-1990 **C L C 78; DAM POP; SSC 13**
See also CA 102; 132; CANR 49; DLB 206

MacLeish, Archibald 1892-1982**CLC 3, 8, 14, 68; DAM POET**
See also CA 9-12R; 106; CANR 33, 63; DLB 4, 7, 45; DLBY 82; MTCW 1

MacLennan, (John) Hugh 1907-1990 **CLC 2, 14, 92; DAC; DAM MST**
See also CA 5-8R; 142; CANR 33; DLB 68; MTCW 1

MacLeod, Alistair 1936-**CLC 56; DAC; DAM MST**
See also CA 123; DLB 60

Macleod, Fiona
See Sharp, William

MacNeice, (Frederick) Louis 1907-1963**C L C 1, 4, 10, 53; DAB; DAM POET**
See also CA 85-88; CANR 61; DLB 10, 20; MTCW 1

MacNeill, Dand
See Fraser, George MacDonald

Macpherson, James 1736-1796 .... **LC 29**
See also Ossian
See also DLB 109

Macpherson, (Jean) Jay 1931- .... **CLC 14**
See also CA 5-8R; DLB 53

MacShane, Frank 1927- .... **CLC 39**
See also CA 9-12R; CANR 3, 33; DLB 111

Macumber, Mari
See Sandoz, Mari(e Susette)

Madach, Imre 1823-1864 .... **NCLC 19**

Madden, (Jerry) David 1933- ....**CLC 5, 15**
See also CA 1-4R; CAAS 3; CANR 4, 45; DLB 6; MTCW 1

Maddern, Al(an)
See Ellison, Harlan (Jay)

Madhubuti, Haki R. 1942-**CLC 6, 73; BLC 2; DAM MULT, POET; PC 5**
See also Lee, Don L.
See also BW 2; CA 73-76; CANR 24, 51, 73; DLB 5, 41; DLBD 8

Maepenn, Hugh
See Kuttner, Henry

Maepenn, K. H.
See Kuttner, Henry

Maeterlinck, Maurice 1862-1949 ... **TCLC 3; DAM DRAM**
See also CA 104; 136; DLB 192; SATA 66

Maginn, William 1794-1842 .... **NCLC 8**
See also DLB 110, 159

Mahapatra, Jayanta 1928- .... **CLC 33; DAM MULT**
See also CA 73-76; CAAS 9; CANR 15, 33, 66

Mahfouz, Naguib (Abdel Aziz Al-Sabilgi) 1911(?)-
See Mahfuz, Najib
See also BEST 89:2; CA 128; CANR 55; DAM NOV; MTCW 1

Mahfuz, Najib .... **CLC 52, 55**
See also Mahfouz, Naguib (Abdel Aziz Al-Sabilgi)
See also DLBY 88

Mahon, Derek 1941- .... **CLC 27**
See also CA 113; 128; DLB 40

Mailer, Norman 1923-**CLC 1, 2, 3, 4, 5, 8, 11, 14, 28, 39, 74, 111; DA; DAB; DAC; DAM MST, NOV, POP**
See also AITN 2; CA 9-12R; CABS 1; CANR 28, 74; CDALB 1968-1988; DLB 2, 16, 28, 185; DLBD 3; DLBY 80, 83; MTCW 1

Maillet, Antonine 1929- . **CLC 54, 118; DAC**

See also CA 115; 120; CANR 46, 74; DLB 60; INT 120

Mais, Roger 1905-1955 .... **TCLC 8**
See also BW 1; CA 105; 124; DLB 125; MTCW 1

Maistre, Joseph de 1753-1821 .... **NCLC 37**

Maitland, Frederic 1850-1906 .... **TCLC 65**

Maitland, Sara (Louise) 1950- .... **CLC 49**
See also CA 69-72; CANR 13, 59

Major, Clarence 1936-**CLC 3, 19, 48; BLC 2; DAM MULT**
See also BW 2; CA 21-24R; CAAS 6; CANR 13, 25, 53; DLB 33

Major, Kevin (Gerald) 1949- .. **CLC 26; DAC**
See also AAYA 16; CA 97-100; CANR 21, 38; CLR 11; DLB 60; INT CANR-21; JRDA; MAICYA; SATA 32, 82

Maki, James
See Ozu, Yasujiro

Malabaila, Damiano
See Levi, Primo

Malamud, Bernard 1914-1986**CLC 1, 2, 3, 5, 8, 9, 11, 18, 27, 44, 78, 85; DA; DAB; DAC; DAM MST, NOV, POP; SSC 15; WLC**
See also AAYA 16; CA 5-8R; 118; CABS 1; CANR 28, 62; CDALB 1941-1968; DLB 2, 28, 152; DLBY 80, 86; MTCW 1

Malan, Herman
See Bosman, Herman Charles; Bosman, Herman Charles

Malaparte, Curzio 1898-1957 .... **TCLC 52**

Malcolm, Dan
See Silverberg, Robert

Malcolm X .... **CLC 82, 117; BLC 2; WLCS**
See also Little, Malcolm

Malherbe, Francois de 1555-1628 .... **LC 5**

Mallarme, Stephane 1842-1898 **NCLC 4, 41; DAM POET; PC 4**

Mallet-Joris, Francoise 1930- .... **CLC 11**
See also CA 65-68; CANR 17; DLB 83

Malley, Ern
See McAuley, James Phillip

Mallowan, Agatha Christie
See Christie, Agatha (Mary Clarissa)

Maloff, Saul 1922- .... **CLC 5**
See also CA 33-36R

Malone, Louis
See MacNeice, (Frederick) Louis

Malone, Michael (Christopher) 1942-**CLC 43**
See also CA 77-80; CANR 14, 32, 57

Malory, (Sir) Thomas 1410(?)-1471(?)**LC 11; DA; DAB; DAC; DAM MST; WLCS**
See also CDBLB Before 1660; DLB 146; SATA 59; SATA-Brief 33

Malouf, (George Joseph) David 1934-**CLC 28, 86**
See also CA 124; CANR 50, 76

Malraux, (Georges-)Andre 1901-1976**CLC 1, 4, 9, 13, 15, 57; DAM NOV**
See also CA 21-22; 69-72; CANR 34, 58; CAP 2; DLB 72; MTCW 1

Malzberg, Barry N(athaniel) 1939- ... **CLC 7**
See also CA 61-64; CAAS 4; CANR 16; DLB 8

Mamet, David (Alan) 1947-**CLC 9, 15, 34, 46, 91; DAM DRAM; DC 4**
See also AAYA 3; CA 81-84; CABS 3; CANR 15, 41, 67, 72; DLB 7; MTCW 1

Mamoulian, Rouben (Zachary) 1897-1987
CLC 16
See also CA 25-28R; 124

Mandelstam, Osip (Emilievich) 1891(?)-1938(?)
TCLC 2, 6; PC 14
See also CA 104; 150

Mander, (Mary) Jane 1877-1949 ... **TCLC 31**
See also CA 162

Mandeville, John fl. 1350- .... **CMLC 19**

See also DLB 146

Mandiargues, Andre Pieyre de .... **CLC 41**
See also Pieyre de Mandiargues, Andre
See also DLB 83

Mandrake, Ethel Belle
See Thurman, Wallace (Henry)

Mangan, James Clarence 1803-1849**NCLC 27**

Maniere, J.-E.
See Giraudoux, (Hippolyte) Jean

Mankiewicz, Herman (Jacob) 1897-1953
TCLC 85
See also CA 120; 169; DLB 26

Manley, (Mary) Delariviere 1672(?)-1724**L C 1, 42**
See also DLB 39, 80

Mann, Abel
See Creasey, John

Mann, Emily 1952- .... **DC 7**
See also CA 130; CANR 55

Mann, (Luiz) Heinrich 1871-1950 ... **TCLC 9**
See also CA 106; 164; DLB 66, 118

Mann, (Paul) Thomas 1875-1955 **TCLC 2, 8, 14, 21, 35, 44, 60; DA; DAB; DAC; DAM MST, NOV; SSC 5; WLC**
See also CA 104; 128; DLB 66; MTCW 1

Mannheim, Karl 1893-1947 .... **TCLC 65**

Manning, David
See Faust, Frederick (Schiller)

Manning, Frederic 1887(?)-1935 ... **TCLC 25**
See also CA 124

Manning, Olivia 1915-1980 .... **CLC 5, 19**
See also CA 5-8R; 101; CANR 29; MTCW 1

Mano, D. Keith 1942- .... **CLC 2, 10**
See also CA 25-28R; CAAS 6; CANR 26, 57; DLB 6

Mansfield, Katherine**TCLC 2, 8, 39; DAB; SSC 9, 23; WLC**
See also Beauchamp, Kathleen Mansfield
See also DLB 162

Manso, Peter 1940- .... **CLC 39**
See also CA 29-32R; CANR 44

Mantecon, Juan Jimenez
See Jimenez (Mantecon), Juan Ramon

Manton, Peter
See Creasey, John

Man Without a Spleen, A
See Chekhov, Anton (Pavlovich)

Manzoni, Alessandro 1785-1873 .... **NCLC 29**

Map, Walter 1140-1209 .... **CMLC 32**

Mapu, Abraham (ben Jekutiel) 1808-1867
NCLC 18

Mara, Sally
See Queneau, Raymond

Marat, Jean Paul 1743-1793 .... **LC 10**

Marcel, Gabriel Honore 1889-1973 . **CLC 15**
See also CA 102; 45-48; MTCW 1

Marchbanks, Samuel
See Davies, (William) Robertson

Marchi, Giacomo
See Bassani, Giorgio

Margulies, Donald .... **CLC 76**

Marie de France c. 12th cent. - **CMLC 8; PC 22**
See also DLB 208

Marie de l'Incarnation 1599-1672 ...... **LC 10**

Marier, Captain Victor
See Griffith, D(avid Lewelyn) W(ark)

Mariner, Scott
See Pohl, Frederik

Marinetti, Filippo Tommaso 1876-1944**TCLC 10**
See also CA 107; DLB 114

Marivaux, Pierre Carlet de Chamblain de 1688-1763 .... **LC 4; DC 7**

Markandaya, Kamala .... **CLC 8, 38**
See also Taylor, Kamala (Purnaiya)

Markfield, Wallace 1926- .... **CLC 8**

See also CA 69-72; CAAS 3; DLB 2, 28

Markham, Edwin 1852-1940 .... **TCLC 47**
See also CA 160; DLB 54, 186

Markham, Robert
See Amis, Kingsley (William)

Marks, J
See Highwater, Jamake (Mamake)

Marks-Highwater, J
See Highwater, Jamake (Mamake)

Markson, David M(errill) 1927- .... **CLC 67**
See also CA 49-52; CANR 1

Marley, Bob .... **CLC 17**
See also Marley, Robert Nesta

Marley, Robert Nesta 1945-1981
See Marley, Bob
See also CA 107; 103

Marlowe, Christopher 1564-1593 **LC 22, 47; DA; DAB; DAC; DAM DRAM, MST; DC 1; WLC**
See also CDBLB Before 1660; DLB 62

Marlowe, Stephen 1928-
See Queen, Ellery
See also CA 13-16R; CANR 6, 55

Marmontel, Jean-Francois 1723-1799 .. **LC 2**

Marquand, John P(hillips) 1893-1960**CLC 2, 10**
See also CA 85-88; CANR 73; DLB 9, 102

Marques, Rene 1919-1979 ..... **CLC 96; DAM MULT; HLC**
See also CA 97-100; 85-88; DLB 113; HW

Marquez, Gabriel (Jose) Garcia
See Garcia Marquez, Gabriel (Jose)

Marquis, Don(ald Robert Perry) 1878-1937
TCLC 7
See also CA 104; 166; DLB 11, 25

Marric, J. J.
See Creasey, John

Marryat, Frederick 1792-1848 .... **NCLC 3**
See also DLB 21, 163

Marsden, James
See Creasey, John

Marsh, (Edith) Ngaio 1899-1982 **CLC 7, 53; DAM POP**
See also CA 9-12R; CANR 6, 58; DLB 77; MTCW 1

Marshall, Garry 1934- .... **CLC 17**
See also AAYA 3; CA 111; SATA 60

Marshall, Paule 1929- .. **CLC 27, 72; BLC 3; DAM MULT; SSC 3**
See also BW 2; CA 77-80; CANR 25, 73; DLB 157; MTCW 1

Marshallik
See Zangwill, Israel

Marsten, Richard
See Hunter, Evan

Marston, John 1576-1634**LC 33; DAM DRAM**
See also DLB 58, 172

Martha, Henry
See Harris, Mark

Marti, Jose 1853-1895**NCLC 63; DAM MULT; HLC**

Martial c. 40-c. 104 .... **PC 10**

Martin, Ken
See Hubbard, L(afayette) Ron(ald)

Martin, Richard
See Creasey, John

Martin, Steve 1945- .... **CLC 30**
See also CA 97-100; CANR 30; MTCW 1

Martin, Valerie 1948- .... **CLC 89**
See also BEST 90:2; CA 85-88; CANR 49

Martin, Violet Florence 1862-1915 **TCLC 51**

Martin, Webber
See Silverberg, Robert

Martindale, Patrick Victor
See White, Patrick (Victor Martindale)

Martin du Gard, Roger 1881-1958 **TCLC 24**
See also CA 118; DLB 65

Martineau, Harriet 1802-1876 .... **NCLC 26**
See also DLB 21, 55, 159, 163, 166, 190; YABC 2

Martines, Julia
See O'Faolain, Julia

Martinez, Enrique Gonzalez
See Gonzalez Martinez, Enrique

Martinez, Jacinto Benavente y
See Benavente (y Martinez), Jacinto

Martinez Ruiz, Jose 1873-1967
See Azorin; Ruiz, Jose Martinez
See also CA 93-96; HW

Martinez Sierra, Gregorio 1881-1947**TCLC 6**
See also CA 115

Martinez Sierra, Maria (de la O'LeJarraga) 1874-1974 ....
TCLC 6
See also CA 115

Martinsen, Martin
See Follett, Ken(neth Martin)

Martinson, Harry (Edmund) 1904-1978**C L C 14**
See also CA 77-80; CANR 34

Marut, Ret
See Traven, B.

Marut, Robert
See Traven, B.

Marvell, Andrew 1621-1678 ... **LC 4, 43; DA; DAB; DAC; DAM MST, POET; PC 10; WLC**
See also CDBLB 1660-1789; DLB 131

Marx, Karl (Heinrich) 1818-1883 . **NCLC 17**
See also DLB 129

Masaoka Shiki .... **TCLC 18**
See also Masaoka Tsunenori

Masaoka Tsunenori 1867-1902
See Masaoka Shiki
See also CA 117

Masefield, John (Edward) 1878-1967**CLC 11, 47; DAM POET**
See also CA 19-20; 25-28R; CANR 33; CAP 2; CDBLB 1890-1914; DLB 10, 19, 153, 160; MTCW 1; SATA 19

Maso, Carole 19(?)- .... **CLC 44**
See also CA 170

Mason, Bobbie Ann 1940-**CLC 28, 43, 82; SSC 4**
See also AAYA 5; CA 53-56; CANR 11, 31, 58; DLB 173; DLBY 87; INT CANR-31; MTCW 1

Mason, Ernst
See Pohl, Frederik

Mason, Lee W.
See Malzberg, Barry N(athaniel)

Mason, Nick 1945- .... **CLC 35**

Mason, Tally
See Derleth, August (William)

Mass, William
See Gibson, William

Master Lao
See Lao Tzu

Masters, Edgar Lee 1868-1950 **TCLC 2, 25; DA; DAC; DAM MST, POET; PC 1; WLCS**
See also CA 104; 133; CDALB 1865-1917; DLB 54; MTCW 1

Masters, Hilary 1928- .... **CLC 48**
See also CA 25-28R; CANR 13, 47

Mastrosimone, William 19(?)- .... **CLC 36**

Mathe, Albert
See Camus, Albert

Mather, Cotton 1663-1728 .... **LC 38**
See also CDALB 1640-1865; DLB 24, 30, 140

Mather, Increase 1639-1723 .... **LC 38**
See also DLB 24

Matheson, Richard Burton 1926- ..... **CLC 37**
See also CA 97-100; DLB 8, 44; INT 97-100

Mathews, Harry 1930- .... **CLC 6, 52**
See also CA 21-24R; CAAS 6; CANR 18, 40

Mathews, John Joseph 1894-1979 .. **CLC 84; DAM MULT**
See also CA 19-20; 142; CANR 45; CAP 2; DLB 175; NNAL

Mathias, Roland (Glyn) 1915- .... **CLC 45**
See also CA 97-100; CANR 19, 41; DLB 27

Matsuo Basho 1644-1694 .... **PC 3**
See also DAM POET

Matthesun, Rodney
See Creasey, John

Matthews, Greg 1949- .... **CLC 45**
See also CA 135

Matthews, William (Procter, III) 1942-1997 **CLC 40**
See also CA 29-32R; 162; CAAS 18; CANR 12, 57; DLB 5

Matthias, John (Edward) 1941- .... **CLC 9**
See also CA 33-36R; CANR 56

Matthiessen, Peter 1927-**CLC 5, 7, 11, 32, 64; DAM NOV**
See also AAYA 6; BEST 90:4; CA 9-12R; CANR 21, 50, 73; DLB 6, 173; MTCW 1; SATA 27

Maturin, Charles Robert 1780(?)-1824**NCLC 6**
See also DLB 178

Matute (Ausejo), Ana Maria 1925- .. **CLC 11**
See also CA 89-92; MTCW 1

Maugham, W. S.
See Maugham, W(illiam) Somerset

Maugham, W(illiam) Somerset 1874-1965 **CLC 1, 11, 15, 67, 93; DA; DAB; DAC; DAM DRAM, MST, NOV; SSC 8; WLC**
See also CA 5-8R; 25-28R; CANR 40; CDBLB 1914-1945; DLB 10, 36, 77, 100, 162, 195; MTCW 1; SATA 54

Maugham, William Somerset
See Maugham, W(illiam) Somerset

Maupassant, (Henri Rene Albert) Guy de 1850-1893 ....
NCLC 1, 42; DA; DAB; DAC; DAM MST; SSC 1; WLC
See also DLB 123

Maupin, Armistead 1944-**CLC 95; DAM POP**
See also CA 125; 130; CANR 58; INT 130

Maurhut, Richard
See Traven, B.

Mauriac, Claude 1914-1996 .... **CLC 9**
See also CA 89-92; 152; DLB 83

Mauriac, Francois (Charles) 1885-1970 **C L C 4, 9, 56; SSC 24**
See also CA 25-28; CAP 2; DLB 65; MTCW 1

Mavor, Osborne Henry 1888-1951
See Bridie, James
See also CA 104

Maxwell, William (Keepers, Jr.) 1908-**CLC 19**
See also CA 93-96; CANR 54; DLBY 80; INT 93-96

May, Elaine 1932- .... **CLC 16**
See also CA 124; 142; DLB 44

Mayakovski, Vladimir (Vladimirovich) 1893-1930 .... **TCLC 4, 18**
See also CA 104; 158

Mayhew, Henry 1812-1887 .... **NCLC 31**
See also DLB 18, 55, 190

Mayle, Peter 1939(?)- .... **CLC 89**
See also CA 139; CANR 64

Maynard, Joyce 1953- .... **CLC 23**
See also CA 111; 129; CANR 64

Mayne, William (James Carter) 1928-**CLC 12**
See also AAYA 20; CA 9-12R; CANR 37; CLR 25; JRDA; MAICYA; SAAS 11; SATA 6, 68

Mayo, Jim
See L'Amour, Louis (Dearborn)

Maysles, Albert 1926- .... **CLC 16**

See also CA 29-32R

Maysles, David 1932- .... **CLC 16**

Mazer, Norma Fox 1931- .... **CLC 26**
See also AAYA 5; CA 69-72; CANR 12, 32, 66; CLR 23; JRDA; MAICYA; SAAS 1; SATA 24, 67, 105

Mazzini, Guiseppe 1805-1872 .... **NCLC 34**

McAuley, James Phillip 1917-1976 .. **CLC 45**
See also CA 97-100

McBain, Ed
See Hunter, Evan

McBrien, William Augustine 1930-.. **CLC 44**
See also CA 107

McCaffrey, Anne (Inez) 1926-**CLC 17; DAM NOV, POP**
See also AAYA 6; AITN 2; BEST 89:2; CA 25-28R; CANR 15, 35, 55; CLR 49; DLB 8; JRDA; MAICYA; MTCW 1; SAAS 11; SATA 8, 70

McCall, Nathan 1955(?)- .... **CLC 86**
See also CA 146

McCann, Arthur
See Campbell, John W(ood, Jr.)

McCann, Edson
See Pohl, Frederik

McCarthy, Charles, Jr. 1933-
See McCarthy, Cormac
See also CANR 42, 69; DAM POP

McCarthy, Cormac 1933- **CLC 4, 57, 59, 101**
See also McCarthy, Charles, Jr.
See also DLB 6, 143

McCarthy, Mary (Therese) 1912-1989**CLC 1, 3, 5, 14, 24, 39, 59; SSC 24**
See also CA 5-8R; 129; CANR 16, 50, 64; DLB 2; DLBY 81; INT CANR-16; MTCW 1

McCartney, (James) Paul 1942- **CLC 12, 35**
See also CA 146

McCauley, Stephen (D.) 1955- .... **CLC 50**
See also CA 141

McClure, Michael (Thomas) 1932-**CLC 6, 10**
See also CA 21-24R; CANR 17, 46; DLB 16

McCorkle, Jill (Collins) 1958- .... **CLC 51**
See also CA 121; DLBY 87

McCourt, Frank 1930- .... **CLC 109**
See also CA 157

McCourt, James 1941- .... **CLC 5**
See also CA 57-60

McCoy, Horace (Stanley) 1897-1955**TCLC 28**
See also CA 108; 155; DLB 9

McCrae, John 1872-1918 .... **TCLC 12**
See also CA 109; DLB 92

McCreigh, James
See Pohl, Frederik

McCullers, (Lula) Carson (Smith) 1917-1967 **CLC 1, 4, 10, 12, 48, 100; DA; DAB; DAC; DAM MST, NOV; SSC 9, 24; WLC**
See also AAYA 21; CA 5-8R; 25-28R; CABS 1, 3; CANR 18; CDALB 1941-1968; DLB 2, 7, 173; MTCW 1; SATA 27

McCulloch, John Tyler
See Burroughs, Edgar Rice

McCullough, Colleen 1938(?)- **CLC 27, 107; DAM NOV, POP**
See also CA 81-84; CANR 17, 46, 67; MTCW 1

McDermott, Alice 1953- .... **CLC 90**
See also CA 109; CANR 40

McElroy, Joseph 1930- .... **CLC 5, 47**
See also CA 17-20R

McEwan, Ian (Russell) 1948- .... **CLC 13, 66; DAM NOV**
See also BEST 90:4; CA 61-64; CANR 14, 41, 69; DLB 14, 194; MTCW 1

McFadden, David 1940- .... **CLC 48**
See also CA 104; DLB 60; INT 104

McFarland, Dennis 1950- .... **CLC 65**
See also CA 165

14, 34, 39; **DAM POET**
  See also CA 1-4R; 116; CANR 2, 55; DLB 48
Militant
  See Sandburg, Carl (August)
Mill, John Stuart 1806-1873 .... **NCLC 11, 58**
  See also CDBLB 1832-1890; DLB 55, 190
Millar, Kenneth 1915-1983 .... **CLC 14; DAM POP**
  See also Macdonald, Ross
  See also CA 9-12R; 110; CANR 16, 63; DLB 2; DLBD 6; DLBY 83; MTCW 1
Millay, E. Vincent
  See Millay, Edna St. Vincent
Millay, Edna St. Vincent 1892-1950 **TCLC 4, 49; DA; DAB; DAC; DAM MST, POET; PC 6; WLCS**
  See also CA 104; 130; CDALB 1917-1929; DLB 45; MTCW 1
Miller, Arthur 1915- **CLC 1, 2, 6, 10, 15, 26, 47, 78; DA; DAB; DAC; DAM DRAM, MST; DC 1; WLC**
  See also AAYA 15; AITN 1; CA 1-4R; CABS 3; CANR 2, 30, 54, 76; CDALB 1941-1968; DLB 7; MTCW 1
Miller, Henry (Valentine) 1891-1980 **CLC 1, 2, 4, 9, 14, 43, 84; DA; DAB; DAC; DAM MST, NOV; WLC**
  See also CA 9-12R; 97-100; CANR 33, 64; CDALB 1929-1941; DLB 4, 9; DLBY 80; MTCW 1
Miller, Jason 1939(?)- .... **CLC 2**
  See also AITN 1; CA 73-76; DLB 7
Miller, Sue 1943- .... **CLC 44; DAM POP**
  See also BEST 90:3; CA 139; CANR 59; DLB 143
Miller, Walter M(ichael, Jr.) 1923- **CLC 4, 30**
  See also CA 85-88; DLB 8
Millett, Kate 1934- .... **CLC 67**
  See also AITN 1; CA 73-76; CANR 32, 53, 76; MTCW 1
Millhauser, Steven (Lewis) 1943- **CLC 21, 54, 109**
  See also CA 110; 111; CANR 63; DLB 2; INT 111
Millin, Sarah Gertrude 1889-1968 ... **CLC 49**
  See also CA 102; 93-96
Milne, A(lan) A(lexander) 1882-1956 **TCLC 6, 88; DAB; DAC; DAM MST**
  See also CA 104; 133; CLR 1, 26; DLB 10, 77, 100, 160; MAICYA; MTCW 1; SATA 100; YABC 1
Milner, Ron(ald) 1938- **CLC 56; BLC 3; DAM MULT**
  See also AITN 1; BW 1; CA 73-76; CANR 24; DLB 38; MTCW 1
Milnes, Richard Monckton 1809-1885 **N C L C 61**
  See also DLB 32, 184
Milosz, Czeslaw 1911- **CLC 5, 11, 22, 31, 56, 82; DAM MST, POET; PC 8; WLCS**
  See also CA 81-84; CANR 23, 51; MTCW 1
Milton, John 1608-1674 **LC 9, 43; DA; DAB; DAC; DAM MST, POET; PC 19; WLC**
  See also CDBLB 1660-1789; DLB 131, 151
Min, Anchee 1957- .... **CLC 86**
  See also CA 146
Minehaha, Cornelius
  See Wedekind, (Benjamin) Frank(lin)
Miner, Valerie 1947- .... **CLC 40**
  See also CA 97-100; CANR 59
Minimo, Duca
  See D'Annunzio, Gabriele
Minot, Susan 1956- .... **CLC 44**
  See also CA 134
Minus, Ed 1938- .... **CLC 39**
Miranda, Javier
  See Bioy Casares, Adolfo

Mirbeau, Octave 1848-1917 .... **TCLC 55**
  See also DLB 123, 192
Miro (Ferrer), Gabriel (Francisco Victor) 1879-1930 .... **TCLC 5**
  See also CA 104
Mishima, Yukio 1925-1970 **CLC 2, 4, 6, 9, 27; DC 1; SSC 4**
  See also Hiraoka, Kimitake
  See also DLB 182
Mistral, Frederic 1830-1914 .... **TCLC 51**
  See also CA 122
Mistral, Gabriela .... **TCLC 2; HLC**
  See also Godoy Alcayaga, Lucila
Mistry, Rohinton 1952- .... **CLC 71; DAC**
  See also CA 141
Mitchell, Clyde
  See Ellison, Harlan (Jay); Silverberg, Robert
Mitchell, James Leslie 1901-1935
  See Gibbon, Lewis Grassic
  See also CA 104; DLB 15
Mitchell, Joni 1943- .... **CLC 12**
  See also CA 112
Mitchell, Joseph (Quincy) 1908-1996 **CLC 98**
  See also CA 77-80; 152; CANR 69; DLB 185; DLBY 96
Mitchell, Margaret (Munnerlyn) 1900-1949 **TCLC 11; DAM NOV, POP**
  See also AAYA 23; CA 109; 125; CANR 55; DLB 9; MTCW 1
Mitchell, Peggy
  See Mitchell, Margaret (Munnerlyn)
Mitchell, S(ilas) Weir 1829-1914 ... **TCLC 36**
  See also CA 165; DLB 202
Mitchell, W(illiam) O(rmond) 1914-1998 **CLC 25; DAC; DAM MST**
  See also CA 77-80; 165; CANR 15, 43; DLB 88
Mitchell, William 1879-1936 .... **TCLC 81**
Mitford, Mary Russell 1787-1855 ... **NCLC 4**
  See also DLB 110, 116
Mitford, Nancy 1904-1973 .... **CLC 44**
  See also CA 9-12R; DLB 191
Miyamoto, Yuriko 1899-1951 .... **TCLC 37**
  See also CA 170; DLB 180
Miyazawa, Kenji 1896-1933 .... **TCLC 76**
  See also CA 157
Mizoguchi, Kenji 1898-1956 .... **TCLC 72**
  See also CA 167
Mo, Timothy (Peter) 1950(?)- .... **CLC 46**
  See also CA 117; DLB 194; MTCW 1
Modarressi, Taghi (M.) 1931- .... **CLC 44**
  See also CA 121; 134; INT 134
Modiano, Patrick (Jean) 1945- .... **CLC 18**
  See also CA 85-88; CANR 17, 40; DLB 83
Moerck, Paal
  See Roelvaag, O(le) E(dvart)
Mofolo, Thomas (Mokopu) 1875(?)-1948 **TCLC 22; BLC 3; DAM MULT**
  See also CA 121; 153
Mohr, Nicholasa 1938- **CLC 12; DAM MULT; HLC**
  See also AAYA 8; CA 49-52; CANR 1, 32, 64; CLR 22; DLB 145; HW; JRDA; SAAS 8; SATA 8, 97
Mojtabai, A(nn) G(race) 1938- **CLC 5, 9, 15, 29**
  See also CA 85-88
Moliere 1622-1673 **LC 10, 28; DA; DAB; DAC; DAM DRAM, MST; WLC**
Molin, Charles
  See Mayne, William (James Carter)
Molnar, Ferenc 1878-1952 .. **TCLC 20; DAM DRAM**
  See also CA 109; 153
Momaday, N(avarre) Scott 1934- **CLC 2, 19, 85, 95; DA; DAB; DAC; DAM MST,**

MULT, NOV, POP; PC 25; WLCS
  See also AAYA 11; CA 25-28R; CANR 14, 34, 68; DLB 143, 175; INT CANR-14; MTCW 1; NNAL; SATA 48; SATA-Brief 30
Monette, Paul 1945-1995 .... **CLC 82**
  See also CA 139; 147
Monroe, Harriet 1860-1936 .... **TCLC 12**
  See also CA 109; DLB 54, 91
Monroe, Lyle
  See Heinlein, Robert A(nson)
Montagu, Elizabeth 1720-1800 .... **NCLC 7**
Montagu, Mary (Pierrepont) Wortley 1689-1762 .... **LC 9; PC 16**
  See also DLB 95, 101
Montagu, W. H.
  See Coleridge, Samuel Taylor
Montague, John (Patrick) 1929- **CLC 13, 46**
  See also CA 9-12R; CANR 9, 69; DLB 40; MTCW 1
Montaigne, Michel (Eyquem) de 1533-1592 **LC 8; DA; DAB; DAC; DAM MST; WLC**
Montale, Eugenio 1896-1981 **CLC 7, 9, 18; PC 13**
  See also CA 17-20R; 104; CANR 30; DLB 114; MTCW 1
Montesquieu, Charles-Louis de Secondat 1689-1755 .... **LC 7**
Montgomery, (Robert) Bruce 1921-1978
  See Crispin, Edmund
  See also CA 104
Montgomery, L(ucy) M(aud) 1874-1942 **TCLC 51; DAC; DAM MST**
  See also AAYA 12; CA 108; 137; CLR 8; DLB 92; DLBD 14; JRDA; MAICYA; SATA 100; YABC 1
Montgomery, Marion H., Jr. 1925- .... **CLC 7**
  See also AITN 1; CA 1-4R; CANR 3, 48; DLB 6
Montgomery, Max
  See Davenport, Guy (Mattison, Jr.)
Montherlant, Henry (Milon) de 1896-1972 **CLC 8, 19; DAM DRAM**
  See also CA 85-88; 37-40R; DLB 72; MTCW 1
Monty Python
  See Chapman, Graham; Cleese, John (Marwood); Gilliam, Terry (Vance); Idle, Eric; Jones, Terence Graham Parry; Palin, Michael (Edward)
  See also AAYA 7
Moodie, Susanna (Strickland) 1803-1885 **NCLC 14**
  See also DLB 99
Mooney, Edward 1951-
  See Mooney, Ted
  See also CA 130
Mooney, Ted .... **CLC 25**
  See also Mooney, Edward
Moorcock, Michael (John) 1939- **CLC 5, 27, 58**
  See also AAYA 26; CA 45-48; CAAS 5; CANR 2, 17, 38, 64; DLB 14; MTCW 1; SATA 93
Moore, Brian 1921- **CLC 1, 3, 5, 7, 8, 19, 32, 90; DAB; DAC; DAM MST**
  See also CA 1-4R; CANR 1, 25, 42, 63; MTCW 1
Moore, Edward
  See Muir, Edwin
Moore, G. E. 1873-1958 .... **TCLC 89**
Moore, George Augustus 1852-1933 **TCLC 7; SSC 19**
  See also CA 104; DLB 10, 18, 57, 135
Moore, Lorrie .... **CLC 39, 45, 68**
  See also Moore, Marie Lorena
Moore, Marianne (Craig) 1887-1972 **CLC 1, 2, 4, 8, 10, 13, 19, 47; DA; DAB; DAC; DAM MST, POET; PC 4; WLCS**
  See also CA 1-4R; 33-36R; CANR 3, 61;

Northrup, B. A.
See Hubbard, L(afayette) Ron(ald)
North Staffs
See Hulme, T(homas) E(rnest)
Norton, Alice Mary
See Norton, Andre
See also MAICYA; SATA 1, 43
Norton, Andre 1912- .... CLC 12
See also Norton, Alice Mary
See also AAYA 14; CA 1-4R; CANR 68; CLR 50; DLB 8, 52; JRDA; MTCW 1; SATA 91
Norton, Caroline 1808-1877 .... NCLC 47
See also DLB 21, 159, 199
Norway, Nevil Shute 1899-1960
See Shute, Nevil
See also CA 102; 93-96
Norwid, Cyprian Kamil 1821-1883 NCLC 17
Nosille, Nabrah
See Ellison, Harlan (Jay)
Nossack, Hans Erich 1901-1978 .... CLC 6
See also CA 93-96; 85-88; DLB 69
Nostradamus 1503-1566 .... LC 27
Nosu, Chuji
See Ozu, Yasujiro
Notenburg, Eleanora (Genrikhovna) von
See Guro, Elena
Nova, Craig 1945- .... CLC 7, 31
See also CA 45-48; CANR 2, 53
Novak, Joseph
See Kosinski, Jerzy (Nikodem)
Novalis 1772-1801 .... NCLC 13
See also DLB 90
Novis, Emile
See Weil, Simone (Adolphine)
Nowlan, Alden (Albert) 1933-1983 CLC 15;
DAC; DAM MST
See also CA 9-12R; CANR 5; DLB 53
Noyes, Alfred 1880-1958 .... TCLC 7
See also CA 104; DLB 20
Nunn, Kem .... CLC 34
See also CA 159
Nye, Robert 1939- .. CLC 13, 42; DAM NOV
See also CA 33-36R; CANR 29, 67; DLB 14;
MTCW 1; SATA 6
Nyro, Laura 1947- .... CLC 17
Oates, Joyce Carol 1938-CLC 1, 2, 3, 6, 9, 11,
15, 19, 33, 52, 108; DA; DAB; DAC; DAM
MST, NOV, POP; SSC 6; WLC
See also AAYA 15; AITN 1; BEST 89:2; CA 5-
8R; CANR 25, 45, 74; CDALB 1968-1988;
DLB 2, 5, 130; DLBY 81; INT CANR-25;
MTCW 1
O'Brien, Darcy 1939-1998 .... CLC 11
See also CA 21-24R; 167; CANR 8, 59
O'Brien, E. G.
See Clarke, Arthur C(harles)
O'Brien, Edna 1936- CLC 3, 5, 8, 13, 36, 65,
116; DAM NOV; SSC 10
See also CA 1-4R; CANR 6, 41, 65; CDBLB
1960 to Present; DLB 14; MTCW 1
O'Brien, Fitz-James 1828-1862 ..... NCLC 21
See also DLB 74
O'Brien, Flann .... CLC 1, 4, 5, 7, 10, 47
See also O Nuallain, Brian
O'Brien, Richard 1942- .... CLC 17
See also CA 124
O'Brien, (William) Tim(othy) 1946- . CLC 7,
19, 40, 103; DAM POP
See also AAYA 16; CA 85-88; CANR 40, 58;
DLB 152; DLBD 9; DLBY 80
Obstfelder, Sigbjoern 1866-1900 ... TCLC 23
See also CA 123
O'Casey, Sean 1880-1964 CLC 1, 5, 9, 11, 15,
88; DAB; DAC; DAM DRAM, MST;
WLCS
See also CA 89-92; CANR 62; CDBLB 1914-
1945; DLB 10; MTCW 1

O'Cathasaigh, Sean
See O'Casey, Sean
Ochs, Phil 1940-1976 .... CLC 17
See also CA 65-68
O'Connor, Edwin (Greene) 1918-1968CLC 14
See also CA 93-96; 25-28R
O'Connor, (Mary) Flannery 1925-1964 C L C
1, 2, 3, 6, 10, 13, 15, 21, 66, 104; DA; DAB;
DAC; DAM MST, NOV; SSC 1, 23; WLC
See also AAYA 7; CA 1-4R; CANR 3, 41;
CDALB 1941-1968; DLB 2, 152; DLBD 12;
DLBY 80; MTCW 1
O'Connor, Frank .... CLC 23; SSC 5
See also O'Donovan, Michael John
See also DLB 162
O'Dell, Scott 1898-1989 .... CLC 30
See also AAYA 3; CA 61-64; 129; CANR 12,
30; CLR 1, 16; DLB 52; JRDA; MAICYA;
SATA 12, 60
Odets, Clifford 1906-1963CLC 2, 28, 98; DAM
DRAM; DC 6
See also CA 85-88; CANR 62; DLB 7, 26;
MTCW 1
O'Doherty, Brian 1934- .... CLC 76
See also CA 105
O'Donnell, K. M.
See Malzberg, Barry N(athaniel)
O'Donnell, Lawrence
See Kuttner, Henry
O'Donovan, Michael John 1903-1966CLC 14
See also O'Connor, Frank
See also CA 93-96
Oe, Kenzaburo 1935- CLC 10, 36, 86; DAM
NOV; SSC 20
See also CA 97-100; CANR 36, 50, 74; DLB
182; DLBY 94; MTCW 1
O'Faolain, Julia 1932- .... CLC 6, 19, 47, 108
See also CA 81-84; CAAS 2; CANR 12, 61;
DLB 14; MTCW 1
O'Faolain, Sean 1900-1991 CLC 1, 7, 14, 32,
70; SSC 13
See also CA 61-64; 134; CANR 12, 66; DLB
15, 162; MTCW 1
O'Flaherty, Liam 1896-1984CLC 5, 34; SSC 6
See also CA 101; 113; CANR 35; DLB 36, 162;
DLBY 84; MTCW 1
Ogilvy, Gavin
See Barrie, J(ames) M(atthew)
O'Grady, Standish (James) 1846-1928T C L C
5
See also CA 104; 157
O'Grady, Timothy 1951- .... CLC 59
See also CA 138
O'Hara, Frank 1926-1966 . CLC 2, 5, 13, 78;
DAM POET
See also CA 9-12R; 25-28R; CANR 33; DLB
5, 16, 193; MTCW 1
O'Hara, John (Henry) 1905-1970CLC 1, 2, 3,
6, 11, 42; DAM NOV; SSC 15
See also CA 5-8R; 25-28R; CANR 31, 60;
CDALB 1929-1941; DLB 9, 86; DLBD 2;
MTCW 1
O Hehir, Diana 1922- .... CLC 41
See also CA 93-96
Okigbo, Christopher (Ifenayichukwu) 1932-
1967 . CLC 25, 84; BLC 3; DAM MULT,
POET; PC 7
See also BW 1; CA 77-80; CANR 74; DLB 125;
MTCW 1
Okri, Ben 1959- .... CLC 87
See also BW 2; CA 130; 138; CANR 65; DLB
157; INT 138
Olds, Sharon 1942- .... CLC 32, 39, 85; DAM
POET; PC 22
See also CA 101; CANR 18, 41, 66; DLB 120
Oldstyle, Jonathan
See Irving, Washington

Olesha, Yuri (Karlovich) 1899-1960 .. CLC 8
See also CA 85-88
Oliphant, Laurence 1829(?)-1888 .. NCLC 47
See also DLB 18, 166
Oliphant, Margaret (Oliphant Wilson) 1828-
1897 .... NCLC 11, 61; SSC 25
See also DLB 18, 159, 190
Oliver, Mary 1935- .... CLC 19, 34, 98
See also CA 21-24R; CANR 9, 43; DLB 5, 193
Olivier, Laurence (Kerr) 1907-1989 . CLC 20
See also CA 111; 150; 129
Olsen, Tillie 1912-CLC 4, 13, 114; DA; DAB;
DAC; DAM MST; SSC 11
See also CA 1-4R; CANR 1, 43, 74; DLB 28,
206; DLBY 80; MTCW 1
Olson, Charles (John) 1910-1970CLC 1, 2, 5,
6, 9, 11, 29; DAM POET; PC 19
See also CA 13-16; 25-28R; CABS 2; CANR
35, 61; CAP 1; DLB 5, 16, 193; MTCW 1
Olson, Toby 1937- .... CLC 28
See also CA 65-68; CANR 9, 31
Olyesha, Yuri
See Olesha, Yuri (Karlovich)
Ondaatje, (Philip) Michael 1943-CLC 14, 29,
51, 76; DAB; DAC; DAM MST
See also CA 77-80; CANR 42, 74; DLB 60
Oneal, Elizabeth 1934-
See Oneal, Zibby
See also CA 106; CANR 28; MAICYA; SATA
30, 82
Oneal, Zibby .... CLC 30
See also Oneal, Elizabeth
See also AAYA 5; CLR 13; JRDA
O'Neill, Eugene (Gladstone) 1888-1953TCLC
1, 6, 27, 49; DA; DAB; DAC; DAM DRAM,
MST; WLC
See also AITN 1; CA 110; 132; CDALB 1929-
1941; DLB 7; MTCW 1
Onetti, Juan Carlos 1909-1994 ... CLC 7, 10;
DAM MULT, NOV; SSC 23
See also CA 85-88; 145; CANR 32, 63; DLB
113; HW; MTCW 1
O Nuallain, Brian 1911-1966
See O'Brien, Flann
See also CA 21-22; 25-28R; CAP 2
Ophuls, Max 1902-1957 .... TCLC 79
See also CA 113
Opie, Amelia 1769-1853 .... NCLC 65
See also DLB 116, 159
Oppen, George 1908-1984 ...... CLC 7, 13, 34
See also CA 13-16R; 113; CANR 8; DLB 5,
165
Oppenheim, E(dward) Phillips 1866-1946
TCLC 45
See also CA 111; DLB 70
Opuls, Max
See Ophuls, Max
Origen c. 185-c. 254 .... CMLC 19
Orlovitz, Gil 1918-1973 .... CLC 22
See also CA 77-80; 45-48; DLB 2, 5
Orris
See Ingelow, Jean
Ortega y Gasset, Jose 1883-1955 .... TCLC 9;
DAM MULT; HLC
See also CA 106; 130; HW; MTCW 1
Ortese, Anna Maria 1914- .... CLC 89
See also DLB 177
Ortiz, Simon J(oseph) 1941- .. CLC 45; DAM
MULT, POET; PC 17
See also CA 134; CANR 69; DLB 120, 175;
NNAL
Orton, Joe .... CLC 4, 13, 43; DC 3
See also Orton, John Kingsley
See also CDBLB 1960 to Present; DLB 13
Orton, John Kingsley 1933-1967
See Orton, Joe
See also CA 85-88; CANR 35, 66; DAM

DRAM; MTCW 1

Orwell, George . TCLC **2, 6, 15, 31, 51; DAB; WLC**
See also Blair, Eric (Arthur)
See also CDBLB 1945-1960; DLB 15, 98, 195

Osborne, David
See Silverberg, Robert

Osborne, George
See Silverberg, Robert

Osborne, John (James) 1929-1994CLC **1, 2, 5, 11, 45; DA; DAB; DAC; DAM DRAM, MST; WLC**
See also CA 13-16R; 147; CANR 21, 56; CDBLB 1945-1960; DLB 13; MTCW 1

Osborne, Lawrence 1958- .... CLC **50**

Oshima, Nagisa 1932- .... CLC **20**
See also CA 116; 121

Oskison, John Milton 1874-1947 .. TCLC **35; DAM MULT**
See also CA 144; DLB 175; NNAL

Ossian c. 3rd cent. - .... CMLC **28**
See also Macpherson, James

Ossoli, Sarah Margaret (Fuller marchesa d') 1810-1850
See Fuller, Margaret
See also SATA 25

Ostrovsky, Alexander 1823-1886NCLC **30, 57**

Otero, Blas de 1916-1979 .... CLC **11**
See also CA 89-92; DLB 134

Otto, Rudolf 1869-1937 .... TCLC **85**

Otto, Whitney 1955- .... CLC **70**
See also CA 140

Ouida .... TCLC **43**
See also De La Ramee, (Marie) Louise
See also DLB 18, 156

Ousmane, Sembene 1923- .... CLC **66; BLC 3**
See also BW 1; CA 117; 125; MTCW 1

Ovid 43B.C.-18(?)CMLC **7; DAM POET; PC 2**

Owen, Hugh
See Faust, Frederick (Schiller)

Owen, Wilfred (Edward Salter) 1893-1918 TCLC **5, 27; DA; DAB; DAC; DAM MST, POET; PC 19; WLC**
See also CA 104; 141; CDBLB 1914-1945; DLB 20

Owens, Rochelle 1936- .... CLC **8**
See also CA 17-20R; CAAS 2; CANR 39

Oz, Amos 1939-CLC **5, 8, 11, 27, 33, 54; DAM NOV**
See also CA 53-56; CANR 27, 47, 65; MTCW 1

Ozick, Cynthia 1928- CLC **3, 7, 28, 62; DAM NOV, POP; SSC 15**
See also BEST 90:1; CA 17-20R; CANR 23, 58; DLB 28, 152; DLBY 82; INT CANR-23; MTCW 1

Ozu, Yasujiro 1903-1963 .... CLC **16**
See also CA 112

Pacheco, C.
See Pessoa, Fernando (Antonio Nogueira)

Pa Chin .... CLC **18**
See also Li Fei-kan

Pack, Robert 1929- .... CLC **13**
See also CA 1-4R; CANR 3, 44; DLB 5

Padgett, Lewis
See Kuttner, Henry

Padilla (Lorenzo), Heberto 1932- ..... CLC **38**
See also AITN 1; CA 123; 131; HW

Page, Jimmy 1944- .... CLC **12**

Page, Louise 1955- .... CLC **40**
See also CA 140; CANR 76

Page, P(atricia) K(athleen) 1916- CLC **7, 18; DAC; DAM MST; PC 12**
See also CA 53-56; CANR 4, 22, 65; DLB 68; MTCW 1

Page, Thomas Nelson 1853-1922 .... SSC **23**

See also CA 118; DLB 12, 78; DLBD 13

Pagels, Elaine Hiesey 1943- .... CLC **104**
See also CA 45-48; CANR 2, 24, 51

Paget, Violet 1856-1935
See Lee, Vernon
See also CA 104; 166

Paget-Lowe, Henry
See Lovecraft, H(oward) P(hillips)

Paglia, Camille (Anna) 1947- .... CLC **68**
See also CA 140; CANR 72

Paige, Richard
See Koontz, Dean R(ay)

Paine, Thomas 1737-1809 .... NCLC **62**
See also CDALB 1640-1865; DLB 31, 43, 73, 158

Pakenham, Antonia
See Fraser, (Lady) Antonia (Pakenham)

Palamas, Kostes 1859-1943 .... TCLC **5**
See also CA 105

Palazzeschi, Aldo 1885-1974 .... CLC **11**
See also CA 89-92; 53-56; DLB 114

Paley, Grace 1922-CLC **4, 6, 37; DAM POP; SSC 8**
See also CA 25-28R; CANR 13, 46, 74; DLB 28; INT CANR-13; MTCW 1

Palin, Michael (Edward) 1943- .... CLC **21**
See also Monty Python
See also CA 107; CANR 35; SATA 67

Palliser, Charles 1947- .... CLC **65**
See also CA 136; CANR 76

Palma, Ricardo 1833-1919 .... TCLC **29**
See also CA 168

Pancake, Breece Dexter 1952-1979
See Pancake, Breece D'J
See also CA 123; 109

Pancake, Breece D'J .... CLC **29**
See also Pancake, Breece Dexter
See also DLB 130

Panko, Rudy
See Gogol, Nikolai (Vasilyevich)

Papadiamantis, Alexandros 1851-1911T C L C **29**
See also CA 168

Papadiamantopoulos, Johannes 1856-1910
See Moreas, Jean
See also CA 117

Papini, Giovanni 1881-1956 .... TCLC **22**
See also CA 121

Paracelsus 1493-1541 .... LC **14**
See also DLB 179

Parasol, Peter
See Stevens, Wallace

Pardo Bazan, Emilia 1851-1921 .... SSC **30**

Pareto, Vilfredo 1848-1923 .... TCLC **69**

Parfenie, Maria
See Codrescu, Andrei

Parini, Jay (Lee) 1948- .... CLC **54**
See also CA 97-100; CAAS 16; CANR 32

Park, Jordan
See Kornbluth, C(yril) M.; Pohl, Frederik

Park, Robert E(zra) 1864-1944 ...... TCLC **73**
See also CA 122; 165

Parker, Bert
See Ellison, Harlan (Jay)

Parker, Dorothy (Rothschild) 1893-1967C L C **15, 68; DAM POET; SSC 2**
See also CA 19-20; 25-28R; CAP 2; DLB 11, 45, 86; MTCW 1

Parker, Robert B(rown) 1932-CLC **27; DAM NOV, POP**
See also BEST 89:4; CA 49-52; CANR 1, 26, 52; INT CANR-26; MTCW 1

Parkin, Frank 1940- .... CLC **43**
See also CA 147

Parkman, Francis, Jr. 1823-1893 .. NCLC **12**
See also DLB 1, 30, 186

Parks, Gordon (Alexander Buchanan) 1912-

CLC **1, 16; BLC 3; DAM MULT**
See also AITN 2; BW 2; CA 41-44R; CANR 26, 66; DLB 33; SATA 8

Parmenides c. 515B.C.-c. 450B.C. CMLC **22**
See also DLB 176

Parnell, Thomas 1679-1718 .... LC **3**
See also DLB 94

Parra, Nicanor 1914- ...... CLC **2, 102; DAM MULT; HLC**
See also CA 85-88; CANR 32; HW; MTCW 1

Parrish, Mary Frances
See Fisher, M(ary) F(rances) K(ennedy)

Parson
See Coleridge, Samuel Taylor

Parson Lot
See Kingsley, Charles

Partridge, Anthony
See Oppenheim, E(dward) Phillips

Pascal, Blaise 1623-1662 .... LC **35**

Pascoli, Giovanni 1855-1912 .... TCLC **45**
See also CA 170

Pasolini, Pier Paolo 1922-1975 . CLC **20, 37, 106; PC 17**
See also CA 93-96; 61-64; CANR 63; DLB 128, 177; MTCW 1

Pasquini
See Silone, Ignazio

Pastan, Linda (Olenik) 1932- CLC **27; DAM POET**
See also CA 61-64; CANR 18, 40, 61; DLB 5

Pasternak, Boris (Leonidovich) 1890-1960 CLC **7, 10, 18, 63; DA; DAB; DAC; DAM MST, NOV, POET; PC 6; SSC 31; WLC**
See also CA 127; 116; MTCW 1

Patchen, Kenneth 1911-1972 ... CLC **1, 2, 18; DAM POET**
See also CA 1-4R; 33-36R; CANR 3, 35; DLB 16, 48; MTCW 1

Pater, Walter (Horatio) 1839-1894 .. NCLC **7**
See also CDBLB 1832-1890; DLB 57, 156

Paterson, A(ndrew) B(arton) 1864-1941 TCLC **32**
See also CA 155; SATA 97

Paterson, Katherine (Womeldorf) 1932-C L C **12, 30**
See also AAYA 1; CA 21-24R; CANR 28, 59; CLR 7, 50; DLB 52; JRDA; MAICYA; MTCW 1; SATA 13, 53, 92

Patmore, Coventry Kersey Dighton 1823-1896 NCLC **9**
See also DLB 35, 98

Paton, Alan (Stewart) 1903-1988 CLC **4, 10, 25, 55, 106; DA; DAB; DAC; DAM MST, NOV; WLC**
See also AAYA 26; CA 13-16; 125; CANR 22; CAP 1; DLBD 17; MTCW 1; SATA 11; SATA-Obit 56

Paton Walsh, Gillian 1937-
See Walsh, Jill Paton
See also CANR 38; JRDA; MAICYA; SAAS 3; SATA 4, 72

Patton, George S. 1885-1945 .... TCLC **79**

Paulding, James Kirke 1778-1860 ... NCLC **2**
See also DLB 3, 59, 74

Paulin, Thomas Neilson 1949-
See Paulin, Tom
See also CA 123; 128

Paulin, Tom .... CLC **37**
See also Paulin, Thomas Neilson
See also DLB 40

Paustovsky, Konstantin (Georgievich) 1892-1968 .... CLC **40**
See also CA 93-96; 25-28R

Pavese, Cesare 1908-1950 ... TCLC **3; PC 13; SSC 19**
See also CA 104; 169; DLB 128, 177

Pavic, Milorad 1929- .... CLC **60**

25

Pix, Mary (Griffith) 1666-1709 .... **LC 8**
See also DLB 80
Pixerecourt, (Rene Charles) Guilbert de 1773-1844 ....
NCLC 39
See also DLB 192
Plaatje, Sol(omon) T(shekisho) 1876-1932
TCLC 73; BLCS
See also BW 2; CA 141
Plaidy, Jean
See Hibbert, Eleanor Alice Burford
Planche, James Robinson 1796-1880**NCLC 42**
Plant, Robert 1948- .... **CLC 12**
Plante, David (Robert) 1940- **CLC 7, 23, 38; DAM NOV**
See also CA 37-40R; CANR 12, 36, 58; DLBY 83; INT CANR-12; MTCW 1
Plath, Sylvia 1932-1963 **CLC 1, 2, 3, 5, 9, 11, 14, 17, 50, 51, 62, 111; DA; DAB; DAC; DAM MST, POET; PC 1; WLC**
See also AAYA 13; CA 19-20; CANR 34; CAP 2; CDALB 1941-1968; DLB 5, 6, 152; MTCW 1; SATA 96
Plato 428(?)B.C.-348(?)B.C. .... **CMLC 8; DA; DAB; DAC; DAM MST; WLCS**
See also DLB 176
Platonov, Andrei .... **TCLC 14**
See also Klimentov, Andrei Platonovich
Platt, Kin 1911- .... **CLC 26**
See also AAYA 11; CA 17-20R; CANR 11; JRDA; SAAS 17; SATA 21, 86
Plautus c. 251B.C.-184B.C. .. **CMLC 24; DC 6**
Plick et Plock
See Simenon, Georges (Jacques Christian)
Plimpton, George (Ames) 1927- .... **CLC 36**
See also AITN 1; CA 21-24R; CANR 32, 70; DLB 185; MTCW 1; SATA 10
Pliny the Elder c. 23-79 .... **CMLC 23**
Plomer, William Charles Franklin 1903-1973
CLC 4, 8
See also CA 21-22; CANR 34; CAP 2; DLB 20, 162, 191; MTCW 1; SATA 24
Plowman, Piers
See Kavanagh, Patrick (Joseph)
Plum, J.
See Wodehouse, P(elham) G(renville)
Plumly, Stanley (Ross) 1939- .... **CLC 33**
See also CA 108; 110; DLB 5, 193; INT 110
Plumpe, Friedrich Wilhelm 1888-1931**TCLC 53**
See also CA 112
Po Chu-i 772-846 .... **CMLC 24**
Poe, Edgar Allan 1809-1849**NCLC 1, 16, 55; DA; DAB; DAC; DAM MST, POET; PC 1; SSC 1, 22; WLC**
See also AAYA 14; CDALB 1640-1865; DLB 3, 59, 73, 74; SATA 23
Poet of Titchfield Street, The
See Pound, Ezra (Weston Loomis)
Pohl, Frederik 1919-............ **CLC 18; SSC 25**
See also AAYA 24; CA 61-64; CAAS 1; CANR 11, 37; DLB 8; INT CANR-11; MTCW 1; SATA 24
Poirier, Louis 1910-
See Gracq, Julien
See also CA 122; 126
Poitier, Sidney 1927- .... **CLC 26**
See also BW 1; CA 117
Polanski, Roman 1933- .... **CLC 16**
See also CA 77-80
Poliakoff, Stephen 1952- .... **CLC 38**
See also CA 106; DLB 13
Police, The
See Copeland, Stewart (Armstrong); Summers, Andrew James; Sumner, Gordon Matthew
Polidori, John William 1795-1821 . **NCLC 51**

See also DLB 116
Pollitt, Katha 1949- .... **CLC 28**
See also CA 120; 122; CANR 66; MTCW 1
Pollock, (Mary) Sharon 1936-**CLC 50; DAC; DAM DRAM, MST**
See also CA 141; DLB 60
Polo, Marco 1254-1324 .... **CMLC 15**
Polonsky, Abraham (Lincoln) 1910- **CLC 92**
See also CA 104; DLB 26; INT 104
Polybius c. 200B.C.-c. 118B.C. ...... **CMLC 17**
See also DLB 176
Pomerance, Bernard 1940- .... **CLC 13; DAM DRAM**
See also CA 101; CANR 49
Ponge, Francis (Jean Gaston Alfred) 1899-1988
CLC 6, 18; DAM POET
See also CA 85-88; 126; CANR 40
Pontoppidan, Henrik 1857-1943 .... **TCLC 29**
See also CA 170
Poole, Josephine .... **CLC 17**
See also Helyar, Jane Penelope Josephine
See also SAAS 2; SATA 5
Popa, Vasko 1922-1991 .... **CLC 19**
See also CA 112; 148; DLB 181
Pope, Alexander 1688-1744 **LC 3; DA; DAB; DAC; DAM MST, POET; WLC**
See also CDBLB 1660-1789; DLB 95, 101
Porter, Connie (Rose) 1959(?)- .... **CLC 70**
See also BW 2; CA 142; SATA 81
Porter, Gene(va Grace) Stratton 1863(?)-1924
TCLC 21
See also CA 112
Porter, Katherine Anne 1890-1980**CLC 1, 3, 7, 10, 13, 15, 27, 101; DA; DAB; DAC; DAM MST, NOV; SSC 4, 31**
See also AITN 2; CA 1-4R; 101; CANR 1, 65; DLB 4, 9, 102; DLBD 12; DLBY 80; MTCW 1; SATA 39; SATA-Obit 23
Porter, Peter (Neville Frederick) 1929-**CLC 5, 13, 33**
See also CA 85-88; DLB 40
Porter, William Sydney 1862-1910
See Henry, O.
See also CA 104; 131; CDALB 1865-1917; DA; DAB; DAC; DAM MST; DLB 12, 78, 79; MTCW 1; YABC 2
Portillo (y Pacheco), Jose Lopez
See Lopez Portillo (y Pacheco), Jose
Post, Melville Davisson 1869-1930 **TCLC 39**
See also CA 110
Potok, Chaim 1929- ... **CLC 2, 7, 14, 26, 112; DAM NOV**
See also AAYA 15; AITN 1, 2; CA 17-20R; CANR 19, 35, 64; DLB 28, 152; INT CANR-19; MTCW 1; SATA 33
Potter, (Helen) Beatrix 1866-1943
See Webb, (Martha) Beatrice (Potter)
See also MAICYA
Potter, Dennis (Christopher George) 1935-1994
CLC 58, 86
See also CA 107; 145; CANR 33, 61; MTCW 1
Pound, Ezra (Weston Loomis) 1885-1972**CLC 1, 2, 3, 4, 5, 7, 10, 13, 18, 34, 48, 50, 112; DA; DAB; DAC; DAM MST, POET; PC 4; WLC**
See also CA 5-8R; 37-40R; CANR 40; CDALB 1917-1929; DLB 4, 45, 63; DLBD 15; MTCW 1
Povod, Reinaldo 1959-1994 .... **CLC 44**
See also CA 136; 146
Powell, Adam Clayton, Jr. 1908-1972**CLC 89; BLC 3; DAM MULT**
See also BW 1; CA 102; 33-36R
Powell, Anthony (Dymoke) 1905-**CLC 1, 3, 7, 9, 10, 31**
See also CA 1-4R; CANR 1, 32, 62; CDBLB 1945-1960; DLB 15; MTCW 1

Powell, Dawn 1897-1965 .... **CLC 66**
See also CA 5-8R; DLBY 97
Powell, Padgett 1952- .... **CLC 34**
See also CA 126; CANR 63
Power, Susan 1961- .... **CLC 91**
Powers, J(ames) F(arl) 1917-**CLC 1, 4, 8, 57; SSC 4**
See also CA 1-4R; CANR 2, 61; DLB 130; MTCW 1
Powers, John J(ames) 1945-
See Powers, John R.
See also CA 69-72
Powers, John R. .... **CLC 66**
See also Powers, John J(ames)
Powers, Richard (S.) 1957- .... **CLC 93**
See also CA 148
Pownall, David 1938- .... **CLC 10**
See also CA 89-92; CAAS 18; CANR 49; DLB 14
Powys, John Cowper 1872-1963**CLC 7, 9, 15, 46**
See also CA 85-88; DLB 15; MTCW 1
Powys, T(heodore) F(rancis) 1875-1953
TCLC 9
See also CA 106; DLB 36, 162
Prado (Calvo), Pedro 1886-1952 ... **TCLC 75**
See also CA 131; HW
Prager, Emily 1952- .... **CLC 56**
Pratt, E(dwin) J(ohn) 1883(?)-1964 **CLC 19; DAC; DAM POET**
See also CA 141; 93-96; DLB 92
Premchand .... **TCLC 21**
See also Srivastava, Dhanpat Rai
Preussler, Otfried 1923- .... **CLC 17**
See also CA 77-80; SATA 24
Prevert, Jacques (Henri Marie) 1900-1977
CLC 15
See also CA 77-80; 69-72; CANR 29, 61; MTCW 1; SATA-Obit 30
Prevost, Abbe (Antoine Francois) 1697-1763
LC 1
Price, (Edward) Reynolds 1933-**CLC 3, 6, 13, 43, 50, 63; DAM NOV; SSC 22**
See also CA 1-4R; CANR 1, 37, 57; DLB 2; INT CANR-37
Price, Richard 1949- .... **CLC 6, 12**
See also CA 49-52; CANR 3; DLBY 81
Prichard, Katharine Susannah 1883-1969
CLC 46
See also CA 11-12; CANR 33; CAP 1; MTCW 1; SATA 66
Priestley, J(ohn) B(oynton) 1894-1984**CLC 2, 5, 9, 34; DAM DRAM, NOV**
See also CA 9-12R; 113; CANR 33; CDBLB 1914-1945; DLB 10, 34, 77, 100, 139; DLBY 84; MTCW 1
Prince 1958(?)- .... **CLC 35**
Prince, F(rank) T(empleton) 1912- .. **CLC 22**
See also CA 101; CANR 43; DLB 20
Prince Kropotkin
See Kropotkin, Peter (Aleksieevich)
Prior, Matthew 1664-1721 .... **LC 4**
See also DLB 95
Prishvin, Mikhail 1873-1954 .... **TCLC 75**
Pritchard, William H(arrison) 1932- **CLC 34**
See also CA 65-68; CANR 23; DLB 111
Pritchett, V(ictor) S(awdon) 1900-1997 **CLC 5, 13, 15, 41; DAM NOV; SSC 14**
See also CA 61-64; 157; CANR 31, 63; DLB 15, 139; MTCW 1
Private 19022
See Manning, Frederic
Probst, Mark 1925- .... **CLC 59**
See also CA 130
Prokosch, Frederic 1908-1989 ...... **CLC 4, 48**
See also CA 73-76; 128; DLB 48
Propertius, Sextus 50(?)B.C.-15(?)B.C.**CMLC**

DLB 9, 22, 102; DLBD 17; JRDA; MAICYA; SATA 100; YABC 1

Ray, Satyajit 1921-1992 .. **CLC 16, 76; DAM MULT**
See also CA 114; 137

Read, Herbert Edward 1893-1968 ..... **CLC 4**
See also CA 85-88; 25-28R; DLB 20, 149

Read, Piers Paul 1941- .... **CLC 4, 10, 25**
See also CA 21-24R; CANR 38; DLB 14; SATA 21

Reade, Charles 1814-1884 .... **NCLC 2, 74**
See also DLB 21

Reade, Hamish
See Gray, Simon (James Holliday)

Reading, Peter 1946- .... **CLC 47**
See also CA 103; CANR 46; DLB 40

Reaney, James 1926- .. **CLC 13; DAC; DAM MST**
See also CA 41-44R; CAAS 15; CANR 42; DLB 68; SATA 43

Rebreanu, Liviu 1885-1944 .... **TCLC 28**
See also CA 165

Rechy, John (Francisco) 1934- **CLC 1, 7, 14, 18, 107; DAM MULT; HLC**
See also CA 5-8R; CAAS 4; CANR 6, 32, 64; DLB 122; DLBY 82; HW; INT CANR-6

Redcam, Tom 1870-1933 .... **TCLC 25**

Reddin, Keith .... **CLC 67**

Redgrove, Peter (William) 1932- ..**CLC 6, 41**
See also CA 1-4R; CANR 3, 39; DLB 40

Redmon, Anne .... **CLC 22**
See also Nightingale, Anne Redmon
See also DLBY 86

Reed, Eliot
See Ambler, Eric

Reed, Ishmael 1938-**CLC 2, 3, 5, 6, 13, 32, 60; BLC 3; DAM MULT**
See also BW 2; CA 21-24R; CANR 25, 48, 74; DLB 2, 5, 33, 169; DLBD 8; MTCW 1

Reed, John (Silas) 1887-1920 .... **TCLC 9**
See also CA 106

Reed, Lou .... **CLC 21**
See also Firbank, Louis

Reeve, Clara 1729-1807 .... **NCLC 19**
See also DLB 39

Reich, Wilhelm 1897-1957 .... **TCLC 57**

Reid, Christopher (John) 1949- .... **CLC 33**
See also CA 140; DLB 40

Reid, Desmond
See Moorcock, Michael (John)

Reid Banks, Lynne 1929-
See Banks, Lynne Reid
See also CA 1-4R; CANR 6, 22, 38; CLR 24; JRDA; MAICYA; SATA 22, 75

Reilly, William K.
See Creasey, John

Reiner, Max
See Caldwell, (Janet Miriam) Taylor (Holland)

Reis, Ricardo
See Pessoa, Fernando (Antonio Nogueira)

Remarque, Erich Maria 1898-1970 **CLC 21; DA; DAB; DAC; DAM MST, NOV**
See also AAYA 27; CA 77-80; 29-32R; DLB 56; MTCW 1

Remington, Frederic 1861-1909 .... **TCLC 89**
See also CA 108; 169; DLB 12, 186, 188; SATA 41

Remizov, A.
See Remizov, Aleksei (Mikhailovich)

Remizov, A. M.
See Remizov, Aleksei (Mikhailovich)

Remizov, Aleksei (Mikhailovich) 1877-1957 **TCLC 27**
See also CA 125; 133

Renan, Joseph Ernest 1823-1892 .. **NCLC 26**

Renard, Jules 1864-1910 .... **TCLC 17**
See also CA 117

Renault, Mary .... **CLC 3, 11, 17**
See also Challans, Mary
See also DLBY 83

Rendell, Ruth (Barbara) 1930- . **CLC 28, 48; DAM POP**
See also Vine, Barbara
See also CA 109; CANR 32, 52, 74; DLB 87; INT CANR-32; MTCW 1

Renoir, Jean 1894-1979 .... **CLC 20**
See also CA 129; 85-88

Resnais, Alain 1922- .... **CLC 16**

Reverdy, Pierre 1889-1960 .... **CLC 53**
See also CA 97-100; 89-92

Rexroth, Kenneth 1905-1982**CLC 1, 2, 6, 11, 22, 49, 112; DAM POET; PC 20**
See also CA 5-8R; 107; CANR 14, 34, 63; CDALB 1941-1968; DLB 16, 48, 165; DLBY 82; INT CANR-14; MTCW 1

Reyes, Alfonso 1889-1959 .... **TCLC 33**
See also CA 131; HW

Reyes y Basoalto, Ricardo Eliecer Neftali
See Neruda, Pablo

Reymont, Wladyslaw (Stanislaw) 1868(?)-1925 **TCLC 5**
See also CA 104

Reynolds, Jonathan 1942- .... **CLC 6, 38**
See also CA 65-68; CANR 28

Reynolds, Joshua 1723-1792 .... **LC 15**
See also DLB 104

Reynolds, Michael Shane 1937- .... **CLC 44**
See also CA 65-68; CANR 9

Reznikoff, Charles 1894-1976 .... **CLC 9**
See also CA 33-36; 61-64; CAP 2; DLB 28, 45

Rezzori (d'Arezzo), Gregor von 1914-1998 **CLC 25**
See also CA 122; 136; 167

Rhine, Richard
See Silverstein, Alvin

Rhodes, Eugene Manlove 1869-1934**TCLC 53**

Rhodius, Apollonius c. 3rd cent. B.C.-**C M L C 28**
See also DLB 176

R'hoone
See Balzac, Honore de

Rhys, Jean 1890(?)-1979 **CLC 2, 4, 6, 14, 19, 51; DAM NOV; SSC 21**
See also CA 25-28R; 85-88; CANR 35, 62; CDBLB 1945-1960; DLB 36, 117, 162; MTCW 1

Ribeiro, Darcy 1922-1997 .... **CLC 34**
See also CA 33-36R; 156

Ribeiro, Joao Ubaldo (Osorio Pimentel) 1941- **CLC 10, 67**
See also CA 81-84

Ribman, Ronald (Burt) 1932- .... **CLC 7**
See also CA 21-24R; CANR 46

Ricci, Nino 1959-................................. **CLC 70**
See also CA 137

Rice, Anne 1941- .... **CLC 41; DAM POP**
See also AAYA 9; BEST 89:2; CA 65-68; CANR 12, 36, 53, 74

Rice, Elmer (Leopold) 1892-1967 **CLC 7, 49; DAM DRAM**
See also CA 21-22; 25-28R; CAP 2; DLB 4, 7; MTCW 1

Rice, Tim(othy Miles Bindon) 1944- **CLC 21**
See also CA 103; CANR 46

Rich, Adrienne (Cecile) 1929-**CLC 3, 6, 7, 11, 18, 36, 73, 76; DAM POET; PC 5**
See also CA 9-12R; CANR 20, 53, 74; DLB 5, 67; MTCW 1

Rich, Barbara
See Graves, Robert (von Ranke)

Rich, Robert
See Trumbo, Dalton

Richard, Keith .... **CLC 17**
See also Richards, Keith

Richards, David Adams 1950- **CLC 59; DAC**
See also CA 93-96; CANR 60; DLB 53

Richards, I(vor) A(rmstrong) 1893-1979**C L C 14, 24**
See also CA 41-44R; 89-92; CANR 34, 74; DLB 27

Richards, Keith 1943-
See Richard, Keith
See also CA 107

Richardson, Anne
See Roiphe, Anne (Richardson)

Richardson, Dorothy Miller 1873-1957**TCLC 3**
See also CA 104; DLB 36

Richardson, Ethel Florence (Lindesay) 1870-1946
See Richardson, Henry Handel
See also CA 105

Richardson, Henry Handel .... **TCLC 4**
See also Richardson, Ethel Florence (Lindesay)
See also DLB 197

Richardson, John 1796-1852**NCLC 55; DAC**
See also DLB 99

Richardson, Samuel 1689-1761**LC 1, 44; DA; DAB; DAC; DAM MST, NOV; WLC**
See also CDBLB 1660-1789; DLB 39

Richler, Mordecai 1931-**CLC 3, 5, 9, 13, 18, 46, 70; DAC; DAM MST, NOV**
See also AITN 1; CA 65-68; CANR 31, 62; CLR 17; DLB 53; MAICYA; MTCW 1; SATA 44, 98; SATA-Brief 27

Richter, Conrad (Michael) 1890-1968**CLC 30**
See also AAYA 21; CA 5-8R; 25-28R; CANR 23; DLB 9; MTCW 1; SATA 3

Ricostranza, Tom
See Ellis, Trey

Riddell, Charlotte 1832-1906 .... **TCLC 40**
See also CA 165; DLB 156

Riding, Laura .... **CLC 3, 7**
See also Jackson, Laura (Riding)

Riefenstahl, Berta Helene Amalia 1902-
See Riefenstahl, Leni
See also CA 108

Riefenstahl, Leni .... **CLC 16**
See also Riefenstahl, Berta Helene Amalia

Riffe, Ernest
See Bergman, (Ernst) Ingmar

Riggs, (Rolla) Lynn 1899-1954 ..... **TCLC 56; DAM MULT**
See also CA 144; DLB 175; NNAL

Riis, Jacob A(ugust) 1849-1914 ..... **TCLC 80**
See also CA 113; 168; DLB 23

Riley, James Whitcomb 1849-1916**TCLC 51; DAM POET**
See also CA 118; 137; MAICYA; SATA 17

Riley, Tex
See Creasey, John

Rilke, Rainer Maria 1875-1926**TCLC 1, 6, 19; DAM POET; PC 2**
See also CA 104; 132; CANR 62; DLB 81; MTCW 1

Rimbaud, (Jean Nicolas) Arthur 1854-1891 **NCLC 4, 35; DA; DAB; DAC; DAM MST, POET; PC 3; WLC**

Rinehart, Mary Roberts 1876-1958**TCLC 52**
See also CA 108; 166

Ringmaster, The
See Mencken, H(enry) L(ouis)

Ringwood, Gwen(dolyn Margaret) Pharis 1910-1984 .... **CLC 48**
See also CA 148; 112; DLB 88

Rio, Michel 19(?)- .... **CLC 43**

Ritsos, Giannes
See Ritsos, Yannis

Ritsos, Yannis 1909-1990 .... **CLC 6, 13, 31**
See also CA 77-80; 133; CANR 39, 61; MTCW 1

See Lovecraft, H(oward) P(hillips)
Rowson, Susanna Haswell 1762(?)-1824
NCLC **5, 69**
See also DLB 37, 200
Roy, Arundhati 1960(?)- .... CLC **109**
See also CA 163; DLBY 97
Roy, Gabrielle 1909-1983 CLC **10, 14; DAB;**
DAC; DAM MST;
See also CA 53-56; 110; CANR 5, 61; DLB 68;
MTCW 1; SATA 104
Royko, Mike 1932-1997 .... CLC **109**
See also CA 89-92; 157; CANR 26
Rozewicz, Tadeusz 1921- .. CLC **9, 23; DAM**
POET
See also CA 108; CANR 36, 66; MTCW 1
Ruark, Gibbons 1941- .... CLC **3**
See also CA 33-36R; CAAS 23; CANR 14, 31,
57; DLB 120
Rubens, Bernice (Ruth) 1923-.... CLC **19, 31**
See also CA 25-28R; CANR 33, 65; DLB 14,
207; MTCW 1
Rubin, Harold
See Robbins, Harold
Rudkin, (James) David 1936- .... CLC **14**
See also CA 89-92; DLB 13
Rudnik, Raphael 1933- .... CLC **7**
See also CA 29-32R
Ruffian, M.
See Hasek, Jaroslav (Matej Frantisek)
Ruiz, Jose Martinez .... CLC **11**
See also Martinez Ruiz, Jose
Rukeyser, Muriel 1913-1980CLC **6, 10, 15, 27;**
DAM POET; PC 12
See also CA 5-8R; 93-96; CANR 26, 60; DLB
48; MTCW 1; SATA-Obit 22
Rule, Jane (Vance) 1931- .... CLC **27**
See also CA 25-28R; CAAS 18; CANR 12; DLB
60
Rulfo, Juan 1918-1986 ...... CLC **8, 80; DAM**
MULT; HLC; SSC 25
See also CA 85-88; 118; CANR 26; DLB 113;
HW; MTCW 1
Rumi, Jalal al-Din 1297-1373 .... CMLC **20**
Runeberg, Johan 1804-1877 .... NCLC **41**
Runyon, (Alfred) Damon 1884(?)-1946T C L C
10
See also CA 107; 165; DLB 11, 86, 171
Rush, Norman 1933-.......................... CLC **44**
See also CA 121; 126; INT 126
Rushdie, (Ahmed) Salman 1947- CLC **23, 31,**
55, 100; DAB; DAC; DAM MST, NOV,
POP; WLCS
See also BEST 89:3; CA 108; 111; CANR 33,
56; DLB 194; INT 111; MTCW 1
Rushforth, Peter (Scott) 1945- .... CLC **19**
See also CA 101
Ruskin, John 1819-1900 .... TCLC **63**
See also CA 114; 129; CDBLB 1832-1890;
DLB 55, 163, 190; SATA 24
Russ, Joanna 1937-............................ CLC **15**
See also CANR 11, 31, 65; DLB 8; MTCW 1
Russell, George William 1867-1935
See Baker, Jean H.
See also CA 104; 153; CDBLB 1890-1914;
DAM POET
Russell, (Henry) Ken(neth Alfred) 1927-C L C
16
See also CA 105
Russell, William Martin 1947- .... CLC **60**
See also CA 164
Rutherford, Mark .... TCLC **25**
See also White, William Hale
See also DLB 18
Ruyslinck, Ward 1929-...................... CLC **14**
See also Belser, Reimond Karel Maria de
Ryan, Cornelius (John) 1920-1974 ..... CLC **7**
See also CA 69-72; 53-56; CANR 38

Ryan, Michael 1946-............................ CLC **65**
See also CA 49-52; DLBY 82
Ryan, Tim
See Dent, Lester
Rybakov, Anatoli (Naumovich) 1911-1998
CLC **23, 53**
See also CA 126; 135; 172; SATA 79
Ryder, Jonathan
See Ludlum, Robert
Ryga, George 1932-1987CLC **14; DAC; DAM**
MST
See also CA 101; 124; CANR 43; DLB 60
S. H.
See Hartmann, Sadakichi
S. S.
See Sassoon, Siegfried (Lorraine)
Saba, Umberto 1883-1957 .... TCLC **33**
See also CA 144; DLB 114
Sabatini, Rafael 1875-1950 .... TCLC **47**
See also CA 162
Sabato, Ernesto (R.) 1911-CLC **10, 23; DAM**
MULT; HLC
See also CA 97-100; CANR 32, 65; DLB 145;
HW; MTCW 1
Sa-Carniero, Mario de 1890-1916 . TCLC **83**
Sacastru, Martin
See Bioy Casares, Adolfo
Sacher-Masoch, Leopold von 1836(?)-1895
NCLC **31**
Sachs, Marilyn (Stickle) 1927- .... CLC **35**
See also AAYA 2; CA 17-20R; CANR 13, 47;
CLR 2; JRDA; MAICYA; SAAS 2; SATA 3,
68
Sachs, Nelly 1891-1970 .... CLC **14, 98**
See also CA 17-18; 25-28R; CAP 2
Sackler, Howard (Oliver) 1929-1982 CLC **14**
See also CA 61-64; 108; CANR 30; DLB 7
Sacks, Oliver (Wolf) 1933-................... CLC **67**
See also CA 53-56; CANR 28, 50, 76; INT
CANR-28; MTCW 1
Sadakichi
See Hartmann, Sadakichi
Sade, Donatien Alphonse Francois, Comte de
1740-1814 ....
NCLC **47**
Sadoff, Ira 1945- .... CLC **9**
See also CA 53-56; CANR 5, 21; DLB 120
Saetone
See Camus, Albert
Safire, William 1929- .... CLC **10**
See also CA 17-20R; CANR 31, 54
Sagan, Carl (Edward) 1934-1996CLC **30, 112**
See also AAYA 2; CA 25-28R; 155; CANR 11,
36, 74; MTCW 1; SATA 58; SATA-Obit 94
Sagan, Francoise .... CLC **3, 6, 9, 17, 36**
See also Quoirez, Francoise
See also DLB 83
Sahgal, Nayantara (Pandit) 1927- .... CLC **41**
See also CA 9-12R; CANR 11
Saint, H(arry) F. 1941- .... CLC **50**
See also CA 127
St. Aubin de Teran, Lisa 1953-
See Teran, Lisa St. Aubin de
See also CA 118; 126; INT 126
Saint Birgitta of Sweden c. 1303-1373C M L C
24
Sainte-Beuve, Charles Augustin 1804-1869
NCLC **5**
Saint-Exupery, Antoine (Jean Baptiste Marie
Roger) de 1900-1944TCLC **2, 56; DAM**
NOV; WLC
See also CA 108; 132; CLR 10; DLB 72;
MAICYA; MTCW 1; SATA 20
St. John, David
See Hunt, E(verette) Howard, (Jr.)
Saint-John Perse
See Leger, (Marie-Rene Auguste) Alexis Saint-

Leger
Saintsbury, George (Edward Bateman) 1845-
1933 .... TCLC **31**
See also CA 160; DLB 57, 149
Sait Faik .... TCLC **23**
See also Abasiyanik, Sait Faik
Saki .... TCLC **3; SSC 12**
See also Munro, H(ector) H(ugh)
Sala, George Augustus .... NCLC **46**
Salama, Hannu 1936- .... CLC **18**
Salamanca, J(ack) R(ichard) 1922-CLC **4, 15**
See also CA 25-28R
Sale, J. Kirkpatrick
See Sale, Kirkpatrick
Sale, Kirkpatrick 1937- .... CLC **68**
See also CA 13-16R; CANR 10
Salinas, Luis Omar 1937- ...... CLC **90; DAM**
MULT; HLC
See also CA 131; DLB 82; HW
Salinas (y Serrano), Pedro 1891(?)-1951
TCLC **17**
See also CA 117; DLB 134
Salinger, J(erome) D(avid) 1919-CLC **1, 3, 8,**
12, 55, 56; DA; DAB; DAC; DAM MST,
NOV, POP; SSC 2, 28; WLC
See also AAYA 2; CA 5-8R; CANR 39; CDALB
1941-1968; CLR 18; DLB 2, 102, 173;
MAICYA; MTCW 1; SATA 67
Salisbury, John
See Caute, (John) David
Salter, James 1925- .... CLC **7, 52, 59**
See also CA 73-76; DLB 130
Saltus, Edgar (Everton) 1855-1921 . TCLC **8**
See also CA 105; DLB 202
Saltykov, Mikhail Evgrafovich 1826-1889
NCLC **16**
Samarakis, Antonis 1919- .... CLC **5**
See also CA 25-28R; CAAS 16; CANR 36
Sanchez, Florencio 1875-1910 .... TCLC **37**
See also CA 153; HW
Sanchez, Luis Rafael 1936- .... CLC **23**
See also CA 128; DLB 145; HW
Sanchez, Sonia 1934-.... CLC **5, 116; BLC 3;**
DAM MULT; PC 9
See also BW 2; CA 33-36R; CANR 24, 49, 74;
CLR 18; DLB 41; DLBD 8; MAICYA;
MTCW 1; SATA 22
Sand, George 1804-1876NCLC **2, 42, 57; DA;**
DAB; DAC; DAM MST, NOV; WLC
See also DLB 119, 192
Sandburg, Carl (August) 1878-1967CLC **1, 4,**
10, 15, 35; DA; DAB; DAC; DAM MST,
POET; PC 2; WLC
See also AAYA 24; CA 5-8R; 25-28R; CANR
35; CDALB 1865-1917; DLB 17, 54;
MAICYA; MTCW 1; SATA 8
Sandburg, Charles
See Sandburg, Carl (August)
Sandburg, Charles A.
See Sandburg, Carl (August)
Sanders, (James) Ed(ward) 1939- .. CLC **53;**
DAM POET
See also CA 13-16R; CAAS 21; CANR 13, 44;
DLB 16
Sanders, Lawrence 1920-1998CLC **41; DAM**
POP
See also BEST 89:4; CA 81-84; 165; CANR
33, 62; MTCW 1
Sanders, Noah
See Blount, Roy (Alton), Jr.
Sanders, Winston P.
See Anderson, Poul (William)
Sandoz, Mari(e Susette) 1896-1966 .. CLC **28**
See also CA 1-4R; 25-28R; CANR 17, 64; DLB
9; MTCW 1; SATA 5
Saner, Reg(inald Anthony) 1931- .... CLC **9**
See also CA 65-68

Scudery, Madeleine de 1607-1701 .... **LC 2**
Scum
　See Crumb, R(obert)
Scumbag, Little Bobby
　See Crumb, R(obert)
Seabrook, John
　See Hubbard, L(afayette) Ron(ald)
Sealy, I. Allan 1951- .... **CLC 55**
Search, Alexander
　See Pessoa, Fernando (Antonio Nogueira)
Sebastian, Lee
　See Silverberg, Robert
Sebastian Owl
　See Thompson, Hunter S(tockton)
Sebestyen, Ouida 1924- .... **CLC 30**
　See also AAYA 8; CA 107; CANR 40; CLR 17;
　JRDA; MAICYA; SAAS 10; SATA 39
Secundus, H. Scriblerus
　See Fielding, Henry
Sedges, John
　See Buck, Pearl S(ydenstricker)
Sedgwick, Catharine Maria 1789-1867**NCLC 19**
　See also DLB 1, 74
Seelye, John (Douglas) 1931- .... **CLC 7**
　See also CA 97-100; CANR 70; INT 97-100
Seferiades, Giorgos Stylianou 1900-1971
　See Seferis, George
　See also CA 5-8R; 33-36R; CANR 5, 36;
　MTCW 1
Seferis, George .... **CLC 5, 11**
　See also Seferiades, Giorgos Stylianou
Segal, Erich (Wolf) 1937- . **CLC 3, 10; DAM POP**
　See also BEST 89:1; CA 25-28R; CANR 20,
　36, 65; DLBY 86; INT CANR-20; MTCW 1
Seger, Bob 1945- .... **CLC 35**
Seghers, Anna .... **CLC 7**
　See also Radvanyi, Netty
　See also DLB 69
Seidel, Frederick (Lewis) 1936- .... **CLC 18**
　See also CA 13-16R; CANR 8; DLBY 84
Seifert, Jaroslav 1901-1986 .. **CLC 34, 44, 93**
　See also CA 127; MTCW 1
Sei Shonagon c. 966-1017(?) .... **CMLC 6**
Séjour, Victor 1817-1874 .... **DC 10**
　See also DLB 50
Sejour Marcou et Ferrand, Juan Victor
　See Séjour, Victor
Selby, Hubert, Jr. 1928-**CLC 1, 2, 4, 8; SSC 20**
　See also CA 13-16R; CANR 33; DLB 2
Selzer, Richard 1928- .... **CLC 74**
　See also CA 65-68; CANR 14
Sembene, Ousmane
　See Ousmane, Sembene
Senancour, Etienne Pivert de 1770-1846
　NCLC 16
　See also DLB 119
Sender, Ramon (Jose) 1902-1982**CLC 8; DAM MULT; HLC**
　See also CA 5-8R; 105; CANR 8; HW; MTCW
　1
Seneca, Lucius Annaeus 4B.C.-65 . **CMLC 6; DAM DRAM; DC 5**
Senghor, Leopold Sedar 1906- **CLC 54; BLC 3; DAM MULT, POET; PC 25**
　See also BW 2; CA 116; 125; CANR 47, 74;
　MTCW 1
Serling, (Edward) Rod(man) 1924-1975**CLC 30**
　See also AAYA 14; AITN 1; CA 162; 57-60;
　DLB 26
Serna, Ramon Gomez de la
　See Gomez de la Serna, Ramon
Serpieres
　See Guillevic, (Eugene)
Service, Robert

　See Service, Robert W(illiam)
　See also DAB; DLB 92
Service, Robert W(illiam) 1874(?)-1958**TCLC 15; DA; DAC; DAM MST, POET; WLC**
　See also Service, Robert
　See also CA 115; 140; SATA 20
Seth, Vikram 1952-**CLC 43, 90; DAM MULT**
　See also CA 121; 127; CANR 50, 74; DLB 120;
　INT 127
Seton, Cynthia Propper 1926-1982 .. **CLC 27**
　See also CA 5-8R; 108; CANR 7
Seton, Ernest (Evan) Thompson 1860-1946
　TCLC 31
　See also CA 109; DLB 92; DLBD 13; JRDA;
　SATA 18
Seton-Thompson, Ernest
　See Seton, Ernest (Evan) Thompson
Settle, Mary Lee 1918- .... **CLC 19, 61**
　See also CA 89-92; CAAS 1; CANR 44; DLB
　6; INT 89-92
Seuphor, Michel
　See Arp, Jean
Sevigne, Marie (de Rabutin-Chantal) Marquise de 1626-1696 .... **LC 11**
Sewall, Samuel 1652-1730 .... **LC 38**
　See also DLB 24
Sexton, Anne (Harvey) 1928-1974**CLC 2, 4, 6, 8, 10, 15, 53; DA; DAB; DAC; DAM MST, POET; PC 2; WLC**
　See also CA 1-4R; 53-56; CABS 2; CANR 3,
　36; CDALB 1941-1968; DLB 5, 169;
　MTCW 1; SATA 10
Shaara, Michael (Joseph, Jr.) 1929-1988**CLC 15; DAM POP**
　See also AITN 1; CA 102; 125; CANR 52;
　DLBY 83
Shackleton, C. C.
　See Aldiss, Brian W(ilson)
Shacochis, Bob .... **CLC 39**
　See also Shacochis, Robert G.
Shacochis, Robert G. 1951-
　See Shacochis, Bob
　See also CA 119; 124; INT 124
Shaffer, Anthony (Joshua) 1926- .... **CLC 19; DAM DRAM**
　See also CA 110; 116; DLB 13
Shaffer, Peter (Levin) 1926-**CLC 5, 14, 18, 37, 60; DAB; DAM DRAM, MST; DC 7**
　See also CA 25-28R; CANR 25, 47, 74; CDBLB
　1960 to Present; DLB 13; MTCW 1
Shakey, Bernard
　See Young, Neil
Shalamov, Varlam (Tikhonovich) 1907(?)-1982
　CLC 18
　See also CA 129; 105
Shamlu, Ahmad 1925- .... **CLC 10**
Shammas, Anton 1951- .... **CLC 55**
Shange, Ntozake 1948-**CLC 8, 25, 38, 74; BLC 3; DAM DRAM, MULT; DC 3**
　See also AAYA 9; BW 2; CA 85-88; CABS 3;
　CANR 27, 48, 74; DLB 38; MTCW 1
Shanley, John Patrick 1950- .... **CLC 75**
　See also CA 128; 133
Shapcott, Thomas W(illiam) 1935- .. **CLC 38**
　See also CA 69-72; CANR 49
Shapiro, Jane .... **CLC 76**
Shapiro, Karl (Jay) 1913-**CLC 4, 8, 15, 53; PC 25**
　See also CA 1-4R; CAAS 6; CANR 1, 36, 66;
　DLB 48; MTCW 1
Sharp, William 1855-1905 .... **TCLC 39**
　See also CA 160; DLB 156
Sharpe, Thomas Ridley 1928-
　See Sharpe, Tom
　See also CA 114; 122; INT 122
Sharpe, Tom .... **CLC 36**
　See also Sharpe, Thomas Ridley

　See also DLB 14
Shaw, Bernard .... **TCLC 45**
　See also Shaw, George Bernard
　See also BW 1
Shaw, G. Bernard
　See Shaw, George Bernard
Shaw, George Bernard 1856-1950**TCLC 3, 9, 21; DA; DAB; DAC; DAM DRAM, MST; WLC**
　See also Shaw, Bernard
　See also CA 104; 128; CDBLB 1914-1945;
　DLB 10, 57, 190; MTCW 1
Shaw, Henry Wheeler 1818-1885 .. **NCLC 15**
　See also DLB 11
Shaw, Irwin 1913-1984 **CLC 7, 23, 34; DAM DRAM, POP**
　See also AITN 1; CA 13-16R; 112; CANR 21;
　CDALB 1941-1968; DLB 6, 102; DLBY 84;
　MTCW 1
Shaw, Robert 1927-1978 .... **CLC 5**
　See also AITN 1; CA 1-4R; 81-84; CANR 4;
　DLB 13, 14
Shaw, T. E.
　See Lawrence, T(homas) E(dward)
Shawn, Wallace 1943- .... **CLC 41**
　See also CA 112
Shea, Lisa 1953- .... **CLC 86**
　See also CA 147
Sheed, Wilfrid (John Joseph) 1930-**CLC 2, 4, 10, 53**
　See also CA 65-68; CANR 30, 66; DLB 6;
　MTCW 1
Sheldon, Alice Hastings Bradley 1915(?)-1987
　See Tiptree, James, Jr.
　See also CA 108; 122; CANR 34; INT 108;
　MTCW 1
Sheldon, John
　See Bloch, Robert (Albert)
Shelley, Mary Wollstonecraft (Godwin) 1797-1851**NCLC 14, 59; DA; DAB; DAC; DAM MST, NOV; WLC**
　See also AAYA 20; CDBLB 1789-1832; DLB
　110, 116, 159, 178; SATA 29
Shelley, Percy Bysshe 1792-1822 . **NCLC 18; DA; DAB; DAC; DAM MST, POET; PC 14; WLC**
　See also CDBLB 1789-1832; DLB 96, 110, 158
Shepard, Jim 1956- .... **CLC 36**
　See also CA 137; CANR 59; SATA 90
Shepard, Lucius 1947- .... **CLC 34**
　See also CA 128; 141
Shepard, Sam 1943-**CLC 4, 6, 17, 34, 41, 44; DAM DRAM; DC 5**
　See also AAYA 1; CA 69-72; CABS 3; CANR
　22; DLB 7; MTCW 1
Shepherd, Michael
　See Ludlum, Robert
Sherburne, Zoa (Morin) 1912- .... **CLC 30**
　See also AAYA 13; CA 1-4R; CANR 3, 37;
　MAICYA; SAAS 18; SATA 3
Sheridan, Frances 1724-1766 .... **LC 7**
　See also DLB 39, 84
Sheridan, Richard Brinsley 1751-1816**NCLC 5; DA; DAB; DAC; DAM DRAM, MST; DC 1; WLC**
　See also CDBLB 1660-1789; DLB 89
Sherman, Jonathan Marc .... **CLC 55**
Sherman, Martin 1941(?)- .... **CLC 19**
　See also CA 116; 123
Sherwin, Judith Johnson
　See Johnson, Judith (Emlyn)
Sherwood, Frances 1940- .... **CLC 81**
　See also CA 146
Sherwood, Robert E(mmet) 1896-1955**TCLC 3; DAM DRAM**
　See also CA 104; 153; DLB 7, 26
Shestov, Lev 1866-1938 .... **TCLC 56**

5, 6

Slesinger, Tess 1905-1945 .... **TCLC 10**
See also CA 107; DLB 102

Slessor, Kenneth 1901-1971 .... **CLC 14**
See also CA 102; 89-92

Slowacki, Juliusz 1809-1849 .... **NCLC 15**

Smart, Christopher 1722-1771 .. **LC 3; DAM POET; PC 13**
See also DLB 109

Smart, Elizabeth 1913-1986 .... **CLC 54**
See also CA 81-84; 118; DLB 88

Smiley, Jane (Graves) 1949-**CLC 53, 76; DAM POP**
See also CA 104; CANR 30, 50, 74; INT CANR-30

Smith, A(rthur) J(ames) M(arshall) 1902-1980 **CLC 15; DAC**
See also CA 1-4R; 102; CANR 4; DLB 88

Smith, Adam 1723-1790 .... **LC 36**
See also DLB 104

Smith, Alexander 1829-1867 .... **NCLC 59**
See also DLB 32, 55

Smith, Anna Deavere 1950- .... **CLC 86**
See also CA 133

Smith, Betty (Wehner) 1896-1972 .... **CLC 19**
See also CA 5-8R; 33-36R; DLBY 82; SATA 6

Smith, Charlotte (Turner) 1749-1806 **NCLC 23**
See also DLB 39, 109

Smith, Clark Ashton 1893-1961 .... **CLC 43**
See also CA 143

Smith, Dave .... **CLC 22, 42**
See also Smith, David (Jeddie)
See also CAAS 7; DLB 5

Smith, David (Jeddie) 1942-
See Smith, Dave
See also CA 49-52; CANR 1, 59; DAM POET

Smith, Florence Margaret 1902-1971
See Smith, Stevie
See also CA 17-18; 29-32R; CANR 35; CAP 2; DAM POET; MTCW 1

Smith, Iain Crichton 1928-1998 .... **CLC 64**
See also CA 21-24R; 171; DLB 40, 139

Smith, John 1580(?)-1631 .... **LC 9**
See also DLB 24, 30

Smith, Johnston
See Crane, Stephen (Townley)

Smith, Joseph, Jr. 1805-1844 .... **NCLC 53**

Smith, Lee 1944- .... **CLC 25, 73**
See also CA 114; 119; CANR 46; DLB 143; DLBY 83; INT 119

Smith, Martin
See Smith, Martin Cruz

Smith, Martin Cruz 1942- ..... **CLC 25; DAM MULT, POP**
See also BEST 89:4; CA 85-88; CANR 6, 23, 43, 65; INT CANR-23; NNAL

Smith, Mary-Ann Tirone 1944- .... **CLC 39**
See also CA 118; 136

Smith, Patti 1946- .... **CLC 12**
See also CA 93-96; CANR 63

Smith, Pauline (Urmson) 1882-1959**TCLC 25**

Smith, Rosamond
See Oates, Joyce Carol

Smith, Sheila Kaye
See Kaye-Smith, Sheila

Smith, Stevie .... **CLC 3, 8, 25, 44; PC 12**
See also Smith, Florence Margaret
See also DLB 20

Smith, Wilbur (Addison) 1933- .... **CLC 33**
See also CA 13-16R; CANR 7, 46, 66; MTCW 1

Smith, William Jay 1918- .... **CLC 6**
See also CA 5-8R; CANR 44; DLB 5; MAICYA; SAAS 22; SATA 2, 68

Smith, Woodrow Wilson
See Kuttner, Henry

Smolenskin, Peretz 1842-1885 .... **NCLC 30**

Smollett, Tobias (George) 1721-1771**LC 2, 46**
See also CDBLB 1660-1789; DLB 39, 104

Snodgrass, W(illiam) D(e Witt) 1926-**CLC 2, 6, 10, 18, 68; DAM POET**
See also CA 1-4R; CANR 6, 36, 65; DLB 5; MTCW

Snow, C(harles) P(ercy) 1905-1980**CLC 1, 4, 6, 9, 13, 19; DAM NOV**
See also CA 5-8R; 101; CANR 28; CDBLB 1945-1960; DLB 15, 77; DLBD 17; MTCW 1

Snow, Frances Compton
See Adams, Henry (Brooks)

Snyder, Gary (Sherman) 1930-**CLC 1, 2, 5, 9, 32; DAM POET; PC 21**
See also CA 17-20R; CANR 30, 60; DLB 5, 16, 165

Snyder, Zilpha Keatley 1927- .... **CLC 17**
See also AAYA 15; CA 9-12R; CANR 38; CLR 31; JRDA; MAICYA; SAAS 2; SATA 1, 28, 75

Soares, Bernardo
See Pessoa, Fernando (Antonio Nogueira)

Sobh, A.
See Shamlu, Ahmad

Sobol, Joshua .... **CLC 60**

Socrates 469B.C.-399B.C. .... **CMLC 27**

Soderberg, Hjalmar 1869-1941 ..... **TCLC 39**

Sodergran, Edith (Irene)
See Soedergran, Edith (Irene)

Soedergran, Edith (Irene) 1892-1923 **TCLC 31**

Softly, Edgar
See Lovecraft, H(oward) P(hillips)

Softly, Edward
See Lovecraft, H(oward) P(hillips)

Sokolov, Raymond 1941- .... **CLC 7**
See also CA 85-88

Solo, Jay
See Ellison, Harlan (Jay)

Sologub, Fyodor .... **TCLC 9**
See also Teternikov, Fyodor Kuzmich

Solomons, Ikey Esquir
See Thackeray, William Makepeace

Solomos, Dionysios 1798-1857 .... **NCLC 15**

Solwoska, Mara
See French, Marilyn

Solzhenitsyn, Aleksandr I(sayevich) 1918-**CLC 1, 2, 4, 7, 9, 10, 18, 26, 34, 78; DA; DAB; DAC; DAM MST, NOV; SSC 32; WLC**
See also AITN 1; CA 69-72; CANR 40, 65; MTCW 1

Somers, Jane
See Lessing, Doris (May)

Somerville, Edith 1858-1949 .... **TCLC 51**
See also DLB 135

Somerville & Ross
See Martin, Violet Florence; Somerville, Edith

Sommer, Scott 1951- .... **CLC 25**
See also CA 106

Sondheim, Stephen (Joshua) 1930- . **CLC 30, 39; DAM DRAM**
See also AAYA 11; CA 103; CANR 47, 68

Song, Cathy 1955- .... **PC 21**
See also CA 154; DLB 169

Sontag, Susan 1933-**CLC 1, 2, 10, 13, 31, 105; DAM POP**
See also CA 17-20R; CANR 25, 51, 74; DLB 2, 67; MTCW 1

Sophocles 496(?)B.C.-406(?)B.C. ... **CMLC 2; DA; DAB; DAC; DAM DRAM, MST; DC 1; WLCS**
See also DLB 176

Sordello 1189-1269 .... **CMLC 15**

Sorel, Georges 1847-1922 .... **TCLC 91**

See also CA 118

Sorel, Julia
See Drexler, Rosalyn

Sorrentino, Gilbert 1929-**CLC 3, 7, 14, 22, 40**
See also CA 77-80; CANR 14, 33; DLB 5, 173; DLBY 80; INT CANR-14

Soto, Gary 1952- **CLC 32, 80; DAM MULT; HLC**
See also AAYA 10; CA 119; 125; CANR 50, 74; CLR 38; DLB 82; HW; INT 125; JRDA; SATA 80

Soupault, Philippe 1897-1990 .... **CLC 68**
See also CA 116; 147; 131

Souster, (Holmes) Raymond 1921-**CLC 5, 14; DAC; DAM POET**
See also CA 13-16R; CAAS 14; CANR 13, 29, 53; DLB 88; SATA 63

Southern, Terry 1924(?)-1995 .... **CLC 7**
See also CA 1-4R; 150; CANR 1, 55; DLB 2

Southey, Robert 1774-1843 .... **NCLC 8**
See also DLB 93, 107, 142; SATA 54

Southworth, Emma Dorothy Eliza Nevitte 1819-1899 ....

NCLC 26

Souza, Ernest
See Scott, Evelyn

Soyinka, Wole 1934-**CLC 3, 5, 14, 36, 44; BLC 3; DA; DAB; DAC; DAM DRAM, MST, MULT; DC 2; WLC**
See also BW 2; CA 13-16R; CANR 27, 39; DLB 125; MTCW 1

Spackman, W(illiam) M(ode) 1905-1990**CLC 46**
See also CA 81-84; 132

Spacks, Barry (Bernard) 1931- .... **CLC 14**
See also CA 154; CANR 33; DLB 105

Spanidou, Irini 1946- .... **CLC 44**

Spark, Muriel (Sarah) 1918-**CLC 2, 3, 5, 8, 13, 18, 40, 94; DAB; DAC; DAM MST, NOV; SSC 10**
See also CA 5-8R; CANR 12, 36, 76; CDBLB 1945-1960; DLB 15, 139; INT CANR-12; MTCW 1

Spaulding, Douglas
See Bradbury, Ray (Douglas)

Spaulding, Leonard
See Bradbury, Ray (Douglas)

Spence, J. A. D.
See Eliot, T(homas) S(tearns)

Spencer, Elizabeth 1921- .... **CLC 22**
See also CA 13-16R; CANR 32, 65; DLB 6; MTCW 1; SATA 14

Spencer, Leonard G.
See Silverberg, Robert

Spencer, Scott 1945- .... **CLC 30**
See also CA 113; CANR 51; DLBY 86

Spender, Stephen (Harold) 1909-1995**CLC 1, 2, 5, 10, 41, 91; DAM POET**
See also CA 9-12R; 149; CANR 31, 54; CDBLB 1945-1960; DLB 20; MTCW 1

Spengler, Oswald (Arnold Gottfried) 1880-1936 **TCLC 25**
See also CA 118

Spenser, Edmund 1552(?)-1599**LC 5, 39; DA; DAB; DAC; DAM MST, POET; PC 8; WLC**
See also CDBLB Before 1660; DLB 167

Spicer, Jack 1925-1965 **CLC 8, 18, 72; DAM POET**
See also CA 85-88; DLB 5, 16, 193

Spiegelman, Art 1948- .... **CLC 76**
See also AAYA 10; CA 125; CANR 41, 55, 74

Spielberg, Peter 1929- .... **CLC 6**
See also CA 5-8R; CANR 4, 48; DLBY 81

Spielberg, Steven 1947- .... **CLC 20**
See also AAYA 8, 24; CA 77-80; CANR 32; SATA 32

Spillane, Frank Morrison 1918-
See Spillane, Mickey
See also CA 25-28R; CANR 28, 63; MTCW 1;
SATA 66
Spillane, Mickey .... **CLC 3, 13**
See also Spillane, Frank Morrison
Spinoza, Benedictus de 1632-1677 .... **LC 9**
Spinrad, Norman (Richard) 1940- ... **CLC 46**
See also CA 37-40R; CAAS 19; CANR 20; DLB
8; INT CANR-20
Spitteler, Carl (Friedrich Georg) 1845-1924
TCLC 12
See also CA 109; DLB 129
Spivack, Kathleen (Romola Drucker) 1938-
CLC 6
See also CA 49-52
Spoto, Donald 1941- .... **CLC 39**
See also CA 65-68; CANR 11, 57
Springsteen, Bruce (F.) 1949- .... **CLC 17**
See also CA 111
Spurling, Hilary 1940- .... **CLC 34**
See also CA 104; CANR 25, 52
Spyker, John Howland
See Elman, Richard (Martin)
Squires, (James) Radcliffe 1917-1993 **CLC 51**
See also CA 1-4R; 140; CANR 6, 21
Srivastava, Dhanpat Rai 1880(?)-1936
See Premchand
See also CA 118
Stacy, Donald
See Pohl, Frederik
Stael, Germaine de 1766-1817
See Stael-Holstein, Anne Louise Germaine
Necker Baronn
See also DLB 119
**Stael-Holstein, Anne Louise Germaine Necker
Baronn** 1766-1817 .... **NCLC 3**
See also Stael, Germaine de
See also DLB 192
Stafford, Jean 1915-1979 **CLC 4, 7, 19, 68; SSC
26**
See also CA 1-4R; 85-88; CANR 3, 65; DLB 2,
173; MTCW 1; SATA-Obit 22
Stafford, William (Edgar) 1914-1993 **CLC 4,
7, 29; DAM POET**
See also CA 5-8R; 142; CAAS 3; CANR 5, 22;
DLB 5, 206; INT CANR-22
Stagnelius, Eric Johan 1793-1823 . **NCLC 61**
Staines, Trevor
See Brunner, John (Kilian Houston)
Stairs, Gordon
See Austin, Mary (Hunter)
Stannard, Martin 1947- .... **CLC 44**
See also CA 142; DLB 155
Stanton, Elizabeth Cady 1815-1902 **TCLC 73**
See also CA 171; DLB 79
Stanton, Maura 1946- .... **CLC 9**
See also CA 89-92; CANR 15; DLB 120
Stanton, Schuyler
See Baum, L(yman) Frank
Stapledon, (William) Olaf 1886-1950 **T C L C
22**
See also CA 111; 162; DLB 15
Starbuck, George (Edwin) 1931-1996 **CLC 53;
DAM POET**
See also CA 21-24R; 153; CANR 23
Stark, Richard
See Westlake, Donald E(dwin)
Staunton, Schuyler
See Baum, L(yman) Frank
Stead, Christina (Ellen) 1902-1983 **CLC 2, 5,
8, 32, 80**
See also CA 13-16R; 109; CANR 33, 40;
MTCW 1
Stead, William Thomas 1849-1912 **TCLC 48**
See also CA 167
Steele, Richard 1672-1729 .... **LC 18**

See also CDBLB 1660-1789; DLB 84, 101
Steele, Timothy (Reid) 1948- .... **CLC 45**
See also CA 93-96; CANR 16, 50; DLB 120
Steffens, (Joseph) Lincoln 1866-1936 **T C L C
20**
See also CA 117
Stegner, Wallace (Earle) 1909-1993**CLC 9, 49,
81; DAM NOV; SSC 27**
See also AITN 1; BEST 90:3; CA 1-4R; 141;
CAAS 9; CANR 1, 21, 46; DLB 9, 206;
DLBY 93; MTCW 1
Stein, Gertrude 1874-1946**TCLC 1, 6, 28, 48;
DA; DAB; DAC; DAM MST, NOV, POET;
PC 18; WLC**
See also CA 104; 132; CDALB 1917-1929;
DLB 4, 54, 86; DLBD 15; MTCW 1
Steinbeck, John (Ernst) 1902-1968**CLC 1, 5, 9,
13, 21, 34, 45, 75; DA; DAB; DAC; DAM
DRAM, MST, NOV; SSC 11; WLC**
See also AAYA 12; CA 1-4R; 25-28R; CANR
1, 35; CDALB 1929-1941; DLB 7, 9; DLBD
2; MTCW 1; SATA 9
Steinem, Gloria 1934- .... **CLC 63**
See also CA 53-56; CANR 28, 51; MTCW 1
Steiner, George 1929- ... **CLC 24; DAM NOV**
See also CA 73-76; CANR 31, 67; DLB 67;
MTCW 1; SATA 62
Steiner, K. Leslie
See Delany, Samuel R(ay, Jr.)
Steiner, Rudolf 1861-1925 .... **TCLC 13**
See also CA 107
Stendhal 1783-1842**NCLC 23, 46; DA; DAB;
DAC; DAM MST, NOV; SSC 27; WLC**
See also DLB 119
Stephen, Adeline Virginia
See Woolf, (Adeline) Virginia
Stephen, SirLeslie 1832-1904 .... **TCLC 23**
See also CA 123; DLB 57, 144, 190
Stephen, Sir Leslie
See Stephen, SirLeslie
Stephen, Virginia
See Woolf, (Adeline) Virginia
Stephens, James 1882(?)-1950 .... **TCLC 4**
See also CA 104; DLB 19, 153, 162
Stephens, Reed
See Donaldson, Stephen R.
Steptoe, Lydia
See Barnes, Djuna
Sterchi, Beat 1949- .... **CLC 65**
Sterling, Brett
See Bradbury, Ray (Douglas); Hamilton,
Edmond
Sterling, Bruce 1954- .... **CLC 72**
See also CA 119; CANR 44
Sterling, George 1869-1926 .... **TCLC 20**
See also CA 117; 165; DLB 54
Stern, Gerald 1925- .... **CLC 40, 100**
See also CA 81-84; CANR 28; DLB 105
Stern, Richard (Gustave) 1928- .... **CLC 4, 39**
See also CA 1-4R; CANR 1, 25, 52; DLBY 87;
INT CANR-25
Sternberg, Josef von 1894-1969 .... **CLC 20**
See also CA 81-84
Sterne, Laurence 1713-1768 ... **LC 2, 48; DA;
DAB; DAC; DAM MST, NOV; WLC**
See also CDBLB 1660-1789; DLB 39
Sternheim, (William Adolf) Carl 1878-1942
TCLC 8
See also CA 105; DLB 56, 118
Stevens, Mark 1951- .... **CLC 34**
See also CA 122
Stevens, Wallace 1879-1955 **TCLC 3, 12, 45;
DA; DAB; DAC; DAM MST, POET; PC
6; WLC**
See also CA 104; 124; CDALB 1929-1941;
DLB 54; MTCW 1
Stevenson, Anne (Katharine) 1933-**CLC 7, 33**

See also CA 17-20R; CAAS 9; CANR 9, 33;
DLB 40; MTCW 1
Stevenson, Robert Louis (Balfour) 1850-1894
**NCLC 5, 14, 63; DA; DAB; DAC; DAM
MST, NOV; SSC 11; WLC**
See also AAYA 24; CDBLB 1890-1914; CLR
10, 11; DLB 18, 57, 141, 156, 174; DLBD
13; JRDA; MAICYA; SATA 100; YABC 2
Stewart, J(ohn) I(nnes) M(ackintosh) 1906-
1994 .... **CLC 7, 14, 32**
See also CA 85-88; 147; CAAS 3; CANR 47;
MTCW 1
Stewart, Mary (Florence Elinor) 1916-**CLC 7,
35, 117; DAB**
See also CA 1-4R; CANR 1, 59; SATA 12
Stewart, Mary Rainbow
See Stewart, Mary (Florence Elinor)
Stifle, June
See Campbell, Maria
Stifter, Adalbert 1805-1868**NCLC 41; SSC 28**
See also DLB 133
Still, James 1906- .... **CLC 49**
See also CA 65-68; CAAS 17; CANR 10, 26;
DLB 9; SATA 29
Sting 1951-
See Sumner, Gordon Matthew
See also CA 167
Stirling, Arthur
See Sinclair, Upton (Beall)
Stitt, Milan 1941- .... **CLC 29**
See also CA 69-72
Stockton, Francis Richard 1834-1902
See Stockton, Frank R.
See also CA 108; 137; MAICYA; SATA 44
Stockton, Frank R. .... **TCLC 47**
See also Stockton, Francis Richard
See also DLB 42, 74; DLBD 13; SATA-Brief
32
Stoddard, Charles
See Kuttner, Henry
Stoker, Abraham 1847-1912
See Stoker, Bram
See also CA 105; 150; DA; DAC; DAM MST,
NOV; SATA 29
Stoker, Bram 1847-1912**TCLC 8; DAB; WLC**
See also Stoker, Abraham
See also AAYA 23; CDBLB 1890-1914; DLB
36, 70, 178
Stolz, Mary (Slattery) 1920- .... **CLC 12**
See also AAYA 8; AITN 1; CA 5-8R; CANR
13, 41; JRDA; MAICYA; SAAS 3; SATA 10,
71
Stone, Irving 1903-1989 ..**CLC 7; DAM POP**
See also AITN 1; CA 1-4R; 129; CAAS 3;
CANR 1, 23; INT CANR-23; MTCW 1;
SATA 3; SATA-Obit 64
Stone, Oliver (William) 1946- .... **CLC 73**
See also AAYA 15; CA 110; CANR 55
Stone, Robert (Anthony) 1937-**CLC 5, 23, 42**
See also CA 85-88; CANR 23, 66; DLB 152;
INT CANR-23; MTCW 1
Stone, Zachary
See Follett, Ken(neth Martin)
Stoppard, Tom 1937-**CLC 1, 3, 4, 5, 8, 15, 29,
34, 63, 91; DA; DAB; DAC; DAM DRAM,
MST; DC 6; WLC**
See also CA 81-84; CANR 39, 67; CDBLB
1960 to Present; DLB 13; DLBY 85; MTCW
1
Storey, David (Malcolm) 1933-**CLC 2, 4, 5, 8;
DAM DRAM**
See also CA 81-84; CANR 36; DLB 13, 14, 207;
MTCW 1
Storm, Hyemeyohsts 1935- ...... **CLC 3; DAM
MULT**
See also CA 81-84; CANR 45; NNAL
Storm, Theodor 1817-1888 .... **SSC 27**

Storm, (Hans) Theodor (Woldsen) 1817-1888
NCLC 1; SSC 27
See also DLB 129

Storni, Alfonsina 1892-1938. TCLC 5; DAM
MULT; HLC
See also CA 104; 131; HW

Stoughton, William 1631-1701 .... LC 38
See also DLB 24

Stout, Rex (Todhunter) 1886-1975 ..... CLC 3
See also AITN 2; CA 61-64; CANR 71

Stow, (Julian) Randolph 1935- .. CLC 23, 48
See also CA 13-16R; CANR 33; MTCW 1

Stowe, Harriet (Elizabeth) Beecher 1811-1896
NCLC 3, 50; DA; DAB; DAC; DAM MST,
NOV; WLC
See also CDALB 1865-1917; DLB 1, 12, 42,
74, 189; JRDA; MAICYA; YABC 1

Strachey, (Giles) Lytton 1880-1932TCLC 12
See also CA 110; DLB 149; DLBD 10

Strand, Mark 1934- CLC 6, 18, 41, 71; DAM
POET
See also CA 21-24R; CANR 40, 65; DLB 5;
SATA 41

Straub, Peter (Francis) 1943- . CLC 28, 107;
DAM POP
See also BEST 89:1; CA 85-88; CANR 28, 65;
DLBY 84; MTCW 1

Strauss, Botho 1944- .... CLC 22
See also CA 157; DLB 124

Streatfeild, (Mary) Noel 1895(?)-1986CLC 21
See also CA 81-84; 120; CANR 31; CLR 17;
DLB 160; MAICYA; SATA 20; SATA-Obit
48

Stribling, T(homas) S(igismund) 1881-1965
CLC 23
See also CA 107; DLB 9

Strindberg, (Johan) August 1849-1912TCLC
1, 8, 21, 47; DA; DAB; DAC; DAM DRAM,
MST; WLC
See also CA 104; 135

Stringer, Arthur 1874-1950 .... TCLC 37
See also CA 161; DLB 92

Stringer, David
See Roberts, Keith (John Kingston)

Stroheim, Erich von 1885-1957 ..... TCLC 71

Strugatskii, Arkadii (Natanovich) 1925-1991
CLC 27
See also CA 106; 135

Strugatskii, Boris (Natanovich) 1933-CLC 27
See also CA 106

Strummer, Joe 1953(?)- .... CLC 30

Stuart, Don A.
See Campbell, John W(ood, Jr.)

Stuart, Ian
See MacLean, Alistair (Stuart)

Stuart, Jesse (Hilton) 1906-1984CLC 1, 8, 11,
14, 34; SSC 31
See also CA 5-8R; 112; CANR 31; DLB 9, 48,
102; DLBY 84; SATA 2; SATA-Obit 36

Sturgeon, Theodore (Hamilton) 1918-1985
CLC 22, 39
See also Queen, Ellery
See also CA 81-84; 116; CANR 32; DLB 8;
DLBY 85; MTCW 1

Sturges, Preston 1898-1959 .... TCLC 48
See also CA 114; 149; DLB 26

Styron, William 1925-CLC 1, 3, 5, 11, 15, 60;
DAM NOV, POP; SSC 25
See also BEST 90:4; CA 5-8R; CANR 6, 33,
74; CDALB 1968-1988; DLB 2, 143; DLBY
80; INT CANR-6; MTCW 1

Su, Chien 1884-1918
See Su Man-shu
See also CA 123

Suarez Lynch, B.
See Bioy Casares, Adolfo; Borges, Jorge Luis

Suckow, Ruth 1892-1960 .... SSC 18

See also CA 113; DLB 9, 102

Sudermann, Hermann 1857-1928 .. TCLC 15
See also CA 107; DLB 118

Sue, Eugene 1804-1857 .... NCLC 1
See also DLB 119

Sueskind, Patrick 1949- .... CLC 44
See also Suskind, Patrick

Sukenick, Ronald 1932- .... CLC 3, 4, 6, 48
See also CA 25-28R; CAAS 8; CANR 32; DLB
173; DLBY 81

Suknaski, Andrew 1942- .... CLC 19
See also CA 101; DLB 53

Sullivan, Vernon
See Vian, Boris

Sully Prudhomme 1839-1907 .... TCLC 31

Su Man-shu .... TCLC 24
See also Su, Chien

Summerforest, Ivy B.
See Kirkup, James

Summers, Andrew James 1942- .... CLC 26

Summers, Andy
See Summers, Andrew James

Summers, Hollis (Spurgeon, Jr.) 1916-CLC 10
See also CA 5-8R; CANR 3; DLB 6

Summers, (Alphonsus Joseph-Mary Augustus)
Montague 1880-1948 .... TCLC 16
See also CA 118; 163

Sumner, Gordon Matthew .... CLC 26
See also Sting

Surtees, Robert Smith 1803-1864 .. NCLC 14
See also DLB 21

Susann, Jacqueline 1921-1974 .... CLC 3
See also AITN 1; CA 65-68; 53-56; MTCW 1

Su Shih 1036-1101 .... CMLC 15

Suskind, Patrick
See Sueskind, Patrick
See also CA 145

Sutcliff, Rosemary 1920-1992CLC 26; DAB;
DAC; DAM MST, POP
See also AAYA 10; CA 5-8R; 139; CANR 37;
CLR 1, 37; JRDA; MAICYA; SATA 6, 44,
78; SATA-Obit 73

Sutro, Alfred 1863-1933 .... TCLC 6
See also CA 105; DLB 10

Sutton, Henry
See Slavitt, David R(ytman)

Svevo, Italo 1861-1928 . TCLC 2, 35; SSC 25
See also Schmitz, Aron Hector

Swados, Elizabeth (A.) 1951- .... CLC 12
See also CA 97-100; CANR 49; INT 97-100

Swados, Harvey 1920-1972 .... CLC 5
See also CA 5-8R; 37-40R; CANR 6; DLB 2

Swan, Gladys 1934- .... CLC 69
See also CA 101; CANR 17, 39

Swarthout, Glendon (Fred) 1918-1992CLC 35
See also CA 1-4R; 139; CANR 1, 47; SATA 26

Sweet, Sarah C.
See Jewett, (Theodora) Sarah Orne

Swenson, May 1919-1989CLC 4, 14, 61, 106;
DA; DAB; DAC; DAM MST, POET; PC
14
See also CA 5-8R; 130; CANR 36, 61; DLB 5;
MTCW 1; SATA 15

Swift, Augustus
See Lovecraft, H(oward) P(hillips)

Swift, Graham (Colin) 1949- ...... CLC 41, 88
See also CA 117; 122; CANR 46, 71; DLB 194

Swift, Jonathan 1667-1745 ..... LC 1, 42; DA;
DAB; DAC; DAM MST, NOV, POET; PC
9; WLC
See also CDBLB 1660-1789; CLR 53; DLB 39,
95, 101; SATA 19

Swinburne, Algernon Charles 1837-1909
TCLC 8, 36; DA; DAB; DAC; DAM MST,
POET; PC 24; WLC
See also CA 105; 140; CDBLB 1832-1890;
DLB 35, 57

Swinfen, Ann .... CLC 34

Swinnerton, Frank Arthur 1884-1982CLC 31
See also CA 108; DLB 34

Swithen, John
See King, Stephen (Edwin)

Sylvia
See Ashton-Warner, Sylvia (Constance)

Symmes, Robert Edward
See Duncan, Robert (Edward)

Symonds, John Addington 1840-1893 N C L C
34
See also DLB 57, 144

Symons, Arthur 1865-1945 .... TCLC 11
See also CA 107; DLB 19, 57, 149

Symons, Julian (Gustave) 1912-1994 CLC 2,
14, 32
See also CA 49-52; 147; CAAS 3; CANR 3,
33, 59; DLB 87, 155; DLBY 92; MTCW 1

Synge, (Edmund) J(ohn) M(illington) 1871-
1909 ... TCLC 6, 37; DAM DRAM; DC 2
See also CA 104; 141; CDBLB 1890-1914;
DLB 10, 19

Syruc, J.
See Milosz, Czeslaw

Szirtes, George 1948- .... CLC 46
See also CA 109; CANR 27, 61

Szymborska, Wislawa 1923- .... CLC 99
See also CA 154; DLBY 96

T. O., Nik
See Annensky, Innokenty (Fyodorovich)

Tabori, George 1914- .... CLC 19
See also CA 49-52; CANR 4, 69

Tagore, Rabindranath 1861-1941TCLC 3, 53;
DAM DRAM, POET; PC 8
See also CA 104; 120; MTCW 1

Taine, Hippolyte Adolphe 1828-1893 . N C L C
15

Talese, Gay 1932- .... CLC 37
See also AITN 1; CA 1-4R; CANR 9, 58; DLB
185; INT CANR-9; MTCW 1

Tallent, Elizabeth (Ann) 1954- .... CLC 45
See also CA 117; CANR 72; DLB 130

Tally, Ted 1952- .... CLC 42
See also CA 120; 124; INT 124

Talvik, Heiti 1904-1947 .... TCLC 87

Tamayo y Baus, Manuel 1829-1898 NCLC 1

Tammsaare, A(nton) H(ansen) 1878-1940
TCLC 27
See also CA 164

Tam'si, Tchicaya U
See Tchicaya, Gerald Felix

Tan, Amy (Ruth) 1952-CLC 59; DAM MULT,
NOV, POP
See also AAYA 9; BEST 89:3; CA 136; CANR
54; DLB 173; SATA 75

Tandem, Felix
See Spitteler, Carl (Friedrich Georg)

Tanizaki, Jun'ichiro 1886-1965CLC 8, 14, 28;
SSC 21
See also CA 93-96; 25-28R; DLB 180

Tanner, William
See Amis, Kingsley (William)

Tao Lao
See Storni, Alfonsina

Tarassoff, Lev
See Troyat, Henri

Tarbell, Ida M(inerva) 1857-1944 . TCLC 40
See also CA 122; DLB 47

Tarkington, (Newton) Booth 1869-1946TCLC
9
See also CA 110; 143; DLB 9, 102; SATA 17

Tarkovsky, Andrei (Arsenyevich) 1932-1986
CLC 75
See also CA 127

Tartt, Donna 1964(?)- .... CLC 76
See also CA 142

Tasso, Torquato 1544-1595 .... LC 5

See also CA 13-16R; CAAS 22; CANR 5, 21, 44, 67; DLB 175; NNAL

Vizinczey, Stephen 1933- .... **CLC 40**
See also CA 128; INT 128

Vliet, R(ussell) G(ordon) 1929-1984 **CLC 22**
See also CA 37-40R; 112; CANR 18

Vogau, Boris Andreyevich 1894-1937(?)
See Pilnyak, Boris
See also CA 123

Vogel, Paula A(nne) 1951- .... **CLC 76**
See also CA 108

Voigt, Cynthia 1942- .... **CLC 30**
See also AAYA 3; CA 106; CANR 18, 37, 40; CLR 13, 48; INT CANR-18; JRDA; MAICYA; SATA 48, 79; SATA-Brief 33

Voigt, Ellen Bryant 1943- .... **CLC 54**
See also CA 69-72; CANR 11, 29, 55; DLB 120

Voinovich, Vladimir (Nikolaevich) 1932-**CLC 10, 49**
See also CA 81-84; CAAS 12; CANR 33, 67; MTCW 1

Vollmann, William T. 1959- ..**CLC 89; DAM NOV, POP**
See also CA 134; CANR 67

Voloshinov, V. N.
See Bakhtin, Mikhail Mikhailovich

Voltaire 1694-1778 . **LC 14; DA; DAB; DAC; DAM DRAM, MST; SSC 12; WLC**

von Aschendrof, BaronIgnatz
See Ford, Ford Madox

von Daeniken, Erich 1935- .... **CLC 30**
See also AITN 1; CA 37-40R; CANR 17, 44

von Daniken, Erich
See von Daeniken, Erich

von Heidenstam, (Carl Gustaf) Verner
See Heidenstam, (Carl Gustaf) Verner von

von Heyse, Paul (Johann Ludwig)
See Heyse, Paul (Johann Ludwig von)

von Hofmannsthal, Hugo
See Hofmannsthal, Hugo von

von Horvath, Odon
See Horvath, Oedoen von

von Horvath, Oedoen
See Horvath, Oedoen von

von Liliencron, (Friedrich Adolf Axel) Detlev
See Liliencron, (Friedrich Adolf Axel) Detlev von

Vonnegut, Kurt, Jr. 1922-**CLC 1, 2, 3, 4, 5, 8, 12, 22, 40, 60, 111; DA; DAB; DAC; DAM MST, NOV, POP; SSC 8; WLC**
See also AAYA 6; AITN 1; BEST 90:4; CA 1-4R; CANR 1, 25, 49, 75; CDALB 1968-1988; DLB 2, 8, 152; DLBD 3; DLBY 80; MTCW 1

Von Rachen, Kurt
See Hubbard, L(afayette) Ron(ald)

von Rezzori (d'Arezzo), Gregor
See Rezzori (d'Arezzo), Gregor von

von Sternberg, Josef
See Sternberg, Josef von

Vorster, Gordon 1924-........................ **CLC 34**
See also CA 133

Vosce, Trudie
See Ozick, Cynthia

Voznesensky, Andrei (Andreievich) 1933-
CLC 1, 15, 57; DAM POET
See also CA 89-92; CANR 37; MTCW 1

Waddington, Miriam 1917- .... **CLC 28**
See also CA 21-24R; CANR 12, 30; DLB 68

Wagman, Fredrica 1937- .... **CLC 7**
See also CA 97-100; INT 97-100

Wagner, Linda W.
See Wagner-Martin, Linda (C.)

Wagner, Linda Welshimer
See Wagner-Martin, Linda (C.)

Wagner, Richard 1813-1883 .... **NCLC 9**
See also DLB 129

Wagner-Martin, Linda (C.) 1936- .... **CLC 50**
See also CA 159

Wagoner, David (Russell) 1926- **CLC 3, 5, 15**
See also CA 1-4R; CAAS 3; CANR 2, 71; DLB 5; SATA 14

Wah, Fred(erick James) 1939- .... **CLC 44**
See also CA 107; 141; DLB 60

Wahloo, Per 1926-1975 .... **CLC 7**
See also CA 61-64; CANR 73

Wahloo, Peter
See Wahloo, Per

Wain, John (Barrington) 1925-1994 . **CLC 2, 11, 15, 46**
See also CA 5-8R; 145; CAAS 4; CANR 23, 54; CDBLB 1960 to Present; DLB 15, 27, 139, 155; MTCW 1

Wajda, Andrzej 1926- .... **CLC 16**
See also CA 102

Wakefield, Dan 1932- .... **CLC 7**
See also CA 21-24R; CAAS 7

Wakoski, Diane 1937- **CLC 2, 4, 7, 9, 11, 40; DAM POET; PC 15**
See also CA 13-16R; CAAS 1; CANR 9, 60; DLB 5; INT CANR-9

Wakoski-Sherbell, Diane
See Wakoski, Diane

Walcott, Derek (Alton) 1930-**CLC 2, 4, 9, 14, 25, 42, 67, 76; BLC 3; DAB; DAC; DAM MST, MULT, POET; DC 7**
See also BW 2; CA 89-92; CANR 26, 47, 75; DLB 117; DLBY 81; MTCW 1

Waldman, Anne (Lesley) 1945-........... **CLC 7**
See also CA 37-40R; CAAS 17; CANR 34, 69; DLB 16

Waldo, E. Hunter
See Sturgeon, Theodore (Hamilton)

Waldo, Edward Hamilton
See Sturgeon, Theodore (Hamilton)

Walker, Alice (Malsenior) 1944- **CLC 5, 6, 9, 19, 27, 46, 58, 103; BLC 3; DA; DAB; DAC; DAM MST, MULT, NOV, POET, POP; SSC 5; WLCS**
See also AAYA 3; BEST 89:4; BW 2; CA 37-40R; CANR 9, 27, 49, 66; CDALB 1968-1988; DLB 6, 33, 143; INT CANR-27; MTCW 1; SATA 31

Walker, David Harry 1911-1992 .... **CLC 14**
See also CA 1-4R; 137; CANR 1; SATA 8; SATA-Obit 71

Walker, Edward Joseph 1934-
See Walker, Ted
See also CA 21-24R; CANR 12, 28, 53

Walker, George F. 1947- . **CLC 44, 61; DAB; DAC; DAM MST**
See also CA 103; CANR 21, 43, 59; DLB 60

Walker, Joseph A. 1935- .... **CLC 19; DAM DRAM, MST**
See also BW 1; CA 89-92; CANR 26; DLB 38

Walker, Margaret (Abigail) 1915-1998**CLC 1, 6; BLC; DAM MULT; PC 20**
See also BW 2; CA 73-76; 172; CANR 26, 54, 76; DLB 76, 152; MTCW 1

Walker, Ted .... **CLC 13**
See also Walker, Edward Joseph
See also DLB 40

Wallace, David Foster 1962- ..... **CLC 50, 114**
See also CA 132; CANR 59

Wallace, Dexter
See Masters, Edgar Lee

Wallace, (Richard Horatio) Edgar 1875-1932
TCLC 57
See also CA 115; DLB 70

Wallace, Irving 1916-1990 **CLC 7, 13; DAM NOV, POP**
See also AITN 1; CA 1-4R; 132; CAAS 1; CANR 1, 27; INT CANR-27; MTCW 1

Wallant, Edward Lewis 1926-1962**CLC 5, 10**

See also CA 1-4R; CANR 22; DLB 2, 28, 143; MTCW 1

Wallas, Graham 1858-1932 .... **TCLC 91**

Walley, Byron
See Card, Orson Scott

Walpole, Horace 1717-1797 ....**LC 49**
See also DLB 39, 104

Walpole, Hugh (Seymour) 1884-1941**TCLC 5**
See also CA 104; 165; DLB 34

Walser, Martin 1927-......................... **CLC 27**
See also CA 57-60; CANR 8, 46; DLB 75, 124

Walser, Robert 1878-1956 **TCLC 18; SSC 20**
See also CA 118; 165; DLB 66

Walsh, Jill Paton .... **CLC 35**
See also Paton Walsh, Gillian
See also AAYA 11; CLR 2; DLB 161; SAAS 3

Walter, Villiam Christian
See Andersen, Hans Christian

Wambaugh, Joseph (Aloysius, Jr.) 1937-**C L C 3, 18; DAM NOV, POP**
See also AITN 1; BEST 89:3; CA 33-36R; CANR 42, 65; DLB 6; DLBY 83; MTCW 1

Wang Wei 699(?)-761(?) .... **PC 18**

Ward, Arthur Henry Sarsfield 1883-1959
See Rohmer, Sax
See also CA 108

Ward, Douglas Turner 1930- .... **CLC 19**
See also BW 1; CA 81-84; CANR 27; DLB 7, 38

Ward, Mary Augusta
See Ward, Mrs. Humphry

Ward, Mrs. Humphry 1851-1920 .. **TCLC 55**
See also DLB 18

Ward, Peter
See Faust, Frederick (Schiller)

Warhol, Andy 1928(?)-1987 .... **CLC 20**
See also AAYA 12; BEST 89:4; CA 89-92; 121; CANR 34

Warner, Francis (Robert le Plastrier) 1937-
CLC 14
See also CA 53-56; CANR 11

Warner, Marina 1946- .... **CLC 59**
See also CA 65-68; CANR 21, 55; DLB 194

Warner, Rex (Ernest) 1905-1986 ...... **CLC 45**
See also CA 89-92; 119; DLB 15

Warner, Susan (Bogert) 1819-1885 **NCLC 31**
See also DLB 3, 42

Warner, Sylvia (Constance) Ashton
See Ashton-Warner, Sylvia (Constance)

Warner, Sylvia Townsend 1893-1978 **CLC 7, 19; SSC 23**
See also CA 61-64; 77-80; CANR 16, 60; DLB 34, 139; MTCW 1

Warren, Mercy Otis 1728-1814 ..... **NCLC 13**
See also DLB 31, 200

Warren, Robert Penn 1905-1989**CLC 1, 4, 6, 8, 10, 13, 18, 39, 53, 59; DA; DAB; DAC; DAM MST, NOV, POET; SSC 4; WLC**
See also AITN 1; CA 13-16R; 129; CANR 10, 47; CDALB 1968-1988; DLB 2, 48, 152; DLBY 80, 89; INT CANR-10; MTCW 1; SATA 46; SATA-Obit 63

Warshofsky, Isaac
See Singer, Isaac Bashevis

Warton, Thomas 1728-1790 .....**LC 15; DAM POET**
See also DLB 104, 109

Waruk, Kona
See Harris, (Theodore) Wilson

Warung, Price 1855-1911 .... **TCLC 45**

Warwick, Jarvis
See Garner, Hugh

Washington, Alex
See Harris, Mark

Washington, Booker T(aliaferro) 1856-1915
TCLC 10; BLC 3; DAM MULT
See also BW 1; CA 114; 125; SATA 28

Washington, George 1732-1799 .... **LC 25**
See also DLB 31

Wassermann, (Karl) Jakob 1873-1934 **T C L C 6**
See also CA 104; 163; DLB 66

Wasserstein, Wendy 1950- ... **CLC 32, 59, 90; DAM DRAM; DC 4**
See also CA 121; 129; CABS 3; CANR 53, 75; INT 129; SATA 94

Waterhouse, Keith (Spencer) 1929- . **CLC 47**
See also CA 5-8R; CANR 38, 67; DLB 13, 15; MTCW 1

Waters, Frank (Joseph) 1902-1995 .. **CLC 88**
See also CA 5-8R; 149; CAAS 13; CANR 3, 18, 63; DLBY 86

Waters, Roger 1944- .... **CLC 35**

Watkins, Frances Ellen
See Harper, Frances Ellen Watkins

Watkins, Gerrold
See Malzberg, Barry N(athaniel)

Watkins, Gloria 1955(?)-
See hooks, bell
See also BW 2; CA 143

Watkins, Paul 1964- .... **CLC 55**
See also CA 132; CANR 62

Watkins, Vernon Phillips 1906-1967 **CLC 43**
See also CA 9-10; 25-28R; CAP 1; DLB 20

Watson, Irving S.
See Mencken, H(enry) L(ouis)

Watson, John H.
See Farmer, Philip Jose

Watson, Richard F.
See Silverberg, Robert

Waugh, Auberon (Alexander) 1939- .. **CLC 7**
See also CA 45-48; CANR 6, 22; DLB 14, 194

Waugh, Evelyn (Arthur St. John) 1903-1966 **CLC 1, 3, 8, 13, 19, 27, 44, 107; DA; DAB; DAC; DAM MST, NOV, POP; WLC**
See also CA 85-88; 25-28R; CANR 22; CDBLB 1914-1945; DLB 15, 162, 195; MTCW 1

Waugh, Harriet 1944- .... **CLC 6**
See also CA 85-88; CANR 22

Ways, C. R.
See Blount, Roy (Alton), Jr.

Waystaff, Simon
See Swift, Jonathan

Webb, (Martha) Beatrice (Potter) 1858-1943 **TCLC 22**
See also Potter, (Helen) Beatrix
See also CA 117; DLB 190

Webb, Charles (Richard) 1939- .... **CLC 7**
See also CA 25-28R

Webb, James H(enry), Jr. 1946- .... **CLC 22**
See also CA 81-84

Webb, Mary (Gladys Meredith) 1881-1927 **TCLC 24**
See also CA 123; DLB 34

Webb, Mrs. Sidney
See Webb, (Martha) Beatrice (Potter)

Webb, Phyllis 1927- .... **CLC 18**
See also CA 104; CANR 23; DLB 53

Webb, Sidney (James) 1859-1947 .. **TCLC 22**
See also CA 117; 163; DLB 190

Webber, Andrew Lloyd .... **CLC 21**
See also Lloyd Webber, Andrew

Weber, Lenora Mattingly 1895-1971 **CLC 12**
See also CA 19-20; 29-32R; CAP 1; SATA 2; SATA-Obit 26

Weber, Max 1864-1920 .... **TCLC 69**
See also CA 109

Webster, John 1579(?)-1634(?) ... **LC 33; DA; DAB; DAC; DAM DRAM, MST; DC 2; WLC**
See also CDBLB Before 1660; DLB 58

Webster, Noah 1758-1843 .... **NCLC 30**
See also DLB 1, 37, 42, 43, 73

Wedekind, (Benjamin) Frank(lin) 1864-1918 TCLC 7; DAM DRAM
See also CA 104; 153; DLB 118

Weidman, Jerome 1913-1998 .... **CLC 7**
See also AITN 2; CA 1-4R; 171; CANR 1; DLB 28

Weil, Simone (Adolphine) 1909-1943 **TCLC 23**
See also CA 117; 159

Weininger, Otto 1880-1903 .... **TCLC 84**

Weinstein, Nathan
See West, Nathanael

Weinstein, Nathan von Wallenstein
See West, Nathanael

Weir, Peter (Lindsay) 1944- .... **CLC 20**
See also CA 113; 123

Weiss, Peter (Ulrich) 1916-1982 **CLC 3, 15, 51; DAM DRAM**
See also CA 45-48; 106; CANR 3; DLB 69, 124

Weiss, Theodore (Russell) 1916- **CLC 3, 8, 14**
See also CA 9-12R; CAAS 2; CANR 46; DLB 5

Welch, (Maurice) Denton 1915-1948 **TCLC 22**
See also CA 121; 148

Welch, James 1940- ..... **CLC 6, 14, 52; DAM MULT, POP**
See also CA 85-88; CANR 42, 66; DLB 175; NNAL

Weldon, Fay 1931- . **CLC 6, 9, 11, 19, 36, 59; DAM POP**
See also CA 21-24R; CANR 16, 46, 63; CDBLB 1960 to Present; DLB 14, 194; INT CANR-16; MTCW 1

Wellek, Rene 1903-1995 .... **CLC 28**
See also CA 5-8R; 150; CAAS 7; CANR 8; DLB 63; INT CANR-8

Weller, Michael 1942- .... **CLC 10, 53**
See also CA 85-88

Weller, Paul 1958- .... **CLC 26**

Wellershoff, Dieter 1925- .... **CLC 46**
See also CA 89-92; CANR 16, 37

Welles, (George) Orson 1915-1985 **CLC 20, 80**
See also CA 93-96; 117

Wellman, John McDowell 1945-
See Wellman, Mac
See also CA 166

Wellman, Mac 1945- .... **CLC 65**
See also Wellman, John McDowell; Wellman, John McDowell

Wellman, Manly Wade 1903-1986 .... **CLC 49**
See also CA 1-4R; 118; CANR 6, 16, 44; SATA 6; SATA-Obit 47

Wells, Carolyn 1869(?)-1942 .... **TCLC 35**
See also CA 113; DLB 11

Wells, H(erbert) G(eorge) 1866-1946 **TCLC 6, 12, 19; DA; DAB; DAC; DAM MST, NOV; SSC 6; WLC**
See also AAYA 18; CA 110; 121; CDBLB 1914-1945; DLB 34, 70, 156, 178; MTCW 1; SATA 20

Wells, Rosemary 1943- .... **CLC 12**
See also AAYA 13; CA 85-88; CANR 48; CLR 16; MAICYA; SAAS 1; SATA 18, 69

Welty, Eudora 1909- **CLC 1, 2, 5, 14, 22, 33, 105; DA; DAB; DAC; DAM MST, NOV; SSC 1, 27; WLC**
See also CA 9-12R; CABS 1; CANR 32, 65; CDALB 1941-1968; DLB 2, 102, 143; DLBD 12; DLBY 87; MTCW 1

Wen I-to 1899-1946 .... **TCLC 28**

Wentworth, Robert
See Hamilton, Edmond

Werfel, Franz (Viktor) 1890-1945 ... **TCLC 8**
See also CA 104; 161; DLB 81, 124

Wergeland, Henrik Arnold 1808-1845 **N C L C 5**

Wersba, Barbara 1932- .... **CLC 30**
See also AAYA 2; CA 29-32R; CANR 16, 38; CLR 3; DLB 52; JRDA; MAICYA; SAAS 2; SATA 1, 58; SATA-Essay 103

Wertmueller, Lina 1928- .... **CLC 16**
See also CA 97-100; CANR 39

Wescott, Glenway 1901-1987 .... **CLC 13**
See also CA 13-16R; 121; CANR 23, 70; DLB 4, 9, 102

Wesker, Arnold 1932- .... **CLC 3, 5, 42; DAB; DAM DRAM**
See also CA 1-4R; CAAS 7; CANR 1, 33; CDBLB 1960 to Present; DLB 13; MTCW 1

Wesley, Richard (Errol) 1945- .... **CLC 7**
See also BW 1; CA 57-60; CANR 27; DLB 38

Wessel, Johan Herman 1742-1785 .... **LC 7**

West, Anthony (Panther) 1914-1987 **CLC 50**
See also CA 45-48; 124; CANR 3, 19; DLB 15

West, C. P.
See Wodehouse, P(elham) G(renville)

West, (Mary) Jessamyn 1902-1984 **CLC 7, 17**
See also CA 9-12R; 112; CANR 27; DLB 6; DLBY 84; MTCW 1; SATA-Obit 37

West, Morris L(anglo) 1916- .... **CLC 6, 33**
See also CA 5-8R; CANR 24, 49, 64; MTCW 1

West, Nathanael 1903-1940 **TCLC 1, 14, 44; SSC 16**
See also CA 104; 125; CDALB 1929-1941; DLB 4, 9, 28; MTCW 1

West, Owen
See Koontz, Dean R(ay)

West, Paul 1930- .... **CLC 7, 14, 96**
See also CA 13-16R; CAAS 7; CANR 22, 53, 76; DLB 14; INT CANR-22

West, Rebecca 1892-1983 ... **CLC 7, 9, 31, 50**
See also CA 5-8R; 109; CANR 19; DLB 36; DLBY 83; MTCW 1

Westall, Robert (Atkinson) 1929-1993 **CLC 17**
See also AAYA 12; CA 69-72; 141; CANR 18, 68; CLR 13; JRDA; MAICYA; SAAS 2; SATA 23, 69; SATA-Obit 75

Westermarck, Edward 1862-1939 . **TCLC 87**

Westlake, Donald E(dwin) 1933- **CLC 7, 33; DAM POP**
See also CA 17-20R; CAAS 13; CANR 16, 44, 65; INT CANR-16

Westmacott, Mary
See Christie, Agatha (Mary Clarissa)

Weston, Allen
See Norton, Andre

Wetcheek, J. L.
See Feuchtwanger, Lion

Wetering, Janwillem van de
See van de Wetering, Janwillem

Wetherald, Agnes Ethelwyn 1857-1940 **T CLC 81**
See also DLB 99

Wetherell, Elizabeth
See Warner, Susan (Bogert)

Whale, James 1889-1957 .... **TCLC 63**

Whalen, Philip 1923- .... **CLC 6, 29**
See also CA 9-12R; CANR 5, 39; DLB 16

Wharton, Edith (Newbold Jones) 1862-1937 **TCLC 3, 9, 27, 53; DA; DAB; DAC; DAM MST, NOV; SSC 6; WLC**
See also AAYA 25; CA 104; 132; CDALB 1865-1917; DLB 4, 9, 12, 78, 189; DLBD 13; MTCW 1

Wharton, James
See Mencken, H(enry) L(ouis)

Wharton, William (a pseudonym) **CLC 18, 37**
See also CA 93-96; DLBY 80; INT 93-96

Wheatley (Peters), Phillis 1754(?)-1784 **LC 3; BLC 3; DA; DAC; DAM MST, MULT, POET; PC 3; WLC**
See also CDALB 1640-1865; DLB 31, 50

Wheelock, John Hall 1886-1978 .... **CLC 14**
See also CA 13-16R; 77-80; CANR 14; DLB 45

White, E(lwyn) B(rooks) 1899-1985 **CLC 10,**

34, 39; DAM POP
See also AITN 2; CA 13-16R; 116; CANR 16, 37; CLR 1, 21; DLB 11, 22; MAICYA; MTCW 1; SATA 2, 29, 100; SATA-Obit 44

White, Edmund (Valentine III) 1940-CLC 27, 110; DAM POP
See also AAYA 7; CA 45-48; CANR 3, 19, 36, 62; MTCW 1

White, Patrick (Victor Martindale) 1912-1990 CLC 3, 4, 5, 7, 9, 18, 65, 69
See also CA 81-84; 132; CANR 43; MTCW 1

White, Phyllis Dorothy James 1920-
See James, P. D.
See also CA 21-24R; CANR 17, 43, 65; DAM POP; MTCW 1

White, T(erence) H(anbury) 1906-1964 C L C 30
See also AAYA 22; CA 73-76; CANR 37; DLB 160; JRDA; MAICYA; SATA 12

White, Terence de Vere 1912-1994 ... CLC 49
See also CA 49-52; 145; CANR 3

White, Walter F(rancis) 1893-1955 TCLC 15
See also White, Walter
See also BW 1; CA 115; 124; DLB 51

White, William Hale 1831-1913
See Rutherford, Mark
See also CA 121

Whitehead, E(dward) A(nthony) 1933-CLC 5
See also CA 65-68; CANR 58

Whitemore, Hugh (John) 1936- .... CLC 37
See also CA 132; INT 132

Whitman, Sarah Helen (Power) 1803-1878 NCLC 19
See also DLB 1

Whitman, Walt(er) 1819-1892 . NCLC 4, 31; DA; DAB; DAC; DAM MST, POET; PC 3; WLC
See also CDALB 1640-1865; DLB 3, 64; SATA 20

Whitney, Phyllis A(yame) 1903- ..... CLC 42; DAM POP
See also AITN 2; BEST 90:3; CA 1-4R; CANR 3, 25, 38, 60; JRDA; MAICYA; SATA 1, 30

Whittemore, (Edward) Reed (Jr.) 1919-CLC 4
See also CA 9-12R; CAAS 8; CANR 4; DLB 5

Whittier, John Greenleaf 1807-1892NCLC 8, 59
See also DLB 1

Whittlebot, Hernia
See Coward, Noel (Peirce)

Wicker, Thomas Grey 1926-
See Wicker, Tom
See also CA 65-68; CANR 21, 46

Wicker, Tom .... CLC 7
See also Wicker, Thomas Grey

Wideman, John Edgar 1941- CLC 5, 34, 36, 67; BLC 3; DAM MULT
See also BW 2; CA 85-88; CANR 14, 42, 67; DLB 33, 143

Wiebe, Rudy (Henry) 1934- .. CLC 6, 11, 14; DAC; DAM MST
See also CA 37-40R; CANR 42, 67; DLB 60

Wieland, Christoph Martin 1733-1813N C L C 17
See also DLB 97

Wiene, Robert 1881-1938 .... TCLC 56

Wieners, John 1934- .... CLC 7
See also CA 13-16R; DLB 16

Wiesel, Elie(zer) 1928- CLC 3, 5, 11, 37; DA; DAB; DAC; DAM MST, NOV; WLCS
See also AAYA 7; AITN 1; CA 5-8R; CAAS 4; CANR 8, 40, 65; DLB 83; DLBY 87; INT CANR-8; MTCW 1; SATA 56

Wiggins, Marianne 1947- .... CLC 57
See also BEST 89:3; CA 130; CANR 60

Wight, James Alfred 1916-1995
See Herriot, James

See also CA 77-80; SATA 55; SATA-Brief 44

Wilbur, Richard (Purdy) 1921-CLC 3, 6, 9, 14, 53, 110; DA; DAB; DAC; DAM MST, POET
See also CA 1-4R; CABS 2; CANR 2, 29, 76; DLB 5, 169; INT CANR-29; MTCW 1; SATA 9

Wild, Peter 1940- .... CLC 14
See also CA 37-40R; DLB 5

Wilde, Oscar 1854(?)-1900TCLC 1, 8, 23, 41; DA; DAB; DAC; DAM DRAM, MST, NOV; SSC 11; WLC
See also CA 104; 119; CDBLB 1890-1914; DLB 10, 19, 34, 57, 141, 156, 190; SATA 24

Wilder, Billy .... CLC 20
See also Wilder, Samuel
See also DLB 26

Wilder, Samuel 1906-
See Wilder, Billy
See also CA 89-92

Wilder, Thornton (Niven) 1897-1975CLC 1, 5, 6, 10, 15, 35, 82; DA; DAB; DAC; DAM DRAM, MST, NOV; DC 1; WLC
See also AITN 2; CA 13-16R; 61-64; CANR 40; DLB 4, 7, 9; DLBY 97; MTCW 1

Wilding, Michael 1942-...................... CLC 73
See also CA 104; CANR 24, 49

Wiley, Richard 1944- .... CLC 44
See also CA 121; 129; CANR 71

Wilhelm, Kate .... CLC 7
See also Wilhelm, Katie Gertrude
See also AAYA 20; CAAS 5; DLB 8; INT CANR-17

Wilhelm, Katie Gertrude 1928-
See Wilhelm, Kate
See also CA 37-40R; CANR 17, 36, 60; MTCW 1

Wilkins, Mary
See Freeman, Mary Eleanor Wilkins

Willard, Nancy 1936- .... CLC 7, 37
See also CA 89-92; CANR 10, 39, 68; CLR 5; DLB 5, 52; MAICYA; MTCW 1; SATA 37, 71; SATA-Brief 30

William of Ockham 1285-1347 ..... CMLC 32

Williams, Ben Ames 1889-1953 ..... TCLC 89
See also DLB 102

Williams, C(harles) K(enneth) 1936-CLC 33, 56; DAM POET
See also CA 37-40R; CAAS 26; CANR 57; DLB 5

Williams, Charles
See Collier, James L(incoln)

Williams, Charles (Walter Stansby) 1886-1945 TCLC 1, 11
See also CA 104; 163; DLB 100, 153

Williams, (George) Emlyn 1905-1987CLC 15; DAM DRAM
See also CA 104; 123; CANR 36; DLB 10, 77; MTCW 1

Williams, Hank 1923-1953 .... TCLC 81

Williams, Hugo 1942- .... CLC 42
See also CA 17-20R; CANR 45; DLB 40

Williams, J. Walker
See Wodehouse, P(elham) G(renville)

Williams, John A(lfred) 1925-CLC 5, 13; BLC 3; DAM MULT
See also BW 2; CA 53-56; CAAS 3; CANR 6, 26, 51; DLB 2, 33; INT CANR-6

Williams, Jonathan (Chamberlain) 1929- CLC 13
See also CA 9-12R; CAAS 12; CANR 8; DLB 5

Williams, Joy 1944- .... CLC 31
See also CA 41-44R; CANR 22, 48

Williams, Norman 1952- .... CLC 39
See also CA 118

Williams, Sherley Anne 1944-CLC 89; BLC 3;

DAM MULT, POET
See also BW 2; CA 73-76; CANR 25; DLB 41; INT CANR-25; SATA 78

Williams, Shirley
See Williams, Sherley Anne

Williams, Tennessee 1911-1983CLC 1, 2, 5, 7, 8, 11, 15, 19, 30, 39, 45, 71, 111; DA; DAB; DAC; DAM DRAM, MST; DC 4; WLC
See also AITN 1, 2; CA 5-8R; 108; CABS 3; CANR 31; CDALB 1941-1968; DLB 7; DLBD 4; DLBY 83; MTCW 1

Williams, Thomas (Alonzo) 1926-1990CLC 14
See also CA 1-4R; 132; CANR 2

Williams, William C.
See Williams, William Carlos

Williams, William Carlos 1883-1963CLC 1, 2, 5, 9, 13, 22, 42, 67; DA; DAB; DAC; DAM MST, POET; PC 7; SSC 31
See also CA 89-92; CANR 34; CDALB 1917-1929; DLB 4, 16, 54, 86; MTCW 1

Williamson, David (Keith) 1942- ...... CLC 56
See also CA 103; CANR 41

Williamson, Ellen Douglas 1905-1984
See Douglas, Ellen
See also CA 17-20R; 114; CANR 39

Williamson, Jack .... CLC 29
See also Williamson, John Stewart
See also CAAS 8; DLB 8

Williamson, John Stewart 1908-
See Williamson, Jack
See also CA 17-20R; CANR 23, 70

Willie, Frederick
See Lovecraft, H(oward) P(hillips)

Willingham, Calder (Baynard, Jr.) 1922-1995 CLC 5, 51
See also CA 5-8R; 147; CANR 3; DLB 2, 44; MTCW 1

Willis, Charles
See Clarke, Arthur C(harles)

Willis, Fingal O'Flahertie
See Wilde, Oscar

Willy
See Colette, (Sidonie-Gabrielle)

Willy, Colette
See Colette, (Sidonie-Gabrielle)

Wilson, A(ndrew) N(orman) 1950- ... CLC 33
See also CA 112; 122; DLB 14, 155, 194

Wilson, Angus (Frank Johnstone) 1913-1991 CLC 2, 3, 5, 25, 34; SSC 21
See also CA 5-8R; 134; CANR 21; DLB 15, 139, 155; MTCW 1

Wilson, August 1945- ... CLC 39, 50, 63, 118; BLC 3; DA; DAB; DAC; DAM DRAM, MST, MULT; DC 2; WLCS
See also AAYA 16; BW 2; CA 115; 122; CANR 42, 54, 76; MTCW 1

Wilson, Brian 1942-.......................... CLC 12

Wilson, Colin 1931- ....CLC 3, 14
See also CA 1-4R; CAAS 5; CANR 1, 22, 33; DLB 14, 194; MTCW 1

Wilson, Dirk
See Pohl, Frederik

Wilson, Edmund 1895-1972CLC 1, 2, 3, 8, 24
See also CA 1-4R; 37-40R; CANR 1, 46; DLB 63; MTCW 1

Wilson, Ethel Davis (Bryant) 1888(?)-1980 CLC 13; DAC; DAM POET
See also CA 102; DLB 68; MTCW 1

Wilson, John 1785-1854 .... NCLC 5

Wilson, John (Anthony) Burgess 1917-1993
See Burgess, Anthony
See also CA 1-4R; 143; CANR 2, 46; DAC; DAM NOV; MTCW 1

Wilson, Lanford 1937- CLC 7, 14, 36; DAM DRAM
See also CA 17-20R; CABS 3; CANR 45; DLB 7

CLC 1, 3, 13, 26, 51; **DAM POET**
See also CA 81-84; CANR 33, 54; MTCW 1
Yezierska, Anzia 1885(?)-1970 .... **CLC 46**
See also CA 126; 89-92; DLB 28; MTCW 1
Yglesias, Helen 1915- .... **CLC 7, 22**
See also CA 37-40R; CAAS 20; CANR 15, 65;
INT CANR-15; MTCW 1
Yokomitsu Riichi 1898-1947 .... **TCLC 47**
See also CA 170
Yonge, Charlotte (Mary) 1823-1901**TCLC 48**
See also CA 109; 163; DLB 18, 163; SATA 17
York, Jeremy
See Creasey, John
York, Simon
See Heinlein, Robert A(nson)
Yorke, Henry Vincent 1905-1974 ...... **CLC 13**
See also Green, Henry
See also CA 85-88; 49-52
Yosano Akiko 1878-1942 .... **TCLC 59; PC 11**
See also CA 161
Yoshimoto, Banana .... **CLC 84**
See also Yoshimoto, Mahoko
Yoshimoto, Mahoko 1964-
See Yoshimoto, Banana
See also CA 144
Young, Al(bert James) 1939-**CLC 19; BLC 3;**
DAM MULT
See also BW 2; CA 29-32R; CANR 26, 65; DLB
33
Young, Andrew (John) 1885-1971 ...... **CLC 5**
See also CA 5-8R; CANR 7, 29
Young, Collier
See Bloch, Robert (Albert)
Young, Edward 1683-1765 .... **LC 3, 40**
See also DLB 95
Young, Marguerite (Vivian) 1909-1995 **C L C**
82
See also CA 13-16; 150; CAP 1
Young, Neil 1945- .... **CLC 17**
See also CA 110
Young Bear, Ray A. 1950- ...... **CLC 94; DAM**
MULT
See also CA 146; DLB 175; NNAL
Yourcenar, Marguerite 1903-1987**CLC 19, 38,**
50, 87; DAM NOV
See also CA 69-72; CANR 23, 60; DLB 72;
DLBY 88; MTCW 1
Yurick, Sol 1925- .... **CLC 6**
See also CA 13-16R; CANR 25
Zabolotsky, Nikolai Alekseevich 1903-1958
TCLC 52
See also CA 116; 164
Zamiatin, Yevgenii
See Zamyatin, Evgeny Ivanovich
Zamora, Bernice (B. Ortiz) 1938- .. **CLC 89;**
DAM MULT; HLC
See also CA 151; DLB 82; HW
Zamyatin, Evgeny Ivanovich 1884-1937
TCLC 8, 37
See also CA 105; 166
Zangwill, Israel 1864-1926 .... **TCLC 16**
See also CA 109; 167; DLB 10, 135, 197
Zappa, Francis Vincent, Jr. 1940-1993
See Zappa, Frank
See also CA 108; 143; CANR 57
Zappa, Frank .... **CLC 17**
See also Zappa, Francis Vincent, Jr.
Zaturenska, Marya 1902-1982 ...... **CLC 6, 11**
See also CA 13-16R; 105; CANR 22
Zeami 1363-1443 .... **DC 7**
Zelazny, Roger (Joseph) 1937-1995 .**CLC 21**
See also AAYA 7; CA 21-24R; 148; CANR 26,
60; DLB 8; MTCW 1; SATA 57; SATA-Brief
39
Zhdanov, Andrei Alexandrovich 1896-1948
TCLC 18
See also CA 117; 167

Zhukovsky, Vasily (Andreevich) 1783-1852
NCLC 35
See also DLB 205
Ziegenhagen, Eric .... **CLC 55**
Zimmer, Jill Schary
See Robinson, Jill
Zimmerman, Robert
See Dylan, Bob
Zindel, Paul 1936-**CLC 6, 26; DA; DAB; DAC;**
DAM DRAM, MST, NOV; DC 5
See also AAYA 2; CA 73-76; CANR 31, 65;
CLR 3, 45; DLB 7, 52; JRDA; MAICYA;
MTCW 1; SATA 16, 58, 102
Zinov'Ev, A. A.
See Zinoviev, Alexander (Aleksandrovich)
Zinoviev, Alexander (Aleksandrovich) 1922-
CLC 19
See also CA 116; 133; CAAS 10
Zoilus
See Lovecraft, H(oward) P(hillips)
Zola, Emile (Edouard Charles Antoine) 1840-
1902**TCLC 1, 6, 21, 41; DA; DAB; DAC;**
DAM MST, NOV; WLC
See also CA 104; 138; DLB 123
Zoline, Pamela 1941- .... **CLC 62**
See also CA 161
Zorrilla y Moral, Jose 1817-1893 .... **NCLC 6**
Zoshchenko, Mikhail (Mikhailovich) 1895-1958
TCLC 15; SSC 15
See also CA 115; 160
Zuckmayer, Carl 1896-1977 .... **CLC 18**
See also CA 69-72; DLB 56, 124
Zuk, Georges
See Skelton, Robin
Zukofsky, Louis 1904-1978**CLC 1, 2, 4, 7, 11,**
18; DAM POET; PC 11
See also CA 9-12R; 77-80; CANR 39; DLB 5,
165; MTCW 1
Zweig, Paul 1935-1984 .... **CLC 34, 42**
See also CA 85-88; 113
Zweig, Stefan 1881-1942 .... **TCLC 17**
See also CA 112; 170; DLB 81, 118
Zwingli, Huldreich 1484-1531 .... **LC 37**
See also DLB 179

Literary Criticism Series
Cumulative Topic Index

This index lists all topic entries in Gale's *Classical and Medieval Literature Criticism, Contemporary Literary Criticism, Literature Criticism from 1400 to 1800, Nineteenth-Century Literature Criticism,* and *Twentieth-Century Literary Criticism.*

Topic Index

Topic Index

Twentieth-Century Literary Criticism
Cumulative Nationality Index

Robinson, Edwin Arlington 5
Roelvaag, O(le) E(dvart) 17
Rogers, Will(iam Penn Adair) 8, 71
Roosevelt, Theodore 69
Rourke, Constance (Mayfield) 12
Runyon, (Alfred) Damon 10
Saltus, Edgar (Everton) 8
Santayana, George 40
Schoenberg, Arnold 75
Sherwood, Robert E(mmet) 3
Slesinger, Tess 10
Stanton, Elizabeth Cady 73
Steffens, (Joseph) Lincoln 20
Stein, Gertrude 1, 6, 28, 48
Sterling, George 20
Stevens, Wallace 3, 12, 45
Stockton, Frank R. 47
Stroheim, Erich von 71
Sturges, Preston 48
Tarbell, Ida M(inerva) 40
Tarkington, (Newton) Booth 9
Taylor, Frederick Winslow 76
Teasdale, Sara 4
Tesla, Nikola 88
Thomas, M. Carey 89
Thurman, Wallace (Henry) 6
Twain, Mark 6, 12, 19, 36, 48, 59
Van Dine, S. S. 23
Van Doren, Carl (Clinton) 18
Veblen, Thorstein B(unde) 31
Washington, Booker T(aliaferro) 10
Wells, Carolyn 35
West, Nathanael 1, 14, 44
Whale, James 63
Wharton, Edith (Newbold Jones) 3, 9, 27, 53
White, Walter F(rancis) 15
Williams, Ben Ames 89
Williams, Hank 81
Wilson, (Thomas) Woodrow 79
Wister, Owen 21
Wolfe, Thomas (Clayton) 4, 13, 29, 61
Woodberry, George Edward 73
Woollcott, Alexander (Humphreys) 5
Wylie, Elinor (Morton Hoyt) 8

ARGENTINIAN
Arlt, Roberto (Godofredo Christophersen) 29
Guiraldes, Ricardo (Guillermo) 39
Hudson, W(illiam) H(enry) 29
Lugones, Leopoldo 15
Storni, Alfonsina 5

AUSTRALIAN
Baynton, Barbara 57
Franklin, (Stella Maria Sarah) Miles (Lampe) 7
Furphy, Joseph 25
Ingamells, Rex 35
Lawson, Henry (Archibald Hertzberg) 27
Paterson, A(ndrew) B(arton) 32
Richardson, Henry Handel 4
Warung, Price 45

AUSTRIAN
Beer-Hofmann, Richard 60
Broch, Hermann 20
Freud, Sigmund 52
Hofmannsthal, Hugo von 11
Kafka, Franz 2, 6, 13, 29, 47, 53
Kraus, Karl 5
Kubin, Alfred (Leopold Isidor) 23
Meyrink, Gustav 21
Musil, Robert (Edler von) 12, 68
Perutz, Leo(pold) 60

Roth, (Moses) Joseph 33
Schnitzler, Arthur 4
Steiner, Rudolf 13
Stroheim, Erich von 71
Trakl, Georg 5
Weininger, Otto 84
Werfel, Franz (Viktor) 8
Zweig, Stefan 17

BELGIAN
Bosschere, Jean de 19
Lemonnier, (Antoine Louis) Camille 22
Maeterlinck, Maurice 3
van Ostaijen, Paul 33
Verhaeren, Emile (Adolphe Gustave) 12

BRAZILIAN
Andrade, Mario de 43
Cunha, Euclides (Rodrigues Pimenta) da 24
Lima Barreto, Afonso Henrique de 23
Machado de Assis, Joaquim Maria 10
Ramos, Graciliano 32

BULGARIAN
Vazov, Ivan (Minchov) 25

CANADIAN
Campbell, Wilfred 9
Carman, (William) Bliss 7
Carr, Emily 32
Connor, Ralph 31
Drummond, William Henry 25
Duncan, Sara Jeannette 60
Garneau, (Hector de) Saint-Denys 13
Grove, Frederick Philip 4
Innis, Harold Adams 77
Knister, Raymond 56
Leacock, Stephen (Butler) 2
McCrae, John 12
Montgomery, L(ucy) M(aud) 51
Nelligan, Emile 14
Pickthall, Marjorie L(owry) C(hristie) 21
Roberts, Charles G(eorge) D(ouglas) 8
Scott, Duncan Campbell 6
Service, Robert W(illiam) 15
Seton, Ernest (Evan) Thompson 31
Stringer, Arthur 37
Wetherald, Agnes Ethelwyn 81

CHILEAN
Huidobro Fernandez, Vicente Garcia 31
Mistral, Gabriela 2
Prado (Calvo), Pedro 75

CHINESE
Liu, E 15
Lu Hsun 3
Su Man-shu 24
Wen I-to 28

COLOMBIAN
Rivera, Jose Eustasio 35

CZECH
Capek, Karel 6, 37
Freud, Sigmund 52
Hasek, Jaroslav (Matej Frantisek) 4
Kafka, Franz 2, 6, 13, 29, 47, 53
Nezval, Vitezslav 44

DANISH
Brandes, Georg (Morris Cohen) 10
Hansen, Martin A(lfred) 32

Jensen, Johannes V. 41
Nexo, Martin Andersen 43
Pontoppidan, Henrik 29

DUTCH
Couperus, Louis (Marie Anne) 15
Frank, Anne(lies Marie) 17
Heijermans, Herman 24
Hillesum, Etty 49
Schendel, Arthur van 56

ENGLISH
Alexander, Samuel 77
Barbellion, W. N. P. 24
Baring, Maurice 8
Baring-Gould, Sabine 88
Beerbohm, (Henry) Max(imilian) 1, 24
Bell, Gertrude (Margaret Lowthian) 67
Belloc, (Joseph) Hilaire (Pierre Sebastien Rene Swanton) 7, 18
Bennett, (Enoch) Arnold 5, 20
Benson, E(dward) F(rederic) 27
Benson, Stella 17
Bentley, E(dmund) C(lerihew) 12
Beresford, J(ohn) D(avys) 81
Besant, Annie (Wood) 9
Blackmore, R(ichard) D(oddridge) 27
Blackwood, Algernon (Henry) 5
Bramah, Ernest 72
Bridges, Robert (Seymour) 1
Brooke, Rupert (Chawner) 2, 7
Burke, Thomas 63
Butler, Samuel 1, 33
Butts, Mary 77
Byron, Robert 67
Carpenter, Edward 88
Chesterton, G(ilbert) K(eith) 1, 6, 64
Childers, (Robert) Erskine 65
Coleridge, Mary E(lizabeth) 73
Collingwood, R(obin) G(eorge) 67
Conrad, Joseph 1, 6, 13, 25, 43, 57
Coppard, A(lfred) E(dgar) 5
Corelli, Marie 51
Crofts, Freeman Wills 55
Crowley, Aleister 7
Dale, Colin 18
Delafield, E. M. 61
de la Mare, Walter (John) 4, 53
Dobson, Austin 79
Doughty, Charles M(ontagu) 27
Douglas, Keith (Castellain) 40
Dowson, Ernest (Christopher) 4
Doyle, Arthur Conan 7
Drinkwater, John 57
Eddison, E(ric) R(ucker) 15
Elaine 18
Elizabeth 41
Ellis, (Henry) Havelock 14
Firbank, (Arthur Annesley) Ronald 1
Ford, Ford Madox 1, 15, 39, 57
Freeman, R(ichard) Austin 21
Galsworthy, John 1, 45
Gilbert, W(illiam) S(chwenck) 3
Gill, Eric 85
Gissing, George (Robert) 3, 24, 47
Glyn, Elinor 72
Gosse, Edmund (William) 28
Grahame, Kenneth 64
Granville-Barker, Harley 2
Gray, John (Henry) 19
Gurney, Ivor (Bertie) 33
Haggard, H(enry) Rider 11
Hall, (Marguerite) Radclyffe 12

Hardy, Thomas **4, 10, 18, 32, 48, 53, 72**
Henley, William Ernest **8**
Hilton, James **21**
Hodgson, William Hope **13**
Hope, Anthony **83**
Housman, A(lfred) E(dward) **1, 10**
Housman, Laurence **7**
Hudson, W(illiam) H(enry) **29**
Hulme, T(homas) E(rnest) **21**
Hunt, Violet **53**
Jacobs, W(illiam) W(ymark) **22**
James, Montague (Rhodes) **6**
Jerome, Jerome K(lapka) **23**
Johnson, Lionel (Pigot) **19**
Kaye-Smith, Sheila **20**
Keynes, John Maynard **64**
Kipling, (Joseph) Rudyard **8, 17**
Laski, Harold **79**
Lawrence, D(avid) H(erbert Richards) **2, 9, 16, 33, 48, 61**
Lawrence, T(homas) E(dward) **18**
Lee, Vernon **5**
Lee-Hamilton, Eugene (Jacob) **22**
Leverson, Ada **18**
Lewis, (Percy) Wyndham **2, 9**
Lindsay, David **15**
Lowndes, Marie Adelaide (Belloc) **12**
Lowry, (Clarence) Malcolm **6, 40**
Lucas, E(dward) V(errall) **73**
Macaulay, Rose **7, 44**
MacCarthy, (Charles Otto) Desmond **36**
Maitland, Frederic **65**
Manning, Frederic **25**
Meredith, George **17, 43**
Mew, Charlotte (Mary) **8**
Meynell, Alice (Christina Gertrude Thompson) **6**
Middleton, Richard (Barham) **56**
Milne, A(lan) A(lexander) **6, 88**
Moore, G. E. **89**
Morrison, Arthur **72**
Murry, John Middleton **16**
Nightingale, Florence **85**
Noyes, Alfred **7**
Oppenheim, E(dward) Phillips **45**
Orwell, George **2, 6, 15, 31, 51**
Ouida **43**
Owen, Wilfred (Edward Salter) **5, 27**
Pinero, Arthur Wing **32**
Powys, T(heodore) F(rancis) **9**
Quiller-Couch, Arthur (Thomas) **53**
Richardson, Dorothy Miller **3**
Rohmer, Sax **28**
Rolfe, Frederick (William Serafino Austin Lewis Mary) **12**
Rosenberg, Isaac **12**
Ruskin, John **20**
Rutherford, Mark **25**
Sabatini, Rafael **47**
Saintsbury, George (Edward Bateman) **31**
Saki **3**
Sapper **44**
Sayers, Dorothy L(eigh) **2, 15**
Shiel, M(atthew) P(hipps) **8**
Sinclair, May **3, 11**
Stapledon, (William) Olaf **22**
Stead, William Thomas **48**
Stephen, Leslie **23**
Strachey, (Giles) Lytton **12**
Summers, (Alphonsus Joseph-Mary Augustus) Montague **16**
Sutro, Alfred **6**
Swinburne, Algernon Charles **8, 36**
Symons, Arthur **11**

Thomas, (Philip) Edward **10**
Thompson, Francis Joseph **4**
Tomlinson, H(enry) M(ajor) **71**
Upward, Allen **85**
Van Druten, John (William) **2**
Wallace, (Richard Horatio) Edgar **57**
Wallas, Graham **91**
Walpole, Hugh (Seymour) **5**
Ward, Mrs. Humphry **55**
Warung, Price **45**
Webb, (Martha) Beatrice (Potter) **22**
Webb, Mary (Gladys Meredith) **24**
Webb, Sidney (James) **22**
Welch, (Maurice) Denton **22**
Wells, H(erbert) G(eorge) **6, 12, 19**
Williams, Charles (Walter Stansby) **1, 11**
Woolf, (Adeline) Virginia **1, 5, 20, 43, 56**
Yonge, Charlotte (Mary) **48**
Zangwill, Israel **16**

ESTONIAN
Talvik, Heiti **87**
Tammsaare, A(nton) H(ansen) **27**

FINNISH
Leino, Eino **24**
Soedergran, Edith (Irene) **31**
Westermarck, Edward **87**

FRENCH
Alain **41**
Alain-Fournier **6**
Apollinaire, Guillaume **3, 8, 51**
Artaud, Antonin (Marie Joseph) **3, 36**
Barbusse, Henri **5**
Barres, (Auguste-) Maurice **47**
Benda, Julien **60**
Bergson, Henri(-Louis) **32**
Bernanos, (Paul Louis) Georges **3**
Bernhardt, Sarah (Henriette Rosine) **75**
Bloy, Leon **22**
Bourget, Paul (Charles Joseph) **12**
Claudel, Paul (Louis Charles Marie) **2, 10**
Colette, (Sidonie-Gabrielle) **1, 5, 16**
Coppee, Francois **25**
Daumal, Rene **14**
Desnos, Robert **22**
Drieu la Rochelle, Pierre(-Eugene) **21**
Dujardin, Edouard (Emile Louis) **13**
Durkheim, Emile **55**
Eluard, Paul **7, 41**
Fargue, Leon-Paul **11**
Feydeau, Georges (Leon Jules Marie) **22**
France, Anatole **9**
Gide, Andre (Paul Guillaume) **5, 12, 36**
Giraudoux, (Hippolyte) Jean **2, 7**
Gourmont, Remy (-Marie-Charles) de **17**
Huysmans, Joris-Karl **7, 69**
Jacob, (Cyprien-)Max **6**
Jammes, Francis **75**
Jarry, Alfred **2, 14**
Larbaud, Valery (Nicolas) **9**
Leautaud, Paul **83**
Leblanc, Maurice (Marie Emile) **49**
Leroux, Gaston **25**
Loti, Pierre **11**
Martin du Gard, Roger **24**
Melies, Georges **81**
Mirbeau, Octave **55**
Mistral, Frederic **51**
Moreas, Jean **18**
Nizan, Paul **40**
Peguy, Charles Pierre **10**

Peret, Benjamin **20**
Proust, (Valentin-Louis-George-Eugene-) Marcel **7, 13, 33**
Rachilde **67**
Radiguet, Raymond **29**
Renard, Jules **17**
Rolland, Romain **23**
Rostand, Edmond (Eugene Alexis) **6, 37**
Roussel, Raymond **20**
Saint-Exupery, Antoine (Jean Baptiste Marie Roger) de **2, 56**
Schwob, Marcel (Mayer Andre) **20**
Sorel, Georges **91**
Sully Prudhomme **31**
Teilhard de Chardin, (Marie Joseph) Pierre **9**
Valery, (Ambroise) Paul (Toussaint Jules) **4, 15**
Verne, Jules (Gabriel) **6, 52**
Vian, Boris **9**
Weil, Simone (Adolphine) **23**
Zola, Emile (Edouard Charles Antoine) **1, 6, 21, 41**

GERMAN
Andreas-Salome, Lou **56**
Auerbach, Erich **43**
Barlach, Ernst **84**
Benjamin, Walter **39**
Benn, Gottfried **3**
Borchert, Wolfgang **5**
Brecht, (Eugen) Bertolt (Friedrich) **1, 6, 13, 35**
Carossa, Hans **48**
Cassirer, Ernst **61**
Doblin, Alfred **13**
Doeblin, Alfred **13**
Einstein, Albert **65**
Ewers, Hanns Heinz **12**
Feuchtwanger, Lion **3**
Frank, Bruno **81**
George, Stefan (Anton) **2, 14**
Goebbels, (Paul) Joseph **68**
Haeckel, Ernst Heinrich (Philipp August) **83**
Hauptmann, Gerhart (Johann Robert) **4**
Heym, Georg (Theodor Franz Arthur) **9**
Heyse, Paul (Johann Ludwig von) **8**
Hitler, Adolf **53**
Horney, Karen (Clementine Theodore Danielsen) **71**
Huch, Ricarda (Octavia) **13**
Kaiser, Georg **9**
Klabund **44**
Kolmar, Gertrud **40**
Lasker-Schueler, Else **57**
Liliencron, (Friedrich Adolf Axel) Detlev von **18**
Luxemburg, Rosa **63**
Mann, (Luiz) Heinrich **9**
Mann, (Paul) Thomas **2, 8, 14, 21, 35, 44, 60**
Mannheim, Karl **65**
Michels, Robert **88**
Morgenstern, Christian **8**
Nietzsche, Friedrich (Wilhelm) **10, 18, 55**
Ophuls, Max **79**
Otto, Rudolf **85**
Plumpe, Friedrich Wilhelm **53**
Raabe, Wilhelm (Karl) **45**
Rilke, Rainer Maria **1, 6, 19**
Simmel, Georg **64**
Spengler, Oswald (Arnold Gottfried) **25**
Sternheim, (William Adolf) Carl **8**
Sudermann, Hermann **15**
Toller, Ernst **10**
Vaihinger, Hans **71**
Wassermann, (Karl) Jakob **6**
Weber, Max **69**

Nationality Index

ISBN 0-7876-2748-8

90000